MW01106610

Advances in Information Systems Development

Bridging the Gap between Academia and Industry

Volume 1

Advances in Information Systems Development

Bridging the Gap between Academia and Industry

Volume 1

Edited by

Anders G. Nilsson and **Remigijus Gustas**
Karlstad University
Karlstad, Sweden

Wita Wojtkowski and **W. Gregory Wojtkowski**
Boise State University
Boise, Idaho, USA

Stanisław Wrycza
University of Gdansk
Gdansk, Poland

Jože Zupančič
University of Maribor
Kranj, Slovenia

 Springer

Anders G. Nilsson
Karlstad University
Universitetsgatan 2
SE-651 88 Karlstad
Sweden
anders.nilsson@kau.se

Wita Wojtkowski
Boise State University
1910 University Drive
Boise, Idaho 83725
USA
wwojtkow@boisestate.edu

Stanisław Wrycza
University of Gdansk
ul. Armii Krajowej 119/121
PL-81-824 Sopot
Poland
swrycza@univ.gda.pl

Remigijus Gustas
Karlstad University
Universitetsgatan 2
SE-651 88 Karlstad
Sweden
remigijus.gustas@kau.se

W. Gregory Wojtkowski
Boise State University
1910 University Drive
Boise, Idaho 83725
USA
gwojtkow@boisestate.edu

Jože Zupančič
University of Maribor
Systems Development Laboratory
SI-6400 Presernova 11
Slovenia
joze.zupancic@fov.uni-mb.si

Proceedings of the 14th International Conference on Information Systems Development—Bridging the Gap between Academia and Industry (ISD 2005), held in Karlstad, Sweden, August 14–17, 2005.

Volume (1): Part 1 of a two-volume set.

Library of Congress Control Number: 2005937686

ISBN-10: 0-387-30834-2
ISBN-13: 978-0387-30834-0

Preface

This publication is an outcome of the Fourteenth International Conference on Information Systems Development, ISD'2005, held in Karlstad, Sweden during 14-17 August 2005. The theme for the ISD'2005 conference was "Advances in Information Systems Development: Bridging the Gap between Academia and Industry". This conference continues the fine tradition of the first Polish – Scandinavian Seminar on Current Trends in Information Systems Development Methodologies, held in 1988, Gdańsk, Poland. Through the years this seminar has evolved into the "International Conference on Information Systems Development (ISD)" as we know today. This ISD conference compliments the network of general Information Systems conferences, e.g. ICIS, ECIS, AMCIS, PACIS and ACIS.

Information Systems Development (ISD) progresses rapidly, continually creating new challenges for the professionals involved. New concepts, approaches and techniques of systems development emerge constantly in this field. Progress in ISD comes from research as well as from practice. The aim of the Conference is to provide an international forum for the exchange of ideas and experiences between academia and industry, and to stimulate exploration of new solutions. The Conference gives participants an opportunity to express ideas on the current state of the art in information systems development, and to discuss and exchange views about new methods, tools and applications. ISD as our professional and academic discipline has responded to these challenges. As a practice-based discipline, ISD has always promoted a close interaction between theory and practice that has been influential in setting the ISD agenda. This agenda has largely focused on the integration of people, business processes and information technology (IT) together with the context in which this occurs.

The ISD conference provides a meeting point or venue for researchers and practitioners. They are coming from over 30 countries representing all continents in the world. The main objective of the conference is to share scientific knowledge and interests and to establish strong professional ties among the participants. This year, the ISD'2005 conference provided an opportunity to bring participants to the newly established Karlstad University in Sweden. Karlstad University is well known for its multidisciplinary research and education programs as well as the close cooperation with the local industry of the Värmland region. The ISD'2005 conference was organised around seven research tracks. This Springer book of proceedings, published in two volumes, is organised after the following conference tracks including a variety of papers forming separate chapters of the book:

- Co-design of Business and IT
- Communication and Methods
- Human Values of Information Technology
- Service Development and IT
- Requirements Engineering (RE) in the IS Life-Cycle
- Semantic Web Approaches and Applications
- Management and IT (MIT)

Three invited keynote speeches were held during the ISD'2005 conference by very prominent authorities in the field: Prof Göran Goldkuhl, CEO Hans Karlander and Prof Bo Edvardsson. In parallel with the conference we held a practical Workshop for the ISD delegates including presentation of a professional E-portal from the Wermland Chamber of Commerce.

The conference call for papers attracted a high number of good quality contributions. Of the 130 submitted papers we finally accepted 81 for publication, representing an acceptance rate of approximately 60%. In addition we had a pre-conference opportunity for promoting and supporting researchers in their professional careers. The pre-conference comprised 25 papers which are published in separate proceedings from Karlstad University Press. We had a best paper award appointment of four papers from the pre-conference offered to join this Springer book of proceedings. All together we have 89 contributions (88 papers and one abstract) published as chapters in this book. The selection of papers for the whole ISD'2005 conference was based on reviews from the International Program Committee (IPC). All papers were reviewed following a "double blind" procedure by three independent senior academics from IPC. Papers were assessed and ranked from several criteria such as originality, relevance and presentation.

We would like to thank the authors of papers submitted to ISD'2005 conference for their efforts. We would like to express our thanks to all program chairs, track chairs and IPC members for their essential work. We would also like to thank and acknowledge the work of those behind the scenes, especially Niklas Johansson for managing the web-site and submission system MyReview and Jenny Nilsson for all valuable help with editing the papers according to the Springer book template. We are also grateful to Karlstad University in particular to Rector Christina Ullenius, Dean Stephen Hwang and Head of Division Stig Håkangård for their support with resources to be able to make the local arrangements.

Karlstad in August 2005

Anders G. Nilsson and **Remigijus Gustas**
Conference Chairs ISD'2005

Conference Organisation

General Chair

Anders G. Nilsson, Karlstad University, Sweden

Program Co-Chairs and Proceedings Editors

Anders G. Nilsson, Karlstad University, Sweden
Remigijus Gustas, Karlstad University, Sweden
Wita Wojtkowski, Boise State University, Idaho, USA
W. Gregory Wojtkowski, Boise State University, Idaho, USA
Stanisław Wrycza, University of Gdańsk, Poland
Jože Zupančič, University of Maribor, Kranj, Slovenia

Track Chairs

Sten Carlsson, Karlstad University, Sweden *(Workshops for Industry)*
Sven Carlsson, Lund University, Sweden *(Management and IT)*
Rodney Clarke, University of Wollongong, Australia *(Communication & Methods)*
Olov Forsgren, University College of Borås, Sweden *(Co-design)*
Odd Fredriksson, Karlstad University, Sweden *(Service Development)*
Göran Goldkuhl, Linköping University, Sweden *(Co-design)*
John Sören Pettersson, Karlstad University, Sweden *(Human Values of IT)*
Birger Rapp, Linköping University, Sweden *(Management and IT)*
William Song, University of Durham, United Kingdom *(Semantic Web)*
Benkt Wangler, University of Skövde, Sweden *(Requirements Engineering)*

International Program Committee (IPC)

Gary Allen, University of Huddersfield, United Kingdom
Erling S. Andersen, Norwegian School of Management, Oslo, Norway
Karin Axelsson, Linköping University, Sweden
Janis Barzdins, University of Latvia, Riga, Latvia
Juris Borzovs, University of Latvia and Riga Technical University, Latvia
Frada Burstein, Monash University, Melbourne, Australia
Rimantas Butleris, Kaunas Technical University, Lithuania
Albertas Caplinskas, Institute of Mathematics and Informatics, Vilnius, Lithuania
Antanas Cenys, Semiconductor Physics Institute, Vilnius, Lithuania

Deren Chen, Zhejiang University, Hangzhou, China
Heitor Augustus Xavier Costa, Universidade Federal de Lavras, Brazil
Stefan Cronholm, Linköping University, Sweden
Darren Dalcher, Middlesex University, London, United Kingdom
Dalé Dzemydiené, Law University, Vilnius, Lithuania
Owen Eriksson, Dalarna University College, Borlänge, Sweden
Jørgen Fischer Nilsson, Technical University of Denmark, Lyngby, Denmark
Julie Fisher, Monash University, Melbourne, Australia
Guy Fitzgerald, Brunel University, Middlesex, United Kingdom
Chris Freyberg, Massey University, Palmerston North, New Zealand
Janis Grundspenkis, Riga Technical University, Latvia
Hele-Mai Haav, Tallinn University of Technology, Estonia
G. Harindranath, University of London, United Kingdom
Igor Hawryszkiewycz, University of Technology, Sydney, Australia
Alfred Helmerich, Research Institute of Applied Technology, Munich, Germany
Joshua Huang, E-Business Technology Institute, Hong Kong, China
Juhani Iivari, University of Oulu, Finland
Mirjana Ivanovic, University of Novi Sad, Serbia and Montenegro
Marius A. Janson, University of Missouri - St. Louis, USA
Nimal Jayaratna, Curtin University, Perth, Australia
Roland Kaschek, Massey University, Palmerston North, New Zealand
Karlheinz Kautz, Copenhagen Business School, Denmark
Marite Kirikova, Riga Technical University, Latvia
Jerzy A. Kisielnicki, Warsaw University, Poland
Gábor Knapp, Budapest University of Technology and Economics, Hungary
John Krogstie, Norwegian University Science/Technology, Trondheim, Norway
Rein Kuusik, Tallinn University of Technology, Estonia
Sergei Kuznetsov, Russian Academy of Science, Moscow, Russia
Michael Lang, National University of Ireland, Galway, Ireland
Xiaoming Li, Peking University, Beijing, China
Mikael Lind, University College of Borås, Sweden
Henry Linger, Monash University, Melbourne, Australia
Björn Lundell, University of Skövde, Sweden
Audrone Lupeikiene, Institute of Mathematics and Informatics, Vilnius, Lithuania
Kalle Lyytinen, Case Western Reserve University, Cleveland, Ohio, USA
Leszek A. Maciaszek, Macquarie University, Sydney, Australia
Gábor Magyar, Budapest University of Technology and Economics, Hungary
Yannis Manolopoulos, Aristotle University, Thessaloniki, Greece
Majed Al-Mashari, King Saud University, Riyadh, Saudi Arabia
Heinrich C. Mayr, University of Klagenfurt, Austria
Ulf Melin, Linköping University, Sweden
Elisabeth Métais, CNAM University, Paris, France
Robert Moreton, University of Wolverhampton, United Kingdom
Pavol Navrat, Slovak University of Technology, Bratislava, Slovakia
Lina Nemuraite, Kaunas Technical University, Lithuania
Ovidiu Noran, Griffith University, Brisbane, Australia

Jacob Nørbjerg, Copenhagen Business School, Denmark
Eugene K. Ovsyannikov, The Academy of Sciences, St. Petersburg, Russia
Jari Palomäki, Technical University of Tampere/Pori, Finland
Malgorzata Pankowska, University of Economics in Katowice, Poland
George A. Papadopoulus, University of Cyprus, Nicosia, Cyprus
Anne Persson, University of Skövde, Sweden
Alain Pirotte, University of Louvain, Belgium
Jaroslav Pokorný, Charles University in Prague, Czech Republic
Boris Rachev, University of Rousse and Technical University of Varna, Bulgaria
Vaclav Repa, Prague University of Economics, Czech Republic
Kamel Rouibah, College of Business Administration, Safat, Kuwait University
David G. Schwartz, Bar-Ilan University, Ramat Gan, Israel
Zhongzhi Shi, Institute of Computing Technology, CAS, Beijing, China
Timothy K. Shih, Tamkang University, Tamsui, Taipeh Hsien, Taiwan
Klaas Sikkel, University of Twente, Netherlands
Guttorm Sindre, Norwegian University Science/Technology, Trondheim, Norway
Larry Stapleton, Waterford Institute of Technology, Republic of Ireland
Eberhard Stickel, Bonn University of Applied Sciences, Germany
Uldis Sukovskis, Riga Technical University, Latvia
Bo Sundgren, Statistics Sweden and Stockholm School of Economics, Sweden
Arne Sølvberg, Norwegian University Science/Technology, Trondheim, Norway
Janis Tenteris, Riga Technical University, Latvia
Jacek Unold, Wrowlaw University of Economics, Poland
Olegas Vasilecas, Vilnius Gediminas Technical University, Lithuania
Jiri Vorisek, Prague University of Economics, Czech Republic
Gottfried Vossen, University of Münster, Germany
Gert-Jan de Vreede, University of Nebraska at Omaha, USA
Roel Wieringa, University of Twente, Netherlands
Carson C. Woo, University of British Columbia, Vancouver, Canada
Aoying Zhou, Fudan University, Shanghai, China
Hai Zhuge, Institute of Computing Technology, CAS, Beijing, China

Organising Committee

Anders G. Nilsson, Karlstad University, Sweden *(Chair)*
Remigijus Gustas, Karlstad University, Sweden *(Movie Production)*
Niklas Johansson, Karlstad University, Sweden *(IT Resources)*
Ulrika Mollstedt, Karlstad University, Sweden *(Marketing)*
Jenny Nilsson, Karlstad University, Sweden *(Editing Work)*
Kurt Samuelsson, Karlstad University, Sweden *(Photographing)*
Maria Kull, Karlstad University, Sweden *(Conference Services)*
Helena Persson, Karlstad University, Sweden *(Conference Services)*
Ximena Dahlborn, Karlstad University, Sweden *(Communication)*
Nina Sundelin, Karlstad University, Sweden *(Accounting)*

Sponsors

The organisers would like to thank the following for their support:

Karlstad University
Rector's Office, Faculty Board, Division for Information Technology

City of Karlstad
Karlstads kommun

Compare Karlstad
Competence Area network for IT companies in Karlstad

Elite Hotels of Sweden
Stadshotellet Karlstad

Contents

Volume 1

Keynote Speeches

Co-design of Business and IT

Communication and Methods

Human Values of Information Technology

Service Development and IT

Volume 2

Service Development and IT (cont.)

Requirements Engineering (RE) in the IS Life-Cycle

Semantic Web Approaches and Applications

List of Authors

Change Analysis – Innovation and Evolution

Göran Goldkuhl and Annie Röstlinger

Department of Computer and Information Science,
Linköping University, Sweden (ggo, aro)@ida.liu.se

Introduction

Is information systems development (ISD) an organisationally legitimate and appropriate change measure? This is a fundamental question for information systems (IS) practitioners and researchers. It is one possible question that a change analysis (CA) tries to answer. Before one starts to develop or procure an information system, one needs to be sure that this kind of measure really will solve problems and realise goals. Change analysis is an investigation with the purpose to perform a diagnosis of a current organisational situation and a determination of appropriate change measures. A basic idea of CA is not to take ISD or any other type of change for granted. Determined change measures should be well-founded through an unbiased analysis.

Change analysis was originally developed around 1975 and was at that time an innovation in the area of information systems development and organisational change. The concept of change analysis was originally developed by Göran Goldkuhl, Mats Lundeberg and Anders G Nilsson in the ISAC research group at Stockholm University. This concept was operationalised into the method change analysis/ISAC (Lundeberg et al, 1978; 1981). In the beginnings of the 80'ies the CA concept was brought further by the works of Göran Goldkuhl and Annie Röstlinger. Partially inspired by the ISAC method, we started to develop the change analysis/SIMM method. This method has now evolved over 25 years through research, application and education.

In this paper we will describe the basic idea of CA as it emerged during the 70'ies in the ISAC group and the continual evolution of change analysis/SIMM from the beginning of the 80'ies up until now. During the 80'ies there was a heavy focus on considering change analysis as an organisational problem solving process. Several important description techniques were developed to support collective problem solving. Much effort was put into structuring the change analysis process encouraging both critical reflection and creativity.

In the early 90'ies the method was influenced by business process thinking. Process oriented notations were developed and included in the method. Important at this stage was the development of a generic business interaction model, called the BAT model (Goldkuhl, 1996). This meant also an introduction of theoretical models to be used as a driver for inquiries. During the late 90'ies this was even sharpened through the introduction of workpractice theory and its generic practice model (Goldkuhl & Röstlinger, 2003).

The structure of the CA/SIMM has evolved over the years. As more and more parts were included, we needed to make the structure more flexible. The method evolved during the 90'ies from a monolithic method structure to a flexible configuration of method components.

CA has during 30 years evolved as a perspective and a method. Some highlights from this evolution will be showed in this paper. It is beyond the scope of this paper to make any comparison with other methods. We will focus on how change analysis originated and how it has evolved since its inception.

Change Analysis as Choice of Change Measures

The use of information technology (IT) for improving organisations is today so extensive that we simply tend to take it for granted. However, the use of IT is not the only proper answer to the question "how to improve an organisation". There are other types of change measures. Development of information systems should not be taken for granted as the change measure, although it many times is an appropriate type of change.

The concept of change analysis was introduced by Lundeberg, Goldkuhl & Nilsson (1978, 1981) as a way to avoid an un-reflected decision on information systems development. One main ground and experience for this was a large action research project in mid of 70'ies. We participated and tested some of the ISAC methods for early ISD in a project in a large Swedish enterprise. After many problems in this project we eventually found out that the ISD project actually was a pseudo endeavour in order to avoid a basic conflict in the enterprise. After finding out this we first got very upset, but later we were grateful for this experience and the emerging insight: Perform always a change analysis before one starts the development of an IS.

Change analysis is to be seen as a separate activity to investigate some organisational situation in order to arrive at informed choices of action. The decided change measures should be seen as proper ways of resolving problems and obtaining the goals of the organisation. Not any change measure should be taken for granted. The understanding of different problems should guide the search for proper changes. CA should be performed in an unbiased way, which means that CA should be performed without any particular solution bias.

In relation to ISD, change analysis is seen as a separate and preceding step. Change analysis can lead to a decision to develop an information system, but it may also lead to other change measures as well as the decisions of not making any changes at all or even to the decision to close down some part of the enterprise (figure 1). If ISD is chosen as a change measure in CA, there may also be other complementary changes decided upon. This is important since IS should not be seen as a universal solution. There might be other types of problems, which need other appropriate solutions. The result of a change analysis might many times be a "package" of change measures, which complement and support each other.

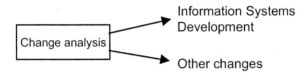

Fig. 1. Change analysis as a choice of change measures

Change Analysis as Organisational Problem Solving

Research on CA was brought further 1981 in the Human-Infological research group (HUMOR). We stared to develop the method Change Analysis/SIMM. This research continued 1990 in the research network VITS (www.vits.org).

One purpose of using CA is to create changes in organisations, i.e. changes which can be implemented as solutions of different problems. Change analysis is therefore a method for problem solving. A CA process starts with vague ideas of problems. During the CA-work the problems are considered in a thorough way to get verified, balanced and structured problem descriptions.

We conceive the process of problem solving as a creative interaction and communication process. A process with different actors involved, actors with different understandings of the workpractice as well as different understandings of goals and values (Goldkuhl & Röstlinger, 1984; 1988). A well performed problem solving process increases the opportunity to reach excellent solutions. Excellent solutions are measures that really improve the workpractice when they are implemented. According to the intentions of CA involved actors can take part in a joint problem solving process. The participation is supported by use of communication instruments in form of structured documentation (e.g. graphical diagrams). This participation of different actors facilitates the use of the work knowledge of different actors and also makes the problem solving process being transparent, well-founded and balanced. In the method design of CA we have been influenced by general models of problem solving and the phases of preparation, incubation, illumination and verification (Harman & Rheingold, 1984) can be traced in the CA-method.

Problem resolving starts with a problem, i.e. an apprehension that a problematic situation exists. Someone conceives an important difference between the actual and the desired situation, where the deviation is the problem (Dewey, 1938; Schön, 1983). But it is not only one simple problem; we often have to deal with many problems in a complex pattern. We early introduced problem diagrams as a way to handle the need for structuring complex problem situations including various problems (Röstlinger, 1981; Goldkuhl & Röstlinger, 1993). With problem diagrams a problem can be related to other problems in the problematic situation. One problem can have the function of either cause or effect or both cause and effect. A deeper understanding of the different problems and their functions gives prerequisites for finding critical problem causes and in that way getting appropriate solutions of problems. Problem analysis with problem diagrams explicitly emphasise the problem solving dimension of the CA-work.

In order to improve workpractices it is important to reduce problems but not to reduce the strength. In fact it is important to get knowledge of strong points in the organisation. Not to do these strengths away but instead they are essential to keep and improve. Strength diagrams (Röstlinger, 1993) are constructed in the same way as problem diagrams. Different strong points are identified and related in order to find critical causes and effects. By problem analysis and strength analysis the CA-work can focus on both negative and positive aspects related to the organisation and the problematic situation.

To determine if something is a problem or a strength and if a measure is a god or a bad one, it is important to have reference points to compare with. Workpactice goals are such reference points. A goal expresses what is desired. In CA it is therefore important to focus on goals; both to identify existing goals, explicit as well as implicit goals, and also to modify and develop new goals. In CA we work with goal diagrams as an analysis instrument to relate goals in terms of main goals and sub goals, and to detect conflicts between different goals (Goldkuhl & Röstlinger, 1988). It is important to settle goals for the future workpractice in order to decide on suitable measures.

One important part of the CA-work is to get knowledge of what problems to reduce and what strengths to use. This is called change requirements and is a step forward to the measures. A certain change measure is a concrete way to improve the workpractice, but there can be several different ways of improvement for one change requirement. It is important to have the possibilities to choose between different ways of change actions. Therefore identification and formulation of change requirements are important before the treatment of measures. This part of the CA is summarised in a document called condensed evaluation and is including the most important goals, problems and strengths together with the formulated change requirements.

To formulate change requirements is the final step in the diagnosis phase of the CA process (Goldkuhl & Röstlinger, 2003). A performed diagnosis should lead forward to a decision of what to do if something really needs to be done. A diagnosis giving adequate information about significant aspects of the workpractice is a prerequisite for useable measures that fulfil goals by resolving problems and maintaining and developing strengths.

Change Analysis as Business Process Development

Already in 1986, some years before the business process wave started, the first steps in this direction were taken for the CA/SIMM method. Up until then, we had used the Activity graphs from ISAC (Lundeberg et al, 1981) as a method part in CA/SIMM. The working procedure of ISAC A-graphs was a top-down de-compositional approach based on systems theory. During a large industrial project in 1986, a new alternative notation was developed (action diagrams), which replaced A-graphs. Instead of a de-compositional approach, we chose to work mainly "bottom-all"; modelling actions and the flow of information and material (Goldkuhl, 1992). Action diagrams use the basic modelling concepts of action, performer and object.

Action diagrams became very appropriate for a horizontal analysis of business activities; as a kind of workflow analysis that has become a backbone for process oriented approaches. One main trigger for this kind of process orientation was the seminal paper by Hammer (1990). A focus on horizontal business processes and on customer satisfaction has since then influenced development of organisations and information systems.

CA/SIMM emerged during the 90'ies as a method for business process development (Lind, 1996; Röstlinger et al, 1997; Lind & Goldkuhl, 1997; Christiansson, 1998).

The conception of a business process is of course vital for such methods. In many business process approaches there seems to be a bias towards "business processes as transformation of input objects to output objects for customers". This transformation view has been challenged by a coordination view, where the interaction between customers and suppliers is emphasised (Keen, 1997). In CA/SIMM we adopt a combined view, acknowledging business processes as both workflow and interaction (Goldkuhl & Röstlinger, 2003).

A theoretical basis for the business process analysis in CA/SIMM inquiries emerged through the BAT model (Goldkuhl, 1996; Goldkuhl & Lind, 2004). BAT (Business interAction & Transaction framework) describes in different generic models how a customer and a supplier interact with each other. The BAT models describe business interaction in terms of generic business phases where business proposals, commitments, fulfilments and assessments are exchanged between customer and supplier (figure 2). BAT can be used as a template or a reference model when analyzing business processes in a CA. It helps the participants to direct their attention towards important aspects; as e.g. how proposals are made, how customers and suppliers come to agreements through negotiation and contracting, how agreements are fulfilled in delivery and payment processes, how both customers and suppliers get satisfied through a business transaction.

A business process oriented CA is operationalised through different modelling techniques. Action diagrams, mentioned above, play an important role. This notation makes it possible to obtain a very detailed and comprehensive process model of the organisation describing sequences, conditions, alternatives, triggers and other parts of the action logic. The detailed process descriptions in action diagrams can be abstracted and aggregated to process diagrams. These describe sequential sub-processes but also alternative variant processes (Lind & Goldkuhl, 1997). Process diagrams are often structured according to the phase structure of the BAT model. The interaction between customer and supplier is modelled in cowork diagrams (Röstlinger et al, 1997). This notation describes, in an essential way, how customer and supplier create and fulfil business agreements. In these ways CA/SIMM can be used to analyse and (re)design business processes as both interaction and workflow.

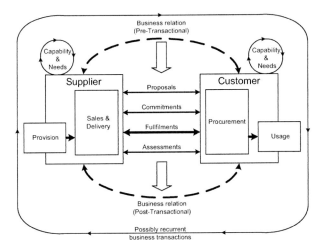

Fig. 2. BAT business transaction model (Goldkuhl & Lind, 2004)

Change Analysis as Practice-Theory Driven Development

Theoretical and methodological development concerning CA/SIMM went on hand in hand. As described above, there was an integral development of the business process notion and supporting modelling techniques. The combined business process view (transformation and coordination) was further developed during the late 90'ies. This combined view was the first step towards a multi-functional view of organisations as practice systems (Goldkuhl et al, 2002). Other important aspects of organisations were added and integrated towards one comprehensive and generic model of workpractices (ibid; Goldkuhl & Röstlinger, 2003).

The generic workpractice model (figure 3) describes a workpractice in terms of actions, actors and action objects as results and preconditions. It acknowledges a workpractice as a transformative practice, i.e. transforming some "raw material" (base) into some product (result) aimed for the clients ("customers") of the practice. It also acknowledges a workpractice as governed by a horizontal coordination, i.e. some assignments (product order) from the clients or some proxy. These two aspects are covered by the combined business process view as described above. Besides these there are several other aspects that are important for workpractices. There is also a vertical coordination, with assignments from management. Instruments and descriptive and procedural knowledge are utilised in the workpractice. We also acknowledge the normative context consisting of norms and judgements that govern the workpractice. Financial flows play also essential roles.

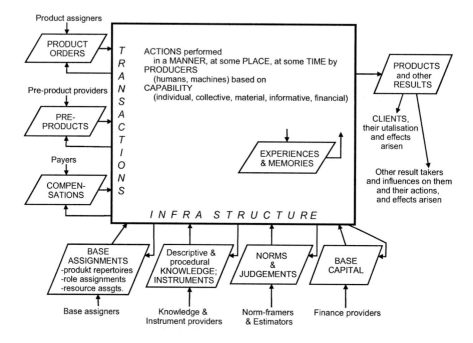

Fig. 3. The generic model of workpractices

A workpractice consists of actions performed by human and artificial producers. Such actions, situated in time and place, are carried out according to the institutionalised manner of the workpractice. Actions within a workpractice are based on performers' capabilities that are established and evolving through a continual learning and conscious development.

This workpractice theory affects CA/SIMM in several ways. At a very early stage of a CA process, workpractice definitions are made (ibid). The different categories of the generic workpractice model are used as a template. The workpractice definitions will guide the CA inquirers to focus crucial aspects of the workpractice. To perform a CA/SIMM inquiry has now become not only method-driven but also theory-driven.

The introduction of workpractice theory has made CA more focused. Later parts of CA, as e.g. problem analysis and strength analysis will be governed and informed by the workpractice definitions made. This makes it appropriate to direct attention towards important workpractice characteristics, as e.g. product quality, clarity and reciprocity in assignments, efficiency in transformation, coordination and interoperability between different sub-practices, adequacy and congruence of capabilities, continual learning, relations and congruencies between different assignments and different norms.

Change Analysis as Flexible Use of Method Components

The CA method implies prescriptions for use by the CA investigator. The method tells the method user something about what to do and how to do it when investigating workpractices. But also important is when to do it, i.e. in what order shall something be done. The original CA/SIMM had a rather strict sequential order of work steps. The norm was to start with problems then continue with actions/processes and goals and end up with change requirements and change measures. The method structure was fixed and the method was treated as a monolith, i.e. one integrated wholeness with predetermined work steps.

Over the years we have expanded the CA method. Gradually more and more aspects have been incorporated within the method. With many aspects and many types of notations it was no longer so obvious to perform the inquiry by steps taken always in the same order. We also noticed that different actors used CA/SIMM in quite different ways. In 1988 a book on change analysis was published in Swedish (Goldkuhl & Röstlinger, 1988). This book increased the use of CA/SIMM and also the use of CA/SIMM by different actors and in different situations. We always have recommended a situationally adapted use of CA/SIMM. It is important to focus the issue at stake and to put the studied workpractice in the foreground and the method use in the background.

All these things together increased the need for a more open and flexible structure of the CA/SIMM method. But the need for a redesigned method also forced us to direct attention to the method concept. What is a method for workpractices investigation and development? According to our view a method implies prescriptive rules to support actors performing investigations. These rules are based on some perspective and purposes. A method can consist of separate method components. Each component consists at least of procedural rules (what and how to do), notational rules (what and how to document), concepts (what and how to talk and think about a phenomenon/a task/an issue); Röstlinger & Goldkuhl (1994). Confer figure 4.

This clarification of the method concept was important for the way we changed CA/SIMM. The method changed from a monolithic method structure to a more flexible configuration consisting of different method components. The CA/SIMM was now designed as a basic block structure related in sequence including decision points together with different flexible components (figure 5); cf also Goldkuhl & Röstlinger (2003).

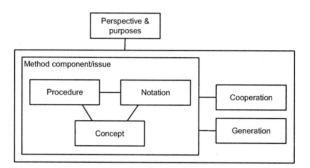

Fig. 4. Method concept

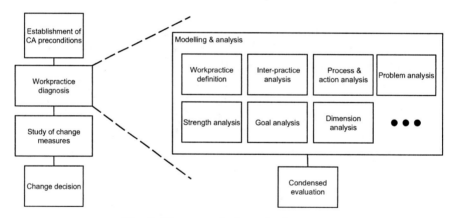

Fig. 5. Change analysis method structure

The main basic blocks are "workpractice diagnosis" and "study of change measures". Each block contains of several separate method components. The investigators have the possibility to choose between the different components in order to get the best support in the current inquiry situation. E.g. in the block workpractice diagnosis there are among others the components workpractice definition, inter-practice analysis and processes & action analysis. These components imply different foci on the workpractice and they can partly be used as complement as well as substitute to each other.

The more flexible structure with basic exchangeable method components gave the CA method a more generic function. CA/SIMM and different generic parts of CA/SIMM can be used by many different actors in a variety of inquiry situations. Different aspects are differently important in different situations. The purpose is to support an efficient and situationally adapted use of the components. The use of CA/SIMM shall enhance a focused creativity and it shall contribute to a transparent inquiry including both communicative quality and decision rationality (Habermas, 1984; Goldkuhl & Röstlinger, 1984; 1988; Forester, 1999).

Conclusions

The CA/SIMM method has evolved over many years. Through many publications and education at several universities the method has been widely spread and used. It has been used by many practitioners in many real life applications and in many different settings.

The method has also been used and tested by us and several research colleagues in many action research projects. Besides this empirical grounding, we have also performed internal grounding (continual revision of concepts and structure in order to make the method more coherent) and theoretical grounding (relating the method explicitly to different theoretical sources). It is through this kind of combined empirical, internal and theoretical grounding (Goldkuhl, 2004) that the CA/SIMM method has evolved over the years.

References

Christiansson MT (1998) Interaction Analysis – An Important Part of Inter-Organisational Business and IS Development. In: Proc of the 3rd Intl Workshop on the Language Action Perspective, Jönköping Int. Business School

Dewey J (1938) Logic: The Theory of Inquiry. Henry Holt, New York

Forester J (1999) The Deliberative Practitioner – Encouraging participatory planning processes. MIT Press, Cambridge, Mass.

Goldkuhl G (1992) Contextual Activity Modelling of Information Systems. In: Proc of the 3rd International Working Conference on Dynamic Modelling of information systems, Noordwijkerhout

Goldkuhl G (1996) Generic Business Frameworks and Action Modelling. In: Proc of Language Action Perspective'96, Springer Verlag

Goldkuhl G (2004) Design Theories in Information Systems – a Need for Multigrounding. Journal of IT Theory and Application (JITTA), 6(2) pp 59-72

Goldkuhl G, Lind M (2004) Developing e-Interactions – a Framework for Business Capabilities and Exchanges. In: Proc of the 12th European Conference on Information Systems (ECIS2004), Turku

Goldkuhl G, Röstlinger A (1984) The Legitimacy of Information Systems Development – a Need for Change Analysis. In: Proc of IFIP Conference Human-Computer Interaction, London

Goldkuhl G, Röstlinger A (1988) Förändringsanalys - Arbetsmetodik och förhållningssätt för goda förändringsbeslut. Studentlitteratur, Lund [In Swedish]

Goldkuhl G, Röstlinger A (1993) Joint Elicitation of Problems: An Important Aspect of Change Analysis. In: Avison D et al (eds) Human, Organizational and Social Dimensions of Information Systems Development, North-Holland

Goldkuhl G, Röstlinger A (2003) The Significance of Workpractice Diagnosis: Socio-Pragmatic Ontology and Epistemology of Change Analysis. In: Proc of the Intl workshop on Action in Language, Organisations and Information Systems (ALOIS-2003), Linköping University

Goldkuhl G, Röstlinger A, Braf E (2002) Organisations as Practice Systems – Integrating Knowledge, Signs, Artefacts and Action. In: Liu K et al (eds) Organisational Semiotics: Evolving a Science of IS, Kluwer, Boston

Habermas J (1984) The Theory of Communicative Action 1- Reason and the Rationalization of Society, Polity Press, Cambridge

Hammer M (1990) Reengineering Work: Don't Automate, Obliterate. Harvard Business Review, pp 104-112

Harman W, Rheingold H (1984) Higher Creativity. Tarcher, Los Angeles

Keen PGW (1997) The Process Edge. Harvard Business School Press

Lind M (1996) Business Process Thinking in Practice. In Proc of 19th IRIS-Conference, Göteborg University

Lind M, Goldkuhl G (1997) Reconstruction of Different Business Processes - a Theory and Method Driven Analysis. Proc of the 2nd Intl Workshop on Language Action Perspective (LAP97), Eindhoven University of Technology

Lundeberg M, Goldkuhl G, Nilsson A (1978) A systematic approach to information systems development - I. Introduction; - II. Problem and data oriented methodology, Information Systems, vol 4, pp 1-12, 93-118

Lundeberg M, Goldkuhl G, Nilsson A (1981) Information Systems Development - A Systematic Approach. Prentice-Hall, Englewood Cliffs

Röstlinger A (1982) Problem Analysis - a Methodological Outline. In Goldkuhl G, Kall C-O (eds) Report from the 5th Scandinavian Research Seminar on Systemeering, Chalmers Unversity of Technology, Göteborg

Röstlinger A (1993) Styrkeanalys – Ett arbetssätt för att tillvarata positiva aspekter i verksamheter, VITS, IDA, Linköping University [In Swedish]

Röstlinger A, Goldkuhl G (1994) Generisk flexibilitet – På väg mot en komponentbaserad metodsyn, VITS, IDA, Linköping University [In Swedish]

Röstlinger A, Goldkuhl G, Hedström K, Johansson R (1997) Processorienterat förändringsarbete inom omsorgen. Kvalitet 97, Göteborg [In Swedish]

Schön D (1983) The reflective practitioner – How Professionals Think in Action. Basic Books, New York

The Computer – The Businessman's Window to His Enterprises

Hans Karlander

Procuritas Partners KB, Stockholm, Sweden (www.procuritas.com)
karlander@procuritas.se

Background

Hans Karlander has a Master of Science in Economics and Business Administration from the Stockholm School of Economics. Hans Karlander is co-owner and managing partner of Procuritas and joined the partnership in 1995. Karlander started his career at Electrolux in 1977 and has since then among other been Executive Vice President at IndustriFinans, Executive Vice President at Swedbank and Under-Secretary of State at the Swedish Ministry of Industry and Commerce before joining Procuritas.

Hans Karlander is invited as key note speaker to represent the business world at the information systems development conference ISD'2005. Drawing from real-life experience insight is given into the life of an ordinary computer user as well as an introduction to the large and growing private equity industry. Thoughts and rationale behind investments in companies and how IT is used to create value are presented.

Procuritas

The large increase in pension capital worldwide has changed the financial landscape fundamentally. Enormous sums of money have been accumulated and are under management. Today, as an illustration, 40 percent of American common stock is owned by pension funds and retirement funds. Asset management is based on modern theories developed by Markowitz, Nobel laureate for his theories on portfolio selection. Capital is allocated into different classes and sub-classes, of which private equity is a sub-class to alternative investments. Pension funds globally invested over 62 billion US dollars in the alternative asset class during 2004, including 17 billion dollars in private equity. In the US, some eight percent of assets under management by institutional investors are placed in private equity. This is expected to increase by one percentage point during 2005, translating into an additional 160 million dollars allocated to private equity. Europe is following the US example.

Private Equity refers to active ownership in non-listed companies through majority positions as opposed to the sleeping ownership of latent institutions in listed companies. Solid businesses with great potential are acquired and held for a period of normally five to six years, representing an active development cycle, during which pressure is put on creating value in the company. It is worth noting that by creating value for investors in the form of financial return on their investments, value is also created for a number of parties as employments become safer, local suppliers get larger orders, distributors receive increased business, and the municipality can collect more income. In order to build a more valuable company information technology is used in two steps. Firstly as a tool for coordinating activities and additionally to create value by itself. It is in this setting that Procuritas acts.

Procuritas was founded in 1986 as the first Nordic private equity company. Procuritas buys, develops, and subsequently sells companies. The company has 25 employees in Stockholm and Copenhagen and is owned by seven partners. Procuritas has over 350 million euro under management that is invested into the so called "mid-segment" of the market – well established companies with proper businesses, but smaller than the giants. Currently Procuritas owns ten corporate groups with combined sales of almost two billion euro with over 12 000 employees. The specialised niche in which Procuritas is active is called management buyouts (MBO). In an MBO, a company is acquired together with the management of the company, aligning management interests with the owners'.

Value Creation

In traditional early-1990's MBOs a large part of the value created originated from financial improvements, and less from operational optimisation and strategic development. However, high historical profitability in the private equity industry has attracted competition and led to a maturing of the industry. The globalisation trends have also reached the private equity industry with international actors entering local markets. The inflow of more private equity funds increases the supply of capital while increasing the demand for acquisition targets. In line with classical economic theory this means it is no longer possible to buy cheap and earn money through only financial leverage and general strategies. Today, genuine insight into the companies' operations and development potential is required to add value. To understand the development potential it is imperative to get a deeper understanding of all aspects of the operations of a company, of which IT is one parameter of great importance, before the acquisition. Therefore, when analysing a potential investment it is vital to understand the current level of IT used, and how IT can be utilised to improve the existing business, manage the investment and subsequently develop services, new products and the business itself.

Relating back to Markowitz (1991), a rational investor maximises the expected return at a given risk level. As private equity investments are riskier than, say, government bonds, investors require a higher return on their money. Typically, investors demand a yearly return of 20 to 25 percent from private equity investments. To meet this target, real value must be created in the investment targets. There are many factors that make an investment attractive, e.g. unique products, interesting markets with growth potential and experienced management with proven results. The single most important factor for creating value is active ownership. It is only through acquiring majority positions in un-listed companies that the owners have the power to really change the company and reach the financial goals. By removing a company from the stock exchanges, fundamental improvements and restructurings can be undertaken without having to worry about meeting the quarterly financial targets set up by the market. Instead the owners can focus on long-term returns rather than short-term. One of the most important tools for an active owner to meet these goals is information technology. However, IT on its own does not automatically add value, but must be used as support for the owner and management.

The business of a company is built up by numerous activities, ranging from the actual production of the products (for a manufacturing company) and logistics systems to marketing and human resource management. In line with classical Michael Porter competition theory, each individual activity can largely be copied by competitors, but it is the specific combination of activity sets that makes a company unique (Porter 1980, 1985). Information technology is often vital to coordinate activities and create a strong, competitive company.

Prerequisites for Successful IT Investments

To meet the return targets and create so much value in a relatively short period of time demands a clear strategy and IT as a part of this, creating durable companies with a competitive advantage. Procuritas is not involved in "day-trading" or speculation – high demands are placed and real value must be created to deliver superior returns to investors.

In the real world, the majority of IT investments are locked into operating and maintaining existing applications. Only ten percent are available for investment outside existing applications, and it is these ten percent that can be invested into new means of creating value, rather than optimising existing processes. Also, a very large share of investments, including but not limited to IT, create no or even destroy value. Surveys by Kaplan and Norton (2004) show that as much as 70 percent of organisations that introduce CRM software cannot show results from these investments. To capture the full potential benefits, each investment, IT or not, must be accompanied by organisational change and development of human capital competencies.

The levels of IT investments are twofold: the first level utilising information technology to improve and coordinate existing activities and the second level using IT to create value by itself. Common to both levels is that data gathering and processing only have a value if the information is correctly interpreted and used. Translated into Procuritas' endeavours, a successful IT investment can only be reached through: (i) strong leadership by management and board of directors; (ii) insight into that implementation of IT must have personnel and organisational consequences; and (iii) the above being used as a strategic goal.

Good to Great

Starting with the first point above, the importance of leadership is analysed. With data transactions becoming virtually instantaneous and cost free, the management of multinational corporations is facilitated. Together with reduced transportation costs (sending a container from China to Europe costs around 1 000 dollars) and movements towards free trade, the geographical location of a company has less relevance. The world is full of good companies, but through the increasing internationalisation and competition from China and India, good is simply not good enough. The old economies have to move from good to great in order to survive. This is true for all sectors that face international competition. Also within the academia, researchers are faced with direct competition from the Far East within their own fields of expertise. Also, it is up to the researchers to provide solutions for the old Western economies if we are to continue to move up the food chain, or at least maintain our positions.

"I have but the simplest taste – I am always satisfied with the best"
– Oscar Wilde

Instead of comparing with best practice the new "buzz-word" is next practice as put forward by professors Prahalad and Ramaswamy (2004) in a recent book. This means that when comparing to the best practice one can only become second best. It is only by striving to develop the next practice through innovation that a company can excel. Jim Collins (2001), author of the best selling book *From Good to Great* started with 1 435 large US companies, examined their performance over 40 years and subsequently found eleven companies that became great and outperformed the others. To be classified as great, a company had to produce average cumulative stock returns several times greater than the general market over a sustained period of time (15 years). He named these eleven companies the Good-to-Great companies and compared them to see what they had in common.

Collins (2001) found seven principles that the group of great companies all had in common: level 5 leadership, disciplined thought, confrontation of brutal facts, hedgehog concept, culture of discipline, flywheel momentum, and preservation of core and stimulation of progress. The common denominator is leadership. It is at the highest level of leadership that a person can take a company from "merely" being good to really being great. One of Collin's key points is *first who – then what*; leadership should come before strategy. It is more important to decide on who should carry out a task than what the actual task should be. In fact, everything is secondary to leadership. Only in the hands of a competent leader, can IT provide the information necessary to form rational decisions and also enable the control of a large organisation and coordination of numerous activities.

Information Technology Investments in the Real World

Continuing with the second and third points relating to the prerequisites for successful IT investments, some concepts must be introduced. Kaplan and Norton (2004) define "information capital" as databases, information systems, networks, and technology infrastructure. Information capital is further divided into four categories: transformational applications, analytic applications, transaction processing applications and technology infrastructure. This concept is used as a reference point henceforth when discussing the use of information technology in the Procuritas portfolio companies.

Before Procuritas makes an acquisition, the level of IT in the company is analysed. Furthermore, the effectiveness of management and its ability to implement what Procuritas perceives as important are evaluated. There are two central points when analysing the level of information technology: IT as support for increasing efficiency of the current operations, including financial control and rationalisations, and how a new strategic course for the company can be set and given strategic IT support.

Table 1a. The Procuritas portfolio companies per July 2005

	DISA	Expan	Thermia
Industry	Moulding machines	Building material	Energy
Turnover	€155M	€77M	€55M
Employees	342	599	345
Geographical areas of operations	Global	Denmark Germany	Sweden Finland
International exposure	Global	Denmark Germany	Europe

Table 1b. The Procuritas portfolio companies per July 2005

	Wermland Paper	Brio Educational + Printel	Bravida
Industry	Kraft paper	Wholesaler of provisions to pre-schools and schools	Installation services
Turnover	€100M	€90M	€998M
Employees	418	186	8 500
Geographical areas of operations	Sweden	Sweden Norway Denmark Finland	Sweden Norway Denmark
International exposure	Global	Nordic region	Sweden Norway Denmark

Table 1c. The Procuritas portfolio companies per July 2005

	Sandå	Axenti	NSG
Industry	Painting	Manufacturing conglomerate	Car transportation
Turnover	€74M	€50M	€43M
Employees	1 200	235	389
Geographical areas of operations	Sweden	Sweden Norway Denmark Finland	Sweden Denmark
International exposure	Sweden	Global	Sweden Denmark

The portfolio companies of Procuritas cover a wide range of industries and face varying degrees of internationalisation (see Table 1a-c). These companies naturally rely on IT to different extents and vary in how far they have come in their strategic positions. As the companies have little in common (other than being, hopefully, good investments) they have different levels of IT, different needs and different opportunities. An example of the diversity is the variety in business lines: there are four manufacturing companies, three service companies, one company within wholesale and one processing company. Also, the companies face varying degrees of internationalisation: for example DISA has production, procurement and sales worldwide while Sandå is a strictly local Swedish business. To illustrate how information technology is viewed in a typical investment case, the acquisition of Wermland Paper is analysed.

Wermland Paper comprises two mills in the forests of Värmland. Together they have a turnover of 100 million euro with over 400 employees. The mills produce unbleached kraft paper, used for among other carrier bags, packaging and masking paper. Within unbleached kraft paper, Wermland Paper is active on three substantially different markets. After two decades of large profits, the two paper mills had faced gradual reduction in profitability during the four years prior to the sale of the company in 2003. Procuritas' investment hypothesis was that it should be possible to bring the mills back to the traditional profitability levels. Bearing this in mind an extensive pre-acquisition company analysis was undertaken.

Just like it is not the individual activities by a company but rather the entire set of activities that make it unique, individual components of a pre-acquisition analysis are normally not difficult to obtain; there are always experts that can be hired as consultants to provide specific information.

Rather, it is putting all the pieces of information together and forming a solid opinion on whether the company should be acquired or not that makes the analysis inimitable.

The Wermland Paper analysis showed a great potential for cost reductions, a neglected market side and lack of strategy for the future. Also, it was found that the pulp and paper industry stands before great changes: South-East Asia and Eastern Europe are surging as competitors, and the markets in Europe and the US are changing profoundly. The Wermland Paper mills have developed well without extensive investments in IT, but in order to stay competitive and survive in the new market conditions, Wermland Paper needed a clear strategy with IT implemented to a much larger extent. Swedish industry has a high level of investments into information technology, and especially the forest and paper industry early implemented IT. However, in this industry dominated by engineers, IT has mostly been implemented in production, while neglected in marketing, finance and management. This also became evident in the pre-acquisition analysis of Wermland Paper, where IT was found to suffice as production support, but poor for financial control and non-existent towards customers.

In the investment case an eight point programme was identified to improve the low profitability of the company. Part of this programme included *transaction process* applications such as quality control systems and manufacturing resource planning as well as *analytic* applications, e.g. inventory analysis. Less than two years down the road, the effects of the programme are evident. By implementing IT on the operational level, personnel has been reduced by twelve percent, inventory has been greatly lowered and cost reductions amounting to some ten percent of revenues have been realised. Maintaining the strong focus by management and the active owners on the strategy laid out at acquisition, the eight point programme continues with further investments in for example supply-chain-management, manufacturing and financial management. Once profitability is up and "the fire has been put out" the attention can be drawn to creating further value through investing in *transformational* applications. A central component for these applications is a portal that brings together for example just-in-time delivery systems and packaging tracking. With the support of IT, the organisation has also become less hierarchical. Production managers can now directly access information such as costs and prices for their own accounts. These accounts are also linked to individual budgets so that it is clearer on a lower level, and to more people, how specific units and projects are faring.

To conclude, in a short period of time, remarkably large rationalisations have been made possible through *transaction processing* applications. However, the most important need for the company was new, strong leadership. In conjunction with the acquisition, a new CEO was recruited and since then new management has been built, together with a new and qualified board of directors. Management and board of directors have now started working in strategies that among other include *transformational* applications, such as the portal mentioned above.

Looking at the rest of the Procuritas portfolio, it is evident that depending on how far the companies have come in their development, value creating information technology applications play varying roles. In the three service companies, transaction processing applications are difficult to implement while in the other companies (manufacturing, processing and wholesale) transaction processing applications are vital for cost reductions. In all companies, analytic applications are important for Procuritas as owners, as correct information is essential to manage the companies.

Conclusions

As active private equity owners, the first level of information technology investments, *transaction processing* applications, and to some extent *analytic* applications, can be implemented to under a strong management rather quickly increase profitability. These types of IT-applications generally contribute to enhanced productivity and thus increased profits. However, IT investments create no, or even destroy, value if uncoupled with a clear strategy of what the company should achieve. To ensure that relevant strategies come into place, there must be active owners that put the proper management into place together with a competent board. In the words of Jim Collins (2001), who must come before what, relying on meritocracy when recruiting (whether internal or external). Information technology is an important tool in the world of private equity, but only as a component, and always subordinated to leadership. Management must secure the implementation of the strategy and IT investment(s) both through adapting the organisation and the human resources. By providing a clear strategy and supporting management, private equity companies enable successful implementation of *transformational* applications that support new business models, generate new revenue and contribute to value creation.

In preparation for this speech the present thinking on business strategy, governance and the role of IT has been consulted. It is somewhat gratifying to find that the methods developed by Procuritas are in line with what academia endorses. One can see that what has always been perceived as important by successful private equity firms is confirmed by modern management and governance research. The map seems to coincide with reality.

References

Collins J (2001) Good to Great – Why Some Companies Make the Leap and Others Don't. HarperCollins Publishers, New York
Kaplan RS, Norton DP (2004) Strategy Maps: Converting Intangible Assets into Tangible Outcomes. Harvard Business School Press, Boston Massachusetts
Markowitz HM (1991) Portfolio Selection: Efficient Diversification of Investments. Blackwell Publishers, Oxford UK, 2nd edn
Porter ME (1980) Competitive Strategy – Techniques for Analyzing Industries and Competitors. The Free Press, New York
Porter ME (1985) Competitive Advantage – Creating and Sustaining Superior Performance. The Free Press, New York
Prahalad CK, Ramaswamy V (2004) The Future of Competition: Co-Creating Unique Value with Customers. Harvard Business School Press, Boston Massachusetts

Challenges in New Service Development and Value Creation through Service

Bo Edvardsson, Anders Gustafsson and Bo Enquist

Service Research Center/CTF, Karlstad University, Sweden
(Bo.Edvardsson, Anders.Gustafsson, Bo.Enquist)@kau.se

Introduction and Aim

Many companies are at a crossroad where they try to stay competitive by creating customer value through service development. This combination produces the prerequisites that are necessary for favorable customer experiences. Our focus is not on issues directly related to the new service development process as such, which has often been the case in the service literature (Gupta and Wilemon 1990; Martin and Horne 1993, 1995; Edvardsson et al., 1995, 2000; John and Storey 1998; Scheuing and Johnson 1989; Kelly and Storey 2000). First we focus on challenges in the new business landscape where service competition, IT, and value creation through service, put pressure on companies and markets to develop service offerings preferred by demanding customers. Secondly, we focus on service value creation through favorable customer experiences.

Our aim is to identify and discuss success factors in new service development as a basis for future research. The point of departure is the service research literature and the results from our studies on the development and design of new services. The empirical illustrations are mainly from IKEA, a company we have studied during the last four years.

We begin the article with a discussion on service competition and service strategy. We continue with a discussion on the experience concept and experience-based service value. In the third section we focus on success factors when developing new services, and finally we present some food for thought about challenges companies can expect in the future.

Service Competition and Strategy

Companies are searching for new and improved ways to differentiate their market offerings in order to stay competitive and make a profit (Shaw and

Ivins 2002). We argue that the move toward services is a fundamental re-action to the evolution of competition and one of the major ways for com-panies to differentiate their market offerings, customer relationships, and organizations by creating new customer value through service. Technology infusion in service organizations is one fundamental trend in service com-petition which has resulted in Self-Service Technology (SST) and a wide range of other applications of Information and Communication Technolo-gies (ICT). Many e-services can be discussed in terms of network external-ities (Liebowitz and Margolis 2004). IBM has substituted its 'e' (since e-business is almost ubiquitous and everyone knows what it is) with 'on', to symbolize its 'on demand business services'. Many services become time and place independent so that customers can use or consume services at a time and place of their convenience.

Grove et al., (2003) found in their study that there is a need to explore the growing interplay between services and information technology, and particularly the Internet and e-commerce that it has spawned. The experts suggest that there is a need to explore, in more detail, the role that technol-ogy plays in the communication, delivery, sale, and support of services, the nature of the e-service encounter, the nature of service excellence when the service is technology-based, and the impact of high-technology service dimension on the demand for high-touch features. Nilsson (2005) dis-cusses the future of information systems development (ISD) and argues that

"ISD will be oriented to model how companies will operate in the on-coming virtual markets. The modeling area of interest will become how different kinds of inter-organizational IT-systems can support electronic commerce and web-based business solutions" (p. 31).

We often hear about service infusion in manufacturing. For instance, Ford Motor Company claims that:

"If you go back to even a very short while ago, our whole idea of a customer was that we would wholesale a car to a dealer, the dealer would then sell the car to the customer, and we hoped we never heard from the customer – because if we did, it meant something was wrong".

Ford continues and states:

"Today we want to establish a dialogue with the customer throughout the entire ownership experience. We want to talk to and touch our custom-ers at every step of the way. We want to be a consumer products and ser-vices company that just happens to be in the automotive business" (Garten 2001 p. 137).

We believe that service and service constellations, including favorable customer experiences but not physical goods, are fueling modern economic growth. A physical product of good quality can be seen as a prerequisite. It is an entry ticket for a company to start to compete. But there are other traits necessary for success in a market. Even the niches become host to similar competitors where quality is a given and price is the main way to compete. New technology and service outsourcing is making it possible to produce services in parts of the world where labor is cheaper.

Products become platforms for services and experiences which render value. This evolution has forced companies to look downstream, or down the value chain, to the possibility of competing through the services that surround their products or use the products as resources in service and experience concepts. Rather than sell the cake mix, you help the customers create a memorable birthday party. For a company to go from a pure product company to a company that stages services and experiences is quite a challenge.

A company needs to develop new service processes and a service structure that contains and supports a number of different and changing customer processes. This will affect the supplier relationship. A company will have to think in terms of allied production, by not only working closely together, but also relying on suppliers to invent and deliver superior value to the company's customers. In other words, outsource everything that is not a core component of the company. A key term is networking, where different competencies are combined to deliver superior value to customers.

Furthermore, companies too often become locked into their own business models. These companies are reluctant to modify their own business by installing new technology, products, services, or distribution channels. They become so focused on providing customers with what they wanted yesterday that they miss the opportunities to create markets for tomorrow. We suggest that improving the prerequisites for new service development processes is one of the ways to stay in business. We will focus on the creation of favorable customer experiences and experience-based value. The focus is not only on value from physical products and services per se but also on experiences. Customers become co-creators of attractive experiences which may result in lasting customer value and long-term relationships. 'Value-in-use' (Vargo and Lusch 2004a, b) and 'consumption judgments' are related concepts. In both cases the traditional focus on cognitive evaluation has been extended to include service-elicited emotions and experiences.

The Experience Concept and Experience-Based Service Value

In their book "The Future of Competition", Prahalad and Ramaswamy (2004) focus on co-creating unique value with customers, and argue that "value is now centered in the experiences of consumers" (p. 137) and not just embedded in products and services. Customer delight and customer perceived value are linked to memorable, *favorable customer experiences* (Pine and Gillmore 1999; Johnson and Gustafson 2000; Berry et al., 2002).

Customers must experience the intangible service in order to understand it. Unlike goods, the intangibility of services makes it more difficult for customers to imagine, desire, and thus assess the value. Customers purchasing professional tax advice have no knobs to turn, buttons to push, or pictures to see. Customers' perceptions of risk tend to be high for services because services cannot be touched, smelled, tasted, or tried on before purchase. Customers can test-drive a new automobile and kick the tires, but to try a new vacation resort they must first register as guests (Reichheld and Sasser 1990).

Traditionally, the experience concept is used to describe and understand experience-intensive situations, where people integrate what they perceive and encounter according to a script during and after consumption. Customers' fantasies are staged and, at least to some extent, controlled in relation to attractive solutions where products and services become platforms for experiences, not just a means to an end in a logical and calculative way.

We define a service experience as the service encounter and/or service process that creates the customer's cognitive, emotional, and behavioral responses resulting in a mental mark or a memory (in line with Johnston and Clark 2000). Some of the experiences are especially favorable and others are particularly unfavorable. Both tend to stay in the customer's (long-term) memory. We call these experiences memorable.

Berry et al., (2002) emphasize the necessity of "managing the total customer experience" when discussing service experiences. They advocate recognizing clues of experience related to functionality and clues of experience related to emotions. According to Voss (2003), organizations focus to a higher degree on experiences to engage customers, to create and support brands, and to differentiate themselves (ibid. p. 26).

Customers respond to an event in certain ways in order to maintain positive emotions and to avoid negative emotions (Stauss and Neuhaus 1997).

"During the consumption experience, various types of emotions can be elicited, and these customer emotions convey important information on how the customer will ultimately assess the service encounter and subsequently, the overall relationship quality" (Wong 2004 p. 369).

Hence, the more we know about drivers of negative and positive customer emotions, the better we understand the focus in developing new services with designed-in experiences, and the better we can manage service competition. Emotions are expressed at critical incidents when customers perceive disappointment or delight. Customer feed-back, complaints, and praise (or compliment) contain information about positive and negative emotions. Emotions are evoked during service consumption or use. The narrative approach is a useful way of collecting data; it describes customers' emotions when exposed to situations creating both favorable and unfavorable customer experiences.

Critical Success Factors When Developing New Services

Our findings, from a number of research projects and publications (Edvardsson et al., 1995, 2000; Johnson and Gustafsson 2000; Gustafsson and Johnson 2003) about how to successfully develop and launch new services, are suggested below.

1. Develop a Deep and Thorough Understanding of the Customer and what Creates Value through the Lens of the Customer

Understanding the customer is the key to commercial success. To survive, you need to *understand* the problems and needs of the customers who use your products and services, and to use that information to create a competitive advantage. It is not enough to simply organize a couple of focus groups and assume that you understand your customers' needs. Understanding requires a much deeper knowledge of the following:

- customers' needs, priorities, requirements, expectations, and preferences
- customers' service context, or when, what, how, why, and where the service is used
- customers' knowledge and capability to use the service
- customers' values and cognitive structures
- customers' experiences, emotions, and behaviors when using the services

Unfortunately, many companies outsource the task of collecting and interpreting customer information and thus introduce a filter. We argue that it is extremely important for companies to develop their own skills for understanding customers, and thereby take charge of one of their most important assets.

IKEA emphasizes the lens of the customer, the language of the customer, and the solutions to real life problems. IKEA focuses on total customer experiences and how they are formed during use and consumption. These experiences are filled with emotional energy since they are established during periods of tension and adventure. They are articulated and may be objectified during an institutionalization process that turns them into identity carrying traditions. Some become narratives and thus reproduce the company culture.

2. Create a Customer-Centric Service Culture and Strategy within the Company

Unfortunately, it is not enough to just gain a deep understanding of the customers' needs, expectations, usability process, quality perceptions, and values. The real challenge is to create a service strategy and a culture within a company which is in line with customers' value perceptions and priorities. This lays the foundation for, and gives support to, realizing powerful service concepts where the technical infrastructure often plays a key role. Service concepts and the latest technology itself, however, will not be enough. Services always rely on service encounters and moments of truth where people interact. Personal interactions, both inside the company and with external customers, always play a key role in creating loyal and profitable customer relationships. IKEA suggests that the values of the customers need to be understood and through design, advertising, catalogues, development teams etc., the furniture becomes a physical artifact which represents and expresses these core customer values. This is important to attract, touch, and retain customers.

3. Stay Focused on your Customers

Building and maintaining a service advantage require market segmentation. Your ability to build the culture, and subsequently link activities, depends on remaining strategically focused on a particular customer population.

How does IKEA address the question of staying focused on the customers? IKEA focuses on designing "solutions to real life problems". The focus is not on the furniture as such but on the value in use at home that addresses "every day life needs". Functional quality is important because design creates attraction but the total customer experience in the form of individualized customer solutions is the acid test.

4. Apply a Multi-Method Approach

In some cases it is enough to simply ask customers what they want and then design and offer what they require. In many cases, however, customers have difficulty explaining what they want in order to direct the service development processes, especially when developing innovative new services. In order to collect all the different data needed to get to know the customer, a multi-method approach is needed. Surveys and customer satisfaction studies based on verbal methods are simply not enough. A number of methods are needed to capture different, relevant, and important aspects of the customers' needs, value-drivers, and usability process in great detail.

5. Involve the Customer in the Development Process

Many new services are technology driven rather than customer driven. Furthermore, these new services do not seem to be tested in a systematic way before they are launched. This may be due to a lack of customer-centric culture in many companies. We are surprised to find that only a few of the service companies we have studied over the years proactively involve demanding and knowledgeable customers in project teams and new service development processes. In the automobile industry, for example, customers are heavily involved when new cars are being developed. During the past 25 years Honda has worked very closely with customers in different phases of the development process. The customers even have a veto right, which means that the project must get their acceptance to continue from one phase to the next. In contrast, service companies seem to rely more on simple verbal input or feedback from customers.

Our studies show that many of the most successful organizations work in close cooperation with real and demanding customers on their premises. This approach makes efficient use of a company's resources, reaches better results, and is faster. Having highly motivated and engaged customers in the process may prove to be important in the launching of a new service in a timely fashion. The Internet is an excellent tool for involving customers and enabling companies to have easy and direct access to almost anyone in the world.

In IKEA, touch-points are important for creating great experiences and mental marks. Customers are involved in creating these touch-points and in managing experience design. IKEA customers are involved by designing their own solutions, assembling the furniture, using the catalogue, using the Internet, getting advice from professionals, e.g., architects in the store, and using technology to simulate the solution and test it before purchase and consumption. Work IKEA is a good example. You can design your own ideal workplace with the IKEA free internet 3D planner, but you can also talk to an IKEA expert who is ready to listen and give advice.

6. Appoint Multi-Teams

Successful service development requires organizations to first choose working methods and to determine the role of the project manager (leadership, responsibilities, and authorities). Thereafter, development activities are usually organized into project teams. We argue that a close and working cooperation between functions, professional groups, and customers within the organization is a key success factor. Such multi-teams should include people with different kinds of experiences and expertise such as sales people, customer service employees, computer software specialists, net-services, and technicians. The teams may benefit from including external experts from partner companies and research institutions.

The primary benefits of using multi-teams are increased communication and the ability to view the opportunity or problem from many different perspectives. The use of multi-teams not only brings in expertise and knowledge, but also results in team members taking information back to share with their own functional area or organization. Once a consensus is reached at a meeting that involves many different parties, they also take responsibility for the decision.

7. Manage Internal and External Communication

New services are becoming more complicated and are often based on a technical solution. Consequently, more people are involved in projects today and companies frequently need to work within in a network to complete the new service. Internal and external communication is crucial for the success of a new service development project. Lufthansa has developed an interesting approach where posters or learning maps are used to illustrate the customer process, provide information on how customers come in contact with the company, list their goals, and state the type of customers they have. Information is available and interactive systems make communication with the customers possible before, during, and after, for example, a visit to the store.

8. Appoint a Project Leader with the Skills to Lead, Coach, and Develop Team Members

It is rare in today's business environment to have project managers who are both strong leaders and responsible for all the important project decisions. To handle a multi-team, a talented individual is required with the skills to lead, coach, and develop team members. Empowering the team is extremely important. A leader must be agile and flexible enough to meet the challenges facing the organization. A team-based approach for developing new services also requires methods and structures that work on projects in a customer-centric way. If the team loses sight of the customer, the end results are jeopardized. The product/concept developer in IKEA has the role as a coach and "design developer". Their result will be audited from a customer value perspective.

9. Take on a Holistic Approach

Time to market is a key success factor. In order to keep the development time to a minimum, it is necessary to work on different issues at the same time using a holistic approach with a number of parallel and simultaneous activities, rather than using a sequential approach in which one problem is solved at a time. Taking a holistic view also means widening the scope, looking at the total offering, and looking at both the cognitive and emotional assessment of the service experience.

In IKEA the holistic approach is customer based. Traditional show rooms in which furniture is displayed become experience rooms where solutions to real life problems express the holistic approach. Examples of total customer solutions are complete kitchens, living rooms, and bedrooms. The Communications Manager for Sweden provides us with his view of this expertise; he gives the expression "a holistic view" a specific IKEA meaning.

10. Focus on the Whole Integrated Customer Solution and the Service Experience

Integrated customer solutions are usually further developments of existing services and are only to some extent based on radically new service offerings. Many new services are inspired by, or more or less copied from, competitors. Most new products and services previously existed in some form. From the customer's perspective, services are most often packages or functions that form integrated customer solutions. These must be understood by the customer and also easy to use. For some services a physical product provides the platform for the service, such as a washing machine for laundry services. In the telecom field, the customer's technical infrastructure may be crucial.

When a new service is developed it is important that it fits into a larger context. New services are natural extensions of existing ones, and not separate parts. In the world of physical goods, competitors may use either segmentation or differentiation to compete. Segmentation means focusing on a subset of the market, or market segment, to better serve their needs. Successful service companies combine segmentation and differentiation as part of their "seamless system" of linked activities.

11. Monitor and Understand Market and Future Trends

New markets are opening up (e.g. China, India, and Eastern Europe) while other markets are becoming more competitive (e.g. telecommunications, airlines, and electricity) or evolving (e.g. call centers, computer solutions, and PC software). As a result, companies are constantly discovering new customer needs. To further complicate the picture, the Internet is opening up new ways to trade. A consumer will soon be able to buy a product from the least expensive source. This means that customers will alter their behavior therefore it is important to understand these new trends. One trend is for customers to want more control. Some factors feed this desire:

- advances in communications and information technology that are constantly and drastically reducing the cost of information
- substantially higher levels of education
- availability of more information through expanded media and sophisticated customer data-bases
- a widespread distrust of experts and of authority in general
- a strong consumer-advocacy movement
- a resistance to arbitrary pricing practices

Challenges for Companies in the Future

To forecast development in the field of new service development is not easy, and may be impossible. However, we would like to suggest some food for thought. Service innovations, service design, and new service development will be critical for company growth, competitiveness, and profitability. Various technology enablers will fuel this development and high tech will be combined with high touch services. More services will be carried out by customers at a time and place of their convenience. The global service market place will be replaced with the global service resource space. Time and place will have a completely new meaning and the borderless, virtual, and networked organization will be a reality. Customers become co-creators and are provided with capabilities and resources to serve themselves in completely new ways. This will change the game of marketing and management. The empowered and creative customer will compete with other market actors to design, create, and provide solutions and experiences in a resource efficient way combined with social and environmental responsibility.

References

Berry L, Carbone L, Haeckel S (2002) Managing the total customer experience. MIT Sloan Management Review, spring 2002

Edvardsson B, Enquist B, Johnston B (2004) Co-creating Customer Value through Hyperreality in the Pre-purchase Service Experience. Working paper. Service Research Center, University of Karlstad Sweden

Edvardsson B, Gustafsson A, Johnson M, Sandén B (2000) Service development and Innovation in the New Economy. Studentlitteratur, Lund.

Edvardsson B, Gustafsson A, Roos I (2005) Service Portraits in Service Research – A Critical Review. Int. J. of Service Industry Management. Forthcoming

Edvardsson B, Enquist B (2002) Service Culture and Service Strategy - The IKEA Saga. The Service Industries Journal, vol 22, no 4, pp 153-186

Edvardsson B, Haglund L, Mattsson J (1995) Analysis, Planning, Improvisation and Control in the Development of New Services. Int. Journal of Service Industry Management, vol 6, no 3, pp 24-35

Garten J (2001) The Mind of the CEO. Basic Books, New York

Grove SJ (2003) The future of services marketing: forecasts from ten services experts. Journal of Services Marketing, vol 17, no 2, pp 107-121

Gupta A, Wilemon DL (1990) Accelerating the Development of Technology-Based New Products. California Management Review, vol 32, no 2, Winter, pp 24-44

Gustafsson A, Johnson M (2003) Competing in a Service Economy: How to Create a Competitive Advantage through Service Development and Innovation. Jossey-Bass, San Francisco

Johne A, Storey C (1998) New Service Development: a Review of the Literature and Annotated Bibliography. European Journal of Marketing, vol 32, no 3/4, pp 184-251

Johnson M, Gustafsson A (2000) Improving Customer Satisfaction, Loyalty, and Profit. An Integrated Measurement and Management System, Jossey Bass Inc., San Francisco California

Johnston R, Clark G (2001) Service Operations Management. Prentice Hall, London

Kelly D, Storey C (2000) New Service Development: Initiation Strategies. Int. Journal of Service Industry Management, vol 11, no 1, pp 45-62

Liebowitz SJ, Margolis SE (2004) Network Externalities. http://www.utdallas.edu/ liebowit/palgrave/network.html.

Martin CR, Horne DA (1993) Service Innovations: Successful versus Unsuccessful Firms. Int. Journal of Service Industry Management, vol 4, pp 48-64

Martin CR, Horne DA (1995) Level of Success Inputs for Service Innovations in the Same Firm. Int. J. of Service Industry Management, vol 6, no 4, pp 40-56

Nilsson AG (2005) Information Systems Development (ISD) – Past, Present, Future Trends". Proceedings of the 13th International Conference on Information Systems Development – ISD 2004, Vilnius Lithuania. In: Vasilecas O, Caplinskas A, Wojtkowski W, Wojtkowski WG, Zupancic, J, Wrycza S (2005) Information Systems Development: Advances in Theory, Practice, and Education. Springer, New York, pp 29-40

Pine BJ, Gilmore JH (1999) The experience economy – Work is theatre & every business a stage. Harvard business school press, Boston Massachusetts

Prahalad CK, Ramaswamy V (2004) The Future of Competition – Co-Creating Unique Value with Customers. Harvard Business School Press, Boston

Reichheld F, Sasser EW (1990) Zero Defections: Quality comes to Services. Harvard Business Review, September-October, pp 105-111

Shaw C, Ivins J (2002) Building Great Customer Experiences. Palgrave, London

Stauss B, Neuhaus P (1997) The Qualitative Satisfaction Model. International Journal of Service Industry Management, vol 8, no 3. pp 236-249

Vargo SL, Lusch RF (2004a) Evolving to a New Dominant Logic of Marketing. Journal of Marketing, vol 68, January, pp 1-17

Vargo SL, Lusch RF (2004b) The Four Service Marketing Myths – Remnants of a Goods-Based, Manufacturing Model. Journal of Service Research, vol 6, no 4, pp 324-335

Voss C (2003) The Experience Profit Cycle Research Report. Center for Operations and Technology Management, London Business School London

Wong A (2004) The Role of Emotions in Service Encounters. Managing Service Quality, vol 14, no 5, pp 365-376

Churchmanian Co-design – Basic Ideas and Application Examples

Olov Forsgren

School of Business and Informatics, University College of Borås, Sweden.
olov.forsgren@hb.se

Introduction

C West Churchman devoted his life to a new philosophy of knowledge. He called it "systems thinking or the systems approach". I had the privilege to be part of this work from 1973 when I first was advised to meet with him. There are many good stories about the start of this new philosophy of knowledge, including writings of Churchman himself. In this text I am not going to repeat those stories. Instead, the main focus is to discuss some results and implications when we start to use this new philosophy of knowledge in practice.

First I should say that I really disliked Churchman's label, "systems thinking and systems approach", because most researchers and philosophers that place themselves as systems thinkers have very little in common with Churchman's ideas. To make it simple, most systems people I have met are analytic in their thinking. In their thinking the world start to be so complex that we have to divide it into subsystems, and subsystems of subsystems (and so on) in order to be able to overview the different parts and processes and their relations. As an example, Simon at one time was a well known systems thinker, but as Ulrich pointed out [1] Churchman had radically different basic ideas to what Simon had. I prefer to say that Churchman was the first co-design thinker. His basic idea was that we can design an infinite number of views of reality; some more detailed, others more an overview. But Churchman said this is not enough. We can also "calibrate" the viewing instrument and decide which of all the possible views that should be implemented. It is both a design process and a Co-process to select the best possible of many views. In this sense Churchman was the first co-designer.

Churchman was often criticised for a lack of practical examples of co-design thinking. In the beginning of the 1980's, I was able to attend a talk by Churchman at Stanford. A large audience was listening and at the end there was time for questions. As I remembered there was only one serious question. The question was phrased like this – "Now you have been preaching for more than fifteen years about these ideas, can you mention any example of how these ideas have been used in practice, or is it, as many of us think – just empty talk?" Churchman's answer to that question was. –"There are many examples, but the closest to you all is the American constitution. This is a really good example because it has been in use for a while and many of us would agree that it works." This was a perfect answer and the critical people were very quiet afterwards. After the talk he admitted "It was a good question – implementation is our weakest side, but on the other hand this is early in the process".

From my point of view there are now many examples of successful implementation of co-design thinking. Pioneers in this work are Ackoff [2], Checkland [3], Mitroff and Mason[4]. Their approaches have stimulated good implementation work all over the world today. But it is more than that. There is a slow change in world view coming along on all levels of human behaviour. I remember once at a seminar Capra talked about his way of working with physics. Churchman's comment was "It is a shame that he is coming here telling us about implications of the systems approach". There are now many researchers with work along in this route of thinking which is summarized well by the philosopher von Wright as "the analytic thinking of knowledge is dead in the philosophical conversation, instead we can see growing co-evolutionary thinking approaches. [5] I think the best summary of this movement is formulated by Churchman in my translation as: "When for the first time you can see the world from the view of someone else..." you have started to be a co-designer. [6]

Co-design in Practice

In a way, Churchman's formulation is really practical. For more than twenty years, I have been working with small and large companies and organisations in different projects where we have tried out co-design thinking in practice. This includes management models as well as software development. I will tell a bit more about that later, but still I think Churchman's formulation is the most important.

I do not know how many times I have heard statements such as "Yes, I realise there are different perspectives on this, but we also have to count the hard facts." From my point of view in general, educated people from universities are the most hard fact and empirically grounded theory oriented. For them, "perspectives" is sloppy language use which has nothing to do with scientific-based thinking.

It is like an enormous thinking barrier standing there. It takes time, energy and boldness to come to a point where you see that all hard facts come out of co-designed measurement scales (perspectives) implemented in instruments and software. When people break this barrier, sometimes it can be rather dramatic. I once saw a rather recognised professor with tears in his eyes declare that he suddenly realised that most of his earlier work was a waste of time. More common is a reaction of anger combined with arguments like: "Applying this relativistic thinking will cause a collapse of our culture – the whole school system based on the idea of educating the truth to our children will turn into chaos."

After working with these ideas in more than 25 years I am still impressed by the curage it takes to dare to think co-design. Donald Schöön once told me that he did not dare to tell most other researchers at MIT about his co-design ideas. They will just think I am out of my mind, he told me. At that time we were discussing the idea that from a co-design perspective also politics has to be an integrated part. In many places it is almost dangerous to express such ideas. We have been so nurtured with ideas and practice reflecting a complete separation between the scientists producing understanding of the world and the politicians making decisions about how to act based on proper understanding. May be relativistic perspective thinking is one step on the way to co-design thinking. The relativist says "there are an infinite number of ways to describe an apartment or a dead human being". The co-designer agrees but he also says "if the human culture is going to develop, someone has to decide on which description to use, and that is an act of politics, ethics and aesthetics.

It really amazes me to listen to all these "half way" Co-design thinking approaches. The line of argumentation is this. Yes we can see the existence of different "co-designed" perspectives or frameworks and our job as co-design researchers is to find out in which perspective we can find the deepest and most proper understanding. In line with this thinking are expressions like "it is an advantage to use a scientific and more precise language". It seems like people using these expressions never seriously have reflected on the relation between precision and the used scale or framework. From my point of view this type of thinking is even less developed than the relativistic thinking.

Interestingly there are now starting to grow many scientific conferences and meetings where the basic underlying philosophy is direct relativistic multi-perspective and multi-disciplinary thinking. This is not at all in line with co-design thinking. Co-design thinking is not relativistic. We can design an infinite number of measurement scales (perspectives), but we have to select which of all the possible scales we are going to use in a specific situation. Otherwise we can not act. May be Churchman was not so clear about this. His main point in his earlier writings was to challenge the dominating perspective in a dialectical approach. But Churchman also had ideas about calibration as the complementary side of bringing in new perspectives into a conversation. In calibration, we have to agree on which measurement scale to use. A good example is what scale to use if we are going to decide if a human being is dead or alive. It is possible to use an infinite number of scales, but we have to use one of them when are going to determine if a human being is dead. Different scales influence different people in different ways. In recent years we have had such a discussion. Are we are going to use brain-dead or heart-dead as the scale in action? For the moment at least, in Sweden, brain-dead is the scale in action making it possible to perform more successful organ transplantations. This example also gives us a hint about co-design thinking in action.

Coming so far, I have to comment on another thinking barrier, related to co-design thinking that creates a lot of frustration, anger, and fear. The argument this time sounds like: "Only God can decide what is to be regarded as dead or living and every attempt to try to put you in God's position will just lead to catastrophe." At one conversation on this topic an old professor looked at me and said "You must be sent by the devil himself". Churchman himself struggled a lot with this, as he called it the guarantor problem. My position is that co-design thinking tries to consider, and when possible also involve all people that can be influenced by some perspective embedded in actions and technology, simply because each individual in co-design thinking represent a piece of God.

In summary, I believe that there is a number of ways to lead people into the application of co-design thinking. Most important is still to be able to cross the real fundamental thinking barriers. After passing these thinking barriers, almost everything you do is co-design in practice.

Co-design Applied to e-Government

From the view of Churchman, Co-design behaviour has its origins in the philosophy of Kant [7]. To solve the philosophical dispute between the idealists focusing on ideas as the essence of the world, and the realists focusing on reality as the essence of the world, Kant proposed that we need a' priori ideas to interpret the real world. This idea, that today we refer to as perspective, was much more elaborated by another philosopher, Singer.[8] He expressed the same idea in a different language. He said that we need to design measurement scales to be able to measure, or in other terms, we need to create good questions to get good answers.

Subsequently Churchman, [9] clarified the direct connection between a measurement scale, an idea and a hope for the future. We, for instance, can "measure" day care centres for children so that parents can choose between them. But more important Churchman also proposed that we have to design the measurement scale taking into account that different people have different hopes for the future and that their hopes change over time.

For example, when council staff measure, or describe, a day care centre s/he has to think about whom s/he is talking to: is it a family with several children, with disabled children, a family with strong environmental concerns, a family where the parents work long hours, etc. The design of the measurement scale becomes a co-designed system between different interests. This co-designed measurement scale/view directly influences the design of the day care centre database and the presentation of measurement results for the public, e.g., one component in what we today call e-government and e-services. [10] An e-service informing about staff knowledge in different languages is based on the clients question or hope for the future of being able to use a specific language. Views not only influence the design of information and services, but also often influence the design of the service or business itself. A smart manager of a day care centre who often gets a question about the knowledge in a special language can make a decision to hire staff with that skill and make this into a speciality or business idea. With these background ideas, we started in the beginning of the 1990's to develop the first e-government prototypes "Live-better, Home-Samit and Learn-Samit". Inspired by that a number of pilot projects started in a few Swedish cities. I joined a strong pioneering group in Kista, the Silicon Valley of Sweden, and together we built the first real Co-design e-government systems in the middle of the 90's. [11]

One important aspect of co-design applied in e-government is that the result hardly can be classified in the distinctions government, learning and democracy. In "Kista.com" portal all these aspects were integrated. In the beginning, we worked with a first stakeholder model. The model were discussed and decided by the Board. Based on this model a first set of services were created. One of these services was the e-Parliament where the citizens could have opinions and proposals about the services in Kista. Another part of the Kista portal was a user panel also evaluating new possible and implemented services. New proposals about stakeholders and services led into co-design projects and after decision in the Board also in some cases new services were implemented. It was government, learning and democracy at once. But more than also business were involved. Many questions were about how to present local business as a part of the local services. Finally, it was also another type of "business". Also for a physical community it is important to show a good web front end in order to stimulate tourism and new inhabitants.

Co-design Applied to e-Business

The following small scenario gives some hints about how the co-design thinking also can improve e-business. All tailors know by experience that there are a few key measurements to perform on the body of a customer in order to be able to produce a perfect fitting dress. In this scenario the tailor, together with a co-designer, created a self measurement system easy to perform by everybody. This idea, together with the possibility for mail order companies to store a large variety of sizes, opens up the possibility of e-tailors on the Internet. As a customer you just perform the self-measurement and give the results in the e-tailor portal. As a result the e-tailor company will send you a perfect fitting tailor-made dress for a lower price than a regularly purchased dress.

Both examples above are happening today and they show the basic ideas of co-design thinking in action. In summary, the examples tell us that it is a waste of energy, and from a co-design point of view, naïve, to try to analyse a day care centre or a human body into its smallest detail. These details are infinite since they depend on designed measurement scales. Instead we have to focus the energy on designing measurement scales that in use can satisfy some hope for a future better life for some people.

If these examples demonstrate the basic ideas, there are also examples of application areas with more visible impact. A few years ago we started work with large Swedish banks and large companies such as Nokia, Volvo and Ikea with the same underlying ideas, but with a different focus. In these companies we focus a financial situation (bank), a transport situation (Volvo) or a living situation (Ikea). One important consequence of co-design thinking is that the company or bank has to integrate all resources in the answer/service offer as a response to the selected customer questions/requests/views. This also means that there has to be an integrating steering body within the company with power to create synergies between the customer contact channels, such as shop, advertisement, Web-portal, catalogue and so on. In most companies this causes a large reorganisation need. From my point of view Ikea is far on the way in this development process. As a result of the earlier mentioned work in Kista, we have now also for some years been working with some large cities in Europe within the European framework research programmes. The basic underlying co-design philosophy has been the same, but in these examples the services have included all sorts of citizen questions and needs.

A special application with strong potential impact is the creation of the Stockholm Challenge award as a modern IT-Nobel-prize. As the examples show, a co-design situation is an ideal in itself. It is a co-evolving system creating value to its stakeholders. From a co-design perspective this ideal or view can be applied as a frame of measurement itself. The measurement shows how close to a co-design ideal a project is. If we than add a prize for the project closest to the ideal we have created a co-design driving system with great potential.

Some Strategies for Implementation of Co-design Ideas

As I mentioned earlier Churchman admitted that implementation was the weak side of the systems approach. On the other hand when we observe how many thinkers and practitioners around the world saying that they have been influenced by Churchman or/and his students, it is also possible to say that implementation is rather strong. It is interesting to notice that Churchman and his best known student Ackoff has used two rather opposite strategies in their attempts to involve more people trying out the "systemic" ideas as Ackoff calls them. Churchman is fundamentally unsure – questioning everything from still another perspective, and another and... Ackoff on the other hand is fundamentally sure – with a clear argumentation he paints a new systemic landscape. Within this landscape the idea of new perspectives connected to ideals are fundamental. It looks to me that Churchman all the time tries to go outside the boundaries of his own thinking. That is why it is hard to know if he regard the "enemies of the systems approach" really are the enemies or if they are just new perspectives that have to be "swept in". For Ackoff it seems enough to clear his own mind not trying to break out of it.

My approach may be a bit closer to Ackoff even if I regard myself to be a Churchmanian. It is part of the co-design approach to create new perspectives and to involve new stakeholders with new perspectives into conversation and action. But there is also a strong breaking out component in co-design thinking. This breaking out component is an awareness of other languages to express perspectives. There is the well known body and action language all the way from habits to dance and exercise in all forms. There is also the possibility to use all kinds of artefacts and paintings to express perspectives.

Also here it is possible to view Ikea as a good example of applying co-design thinking. It is an attempt to integrate perspectives in language and pictures in the catalogue and web with the stores and the management style. Included are also the offices and to some part also openness to find new ways of express what Ikea stands for.

One way is to express this idea is to refer back to the expression "the mouth was saying one thing but the eyes another thing". The idea of co-design is to be aware of as many expressions as possibly and to form them together into a genuine good living experience.

Saying that, one crucial question is, how do we dare to try out new expressions? Or, how do we dare to listen to strange enemies? It reminds about the first big step for the baby to move from milk to other types of food. You have to dare to try to be able to include another perspective or aspect of life. As another example many people have difficulties to try the Swedish delicates fermented herring because they think the smell is awful. In that way they will miss one of the top food experiences I think. European collaboration is from my point of view to some part to try out and to get inspired by local specialities.

Also here there is a limit – you can not try out everything and some – a lot of experiences can also be dangerous for yourself and your friends. The first time I heard about Churchman was as a deep thinking man sitting in a bathtub with a view over the ocean being served with drinks and drugs by his wife. Later Churchman had to realise he was an alcoholic and we once talked about the problem of how to know when a new experience starts to become dangerous. I remember his question: "You are strange - how can you stop drinking when it tastes better the more you drink?" From my view Churchman was trapped into a dangerous experience. Later he got help from the AA movement and he started to see that organisation as a strong model for rescuing organisations. During the last years of his life he used this experience in reflections about science as a dangerous trap. Much more can be said about this but my point here is to say that Churchman really tried to include new experiences expressed in various languages, and he didn't just talk about it he also to some part also lived it.

The Surf Wave Strategy

To summarize, the co-design approach I have used and exemplified with Ikea example can be described with a surf wave metaphor, a question of timing. Based on old experiences you just know when it is time to try to involve a new perspective or experience. If you start too early or paddle too hard you will run into a dangerous trap. On the other hand if you start too late or paddle too slow you will be too late to have any impact with the involvement of a new perspective.

A strange experience I have is also that it is easier to work with the front wave development together with companies and organisations than what it is with the scientific community. From this perspective the scientific community is more conservative. A company can say – we do not exactly understand, but lets try it out so may be we can learn. The scientific community is more of the view that "this is not our perspective so it must be wrong".

To this can be added, and demonstrated with the Ikea example, that new perspectives and experiences can have all different forms. In practice this have had the implication that the co-design projects I have been part of involves not just pure formal language modelling but also trying to find out good working conditions involving as many good perspectives as possible. The ideal result can be summarized with the word fun. It is fun to surf a wave.

An important aspect of this strategy is the paddling part of the wave metaphor. How hard to introduce new perspectives, it is a balance between too much push and too little push. This is not an easy task. My attempts have always been in line with Schön's "leading subsystems" approach. [12] Start with small examples and let these examples stimulate a change with more impact. This strategy is also to some part reflected in the structure of this text in which I try to move in small steps from small limited examples into examples with more impact and importance.

Of course there are other strategies when it comes to implementation of co-design thinking. Here I will shortly mention the three most important I have worked with. The guideline approach, the review approach and the award approach.

The Guideline Design Approach

This approach is basically to hand out some guidance thought steps models and tools that can be used in order to support people or companies that want to try to work as co-designers. One critical question here is how detailed the guidelines should be. If you make them too detailed, there is a great risk that people will not use them, and if they are too little detailed, people may be feeling lost. Albinsson has been working with these ideas in many companies and organisations in Sweden. [13]

The question reminds me about some of the golf coaches I have experienced. I specially remember Sven Tumba Johansson, a legend in Sweden, now living in Florida. He told me "You have to understand there is simply just one rule you have to know to be a good golfer. You have to move away from a feeling that you hit the ball into a feeling that you drop the ball. The golf club is doing the work and you just decide where you want to drop the ball, that's it. If you have this feeling in your body you can master most of the almost infinite number of situations you will get into." At least for me, that introduction strategy worked to my satisfaction.

I realise that I, to a great extent, have used the Tumba strategy in my work with coaching people in companies and organisations to be co-designers. Maybe I have taken this strategy one step further in that I have tried to adapt to the local culture and the use of wolds in that culture. I have almost never talked about co-design thinking. Instead I have engaged with the people formulating the basic ideas in a language fitting into this specific situation. I have made them into co-designers of their own co-design guidelines. An example is the work with Volvo. In that context, we worked with guidelines for development of a new "sale support system". Inspired with work from Ikea where we worked with "buy support systems", we at one point suggested to change the name at Volvo to "buy support system". This was just an impossible suggestion. I do not have to tell you that we never tried to use the term co-design system, even if the basic idea was that the buyer and the dealer together were co-designing the best possible car for the buyer.

The Review Design Approach

At IIASA I was using an evaluation/review- design for introducing the co-design ideas in relation to an environment management system in Europe. The idea is simple. As I have described above, in every question is embedded a perspective and a hope for the future. So if we use this idea and then put the co-design view itself into the question with the hope that the respondent will start to reflect in line with the co-design ideas. As an example in the environmental case you can ask. "Which stakeholders were involved in the co-design of the co-design of the environmental measuring systems? How were they involved? What kind of hopes for the future did they have? And so on. [14]

In review setting you can just tick the box for every answer. If they have no answer, or the answer is – we have never thought about this – there is no tick in the box. In summary the result of the IIASA case was that there was no tick in the box since the environmental models were created by the scientists in an analytical mode of thinking. My conclusion was that from a co-design point of view this environmental system represented low quality. They also completely failed because they were never used. This review-design strategy is to a high degree successfully used by the ISO-standardisation groups even if they, for the most part, seem unconscious about the designed perspective that is embedded in the review questions.

The Award Design Approach

In the earlier mentioned Stockholm Challenge award, a quite similar co-design of co-design introduction approach was used. In this case the review questions were complemented with an international experienced jury that could use the questions as guidelines for their evaluation. Also an award was set up with a similar ceremony as the Nobel prize ceremony. Complementary to this, all nominated projects were invited to a conversation about exchange of experiences and challenges for the future. The Stockholm Challenge award was a success and between 600 and 900 projects from all over the world were evaluated each year from 1999-2003.

End Remark

I know many co-design thinkers, like Churchman were, are rather or very pessimistic about the future of academic research. What they see is scientific production counted in overwhelming numbers of papers accepted in a narrow community with the same or similar views – with little or no connection to attempts to solve any problems for anyone in practice. I am not that pessimistic – of course it is ridiculous to count scientific progress in the number of papers, but on the other hand I can feel a change is under way. In the European Union this change is very much pushed by the framework research programmes. Universities all over the world try to be more in connection to the world outside. A co-design wave is starting to build up and I think its time to start paddling. The Karlstad conference is an important opportunity for this.

References

[1] Ulrich W (1980) The Metaphysics of Design: A Simon-Churchman "Debate". Vol 10, no 2, pp 35-40
[2] Ackoff RL (1981) Creating the Corporate Future. Wiley New York
[3] Checkland PB (1988) Soft Systems Methodology: An Overview. Journal of Applied Systems Analysis, no 15, pp 27-30

[4]   Mitroff II, Mason RO (1981) Creating a Dialectical Social Science. Reidel Dordrecht
[5]   von Wright GH (1989) Science, Reason and Value. The Royal Swedish Academy of Sciences Stockholm
[6]   Churchman CW (1968) The Systems Approach. Dell Publishing Co Inc NY
[7]   Kant I (1987) Critique of Judgement. Hackett Publishing Company Indianapolis
[8]   Singer EA Jr (1959) Experience and Reflection. University of Pennsylvania Press Philadelphia
[9]   Churchman CW (1971) The Design of Inquiring Systems: Basic Principles of Systems and Organization. Basic Books New York
[10] Grönlund Å, Forsgren O, ao (2000) Managing Electronic Services. Springer London
[11] Forsgren O (2001) The e-Power, Integrating e-Commerce, e-Government and e-Learning into Constructive Learning Networks. Paper Presented at the 31st Annual Conference of the International Society for Systems Research. Asilomar California
[12] Schön D (1973) Beyond the Stable State. Norton New York
[13] Albinsson L, Forsgren O (2004) On the Co-Design of Electronic Assistants Serving Elderly People – Methods, Results and Reflections about the EU-Project Avanti from a Systemic Co-Design Perspective. Paper Presented at the Third International Conference on Systems Thinking in Management. Philadelphia Pennsylvania May 19-21 2004
[14] Forsgren O (1988) Samskapande Datortillämpningar: En systemteoretisk ansats för lösning av vissa förändringsproblem vid administrativ datoranvändning (Co-Designing Computer Applications). Doctoral Thesis Department for Informatics Umeå University

The Ideal Oriented Co-design Approach Revisited

Christina Johnstone

School of Business and Informatics, University College of Borås, Sweden.
cjohnsto@algonet.se

Introduction

There exist a large number of different methodologies for developing information systems on the market. This implies that there also are a large number of "best" ways of developing those information systems. Avison and Fitzgerald (2003) states that every methodology is built on a philosophy. With philosophy they refer to the underlying attitudes and viewpoints, and the different assumptions and emphases to be found within the specific methodology.

One rather new philosophy concerning the system development area is the Co-design philosophy. This philosophy has its origin from late C West Churchman and his philosophy of knowledge, a philosophy he labelled as systems thinking or the systems approach. The name Co-design is from Olov Forsgren who has grounded the Co-design philosophy mainly on Churchman and his work. The main idea in Co-design is that the world consists of infinite views of reality. In order to create new perspectives on the system about to be developed, every stakeholder expected to be affected by the system has to be involved and all kinds of artefacts and paintings have to be used to express those perspectives.

But when looking for methodologies or guidelines built on those assumptions and on the Co-design approach - it is not easy to find any. In this paper I therefore will describe the Co-design approach and analyze the philosophy on which it is grounded. I will also describe and analyze the Ideal oriented Co-design approach which could be seen as one way to use the Co-design spirit in practice. I also give some suggestions how to improve this Ideal oriented co-design approach to make it easier to adopt.

Brief Description of Co-design

Forsgren (2004) states that late C West Churchman was the world first co-design thinker. Churchman himself did not use the term co-design. Instead he called his philosophy of knowledge for systems thinking or the systems approach. Churchman was inspired by the philosopher Edgar Singer. Singer told us that if we want to get a good answer, we first have to create a good question. Otherwise we shouldn't be able to design the measurement scales necessary in order to be able to measure (Forsgren, 2004). For example when an organization thinking of adopting or purchasing a methodology they have to measure methodologies for system development, so they can choose between them. The measurement scale allows the organization to know how well the methodology is working and meeting the needs of its users. Churchman says that the measurements need a teleological view, which means that the purpose of the measurement has to be defined.

His reason for this is that: "…measurements are a specific type of information which co-determine decision in a wide variety of contexts." (1971, p.93). To measure something, the object being measured must be specified, and so must its properties. According to this, Churchman also points out that all measurement involves prediction.

West Churchman and Russel Ackoff (Forsgren 2004) found out that there was a direct connection between these measurements scales and an idea and a hope for the future. From this aspect Forsgren points out that when designing those measurements scales one must take into account that different people have different hopes for the future and that those hopes are changing over time. Forsgren also argues that those measurements scale not are to be seen as relativistic. There can be an infinite number of measurements scales or perspectives. But the stakeholders have to select which of all possible scales to be used in a specific situation. Churchman called this action for calibration.

Churchman (1971) states that human knowledge does not come in pieces. To understand an aspect of nature it has to be seen through all ways of imaginary. Bausch (2004) interpretation of this statement is that a person refines his solid opinion by sweeping in multiple and divergent viewpoints in order to gain a rounded appreciation of a topic. Forsgren (2004) calls this approach for co-design and defines a co-designer as a person that can see the world from the view of someone else.

Bausch (2004) claims that for Churchman, human bias was an essential aspect. Churchman's idea was that system theorists should try to weave all matters of human concern into one grand imagery or purpose behaviour.

They should also seek to tie all different goals together without making it inexplicable to the people involved. Churchman also argued that a real system theorist is interested in how we know, plan, make decision and make sure that those decisions are ethical.

Co-design in the Light of Philosophy

Avison and Fitzgerald (2003) think it is important that an organization, when it is about to adopt or purchase a methodology, puts efforts on making sure that they choose the one that corresponds to their needs. They therefore suggest their "Framework for comparing methodologies" as a tool for understanding different methodologies but also as a tool for comparisons. In this chapter, I will use their framework (Fig. 1) as a way to describe the philosophy of Co-design and as a tool to look at the Ideal oriented Co-design approach in the perspective of improving the approach.

1	**Philosophy**
	(a) Paradigm
	(b) Objectives
	(c) Domain
	(d) Target
2	**Model**
3	**Techniques and tools**
4	**Scope**
5	**Outputs**
6	**Practice**
	(a) Background
	(b) User base
	(c) Participants
7	**Product**

Fig. 1. The Framework for comparing methodologies (Avison & Fitzgerald, 2003)

The Paradigm Element

A paradigm in this perspective is a specific way of thinking about problems but also a foundation of practices for the future. Avison and Fitzgerald (2003) define two paradigms which they think is relevant for system development methodologies; the science paradigm and the systems paradigm. The authors also include that a philosophy consist both of ontological and epistemological assumptions. Translating this into a modelling situation one can say that ontology is about what to model, whilst epistemology is about how to model.

In their book Avison and Fitzgerald use a model, developed by Lewis in 1994, showing the connections between ontology and epistemology (Fig. 2). In this model Ontology contains a scale between Realism and Nominalism. Realism argues that there exist immutable objects and structures in the universe that are independent of the observer's appreciation of them.

Nominalism argues that those objects cannot be immutable instead they are social structured. (Avison and Fitzgerald 2003) The scale of Epistemology also has two positions. On one side of the scale is the Positivism which implies that there exist causal relationships which can be scientific measured. On the other end is the Interpretivism which argues that there is no single truth that can be proven by such an investigation.

Figure 2 also shows the positions of the different aspects in Epistemology and Ontology and their relationship towards each other in the terms of objectivism and subjectivism. An Objectivist approach to a system development process, according to Avison and Fitzgerald (2003), is built on the assumptions that there are true facts existing which are immutable. This could be a proper approach when modelling

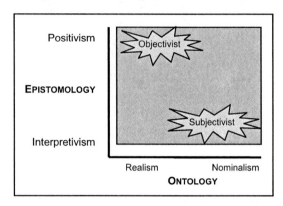

Fig. 2. Framework for analysing the underlying philosophies of methodologies (Avison & Fitzgerald 2003)

entities for a database. A subjective approach look at the data collected as a perception of data constructed by the viewer. This approach could be proper when for example designing a user interface.

The Paradigm of Co-design

Co-design can be described as a holistic approach since it tries to sweep in all the different views that can affect the systems and its different stakeholders. From this perspective it could be viewed as soft systems thinking. But it also argues for defined measurement scales that define and measure for example the artefacts, the services or the activities in focus. It seems that the co-design tries to bridge two different kinds of views on how to best develop an information system.

It is also possible to describe Co-design as an epistemological approach since Churchman himself thought of his idea as a philosophy of knowledge. Using Lewis scale of Epistemology when defining the philosophy of Co-design in the terms of Interpretivism and Positivism, I think the idea of Co-design is to cover the more evolutionary way of knowledge creation. With this I mean that Co-design is more Interpretivistic than Positivistic. Forsgren's argument that appropriate members of the organization and its stakeholders must be participating in the development work, to catch every view important for the system being developed, is an approach that also implies that there not only exists one truth.

On the other hand, since the idea of Co-design is to sweeping in the different stakeholders opinions, the philosophy probably also consider to incorporate the fact that some of the stakeholders believe that knowledge is a result of examining the one and only truth. I think that the philosophy of Co-design tries to handle both Interpretivism and Positivism. For example the calibration of the measurements scale could be described as evolutionary and implies that it is to be categorized as Interpretivism. But the result of the calibration has to be judged as a truth which then will be used in a specific situation by specific users. Therefore the calibration also could be seen as a positivistic action.

Co-design, in the way Forsgren describes it (2004), has a Humanistic perspective, which implies that the human is the active part in the information system, not the system itself. This view is what I define as an ontological perspective. With Humanistic perspective I refer to Nurminen (1988) who argues that the humanistic perspective emphasis on individuals. Knowledge is seen as situated, the user is seen as a human actor of both job and the Information System and the tasks is performed by human actors using tools. This perspective also thinks that the system development is evolutionary.

Nurminen (1988) have also defined a System theoretical perspective and a Socio-technical perspective. The system theoretical perspective does emphasis on technical formal aspects. Knowledge is seen as objectivistic and users, if there are any, are rational and mechanical. This perspective sees tasks as performed by machines and the communication is with a machine. The system development process is argued to be a lifecycle. In Lewis model this could be compared with Realism. The Socio-technical perspective does emphasis on interaction between human and computer, knowledge is seen as instrumental and the users are seen as active users of the information system. This perspective thinks the actors are communicating with a user-friendly machine and the users are participating in the system development process.

Using Nurminens' definitions above one could argue that Co-design not only is Humanistic but also has a socio-technical perspective. This since it argues that the stakeholders should participate in the development process. But I think that Co-design want something more from the stakeholder than just participation when the developers need their stakeholders' opinion about the user interface etc. The Co-design is said to be driven by the stakeholders and the stakeholders are involved throughout the process. From my point of view it depends to be closer to the Humanistic side. But once again, the fundamental idea of Co-design is to look at the development process from every angel possible. So according to Lewis scale on Ontology I would say that a real Co-designer must cope with the whole scale, even the System theoretical perspective, just because the idea of Co-design is to get the differing perspectives of the world being defined.

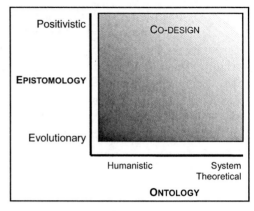

Fig. 3. A way to look at Co-design relating Epistemology and Ontology

If using Lewis model – taking away the subjectivist and objectivistic approach and instead use the terms from the co-design philosophy and Nurminen - the figure, from my point of view, will look little different. In this figure I show that the darker areas have more of a genuine co-design approach than the lighter one. Even if the whole range could be seen as Co-design. (Fig. 3).

The Objective of Co-design

This sub element objective related to philosophy, analyzes the objective of the methodology. For example if the methodology will develop a computerized information system or if the methodology has a wider view and not only force the development of an information system but also have the goal to improve the organization as well. Avison and Fitzgerald (2003) are of the opinion that this is a very important aspect to consider, when choosing a methodology. A methodology that concerns itself solely with providing an IT solution is quite a different methodology from one that does not.

Co-design according to Forsgren (2004) is a moral and political question because its objective is to support the ideal life of somebody. This means that the underlying assumption is to both develop a computerized information system and to improve the organization as well. But this only if it will support those who are affected by the system and result in a good world for "the future generations to live in". This is a huge objective and not that easy to grasp developers, designers or the organization itself. The objective of Co-design is to be seen as long-termed or long-ranged, putting in more aspects than Avison and Fitzgerald describes in their framework.

The Co-design Domain

The third sub element related to philosophy is about the domain of situations the methodology address. It differs from the object element in the way that this is focusing on the areas where for example the information system is about to support the users or which part of the organisation is to be improved. Avison and Fitzgerald (2003) relates this element to what information is needed and the strategy needed to get this information in order to be able to develop the desired system or to do the desired improvements. For example, the strategy and information needed will be different if the methodology seeks to identify the overall planning and organisation, than if the methodology concentrates on solving one specific and pre-identified problem.

The Co-design domain has, from my point of view, no restrictions. It could focus on just a specific and pre-identified problem but it could as well try to identify the overall planning and organisation for the desired future. In fact this means that, even if the system about to be developed just will handle the pre-defined problem or if it will be an overall solution improving the organisation, the co-design process will be the same: Involve all the different stakeholders, let them together define the measurement scales, let them together decide the measurement scale to be used and then together develop the desired future.

The Co-design Target

The fourth sub element related to philosophy is about the applicability of the methodology. Avison and Fitzgerald (2003) think this aspect is important because some methodologies are specifically targeted at particular types of problems, environments or size of organizations - while others are said to have a general purpose. This means that there are methodologies that only can be used when developing special applications while others can be used when developing more general applications.

Even from this target perspective I think there are no limitations concerning the Co-design target. Since the Co-design approach is about to sweep in every perspective important for the system, from every stakeholder affected by the system, the Co-design approach could be used both for bespoke systems and for more general web-based systems. I think this wide range of target for the Co-design approach is where Forsgren (2004) found the big thinking barriers among both developers and designer of information systems. This because the developers and designers first have to take into account many different measurement scales and than manage to calibrate them in cooperation with the stakeholders. They also have to be prepared for the reality that those stakeholders, involved in the development process, probably will change their measurements scale when their hopes for their future change. This type of situations and questions I don't think the developers or designers are prepared for to handle, when they leave their education in informatics.

Brief Description of Ideal Oriented Co-design Approach

Ideal oriented Co-design approach has evolved from theories. The philosophy is from Churchman and his idea about system thinking. The Ideal approach is then formulated by Albinsson and Forsgren (2004) upon their experience from different research and design projects. The practice is though built on the theories. Albinsson and Forsgren (2004) states that in a development process it is crucial that the methodology used has an approach that handles the dynamics of requirement. Their suggestion is to use the Ideal oriented Co-design approach. The authors argue that the Ideal approach is not to be declared as a complete systems development methodology or a project management methodology. Instead it should be seen as a pointer to critical qualities of system development.

Albinsson and Forsgren (2004), has learned through experience that the stakeholders view on the project during its lifecycle will change; a change that may affect scope, goals or even the existence of the project. Therefore the approach put a great effort on the stakeholders and how to know and engage the most important stakeholders. It is also important to make it possible for the stakeholders to discuss about the future and those things they don't know the existence of or have words for. The authors suggest using mini-scenarios to facilitate the communication between developers, designers and stakeholders. They also suggest mock-ups as a way to visualize the systems and its user interaction.

The Ideal oriented Co-design approach is visualized as a road with different number of lines which in different phases of the process have different width. The different lanes are supposed to be dynamic and co-exist with the other lanes and with other methodologies. They also have to run parallel during the whole process. The authors also state that the realization part is the one that demands the most resources. But they don't describe how to perform this phase, only that there exists many approaches and methodologies that handles system development. Generally there are no models, techniques or tools described how to be used in the description of the Ideal oriented Co-design approach. I would say that the descriptions of the approach is more like advises of how to think about the different phases in a system development project, than a hands-on description over how to actually perform a development process with a Co-design approach.

Reflections and Suggestions to Improve the Ideal Oriented Co-design Approach

In this paper I have focused on describing the Co-design philosophy and how it could be used in practice by also describing the Ideal oriented Co-design approach. From the analysis I will now reflect and give some suggestions on how to improve the Ideal oriented Co-design approach.

From a Pointer to a Toolbox

Ideal oriented Co-design approach does not want to be seen as a methodology, but rather as a pointer to critical aspects in the system development process. I understand that distinction because the Co-design approach includes so many more dimension than just data based information system. But when Albinsson and Forsgren arguing for the approach to be just a pointer, I think there is a risk that the developers and designers will handle the approach as just theories and do not put any efforts on those aspects in their practical work of building information systems. The lack of concrete methodologies, which address the Co-design approach, may also have the consequences that the developers and designers never will be confronted with the Co-design philosophy. It could also get the consequence that the Co-design approach neither is mentioned or used in education and training.

Since the world also is known to be changing continually, as well as the stakeholders need and hope for the future is changing, I also think there rather is a need for a toolbox than a specific Co-design methodology. I'm not myself an advocate of using one specific methodology and only hold on to that during the system development process. This because I think that different stakeholder, different time, different circumstances, different environments, different question and so on, will shape unique contexts. These different contexts demands adjusted methodologies, techniques and tools. My suggestion is therefore that the Ideal approach put together the best from a lot of methodologies, techniques and tools, which all fit into the Co-design philosophy and marketing itself as the toolbox to be used by those who want to join the Co-design approach.

Probably the question will appear how can some one selects the best or the appropriate from the toolbox. This question can however never be answered by the toolbox, since the craftsmen themselves from their experience, knowledge and competence must take response for their work.

Take the Best from the Best

The Ideal oriented Co-design approach is mainly evolved from Church-man's ideas of systems thinking. When describing the approach the most efforts are put on how to think instead of how to do. This implies that it still is more of a theoretical approach than a practical one. I think it is of great value to explicitly have these - I call the guidelines - when develop-ing information systems, but since I'm arguing for a toolbox I also want to see hands-on descriptions of how to use different techniques and tools with the Co-design approach as a basis. This off course, demands that there is a decision and ambition to evolve the Ideal oriented Co-design approach into a more practical approach.

When looking for those techniques and tools which contribute to the Co-design approach, one idea is to look among the followers of Church-man and not only on Churchman himself. I found that many ideas in the Ideal oriented Co-design approach are similar to those in the methodology Interactive Planning. This methodology has been developed by Russell Ackoff, who was a former student to Churchman. Another follower of Churchman is Peter Checkland, who developed the Soft System Method-ology (Checkland & Scholes 1990). In this methodology there are tech-niques as Rich Pictures, CATWOE and Root definitions, which in one way could be said to be built on the Co-design philosophy. But from my point of view they have to be explicit claimed and perhaps also described how to be used form the view of the Ideal oriented Co-design approach. There are more adopters of the Churchmanian philosophy, so probably there also will be other methodologies, techniques and tools that already are grounded in the Co-design spirit. Perhaps they just need a little adjustment to the Ideal oriented Co-design approach and they could also be put into the toolbox.

When looking closer to the description of the Ideal oriented Co-design approach, Albinsson and Forsgren let us know that mock-ups, prototypes, animation, testing and technologies for realization have to be used. The de-scription also implies that the scenarios, that are developed, have to be evaluated. All those techniques and models to be used I think must be de-scribed how to be used in the spirit of Co-design. One suggestion could be to look at the toolbox the same as to a solution sharing community. What I mean is that different developers could contribute to the growth of a Co-design toolbox by putting their techniques, tools and models into the box. Then the toolbox itself will act in a Co-design spirit.

Position Co-design towards other Approaches

Today many system approaches, other than Co-design, are using the word design with an understatement of involving the stakeholders. There are for example the Participatory design, the Cooperative design, the Interaction design and the Human centred design. Due to the essence of the Co-design philosophy all those other approaches have to be positioned toward the Co-design approach and reflected on in which way they contribute or not to the Co-design philosophy. From the description of the Ideal oriented Co-design approach I learned that the approach not only considers the technical aspects of a system but also organizational, managerial, moral and political aspects. I think these are important aspects and therefore have to be declared in order to facilitate for the developers and designers in their decision to adopt the Co-design philosophy and approach and not one of the others into their repertoire.

Improving the Road Metaphor

Albinsson and Forsgren use the metaphor of a road with three co-existing lines, when they describe the Ideal oriented Co-design approach. With this metaphor they want to visualize that different concerns run parallel in the process and that all lines do go all the way from the start of the process to the end. As the developers and designers drive the project along the road, it is possible to drive in different speed at different points along the road. This far I think the metaphor is alright, but when one of the lanes brakes up into two tracks, the metaphor – like a car – also get a breakdown. Even if it is just a metaphor I think it has to be improved.

  My interpretation is that the intention with breaking up one of the lines into two tracks is that along this so called consequence line; there will sometimes be need for using the decision track. Meantime the realization track, which is the other track, will go on continuously, just slowing down when considering the outcome of the decision track. To maintain the intention in this and the other lanes I can see two solutions. The first one is just to use four lanes instead of just three. But I guess that Albinsson and Forsgren already considered this and also have removed that possibility because decisions are not to be taken all the time. In the second solution I will suggest that this third lane get halting-places along the way. When there is a need for decisions the project drivers can turn over and halt during the time the decisions are considered. If there are no need for decisions the project just roll on.

But there is also another problem with the metaphor concerning the description of the Ideal oriented Co-design approach. Albinsson and Forsgren have through experience learned that the process need about three iteration to result in a reasonable, acceptable and stable design. The fact that they use the term iteration implies that there are recurrent activities in the software development process. If this is the intention, the metaphor should have had the look of a racing track instead of an ongoing road. But I don't think the authors mean iterations as it used in for example the methodology Rational Unified Process: RUP (Kruchten 1999). My interpretation of their description is that the Ideal oriented Co-design approach has an evolutionary approach which also the metaphor of the ongoing road implies. When talking about iteration I will instead suggest that the three lines in the metaphor pass through different landscapes. The first requires a sketch or a mock-up to make it possible for the drivers to be able to leave the area. The second requires a prototype and the third a deployable system. I think that putting in landscapes along the road of the development process, will make the metaphor dynamic. It is possible to put in new landscapes along the road, but also to alternate landscapes; without taking away the intentions of the three lanes. It is also possible to use the landscapes as a way to get new perspectives on the system about to be developed.

References

Albinsson L, Forsgren O (2004) Who's at the Wheel of User Driven Projects when User can't Drive? Presented at the Third International Conference on Systems Thinking in Management. University of Pennsylvania

Avison D, Fitzgeral G (2003) Information Systems Development: Methodologies, Techniques and Tools. McGraw-Hill London

Bausch K (2004) Be Your Enemy. In: C. West Churchman Legacy and Related Works. Vol 1. Rescuing the Enlightenment from Itself: Implications for Re-Working Democracy

Checkland P, Scholes J (1990) Soft System Methodology in Action. John Wiley & Sons Ltd Chichester

Churchman W (1971) The Design if Inquiring Systems. Basic Principles of Systems and Organization. Basic Books New York

Forsgren O (2004) Co-Design in Practice Building on the Churchmanian Philosophy of Knowledge. In: C. West Churchman Legacy and Related Works. Vol 1. Rescuing the Enlightenment from Itself: Impl for Re-Working Democracy.

Kruchten P (1999) The Rational Unified Process An Introduction. Addison Wesley Massachusetts

Nurminen M (1988) People or Computers: Three Ways of Looking at Information Systems. Studentlitteratur Lund

What's in It for Me? Co-design of Business and IS

Sandra Haraldson and Jan Olausson

School of Business and Informatics, University College of Borås, Sweden. (sandra.haraldson, jan.olausson)@hb.se

Introduction

Information systems development (ISD) of today is too limited, with a tendency to focus on the information systems as such. It has been claimed that system development could be seen as business development (cf. Winograd & Flores, 1986). When studying approaches to ISD one could however question how system development as business development is promoted (cf. Kruchten, 1999; Jacobson et al, 1995). Lately, a strong emphasis has been put upon successful IS project at the cost of not being able to focus enough on the business (context).

Several IS development methods uses business analysis in order to secure the projects knowledge about the context that the IS should support. But is it enough performing a business analysis and not consider the business perspective in the following phases of the system development process, and what perspectives should be included performing the business analysis? From a Scandinavian perspective use oriented design has been strongly emphasized. Is this isolation towards IS use enough to facilitate simultaneous development of IS and business? During the later years a co-design perspective (Forsgren, 2004; Rowe, 2005) on business and IS has been put forward.

In contemporary organizational change approaches, such as Business Process Reengineering (BPR) and Total Quality Management (TQM), the process notion is focused. Several different methods for process modelling exist and different methods are based on different conceptual frameworks and thus different process notions. Two views can be identified – the transformative and the communicative view (Keen, 1997; Goldkuhl & Lind, 2004). The transformative view can be regarded as a "manufacturing" view concerned with describing the transformation of input into output. This is of course important to describe, but in many situations it is apparently not sufficient, especially in the ISD area. This narrow view is challenged in Language/Action (L/A) approaches for business modelling; cf. e.g. Action Workflow (Medina-Mora et al, 1992) and DEMO (Dietz,

1999). This view is based on the idea that communication is not just transfer of information. When you speak, you also act (Austin, 1962, Searle, 1969). By using a communicative view on processes, the organizations' establishment and fulfillment of commitments are emphasized.

In this paper we are inspired by use centered design (cf. Arvola, 2004; Ehn & Löwgren, 1997; Holmlid, 2002). These theories emphasize the usage in the design process and derive from the work oriented design approach (cf. Ehn, 1988). Lately, several researchers have studied use in relation to information systems development (Olausson & Haraldson, 2005; Arvola, 2004; Ågerfalk, 2003; Holmlid, 2002). Information systems are part of a business structure, and the IS has no value in itself. It is when the IS is used, the value arises. In this paper IS use refers to a use situation, where the IS is an instrument humans use acting in business processes. We focus on digital artifact as IS for business processes, i.e. process oriented IS, and not digital artifacts in general.

As information system developers we want to enable design of process oriented IS, i.e. sufficient support for business processes. We have been conducting five process modeling projects, involving different organizations, and the cases have showed that IS do not support the business processes to a desirable extent. This paper put forward aspects that enables the designer to develop process oriented IS, where a co-design approach is considered as a mean for the development of such systems.

We adopt three use situations; (1) product utilization, (2) customer interaction and (3) IS use, identified and presented by Olausson & Haraldson (2005). The authors mean that these aspects are necessary to consider by the designer, in order to design process oriented IS.

Further, we build this paper on three foundations; (1) Businesses should be process oriented. (2) Business and Information systems should be developed in concert (i.e. co-designed). (3) Use is an important aspect when designing information systems.

In this paper we elaborate on the idea of the use situations as a co-design approach to IS development. It is our understanding that business characteristics, such as property of products, influence the business processes and therefore the perceptions of the different use situations.

We use four scenarios to illustrate the interrelationship between the use situations, based on different business characteristics and we conclude by comment on the implications for IS development.

The purpose of this paper is to explore how a co-design oriented approach to IS and business development can serve as a foundation for design of process oriented IS. To summarize; based on the knowledge of how to interpret use in co-design, *how are the different use situations interrelated and affected by different business characteristics?*

Co-Design of Business and IS

Information systems as a discipline is concerned with designed artifacts. The practice of information system is interplay between design and usage of such systems (Goldkuhl, 2004). Design as process, the IS development, and design as product, the developed IS, need to be addressed. Design is interpreted in a broad sense, involving "solving problems, creating something new or transforming less desirable situations to preferred situations" (Friedman, 2003, p. 507).

In order to design information systems it is important to understand the usage of the system and the role it has performing the business, to understand the IS as a part of the larger business structure. But during the design the IS and business have to be treated as different objects in order to reduce complexity of the design. Business development and IS development also derives from two different traditions. Business development according to Hammer (1996) and Davenport (1993), stresses business processes and the advantage with such a perspective are a clear focus on value creating activities and the customer. In this view the IT-system is, in the design situation, considered to be an enabler for business development. IS development takes, on the other hand, the system as a starting point and acknowledge the business only as the systems environment (e.g. Langefors, 1973). In our opinion, it is important to understand the business processes since the IS should support them. But, it is also important to acknowledge IT as a driver for business change. In the design process this implies a continuous shift in focus from IT to business processes and back, in order to co-design.

Further, IS development in itself can be dealt with from different perspectives. One is the L/A perspective mentioned above. Within the L/A community IS are regarded as communication and action systems. LAP approaches have been proven to be powerful for developing and understanding the role of IS in organizations, cf. e.g. Action Workflow (Medina-Mora et al, 1992) and DEMO (Dietz, 1999). These approaches are also to prefer since they include a customer orientation and emphasize commitments made by different parties.

Customer orientation implies a focus on the ones the organization produces value for. In order to ensure such value creation, it is essential that actions are performed with quality. In order to ensure high quality in organizations (meeting the customers expectations) there is a need to focus on the product produced for the customer, and how this is produced (transformative aspects). As a mean to reach this focus, it is important to acknowledge the communication within the organization as well as the interaction between the organization and the customer (communicative and co-ordinative aspects). A successful process of establishing commitments and fulfilling these commitments, determines communication quality.

In order to produce a co-designed product (for an elaboration on the concept of co-design see Olausson & Haraldson, 2005) it is necessary to consider stakeholders, of which the client is the most important. By considering the client, the use of the product are emphasized, and not the product as such (see Dahlbom, 2002). When adopting a *co-design approach* (Olausson & Haraldson, 2005), the designer has to take into consideration the ones affected by the design and by the usage. When designing a new information system, the existing systems must be taken into consideration. The old can then be seen as stakeholder in the design process.

A co-design approach implies a view on information systems, where the artifact must be considered in relation to its usage and effects on others besides the direct user (ibid.). Usage can only be comprehended indirectly through the operations by which they make sense to the persons involved (Gauthier, 1999). Goldkuhl & Röstlinger (2002), Dahlbom (2002) and Gauthier (1999), among others, acknowledge consideration to the usage and the identification of other stakeholders besides the client.

Three Use Situations

The design situation as such is complex, there are many aspects to reflect upon and several roles involved. Each use situation involves several roles, which are to be seen as stakeholders, with interest to either the product produced or the design process. The consideration to different aspects and interests could be done by several designers and in different ways. The important thing, at this point, is not how the consideration is done but that these aspects are acknowledged in some way in the process and that the designer makes active choices. Which interests the designers choose to consider depends on many factors such as influence, power etc. We do not elaborate on these aspects in this paper, but do acknowledge the importance and put them forward as further research.

A simultaneous development of business and IS implies consideration to different use situations (Olausson & Haraldson, 2005). Firstly, the use of business products has to be considered (*Product utilization – in figure 1*). In order to design good businesses, customers' satisfaction must be prioritized. Customers assess the product in the use situation. The customer would be unsatisfied if the product in use is different from the expectations, regarding the product. The possible use of the products must be reflected in the design of the business processes and therefore in the design of the IS.

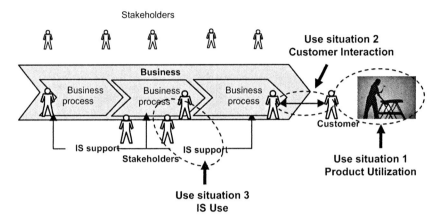

Fig. 1. Three use situations in co-design of business and IS (adapted from Olausson & Haraldson, 2005)

The second use situation (*Customer interaction - in figure 1*) is the use of the organization. Clients interact with the organization in order to fulfill a need, through using a service or purchasing a product, provided by the business. In the interaction, the organization and the customer need to understand the each others expectations. The organization must be able to understand the customer's expectations regarding the product, which means that the customer must be able to express the needs. The organization also has to express their expectations concerning customer's future actions, such as payments. The understanding of these expectations serves as a base for the commitment. In order to arrive at communication quality there is a need to distinguish between the organization as an actor and the agents within the organization, acting on behalf of the organization (Ahrne, 1994; Taylor, 1993).

The commitment is to be seen as establishment of expectations regarding the parties' future actions (Haraldson & Lind, 2005). The customer has certain expectations on the product and on the organization and the supplier has certain expectations on the customer's behavior. Of course there are other stakeholders to the business as such, all with different interests about how the business should act and behave, which we do not reflect upon in this paper. In use situation the client could be seen both as an indirect user to the developed IS and as a direct user of the developed organization.

The customer is an indirect user of the system through information provided by the business actors, in terms of product information such as availability and deliverance. The customer is also a direct user of the organization. For example, when the customer enters a store, (s)he interacts with the organization. If the customer does not get certain product information the organization can fail in fulfilling customer needs and meet the customer expectations. Other stakeholders to this situation are of course business actors, who acts based on the commitment established between the customer and the organization.

The third situation, is the use of the information system (*IS use - in figure 1*). The users of the developed system are the business actors. It is essential to understand the business processes and what support (in terms of information system) actors need performing the business. This, as well as the comprehension of the interaction between business actors and the information system, is necessary aspects when designing process oriented IS.

We believe that consideration to the three use situations provides a possibility to describe and handle the complexity of the design situation. We can describe it by acknowledge the three use situations, but in order to handle it we need guidelines how to behave. A framework is purposed as further research, at the end of this paper.

Four Scenarios

As mentioned earlier, we use four scenarios in order to clarify the three use situations and to identify business aspects that could influence the perception of the use. We refer to the four scenarios as; the bike store, the e-business, the hairdresser's and the e-service.

The first business, the bike store, is a regular store with the business concept of selling bikes to everyday people. The practice is constituted of several business processes; warehousing, sales and procurement among others. Potential customers have to enter the store in order to purchase a bike. In the store there are selections of bikes in display, and there are several variants kept in stock. The customer interacts with the organization through the sales personal. The sales personal are dependent on the IS during the interaction in order to provide the customer with valid information.

The second scenario is an e-business, selling home electronics via an internet store. In this example, the IS is used during the interaction between the customer and the organization. Potential customers need to enter the business web site in order to purchase the electronics. The web site is the only possible way for customers to purchase products.

The third scenario is a hairdresser's, who uses a scheduling system in order to plan the business. The hairdresser and the customer interact in the scheduling situation and the hairdresser uses the system in order to see time available and to make the time reservation. The information in the system then functions as a base when confirming the customer reservation.

The last scenario (e-service) is a bank providing services including paying invoices over the Internet. The bank also provides a number of additional services, not focused in this paper. The interaction between the bank and the customer goes via the bank web site.

Three Use Situations in Four Scenarios

As mentioned above, a simultaneous development of business and IS implies consideration to different use situations. In the sections below, the business characteristics in each scenario are emphasized. The first scenario is therefore the richest and the following stresses the aspects not included in the bike store scenario.

Three Use Situations in the Bike Store

The first use situation (*Product utilization - in figure 1*) implies the use of the business product. In order to design a good business, customers' satisfaction must be prioritized. Customers assess the product in the use situation and the customer would be unsatisfied if the product in use is different from the expectations, regarding the product. The possible use of the products must be reflected in the design of the business processes, and therefore in the design of the IS. The customer's as well as the organization's expectations about future actions should be established, and reflected in the commitment made by the two parties. This is made in the second use situation (*Customer interaction - in figure 1*), which refers to the use of the organization. The customer interacts with the organization in order to fulfill a need, through purchasing a product or a service provided by the business. Here, we refer to the customer entering the store in order to purchase a new bike. The customer is an indirect user of the system through information provided by the sales personal, in terms of product information such as availability and deliverance. The customer is also a direct user of the organization. When the customer enters the store, (s)he interacts with the organization. If the salesman is unable to get the certain product information, s(he) can not neither mediate the information to other business actors, nor provide the customer with sufficient information. The organization may thereby fail to fulfill customer needs and meet the customer expectations. Other stakeholders are the business actors, who act based on the commitment made by the two parties.

The third use situation is the use of the information system (*IS use - in figure1*). The IS users are the business actors, i.e. the warehouse, production and sales personal. It is essential to understand the business processes and what support (in terms of information system) the actors need performing the business actions. This, as well as the comprehension of the interaction between the business actors and the IS, are necessary aspects in order to design process oriented IS. The use, in this third use situation, reflects the personal working with warehousing and sales, interacting with the system in order to create customer value.

Three Use Situations in the E-Business

In this business, the second use situation is an aspect of IS use (*IS use - in figure 1*), were the customer interaction (*Customer interaction - in figure 1*) is one possible use of the IS. Therefore, the use of IS implies both customer using the web site in order to purchase home electronics and the internal business actors interaction with the IS in order to perform the business processes.

The IS designers have to consider the first use situation (*Product utilization - in figure 1*) when designing the web site. The interaction patterns constitute the service use, where the customer uses the IS and where the commitments are made. One stakeholder that clearly affects the interaction pattern is the supplier or base provider. If the e-businesses' and suppliers' IS are integrated it is possible to provide the e-business, and by that the customer, with stock information. By that the e-business could minimize their stock levels. Further, based on the information received, the e-business can offer the customer valid product information.

Three Use Situations at the Hairdresser's

At the hairdresser's, the customer interacts with the organization through both telephone i.e. when reserving time, and when utilizing the service i.e. getting the hair done. This implies the customer interaction to be two folded. The first use situation *(IS use – in figure 1)* appears when the business actor scheduling the customer. In this case, the second and third use situation occurs at the same time *(Customer interaction and product utili-*

zation – in figure 1). When the customer utilize the service (s)he also interacts with the organization. Designing an IS for the hairdresser's, implies understanding for the simultaneous use. If not considering these characteristics there could be consequences, such as double booking. Some acts take more time to perform and sometimes certain equipment is needed. In order to perform the business efficient, coordination is required. It is therefore essential that the person who makes the time reservation, perceives the customer's needs and that the system supports this action by allowing the expectations to be mediated and used as a base when the service is provided.

Three Use Situations in the e-Service Business

In the e-service business the customer interacts with the banks web site in order to pay invoices *(Customer interaction – in figure 1)*. In this case the actions' includes all three use situations. The customer uses the IS performing the payment *(IS use – in figure 1)*, (s)he interacts with the organization as well as utilizing the service at the same time, i.e. the customer utilize the service, interacting with the organization *(Customer interaction and product utilization – in figure 1)*.

What's In It for Me?

Developing process oriented IS is a matter of considering use situations. Process orientation is about providing value for customers, where value is constituted by use experience. Value adding activities in process oriented theories, refers to customer satisfaction (cf. Davenport, 1993). Customer satisfaction, drive the designer to ask the question "What's in it for me?" from a customer perspective. But, as we discussed above, the customer view is not enough, the designer has to consider other stakeholders as well. Further, this implies that *"me"* refers to different subjects depending on which use situation the designer considers. *"Me"* can also imply different stakeholders in the same use situation.

Characteristics in the four scenarios can be divided in two main groups; products/services and digital/non digital. If the business regards services the product utilization and customer interaction overlaps, and if the customer interaction is digital (e.g. e-commerce) it overlaps with the IS use.

Depending on business characteristics the use situations arise in different constellations. In the first scenario the use situations are evaluated separately. IS use, customer interaction and product utilization all occurs separated from each other. In the second scenario, the second and third use situation overlaps. The customer uses the IS for placing the order (interacting with the organization). In the third scenario the service utilization requires interaction with the organization. And finally, the last scenario illustrates how all use situations are consolidated into one. What implications does this variation of use situation have on the co-design approach?

Well, the designer has to consider the customer variation concerning different use property. There are different stakeholders to each use situation and each stakeholder has different perceptions regarding the use. A designer has to identify stakeholders in order to choose which interest to consider, i.e. making an active choice. It is also important for the designer to understand the notion of each use situation and how they interrelate. This perception affects the co-design and the possibility to meet stakeholders' expectations (above all the customers'). Therefore, the question "What's in it for me?" is a key question for designers. By consider stakeholders, the designer could identify perceptions of use, which enables design of process oriented IS.

From a designer's point of view, developing an IS for the fourth scenario (i.e. the e-service) might be easiest. The three use situations are consolidated into one and could therefore be regarded as one "single" situation. On the other hand, the demands put on this "single" use situation are higher, because the customer assesses the three use situations by experience one. For example, a bike purchase implies several ways for the business to influence the customer, such as correct stock information, knowledgeable sales personal and suitable products. In the bike store scenario, each use situation is assessed separately. In relation, the e-service only has one opportunity to influence the customer. The customer assesses all three use situations by one interaction.

In this paper we emphasis how the three use situations are affected by business characteristics and in the four scenarios, business characteristics vary and results in different business and IS requirements.

Our contribution in this paper is a further development of a co-design approach, by illustration of how the use situations are affected and dependent on different business characteristics.

As further research we propose development of a framework for how to act in line with a co-design approach to IS development. Other research questions that are important to address is the influence and power different stakeholder has in this approach.

References

Ågerfalk P (2003) Information Systems Actability – Understanding Information Technology as a Tool for Business Action and Communication. Doctoral Dissertation No 7 Linköping Studies in Information Science Linköping University Linköping Sweden

Ahrne G (1994) Social Organizations. Interaction Inside, Outside and Between Organization. Sage London

Arvola M (2004) Shades of Use – The Dynamics of Interaction Design for Sociable Use. Doctoral Dissertation No 900 Linköping Studies in Science and Technology Linköping University Linköping Sweden

Austin JL (1962) How to do Things with Words. Oxford University Press

Dahlbom B (2002) The Idea of An Artificial Science. In: Dahlbom B, Beckman S, Nilsson GB (eds) Artifacts and Artificial Science. Almqvist & Wiksell International Stockholm

Davenport TH (1993) Process Innovation – Reengineering Work through Information Technology. Harvard Business School Press Boston

Dietz JLG (1999) Understanding and Modelling Business Processes with DEMO, Proc of the 18th Int Conference on Conceptual Modeling (ER'99) Paris

Ehn P (1988) Work-Oriented Design of Computer Artefacts. Almqvist & Wiksell Stockholm Sweden

Ehn P, Löwgren J (1997) Design for Quality-In-Use: Human-Computer Interaction Meets Information Systems Development. In: Helander M, Landauer T, Prabhu P (eds) Handbook of Human-Computer Interaction. Second Completely Revised Edition. Elsevier Amsterdam Netherlands

Forsgren O (2004) Digital Commons and e-Service Co-Design Platforms – Theory, Challenges and a Framework Model. Presented at eChallenges E-2004 Vienna

Friedman K (2003) Theory Construction in Design Research: Criteria, Approaches, and Methods. Design Studies, vol 24, pp 507-522

Goldkuhl G (2004) Design Theories in Information Systems – a Need for Multigrounding. Journal of Information Technology Theory and Application (JITTA), vol 6, no 2, pp 59-72

Goldkuhl G, Lind M (2004) Developing e-Interactions – a Framework for Business Capabilities and Exchanges. Proc of the 12th European Conference on information systems (ECIS2004) Turku

Goldkuhl G, Röstlinger A (2002) The Practice of Knowledge – Investigating Functions and Sources, Accepted to the 3rd European Conference on Knowledge Management (3ECKM) 24-25 September 2002 Dublin

Gauthier P (1999) Technological Intervention and the Malady of Happiness. Design Issues, vol 15, no 2

Hammer M (1996) Beyond Reengineering – How the Process-Centred Organization is Changing Our Work and Our Lives. HarperCollins Business London

Haraldson S, Lind M (2005) Broken Patterns. Proc of the 10th International Working Conference on The Language Action Perspective on Communication Modelling LAP 2005 Kiruna

Holmlid S (2002) Adapting Users: Towards a Theory of Use Quality. Doctoral Dissertation no 765 Linköping Studies in Science and Technology Linköping University Linköping Sweden

Jacobson I, Ericsson M, Jacobson A (1995) The Object Advantage – Business Process Reengineering with Object Technology. ACM Press

Keen PGW (1997) The Process Edge – Creating Value where IT Counts. Harvard Business School Press Boston

Kruchten P (1999) The Rational Unified Process: an Introduction.Addison-Wesley

Langefors B (1973) Theoretical Analysis of Information Systems. Fourth Edition. Studentlitteratur Lund

Medina-Mora R, Winograd T, Flores R, Flores F (1992) The Action Workflow Approach to Workflow Management Technology. Proc of the Conference on Computer-Supported Cooperative Work CSCW'92

Olausson J, Haraldson S (2005) Process Oriented IS – Co-Design of Business and IS. Proc of the International Workshop on Communication and Coordination in Business processes CCBP 2005 Kiruna

Rowe D (2004) Open Applications and Solution Sharing for Goverments. Presented at eChallenges E-2004 Vienna

Searle JR (1969) Speech Acts: An Essay in the Philosophy of Language. Cambridge University Press London

Taylor JR (1993) Rethinking the Theory of Organizational Communication: How to Read an Organisation. Ablex Norwood NJ

Winograd T, Flores F (1986) Understanding Computers and Cognition: A New Foundation for Design. Ablex Norwood NJ

Modelling of Reusable Business Processes: An Ontology-Based Approach

Donatas Ciuksys and Albertas Caplinskas

Institute of Mathematics and Informatics, Vilnius, Lithuania.
donatas.ciuksys@maf.vu.lt, alcapl@ktl.mii.lt

Introduction

Reuse is one of most important issues in information systems (IS) engineering. Information systems mostly are used to support some business and must be aligned with supported business in all aspects. From the point of view of IS engineering, any business can be considered as a system that can be decomposed into two interrelated, however, relatively independent layers: basic entities that usually are referred as *registered units* (Caplinskas and Vasilecas 1998) and processes in which some basic entities are acting as actors. Other basic entities are used as process resources or manipulated by the processes as objects processed performing business transactions (business objects). Although each business process has its own view on basic entities, such entities also have some process-independent ontological properties. In information systems ontological properties of basic entities are registered and stored in process-independent databases called *registers* (Caplinskas and Vasilecas 1998). The notion of register comprises also service required to create and maintain appropriate database. In this paper we use term *application domain* to refer to the knowledge about basic entities and their ontological properties, and term *problem domain* to refer to the knowledge about a particular business process including knowledge about the specific, required only in the context of this process, properties of basic entities. So, in the proposed terms, each IS has one application domain and a number of problem domains. Application domain is implemented by a number of registers and each problem domain by an appropriate *functional subsystem* of IS. We suppose that registers are implemented as components and are shared by many different subsystems.

Ontologies in IS engineering are used to support both application domain knowledge (domain concepts) reuse and process domain knowledge (process concepts) reuse. Usually, however, both kind of knowledge are mixed, interrelated and business processes are described in terms of particular application domain. On the other hand, it is possible to separate knowledge about business entities and business processes, to generalise process knowledge, describe processes in terms of abstract roles (actors, resources, business objects, et cetera) played by basic entities but not directly in terms of basic entities themselves. In other words, it is possible to describe generic business processes and reuse such generic processes in different application domains. This idea has been proposed in (Caplinskas 2003) and elaborated in details in (Caplinskas and Ciuksys 2004). The main purpose of this paper is to propose ontology-based approach to domain engineering that enables process knowledge reuse. The research is still in progress. The main contribution of the paper is proposal how to separate business process and application domain knowledge during the engineering for reuse, how to combine business process knowledge and application domain ontologies during the engineering with reuse in a particular application domain and how, during this process, to associate problem domain knowledge with reusable domain-independent software components in order to build the functional subsystem supporting corresponding business process.

The rest of the paper proceeds as follows. The paper starts by discussing the notion of generic business process. After this reusable top-level ontologies are proposed. Then the main ideas of engineering with reuse in the proposed approach are illustrated with a particular example. Finally, paper ends with conclusions.

Generic Business Process

The notion of a generic business process is similar to the notion of generic task (Chandrasekaran 1986). A generic business process is an abstraction used to describe the family of particular processes. We suppose that generic processes have hierarchical structure and that different levels of the hierarchy describe the process with different granularity. Like the feature models (Kang et al. 1990), it consists of variable components (variabilities) and components included into each process of the family (communalities). Generic processes are described in terms of abstract roles (actors, inputs, outputs, resources, et cetera). They are designed with the intention to generate particular processes, that is, processes in which some basic entity of a particular application domain (or a group of such entities) is *assigned* to each process role. We say that particular process is created by the *location* of a generic process in a particular application domain. Apart of the assignment of roles, the location of a generic process in an application domain provides its *configuration* and its *refinement*. The purpose of configuration is to reject variabilities that are not relevant to the application domain. The purpose of the refinement is to decide about the granularity of the process.

We suppose that generic business processes are *role-limiting* processes. It means that for each role the properties of the basic entities that can candidate to play this role are defined by the set of constraints. On the other hand, we suppose that basic entities must be classified into subclasses of pretenders to play different roles. Although often role assignment is quite simple and takes down merely to the analysis of terminological differences between definitions in domain and process models, sometimes there exists significant semantic difference between roles and basic entities. In such cases, the mapping requires use of transformation rules that should be part of process location requirements.

A particular process (process located in a particular application domain) still is an abstraction because it describes a number of process instances all of which are intended to achieve the same goal.

Ontologies for Reuse

To be reused in different application domains, the business process software must be designed for reuse. It means that it must implement generic business process, more exactly, family of business processes. The proposed reuse approach attempts to combine domain-engineering techniques and ontology-based IS engineering techniques. This approach splits domain-engineering activities into two parallel groups of activities: process domain engineering and application domain engineering. Process domain engineering can be done in at least two different ways.

One approach is to extend the process domain analysis with additional activities for the development of business process ontology and to use this ontology to produce a model of generic business process. Process ontology should define concepts required to model business process, that is, it should specify primitives that constitute a generic process and define the roles played by the basic entities in the process. It also should serve as an interface to evaluate whether an application domain conforms to the structure of knowledge used by the process. Generic business model should describe the family of business processes having common aspects, predicted variability and granularity levels. Generic business model, in contradistinction to process ontology, includes high-level control knowledge. Control knowledge specifies the ordering of the generic process's steps, that is, how the process activities can be combined to generate process outputs. During the process domain design *generic process architecture* is produced. Generic process architecture is a parameterized scheme that describes the structural properties and components of appropriate functional subsystem. Components are described in the terms of roles. Generic architecture is the scheme that can be used to produce generic components (that is, parameterised components that include foreseen variabilities and granularity levels) as well as other reusable assets. Allowed sequencing of components is defined by a special component or in some other way. Reusable process assets are produced during the process domain implementation phase. The inputs for application engineering (that is, for engineering with reuse) phase are generic process architecture, application domain ontology, reusable process assets, UML™[1] platform profile and requirements describing implementation constraints. UML™ platform profile defines stereotypes necessary to express subsystem architecture in terms of a particular software platform (.NET, J2EE®[2], et cetera). The main shortcoming of this approach is that the control knowledge is being used in a very early phase (during process domain design) and cannot be adjusted later. As a consequence, the system produced in such a way often requires essential real-world business process's changes, because there is no way to change control knowledge in order to adapt it to real-world business process (control knowledge is hard-coded within generic process components). As a matter of facts, this is one of the most important disadvantages of ERP packages.

Another approach (Fig. 1) provides that process ontology is the only artefact developed during the process domain analysis phase. The only result of the process domain design in this approach is a parameterized scheme describing the structural properties and components of functional subsystem. In this case, reusable assets produced during process domain implementation phase do not include any control knowledge. Control knowledge is considered as a part of implementation requirements and is used during application engineering phase only. Thus, this approach eliminates disadvantages of the first approach.

At least two ontologies are necessary to support the proposed approach:

- application domain ontology, and
- business process ontology.

---

[1] UML™ is a trademark of Object Management Group, Inc.
[2] J2EE® is a registered trademark of Sun Microsystems, Inc.

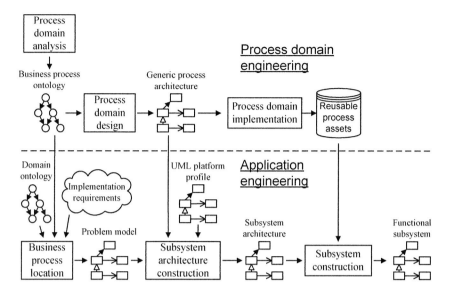

Fig. 1. Business process reuse

Application domain ontology captures domain knowledge independently of its use. To be useful for application engineering purposes however, domain knowledge should be organised in some special way. In addition, both application domain ontology and business process ontology should be described by some common system of metaconcepts. It means that some higher-level ontology must be developed. We call this ontology upper-level ontology (Fig. 2)

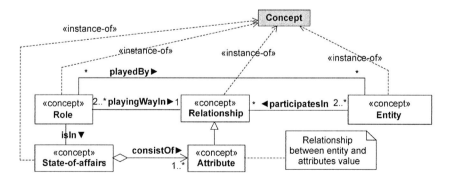

Fig. 2. Upper-level ontology

The upper-level ontology introduces generic concepts that are shared by all lower-level ontologies and reflect underlying theory about the nature of enterprise's social reality (discourse of interest). It is functional or, in other words, designed for specific purposes of enterprise information system design. This ontology has been influenced strongly by ideas beyond Uschold's enterprise ontology (Uschold et al. 1998). The most important difference between Uschold's enterprise ontology and our upper-level ontology is that we allow states for roles. Concepts defined by upper-level ontology are shared across all IS domains.

It should be noted that indeed we have three metalevels. In upper-level ontology two metalevels are present. The top level provides only one concept "concept" that is used to define second level concepts "entity", "relationship", "role", and "state-of-affairs". These concepts, in turn, are used to define third level concepts in application domain ontology and in business process ontology. In other words, we follow scheme provided by MOF^{TM}3 standard (Object Management Group, Inc. 2002). Following this approach instances of metaconcepts are concepts themselves. It means that concepts of lower level are instances of concepts of the higher level. Concepts that belong to the same level in ontology can be specialised using generalisation (that is, class/subclass) relationship.

One more note is that in this paper, for the sake of simplicity, we visualise the proposed ontologies using UML™-like diagrams (actually in our research we describe ontologies using OWL (World Wide Web Consortium 2004). It means that we use UML™-like language to describe ontologies. Because UML™ does not provide metamodelling facilities, our diagrams should not be considered as proper UML™ diagrams.

Application domain ontology (Fig. 3) introduces general concepts that are shared by application domains across all enterprises. This ontology provides categorisation of basic entities in two, possibly overlapping, categories: active entities and passive entities.

Active entities are possible candidates to play active roles (that is, to be actors) in business processes. They must have capabilities required to achieve some business goals or subgoals. Business goal is a state of passive entity that candidates to play output role in some business process. A special kind of capability is to be able to use some tools. Such organisation of knowledge in the application domain significantly facilitates mapping of actor roles to application domain entities.

---

3 MOF^{TM} is a trademark of Object Management Group, Inc.

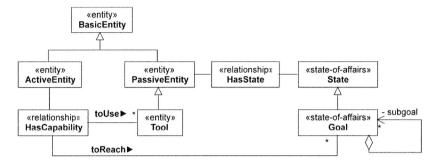

Fig. 3. Top-level ontology of application domain; concepts of this ontology are instances of upper-level ontology's concepts (shown as stereotypes)

In business processes, goals, subgoals and passive entities (including tools) candidate to play the roles of role states, inputs, outputs and resources/instruments (Fig. 4). Outputs (in some role state) must be mapped on physical objects with goals as their possible states. Such mappings should be provided as part of implementation requirements. The special kind of passive entities are tools. In business processes they candidate to play the roles of instruments. Instrument is the subclass of resource. Resources can be mapped into passive entities by matching of their attributes.

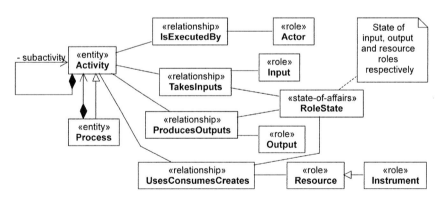

Fig. 4. Business process top-level ontology[4]

---

[4] The figure 4 and further figures do not show names of links between concepts because stereotypes fully define the meaning of links.

Process Knowledge Reuse

The main idea for engineering with reuse (Fig. 1) in our approach is:

- using implementation requirements, to configure reusable software components (that is, to remove non required variable features),
- combining application domain ontology and business process ontology to produce problem domain model and, using this model, to assign basic entities to business process roles and to store links between role names and entity names in configuration of name server,
- using problem domain model, to refine reusable software components up to required level of granularity,
- combining problem domain model and control knowledge to generate process specification (that is, process description in some process orchestration language) for a process execution engine.

It is assumed that the produced system will run in a component environment orchestrated by some BPM platform (Huntress 2004).

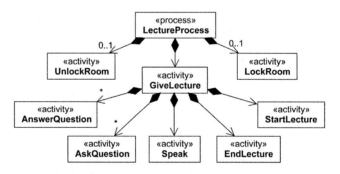

Fig. 5. Activity concepts of the "Lecture" process

Let us explain the proposed ideas in more detail using as an example a simplified lecture process. This process is considered as a generic process. It means that it can be reused in different universities, colleges as well as to give presentation at conferences. At the generic level, it can be seen as a process in which *speakers* tell something to *listeners*. A fragment of the ontology of this process is shown in Fig. 5. Ontology defines main activities of this process. Some activities are optional, as marked by multiplicities "0..1" or "*". For example, activity "UnlockRoom" is optional, meaning that there can be domains where the room should not be locked/unlocked before/after lecture. This activity is executed by the actor

"Keyholder" (Fig.6). The input of the process is "LockedRoom", and it must be in the state "Locked". The instrument "UnlockingInstrument" is provided to unlock the room (that is, to change its state). All names are role names. Process ontology does not include any control knowledge (that is, sequencing of activities).

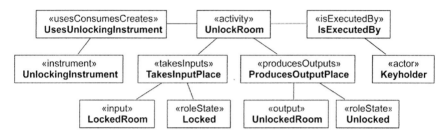

Fig. 6. A fragment of ontology for the activity "UnlockRoom"; it shows roles for actor, input, output and instrument

Control knowledge for generic lecture process is defined separately (Fig. 7). It is a part of implementation requirements. For the sake of simplicity, the figure does not show the activity "GiveLecture" itself. In general case, control knowledge has a hierarchical structure because any non elementary subactivity (in our example the subactivity "GiveLecture") has its internal control flow. The Fig. 7 presents the result of evaluation of the whole hierarchy. Control knowledge should be expressed in some process orchestration language, for example, BPEL4WS (Andrews et al. 2003), and intended to be executed by some process execution engine.

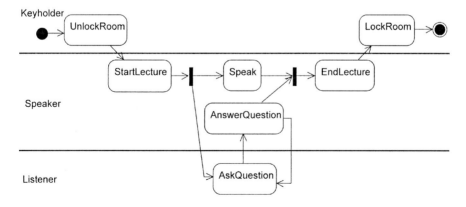

Fig. 7. Control knowledge for the lecture process

It is supposed that, at the information system level, each business process is supported by an appropriate information process. However, not all process activities must be supported by IS. During process domain implementation phase each activity that must be supported by IS is implemented as a reusable process asset. During application engineering phase assets are transformed to process components for a given platform, for example, Enterprise JavaBeans[5] (Sun Microsystems, Inc. 2003). Process execution engine calls these components in a sequence defined by process orchestration language. Such an approach looses coupling between components and facilitates the reuse of process components. Application domain entities are not referenced by process components directly. When needed, reference is provided by name server (role-name must be given as a parameter).

Fig. 8 shows a fragment of application domain ontology for a particular university. In this domain, the entity "Watchman" (an agent) has capability to use the entity "Key" (a tool). The entity "Watchman" is related to subgoals "UnlockedClassroom" and "LockedClassroom". Both subgoals define the states for instances of the entity "Classroom". The entity "Lecturer" is related to goal "LectureIsGiven" that defines the state for instances of the entity "LectureObject".

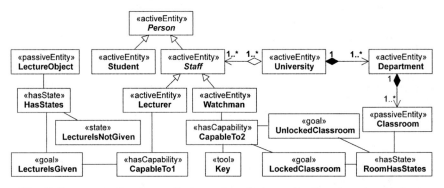

Fig. 8. Fragment of some particular university's application domain ontology

Fig. 9 shows goal hierarchy. The goal "LectureIsGiven" is the main goal and it has two subgoals: "UnlockedClassroom" and "LockedClassroom". Fig. 10 shows how domain entities are mapped to the roles of the activity "UnlockRoom". Firstly, hierarchy of role states of outputs is matched with goals hierarchy and the roles "LockedRoom" and "UnlockedRoom" are mapped to the entity "Classroom". Then the role "UnlockingInstrument" is

---

[5] Enterprise JavaBeans[®] is a registered trademark of Sun Microsystems, Inc.

mapped to the entity "Key". Finally, the role "Keyholder" (actor) is mapped to the entity "Watchman" (agent that will execute "UnlockRoom" activity).

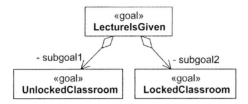

Fig. 9. Goal hierarchy

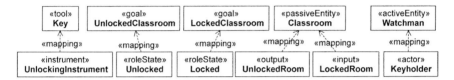

Fig. 10. Mapping of application domain entities to the roles of the activity "UnlockRoom"

Conclusions

Combining domain-engineering techniques with ontology-based approaches to IS engineering, it is possible to separate application domain knowledge and generic knowledge about business processes, and reuse process knowledge in a number of different information systems. Uschold's enterprise ontology (Uschold et al. 1998) provides an appropriate basis to model application domain knowledge as well as knowledge about business processes. Modern component environments and BPM platforms allow modifying traditional domain-engineering techniques in such ways that facilitate the reuse of process knowledge significantly. The paper only sketches the proposed approach. The research is still in progress. Further research intends to elaborate the proposed algorithm in detail, especially for the situations when the role should be mapped to the group of entities. It is also planed to elaborate further techniques to refine generic process, to produce assets and to generate process execution specifications for process execution engine.

References

Andrews T et al (2003) Business Process Execution Language for Web Services (BPEL4WS) version 1.1. www6.software.ibm.com/software/developer/library/ws-bpel11.pdf

Caplinskas A (2003) An Ontology-based Approach to Enterprise Engineering. Computer Science Reports, vol 14/ 03, pp 22-26

Caplinskas A, Ciuksys D (2004) Ontologies, Knowledge Reuse and Domain Engineering Techniques in Information Systems Engineering. Proc of the Thirteenth International Conference on Information Systems Development: Advances in Theory, Practice and Education. Vilnius Lithuania September 9-11

Caplinskas A, Vasilecas O (1998) Registers and Register – Based Information Systems. Proc of the Third International Baltic Workshop "BalticDB&IS'98". Riga Latvia April 15-17 1998

Chandrasekaran B (1986) Generic Tasks in Knowledge-Based Reasoning: High-level Building Blocks for Expert System Design. IEEE Expert, vol 1, no 3, pp 23-30

Huntress J (2004) BPM Can Enable Process Agility Which Can Enable Enterprise Agility. BPM Institute. www.bpminstitute.org/article/article/bpm-can-enable-process-agility-which-can-enable-enterprise-agility/news-browse/1.html

Kang K, Cohen S, Hess J, Novak W, Peterson A (1990) Feature-Oriented Domain Analysis (FODA) Feasibility Study. Technical Report CMU/SEI-90-TR-21 SEI Carnegie Mellon University Pittsburgh Pennsylvania

Object Management Group Inc (2002) Meta-Object Facility (MOF) specification, version 1.4. www.omg.org/cgi-bin/doc?formal/2002-04-03

Sun Microsystems Inc (2003) Enterprise JavaBeans, version 2.1. www.jcp.org/en/jsr/detail?id=153

Uschold M, King M, Moralee S, Zorgios Y (1998) The Enterprise Ontology. In: Uschold M, Tate A (eds) The Knowledge Engineering Review. Vol 13 Special Issue on Putting Ontologies to Use

World Wide Web Consortium (2004) Web Ontology Language (OWL). www.w3.org/2004/OWL/

Product Characteristics Influencing Customer Communication Media Portfolio in Distance Selling Settings

Karin Axelsson[1] and Britt-Marie Johansson[2]

[1] Department of Computer and Information Science, Linköping University, Sweden. karax@ida.liu.se
[2] Department of Informatics, Jönköping International Business School, Sweden. jobm@ihh.hj.se

Introduction

There has been a rapidly increasing establishment of distance selling businesses the last ten years. Many of those organisations have chosen Internet as their primary (and sometimes only) customer communication medium. Others have chosen to offer their customers a wide range of communication media. There are reasons for both these decisions, but both choices may also cause problems. Organisations that only offer one way of communication might exclude some customer groups, since different customers prefer different media. Organisations that allow many communication media might, on the other hand, be trapped in this generosity, since each medium added to the communication media portfolio means more channels to maintain.

There are several theories that try to explain why people choose to communicate through a certain medium and not others. One of the most referred, although highly criticised, theories is the media richness theory (Daft & Lengel, 1986). Its purpose is to explain managers' choice of communication media and to explore how to make communication more effective by choosing the appropriate communication medium. Our paper focuses on aspects that are central in media richness theory, but we are taking the criticism towards this theory into account; that there is not one effective way to communicate for all people or in all contexts (see Markus, 1994; Yates & Orlikowski, 1992; Carlsson & Zmud, 1999). Instead of adopting media richness theory as a guide when discussing how a communication media portfolio should be developed, we are interested in how different product types might affect the customer communication. Nevertheless, there are similarities between what we try to understand and the knowledge objects of media richness theory.

In this paper we will discuss the thesis that a distance selling company should let their product type(s) influence the customer communication portfolio. We are using a product classification scheme by Goldkuhl and Röstlinger (2000) in order to classify products in two distance selling companies. We have conducted case studies in these two organisations (the Photo Company and the CD Company) and have found typical questions and problems that the customers have in each case. By comparing these problems to the different product types we aim at finding some illustrations of how the product type affects which customer communication media that are more or less feasible. The purpose of the paper is to shed some light on important issues to consider for companies when deciding which customer communication media they should include in their portfolio and which media they should leave out.

Product Classification

There is a classical division between goods and services, in literature as well as in daily conversations. The product a customer buys is either a physical "thing" or an immaterial "assistance" of some kind. Service marketing is a research field that has focused on the characteristics of services in comparison to characteristics of goods (Grönroos, 1990). Grönroos (ibid.) defines services to be intangible (immaterial), inseparable in production and consumption, heterogeneous and perishable (i.e. having no separate and lasting evidence). These characteristics have, however, been questioned by Goldkuhl and Röstlinger (2000), who criticise the division between goods and services as being outdated. Instead, they state that the notion of action is important when characterising goods and services. They base their objections on a pragmatic perspective, which means that actions are performed by an actor who has certain intentions (von Wright, 1963). Each action results in something. There are material actions which give rise to material results, other actions are of a communicative nature and many actions are social. This pragmatic ground implies that we need a more detailed division of products, than just to distinguish between goods and services. (Goldkuhl & Röstlinger, 2000)

In order to better understand the characteristics of pragmatism we refer to Goldkuhl (2004) who explores the meanings of pragmatism and its consequences for information systems research. He formulates six aspects that distinguish pragmatic research; an interest for actions, an interest for actions in their practice context, an acknowledgement of action permeation on knowledge, an interest for practical consequences of knowledge, an interest in what works and what does not work, and an acknowledgement of the full dialectics between knowledge and action; i.e. proper action is knowledgeable action and proper knowledge is actable knowledge (ibid.).

We will not go into detail about Goldkuhl's and Röstlinger's criticism of Grönroos' service characteristics in this paper. In short, they use arguments from the pragmatic perspective to show that services are not always intangible, inseparable in production and consumption, heterogeneous, or perishable. The result of their critical investigation is, thus, that these aspects are not determinant characteristics for services. Goldkuhl's and Röstlinger's criticism follows previous critique of the division of goods and services made by von Wright (1995) and Castells (1996). As an alternative to the common division of goods and services, Goldkuhl and Röstlinger (2000) formulate a product classification consisting of four main product classes and eight sub-classes: Provided goods (Goods for transfer and Temporarily provided goods), Treatment (Treatment of client's property and Treatment of client), Transportation (Transportation of client's property and Transportation of client), and Presentation (Exhibition of goods and Presentation of producer).

This classification builds on the notion that both goods and services might have either a material or immaterial character; i.e. there are both material and immaterial goods as well as services. It also builds on a division between four use situations; material use, informative use, experiential use, and financial use, in order to characterise differences in anticipated customer use and potential satisfaction. Goldkuhl and Röstlinger claim these to be generic producing acts and products. (ibid)

A reason to use this classification scheme is that we find Goldkuhl's and Röstlinger's pragmatic arguments attractive since we agree with the notion of actions as important objects to focus on, in order to understand situations and contexts. The basic standpoint of the classification scheme is the two actor roles of the producer and the customer. The producer performs actions that result in a product, intended for the customer. The customer performs actions of consumption when receiving and using the product. There will be customer effects of the product and its use; the customer might be satisfied or not. There might also be producer effects when the acts, the results, and the customer reactions retroact on the producer, which is an example of the reflexive and learning aspect of action (ibid.).

In table 1, the product classification scheme is illustrated with examples of each class. The product classes are ideal types. In reality many products are multifunctional, since they fulfil several purposes (ibid.).

Table 1. Product classification scheme (Goldkuhl & Röstlinger, 2000:8)

	Material	Informative	Experiential	Financial
Goods for transfer	Goods purchased for material use	Goods purchased for informative use	Goods purchased for experiential use	Goods/financial means purchased in purpose of exchange/returns
Example	Purchased car	Purchased textbook	Purchased video film (action)	Bond
Temporarily provided goods	Goods rented/ borrowed for material use	Goods rented/ borrowed for informative use	Goods rented/ borrowed for experiential use	Goods/financial means borrowed in purpose of exchange/returns
Example	Rented car, rental of washing facilities for car	Book (non-fiction) borrowed from library	Rented video film, game session in squash hall	Loan of money
Treatment of client's property	Clients' property treated with material aim	Clients' property treated with informative aim	Clients' property treated with experiential aim	Clients' property treated with financial aim
Example	Car repair service	Auditing, vehicle test	Copying of photos or film	Stock administration
Treatment of client	Client treated for physical effect	Client treated for increase in knowledge	Client treated for experiential enhancement	Client treated for economic influence
Example	Eye operation	Eye examination, training	Psychotherapy	Personal insurance
Transportation of client's property	Client's property/material transported with material purpose	Client's property/information transported with informative purpose	Client's property/information transported with experiential purpose	Client's property/financial means transported with economic purpose
Example	Transportation of furniture	Telephony, mail, e-mail, telefax	Telephony, mail, e-mail, telefax	Order for payment, withdrawal from account

Table 1. (cont.)

	Material	Informative	Experiential	Financial
Transporta-tion of client	Client trans-ported with purpose to change loca-tion	Client trans-ported with informative purpose	Client trans-ported with experiential purpose	
Example	Bus journey	Driving lesson	Cruise	
Exhibition of goods		Goods exhib-ited with informative purpose	Goods exhib-ited with experiential purpose	
Example		Television broadcast documentary	Art exhibi-tion, enter-tainment film	
Presentation of producer		Producer presentation with informa-tive purpose	Producer presentation with experien-tial purpose	
Example		Lecture given by public lecturer	Theatre performance	

Research Method

We have performed two qualitative, interpretive case studies in distance selling businesses in order to analyze the customer communication media portfolio and the effect of product characteristics. The methods used to collect data about the companies, the way they communicate, their experiences, and opinions of customer communication, etc. are interviews, observations, and examination of different documents such as data stored in databases, publications, marketing documents, and policy documents. This method triangulation has been necessary to get a truthful view of both the companies' and the customers' perspectives on customer communication.

In both companies interviews with the managers of the customer service departments were followed by observations of the employees attending the different communication media. The observations entailed listening to telephone calls from customers, observing the registration of order forms and answering of e-mails as well as letters and faxes. During the observations we also asked the employees about observed events. As the questions were posed in the working environment they were used as complement to the prepared question guides used during the interviews. The observations were followed by further interviews with the managers of the customer service departments as well as interviews with employees. These, in turn, were followed by new observations and so on until a state of redundancy was reached, i.e. a state where new data did not add any further findings.

Empirical Cases

The two studied cases show several differences compared to each other, which make them suitable to use. We are going to examine the cases in order to find what kind of typical questions customers in each case pose to the company. By doing so we aim at finding examples of what kind of problems a specific product type may cause the customers. The studied cases are a company that sells CDs and a company that develops digital photos. As the companies participated in this study on the condition of anonymity they are named by their products, i.e. the CD Company and the Photo Company. Common for the two cases are that neither of them has any physical shop and they have no face-to-face communication with their customers.

The CD Company

The case study at the CD Company was carried out between fall 2000 and spring 2002. The CD Company is a retailer, selling music CDs on the Swedish and the Norwegian market. The company was founded by the present CEO some thirty years ago and is now a subsidiary in a corporation with several mail order companies in several countries in Europe. The company has approx. 30 employees.

To purchase from the company, customers are required to register and become members of the customer club. All members receive a monthly magazine with a mandatory offer. The customers will receive the offer if they do not turn it down. Customers can also order other products, which are offered in the magazine and on the company's Internet site. The CD Company offers their customers the following communication media; telephone, fax, letter, membership coupons and order forms, e-mail, voice response system, and web-based interface.

Some of these media are offered for any business action (such as posing questions or making complaints) and other media are only offered for placing orders and turning down the offer of the month. In table 2 we illustrate each communication medium's different usage possibilities in a business action matrix (Johansson & Axelsson, 2005).

Table 2. Business action matrix of the CD Company

	Tele-phone	Fax	Letter	Membership coupons, order forms	E-mail	Voice re-sponse system	Web-inter-face
Placing or-der	x	x	x	x	x	x	x
Turning down man-datory offer	x	x	x	x	x	x	x
Posing questions	x	x	x		x		FAQ
Making complaints	x	x	x		x		

The company sells music CDs; a product that according to the product classification scheme is *goods purchased for experiential use*. This means that the CD is a material product, but it is not until the customer listens to the music that she gets any real use of the product. The customer experiences something when listening; she is either pleased or dissatisfied with the outcome. The product is standardized; i.e. each item is similar and there are no ways for customers to influence the product.

Typical Customer Questions and Problems in the CD Company

Most questions and problems presented from the CD Company's customers are common to any mail order company. Some of them relate to when products, currently out of stock, will be delivered, how to return a delivered product, how long the delivery time will be, if it is possible to defer the payment for delivered products. Specific questions concerning the product are e.g. if a recently released CD is sold by the company or in what CD a specific song is to be found. The most complicated questions are when a customer needs help with finding out who the artist of a certain song is or the name of a song heard on the radio or on the television.

The company is very positive to their customers using the voice response system. By the voice response system the customers serve themselves which gives the employees more time to attend other matters. Another appreciated communication media, from the company's perspective, is the e-mail as e-mails can be attended to at any hour and from anywhere.

The Photo Company

The second case is a company offering several photo services by mail order. The company was founded about 30 years ago in Sweden, but is now a subsidiary of a larger European corporation dedicated to the photo business. The Photo Company has approx. 130 employees and serves the Nordic market. All production is placed in Sweden. The product in focus in this paper is the development of digital photos (the company also develops photos from traditional roles of film). The case study at the Photo Company was carried out during the autumn and the winter of 2004.

When placing an order, the digital pictures can be sent by mail on memory cards, on CDs or be uploaded on the company's web site. When sending items by mail the customers can use a certain photo envelope to put the items in. These envelopes are sent to potential and current customers as a recurrent marketing action. Some customers even send their digital pictures attached to e-mails, but that is not a communication alternative marketed by the company. The fastest way to send digital pictures is by uploading them to the customer's personal page on the company's web site.

The Photo Company offers their customers the following communication media; telephone, fax, letter, order forms (photo envelopes), e-mail, and web-based interface.

Some of these media are offered for any business action (such as posing questions or making complaints) and other media are only offered for sending the electronic files for developing photos. In table 3 we illustrate each communication medium's different usage possibilities in a business action matrix.

According to the product classification scheme the product is *client's property treated with experiential aim.* This means that the customer sends a piece of her property to the company; i.e. a memory card, a CD, or by uploading an electronic file. The company delivers photos from this property (either on paper or in digital form), which the customer uses by looking at the pictures, showing them for friends, giving them away as presents, etc. Thus, the product is used in an experiential way. The customer might be pleased or dissatisfied with the quality of the pictures, but also with the photographed subject which might bring good memories from a holiday.

Table 3. Business action matrix of the Photo Company

	Tele-phone	Fax	Letter	Order forms, photo envelopes	E-mail	Web-interface
Placing order (memory card)			x	x		
Placing order (CD)			x	x		
Placing order (upload electronic files)					x	x
Posing questions	x	x	x		x	FAQ
Making complaints	x	x	x		x	

Typical Customer Questions and Problems in the Photo Company

The increased adoption of digital photo technology has changed the situation for the Photo Company in many aspects. They get many and often very time consuming customer questions about digital photos. Customers need help with their computing settings, the application to edit the digital photos and how to upload their photos on the company's web site.

Apart from these questions, there are also common questions about why a picture did not come out as good as expected. The employee then has to ask the customer about light conditions when the photo was taken, if a flash was used, if the photos the customer is not satisfied with were taken outdoors, and so on. Sometimes unsuccessful photos are the result of the photographer's inexperience and sometimes the result of low quality of the camera used. In these cases the matter is delicate to discuss with the customer. As the questions from customers often are complicated, the Photo Company prefers telephone questions instead of questions posed on e-mail. If a customer has problems when downloading the photos on the web, this could be due to many different reasons. All these reasons, thus, have to be explained in the e-mail, which takes a lot of time in each case.

Sometimes the customers do not receive the photos they expect. The Photo Company has a department dedicated to tracking lost photos or mapping returned photos with customers missing their photos. Many times they have to call the customers and ask them about details in the photos, to make sure they will send the right ones.

Discussion

Our two cases give us good examples of the similarities and differences between the studied products. The CD Company's product is a material and standardised product. In this case, the order process might be handled by many different communication media, but the delivery process always needs to include physical logistics for the product to reach the customer.

The Photo Company, on the other hand, has a product which could be both material and digital, depending on which media the customer chooses to have the photos delivered on (paper or disc). The order process is more complex in this case, since the order includes a delivery from the customer. The product cannot be produced without a treatment of the customer's property, i.e. its digital pictures. The Photo Company has not got a true digital product, though, since there is always some material element in the process; the customer might send a material storage of the electronic files (a memory card e.g.) or the company delivers the photos on a material disc. This is an important distinction, since it is only true digital products that could be handled in a totally digital business process. In our cases there is always some element of physical delivery, which affects the communication media chosen.

The similarity between the studied products is that both have an experiential purpose. The difference when it comes to experiencing the products is that the customer is a "passive" listener when using the CD, but she affects the quality of the photos taken. Thus, she is involved in the product quality in this case. This also results in a more or less complex process if the customer is not satisfied with the product or the delivery process. The CD can easily be replaced by another copy if broken under transport or exchanged to another artist if not satisfactory. In the Photo Company there is a much more complex process if the customer is not satisfied with the product quality, since it might be due to the photographer's skills. If the products are not delivered it is also complex to investigate which motives that have been delivered by the customer but not developed by the company. These examples of varying complexity affect feasible communication media for this interaction. Standardised and automatic media (e.g. web interface or voice response system) might be a good choice for the CD Company, but the Photo Company probably would get much extra work if they were not able to talk directly to their customers in problematic cases. When it comes to uploading the electronic files, on the other hand, the web interface is the most convenient medium for the Photo Company. The findings above also indicate that a voice response system is not of much use in cases where the customer needs to contribute with some piece of property in order for the product to be produced, as in the Photo Company.

The fact that there are many alternative operative systems, web browsers and other settings in the customers' computers makes it often difficult to communicate by e-mails, in the Photo Company, where the customer needs a certain application to be able to edit and upload the files at the web site. Telephone is, thus, a faster communication medium, which allows the company to ask detailed questions about computer settings, whether the customer has tested other alternatives etc. Employees have the same applications and are able to solve the problems by guiding the customer through each step. In this case direct contact through telephone is highly appreciated by both company and customers. Compared to the Photo Company, the CD Company has less complex customer questions to handle, which makes e-mail a favoured medium in this case.

Conclusion

The main lesson learned in this paper is that distance selling companies should let the product type influence the communication media portfolio. Our use of the product classification scheme by Goldkuhl and Röstlinger (2000) shows that this is a feasible classification for this purpose.

The main motive for choosing Goldkuhl's and Röstlinger's product classification scheme is that we find this classification detailed enough to give us proper help when classifying product types in our case studies. The detailed product classes imply a thorough conceptualisation, which is useful. The common division of products and services would have been much too blunt for this purpose. The fact that only one class (goods for transfer) treats goods in a traditional sense, although there are elements of goods in some of the other classes, implies that this classification is much more exhaustive than earlier attempts to distinguish between goods and services. If we relate this to distance selling settings, we claim that many of the B2C organisations that we find on Internet offer products that are a mixture of goods and services. This is another important motive for us to use this classification scheme. The classification scheme also highlights the intentions behind different actions, which we see as very important to take into account when making decisions about which communication media to include or exclude in the communication media portfolio.

There are of course other aspects to take into account when developing a customer communication media portfolio, besides product type. Our aim in this paper has, however, been to highlight that product type is one important aspect, that should not be neglected in this context. In both case studies we have analysed a product which is used in an experiential way. Thus, we need further studies to expand the scope and look at distance selling businesses that sell products for material, informative, and financial use as well. Such studies would be interesting since other product types might give us insights that we have failed to recognise in this paper. The findings would also gain in generalisation if studies covering all product classes in the classification scheme were conducted.

References

Carlson J R, Zmud R W (1999) Channel Expansion Theory and the Experimental Nature of Media Richness Perceptions. Academy of Management Journal, vol 42, no 2, pp 153-170

Castells M (1996) The Information Age. Economy, Society and Culture. Volume 1, The Rise of the Network Society. Blackwell, Oxford

Daft RL, Lengel RH (1986) Organizational Information Requirements, Media Richness and Structural Design. Management Science, vol 32, no 5, pp 554-571

Goldkuhl G (2004) Meanings of Pragmatism: Ways to Conduct Information Systems Research. Presented at the 2nd International Conference on Action in Language, Organisations and Information Systems (ALOIS 2004). Linköping, Sweden 17-18 March 2004

Goldkuhl G, Röstlinger A (2000) Beyond Goods and Services – An Elaborate Product Classification on Pragmatic Grounds. Presented at The Seventh International Research Symposium on Service Quality (QUIS 7), Karlstad, Sweden, June 13-16 2000

Grönroos C (1990) Service Marketing and Management. Managing the Moments of Truths in Service Marketing. Lexington Books, Lexington

Johansson B-M, Axelsson K (2005) Analysing Communication Media and Actions – Extending and Evaluating the Business Action Matrix. In: Bartman D et al. (eds) Proc of the 13th European Conference on Information Systems (ECIS2005), Regensburg, Germany 26-28 May 2005

Markus ML (1994) Electronic Mail as the Medium of Managerial Choice. Organization Science, vol 5, no 4, pp 502-527

von Wright GH (1963) Norm and Action. Routledge & Kegan Paul, London.

Yates J, Orlikowski WJ (1992) Genres of Organizational Communication: An Approach to Studying Communication and Media. The Academy of Management Review, vol 17, no 2, pp 299-326

Process Maturity and Organizational Structure as a Framework for Performance Improvements

Rok Škrinjar, Vlado Dimovski, Miha Škerlavaj and Mojca Indihar-Štemberger

Faculty of Economics, University of Ljubljana, Slovenia. (rok.skrinjar, vlado.dimovski, miha.skerlavaj, mojca.stemberger)@ef.uni-lj.si

Introduction

Business and technological change threatens organizational sustainability, which depends on a balance between change and order. Few organizations can control the forces that affect them, but they can control the way in which they deal with those forces. Organizations today face increasing pressures to integrate their processes across disparate divisions and functional units, in order to remove inefficiencies as well as to enhance manageability. Although many enterprises acknowledge the need to be quick and responsive in a global economy and market that is constantly changing, many are not adequately structured to do so. The functional/divisional organizational structure, the legacy form industrial age and one of the major agility inhibitors, is still predominant.

In the paper we develop a process-structure development model that serves as a framework for organizational development. Model is built using capability maturity model and evolution of organizational structures model. Any change initiative based on only one of the models is too narrow in its nature so the results are innately subordinate, and are often far from what has been planned and anticipated. By combining the two we suggest that for optimal gains changes must occur simultaneously.

Framework should also be considered when new information technology is deployed in an organization. Neglecting the processes and/or structures might severely limit the benefits of any new technology, software, hardware or an integrated solution. Information technology should never be considered in isolation from such concepts as it, by itself, can not improve the organizational performance.

The structure of the paper is as follows. First, we present some of business renovation methodologies, examine their success rate and review the literature on the critical success factors of BPR. Next, we introduce the capability maturity model used to assess the process maturity. In the next section the evolution of organizational structures is briefly discussed and subsequently the process-oriented organizational structure is thoroughly presented. Next we present our synthesized model of process-structure development. In the last section main practical implications are described, limitations of the model are exposed and recommendations for future research are outlined.

From Functions to Processes

To cope with the challenges organizations must accept process-based management principles. Process is one or more tasks that add value by transforming a set of inputs into a specific set of outputs (goods or services) for another person (customer) by a combination of people, methods, and tools (Tenner and DeToro 1997). The process paradigm implies a new way of looking at organizations based on the processes they perform rather than the functional units, divisions or departments they are divided into. The perceived need for such a shift in organizational design stems from the fact that, despite the changes in contemporary economic and social environments, management values and principles from the industrial revolution still determine the organizational structure of many modern firms. This has resulted in companies being organized around functional units (departments or divisions), each with a highly specialized set of responsibilities. In such form of vertical organization units become centers of expertise that build up considerable bodies of knowledge in their own subjects, but even the simplest business tasks tend to cross functional units and require the co-ordination and co-operation of different parts of the organization (Giaglis et al. 1999 taken from Blacker 1995).

To be a truly world-class organization, the company needs to work as a team and all the functional areas of the business need to be properly integrated, with each understanding the importance of cross functional processes. As the basis of competition changes from cost and quality to flexibility and responsiveness, the value of process management is now being recognized (O'Neill and Sohal 1999).

The transition from functional/divisional organizational to process design can take many forms. Business process (re)design is one of the most common forms of organizational change (Smith 2003). Business process redesign is any planned change in a business process to permanently improve the functioning of that process. The change may involve redefining the steps in the process, applying new technology (including software and hardware), redefining performance standards, improving the quality of inputs, training the personnel responsible for the process, enhancing management's control over the process, and enhancing the alignment among processes.

Business process redesign was a major trend in the 1990s. Many authors and researchers tackled the subject and developed their own understanding and management guidelines on the issue. As a result there are many terms that describe the same general idea. O'Neil and Sohal (1999), reviewing the literature on the subject of business process reengineering, cited the following variations: business process improvement, core process redesign, process innovation, business process transformation, breakpoint business process redesign, organizational reengineering, business process management, business scope redefinition, organizational change ecology, and structured analysis and improvement.

Putting the terminology aside, all of the ideas provided above had the basic aim of bridging the problems organizations faced and improving their performance. Selection of the improvement approach that is appropriate for each process at any given time is based on three factors: the importance and opportunity associated with closing a performance gap and the feasibility of the improvement effort. Wide areas of organizational changes span from an ongoing continuous improvement efforts (e.g. TQM) to occasional breakthrough reengineering projects (e.g. BPR).

Business process reengineering on one side is the fundamental rethinking and radical redesign of business processes to achieve dramatic improvements in critical measures of performance, such as cost, quality, service and speed (Hammer and Champy 1993). Continuous improvement on the other end of the spectrum accents improvements efforts that are more frequent (ongoing) but have smaller, more incremental impact on firm's operations.

During the 1990s many firms undertook the BPR projects and despite its promising scheme the success rate was well below the desired one. Different studies report different failure rates of BPR project and span from 70% (Champy 1995) to almost 80% (Smith 2003) failure rate. Such results fueled new studies in order to identify reasons for failure.

Determining the critical success factors (CSF) of business process reengineering emerged as a response to low success rates of BPR projects. Many authors approached the subject and the list of CSFs appeared. As the list grew so did the need to synthesize the CSF framework. Guimaraes (1997) categorizes CSF into 6 categories: [1] External, [2] Employee empowerment, [3] Operational, [4] Communication, [5] Methods and Tools, [6] Leadership. Sung and Gibson segment CSF as [1] Strategic, [2] Organizational [3] Methodological [4] Technological and Educational. Al-

Mashari and Zairi (1999) cite 5 dimensions. One of common characteristics of any CSF framework we have found is the fact that organizational factors are highly neglected or are absent altogether.

Practitioners, next to the academics, similarly fail to recognize the significance of structural elements in redesign projects. In their empirical study of Korean firms Sung and Gibson (1998) found that managers attribute the least importance to organizational factors. Further more, they are the least prepared for organizational changes needed to support the BPR project and maintain the redesigned processes.

What the majority have overlooked or barely touched upon is to our opinion one of the key reasons for BPR project failures. Factors of organizational structure design are of paramount importance in delivering successful BPR projects as well as sustaining the gains in business performance. In support of this statement, Sung and Gibson (1998) showed the positive association between BPR and business performance in their study. In our opinion the organizational design changes should go hand in hand with BPR efforts. Implementing new processes can not take place in a rigid environment of functional organizational structure. Instead, corresponding structural changes must reflect the new processes and support and enable their implementation. Process-oriented organization is one such organizational design that enables new work practices and is presented in the following sections.

The Evolution of an Organization's Understanding of Processes

The transition to process-oriented organization starts with the understanding of business processes. Although majority of organizations have some sort of documentation describing their processes (Škerlavaj 2003) it is mainly in the function of ISO9000 quality standard. This documentation is of limited real value for the organizational redesign purposes. Furthermore, it does not enlighten the true functioning of the organization and in that respect does not help managers and employees better understand the business processes within the organization.

To analyze firm's understanding of their processes we propose the use of the adapted Capability Maturity Model (CMM) (Harmon 2003) that was designed as a reference model of the stages that organizations go through as they move from immature to mature in their understanding and management of processes. CMM identifies five levels or steps that describe how organizations typically evolve from immature to mature organizations as follows:

- Level 1 – Initial: The processes are ad hoc, few activities are explicitly defined and success depends on individual effort and heroics. Entrepreneurial organizations and new divisions do things anyway they can to get started.
- Level 2 – Repeatable: At this level, basic project management processes are established to track costs, and to schedule. As the organizations become more mature they begin to conceptualize business processes and seek to organize them, repeat successes, and measure them.
- Level 3 – Defined: Processes are documented and standardized throughout an organization.
- Level 4 – Managed: Detailed measures of process and product quality are defined. Both processes and products are quantitatively understood and controlled.
- Level 5 – Optimizing: Organizations at this level routinely expect managers end employees to improve processes. They understand their processes well enough that they can conduct systematic experiments to determine if changes will be useful or not.

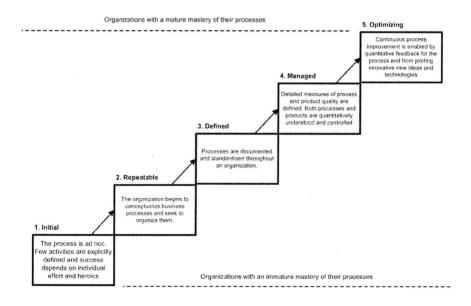

Fig. 1. Five levels of capability maturity model

At each stage certain process management practices have to be implemented before moving to higher capability level (Jung 2004). Jiang et al. (2004) showed that managerial activities at higher levels related positively to software development projects' performance measures. The purpose of the model is to assess at which stage the organization is and to assist in developing a road map to help them where they want to go. Process maturity is the foundation for process-oriented organization as processes themselves take the central role in it. Figure 1 outlines the levels of process maturity.

It should be stressed, however, that implementing CMM takes a lot of effort and requires many resources. It has also been shown that the benefits are only realized after level 3 has been reached (Jiang et al. 2004). Considering the findings of Herbsleb et al. (1997) that it takes between 21 to 37 months to move from one level to another, managers should carefully plan the CMM implementation activities.

Process Oriented Organization

The evolution of the organization can also be viewed as the progress in the organizational design and structure changes. Figure 2 depicts the organizational design development from classical hierarchal type (like functional and divisional organizational structure) trough process-oriented (also termed horizontal organization) to the learning organization, the highest developmental stage of organizational design to date. The main problems encountered in typical vertical organizations (phase one) are the lack of cooperation and coordination between functional departments that function almost in seclusion from other departments. This leads organizations to form project teams, which are responsible for temporally linking previously isolated departments. The result is improved horizontal coordination, however the benefits are limited in time scope as team formation is usually attached to a specific project and is disassembled after the completion of project. The third phase, as its name implies, focuses on core processes and this is the focal point of this paper. The last phase is the learning organization, which is at this moment the most advanced organizational form capable of providing the framework for optimal performance and competitive advantage attainment. The process-oriented organization is not only a step on the path to the learning organization, but is at the same time one of its constituting elements for implementation.

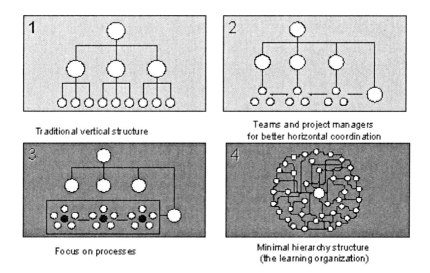

Fig. 2. Evolution of organizational structures

Basic Principles of Process-Oriented Organization

Principles of process-oriented organization (Ostroff 1999) describe their fundamental characteristics and can broadly be divided in two groups. The first group is the design principles. The central principle (1) is to organize work around cross-functional core processes, (which create the value proposition – defined as a set of benefits company offers at a price attractive to customers and consistent with its financial goals) not tasks or functions. The aim is to maximize the horizontal coordination of workers that take part in the core process, which results in better communication and coordination that in turn leads to performance improvements. New horizontal organizational structure emerges as the barriers that existed between functional silos are removed.

The second (2) principle stresses the importance of process owners or managers. They take the responsibility for the core process in its entirety and have to, therefore, be competent in different fields and areas in the organization and have a mixture of authority and persuasion skills.

Next principle (3) of the process-oriented organization is teams. They (more than individuals) are the cornerstone of organizational design and performance. Teamwork encourages creative solution seeking for the problems that organization faces on the daily basis. The fourth (4) principle advocates decreasing hierarchy by eliminating non-value-added work and by giving team members who are not necessarily senior managers the authority to make decisions directly related to their activities within the value chain. (5) Integration with customers and suppliers for tighter and more effective relationships is the fifth design principle of the process-oriented organization.

Changing the organizational design is a daunting and complex undertaking. By following the implementation principles the plausibility of successful restructuring increases. These principles are (Ostroff 1999): (1) empowerment of people by giving them the tools, skills, motivation, and authority to make decisions essential to the team's performance. (2) Use of information technology to help people reach performance objectives and deliver the value proposition to the customer. (3) Emphasis of multiple competencies and training people to handle issues and work productively in cross-functional areas within the new organization. (4) Promotion of multi-skilling, the ability to think creatively and respond flexibly to new challenges that arise in the work that teams do. (5) Educating people trained primarily in specific functions or departments to work in partnership with others. (6) Measurement of end-of-process performance objectives (which are driven by the value proposition), as well as customer satisfaction, employee satisfaction, and financial contribution. And finally (7) Building a corporate culture of openness, cooperation, and collaboration, a culture that focuses on continuous performance improvement and values employee empowerment, responsibility, and wellbeing.

Table 1. Advantages and disadvantages of process-oriented organization

Advantages	Disadvantages
Ensures flexibility and quick responses to the changes of customer needs.	Defining and mapping of the key business processes can be cumbersome and complicated.
Focuses on the creation of added value.	It requires the changes in corporate culture, work place design, management philosophy, measurement and reward systems.
Employees have broader view of the organizational goals and objectives.	Traditional managers may refuse to give up the power and authority.
Focuses on team work and cooperation.	It requires training and reeducation of employees in order for them to effectively work in the environment of horizontal teams.
Satisfied employees – higher authority, responsibility and decision-making.	It can limit the development of highly specialized functional knowledge.

Process-oriented organization has many advantages over functional/divisional organizational structure. However, as any other organizational form it is not flawless. Managers and consultants need to be aware of this when selecting their business model. See table 1 for the most important advantages and disadvantages of a process oriented organization.

Process Structure Development Model

By examining the literature and studies on relevant subjects we have now prepared the tools for our model building. The environmental changes that threaten the very being of any organization must be dealt with in a complex manner, considering all relevant factors. BPR in it self was not the answer to the problems of rigidness of industrial like companies in information age. Projects systematically failed as the desired performance improvements were not reached. The key reason was that BPR was considered too narrowly and neglected organizational factors. The changes in the processes were not reflected in the changes in organizational structure. Organizational design and organizational culture remained unchanged, blocking the success of the BPR efforts.

We consider the learning organization to be the most appropriate organizational form for the information age. The positive impact of the learning organization on company performance was proved empirically (Škerlavaj 2003) on the sample of 220 Slovenian companies. The study showed that companies with better organizational learning processes consistently outperformed companies that had less developed systems to reinforce organizational learning. Later kind of firms were trailing behind in financial indicators as well as non-financial indicator such as employee and customer satisfaction. To reach the highest developmental stage, companies must evolve through several stages. Process-oriented organization is one such stage that also takes the central role in the learning organization as one of its constituting elements.

Business process renovation is only the first albeit necessary and crucial aspect of the evolution. In order for companies to transform themselves they must survey their existing work practices, adapt and restructure them as it best fits their environment and the strategic position they have chosen to follow. Capability maturity model serves as a measurement framework that can be used to asses the state of the process understanding and process management capacity of any given firm. The higher the level a firm reaches on the CMM model more mature it is in the aspect of business processes. The more mature a company is the closer it is to its optimal process performance. The second aspect of the firm's evolution is the evolution of its organizational structure. The model described in previous section serves as a framework for assessing the state of company's organizational structure and as a signpost to where they can and want to go.

We believe that the key to company's success lies in the combination of both frameworks. We synthesize them and present the process-structure development model (figure 3) upon which we base our proposition: *Companies must acknowledge both aspects of the model (process maturity and organizational design) if they want to successfully adapt to environmental changes, improve their performance, and sustain the competitive advantage in both financial as well as non-financial terms.*

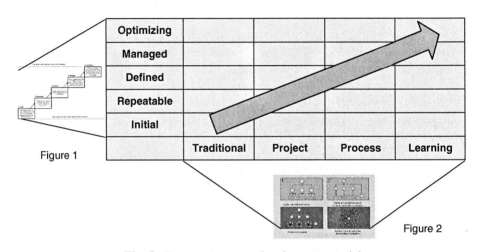

Fig. 3. Process-structure development model

Focusing only on process renovation while staying on the first evolutionary stage will not yield the outcome anticipated. Conversely, solely centering on changing the organizational structure and abandoning the process maturity concept will again prove to be futile. The process-oriented organizational design is well equipped to support the realization of the mature processes and in conjunction with corresponding structure deliver the benefits stated in our hypothesis. By defining new roles and responsibilities coupled with the decision making authority empowered workers continually strive to improve the process performance thereby retaining them in the optimal or near optimal state. Process owners oversee these courses of action and support their execution. Process-oriented organizational design is therefore an appealing concept that should be considered and adopted by organizations facing organizational problems or attempting to stay ahead of the competition.

Conclusion

The proposition stated in previous section has some very practical implications for managers and consultants responsible for business improvements. It should be clear that business change initiatives are complex undertakings and should be approached as such. Furthermore, business process reengineering itself is not sufficient for any long-term gains. It should be coupled with the appropriate structural changes for the benefits to manifest themselves. Managers should recognize the new process paradigm and the process-oriented organizational design as the implementation of this paradigm. Thorough understanding of the concepts presented in this paper will help them in advancing their organization on the way to the current optimal state suggested in our process-structure development model which is a learning organization with mature processes. By achieving this level many of the internal inefficiencies are eliminated and most of the environmental pressures are under control.

While we suggest practical implications of the findings it should be stressed that it is not without limitations. The most crucial one is that the process-structure development model has not been empirically tested. This is left for the future research. Our proposition has to be refined and defined more precisely so it can be measured empirically. Moreover, measures for process maturity and organizational structure need to be devised and formalized. Empirical study designed to measure the constructs of process maturity and organizational structure to test the hypothesis developed on basis of our proposition must be conducted so the validity of the model is either confirmed or rejected.

Despite the limitations the paper presents organizational changes in a new light. It combines different management theories and presents them in a new setting. The real value of paper's contribution will need to be assessed by scrutiny and constructive criticism of fellow academics and researchers. Their valuable feedback will act as an input for fine-tuning of the model and important guideline for empirical study.

References

Al-Mashari M, Zairi M (1999) BPR Implementation Process: An Analysis of Key Success and Failure Factors Business. Process Management Journal, vol 5, issue 1, pp 87-91

Blacker K (1995) The Basics of Business Process Re-Engineering. Edistone Books Birmingham

Giaglis GM, Paul RJ, Hlupic V (1999) Integrating Simulation in Organizational Design Studies. Int. Journal of Information Management, vol 19, pp 219-236

Guimaraes T (1997) Empirically Testing the Antecedents of BPR Success. International Journal of Production Economics, vol 50, pp 199-210

Hammer MH, Champy J (1993) Reengineering the Corporation: A Manifesto for Business Revolution. Harper Business New York

Harmon P (2003) Business Process Change a Manager's Guide to Improving, Redesigning and Automating Processes. Morgan Kaufman Publ. San Francisco

Herbsleb JD, Zubrov D, Goldenson DR, Hayes W, Paulk M (1997) Software Quality and the Capability Maturity Model. Communication of the ACM, vol 40, no 6, pp 30-40

Jiang JJ, Klein G, Hwang HG, Huang J, Hung SY (2004) An Exploration of the Relationship between Software Development Process Maturity and Project Performance. Information and Management, vol 41, pp 279-288

Jung HW (2004) Evaluating the Ordering of the SPICE Capability Levels: An Empirical Study. Information and Software Technology, vol 47, pp 141-149

Ostroff F (1999) The Horizontal Organization. Oxford University Press Oxford

O'Neill P, Sohal AS (1999) Business Process Reengineering: A Review of Recent Literature. Technovation, vol 19, pp 571-581

Smith M (2003) Business Process Design: Correlated of Success and Failure. The Quality Management Journal, vol 10, no 2

Sung TK, Gibson DV (1998) Critical Success Factors for Business Reengineering and Corporate Performance: The case of Korean Corporations. Technological Forecasting and Social Science, vol 58, pp 297-311

Škerlavaj M (2003) Vpliv informacijsko-komunikacijskih tehnologij in organizacijskega učenja na uspešnost poslovanja: teoretična in empirična analiza. Ekonomska fakulteta, Ljubljana

Tenner AR, DeToro IJ (1997) Process Redesign, The Implemantation Guide for Mangers. Addison-Wesley Reading MA

Modeling Business Processes in Public Administration

Vaclav Repa

Department of Information Technologies, University of Economics, Prague, Czech Republic. repa@vse.cz

Introduction

During more than 10 years of its existence business process modeling became a regular part of organization management practice. It is mostly regarded as a part of information system development or even as a way to implement some supporting technology (for instance workflow system). Although I do not agree with such reduction of the real meaning of a business process, it is necessary to admit that information technologies play an essential role in business processes (see [1] for more information). Consequently, an information system is inseparable from a business process itself because it is a cornerstone of the general basic infrastructure of a business. This fact impacts on all dimensions of business process management. One of these dimensions is the methodology that postulates that the information systems development provide the business process management with exact methods and tools for modeling business processes. Also the methodology underlying the approach presented in this paper has its roots in the information systems development methodology.

The field of public administration traditionally interests researchers of management theory. Unlike market-oriented businesses, this area poses considerably harder problems with application of general management principles. The cause is in particular the absence of market. This absence leads to the need for using great portion of abstraction to implement those principles. Questions as "who is a customer?" or "what is the customer's interest?" are typically not easy to answer in this area[1]. The difficulty of using general management practices in this business is visible especially in connection with business processes, namely with their reengineering.

---

[1] For illustration just try to answer these questions in the case of the process of law violation administration. It is absurd to suppose the violator is a customer because his interest is diametrically different from the interest of the community (which is the real customer in this case).

These problems manifest themselves specifically in identifying core processes.

The paper is organized into two main sections. The first section deals with the topic of modeling business processes in general, without respect to the specific features of public administration. It explains the roots of the problem of modeling business processes, the basic principles, and the methodology used.

It also argues for a two-dimensional view of the Real World. Specific where attention is paid to the relationships between two basic types of the Real World processes – on one hand the processes of life cycles of real world classes, and on the other hand the business processes themselves.

The second section focuses on specific features of business processes modeling in the field of public administration. It introduces the concept of Life Events, as it is frequently called, and emphasizes its close connection to the concept of Class Life Cycle as well as its substantial role in the process of discovering core processes in the public administration. Because of the specific characteristics of the public administration area discussed above, this part of the paper addresses the practices that are still not often applied in this field.

Modeling Business Processes

Basic Principles and Methodology

The crucial principle of information system (IS) development is the **Principle of Modeling**. This principle expresses the presumption that the implementation of the business system in the organization must encompass the real facts that exist outside of - and independently on - the organization. Because these real facts influence substantially the possibility of the organization to reach its objectives, they are regarded as relevant. These facts are visible in the form of specific and critical values of so-called "critical factors". We can model each real world object that plays any important role in the business system as a collection of attributes that express these critical factors. We call such an object a business object. Critical changes of the critical factor values are recognized as (external) events. Whenever a business process is initiated, it is due to an event that is called a process trigger.

The principle of modeling states that the system of business processes in the organization is a **model of relationships between objectives and critical events**, and the mutual relationships among these objectives and among these events. The purpose of each business process in the organization is to ensure the proper reaction to a particular event. Essential relationships among the organization's objectives, the critical factors and the events are expressed in the form of relationships among particular processes. Products of these processes as well as their actors, goals, problems, circumstances and other aspects should correspond to the relevant business objects.

In the field of business modeling the purpose of the principle of modeling is:

- it defines the basis for the analysis (what is the essential substance to be analyzed),
- it leads to creation of such system of business processes which:
  - is able to react on each substantial change requiring also the change in business processes (changes of goals, objectives and critical factors),
  - is optimal - it consists of all processes which are necessary in given business conditions and only of those processes.

Information system, as an infrastructure for the business system, has to be based on the same objective model of the real world as it is mentioned above. Such objective model of the real world is traditionally called conceptual model. The concept *conceptual* expresses the fact that the data in the information system should describe the essential characteristics of the real world: objects and their mutual relationships.

Regarding the conceptual point of view together with principles of object orientation[2] one has to stop taking the object's methods just as a heap of procedures usable for communication with other objects. It is necessary to seek for the wider sense of them as a whole – seek for the substance of their synergy. Such "superior sense" of the object's methods is represented by the *object life cycle*.

Figure 1 illustrates the object life cycle as a complement to the Class Diagram. It is good visible that all methods of the conceptual object should be ordered into one algorithm that for each method defines its place in the process of the object's life. This placement of the method in the object life defines the conceptual sense of the method[3].

---

[2] Primarily the principle of natural unity of data and operations.

[3] In this sense it is obviously absurd to take into the account such methods as *give list* or *send status* as well as it is absurd to speak about "sending messages" between objects (discussion between the Order and the Goods in this example). Such a point of view is suitable for the model of objects in a program system, but in case of conceptual objects it is obviously improper.

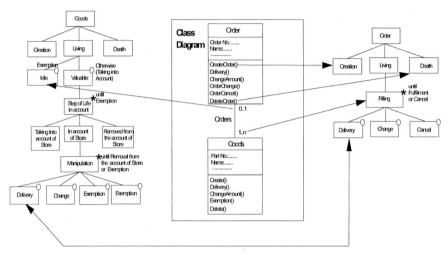

Fig. 1. Object Life Cycles versus Object Model

Two Basic Dimensions of the Real World

According to the principle of modeling, the information system has to be based upon the model of the *real world*. The term real world we understand as the objective substance of the activities to be supported by the information system and of the facts to be stored in its database.

Thus data, stored in the information system, should express the existence of the real objects and their relationships. Functionality of the system then should follow from the way which these objects are manipulated – from business processes. Of course, the way which the objects are manipulated always has to respect their *business nature*, i.e. their natural dynamics – life cycles.

So there are two kinds of the *real world dynamics* to be analyzed:

- Dynamics of the real world objects and their relationships given by their conceptual nature (real world conditions and constraints)
- Dynamics of the business activities given by the conceptual nature of the business processes (business nature).

As it is visible from the discussion above there are two basic orthogonal views of the "real world" (See Figure 2):

- Object view which emphasizes the substance of the real world,
- Process view that emphasizes the real world behavior.

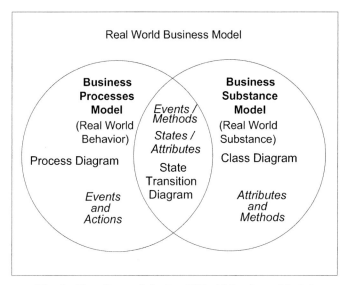

Fig. 2. Two Parts of the Real World Business Model

The first view (Business Substance Model) represents **objects and their mutual relationships** consisting of attributes and methods.

The second view (Business Process Model) represents **business processes** consisting of events and actions.

Of course, the model of objects also describes the behavior - in the form of entity life algorithms (ordering of methods). Such behavior is seen from the point of view of objects and their relationships. It says nothing about the superior reasons for it. Thus the **behavior of objects should be regarded as the structural aspect of the real world**.

Business Processes versus Class Life Cycles

The significant aspect of the real world behavior, seen from the process point of view, which is not present in the object point of view, is that there has to be the superior reason for the real world behavior, independent of the object life rules. In practice it means that for each business process some reason in the form of the goal, objective, and/or external input event (customer requirement) must exist. Business process as the collection of actions, chronologicky ordered and influencing objects (their internal states and their mutual behavior), is something more than just an amorphous heap of the actions.

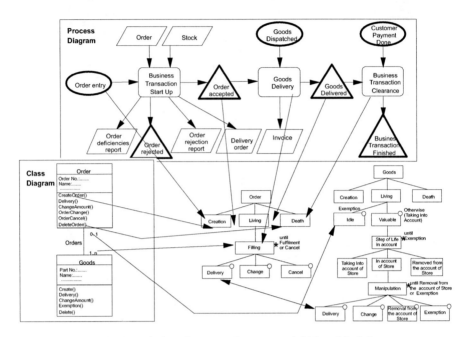

Fig. 3. Relations between Process and Object Models

Similarly to the structural modeling of the real world (Business Sub-stance Model), even for the behavioral model (Process Model) it is necessary to describe the principles and general rules, and develop the tool (diagrammatic technique) which reflects them. [6] roughly states basic principles and general rules of process modeling and contains also basic specification of needed diagrammatic tool – Process Diagram - in the form of Business Process Meta-Model. Following examples use the notation of that Process Diagram.

Figure 3 illustrates how the process model explains dependencies between objects and their life cycles giving them the higher sense. This explanation is based on the perception of object actions in terms of reasons for them – events and process states. Objects are playing roles of attendees or victims (subjects) of processes. For completeness it is necessary to regard the fact that one object typically occurs in more processes as well as one process typically combines the attendance of more objects. The orthogonality of those two points of view is also typical and substantial – it gives the sense to this coupling.

Unfortunately, the Structure Diagram used for description of objects life cycles at Figure 3 is not the regular diagram of the UML. UML prefers unstructured way of describing the context as it follows from historical circumstances (see [4] for instance)[4].

Life Events

The concept of **Life Events** is often used in the context of the process-oriented view on the public administration. This concept represents the view of public administration activities in their natural consequences. These "natural consequences" are always given by the situation in life of the public authority's "customer" – a *citizen*. And life situations of a citizen are in fact very close to the main goal and objective reason for the public administration activities. It is obvious that such view has very much to do with the main principle of business process reengineering – ordering activities according to the main goals, which have to be directly connected with natural strategic goals of the organization – consequently always following from the **customer needs**.

Figure 4 illustrates relationships between most frequent views on the activities of the public authority[5]. It shows two different viewpoints:

- Point of view of the public authority typically emphasizes the "technical" aspects of processes. Clerks use looking at their daily work in terms of individual activities, responsibilities and competences which are connected with their positions. Another alternative view from the same viewpoint is typical for the situation where the Authority owns high-quality information system – the daily work of each clerk is than viewable thru the set of applications or sub-systems / databases.
- Point of view of the citizen represents quite different approach. Nobody visits the Authority of one's own will. The citizen's visit is always caused by some problem, situation – life event. The citizen typically does not care of competences of individual clerks or information systems. The citizen has problem which requires the solution.

---

[4] Properly speaking the UML is just the language, not methodology. It has all possibilities to specify context and the way of modeling is always the point of methodology. Nevertheless as it does not allow "structured" description of an algorithm its possibilities to describe life cycles of objects are appreciable limited. Structured description of the process is namely suitable (and natural) when the process expresses the life of the object.

[5] Note: this figure is just an illustration of the idea; unreadable texts as well as the process diagram are used as symbols and are not meaningful.

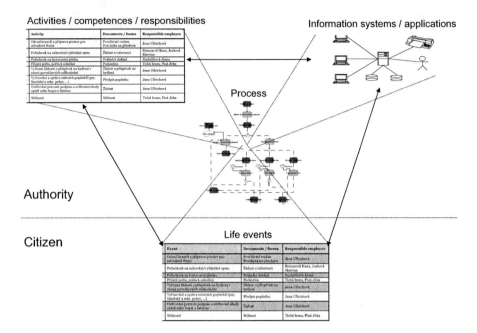

Fig. 4. Different views on public administration process

Looking at the public administration in terms of business processes represents the third view which connects both different views discussed above. Such view respects the technology aspects of the administration (including legislation and organization of the Authority) as well as the needs of the customer (represented by the Citizen at the figure 4). Life events thus represent the needs (problems) of citizens (customers in general) and triggers of administrative activities at once.

Deriving Life Events from Life Cycles of Crucial Classes

Life events became one of the most important subjects of the eGovernment activities. There are several standard classifications of life events as a reaction on the fact that the standardization is very natural in the area of public administration. These standards are of different quality – from simple description of routine activities of clerks till the lists of life events carefully analyzed as core representatives of the public administration activities. One of the most interesting classifications becomes from the *LEAP project*.

LEAP (Life Events Access Project) [5] is a partnership project between British Councils. According to its mission statement "LEAP aims to utilize knowledge management in order to improve service provision to customers. The LEAP consortium will use new information and communication technologies to develop services to best meet the needs of customers and clients." In this project life events are derived from the conception of the standard life cycle of a citizen.

Figure 5 shows the simplified example of the Citizen life cycle description using the Statechart notation from UML [8]. The example comes from the *Reference Public Administration Business Processes Model* project mentioned in Conclusions. Each transition between particular states is described by the triggering event together with the transition action. The transition action should correspond to the action of some business process.

It is obvious that such description of the object life cycle is the good basis for analyzing the crucial life events in order to constitute the interface between the authority and its customers.

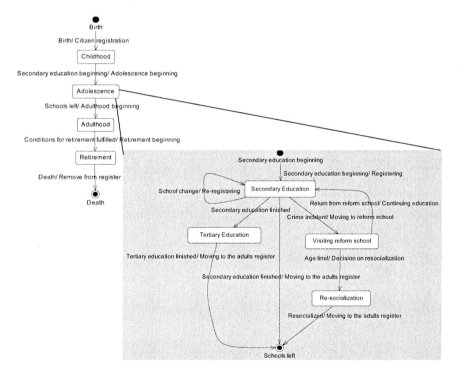

Fig. 5. Example of the Citizen life cycle description

Discovering Core Processes from Crucial Life Events

According to the theory and sense of business processes reengineering core processes in the organization have to deal directly with customer needs[6] [1]. Such process always begins with the event representing the crucial need of customer and ends with fulfilling this need.

As it is stated in the previous section life events represent important situations in life of a citizen. It is obvious that the **crucial life events** should be candidates for the **triggers of** crucial business processes – **core processes of the Authority**.

As it is discussed above in the Introduction *Citizen* is not the only type of the public authority's "customer". Therefore not only citizen-oriented life events should be taken into the account in the process of discovering core processes. For the most important processes their "customer" is the community. As the main subject of the work of the Representation is the needs and requirements of the community, the primary "customer" of the Authority should be the community instead of a citizen. The global mission of the Authority (in the democratic political system, of course) is not fulfilling the needs of an individual but fulfilling the needs of all citizens – the community (respecting individual needs, of course).

Concluding from previous paragraph one can find that in the process of discovering core processes of the authority we also need to consider, besides the *citizen*, the events from lives of some other objects. Typical objects, closely connected with fulfilling the needs of the community, are *Ground Plan*, *Financial Plan*, *Business Environment Development Plan*, and *Social Development Plan*. Life cycles of these objects address such events as "Request for change in the Ground Plan", "Investment intention", and "Social program proposal", etc. Such events seem to be the right candidates for triggers of core community processes.

Moreover, processes following from life events of above mentioned objects are always in close connection with strategy-level decisions. Examples of such processes are: "Realization of the Change of the Ground Plan" or "Realization of the Social Development Action", etc. Such processes are not clearly processes of the authority but rather the processes of the community because their key actors are not just clerks but also community representatives and citizens.

On the other hand there are also core processes which's triggers are coming from life cycles of other objects existing in the area of public ad-

---

[6] Original literature uses the term "customer requirements". Respecting the specificities of public administration field discussed above in the introduction the term "customer needs" seems to be more suitable here.

ministration which are crucial especially from the citizen point of view. One example of all such objects is the *Construction* which's life cycle contains events playing important roles in core processes. In this case it is the core process *House Building* with supporting processes *Building Permission* or *House Inspection* for example.

Discovering core processes from crucial life events, what is the subject of this section, thus requires at first **careful discovering of crucial classes** and actors whose life events are the representatives of core processes triggers.

Conclusions and Further Work

This paper emphasizes the importance of the modeling life cycles of objects as a natural complement to the business process description. It shows the practical significance of this two-way description of the Real World dynamics in the field of public administration processes and discloses the concept of *life events,* wide-spread in the area of eGovernment activities, as a specific manifestation of the same approach. Life events are also identified as the right basis for discovering core processes in the field of public administration.

Theoretical parts of this paper bear on the results of the project *Open-Soul.* The project is aimed on the development of the Business Processes Modeling Methodology based on the formal business process meta-model. For more information see http://opensoul.panrepa.org/.

Application of the theory in the field of public administration bears on the experience from the project *PARMA* (Public Administration Reference Model Architecture) which is not public at the moment (it is planned to be opened soon - after the completion of the first release of the reference model). The project is aimed on the development of the general reference model of a public authority processes and objects. At the current stage the project is aimed on the local authority processes where just life events play the significant role.

References

[1] Hammer M, Champy J, (1993) Reengineering the Corporation: A Manifesto for Business Revolution. Nicholas Brealey Publishing London
[2] Jackson MA (1975) Principles of Program Design. Academic Press London
[3] Jackson MA (1982) System Development. Prentice-Hall Inc Englewood Cliffs NJ

[4] Kobryn C (2000) Introduction to UML: Structural Modeling and Use Cases. Object Modeling with OMG – UML Tutorial Series. www.omg.org

[5] LEAP Project. www.leap.gov.uk/

[6] Repa V, Matula M (2002) Business Processes Modeling with the UML. Research Paper, Prague University of Economics Prague Czech Republic

[7] Repa V (2000) Process Diagram Technique for Business Processes Modeling. Proc of the ISD2000 International Conference. Kluwer Academics Kristiansand Norway

[8] UML (2003) OMG Unified Modeling Language Specification, v. 1.5. (Current version). Object Management Group March 2003

Facilitating Learning in SPI through Co-design

Ulf Seigerroth[1] and Mikael Lind[2]

[1] Jönköping International Business School, Sweden.
ulf.seigerroth@ihh.hj.se
[2] School of Business and Informatics, University College of Borås,
Sweden. mikael.lind@hb.se
[1][2] The research group VITS, Linköping University, Sweden

Introduction

Information system development (ISD) is not a stable discipline. On the contrary, ISD must constantly cope with rapidly changing and diversifying technologies, application domains, and organizational contexts [14]. ISD is a complex and a multi dimensional phenomenon [5, 15]. As a consequence of this Software Process Improvement (SPI) can also be regarded as a complex and multi dimensional phenomenon [16]. Problems that are accentuated in relation to SPI are: SPI is in its current shape a quite young discipline [15], there is a sparse amount of SPI-theories that can guide SPI initiatives [19], SPI-initiatives often focus on the system development (SD)-process, methods and tools which is a narrow focus that leave out important aspects such as business orientation [6], organization and social factors [4, 5] and the learning process [19]. Arguments have therefore been raised that there is a need for both researchers and practitioners to better understand SD-organisations and their practice [5].

In order to succeed with SPI Mathiassen et.al [16] argues for five principles that the SD-organization must adopt; 1) Focus on problems, 2) Emphasize knowledge creation, 3) Encourage participation, 4) Integrate leadership, and 5) Plan for continuous improvements. Ravichandran [19] also discuss critical factors for SPI initiatives, but from an organizational learning perspective, 1) development process must be designed so that it reflects the state-of-the-art, 2) mechanisms to promote learning by sharing and reuse of procedural and declarative knowledge must be established, 3) mechanisms for learning through systematic analysis should be implemented, and 4) evolved performance standards should be used to control the development process.

It is obvious that there are a number of factors that we need to deal with in order to succeed with SPI initiatives. We see the combination of both focusing development and learning as critical, and in doing so we also see a co-design perspective as an important driver. Co-design is emphasised through the need for joint participation (research and practice) and how this can be organised in order to succeed with SPI. There have been arguments raised that there is a need to increase the reflective work in the SPI domain [13]. Therefore, descriptive studies of SPI-initiatives carried out by trained independent researchers are encouraged [13]. We interpret this as a call for co-design where researchers are involved in both the actual SPI-initiative as well as being producers of reflective research. This paper is therefore an initial step in that direction. The research question in this paper is therefore: *How is learning in SPI facilitated through co-design?*

This paper is based on an action research project where we as researchers have been involved in an SPI-initiative as external consultants, inline with the conceptualisation of action research by Cronholm and Goldkuhl [8]. As action researchers we have conducted fieldwork from a clinical perspective [20] with the characteristics to get involved with the practice in order to solve some problem. The empirical base for this paper is operative SPI-project results, log books, field notes and observations.

The structure of this paper will be according to the following. In the next chapter we will present a narrative story of the actual SPI-project. In the third chapter we present our theoretical base. In the last chapter we will then discuss aspects and implication of SPI-initiatives in terms of development of the SD-practice and the multiple learning situations. This will be done by presenting a initial framework for SPI-initiatives where learning aspects are emphasised.

Researchers Coming into Practice

General Description

During 2003 and 2004 we were involved in an action research project with a SD consultancy firm. The purpose with the project was to develop and implement instruments in order to establish congruency in their SD process to ensure that delivered IT-systems harmonised with the actual business. The vision for the consultancy firm is to provide enterprise systems and e-solutions to customers.

What Did We Do

The main structure for the project was divided into three phases, 1) project preparation, 2) project execution, and 3) project conclusion and maintenance. During the preparation phase we had a number of meetings between us as researchers and the project leader at the consultant firm. The project leader had a managing position at the consultancy firm. The main purpose for these meetings was to discuss content, approach and cooperation procedures for the project. The result of these meetings was a schedule with a number of meetings over a time period of one year. These meetings also resulted in a guiding agenda and action plan for the project.

During the execution phase there were a mixture of joint meetings, individual and group based work in between. We performed eight joint meeting, one day each. For the joint meetings we had a predetermined agenda which continuously was adapted depending on the progress in the project. The agenda for each meeting was a mixture of theoretical and practical issues that were to be handled. It was therefore a number of items on the agenda that returned regularly. Such items were introduction, theory injection, case notation, the handbook, and modelling tools. Every meeting started with an introduction by the project leader. During this introduction, the project leader, made a recapitulation of the project and its current status. He also presented the agenda for the meeting and there was a discussion about the status of the assignments that we had agreed upon at the previous meeting. The joint meetings were performed in a co-design manner – both as a mean for joint knowledge creation and to arrive in mutual agreements. In order to create real results and learning in the SD-practice the assignments always consisted of practical application of theories, notation, and/or modelling tools that we had elaborated on during the previous meeting. Depending on how the assignment had been carried out we sometime had to revise the agenda for the meeting. The practical application of new knowledge (theories, notation, and/or modelling tools) was mostly conducted between the meetings and was mainly done in two ways; 1) reconstruction of an old or an ongoing project with the use of new gained knowledge or 2) application of new knowledge in a real ongoing project. The purpose with this procedure was to gain experiences that could serve as input for the next meeting, and development of the handbook where different types of guidelines were formalised and documented. Examples of input to meetings were new process diagrams based on a certain notation technique and reflections about theories that were used to identify variant processes, for instance product theory and theory of practice, see also theoretical injection below.

The process with development of the handbook was a successive and incremental process where the handbook was supposed to serve as an intellectual capital and guiding standard for the SD-practice. The handbook was storied electronically so that it also could be accessed from outside of the office. The handbook had a structure with a number of headings with drill down possibilities and cross references. Example of headlines in the handbook were; theories, cases, modelling tools, notation.

During the joint meetings we also had theoretical injections. This was a mixture of lectures and discussions where both we as researchers and others introduced and presented theories, notation techniques, and modelling tools that could serve as a base and inspiration for development of their practice. One could say that these instruments were drivers in the co-design process. These theoretical injections could result in either development of formalized work descriptions in the handbook (espoused theories) or, not so obvious, development on a personal level (theory in use) [9]. The lectures and discussions always had the primary focus of how this could be beneficial for the consultant firm and their projects.

An important part of the theoretical injections was the joint learning. We will now therefore describe what type of theories that we injected, give examples of where in the process they were injected, why we choose a certain theory and what it resulted in. Theories that were injected can be characterized as follows; *Concepts that we need to attend to during change and investigations*, *Process analysis in its context*, *Process theory*, *Approach for process analysis*, *Method theory*, *Team based reconstruction and dynamic agendas*, *Theory of practice,* and *Change work and change methods beyond process analysis.* This list also represents the main order in which these theories were injected over the year.

At the first meeting we performed the first theory injection, *Concepts that we need to attend to during change and investigations.* This was a presentation that addressed concepts that we, as researchers, considered as important to deal with during this SPI initiative. First we presented our view on, what is an investigation, and how we can use theories, methods, tools and experiences as guiding support in this type of situations. We also presented three other concepts that we believed were important. The first concept was a trinity of *process thinking*, *methods* and *change work* and how they are related and how these should be handled as a whole. In this case process thinking is a common perspective that can be applied during SD or change work in order to describe and perceive an organisation. Methods can be used as support for conducting change work and there are methods that, for instance, are dedicated for SD or change work in general. Change work is then a wide concept where you generate change needs and change measures. The next concept elaborated on *notation, work proce-*

dure, cooperation procedure and *approach for method supported work.* According to our view we argued for that these parts also are related and should be handled as a whole. Notation and work procedure are important parts of a method component and they give guidelines about *how* to document and *how* a certain aspect of the investigation should be conducted. Cooperation procedures accentuate suitable ways to conduct an activity, interviews, individual work, group work, seminars etc. Approaches elaborated on different ways to perform change work; Top-Down, Bottom-Up, Bottom-All. The last concepts that were introduced elaborated on *process* and IT *systems* and how these two are related. IT systems are for instance supposed to support different actions that are performed. Therefore we need to have knowledge about what actions that are performed and how they are related, the process view. The process also helps us to identify functionality in an IS. These concepts were introduced in order to set an initial frame and content for the project. The purpose was also to initiate a more conceptual and reflective thinking in the consultancy firm about their own SD practice. This resulted in a lot of discussions about how this could/should be translated into their operative SD practice. An important result was also that we, in the project group, developed an agreement on that there was a need to have an interchange between theory and practice. Following this initial presentation we had theoretical injections founded in the theories mentioned above. These theoretical injections were intertwined with other project activities. These theories are to be seen as a meta-language for driving the development and learning process forward. This meta-language was an instrument for shifting to discourse [12] and consists of important primitives for handling the change process, i.e. concepts for epistemological dimensions.

We have said that learning is an important part of an SPI initiative. An other example of this is one application of a modelling technique that we used during the project. The purpose with this modelling exercise was first to identify the total portfolio of concepts that ought to be addressed during modelling, i.e. from scope modelling to detailed design. During this process there are a number of levels that the consultant goes through in order to reach detailed system design; level 1: Enterprise Map, level 2: Main Business Processes, level 3: Process, level 4: Sub Processes (logic sequence of activities), and level 5: Task/User Scripts. After that we had identified and defined these concepts we modelled the relations between these concepts. This resulted in a total concept model (a business ontology) that described what concepts that needed to be modelled during the process. This ontology should also to be seen as a meta language for driving the development and learning process forward. What we also did was that we now were able to identify what concept that needed to be modelled on each level

(level 1- 5) and that we were able to clarify the relation between these levels. It was important to clarify how models on an upper level were a rational result and a prerequisite to be able to model the next more detailed level. Now we knew what concepts or primitives that they needed to model through out the whole process. In this case the modelling exercise proved itself to be a fruitful tool for learning on both sides. We as action researchers as well as the practitioners learned what primitives was necessary model on each level and how different levels are related, i.e. how a superior modelling level will have impact in the final IT-solution. In the end of the execution phase we also performed a (simulated) team based reconstruction in the working group reflecting the newly introduced concepts. This was made with the purpose to learn how to practically conduct a modelling seminar in terms of how to make use of theories, methods and suitable work procedures.

In the finishing and maintenance phase we spend a half day to evaluate what results we had produced, the status of these results and how we should continue. We decided to have a meeting every quarter to discuss what the consultant firm had done in terms of development of the SD-practice. We as researcher should in this part just be involved as external reviewers who can serve as a communicative partner and quality reviewer in the process.

Learning in a SPI-Setting

Guidelines for SPI Initiatives

In the context of SPI initiatives we can observe guidelines that specially focus on this area. Three researchers that give recommendations concerning SPI initiatives is Mathiassen et.al [16]. They say that focus on existing problems is the key to succeed with a SPI initiative, see also "the High Way Initiative" which is an advocated approach for SPI initiatives [6]. In our project we had a number of specific problems that needed to be addressed, for example; no common principles for business modelling and no conformity in results of business modelling. When dealing with specific problems there are no standard solutions [16]. Those who are involved in the SPI-initiatives must take into consideration practice specific traditions, values and abilities [16]. Furthermore, people have different opinions about what is problematic and what is not. Therefore the big challenge is to understand and bridge over differences between formal practice and real practice [16], see also espoused theories and theories-in-use by Argyris and Schön [2], who advocate a problem driven approach. In our project there were gaps between prescribed work procedures and methods and the way that the practitioners really worked. This we needed to learn more about. Another thing that is emphasised as crucial during SPI initiatives is knowledge creation [16]. The main message is that there is a need to elucidate and share knowledge about existing SD practice i.e. to learn about existing practice. This knowledge need to be both declarative (know-what) as well as procedural (know-how) [19]. The necessity to deal with development and sharing of knowledge during SPI-initiatives is also accentuated by Meehan and Richardson [17] and Pourkomeylians [18]. In our project there have been a continuous need for mutual learning both for us as researchers and for the practitioners. The need for learning has comprised aspects such as; new theories, prescribed work procedures and work procedures really in use. Encouragement and impetus structures for participation are also emphasised as important ingredient to make SPI happen [16, 6, 7]. This was also an obvious issue in our project. The participants must find it worth wile to be engaged in the project. Even if the participants have learned about existing problems they also need to learn about the benefits (goals) that the project aims to achieve. To avoid dysfunctional effects, these benefits also need to be put in a larger context. The goal for the SPI- initiatives can not be the SD-practice by itself [16]. There is also a need for the SD-practice harmonises with strategic goals for the practice as a whole. To achieve this, it is necessary to involve management who can give information and communicate strategic goals.

A conclusion from this section is that there are a number of aspects that the members in a SPI initiative (researchers and practitioners) have to learn about. We would say that SPI is very much about learning, learning about the actual SD-practice and the SPI initiative itself. This is also confirmed by Ravichandran [19] when he describes SPI-initiatives as organisational learning. We can summarise these learning aspects as; *the actual situation, actual problems, formal and informal work procedures, new theories, project goals and strategic goals.*

Foundation for Used Theories as Meta-Languages

As indicated in the section about the empirical case two related meta-languages were used as instruments for driving the co-design process forward resulting in well-founded development measures. The two related meta-languages could be seen as two dimensions – an epistemological dimension (how to facilitate the knowledge creation process) and an ontological dimension (how to interpret the "world"). The joint development and learning has been facilitated through abstraction and discourse [9]. The theories used for the theory injection has relationships to each other. They are founded in the ontological and epistemological stance advocated for in socio-instrumental pragmatism (SIP) [10]. The basic concept of socio-instrumental action is action. An action is a purposeful and meaningful behavioural of a human being. A human intervenes in the world in order to create some differences. An important distinction is made between the action result and the effects of the action [23]. The action result lies within the range of the actor and the action effects may arise as consequences outside the control of the actor. Actor relationships between the intervening actor and the recipient are established through social actions [12]. An organisation consists of humans, artefacts and other resources, and actions performed. Humans perform action in the name of the organisation [1, 22]. Actions are performed within the organisation – internal acts and there are also external acts towards other organisations (e.g. customers or suppliers). Humans act in order to achieve ends [23, 10]. Human action often aims at making material changes. Humans do however not only act in the material world – they also act communicatively towards other humans. Austin [3] and Searle [21] mean that to communicate is also to act. Human action can therefore have impact in the social world as well as in the material world.

The used theories are aggregates of this generic model; both in terms of ways to acknowledge the world (in theories such as theory of practice and process theory), and ways to conduct knowledge development (in theories such as change management, team based reconstruction and method theory). For further details confer Goldkuhl and Röstlinger [10, 11].

Discussion and Conclusion: Multiple Learning During SPI Initiatives

We have earlier presented a number of aspects (theoretical and empirical) that we have to learn about during SPI initiatives; *the actual situation, actual problems, formal and informal work procedures, new theories, project goals and strategic goals*. The question is now, how we can organise different activities in order to facilitate mutual learning? First of all we se a need for a co-design perspective with integrated leadership and participation where we have the meeting between researchers and practitioners and how both sides are involved in co-designing the "new" SD-practice, for co-design also cf. Olausson and Haraldson [24]. Practitioners have knowledge about exiting practice but this need to be challenged and collided, mostly by the external part, with new perspectives, theories, methods and experiences from other SD practices in order to get ideas of how to improve the existing SD-practice, se Fig 1 below.

In the process of developing the SD-practice we argue for a number of activities that we have found fruitful for learning, evaluation and designing the SD-practice. These activities are; *theoretical injections, relating to real situations, carry out assignments, usage of instruments* and *mutual evaluation and feedback*. Theoretical injections are good for introducing alternative perspectives, theories, methods and experiences. These injections must, however be discussed and elaborated on in relation to characteristics for the actual SD-practice and their projects. In order to learn more and to test injected theories they need to be applied in some way. This can be done by giving assignments to project members where they are supposed to use different instruments (perspectives, theories, methods) as support to accomplish the assignment. When this is done they report back the results and experiences to the project group. This is also a kind of injection that helps the project group to learn about the usefulness of tested theories. During this presentation the project group will conduct a mutual evaluation about the usefulness and need for possible modifications.

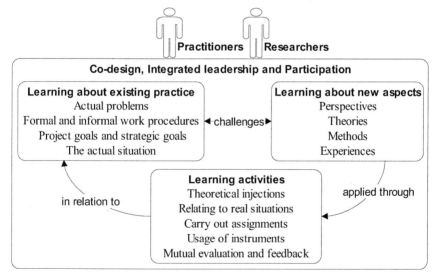

Fig. 1. Framework for facilitating learning during SPI

The framework above accentuates the need of learning on both sides, the research practice and the business practice. This has earlier been elaborated on by Cronholm and Goldkuhl [8] where they conceptualise this as

two interlinked parts with a cross section in action research; theoretical research practice, business change practice/empirical research practice and
regular business practice. We therefore argue for that there is a need for an
interplay between the focus on the SD-practice and the reflection arena.

In this paper we have analysed our experiences from one SPI initiative
that we have been involved in. Our main conclusion is that it's not enough
to just focus on the SD-practice! There should also be a focus on learning.
Such learning focus can be facilitated through a co-design oriented approach, in which a number of different stakeholders' interests have been
taken into consideration during joint meetings.

We believe that there is a need to make a difference both in the material
and the social world. In the material world through that we focus on the
SD-practice and develop guidelines and knowledge that can be used as
support in their regular work. But if these guidelines shall be used, they
also need to have made a difference in the social world. They need to be
accepted and their usefulness must be understood and proven. This means
that there is a need to develop the inter-subjective arena between employees in the SD practice. When it comes to external influences, such as theoretical injections, we can conclude some characteristics. The theories,
which are considered as meta-languages, that are used should have relations to each other, for instance that they are based on the same ontological
foundation. There should also bee a purpose for why a certain theory is
used at a certain point in the process. We can also see that development of
the SD-practice and reflection must go hand in hand. This is for instance
important in order to decide how and when different theories can be used.

References

[1]   Ahrne G (1994) Social Organizations. Interaction Inside, Outside and Be-
      tween Organization, Sage London
[2]   Argyris C, Schön DA (1996) Organisational Learning: A theory of action
      perspective. Addison-Wesley Reading
[3]   Austin JL (1962) How to Do Things With Words. Oxford University Press
[4]   Baddoo N, Hall T (2002) Practitioner Roles in Software Process Improve-
      ment: An Analysis using Grid Technique. Journal Software Process Im-
      provement and Practice, vol 7, pp 17-31 (DOI: 10.1002/spip.151)
[5]   Butler T, Fitzgerald B (1997) An Empirical Model of the Information Sys-
      tems Development Process. Proc of Fifth International Conference on Infor-
      mation Systems Methodologies
[6]   Börjesson A (2003) Making SPI Happen: The Impact of Iterations in Imple-
      menting Success. Proc of 26th Information Systems Research Seminar in
      Scaninavia, August 9-12, Haikko Manor Finland

[7]   Börjesson A, Mathiassen L (2004) Making SPI Happen: The Roads to Process Implementation. Proc of the 12th European Conference on Information Systems, June 14-16, Turku Finland

[8]   Cronholm S, Goldkuhl G (2003) Understanding the Practices of Action Research. 2nd European Conference on Research Methods in Business and Management (ECRM2003) Reading UK

[9]   Goldkuhl G, Lind M, Seigerroth U (1998) Method Integration: the Need for a Learning Perspective. IEE Proc – Software, Special Issue on Information Systems Methodologies, vol 145, no 4, pp 113-118

[10] Goldkuhl G, Röstlinger A (2002) Towards an Integral Understanding of Organisations and Information Systems: Convergence of Three Theories. Proc of the 5th International Workshop on Organisational Semiotics, Delft

[11] Goldkuhl G, Röstlinger A (2003) The Significance of Workpractice Diagnosis: Socio-Pragmatic Ontology and Epistemology of Change Analysis. Accepted to the International Workshop on Action in Language, Organisations and Information Systems (ALOIS-2003), Linköping University

[12] Habermas J (1984) The Theory of Communicative Action 1, Reason and the rationalization of society. Beacon Press

[13] Hansen B, Rose J, Tjørnehøj G (2004) Prescription, Description, Reflection: the Shape of the Software Process Improvement Field. Internationa Journal of Information management, vol 24, pp 457-472

[14] Kautz K, Norbjerg J (2003) Persistent Problems in Information Systems Development. The Case of the World Wide Web. Proc of the 11th European Conference on Information Systems (ECIS 2003) Naples

[15] Mathiassen L (1997) Reflective Systems Development – Position Summary. Department of Computer Science Aalborg University Denmark

[16] Mathiassen L, Pries-Heje J, Ngwenyama O (2002) Improving Software Organizations – From Principles to Practice. Adisson-Wesley

[17] Meehan B, Richardson I (2002) Identification of Software Process Knowledge Management. Journal of Software Process Improvement and Practice, vol 7, pp 47-55 (DOI: 10.1002/spip.154)

[18] Pourkomeylian P (2002) Software Practice Improvement. Gothenburg Studies in Informatics Report 22 Doctoral Dissertation Gothenburg University

[19] Ravichandran T (2000) Software Process Management – An Organizational Learning Perspektive. Proc of 8th European Conference of Information Systems (ECIS 2000) Track Development Methodologies II

[20] Schein EH (1987) The Clinical Perspective in Fieldwork, Qualitative Research Methods Series 5. A Sage University Paper Sage Publications USA

[21] Searle JR (1969) Speech Acts. An Essay in the Philosophy of Language, cambridge University Press London

[22] Taylor JR (1993) Rethinking the Theory of Organizational Communication: How to Read an Organisation. Ablex Norwood

[23] von Wright GH (1971) Explanation and Understanding. Rouledge & Kegan Paul London

[24] Olausson J, Haraldson S (2005) Process Oriented IS – Co-Design of Business and IS. Accepted to the International Workshop in Communication and Co-ordination in Business Processes (CCBP 2005), June 22 2005 Kiruna Sweden

Feasibility Study: New Knowledge Demands in Turbulent Business World

Renate Sprice and Marite Kirikova

Riga Technical University, Latvia. renate_sprice@navigator.lv, marite@cs.rtu.lv

Introduction[1]

Feasibility study is one of the early activities in information systems (IS) development when important decisions regarding choice among several possible systems development alternatives are to be made. In times of relatively stable business environment and waterfall model as a systems development approach, the role and methods of feasibility study where quite clear (Kendall and Kendall 1995). However, new software development methods and the necessity to develop more rapidly new IS or their parts may challenge the possibility to evaluate project feasibility in the early stages of IS development.

In relatively stable environment the main methods of feasibility study were economic ones based on the statistical analysis of an organisation. These methods were accompanied by the evaluation of some other feasibility perspectives such as technical feasibility and operational feasibility. In order to use these methods and perform statistical analysis mainly historical knowledge about organization and IS projects was utilized. Nowadays, in turbulent business environment statistics based evaluations may not always predict future benefits and losses correctly. Changes in organisational environment require to take into consideration their potential impact on future IS (Kendall and Kendall 2002). Therefore it is necessary to reconsider the scope of knowledge needed for feasibility study in order to analyse feasibility of IS projects correctly.

This paper looks at feasibility study in turbulent business environment from two perspectives: both theoretical and practical. From the theoretical perspective, the paper applies systems theory to reveal IS project feasibil-

---

[1] This work has been partly supported by the European Social Fund within the National Programme "Support for the carrying out doctoral study programm's and post-doctoral researches" project "Support for the development of doctoral studies at Riga Technical University"

ity study factors, which describe knowledge required for feasibility study relevant in rapidly changing environment. From the practical perspective, the paper analyses existing feasibility study methods and their potential to provide knowledge about theoretically important factors. The paper compares feasibility analysis knowledge dimensions relevant in relatively stable environment to the knowledge dimensions important in turbulent environment and suggests an organised set of factors to be considered for IS project feasibility analysis.

The paper is organised as follows. In Section 2 demands of knowledge for feasibility study in turbulent environment are analysed and the set of relevant feasibility study factors revealed and compared to "classical" feasibility study factors. In Section 3 a survey of 27 feasibility study methods from a historical perspective and analysis of their capacity to cover the theoretical feasibility study factors are presented. This section analyses applicability of different feasibility study methods in turbulent organisational environment. In Section 4 a simple feasibility study method FEASIS, which utilizes all identified feasibility factors relevant in turbulent environment, is discussed. In Section 5 brief conclusions are presented.

Feasibility Study in Turbulent Environment: the Systems Perspective

Turbulent organisational environment is dynamic, continually changing, unpredictable, and uncertain (Bordia et al. 2004, Knoll et al. 1994, Milliken 1987, Burns and Stalker 1961). It has such features as unpredictability, turnover, and absence of pattern in the changes that occur in market conditions or technologies (Bordia et al 2004). Moreover, changes in turbulent environment may happen faster than organisations are able to meet these changes. No doubt, turbulent environment is a challenge for most of organisational processes including the process of the IS development. Feasibility study, in turn, is one of the IS development subprocesses, which requires knowledge that enables organisation to make the best choice from several IS project alternatives.

Previously, in relatively stable environment relatively static organisations selected IS projects on the basis of knowledge about economical, operational, and technical feasibility (Kendall and Kendall 1995). In feasibility study the main objects of interest were the proposed IS and its development project. In turbulent environment the feasibility study becomes more complex. First, project feasibility study should be done in a shorter period of time and more often, because of more frequent changes in organisational strategies, goals, processes, structure, and knowledge (Hartmann and Froster 1997). Second, the spectrum of objects of interest in feasibility study becomes larger, because of the necessity to acquire and start to use IS faster, which requires a reasonably good fit between the IS, organisation and its external environment (Sprice 2002, Sprice 2003).

From the system theory point of view the IS is a subsystem of an organisation, the organisation, in turn, is a subsystem of its external environment (Skyttner 1996). Therefore changes that can influence the IS may be considered on two levels of abstraction, namely – organisational level and environmental level (Fig. 1). Organisational environment is composed of two interrelated levels, namely, *task environment* and *social environment* (Bayars 1996, Jackson 2000, Skyttner 1996).

Fig. 1. Organisation and its environmental levels

Task environment consists of customers, suppliers, alliances, governmental bodies, competitors. Social environment contains the following elements: social factors, economical factors, political factors and technological factors (Wheelen and Hunger 2002). The main change drivers, such as economical globalisation, political globalisation, technical progress, and sociological issues, are rooted in social environment (Turban et al. 2001). These change drivers initiate changes in task environment; thus, the organisation is influenced by its social environment and task environment, as well (Fig. 1). In many cases an organisation is a member of the inter-organisational network (Hatch 1997). It means that an organisation can be influenced by other organisations belonging to this network and the organisation has to be able to adapt to these organisations and their subsystems. For example, the IS of one organisation should fit the IS of another organisation if these organisations exchange data by using their IS.

To reveal all factors important for feasibility study in turbulent environment we assume that:

1. all factors relevant in stable organisational environment are to be taken into consideration also in turbulent environment (the main objects of interest: IS and IS development project);
2. additional feasibility factors should be derived from the impact of environmental factors on organisations and their subsystems (main objects of interest: organisation, task environment, and social environment).

In order to find out which organisational subsystems must be analysed from the system theory point of view, main organisational issues, such as goals, structure, processes, management and control, and resources were organised in interrelated subsystems so that changes in one of the subsystems can be transparently tracked in other subsystems. Thus, the factors were derived on the basis of analysis of mutual relationships between the following organisational subsystems: goals subsystem, technological subsystem, subsystem of organisational structure, subsystem of resources, process subsystem (including management and control), IS (i.e., subsystem), and knowledge subsystem, as well as on the basis of analysis of the impact of constituents of task and social environments on those organisational subsystems.

Altogether forty-six factors required for feasibility study were identified. The factors are organised in five levels of abstraction where each abstraction level refers to each object of interest given above, namely, IS level (ISL), IS project level (PL), organisational level (OL), task environmental level (TL), and social environmental level (SL) (Fig. 2). Each factor requires knowledge on a particular level of detail and abstraction, e.g., knowledge about ISL factors is needed on a higher level of detail and concreteness than knowledge about TL or SL factors.

The following three groups of factors are considered to compare the knowledge needed for feasibility analysis in relatively stable environment and the knowledge needed for feasibility study in turbulent environment:

1. factors relevant in both cases and requiring knowledge on the same level of detail and concreteness in stable and turbulent environment;
2. factors relevant in both cases, but in turbulent environment requesting knowledge on a higher level of detail and concreteness than in relatively stable organisational environment;
3. factors relevant in turbulent environment.

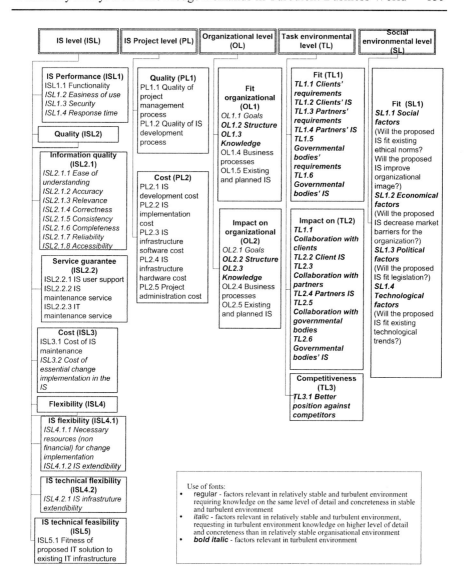

Fig. 2. IS project alternative feasibility factors

Factors reflected in Fig. 2 show that the knowledge needed for analysis of feasibility of IS project alternatives in turbulent environment is considerably richer than the knowledge needed for this activity in relatively stable organisational environment.

First, besides factors relevant in stable environment the following knowledge is needed:

- knowledge about organisational structure and organisational knowledge (OL);
- knowledge about client, partner, and governmental IS and requirements, as well as knowledge about competitors IS (TL);
- knowledge about social and ethical norms and legislation issues and technological trends (SL).

Second, deeper knowledge in comparison with relatively stable environment is needed with respect to such ISL factors as IS performance, IS quality, IS costs, and IS flexibility.

In order to perform feasibility study not only *the set of factors* but also *the method* of evaluation of IS project alternatives is needed. Section 3 provides analysis of existing methods suitable for feasibility study with respect to their capacity to utilize knowledge requested by all forty-six identified feasibility factors relevant in turbulent environment.

Analysis of Feasibility Study Methods

In this section the feasibility study methods are surveyed from the following two perspectives:

1. their capacity to cover theoretical feasibility study factors presented in Section 2 (Table 1);
2. historical perspective (Fig. 3).

Table 1 amalgamates twenty-eight feasibility study methods. Each method (column 2) has its sequential number (column 1), which is used to refer to a particular method further in the text. Column 3 shows how many feasibility factors out of forty-six identified ones the method directly considers. Column 4 shows how many factors the method considers and could consider.

Feasibility study methods with 0 in the third column are the ones which do not prescribe particular analysis factors. The choice of the factors is left to the user of the method. Some methods prescribe particular feasibility factors, the scope of which may or may not be extendable. None of the methods currently utilize all forty-six factors; however, there are two methods, which have a potential to utilize all these factors.

Table 1. Feasibility study methods:coverage of feasibility factors

Nr	Method	Covered factors	Potential factors
1	Graphical judgement (Kendall & Kendall 2002)	0	8
2	The method of least squares (Efunda 2005)	0	8
3	Moving averages (Kendall & Kendall 2002)	0	8
4	Break-even analysis (BreakEven 2005)	0	8
5	Payback (Toolkit 2005)	0	8
6	Cash-flow analysis (Ward 2004)	0	8
7	Net Present value (Remenyi 1999)	0	8
8	Internal Rate of Return (Brav et al. 1999)	0	8
9	Profitability Index (Remenyi 1999)	0	8
10	Real Options Theory (Asundi & Kazman 2004)	0	8
11	Portfolio (Asundi & Kazman 2004)	0	8
12	Scoring models (Turban 2001)	0	44
13	Analytical Hierarchy Process (Sarkis & Sundar-raj 2003)	0	44
14	Critical Success factors (Turban 2001)	3	3
15	Balanced Score Card (Alleman 2003)	6	39
16	Multi-criteria utility theory (Stewart & Mohamed 2002)	11	20
17	Information economics (Lere & Gaumnitz 2003)	15	15
18	Application Development Project Estimation (Brandon 2004)	15	15
19	COCOMO (Costar 2004)	1	1
20	Total cost of ownership (Turban 2001)	0	7
21	Rapid economic justification (Micro 2005)	15	17
22	PORE (Procurement – Oriented Requirements Engineering) (Sommerville 2005)	5	5
23	IEEE Recomended Practice for Software Acquisition (IEEE Std 1062, 1998) (IEEE_1062 1998)	20	20
24	Value analysis (Turban 2001)	15	29
25	E-commerce evaluation method (Lu 2003)	11	11
26	OAR method (OAR 2004)	12	12
27	Value Based Software Reuse Investment (VBRI) (Favaro et al. 1998)	2	2
28	Information Systems work and Analysis of Change (ISAC) (Avison & Fitzgerald 2003)	12	38

All these methods are developed in different time periods. It is interesting to see, whether there is a relationship between the time of appearance of the method and the scope of factors prescribed by the method. Fig. 3

shows the answer to this question. According to Fig. 2, there are 23 factors on IS level, 7 factors on PL, 5 factors on OL, 7 factors on TL, and 4 factors on SL. Project feasibility study methods M1-M13 do not prescribe any particular evaluation factors, therefore they are not included in Fig. 3.

Fig. 3 reflects IS project feasibility study methods and the number of factors that are covered by a specific method against all factors on a particular level of abstraction, e.g. M16 - method number 16 - Multi-criteria utility theory (Table 1) on the IS level (IS) cover 4 evaluation factors of twenty-three possible factors.

Fig. 3 shows that there is a tendency in methods with later dates of appearance to cover more factors on lower level abstraction levels then earlier methods, as well as to cover more factors on higher levels of abstraction than earlier methods. However, none of the methods cover all factors.

	1980-1985	1985-1990	1990-1995	1995-2000	2000-2005
SL					
TL					M25(3/7)
OL	M28*(2/5) M14(2/5) M17(5/5)		M15(5/5)	M22(1/5) M27(2/5)	M26(1/5) M25(2/5) M16(2/5) M21(5/5) M18(3/5)
PL	M28*(5/7) M24(7/7) M19(1/7) M17(5/7)				M26(4/7) M16(5/7) M21(5/7) M18(7/7)
IS	M28*(5/23) M14(1/23) M24(8/23) M17(5/23)		M15(1/7)	M22(4/23) M23(20/23)	M25(6/23) M16(4/23) M26(7/7) M21(7/23) M18(5/23)

Fig. 3. Coverage of feasibility factors by methods: historical perspective. *M28 is developed in 70th

We assume that the later period on the X axis refers to a more turbulent organisational environment. In this context Fig. 3 also shows the following:

- Richer knowledge on ISL factors is used in methods that have been developed during the period of more turbulent organisational environment.
- Most of the project level factors are covered by early feasibility study methods. Therefore we can conclude that these factors are almost equally important in both stable and turbulent environments.
- Organisational level factors are more comprehensively covered by recently developed feasibility study methods (years 2000-2005).

Task environmental level factors are scarcely covered by existing feasibility study methods while social environmental level factors are not covered at all.

Regarding the potential of the methods to cover forty-six feasibility factors (Table 1, column 4) we can see that only two methods can utilize all knowledge needed for feasibility study in turbulent environment, namely, Analytical Hierarchy Process and Balanced Score Card. However both methods require quite sophisticated knowledge with respect to the use of methods. Moreover the Balanced Score Card requires the use of quantitative measures that may not be available in all organisations, i.e. it utilizes rather explicit than tacit knowledge with respect to the IS projects alternatives. Complexity of those methods may hinder their use for practical application of identified feasibility factors. On the other hand, several methods potentially could be combined to cover all factors. But combinations of methods require additional research with respect to their compatibility. Therefore practical applicability of all factors was tested using new IS feasibility study method **Feas**ible **I**nformation **S**ystem (FEASIS), which was developed for utilization of both explicit and tacit knowledge about all identified feasibility study factors. The method is briefly described in Section 4.

Information System Project Alternative Feasibility Method FEASIS

The feasibility study method FEASIS is developed in order to provide both the framework of analysis and cognitive aid in the utilization of tacit and explicit knowledge about IS alternatives. It covers all forty-six feasibility factors.

The feasibility factors are presented in the form of a table with three columns (Fig. 4). The first column contains the evaluation factors organised on five abstraction levels (Section 2). The second column contains "cognitive aid" - questions that help to better understand what should be evaluated. The third column contains rules how to evaluate each factor according to answers to the questions.

Simple equations and normalisation procedures are used to calculate the total score for each alternative. The alternative with the higher score can be considered as the best one.

FEASIS was applied in two small organisations. At the first attempt FEASIS was used without a "cognitive aid". However, it was difficult to use the method without consulting the method's developer. Therefore the method was extended by adding questions. The second application of the method was successful. This allows to assume that it is possible to utilize both tacit and explicit knowledge in IS project feasibility study. More experiments are needed to prove that this assumption is correct.

Factor	Question	Possible values
Organizational level (OL)		
Fit and impact on organizational business processes	Does the proposed systems functionality fit business processes that are going to be supported by information system?	• If the answer to the first question is negative, the rating of the factor can be between <1>and <2>
	Does the proposed system fit the written procedures regarding business processes that are going to be supported by information system?	• If 2.-4. questions have at least 2 positive answers, the rating of the factor can be between <3> and <5>
	Does the proposed system support data flows related (existing and planed) to business processes?	• If all questions have positive answers, the rating can be between <4> and <5>.
	Does the proposed system support business process (existing or planned)?	• If no question has positive answer, the rating can be <1>

Fig. 4. FEASIS example for the evaluation factor "Fit and impact on the organisational business processes"

Conclusion

Knowledge needed for feasibility study in turbulent environment is richer than knowledge needed in relatively stable environment, especially regarding the organizational internal and external environment. Therefore more evaluation factors are to be used for performing the feasibility study in turbulent environment (additional twelve factors). The study of the existing feasibility study methods shows that none of them covers all required evaluation factors. There are two methods that can potentially cover all factors, however these methods are quite complex and are not easy to be introduced in all, especially small organisations because of specific knowledge needed to utilize these methods. Organisation could integrate several methods of feasibility study and/or expand one method with additional evaluation factors, but it requires a good expertise on all peculiarities of these methods. For small organisations, which base their decisions on tacit knowledge rather than on explicit one, the FEASIS method may be recommended, as it is simple, utilizes forty six feasibility factors, and provides questions based cognitive aid for feasibility study. More detailed evaluation of FEASIS from the theoretical and practical perspective should be done in the future.

References

Alleman GB (2003) Using Balanced Scorecard to Build a Project Focused IT Organisation Driving High Performance Teams. Balanced Scorecard Conference IQPC, San Francisco, Oct 28-30 2003.
www.niwotridge.com/PDFs/Using%20Balanced%20Scorecard%20to%20Build%20a%20Proj.PDF (14.12.2004)

Asundi J, Kazman R (2004) A Foundation for the Economic Analysis of Software Architectures. www.cs.washington.edu/homes/taoxie/realoptionse.htm (14.12.2004)

Avison D, Fitzgerald G (2003) Information System Development: Methodologies, Techniques and Tools. McGraw-Hill Education

Bayars L (1996) Strategic Management. Chicago

Bordia P, Hobman E, Jones E, Gallois C, Callan VJ (2004) Uncertainty During Organisational Change: Types, Consequences, and Management Strategies. Journal of Business and Psychology, vol 18, no 4, pp 507-532

Brandon M (2004) Guide to Application Development Project Estimation. White Paper Info-Tech Research Group

Brav A, Harvey CR, Gray S, Maug E (1999) Global Financial Management Valuation of Cash Flows Investment Decisions and Capital Budgeting

BreakEven (2004) The Method Break Even.
www.businessknowhow.com/startup/break-even.htm (14.12.2004)

Burns T, Stalker G (1961) The Management of Innovation. London Tavistock

Costar (2004) COCOMO Description. www.softstarsystems.com/overview.htm (28.12.2004)

Efunda (2004) The Method of Least Squares.
www.efunda.com/math/leastsquares/leastsquares.cfm (14.12.2004)

Favaro JM, Favaro KR, Favaro PF (1998) Value Based Software Reuse Investment. Annals of Software Engineering 5 J AG Science Publishers, pp 5-52

Hartmann M, Froster T (1997) Turbulent Environment. Proc of IFAC Automated Systems Based on Human Skill. Kranjska gora Slovenija

Hatch MJ (1997) Organization Theory. Oxford University Press Inc New York

IEEE_1062 (1998) IEEE Std 1062 IEEE Recommended Practice for Software Acquisition, Software. The Institute of Electrical and Electronics Engineers Inc

Jackson MC (2000) System Approaches to Management. Kluwer Academic Plenum Publisher New York

Kendall KE, Kendall JE (1995) Systems Analysis and Design. Pearson Education Inc Upper Saddle River New Jersey

Kendall KE, Kendall JE (2002) Systems Analysis and Design. Pearson Education Inc Upper Saddle River New Jersey

Knoll K, Jarvenpaa SL (1994) Information Technology Alignment or „Fit" in Highly Turbulent Environments: the Concept of Flexibility. ACM

Lere JC, Gaumnitz BR (2003) The Impact of Codes of Ethics on Decision Making: Some Insights from Information Economics. Journal of Business Ethics, no 48, pp 365-397

Lu J (2003) A Model for Evaluating E-Commerce Based on Cost/Benefit and Customer Satisfaction. Information System Frontiers, vol 5, no 3, pp 265-277

Microsoft (2005) Microsoft Business Value An Introduction to the Microsoft ® REJ™ Framework. www.microsoft.com (14.01.2005)

Milliken FJ (1987) Three Types of Perceived Uncertainty About the Environment: State, Effect, and Response Uncertainty. Academy of Management Review. vol 12, no 1, pp 133-143

OAR (2004) Description of OAR method. www.sei.cmu.edu/reengineering/oar_method.html (20.11.2004)

Remenyi D (1999) IT Investment: Making a Business Case. Butterworth-Heinemann ©

Sarkis J, Sundarraj RP (2003) Evaluating Componentized Enterprise Information Technologies: A Multiattribute Modelling Approach. Information System Frontiers, vol 5, no 3, pp 303-319

Skyttner L (1996) General Systems Theory: An Introduction. Antony Rowe Ltd ChippenhamWiltshire Great Britain

Sommerville I (2005) Integrated Requirements Engineering. Lancaster University UK. www.comp.lancs.ac.uk/computing/resources/IanS/Ian/Research/Papers-PDF/Misc-Invited/IntegratedReqEng.pdf (25.01.2005)

Sprice R (2002) Estimation of Project Feasibility in Changeable Environment. Proc of Riga Technical University Computer Science Series Applied computer Systems, vol 13. Riga Technical University Riga

Sprice R (2003) The Organization – the Environment of the Information System Project. Proc of Riga Technical University

Stewart R, Mohamed S (2002) IT/IS Projects Selection Using Multi-Criteria Utility Theory. Logistic Information Management, vol 15, no 4, pp 254-270

Toolkit (2004) Payback Method. www.toolkit.cch.com/text/P06_6510.asp (14.12.2004)

Turban E, McLean E, Wetherbe J (2001) Information Technology for Management. Second Edition Update. John Wiley & Sons

Ward S (2004) Cash Flow Definition. (14.12.2004) http://sbinfocanada.about.com/cs/management/g/cashflowanal.htm

Wheelen TL, Hunger JD (2002) Strategic Management and Business Policy. Pearson Education Inc Upper Saddle River New Jersey

Co-design as Proposals, Assessments and Decisions – Stakeholder Interaction in Information Systems Development

Ulf Larsson

Jönköping International Business School, Sweden. laru@jibs.hj.se

Introduction

The ISD process has, historically, been done with a varied degree of involvement from stakeholders of the work practice. However, the importance of active stakeholder participation in the development process has been emphasised in books and articles over the past couple of decades, ([1]; [2]). This is due to the increased diversity of the stakeholders of computerized information systems and the increased level of computer literacy among them.

This paper will begin with an overview of how users, as a main stakeholder group, participate in the ISD process. The main focus of the article is the presentation of empirical studies of interaction between the stakeholders, i.e. users and designers, in two ISD processes.

Stakeholder Participation in the ISD Process

Stakeholder participation, eg. by end-users, has been considered critical for the successful development and implementation of information systems by a number of different researchers ([3]; [4]; [5]; [6]) and has also been considered good and a natural maturity of the ISD process. According to [7], stakeholder participation is encouraged in order to gain a correct understanding of user requirements, to potentially ensure user commitment and to avoid user resistance. These views of the reasons for user participation, however, have been criticized for being manipulative towards users by not allowing them real decision making power in the ISD process, e.g. [8].

In their comprehensive account of ISD from a historical perspective, [1] identifies three chronological phases of ISD, each of which is identified by a category of major constraints thwarting the development process and thus the benefits of supporting computer-based systems in the work practice. In the two first phases, the constraints pertain to hardware and software respectively. The hardware constraints of the first phase of systems development, from the late 1940s to the middle of the 1960s, concern costs of hardware and its limitations regarding capacity and reliability. The software constraints of the second phase (mid 1960s to the end of the 1970s) concerns productivity of systems developers and the difficulty of delivering reliable systems on time and within budget. This has commonly been referred to as "the software crises" within ISD.

In the third phase, beginning in the early 1980s, "user relations" emerged as the major constraint for ISD. User relations imply system quality problems stemming from an inadequate perception of stakeholder demands and inadequately servicing their needs, i.e. not meeting stakeholder requirements for a useful and usable work support of IT-artefacts. This constraint was present, though not prominent, already in the earlier phases. However, as the experience of stakeholders increased, demands for more complex applications grew, and the systems began to be judged on their usefulness, i.e. not just constituting automated imitations of formerly manual tasks. This included the ease of use in supporting the specific work tasks as well as the general aims of users when applied on more sophisticated tasks. Because applications became less structured as they increasingly handled managerial or planning oriented tasks, the ability of the ISD-process to unambiguously specify the requirements of the systems decreased. From his research, [2] confirms that the problem of handling user relations in an adequate way continues to be the prime constraint of ISD also after the 1980s.

In order to deal with the problems of meeting and understanding user requirements a number of strategies have been pursued. One such strategy presented by [1] is to focus on breaking down the barrier between users and developers by focusing on creating a common platform or scene within a project group where users and developers are enabled to communicate on equal terms. Two examples of strategies within this approach are the socio-technical and democratic approaches. The socio-technical approach, permeating the development method ETHICS developed by researchers at the Tavistock Institute ([9]), and focusing on ISD as a parallel work of both technical and human aspects in using information systems through participation of a wide range of interested parties. The democratic approach is building on political-conscious class division of the relations within a project group ([10]). The so-called Scandinavian approach to ISD and the development of Participatory Design have been influential in certain ISD projects. However, as [2] suggests, some have seen the democratic approach mainly as academically led action research projects with the main aim of creating group processes for change work that fills democratic demands for all participants rather than aiming primarily at making qualitative software.

The Need for Further Studies of the Stakeholder-Developer Interaction

Since the 1980s the strategies for solving problems of stakeholder participation in ISD have been refined and new strategies have been formed. Studies show that there is a lack of empirical research on the actual communication process between the stakeholders in ISD. [11] states that the interaction between the participants has not been the focus of much study compared to other parts within the ISD-process. [12] concludes, relating to the dialogue between stakeholders and systems developers, that the methods available to study the stakeholder situation may be satisfying but he questions if there is sufficient support in present methods for the stakeholder to create the synthesis in her mind between the manual tasks at hand and the proposed computerized system meant to support them. The form of cooperation needed to aid the communication of such learning has been pushed to the background in favour of the development of the formal documentation within the methods.

The language used by the participants in the ISD process is not only important for the elicitation of requirements for a potential system but, as e.g. [13] shows, can also be analysed and the result used to make the participants *"aware of patterns of work practice and conceptual structures they are not paying attention to during daily work"* [13], page 118.

There appears to be a genuine need for studies on the actual interaction between the stakeholders in the ISD process. Several studies have been made on establishing factors that influence the outcome of an ISD-process, either positively or negatively. User influence and user participation are two such factors. However, not so many empirical studies have been made to characterize the interaction within the ISD-process between the various actors from both the stakeholder- and developer-side, according to [14].

Case Studies and Related Work

Given the need for a study of the actual interaction between the various actors in the ISD process, i.e. what the participants say to each other and how they co-design together during project group sessions, the author has analysed a number of dialogue sequences of video recorded ISD processes that have been made accessible.

The empirical material is, partly, made up of sessions held during an ISD project within an elderly care unit of a Swedish municipality. This ISD process covers 15 meetings during a time span of about a year. In total 17 hours of video taped sessions. The video recordings were made for research purposes and the ISD-project has been used as empirical base in other research projects, e.g. [15] and [16].

The videotaped sessions were held in various constellations of stakeholders from the work practice and from the system developer practice. The sessions were also held with various foci, e.g. design-oriented talks, prototype testing and user training. Sessions of interest in this paper concerns the design-oriented talks and the prototype testing as they are focused on design aspects of the system to be built. These are the types of sessions where interaction between actor roles is the most frequent. By actor roles is meant system developers, nurses and a manager of the nursing unit. The two latter being the future end-user groups of the system. The ISD process is based, implicitly, on the cooperative approach following the Scandinavian Participatory Design-approach.

The empirical material to this paper also comes from an ISD process within a Swedish government office where an information system was developed in order to replace a number of smaller systems presently in use. Like the previous process within the elderly care, a number of prototype based sessions were video taped. In total nine session and about 20 hours of material was made available. The actors in this process was system developers, both internal staff from the IT section of the government office and an external consultants, and users. Some of the users were also system administrators of the systems to be replaced.

In order to study the interaction between the stakeholders, a number of sequences of talk within the sessions were selected based on the criteria of being directed towards a design solution. These talk sequences were transcribed. Each sequence was made up of utterances. An utterance is one actor's contribution to the dialogue. On average, a talk sequence include 15-20 utterances.

In an earlier study, [17], an analysis was made, based on some of the transcribed talk sequences, to discover design promoting characteristics of the interaction between the actors in the process, i.e. features of the interaction between developers and work practice stakeholders that appear to have a positive influence on the development of the design of the information system.

In [18] a further analysis was done on one of the talk sequences. The analysis revealed how design solutions gradually evolve and mutual understanding progressively is reached through iterations. Also, the analysis show how implicit criteria of both IT-design logic and work practice knowledge guide the way solutions to design problems are suggested and decided on.

Result and Analysis

Following on, and building on, the study in [18] this paper aim at illustrating three types of actions involved in design discussions concerning an IT system: proposing a solution, assessing a solution proposal and deciding on a solution. Occurrences of the three action types emerge in discussions among stakeholders as design problems are presented and the need for a solution is called for, a form of co-design. This is often done in iteratively as Figure 1 below suggests.

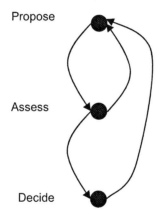

Fig. 1. Model for design decisions. Adopted from [18]

In this paper two examples will be given to illustrate the three action types. The first example (see Table 1) is taken from a talk sequence named Alarm Number from the ISD project within the elderly care. This sequence contains a discussion between one of the nursing staff (Vilma) and two designers (Stig and Sten) on how to solve the design problem of a proper identification concept to use for patients in a search field in order to be able to look up the information on the patients and then register new information about the patients condition in the journal. Prior to the first utterance in the talk sequence a unique personal ID-number was suggested by the designers as a proper identification concept to use. The talk sequence reads as follows:

Table 1. Talk sequence Alarm Number

No.	Actor	Utterance
1	Vilma	But, I think there could be problems. I mean, it's easy to mix personal ID-numbers.
2	Stig	But, do you remember the names, or do you use the personal ID-number?
3	Vilma	No, it's the names
4	Stig	OK, so it's the names
5	Sten	But, how do you know that it's correct in the Journal then?
6	Vilma	Her personal ID-number is in the Journal, you know.
7	Sten	But, you may have two Anna Karlsson?
8	Vilma	The address! She can be identified on her address, you see.
9	Sten	The address. So it's on the address you identify?
10	Stig	Would you like this? Would it be…
11	Vilma	Yes, why not. But you see, 59, that's of course the whole house over there.
12	Stig	OK, so it does not help?
13	Vilma	No, not really. They all live at address 59 over there.
14	Sten	Is it the Alarm number?
15	Vilma	Well yes, the Alarm number is of course better!
16	Stig	Should we decide on the Alarm number?
17	Vilma	Yes, the Alarm number is terrific!

In utterance number 1 of Table 1 the nurse is assessing the suggested identification concept but is not readily accepting it as she sees a problem from a work practice point of view. Her assessment leads to a deepened assessment in utterance 2 when one of the designers seeks to find out the normal work practice for identifying patients in the (manual) journals. Utterance 3 and 4 can be said to, implicitly, constitute a new and joint solution proposal for the problem. In assessing 'name' as identification concept, the second designer (Sten) in utterance 5 and 7 call into question the appropriateness of the concept suggested. He questions both the correctness of the names in the Journal as well as the duplicity of names.

This makes the nurse propose another potential identification concept, the patient's address at the elderly care centre (utterance 8). The designers assess the suitability of the suggested concept by eliciting questions (utterance 9-10). Initially in utterance 11, the nurse appears to confirm that the group has arrived at a suitable concept, but in her assessment she reflects on work practice implications of the design proposal and realizes some problems in using the address. Thus, the proposal is rejected in the joint assessment of the nurse and a designer (utterance 12-13). Another proposal is put forward by one of the designers (utterance 14) in the form of a question. This proposal receives an immediate positive assessment (utterance 15) and, finally, a decision can be made (utterance 16-17).

In this sequence we can see several strategies employed in order to propose and assess solutions. Proposals are made both individually and joint by two stakeholders. Furthermore, proposals are made both in the form of questions (utterance 14) and exclamations (utterance 8). Assessments can be made in the form of reflections that can be clear (utterance 1) or vague (utterance 11), or in the form of questions. A questions can in itself be an assessive act (utterance) or it can combine with one or several utterances to constitute an assessive act (utterance 5-7).

Decisions often appear to be made implicitly. Few times in the talk sequences studied there are explicit statements made like "We decide to…" or "The decision is to…". Rather, decisions are often made by the absence of further questions or comments. However, in the talk sequence in Table 1 the decision is made quite explicitly (utterances 16-17) where the affirmative answer in the last utterance confirms the decision.

The second example (see Table 2) is taken from a talk sequence named "Confirm button" from the ISD project within the government office. This sequence contains a discussion between one of the users (Anders) and three designers (David, Doris and Dan) on how to design a simplified function for confirming an order in a part of the new system This second talk sequence is more extensive then the first one and reads as follows:

Table 2. Talk sequence Confirm button

No.	Actor	Utterance
1	David	[If you continue] you will get all the information on the order so you can check and make changes, and this is where the Confirm button comes in.
2	Anders	Yes! That's where I want the Confirm button. That's when I want it visible.
3	Doris	Yes, and the question is: Do we want to steer the navigation so that if you come to it via the Search-form you want the button activated. If you come directly to this form then it should not be activated. Is that how you want it?
4	Anders	Yeah.
5	Doris	OK. Why not always make it active?
6	Dan	Should one be able to confirm it at once? If you have the order open…

Table 2. (cont.)

7	Anders	Yes, that's right! Actually, I then could confirm and send it straight away.
8	Dan	You could first save, then confirm and save again and you're done with it. We could add the control…
9	Doris	If would even be possible to first confirm and then save.
10	Dan	Yes.
11	Anders	Yes. I only want to click once
12	Dan	Yes. If we should allow that, yes
13	Doris	But there aren't so many of you working on this so it ought to be OK
14	David	It's not that you then start to fiddle with it and think that…?
15	Doris	Cheat?
16	David	…"we don't bother about"…Yes, exactly.
17	Anders	"We don't bother to double-check?"
18	David	Yes. "We confirm straight away"
19	Doris	You can do that today also.
20	Dan	You can actually do that here as well.
21	David	Yes. Just that it is unnecessary to look them up.
22	Doris	No, it's just that…maybe you are not cheating…
23	Anders	Yes, but then…Well…
24	Doris	That is a manual routine
25	Anders	Yes, when I'm registering it…I mean, it needs to be activated, not just Save. We do that with…it's the tab function for Save, isn't it?
26	Doris	Yes
27	David	Yes, or Save is Alt+S. So it's only shortcuts to use. So it's quick.
28	Anders	Yes
29	Doris	It is good that you need to press Confirm in order to change it, so that you don't accidentally…
30	Anders	No, that's the thing. I should not just accidentally do it.
31	Doris	No, and you don't do that, because at a certain point you must confirm.
32	Anders	Yes. Then it's OK
33	David	I understand how you think, Anders. Maybe you don't…well, you just happen to press Alt+G instead of Alt+S and you don't realize that the state has been changed to Confirmed. Then you think: "Did I really press Save?"
34	Doris	But you could easily add a small window saying "Do you want to confirm this change? Yes or No" So that you get a…if you happen to press Confirm.
35	Dan	In the case when you haven't answered…

Table 2. (cont.)

36	Doris	That's right
37	Anders	Yes
38	Dan	…earlier.
39	Doris	Yes, and then you'll get the small warning.
40	Anders	Yes, but that's actually when I enter the Registering Order form. That's when I ought to get a warning if I try to confirm it already at that time.
41	Doris	Yes, I think so.
42	Anders	But I should not get a warning if I come via the Search form.
43	Dan	But if you enter the form and clicks on Save and then on Confirm and Save again. Would you like a warning then, as well?
44	Anders	No, because then it's like…then it's actively done.
45	Dan	OK. So when it's not saved we warn if you change the state of it, and if it is saved once then you just continue.
46	Anders	Yes
47	Doris	Great!
48	David	Yes.

In utterance number 2 of Table 2 the user is proposing a simplification of the process of confirming an order by designing a click-able button on the form to be visible when arriving at the Order form via the Search form. In utterance 3 a designer assess the proposal by asking questions to clarify the proposal. After receiving a positive feed back from the user two of the designers jointly propose a slightly different solution in utterances 5 and 6. The user's assessment of the revised proposal in utterance 7 is an immediate and positive response. His utterance also indicates an elaboration on the benefits of the proposal. Again, the designers in utterances 8 and 9 make a joint proposal, which is adding to and strengthening the previous proposal. In the new proposal regulations within the organisation on how an order needs to be verified is taken into consideration. In utterance 11 the user assess the proposal positively and at the same time clarifies the expected benefit of the original proposal, which appears to be somewhat contrary to the regulations. The designers in the following two utterances assess this contradiction.

In utterances 14-32 further assessments on the practical implications of not following the regulations are made and discussed by all three designers and the user. These assessments concern both the temptation to wilfully work around the regulations and to accidentally do it. The proposed solution by a designer in utterance 34 is to use a warning message to alert the user when clicking the Confirm button. This proposal follows the consent by the user in utterance 32 that, together with the proposal in utterance 34, implicitly can be interpreted as a decision to include the Confirm button. This interpretation is strengthened by the content of the rest of the utterances in the talk sequence that concerns the conditions for when the warning message is to be displayed. These conditions are clarified through a number of proposals and assessments in utterances 35-44 made by both the designers and the user. In utterance 45 one of the designers sums up the proposal and in utterances 46-48 the affirmative responses becomes an implicit decision point after which the discussion continues on another issue, i.e. a new talk sequence is opened.

As with the first talk sequence, an in depth study of the turn taking in the dialogue of the talk sequence Confirm button reveals a number of ways in which the three action types proposing solutions, assessing the proposals and deciding are performed as strategies in order to reach design decisions. Proposals are suggested both individually as well as jointly by several participants. Proposals can be made through questions or declarative statements. Some proposals are strengthening earlier proposals, whereas others are new. Assessments are sometimes based on individual preferences and knowledge of the practical use of the present systems. Other times they are based on regulations that governs the work practice of the organisation. Decisions in this talk sequence are made implicitly when agreements are reached.

Conclusion

It is important to emphasize that the analyses made above are based on the author's interpretative study, i.e. an analysis made by another researcher may focus on other aspects of the dialogue and thus look differently.

The three action types of proposing solutions to design problems, assessing the proposed solutions and making design decisions can be derived when making detailed interpretative studies of talk sequences in ISD processes. The studies of the two samples of talk sequences in this paper indicate that there are variations of complex strategies for co-design used by the stakeholders in order to effectuate the three action types of the decision making process. Furthermore, the studies indicate that the co-design process is not a linear one but rather an iterative process where solutions are proposed, assessed, rejected, adjusted solutions proposed and assessed again in several turns before reaching a (often implicit) decision.

References

[1] Friedman A, Cornford D (1989) Computer Systems Development – History, Organization, and Implementation. John Wiley & Sons Ltd Chichester

[2] O'Neill E (2001) User-Developer Cooperation in Software Development – Building Common Ground and Usable Systems. Springer-Verlag London

[3] Mumford E, Weir M (1979) Computer Systems in Work Design – the ETHICS Method. Associated Business Press London

[4] Ives B, Olson M (1984) User Involvement and MIS Success: a Review of Research. Management Science, vol 30, pp 586-603

[5] Kappelman L, McLean E (1991) The Respective Roles of User Participation and User Involvement in Information Systems Implementation Success. Proc of the twelfth International Conference on Information Systems

[6] Hartwick J, Barki H (1994) Explaining the Role of User Participation in Information Systems Use. Management Science, vol 40, pp 440-465

[7] Cavaye ALM (1995) User Participation in Development Revisited. Information & Management, vol 28, pp 311-323

[8] Greenbaum J, Kyng M (1991) Preface: Memories of the Past. In: Greenbaum J, Kyng M (eds) Design at Work. Lawrence Erlbaum Ass Publ Hillsdale

[9] Mumford E (1993) The Participation of Users in Systems Design – an Account of the Origin, Evolution and Use of the ETHICS Method. In: Schuler D, Namioka A (eds) Participatory Design: Principles and Practices. Lawrence Erlbaum Hillsdale

[10] Ehn P (1988) Work-Oriented Design of Computer Artifacts. Arbetslivscentrum Stockholm

[11] Gallivan MJ, Keil M (2003) The User-Developer Communication Process: a Critical Case Study. Information Systems Journal, vol 13, pp 37-68

[12] Carlsson S (2000) Lärande systemutveckling och samarbetsformer. Karlstad University Press Karlstad (in Swedish)

[13] Holmqvist B, Andersen PB (1991) Language, Perspectives and Design. In: Greenbaum J, Kyng M (eds) Design at Work. Lawrence Erlbaum Ass Publishers Hillsdale

[14] Newman M, Robey D (1992) A Social Process Model of User-Analyst Relationships. MIS Quarterly, June 1992

[15] Cronholm S, Goldkuhl G, Hedström K, Pilemalm M-L (2003) Handlingsbart IT-system för kvalitetssäkring och individualisering av äldreomsorg. KvalitetsMässan Göteborg (in Swedish)

[16] Hedström K (2004) Spår av datoriseringens värden – Effekter av IT i äldreomsorg. Dissertation No. 9 Linköping Studies in Information Science Linköping University Sweden (in Swedish)

[17] Larsson U (2004) Designarbete i dialog – karaktärisering av interaktionen mellan användare och utvecklare i en systemutvecklingsprocess. Licentiatavhandling FiF 77 Institutionen för datavetenskap Linköping University Sweden (in Swedish)

[18] Goldkuhl G, Larsson U (2004) IT-design i verksamhetskontexter – kunskap i handling vid professionella möten. In: Jernström E, Säljö R (eds) Lärande i arbetsliv och var dag. Brain Books Jönköing Sweden (in Swedish)

Inter-Activities Management for Supporting Cooperative Software Development

Arnaud Lewandowski and Grégory Bourguin

Laboratoire d'Informatique du Littoral, Université du Littoral Côte d'Opale (ULCO), France. (lewandowski, bourguin)@lil.univ-littoral.fr

Introduction

Systems supporting Computer Supported Cooperative Work (CSCW) are more and more omnipresent. As technologies continuously evolve, users are looking for new supports for their activities, which are intrinsically cooperative and imply many actors, distributed through space and time.

The software development domain, which provides such new tools as well as uses them, does not escape from this rule. Systems are more and more complex, and their development requires the cooperation of many actors, with different roles and different cultures. Anyway, many studies of common practices that occur during software development illustrate how this cooperative dimension holds a strong place in this field [9][11][16]. Actually, the necessity to take into account this dimension in environments supporting software development has been underlined for a long time [18]. However, one can notice that the current systems supporting software development do not bring to the fore, or according to recent work on CSCW, support poorly the cooperative dimension of these activities.

We have been working for several years on the problems tied to the creation of global and integrated CSCW environments. Our work is inspired by some results coming from the Social and Human Sciences (SHS), especially the Activity Theory (AT), and aims at proposing tailorable models and systems, in accordance with the expansive properties of every human activity. These thoughts led us to define the Coevolution [4] principle, which is integrated in the growing platform named CooLDA [2].

This paper presents a proposition to better take into account the cooperative dimension in software development tools, while integrating our previous results about tailorability. This work is realized through the CoolDev project (Cooperative Layer for software Development), supported by the French research ministry. The first part of this paper presents the implications tied to the support of software development cooperative activities, by integrating the results of our work in the CSCW domain. The second part presents the solution we propose, through a cooperative extension to the Eclipse platform. Finally, the third part presents the orientations we take, with regard to the results presented in this paper.

Cooperative Software Development

Software development environments generally provide a poor support to the cooperative dimension of this activity. From our point of view, adding a cooperative dimension does not simply consist in plugging specific communication tools, such as an IRC (Internet Relay Chat), that will bring a new coloration in the environment. We have been working since years in the CSCW field, and we have to integrate as many results we obtained in this field as possible, if we want our cooperative software development environment to be a 'good' CSCW environment too.

CSCW, Tailorability and Coevolution

For years, the CSCW research has identified the need for tailorability in the systems. This necessity has been brought to the fore by many empirical and theoretical results, based on several theories coming from the Social and Human Sciences, like Situated Action [17], Ethnomethodology [6], or Activity Theory (AT) [1]. Besides, our research is founded on the AT, which has been broadly used in the domain over the last ten years [10][13].

The AT provides a lot of information that can help systems designers to better understand the human activities they try to support. We cannot explain in this paper all the results we obtained by founding our research on this theory, neither detail the links between the choices we have made and the AT. Further information can be found in [2] and [3]. However, in order to facilitate the understanding of the paper, we have to briefly remind some of the basic elements of the AT that found our general reasoning.

We use the basic structure of an activity proposed by Engeström [7]. This structure presents the human activity as an interdependent system involving a subject that realizes the object of the activity, and the community of subjects who are concerned with this realization. Relations between the subject, the object and the community are mediated. In particular, the subject uses tools to realize the object of his activity. Rules determine what means belonging to the community, and a division of labor describes how the work is shared up by the members of the community. Furthermore, this structure as a whole is dynamic and continually evolves during the realization of the activity. For example, subjects may transform the mediating elements, such as tools, as new needs emerge. Subjects themselves evolve during the activity, acquiring skills and developing some experience of its realization. Thus, when subjects transform the elements participating in their activity, the experience they acquired crystallizes in these elements. This experience, 'written' in the transformed artifacts, becomes available for others, which can use it in other activities.

Thus, a system that supports a specific activity is a mediator of it. It may contain a representation of it: the subject and the community are represented; roles inside the system reflect the division of labor, etc. The system does not contain the activity, but rather takes part in it. Therefore, it has to be tailorable: it must provide the means to adapt it during the activity it is involved in. Finally, this tailorability can be associated with some mechanisms of experience crystallization and reuse. All these elements brought us to the Coevolution principle [4]. In this approach, a system has to support not only the activity it is designed for, but also its own (re)design cooperative activity.

Shortcomings of the Existing Platforms

Today, many platforms support software development cooperative activities. Among them, we have taken an interest in some web portals and some integrated development environments (IDE) widely used.

Web portals, like SourceForge (http://sourceforge.net) and Freshmeat (http://freshmeat.net), provide a global environment that integrates many tools, such as planning tools, concurrent versions systems and document sharing tools, forums, and bug reporting tools, for example. These integrated tools aim at supporting some cooperative activities tied to the software development process. However, those web environments present some drawbacks, especially with regards to tailorability. Indeed, the latter is in most cases greatly reduced, since the available tools are defined *a priori* in the system. The dynamic integration of new tools is generally not possible, or in best cases, is hardly accessible to end users.

Integrated Development Environments (IDE), such as NetBeans (www.netbeans.org) or Eclipse (www.eclipse.org), also integrate sets of tools dedicated to support producing code activities. Unfortunately, most of the IDE only focus on these producing code activities, and avoid or forsake their cooperative dimension. Actually, such IDE just provide gates towards a common repository – such as CVS (Concurrent Versions System [8]) – which supports and manages documents sharing, but not the communication between developers. A few collaborative extensions to Eclipse try to palliate this lack [5]. But from our point of view, this kind of extensions – that just provides some collaborative functionalities like an IRC, for example – still remains superficial, and does not tend to take into account the cooperation at a global level. Eclipse has not been designed in that orientation, and it does not manage any notion of role, or something like this that takes into account the status of a user in the global cooperative activity he participates in. As a result, the user has to integrate the tools (plug-ins) he needs himself, and to configure them himself, according to his role in the real activity supported.

In practice [19], due to the lack of tailorability and of cooperative support in commonly used platforms, the actors of software development use in a complementary way many tools (IDE, web portals, synchronous discussion tool, etc.), each one supporting one or more (sub)activities. Faced with such statements, we aim at proposing a platform that palliates these needs: a tailorable platform supporting software development cooperative activities, inspired by our previous work on the Coevolution principle.

CooLDev: Cooperation under Eclipse

The CooLDev project has been initiated with the support of the French research ministry. The project is directly inspired by results obtained during the DARE project [3], that evolved until becoming CooLDA [2] (Cooperative Layer supporting Distributed Activities), the generic underlying platform on which CooLDev lays.

Our Approach: Managing Inter-Activities

A major choice in our reasoning to design a CSCW environment is to consider that many tools already exist, and are useful in supporting some activities we are interested in. Thus, our main goal is not to create such tools, like a new discussion tool, or a new code editor. Rather, we want to create an environment that integrates these many tools. From our point of view, each tool supports one kind of activity. When several tools are used in parallel by a group of actors, they generally serve a more global activity than the original activity there were designed for. The Figure 1a illustrates this idea: a group uses in parallel an IRC, a CVS, a code editor, and an annotation tool. Each of these tools supports a particular activity (discussion for the IRC, etc.) but they do not know each other. However, they are used in a complementary way by the group since they are used in the context of a global cooperative activity: software development. In such a case, the coherence of the environment is mainly mentally managed by the users. Then, our purpose is to provide an environment that can create the context of use of the different tools involved in a global cooperative activity, for example a software development activity, managing the links between its different (sub-)activities. Assuming that each tool supports a specific activity, our environment is intended to manage what we call inter-activities.

To achieve this, we have created an activity model (cf. Figure 1b) allowing the specification of the links of the inter-activities. Each activity is linked to a resource that proposes operations. A resource corresponds to a software tool, like an IRC client, for example. A user is an actor in the activity, as he plays a role in it, role that allows him to do actions. An activity can be linked to other ones, when the role of one of its actors implies that this user plays another role in another activity. Finally, an activity is an instance of a task, which constitutes an activity model, or pattern. As we will see later, the task is intended to crystallize the experience of the actors.

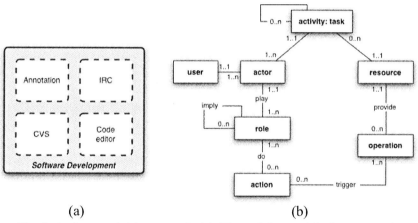

(a)   (b)

Fig. 1. An inter-activities example (a). The activity model of CooLDA (b)

Choosing Eclipse

Our work in the software development field led us to look closer at the Eclipse platform, that has been adopted by many developers. The success of Eclipse has been a driving force for the development of many tools, that can be integrated into the platform as plug-ins. As we have underlined before, we do not aim at developing new tools, but at giving the means to articulate them in a global cooperative activity. From this viewpoint, Eclipse is very interesting. Indeed, Eclipse is much more than a simple IDE: it was originally conceived as a universal platform for tools integration [14].

Thus, the platform is constructed around the OSGi standard framework [15], which supports the dynamic discovery, installation and activation of plug-ins. Apart from this minimal kernel managing the basic integration mechanisms, all the proposed functionalities are provided through plug-ins or sets of plug-ins. Thus, from our viewpoint, what makes the success of Eclipse is that it has been principally conceived in terms of tailorability. The end user can adapt the environment according to his emergent needs. He can discover and dynamically integrate tools available on the network and that can help him to realize his activity.

Another element in Eclipse, which is in tune with our work inspired by the AT, is the perspectives mechanism. A perspective corresponds to a particular point of view on the working environment (and the activated plug-ins) during the realization of a kind of activity. This point of view manages the plug-ins activation and arrangement at the user interface level. Eclipse lets the user create and modify his own perspectives, saving his preferences for a kind of activity. From our viewpoint, the perspectives provide a powerful mean to crystallize the user's experience. However, one can notice that perspectives can activate only plug-ins that are available on the user's station. In other words, if a plug-in is referenced by a perspective but is not installed, it will be skipped.

Finally, thanks to its introspection mechanisms, and as we will present it thereafter, Eclipse framework provides very useful means to specify and to support the inter-activities. These mechanisms let us dynamically create the links, until now not supported, that exist between the (sub-)activities supported by the activated plug-ins in a global cooperative activity.

Managing Inter-Activities

At the time we are writing, Eclipse does not provide the cooperative dimension we need. Our contribution lies within several levels: first, it consists in extending the Eclipse framework by integrating the elements of our model of activity. According to this model, each plug-in supports one activity. We propose to manage the inter-activities thanks to a meta plug-in named CooLDev, whose role is to articulate the other plug-ins in the context of global cooperative activities. This meta plug-in is connected to a server that manages the persistence of the instances of our model. The Figure 2 presents an example of such a cooperative global environment for software development, that integrates the mechanisms we now describe.

Because of our meta plug-in, the user has to identify himself to launch Eclipse, in the same way as other CSCW tools. Thanks to this, we can retrieve information concerning the role of the user in the appropriate global activity. This role is an instance of a type of role that can be shared by several actors. It allows the meta plug-in to configure the user's working environment. To do this, we have extended Eclipse perspectives, in the context of a cooperative activities management: perspectives are shared by users playing the same role, and as we will see later, can also reflect the user's preferences in his role. Moreover, as we underlined in previous part, when a perspective tries to activate an unavailable plug-in, this latter is skipped. In case of a standard use of Eclipse, this is acceptable, since things go otherwise: installed plug-ins are packaged with some perspectives, suitable for their utilization. In the context of CooLDev, it is the role of the user, and consequently his perspective, that determines which plug-ins will be used in a particular activity. Thus, we have extended the basic perspective mechanism so that it can automatically download plug-ins that are specified in the perspective but not installed on the user's station.

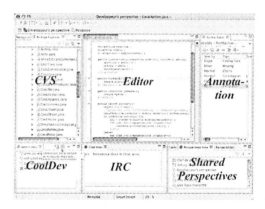

Fig. 2. An example of a global cooperative environment

Even if the tools that support the user's activities are instantiated by these extended perspectives, it is not enough to support the inter-activities as we define it. We use our model to specify the actions that have to be processed by a role when its user joins the activity. These actions configure the plug-ins for this user. For example, when a user joins a code reviewing activity, in a development project, our plug-in uses the user's role to instantiate a CVS plug-in, an IRC plug-in, a code editor and an annotation tool. For the user to avoid identifying another time in the IRC (he has already identified himself while connecting to our environment), we have to indicate to this plug-in what is its configuration (pseudo, server, etc.). From our model's point of view, the user's role realizes actions that trigger operations on the linked plug-in. Technically speaking, the operations are mapped on methods provided by the plug-in and discovered by CooLDA, using introspection mechanisms.

Managing Tailorability

As CooLDev focuses on the inter-activities management, the tailorability it provides sits at this level. First, we take benefit from the tailorability in Eclipse, and we extend it in a cooperative context. Thanks to the plug-ins and perspectives mechanisms, each user can customize his environment by adding, removing and arranging tools that serve his activity. However, in the global cooperative activity, a particular perspective reflects not only the user's preferences, but also his role. Thus, it crystallizes the experience developed in his function. We have set up a mechanism that allows the user to generalize this perspective at the role level. This feature is presented in Figure 3a. Of course, in the framework of the Coevolution principle (that is a cooperative management of the system adaptation), this action can be proposed only to users with a specific role. One can also imagine that the decision to generalize a particular extended perspective in a role has to be negotiated between actors. Thus, when a new user joins an activity with a particular role, he retrieves the experience of users that have already played the same role. Finally, if the scenario set up in the activity permits it, the user can again modify his own perspective, and so on.

(a)   (b)

Fig. 3. Zoom on the CooLDev view and on the mechanism that generalizes a perspective at the role level (a), and on the shared perspectives view (b)

In order to complete the mechanism that generalizes a perspective at the role level, we have developed a tool allowing actors to share their perspectives. This feature is presented in Figure 3b. Thanks to this mechanism, actors can share extended perspectives without having to crystallize them in their role model, which would be constraining for actors who just want to test perspectives, or to share a viewpoint for a short while before deciding to crystallize it.

We have also introduced tools that provide tailorability at finer levels of the inter-activities management. Thanks to the introspection mechanism of our model of activity, it is possible to (re)define during the activity the elements that participate in it, like for example the actions for each role. The lowest abstraction level is the one of operations that define the links between the actions (of a role) and the methods (provided by a plug-in).

CooLDA is able to dynamically retrieve these methods, allowing to (re) define the operations used in the specification of the roles' actions. We are aware that the abstraction level of this kind of tailorability is still hardly within the reach of every end user. However, implementing these mechanisms helps us, at first, to verify the technical feasibility of such an approach. We are now working on user interfaces of higher abstraction level, to give end users the means to access this inter-activities management.

More generally speaking, the evolution of an activity – its tools (integrated plug-ins, operations) and roles (extended perspectives, actions) – is synthesized in a model of activity that we call *task*. A task forms thus a model that has crystallized the experience developed cooperatively by users during their global activity, and that can be re-instantiated in order to support other similar activities. These latter, evolving in turn, will be able to modify their task, or to create new ones. Even if very interesting, this reflexive approach, developed in the framework of the DARE project [3], raises also many problems. We can not develop them here, but one can refer to [2] to discover the many stakes in it that we have already identified.

The mechanisms described here present the tailorability and crystallization currently provided in our support. These mechanisms are not at the same abstraction level. As underlined by Morch [12], the tailorability level increases proportionately to its difficulty of access for end users. The basic integration of tools and the mechanisms tied to the extended perspectives are more directly aimed at end users. The evolution of roles and actions are aimed at CoolDev specialists, and the definition of operations by introspection on methods at developers. At first, we will package CoolDev with a set of predefined tasks. Users will then be able to adapt these tasks according to their needs, providing thus new activity patterns. The many abstraction levels, and the cooperative dimension of the supported activities let us hope that the end users, interested in the tailorability levels they will be able to reach, will increase their experience towards the system, and will become more and more expert of it, being able to access more advanced levels of tailorability. They will be able then to share this experience through the system, meeting the Coevolution principle.

Perspectives

Towards a Finer Inter-Activities Management

The current version of CooLDev contextualizes activities supported by 'isolated' tools in the framework of a global cooperative activity. However, in the long run, our aim is to provide more advanced mechanisms. For instance, it could be interesting to catch events coming from an activity, to give them a sense in the global activity and to act according to it in the other linked activities. For example, one can imagine an activity where a reviewer is annotating a file. The fact that he saves his work generates an event in the annotation activity; this changes the state of the global activity, and may warn the developers by displaying a message in the IRC. We have already begun this work and verified the technical feasibility of such an approach. Even if this level seems interesting, the main problem stands in the semantic of events. Indeed, in order to give a sense to an event in the global activity, one must be able to understand this event in the activity it comes from. As CooLDA integrates dynamically tools that it does not know *a priori*, this semantic problem is very meaningful. That is why we work on a proposition to extend the plug-ins model, in order to add a semantic level that should facilitate a finer integration by end users.

Experiments in Real Situations

In order to evaluate the use of the given tailorability, we have to experiment the platform in real projects. At first, we plan to use CooLDev in the context of development projects realized cooperatively by teams of students. With such real tests, we will be able to verify the stability of the system, with regards to its reflexive properties, from a technical and – especially – a human viewpoint. Indeed, the Coevolution principle has been defined upon results based on the AT. We have proposed a system that can be adapted to the emergent needs of the users during their activity. For the system to be 'correctly' adapted, the activity must pass by stable stages, allowing users to increase their experience. So we want to verify that the human dimension brought to the fore in CooLDev (the system is adaptable, but not self-adaptive) permits, not a continuous evolution of the environment, but rather the crystallization of a true experience for end users.

Coevolution in Web Portals

The Eclipse platform is well suited for our needs in the context of software development, since many plug-ins supporting related activities are already available. Actually, new generations of web portals, thanks to the web services normalization, provide some properties that are close to those we set up. However, the underlying models of such portals seem to present some shortcomings, with regards to the principles we want to manage; especially, they do not consider the activity consisting in the evolution of the environment as a fully-cooperative activity, which seems to be harmful for supporting the Coevolution, as we have underlined in [2]. Therefore, we are studying the possibilities and limitations of these technologies, in order to use them in the scope of our work, even if, due to the nature of the available components, the application field will certainly differ from the one we are currently focused on, namely software development.

Conclusion

As software development is today a strongly cooperative activity, we focused in this paper on the means that can support it. We have been working for many years in the CSCW research domain, trying to take benefit from SHS theories, especially the Activity Theory (AT). This work has led us to identify the crucial need for tailorability in cooperative environments, and to define the Coevolution principle. By studying several platforms broadly used by developers, we have identified their shortcomings, in line with the stakes defined in the CSCW field. Therefore, we have proposed a solution that consists in an extension of the Eclipse platform which is already broadly used for software development, but which does not integrate the cooperative dimension of such activities at a global level.

Basing on results coming from the AT and on Eclipse properties, we propose a model of activity and a meta plug-in that contextualizes the activities supported by plug-ins. We aim at creating a tailorable support for managing the inter-activities and setting up the Coevolution: the system must support software development cooperative activities and its own cooperative (re)design (meta)activity, while fostering crystallization and sharing of the experience developed by its users. Our proposition brings several levels of tailorability, that are intended both to end users and to users which have developed more advanced skills concerning our platform.

Although it already provides a tailorable support for the inter-activities management, our proposition needs to be developed further and to be tested in real situations. We have to work on raising its abstraction level. In order to achieve this, we plan to pursue our efforts and to look closer at the problem of the semantic associated to components (plug-ins, JavaBeans or Web services) available on the Internet. Indeed, even if there exist solutions trying to palliate this problem, one must agree that most of the existing component models are intended to software developers, whereas the results of studies in many fields show that the means for discovering, and dynamically and finely integrating tools would be useful for end users, as it would take into account *in situ* their emergent needs.

References

[1] Bedny G, Meister D (1997) The Russian Theory of Activity, Current Applications to Design and Learning. Lawrence Erlbaum Associates Publishers
[2] Bourguin G (2003) Les leçons d'une expérience dans la réalisation d'un collecticiel réflexif. In: Actes de la 15ème conférence francophone IHM 2003 Caen ACM International Conference Proceedings Series, pp 40-47
[3] Bourguin G (2000) Un support informatique à l'activité coopérative fondé sur la Théorie de l'Activité : le projet DARE. Ph. D. Thesis, Informatique, n°2753, Université des Sciences et Technologies de Lille France
[4] Bourguin G, Derycke A, Tarby JC (2001) Beyond the Interface: Co-evolution inside Interactive Systems – A proposal Founded on Activity Theory. People and Computer, no 15, Interaction without Frontiers, proc of HCI'2001 Blandford Vanderdonckt, pp 297-310
[5] Cheng L, Hupfer S, Ross S, Patterson J (2003) Jazzing up Eclipse with Collaborative Tools. Proc of the 2003 OOPSLA Workshop on Eclipse Technology eXchange, Anaheim California, pp 45-49
[6] Dourish P, Button G (1998) On "Technomethodology": Foundational Relationships between Ethnomethodology and System Design. Human-Computer Interaction, no 13, pp 395- 432
[7] Engeström Y (1987) Learning by Expanding. Orienta-konsultit Helsinki
[8] Krause R (2001) CVS: An Introduction. Linux journal, vol 87, no 3
[9] Kraut RE, Streeter LA (1995) Coordination in Software Development. Communications of the ACM, vol 38, no 3, pp 69-81
[10] Kuutti K (1993) Notes on Systems Supporting "Organisational Context" – An Activity Theory Viewpoint. COMIC European project D1.1, pp 101-117
[11] Lethbridge T, Singer J (2002) Studies of the Work Practices of Software Engineers. In: Erdogmus H, Tanir O (eds) Advances in Software Engineering: Comprehension, Evaluation, and Evolution. Springer-Verlag, pp 53-76
[12] Morch A (1997) Method and Tools for Tailoring of Object-oriented Applications: An Evolving Artifacts Approach, Part 1. Dr. Scient. Thesis Research Report 241 Department of Informatics University of Oslo Norway
[13] Nardi B (1996) Context and Consciousness: Activity Theory and Human-Computer Interaction. MIT Press Cambridge

[14] Object Technology International Inc (2003) Eclipse Platform Technical Overview. www.eclipse.org/
[15] OSGi Alliance (2004) About the OSGi Service Platform. Technical paper
[16] Pavlicek RG (2000) Embracing Insanity: Open Source Software Development. Sams Publishing Indianapolis
[17] Suchman L (1987) Plans and Situated Actions. Cambridge University Press Cambridge UK
[18] Vessey I, Sravanapudi AP (1995) CASE Tools as Collaborative Support Technologies. Communications of the ACM, vol 38, no 1, pp 83-95
[19] Wester M (2003) An End-User View of the Collaborative Software Development Market. Market Research Report IDC #30608, vol 1. www.collab.net

The Socialization of Virtual Teams: Implications for ISD

Brenda Mullally and Larry Stapleton

I.S.O.L Research Group, Waterford Institute of Technology (WIT), Republic of Ireland. (Bmullally, lstapleton)@wit.ie

Introduction

Studies show that Information Systems Development (ISD) projects do not fulfil stakeholder expectations of completion time, quality and budget. Ovaska's (2005) study shows that development is more about social interaction and mutual understanding than following a prescribed method. Systems development is a social process where interactions help to make sense of the reality within which the system is developed (Hirschheim et al., 1991). Research concentrates on methodology when in fact method may not be the primary problem. Authors have called for further research to investigate the true nature of the current systems development environment in real organisational situations (Fitzgerald, 2000).

Advances in technology, availability of resources and globalisation has lead to development teams spread across countries and continents. These virtual teams suffer from the lack of face-to-face contact necessary for effective operation. The literature lacks a coherent framework that addresses the problems faced by virtual ISD teams. Consequently, a preliminary conceptual framework for effective virtual ISD is presented in this paper. The paper is organised into several sections, the first outlines the paradigmatic influences on methodologies, the use of virtual teams for software development and the impact of virtuality on the tasks necessary to perform ISD. The later section describes the use of socialisation tactics to improve the effectiveness of these teams and poses future research questions.

ISD: A Review of the Literature

The information systems development discipline has a history that includes the constant creation and redevelopment of methodologies. Systems development in the 1960's resulted in a 'software crisis'. In response, ISD approaches emerged that aimed to help the development process by meeting costs and time constraints. Iivari and Hirschheim (1996) define an ISD approach as a category of methodologies by common features. It has concepts and principles originating from a paradigm and can comprise of one or more methodology. A methodology or method is a set of goal-orientated procedures supported by tools and techniques.

Research supports the principle that established paradigms exist in the ISD discipline. Hirschheim and Klein (1989) highlighted the influence of implicit and explicit assumptions on ISD. These assumptions influence the process of seeking and dealing with information. Each ISD approach brings with it epistemological assumptions relating to the generation and acquisition of knowledge, and ontological assumptions relating to the representation of the physical and social reality within which we exist. Further studies conducted provide a comprehensive breakdown of the alternative paradigms (Avison and Fitzgerald, 2003). These challenge the paradigmatic foundations of the early approaches. Providing an alternative to the functionalist view of information, the positivist epistemology and the structuralist view of organisations. However, many methodologies still fall under the functionalist paradigm and continue to consider social issues a lesser priority than technical issues. ISD in practice uses methodologies in a pragmatic way (Fitzgerald, 1997). This involves the use of tools and techniques that are appropriate to the situation. Methodologies alone will not result in successful ISD; it is necessary for the practitioner to have certain skills. The following competencies are essential for ISD; communication, negotiation, business knowledge and the ability to establish interpersonal relationships (Lee et al., 2002; Tan, 1994). The prioritisation of these competencies may be influenced by the paradigmatic assumptions, relegating social competencies in favour of technical ones.

Advances in technology, availability of resources and globalisation has lead to development teams spread across countries and continents. Since the late 1990's the virtual team as an organisational model is more and more popular (Cramton and Webber, 2005). In the context of this paper, a virtual team exists across organisational boundaries and performs interdependent tasks with responsibility for the outcomes. Geographic dispersion is inherent of a virtual team, resulting in a reliance on technology-mediated communications to accomplish tasks. The majority of virtual team communication exists through email, voicemail, fax, teleconference, videoconference, online collaborative tools and telephone. Teams may meet face-to-face but the coordination and collaboration of work carried out bears a heavy reliance on technology. An understanding of problems encountered by virtual teams helps to appreciate the impact these problems can have on ISD competencies.

ISD Competencies and Virtual Team Complications

By definition, communication in virtual teams must take place predominantly through computer-mediated communication (CMC). Communication and coordination are identified as key contributors to the success of ISD (McManus and Wood-Harper, 2003). Habermas's critical social theory of the 'ideal speech situation' forms the basis for Hirschheim and Klien's (1994) theory that if rational discourse takes place through clear communication, discussions would be more effective. Rational discourse involves two or more individuals communicating without deceiving themselves or others. Deception or distortion occurs due to linguistic barriers such as limitations of language, and social barriers such as inequalities of power and education or resources. The elimination of status, position, class or appearance through email or teleconferencing helps to reduce social barriers. Linguistic barriers may be reduced through improved social ties (Cramton and Webber, 2005). Social ties develop through the sharing of information that is local to the team members' context along with constraints and differences across locations. These social ties create familiarity and understanding between team members thus increasing levels of interaction, the ability to express information, and correctly interpret feedback from others. It is more likely that virtual teams be effective when members have strong social links. Those teams that do not have strong links require more structured management and coordination (Kiesler and Cummings, 2002).

Virtual teams depend on the written word as one of the main forms of communication. There is much literature on the negative affects of CMC on the written word. (Mannix et al., 2002; Sproull and Kiesler, 1991). Participants interpret a message through the meanings of words as well as facial expression, body language and intonation. These indicators of meaning are lacking in CMC. Problems of mutual understanding between team members, differing interpretations of the meaning of silence, the constant unequal distribution of information, misattribution (Cramton, 2001), group identity (Armstrong and Cole, 2002) and conflict (Mannix et al., 2002) can occur as a result.

A lack of situational knowledge can cause participants to reach inaccurate conclusions regarding the behaviour of others. The human instinct is to attribute behaviour to a person's personality rather than their situation. Virtual teams are often groups of people who have not worked together in the past. Group identity is slow to develop and in some circumstances, members do not feel part of the group at all. Virtual teams encounter more frequent and faster developing forms of conflict than proximate teams (Sproull and Kiesler, 1991) and allow conflict to linger due to the lack of face-to-face interaction normally used to recognise and resolve conflict. Conflict during ISD can lead to delays in decision-making. Virtual teams may lack the ability to demonstrate and develop their competencies in communication, negotiation and interaction as they lack knowledge of other's skills, perspectives, interpersonal styles and work environment.

This paper concentrates on applying socialisation theory to the virtual ISD team context. The key problem areas for virtual team members are team solidarity, equal dissemination of information, trust, conflict and mutual understanding. Many of these problems cause failures in ISD but are significant benefits of socialisation theory. The following section describes the socialisation process and the tactics available to the virtual ISD team.

Socialisation in the Context of ISD

Socialisation is the process of 'learning the ropes' through training, mentoring, role models and other tactics (Schein, 1988). Organisational socialisation concerns the assimilation of newcomers into the organisation i.e. learning what is important in the organisation in terms of task, behaviour and role. Work group socialisation relates to familiarisation with the work and social environment within which the newcomer conducts their work. A new member must learn the value system, norms, and appropriate behaviour of the work group. According to Schein (1988) "the speed and effectiveness of socialization determine employee loyalty, commitment, productivity, and [staff] turnover". The initial emphasis during the 1960's was that the organisation demonstrates and ensures compliance by the newcomer to the rules and procedures of the organisation through the socialisation process. This view then developed into a socialisation process that could be designed through the use of tactics developed by Van Maanen & Schein (1979) to produce particular outcomes. Studies conducted in the late 90's show strong links between these tactics and performance outcomes. Mignerey et al (1995) linked specific socialisation tactics with communication and attributional satisfaction, demonstrating that socialisation is needed for effective communication.

The concentration of research has been in the area of organisational socialisation. Researchers of work group socialisation Moreland and Levine (1999) believe that socialisation occurs primarily in work groups and that it has a stronger impact on the behaviour of most employees. Research also provides findings that support this argument, for example an early study found that daily interaction with peers was the most important factor in helping newcomers to feel effective (Louis et al., 1983). Ostroff and

Kozlowski (1992) found that newcomers relied primarily upon the observation of others, followed by supervisors and co-workers as a means to acquiring information. Given the current trends in organisational team working, there have been recent calls for further research in the area of work group socialisation (Ahuja and Galvin, 2003).

Van Maanen & Schein's (1976) organisational socialisation model has been tested and its findings offer an explanation of how particular tactics influence the role orientation of newcomers. The use of tactics therefore may influence the ability to communicate, understand and interact thus affecting the success of ISD. This paper attempts to add to Van Maanen & Schein's (1976) theory, by applying it to the development of information systems in the virtual team environment. Following on from this line of enquiry this paper posits that the use by a virtual team of the chosen methodology will affect the socialisation tactics used, as the methodological assumptions, epistemology and ontology will influence the process of socialisation and the choice of tactics. It may also be the case that socialisation tactics influence the use of the methodology. The following section unpacks these tactics in relation to a virtual ISD team. This model has received little attention from ISD theorists but may have some theoretical power in determining effective socialisation tactics during the ISD process.

Collective vs. Individual

Collective socialisation occurs when a group of new members collectively share the same experience for example, training or induction. Individual socialisation involves each new member experiencing socialisation independently of others as in apprenticeships. Collective socialisation results in cohesiveness and collective understanding through the sharing of the experience. This can lead to the establishment of a history, something that is typically delayed for virtual teams (Armstrong and Cole, 2002). Stage (1991) describes methodologies as tools that allow knowledge to be stored, systematised, disseminated and exchanged. Collective socialisation would encourage team members to collectively identify the ways in which they intend to use the tool as a means to store or disseminate knowledge. Collective socialisation is a tool that can improve the shared understanding between virtual team members. Individual socialisation encourages independent behaviour and the ability to use one's own initiative. Teams working towards a common goal require a degree of independence. However interdependence and the formation of trust within a team are essential to functioning effectively.

Formal vs. Informal

Formal socialisation occurs when new members are set aside from the rest of the organisation and put through experiences specifically designed for the new members. This is to clarify the role of the new members within the organisation. Informal socialisation tactics do not highlight the newcomers role specifically, nor demonstrate the difference between the new member and existing organisation members (Van Maanen and Schein, 1979). New roles are learned through experience on the job and work assignments. Formal tactics are used in situations where it is important that new members learn the correct attitudes and values associated with their new role. Teams using methodologies based on the functionalist paradigm require team member roles to be clear and established early in the project; analysts, programmers and testers are designated specific responsibilities. Research shows that virtual teams have difficulty identifying who is part of the team (Mortensen and Hinds, 2002). Formal tactics can be used to establish an understanding of team roles and responsibilities. Informal tactics require the new member to be the instigator of socialisation, seeking out the information. Consequently mistakes can be costly as the information may be incorrect and require face-to-face meetings to rectify the problems caused (Van Maanen and Schein, 1979).

Sequential vs. Random

In most professional training, there are events or steps through which the candidate progresses, at the end of which they take on the professional role. Sequential socialisation refers to the degree to which the organisation specifies a sequence of steps leading to the intended role. Random socialisation involves unknown steps that lead to the role (Van Maanen and Schein, 1979). ISD teams may benefit from a sequence of training steps that, when completed, provides the team member with the skills to perform in their given role. This may include training in communications, problem solving, ISD methodologies and the problem domain technologies. Wegner's (1986) work on transactive memory demonstrates the need to share knowledge amongst team members. When team members know more about each other, the planning of work, the anticipation of behaviour and the assigning of tasks is more effective (Moreland and Levine, 1999). Random socialisation could result in varying abilities and skills of team members in the same role. In a co-located environment, the lack of skills would be apparent through face-to-face meetings. In ISD, the interdependence between tasks requires collaboration. The assumption is that the other team members have the skills and ability to perform.

Fixed vs. Variable

Fixed or variable socialisation determines the degree to which the organisation has the steps of the socialisation process timetabled. Fixed socialisation allows the new member to know exactly when and for how long each step will take. Variable socialisation provides the new member with some idea of the timetable but it is not precise or fixed in any way. ISD exists in a changeable environment with uncontrollable factors affecting the movement of resources. Many ISD projects now are of a shorter life span (Fitzgerald, 2000) and the use of fixed timetabled steps may be limited. However, variable socialisation tactics do not instil cohesiveness and solidarity within a team. If the timetable for socialisation is not clear then ISD team members may be hesitant to converse freely with each other. The establishment of trust in co-located teams is linked with the strength of identification with a group and its members (Kramer et al., 1999). Research found that socialisation, communication and participation practices create an environment that is both controlled and trusting (O'Leary et al., 2002). In a virtual team, members must collaborate with unfamiliar team members. Fixed socialisation tactics may help to create a trusting environment where virtual ISD teams can work effectively.

Serial vs. Disjunctive

Serial socialisation occurs when an established member of the team acts as the role model for the new recruit. In this way the teams norms, attitudes and behaviour pass to the new recruit. Disjunctive socialisation is when no role model or established member is responsible for the new recruit (Van Maanen, 1976). Mentoring for team members involved in ISD may help to create greater understanding of the problem domain, the application of a methodology and the approach to problem solving. Extreme programming involves constant interaction and sharing of information. This method could be adapted to incorporate mentoring functions. However, the lack of visual observation inherent in virtual teams, impedes distance mentoring (Armstrong and Cole, 2002) Distance-mentoring techniques such as programming while being observed on-line and collaborative analysis may be suitable for ISD. It may be the case that disjunctive socialisation is common due to the infancy of the virtual team as a new organisational work unit. Many of those joining a virtual team may in fact have never worked in that type of environment previously and therefore cannot act as mentors.

Investiture vs. Divestiture

This tactic determines the acceptance or rejection of the new members personality and attitudes through positive or negative support by the established members of the organisation (Jones, 1986). Investiture socialisation aims to accept and confirm the positive benefits gained through the new member's personal characteristics. The investiture tactic says to the recruit "We like you just as you are" (Van Maanen and Schein, 1979). The organisation or team in this instance does not want to change the new member. Carefully selected members will already conform to the set of beliefs and attitudes established by the team. Divestiture socialisation aims to disconfirm the perceptions and beliefs a new recruit holds. Jones (1986) argued that divestiture tactics lead new members to question situations and evaluate the influence of established members on their perception of a situation.

Socialisation Framework

Figure 1 is a conceptual ISD socialisation framework developed by the author. It represents the reciprocal relationship between ISD methodologies and socialisation tactics, highlighting their affect on ISD success. This is a working theoretical framework that is to be informed by a future pilot study. The key practical implication of this framework is to support the establishment and effective operation of virtual ISD teams using methodologies and socialisation tactics. The framework categorises socialisation tactics and methodologies into structured and unstructured. The choices made in these areas affect the success of virtual ISD.

There is a danger that development teams concentrate on the methodology in terms of deadlines and documentation to the detriment of conversing with users, and understanding their needs (Wastell, 1996). The combined approach of methodology and socialisation is a new area of investigation. There is a need for future empirical work to support the theory that socialisation in virtual ISD teams will benefit the use of methodologies and the success of ISD.

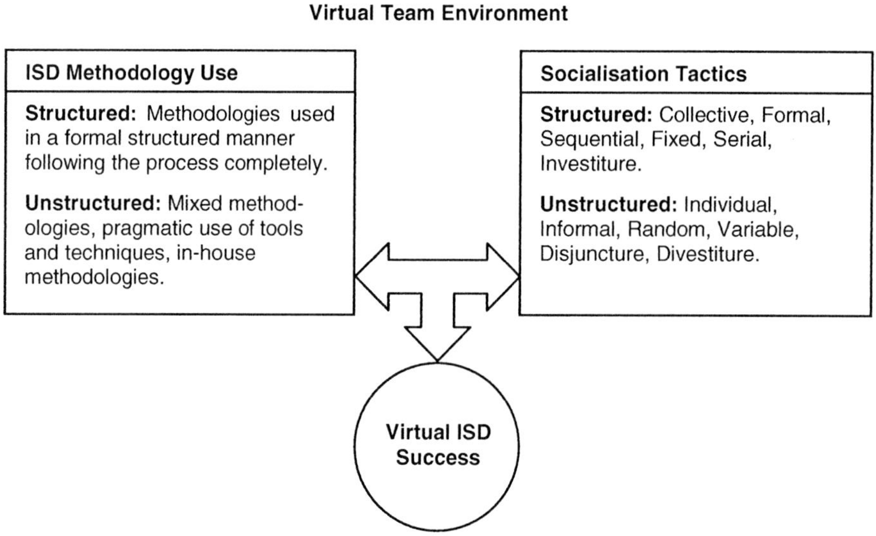

Virtual Team Environment

Fig. 1. Information Systems Development Socialisation Framework

Conclusion and Future Research

Development teams are required to work effectively together in order to maximise the benefits of using an ISD methodology. Virtual team research has shown that many problems exist for those teams working in a virtual environment (Hinds and Kiesler, 2002; Sproull and Kiesler, 1991; Sproull and Finholt, 1990). It is important that the social aspects of development are recognised in the field of ISD research and considered in the use of ISD methodologies. People, not methodologies, develop information systems. Many ISD methodologies concentrate on the technical, rational and functional aspects of development without concentrating on the contextual use of the method. Situations occur where face-to-face meetings are not feasible, predominately written communication occurs. Task assignments, status reports, checklists and specifications are examples of technical information available to all members of an ISD team. This type of information is easy to distribute across computer mediated means and the content is less ambiguous than subjective descriptions of requirements (Ahuja and Galvin, 2003). Social information is more difficult to transmit and is typically learned through observation (Ostroff and Kozlowski, 1992). Newcomers require social information to understand the team norms, attitudes and values. Without the socialisation of team members, miscommunication and inaccurate understanding or interpretation of documents may occur. ISD is a complex process during which coordination and excellent communication is essential. Evidence suggests that virtual teams are not socialised enough during the ISD process to gain the maximum advantages of being virtual (Cramton and Webber, 2005; Ovaska, 2005).

Past research in the virtual team arena has concentrated on small teams of students. This research aims to extend the generalisability of the study by using organizational teams thus reducing the data base bias . This study recognises the social nature of ISD, where the virtual team continuously interacts throughout the creation of the information system. A pluralist approach that recognises both the subjective nature of reality through meanings and interactions, and the objective nature of reality through facts and measures is appropriate to this study of the social aspects of ISD. The influence of the positivist paradigm may be seen in the collection of data on the methodologies and tactics used. The interpretivist paradigm will influence the collection of subjective data on the outcomes and changes in the team's interpersonal relationships. Consequently, it is clear that both qualitative and quantitative methods are appropriate to this study. The next step is to take the theoretical framework for ISD socialisation and test it in the field.

References

Ahuja MK, Galvin JE (2003) Socialization in Virtual Groups. Journal of Management, vol 29, Iss 2, pp 161-185

Armstrong DJ, Cole P (2002) Managing Distances and Differences in Geographically Distributed Work Groups. In: Hinds PJ, Kiesler S (eds) Distributed Work. MIT Press London

Avison DE, Fitzgerald G (2003) Where Now for Development Methodologies? Communications of the ACM, vol 46, Iss 1, pp 79-82

Cramton CD (2001) The Mutual Knowledge Problem and its Consequences for Dispersed Collaboration. Organization Science, vol 12, Iss 3, p 346

Cramton CD, Webber SS (2005) Relationships Among Geographic Dispersion, Team Processes, and Effectiveness in Software Development Work Teams. Journal of Business Research, vol 58, Iss 6, p 758

Fitzgerald B (1997) The Use of Systems Development Methodologies in Practice: a Field Study. Info Systems Journal, vol 7, pp 201-212

Fitzgerald B (2000) Systems Development Methodologies: the Problem of Tenses. Information Technology & People, vol 13, Iss 3, pp 174-185

Hinds PJ, Kiesler S (2002) Distributed Work. MIT Press London

Hirschheim R, Klein H (1989) Four Paradigms of Information Systems Develo-
ment. Communications of the ACM, vol 32, Iss 10

Hirschheim R, Klein HK (1994) Realizing Emancipatory Principles in Information
Systems Development: The Case for ETHICS. MIS Quaterly, vol 18, Iss 1, pp
83-110

Hirschheim R, Klein HK, Newman M (1991) Information Systems Development
as Social Action: Theoretical Perspective and Practice. International Journal
of Management Science, vol 19, Iss 6, pp 587-608

Iivari J, Hirschheim R (1996) Analyzing Information Systems Development: A
Comparison and Analysis of Eight ISD Deveopment Approaches. Information
Systems, vol 21, Iss 7, pp 551-575

Jones GR (1986) Socialization Tactics, Self-Efficacy, and Newcomers' Adjustments to Organizations. Academy of Management Journal, vol 29, Iss 2, pp
262-279

Kiesler S, Cummings JN (2002) What Do We Know about Proximity and Distance in Work Groups? A Legacy of Research. In: Hinds PJ, Kiesler S (eds)
Distributed Work. MIT Press London

Kramer RM, Hanna BA, Su S, Wei J (1999) Collective Identity, Collective Trust,
and Social Capital: Linking Group Identification and Group Cooperation. In:
Turner M (ed) Groups at Work, Theory and Research, Erlbaum Mahwah NJ

Lee S, Koh S, Yen D, Tang H-L (2002) Perception Gaps between IS Academics
and IS Practitioners: an Exploratory Study. Information & Management, vol
40, pp 51-61

Louis MR, Posner BZ, Powell GN (1983) The Availability and Helpfulness of Socialization Practices. Personnel Psychology, vol 36

Mannix EA, Griffith T, Neale MA (2002) The Phenomenology of Conflict in Distributed Work Teams. In: Hinds PJ, Kiesler S (eds) Distributed Work. MIT
Press London

McManus J, Wood-Harper T (2003) Information Systems Project Management:
The Price of Failure. Mangement Services, vol 47, Iss 5, p 16

Mignerey JT, Rubin RB, Gorden WI (1995) Organisational Entry: An Investigation of Newcomer Communication Behavior and Uncertainty. Communication Research, vol 22, Iss 1, pp 54-85

Moreland RL, Levine JM (1999) Socialization in Organizations and Work Groups.
In: Turner ME (ed) Groups at Work: Theory and Research. Lawrence Erlbaum Assoc NJ

Mortensen M, Hinds PJ (2002) Fuzzy Teams: Boundary Disagreement in Distributed and Collocated Teams. In: Hinds PJ, Kiesler S (eds) Distributed Work.
MIT London

O'Leary M, Orlikowski W, Yates J (2002) Distributed Work over the Centuries:
Trust and Control in the Hudson's Bay Company 1670-1826. In: Hinds PJ,
Kiesler S (eds) Distributed Work. MIT Press London

Ostroff C, Kozlowski SWJ (1992) Organizational Socialization as a Learning
Process: The Role of Information Acquisition. Personnel Psychology, vol 45,
Iss 4, p 849

Ovaska P (2005) Working with Methods: Observations on the Role of Methods in Systems Development. In: Vasilecas O (ed) Information Systems Development: Advances in Theory, Practice and Education. Springer

Schein EH (1988) Organizational Socialization and the Profession of Management. Sloan Management Review, vol 30, Iss Fall, pp 53-65

Sproull L, Finholt TA (1990) Electronic Groups at Work. Organization Science, vol 1, Iss 1

Sproull L, Kiesler S (1991) Connections. New Ways of Working in the Networked Organization. MIT Press London

Stage J (1991) The Use of Descriptions in the Anlaysis and Design of Information Systems. In: Stamper RK, Kerola P, Lee RT, Lyytinen K (eds) Collaborative Work, Social Communications and Information Systems. Elsevier Science Amsterdam

Tan M (1994) Establishing Mutual Understanding in Systems Design. An Empirical Study. Journal of Management Information Systems, vol 10, Iss 4, pp 159-182

Van Maanen J (1976) Breaking In: Socialization to work. In: Dubin R (ed) Handbook of Work, Organization and Society. Rand McNally Chicago

Van Maanen J, Schein EH (1979) Toward a Theory of Organizational Socialization. In: Straw B (ed) Research in Organisational Behaviour. JAI Press CT

Wastell DG (1996) The Fetish of Technique: Methodology as a Social Defence. Information Systems Journal, vol 6, Iss 1, pp 25-40

Wegner DM (1986) Transactive Memory: A Contemporary Analysis of the Group Mind in Theories of Group Behaviour. In: Mullen B, Goethals GR (eds) Theories of Group Behaviour. Springer-Verlag New York, pp 185-208

Providing a Correct Software Design in an Environment with Some Set of Restrictions in a Communication between Product Managers and Designers

Deniss Kumlander

Department of Informatics, Tallinn University of Technology, Estonia.
kumlander@gmail.com

Introduction

Today importance of providing software design that as much as possible corresponds to an initial requirement is well known. It can save a lot of resources, which is extremely important in nowadays environment when a competition among software companies becomes higher and higher.

There are a lot of papers that concentrate on an automated design check and a design verification from a "programming" point of view, i.e. if this can be programmed, for instance Dinh-Trong (2004), and much less about design problems that arise due a lack of a communication between a designer and a product manager, although some exists - see Rauterberg and Strohm (1992). Usually a communication problem is examined from a cultural difference point of view that could be also a reason of a communication gap, but there are more and more companies, which are distributed among two or more locations and this physical distance, from our point of view, could be a reason of even a bigger communication gap. Here we are not going to research a case when the product manager is not willing to communicate (share information) with others. This is an obligatory requirement.

In this paper we use a "product manager" term to identify a person who is responsible for defining a task and setting requirements. There are different names for this person in different methodologies and therefore you can call him using another term, but it will not change anything in the scope of this paper. Usually this person is acting as a software company customer representative. He or she usually has a very deep knowledge of an area where software to be applied and has a small or none knowledge of software design and programming. This person is a key figure in deciding if designed software corresponds to user needs or to defined requirements for a software project.

In this paper we research what are common communication problems and how it is possible to overtake them. We also give an overview of two real companies having such problems and ways they try to solve those.

Environment

Nowadays globalization and European Union allows decentralizing a software company. Reasons of that can be the following:

- Cheaper software production for a decentralized company;
- Unequal distribution of a skilled personal (programmers etc) and market on which a product can be sold;
- Decentralizing due buying a company locating in another geographical place;
- A company daughters/branches have to work together, for example, initially each group was independent but starting from some moment they have to integrate their software. Quite often such daughter-companies or branches that work on the same project are called "sites";
- Globalization of operations, i.e. need to extent business to other countries;
- Need to cooperate with partners in other countries, integrate software etc.

There are a lot of companies that moved their software either to East Europe, India, Chine and other geographical areas with low development costs or offshore. We will analyze two companies later in the "Case company analyses" section, which are very good representatives from some of those groups.

Product manager in both cases are acting in different countries in compare to location of software designers. Usually product managers locate in a country or countries, where a product is sold or where the central company management locates. A common characteristic of those cases is an existence of a certain distance between those key persons. This distance restricts possibilities to communicate or in other words produce some communication gaps that we will review in the next section. Of course usually companies use to get together a team to have a product meeting during which requirements are discussed and set. Even in this situation the distance is still there after a meeting and can play its negative role. Among others, it might be a lot of small things that will require communication like discussing on the details that were uncovered during the initial meeting. Those meeting cannot be a "treatment" also for cases of applying "iterational", which is described by Boehm (1988) and Reed (1999), or extreme programming with frequent releases.

Communication Gaps

Communication gaps for the decentralized company basically are produced by a physical distance between a product manager's workplace and a designer's workplace. The designer in this situation cannot just walk to the program manager office, talk face-to-face and ask to review software or do other things the designer needs to be done.

Besides such a distance force them also to communicate in a "none-visual" manner that usually makes a communication between two different people much more problematic. Generally there is always a problem in the communication between any two persons that are explained by a difference in experience, skills, available information, life's and work's environments and culture backgrounds. A lot of researches also prove that "visual" feedback is a very important communication channel between any persons. Different articles say that it provides from 20% to 40% of information – see Hadelich et al. (2004) or Ludlow and Panton (1995). So, lacking of "visual" feedback of an opponent reaction makes the communication problem deeper since so important information is hidden.

Another common problem is an impossibility of a "full" communication, like to draw a diagram immediately, show by hands a data flow on it etc. There are different software vendors that try to solve this problem by software targeted to share applications or painting applications, but this software sometimes cannot be used. For example if a person does not have an access (now or at all) to such application or network communication is pure. Besides those applications are lacking functionality i.e. do not provide all we need.

So far we have identified the next "communication" problems that can arise in the decentralized company:

- Impossibility to do/force to do something if it is needed;
- Loss of information during a communication, for example by using "none visual" channels;
- Inability to use some types of actions to explain, like to show a printed document, to draw a diagram right now etc.

All those reasons cause a certain probability that a design will not correspond to requirements.

Communication Problems from Software Design Point of View

We have identified during our research and experience in some companies that listed earlier communication problems can produce the following "design" problems while are applied to the software design area:

- Time lag / delays in the communication process

Under the "time lag" term we mean certain pauses in the communication between a product manager and a designer that occurs after a question is sent and before an answer is received. Those pauses are a very common issue when an offline communication is used and there is no way to avoid the offline communication since online mode (phone etc.) cannot be use by some reasons. Especially it is true for companies, which branches are operating in significantly different time zones. Besides some questions need a time to thing about an answer or to collect additional information and therefore cannot be answered immediately. The size of the time lag could be from hours to days or even weeks. This slow down the communication and decrease wishes to ask some detail – due that the design in details could be significantly "faulty".

- Inability of a product manager to provide a full info

  – Restriction due need of impersonal communication
  – Product manager does not have a complete picture of a desired system and this problem is not identified due problems in the communication
  – Pure requirements' documentation that leaves enough space for misinterpretations

This is a case when the communication problem makes general problem of a pure specification much deeper. The problem of transferring correctly information from the product manager to the designer exists because some information is lost due impersonal communication, time lag etc. If the product manager has an incomplete picture then his ability to explain something to the designer reduce dramatically, especially in the impersonal communication. Beside product managers tend to leave some details unspecified to have enough space to maneuver later.

Another problem can be in different understanding of the same terms or design elements, which is also sometimes quite common.

All those reasons lead to incorrect, incomplete design.

- Inability to force reviewing of a design or a code

A common problem for designers locating far away from a product manager is inability to force the project manager to do things that have to be done. Project managers usually are very busy persons and tend to postpone any activities that are asked remotely, i.e. if nobody is rushing into the office and ask if a code or design was reviewed. The smallest consequence of that is a delay of the project release, and the bigger one is need to redesign and rebuild it partly or even fully. In the worst case reviewing is postponed as much as possible and problems are explored in the day before a release day.

- Unexpected changes of requirements in the middle of a project

If you are not working on a site when those changes are growing, then you could be the last person, who will be informed that there is a decision to do some changes. Being on a big distance means not to hear things discussed among main office workers. It also means not to be asked some "simple" questions that will later be a core of a project change just due inability (different time zones) or "complexity" of sending emails in compare with such an "easy" question/detail that is discussed.

An effect of this unexpected change in the middle of a project could be different. Sometimes it means that you have to redesign fully a system and this case is quite common – circa 25% of unexpected changes from our practice were those. Other changes force to review and change the design that can lead in the end of ends to a total mess in the design documents. If such changes occur in the end phase of a project then it is common to make the design to correspond to software than vise versa.

- Pure communication between different sites involved into the same design work

It could happen if persons involved into the design persons are never met before face-to-face and therefore they are not so strong in the communication.

Any particular company could have its own set of the listed problems. Moreover by a Pareto principle it is highly probable that the company will benefit mostly from solving circa 20% of those problems, while remaining 80% will not be so important.

Possible Ways to Avoid or Solve Communication Problems

Here we are giving an overview of methods to solve or avoid problems listed earlier.

- Define rules and good practices, define processes in the development as clear and simple as possible

The most common problem is lack of rules and good practices that demand to document some phases of the design process. If nobody is responsible for reviewing a design or such responsibility is shared among two or more persons then nobody will do it and errors that are easy to fix on first stages will become a problem later. Those rules should be as clear and as simple as possible. There is no need to produce an unhelpful bureaucracy. Besides, worker should be informed on those rules or trained to follow, otherwise those rules will not work. The best case is when workers are involved into formulating them since then they will surely follow rules they made, they will know while it is done in one or another way etc.

- Each specification has to be rewritten by your using your wording and send back to verify that you have understood everything correctly

Nothing can be written correctly if you do not understand what you are writing. So, if the designer does not have enough information then he will not be able to reformulate requirements using own wording. Besides such reformulation can also force the designer to think or plan already on a functional requirements stage and it will help to identified missed / unspecified issues.

- Force to underwrite a project specification – especially your/designer variant.

The designer has to ensure that his document was read and accepted. It will secure his future work from product managers' sentences like: "Well, really we have planned to do it in another way and we have explained it to you!". If the design corresponds to the underwritten specification then each design change should be seen as a reformulation rather that fixing designers errors. There is also an advantage for project managers as well since such document make him to:

1. Rethink functional specifications basing on different formulations of those;
2. Develop own communication skills if the designer misunderstood anything.

- Iterational development, shorter development circles

Divide your project into a set of steps/iterations, for example, ones a month. As the output of each development iteration, the development team has to release a part of software (iteration's features) and ask the product manager to review it. In some case the rule could be that the product managers need to make a demo of working system to the customers. This is an instrument that could help to identify design errors as soon as possible. Prototyping is a one example of iterational development, although the iterational development extends iterations to the whole project, while prototyping mean just an isolate iteration on the project start stage. Besides customers and the product manager fill much more comfortable since they have a better understanding of the work progress.

The iterational software development as an instrument to prevent/check design errors requires setting rules forcing product managers or customers to review the software, otherwise design will not be validated.

Another advantage of that: requirements defined for one month work is much clearer than the same specification for one year work.

- Regular meetings between designers and product managers handling the list of open issues.

Daily 30 minutes meeting with the clear list of follow up for each participant till the next meeting the day after. All the clarifications on requirements like a detailed description of the workflows need to be documented for the future reference.

- Better preparations for each meeting

  - All the documentation needs to be distributed in advance before the meeting.
  - Everybody should think about goals and review previous meeting notes to find, which issues are pending.
  - Good timing for the meetings with respect of the time difference.

Generally saying, each meeting participant should be ready to solve problems. He or she should not be too tired or sleepy, should have enough information and have to do his/her home work. Some informal phrases during such meetings could improve the communication between sites, although face-to-face meetings of course are much more efficient if those can be held.

Case Company Analyses

Unfortunately we are not able to provide full names of companies to be described due confidentiality reasons. From another point of view, those companies are very typical and therefore this extends our examples to hundreds similar companies.

Company "A" – a Small One

This company is a quite small one and was decentralized since its market is located in West-Europe and skilled (and cheaper) developers were found in Eastern Europe. The number of workers during the researched period is 23.

This company is a small one and therefore is using its small size to be flexible and quick in reactions. Unfortunately such strong side of the company is also its weakness. We have identified the following problems before we started to consult them:

- Quite often a design was compromised because of wishes to have a "flexibly" design – a lot of projects had unfixed details even on the development phase.
- Product managers have to be salesmen as well and are involved into different projects, therefore their responses/reviews used to be quite randomly distributed in a time frame from a day to weeks.
- Lack of rules and requirements on the documentation.
- Sometimes requirements are "unstable", i.e. in each forth project requirements were reformulated and this led to redesign of the project.

The goal of this company is not to lose its flexibility and simultaneously improve the software development process to reduce improperly spent time on a work that has to be redone later due errors in a design or changes in requirements. It means that they need to prevent or avoid errors in the design or errors in requirements as much as possible, i.e. decrease need to redesign due errors, but still have a possibility to fulfill requirements demanded by customers during any phase.

The best "treatments" that we have identified for this case are:

- Defined rules and documents that should be complete during each step of any project – this force all involved into a project think twice as well as documents requirements details. "Project charter", a document that concentrates specifications and design as described by Reed (1999), has to be written by a designer and underwritten by a product manager.

- The iterational model of software developing is applied – this helps to be flexible, eliminate design errors on early stages, and provides possibility to redesign software parts to be released later.
- Defined a special person at the product managers' office that should help the designer to force product managers to review documents and releases. This type of work does not require spending a lot of hours on it.

Those routines helped the company to improve software development routine and dramatically reduced "improperly" spent time increasing productivity.

Company "B" – a Big One

This company operates globally and has a lot of branches. We are going to describes problems and solutions that were used in a project managed from US, designed and developed in Europe and co-designed and co-developed in India (the project included an integration of India and Europe software that used to be independent). The total size of a project team is around 250.

The strong side of the company is huge resources, quite skilled personal and quite a good design work.

We have identified the following problems before we started to consult them:

- Bad movement of information between sites.
- Bad communication between developers' teams.
- Design documentation is purely used that lead to rebuilding of it because of already written software (to meet a time schedule).
- Problem in communication because of sufficiently different time zones.
- Unexpected redesigns.
- A lot of pending issues that exist since team members are sending a problem from one to another rather than solving it.
- As a result - slow developing, compromised design and a lot of errors.

The goal of our project was to change work habits, improve the communication and reduce a number of problems in designs that affects later time schedules.

The following changes were done:

- Regular meetings are started to bring all together, solve pending issues and improve the communication between team members and provide information to others as soon as possible. This also required a proper choosing of a meeting time and a lot of forces to make all to prepare for those meetings.
- Designers and developers' leaders from all sites where asked to underwrite design documents and write opinions on that. That made them to read and follow designs and number of the later design changes because of already existing code was sufficiently reduced.
- Designers meetings (before each project start) are started. This brings all together improving communication between team members, since they can talk face-to-face. Besides each design is discussed a lot at the starting point of a project and this improved a lot the quality of the design

Those procedures and rules helped to decrease a number of errors in a project's design and decrease an overall software development time. The number of stresses decreased also, and this improved conditions of their work environment and also increased productivity and general satisfaction of workers.

Conclusion

In this paper we have tried to identify what are common communication problems between a designer and a product manager for a decentralized company. The identified problems can easily lead to lose of time since improper designed software will need to be rewritten. Today's software companies' tight competition requires careful evaluating of the following communication problems:

- Time lag / delays in the communication process;
- Inability of a product manager to provide a full info;
- Inability to force reviewing of a design or a code;
- Unexpected changes of requirements in the middle of a project;
- Pure communication between different sites involved into the same design work.

Besides we listed possible ways to solve such problems, although each company should decide itself which of them can be applied for their case. The following principles how to solve communication problems are identified:

- Define rules and good practices, define processes in the development as clear and simple as possible;
- Each specification has to be rewritten by you using your wording and send back to verify that you have understood everything correctly;
- Force to underwrite a project specification – especially your/designer variant;
- The iterational development, shorter development circles;
- Regular meetings between designers and product managers handling a list of open issues;
- Better preparations for each meeting.

The last part of the paper contains two real examples of companies having such problems and descriptions how those problems are dealt with. Applying those principles to the reviewed companies helped them a lot.

References

Boehm BW (1988) A Spiral Model of Software Development and Enhancement. Computer, May, pp 61-72

Dinh-Trong TT (2004) A Systematic Approach to Testing UML Design Models. Doctoral Symposium, 7th International Conference on the Unified Modeling Language (UML). Lisbon Portugal

Hadelich K, Branigan H, Pickering M, Crocker M (2004) Alignment in Dialogue: Effects of Visual versus Verbal-feedback. Proc of the 8th Workshop on the Semantics and Pragmatics of Dialogue, Catalog'04. Barcelona Spain

Ludlow R, Panton F (1995) The Essence of Effective Communication. Prentice Hall

Rauterberg M, Strohm O (1992) Work Organisation and Software Development. Annual Review of Automatic Programming, vol 16, pp 121-128

Reed PR (1999) Developing Applications with Visual Basic and UML. Addison-Wesley Professional

New Document Concept and Metadata Classification for Broadcast Archives

István Szakadát[1] and Gábor Knapp[2]

[1] Budapest University of Technology and Economics (BME), Hungary.
syi@axelero.hu.
[2] National Audiovisual Archive (NAVA), Hungary. knapp@nava.hu

Introduction

It is evident that document is the central concept in any archive, and the basic task is to make these documents searchable and retrievable. Textual documents can be full text indexed therefore they can be searched with the help of very efficient search engines like Google, however non-textual documents as still images, moving images, sounds or mixed audiovisual documents require associated textual information, metadata to make search possible.

Several document definitions and metadata exchange schemes can be found for all types of documents. However, when we started to design the information system for the Hungarian National Audiovisual Archive (NAVA) that was established to be the digital legal deposit of the Hungarian related broadcast audiovisual programs, we have to face some inevitable problems. The main questions were: how to define the bibliographic unit, the document in broadcast environment and which standardized metadata scheme can serve most efficiently the archival processes?

This paper describes the selection process that lead to the multilevel, multidimensional document model and classified metadata scheme that proved to be adequate both for archival and retrieval purposes. The concepts introduced can be useful for all kinds of document archives to extend their capabilities.

Basic Data Model

The audiovisual archive's basic data model is very simple. The three main entities are the Document, Agent and Event. There are relations defined between Document and Agent (e.g. Writer, Director, Actor), between

Agent and Event (got a prize), Document and Event (about the 2nd World War). And there are also internal relations among Document, Event and Agent.

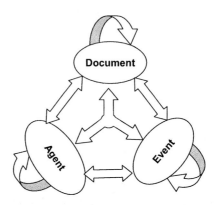

Fig. 1. The basic data model

Using this simple model and applying the principles of the Dublin Core Metadata Initiative a data structure of more than a hundred tables was designed. That is very useful for precise description and refined search, however metadata association is not an easy task. To exploit the strength of the model, efficient support should be provided for the archivists. In the case of Agent and Event the techniques of authority lists could be adapted, however the document concept and the document-document relationship has to be revised for broadcast audiovisual content.

What is a 'Document'?

Studying reference works and searching the web, several definitions can be found for the concept of the *document*. The large number of definitions shows that the problem isn't solved yet.

Problems with Document Definition

Let us see some typical approaches for document definition:

- "A document is a writing that contains information" [1]
- "A physical entity of any substance on which is recorded all or part of a work or multiple works" [2]

- "Recorded information or object which can be treated as a unit" [3]
- "An information resource is defined to be anything that has identity" [4]

Any definition referring to writing is inadequate for audiovisual material. Physical objects also can hardly be associated to documents in a digital environment, because storage systems with hundreds of terabytes capacity don't make the physical distinction of logical units possible. The last two definitions use the tricky solution of the problem: the obscure concept of 'document' is defined by the similarly obscure concept of 'unit' or 'resource', respectively.

Conventional archives like libraries have already solved some definition problems with series and periodicals or compound volumes, but they have the book, the physical object as a starting point. In the case of broadcast audiovisual programs only the practically infinite media stream can be considered as physical reality, all program items can be identified technically as a time interval in the stream by a more or less arbitrary human decision. Broadcast items are typically multiple level compounded documents, and can be elements of several series, so the solutions used by librarian practice can be used only partially. Preliminary program guides can help to select basic units of the stream, but these guides are usually not exact by time and not detailed enough. Human processing time for the audiovisual units is critical, because the stream flows, so the birth of new documents is continuous. However filling the transmission time with all original items is almost impossible for the broadcasting companies, thus replaying, reusing of items is a general practice, so the number of documents to be processed is less than it can be expected by technical calculations.

To summarize the broadcast document model requirements, it has to be able to:

- Define exact technical parameters, because recorders and encoders do need exact commands, algorithms.
- Enable multilevel hierarchy or relations to make any level of itemization possible.
- Support processing by the exploitation of document-document relations, identity, similarities and inheritance.

Identifying Documents in Broadcast Environments

For a real archive a practical, method oriented definition is have to be given, omitting undefined or obscure concepts.

The birth of a document is its first transmission, broadcasting to the public. The document's source (by the definition of the DCMI [4]), so the recorded sub-stream itself technically can be identified by the frequency, the transmission network (including geographical location) and the time interval. The first two parameters can be considered as static (at least rarely changing), so the key issue is the determination of the time interval. In NAVA the raw recordings are available for about ten days (then the cyclic buffer overwrites unsaved data), so the time for archiving limited.

As the first step, to take the authors intention into account, the program guide's items are used as the rough selection points. It has to be mentioned, that the program guides don't include any reference to the advertisements, program recommendations that wedged between program items, so the staring points of the interval van differ significantly. By the definition used in our archive, the first level document starts at the beginning frame of the program item and lasts until the first frame of the following, preliminary announced program item. The first level of the document delimitation often includes several foreign parts and most often defines a multilevel compounded document. The basic metadata are associated to the first level documents based on preliminary information, so at the end of the first step practically an interactive program guide is obtained.

After the first step we arrive to a decision point. Because the capacity of the storage system, and therefore the processing time is limited, we have to decide that a certain first level document has to be included in the long term archive or not. If the preservation is refused, the processing is finished, but if it is enabled (the program is considered as Hungarian related, and not yet processed), the first level document is stored in the long term archive (to be retained for 'eternity'). Obviously valuable data can be lost, because seemingly neutral program items can contain Hungarian relations (contributors, locations, events), or the already processed document occurs in a definitely different context, but we have to live with this limitations.

The second step is the further partitioning of the selected first level documents. We have now more time, the selected first level documents are retained for ever. Generally the selected document has several compounds. According to our model these compounds can be selected as parts of the *whole* document, and treated as new, independently described documents inherently related to the parent document. (The relation type determines the metadata inheritance or import rules.)

After the second step, since the document is archived, third, fourth and more steps can be done for more and more refine the resolution to reach the desired level.

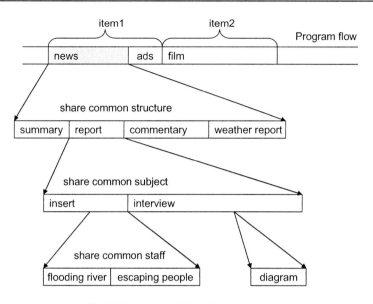

Fig. 2. Document identification process

The document hierarchy is illustrated on the figure. This simple example shows that a single news magazine can generate dozens of documents with different staff, different subject, different structure, however sharing some common properties. Extrapolating this tendency to a 24-our program flow, we can calculate with hundreds of separate documents on a single day, on a single television or radio channel, each has its own metadata set.

What does Metadata Describe?

Metadata provide information about information (or more precisely data about document) by definition. Several standardized metadata schemes exist such as MARC in libraries or Dublin Core in the world of digital documents. Metadata are classified by Gilliland-Swetland [5] as administrative, descriptive, technical, preservation and use categories. However the mentioned examples stand mainly for the descriptive metadata class. In an operational environment other metadata categories are to be used intensively to control workflow, or standard descriptive metadata are associated with a new meaning.

It was mentioned earlier that in audiovisual broadcast archives the time factor is of the key success factors due to the enormous quantity of documents. A lot of human effort can be saved by the utilization of the relations among documents. Even in the librarian world the role of document-document relations is increasing. The number of pre-defined relation types is growing [6], or additional document levels are defined to join documents that cannot be hold together using the one level model [7].

In the following chapters we give a few examples on the utilization of the *Relation* metadata field for enhancing effectiveness of processing but maintaining the original meaning as well.

Relation traditionally means a semantic connection between things (of course between documents), however it can serve as a very efficient tool also to help managing (making suggestions or even automatical filling) metadata values, and on the contrary, the similarities in metadata values can suggest the existence of a special relation between documents.

Document Relationship – Virtual Documents

Virtual documents are documents that have metadata, but no essence in the digital repository, virtual documents are pure metadata sets that are not associated directly to a media stream.

Using virtual documents can play extremely useful role in describing periodicals and series. If a program has a regular staff, and it runs daily, the staff has to be filled at the virtual document level and different series members inherit these metadata through the IsMemberOf relation type. Only the specific characteristics (guests, subject) have to be recorded for the actual item. For example the metadata of Star Track can be normalized like a well structured relational database using three hierarchy levels minimizing human processing time, and minimizing the number of potential errors.

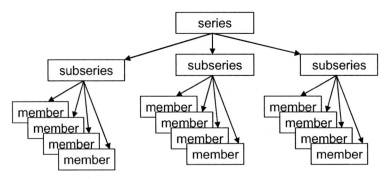

Fig. 3. Inheritance from series

The same hierarchical structure, but a theoretically different situation can be found in the four-level document model of the International Federation of Library associations [7]. This model distinguishes stages according the logical distance from theoretical authoring (Work) through the materialization process (Expression, Manifestation) to the physical object (Item). In broadcast archives replays can be considered as items of the same Manifestation, so all metadata of the Manifestation level except timing can be inherited to items through the IsExemplifiedBy relation. The several (shorter or longer) versions of a commercial are examples of the Expression to Manifestation relationship, like different editions of a novel. The associated relation is IsEmbodiedIn and almost all metadata can be inherited except duration and time. The application of the Work to Expression relationship often goes beyond the limits of the audiovisual archive. The IsRealizedThrough relation can link documents that have the same origin. Several treatments (drama, ballet, orchestral music) of the story of Romeo and Juliet can share the same content description using the Work concept. The Work, Expression and Manifestation are always a virtual documents, the only physical entity is Item.

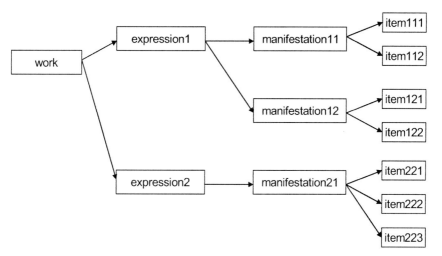

Fig. 4. The Work-Expression-Manifestation-Item levels

The utilization of logical document relations and inheritance is very useful to shorten processing time (and save storage capacity), but there is no common rule for the extent of inheritance. From case to case the fields to be inherited and the fields with prohibited inheritance have to be carefully selected.

Document Types – Document Templates

Virtual documents described in the previous chapter were applicable if there were a logical, intentional, strong relation between documents. This means, that not only the metadata structure, but subset of metadata values is the same. However there are slight relationships that also can be exhausted.

The Type metadata, as used by DCMI, is used to determine the properties of the content. In the Dublin Core Type Vocabulary a general, but rather course typology is given restricted only for the basic types. In the case of audiovisual content Type is often associated more or less with Genre. In the practice of broadcast companies the theoretical genre and the intended audience is often confused. The European Broadcasting Union's P/META project [8] gave a clear vision and a four dimension encoding scheme to solve these problems. The following dimensions were separated:

- the broadcaster's intention,
- the formal structure,
- the content and
- the relevant groups.

If we study the programs of the same or similar formal structure, several similarities can be noticed also in the main metadata groups and fields.

Determining and considering the formal structural type of the document, common templates can be used. These templates utilize only a small part of the whole model, so filling fields is much easier and faster. At the application level document templates can be derived from real documents, retaining only the filled fields of the model.

Looking for Similarities – Embedded Search

The methods described in the previous chapters are usable only if the archivist has the knowledge of the essential logical or the formal relations. Certainly this knowledge develops after a while, but the large number of documents makes the decisions difficult. The content management system of our archive helps this process by software tools.

Let's suppose that the archivist responsible for a program item doesn't recognize any essential or formal relations, considers the document as a standalone, new item and starts to fill the fields of the entire model. After completing the formal section of metadata set a background process starts and looks for similar documents. If a certain correspondence is found a special relationship and a document template is offered to the user. The keyword is the 'certain correspondence'. The adequate measure of similarity should be derived from best practice, however the categories can be presented according to the model.

Table 1. Cases of similarity

Correspondence	Technique/relation
Same format fields are filled	Same Type
Same values in the same fields	Serial member or Same Item
Similar values in content fields	Expressions or Manifestations of the same Work

Conclusion

One of the main problems of the operation of audiovisual archives rises from the large number of individually retrievable documents. This large number arises from the nature of broadcasting, the use of complex, multiple level compounded program items. However analyzing the structure and the elements of the program flow several identical or similar documents or document variations can be found.

Based on the document-document relation models borrowed from the librarian practice and adapted for broadcast environment, an efficient tool was conceptualized and experimentally implemented to help archivist to recognize and utilize relations, and spare processing time, reduce database size and minimize storage capacity without any restrictions to the usability of the archive.

References

[1] Wikipedia, the Free Encyclopedia. www.en.wikipedia.org
[2] U.S. National Archives and Records Administration. www.archives.gov
[3] National Archives of Australia. www.naa.gov.au
[4] Dublin Core Metadata Initiative. www.dublincore.org
[5] Gilliland-Swetland AJ (2000) Setting the Stage Introduction to Metadata. www.getty.edu/research/conducting_research/standards/intrometadata/2_arti cles/gill/index.html
[6] The European Library Project. www.europeanlibrary.org/
[7] Functional Requirements for Bibliographic Records IFLA (1998)
[8] The EBU Metadata Exchange Scheme. EBU Tech 3295

Class Model Development Using Business Rules

Tomas Skersys and Saulius Gudas

Kaunas University of Technology, Lithuania. tomas.skersys@ktu.lt, gudas@soften.ktu.lt

Introduction[1]

New developments in the area of computer-aided system engineering (CASE) greatly improve processes of the information systems development life cycle (ISDLC). Much effort is put into the quality improvement issues, but IS development projects still suffer from the poor quality of models during the system analysis and design cycles. At some degree, quality of models that are developed using CASE tools can be assured using various automated model comparison, syntax checking procedures. It is also reasonable to check these models against the business domain knowledge, but the domain knowledge stored in the repository of CASE tool (enterprise model) is insufficient (Gudas et al. 2004). Involvement of business domain experts into these processes is complicated because non-IT people often find it difficult to understand models that were developed by IT professionals using some specific modeling language.

From our point of view one of the most promising techniques to verify Class model (CM) against the business domain knowledge is the business rules (BR) approach (Ross 2003, Dorsey 2002, Hay and Healy 2000). Business rules are among the main elements composing the core of structured business domain knowledge; moreover, BR can be understood and therefore verified by business domain experts. However, clearly expressed, formalized BR are still not commonly used in novel CASE systems.

As far as BR are not realized as a separate component of the CASE system repository, there is no possibility to uniquely identify and use them in other phases of the ISDLC. Another reason is that most of the CASE tools are mainly based on the modeling languages that are not well suited for BR modeling. UML is the most widely used object-oriented modeling language and it also lacks support for business rules modeling (Haggerty 2000). Nevertheless, it should be pointed out that the OMG group has al-

---

[1] The work is supported by Lithuanian State Science and Studies Foundation according to Eureka programme project "IT-Europe" (Reg. No 3473)

ready begun an initiative to find ways of BR integration with the OMG standards (UML and MDA in particular) (OMG 2002, OMG 2003).

The approach for BR integration in the IS development process was already proposed in (Skersys and Gudas 2004). This paper is focused on the principles of BR-based UML Class model verification. The Business rules meta-model, extended UML Class meta-model are presented, and formalized steps are developed to verify an extended UML Class model.

Business Rules Meta-model

For BR representation and management activities it is essential to store BR in a separate Business rules repository (Herbst and Myrach 1997, Kapocius and Butleris 2002, Plotkin 1999). None of the analyzed repository models provide a mechanism for structuring BR, i.e. there are no constructs for the decomposition of business rule to its atomic elements defined in those repositories. Moreover, for the purposes of IS development the BR repository must be integrated with other business objects via constructs of the Enterprise model (EM) (Gudas et al. 2004, Skersys and Gudas 2004).

Business rules meta-model defines the structure of BR repository (BRR). Proposed BR repository model is depicted in Fig. 1.

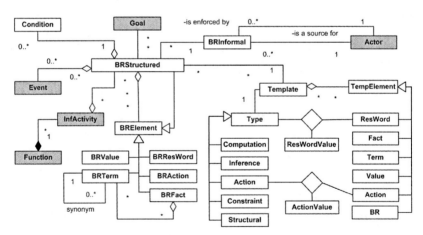

Fig. 1. Business rules repository model (UML notation)

Constructs of the Business rules repository model are as follows:

- *BRInformal, BRStructured* represent BR written in natural language and structured (formalized) forms respectively. Informal BRs (*BRInformal*) are gathered from the sources (*Actor*) within the organization. A structured BR (*BRStructured*) is extracted from the informal rule (informal BR may be transformed into one or more structured BR). Structured BR may have events (*Event*) that initiate this rule, and pre-conditions (*Condition*) that must hold true in order to process the rule. A rule is a part of an information activity (*InfActivity*) that is also the element of the Enterprise model (EM elements are darkened in Fig. 1) (Gudas et al. 2004).

- BR is a composition of certain elements (*BRElement*). Elements may be:
  - Business rule itself (*BRStructured*);
  - Term (*BRTerm*) – a word or phrase that is relevant to business;
  - Fact (*BRFact*) – a statement that asserts a relationship between two (or more) terms;
  - Reserved word (*BRResWord*) – a reserved symbol, word or phrase that has particular, well-defined meaning in a business rule;
  - Value (*BRValue*) – a particular symbolic or numerical value in a business rule;
  - Action (*BRAction*) – an action that can be performed with business object.

In the context of this paper two features of *BRResWord* will be used: *Meaning* and *Type*. Values assigned to *Meaning* can be *Relationship* or *Feature*; values of *Type* can be *Association, Aggregation, Composition* or *Generalization*.

- We propose to structure BR using a predefined system of templates (Sec. "Business rules formalization using templates"). Therefore, BRR model contains elements aimed to implement this feature: Template (*Template*), Template element (*TempElement*). Template includes elements of the following types: Value (*Value*), Reserved word (*ResWord*), Action (*Action*), Fact (*Fact*), Term (*Term*), Business rule (*BR*).
- Business rules templates have to be classified in order to define their structure. This classification is close to the ones presented in (Von Halle, 2001, Kadir and Loucopoulos 2003).Type of the template itself is defined by the *Type*: Computation (*Computation*), Inference (*Inference*), Action (*Action*), Constraint (*Constraint*), Structural (*Structural*). The classification of templates coincides with the classification of business rules (Table 1).

The BR repository presented in Fig. 1 plays a major role in the BR-based Class model verification process.

Table 1. The classification of business rules

Type	Definition
Term	A word or phrase that is relevant to the business.
Fact (Structural)	A statement that asserts a meaningful relationship between two (or more) terms.
Constraint	A statement that specifies a mandatory feature of the business entity.
Inference	A statement where logic operations are used to derive a new fact.
Action assertion	A statement that defines conditions for the initiation of a certain business action.
Computation	A statement that derives a value of the fact by using a certain algorithm.

Business Rules Formalization Using Templates

Today most of the IT specialists agree that one of the major problems in the area of IS engineering is the communication gap between the business people and systems developers (Ross and Lam 2001a). Communicating requirements through the formalized business rules narrows this gap.

Business rules structuring using templates is an acceptable way of BR formalization (Skersys and Gudas 2004). National (i.e., Lithuanian) language-based templates were developed with respect to the basic recommendations on BR templates construction (Ross and Lam 2001b, Reeder 2002) – this is important in order to reach maximum compatibility with the English-based template analogues. Consequently, this will let to minimize efforts of mapping structured BR to other formalized forms and reach the implementation level of the rules. Business rules templates were developed on the basis of elements that define the structure of the Template (*Template*) in the BR repository model (Fig. 1). Basic structures of the classified BR templates (EBNF notation) are as follows:

<Template_Fact>::=<Term><ResWord><Term> – template for a Fact;

<Template_Constraint>::= (<Fact>|<Term>)<ResWord> {[<ResWord>]| [<ResWord><Value>]} [(<Fact>|<Term>|<Value>)] – the template for a Constraint;

<Template_Inference>::=<ResWord><Fact><ResWord>(<Fact>|<Value>) [{<ResWord><Fact><ResWord>(<Fact>|<Value>)}]<ResWord><Fact> <ResWord>(<Fact>| <Value>) – the template for an Inference BR.

<Template_Action>::=<ResWord><Fact><ResWord>(<Fact>|<Value>) [{<ResWord> <Fact><ResWord>(<Fact>|<Value>)}]<ResWord><Action> (<Term>|<Fact>|
) – the template for an Action BR.

<Template_Computation>::=<Fact><ResWord>(<Fact>|<Value>){[<ResWord> (<Fact>|<Value>)]} – the template for a Computation BR.

Extended UML Class Meta-model

Objects and classes are core concepts for the object-oriented (OO) system analysis and design, and a Class model is the most often used model for visual representation of static aspect of classes. Class models in OO methods are typically used: as domain models to explore domain concepts; as conceptual/analysis models to analyze requirements; as system design models to depict detailed design of OO software (Ambler 2003). Class model is also a part of OMG standard, namely Unified Modeling Language (UML). Class model in UML-based CASE systems serves as a main source of knowledge for the development of information system prototype: database specification, graphical user interface (GUI), application code.

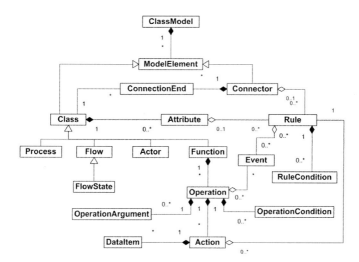

Fig. 2. Extended UML Class meta-model (UML notation)

However, from our point of view it is important to note that UML meta-model does not have sufficient set of constructs for business modeling. The construct of business rules is also omitted UML meta-model even though BR is recognized as one of the main aspects of business modeling. We have proposed extended UML Class meta-model (Fig. 2) that is based on the core of the UML meta-model, but also incorporates constructs from the Enterprise meta-model (Gudas et al. 2004) and BR meta-model (see Sec. "Business rules meta-model" and (Skersys and Gudas 2004) for more details on BR meta-model).

Constructs of the extended UML Class meta-model are as follows:

- Class model (*ClassModel*) is composed of the model elements (ModelElement). Class model elements can be either classes (*Class*) or relationships (*Connector*) that relate these classes to each other. Each relationship has at least two connection ends (*ConnectionEnd*) and also may have some constraints or structural rules (*Rule*) that specify that relationship.
- Traditionally, classes have attributes and operations. We enriched construct *Class* with certain subtypes: *Process, Flow, Actor* and *Function*. Such classification is based on the specification of the Enterprise model introduced in (Gudas et al. 2004). The classification of classes is not a new idea – P. Coad's UML modeling in color (Coad et al. 1999), Robustness diagrams are just a few examples. Techniques that classify classes pursue certain practical goals. In our case this classification is made in order to make a close link between the business environment (Enterprise model) and the IS design models (in this case, extended UML Class model).
- Classes of type *Flow* may have states (*FlowState*).
- In our Class meta-model each class may have attributes (*Attribute*), but the operation level (*Operation*) is specific only to the *Function* type classes. Construct *Operation* represents algorithmically-complex operations (Coad and Yourdon 1991), and algorithmically-simple operations (such as Create, Connect, Access, Release) are not modeled in order to reduce the complexity of the class models. Classes of type *Function* are at some degree similar to the controller type classes in Robustness diagrams. Class' attribute (*Attribute*) may have number of constraining rules (*Rule*).
- Class operation (*Opperation*) is composed of actions (*Action*) and may have arguments (*OperationArgument*) and conditions (*OperationCondition*) that must be true in order to fire the operation.
- Structure of the action may contain certain data items (*DataItem*) from the Data base (BD) of the system. Action represents single business rule (*Rule*) of type *Computation, Action assertion* or *Inference* (Table 1). These rules may have certain conditions (*RuleCondition*) that need to be true for the business rule to fire out. Rules may be triggered by the events (*Event*).

UML Class Model Development Using Business Rules

Mappings between BR and Class Meta-models

Building the Class model (CM) for a problem domain is among the main objectives of the OO software development. Nevertheless, there is still no clear, well-developed process proposed to help the software engineers solve this problem successfully (Dong et al. 2003, Wahono and Far 2002). It is a common practice when system designer develops models of the system by analyzing earlier created models and relying on his own experience and knowledge about the problem domain. In other words, transition from stage to stage in the ISDLC is done empirically. In such situation model verification and approval by business domain experts becomes a very important activity. Yet there is no CASE tool or method that could propose a sufficient technique of UML CM (or other IS model) verification against the business domain knowledge approved by business expert.

Making reference to the OMG's Model Driven Architecture (MDA) (Mellor et al. 2004), verification of the Domain model (in our case represented as a Class model) must be done on the platform-independent level, and this is the level where business rules naturally reside.

Table 2 presents relationships between the Business rules meta-model (BRMM, Fig. 1) and extended UML Class meta-model (CMM, Fig. 2). This is done by showing how elements of the BRMM map to the elements of the CMM (φ: <BRMM> $\rightarrow$ <CMM>).

Table 2. BRMM to CMM mappings (BRMM $\rightarrow$ CMM)

BR meta-model element	Mapping	Extended UML Class meta-model element
<BRMM.BRStructured>	$\varphi 1$	<CMM.Rule>
<BRMM.Condition>	$\varphi 2$	<CMM.RuleCondition>
<BRMM.Event>	$\varphi 3$	<CMM.Event>

Formalized business rule (*CMM.Rule* in Table 2) can be applied either to specify (or constrain) attribute of the class or relationship between two specific classes, or to specify the action (in platform independent manner) that is a composing part of the operation of the class. In the Class meta-model (Fig. 2) construct *Rule* is related with the *Attribute, Relationship* and *Action* via the aggregation relationship.

Algorithm of Class Model Enhancement

The algorithm of business rules-based enhancement of Class model (CM) represents the activities of model verification against the knowledge of business domain and model augmentation. Knowledge of business domain is expressed in a form of structured business rules. The algorithm is composed of three steps:

- **Step 1.** Verification and specification of *relationships* among the classes of the CM (Fig. 3). Missing relationships are identified and inserted into the model during the interactive communication with model developer. Additionally, the model is augmented with the *roles* that classes play communicating with each other; *types* and *cardinalities* of these relationships are also specified. Business rules of types *Constraint* and *Structural (Fact)* are used in the first step of the algorithm.
- **Step 2.** Verification and specification of classes' *attributes* (Fig. 4). Attributes are verified against the *Constraint* and *Structural (Fact)* type business rules. Missing attributes are also identified and assigned to the classes of CM.
- **Step 3.** The *composition of classes' operations* (methods) is defined in the third step. In traditional and object-oriented IS development methods business logic is usually buried within lines of application code – this causes a lot of problems in rapidly changing business environments (Skersys and Gudas 2004). In business rules-extended IS development process every line of code that expresses business logic can be identified and tracked. This can be achieved because these lines of procedural code are the implementation of particular business rules that are stored and managed separately from the application code itself. Computation, inference and action assertion business rules compose the core of application. On the platform independent CM development stage we suggest to fill the content of the class' operation with structured rules represented in platform independent manner. Such specification can be elaborated and transformed into procedural code in later stages of ISDLC.

Principles of the first two steps are presented in Fig. 3 and Fig. 4 respectively; the first step is also illustrated with example in section "Description of the Algorithm".

The example is written in English. However, in real situation problem domain should be specified and modeled using national language, in order to reach the best understanding among business experts and system development team. In general, the proposed BR repository allows the construction of BR in any language.

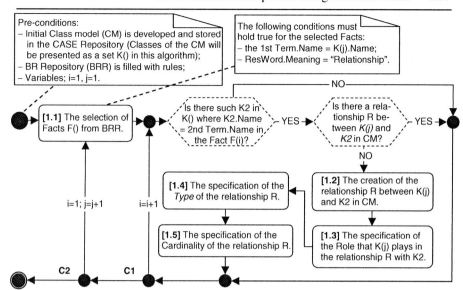

Fig. 3. Business rules-based specification of relationships among the classes of the Class model

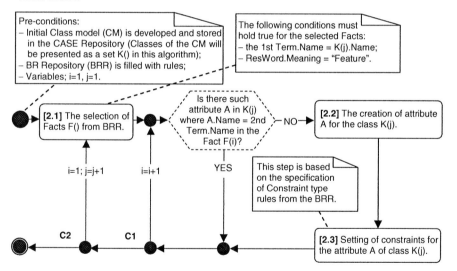

Fig. 4. Business rules-based specification of classes' attributes of the Class model

Description of the Algorithm

Let's consider BR repository filled with business rules (Table 3) and the initial Class model which we want to enhance (Fig. 5). The presented set of rules is just enough to illustrate the main principles of the algorithm. The enhanced Class model is depicted in Fig. 6.

Table 3. List of business rules stored in BR repository

No.	Business rule	Comments
1.1	Shipping department performs Product ship-	List of Facts describing
1.2	ment.	relationships and roles
1.3	Shipping department reports to Head office. Product shipment is performed by Shipping department.	among business objects.
2.1	Workload schedule is composed of exactly three Scenarios.	List of Constraints describing cardinalities of
2.2	Scenario belongs to exactly one Workload schedule.	relationships among business objects.
3.1	Scenario has a feature Scenario ID.	This is a list of Facts de-
3.2	Scenario has a feature Scenario instructions.	scribing features (attrib-
3.3	Scenario has a feature Estimated duration.	utes) of business objects in the business domain.
4.1	Scenario Scenario ID is unique.	This is a list of rules de-
4.2	Scenario Estimated duration must be greater than zero.	scribing Constraints on business objects' attributes.

Let us briefly go through the first part of the algorithm (Fig. 3):

- *Step 1.1.* A set of Facts $F()$ is selected from the BR Repository. Selected Facts are related with a certain class $K(j)$ of CM through the Fact's first Term *Name*; second condition is that the *Meaning* of the reserved word *ResWord* of these Facts is *"Relationship"*.
- In our case let us assume that K(1) = "Shipping department". Then F(1)= "Shipping department performs Product shipment." and F(2) = "Shipping department reports to Head office.".
- If there is a class *K2* in the CM where the *Name* of *K2* equals to the Fact's $F(i)$ second Term *Name* of the Fact $F(i)$, one proceeds to the next step. If there is no such *K2* then the Fact $F(i)$ is skipped and the next Fact from the set $F()$ is selected $(F(i+1))$ and the step is repeated.
- In our case only the Fact $F(1)$ satisfies the condition. $F(2)$ is skipped because second Term *Name* of the $F(2)$ is *"Head office"* and there is no such class *"Head office"* in the Class model *"Schedule processing"*.
- If there is a class *K2*, the algorithm checks if there is a relationship between the classes $K(j)$ and *K2* already exist in the Class model. If so, one proceeds to the step 1.3, otherwise, step 1.2 is the next one.

- In our case there is a relationship between the classes *"Shipping department"* and *"Product shipment"* therefore one proceeds to the step 1.3.
- *Step 1.2.* One proceeds to the step 1.2 when there is no relationship between $K(j)$ and $K2$ in the CM detected and the suggestion to create this relationship on the basis of $F(i)$ is accepted by the system analyst. One proceeds to the step 1.3 after the relationship between $K(j)$ and $K2$ is created.
- *Steps 1.3, 1.4.* The *Role* of $K(j)$ in the relationship with $K2$ and the *Type* of that relationship is characterized by a *Reserved word* (*ResWord*) in $F(i)$. The results of these steps are marked with tag 1 in Fig. 6.
- In our example *ResWord Name* of $F(1)$ is equal to *"performs"* – this is the *Role* that the class *"Shipping department"* plays in the relationship with the class *"Product shipment"*. *Type* of the *ResWord* was *"Association"*.
- *Step 1.5.* Cardinalities of the relationships among the classes are specified in Step 1.4. It is done on the basis of Constraint type business rules stored in BRR. Constraints are selected using a simple condition – a rule must implement some constraint between two business objects that are represented as classes in the Class model. In our case Constraints 2.1 and 2.2 (Table 4) are selected because they implement constraints on the cardinality of the relationship between the existing classes of the Class model (see tag 2 in Fig. 6).

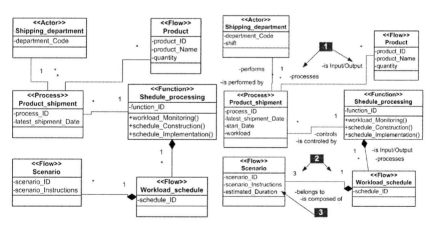

Fig. 5. The initial UML Class model "Schedule processing"

Fig. 6. The final UML Class model "Schedule processing"

- The inner cycle C1 of the algorithm (Fig. 3) closes with the conditional check if all the Facts from the set $F()$ are reviewed. Otherwise, one begins a new cycle with the new Fact $F(i+1)$.
- The outer cycle C2 closes with the conditional check if all the Classes from the Class model are reviewed. If not, one begins a new cycle with the Class $K(j+1)$. Otherwise, the first part of the algorithm is finished.

The second part of the Class model enhancement algorithm is depicted in Fig. 4. Rules that are used in this part are also presented in Table 3 (rules 3.1-4.2). Results received after the execution of this part are marked with the tag 3 in Fig. 6.

Conclusions

The UML meta-model does not distinguish business rules as a separate construct. This makes it problematic to use UML as a modeling language in IS development projects for agile, ever-changing business environments. In order to apply business rules-extended approach for IS development purposes BR repository model and extended UML Class meta-model were proposed and discussed in this paper.

We have provided a set of structured templates for business rules specification. The templates are used for business rules construction into formalized, national language-based sentences. This should break the language barrier and improve the quality of communication between the business people and system developers.

Basic steps of the UML Class model enhancement using formalized business rules are described and fragmentally illustrated by example.

References

Ambler SW (2003) The Elements of UML Style. Cambridge University Press

Coad P, Lefebvre E, De Luca J (1999) Java Modeling in Color with UML: Enterprise Components and Process. Yourdon Press Prentice Hall

Coad P, Yourdon E (1991) Object-Oriented Analysis. 2nd ed. Yourdon Press

Dong L, Subramaniam K, Eberlein A, Far BH (2003) Automating Transition from Use-Cases to Class Model. IEEE Canadian Conference on Electrical and Computer Engineering CCECE 2003

Dorsey P (2002) The Business Rules Approach to Systems Development. BRIM® Information Documents. www.dulcian.com

Gudas S, Skersys T, Lopata A (2004) Framework for Knowledge-based IS Engineering. Proc Advances in Information Systems ADVIS'2004. LNCS 326

Haggerty N (2000) Modeling Business Rules Using the UML and CASE. Business Rules Forum'2000. www.brcommunity.com

Hay D, Healy KA (2000) Defining Business Rules – What are They Really? Final Report – Revision 1.3. The Business Rules Group

Herbst H, Myrach T (1997) A Repository System for Business Rules. Database Application Semantics London

Kadir MN, Loucopoulos P (2003) Relating Evolving Business Rules to Software Design. Proc Software Engineering Research and Practice'03

Kapocius K, Butleris R (2002) The Business Rules Repository for Information Systems Design. Research Communications of 6th East European Conference ADBIS'02. Bratislava

Mellor SJ, Kendall S, Uhl A, Weise D (2004) MDA Distilled: Principles of Model-driven Architecture. Addison-Wesley

Object Management Group – OMG (2002) Business Rules in Models RFI. OMG Document: br/2002-09-13

Object Management Group – OMG (2003) Business Semantics of Business Rules RFP. OMG Document: br/2003-06-03

Plotkin D (1999) Business Rules Everywhere. Intelligent Enterprise, vol 2, no 4, pp 37-44

Reeder J (2002) Templates for Capturing Business Rules. www.brcommunity.com

Ross R (2003) Principles of the Business Rule Approach. Addison Wesley

Ross R, Lam GSW (2001a) The Do's and Don'ts of Expressing Business Rules. The BRS RuleSpeak™ Practitioner Kit. www.brsolutions.com

Ross R, Lam GSW (2001b) RuleSpeak Sentence Templates. The BRS RuleSpeak™ Practitioner Kit. www.brsolutions.com

Skersys T, Gudas S (2004) Business Rules Integration in Information Systems Engineering. Proc Information Systems Development ISD'2004. Technika Vilnius

Von Halle B (2001) Building a Business Rules System. DM Review Magazine, January. www.dmreview.com

Wahono RS, Far BH (2002) A Framework of Object Identification and Refinement Process in Object-Oriented Analysis and Design. Proc Cognitive Informatics ICCI 2002

Ontology-Based Evaluation and Design of Domain-Specific Visual Modeling Languages

Giancarlo Guizzardi, Luis Ferreira Pires and Marten van Sinderen

CTIT, University of Twente, Enschede, The Netherlands.
(guizzard, pires)@cs.utwente.nl, sinderen@ctit.utwente.nl

Introduction

In recent years, increasing attention has been paid to the development of *domain-specific visual modeling languages* (DSVLs). It is believed that these languages can lead to an increase in productivity in the modeling activity and contribute to the production of models that are more flexible, reusable and easier to maintain than models produced by using general-purpose modeling languages (Tolvanen et al 2004). However, in order to be effective, a DSVL must be defined taking into account the needs of its client users. From their perspective, the use of the language should be satisfactory in the following terms: (i) it should easy for a user of the language to communicate, understand and reason with the produced models (*comprehensibility appropriateness*); (ii) The language should be truthful to the domain in reality that it represents (*domain appropriateness*).

In this article, we present an ontology-based method for the evaluation and (re)design of DSVLs that reinforces properties (i) and (ii) above. We start by presenting the different elements of languages design, namely, *syntax*, *semantics* and *pragmatics*. After that, we discuss the subject of *formal ontologies* and its relation to each of these elements and present the proposed method. Finally, we illustrate this method with the design of a visual modeling language in the domain of genealogy.

Elements of Language Design

According to Morris (1938) a language comprises three parts: *syntax, semantics* and *pragmatics*. **Syntax** is devoted to *"the formal relation of signs to one another"*. In order to communicate, agents must agree on a common communication language. This fixes the sets of signs that can be exchanged (syntax) and how these signs can be combined in order to form valid expressions (syntactical rules). The set of available modeling primitives of a language forms the lexical layer and the language **abstract syntax** (typically defined in terms of a **metamodel**) delimits the set of grammatically correct models that can be constructed using this language.

A syntactic item is essential to give a concrete and persistent status to some information, but it is in itself, however, vacuous in terms of meaning. Therefore, participants in a communication process must also share the same meaning for the syntactical constructs being communicated, i.e., they must interpret in a compatible way the expressions of the communication language being used. Thus, to assign meaning to a syntactic sign, a mapping is necessary, between that sign and some entity in reality that it represents. The Semantics of a given syntactic item can then be defined as *"the relation of signs to real world entities they represent"* (Morris, ibid.).

Whilst the abstract syntax defines the rules for the creation of well-formed sentences of a given language, the vocabulary, or **concrete syntax**, provides a concrete representational system for expressing the elements of a given the domain. In sentential languages, there is a clear separation between vocabulary, syntax and semantics. The same does not hold for visual languages. For example, a visual vocabulary may include shapes such as circles, squares, arcs and arrows, all of differing sizes and colors. These objects often fall naturally into a hierarchical typing which almost certainly constrains the syntax and, furthermore, informs the semantics of the system (Gurr 1999). This idea is illustrated by Figure 1 below, in which two different languages are used to express logical syllogisms. The sentential language of Figure 1.a and the graphical language of Figure 1.b are semantically equivalent. Despite that, the inference step that culminates with conclusion (iii) is performed in a much more straightforward way in the language of Euler's circles (Figure 1.b).

Fig. 1. Logical Syllogism represented in (a) a sentential language and (b) in the visual language of Euler's Circles

This classic example shows how semantic information can be directly captured in a visual symbol. Here a sequence of valid operations is performed which cause some consequence to become manifest in a diagram, where that consequence is not explicitly insisted upon by the operations. This is because that the *partial order* properties of the set inclusion relation are represented via the similarly transitive, irreflexive and asymmetric visual properties of proper spatial inclusion in the plane, i.e. the representing relation has the same semantic properties of the represented relation.

In visual languages, intrinsic properties of the representation system can be systematically used to directly correspond to properties in the represented domain. This can lead to major increases in the effectiveness for performing specific tasks of the diagrams produced using this language (Gurr, ibid.). The benefits that can be achieved by exploring the inherent properties of representation systems (as well as the potential traps of ignoring them) are derived from the relation between a representation system of visual syntax and the human users interpreting that representation. Thus, following (Morris, ibid.), if syntax refers to *"the formal relation of signs to one another"*, and semantics to *"the relation of signs to real world entities they represent"*, then **pragmatics** refers to *"the relation of signs to (human) interpreters"*.

Ontology, (Meta)Conceptualization and Language

One of the main success factors behind the use of a modeling language is its ability to provide to its target users a set of modeling primitives that can directly express relevant domain abstractions. Domain abstractions are constructed in terms of concepts, i.e., abstract representations of certain aspects of entities that exist in a given domain that we name here *a domain conceptualization.* An abstraction of a certain *state of affairs* expressed in terms of a set of domain concepts, i.e., according to a certain conceptualization, is termed a *domain abstraction* in this work. Domain abstractions and conceptualizations are intangible entities that only exist in the mind of the user or a community of users of a language. In order to be documented, communicated and analyzed they must be captured, i.e. represented in terms of some concrete artifact. This implies that a language is necessary for representing them in a concise, complete and unambiguous way. The relations between these entities are elaborated in Figure 2, which depicts the distinction between a domain abstraction and its representation, and their relationship with the domain conceptualization and the representation language. In the scope of this work the representation of a domain abstraction in terms of a representation language L is called a *model or specification* and the language L used on its creation is called a modeling (or specification) language.

The position defended here is that a particular model $\mathcal{M}$ (produced in a modeling language $\mathcal{L}$) is considered a adequate model of a domain abstraction $\mathcal{A}$ if it preserves the structure of $\mathcal{A}$. Likewise, we can say that a modeling language $\mathcal{L}$ is appropriate to model a domain $\mathcal{D}$ according to a conceptualization C of $\mathcal{D}$ if $\mathcal{L}$ allows model designers to build models $\mathcal{M}$ which preserve the structure of the domain abstractions articulated with C. We then advocate that the adequacy of a modeling language to represent phenomena in a given domain can be systematically evaluated by comparing, on one hand, a concrete representation of the worldview underlying that language (captured by that language's **metamodel**) to, on the other hand, a concrete representation of a domain conceptualization, or a **domain ontology**. The truthfulness to reality *(domain appropriateness)* and conceptual clarity *(comprehensibility appropriateness)* of a modeling language depend on the level of homomorphism between these two entities. The stronger the match between an abstraction in reality and its representing model, the easier is to communicate and reason with that model.

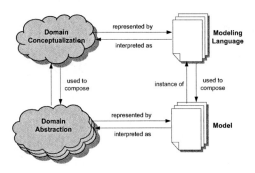

Fig. 2. Relation between conceptualization, abstraction, language and model

In Guizzardi et al. (2005), we have discussed a number of properties that should be reinforced for an isomorphic mapping to take place between an ontology O representing a domain $\mathcal{D}$ and a domain language's metamodel. These properties are briefly discussed in the sequel: **(a) Soundness:** A language $\mathcal{L}$ is *sound* w.r.t. to a domain $\mathcal{D}$ iff every modelling primitive in the language has an interpretation in terms of a domain concept in the ontology O; **(b) Completeness:** A language $\mathcal{L}$ is *complete* w.r.t. to a domain $\mathcal{D}$ iff every concept in the ontology O of that domain is represented in a modelling primitive of that language; **(c) Lucidity:** A language $\mathcal{L}$ is *lucid* w.r.t. to a domain $\mathcal{D}$ iff every modelling primitive in the language represents at most one domain concept in O. **(d) Laconicity:** A language $\mathcal{L}$ is *laconic* w.r.t. to a domain $\mathcal{D}$ iff every concept in the ontology O of that domain is represented at most once in the metamodel of that language.

Unsoundness, Non-Lucidity, Non-Laconicity and *Incompleteness* violate what the philosopher of language H.P.Grice (1975) names *conversational maxims* that states that a speaker is assumed to make contributions in a dialogue which are *relevant, clear, unambiguous*, and *brief, not overly informative* and *true according to the speaker's knowledge*. Whenever models do not adhere to these conversational maxims, *they* can communicate incorrect information and induce the user to make incorrect inferences about the semantics of the domain.

In regards to the property of completeness, when mapping the elements of a domain ontology to a language metamodel we must guarantee that these elements are represented in their full formal descriptions. In other words, the metamodel $\mathcal{MT}$ of language $\mathcal{L}$ representing the domain ontology O must also represent this ontology's full axiomatization. In formal, model-theoretic terms, this means that these entities should have the same set of logical models. In Guizzardi et al. (2005), we discuss this topic in depth and present a formal treatment of this idea. The set of logical models of O represent the state of affairs in reality deemed possible by a given domain conceptualization. In contrast, the set of logical models of $\mathcal{MT}$ stand for the world structures which can be represented by the grammatically correct specifications of language $\mathcal{L}$. In summary, we can state that if a domain ontology O is fully represented in a language metamodel $\mathcal{MT}$ of $\mathcal{L}$, then the only grammatically correct models of $\mathcal{L}$ are those which represent state of affairs in reality deemed possible by the domain conceptualization represented by O.

By representing a domain conceptualization in terms of a concrete artefact (a domain ontology) we can systematically evaluate the adequacy of existing modeling languages to represent phenomena in that domain. However, we can also use the domain ontology as the starting point for the design of new modeling language in that domain. In both cases, the objective is to reach a language metamodel which is isomorphic to an ontology representing a conceptualization of that domain. When this isomorphism is guaranteed, some pragmatic benefits are already achieved. However, additional benefits are achieved when another isomorphism is reinforced, namely, between the language metamodel (describing the language's abstract syntax) and the system of representations that forms the concrete syntax of the language.

Take, for instance, the model depicted in Figure 3. As one can notice, the models of Figures 3.a and 3.b are isomorphic. In this figure the arrow symbol represents the subsumption relation between types. The dashed arrow symbol, in particular, represents a subsumption relation between two different modes of type, namely, a *kind* (e.g., City) and a *phase* type (e.g., Town) (Guizzardi et al., 2004). Phases represent types which are instantiated by an individual only *contingently* (in the modal sense). A kind, in contrast, is instantiated by its instances *necessarily* (again, in the modal sense). For instance, every instance of the type person must be a person, i.e., it cannot cease to be a person without ceasing to exist. However, a person can be a student in a world w and cease to be so in world w' without ceasing to be the same individual (the same person). In this example, the same city *a* can be considered a town in a world w and a metropolis in w', but still maintaining its cross-world identity. Likewise, in Figure 3.b, the color property of a geometric figure is considered one of its contingent properties. Thus, a particular circular form is assumed to be able to change its color while maintaining a continuous visual percept.

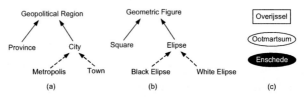

(a)   (b)   (c)

Fig. 3. Examples of (a) a illustrative domain ontology/metamodel; (b) a system of visual syntax isomorphic to the metamodel in (a); (c) a particular valid model according to (a)

This example highlights some important aspects of the approach discussed here. To start with, since ontologies are themselves models, they must also be represented in a certain modeling language. Take for instance, the small geopolitical regions ontology depicted above (Figure 3.a). In terms of Figure 2, this ontology can be considered a representation of a geopolitical regions conceptualization (upper-left corner), and isomorphic to the metamodel of language for describing geopolitical regions (upper-right corner). A possible model in the language defined by this metamodel (bottom-right corner) is the one of figure 3.c. This model represents a state of affairs (bottom-left corner) in which there exists a province named Overijssel, a city named Enschede, which is considered a metropolis, and a city named Ootmartsum, which is considered a town.

However, if we put the ontology of Figure 3.a in the bottom-right corner of Figure 2, then it can be considered as a valid model of a *general ontology representation language* (upper-right corner), containing primitives such as the (dashed) arrows in Figure 3.a. In this case, what should be the domain-independent meta-conceptualization that this general ontology representation language should commit to? We argue that it should be a system of general categories and their ties, which can be used to articulate domain-specific common sense theories of reality. This meta-conceptualization should comprise a number of domain-independent theories (e.g., theory of parts and wholes, types and subsumption, identity, existential dependence, etc.), which are able to characterize aspects of real-world entities irrespective of their particular nature. The development of such general theories of reality is the business of the philosophical discipline of *Formal Ontology*. A concrete artefact representing this meta-conceptualization is named a *Foundational Ontology*.

In a series of papers (e.g., Guizzardi et al., 2004, 2005), we have employed the evaluation method discussed in this section to evaluate and re-design the Unified Modeling Language (UML) for the purpose of conceptual modelling and ontology representation. Following this method, we compare the UML 2.0 metamodel with a philosophically principled foundational ontology. As a result we were able not only to propose a well-founded modeling profile that extends the language, but also to provide real-world semantics for the elements that constitute this profile.

The method proposed here evaluates the quality of domain-specific modelling language w.r.t. a domain ontology. As a consequence, the quality of a modelling language strongly depends on the quality of the ontology in which it is based. For this reason, the use of *suitable* ontology representation language to create these domain ontologies plays an important in this approach. Moreover, as illustrated in Figure 3, a representation language which recognizes more subtle distinctions among domain concept categories, allows for the construction of visual syntaxes which are also sensitive to these distinctions, or as defended by Gurr (1999): the more we know about a domain being represented, the bigger the chance we have of devising pragmatically efficient languages for that domain.

In summary, the approach proposed here for domain-specific visual language evaluation and re-design comprises of: (1) a number of properties that should be reinforced for guaranteeing the isomorphism between: (i) a domain ontology (representing the target domain conceptualization) and a metamodel of the language; (ii) a metamodel of the language (defining its set of valid models) and one representing its system of concrete visual syntax; (2) a general ontology representation language that can be used to construct these domain ontologies.

Example: A DSVL for the Genealogy Domain

In the sequel we illustrate the notions discussed so far with an example in the domain of genealogical relations. A certain conceptualization of this domain can be articulated by considering concepts such as *person, living person, deceased person, father, mother, offspring, fatherOf* and *motherOf*. These concepts are related to each other and have their interpretation constrained by axioms imposed on their definitions. Figure 4 depicts a domain ontology representing a possible conceptualization in this domain. The language used to represent this model is the ontologically well-founded version of UML proposed in (Guizzardi et al., 2004). The diagram on this picture can be complemented by the following axioms: (a) A person x is a *parentOf* person y iff x is *fatherOf* y or x is *motherOf* y; (b) A person x is a *ancestorOf* person y iff x is *parentOf* y or there is a person z such that z is an *parentOf* y and x is *ancestorOf* z; (c) A person cannot be its own ancestor; (d) If a person x is an *ancestorOf* person y then y cannot be an *ancestorOf* x; (d) If a person x is an *ancestorOf* person y and y is an *ancestorOf* person z then x is an *ancestorOf* z.

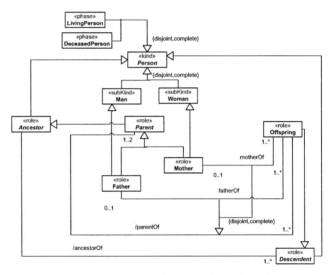

Fig. 4. An ontology for the genealogy domain

By representing a conceptualization of this domain in terms of this concrete artefact we can design a language to express phenomena on this domain capturing characteristics that this conceptualization deems relevant. For instance, according to this domain ontology, Person is an abstract type, i.e., one that cannot have direct instances. This type is partitioned in two independent suptyping structures:

- *Man, Woman:* this partition represents that every individual person (instance of type Person) in the universe of discourse is either a man (an instance of Man) or woman (instance of Woman). Moreover, due to the «subKind» stereotype, it states that every man is *necessarily* a man (in a modal sense). Analogously, the same applies to instances of Woman;

- *LivingPerson, DeceasedPerson:* this partition represents that every individual person in the universe of discourse is either a living person or a deceased one. However, in contrast to the ⟨Man,Woman⟩ partition, an instance of LivingPerson *is not necessarily so* (in the modal sense). That is to say that for every x such that x is LivingPerson there is a counterfactual situation in which x is not a LivingPerson, which in this case, implies that x is a DeceasedPerson in this counterfactual situation. Analogously, the same applies to instances of DeceasedPerson. These facts are implied by the presence of «phase» stereotyped constructs and the associated constraint in the modelling profile used that phases must be defined in a partition (Guizzardi et al., 2004).

A cross-relation of these two partitions give us four concrete types, i.e., types that can have direct instances, let us name them *LivingMan, DeceasedMan, LivingWoman* and *DeceasedWoman*. Every instance of person in a given situation is necessarily an instance of one of these types. A suitable modeling language in this domain must have modelling primitives that conform to these constraints. Other constraints on the possible models according to this ontology include: that every *offspring* can have at maximum one *father* and one *mother*; the *ancestorOf* relation (defined to hold between instances of *Person*) is irreflexive, antisymmetric and antitransitive. The constraints captured in this ontology must be taken into account in design (and evaluation) of a language to model genealogical relations.

By having a conceptualization (abstract entity) represented in terms of domain ontology and, by applying the method discussed in section 3, one can, in a precise manner, design a suitable modeling language for that given domain. In this particular case, we are able to design a language $\mathcal{L}_1$ which structure is isomorphic to the ontology of Figure 4. The primitives of this language are presented in Figure 5.

The following characteristics of language $\mathcal{L}_1$ should be observed: (i) the language contain modeling primitives that represent all concrete classifiers (*LivingMan, DeceasedMan, LivingWoman, DeceasedWoman*) and non-derived relations present in the ontology (*fatherOf, motherOf*). Consequently, we can say that language is expressive enough to model all characteristics of the domain that are considered relevant by the underlying ontology; (ii) there is no case of construct redundancy, construct overload or construct excess; (iii) since the metamodel of this language is identical to the ontology of Figure 4, the well-formedness rules in this metamodel also includes the axioms of that ontology. In other words, the only syntatically valid models in language $\mathcal{L}_1$ are those that represent state of affairs deemed admissible by that ontology. As a consequence, the models depicted in

Figure 6 (a-c) are not syntactically valid in $\mathcal{L}_1$. A valid model in this language is depicted in Figure 6.d.

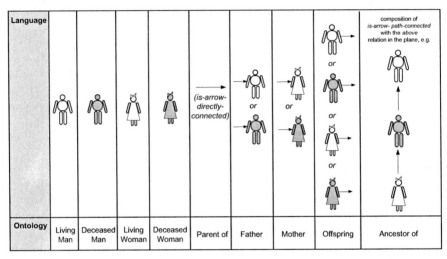

Fig. 5. Domain Concepts and their representing modeling primitives in L1

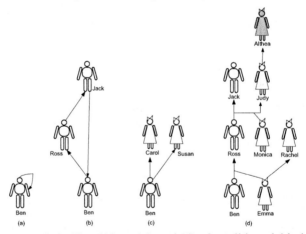

Fig. 6. (a-c) Examples of invalid models and (d) of a valid model in language L1

Another aspect that should be noticed is how the ontology of Fig 4 contributes for the pragmatic efficiency of $\mathcal{L}_1$. By explicitly considering the ontological meta-properties of the domain entities (e.g., if they are instantiated necessarily by their instances of not) we are able to account for other direct aspects of visual syntaxes. In the case of language $\mathcal{L}_1$, the following can be observed.

Firstly, the types Man and Woman are *kinds*. This means that instances of these types will continue to be so as long as they exist in the model. In contrast, an individual man (or woman) can have the (intrinsic) properties of *begin alive* or *being dead* in different situations. In language L_1, the icons used to represent instances of Person maintain the stable visual percept, which represents the dichotomy of the rigid types Man and Woman. The phases living and deceased are represented as variations of this visual percept, that is, the *same* visual percept can appear in different situations as one of these two variations

Secondly, the types modeled as concrete *Roles* in the ontology are Father, Mother and Offspring. *Roles*, like phases, are instantiated by their instances only contingently. Moreover, roles are *relationally dependent* types, i.e., individuals play roles only in a certain context or in relation to another entity (Guizzardi et al., 2004). For instance, the *same* instance *x* of Father can exist in another situation in the model without being a Father. Moreover, to be a Father is to be a Man who has (at least) one Offspring, i.e., for *x* to be a Father he must share a relational property with another individual who is an instance of Offspring. In L_1, the Parent role is represented by the adjacency relation between the icon representing a Person and the arrow-head of the symbol representing the parentOf relation. Additionally, the Offspring role is represented by the adjacency relation between the icon representing a Person and the arrow-tail of the symbol representing the parentOf relation. This representation choice highlights the dependency of these roles on relational properties. Moreover, it allows the modeling that x *qua* Man maintains its identity in the scope of different relations and across different situations.

Thirdly, the *ancestorOf* relation is represented by the above relation in the plane associated with the arrow-path-connectedness, i.e., if x and y are two persons who are path-connect and x is above y in the plane then x is an ancestorOf y. The composed relation *above-path-connect* is also irreflexive, asymmetric and transitive, i.e., a partial order relation. These are exactly the same meta-properties enjoyed by the ancestor relation. For this reason, the conclusion that (x ancestorOf z) if (x ancestorOf y) and (y ancestorOf z) is directly inferred from (x is above-path-connected-to z) if (x above-path-connected-to y) and (y above-path-connected-to z).

Final Considerations

In this paper we argue that formal domain ontologies are suitable as starting point for the design of domain-specific visual languages. We present the different elements of languages design and discuss the relation between ontologies and each of these elements. Additionally, we motivate the need for an ontologically well-justified representation language for the purpose of ontology specification and language conceptual metamodeling.

A number of formal ontologies have been developed during the years, in several important application areas. Motivated by the Semantic Web, we have seen a fast growth on the number of implemented ontologies as well as a diversification of their application domains. We demonstrate that ontology engineering can make important contributions to the area of domain-specific visual modeling languages, and that a suitably represented domain ontology can be used to: (i) provide real-world semantics for a domain language modeling primitives; (ii) delimit the set of models that should be deemed grammatically valid by that language, thus constraining its abstract syntax; and (iii) inform important pragmatic properties that should be reinforced by the language system of concrete visual syntax.

Acknowledgements

This work is part of the Freeband A-MUSE Project (contract BSIK 03025). We would like to thank Gerd Wagner, Nicola Guarino and Chris Vissers for fruitful discussions and for providing valuable input to the issues of this article.

References

Grice HP (1975) Logic and Conversation. In: Cole P, Morgan J (eds) Syntax and Semantics. Vol 3, Speech Acts. Academic Press New York
Guizzardi G, Ferreira Pires L, van Sinderen M (2005) An Ontology-Based Approach for Evaluating Domain Appropriateness and Comprehensibility Appropriateness of Modeling Languages. Proc of the 8th MoDELS. Jamaica
Guizzardi G, Wagner G, Guarino N, van Sinderen M (2004) An Ontologically Well-Founded Profile for UML Conceptual Models. Proc of the 16th CAiSE. Latvia
Gurr CA (1999) Effective Diagrammatic Communication: Syntatic, Semantic and Pragmatic Issues. Journal of Visual Languages and Computing, no 10, pp 317-342
Morris CW (1938) Foundations of a Theory of Signs. Chicago University Press Chicago, pp 77-138
Tolvanen J-P, Gray J, Rossi M (eds) (2004) Domain-Specific Modeling with Visual Languages. Journal of Visual Languages and Computing Elsevier Science

Engagements as a Unifying Concept for Process Integration

Igor T. Hawryszkiewycz

Faculty of Information Technology, University of Technology, Sydney, Australia. igorh@it.uts.edu.au

Introduction

Work processes in any organization now fall into a spectrum that ranges from predefined processes, through team based processes, to highly emergent processes. Process characteristics change across the spectrum. Perhaps one of the most important changes is that collaboration increases as processes become more emergent, because more and more people get involved at each process stage. These for example, include creation of new products and services (Grant, 1996) where new expertise may be needed as ideas evolve. There also tends to be increasing physical separation of people both within and between organizations as such expertise may be at different locations. The tasks become more flexible as people discover new ways to do things and goal congruency between the different process participants diverges.

Another problem is that processes often use different kinds of technologies and are not easily integrated to focus on agreed organizational goals. Thus predefined processes often use workflow technologies, whereas emergent technologies are more likely to use communications technologies such as e-mail or various kinds of groupware. Often such technologies are difficult to integrate. This can lead to coordination problems as participants in different processes are not aware of what is happening in other processes. One question is how to gradually introduce collaboration into organizational processes and ways to integrate collaborative processes into organizational goals.

This paper addresses ways of integrating collaborative activities into business processes by introducing a new perspective to collaboration. This is to define a higher level concept, or composite object, known as an engagement. Conceptually it can be viewed as a composite object (Shanks, Lansley, Weber, 2004) that can be represented in terms of modeling concepts such as entities or relationships. Users can set up engagements to reach local short-term goals within a longer term global context. An engagement in this sense is usually a number of interactions that have a sub-goal, which is part of a wider goal. Such a wider goal is accomplished through a number of engagements. An engagement usually results in someone sharing knowledge or using their tacit knowledge to interpret some part of the current context or to make an intermediate decision. The paper goes further to suggest that engagements will evolve as collaboration intensifies.

There are a number of advantages of using such higher level concepts in collaborative systems. One is to provide a social construct that can be easily understood. Another is to provide a high level object that can be used to identify services at a macro level. Still another, which is shown in this paper, is that engagements as particularly suitable as a way of integrating processes. To achieve this goal requires a way to deliver services that support engagements across a spectrum of processes. The paper claims that engagements provide a basis that ranges from predefined processes to emerging processes. They can apply in local as well as mobile environments. They support communication at a macro level beyond the simple exchange of messages that often characterize e-mail. An engagement is a goal oriented communication that integrates a number of messages into the one engagement. The paper, however, sees that support must be provided to manage engagements and suggests agents as suitable for this purpose.

The paper will first describe why engagements can serve as a useful concept in representing and supporting collaborative processes. It will then provide a more formal definition of engagements and ways to identify them during analysis and design.

Engagements as Part of a Process

The simplest definition of an engagement is two or more people sharing their knowledge to achieve a defined although a short term goal. For example, it may be something like resolving a conflict in a requirements specification. We use the term engagement rather than interaction to imply that an engagement includes more than one person and has a defined objective. It is also possible to view an engagement as a task. A task however can be almost any activity whereas engagements are restricted to collaboration. It should then be possible to create generic engagements that can be easily customized to a variety of processes. A more detailed definition will be given later in the paper. The paper now describes how engagements can be easily integrated into different kinds of processes.

Increasing Collaboration in Predefined Processes

To see how engagement fits into a predefined process consider a normal workflow. Figure 1 shows where engagements can be included in a workflow. In a simple workflow each task is usually performed often by one person taking the task role. For example in Figure 1 where a requisition is made, followed by approval, followed by a part order Usually only one engagement is needed in each step, for example, between team leader and member making a requisition. In general here the task and goal are well defined. All participants at each task work to a common goal and hence the kinds of services provided to support collaboration can also be well-defined.

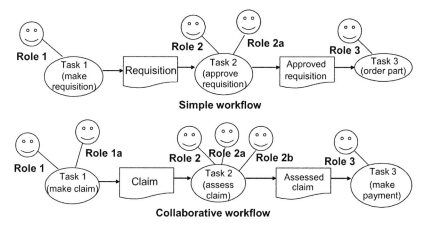

Fig. 1. Extending predefined flows

A more common situation is now one where the task requires some further engagements or agreements between a number of people, each taking a different role. Another example is claims processing, where more than one person is usually involved in claims assessment. Here there is considerable task complexity. As a result, there may be more than one engagement needed to complete an assessment. They can include clarification with claimant, getting an assessment, completing reports and so on. Making a requisition is also an example but the engagement here is often a simple one between a team leader and a team member.

Extending Engagements to Collaboration between Tasks

Earlier research (Hawryszkiewycz, 1996), which reported support for business network formation, is an example of team oriented processes in an interorganizational context. A model of activities in business network formation is illustrated in Figure 2. Brokers are contracted to facilitate the formation of business networks to take advantage of a business opportunity. Network formation includes three main activities, assessing business opportunities, finding business partners to meet them, and making and managing contracts between the business partners.

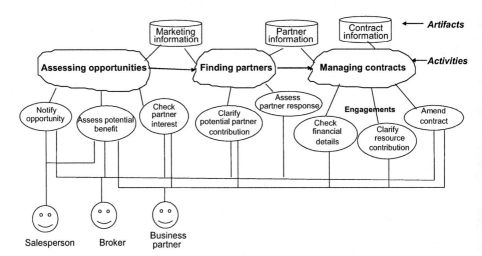

Fig. 2. Conceptual Model of Business Networks

Each of the major activities is more complex than predefined processes. Each activity can have more than one engagement and can involve a number of roles. The three activities, which are shown in Figure 2, are:

- Assessing business opportunities where external contacts notify brokers of business opportunities. The major roles here were the broker, business partner and salesperson,
- Finding partners, who may be willing to form a network to respond to the opportunity. Here brokers explain the opportunities to the business and suggest possible advantages to clients, and
- Managing contracts between business partners.

Figure 2 was the result of a first step in a study to design systems for supporting business network formation. Each of these activities now contains a number of engagements and participants can select services appropriate to the engagement. Further detailed work (Hawryszkiewycz, 1996) on business networks led to the identification of engagements through a questionnaire. Some of these, which are shown by oval shapes in Figure 2, include notifying an opportunity, amending contract documents, or assessing partner interest an opportunity. The difference from the predefined approach now is increased task and goal flexibility. This in turn means that there are many more engagements as well as strong relationships between the engagements, even in different activities. Often different kinds of services are often chosen for each engagement requiring integration between these services. The eventual strategy here concentrated on meeting broker goals by developing a contact service and a portal service to post opportunities.

Emergent Process

Finally emergent processes are generally those where engagements cannot be grouped in a sensible manner. Here engagements tend to emphasize people relationships.

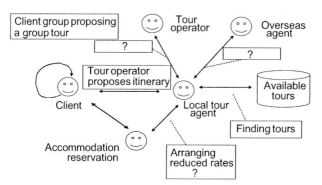

Fig. 3. Engagements in arranging travel

Figure 3 is an example of the kind of engagements that exist when arranging travel. Here there are a number of roles basically responding to events. These are now virtually event driven and the various participants each within own goal respond to these events. The services are virtually randomly chosen and rely on devices available to participants.

Engagements – a More Formal Definition

The paper now defines engagements more formally. An engagement in this paper is made up of a number of interactions to achieve a sub-goal within a larger goal. For example, developing a common document may be an engagement that involves many interactions, such as agreeing on a change, editing and so on. Document development itself is one of the engagements in the entire process. The approach proposed here is to identify communities and roles within these communities. We then define the communications needed between the different roles, and then go into detailed design by identifying engagements followed by providing services to support these engagements.

In theory an engagement can be seen as a composite object. It can be described in a number of ways. One uses existing E-R semantics to illustrate the concepts although ultimately a more collaboratively oriented presentation is preferred. The representation in terms of E-R models is illustrated in Figure 4.

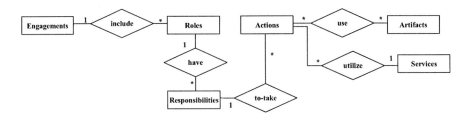

Fig. 4. Defining Engagements

Here an engagement includes number of roles having a number of responsibilities, which are carried out by actions supported by the engagement. Any action must be consistent with the entire context and hence engagement support must include integration with the organizational context. Figure 5 is another example of engagements. There are two activities here. One is where a student submits an assignment for assessment. The other where the assessment is clarified to the student

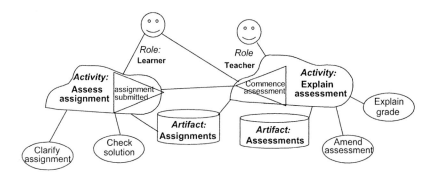

Fig. 5. A concrete example of engagements in education

In summary the main engagement components are:

- Engagement with a defined goal such as "check a solution", or "get client request",
- Roles responsibilities for responsibilities to realize the engagement goal,
- Actions define what must be done to accomplish the engagement goal,
- Services, which are provided to allow users to carry out the actions. These may be chatrooms, discussion databases,
- Artifacts that are used in the actions. These may include the private context is what is directly needed to carry out the function, as well as artefacts in a global context, that may be used as background knowledge in the engagement.

A more formal grammatical definition follows:

Engagement: *Engagement-name;*
Engagement-goal: (Text with keywords);
Activity: activity where engagement takes place;
Engagement-roles: +{<role-name>,+{<responsibilities>}};
Content:
      engagement-content: +{<artifact-name>};
      services: + {<service-name>};
      +actions: {{engagement-artifact:+{artifact-name}}, {services:
        +{<service-name>}}, +{action:{+{<role-
        name>},services:+{service-name}, information:+{artifact-
        name} };

There are also constraints and permissions, as for example, role permissions to access information, and what kind of access is permitted. The kinds of semantics include:

- Create-engagement ,
- Invite people to take up a role,
- Add artefacts to the engagement,
- Alert people of actions taken by others in the engagement,
- Setup services to support actions in the engagement.

The engagement in this case can be seen as collaboration in the small being carried out within a larger framework. The issues then are how to subdivide a process into engagements while maintaining links to the entire context.

Implementing Engagements

The most obvious implementation is to create a separate workspace for each engagement, and then integrate the workspaces into the main work process. Alternatively for emergent processes the implementation may be as a set of workspaces sharing a common database. The workspace would include the elements defined in Figure 4.

The workflow management coalition standards for workflows, for example, include client interfaces, which could be realized as workspaces. Collaborative applications are also realized as workspaces. We have for example carried out a study of services needed by students working on group projects. These include activities such setting up a learning plan, initiating learning activities, and supporting impromptu discussions.

Networking Engagements

In an organization wide solution a particular person may have access to a number of workspaces. These correspond to the activities in which the person participates. Each workspace deals with a separate activity. Thus there may be one workspace called 'MyWork' which identifies all activities for the participant. There are then a number of related workspaces. These include workspaces for different communities such as committees, workspaces for classes, or research projects.

Generic Engagements

One of our goals is to identify generic engagements that can be applicable across many applications. The type of engagements will depend on the type of virtual organization. For example Carmel (1999) identifies a variety of engagements for software development. The high level engagements primarily concerned with developing working relationships between disparate groups. These emphasize team building through building personal bridges between sites and team governance including defining roles and responsibilities.

A similar broadbased study by O'Hara-Devereaux and Johansen (1994) identified a generic set of engagements for team building. These included:

- Orientation to determine the community goal within its environment,
- Trust building to develop confidence in working with other person,
- Goal/Role Clarification to subdivide the work among roles,
- Commitment of people assigned to responsibilities,
- Implementation carrying out the role responsibilities,
- Performance or determining and evaluating outcomes,
- Renewal, or defining the next project.

One conclusion here was that many of the initial stages are best carried out synchronously, whereas the latter are adaptable to asynchronous support. This to some extent supported by outsourcing companies, which in general require requirements to be defined in face to face situations.

Future Work

Engagements are especially useful for extending capabilities for mobile devices. Figure 6 for example illustrates the issues of supporting mobile users within the organizational context. Here different engagement roles (Hawryszkiewycz, Steele, 2005) may be on different mobile devices but their activities are coordinated through the central server.

Extending to Virtual Networks

Work across distance, sometimes known as virtual work, centers on communication services that support people working in knowledge environments towards common goals. Research to date shows that participants most users often resort to e-mail, although research has shown the limitations of engagements that can be supported by e-mail. Cummings (2002), for example, suggests that e-mail on the InterNet can at best support information exchange. Ducheneaut and Bellotti (2001) describe the issues confronting users who wish to go beyond simple exchange. This requires them to set up their own environments on their personal computers, leading to the usual problems of maintaining consistency with duplicated sites. Engagements can provide new insights at this level, particularly in facilitating meaningful relationships between people in virtual organizations.

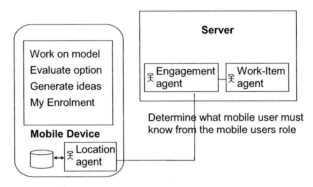

Fig. 6. Application in mobility

Important Considerations in Designing Engagements for Virtual Organizations

So far we have identified the engagements in broad form. Each engagement can be used to identify the best service for the engagement. The choice of services is quite simple as shown in Figure 7. This is simply to list the engagements and services and identify the most appropriate service for each engagement. Figure 7 also shows the services needed for each engagement. These need not be necessary computer services.

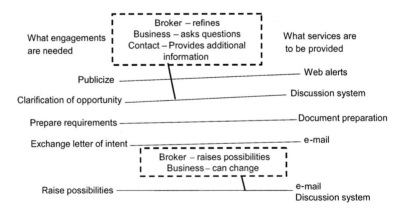

Fig. 7. Detailed Design

Further details are often needed to set up the service. These particularly involve defining roles and their responsibilities within an engagement. The details can also be shown in the way illustrated in Figure 7. Thus for example a coordinator is proposed to coordinate the assessment of a situation and deciding on subsequent action. The identified services are then placed in one workspace.

Adding Agents

Questions then arise as to whether such evolution can be actively supported by software agents. The agents observe the work environment and suggest actions to be taken by participants. Examples can include observing progress of plans and suggesting actions to be taken by participants.

Developing agents specifically for each application is prohibitive and our goal is to identify generic agents that can be used across applications. One objective is to develop reusable agents. One important agent suggested here (Ott and Nastansky 1997) is a broker agent that will assist the construction of teams to meet emerging work objectives. Thus for example there can be agents that manage typical engagements. We have also developed agents to manage progress through project case studies. These initiate activities, monitor their progress, and suggest new engagements and services to expedite project completion.

Summary

This paper introduced the concept of engagements are as way of integrating different kinds of processes. It defined the concept of engagement and showed its application to a range of processes. It then suggested alternate ways to provide services to support engagements. The main alternatives were based on workspaces and the paper described issues in integrating workspaces into processes. It then described future work in this area including mobility and the ways engagements can be used to support virtual organizations.

References

Carmel E (1999) Global Software Teams. Prentice-Hall Upper Saddle River
Cummings JN, Butler B, Kraut R (2002) The Quality of OnLine Social Relationships. Communications of the ACM, vol 45, no 1, pp 103-111

Ducheneaut N, Bellotti V (2001) E-mail as Habitat. Interactions, September-October 2001, pp 30-38

Grant RM (1996) Prospering in Dynamically-Competitive Environments: Organizational Capability as Knowledge Integration. Organization Science, vol 7, no 4, pp 375-387

Hawryszkiewycz IT (1996) Providing Computer Services For Business Networks. Proc of the Ninth International Conference on EDI-IOS. Bled June 1996

Hawryszkiewycz IT (2004) Agent Support for Learner Groups. Proc of the 7th IASTED International Conference on Computers and Advanced Technology in Education. Hawaii

Hawryszkiewycz IT, Steele R (2005) A Framework for Integrating Mobility into Collaborative Business Processes. Proc of the Conference on Mobile Business. July 2005

O'Hara-Devereaux M, Johansen R (1994) GlobalWork: Bridging Distance. Culture and Time Jossey-Bass Publishers San Francisco

Ott M, Nastansky L (1997) Modeling Organizational Forms of Virtual Enterprises. http://fb5www.uni-paderborn.de/winfo2

Shanks G, Lansley E, Weber R (2004) Representing Composites in Conceptual Modeling. Communications of the ACM, vol 47, no 7, pp 77-80

Method Configuration – A Systems Development Project Revisited

Fredrik Karlsson

MELAB, Department of Informatics (ESI), Örebro University, Sweden.
fredrik.karlsson@esi.oru.se

Introduction

Method engineering is a design research discipline with a focus on providing support for method engineers and systems developers. Brinkkemper (1996) defines it as 'the engineering discipline to design, construct and adapt methods, techniques and tools for the development of information systems.' Such support is provided in the form of frameworks (e.g. Ågerfalk and Wistrand, 2003), methods (e.g. Yourdon, 1989), meta-methods (e.g. Harmsen, 1997), and computerized tool support (e.g. Rossi, 1998). Subsequently, as a design science discipline we attempt to support human actions (March and Smith, 1995). Since design is about the artificial (Dahlbom, 2002) it consists of a duality involving both construction and evaluation. However, within the field of method engineering the attention is often given to the former and often with a theoretical focus.

In this paper we focus on evaluation of a meta-method proposed for method configuration. Method configuration, one sub-section of method engineering, is defined as the planned, systematic and reusable adaptation of a specific method, termed base method (Karlsson and Ågerfalk, 2004). The evaluation has a longitudinal characteristic since it covers a timeframe of three years. Furthermore, it involves evaluation on three different layers, which are summarized in Fig. 1. The figure illustrates four layers in total. The top most layer is about meta-method construction, where the development of the evaluated meta-method is done. The meta-method, named Method for Method Configuration (MMC), is used as input for method configuration activities, together with methods and reusable patterns. The reusable patterns are method parts adapted using MMC. The third layer is the systems development where the situational method is used as input. It is turned into method-in-action by the system developers and the final result is often an information system. Finally, at the bottom of Fig. 1 we find the end user practice layer, where the information system is part of the day-to-day practice in a business, supporting end users.

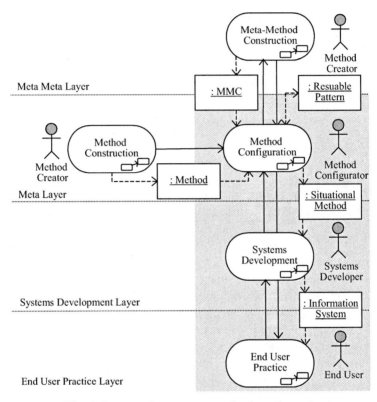

Fig. 1. Layers of concern to method configuration

The four layers in Fig. 1 contain five different roles. They are directly or indirectly affected through MMC or the situational method that is a result from the method configuration activity. The shaded part of the figure demarcates the area of interest for this paper. The roles we center are: method configurator, systems developer and end user.

This paper is organized in six sections, including this opening section. In the following section we discuss the research method adopted for tracking the effects of MMC. In the third section we give a brief introduction to the meta-method, which has been used during method configuration for the current project. In the fourth section we introduce the research site, which later is interwoven with the fifth section that contains a discussion about how the meta-method, the situational method and the information system turned out as support on the different layers discussed above. Finally, we end the paper with the sixth section, containing a short conclusion.

Research Method Adopted

The evaluation of MMC is part of a larger research project on flexible methods, where the aim is to provide method and computerized tool support for method configuration. The meta-method has been developed using collaborative practice research (Mathiassen, 2002), involving practitioners in the grounding processes (Goldkuhl, 1999).

Evaluation of methods and their results are not without difficulties as discussed by Siau and Rossi (1998). They discuss a wide range of evaluation techniques for method research, divided into non-empirical and empirical techniques. In the latter category we find survey, laboratory experiment, field experiment, case study and action research. Collaborative practice research is often termed action research and hence the evaluation part follows this path. The systems development project that is revisited in this paper was originally part of the larger research project, constituting one of the action research cases.

The author has, in line with this idea, been closely involved both as method creator of MMC and in the systems development project, termed Personnel Register System (PRS). The author has acted both as method configurator and project manager in the PRS project, which gave the possibility of close trace of the project and its results. However, at the same time it has been a trade-off between access and the risk of bias.

One major weakness in Siau and Rossi (1998) is that they do not address operationalization of evaluation criteria. Traditionally, evaluation of projects is compared to the initial project goals (Archibald, 1992). However, a project is both a process and a product, which is important in our case since method configuration addresses the way of working during a development process. Hence, the situational method is treated as an intermediate project artifact during the project. Furthermore, the project's final artifact should be judged from how it transforms the situation in the business when it is delivered, not from the initial goals since goals can change along the project. Subsequently, we need to address the relevance of the project's different artifacts in combination with the problem situation to be solved on each layer and the decisions made at each decision point. In addition to the relevance criterion, we have to take the projects constraints into consideration. The most straightforward constraints are time and cost, which become two additional criteria for evaluation of the project.

Relevance can be interpreted as the degree of achieved rationality resonance. Rational resonance is when the user's rationality and the rationality of the artifact overlap (Stolterman and Russo, 1997). Subsequently, it is about focus on goal fulfillment on each of the three layers during the project course. The process for achieving rationality resonance has been operationalized as follows. On the meta layer we compare the support from MMC to the method creator's design decisions and the meta-method's expressed rationale. Moving down one layer, to the systems development layer, we center the situational method as support for the systems developers and end users during systems development. Subsequently, the situational method's rationale is compared to the method configurator's decisions and the situational method's rationale. Finally, PRS is evaluated on the end user practice layer, focusing on the transformation of the initial problem situation. The systems developer's decisions and the design rationale of PRS is compared to the end users' intentions in their day-to-day work after the delivery of PRS.

Different techniques have been used in order to enable the trace of effects. Log books where used to document problems and lessons during the method configuration and systems development activities. The systems development team involved four systems developer who continuously gave feedback on how the situational method supported them. These lessons could later be traced to the possible causes. For example, if parts of the situational method were found inappropriate they could be traced to the meta-method, the systems developer's knowledge about the base method or both.

The information system has been evaluated using interviews with the end users and tracing the need for system maintenance. The former focused on the end users' opinion about the support that PRS offers in their day-to-day work and how the problem situation has been transformed. The latter is an indirect measurement of the end users' opinion based on the degree of reworked functionality that has been necessary after deploying PRS. A low number of changes indicate that rationality resonance exists between the design and the end users' needs.

Method for Method Configuration

In this section we give a brief introduction to MMC, for details see Karlsson and Ågerfalk (2004). The base method's rationale and the characteristics of the development situation types are used as the focal area for classification of the base method's content. Method fragment (Harmsen, 1997) is used as the modularization concept, when parts in the base method are suppressed or added. Furthermore, MMC contains two concepts to facilitate reuse, which is central for method configuration. These conceptual constructs are configuration package and template.

Each development situation type is divided into problems areas based on the characteristics; problems areas which a demarcated part o a situational method should handle. Therefore, we have operationalized characteristics as questions, where each question has a set of possible answers. A possible answer is termed a configuration package. Thus a configuration package contains a set of classified method fragments from the base method's process and product model, and if necessary method fragments from complementing methods.

However, real world projects cannot be captured through one single characteristic. Therefore, we make an abstraction of similar projects into development situation types involving several characteristics. As a consequence we need a combination of configuration packages, to capture a configuration for a development situation type. Configuration templates are used to capture these more complex situations. A configuration template is a combined method configuration, based on configuration packages, for a set of recurrent project characteristics. This can be thought of as a predefined combination of configuration packages common within the organization.

Configuration templates are used to create situational methods with an origin in a base method. A situational method is based on a configuration template through the use of characteristics. Each new project is described using the range of characteristics, operationalized as questions. The project profile is then matched against the profiles of development situation types and their configuration templates.

The Research Site

The research site is from a department at Örebro University. A project team, termed the development team, of four people was assigned to develop a web-based personnel register system. This was a small project of about 350 hours over a period of three calendar months. In addition, up to five end users participated during the project.

Considering the problem situation on the meta layer we can conclude that there existed no structured way of working with method configuration at the university. Subsequently, method configuration was earlier not considered important and no reusable patterns existed. However, the method configurator had earlier experience from both method configuration in general and using MMC.

The following is a short summary of the conditions when the project began and which acted as input for the problem solving process using MMC: An older information system was used for storing information about personnel. This system contained information about employees, such as name, social security number, work and private phone numbers, and home address. During an earlier project when the department's web site was redesigned a discussion got underway about the benefits of a database-driven web-solution for personnel information. The web project found unused potential through coordination of this information. Parts of the information could be useful as contact information on the web site, while other information, such as social security numbers, was for internal department use only. However, integrating this information system with the re-designed web site was beyond the scope of that project. Furthermore, it was not a suitable solution for technical reasons. Thus the development team was assigned to design a new system.

The members of the development team had varying experience of web development and more specifically building component-based solutions combining Active Server Pages (ASP) and COM+. The technical platform for this project was given since the existing web site was built on ASP-technology. The choice of method was Rational Unified Process (RUP). This was a trade-off to the benefit of the academic sphere, based on the use of RUP as the reference method in other parts of the meta-method project. One drawback of this choice was that the development team was fairly inexperienced with the method; this was the first time they used it. Still, this was not perceived as a significant problem since all members of the development team were familiar with many of the artifacts found in RUP, since they are also found in other methods. Furthermore, the development team members had a fairly good knowledge of methods in general. However, RUP was considered a large method, which could cause problems in such a small project.

Evaluation of Support on Three Layers

In this section we discuss the support found on the three layers discussed in the Introduction. It is not possible to present every part of the method configuration and systems development activities due to the limited space in this paper. Consequently, a selection has been made. This selection represents some of the major decisions made during this project and how they later turned out.

The Meta Layer

The method configuration process resulted in a situational method for the devlopment team, based on a set of configuration packages. One example, of such a configuration package concerned the Business Modeling discipline in RUP. Since the web site project preceded the PRS project it existed a good understanding about the organization and its requirements. This discipline was suppressed in this configuration package, based on the method rationale expressed for the Business Modeling discipline and the need expressed by the systems developers. Subsequently, MMC contributed with valuable focus while analyzing the possibilities to achieve rationality resonance between method fragments in RUP and the systems developers' needs and intentions.

As discussed in Section 3, the concept of method fragment was used as the smallest modularization unit in this version of MMC. The author experienced that this concept has both benefits and drawbacks. Using the different layers of the method fragment construct during method configuration is an efficient way of making aggregate classifications. However, the use of the method fragment concept results in tracking of related method fragments both in the hierarchy of fragments and between the process and product model. The result is time consuming and an unnecessary risk arises of fragmented situational methods. Therefore, a change request for later versions of MMC was issued and a concept that treats related method fragments as one single unit has been proposed.

The Systems Development Layer

On the system development layer we identify the problem situation as follows. There was a need to administer and distribute information about personnel at the department with increased efficiency and relevance. The old system often contained incorrect information. This was due to the manual procedures where one person had the responsibility to gather information and keep the register updated. Paper based versions of the personnel information was printed regularly, resulting in circulation of out-of-date information. Furthermore, the paper-based versions were only distributed for internal department use, leaving out one important target group: externals of the department (e.g. students, customers, researchers).

The situational method was designed to target these different user groups. For example, use cases were used to describe the different actors' interactions with the new system. Both the systems developers and the end users expressed that the use of use cases was successful. Hence, we can conclude that rationality resonance occurred between the situational method and the systems developers and the end users. When considering the assumptions behind use cases (Baekgaard, 2005) one can see that their purpose are suitable for the situation. First, the border between the system and the environment was clear. Second, the activities of the actors were well understood. Third, the development team was designing a reactive system since it acts in response to external events in the environment.

The requirements analysis resulted in a solution where department employees had the possibility to access his or her personal data to some extent. This design decision was made in order decentralize how personnel information is to be updated, which was one major problem in the existing system. For the detailed design, the situational method prescribed prototypes and navigation maps. The latter was an extension to RUP, which was made during method configuration. The method rationale in a navigation map is to discuss the navigation structure together with the end users, with the advantage of using a visual overview. The systems developers' intention was to create a navigation structure that felt natural for the end users. This was considered important for the success of the project since the PRS was built as a web application with no possibility of end user education.

During the systems development work it was possible to conclude that the method configurator had given the characteristics of the final artifact too much attention during configuration. It resulted in several challenges and problems during the actual project. First, the workload became distorted since differences existed in the development team members' COM+ experience. Finding a suitable division of the implementations issues became problematic at some stages. Second, the inexperience of COM+ caused a deployment problem. During installation an incorrect option was chosen for the synchronizing support of the installed COM+ components. It resulted in extremely high response times when performing searches in PRS. This flaw resulted in a change request, to improve the response time. Since this problem did not exist in the development environment, the development team compared the two environment settings and the problem was put right after a couple of hours. The occurrence of the deployment problem can be traced back to the situational method and the method configuration. The part of RUP that prescribes defining bill of deployment material had been omitted. The deployment was to be made by the development team, and therefore they found the material unnecessary. Subsequently, during method configuration none of the project members though that rationality resonance would be achieved for this part. However, the communication between team members on how to install the application could have been improved through a short installation instruction. Especially, since the experience of COM+ development differed between the team members. An installation instruction would have eliminated the ambiguity of which synchronizing support to choose.

Summarizing the systems development discussion we can conclude that, despite some minor problems, the PRS project was closed out on time and within budget. From a method configuration point of view it was possible to achieve rationality resonance between the use of use cases, prototypes and navigation maps on the one hand and the systems developers' and the end users' intention on the other hand. An indication of this is the development team who expressed that they found support in the situational method. Furthermore, PRS was found to contain the requested functionality during the acceptance test and as will be discussed in the next section this project has only had few change requests after deployment.

The End User Practice Layer

The PRS has now been operational for almost three years in the department's day-to-day business. During this period of time only two change requests have been issued (after the initial deployment problem). The first one contained a redesign of how the information about phone numbers and addresses was presented. Since the web application was structured into four layers, this change request only affected the presentation layer. Subsequently, it meant a redesign of the HTML content, and it was accomplished within one hour.

The second change request addressed how two search criteria could be combined in the public search engine. This request affected the layer that performed SQL-queries in the database and a minor change in the presentation layer. However, the structure of the retrieved data remained unchanged. The implementation of this change took about two hours.

The PRS transformed the situation with out-of-date information. However, the design decision to decentralize the function to update information has not been entirely satisfactory. The solution do not take into account employees how have low maturity of using computers or who just do not care if their information is correct or not. Still, it reduced the time spent on updating the register and it gave the opportunity to provide information on department's website, which had not been possible before. Furthermore, the distribution of paper versions of personnel information is almost gone. This information is instead provided through the website as public or private information. The latter requires password to access and is for internal department use only.

The public part of the system, which was publishing information on the web, has been exchanged during the last year. The reason was not improper fulfillment of requirements; rather this part of the system was replaced by a university wide system with the same functionality. The new system was part of the university's redesigned website which nowadays is implemented using a content management system. The parts of PRS that addressed the department's internal requirements are still in use.

The change of the problem situation on the end user practice layer has been considered successful, since the time spent on updating personnel information has been reduced while the relevance of the PRS data has increased. Furthermore, the amount of maintenance caused by PRS has been low. The two change requests discussed above have been considered as minor changes.

Conclusions

This paper is about a longitudinal evaluation of method configuration using Method for Method Configuration (MMC) in a systems development project. The evaluation concerns the Personnel Register System (PRS) project and how the delivered result has transformed the initial problem situation. The systems development method for this project was Rational Unified Process (RUP). Since PRS was a small systems development project it was considered a challenge to tailor the method to a supportive situational method.

The evaluation has been performed on three layers: the meta-layer, the systems development layer and the end user practice layer. On each layer the achievement of rationality resonance has been used as the evaluation criterion. Starting on the meta layer we focused the method rationale in MMC and how it supported method configuration actions to deliver a situational method. On the second layer, the rationale of the situational method was focused and how it supported delivery of the PRS. Finally, on the end user practice layer we looked into how the PRS changed the initial problem situation and how the situational method has affected maintenance.

Table 1 contains the lessons learned about the use of MMC. The table is divided into two columns; the leftmost contains the layers while the second column contains the lessons. MMC provided a useful focus when analyzing method parts to suppress, add or emphasize. The major problem that was found concerned the use of the method fragment concept. The use of this concept resulted in tracking related method fragments on different layers and between the process and product model on the same layer. As a solution a redesigned method component concept has been proposed and introduced into MMC. This concept has been reported on in Wistrand and Karlsson (2004).

Table 1. Lesson Learned from the three layers

Layer	Lesson Learned
Method Configuration	1. MMC contributed with a valuable focus while analyzing possibilities to achieve rationality resonance. 2. The layer structure in the method fragment concept is an efficient way to aggregate classifications. 3. The use of the method fragment concept results in tracking of related method fragments, resulting in time consumption and unnecessary risk of fragmented situational methods.
Systems Development	4. Rationality resonance is possible to achieve between prescribed method fragments and the team members intentions. 5. The project team members' experience is important input during method configuration.
End User Practice	6. Giving architectural issues priority in the situational method eased the burden during maintenance.

The project members found the delivered situational method supportive. Subsequently, MMC made it possible to achieve rationality resonance. Furthermore, the project was closed out on time and within budget. However, we can also conclude that the project members' experiences have to receive as much attention as the characteristics of final artifact. Method configuration should therefore be performed interactively with project members to construct a suitable situational method based on multi-perspectives. This can also improve project members' understanding of why parts of a method are included. The problem is to achieve this multi-perspective aspect at reasonable cost.

On the end user practice layer we found a satisfactory transformation of the original problem situation. An indicator is the low number of change requests and the time spent on maintenance. Consequently, the PRS project delivered a successful information system using a tailored version of RUP – a version tailored using MMC.

References

Archibald RD (1992) Managing High-Technology Programs and Projects. John Wiley & Sons, Inc., New York USA

Baekgaard L (2005) From Use Cases to Activity Cases, In: Fitzgerald B (ed) Action in Language, Organisations and Information Systems. Limerick, Ireland,

Brinkkemper S (1996) Method Engineering: Engineering of Information Systems Development Methods and Tools. Information and Software Technology, vol 38, no 4, pp 275-280

Dahlbom B (2002) The Idea of an Artifical Science. In: Nilsson GB (ed) Artifacts and Artificial Science. Almqvist & Wiksell International, Stockholm

Goldkuhl G (1999) The Grounding of Usable Knowledge: An Inquiry in the Epistemology of Action Knowledge. Linköping University, CMTO Research Papers 1999:03, Linköping, Sweden

Harmsen AF (1997) Situational Method Engineering. Doctoral Dissertation, Moret Ernst & Young Management Consultants, Utrecht, The Netherlands

Karlsson F, Ågerfalk PJ (2004) Method Configuration: Adapting to Situational Characteristics While Creating Reusable Assets. Information and Software Technology, vol 46, no 9, pp 619-633

March ST, Smith GF (1995) Design and Natural Science Research on Information Technology. Decision Support Systems, vol 15, pp 251-266

Mathiassen L (2002) Collaborative Practice Research. Information Technology & People, vol 15, no 4, pp 321-345

Rossi M (1998) Advanced Computer Support for Method Engineering: Implementation of Came Environment in Metaedit+. Doctoral Dissertation, University of Jyväskylä, Jyväskylä, Finland

Siau K, Rossi M (1998) Evaluation of Information Modeling Methods: A Review, Proc of the Thirty-First Hawaii International Conference on System Sciences, IEEE Computer Society Press, vol 5, pp 314-322

Stolterman E, Russo NL (1997) The Paradox of Information Systems Methods – Public and Private Rationality. In: The British Computer Society 5th Annual Conference on Methodologies. Lancaster England

Wistrand K, Karlsson F (2004) Method Components – Rationale Revealed. In: The 16th International Conference on Advanced Information Systems Engineering (CAiSE 2004). Riga Latvia

Yourdon E (1989) Modern Structured Analysis. Prentice-Hall, Englewood Cliffs NJ

Ågerfalk PJ, Wistrand K (2003) Systems Development Method Rationale: A Conceptual Framework for Analysis. In: Proc of the 5th International Conference on Enterprise Information Systems (ICEIS 2003). Angers France

Combining Project Management Methods: A Case Study of Distributed Work Practices

Per Backlund and Björn Lundell

University of Skövde, Sweden. (per.backlund, bjorn.lundell)@his.se

Introduction

The increasing complexity of information systems development (ISD) projects call for improved project management practices. This, together with an endeavour to improve the success rate of ISD projects (Lyytinen and Robey 1999; Cooke-Davies 2002; White and Fortune 2002), has served as drivers for various efforts in process improvement such as the introduction of new development methods (Fitzgerald 1997; Iivari and Maansaari 1998).

According to Evaristo et al. (2004) distribution can occur over various dimensions. In situations where ISD methods are to be combined the project management practices will be distributed over different methods, which constitute a matter of coordination. In this paper we focus on distribution over methods and work practices. Hence, we see that there is an inherent complexity in the case presented, which stems from the tension between the method as proposed and the method as used in the organisation (Lundell and Lings 2004).

According to Russo and Stolterman (2000) there is a bias in ISD research towards conceptual/normative studies as opposed to in-depth studies of the actual development process. This bias could be dealt with by carrying out studies of the actual use of ISD methods in empirical settings (Iivari and Maansaari 1998; Iivari 2002; Mustonen-Ollila and Lyytinen 2003). This paper presents a case, forming a study extended over a period of time, which characterises the problems associated with introducing and using a new ISD method. Such a study is feasible since it allows for a deeper understanding of work practices in their context. The result of the study is a set of emerging themes concerning method use.

Background

Project management is an essential issue in ISD (Rose 2001). Since some ISD methods actually contain a separate project management module we have chosen to focus our study on that area. According to Cooke-Davies (2002) and Turner and Muller (2003) the two most important elements of project performance are communication management and risk management. Risk management is also put forward as an important issue in many ISD methods (Cadle and Yeates 2001). Furthermore, Cooke-Davies (2002) emphasizes the human dimension of project success factors since it is humans that carry out every process and thus determine its adequacy. Thus, the introduction of new project management practices is about changing the work practices of people

There are several definitions of the term method (Lings and Lundell 2004). We note that the definition of Avison and Fitzgerald (2003) explicitly mentions project management. A method has a number of components which specify how a project is broken down into stages and what is carried out in each stage. It also specifies how projects should be managed, which people should be involved, and what support tools may be utilised.

It has been claimed that it is favourable to follow a set of best practices which are commonly used in industry (Rational 2002). These best practices are: develop iteratively, manage requirements, use component-based architectures, model visually, verify quality, and control changes to software.

Commercial methods are typically products including manuals, education and training, consultancy support, CASE tools, and different types of templates (Avison and Fitzgerald 2003). RUP is an example of a commercial method in the above terms. It consists of a number of best practices: develop iteratively, manage requirements, use component-based architectures, model visually, verify quality, and control changes to software (Rational 2002). In all, this may be described as a pragmatic view, i.e. use (commercially) proven approaches to software development.

Project management in RUP focuses on providing a framework for managing software-intensive projects; providing practical guidelines for planning, staffing, executing, and monitoring projects; and, providing a framework for managing risk. The management artefact[1] set includes a software development plan, a business case, and various plan and assessment documents.

---

[1] In RUP an artefact is defined as a piece of information that is produced, modified, or used, i.e. it is a tangible product of the project.

In a normal situation of method use, a combination of methods that suits the specific organisation has to be chosen (Nilsson 1999). This results in a distribution over methods and policies (Evaristo et al. 2004), which affects the work situation of the co-workers. Evaristo et al. (2004) describe the concurrent utilisation of methods pertaining to a waterfall life-cycle and an object-oriented life-cycle.

Research Approach and Context for the Study

The study was made at Volvo Information Technology, a company with approximately 4700 employees. The site where the study was conducted employs about 150 people. The reasons for Volvo Information Technology to adopt RUP as the main method in all new application development were: a need to deal with the more rapid changes of the customers' operations; a need for a global and common way of work; and, a need for a modifiable development process (Backlund et al. 2003).

The case was chosen by means of purposeful sampling. We utilise this strategy since a longitudinal study with close access to an organisation is necessary in order to study this type of research question. Hence, we have selected the case based on a long period of prior cooperation. The fact that the project was internal to the organisation made close organisational access and practical planning of the research easier.

The general aim of the project is to replace the numerous system registers in use with one general register, which will aid in making system maintenance more efficient. The project also has two organisational goals: to give the team members an opportunity to *use* RUP in a real project setting; and to *introduce* new technology and a new development tool.

In order to conduct the study of how methods are combined and utilized, one of the researchers followed a development project for six months using an ethnographical approach (Viller and Sommerville 2000; Williamson 2002), complemented by open interviews. One of the authors conducted data collection by observing project meetings and work sessions taking detailed field notes. In total, 15 development team meetings, 3 stakeholder meetings, and 2 tool workshops were attended to. During these sessions the number of participating stakeholders varied. For example: approximately 10 stakeholders participated in team meetings, whereas two stakeholders carried out pair programming sessions. We also had access to 2 versions of the project documentation. Furthermore, the observation data was complemented by informal discussions after each project meeting. In order to validate the field notes 4 interviews (60 to 90 minutes) were carried out with the core group of the project. The interviews were recorded and transcribed and the interviewees were given an opportunity to comment on the transcripts.

The data collected was content analysed (Patton 2002) to identify emerging concepts. These concepts were then organised into categories and a set of themes in order to achieve a better structure of the data. The emerging themes were also used to direct further searches.

The different objects of observation provide complementary views of how the development method was used in the project. Moreover, the different sources cater for source triangulation (Williamson 2002).

Method Combination at the Case Study Site

The following subsections will characterise the mapping between methods, the compatibility between the methods in use, and the utilisation of iterative work practices.

Method Mapping

There is a wide range of methods in use at the IT department. They must be related to each other in order to avoid redundancy and overlap. This is achieved in terms of formulating an explicit mapping between methods in the organisation.

There are several methods complementing RUP. For example there are in-house methods for project management, maintenance and configuration management, application support, quality assurance, and business engineering. The mapping between the different methods can be described in terms of method *structure mapping* and *document mapping*. Method structure mapping refers to how the internal catalogue structures of the methods relate to each other and document mapping refers to how concepts are related to each other in various document types, especially between document types originating from different methods.

Document mapping concerns how different documents are linked to each other. For example, the risk management document identifies the attributes used to describe a risk. The document study reveals one attribute, 'Roadmap of impact', which refers to a specific construct of roadmaps in the in-house module for project management.

Method Compatibility

The term compatibility can be used to describe how different methods fit together. Compatibility between methods is important in situations where an in-house method is to be combined with a new method (Nilsson 1999). One important aspect of the in-house project management method is the system of 'gates', which is a system of checkpoints in the in-house method. The fact that a road map roughly corresponds to the idea of phases in RUP has caused problems concerning compatibility between the in-house method and RUP, which has lead to a perception of the RUP project management set as superfluous. This becomes obvious in small projects with no or few iterations within each phase. The problem can be illustrated by the statement that there is an iteration plan which is more on paper than actually in use. As stated by the project manager, the iteration plan was perceived as adding little value to the actual work situation, even though it was considered an important artefact in the development case.

"I have written an iteration plan according to RUP. But, how shall I put it; it is more on paper than actually in use." (Project manager)

The document study reveals that only a limited part of the management artefact set from RUP is used. The iteration plan is the part of the management artefact set considered most valuable by the stakeholders.

According to the project manager the RUP management artefact set did not have a large impact on project management. This statement is supported by the fact that only a few of the RUP project management artefacts were used.

A closer inspection of the artefacts in use gives that a large part of the development case was duplicated from another project, which led to a situation where the artefact had to be revised throughout the project. The concept of development case is a central aspect in the project adaptation of RUP. Many authors, for example Kruchten (2002), emphasise the need for the adaptation of the development process to the specific project. The project specific process in RUP is described as a development case that provides an overview of the types of documents used in the project.

Iterative Practices

RUP suggests two iteration strategies: wide and shallow; and narrow and deep. The wide and shallow approach is recommended for inexperienced teams. Wide and shallow means that the entire problem domain should be analysed taking only the surface details into account. However, the wide and shallow approach is associated with some pitfalls (Rational 1999). In the case, we find that iterative work and iterative planning are cumbersome for many reasons since it is hard to estimate both the extent and time consumption of an iteration.

The small project scope did not actually call for advanced iteration planning. The project also had a low intensity in terms of hours spent, which resulted in modest progress over a long time period. The need and motivation for iteration planning was low and therefore iterative work was not explicitly applied as described by RUP. Nevertheless, much of the work achieved was iterative in that the team returned to artefacts developing them further, even though this was not explicitly planned.

"To work iteratively, that is something which is hard to grasp /.../ It is not easy for a project manager to control iterative work. Each iteration should end with some kind of release. /.../ An iteration should not only be a time slot where you work towards a deadline and then just go on. /.../ then you tend to go on where you stopped the last time. That is the hard part. In a sense you just move on. You do not rework" (Developer)

The in-house project management method and the project management workflow from RUP are to co-exist. However, there is no exact mapping between iterations and iteration planning in RUP and any specific concept in the in-house project management method.

"Well, the /in-house method for project management/ does not have iterations in exactly the same sense. You rather have road maps between the various gates /typically in the form of a system of check lists/. And that is where you do your planning. But so far, in this project, one iteration has corresponded to one road map. /.../ So, it is possible that you have better use for iteration planning in a project with more iterations. But when one iteration corresponds to one road map you do not really see the need. You rather do the planning for one road map and then you do the follow up. /.../ We have made a mapping so that, for example, the inception phase corresponds to the first road map." (Project manager)

Iterative planning makes better sense in large projects with several iterations in each phase. However, there is still the problem of mapping any concepts in use within different methods to each other.

Emerging Themes and Their Solutions in the Case

The case presented clearly shows the impact of distribution on project management practices in terms of the combination of methods. In the following subsections, a set of emerging themes from the case will be presented and analysed.

The Method Landscape

There is a problem in relating different methods in an organisation to each other. One effect of this problem is that there is a risk for redundant work and inconsistencies. In order to solve the problem of method combination it is vital to make sure that the different methods are explicitly related to each other. In order to ensure a more efficient cohesion the use of explicit connection points may be a good idea. These connection points should also cater for the translation of concepts that differ between the methods. The main characteristic is hence that the method landscape provides an overview of how the various methods in use relate to each other.

In a normal situation of method use, a combination of methods that suits the specific organisation has to be chosen (Nilsson 1999). Nilsson (1999) proposes two different ways of integrating methods: method chains and method alliances. According to Nilsson (1999) there are three directions in method engineering: method fragments, method components, and method integration. Method integration is an effort to combine methods within or along a whole life cycle. Hence, the method mapping in the case should be classified as a method integration effort. The strength of the method landscape is that it explicitly maps the different methods to each other. However, the problem of the exact mapping of low level concepts remains to be dealt with. The method landscape only provides an indication that this needs to be done. To summarize, the overview of methods is emphasised at the cost of the detailed concept level.

Combine Commercial and In-house Methods

In general commercial development methods, such as RUP, can be described in terms of public knowledge available to anyone who is willing to pay for it (Davenport and Prusak 1998). The ability to draw from such sources is a well known knowledge management problem. The analysis of this theme shows the importance of being able to assimilate the knowledge contained in a commercial method and make it a part of the organisational knowledge. It is this combination of external and internal knowledge that adds the competitive advantage.

According to Lyytinen and Robey (1999) externally acquired knowledge seems to add little competitive advantage since it is available to any competitor. On the other hand, Nilsson (1999) argues that established methods should be used since they are continuously refined and improved by method vendors. A critical evaluation of the concept of knowledge work (Alvesson 2001) illustrates that image is an important part of the perception of knowledge intensive organisations; being able to demonstrate that the organisation works according to a certain process may thus be considered as part of the image. Nevertheless, it is not sufficient to say that the work of professionals is only the direct application of a systematic body of formalised knowledge (Alvesson 2001). Rather, the 'Combine commercial and in-house methods' theme shows the advantage of being able to assimilate the knowledge contained in the commercial method by making it part of the organisational knowledge. Hence, the combination of external and internal knowledge constitutes a competitive advantage (Janz et al. 1997; Bell et al. 2002; Backlund 2004). However, we would like to emphasise that such an advantage is dependent on the way in which the combined method is effectively used in practice.

Iterative Work and Holistic Planning

The tension between iterative work and iterative planning illustrates some difficulties which need to be dealt with in project planning. Particularly, there is a problem in projects with low intensity since the work effort tends to be drawn out in time. Iteration planning becomes harder if a project is prolonged. It is often recommended that a new development method should be introduced in pilot projects or low risk projects. These types of projects are typically given a low priority in organisational planning which leads to a situation where the team members have to focus on other tasks (with higher priority) at the same time. One potential solution to this problem is to save time for intense work periods with a low frequency in calendar time instead of spending only a few hours at the time with a high frequency. This will facilitate the planning, implementation, and results of an iteration. However, this entails a risk. If the time that elapses between the working sessions becomes too long iterative work habits will be obstructed. That is, there is a tension between iterative planning and the implementation of iterative work habits that has to be dealt with. Madsen and Kautz (2002) report a similar problem associated with iterative work practices and conclude that it derives from the pressure of fixed contracts.

Holistic estimations are typically based on prior similar projects. The first lesson to learn is that there is a need to identify the known, rather then the unknown, which is difficult with limited experience. Cadle and Yeates (2001) refer to this as the analogy method. The analogy method is reliable but it depends on a knowledge base from which to draw. Consequently, holistic planning is problematic in new environments and when working according to new practices since the knowledge base is limited in terms of the new knowledge needed. Holistic planning thus became cumbersome in the case since it is problematic to obtain an overall view of the project when a new method is introduced as there is little experience from applying it.

Typically, planning an entire project calls for holistic planning approaches, which require more experience and are therefore harder to achieve when the team is new to a method. One potential solution to the problem is to use a well known planning approach to achieve the overall view of the project. The use of the new method will hence be restricted to subsections of the project until it has become internalised. This approach encourages the project to identify the known rather than the new to form a base for planning.

Discussion and Conclusion

In the case, we see that we do not only have to deal with factors concerning distributed environments in which a project takes place; we also have to deal with distribution of methods and work practices within the actual project. The latter becomes clear in distributed organisations when merging knowledge from different sources. These sources are the different methods that have to be combined when introducing new project management practices.

In our study there is evidence of stakeholder experiences to suggest that RUP has both benefits and drawbacks. For example, it seems to be problematic to combine low level concepts of road maps in the in-house method and iterations in RUP. According to Kruchten (2002, p. 703), RUP "is highly customizable to the needs of the adopting organization." However, our study provides evidence to suggest a lack of congruence in the underlying assumptions of the methods, specifically concerning differences between the two methods' process models. This may not be surprising in the light of previous criticism of RUP for its rigidity (Bygstad and Munkvold 2002). We expect such aspects to become even more accentuated when stakeholders engage in a geographically distributed development project.

The case shows that the contribution from RUP in terms of project management was limited in that the organisation only adopted three new artefacts concerning project management. This observation seems to be in line with the view of Lyytinen and Robey (1999) that externally acquired knowledge seems to bring limited competitive advantage. However, Nilsson (1999) claims that established methods should be used since they are continuously improved. To us, it is important to note that it is the way in which the new method can support effective work practices that is important for project success. The extent to which this is achieved through a mixture of influences is of secondary importance. In practice, this may be a balancing act between management push for increased process streamlining and stakeholder pull for support of work practice. To summarise, the issue of method transfer is a complex one (Lings and Lundell 2004).

The case shows that the introduction of an iterative work practice is hard since new methods are typically introduced in low prioritised pilot project. This implies that there is a limited need for advanced iterative planning. Kovács and Paganelli (2003) identify contingency risks and complexity of scope as two important factors to be addressed in project management. However, the way of reducing risk by reducing the complexity of project scope is counterproductive since it reduces the actual need for advanced iteration planning. Therefore, such behaviour will not fully test the new method's process model. On the other hand, this constitutes a reasonable way of dealing with the risk. In turn, this closely relates to the properties of holistic planning as being based on prior similar projects.

Iterative work practices are not truly tested in low priority projects. The case has shown a solution which proposes saving time for intense work periods with a low frequency in calendar time instead of frequent work in short time slots. The stakeholders perceived this as a feasible solution even though it may deviate from the intention of using rapid iterations in an application of RUP. It is unclear whether this adaptation of the process model constitutes an anticipated customisation by the organisation as envisaged by proponents of RUP (e.g. Kruchten 2002).

To summarise our findings, we stress the importance of taking a start in the work practice in terms of a method in use as opposed to method proponents' push for new methods. Any long term change in work practices has to be internalised by the stakeholders in the practical context of method use. Hence, the case study presented here adds to the body of knowledge which distinguishes between the method as used and the method as prescribed by its proponents.

Acknowledgements

This research has been financially supported by the Swedish Knowledge Foundation (KK-stiftelsen) and the European Commission via FP6 Coordinated Action Project 004337 in priority IST-2002-2.3.2.3 'Calibre' (www.calibre.ie).

References

Alvesson M (2001) Knowledge Work: Ambiguity, Image, and Identity. Human Relations, vol 54, no 7, pp 863-886

Avison D, Fitzgerald G (2003) Information Systems Development Methodologies, Techniques and Tools. Third ed. McGraw Hill New York

Backlund P (2004) An Analysis of ISD as Knowledge Work - an Analysis of How a Development Method is Used in Practice. Proc of the Thirteenth International Conference on Information Systems Development (ISD 2004) Advances in Theory, Practice and Education. Vilnius Lithuania.

Backlund P, Hallenborg C, Hallgrimsson G (2003) Implementing the Rational Unified Process - A Case of Knowledge Transfer. Proc of the 11th European Conference on Information Systems (ECIS 2003). Naples Italy

Bell DG, Giordano R, Putz P (2002) Inter-Firm Sharing of Process Knowledge: Exploring Knowledge Markets. Knowledge and Process Management, vol 9. no 1, pp 12-22

Bygstad B, Munkvold BE (2002) Software Engineering and IS Implementation Research: an Analytical Assessment of Current SE Frameworks as Implementation Strategies. In: Kirikova M et al (eds) Information Systems Development: Advances in Methodologies, Components, and Management. Kluwer New York

Cadle J, Yeates D (2001) Project Management for Information Systems. Financial Times Prentice Hall New York

Cooke-Davies T (2002) The "Real" Success Factors on Projects. International Journal of Project Management, no 20, pp 185-189

Davenport TH, Prusak L (1998) Working Knowledge: How Organisations Manage What They Know. Harvard Business School Boston Mass.

Evaristo JR, Scudder R, Desouza KC, Sato O (2004) A Dimensional Analysis of Geographically Distributed Project Teams: a Case Study. Journal of Engineering and Technology Management, vol 3, no 21, pp 175-189

Fitzgerald B (1997) The Use of Systems Development Methodologies in Practice: A Field Study. The Information Systems Journal, vol 7, no 3, pp 201-212

Fitzgerald B, Russo NL, Stolterman E (2002) Information Systems Development: Methods in Action. McGraw-Hill London

Iivari J (2002) The IS Core - VII Towards Information Systems as a Science of Meta-Artifacts. Communications of the Association for Information Systems, no 12, pp 568-581

Iivari J, Maansaari J (1998) The Usage of Development Methods: Are We Stuck to Old Practices? Information and Software Technology, vol 40, pp 501-510

Janz BD, Wetherbe JC, Davis GB, Noe RA (1997) Reengineering the Systems Development Process: The Link between Autonomous Teams and Business Process Outcomes. Journal of Management Information Systems, vol 14, no 1, pp 41-68

Kovács GL, Paganelli P (2003) A Planning and Management Infrastructure for Large, Complex, Distributed Projects - Beyond ERP and SCM. Computers in Industry, no 51, pp 165-183

Kruchten P (2002) Tutorial: Introduction to the Rational Unified Process. Proc of the 24th International Conference on Software Engineering

Lings B, Lundell B (2004) On Transferring a Method into a Usage Situation. In: IFIP Working Group 8.2 - IS Research Methods Conference - Relevant Theory and Informed Practice: Looking Forward from a 20 Year Perspective on IS Research. Kluwer Boston

Lundell B, Lings B (2004). Method in Action and Method in Tool: a Stakeholder Perspective. Journal of Information Technology, vol 19, no 3, pp 215-223

Lyytinen K, Robey D (1999) Learning Failure in Information Systems Development. Information Systems Journal, no 9, pp 85-101

Madsen S, Kautz K (2002) Applying System Development Methods in Practice - The RUP Example. In: Kirikova M et al. (eds) Information Systems Development: Advances in Methodologies, Components, and Management. Kluwer New York

Mustonen-Ollila E, Lyytinen K (2003) Why Organizations Adopt Information System Process Innovations: a Longitudinal Study Using Diffusion of Innovation Theory. Information Systems Journal, vol 13, pp 275-297

Nilsson AG (1999) The Business Developer's Toolbox: Chains and Alliances between Established Methods. In: Nilsson AG, Tolis C, Nellborn C (eds) Perspectives on Business Modelling Understanding and Changing Organisations. Springer Berlin

Patton MQ (2002) Qualitative Research & Evaluation Methods. Third ed. Sage Publications Thousand Oaks

Rational (1999) Rational Unified Process 5.1.1. Rational Corp

Rational (2002) Rational Unified Process. www.rational.com (Retrieved 04-08 2002)

Rose J (2001) Information Systems Development as Action Research in Soft Systems Methodology and Structuration's Theory Current. Ph.D. Thesis Lancaster University Lancaster

Russo NL, Stolterman E (2000) Exploring the Assumptions Underlying Information Systems Methodologies: Their Impact on Past, Present and Future ISM Research. Information Technology & People, vol 13, no 4, pp 313-327

Turner R, Muller R (2003) On the Nature of the Project as a Temporary Organisation. International Journal of Project Management, no 21, pp 1-8

White D, Fortune J (2002) Current Practice in Project Management - an Empirical Study. International Journal of Project Management, vol 20, pp 1-11

Viller S, Sommerville I (2000) Ethnographicaly Informed Analysis for Software Engineers. Int Journal of Human-Computer Studies, vol 53, pp 169-196

Williamson K (2002) Research Methods for Students, Academics and Professionals Information Management and Systems. Second ed. Centre for Information Studies Wagga Wagga

User Research Challenges in Harsh Environments: A Case Study in Rock Crushing Industry

Jarmo Palviainen and Hannele Leskinen

Institute of Software Systems, Tampere University of Technology, Finland. (jarmo.palviainen, hannele.leskinen)@tut.fi

Introduction

Rock crushing is an atypical part of process automation industry. Process automation deals with physical processes that are continuous in time and space and in which the product flows through the operations [3]. The typical areas of the industry are electricity generation and distribution, chemical manufacturing, fabrication of cloth, metal wire, paper etc. Normally these large scale systems are run by automation which is controlled in dedicated control rooms by well trained operators. At the quarries, there are often neither control rooms nor trained operators. In fact, the operators sometimes have no formal or informal training for their task except the help from their coworkers while they are working. In some market areas, the operators cannot even read. The operators are also not necessarily dedicated to operate the process and control the automation system, but to do other tasks and react to alarms and problems when they occur. Also, while most of process automation control is done indoors, this industry operates outdoors and may also have the automation system UI under normal weather conditions, leaving little chance for the operators to use paper and pen or paper manuals.

The level of knowledge of user needs as well designers' abilities to utilize knowledge in user interfaces development defines the level of end user satisfaction. Iterative human-centred methods can substantially help in eliciting and prioritising user requirements. It also increases understanding of users and gives in depth information about users' tasks. It is widely accepted that the methods like Contextual Design (CD) are beneficial in user interface development projects.

This case study was conducted in autumn 2004 for Finnish company Metso Minerals to develop a concept of a new user interface (UI) for the automation system of a cone crusher. The focus was to research the work in context and develop the UI that meets the needs of the end users. Contextual Design (CD), a well specified user centred design method was applied in this project.

The article presents challenges that special circumstances of user environment cause to contextual inquiries (CI) and how the collected user information influenced the UI development. The UI design ended at the concept level giving a base for the future development of UIs.

The design team consisted of people with various backgrounds. Two university researchers had expertise in usability, software engineering, and also some knowledge of automation. Metso Minerals' six design team participants had industrial design, maintenance and automation system design backgrounds. All the Metso Minerals employees had a history of several years in the business.

The Research and the Setting

The targets of this study were the cone crushers and their users. At the quarries, the crushers are used for making rock raw material for constructing. There is normally a minimum of three crushers and a screen either in a separate unit or combined with a crusher.

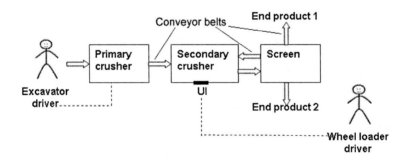

Fig. 1. An illustration of a mobile plant. Arrows describe the movement of rock material. At one site there can be multiple end products at one time. The UI that was designed in this project is located on the side of each crusher.

The crushers are used in stationary and mobile plants. At the stationary plants all the machines have stabile location and raw material is extracted at the site or transported to the quarry. At the mobile plants the whole crushing process consists of individual crushers and screens (see Fig 1). The whole work process starts from setting up the site at a quarry and ends with leaving to the next quarry.

The crushing process consists of tasks of choosing raw material (e.g. different types of stone) and changing the end product qualities (different end product target size and form). The form is not possible to be selected from some group of alternatives but it is a result of the nature of the process. The process includes support functions for the production and work, such as statistical follow-up on the end product amount and quality as well as machine maintenance and repair work.

The Users

The crushers have two types of users: the end users (the operators) and the maintenance people. The operators are willing to manage crushers operation only to some extent. They are controlling the end product quality and the crusher capacity. They are responsible for doing daily maintenance and repair work for machines if required. Maintenance people need the UI when locating and solving crusher related problems.

This research is focusing on studying the needs of the operators. This was considered necessary, because they have various levels of education. Typically their education is at an elementary school level. In the developing countries the users may not have reading skills. The operators may have to start using the machinery with limited training. In addition, the operators have to be able to use the machinery without instruction manuals because of the working conditions and safety of the work.

The operators' work is physically demanding and not always very rewarding, and therefore the labor turnover may be high. The attitude towards the work (e.g. using the safety helmets or avoiding dangerous places) varied a lot.

The Operator's Tasks

The operator's tasks are aligned with the foreman's goals. The high level goal is to achieve the maximum amount of end product at appropriate quality level. There are three types of tasks related to crushers. Firstly, controlling and optimizing the process, which affect crusher capacity (tonnages produced) and product quality. Secondly, diagnosing and fixing problem situations such as broken sensors or wires and thirdly maintaining the machines, for example changing the oil and the filters.

The operators have often a major role which is other than using the crusher(s). For example, at the quarry there may be

- the excavator driver who mainly drives the digger and is usually responsible for the functioning of the primary crusher,
- the wheel loader driver who mainly takes care of the secondary crusher,
- the foreman,
- the field worker who takes care of the crushers and the conveyer belts between them,
- the process controller (in bigger sites), who controls the process as a whole from the controlling 'tower' and
- sometimes there is also the quality controller, who measures the distribution of the different particle sizes in the end product.

Using the crusher UI is intermitted; interaction frequency is less than once an hour if everything is in control. Wrong qualities of the end product or problems in other parts of the system indicate problems in the crusher adjustments. If the crusher is broken or it is overloaded it is signalled to the operator with the alarm lights of the crusher. The operator leaves his other tasks and moves to the crusher to solve the problem situation.

Challenging User Environment

The quarries are dusty and noisy working places. Problem with dust and noise is greater at the mobile plants in which all the equipment and crusher UIs are outside than at the stationary plants where the process can be controlled partly or entirely from a control tower. Dust is fine and obscures the UI, especially when it is raining. Users typically wipe the UI with their hand to see it. Weather conditions vary a lot from cold and rain to boiling hot sunshine.

Because of high noise level ear plugs are required. The operators communicate often with hand signs. At one observation site the process controller in the control tower tried to catch attention of the field operator by irregularly changing the speed of the line feeder feeding rocks into to the crusher. At the visited sites there were no microphones or headsets used for communication. Besides the noise and dust the crushing process causes irregular vibration. Sometimes, due to heavy vibration, reading the UI or pressing a button may be even impossible.

It is not always possible to see the whole process from one spot but the process can be checked one machine at a time. At stationary plants there is a barrack or control tower where the process-controlling devices are located. These barracks have better working conditions such as lower noise level, less dust and no vibration. If there is a barrack the user has visibility at most of the end products and crushers and other equipment.

Fig. 2. Quarries are dusty and noisy working environment

Contextual Design – a Holistic Method for Human-Centred Design

The design team followed the CD process rather strictly. The way the method was altered in this case is explained at the end of this section. Contextual Design method defines a detailed human centred design process, which is illustrated in the figure 3. It also includes a set of communication tools for a development team, and the notations to be used in the process. The CD process is based on Contextual Inquiries, which are a collaborative interviews with the users in natural context of work combined with observation of natural work tasks. It is essential to observe real tasks derived from the users' real work.

There are five different graphical models introduced in CD: flow, sequence, artefact, cultural and physical model. These models are visual representations of what the team interprets based on the observations from contextual inquiries. The models are used as documentation and communication tools during the whole process.

The flow model describes the interactions between users and their co-workers and customers. The sequence model describes the users work and goals chronologically in detail. The artefact model catches the essential features of the documents and other physical or electronic means of transferring or transforming information. The cultural model profiles the policies and the culture of the workplace and the user population. The physical model describes the essence of the physical environment, for example,

270   Jarmo Palviainen and Hannele Leskinen

how computers, machines, and other tools are situated (see Figure 1. for a simplified physical model).

Depending on the focus of the project, some models can be omitted or left to minor consideration. For example, if the project is set to plan a new product it should be using the whole variety of tools offered by the method, but in a case the focus is on designing a single piece of the system, Beyer and Holtzblatt advise to start with only sequence and artefact models [4], [5].

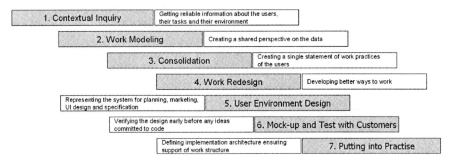

Fig. 3. The phases of the Contextual Design process [4]

After enough knowledge of the context has been gained the team can move on to consolidate the data gathered so far. Based on the data, the team constructs a new way of working, if necessary. How the new way of working is presented in the UI is designed in the phase called User Environment Design (UED). After UED, the team sketches user interface prototypes. Normally, the first ones are low-fidelity prototypes like paper prototypes, which are tested iteratively with the real users. The team handles the results from these tests and may add them into the models made earlier.

Finally, when the prototypes are good enough to meet the usability (and other) requirements of the project, the team plans how to proceed to make the product real (phase 7. Putting into practice in Figure 3.) This may include also planning how to make changes caused by the introduction of new work practices in the processes and even in organizations.

Applying the Contextual Design in the Project

In this case CD was followed until phase 7 (see Figure 3.). After the CIs work modeling was done and the models were consolidated. Work redesign and UED were created, which were good bases for prototyping and prototype testing.

Four inquiries were conducted and interpreted normally the day after the inquiry. The tasks which the users do most often were studied, and the users were observed and interviewed. The CIs were documented with a camcorder, a digital camera and notes were written at the site. Physical models were sketched at the site and artefact models were collected. After the inquiries and work modeling the design team had consolidating and work redesigning sessions and an affinity wall was formed.

Members of the design team read the affinity wall thoroughly and wrote notes and questions on it. The walkthrough took about four days since every member of the design team took turns and commented the previous notes and questions. After the walkthrough the design team had a judgement free visioning session to cultivate new ideas. The problems, possible ideas and improvements were listed on flap board papers. Then the design team discussed technical solutions, which could be used to implement new ideas and improvements. However there were also some ideas that were found almost impossible to solve with the existing knowledge of technical solutions. After brainstorming and analyzing the ideas, the design team revised project goals, documented new ideas for future use and then decided which issues to take into account in the new crusher UI. The UED was developed as a result of this phase.

The navigation model, which means the User Environment Design (UED), was designed on A3 paper with post-it notes. It was updated later during the prototyping phase. After the UED was constructed the team started to sketch UI prototypes.

The first prototype was sketched on A4-papers with a pencil. Later on prototypes were made with post-its, which was found more flexible. Three sessions were used for prototyping. The sessions were a mixture of testing and designing with the user. At the very end of the project also an electronic prototype was made with MS PowerPoint. It did not include all the views and operations of the intended UI, because during the project it was agreed to concentrate on those features which are needed most often. The electronic prototype was tested by two case company employees.

Findings and Results

Automation Design Issues

A typical user centred project would invest remarkably more time on finding an appropriate allocation of function between users and technology [2]. In this particular field the purpose is to automate whatever is possible though this is not usually a wise way to design an automation system.

However, at a quarry the operators are not supposed to control and monitor the machines continuously like in normal process control automation. In fact, they have other tasks to do e.g. driving the excavator or wheel loader.

The two occasions when a task is not automated are those when it is too expensive or when safety issues demand human intervention. For example, when the machine has stopped because of sudden failure of some sensor fault, it must be started manually even if the cause of the stoppage had disappeared by itself. Automatic start might cause human injury if someone is fixing the cause of the problem. Another example is the measuring of the end product (its size distribution) which cannot be done by the system fast and accurately enough though it would remarkably help in making real-time process control adjustments and getting exactly the kind of end product that is demanded. Thus, the operators need to actively control the quality of the end product and react upon it.

The cone crusher operators could use (and some do) the machinery without modern automation system, but it would mean lower productivity and higher rate of failures and maintenance costs. The observed and interviewed users were relatively satisfied with the current automation system. They managed to do the most important tasks they needed to do and the behaviour of the system was understandable enough. Still the design team knows that the operators would get more out of their equipment if they were using it to its full potential. The problem is that the users are not motivated to learn more than what is needed to do the basic operations. Therefore the new UI concept has to be very easy to learn, fast to use and it should lure the user into navigating it just to explore what it has to offer.

The UI Concept

The UI requirements were derived from the CIs and they were processed among the design team. A short survey on an old crusher revealed that terminology and navigation can be improved. The old UI had non-functional views in which it was possible only to navigate to other views. Also some functions, for instance starting and stopping the machinery, required a long navigation path before they could be used.

The navigation structure of the new UI concept is based on the CD method's UED. The UED effectively helped the team to remove hierarchical menu views from the concept and give meaningful and functional purpose for each UI view. Additionally, the findings from the context can be traced from the UI back to the CIs and in other words to the working context.

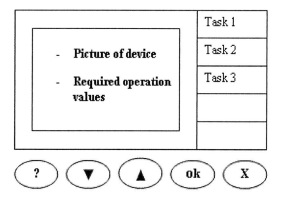

Fig. 4. The sketch of the main view. On the right side of the UI there are navigational buttons. And in the lower row there are stabile functional buttons

The most often needed features should be easy, simple and fast to use in order to accomplish work tasks conveniently. To keep the interface simple the information content of the views was kept in minimum. For instance in the main view of the UI only a simplified layout of machinery, the required devices-related operation values, navigation buttons and functional buttons were used. (Figure 4.) The navigation buttons were placed on the right side of the UI. These navigational buttons can be used to select work related task that the user is willing to accomplish. One of the buttons is Back in the right side. It is used in all the other views except the main view (See Figure 5.). Its function is to return back to the main view. The navigational buttons are based on the UED's grouping of work tasks. The functional buttons have fixed location and function in the lower row. The functional buttons are: Help (presented with ? symbol), decrease value (arrow up) and increase value (arrow down) OK and Cancel (X –symbol).

The design team also noted that the operators could memorize the most common pressing sequences. In fact they did not even look what was on the screen when they made some adjustments. This was taken into account and the required hand movements while pressing buttons to accomplish a certain work task were minimized. For instance it was noted that when the user selects a task to accomplish (such as reading of the log information) in the main view, he does certain subtasks more often than others. Therefore the mostly used subtask button was placed under the same button as the selection of the task in the main view.

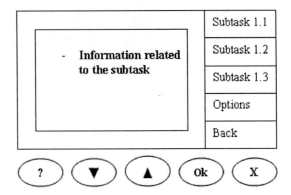

Fig. 5. The sketch of the subtask view. Tools related to the selected subtask can be shown by pressing Options or by pressing the button named according to the subtask. Back returns to the main view.

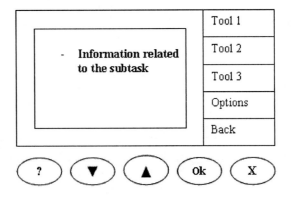

Fig. 6. The sketch of the tools related to a subtask

When the user has decided to do the subtask he typically wants to use some subtask-related tools to operate with the subtask-related information. For instance when reading the log he may want to sort the log according to time. To make usage straight forward, two alternative ways to accomplish the same selection were designed. First, pressing Options in the subtask view shows the selection of tools. Second, the user can press the button that has the name of the subtask to see the subtask related tools. (Figure 5.). Figure 6 shows the view containing the tools of a subtask.

In addition to previously described design issues also terminology was checked to match the terminology of the users. Some obscure terms were still used since they were more or less industry standards. Because of the working conditions the text has to be quite big to read. Long textual information was avoided, because it is not always possible to read it.

Survival Tricks for Contextual inquiry in Demanding Conditions

The quarries were noisy, which meant that voice was inaudible if the distance between people was greater than half a meter. There were typically 3-4 design team members present and only one of them was able to hear what the user was saying. The others made visual observations and the information was shared in a follow-up discussion in a quieter place. The user was asked to take a break when something happened that required some discussion. It is worthwhile to consider headsets and microphones for communicating,.

Practical issues should be taken into account when CIs are conducted in challenging work environments. Everyday things such as contact lenses and a pencil mayt not work because of the fine dust. The notes can be made on transparencies or paper in waterproof ink. This helps to cope with the dust and rain.

Even though some of the advice may seem self evident, we e.g. had to iterate the usage of the video camera several times before we were satisfied with the result. If you cannot afford expensive water and dust proof video equipment, then you have to protect your devices for instance with a plastic bag. The first videotaping failed because a nontransparent plastic bag was used to cover the camera and the cameraman pressed accidentally a button, which stopped the recording. The final version was better, since the transparent plastic bag was wrapped around the camera so that also the LCD screen on the side could be opened to check what was actually going to be recorded.

The presence of some application area specialists (e.g. the company members of the design team) was even more important than in more typical cases, because of the limited hearing and communication with the users. The researcher also needs to be prepared to spend hours without anything to study. The most fruitful times where at the beginning of the day and when the shift was changing.

Conclusions and Future Work

This paper described how the results of field studies gave input to the design of a new UI concept. Some advices are given how to conduct user research in harsh environments. Knowledge of work conditions and users and their motivations and backgrounds affects the UI and it can be designed to match contexts of use. Contextual inquiries are also very beneficial for the company participants, because they have opportunity to study users and machines and understand challenges that the users meet while working at quarries. The UED (also known as the navigation model) that is based on the data from the CD process phases improved the structure and navigation of the UI. In summary, contextual design method also gave structured way for UI concept development which made it possible for all the members of the design team to have influence on the design. Currently a product based on the concept UI is being developed.

It is necessary to find the most suitable usability testing and research methods for this particular application area where embedded systems, moving production machinery and heavy working conditions are present. A new study has just been started on the subject.

References

[1] Beyer H, Holtzblatt K (1998) Contextual Design: Defining Customer-Centered Systems. Morgan Kaufmann Publishers Inc, San Francisco CA
[2] ISO 13407:1999. Human-Centred Design Processes for Interactive Systems
[3] Sheridan TB (2002) Humans and Automation: System Design an Research Issues. John Wiley & Sons Inc, New York
[4] Beyer H, Holtzblatt K (1999) Contextual Design. Interactions, vol 6, Issue 1 Jan/Feb 1999, pp 32-42. Periodical-Issue-Article, ACM Press NY USA
[5] Holzblatt K, Wendell JB, Wood S (2005) Rapid Contextual Design: A How-To Guide to Key Techniques for User-Centered Design. Elsevier San Francisco

Scenarios for Improvement of Software Development Methodologies

Damjan Vavpotič, Marko Bajec and Marjan Krisper

Faculty of Computer and Information Science, University of Ljubljana, Slovenia. (damjan.vavpotic, marko.bajec, marjan.krisper)@fri.uni-lj.si

Introduction and Background

In recent years many initiatives to improve a use of formal software development methodologies (SDM) in organisations have been commenced, nevertheless not many successful. Different studies show that many software development organisations do not own a formal SDM, and only a fraction of organisations that own a formal SDM actually follow it [2, 5, 13, 14].

An important cause for SDM non-adoption is that SDM are not attuned to actual organisation and project needs [3, 4, 5, 6, 10, 11, 13, 15, 17]. E.g., SDM prescribe inappropriate techniques and methods; SDM are too rigid and cannot be adapted to specific project demands; etc. Another reason for non-adoption is SDM do not fit specific social and cultural characteristics of a development team and an organisation [4, 7, 8, 9, 11, 13]. E.g., it is difficult to introduce rigorous SDM into organisations having liberal culture; non-innovative development team will probably reject innovative SDM; etc.

Therefore we believe that each SDM should be considered from two different dimensions: the SDM technical suitability for a given project; and its social suitability for a given development team.

To this end, our work merges efforts from two research areas, method engineering research dealing with technical aspects of SDM construction, and diffusion and adoption of software process innovation research, which covers social aspects of SDM adoption. The aim of method engineering is to construct SDM from a methodology components or fragments. Especially important is situational method engineering that deals with construction of a methodology adapted to a certain project [3, 12, 17]. While method engineering considers every possible technical aspect of SDM construction, it almost completely omits social aspects of its users. To obtain a clear picture of SDM value we also have to consider a research area explaining SDM (non)adoption in software development organisations. It is based mainly on Rogers' diffusion of innovations theory (DOI) that tries to explain why certain innovations spread among their target users and others do not [19]. Researchers in this field consider a SDM as an innovation and try to predict/explain its (non)adoption i.e. to explain target adopter attitudes and their innovation-related behaviour [7, 16, 20].

The first part of the paper briefly introduces a SDM evaluation model. A more detailed description of the evaluation model can be found in [21] (Sect. SDM evaluation model). Using the results of the evaluation model we create suitable scenarios for SDM improvement. The paper focuses on different types of the scenarios and rules for their selection. The paper also presents different strategies that can be used to create the scenarios (Sect. Scenarios and strategies for SDM improvement). The last part of the paper discusses practical application of the evaluation model and the improvement scenarios in a software development organisation (Sect. Practical application).

SDM Evaluation Model

The SDM evaluation model is intended for organisations that do not follow to their SDM completely or not at all. The model enables such organisations to evaluate the suitability of their SDM according to two dimensions. The first dimension is SDM technical suitability. It tells how appropriate the SDM is in technical manner – is the SDM suitable to typical projects that the organisation is taking or to its technical characteristics? (The measurement of this dimension is based on situational method engineering). However, developers would not necessarily adopt even technically efficient and refined SDM. To introduce SDM successfully we must also consider social and cultural characteristics of a development team [18, 20]. SDM social suitability forms the second dimension. The social suitability tells how appropriate the SDM is according to social and cultural characteristics of the development team. These characteristics help to determine the level to which the SDM has been adopted in a certain development team. But again, even if socially appropriate for a given team it is not necessary that the SDM will also technically suit to projects undertaken by the team.

Furthermore, we argue that it is important not only to consider SDM as a whole, but also as a constitution of interconnected elements. We define a SDM element as a constituent part of the SDM and specially focus on SDM elements that can be formalised. The most common SDM elements

that can be formalised include activities, phases, workflows, roles, artefacts, techniques, templates, guidelines, recommendations, etc. [3, 14] An
important advantage when evaluating single SDM element in contrast to
the evaluation of a SDM as a whole is that we get much clearer picture on
which SDM elements are technically sound and well adopted, which elements need readjustments whether technical or social and which elements
should be replaced. Another important advantage when evaluating a single
SDM element is that we can precisely pinpoint the user of the element and
evaluate whether he or she adopted the element or not.

The SDM evaluation model is shown in Fig. 1. It helps to evaluate simultaneously each of the SDM elements according to its technical (horizontal dimension) and social suitability (vertical dimension). Based on this
model four different types of the SDM elements can be distinguished. In
Fig. 1, each of the four element types is positioned in a separate quadrant.

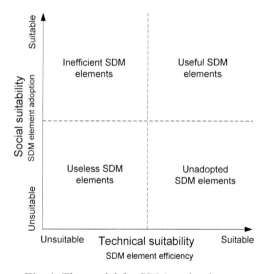

Fig. 1. The model for SDM evaluation

An important part of the evaluation model is also a set of improvement
scenarios that tell how specific elements that are found technically or socially unsuitable can be changed. We expect that using these scenarios a
majority of the less suitable SDM elements can be improved (see Fig. 2),
though some of the elements might still need further improvements or replacement (grey SDM elements in Fig. 2). We intend to use the model iteratively, i.e. after application of improvement scenarios new evaluation
cycle would start and each SDM element would be evaluated again. Itera-

tive approach is especially important since the modifications of a SDM might have side effects, such as some of the previously suitable elements become less suitable in the improved SDM.

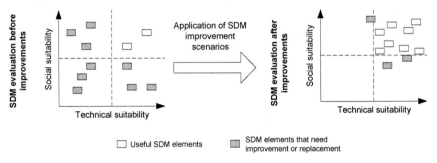

Fig. 2. Improvement of SDM using the evaluation model

Scenarios and Strategies for SDM Improvement

Scenarios for SDM Improvement

The goal of the SDM improvement scenarios is to advise proper actions to improve SDM elements. We distinguish between two types of improvement scenarios:

- The scenarios for improving the adoption of SDM elements: the goal of these scenarios is to improve SDM adoption without having to change the SDM formal description i.e. to persuade the potential adopters to use SDM elements in their existing form.
- The scenarios for improving the SDM elements: these scenarios do not prescribe any step for the introduction of SDM elements. Their purpose is to change the SDM elements themselves to become more suitable for a given development team and/or project. These scenarios are usually used in a combination with the aforementioned adoption scenarios. They can be divided into two sub-types: the scenarios for improving social acceptability and the scenarios for improving technical acceptability of a SDM. The former scenarios adapt SDM elements to follow users' ideas, needs and knowledge. The primary goal of these scenarios is to make the SDM more socially acceptable, but still retain its technical efficiency. The latter scenarios, on the other hand, focus on technical aspect and adapt the SDM elements so that they become more technically suitable for a given organisation and its projects. The main purpose of these

scenarios is to make SDM technically efficient, but preserve its social acceptability.

To select the most suitable (sub)type of the improvement scenario we have to consider the situation of SDM element. One part of the situation is defined by technical and social evaluation of SDM already discussed in the previous sect. Another part of the situation is defined by an additional dimension of changeability that can be divided further into the changeability of a SDM element and the changeability of potential element users. Our definition of changeability is based mostly on research trying to define suitable strategies for IT innovation implementation [1, 19, 20].

- The changeability of a SDM element is defined as a level of difficulty to make changes to a certain SDM element. To determine SDM element changeability we consider the complexity of the SDM element introduction into the target group of users (number of people and on the number of different organisation units that have to adopt the new SDM element), SDM element transferability (i.e. how difficult is it to present the element to the potential adopter and convince him to adopt it), SDM element divisibility (defines whether the element can be introduced by parts or only as a whole), and element technical complexity (i.e. how difficult is it so make changes to the element from technical point of view). E.g. it is easier to convince a smaller number of potential adopters to use a SDM element than a larger number as each of them presents a potential adoption barrier; an element that forms SDM core can be changed only to a minimal extent or not at all; etc.
- The changeability of the potential users delineates the level of difficulty to convince users to utilize a certain SDM element. It depends mostly on SDM users' characteristics (innovativeness, willingness to learn, willingness to cooperate etc.) and organisation's characteristics (organisation culture, management support, possibility of new employments etc.) E.g. it is difficult to train users unwilling to cooperate and learn; when possibility of new employments exists one might choose to employ experts to fill the gaps in the development team proficiency; etc.

The complete evaluation of the SDM element situation enables us to select an appropriate (sub) type of improvement scenario. For the purpose of our research we developed a decision model that fosters the selection of the most suitable scenario (sub)type (see Table 1).

In a case of a technically inefficient SDM element the only suitable scenario type is the improvement of element's technical efficiency. It is rational to improve the adoption and acceptability of technically efficient elements only. The elements that are technically efficient and socially adopted do not need any improvement so the remaining scenarios are intended for technically efficient but unadopted SDM elements. In this case we consider the scenarios for improvement of element adoption and/or acceptability; the selection depends on the dimension of changeability as shown in the table.

Table 1. The Selection of the most suitable scenario type

Technical efficiency	Social adoption	Changeability of SDM element	Changeability of potential users	Most suitable scenario (sub)type
Unsuitable	-	-	-	Technical efficiency
Suitable	Unsuitable	Low	Low	Acceptability, Adoption
Suitable	Unsuitable	Low	High	Adoption
Suitable	Unsuitable	High	Low	Acceptability
Suitable	Unsuitable	High	High	Adoption, Acceptability
Suitable	Suitable	-	-	not needed

The next step is to choose a suitable introduction strategy for adoption improvement scenarios or a suitable improvement strategy for efficiency and acceptability improvement scenarios.

SDM Element Introduction Strategies

In the case of the adoption improvement scenarios the most suitable introduction strategy for a new or an unadopted SDM element has to be selected. We use the following strategies:

- **Support** is a passive strategy that offers information about SDM elements to all potential adopters. It does not prescribe the use of the elements but merely gives the potential users an opportunity to recognise the benefits of use. Users are given an opportunity to informally use and experiment with SDM elements. It is their decision whether to adopt the elements or not.
- **Advocacy** is a more active strategy. A group of pilot users is formed where the use of SDM elements is prescribed. The group is offered appropriate training and support. Members of the pilot group are mostly innovative individuals willing to cooperate. After the elements are adopted by the pilot group members it becomes their responsibility to foster the adoption among other potential users.

- **Total commitment** is best described as simultaneous use of support and advocacy strategies on the entire population of potential adopters. This strategy performs best when the company is completely convinced of certain SDM elements benefits and is prepared to provide all needed resources to encourage their adoption.
- **Combined strategies** are formed of support and advocacy strategies. There are two types of combined strategies: ones that first employ the support strategies and later on the advocacy strategies; and ones that first employ the advocacy strategies and later on the support strategies.

Table 2. The selection of a suitable introduction strategy

Potential adopter's innovativeness	Complexity of SDM element introduction	SDM element type	Most suitable strategy
Non-innovative	Simple	Tool	Advocacy
Non-innovative	Simple	Process	Total commitment
Non-innovative	Complex	Tool	Combined: Support followed by Advocacy
Non-innovative	Complex	Process	Total commitment
Innovative	Simple	Tool	Support
Innovative	Simple	Process	Combined: Support followed by Advocacy
Innovative	Complex	Tool	Combined: Advocacy followed by Support
Innovative	Complex	Process	Combined: Advocacy followed by Support

The decision model (see Table 2) that helps us to choose a proper introduction strategy is based on the model proposed by Agarwal [1]. To select an appropriate introduction strategy the model considers the following criteria: level of potential adopters' innovativeness, the complexity of SDM element introduction and the SDM element type – *a tool* or *a process*. The first two criteria have been discussed in the previous sect. as they are used to determine the changeability also. To determine SDM element type we have to consider elements' influence on users' behaviour and the way they perform their work. SDM elements that have greater influence can be considered as *process* elements (e.g. activities, techniques, program languages, complex tools, etc.). More simple SDM elements (e.g. artefacts, simple tools, simple programming standards etc.) can be considered as *tool* elements. The introduction of process elements requires higher level of commitment compared to introduction of tool elements.

SDM Element Improvement Strategies

To define appropriate scenarios for improving of the technical efficiency or acceptability of the SDM elements we propose the following strategies:

- **User participation** is a strategy that anticipates active cooperation of technically advanced users. Based on their knowledge and experience SDM element improvements are formed. A positive side effect of this strategy is a faster adoption of new or renovated SDM elements by users who participated in their creation [19].
- **Expert knowledge** is a strategy which uses external knowledge (experts, research, literature etc.) to form improvements. The users of a SDM are not involved in the creation of improvements as they do not have enough knowledge or are not willing to participate.
- **Collaboration** is a simultaneous use of user participation and expert knowledge strategies. It is useful especially in cases when the potential users of a SDM element do not have enough knowledge but have some experience and are willing to participate in the improvement of the element. The involvement of users has a positive effect on the adoption.

Table 3. The selection of a suitable improvement strategy

Experi. and knowl. of SDM	Experi. and knowl. in SW development	SDM element type	Most suitable strategy
Inexperienced	Inexperienced	Unprepared	Expert knowledge
Inexperienced	Inexperienced	Prepared	Collaboration
Inexperienced	Experienced	Unprepared	Expert knowledge
Inexperienced	Experienced	Prepared	Collaboration
Experienced	Inexperienced	Unprepared	Expert knowledge
Experienced	Inexperienced	Prepared	Collaboration
Experienced	Experienced	Unprepared	Collaboration
Experienced	Experienced	Prepared	User participation

To select the most suitable improvement strategy we consider the potential users' experience and knowledge in the field of SDM and in the field of software development. We also consider users' preparedness to cooperate in the creation of SDM improvements. In a case experienced users are willing to cooperate, collaboration and user participation strategies are recommended. When users are unwilling to cooperate the strategy of expert knowledge should be employed. Table 3 shows the decision model that helps us choose an appropriate strategy.

Practical Application

The evaluation and improvement model described in this paper was tested in a company that develops software in an object-oriented way. The company uses its own SDM which was specifically tailored to the organisation's needs. The SDM contains 137 elements, which represent basic units for the evaluation. The SDM is relatively non-prescriptive/non-rigorous and is stored in a web-based form so that users can access SDM easily through organisation's intranet.

To gather the required data for the evaluation, a survey among potential users of SDM was conducted. The survey compounded of three parts: the first one concerning methodology social adoption, the second one concerning methodology technical efficiency and the third one concerning a user profile.

Two groups of users were formed that completed different parts of the survey. The first group consisted of all potential users of the SDM. Their task was to evaluate their personal adoption of each SDM element that related to typical roles they had in the company's projects. E.g. analysts had to evaluate all SDM elements related to the analysis, system administrators had to evaluate all elements related to the system administration etc. The second group were advanced users, i.e. experts in a certain field of software development. Their task was to evaluate the technical efficiency of each SDM element. E.g. advanced analysts evaluated technical efficiency of all SDM elements related to the analysis etc.

We received 225 answers, 2 SDM elements remained completely unevaluated. As we discovered later these 2 elements were dealing with database administration, that nobody of the survey participants felt responsible for. Remaining 135 elements were evaluated as follows: 81 were evaluated by both dimensions, 54 were evaluated only by dimension of social adoption. These 54 elements remained partially unevaluated as we could not identify advanced users who would be able to competently evaluate their technical efficiency.

Fig. 3 shows results of the evaluation. Points on the diagram indicate SDM elements. The vertical position represents element's social adoption and the horizontal position element's technical efficiency. Larger size of a point indicates that more elements have the same position (same evaluation).

Two different approaches are used to position an element in the diagram. The first one (left diagram in Fig. 3) is to compute the average of all evaluations for certain SDM element made by different users and position the element accordingly. The second one (right diagram in Fig. 3) is to take only the worst evaluation i.e. to consider only the most dissatisfied user of a certain SDM element. The latter approach is more rigorous as it enables us to identify all improvement opportunities. Using the results of the evaluation we can exactly pinpoint weak SDM elements that need improvement.

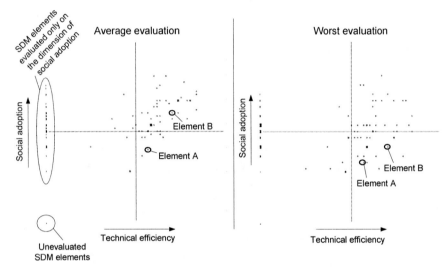

Fig. 3. The evaluation of the organisation's SDM

To explain how to use the results of the evaluation model we will focus on a single SDM element (marked as Element A in Fig. 3). Element A is an artefact in the organisation's SDM. It is a document that shows the logical structure of the system. The following steps demonstrate how to improve Element A using the SDM evaluation model, introduction scenarios and introduction strategies.

1. Element A is evaluated as rather efficient but unadopted. Therefore we could choose either a scenario for improvement of acceptability or a scenario for improvement of adoption (see Table 1). To select one of the two possible scenario types we have to consider the changeability. We evaluate the changeability of the element as high and the changeability of the users as middle. Therefore the primary goal of the scenario should be improvement of the acceptability.
2. It was determined (based on users profiles) users are experienced in software development, but rather inexperienced in SDM and semi-prepared to cooperate. We choose collaboration strategy (see Table 3).

3. Next we consider users proposals for the element improvement. They suggest the element should be simplified since only parts of the element are used. Therefore we form a simplified version of Element A.
4. Finally we recommend the most suitable adoption strategy for the improved Element A. Since potential users are semi-innovative, the element is relatively simple, and its type is a tool we recommend support strategy. Description of the improved element should be accessible to the potential users and they should be noted that an improved version of the element is available.

Similar steps are used to create improvement scenarios for every SDM element that requires improvement. The most problematic is the creation of improvement scenarios for SDM elements that lack the evaluation of technical efficiency. The lack of technically competent users requires technical evaluation to be done by experts. Another problem pose SDM elements, whose evaluations vary considerably (see Element B in Fig. 3) i.e. where a great difference between the worst and the average evaluation exists. This might indicate a diversity of users' needs and/or knowledge. Such elements call for further investigation that in some cases might result in two or more versions of the element adapted to different needs of the users.

Summary and Conclusion

The paper presents an approach to evaluate and improve SDM technical suitability and social adoption in software development organisations. Simultaneous use of the evaluation model and improvement scenarios provides a comprehensive tool for SDM improvement.

We believe the presented approach has a strong potential, but we are also aware that it cannot be used in every software development organisation. Firstly, the organisation must own a formal SDM suitable for adaptation and improvisation, and secondly, SDM users must be willing to participate in SDM evaluation and creation since the application of the approach is based on the user involvement.

References

[1]   Agarwal R, Tanniru M, Wilemon D (1997) Assimilating Information Technology Innovations. IEEE Transac. on Eng. Manag, vol 44, no 4, pp 347-358

[2]   Avison D, Fitzgerald G (2003) Information Systems Development: Method-
      ologies, Techniques and Tools. Third Edition. McGraw-Hill New York
[3]   Brinkkemper S, Saeki M, Harmsen F (1999) Meta-Modelling Based Assem-
      bly Technology for Situational Method Engineering. Information Systems,
      vol 24, no 3, pp 209-228
[4]   Cockburn A (2002) Agile Software Development. Addison-Wesley
[5]   Fitzgerald B (1998) An Empirical Investigation into the Adoption of System
      Development Methodologies. Information & Management, vol 34, pp 317-
      328
[6]   Fitzgerald B, Russo NL, O'Kane T (2003) Software Development: Method
      Tailoring At Motorola. Communications of the ACM, vol 46, no 4, pp 64-70
[7]   Gallivan MJ (2001) Organizational adoption and assimilation of complex
      technological innovations. ACM SIGMIS Database 32(3): 51-85
[8]   Gallivan MJ (2003) The Influence of SW Developers' Creative Style on their
      Attitudes to and Assimil. of a SPI. Information & Management, vol 40, pp
      443-465
[9]   Green GC, Collins RW, Hevner AV (2004) Perceived Control and the Diffu-
      sion of SPI. Journal of High Technology Management Research, vol 15, no
      1, pp 123-144
[10] Henderson-Sellers B (2003) Method Engineering for OO Systems Develop-
      ment. Communications of the ACM, vol 46, no 10, pp 73-78
[11] Highsmith J (2000) Adaptive SW Development. Dorset House Publishing
[12] Hofstede HA, Verhoef TF (1997) On the Feasibility of Situational Method
      Engineering. Information Systems, vol 22, no 6/7, pp 401-422
[13] Huisman M, Iivari J (2002) The Individual Deployment of Systems Devel-
      opment Methodologies. Lecture Notes in Computer Science. Springer 2348,
      pp 134-150
[14] Huisman M, Iivari J (2003) Systems Development Methodology Use in
      South Africa. Proc of the Ninth Americas Conf on Information Systems
[15] Miller G (2001) Sizing up Today's Light. SW proces. IT Professional, vol 3,
      pp 46-49
[16] Niazi M, Wilson D, Zowghi D (2003) A Maturity Model for the Implementa-
      tion of SP Improvement: An Empirical Study. JSS (in press, online dec 2003)
[17] Ralyte J, Deneckere R, Rolland C (2003) Towards a Generic Model for Situ-
      ational Method Engineering. Proc of the 15th ICAISE
[18] Riemenschneider CK, Hardgrave BC, Davis FD (2002) Explaining Software
      Developer Acceptance of Methodologies: A Comparison of Five Theoretical
      Models. IEEE Transactions on SW Engineerin, vol 28, no 12, pp 1135-1145
[19] Rogers ME (2003) Diffusion of Innovations. Free Press New York
[20] Sharma S, Rai A (2003) An Assessment of the Relationship between ISD
      Leadership Characteristics and IS Innovation Adoption in Organizations. In-
      formation & Management, vol 40, pp 391-401
[21] Vavpotič D, Bajec M, Krisper M (2004) Measuring and Improving SDM
      Value by Considering Technical and Social Suitability of its Constituent Ele-
      ments. Proc of the 13th ISD. Vilnius Lithuania

Managing the Collaborative Networks Lifecycle: A Meta-Methodology

Ovidiu Noran

School of Information and Communication Technology, Griffith University, Australia. O.Noran@griffith.edu.au

Introduction

The benefits of using various forms of Collaborative Networks (CNs) to create agile virtual organisations (VO), shop floors and laboratories, or to bring together professionals worldwide in virtual communities are commonly acknowledged in both academia and industry. Currently however, the existing CN knowledge is scattered and overlapping; this is a transitional phase in the maturing of the CN domain and its evolution towards a proper discipline. The progress of the CN research domain (and its practical applications) relies upon the structuring of relevant knowledge into a consistent framework that conveys an unambiguous and agreed-upon collaborative paradigm. The methodological aspect of this integration effort can be significantly supported by the creation of a high-level artefact, able to express and manage existing and emerging knowledge related to the creation and operation of various CN types and their concrete manifestations. The proposed artefact could take the form of a 'to-do list on how to create methods' (thus, a meta-methodology) for specific enterprise architecture (EA) tasks or task types, which typically include the information system (IS) supporting the business.

This paper attempts to summarize the cyclic and reflective action research (AR) that has resulted in the establishment of a meta-methodology prototype for CNs and their specific materialisations. Thus, a brief description of the research question, strategy and design is followed by concise narratives of iterations of the main research cycles that have tested, reflected on, and refined the meta-methodology concept. Subsequently, the paper describes the meta-methodology content evolution during the research life cycle, resulting in a last refinement leading to a working and useful meta-methodology prototype. The paper closes with conclusions on the research performed and with a description of proposed further work.

Meta-methodology Primer

Research Question, Strategy and Design

The main research question of this extensive study was whether a step-by-step method describing the lifecycles of CNs and their manifestations can be built, and what factors influence such an attempt. This topic has provided an opportunity to employ Action Research (AR) (Galliers 1992; Wood-Harper 1985), which allows for practical problem solving and for theory generation and testing (Eden and Chisholm 1993; McKay and Marshall 2001). The practical problem was how to set up CNs and then swiftly create VOs addressing business opportunities requiring competencies unavailable in any single CN participant. The theory generation and testing aspect related to the proposed meta-methodological artefact and the theoretical model adopted: ISO/IS 15704 Annex A: 'Generalised Enterprise Reference Architecture and Methodology' (GERAM) (ISO/TC184 2000).

The research strategy adopted was based on the cyclic and reflective AR concepts described in Checkland's (1991) and McKay and Marshall's (2001) work, with two main cycles involving simulation, field experiments and reflections leading to conceptual work for theory extension. Triangulation was to be used after iterations to check the validity of the results. The critical literature review performed in the research preparation (Noran 2003a) has created an essential deliverable component, i.e. a Structured Repository (SR) of Architecture Framework (AF) elements.

Initially, the researcher saw himself as a facilitator in an anti-positivist stance, guided by an interpretivist paradigm, seeing humans as voluntaristic and organisations as dynamic entities; however, this position was adapted to suit the EA research domain. Thus, the researcher position changed to being a facilitator and a systems expert (Burrell and Morgan 1979; Hirschheim and Klein 1989). A complete research strategy description is beyond the scope of this paper; see (Noran 2004b), (Noran 2004d).

Initial Meta-methodology Concept

Step 1: Identify entities relevant to the specific enterprise engineering task.

Step 2: Construct a business model showing these entities and their relations in the context of their life cycles.

Step 3: 'Read' the life cycle diagrams of the entities to be designed (e.g. CN) phase by phase, noting the relations of each phase with phases of other entities and constructing a list of activities expressing these relations.

These steps can be traced in the final meta-methodology (Figure 1).

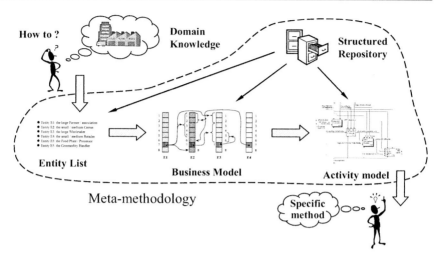

Fig. 1. The meta-methodology concept

The Main Research Cycles

Simulation

The EA area of research involves substantial test turn-around times; thus, such tests must be carefully prepared. The concepts to be tested in the field must be mature, so as to obtain meaningful and potentially convergent results. This can be achieved by simulation, although typically the models thus obtained can only be checked for internal validity (Trochim 2000).

The preliminary meta-methodology prototype has been used to simulate the creation of models for the setup and operation of a virtual transport enterprise called Fresh Produce Virtual Integrated Transport Enterprise (FP-VITE), using an existing reference model (RM) (Chalmeta 2000) and common AF elements. The simulation has applied the steps previously described, producing a list of relevant entities, a business model (Figure 2) and a functional model containing types of activities involved in the life cycle of FP-VITE (Figure 3).

The formalism used in the business model reflects the life cycle view of the modelling framework (MF) belonging to GERA (the reference architecture used in the research, which is a part of GERAM), which allows representing relations between life cycle phases of the relevant entities. The IDEF0 (Integration DEFinition for Function Modelling (NIST 1993)) formalism used in the functional model (Figure 4) controls model consistency and complexity and assists process understanding by showing activity inputs, outputs, controls and required resources. IDEF0 is a functional language belonging to the IDEF family (Menzel and Mayer 1998), equivalent in expressiveness to UML Activity Diagrams (Noran 2003b))

This simulation has validated the applicability of the meta-methodology concept, refined its content and has uncovered some problems as further described. Other details of this simulation are described in (Noran, 2004b).

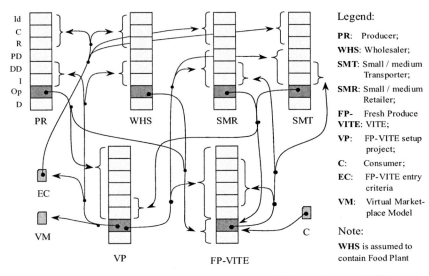

Fig. 2. Business model showing life cycle relations (Noran 2004b)

A First Field Test / Case Study

In this real scenario, the application of the meta-methodology has yielded a design (and partly operation) method for a CN called Service Network Organisation (SNO) and the Service Virtual Enterprises (SVEs) created by this CN (Hartel et al. 2002).

The CN lead partners wished to retain control of the identification and concept phases of the SVEs life cycle, with the rest covered by the CN (see Figure 4).The audience was partly familiar with the IDEF family and with an RM developed by the Globemen consortium (Global Engineering and Manufacturing in Enterprise Networks (Globemen 2000-2002)) using a specialised version of the GERA MF called VERA (Virtual Enterprise Reference Architecture described in Tølle et al. (2002)).

The application of the modified set of meta-methodology steps has resulted in an IDEF0 model of the design methodology for the SNO and the SVEs created by it, based on the Globemen RM (see Figure 5).

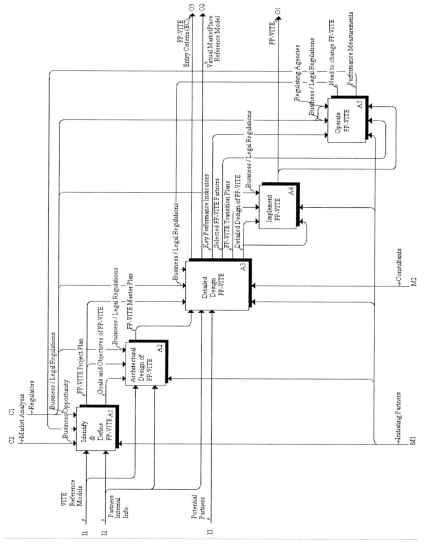

Fig. 3. Create and Operate FP-VITE (IDEF0), first level of detail (Noran 2004b)

The application of the meta-methodology has also produced a model of the decisional aspect of the partners, SNO and potential SVE(s) using GRAI (Graphs with Results and Activities Interrelated (Doumeingts et al. 1998)) Grids and applicable RMs (Olegario and Bernus 2003). Subsequent reflection has proposed changes to the meta-methodology and its SR. The resulting model has been used in the real SNO design with good results.

Space and scope limitations do not allow to present full details of this test; refer to (Bernus et al. 2002), (Noran 2004b).

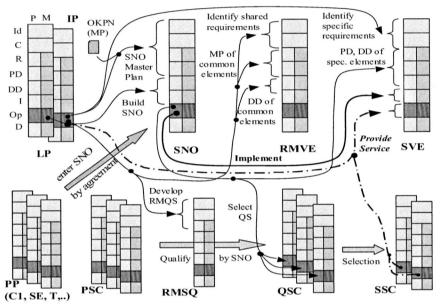

Legend:
LP: Leading Partners; **IP**: Initiating Partner; **PP**: Potential partners; **C1**: Large Customer; **SE**: Service Enterprise; **T**: Telecom Company; **PSC**: Potential Suppliers & Contractors (S&C); **QSC**: Qualified SC; **SSC**: Selected S&C; **SNO**: Service Network Organisation; **SVE**: Service Virtual Enterprise; **RMVE**:VE Reference Model; **RMQSC**: Ref Model Supplier Qualification; **OKPN**: One-kind-of-Product Network; **MP**: Master Plan

Fig. 4. Business model with life cycle relations (based on (Bernus et al., 2002))

The Second Field Test / Case Study

In the second test, the refined meta-methodology has been applied in order to produce guidance for the creation of a VO in the tertiary education sector (Noran, 2004a). Several IT schools of a Faculty within a University wished to form a VO in order to capitalize on their shared knowledge and to present a unique and stronger school image. The schools had different locations, organizational cultures and staff profiles, but similar management models, education profiles and shared a common University infrastructure.

The schools' current (AS-IS) states were not fully understood by stakeholders – and yet, they were to be used to derive their future (TO-BE) states. The business model created (see Figure 6) used a combined representation of the AS-IS and possible TO-BE states.

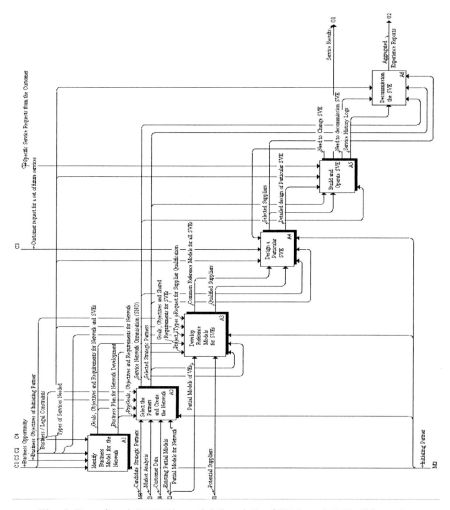

Fig. 5. Functional (IDEF0) model (level 1) of SNO and SVEs life cycles

The main deliverable of this field test was a customised VO creation method expressed in IDEF0 (Figure 7), supplemented by models of decisional and organisational structures (using GRAI Grid) and by high-level models and guidelines for project management, human resources and organisational culture aspects.

These models have used available mainstream reference models whenever possible, e.g. gap analysis concepts from Ansoff's (1965), Howe's (1986) and Kotter's (1996) gradual organisational change process. Details of this experiment are available in (Noran 2004b, 2004c).

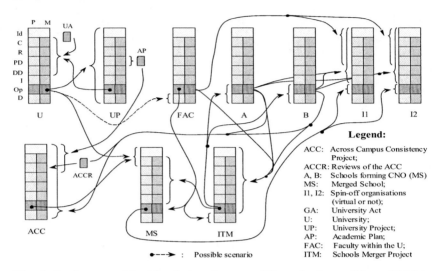

Fig. 6. Business model with relations between life cycle phases (Noran 2004c)

The Meta-methodology Evolution

The number of steps in the meta-methodology has steadily increased, as can be seen from Figure 8; however, it has ultimately converged to a limited set. Thus, the reflection following the first research iteration has proposed an additional meta-methodology step (modelling of aspects other than functional) and has uncovered the needs for step applicability rules, detail levels in models and management (control) view in the business models. It has also found that the business model *quality* is paramount to the usefulness and usability of the main functional model.

Subsequent reflection has proposed *sub-steps* for identifying relevant aspects to be modelled and formalisms and tools to be used, using views (e.g. Function, Information, Organisation, Decision) present in the MFs of the AFs (Zachman (Zachman 1987), ARIS (Scheer 1992, 1999), etc) that had been classified during the critical review phase using GERAM. Initially proposed as separate sub-steps, modelling of additional aspects has become a *sub-step of all* main meta-methodology steps.

The initial SR contained elements grouped by categories with attached applicability rules of the form IF / THEN that had to be sequentially tested by the meta-methodology. Subsequent reflection has identified scalability problems and the need for additional AF elements (e.g. reference models), for generic modelling languages / tools (for non AF-specific elements) and for additional attributes for ranking AF elements by various criteria.

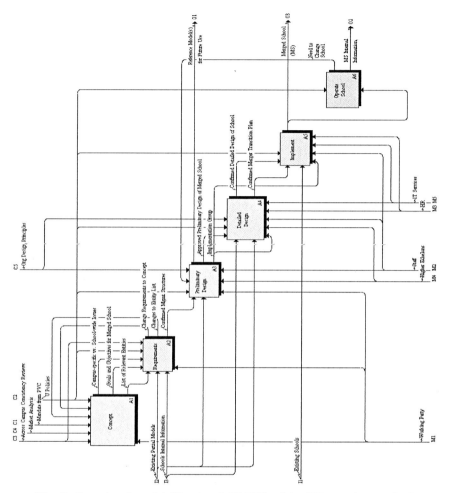

Fig. 7. Functional model (first level, IDEF0) of the VO creation method

Further conceptual development has redesigned the AF elements in the SR to contain prerequisites and modelling outcomes (Figure 9, left), usable by the SR-wide external selection rules.

Final Refinement: The Prototype

Step 1: Identify a list of entities relevant to the EA project. If projects are set up to build the target entity (entities), consider including them;

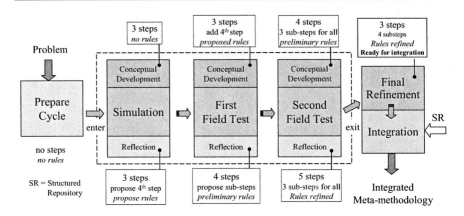

Fig. 8. Evolution of the meta-methodology steps (Noran 2004b)

Step 2: Create a business model showing the relations between the life cycles of the identified entities; for each entity, re-assess the need for its presence in the diagram and the size of the life cycle set being represented;

Step 3: Reading the life cycle diagram of the target entity phase by phase; create a set of activities describing its relations with other entities.

Sub-step 1: Choose to represent the present (AS-IS), future (TO-BE), or both states, separately or combined. The sub-step logic can be embedded in the SR, which advises according to step number and other user answers;

Sub-step 2: Choose aspect to model depending on the current step. This can also be performed by the SR (including any modelling dependencies);

Sub-step 3: Choose modelling formalism and tool depending on the aspect selected and on modelling best-practice criteria (contained in the SR).

The structure of the final SR prototype (Figure 9, left) suits a rule-based expert system implementation. (Noran 2004b) contains further details on the SR structure and on the user interaction with the meta-methodology environment, which integrates the Meta-methodology steps with the SR.

Conclusions and Further Work

This research contributed to the EA body of knowledge by demonstrating the feasibility and usefulness of a meta-methodology for describing the life cycle of CNs and their manifestations. In addition, it has created two practical sets of models and the design specs of a decision support system.

The SR knowledge base members, rules and element representation can be changed to reflect various approaches to enterprise modelling. Interestingly, this makes the meta-methodology applicable to other EA tasks, or even to *any* entity type and task.

Further testing and refinement are needed to completely specify the SR. In addition, the meta-methodology environment needs to be *formalised* in order to enable its implementation (Noran, 2004b).

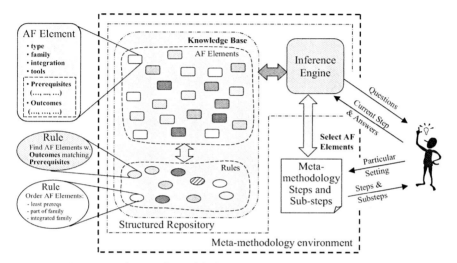

Fig. 9. User interaction with the meta-methodology environment

References

Ansoff H I (1965) Corporate Strategy. McGraw-Hill New York

Bernus P et al. (2002) Using the Globemen Reference Model for Virtual Enterprise Design in After Sales Service. In: Karvoinen I et al. (eds) Globemen VTT Symposium 224 Helsinki Finland, pp 71-90

Burrell G, Morgan G (1979) Sociological Paradigms and Organisational Analysis. Heineman London

Chalmeta R (2000) Virtual Transport Enterprise Integration. Journal of Integrated Design Process Science, vol 4, no 4

Checkland P (1991) From Framework through Experience to Learning: the Essential Nature of Action Research. In: Nissen H-E et al. (eds) Information Systems Research: Contemporary Approaches & Emergent Traditions, Elsevier

CIMOSA Association (1998) CIMOSA – Open System Architecture for CIM, Technical Baseline, ver 3.2.

Doumeingts G et al. (1998) GRAI Grid Decisional Modelling. In: Bernus P et al. (eds) Handbook on Architectures of Information Systems. Springer Verlag, Heidelberg, pp 313-339

Eden M, Chisholm RF (1993) Emerging Varieties of Action Research: Introduction to the Special Issue. Human Relations, vol 46, pp 121-142

Galliers RD (1992) Choosing Information Systems Research Approaches. In: Galliers R (ed) IS Research – Issues, Methods: Alfred Waller Ltd, pp 144-162

Globemen (2000-2002) Global Engineering and Manufacturing in Enterprise Networks – IMS project no. 99004 / IST-1999-60002

Hartel I et al. (2002) Virtual Organisation of the After-sales Service in the One-of-a-kind Industry. In: Camarinha-Matos L (ed) Collaborative Business Ecosystems and VEs (Proc of PROVE02) Sesimbra Portugal, pp 405-420

Hirschheim R, Klein HK (1989) Four Paradigms of Information Systems Development. Communications of the ACM, vol 32, no 10, pp 1199-1216

Howe WS (1986) Corporate Strategy. MacMillan Education, London

ISO/TC184 (2000) Annex A-GERAM: ISO/DIS 15704: Industrial Automation Systems: Reqs for Enterprise-Reference Architectures and Methodologies

Kotter J P (1996) Leading Change. Harvard Business School Press Boston MA

McKay J, Marshall P (2001) The Dual Imperatives of Action Research. IT & People, vol 14, no 1, pp 46-59

Menzel C, Mayer RJ (1998) The IDEF Family of Languages. In: Bernus P et al. (eds) Handbook on Arch Information Systems. Springer Verlag, pp 209-241

NIST (1993) Integration Definition for Function Modelling (IDEF0) (Federal Information Processing Standards 183) Computer Systems Laboratory, NIST

Noran O (2003a) A Mapping of Individual Architecture Frameworks onto GERAM. In: Bernus P et al. (eds) Handbook of Enterprise Architecture. Springer Verlag Heidelberg, pp 65-210

Noran O (2003b) UML vs. IDEF: An Ontology-oriented Comparative Study in View of Business Modelling. Proc of ICEIS 2004 Portugal, pp 674-682

Noran O (2004a) Application of the Meta-methodology for Collaborative Networked Organisations to a School Merger, School of CIT, Griffith University.

Noran O (2004b) A Meta-methodology for Collaborative Networked Organisations, (Doctoral Thesis). School of CIT, Griffith University.

Noran O (2004c) A Meta-methodology for Collaborative Networked Organisations: A Case Study and Reflections. Presented ICEIMT 04, Toronto Canada

Noran O (2004d) Towards a Meta-methodology for Collaborative Networked Organisations. In: Camarinha-Matos L (ed) Proc of PROVE 04. Kluwer Academic Publishers, pp 71-78

Olegario C, Bernus P (2003) Modelling the Management System. In: Bernus P et al. (eds) Handbook on Enterprise Architecture. Springer Verlag Heidelberg

Scheer A-W (1992) Architecture for Integrated Information Systems. Springer-Verlag Berlin, pp 435-500

Scheer A-W (1999) ARIS-Business Process Frameworks. Springer-Verlag Berlin

Tølle M et al. (2002) Reference Models for Virtual Enterprises. In: Camarinha-Matos L (ed) Proc of PROVE02, Sesimbra Portugal, pp 3-10

Trochim WM (2000) The Research Methods Knowledge Base (2nd ed)

Wood-Harper AT (1985) Research methods in IS: Using Action Research. In: Mumford E et al. (eds) Proc of the IFIP WG 8.2 Colloquium. North-Holland Amsterdam, pp 169-191

Zachman J (1987) A Framework for Information Systems Architecture. IBM Syst. Journal, vol 26, no 3, pp 276-292

Modelling Assignments

Jan Olausson and Mikael Lind

School of Business and Informatics, University College of Borås, Sweden.
(jan.olausson, mikael.lind)@hb.se

Introduction

When information systems are specified, developed and evaluated, such systems need to be understood contextually. A vital step during information systems development is therefore business modeling. Critical issues when developing such systems are what aspects to take into consideration. There is a need to understand different aspects of the organization and how the information systems can be supportive and integrating different parts of the organization.

Information system development can be dealt with from different perspectives. One such perspective is the language/action perspective (Austin, 1962; Searle, 1969; Habermas, 1984). The language/action perspective is based on the idea that communication is more the just transfer of information, when you speak, you also act. This implies that the information transferred within and between organizations has to be seen from a perspective where you look at the interchange as different actions, where each actor has an intention with their actions, rather then just a flow of information. Every communicative act has purpose, but also creates expectations. Communicative acts are important for the understanding of how expectations are established, fulfilled and evaluated. An assignment is an expression for one or several actors expectations directed towards another actor. It can be claimed that different types of assignments that are given, taken, forwarded and fulfilled form the backbone of organizational work.

There does not exist any suitable modeling techniques for modeling such essentials. However, there exist modeling techniques, founded in the language/action perspective among other theories, which could be used as a basis for modeling and pinpointing the role of assignments within, and between organizations. Examples of such modeling techniques are action diagrams, co-operation diagrams, co-ordination diagrams and process diagrams (cf. Lind & Olausson, 2004). The purpose of this paper is to elaborate on a suitable theory for understanding assignments within and between organizations as well as evaluating the modeling techniques mentioned above for capturing such theoretical constructs. The research question that drives us is *how should assignments be understood in theory and represented in models for the purpose of business modeling?*

The paper is structured as follows. First we have a discussion concerning the role of theory and method during modeling. Following that we will present a theory about assignment. This theory is followed by a brief example focusing the role of assignment in a mail-order firm. Based on this example some reflections will be made regarding implications for business modeling and how the mentioned models above are suitable to capturing assignments.

Theory and Method Driven Business Modeling

The purpose of business modeling is to generate models of the business in study. Business modeling is about stating and answering questions. The concept of model implies a simplified description of an object, and a business model is therefore a simplified description of a business and illustrates different aspects relevant for the purpose of the model.

Dietz et al (1998) discusses that different driving forces can be used in modeling situations. Dietz et al (1998) claims that both method and theory can in a modeling situation, guide an analyst. Sometimes a theory is the main driving force, where the analyst utilizes the generative power of the theory to put questions. In other situations, a method might be the main driving force. In such a case, the analyst is using the modeling capabilities (notational and procedural rules) of the method as the main question generator. It is however important to note that the business situation being studied must be taken into consideration when generating questions.

One purpose of using methods in the process of business modeling is to document the answers corresponding to the stated questions. Different types of models within the method are used to document answers. Examples of such model types are Action Diagrams, Process Diagrams, Co-operation Diagrams and Co-ordination Diagrams (cf. Lind & Olausson, 2004). Methods are however also used to state accurate questions. Documented answers are important sources of inspiration when stating new questions. Since methods are based on underlying perspectives (Fitzgerald et al, 2002) there is a need for congruence between the perspective, founded in underlying theories, used for stating questions and the perspective used for documenting answers.

A method driven modeling means that a directed attention is obtained. This attention is facilitated by the different questions and description techniques included in the method. A theory contains concepts and categories with clear interrelations. When comparing methods and theories, the latter contains more explicit conceptualizations. On the other hand methods' contains clear normative instructions, which are left out in theories. Through the conceptual richness, a theory driven reconstruction can be very generative by its character (Dietz et al, 1998). It is thus necessary that there exist modeling primitives in the business models for capturing the concepts and categories focused in the theory.

The Theory about Assignments

Co-ordination is a necessity in all social systems, (Alter & Hage, 1993) and organizations exist through co-ordination. This is acknowledged in both classical organizational theory (Mintzberg, 1979) and communication oriented organizational theory (Taylor, 1993). In this paper we adopt a communicative perspective inspired from the language/action perspective (Austin, 1962; Searle, 1969; Habermas, 1984) on co-ordination – co-ordination is performed through communication.

The backbone of co-ordination is different *types of assignments*. Lind & Goldkuhl (2002) have identified three types of assignments for analyzing vertical and horizontal co-ordination; role assignment, external product assignment and internal product assignment. These types of assignments are agreed upon and constituted through social actions (Lind & Goldkuhl, 2002). The utterances are addressed to someone. This addressee is also the one proposed to take action. The *proposed action* is specified (or at least mentioned). When describing the action some other important features are also described. The *beneficiary* of the action is mentioned, i.e. for whom something will be made or to state it otherwise who is in favor of the action. The actions specified also involve a reference to whom the actor shall address his/her action, i.e. the recipient of the action result. This role category is called *next recipient* (to be compared with next-speaker selection) and it must be distinguished from the beneficiary. In some cases, the next recipient and the beneficiary will naturally coincide. The description of the action also involves the kind of action object, which is referred to, i.e. in this case, the *product* to handle. For a deeper communicative action analysis of different organizational assignments, confer Lind & Goldkuhl (2002).

Three different types of assignments need to be acknowledged in order to direct attendance towards vertical and horizontal, as well as internal and external co-ordination. These are:

1. Role assignments (principal - agency relations)
2. Customer orders (customer – supplier relations)
3. Forwarded/transformed orders within an organization (internal process relations)

The first and third assignments are performed within an organization. The first can be seen as a vertical relation and the second and third can be seen as horizontal relations. There are however important differences between external and internal acts/relations. Customer order and forwarded orders are concerned with the particular; a particular customer and a particular product (Lind & Goldkuhl, 2002). There are important differences between a customer order (i.e. external to the organization) and forwarded/transformed internal orders (or requests) that are issued within the organization. The beneficiaries of these different assignment types are, however, always the same, i.e. the customer. One important difference is that in the customer order case the customer is locutor, next recipient as well as beneficiary. This will not be the case with forwarded orders. The locutor will be an internal agent (actor). The next recipient will (often) not be the locutor. The next recipient will be the beneficiary when the product is delivered by the organization, but not for pure internal acts. For such cases the next recipient will be an internal agent (actor).

There are also important differences between principal - agency relations and horizontal relations. Role assignments are internal acts (i.e. made within the organization) and are concerned with the typical (all possible customers and products) (Lind & Goldkuhl, 2002). Role assignments are, as mentioned above directives. However they also have a declarative force since they appoint actors to roles. The differences between the different types of assignments are illustrated in table 1 below.

In order to handle this view of co-ordination there is a need to distinguish between different types of assignments as well as between different types of roles (Lind & Goldkuhl, 2002). There is a need to distinguish between several roles, which go beyond the traditional role repertoire in speech-act based modeling approaches. The roles distinguished by Lind & Goldkuhl (2002) are:

- Requester (locutor)
- Performer (producer)
- Next recipient
- Beneficiary

Table 1. Characterizations of different types of assignments (Lind & Goldkuhl 2002)

Type of assign-ment	Communica-tion place	Organiza-tional dimension	Degree of specificality	Communica-tion roles
Role assignment	Internal	Vertical	Typical products and customers (type level)	Organization (principal) → Agent
External product assignment (Customer order)	External	Horizontal	Particular products and customers (instance level)	Customer → Organization (supplier)
Internal product assignment (For-warded order)	Internal	Horizontal	Particular products and customers (instance level)	Agent → Agent

Assignments are agreed upon and established through interactions. There are thus interactions concerning the vertical co-ordination going on between the principal and agent(s) in order to establish role assignments (see figure 1). These interactions are, as mentioned above, concerned with the typical. There are also interactions between agents within the organiza-tion as well as between agents within the organization and the beneficiary of the organization. These interactions concern internal and external hori-zontal co-ordination, i.e. establishing and fulfilling product assignments.

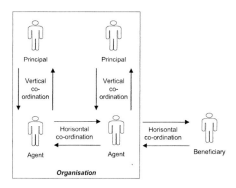

Fig. 1. Horizontal versus vertical co-ordination (Lind & Olausson, 2004)

The propositional content of the vertical co-ordination, what each agent should do, is about the horizontal co-ordination. The sum of all role assignment should thus reflect the total horizontal co-ordination for establishing and fulfilling agreements with the beneficiary of the organization.

Organizational work can be studied from many different perspectives. In this paper we have used the theory of practice (Goldkuhl & Röstlinger, 2002) as the basis for understanding organizational work. According to the theory of practice, a work practice is governed by a number of different pre-conditions and exists in order to produce results for its clients and their utilization of produced products. According to Lind & Olausson (2004), the action performed within a practice can be categorized as being of different kinds. First of all some actions are performed for *potential clients*, i.e. the beneficiary is a potential client, in relation to that some actions are performed for *particular clients*. This definition relies on that when the action is performed the client is known, in other situations the client is a thought one. All co-ordination can therefore not be founded in the external customer order, i.e. the external product assignment. Also the parts of the practice, i.e. some of the sub practices, need to be coordinated initiated by internal assignments.

Three different sub practices can be distinguished founded in the separation between work for potential and particular customers/clients as well as in the separation between operative vs. development-oriented work (Lind, 2003). First there is a delivery practice consisting of both operative and development-oriented actions performed for particular customers/clients. Then there is the providing practice consisting of operative actions performed for potential customers/clients. The third sub practice is the managing and condition-creating practice consisting of development-oriented actions for potential customers.

Understanding Assignments in a Practical Setting

The mail-order firm, at which our analysis has been performed, belongs to a larger owner group of companies (a European group of retail business) that trade in different products such as garments, furniture, gifts and home electronics through the mail distribution channel to different European customer markets. The firm markets and sells garments for the whole family as well as products for the home, leisure and electronics.

The exposure of the product repertoire is done through mail-order catalogues and the e-commerce site. The product repertoire is, in regard to garments, based on season. Products that are directed towards home, leisure and electronics follow the planning and development of the garment assortment, but are not as sensitive to the season as the garments.

The product repertoire consists of own-assortment products, owner-assortment products as well as factory-produced products (not produced in advance). The planning and development of the assortment is governed by internal assignments. The planning and development work is initiated approximately a year prior the start of the season, which means that the mail-order firm handles issues for multiple seasons at the same time. The result of planning and development is mail-order catalogues, i.e. the product repertoire, and made procurements. The goal for a mail-order firm is that there should be products in stock in accordance with the customer order to ensure short lead-times.

This mail-order firm produces a number of different catalogues (one main catalogue, two follow-up catalogues and several sales catalogues) with the purpose of exposing the assortments and thereby selling products to potential customers. The goal is to arrive at a stock-level close to zero at the end of the season. The procurement department defines the product offers for each catalogue. When the product offers has been approved two things happen. First the catalogue department forwards an external assignment to the printing house to print the catalogues. Second the procurement department assigns the marketing department a marketing assignment to market the specific products (via the catalogue) to potential customers. When the printing process is finished, the catalogues are delivered to the distributor of the catalogues. In order for the distributor to deliver the catalogues, this external partner receives addresses from the marketing department in the mail-order firm. In terms of the co-ordination logic the distributor receives through this action an external assignment that instructs the distributor to deliver the catalogues to a number of specific recipients that are the potential customers for the mail-order firms' products.

The particular customer uses different channels (e.g. phone, letter, fax, internet) to place the order based on the offer made by the mail-order firm. The customer order is to be regarded as an external product assignment directed to the customer service. After checking the availability (stock level) the customer service confirms the order by a delivery notice (order confirmation). Since the products can be of different kinds such as own-assortment, owner-assortment orders and factory-produced products the original customer order will be split into different parts depending on the types of products requested by the customer. The different parts of the orders will then be forwarded to their recipients, i.e. to the warehouse, to the owner or to the factory, in order to fulfill the customer order.

The factory order will be delivered directly to the customer. Some orders consisting of both own-assortment and owner-assortment will be, under certain conditions, jointly packed which requires that the mail-order firm has to wait for the owner-assortment products to arrive at the firm before this packing can be made. During execution of the fulfillment phase the warehouse takes on both the role of fulfilling the original customer request (packing and handing over the package to the distributor) and that of acting as a marketing channel (by supplying with extra offers) towards the particular customer to generate new customer orders from him/her.

The payment from the customer can be handled in different ways, either as a C. O .D (cash-on-delivery) or as invoice-based accounts. There is also a material flow going "in reverse", which depicts the handling of products returned by the customer to the mail-order firm. The goods that are returned can either be regarded as condemned products, re-sold through the mail-order logic, sold in the warehouse-shop or be returned to the supplier.

Implications for Business Modeling

The presentation made in section 4 is made from an assignment perspective. This presentation has been made based on the theory of assignment put forward in section 3. These issues, concerning the role of assignments, need to be possible to model. It can be noticed from the empirical illustration above that there is a need to cover different sub-practices and their inter-relations in business models. The overall logic of assignment-based coordination is shown in figure 2. The organization gives the supplier an external product assignment in order to establish the needed preconditions to start the interaction with the specific customer.

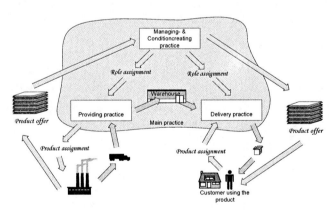

Fig. 2. Overall logic in the sub-practices and the external product assignments

The logic described in figure 2 can look different, like in the empirical illustration above, where the customer order initiates a suborder to the selling organization's supplier. This is the case for owner-assortment products as well as for factory-produced products. In that case the providing practice rather has the role of establishing frame contracts between the supplier and the mail-order company. Based on that frame contract, there will be an interaction between the supplier, the mail-order company and the customer within the scope of the delivery practice. The product order from the customer is forwarded external to the supplier who manufacture the product and sends it to the customer.

When modeling businesses, the modeler has to consider theories, models as well as the modeling situation (Dietz et al, 1998). In order to model a business we therefore propose following toolbox; action diagrams, co-operation diagrams, co-ordination diagrams and process diagrams. These diagrams do however need to be adjusted in order to suit a situation where the logic of assignments is put forward (Olausson, 2005).

In order to get a rich description of the modeled business, the modeler has to use both theories and models to direct attention towards important aspects. The smallest unit of analysis is social action and is modeled in action diagrams. The action diagrams provide a possibility to model the business in detail, but it can be difficult to get an overview. We therefore acknowledge a need to use separate models on different levels of abstractions and different focus (see figure 3).

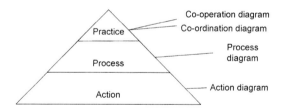

Fig. 3. The main use of the different models

The theory about assignments, described in section 3, and the empirical case, described in section 4, implies a need for the models to describe both role, and product assignments. Desired theoretical constructs must be possible to represent in the business models.

The adjustments in focus, needed for the different business models, are shown in table 2. The table shows the models purpose and focus, bolded indicates the models main focus and italic shows the possibility to model the role of assignments. The models depicted in the table, all has a relative free notion of description and can be used in different levels of abstraction. The models main usage is shown in figure 3. It is however vital that used theory put attention towards assignments during the modeling session. Theory and used methods need to go hand-in-hand.

Table 2. Different models purpose and focus

Model	Purpose	Focus
Co-operation diagram	To create an overview over affected organizations and how these are related through co-operation	Interaction, co-operation, relations, role assignments, product assignments
Co-ordination diagram	To show the product assignment's coordinative effects in the practice	Coordination, product assignments
Process diagram	To create an overview over the existing action logic in the practice and show the result the practice's customer receives	Process, potential/particular, product assignment (towards customer)
Action diagram	to describe and analyze a practice or sub practice through performed actions	Flows, actions, preconditions, result, performer, role assignment, product assignment

In order to secure that the assignments are modeled, we propose the following set of questions:

- What kind of assignments exists in the practice?
- Who gives assignments, e.g. who are assigners?
- Who fulfils the assignment, e.g. who are producers?
- Which kind of product orders exists to the practice? Who orders the product?
- What is the practice product repertoire? Who defines the products?
- Which types of role assignments exists in the practice? Who are role assigners?
- Which types of resource assignments exists in the practice? Who assigns resources?
- Who takes initiative to assignments?
- Who formulate assignment?
- Who is supposed to fulfill the assignment?
- How is the assignment formulated? How is the assignments communicated?

- What strength (power of influence) is in the assignment?
- How do assigner and producer agree upon assignments? How is assignment established?
- How do the producers interpret given assignments?
- Do the different assignments support each other?
- Is there conflicting assignments?
- Is there any forwarding of assignments? Does an assignment generate new/other assignments? How is assignment refined and distributed? Who are involved in the assignment process?

By using the theory and models proposed in this paper the business modeler secure that important aspects is put in focus and is visualized in the models. Since the different models have different focus, the use of them enables a broad coverage of the business in different levels of abstraction.

Conclusions

The logic of dependencies between different types of assignments is essential to understand during information systems development. Such understanding can be achieved through business modeling in which questions are stated and answers are given. Theories are instruments for directing attendance towards desired aspects of an organization and methods are normative instruments for capturing the answers. In this paper we have shown the need for putting forward the role of assignment in different types of sub-practices. Important for arriving at a thorough understanding of the role of assignments are that there exist a congruency between desired theories and the business models used for putting forward these essentials.

A focus on assignments, in the way it has been put forward in this paper, implies a focus on external, internal, horizontal and vertical co-ordination. All these co-ordination mechanisms need to be regarded as complementing each other in order to arrive at a well-coordinated and efficient practice fulfilling the needs of its client. We claim that modeling assignments enhance the understanding of the business process logic. Of course there are other ways to understand the business processes, and following those approaches may arrive in a coordinated and efficient practice, even if they don't explicitly put forward assignments. In those cases well-coordinated and efficient practices are created by chance. If assignments are in focus the creation of a well-coordinated and efficient practice is by intentional and conscious design. For a discussion about intentional design of actable information systems, call for Cronholm & Goldkuhl (2002)

In this paper four different modeling techniques has been briefly discussed and put in relation to proposed theory of assignments. These different modeling techniques have a role in establishing an understanding of different aspects of organizational work at different levels of abstraction.

References

Alter C, Hage J (1993) Organizations Working Together, SAGE Library of Social Research 191. SAGE Publications Newbury Park California

Austin JL (1962) How to do Things with Words. Oxford University Press

Cronholm S, Goldkuhl G (2002) Actable Information Systems – Quality Ideals Put Into Practice. Presented at the Eleventh Conference on Information Systems (ISD 2002) 12-14 September Riga Latvia

Dietz JLG, Goldkuhl G, Lind M, Reijswoud VE (1998) The Communicative Action Paradigm for Business Modelling – A Research Agenda. Proc of the third LAP Conference on The Language Action Perspective on Communication Modelling 25 June 1998 Märsta Sweden

Fitzgerald B, Russo NL, Stolterman E (2002) Information Systems Development – Methods in Action. Mc Graw Hill

Goldkuhl G, Röstlinger A (2002) Towards an Integral Understanding of Organisations and Information Systems: Convergence of Three Theories. Proc of the 5th International Workshop on Organisational Semiotics Delft

Habermas J (1984) The Theory of Communicative Action. Vol one. Reason and Rationalization of Society Beacon Press Boston

Lind M (2003) The Diversity of Work Practices – Challenging the Existing Notion of Business Process Types. Proc of Action in Language, Organisations and Information Systems (ALOIS) Linköping University Linköping Sweden

Lind M, Goldkuhl G (2002) Questioning Two-Role Models or Who Bakes the Pizza? Accepted to the Seventh International Workshop on the Language-Action Perspective on Communication Modeling (LAP 2002) June 12-13 2002 Delft

Lind M, Olausson J (2004) Balancing Horizontal and Vertical Co-ordination in Business Transactions – Towards a Clarification of the Role of IT-systems in an E-commerce Setting. Proc of Action in Language, Organisations and Information Systems (ALOIS) Linköping University Linköping Sweden

Mintzberg H (1979) The Structuring of Organizations. Prentice-Hall Inc New Jersey

Olausson J (2005) Att modellera uppdrag – grunder för förståelse av processinriktade informationssystem i transaktionsintensiva verksamheter. Licentiate Thesis Linköping University

Searle JR (1969) Speech Acts: An Essay in the Philosophy of Language. Cambridge University Press London

Taylor JR (1993) Rethinking the Theory of Organizational Communication: How to Read an Organisation. Ablex Norwood

Collaborative Tools' Quality in Web-Based Learning Systems – A Model of User Perceptions

Paolo Davoli[1] and Matteo Monari[2]

[1] Faculty of Humanities (Literature and Philosophy), University of Modena and Reggio Emilia, Italy. pdavoli@unimore.it
[2] IPLab, Department for Numerical Analysis and Computer Science, Royal Institute of Technology (KTH), Sweden. monari@nada.kth.se

Groupware Evaluation and e-Learning Systems

The importance of collaborative tools is increasing in e-learning practice, both in educational institutions and enterprises. E-learning is nowadays much more than file downloading: both in distance and blended learning, group interactions are showing their didactic relevance. Specific contexts and needs are to be taken into account when evaluating didactic collaborative tools, since they present peculiar aspects. For instance, e-learning platforms are not pure groupware, but didactic systems hosting both groupware facilities and single-user features.

Since the adoption of a software tool is a critical choice with enduring consequences for the adopting institution, its evaluation is of fundamental importance. Anyway, groupware evaluation is known to be a tricky problem (Grudin 1994, Knutilla et al. 2000, Potts Steves et al. 2001, Newman et al. 2003, Neale et al. 2004). We can state that:

- Groupware is a piece of software. An important reference not often considered in groupware evaluation studies is the ISO/IEC 9126-1 standard, which defines a software quality model allowing quality checks for any generic software product (ISO/IEC 2001).
- The large majority of today's groupware systems are Web-based systems, and their evaluation should take into account the peculiarities of Web quality evaluation (for a survey, see Davoli et al. 2005).
- Groupware products entail specific challenges arising from group processes management (Grudin 1994), and adapting traditional evaluation techniques to groupware can be complicated (Knutilla 2000).

According to Pinelle and Gutwin (2000), several methodology problems characterize past groupware evaluations. Among them are: a) the lack of stated measurement goals; b) the limited descriptions of methodologies for data collection and questionnaire contents; c) the focus on specific conclusions rather than on general evaluation; d) the limited number of real world applications considered.

Clear methodologies are still to be established, and we are far from consensus on how a groupware evaluation is to be conducted. A need is felt for using common frameworks across multiple projects (Newman et al. 2003) and evaluating real world systems (Andriessen 2003).

Paper Organization

To face these issues, we developed a model of user quality perceptions for the evaluation of groupware tools embedded in Web-based learning platforms, and tested it in three case studies involving different, widely used both commercial and Open Source systems (*Ping Pong, Blackboard and Moodle*), in Sweden and Italy. Our goal is to provide a) an adaptable low-cost and effective evaluation tool, b) with a clearly stated implementation methodology c) that can be used for real world applications, d) in the e-learning field. The model can be used in conjunction with inspective evaluation methods to provide an integrated view of the software's appropriateness to the context of use

In the following Section 2 we will review some critical issues in the existing literature, highlighting the base of our model. Then, after presenting the model (Section 3), we will describe its implementation methodology for the case studies (Section 4) and discuss the experimental results (Section 5). Finally, some conclusions will be drawn (Section 6). This paper should not be considered as a quality report of the examined systems: our aim was rather to test how the model can help examine and quantitatively assess groupware tools within these e-learning applications.

Related Works and Model Bases

Reference to Standards

User-based and inspector-based evaluations can be used in tandem to gather different and complementary information (Knutilla et al. 2000, Potts Steves et al. 2001, Neale et al. 2004). In both techniques, a certain amount of research arbitrariness is avoidable through clear references to existing specifications. For example, in Web quality evaluation, authors refer to ISO/IEC 9216-1 standard for software quality (ISO/IEC 2001) and to W3 Consortium recommendations (http://w3c.org) (Davoli et al. 2005).

ISO 9126-1 standard deals with six main dimensions of software quality: functionality, reliability, usability, efficiency, maintainability and portability. As far as user perceptions are involved, we claim that mainly functionality and usability are to be taken into account – in fact, the other dimensions refer mainly to technical features that are better examined by specialized inspectors. According to the definitions of the standard:

- *Functionality* is the capability of a software to provide functions which meet stated and implied needs under specified conditions.
- *Usability* is the capability of the software to be understood, learned, used and liked by the user under specified conditions.

When a specific domain is involved, scholars should also refer to agreed specifications in that particular field. As for e-learning, SCORM and IMS (www.imsglobal.org/) specifications are de facto standards, but they do not appear to actually deal with group interactions.

Context, Retroaction and Groupware-Related Problems

Group context and groupware cultural impact are fundamental parameters of groupware evaluations (De Araujo et al. 2002, Neale et al. 2004, Grudin 1994, Knutilla et al. 2000, Eklund et al. 2003). The original *context* always exerts some influence on the adoption of a technology. In the same way, the adoption of a technology always has an impact on the original culture. For example, it may transform the way in which single individuals or entire groups work, as well as their attitudes and expectations, changing the group context. Therefore, we claim that referring to *retroaction* is preferable than referring to impact, because the former better accounts for the circular, dynamic and reciprocal influence between context and technology supported activities.

In addition to context and retroaction issues, *groupware related feelings and problems* (as pointed out by Grudin 1994) should also be considered during an evaluation, since they act on factors related to technology-mediated interaction (e.g. the naturalness of communication).

Groupware Functionality and Usability

In order to evaluate groupware tools, more than traditional usability testing is needed, and the focus on specific groupware processes is required.

Among them are communication, coordination and synchronization, (re)planning, monitoring, assistance, role taking, information sharing and protection (Gutwin and Greenberg 1999, Neale et al. 2004). For these topics, the concept of *groupware usability* was proposed.

Restricting the evaluation to the usability (easiness of use) of tools supporting groupware processes can be limiting, and we suggest that their *functionality* (the degree of support for collaboration processes) should also be taken into account, according to ISO/IEC 9126-1 standard. Moreover, since the collaborative tools we are dealing with are hosted within e-learning systems, the system's *general "classical" usability* is to be considered as well.

A Model of User Perceptions

According to the framework outlined in Sect. 2, we propose a model composed by interacting dimensions, in order to analyze user perceptions of the quality of collaborative tools in e-learning systems.

We suggest that the following dimensions should be taken into account: **D1** – *Context of use*; **D2** – *Retroaction in the context*; **D3** – *Groupware related feelings and problems*; **D4** – *Groupware Functionality*; **D5** – *Groupware Usability*; **D6** – *General system usability*; **D7** – *Class specific activities' Functionality and Usability*; **D8** – *Products*.

A graphical representation of the model is reported in Figure 1, where the reciprocal disposition of the various dimensions indicates their mutual relationships.

Basing on the model in Fig. 1, an effective evaluation should deal with *context* (e.g. trainees' motivations and habits), which is continuously influenced by the *retroaction* exercised by technology mediated group processes. *Groupware functionality* and *groupware usability* (the latter is related to *general usability*) should be taken into account, as well as *specific collaborative activities* implemented in a given educational context (e.g. collaborative writing). *Group related feelings and problems* (situated in an outer belt in the picture) can be considered as issues affecting the overall educational experience. The evaluation may also deal with the *artifacts produced* by the group, even though they are not always mandatory components of educational experiences (in which what matters may be the collaborative process itself and not the final product *per se*).

Each of these dimensions can be examined through several observation variables, for each of whom a user evaluation can be obtained. According to the framework outlined in Sect. 2, we propose the following:

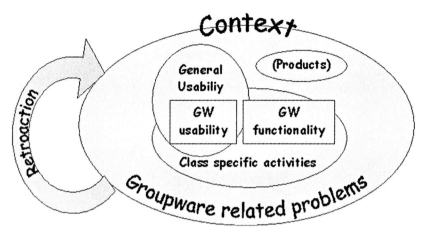

Fig. 1. Graphical representation of user perception model

- **D1. Context**: age, gender, role, motivation, attitude, group size, familiarity with computer technologies and the system, technological resources (e.g. operating systems, available bandwidth).
- **D2. Retroaction**: effects on motivation, collaboration, communication, possible face-to-face meetings and work organization and execution.
- **D3. Groupware related feelings and problems**: balance between extra work and benefits, naturalness of communication, feelings of collaboration, group size appropriateness, possible disruption of social processes, level of use of system functions.
- **D4. Groupware Functionality**: the level of support to teamwork in terms of communication, coordination, monitoring, receiving and providing assistance, identity management, information sharing.
- **D5. Groupware Usability**: level of easiness of use for functions listed in dimension D4.
- **D6. General system usability**: intended in terms of learning, understanding, liking and using the system and its layout, error management, easiness of use of single system functions.
- **D7. Functionality and Usability related to class specific activities**: depending on specific educational processes, e.g. collaborative writing.
- **D8. Products**: level of satisfaction with the artifacts possibly produced by the group, perceived by the trainees themselves or educational staff.

Note that even though dimensions D1-D3 rely on "group" factors, here we focus on the technical features affecting these factors (e.g. familiarity with computer technologies), rather than on group factors *per se* (e.g. leadership dynamics).

Model Implementation

Three Case Studies

The model was applied to the use of collaborative tools by the students of three academic courses, which mixed distance and presence learning at varying levels (blended learning). All the classes conducted collaborative writing activities involving sharing and commenting of written works.

- **Case A.** The course taught at the *Royal Institute of Technology of Stockholm*, Sweden, (about chemistry) was supported by *Ping Pong* (http://www.pingpong.se). The groups had to jointly produce a written report about a case, and post it on the system so that the teacher could read and comment it. A second draft would then be posted by the group and commented by other groups. These discussions will constitute the starting point of in-presence seminars.
- **Case B.** The course at the *University of Gävle*, Sweden, (about creative writing) used *Blackboard* (http://www.blackboard.com). On-line activities consisted in readings and writing assignments, and were accompanied by bimonthly class meetings. Every student was required to post her works on her group's discussion board and comment on the other students' works.
- **Case C.** The module taught at the *University of Modena and Reggio Emilia*, Italy, regarded computer systems for students of Humanities, and was composed by traditional presence lessons and mandatory on-line activities, based on *Moodle* (http://www.moodle.org). Every student was asked to add terms to a collaborative *Glossary tool* provided by the system and to judge other students' definitions, commenting on them and giving grades according to an evaluation scale fixed by the teacher.

User Questionnaire

A questionnaire was derived following the model described in Section 3, incorporating almost all the listed topics (except for dimension *D8 - Products*, which was not relevant in the cases we observed). The time and effort the questionnaire would require to be completed was taken into consideration, by limiting the number and complexity of the (40) questions (Knutilla et al. 2000 and Newman et al. 2003).

Most of the questions were on highly subjective matters (e.g. "How difficult was learning how to operate the system?"), and the users were required to give quantitative answers expressed in a Likert-like scale. Even if

Likert-like scales have some debated issues (Lalla et al. 2004), for our purposes they were simple enough to be understood by all users, and allowed us to capture subjective perceptions in a quantitative and comparable way. A limited amount of open questions was included as well, in order to allow users to account for qualitative factors such as lists of problems, motivations, complaints, etc. and freely motivate the assigned scores. To prevent users from filling questions using "neutral" answers as a shortcut, the scales provided an even number of options (6) forcing users to choose between insufficient and sufficient scores, expressed through linguistic quantifiers graded from a minimum to a maximum (e.g. from "completely useless" to "very useful" graded from 0 to 5).

Score Normalization and Summarization

A total of 74 students filled in the questionnaire. In order to obtain synthetic scores from them, a mean value for each scalar question was calculated for each case study, and normalized to a 0-1 range. Not all of the students accessed all of the platform functions (for example, not all of the students accessed help functions or participants' lists). Hence, in order to obtain comparable data, each activity-specific result was weighted with the number of students who accomplished that activity. Some information (e.g. the answer to questions such as : "how long have you been using the system?") was not expressed directly in a quantitative scale. We categorized it according to reasonable scales, and normalized it to 0-1 range.

At this stage, for each platform we had around thirty normalized values corresponding to the quantitative information drawn from each of the questionnaire's items. The next step was obtaining grouped scores for each evaluation dimension in Section 3. The meaning of scores for dimensions D4-D7 are obvious, while the meaning of scores for dimensions D1-D3 is less obvious. For example, what is the meaning of the score of dimension *D1 – Context of use*? We decided to evaluate:

- D1 – *To what extent the context was favorable to the educational process.* For example, a highly motivated group constituted a more favorable context than a set of low motivated individuals.
- D2 – *The level of positive retroaction on the context.* For example, if users think that using the system to make activities makes them more stimulating we can take this as an indicator of positive retroaction.
- D3 – *To what extent groupware problems were overcome.* For example, if users feel they are working in a collaborating group (despite distance

and mediated communication) this contributes to limit groupware problems.

Dimension *D7 – Class specific processes* was split in two parts and incorporated within dimensions *D4 - Groupware functionality* and *D5-Groupware usability*, according to the graphic model in Fig. 1

The normalized scores were then grouped according to these dimensions and averaged, obtaining a single score for each dimension for each platform. More sophisticated math summarization methods could be adopted while aggregating single normalized scores (e.g. see Davoli et al. 2005). However, for this first stage of model testing, we preferred not to introduce possible biasing features due to possible algorithmic artifacts.

Discussion

For each case study, Figure 2 illustrates the user perceptions of the dimensions composing the model, divided in more group-related (D1-D3) and technical ones (D4-D6) – remember that dimension D7 was incorporated into D4-D5, and D8 was not relevant for the case studies. In the graphs, users' scores are scaled from 0 to 100 (rounded to the nearest integer), and we can consider 60 to be the borderline global score for each dimension.

Dimensions D1-D3

For what concerns dimensions D1, D2 and D3, the three cases obtained different scores. Case A and Case C were characterized by low favorable contexts of adoption (D1), in contrast with case B. For example, the users in Case C were well motivated but unfamiliar with computer technologies, and they had not made a long or intense use of the system

Also the grades for retroaction (D2) are significantly different. In Cases B and C users perceived a sufficient level of positive retroaction on the context of use, while in Case A users expressed an insufficient level of positive retroaction. This last result derives, among other factors, from the low grades given to the system's impact on face-to-face meetings and to the way in which the system improved collaboration.

A comparison of the scores of dimensions D1 and D2 within the same case suggests that a favorable context (D1) and positive retroactions exercised by a tool (D2) do not necessarily depend on each other in a direct way. As is for Case C, even a poor context of adoption can be influenced by a positive retroaction, which may be due (among other factors) to the good levels of functionality and usability of the technology (see below).

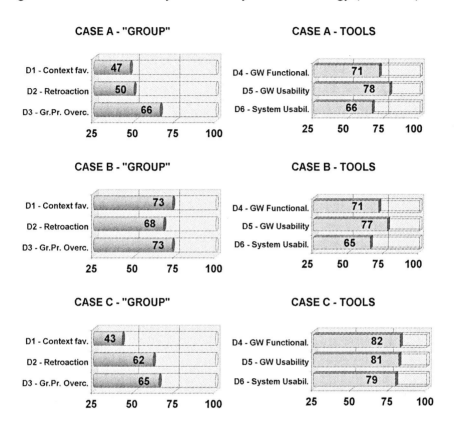

Fig. 2. User perceptions scores for the dimensions composing the model: context favorableness, retroaction on the context, group problems' overcoming, groupware functionality, groupware usability and general system usability. Each row refers to a case study (A, B, C); the left column refers to group-related dimensions (D1-D3); the right column refers to tool-related dimensions (D4-D6)

None of the three cases presented remarkable groupware-related problems (D3). Also in this case, group B obtained the highest score. E.g., its members described the communication that took place on the system as "natural", despite the computer's mediation. "The system has a relaxed atmosphere – almost like sitting in a café" said a user in the open answers.

Dimensions D4-D6 (Incorporating D7)

It should be noted that dimensions D5 and D6 are partially overlapping (see Fig. 1), since groupware usability (D5) can be seen as a specific part of the general usability of the e-learning system (D6).

While the e-learning platform adopted in Case C obtained good user evaluations in all the dimensions we considered, in cases A and B the users pointed out some problems of general usability, assigning borderline scores. These low scores were due mainly to layout and navigation problems, as can be inferred also from the open answers given by the users, who defined the system navigation "not very intuitive", characterized by a "bad overview", that made them "go wrong several times" (Case A).

In cases A and B, the fairly good scores obtained by groupware usability contrast with the (surprisingly) lower ones obtained by general usability, demonstrating once again that groupware usability and general usability should be treated separately.

Always referring to cases A and B, the levels of groupware functionality are slightly lower than those of groupware usability. This may be partially due to the higher technical expertise (and, consequently, higher expectations) characterizing the users of these platforms when compared to those of Case C. For example, some users of group B complained about the system's management of groups and its poor editing functions ("especially important when the format of texts DOES have an influence, as it does with writing", as noted by a user in the open answers). This difference confirms that separating groupware usability and groupware functionality is correct, basing on the ISO 9126-1 standards proposed in Section 3.

It can be pointed out how the grades of dimensions D1-D3 are generally lower than those of dimensions D4-D6 (the former's overall average for the three cases is 61, while the latter's is 74). This suggests that even when users are generally satisfied by the technological features of the adopted systems, the interaction of the software with the context of adoption and its retroaction on the didactic activity may present problematic aspects.

To sum up, Fig. 2 provides a quick and quantitative representation of user perceptions about some important factors in the adoption of cooperative technologies in learning environments, allowing teachers and students to discover critical factors and possibly adopt different strategies.

Conclusions and Further Work

Some of the problems affecting groupware evaluation were assessed, considering the case of collaborative tools hosted within e-learning systems. A model to capture significant users perceptions in such context was proposed. The model implementation was described for three case studies in which well known e-learning platforms were used. Experimental results suggest that even when users are satisfied by technological features, retroaction on didactic practice may present problematic aspects. Altogether, the model:

- a) allows to capture in a quantitative and sensitive way the user perceptions about the adoption of collaborative technologies within e-learning systems and helps to identify specific problems (also through open questions);
- b) relates classical software quality dimensions (e.g. functionality and usability) with group and interaction dimensions (e.g. context and retroaction), as a consequence of their interdependence in computer mediated communication;
- c) allows developers, educators and students to pin point critical factors and consequently change their strategies.

Some research could follow this study, such as a more sophisticated data treatment with fuzzy systems to better manage qualitative user feedback and a proposal of integration of the model with inspector-based techniques.

Acknowledgements

We thank the educators of the three universities involved, as well as the students who patiently answered the questionnaires. Kerstin Severinson Eklundh, Professor in Human-Computer Interaction and research coordinator at the *Interaction and Presentation Laboratory* (*KTH*), is also acknowledged for her support and literature suggestions during experimental work.

References

Andriessen JHE (2003) Working with Groupware, Understanding and Evaluating Collaboration Technology. Springer Verlag New York
Davoli P, Mazzoni F, Corradini E. (2005) Quality Assessment Of Cultural Web Sites with Fuzzy Operators. Journal of Computer Information Systems, vol 46, no 1, pp 44-57
De Araujo RM, Santoro FM and Borges MRS (2002) The CSCW Lab for Groupware Evaluation. In: Haake & Pino (eds) Groupware: Design, Implementation, and Use. CRIWG 2002, LNCS 2440. Springer-Verlag NY

Eklundh KS, Groth K, Hedman A, Lantz A, Rodriguez H, Sallnäs, EL (2003) The World Wide Web as a Social Infrastructure for Knowledge-Oriented Work. In: Herre van Oostendorp (ed) Cognition in a Digital World. Lawrence Erlbaum Associates Mahwah NJ

Grudin J (1994) Groupware and Social Dynamics: Eight Challenges for Developers. Communications of the ACM, vol 37, pp 92-105

Gutwin C, Greenberg S (1999) The Effects of Workspace Awareness Support on the Usability of Real-Time Distributed Groupware. ACM Transactions on Computer-Human Interaction, vol 6, pp 243-281

ISO/IEC 9126-1:2001 (2001) Software engineering – Product Quality – Part 1: Quality model. Geneva, Int'l Org. for Standardization

Knutilla A, Steve M, Allen R (2000) Workshop on Evaluating Collaborative Enterprises – Workshop Report. Proc of the IEEE 9th International Workshops on Enabling Technologies: Infrastructure for Collaborative Enterprises, IEEE Computer Society. Washington DC

Lalla M, Facchinetti G, Mastroleo G (2004) Ordinal Scales and Fuzzy Set Systems to Measure Agreement: An Application to the Evaluation of Teaching Activity. Quantity and Quality, vol 38, pp 577-601

Neale DC, Carroll JM, Rosson MB (2004) Evaluating Computer-Supported Cooperative Work: Models and Frameworks. Proc of the Conference of Computer-Supported Cooperative Work. ACM Press New York

Newman J, Raybourn EM, Huang PH (2003) Evaluating Collaborative Enterprises Workshop Report. Proc of the 12th IEEE International Workshops on Enabling Technologies: Infrastructure for Collaborative Enterprises. IEEE Computer Society, Los Alamitos CA

Pinelle D, Gutwin C (2000) A Review of Groupware Evaluations. Proc of WETICE 2000, Workshops on Enabling Technologies: Infrastructure for Collab Enterprises. IEEE Computer Society, Los Alamitos CA

Potts Steves M, Morse E, Gutwin C, Greenberg S (2001) A Comparison of Usage Evaluation and Inspection Methods for Assessing Groupware Usability. Proc of the 2001 International ACM SIGGROUP Conference on Supporting Group Work. ACM Press New York

The Work that Analysts Do: A Systemic Functional Approach to Elicitation

Rodney J. Clarke

Decision Systems Laboratory, School of Economics and Information Systems, University of Wollongong, Australia. rodney_clarke@uow.edu.au

Introduction: The Work of Analysis as Communication

In this paper we advocate the view of systems analysis as an activity where communication and social interaction within the developer community and between developers, users and other stakeholders is central. Analysis involves a complex bridging process (Quintas 1993) between IS professionals and users implying different backgrounds, knowledge, agendas and social relations of power. We need to study communication in organisational contexts to better understand how we can conduct effective systems analysis and also in order to improve our pedagogic practices. However while there is a general recognition of the importance of communication it is none-the-less a complex social phenomena that is not well understood within the IS discipline and not explicitly addressed in traditional methods and methodologies despite growing interest and recognition in various qualitative, interpretive and ethnographic approaches (Easterbrook 1993).

The primary means for collecting data concerning current and proposed workpractices is through the use of interviews- a primary tool for 'data collection' in all commercial disciplines including Management, Marketing, Economics, Accounting, Industrial Relations as well as Information Systems. While the interview process is central to analysis activities, there is a paucity of information concerning how to accomplish it and in particular how to elicit information from interactants, see for example a folk-linguistic theory of requirements elicitation presented in Burch and Grudnitski (1989, 560). Systems analysts do not have explicit methods that can help them determine the best way to structure interviews, formulate and stage questions, evaluate the completeness of responses, and recover from incomplete responses. Nor are there explicit methods for reviewing the effectiveness of interviews. Consequently, no ongoing professional development or reflexive practice is available to Systems Analysts despite the importance of interviews in development activities.

In this paper we advocate the use of functional linguistic approaches to understanding the work that systems analysts do with a particular interest in elicitation. The theoretical and methodological approach used here is referred to Systemic Functional Linguistics, a semiotic model of language developed by Michael Halliday (1985) and colleagues (Hasan 1985; Martin 1992), has been applied to understanding workpractices associated with systems in organisational contexts (Clarke 2000, 2003) including issues of systems use and renegotiation, system similarity and diachronic change. Interestingly it seems to be a property of communicative and semiotic approaches that the same methods and theories can also be applied at a meta-level- a property which we call metasymmetry. The application of Systemic Functional Linguistics (SFL) concepts to systems analysis activities in context shows the nuances that can occur in particular work situations. In the next section we describe some of the key language resources that are applicable to systems analysis activities, and then in a subsequent section we consider the case of a failed elicitation as a means of revealing how communicative patterns- sometimes referred to as activity sequences or genres- can be gainfully applied to this important aspect of analysis work.

An Orientation to the Systemic Functional Linguistic Approach

SFL is a sophisticated functional and semiotic model of language (Halliday 1985; Hasan 1985; Martin 1992) concerned with the analysis of completed acts of communication (texts) in organisation and institutional settings (contexts). Organisational communication of interest to analysts must take into account the situation specific language associated with particular types of work (registers) and must also be aware of the particular kinds of statements rules, prohibitions, and permissions that distinguish one workplace from another- referred to as social discourse. The text forming properties identified in SFL collectively referred to as texture, play a part in assisting language users including systems analysts in making sense of what is said, heard, written and read. However some language resources are particularly important during systems analysis activities. These can be grouped into five kinds- reference, naming, taxonomy, configuration, and activity sequence, briefly described below:

Reference

The reference system includes those resources collectively referred to as phorocity that describe how 'participants' or people, places, and things get introduced and 'managed' in a text (Eggins 1994, 95). The need for correctly identifying participants occurs in all social occasions including those in which systems analysts 'gather information' about workpractices in workplaces. These social occasions include for example meetings, walk-throughs (spoken-language) or surveys (written language). Whenever we discuss a participant we must provide the reader or listener with information about whether their identity has already been provided (presuming reference) or whether the participant can be considered new for the reader or listener (presenting reference). Where an analyst encounters a presuming referent that is not retrievable, they must utilise their knowledge of language (text) and of situational and cultural contexts to disambiguate it. Analysts will search for situations in which reference can be appropriately recovered in order to identify contrastive, distinctive and functional attributes for candidate participants. If the analyst cannot recover presumed references then this will necessitate further elicitation. For example, during an interview, an analyst can reflect on what a new or otherwise unfamiliar participant might be and use this to provide a follow-up question like 'What do you mean when you say …?', or 'What is a …?'. Analysts correctly employing the reference system will be able to identify the people, places, and things (objects or activities) relevant to particular cultural and situational work contexts.

Naming

It seems trivial to suggest that it is important for analysts to know the correct name for a person, place or thing and yet a considerable number of difficulties for analysts result from just this type of uncertainty. Many language resources are used for naming entities including classifying things into different types as well as other kinds of grammatical and semantic resources. For analysts, questions that can assist in providing the correct names for things include 'What is the correct name for …?', or 'Which one of a possible set of names is this thing- are they different things or synonyms?' Once the correct name for a thing is known it can transformed from the 'everyday' to the 'technical' by means of establishing distinctions or differences between it and other things to which it may be related.

Taxonomy

Our understanding of the social and technical world involves understanding those names or lexical items for things that are relevant to particular social actions and activities (also known as field). It is one thing to know that 'a 68000 chip is a microprocessor'- parenthetically if an Apple Computer salesperson didn't know this then a customer might not value their knowledge! However, it is a more impressive thing to know how this lexical item relates to others in a system of classification; to know that 'a machine with a 68000 family microprocessor a Mac'. If many texts from the same situation are examined, it is possible to build field taxonomies that are represented using the system network notation employed in Figure 1. The lexical items associated with a field are ordered into convenient or observed groups, and possible selection options (paths through the network) can be shown. Over time these systems of classification will be continually modified by adding more options to them (extension), and also by recognising, incorporating and refining the differences between successive options (elaboration). Indeed learning an activity can be represented as extension and elaboration of system networks. Classification is a substantial amount of what we do in systems analysis and also everyday life. Once the relationship between things is known we can start to understand how they enter into processes.

Configuration

Lexical items that are classified into relevant field taxonomies can be used to form messages. Each message will have an agent, utilise a medium of a kind, and exhibit a process. The process is represented by a verb group around which the message or clause will be organised. We can distinguish between different types of processes including material processes, behavioural processes, and mental processes. Material processes express some action going on, some event or something happening, for example "The system is backed up on Friday evening". Behavioural processes concern aspects of behaviour which are in effect psychological processes. Mental processes involve processes of thinking, feeling, or perceiving. Messages can now be assembled to form more complex sequences of activity like those associated with work.

Activity Sequence (Genre)

Goal oriented work can often be characterised by a sequence of functional stages. Likewise when we record and transcribe the language that accompanies work of this type, it also will exhibit a relatively stable and predictable staging. When the pattern of work changes so will the staging of language that accompanies it (see Clarke 2000). Communication about work which is the kind of communication that occurs when workers are trained for a task or when analysts interview workers about their tasks, will also exhibit functional staging that mirrors to a degree the staging of the task. This predictable staging is referred to as an activity sequence or genre. This idea will be explored in the next section.

An Elicitation Incident and its interpretation using Genre

We now concentrate on the use of genres or activity sequences previously introduced. In particular we are interested in using prototypical patterns of communication that are by definition commonly available to all members of an organisational or national culture- the so-called canonical genres. In the first subsection we describe some features common to all genres which make them suitable for use by analysts. In the subsequent subsection we describe a case study involving an interview with a senior manager (anonymous) at an internal warehouse in a large manufacturing company in Australia. Specifically we describe a particular elicitation incident that occurred when conducting the interview. In the final subsection, this elicitation incident is considered from the perspective of genre. These kinds of studies are potential occasions for revealing the social mechanisms through which various kinds of practice are achieved.

Features of Genres

Genres are conventional patterns of communication which are socially endorsed whether within the culture of an organisation or a national. Their purpose is to assist in providing an overall rhetorical organisation to particular types of texts. Genres have the following characteristics. They possess an ordered sequence of elements that represent distinct functions or stages in a text. They are goal-oriented in the sense that all the elements in the sequence must be successfully realised in order for a text to appear complete. Additionally, genres are both associated with and the realisation of a social process.

Each genre has associated with it various textual strategies (Hasan 1985) all of which are useful for the purposes of systems analysis. The first of these is probing where an analyst can request that a response (text) should be 'packaged' to comply with a particular genre. The second strategy is called re-aligning where an analyst for example can re-orient a response which may for some reason not fulfill the appropriate or requested generic conventions. The third feature is called repairing where the analyst can assist in recovering a response, which for some reason or another, could not be provided in accordance with the requested genre. These textual strategies can be used by analysts to elicit texts with specific generic structures and to clarify previous responses as well as to plan subsequent requests for information. In particular, knowledge of the staging of appropriate canonical genres means that an analyst can apply them as heuristics in the field in order to understand important aspects of work including but not limited to:

- Eliciting information about workpractice sequencing: 'What did you do in order to complete … [this particular workpractice]?'
- Determining the identity of workpractice elements: 'If you were going to give a name to that part of … [this particular workpractice], what would you call it?
- Recovery of expected competencies and behaviours of interactants: 'What might you say or do to [a given interactant] who failed to do [this expected behaviour] before [this expected behaviour]?
- Evaluations of the work from the point of view of the participants involved: 'What was difficult about conducting [this particular workpractice]?
- Exploring work experiences: 'Can you tell me about the most difficult [workpractice instance] with which you were involved?

An Elicitation Incident

The author was part of a team engaged in a multimedia case study of warehouse processes in a large manufacturing plant. As part of this case study, interviews were conducted with clients who were involved in various aspects of the workpractices in the warehouse including the Senior Manager in charge of the warehouse, the Operations Manager, and the IT Manager for the warehouse systems. Because we had the funding, the expertise and the equipment, the interviews were recorded by our camera crew. Including the author, two analysts shared the interviews- one would lead and the other would act as a backup. For the purposes of this paper we discuss a single analysis interview which was conducted by my colleague.

Table 1. Senior Manager Systems Analysis Interview. RN stands for Response Number, SMPTE Code is an absolute video time stamp using hours, minutes, and seconds, and a Response Gloss which summarises the details of the response by the interactant

RN	SMPTE Code	Response Gloss
1	0:00:43- 0:02:43	Repairable Items and their status at IDC
2	0:02:48- 0:03:24	Scraping Items
3	0:03:31- 0:03:55	Returned Repairable Items
4	0:04:10- 0:05:01	Decision to Repair an Item
5	0:05:02- 0:05:06	Purchase or Lease Repairable Items
6	0:05:09- 0:06:05	Unique Identification of Repairable Items
7	0:06:08- 0:07:21	Non-repairable Items at IDC
8	0:07:42- 0:08:58	Picking Process
9	0:09:03- 0:09:22	Breakdowns/Issues: SAP & Stock*Man Interaction
10	0:09:38- 0:11:50	Picking Process: Required Information
11	0:12:13- 0:12:59	Item Labels: Common Information
12	0:12:59- 0:13:32	Item Labels: Other Information
13	0:13:57- 0:15:12	Reasons for having a Catalogue Number and a SSN
14	0:15:07- 0:16:03	Structure of the SSN Barcode
15	0:16:13- 0:16:39	ISSUEs
16	0:16:43- 0:17:17	DISPATCHes
17	0:17:21- 0:18:00	Batching Deliveries of ISSUEs to Customers
18	0:18:05- 0:18:18	Standard Delivery Routes for ISSUEs
19	0:18:19- 0:18:48	DISPATCH Deliveries
20	0:18:46- 0:19:04	Costing IDC Services
21	0:19:05- 0:20:26	Scrap Material Storage
22	0:20:32- 0:20:30	Tracking Items to the Delivery Point
23	0:23:35- 0:26:49	Previous System
24	0:26:39- 0:28:28	IDC Operations Room: Personelle
25	0:28:29- 0:29:03	Quarantine Area
26	0:29:20- 0:31:07	SAP System: Raising Orders
27	0:31:10- 0:31:25	SAP System: Accounting
28	0:31:26- 0:31:36	SAP System: Inventory Planning and Management
29	0:31:41- 0:31:45	Inventory Planning and Management Personnel
30	0:31:50- 0:32:46	Performance Reviews of IDC
31	0:33:10- 0:34:25	Stocktake Processes at the IDC
32	0:34:29- 0:36:10	Decision to stock an item in the IDC
33	0:36:12- 0:36:20	Audit trail to Suppliers
34	0:37:20- 0:39:04	Technical Support about Items

The interviewee was the Senior Manager and the topics covered in that interview are listed in Table 1. The first column indicates the topic number in the interview; the second column provides a short form of the SMPTE code which is a broadcast industry standard time code for video production. The third column titled Response Gloss is a short phrase which is based on the theme of the response. The information in Table 1 already provides some useful information. For example there are 34 responses provided by the client in just over 39 minutes- that's fast interviewing and fast answering. For example, RN5 requires all of 4 seconds for the Manager to address. Some responses take longer, RN24 requires almost two minutes for the Manager to address- a lot of text to transcribe for one response. But on balance the length of these responses is short. This is certainly compatible with the fact that this interview was conducted late in the analysis phase. This is evident both in the transcript and the video record of the interview. Despite non-verbally signalling discomfort at being filmed, the interviewee was familiar with and comfortable in the company of the analysts. The relationship between the client and the development team was firmly established, all parties where committed to it, and the project had been proceeding for over a year. The response glosses indicate that many different and seemingly unrelated questions are being asked- the analysts are filling in gaps in their knowledge (for example, RN13). There is some evidence of follow-on questioning (RN12 and RN18), but each of the theme lengths- the number of responses on the same topic- is short.

The workpractices associated with the warehouse involve various ways in which items can be added to the warehouse holdings (inputs) as well as a number of ways in which those holdings can be removed from the warehouse (outputs). The workpractices being studied involved only stocked repairable items, for example engines used in conveyer belts that are not disposable and which are expensive enough to warrant repairing. In order for stored items to be sent out of the warehouse- perhaps to be issued to its customers, or dispatched to a repair shop- the item must first be picked. The incident of interest in this paper occurred at RN8 when the analyst asked the senior manager about this picking process. This should have been a routine question given that this particular manager had worked as a fork lift truck driver for some 15 years. For the last ten years he had been the senior manger of the warehouse and in fact was responsible for the business analysis which resulted in the specification and eventual implementation of the random-warehouse system that we were studying. But when the interviewing analyst elicited information about workpractice sequencing 'How do you pick an item' the manager started confidently enough to explain the sequence of steps, he then paused, corrected himself saying 'no that's not right... next you [use a laser barcode reader to] scan the bay [a location in the warehouse where an item can be stored] then you pick up the palette using the forklift truck and scan the item'. He then stopped, blushed, and asked for time to think about the sequencing. The interviewing analyst attempted to reduce the manager's embarrassment by suggested that the first interpretation was correct. The manager then asked whether the cameraman could erase the response from the video because it was wrong. The cameraman replied that it was not necessary as they could simply repeat the question again and continue from where they had left off. The burning question is what just happened in this micro-encounter? How could an expert interviewee intimately familiar with this work practice get it so wrong? The answer to this question is based on the machinery of generic conventions and has some interesting consequences for analysis practice.

An Interpretation Using Canonical Genre

A probe which seeks a historical recapitulation of an activity in time-order, for example 'what did you just do' or 'how did you do that' is a request to provide a response in the form of a particular canonical genre called a Factual RECOUNT. Note the small capitals are a labelling convention of canonical genres, while the 'Factual' prefix distinguishes it from a similarly structured Narrative RECOUNT. The staging for the genre is provided in Figure 1 based on a digraph representation developed by Clarke (2000). The 'Orientation' is a stage that is used to describe what the RECOUNT is about. This is followed by a set of events in time order followed by an optional Deduction stage.

However as it was not the case that the manager had recently performed this kind of work, the analyst correctly issued the probe 'how are items picked' which is a request to provide a response in the form of a particular canonical genre called a PROCEDURE. This is used to describe how an activity is performed or undertaken in the general case for the purposes of documenting what is common to all picking activities rather than to describing a personal instance of it. The analyst has probed for the correct genre- in fact both Factual RECOUNTs and the PROCEDUREs are activity structured. So what happened to the Senior Manager's knowledge? Management work is not organised around action but abstractions. Our manager will be involved day-to-day with genres that are not organised around activities. When dealing with specific cases, managers will tend to use DESCRIPTIONs as the available non-activity structured complement of a Factual recount. In contrast to Factual RECOUNTs that are organized around events, DESCRIPTIONs are organized around Features, see Fig 1. Furthermore, as the Manager was aware that what was called for was a generalised account their response was not in the form of a DESCRIPTION but organised in the form of a REPORT. REPORTs involve describing entire classes of things. As can be seen from Fig 1, there are two kinds of REPORTs.

Factual RECOUNT
Orientation, Record of Events, (Deduction)

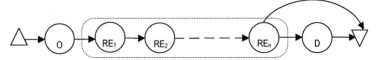

DESCRIPTION
Identification, Feature, (Deduction)

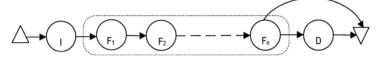

PROCEDURE
Procedural Aim, Instructional Component

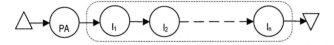

REPORT
Classification Stage: Purpose, Section Preview; Type/Part Stage: Type, Part

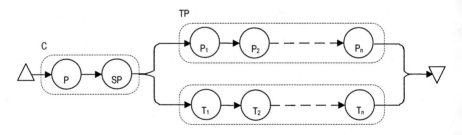

Fig. 1. Genre Digraph representation (after Clarke 2000) of some of the some of the members of the Factual Canonical Genre group (after Martin 1992, 565-568; Eggins and Slade 1996, 236). Refer to text

Part-whole REPORTs are used to distinguish between for example objects, controls or options (parts) that belong to a common group (the whole). Type REPORTs concern objects that are not organised in a part-whole relationship, but can be usefully grouped together at some abstract level. Selecting from the available non-activity structured Factual Genres, the senior Manager selected a Type REPORT and promptly had difficulties because the genre he used to assist him in responding to the request could not help him to package or recollect staging which he had spent a good portion of his working life enacting! This indicates the power that generic social conventions have in communication and understanding.

Conclusions and Further Research

There are a number of immediate outcomes of this research. Systems Analysis activities involving communication between clients and developers and by extension developer-to-developer can be theorised using Systemic Functional Linguistics. Applying SFL methods does appear to assist Systems Analysts during the interviewing process especially in formulating and staging questions, evaluating the completeness of responses, and recovering from incomplete responses. As an illustration of the utility of SFL, methods based on canonical genre were used to understand an elicitation incident occurring during a system analysis interview (reading practices). Importantly canonical genre can be used heuristically by systems analysts in the field as a kind of organisational reading practice. By utilising conventional patterns of meaning, analysts are likely to become familiar with a client's operations. Indeed idiosyncratic interview techniques, whose success relies upon the individual abilities of a gifted analyst, could be replaced with explicit elicitation techniques that could form the basis of new pedagogic practices. Current tertiary educational programmes in systems analysis, emphasis the methods and techniques used to write up deliverables. Coupled with a general unfamiliarity with organisations, students are never actually taught the process of elicitation. SFL based techniques offer the best chance of developing relevant organisational reading practices for analysis students.

References

Burch J, Grudnitski G (1989) Information Systems: Theory and Practice. 5th ed. John Wiley & Sons NY

Clarke RJ (2000) An Information System in its Organisational Contexts: A Systemic Semiotic Longitudinal Case Study. Unpublished PhD Dissertation Department of Information Systems University of Wollongong Australia

Clarke RJ (2003) The Discursive Organisation of Action and Language in Work-practice Descriptions. In: Goldkuhl G, Lind M, Ågerfalk PJ (eds) ALOIS 2003 – Action in Language, Organisations and Information Systems. VITS Research Network Linköping University Sweden 12th-13th March 2003

Easterbrook S (1993) Negotiation and the Role of the Requirements Specification. In: Quintas P (ed) Social Dimensions of Systems Engineering: People, Processes, Policies and Software Development. Ellis Horwood New York

Eggins S (1994) An Introduction to Systemic Functional Linguistics. Pinter Publishers London United Kingdom

Eggins S, Slade D (1997) Analysing Casual Conversation. Cassell London and Washington

Halliday MAK (1985) An Introduction to Functional Grammar. Edward Arnold London

Hasan R (1985) The Structure of a Text. In: Halliday MAK, Hasan R (1985) Language, Context, and Text: Aspects of Language on a Social-Semiotic Perspective. Deakin University Press Geelong Victoria

Martin JR (1992) English Text: System and Structure. John Benjamins Publishing Company Philadelphia/Amsterdam

Quintas P (1993) Introduction – Living the Lifecycle: Social Processes in software and systems development. In: Quintas P (ed) Social Dimensions of Systems Engineering: People, Processes, Policies and Software Development Ellis Horwood Series in Interactive Information Systems. Ellis Horwood Limited London

Sekaran U (1992) Research Methods for Business: A Skill Building Approach. Second ed. John Wiley and Sons USA

Cost Effective Development of Usable Systems: Gaps between HCI and Software Architecture Design

Eelke Folmer and Jan Bosch

University of Groningen, the Netherlands. email@eelke.com, Jan.Bosch@cs.rug.nl

Introduction

A software product with poor usability is likely to fail in a highly competitive market; therefore software developing organizations are paying more and more attention to ensuring the usability of their software. Practice, however, shows that product quality (which includes usability among others) is not that high as it could be. Studies of software projects (Pressman, 2001) reveal that organizations spend a relative large amount of money and effort on fixing usability problems during late stage development. Some of these problems could have been detected and fixed much earlier. This avoidable rework leads to high costs and because during development different tradeoffs have to be made, for example between cost and quality leads to systems with less than optimal usability. This problem has been around for a couple of decades especially after software engineering (SE) and human computer interaction (HCI) became disciplines on their own. While both disciplines developed themselves, several gaps appeared which are now receiving increased attention in research literature. Major gaps of understanding, both between suggested practice and how software is actually developed in industry, but also between the best practices of each of the fields have been identified (Carrol et al, 1994, Bass et al, 2001, Folmer and Bosch, 2002). In addition, there are gaps in the fields of differing terminology, concepts, education, and methods. (Walenstein, 2003). Several problems and solutions have been identified to cover some of these gaps (Constantine et al, 2003, Walenstein, 2003).

Our approach to bridge one of these gaps is based upon the following observation. The software architecture may restrict the level of usability that can be achieved i.e. the quintessential example that is always used to illustrate this restriction is adding Undo. Undo is the ability to reverse certain actions (such as reversing deleting some text in Word). Undo may significantly improve usability as it allows a user to explore, make mistakes and easily go some steps back; facilitating learning the application's functionality. However from experience, it is also learned that it is often very hard to implement undo in application during late stage, because implementing undo requires certain parts of the software architecture to be modified. If this has already been implemented it will affect many parts of existing source code. So adding usability improving solutions during late stage development is to some extent restricted by the software architecture. To cost effectively develop a usable software system one must include creating a software architecture that supports the right level of usability. However, few software engineers and human computer interaction engineers are aware of this restriction leading to avoidable rework. There are several reasons for this, for example user interface designers and software engineers have usually very different backgrounds resulting in a lack of mutual understanding of each others view on technical or design issues. This paper presents a set of "gaps" that explain why explain why usability is not achieved cost effectively in current software development practice. These gaps have been identified in several case studies with software architecture analysis of usability. Some of these problems can be considered as gaps between HCI & SE though not all problems we present here are necessarily gaps between both communities, but rather a failure and shortcoming of the current practice of one community. The next section discusses briefly discusses our assessment technique and the case studies that were performed. In the Sections after that we discuss the problems we identified.

Analysis Method & Case studies

This section briefly introduces our assessment technique and the case studies performed in order to provide the necessary context for understanding the gaps that are presented later on.

SALUTA

In (Folmer et al, 2004) the Scenario based Architecture Level UsabiliTy Analysis (SALUTA) method is presented. A method ensures that some form of reasoning and discussion between different stakeholders about the architecture is taking place at a time it is still cheap to make changes. Until recently no assessment techniques existed that focused on analyzing an architecture for its support of usability. SALUTA is scenario based i.e. in order to assess a particular architecture, a set of scenarios is developed that concretizes the actual meaning of that quality requirement (Bosch, 2000). In our industrial and academic experience with scenario based analysis we have come to understanding that the use of scenarios allows us to make a very concrete and detailed analysis and statements about their impact or support they require, even for quality attributes that are hard to predict and assess from a forward engineering perspective such as maintainability, security and modifiability. SALUTA consists of the following four steps:

1. Create usage profile: a set of scenarios that accurately express the required usability of the system is developed in this step. Usage profile creation does not replace existing requirements engineering techniques. Rather it transforms (existing) usability requirements into something that can be used for architecture assessment.
2. Describe provided usability: Usability analysis requires architectural information that allows the analyst to determine the support for the usage scenarios. In order to do that we need to know which usability improving design solutions may need to be applied during architecture design. This information has been captured in the software - architecture - usability (SAU) framework (Folmer et al, 2003). SALUTA uses the SAU framework to identify which architecture design solutions have been applied in the architecture.
3. Evaluate scenarios: For each scenario, we identify how that scenario may be affected by usability improving design solutions identified in the architecture. We then identify for each scenario, using the SAU framework, how a particular design solution improves or impairs usability (the SAU framework relates these design solutions to particular attributes of usability e.g. learnability, reliability etc.)
4. Interpret the results: after scenario evaluation, the results need to be interpreted to draw conclusions concerning the software architecture. This interpretation very much depends on the goal of the analysis.

A complete overview of our technique and a detailed description of the steps can be found in (Folmer et al, 2004).

Case Studies

In order to validate SALUTA it has been applied at three cases in the domain of web based enterprise systems, e.g. content management- (CMS), e-commerce- and enterprise resource planning (ERP) – systems. From a usability point of view this domain is very interesting: as many different users (e.g. anyone with an internet connection) and usages needs to be supported. In addition, web based systems have become an increasingly popular application format in recent years. Below we briefly discuss the three cases.

- The Webplatform is a web based content management system for one of the largest universities in the Netherlands which enables a variety of (centralized) technical and (de-centralized) non technical staff to create, edit, manage and publish a variety of content (such as text, graphics, video etc), whilst being constrained by a centralized set of rules, process and workflows that ensure a coherent, validated website appearance.
- The Compressor catalogue application is a product developed by the Imperial Highway Group (IHG) for a client in the refrigeration industry. It is an e-commerce application, which makes it possible for potential customers to search for detailed technical information about a range of compressors; for example, comparing two compressors.
- The eSuite product developed by LogicDIS is a system that allows access to various ERP (Enterprise Resource Planning) systems, through a web interface. ERP systems generally run on large mainframe computers and only provide users with a terminal interface. eSuite is built as an web interface on top of different ERP systems.

For each of these cases a set of scenarios was identified that accurately expressed the required usability. Then the architecture was analyzed using the SAU framework which resulted in a set of usability improving design solutions that have been implemented in the architecture. Then the support for each of the scenarios was determined. Finally some action was taken based on the result of the analysis, this was either selecting a particular architecture (Compressor), improving the current architecture design (eSuite). In the Webplatform case no action was taken as implementation of this system had already started but it provided the software architect with valuable insights till which extent certain usability improving design solutions could still be implemented during late stage without incurring great costs. Our impression was that overall the assessment was well received by the architects that assisted the analysis, the assessment emphasized and increased the understanding of the important relationship between software architecture and usability and the results of the assessments were documented and taken into account for future releases and redevelopment of the products. SALUTA may assist a software architect to come up with a more usable first version of a software architecture that might allow for more "usability tuning" on the detailed design level, saving some of the high costs incurring adaptive maintenance activities once the system has been implemented. However, during the definition of our method and the different case studies, we managed to identify several gaps that still need to be bridged before cost effective development of usable systems can be realized. In the next sections these gaps are discussed.

Software Architecture Analysis is an Ad-hoc Activity

Generally, three arguments for defining an architecture are used (Bass et all, 1998). First, it provides an artifact that allows discussion by the stakeholders very early in the design process. Second, it allows for early assessment of quality attributes (Kazman et al, 1998, Bosch, 2000). Finally, the design decisions captured in the software architecture can be transferred to other systems. As identified by (Lassing et all, 2002a) early assessment is least applied in practice. In all organizations where we conducted case studies, architecture assessment was not an explicitly defined process and there was no integration and cooperation with existing (usability) requirements collection techniques. We were called in as an external assessment team mostly at the end of the software architecture design phase and in one case (Webplatform) even after that phase, to assess whether any architecture-usability problems were to be expected. There is no need to assess a software architecture for quality concerns when developers are not aware that the software architecture plays a major role in fulfilling these. The software architecture is often seen as an intermediate product in the development process but its potential with respect to quality assessment still needs to be exploited (Lassing et all, 2002a). In addition for some quality attributes developers have few or no techniques available for predicting them before the system itself is available. Raising the importance of software architecture as an important instrument for quality assessment is an important step forward in bridging this gap. If a software architecture analysis technique such as SALUTA was an integral part of the development process earlier phases or activities would result in the necessary information for creating usage profiles and provide for the necessary architectural descriptions. For example existing usability engineering techniques such as interviews, group discussions, rapid prototyping or observations (Nielsen, 1993, Shneiderman, 1998) typically already provide information such as representative tasks, users and contexts of use and requirements for these scenarios that are needed to create a usage profile. Furthermore, the results of an architecture assessment should influence the architecture design process.

Impact of Software Architecture Design on Usability

One of the reasons to develop SALUTA was to be able to analyze how usability may impact software architecture design. However, we also identified that it worked the other way around; architecture design sometimes leads to usability problems in the interface and the interaction. In the Webplatform case study we identified that the layout of a page (users had to fill in a form) was determined by the XML definition of a specific object. When users had to insert data, the order in which particular fields had to be filled in turned out to be very confusing. Because interface design is often postponed until the later stages of design we run the risk that many assumptions are built into the design of the architecture that unknowingly affect interface/ interaction design and vice versa. Although some prototypes were made for the Webplatform for aesthetic analysis no attention was given to this specific case. In order to deal with this we should not design interfaces and interaction as last but as early as possible to identify what should be supported by the software architecture and how the architecture may affect interface/interaction design. We should not only analyze whether the architecture design supports certain usability solutions but also identify how the architecture design may lead to usability problems. However this is very complex as usability is determined by many factors, issues such as:

- Information architecture: how is information presented to the user?
- Interaction architecture: how is functionality presented to the user?
- System quality attributes: such as efficiency and reliability.

Architecture design does affect all these issues. For example the quality attributes such as performance or reliability are to a considerable extent defined by the software architecture. The software architecture also has major impact on the interaction & information architecture. Designing a usable system is more than ensuring a usable interface; a slow and buggy system architecture with a usable interface is not considered usable on the other hand the most reliable and performing system architecture is not usable if the user can't figure out how to use the system. Currently our work has only focused on how the usability may restrict architecture design. Analyzing how a software architecture may unknowingly affect interface and interaction design is still an open issue.

Technology Driven Design

The software architects we interviewed in the case studies were not aware of the important role the software architecture plays in restricting usability requirements. When designing their systems the software architects had already selected technologies (read features) and had already developed a first version of the system before they decided to include the user in the loop. In one case study (Webplatform) it was already too late to make fundamental changes required to fulfill certain usability requirements. There are two main causes for this problem: First, developers tend to concentrate on the functional features of their architectures and seldom address the ways in which their architectures support quality concerns (Kazman et all, 1994). And second the software engineering community still considers usability to be primarily a property of the presentation of information; the user interface (Berkun, 2002). Designing a usable system is more than ensuring a usable interface; a slow and buggy system architecture with a usable interface is not considered usable, on the other hand the most reliable and performing system architecture is not usable if the user can't figure out how to use the system. Software architects should be aware that the software architecture plays an important role in fulfilling and limiting the level of quality. Second, software architects tend to optimize technological considerations over usability considerations. A software product is often seen as a set of features rather then a set of "user experiences". When design is dominated by a technological view, it's natural for decision makers (including software architects) to optimize technological considerations over all others. In order to change this practice we need to change the attitudes of software engineers e.g. the technological view of a product is only one of many views. The best software comes from teams, or from team leaders, that are able to see the work from multiple perspectives, balancing them in accordance with the project goals, and the state of the project at any given time (Berkun, 2002). Another way to change the attitudes is by making the results of architecture assessment accountable e.g. architectural assessment may save on maintenance costs spent on dealing with usability issues. However at the moment we lack figures to acknowledge this claim. To raise awareness and change attitudes (especially those of the decision makers) we should clearly define and measure the business and competitive advantages of architectural assessment of usability.

Poor Specification of Usability Requirements

Although this gap is well recognized in literature, it is essential for architecture assessment to have specified requirements. In our experience usability requirements are often poorly specified. In all cases we performed, apart from some general usability guidelines (Nielsen, 1993) that had been stated in the functional requirements; no clearly defined and verifiable usability requirements had been collected nor specified. Most software developing companies still underestimate the importance of usability and usability engineering, and postpone the activity of usability requirements collection till there is a running system and assume all usability problems can be easily fixed. Even when usability requirements are specified, they are specified on a rather abstract level. A usability requirement such as: 'the system should be easy to learn' does not state anything about users, contexts of use or tasks for which this requirement should hold. The reason for this abstract specification is that traditionally usability requirements have been specified such that these can be verified for an implemented system. However, such requirements are largely useless in a forward engineering process. For example, we could say that a goal for a system is that it should be easy to learn, or that new users should require no more than 30 minutes instruction, however, a requirement at this level does not help guide the design process. Such requirements can only be measured when the system has been completed. Usability requirements need to take a more concrete form expressed in terms of the solution domain to influence design.

Usability Requirements should be Specified in Terms of the Solution Domain

Usability requirements should be specified in terms of the solution domain. E.g. for a software engineer is much easier to translate a requirement such as "undo is needed in this particular task" to a particular architecture solution then it is for a requirement such as "this task should be error free" or "this task should be easy to learn". In our SAU framework we have captured a number of usability improving solutions which are "architecture sensitive" e.g. hard to retrofit during late stage development. This framework can be used to discuss the architecture support for usability. Architects can check whether particular design solutions need to be implemented and discuss these with usability engineers to identify the increase in usability of the system under analysis. Even in cases where there is no direct need for a particular design solution the usability engineer and software architect may discuss the design solutions in the framework to identify whether particular design solutions may needed to be added to the architecture in the future. In the eSuite case two particular design solutions were implemented in the software architecture to make sure the architecture supported future evolution of usability requirements.

Sharing Design Knowledge

An important gap we identified is the following. Often usability engineers come up with a change request during late stage development which a software engineer cannot implement as this change is too costly to implement. On the other hand when designing an architecture software architects are unaware which usability improving design solutions should be implemented during architecture design. In order to improve upon this situation the relevant design knowledge needs to be shared between both communities. In order to make this design knowledge accessible to both communities we recently decided to coin a new term called "bridging pattern" (Folmer et al, 2005). Bridging patterns extend interaction design patterns, which are well known in HCI community, by adding information on how to generally implement this pattern and sketching out architectural considerations that must be taken into account. Bridging patterns are a first attempt to provide some shared vocabulary (e.g. a Rosetta stone) within both communities to improve current design.

Design for Change

During or after the development usability requirements often change. The context in which the user and the software operate is continually changing and evolving, sometimes users may find new uses for a product, for which the product was not originally intended. New features get added to an existing software product during product evolutions which have different usability requirements. In all case studies we noticed that during development the usability requirements had changed. For example, in the Webplatform case it had initially been specified that the Webplatform should always provide context sensitive help texts, however for more experienced users this turned out to be annoying and led to a usability problem. A system where help texts could be turned off for more experienced users would be much better. After Webplatform had been finished new features (e.g. support & manipulation for streaming video) were added. However these came with new usability requirements (for example the frame rate on a mobile phone should not drop below a certain threshold). The Webplatform software architecture did not sufficiently support these new usability requirements. This example shows that it is hard or even impossible to capture all possible (future) usability requirements during initial design and this may lead to big problems. In order to deal with changing requirements software architectures should provide some flexibility to still be able to cost effectively support future usability requirements. When for example we implement Undo using the Command pattern (Gamma et al 1995) we can easily create new undo actions even for new unforeseen tasks. Determining which design solutions must be implemented during architecture design is still an open issue.

Separation of Concerns

Since software engineers are not usability experts and usability experts are not software engineers, the responsibilities of defining and collecting usability requirements should be separated from the architectural design responsibilities. This requirement very much depends on the size of the software developing organization but in the case studies we performed (varying from small to medium sized organizations) only at one case study these responsibilities were divided. We did not identify any usability engineers trying to design a software architecture but software architects defining usability requirements is not an uncommon practice. A better balancing of the different views of the system (and hence better usability) is achieved when software is designed in multi disciplinary teams.

Conclusions

Architecture analysis of usability is an important tool for cost effective development of usable software. In the context of defining an architecture assessment technique and experiences with performing software architecture analysis of usability in three cases we managed to identify several gaps that still need to be bridged before cost effective development of usable systems can be realized. Because software engineers in industry lacked support for the early evaluation of usability we defined a generalized four-step method for Software Architecture Level UsabiliTy Analysis called SALUTA. Three case studies have been performed in the domain of web based system. With our set of gaps we have focused on the gaps that are of cultural and psychological nature.

- Software architecture analysis is an ad hoc process as the software architecture is only seen as an intermediate product in the development process.
- Not only does usability impact software architecture design but software architecture design may lead to usability problems in the interface and interaction.
- Developers tend to concentrate only on the functional features of their architectures.
- Usability requirements are often poorly specified.
- Usability requirements should be specified in terms of the solution domain in order to help guide the architecture design process.
- The relevant design knowledge needs to be shared between both communities in a form that can be understood by both communities.
- Rather than let change be a big problem we should design an architecture with enough flexibility to support unseen future usability requirements.
- We should have strict separation of concerns concerning usability requirements collection and architecture design.

In our view, the case studies that have been conducted have provided valuable experiences and insights in the relationship between software architecture and usability. By raising:

- The awareness of the importance of the relationship between usability and software architecture.
- The importance of usability as the most important quality attribute.
- The awareness of software architecture as an important instrument to fulfill usability requirements.

Eventually software engineers and usability engineers must recognize the need for a closer integration of practices and techniques leading to cost effective development of usable systems.

References

Bass L, Clements P, Kazman R (1998) Software Architecture in Practice. Addison Wesley Longman

Bass L, Kates J, John BE (2001) Achieving Usability through Software Architecture. Technical Report CMU/SEI-2001-TR-005

Berkun S (2002) The List of Reasons Ease of Use Doesn't Happen on Engineering Projects. www.scottberkun.com/essays/essay22.htm

Bosch J (2000) Design and Use of Software Architectures: Adopting and Evolving a Product Line Approach. Pearson Education (Addison-Wesley and ACM Press)

Caroll JM, Mack RL, Robertson S, Rosson M (1994) Binding Objects to Scenarios of Use. International Journal of Human-Computer Studies, vol 41, no 1-2, pp 243-276

Constantine LL, Biddle R, Noble J (2003) Usage-Centered Design and Software Engineering: Models for Integration. Proc of the ICSE Workshop on Bridging the Gaps between Software Engineering and Human-Computer Interaction

Folmer E, Bosch J (2002) Architecting for Usability; a Survey. Journal of systems and Software, vol 70/1-2, pp 61-78

Folmer E, Gurp Jv, Bosch J (2004) Software Architecture Analysis of Usability. Proc of the 9th IFIP Working Conference on Engineering for Human-Computer Interaction

Folmer E, Gurp Jv, Bosch J (2003) A Framework for Capturing the Relationship between Usability and Software Architecture. Software Process: Improvement and Practice, vol 8, Issue 2, pp 67-87

Folmer E, Welie M, Bosch J (2005) Bridging Patterns - an Approach to Bridge Gaps between SE and HCI. Accepted for the Journal of Information & Software Technology

Gamma E, Helm R, Johnson R, Vlissides J (1995) Design Patterns Elements of Reusable Object-Orientated Software. Addison-Wesley

Kazman R, Abowd G, Webb M (1994) SAAM: A Method for Analyzing the Properties of Software Architectures. Proc of the 16th International Conference on Software Engineering

Kazman R, Klein M, Barbacci M, Longstaff T, Lipson H, Carriere J (1998) The Architecture Tradeoff Analysis Method. Proc of the International Conference on Engineering of Complex Computer Systems. Monterey CA

Lassing N, Bengtsson PO, van Vliet H, Bosch J (2002) Experiences with ALMA: Architecture-Level Modifiability Analysis. Journal of Systems and Software, vol 61, no 1, pp 47-57

Nielsen J (1993) Usability Engineering. Academic Press Inc

Pressman RS, Pres (2001) Software Engineering: A Practitioner's Approach. 5th ed. McGraw-Hill Higher Education

Shneiderman B (1998) Designing the User Interface: Strategies for Effective Human-Computer Interaction. Addison-Wesley

Walenstein A (2003) Finding Boundary Objects in SE and HCI: An Approach through Engineering Oriented Design Theories. Proc of the ICSE Workshop on Bridging the Gaps between Software Engineering and Human-Computer Interaction IEEE

Challenging the HCI Concept of Fidelity by Positioning Ozlab Prototypes

Jenny Nilsson and Joe Siponen

Department of Information Systems, Karlstad University, Sweden.
jenny.nilsson@kau.se, joe.siponen@gmail.com

Introduction

This paper examines how the fidelity concept is used by the HCI community to categorize prototypes. Two fidelity categories are generally used when categorizing prototypes: low-fidelity and high-fidelity. The detailed description of these categories by Rudd et al. (1996) is used to represent the HCI community's view of fidelity as it is often referred to by the HCI community (see for example Preece et al., 2002).

We analyze the fidelity concept by trying to position the Wizard of Oz methodology in the correct fidelity category. This methodology entails that the user believes that he or she is interacting with a computer program when in reality he or she is interacting with a human. There are several ways one can use this methodology. The one we have chosen is the Ozlab system, developed at Karlstad University. It was chosen not only because it fully implements the Wizard of Oz methodology, but also because it extends the modes of human enabled and monitored interactivity to the graphical user interface (GUI). The positioning of the Wizard of Oz methodology is done by positioning the Ozlab prototypes.

The purpose of any prototype is largely defined by the demands posed by the current activities of the software development process. In this paper we focus on the prototyping done when gathering and communicating users' requirements on the proposed system's graphical user interface and functionality. Ozlab and low-fidelity prototypes are exclusively used for this purpose. As a result, a comparison with high-fidelity prototypes in other contexts is not possible.

The paper starts by describing the low and high fidelity categorization. After this it is argued that the advantages and disadvantages of low- and high-fidelity prototypes are directly related to how automatically the prototype responds to the user's actions. The Wizard of Oz methodology and the Ozlab system is then presented before attempting to position an Ozlab prototype in its fidelity category. This positioning leads to another categorization based on the prototype's level of automatic response production.

Characteristics of High- and Low-fidelity Prototypes

Rudd et al. (1996) characterize low-fidelity prototypes as "limited function, limited interaction prototyping efforts [...] constructed for illustrating concepts, design alternatives and screen layouts." These are usually constructed using paper and pencil and other standard office supplies. However, interaction with paper prototypes can also be simulated, for instance Rettig (1994) simulates the interaction flow by having a person act instead of the computer. In response to the user's actions, the person will change between the different papers corresponding to different screen layouts in the system. Input to the system is indicated by, e.g., the user pointing on drawn controls, or writing on the paper sheets.

In contrast to the characterization of low-fidelity prototypes, Rudd et al. (1996) define high-fidelity prototypes as being "fully interactive", meaning that a user can "interact with the user interface as though it is a real product." They further state that these kinds of prototypes look and act so real that the user, in many cases, is unable to tell it apart from the real product. Such high-fidelity prototypes are typically constructed using high-level languages such as SmallTalk, or Visual Basic. Bönisch et al. (2003) have defined an intermediate level of fidelity, where the prototypes are capable of showing part but not all of the interactivity. According to Bönisch et al. (ibid.) these are constructed using tools like Powerpoint®, Hypercard or Tcl/Tk.

In Table 1 we present the advantages and disadvantages of both categories as stated by Rudd et al. (1996).

A Closer Look at the Advantages and Disadvantages

Interestingly, when scrutinizing the different advantages and disadvantages ascribed to both low- and high-fidelity prototyping efforts it becomes apparent that many of these can be explained by *how automatic the response production of a prototype is.*

Table 1. Advantages and disadvantages of high- and low-fidelity prototypes from Rudd et al. (1996)

Type	Advantages	Disadvantages
Low-fidelity prototype	Lower development cost. Evaluate multiple design concepts. Useful communication device. Address screen layout issues. Useful for identifying market requirements. Proof-of-concept.	Limited error checking. Poor detailed specification to code to. Facilitator-driven. Limited utility after requirements established. Limited usefulness for usability tests. Navigational and flow limitations.
High-fidelity prototype	Complete functionality. Fully interactive. User-driven. Clearly defines navigational scheme. Use for exploration and test. Look and feel of final product. Serves as a living specification. Marketing and sales tool.	More expensive to develop. Time-consuming to create. Inefficient for proof-of-concept designs. Not effective for requirements gathering.

In this section we elaborate on the advantages and disadvantages in Table 1 and illustrate how these relate to automatic response production. Note that the quadrants of Table 1 are closely related to each other, where many of the advantages for one type of prototyping are presented as the disadvantages of the other type.

We have divided the advantages and disadvantages into four different subject areas: user-driven-versus-facilitator-driven, development costs, early exploration of the design space and reusability in implementation.

User-Driven-versus-Facilitator-Driven

According to Rudd et al. (1996) a high-fidelity prototype is more **suitable for user testing and exploration** because it "will respond in a manner that represents the behaviour of the eventual product." Their article differentiates between low- and high-fidelity prototypes largely by the manner in which the prototype responds; a high-fidelity responds by itself (i.e. it is **user-driven)** in contrast to low-fidelity prototypes that are **facilitator-**

driven. We believe that what the authors' really are talking about is whether the response production is fully automatic (user-driven) or non-automatic (facilitator-driven). A prototype can thus be thought of as being **completely functional** and **fully interactive** only when its responses are automatically generated.

Given the high degree of autonomy, a high-fidelity prototype can be used to evaluate both **the look and the feel** of the proposed system (not just the look as is the case with low-fidelity prototypes).

Development Costs

Rudd et al. (1996) characterize a high-fidelity prototype as being fully interactive, meaning that a user can expect the prototype to respond to his/her actions automatically (i.e. no human facilitator is needed). In addition of creating a high-fidelity prototype's graphics one also needs to program it to be automatic. It is important to understand that a low-fidelity approach does not mean that the graphics created are of inferior quality – in fact these too are sometimes created on the computer (Rettig 1994). When demonstrating low-fidelity prototypes to clients it is typical that high-fidelity graphics are created simply because, as Rettig (ibid.) puts it, "you want to look sharp." Therefore, the main distinction between low- and high-fidelity prototypes is the degree of automatic response production. The time and money invested in making the prototype act on its own contributes to the **added cost for a high-fidelity prototype**.

It could be argued that in certain kinds of multimedia systems the biggest cost is inflected by the production and/or gathering of the actual media used. However, stock photography or media are typically used when such systems are prototyped. In contrast, it is not possible to purchase "stock" programming in order to make the prototype act automatically. Hence, even when multimedia systems are prototyped the added cost for a high-fidelity prototype is due to the programming required to make the prototype respond automatically to users' actions.

As Rudd et al. (1996) point out a high-fidelity prototyping effort sometimes ends up "requiring many weeks of programming support." The time spent on programming *one* automatic prototype could be used to **evaluate multiple design concepts** if low-fidelity prototyping was used. Myers' & Rosson's (1992) study of 74 software projects has shown that an average of 50.1% of software implementation (i.e. programming) time was used on the user interface, confirming that programming user interfaces is a complex task. The time involved in constructing fully automatic prototypes makes them **inefficient for proof-of-concept designs**.

Implementing automaticity in prototypes influences the cost of a prototype negatively. Cost is then also related to the degree to which a prototype implements automatic behaviour.

Early Exploration of the Design Space

As concerns early communication between stakeholders in a software project, a fully automatic prototype is always at the mercy of its automaticity. It will not allow the developer to fudge even if the discussion demands it. *Fudgeability*, as defined by Cooper & Reimann (2003), in a system is difficult to achieve "because it demands a considerably more capable interface" (ibid., p. 210). Changing a prototype with implemented automaticity is always a matter of reprogramming, debugging, and compiling it again. Another approach involves trying to achieve an overall fudgeability in the prototype's interactivity, but then again this would result in even more time being wasted on programming. A manual prototype on the other hand is inherently fudgeable because the interactions it provides are manually produced. The fudgeable nature of a manual prototype means that one can explore a larger range of design issues than when using an automatic prototype. Constantly having to reprogram an automatic prototype is not cost effective when **identifying market and user requirements** and it will impede early exploration of the design space. The low-fidelity prototypes fudgeable/manual nature makes them ideal **for addressing screen layout issues**. That is, these two advantages are directly related to how automatic the response production of the prototype is.

Reusability in Implementation

Rudd et al. (ibid.) argue that low-fidelity prototypes have **limitations when it comes to depicting navigation and flow** and that high-fidelity prototypes, in contrast, **clearly define the navigational scheme**. Low-fidelity prototypes do not contain detailed enough information about error messages, the layout, or the architecture of help panels (ibid.). The present authors do not believe it has so much to do with the low-fidelity approach per se; rather it is a matter of how high one sets one's goals. A low-fidelity prototype cannot act as a **"living" specification** in the same way as a high-fidelity prototype because every response of the low-fidelity prototype must be produced by a human facilitator. This is a direct consequence of the low-fidelity prototype's manual nature (although one can greatly alleviate this problem by making video recordings of test sessions).

Again, how automatic the response production of a prototype is explains to what extent it can be used as the proposed system's specification.

Finally, a specification in the form of a high-fidelity prototype is an effective **marketing and sales tool**. Its automatic nature allows stakeholders and potential customers to interact with it.

Challenging the Fidelity Concept by Positioning the Wizard of Oz Methodology

The Wizard of Oz Methodology

The Wizard of Oz methodology, first coined by Kelley (1983) as the OZ Paradigm, was originally employed as a non-graphical technique in research concerning natural language interfaces (NLI). The methodology entails that the user believes that he or she is interacting with a computer program when in fact he is interacting with another human, referred to as a *wizard*. The wizard acts instead of the program, giving the user feedback and output when needed. This enables the user to interact with a prototype as if it were a real program, while the wizard produces the responses of the program. Depending on the scenario involved, the wizard could be either hidden, or visible to the user.

This methodology makes it possible for prototypes to simulate the implementation of complex technology, such as speech recognition, without having access to the technology itself, or without having to be hindered by some limitation posed by the technology. In other words, it allows for interaction with programs or technology not yet fully implemented. This enables researchers and product developers to gain early insight to the user's experience without having to fully implement the technology or software.

The Ozlab System and Interaction Shells

The Ozlab system is a simulation-kit for showing a GUI's interactivity in a Wizard of Oz manner. In doing so it extends the Wizard of Oz methodology from a non-graphical technique to letting the wizard control the output in the GUI. This means that one can create prototypes in the Ozlab system, called *interaction shells*, and then fake the interactivity of the prototype in such a way that the user believes the interaction to be automatic. The system was developed within the Centre for HumanIT at Karlstads University by the department of Information Systems in collaboration with the department of Special Education. The Wizard of Oz methodology has previously been used in a GUI setting. However, this use was limited to including new input modalities into an existing software prototype or system (e.g. Dahlbäck et al. 1993; Höysniemi et al. 2004). The unique aspect of the Ozlab system is that one does not require a programmed prototype or system to start user testing. It is used by itself to fake a complete prototype, along with all of the interactions it offers.

The system can be used in any ordinary usability laboratory containing a one-way mirror that enables the wizard to see the user, but prevents the user from seeing the wizard. However, a laboratory is not necessary in order to employ the Ozlab system.

The graphical appearance of the prototype is created using Macromedia's Director. The interaction of the prototype is created live by the wizard during user testing with the help of the Ozlab system. The interaction shells are made by first creating the different graphical elements of the GUI and then laying them out as they would appear in the real program. After the layout is completed, each individual element is prepared for wizard-produced interactivity by attaching so called *behaviours* (i.e. drag-and-droppable code snippets) on them. Currently, Ozlab provides about 20 different behaviours. During the experiment they enable the wizard to manipulate an element in the GUI to behave in a particular way in response to a user's action. Moreover, these behaviours reflect the state of the element as seen on the user's screen. For example, the behaviour "Hideable by the wizard" makes it possible for the wizard to decide when that element should be made visible. This is illustrated in Fig. 1a and 1b which show a frame that is "hideable by the wizard" that is used to highlight one of the '5's in the figures (the third number in the given answer, which is '055').

Wizard's view of the interaction shell: **User's view of the interaction shell:**

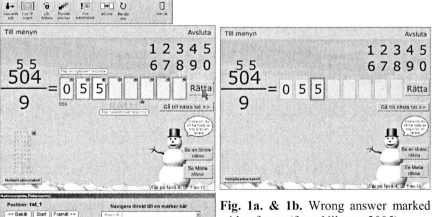

Fig. 1a. & 1b. Wrong answer marked with a frame (from Nilsson, 2005)

As Figure 1a shows, the wizard has access to two control panels that are visible above and below the interaction shell. These control panels can be used by the wizard to control what is shown on the user's screen in several different ways. For instance, in Fig. 1a, two different mouse cursors can be seen in the wizard's view. The larger arrow is green and shows where the user's mouse cursor is located. It becomes red when the user presses the left mouse button.

Interactions Shells – Low- or High-Fidelity?

One would expect that placing Ozlab prototypes (interaction shells) in the correct fidelity category is accomplished easily. On the surface, an interaction shell appears to be of high fidelity if the measure of fidelity is assumed to be based on the user's expectations of an interactive system. Conversely, from the perspective of the developer, the very same prototype would seem to be of low fidelity, because it is incomplete as an automatic system.

As described previously the user's experience of an interaction shell is that it is "real" but the wizard/developer, knowing that the responses were produced by him/her, is of course of another opinion. These opposing perspectives could be explained by one factor, *the dissociation of a prototype's implemented automatic behaviour and what the user perceives as being automatic* in an interaction shell. This dissociation does not exist in traditional prototypes because everything that is perceived as automatic is, in fact, automatic.

Another approach to position interaction shells is to compare an interaction shell's properties to the advantages and disadvantages ascribed to low- and high-fidelity prototypes (see Table 1). Creating an interaction shell is a low-cost effort when compared to high-fidelity prototypes. This in turn makes it possible to evaluate multiple designs concepts. An interaction shell is, just like a low-fidelity prototype, useful for addressing screen layout issues. Additionally, a video recording of an Ozlab simulation session could be utilized as a proof-of-concept.

Comparing with the advantages for high-fidelity prototypes one finds that although interaction shells are not programmed to be interactive and complete in functionality they are at least perceived as such by the user. Therefore, an interaction shell also provides some of the advantages of being user-driven. In addition to mimicking the look and feel of the final product truthfully, it can also be explored and tested. In almost three years of using interaction shells, we have yet to encounter a user who doubted the reality of the interaction (if not made obvious by the test setup).

While screen recordings of a test could be used as a specification, the lack of the ability to interact with the recording means that it cannot be used as a "living" specification in the same way as a traditional high-fidelity prototype. Such a recording can also be used as a marketing and sales tool. In fact, it might be viable to conduct Ozlab simulations at the client's offices, or at a trade show. However, one must conclude that an interaction shell does not live up to all of the advantages of high-fidelity prototypes.

However, it is debatable whether a prototype (regardless of fidelity) ought to (or can) live up to all of the advantages ascribed to high-fidelity prototypes at the same time. We contend that if a prototype fulfils many of these advantages and only has the given disadvantages then one should consider if this is not the actual complete product.

As the above discussion indicates, trying to position interaction shells according to their fidelity is ambiguous owing to the dissociation of perceived and implemented automaticity in interaction shells. The next section will exploit this dissociation for the purpose of presenting another way of categorizing different types of prototypes.

A New Categorisation Based on the Prototype's Level of Automatic Response Production

While the HCI-community has no problem categorizing prototypes according to their fidelity, there is no clear-cut definition of fidelity in this context. The existing definitions of fidelity revolve around the *perceived* fidelity from the user's perspective (see for example Tullis in Rudd et al. 1996). However, frequently, the developers' view of fidelity is used as the standard. This leads to that one and the same prototype can be categorised differently depending on the point of view assumed. Fidelity is, then, something that is perceived and as such it is also a subject to interpretation through our preunderstanding. It is easy to judge a representation's fidelity if the representation has a counterpart in the physical world. However, when developing an interactive system, one does not have the finished system to compare with. As a result, it is difficult to establish the fidelity of a prototype by referring to the final, as-yet-undefined system. For these reasons it is difficult to compare different types of prototypes based on fidelity.

Instead of focusing on fidelity as an approximation of the final system one could think about low- and high-fidelity prototypes as being on a scale that describes how the prototype responds to a user's actions. This scale ranges from a non-automatic to a fully automatic response production.

What Rudd et al. (1996) mean is "interactive" in high-fidelity prototypes is in this context understood as the parts of a prototype that are able to respond automatically to a user's actions. Thus, a high-fidelity prototype is placed towards the fully automatic end of the scale because all of the parts that the user perceives as automatic are indeed automatic (i.e. no human facilitator is needed). The way Rettig (1994) conducts user testing with paper-prototypes is also interactive in this context but because the interaction is mediated by a human facilitator one would place this prototype at the non-automatic part of the scale. Analogously, an interaction shell would also be located towards the non-automatic part of the scale because all of its responses are generated manually by the wizard. Somewhere at the middle one would find prototypes that are semiautomatic needing a human facilitator at times (e.g. to simulate different functions not implemented in the prototype) and at times being automatic. Examples of such prototypes include the experiments conducted by Bönisch et al. (2003), and the Wizard of Oz experiments in a GUI setting that only include a new input modality into an existing software prototype (Höysniemi et al. 2004).

Additionally, a second dimension describing the perceived automaticity is needed. As described previously, a prototype can be perceived as being automatic even if no automatic behaviour was implemented. This is precisely the case with interaction shells, and other Wizard of Oz implementations. This dimension ranges from perceived as manual, to perceived as automatic.

The automaticity plane presented has two axes: implemented and perceived automaticity. However, this plane does not describe the content of the prototype. Therefore, a third dimension is added, *precision.*

Beaudoin-Lafon & Mackay (2003) prefer the term precision instead to fidelity because they feel that precision "refers to the content of the prototype itself, not its relationship to the final, as-yet-undefined system." Precision is described as "the level of detail at which the prototype is to be evaluated" and it is a scale that ranges from rough to highly polished (ibid.). For example, one need not specify the exact wording of a label when the goal is to only address screen layout issues. Beaudoin-Lafon & Mackay (ibid.) also note that precision is something that changes over time as the prototype develops. The medium chosen for the prototype, e.g. paper or a computer, also affects precision. This choice, affects not only the feel of the prototype but also the look, as colours, for example, will look different on a computer screen compared to a paper printout.

The three dimensions described above – implemented automaticity, perceived automaticity, and precision – form a three dimensional model of fidelity in which prototypes could be situated (see Fig. 2).

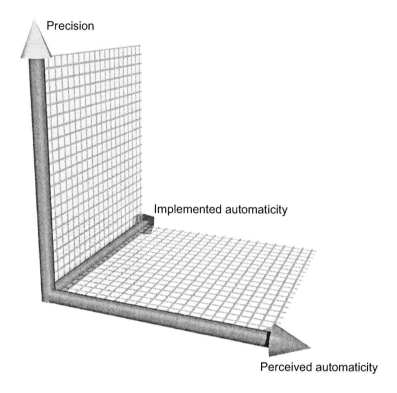

Fig. 2. A three dimensional model of fidelity

Concluding Remarks

It is possible to categorise an Ozlab prototype as being of low- or high-fidelity depending on if it is the user's or the developer's view of fidelity that is used. Interaction shells also share many of the advantages and disadvantages ascribed to both low- and high-fidelity prototypes.

The problems encountered when trying to place interaction shells in a fidelity category arise because of the lack of a clear-cut definition of fidelity within the HCI community. Consequently, we have developed a three dimensional model of fidelity based on the implemented and perceived automaticity, and the precision of a prototype (Fig. 2). This model incorporates both the users' and the developers' view of fidelity, and can be utilized for a more fine-tuned positioning of prototypes.

References

Bönisch B, Held J, Krueger H (2003) Prototyping.ppt – Power Point® for Interface-Simulation of Complex Machines. In: Stephanidis C, Jacko J (eds) Human-Computer Interaction: Theory and Practice (Part II). Lawrence Erlbaum Associates Publishers Mahwah New Jersey

Cooper A, Reimann R (2003) About Face 2.0 – The Essentials of Interaction Design. Wiley Publishing USA

Dahlbäck N, Jönsson A, Arhenberg, L (1993) Wizard of Oz Studies – Why and How. Knowledge-Based Systems, vol 6, no 4, pp 258-266

Höysniemi J, Hämäläinen P, Turkki L (2004) Wizard of Oz Prototyping of Computer Vision Based Action Games for Children. ACM 1-58113-791-5/04/0006

Jacko JA, Sears A, Mahwah NJ (eds) (2003) The Human-Computer Interaction Handbook: Fundamentals, Evolving Technologies and Emerging Applications. Lawrence Erlbaum Mahwah New Jersey

Kelley JF (1983) An Empirical Methodology for Writing User-Friendly Natural Language Computer Applications. Proc of CHI'83

Myers BA, Rosson MB (1992) Survey on User Interface Programming. Proc of CHI'92 The National Conference on Computer-Human Interaction

Nilsson J (2005) Interaktionsdesign av pedagogisk programvara – En experimentell studie av demonstrationer som hjälpfunktioner i ett övningsprogram för mellanstadiebarn (Interaction design of educational software – An Experimental Study of Demonstrations as Help Functions in a Practice Program for Children). Dept. of Information Systems, Karlstad University

Preece J, Rogers Y, Sharp H (2002) Interaction Design: Beyond Human-Computer Interaction. Wiley New York

Rettig M (1994) Prototyping for Tiny Fingers. Communications of the ACM, vol 37, no 4, pp 21-27

Rudd J, Stern K, Isensee S (1999) Low vs. High-fidelity Prototyping Debate. Interactions, January 1996

Rapid Prototyping of User Interfaces in Robot Surgery – Wizard of Oz in Participatory Design

Niklas Larsson[1] and Lennart Molin[2]

[1] Centre for HumanIT, Karlstad University, Sweden.
niklas.larsson@teliamail.com
[2] Department of Information Systems, Karlstad University, Sweden.
lennart.molin@kau.se

Introduction

To specify all the requirements for multimedia systems can be difficult [5]. For the end user it is often hard to articulate the requirements of system interactivity. The developer often has to comprehend both the explicit and implicit demands of the end user. The developer's lack of knowledge of the user's domain could result in a system that is hard to use.

This paper reports on some results and experiences from a project on developing participatory design methodology with the use of Wizard-of-Oz prototyping of graphical user interfaces. The Wizard-of-Oz prototyping method relies on a wizard, hidden from the user, who controls the response to the user's actions (a comprehensive description can be found in [2], [4], [6]).

For this purpose a special software tool called Ozlab has been used [8]. Ozlab makes it possible to use a digital mock-up of an interface in a prototyping session, where a human test manager, the 'wizard', simulates the interaction. No programming of the interaction is necessary because the wizard controls all responses from the computer system.

Ozlab has been used to perform cooperative design sessions with a system for hip surgery. The paper is based on work with multimedia and exploratory requirements activities [5]. Here we highlight the following two questions.

1. Is it possible to strengthen the users' contribution in the design process?
2. How could Ozlab prototyping contribute to system requirements?

A motivation for the questions is that previous research indicates that the user holds a weak position in multimedia design, and that Wizard-of-

Oz prototyping with Ozlab could help the user to be more involved in the development process [6].

We will first describe the research method including background to the project, test setup, brief description of the Ozlab tool and test participants. Then we present results pertaining to each of the two questions. Finally, some remarks related to the results are presented.

Background and Methodology

Wizard-of-Oz prototyping is often used for development of languagebased user interfaces, but Ozlab facilitates interaction which plays on spatial relationships in the on-screen scenes. How would this translate to an application that is dependant on spatial relations in the real world?

In order to explore this, a collaboration with the company Medical Robotics was established. Medical Robotics has developed PinTrace which is a system that helps surgeons to position fixation devices correctly during orthopedic surgery of hip fractures. The system consists of a robot and a computer cabinet and uses information from X-ray images as well as from the surgeon to calculate an image that helps the surgeon to correctly position the fixation instruments. The system also physically guides the surgeon in the drilling process.

To this date, PinTrace is still in a prototype phase but it has been used in surgery approximately 60 times since 1998. During this test phase both users and developers have recognized problems regarding the design of the interface. These problems were discovered during pilot studies and at evaluations after real life surgery:

Ambiguity in work sequence and orientation. The users express difficulties with orientation and work sequence. Certain symbols mean different things at different times which make the user uncertain what to do.

Too many options. Many unnecessary choices can be made and some users explain that they do not know where to start and what the different options are for.

Colour coding. Colours are used to display various types of information to the user. It seems that the user in many cases fail to notice this. Also, even if the different colours are noticed the users express difficulties in the interpretation of its meaning.

The amount of information. The system displays a lot of redundant information. An example is the log where certain internal actions in the system are displayed. This log displays no information that the user could benefit from.

Test Setup

PinTrace consists of two parts, a robot and a computer cabinet. The inter-action with the system is handled through the 19" touch screen on the ro-bot. There is also a trackball and mouse button which is used when more precision is required. The computer cabinet is not used in the interaction with the system during surgery; it simply holds all the electronic equip-ment.

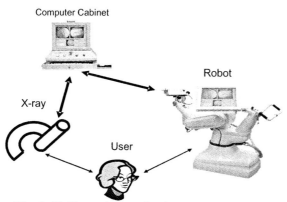

Fig. 1. PinTrace, interaction between components

The thick arrows in figure 1 represent cables that connect the different units. The thin arrows represent the user's interaction with the different units. To the right is the PinTrace robot. The robot is connected to the computer cabinet through a cable. On the cabinet there is a monitor, a key-board and mouse. On the left side of the picture is the X-ray machine. When it is used, pictures are sent to the computer and the surgeon can see them on the robot's 19" display.

To perform the various experiments we had to display the prototype in-terface on the robot's display as well as to record and react to the user's in-teraction with the touch screen of the robot. In order to accomplish this, the system was reconfigured according to the schema pictured below (figure 2).

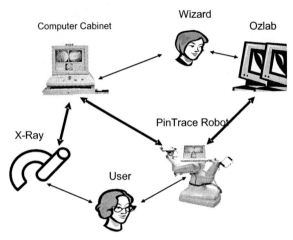

Fig. 2. PinTrace system, connection with Ozlab

Ozlab's mock-up interface is displayed on the robot, but the original system is still fully functional and displayed on the computer cabinet. The user is now able to use the mock-up interface on the robot but the choices he makes will not affect the real system in any way. Potentially the wizard could, by observing the original interface, control the robot according to the user's choices in the mock-up interface. This idea however, was not implemented since it was too difficult for the wizard to control both the robot and the Ozlab functions at the same time. As an alternative we could have used two wizards as described in [7] but coordination would in our case be problematic.

Another difficulty encountered was how to get the X-ray pictures into the mock-up interface. The solution was to use previously stored pictures. It was not possible without serious alteration of the original system to connect the X-ray to the Ozlab system. However, the solution that was implemented did not differ much from the original system from the user's point of view.

The Wizard's View

As already mentioned, the wizard controls the interaction between the user and the system. In the Ozlab environment there are some tools available to the Wizard to help him accomplish this. At the bottom of the screen is the page navigation toolbar which is used to navigate between different screens in the user interface (see fig 3).

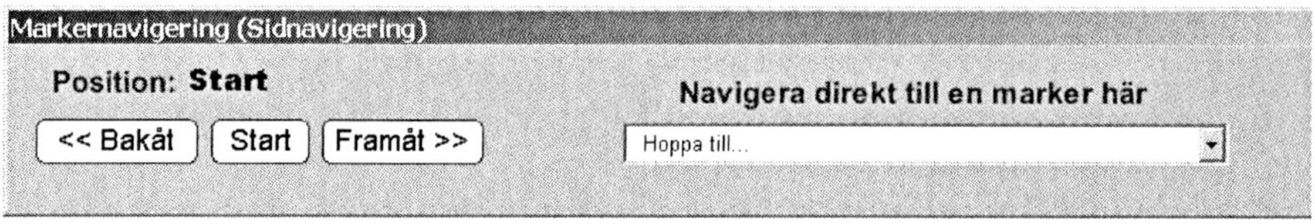

Markernavigering (Sidnavigering)

Position: **Start**

<< Bakåt | Start | Framåt >>

Navigera direkt till en marker här

Hoppa till...

Fig. 3. Page navigation tool bar. Used by the wizard to navigate between scenes

At the top left of the screen there is another set of tools available for the wizard (see fig. 4).

Wizard kontrollpanel

| Visa vänta bild | Frys TP skärm | Lås flyttbara | Återställ objekten | Visa aktivitetslista | Byt skal | Återställ skal | Avsluta |

Fig. 4. Wizard tool bar used to perform additional actions

By using these buttons, the wizard for example may 'freeze' objects that the user normally should be able to move, or he can reposition movable objects to their initial position. The wizard can also hide or show objects to the user, this is done by clicking on the specific object. (The interaction as described here is controlled by the wizard.) There is however a couple of pre-programmed features involved. These features are mostly related to actions from the user that demands an immediate response from the system. The system could for example be made to make a sound or switch an image as the user presses a button.

Test Participants

The results presented in this paper are based on 29 test sessions. Often a designer or a research assistant accompanied the user during the experiments. The users were encouraged to describe and discuss the procedure and all sessions were recorded on video tape for later analysis.

The first experiment took place 2003-05-09 and the experiments continued to 2004-10-05. Fifteen persons have participated and 29 tests were performed, divided into 19 different occasions. The test participants had different backgrounds. There were seven nurses, three orthopedist, one developer, one project assistant, two students and one teacher participating. Prior experience in working with PinTrace differed amongst the participants. The orthopedists had done several simulations and also some real operations while some of the nurses, students and the teacher had no prior experience. All the tests were performed with the test persons fully aware of the fact that the wizard was controlling the responses of the system.

Data from such tests can be collected in several ways:

- Observations done by the Wizard
- Interviews with the users during and after the test
- Video recording of the touch screen and of the dialogue.
- Recording of the screen either through a VHS-recorder or through a special program which captures the screen and the movements.

We used the first three alternatives. The wizard follows the user interaction by observing the Ozlab-screen which shows a copy of the user screen. This is necessary in order for the wizard to interact with the user and interpret user behaviour.

Interviews with the users were carried out during and after the experiments. A constructive dialogue between user and wizard facilitated the articulation of ideas concerning modifications and improvements of the user interface.

Video recordings were used for analysis after the experiments. This was done by the wizard alone as well as in collaboration with the user.

Due to the high screen resolution of the interface, we were not able to use the last method described. The VHS-recorder could not capture the whole screen at once. A special programme was able to this, but the file size grew too large to handle with existing equipment. Since we captured the screen with the video camera it was not deemed necessary to use this alternative.

Results

In this part we will try to answer the two questions posed in the introduction. Examples from the experiments are given to illustrate the analysis.

Is It Possible to Strengthen the Users Contribution in the Design Process?

In one part of a test session the participant is supposed to place five different objects on top of an X-ray image of the patient's hip bone. The objects are used by the system to calculate the exact position where to drill. When the test person tries to rotate one of the objects she discovers that this is not possible in the mock up interface. She comments on this with the expression: "it hurts my soul".

The function to rotate objects exists in the original interface but is not possible to reproduce in the Ozlab environment. Even though the test participant knows that she is working with a prototype she has difficulties in accepting that the objects are not placed precisely right.

The experiments gave numerous examples similar to the one just described, where the user expresses her 'feeling' of the system. The possibility for the users to get this feeling of the system could make it easier for them to comment on overall experience of the system. It is not possible from this study to draw the conclusion that Ozlab tests always makes the participants comment on the experience. However, the idea could be illustrated with the simile of buying a car. When one buys a car, if the sales person describes the functions and performance of the car it is still difficult to make a correct judgement of the overall performance. It is only after a test drive and the combination of all the different impressions, that one can get a good 'feel' of the car. Ozlab prototyping can be described as a test drive where the developer and user could discuss the overall impressions while 'driving'.

In another experiment the user comments on some different weaknesses of the prototype. She gives some suggestions for improvements in some aspects. The test person is eager to see the results of the suggestion and asks if it will take long to implement. The alteration is made in approximately ten minutes and it is then possible to perform a new test run.

The possibility of modifying a prototype according to the users' suggestions helps giving them a feeling of control. They are able to see their suggestions take shape and this could notably motivate them and possibly strengthen the collaboration between the users and the developers. Suggestions from the users often concerned overall design issues such as the workflow order or removal and adding of different functions. These alterations would take considerable amount of time to implement in a programmed prototype. It is not possible to estimate the time required since it depends on many factors, but it could range from a couple of hours to several days.

There are many advocates for greater user involvement in the development process. It is a great challenge to create an experiment that gives the users a possibility to contribute to the process and the final product [1]. The participants in the experiments showed a lot of interest. One user simulated a sound that the robot makes during movement in the PinTrace system. In general, the users seemed to enjoy themselves during the experiments. Together with the feeling of control, this could motivate them to play a greater part in the development process.

How Could Ozlab Prototyping Contribute to System Requirements?

A requirements specification should be comprehensible for both users and developers. Ozlab can be used to visualize the users' precognition, which makes it easier for the developers to understand the users' line of thought.

As an example of this the first prototype included a help function but during tests no participant used it. When asked about it, some users had not even noticed that there existed a help function. One person answered: "No, I don't use that, you never get the right answer". Another user expressed: "The idea is good but I have no need for it".

To draw conclusions from this example is difficult. One user said that the function could be useful but none of them tried it. To draw the conclusion that the help function is unnecessary would be too hasty. We would have to perform more tests to evaluate this. The test could however, with a little alteration, guide us in the design of a help function according to the users' demands.

Another example is the navigation indicator implemented in the early prototype. One of the complaints of the existing PinTrace interface was that it was hard to know what to do next. To counter this, the navigation indicator was implemented. It consisted of a 'time axis' that explained where the user was in the process, which step was next and where the user had been. The result regarding this function differed from the intended use. The general opinion was that the function was not necessary because the new interface was much easier to navigate through than the original. One test person tried to use the time axis to shift scenes (i.e. to navigate between pages). The wizard rejected this attempt and thereby missed the opportunity to allow for unintended use of this feature. This could serve as a reminder of the difficulty in predicting the user's behaviour.

Ozlab prototyping can be a way of visualizing and testing a systems interactive quality before the final product is completed. This can help both the developer and the user to discover implicit demands and express them. An example from the study will illustrate this. The user was encouraged to place five different objects on the screen. This was accomplished by pressing five buttons on the right hand side of the screen. The developers had spent some time beforehand, debating on which was the correct order to place the objects. During the test the user explained that the order in which the objects were placed really made no difference. Instead, the important thing was that the objects could be placed rapidly. This helped the developer to prioritize different requirements. In this way he can concentrate on the most important requirement from the user's point of view.

We also noticed that Ozlab prototyping could be a way to validate already explicit requirements. A breakdown could depend on user requirements that are not fulfilled. Even though requirements are explicit it is not certain that either users or developers fully understand them. An example from the study can illustrate this:

During a test, the user complained about a lack of detail in the X-ray pictures. This led to a discussion between the assistant and the user about the importance of good quality X-ray pictures. The user explained the need to be able to manipulate and enhance pictures in different ways. Since the X-ray machine sometimes produce dark or blurry images, functions to correct this within the system are needed. The result from the test was that detail of requirements increased since the user was able to describe specific functions, and the wizard better understood the importance of the X-ray pictures.

Finally, let us look at possible consequences of user involvement. In one experiment a user comments: "you can do this quickly after a while". An alternative use for Ozlab prototyping [8] was demonstrated during the tests. Because the Ozlab prototype can be made to behave according to any specification. The prototypes can be used as a learning tool for future users of the system. This can, on the other hand be a risk when one wants to evaluate the system specification. As the users who has participated in a participatory design process get more and more involved in the development, chances are that they might not be representative of other end users of the final product. As mentioned, Ozlab can be a way to practice using the proposed system, but this involvement together with developers could also lead to a lack of awareness of certain demands or weaknesses of the prototype. Of course, one obvious solution to this problem is to introduce new test persons during the whole prototyping phase. This possibility was not utilized in the experiments reported above, and will not be commented on here.

Final Viewpoints

A fundamental aspect in Wizard of Oz prototyping is to involve the end user in the development process [4]. To strengthen the user's role would therefore be implicit and a part of the prerequisites of using the method. The collaboration between developers and users can, with Ozlab prototyping be encouraged in many different ways. Different forms of collaboration can take place through the whole chain of the development process. In [3] Gulliksen and Göransson declare that different prototyping activities are necessary through both system development as well as modelling of other activities. Seminars, planning, preparation, tests, and further development of the prototypes, Ozlab prototyping could be considered as a hub around which it all revolves.

Ozlab prototyping can serve as an arena of discussion for the developer and the user. In [9] Winograd & Flores describe some differences between developers and users in the way that they look at the system. They underline the importance of the developers understanding the user's perspective or domain. An understanding that could come from a creative and open discussion between the different actors in the development process. The discussion can benefit from the possibility to switch between test and analysis at a rapid phase. The simulation of the prototype helps to articulate different perspectives concerning interface development, since the user and the developer looks at the process with different kinds of expertise. A discussion that has its origin in a prototype should have better chances to stay in the user's domain since there is something for both developer and user to adhere to.

Acknowledgements

The experiments with Ozlab prototyping reported here were performed 2003-2004 as a project within MTiV (Medicinsk Teknik i Värmland) which during this period was an EU-supported regional competence cluster project in the field of medical technology.

References

[1] Bødker S, Ehn P, Sjögren D, Sundblad Y (2000) Co-Operative Design – Perspectives on 20 Years with 'the Scandinavian IT Design Model'. Proc of NordiCHI2000 October 2000 Stockholm

[2] Dahlbäck N, Jönsson A, Ahrenberg L (1993) Wizard of Oz Studies – Why and How. Knowledge-Based Systems, vol 6, no 4, pp 258-266

[3] Gulliksen J, Göransson B (2002) Användarcentreradsystemdesign. Studentlittratur Lund

[4] Kelley JF (1984) An Iterative Design Methodology for User-Friendly Natural Language Office Information Applications. ACM Transactions on Office Information Systems, vol 2, no 1, pp 26-41

[5] Molin L (2005) Multimedia Development – An Investigation of Four Aspects of Multimedia Development with an Emphasis on Exploratory Requirements Activities. In Swedish. Karlstad University Studies

[6] Molin L, Pettersson JS (2003) How Should Interactive Media be Discussed for Successful Requirements Engineering? In: Burnett R, Brunström A, Nilsson AG (eds) Perspectives on Multimedia – Communication, Media and Information Technology. Wiley New York

[7] Pettersson JS (2003) Ozlab – A System Overview with an Account of Two Years of Experiences. In: Pettersson JS (ed) Humanit 2003. Karlstad University Studies 2003:26 Karlstad

[8] Pettersson JS, Siponen J (2002) Ozlab – A Simple Demonstration Tool for Prototyping Interactivity. Proc of NordiCHI Aarhus Denmark 19-23 October 2002

[9] Winograd T, Flores F (1986) Understanding Computers and Cognition: A New Foundation for Design. Ablex Publishing Corporation Norwood

Designing Simulation-Games for Organizational Prototyping

Joeri van Laere[1], Gert Jan de Vreede[2] and Henk G. Sol[3]

[1] University of Skövde, Sweden. joeri.laere@his.se
[2] University of Nebraska at Omaha, USA. gdevreede@mail.unomaha.edu
[3] Universities of Groningen and Delft, the Netherlands. h.g.sol@rug.nl

Introduction

Studies that analyze the value and success of ICT adoption and use in organizations have created a far from unified picture of the impact of ICT on organizational performance. Although organizational employees more and more often operate in distributed work settings and ICT potentially offers opportunities and benefits (Haywood 1998), many organizations struggle to integrate organizational structures, daily work practices and the development of supporting ICT (Orlikowski 1992; Orlikowski & Barley 2001). Successful ICT adoption often depends on social factors, rather than technological. ICT must 'fit' in the organization; it needs to be embedded in culture and work practices (Orlikowski et al 1995; Robertson et al 2000).

The multi-disciplinary research community Computer Supported Cooperative Work (CSCW) attempts to connect organization and ICT by combining ethnography and systems design in ICT development and organizational change. Building upon the cooperative prototyping approach of Bødker & Grønbæk (1991), Bardram (1996) introduces the concept 'organizational prototyping' as "a dual process of both adapting the tool to the organization and adapting the work practice to conditions of the tool" (p. 75). He describes how organizational prototyping sessions have been organized as part of the design process of an alternative information system in an engineering company (Bardram 1996) and in a hospital context (Bradram 1997). In these sessions a prototype of the information system is demonstrated and potential usage scenarios are discussed with the organizational employees. After the sessions the information system and the work processes are adapted. Similarly, Smeds & Alvesalo (2003, p. 365) define their business process simulation method as "a structured, directed and visualized group discussion about the activities, tasks and information flows in a selected business process. A group of up to 50 people discusses in front of a visual process model their practices and interactions in the process, and negotiates their roles and identities in the process design. Real case projects are systematically talked through in a process oriented way to enlighten the reality in the process and to bring into negotiation the tacit experiental knowledge of the participants."

Below we discuss the use of two simulation-games for organizational prototyping in a change process in the Amsterdam Police Force. We argue that this approach differs from those of Bardram and Smeds as the emphasis on our approach is more on 'playing and discussing' rather than only on 'discussing' work practices and ICT characteristics. Our hypothesis is that our approach enables better discrimination between 'espoused theories' and 'theories in use' (Argyris & Schön 1981) as participants in our sessions first act (play) and later discuss.

In this paper we focus on the **process** of developing the simulation-games and on design choices in game development, rather than on the outcomes of the prototyping sessions (which are recommendations for ICT design and organizational development). Other articles often focus on the outcomes of the sessions, leaving less room for an elaborate discussion of the (complex) design of the game itself. Our aim is to inform how simulation-games for organizational prototype sessions are developed and to explain which considerations need to be taken into account during design. We present our research design, design of the games and experiences from testing and playing the games. We conclude with a discussion of the impact of design choices on game functionality and a reflection of differences between the two games.

Research Design

The development and application of the simulation-games has been part of a larger study on the impact of ICT on coordination in the Amsterdam Police Force (Laere 2003). Early in this research we analyzed current work and coordination practices in an observatory case study. Later we developed new coordination scenarios and organized organizational prototyping sessions in an action research. Action research can be defined as "an inquiry into how human beings design and implement action in relation to one another" (Argyris et al 1982). It is intended to have the dual outcomes of action (or change) and research (understanding). An action researcher participates or intervenes in the phenomenon studied in order to apply a theory to practice and evaluate its worth (Checkland 1981). We wanted to investigate how to develop simulation-games that are suited for organizational prototyping. We developed two simulation-games and organized respectively 9 and 2 prototyping sessions with them. During the design process and the sessions we gathered feedback on the design choices we made and on the impact of these choices on the characteristics and functionality of the two games. In this paper we present our own reflections and comments from police officers who participated in the design of the games or in the prototyping sessions.

Game Design

The two games we developed each focus on a particular part of the coordination problems in the police organization. The 32 autonomous neighbourhood teams of the Amsterdam Police Force need to utilize each other's knowledge and expertise to deal with the variety and complexity of their daily work assignments. But despite the creation of organisation wide knowledge networks, communication and coordination between the neighbourhood teams is disappointing. We investigated how coordination in the knowledge networks could be improved with the help of information and communication technologies (ICT) and used the prototyping sessions to analyze, evaluate and improve future coordination scenarios in the knowledge networks. In the first game the central question is why members of neighbourhood teams do or do not choose to make use of the knowledge and experience of other neighbourhood teams and by what media (intranet, phone, e-mail, bulletin board) they consult organizational knowledge if they want to. In the second game the focus is on the internal organization of the knowledge networks. These consist of one central coordinator and for the rest of decentralized experts who are a member of neighbourhood teams and as such only part of their work time available for the knowledge network. Central question in the second game is how each knowledge network updates knowledge and experience on their intranet site and how they make sure that questions posted on their bulletin board are answered correctly and in time.

We develop a simulation-game in 7 steps which we execute iteratively rather than sequentially (Caluwe et al 1996): 1) analyse processes and mechanisms, 2) draw up a functional set of requirements, 3) design an integral framework, 4) draw up a game-technical set of requirements, 5) construct a prototype, 6) test the prototype, 7) finalize the game. Employees from the police force participated in the design team and intermediate results of the design process have been shared with a larger group of potential users. In this section we describe steps 1 to 5 for each game.

Game 1: Collaboration between Neighbourhood Teams

Processes and Mechanisms

The neighbourhood teams have the following basic tasks: 1) emergency service, 2) take down notifications, 3) criminal investigation, 4) project work, 5) surveillance, and 6) community policing. As all police officers are generalists who need to be able to deal with any problem, specialized expertise can be needed at any given time. However, local experts may not be present, handbooks may be inaccessible or out of date and geographically distributed experts are hard to contact.

Functional Requirements

The central issue in the game is whether police officers will more often consult distributed expertise at other neighbourhood teams when they can access more media like intranet, e-mail (currently not accessible outside the office) and a bulletin board (currently not available at all) and when they are stimulated to do so (by a different culture and management style). Furthermore police officers participating in the game need to get instantaneous feedback on their performance, so they can experience whether consulting knowledge leads to better performance.

Integrated Framework

Figure 1 gives an overview of the interactions between the different roles.

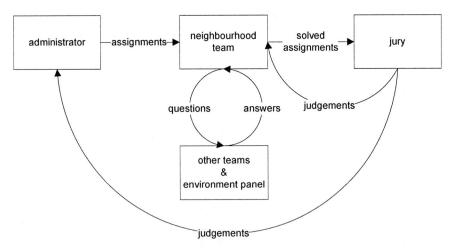

Fig. 1. Integrated framework for the neighbourhood collaboration game

In the game police officers in 3 to 5 neighbourhood teams get assignments from the game administrators and when solving these assignments they are stimulated to use the following coordination options besides relying on their own expertise: a) searching the intranet, b) contacting the central knowledge centre, c) contact an individual expert, d) post a question a bulletin board. The teams consist of 2 or 3 police officers and are a mix of generalists and experts. They can consult one and another or an 'environment panel' who represent the any other party in the police organization they would like to contact. Their assignments are judged by a jury who gives quantitative (a mark between 1 and 5) as well as qualitative feedback (argumentation on both solution content and process). To ease the knowledge search process police officers are provided with an up to date database with all experts, their expertise, phone numbers and e-mail addresses (currently not available), and they can use a search tool that can locate an expert who has the desired expertise and who is currently available.

Game Technical Requirements

Caluwe et al (1996) states that gaming-simulation for organizational change asks for a strong similarity with the organizational **reality**. The content of the assignments and the coordination mechanisms in our game are very close to reality. The main reduction from reality is that assignments are not incidents that are really occurring, but descriptions of situations on paper. The motivation for this is that the focus and challenge of the simulation-game should be on locating, consulting and applying distributed expertise, and not on solving the problems. The neighbourhood team game is kept as **simple** as possible in structure and interfaces. The administrators can vary complexity by sending more complex assignments. By varying the complexity the administrators can prevent that the game is too difficult in the beginning, and too simple after a while when the 'tricks' have been discovered. In the game there are two playing **cycles** both followed by a **debriefing**. In both cycles the participants are invited to try out the new working method. In the debriefing the coordination scenarios, organizational requirements and the ICT tools are evaluated. To make sure that during the debriefings attention can be given to each participant's opinion, a maximum of about 15 **participants** (5 teams with 3 members) is recommended. Furthermore a minimum of 6 to 8 (3 or 4 teams with 2 members) is needed to assure enough dynamism and complexity. Literature (Caluwe et al 1996; Greenblat 1988) strongly recommends that a simulation-game is played in **one room**. This enables control, manageability and face-to-face briefing and debriefing. However, a particular feature of our problem situation is that expertise is distributed over geographically dispersed teams. Therefore we prefer to place the neighbourhood teams in separate rooms. Flex-workplaces at the head office of the police department provided for a nice compromise. Some small rooms separated by glass walls served as team offices. In this way communication between teams was limited to phone and e-mail, while everyone had an overview of all participants. **Computer use** in simulation-games is strongly discouraged by experienced game designers (Caluwe et al 1996; Elgood 1988) Computers may inhibit participant's desire to change game processes, intensive focus on computer use can limit social interaction and computer failure may disturb the game or make continuation impossible. In our case the elements e-mail communication, intranet consultation and bulletin board discussions are crucial elements of the new working method that require computer use in the game. In addition we use the computer for distributing assignments, gathering answers, distributing assessments and calculation of scores.

Prototype Construction

For the development of the computer support for the game we choose to use MS Access because this software is available on the police computer network and because it supports building of a relational database (team, assignment, approach, coordination strategy, assessment, score et cetera). Game participants can make use of the existing intranet and e-mail facilities. The bulletin board feature as well as an overview of experts and their skills are developed in the MS Access environment. By interviewing some experts in the police organization we develop about 60 assignments varying in topic and complexity. For each assignment a 'standard-solution' is described to support the jury in the assessment process.

Game 2: Coordination in Knowledge Networks

Processes and Mechanisms

Currently the content and structure of the regional projects' intranet sites are not linked to the questions that neighbourhood team police officers have in daily practice. Furthermore it is not clear how quality and speed of answers on the bulletin board need to be guaranteed. It is obvious that the regional coordinator of a certain topic cannot perform these tasks alone. Often he is not an in-depth expert on the topic, but rather a good coordinator and manager. Besides he cannot look after the questions and answers on the bulletin board 24 hours a day, 7 days a week. Consequently it seems that the distributed experts working at the neighbourhood teams, who are members of the regional project, need to play a role in maintaining the intranet site and guaranteeing answering speed and quality on the bulletin board.

Functional Requirements

Key challenge in this game is how a regional project can organize the maintenance of the intranet and the bulletin board so that both speed and quality of knowledge exchange are guaranteed. The central coordinator and the distributed experts must decide what subtasks they execute centrally and what they organize decentralized and they have to learn to deal with problems of control (who has the overview whether all tasks are executed in time) and communication (how to discuss complex issues by mail or phone). Instant feedback on performance (good and up to date intranet site, response time and response quality on bulletin board) is important so police officers can judge whether their choices deliver the expected results.

Integrated Framework

From the beginning it has been clear that this second game is more complicated than the first. Instead of one process where a neighbourhood team can chose five alternatives of consulting knowledge, the knowledge networks face 5 different tasks: a) verify intranet changes before publishing, b) publish changes on intranet, c) verify intranet changes after publishing, d) moderate bulletin board and e) verify answers on bulletin board. For each of these 5 tasks they have to decide whether they will organize them more or less centralized or decentralized. Figure 2 shows all possible variants of the five tasks, for instance, a regional project can choose to change the intranet site themselves or they can choose for the option that a central administrative unit carries out these changes for them. Besides the game administrators generate 'new knowledge', 'comments on intranet sites', 'questions on bulletin boards' and 'wrong answers to questions on bulletin boards' which require actions from different players in the game. Judging each other's performance is included as a separate task for neighbourhood teams (acknowledging that judging another creates learning experiences for oneself), so there is not a separate jury like in the first game. A set of indicators is developed for each role to give them insight what tasks need to be addressed first. Examples are "amount of intranet comments not judged yet", "amount of proposals for intranet change not yet verified", "amount of questions unanswered", "amount of answers not yet verified" and "amount of assessment-requests not yet distributed".

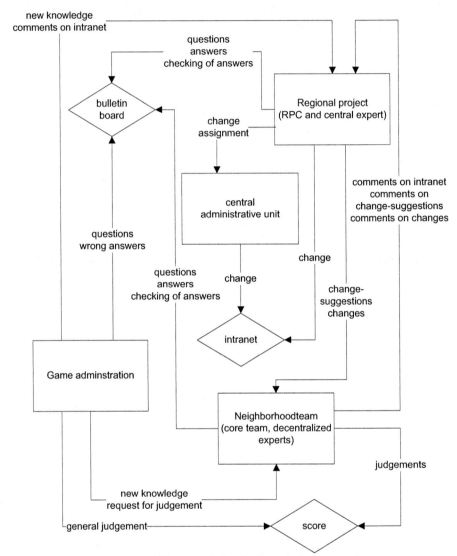

Fig. 2. Integrated framework for the knowledge network game

Game Technical Requirements

A lot of the design decisions with regard to for instance amount of realism in assignments, amount of players, location (flex-workspaces), computer use for logistics and criteria statistics are similar to those in the first game. The major difference is the larger complexity of this game. Besides briefing, playing rounds and debriefing there are smaller planning and reflection rounds just before a play round where members of regional projects decide how to organize their coordination in the next play round. To make sure that debriefings are manageable the maximum amount of participants is again 15. This results in 3 regional projects consisting of 5 actors (a regional project coordinator, a central expert and 3 experts that work decentralized on a neighbourhood team). This is also the minimum, as 3 regional projects are needed to provide enough dynamism and complexity. The actors are distributed over a limited set of computers (where they can access e-mail, intranet and the bulletin board) to resemble their limited availability in practice. Depending on how they allocate their tasks (more or less centralized) the distribution of police officers over workstations may change from play round to play round. This larger complexity is necessary to capture the complexity of the coordination problem we simulate. We strived for more simplicity by reducing the amount of tasks from 12 to 5.

Prototype Construction

This game is again developed in MS Access. A copy of the police intranet is available where the players that have publishing tasks can change the intranet sites with MS Frontpage. These changes are immediately visible for the other players. The Access database consists of different menus for different players. Given the login-name of the player behind the PC the forms are dedicated to that user. This can for instance imply that some optional buttons are not available, but also permissions on the bulletin board may differ (for instance an expert Firearms is allowed to approve answers on the bulletin board considering Firearms, but not those considering Youth). Furthermore the game administrators can enter what division of labour has been chosen by each regional project and these modifications can also influence the appearance of players' menus and their permissions. Knowledge developments, intranet comments, bulletin board questions and (false) answers for each topic area are again gathered by interviewing experts within the police force. An important observation in the development of the second game was that the more complicated structure leads to a much longer and more complicated design process. In the first game a student developed the game in Access from the description of functional requirements and one or two discussions with the researcher. In the second case numerous joint meetings were necessary to arrive at a prototype.

Game Experiences

Testing and Playing Game 1

The first test is a very positive experience. Although the developers focus attention on "trying out all the buttons" the police officers soon start to really play the game. They are eager to find the best solutions or to tease each other ("sorry, our youth expert is currently sick at home, please try another team").They also stress that there is no need for video films or role-playing to illustrate assignments. Their vivid imagination is sufficient. Adjustments to the original design are the simplification of some of the interfaces and changes in some of the assignments because there are flaws in the problem formulation. Putting time constraints for some of the assignments to see what coordination strategy will be chosen under time pressure proves to be counterproductive. Police officers argue that this will harm the key learning opportunity of the game: discovering the value of different coordination strategies. They emphasize that the absence of time pressure is a very valuable aspect of the game in comparison to daily practice.

The neighbourhood team collaboration game has been played in nine organizational prototyping sessions. The game proves to be a well-balanced instrument. Unanimously the participating police officers judge the assignments as realistic and they had a lot of joy in playing the game and exploring new ways of coordination. The evaluation in the debriefings, which take a similar amount of time compared to playing, generate numerous detailed comments on ways how to improve the suggested new coordination scenarios as well as the ICT tools. An inevitable change of location (once) creates two learning experiences for the game developers. First we have a lot of problems with the game because the Access database file has to be installed in another directory of the police network, which has insufficient memory to update it, so we cannot play at all. A delay of two hours confronts us with the drawbacks of a computer supported game. Nonetheless the benefits of logistics and score calculation are very clear in all other instances. A second surprising observation is that it does not really matter that all teams are playing in one large room. They 'simulate' distance anyway, and phone or mail each other although they are only 3 meters apart.

Testing and Playing Game 2

Testing of this game is a more or less continuous process during design due to the complicated structure. Each time changes are made the overall functioning has to be tested for consistency. Also, access to the 'intranet copy' on the police network for all player logins has to be tested numerous times. The focus is thus primarily on technical issues.

When playing this game some of the police officers indicate that they are a little bit overwhelmed by the possible options for labour division and by the complexity of the simulation-game. A major complaint is that it is sometimes not clear what other actors can see or cannot see (although this is mere a characteristic of the coordination problems than a design fault). Despite these undesirable IT-troubles the participating police officers express that the simulation-games are instructive. Furthermore experts in neighbourhood teams are so busy commenting on and questioning other knowledge networks, maintaining their intranet site and moderating their bulletin board, that they lack time to assess performances of others. As a result the scores severely lag behind performance and there is no direct feedback on performance. The researcher perceives this as a major shortcoming, but the participating police officers argue that the indicators (e.g. amount of questions unanswered and amount of answers not yet verified) do provide direct feedback on performance.

Discussion

In developing games for organizational prototyping we adopted the 7 step approach of Caluwe et al (1996). This approach and the numerous recommendations for design choices proved to be very valuable. Overall we observe that the simulation-games served as valuable elements in the organizational prototyping sessions. This is illustrated by the numerous design recommendations that followed from the debriefings of the simulation-games. The comments in these evaluative discussions are much more detailed than in the earlier redesign discussions and the introductory briefings. Besides this design interest participating police officers reported that the games also had an awareness and training interest.

The major design issue we faced is perfectly illustrated by the different experiences we had with the two games. The first game proved to be well-balanced: it was easy to understand, functional and creating a lot of learning experiences. The second game was more complex to develop and more complex to play. Some police officers reported that this complexity hampered their learning. As we already have put much effort in simplifying the second game we think that further simplification would harm the validity of the simulation. A suggestion to overcome this dilemma would be to play the same game several times with the same group of participants and slowly increase the level of complexity. For example first only focusing on the intranet part or the bulletin board part and later combining it. In that way police officers would get used to the basic functionalities and as a result could pay more attention to the real coordination challenges that are in the game.

Conclusion and Future Research

This discussion of the design of simulation-games for organizational prototyping has shown the value of the design approach of Caluwe et al (1996) and has delivered insights in some of the design choices they touch upon. Finding the right balance between realism/validity on one hand and not too much complexity on the other hand proved to be the major design challenge. Furthermore some surprising results were that distributed work can perfectly be simulated in one location, that computer support does not distract from learning objectives when the technology functions properly, and that time constraints may inhibit learning. Future research will further explore to what extent our use of simulation-games differs from the organizational prototyping discussions reported by Bardram and Smeds.

References

Argyris C, Schon D (1978) Organisational Learning: A Theory of Action Perspective. Reading Mass Addison Wesley

Argyris C, Putnam R, McLain Smith D (1982) Action Science, Concepts, Methods and Skills for Research and Intervention. Jossey-Bass San Francisco

Bardram JE (1996) Organisational Prototyping: Adopting CSCW Applications in Organisations. Scandinavian J. of Information Systems, vol 8, no 1, pp 69-88

Bardram JE (1997) Plans as Situated Action: An Activity Theory Approach to Workflow Systems. Proc of ECSCW, Kluwer Academic Publ Lancaster UK

Bødker S, Grønbæk K (1991) Design in Action: From Prototyping by Demonstrating to Cooperative Prototyping. In: Greenbaum K, Kyng M. Design at Work: Cooperative Design of Computer Systems. Lawrence Erlbraum NJ

Caluwe L de, Geurts J, Buis D, Stoppelenburg A (1996) Gaming: Organisatieverandering met Spelsimulaties. Delwel 's Gravenhage Twijnstra Gudde Amersfoort the Netherlands (in Dutch)

Checkland PB (1981) Systems Thinking, Systems Practice. John Wiley and Sons Chichester UK

Elgood C (1988) Handbook of Management Games. Aldershot Gower

Greenblat CS (1988) Designing Games and Simulations: An Illustrated Handbook. Sage Publications Inc. Newbury Park CA

Haywood M (1998) Managing Virtual Teams: Practical Techniques for High-Technology Project Managers. Artech House London

Laere J van (2003) Coordinating Distributed Work, Exploring Situated Coordination with Gaming-Simulation, Doctoral dissertation, Delft University

Orlikowski WJ (1992) Learning Form Notes, Organisational Issues in Groupware Implementation. Proc of CSCW, pp 362-269

Orlikowski WJ, Yates J, Okamura K, Fujimoto M (1995) Shaping Electronic Communication: the Metastructuring of Technology in the Context of Use. Organization Science, vol 6, no 4, pp 423-444

Orlikowski WJ, Barley SR (2001) Technology and Institutions: What Can Research on Information Technology and Research on Organizations Learn from Each Other? MIS Quarterly, vol 25, no 2, pp 145-165

Robertson M, Sorensen C, Swan J (2000) Facilitating Knowledge Creation with Groupware: a Case Study of a Knowledge Intensive Firm. Proc of HICSS-33, January 2000 Hawaii (CD-ROM) IEEE

Smeds R, Alvesalo J (2003) Global Business Process Development in a Global Community of Practice. Production Planning and Control, vol 14, no 4, pp 361-371

The Role of End-Users for Wireless Information Systems Usage

Pablo Valiente

Department of Information Management, Stockholm School of Economics, Sweden. pablo.valiente@hhs.se.

Introduction

This paper is about innovation processes studied in the light of the involvement of users during the development, implementation and usage of wireless information systems in organizations. The coincident appearance of a widely popular innovation, wireless information systems and the renewed interest for socio-technical aspects of information systems development (Wallace, Keil et al. 2004), provides the opportunity to further develop the understanding of user involvement in technology management processes.

At the organizational level, a similar pattern is observed as one of the most central challenges when innovating organizational processes with new technology are not usually the technological problems that need to be solved. A more frustrating part of the process is to understand what the end users of the system really need, i.e. their both expressed, unexpressed, uncertain and unidentified needs (Leonard-Barton 1998, p.183ss). Independently of how good the technical solutions are, if technology does not provide value to the end-users, it will not be accepted nor used. Although the problem of understanding the users' needs is not a unique issue to the implementation of wireless information systems there are a number of topics that make it specially challenging and they will be developed here.

The involvement of users in the development of new products and processes has been widely documented, however there is still much we do not know about how and why user participation sometimes delivers benefits and sometimes not (Leonard-Barton 1998 p.94; Gallivan and Keil 2003). User involvement from a product development approach in marketing has been widely documented and described. The best-known research in the area of customer innovation is probably that of von Hippel (e.g. 1982, 1986, 1988). Here the focus is however on adopting information systems at the organizational level. Nevertheless the marketing area has been a source of inspiration for this work.

Therefore in this paper different types of involvement will be investigated. The aim of this paper is thus to investigate underlying dimensions of mobile user involvement.

Methodology

This paper uses a single case study that describes user involvement during the implementation of a wireless information system at Graninge Timber AB, a forestry and sawmill company located in the Northern part of Sweden. The company implemented a wireless information system to improve their supply chain management. Although the description included in this paper describes the process during the early 1990s the company has gone through some mergers and acquisitions still being object of research.

Several data collection methods were used, including interviews, secondary source material and system documentation. Furthermore, case study reports were reviewed by the interviewees. The description included in this paper borrows heavily from Nilsson (2000). During the process to develop the conceptual results presented in the paper, the analysis has been carried out iteratively between theory and practice. The primary objective with the case was to use it for illustrational purposes. However, it has also improved the final results.

Although user involvement is an important issue independently of the technology being studied, this paper will specifically focus on the management of wireless information systems (WIS) for mobile workforces. As wireless information systems are but a sub-category of information systems, we will now briefly discuss some distinctive characteristics of a wireless information system. (a) The novelty of the technology makes user involvement a central issue. In fact, during the early phases of their development, technologies are formed in close collaboration with the users. As technology matures the technology commoditization process shifts the locus of development from users to vendors; (b) Invalidation of the unity of time and place. This general feature on the hands of mobile workforces particularly means ubiquity data access. New opportunities appear for the users as people are able to access data at different locations. On the other hand the invalidation of time and place enables the development of navigational monitoring systems, i.e. systems that make usage more easily monitored. In addition, the implementation of WIS reduces work freedom. Workers have to adhere to the fixed pace as the reduction of inventory buffers makes workers increasingly dependent on work-flow time-sequencing that is governed by the technology employed; and (c) Complexity of the system. Wireless information systems consist of interconnected parts interacting with each other in such a way as to produce unpredictable outputs. They combine both services and products including hardware, software and network equipment as a whole. This complexity makes integration between the work system and the technical system more intricate.

Mobile User Engagement for Innovation

This section starts with one clarification about terminology being used in the remaining of the paper. Although the term user involvement has been used so far, Barki and Hartwick's (1989) distinction between user participation and user involvement introduces a subtle but important distinction for our purpose. *Involvement* is described as a subjective psychological state, reflecting the importance and personal relevance of an issue (psychology), of a product (marketing) or of one's job (organizational behaviour) or finally of a system to its user (IS) whereas *participation* can be defined as the activities that users or their representatives perform in the system development process. The later introduction of the term *engagement* by Hwang and Thorn (1999) as a common term to refer to the two above will be used in the rest of the paper (cf. Figure 1 below).

Fig. 1. Distinction between participation and involvement

There are a number of reasons for engaging users in the implementation of new technological systems in organizations. Some of these are reduction of risks; rapid diffusion of systems (Alam and Perry 2002); catalyst for new ideas (Magnusson 2003); user education (Alam and Perry 2002) or mutual learning (Magnusson 2003) in the form of input provisioning during the systems design process (Hwang and Thorn 1999).

The main goal for involving users in the adoption process of new technological systems within the area of information systems research has been the successful implementation of technology. Thus, the main dependent variable studied has often been *system success,* representing the overall goal for involving users in the design process (Tait and Vessey 1988) (Hwang and Thorn 1999). Salem (1996 p.145), for example, explains that: 'It is intuitively appealing that user participation leads to system success".

A discussion along three mobile-related key elements of user involvement in Alam et al's (2002) follows here.

a. Type of user: For delimitation purposes it may be informative to include the distinction used in the marketing area between customers and consumers (cf. Magnusson 2003 p.23). Users of a certain system can be represented by customers, consumers or employees. There are two central dimensions in this distinction. First depending if the user is internal or external to the producing organization you can distinguish between customer and employees. Second, depending on who consumes the acquired product you can distinguish between customers and consumers.

Along the first dimension, a central issue in connection to user engagement appears. Employees are in general more accessible to the innovating organization than its customers. Therefore expensive focus-groups interviews or field experiments with customers are seldom required in this particular case. Nevertheless the versatility of usage patterns and contexts in which usage takes place poses other types of constraints such as the difficulty of directly observing mobile users. In addition whereas customers often decide on the adoption of a product by themselves, employees are supposed to adopt new technology based on someone else's decision, such as the implementation of a new corporate e-mail system.

Table 1. Focusing the research

	User	Non-User
Pay	Consumer	Organizational Customer
Doesn't Pay	Employee	N/A

Another important distinction is that customers often pay for the usage of a product whereas employees get paid. When the customer and the user is the same individual, s/he can be referred to as a consumer. In the present study the focus is placed on the special case when the customers (organizations paying for the systems) are separated from the users represented by the firm's employees as illustrated in Table 1.

b. Stages of engagement: Another important issue is to determine when user participation can be advantageous. Should users be involved in the pre-development stages or is engagement more convenient at later stages instead? This issue connects to the life cycle of the system. Robey and Farrow (1982) make an analysis based on three different phases: (1) Initiation; (2) Design; and (3) Implementation. They admit the need to differentiate between phases where different types of activities take place. Barki and Hartwick (1994) similarly to Robey and Farrow (1982) ground their discussion about user involvement in conflict resolution. Through participation and influence conflict arises which can be solved through different resolution mechanisms so that user involvement thus becomes an arena for bargaining (McKeen et al 1994). Hartwick and Barki (1994) explain that participation is required especially during the system development stage (or the ISD phase). However according to the authors, during the pre-development phase and post-implementation stages it is more appropriate to aim at involvement. According to this view on user engagement, a sketch model can be developed as in Figure 2.

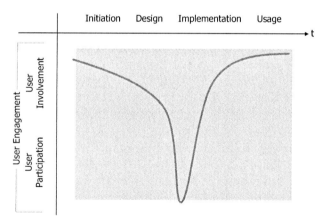

Fig. 2. A life-cycle approach to stages of engagement

The involvement in the post-implementation phase has to do with the attitude towards the system. Positive attitude will increase importance and personal relevance of the system to the user, particularly as we deal with mobile users who are more difficult to map out due to their higher degree of location diversity.

c. Mode of engagement: Next step would be to fill participation and involvement with content: what do these terms really mean? The mode of involvement is thus related to *what* or *how* questions, such as what types of activities are performed in the involvement process at the different stages of development and use.

Newman and Robey (1992) introduce a relevant distinction, namely that of *analyst-led development* and *user-led development* as the extremes of a continuum and in between *joint-system development*. They introduce the term *equivocation* also to refer to a fourth state arising as a consequence of communication problems. According to the authors the first mode of involvement is characterized by the use of structured and formal development methods whereas user-led development is characterized by high level development tools. The joint-system development is characterized by the use of prototyping as an effective method for information systems development. Alam et al (2002) describes a number of activities that are useful in our particular context although they are borrowed from the marketing research area. These are face to face interviews, user visiting and meetings, brainstorming, focus-groups, observation and feedback, ethnography, etc.

It is now due time to look at the case of Graninge before analysing mobile user engagement for innovation.

The Case

Graninge Timber AB is a forestry and sawmill company located in the Northern part of Sweden. The company implemented a wireless information system to improve their supply chain management. The project (SKINFO) started late 1980s when the company became interested in using radio-technology to enhance coordination between units operating in the forest (harvesters and forwarders) and the main office for management and planning of transports. The company experienced a number of problems that led to the implementation of a company wide solution.

Ideas about how to utilize wireless data communication in the supply chain management started to appear around 1988-1989 when a radio workgroup was appointed responsible for analyzing the problem of work coordination to reduce time spent searching for saw logs out in the forest. This pre-phase was called the mobility quest phase.

At the same time, SkogForsk (the Forestry Research Institute of Sweden) and Telia (incumbent telecom operator in Sweden) approached Graninge back in 1990 who during the mobility quest phase had allocated some money budgeted for wireless data communication projects. Skogforsk had previously approached Domänverket (now Sveaskog AB) another Swedish forestry and sawmill company but negotiations between them did not work out. Graninge had moreover some enthusiastic persons or even visionaries during this period hungry to launch new projects that could make the supply-chain more effective.

The initial formal project included a pre-study (pilot) and a second phase for implementing and rolling-out the solution. In the pilot participants from Graninge, Telia and SkogForsk were put together. Moreover as the team lacked competence in information system integration Telesoft Uppsala was invited to join the project team by Telias initiative. The project started around 1990 and in May 1995 it was officially completed.

a. The Pilot: The pilot project consisted of a steering committee with participants from the main actors established; a project team with users from Bollstabruk sawmill (3 work leaders and a representative from the head office); system developers and a project manager from Skogforsk. In addition the pilot was carried out in close cooperation with nine operators. They developed the system for three machines (one harvester and two forwarders). The project group included three operators per machine from the Wilhelmina forest district that worked in shifts from 6 a.m. to noon. One of the project leaders was clearly an enthusiastic person that could take the computers home to test functionality including weekends. He was then nearly 60 years old but very active.

During this phase a functional system was developed and ready for being implemented on full-scale already 1992. The pilot included a definition phase consisting of mapping current operations (IPUV) and a design phase when the specification for the base system was developed and designed. Some add-on functionality was also discussed. However due to time constraints it was never implemented. During this phase Telesoft advised the project team to choose a HuskyHunter16 as the wireless vehicle computer.

Activities connected to the development of the information system at the sawmill were carried out by SkogForsk resulting in the software package *Local Info*. Changes and modifications were made during the pilot in close co-operation with the end-users. The system development activities for the mobile side were carried out by Telesoft. They developed a prototype to get feedback from machine operators on the interface and functionality at an early stage of the pilot. The first prototype without radio communication was ready already at the end of 1990.

As Nilsson (2000) points out: "Bierger Risberg described the project participants as real enthusiasts who sacrificed nights, weekends and even holidays. Without the enthusiasm and will to sacrifice leisure time among these people the project would never have come off".

During the pilot there were technical problems with radio communication. A number of complaints from the users of the system emerged as it was considered cumbersome and difficult to use. The project went through a hard time and only thanks to the enthusiasm from key individuals the project survived.

Users were from the beginning involved in the design of interfaces and routines. They carried out the testing of the prototype so that additional development could be made before the equipment was tested in the final pilot. The specification of the system was difficult due to the fact that previous experience did not exist within the area of the forest sector. During the project users had the opportunity to give their viewpoints about the systems. One example is that during the work with the detailed specification of the routines for the vehicle computer the need for a possibility to print out salary cards in the machine was realised. This function was then added. Also the database in the office was compressed to enable quicker data processing when calculating bonuses.

b. Roll-out: The pilot was finalized in 1992 but the organization delayed the full roll-out decision more than one year. It was not before 1993 that the decision to go-ahead was taken. The decision included the total workforce of approximately 100 machine operators that would start using the new system for reporting activities. For many of these Skinfo was their first contact with IT. Some did not even know what a keyboard was. This period was before the Internet became widespread.

The company divides the woodland in five districts that needed to be upgraded to the new system. The roll-out was carried out one at a time. First representatives from Ericsson visited machine operators and installed the computers in the harvesters and forwarders. Then the project leader from Skogforsk, Bertil Lidén, visited all machine operators and installed the software and demonstrated the application for the users. After that they could play around with the system a couple of days before an indoor training session was arranged. All machine operators were visited during the roll-out. It was relatively little training: one half-day indoors to demonstrate the functionality. Additional testing was provided and finally a final meeting to resolve specific problems was arranged. All together the training session covered one full-day.

Work-leaders in each district were responsible for roll-out and acted as ambassadors for the project. They were responsible for helping with the roll-out and took care of problems that could develop in the field. One issue that emerged was the fact that people often are afraid of admitting they do not understand. Especially as Skinfo meant such a new concept for end-users often they adopted the strategy to keep silent.

c. Usage: Bertil Lidén tells with pleasure one story from a machine operator who commented for one of his colleagues that now he felt himself a part of the IT-society. Skinfo had increased his status. He felt himself upgraded. Operators now were able to send fax and to some extent messages could be sent between machines acting as a rudimentary and very primitive form of e-mail system. However this meant some first contact with the IT-era. The work was made more interesting to machine operators.

Nevertheless the first step is not equally big for all people. Thus the implementation had to proceed slowly and with parallel systems initially. This was however not always the case and due to rapid implementations the users often cursed SKINFO for problems despite the fact that failures depended on the users.

Regarding the usage, operators were obliged to send rapports to the sawmill. This fact encouraged usage and increased the technical skills of the operators. "This is similar to playing piano, you have to train again and again" said Bertil Lidén. In the long run this had a positive effect. Through the usage of the system increased information was available. This was to such an extent that the competitive spirit between operators in different districts developed. By knowing the number of fallen trees competitions between the districts were arranged. This increased the spirit of the workers in the districts.

Discussion and Results

The description above is an example of an organizational innovation process where a wireless information system was implemented at an early stage. In the late 1980s there was limited experience about the usage of wireless data communication. Skinfo represents therefore an early example of a project that benefited from heavy user engagement. Obviously, the case would be different if dealing with mature technological innovations being out of the scope for this paper. Even though the case is 15 years old, we can still see similar patterns in many recent implementations of wireless information systems as an indication that some of the issues raised in the paper are still relevant.

Let us now proceed to the analysis of the different aspects of the Skinfo-engagement presented above. First, the Graninge case illustrates the importance of visionaries to give a flying start to the whole project. Often these visionaries inject new live during the initial phases of the process. However, as evident, their engagement is not limited to the initial phases of the innovation process. Moreover this engagement is based not so much on concrete activities but on enthusiasm and encouragement. This is especially important in the case where development is led by experts and the workers' involvement in decision making is only limited to consultation. It is doubtful that system design methods carried out by experts and presented in an authoritative way will lead to participation in and ownership of the resulting work processes (Niepce and Molleman 1998). Most adequate design comes from those whose jobs are under review. In the case of WIS, where technology has centralizing effects and strong influence on work-flow activities becoming more interdependent, it is doubtful to succeed if such design methods carried out by experts alone are employed.

Furthermore, the Graninge case showed an example of ongoing changes made by users as a result of engagement by participating in concrete development activities. This was in addition carried out early in the pilot phase. The functionality added to support salary cards illustrates this fact. This could be understood as an unplanned change requirement that became evident along the process. The need for circles of experimentation and learning is thus illustrated.

Prototyping was moreover considered necessary in the case above as a powerful method during development. Nevertheless the choice of site to test prototypes is also critical (Leonard-Barton 1998 p.96). Through prototyping and continuous evaluations in close cooperation with users the risk for *overshooting* is decreased. The absence of users in such a process may lead to the development of too much functionality that may never come into usage. This is often driven by the comparison of old with new technologies leading customers to demand better and better versions of what they already have.

Another interesting fact from the case is that the design process started by re-designing existing activities and people's roles. People with interdependent tasks had to be interconnected. In the case of mobile workforces the data requirements are truly complex. The larger level of complexity appointed as a way of introduction may not be solved by just putting persons with similar tasks together as this in many cases may not be possible at all. However a difficulty also observed above is the versatility of user patterns of mobile workforces. This makes the mapping of current operations more difficult.

Furthermore, the issue of first-step balance was also raised in the case description. This in relation to the implementation phase (called roll-out in the case) means that the first step is not equally big for everyone. For example the amount of effort necessary to understand the concept of data transfer is not equally big for all members of the organization. Especially in the case of Graninge, the concept of mobile data was unknown to some part of the organization, unclear to others and within the pilot team we could find experts in the area.

According to the role of human resources during the system development phase, it is important that the means utilized, i.e. the information systems, fit the ends. One such type of fit is between the work system and the technical system. In our particular case, as the implementation of WIS makes the workflow both more effective and technology dependent. Stress factors due to technology illiteracy may thus appear. In the case we see the *keep silent* reaction of some machine operators. This is evident during the implementation and the usage phases of the system implementation process. When machine operators feel that technology overwhelms them instead of influencing the development and implementation process, the keep silent position is adopted.

This is extra critical in the case of WIS due to the risk of revelation of patterns that makes work/usage more easily monitored and therefore the boundaries of privacy traversed. This fact was not directly observed in the Graninge case. An explanation for this may be the training sessions during the roll-out phase.

These are just but some examples taken from the Graninge case. These have been distributed in the model developed earlier in order to illustrate how different activities vary during the process (cf. Figure 3).

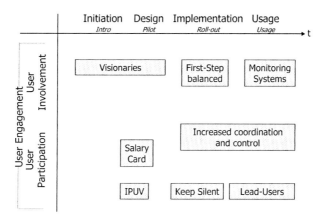

Fig. 3. The Graninge case from a user-engagement perspective

An observation that can be made out of Figure 3 is that both involvement and participation are present along the different phases of the innovation's life-cycle. Earlier contributions such as Hartwick and Barki's (1994) intention to separate participation and involvement may be completed with a view where both are required but where the degree of engagement may be different. Moreover, in connection to the issue of innovation introduced above user engagement particularly means that innovation processes should not be regarded as a development process alone but a technology appropriation and the related social practices of usage associated to the process.

As far as the mobile users concern, the conclusions of this research in process is that there is a need to understand the workplace environment of the users. Researchers should be involved in the development of prototypes after observing the users. Their empirical setting is however based on the establishment of meetings. In the case of mobile users this observation may become more complicated as the variety of locations may impose certain restrictions.

A couple of new ways for developers to become users and for user to understand developers were described in the paper. This is for example done by applying *use cases* as a way to freeze change requirements from mobile users. However a deep training in these use cases is necessary as the users being located in the field may have a more reduced access to tacit/know-how experience. Considering the impact and benefits achieved in the project, Graninge has become a best-practice example because of its pioneer-role in wireless data communication and user involvement.

References

Alam I, Perry C (2002) A Customer-Oriented New Service Development Process. Journal of Services Marketing, vol 16, no 6, pp 515-534

Barki H, Hartwick J (1989) Rethinking the Concept of User Involvement. MIS Quarterly, vol 13, Issue 1, p 53

Barki H, Hartwick J (1994) User Participation, Conflict, and Conflict Resolution: The Mediating Roles of Influence. Information Systems Research, vol 5, Issue 4, p 422

Gallivan MJ, Keil M (2003) The User-Developer Communication Process: a Critical Case Study. Information Systems Journal, vol 13, no 1, pp 37-68

Hwang MI, Thorn RG (1999) The Effect of User Engagement on System Success: A Meta-Analytical Integration of Research Findings. Information & Management, vol 35, no 4, pp 229-236

Leonard-Barton D (1998) Wellsprings of Knowledge: Building and Sustaining the Sources of Innovation / Dorothy Leonard-Barton. Harvard Business School Press Boston Mass

Magnusson PR (2003) Customer-Oriented Product Development: Experiments Involving Users in Service Innovation. Economic Research Institute Stockholm School of Economics (EFI) Stockholm Sweden

McKeen JD, Guimaraes T, Wetherbe JC (1994) The Relationship between User Participation and User Satisfaction. MIS Quarterly, vol 18, Issue 4, p 427

Mölleryd BG (1999) Entrepreneurship in Technological Systems: the Development of Mobile Telephony in Sweden. Economic Research Institute (EFI)

Nilsson G (2000) Creating Meaning with a New Technology: Translation of Mobile Data Technology. Master Thesis Stockholm School of Economics
Overby S (2003) 3 Involve User Representatives; How to Work User Preferences into IT Initiatives. CIO Framingham, vol 16, Issue 12, p 1
Overby S, Varon E (2003) Our Best Practices – CIOs Say That to Be an Effective CIO, You Need to Do Six Things. CIO Framingham, vol 16, Issue 12, p 1
Robey D, Farrow D (1982) User Involvement in Information System Development: A Conflict Model and Empirical Test. Management Science, vol 28, Issue 1, p 73
Von Hippel E (1982) Get New Products from Customers. Harvard Business Review, vol 60, no 2, pp 791-805
Von Hippel E (1986) Lead Users: A Source of Novel Product Concepts. Management Science, vol 32, pp 791-805
Von Hippel E (1988) The Sources of Innovation. Oxford University Press NY
Wallace L, Keil M, Rai A (2004) How Software Project Risk Affects Project Performance: An Investigation of the Dimensions of Risk and an Exploratory Model*. Decision Sciences, vol 35, no 2, pp 289-322

Maintaining Compatibility in an Innovation Infrastructure

Steinar Kristoffersen

Department of Informatics, University of Oslo, Norway.
steinar.kristoffersen@ifi.uio.no

Introduction

Wearable computing has tremendous potential to transform the way we work. The creative and successful miniaturization of computers has made ubiquitous computing a realistic possibility [1, 2]. Deregulation of tele-communications, together with the compelling idea of convergence of computer science, telecommunications and media, open up for wider deployment of such solutions.

It is often assumed that it is certainly not an excuse that the technology is not yet available, because in terms of hardware almost everything that we need is *commercially available off-the shelf* (COTS) [3]. However, users have not extensively adopted wearable computers, and most projects never manage (or aim at) building production quality systems.

This paper explores this problem by looking at an industrial case-study. It describes the development of NORMANS, a complete example of a wearable system ranging from clothing to computers. It was implemented mainly from commercial off-the shelf components and, as it turned out, its success *and* failure can be explained with reference to the surrounding, socio-technical *innovation infrastructure*.

Wearable Computing

Wearable computing typically involves usage scenarios in which the human-computer interface is "continuously worn" [4]. Such systems are generally envisaged as comprising head-mounted displays, various-size keyboards attached to the body and CPUs carried in rucksacks. More importantly, however, wearable computing should blend seamlessly into the background as an:

"intelligent assistant that augments memory, intellect, creativity, communication and physical senses and abilities [4, p. 44]."

This means that it needs to be able to provide constant access to relevant data, represent and react to context, and augment the perception and interaction of the user with the environment. There is, intuitively, a great potential of wearable computing for many 'in-the-field' applications. At the same time, responsive and physically-oriented tasks require unhindered mobility [5]. It should disappear into the background to let the user concentrate 100% on the task at hand.

Unfortunately, however, one cannot easily optimise a wearable solution entirely in the direction of supporting immersion, e.g., since, unavoidably, a host of practical problems will have to be solved: Network capacity must be balanced against transmitter reach and energy consumption, and regardless; users will sooner or later find themselves in a situation in which there is no network coverage [6]. The equipment may have to be carried a long way and hardware is exposed to the vibrations, heat and sunlight of outdoor circumstances [7]. Creating an appealing and efficient interface is therefore always one of the biggest challenges in wearable computing.

Research Background and Problem

Looking back, NORMANS was very much a success in terms of its functional achievements. However, it did not succeed in pressing forward from its research setting. The NORMANS system is (in this respect, even) a representative example of wearable computing. In terms of its ambitions as a project contributing to support the next-generation, land based soldier, moreover, this was not a singular project: "There is no shortage of portable, yet potent information technologies to support mobile Marines and sailors. [8, p. 199]."

Whilst the projects described by Murray [8] saw it as their role to exploit "breakthrough" technologies originating from the commercial sector in military applications, NORMANS addressed the problem (perhaps much more widely recognized in wearable computing altogether) of *rapidly getting to a stage in which usability testing could realistically be carried out, using mainly commercially available off-the-shelf components.* However, we have found modest (to say the least) evidence of a COTS-approach actually leading to faster deployment, even though "the technology is already here".

This problem was addressed using a set of empirically-founded research methodologies: Participant observation and participatory design (similar to e.g., [9]), construction, field-studies and technical evaluation, and, finally, ethnographically-inspired documentation studies (see e.g., [10]).

Our findings indicate that one has to look more closely at the conceptual underpinnings and the methodological approaches to developing wearable computer-systems. Most importantly, the systematic work of maintaining the compatibility between components (COTS) or otherwise, in a highly innovative and experimental systems development environment, requires meticulous care. Having established this requirement, in future research we aim to reason more precisely about this type of compatibility within an innovation infrastructure for wearable computing.

The System

The aim of the NORMANS project was to contribute to develop, evaluate and recommend a fully integrated tactical system that could enable modern combat operations, even in an arctic environment. Emphasis was very much on a "small units' scenario", in which every soldier will have to carry their own equipment and supplies. The overall idea was to provide every member of a squad (which is, in this context, a unit of 10-12 soldiers) with a lightweight wearable computer system that included location and communication services.

Given these requirements, the computers themselves had to be integrated into the uniform, in order to make them easy to carry and blend into the working environment of the soldier. The unit would not have a traditional display, except for the squad leader who might need to be carrying an additional PDA *(Personal Digital Assistant)* with administrative software (e.g., for route planning). Instead a visual interface would have to be overlaid in the sights of the weapon system, or, indeed have head-mounted display for the interface, e.g., overlaid in the visor or separately in a pair of glasses.

Summarizing briefly, the wearable components of the NORMANS implementation were:

- A new composite helmet with an integrated drinking system and improved ventilation.
- A new uniform with better functionality and protection against ABC *(Atomic, Bacteriological and Chemical attacks)*.
- Improved camouflage patterns and climatic as well as laser- and electromagnetic-attack protection.
- Better and lighter ballistic protection (bullet-proof west).
  The project's main hardware components were:

- Optical sights for the weapon.
- A controller pad mounted on front grip of the weapon, as well as one attached on the harness.
- A *Global Positioning System* (GPS).
- Multiple CPUs (at the time, typically, StrongARM 203 Mhz) connected through USB.
- A WLAN 802.11b (modified to broadcast in UHF), as well as an "ordinary" multi-role radio (long range).

Fig. 1. NORMANS "wearables", with the administrative PDA

The project's main software component was an electronic map system, fully integrated with the GPS. It included:

- A TCP-based communication system.
- An inter-squad IP-radio across modified 802.11b WLAN.
- A distributed location system based on UTM (*Universal Transverse Mercator*) co-ordinates, showing every members position. Locations were overlaid on the map.
- Route planning systems, to show the squad members the intended path (as a line on the map). Routes are overlaid on the map. One example is shown in figure 2 below, which shows the route planning component user interface, with position indicators for the squad.
- A reference system showing other units in the landscape. This software subsystem aimed to ensure compatibility with the units of other collabo-

rating forces, since it follows a NATO standard notation. Everything was overlaid on a satellite photo.

The NORMANS system addresses many of the core research questions from ubiquitous computing and CSCW (*Computer-Supported Cooperative Work*), typically related to the situational awareness of the user: Where am I (physically as well as in terms of the flow of work)? Can I find out where my friends are and what do they do now? How can we coordinate our work and use plans efficiently? *Etc.*

Moreover, NORMANS offered incorporated communication support, via the IP-radio and connection through a multi-role, long-range radio back to the headquarters.

The full integration of the wearable computer system's display in the weapon system's sights, and thus, the support for target acquisition and reporting was never finished. Experiments were carried out, but not fully implemented, of integrated magneto-acoustical ground sensors with the system.

Multiple field trials were carried out, and many observers judged that in terms of the functionality that NORMANS offered, it would have to be termed a success. The following section summarizes the most important experiences.

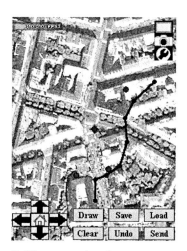

Fig. 2. The route planning component

Project Experiences

The project comprised approximately 10 industrial partners, with responsibilities ranging from clothing to computers. It had a clear philosophy towards using commercially-available components to the extent that it was at all possible. Technical development was supposed to take place for applications and communication systems, mainly; it was intended to test the concept of wearable computing rather than to develop new hardware.

Simplicity and smoothness of in-field operation was emphasized from the very beginning. The result was that the 'man-machine interface' of the system was implemented in dedicated hardware, based on some of the project members' previous military experience. It was conceived as two very simple control pads; one *4-button set* in the harness and another identical set in the front-grip of the weapon system. The users found the control pads robust, silent and easy to use for simple operations, such as stopping and starting the system, as well as controlling radio and map application "output" functionality (toggling backlights and zoom). The evaluation in use was very encouraging.

One COTS PDA had been modified to use a simple, proprietary monochromatic display instead of the standard touch-screen. It was sufficient to display positions from the GPS; however, on a technical level, compatibility with hardware was an issue throughout the project, which had to implement device drivers for each new combination of hardware. Replacing hardware as specifications evolved was a central issue in the software development project. Albeit simple in conceptual terms it is inevitably a real challenge in developing this class of systems to anticipate, specify and verify purely technical compatibility.

Route planning required more advanced input mechanisms and is even more deeply integrated into the strategic military organization. The former made it necessary to implement a separate administrative interface. For this, in contrast to the proprietary monochromatic display, the project used a COTS *HP iPaq*. It did not work as well as hoped. The administrative PDA was connected to the "display-less" wearable PDA directly via USB *(Universal Serial Bus)*, and that turned out to be unstable. The device driver might have been unsuitable, but it is also a possibility of the COTS equipment not working properly in relatively low temperatures.

Perhaps more problematic still, this design assumes naively that it will be possible to switch between two entirely separate *modes* of work-in-the-field for the squad leader. In practice, the "state of affairs" is likely to change too fast and escalate continually (rather than discretely) from an administrative into an operative situation, not to mention the fact that in battle the squad leader may become incapacitated. Thus, ensuring compatibility between i) different stages in dynamically evolving use situations and ii) multifarious interfaces, seems to be an important non-functional requirement. Soldiers enjoyed having status information about themselves *and their system* on their own display, which may be a related issue. System status is usually considered much more administrative than operational. However, in field operations, knowing, e.g., the amount of power left on the battery soon becomes operational information.

On the macro level, compatibility with outside CCIS *(Command and Control information System)* turned out to be important, and will have to be supported in future versions.

Fig. 3. Realistic evaluation

For each squad member, the WLAN-based IP-radio, i.e., the *speech interface* was most crucial. Well known from the HCI (*Human-Computer Interaction*) and CSCW research fields, clear and timely voice is essential to communication [11]. Users expected the WLAN-based radio to furnish enormous advantages in terms of improving efficiency on the battlefield. Due to the computational capabilities of digital audio (e.g., noise cancellation algorithms), it was thought, intuitively, that the performance of this infrastructure would be better than that of analogue radio, for instance with respect to being able to handle variable-dB voice input. This was not implemented, however, and therefore the voice codec was just as poorly dealing with shouting and whispering as traditional radio. In addition, there was a slight delay of compression and transmission that users were not accustomed to. Therefore, the first part (a word or two) of commands often disappeared, which of course was not satisfactory.

Transmission of radio and voice signals in built-up areas was difficult. The project engineers attempted to modify the WLAN-hardware to broadcast in a lower-frequency band instead, in order to gain reach and save battery-consumption with a UHF-WLAN. This did not fit well with the firmware of the cards, however, and it was suspected that the collision detection algorithms had been optimized to the 11 megabit/second bandwidth of the original of 2.4GHz connection. This was not verified by us; however, it shows clearly the importance of compatibility between firmware, hardware and software and the depth and nuances of the concept since it clearly goes beyond was is simply working: Compatibility needs to signify that components work well together with the context of user expectations and *use situation* constraints.

The data interface of the IP-radio worked well, and data payload as well as control information flowed freely across the modified UHF WLAN. The data interface between the IP-radio and the long range radio remained incompatible, however. It only sporadically managed to transmit data. It was believed that the USB-based connection between them was to blame, but other explanations (such as the TCP/IP 'slowstart' algorithm vs. the projects proprietary communication module) are also possible.

Results

Looking back at the case of NORMANS, we find that many of the challenges undertaken in the project can be related to a notion of maintaining compatibility, a few examples of which are shown in table 1 below.

Such problems have to be seen as inevitable. The project aimed to develop highly sophisticated innovation systems and therefore one could not foresee all requirements, consequences and user responses to the choice of hardware or software solutions. At the same time, such problems are sometimes fatal to the innovation of such technologies. Since we are (usually) trying to be ground-breaking—not only in terms of technology, but also in user-functionality—we cannot expect that the budgets (of money, human resources and systemic 'patience') to be unlimited. Therefore, a systematic approach to resolving compatibility problems and the continuance of solutions should have a high priority in such projects. In further research, we shall look at how such phenomena can be more precisely modelled and reasoned about.

Table 1. Some examples of (in)compatibility *break-downs* in the project

Situation	Incompatibility
Technical integration of COTS components	Between OS (operating systems), OS versions, device drivers and physical links, and between programmable and non-programmable devices
Network management	Collision detection of WLAN hardware incompatible with UHF-modification
Microphone technology itself could not handle whispering and shouting	No match between hardware (microphone) and noise cancellation in software
Digital radio not "always better" than analogue	User expectations not clearly expressed in requirements
Cabled connection erroneous	Problems with TCP/IP across USB?
Stage-wise incompatibility of user scenarios	The rapid and continuous change of operations from "soldiering" to administration
International collaboration	Symbolic and graphical information have to be exchanged between systems from various NATO-countries
Command-and-control	Lack of integration with higher-echelon CCIS-systems

Discussion

For many reasons, army settings have been ripe with ideas and examples of wearable computing for soldiers and sailors. It clearly represents a line of work in which interaction is already augmented with advanced instruments and tools for communication, planning, monitoring, etc, so people are used to advanced technology. Moreover, soldiers usually have to carry their own gear and sometimes they end up in situations which definitely do not allow any "office style" interaction with their computers. Developing such systems, however, is far from trivial.

The NORMANS project experienced challenges with respect to packet loss and collisions as well as integration with the multi-role long-rang radio (data transmission was not achieved). This is exactly similar to what Zieniewicz et al. describes for the LandWarrior system [12], the current version of which comprises multiple integrated subsystems. The importance of integration into the wider communication system is clearly recognized, as the US army already plans to issue a multi-role radio that is interoperable with the higher-echelon radios of larger units.

Davies and Gellersen summarize landmark research in wearable computing and identify many new areas of research, especially linked to the complicated deployment of such systems "beyond the laboratory" [13]. They point to aspects such as creating an open distributed environment for ubiquitous computing, with support for adaptation and dynamic reconfiguration (e.g., through reflective middleware platforms) and the need for very low-overhead system management, which is exacerbated by the need to support mobility beyond single administrative domains. Another research topic pointed to in their paper is whether or not it is possible to proactively and dynamically reassign system components to user tasks *in anticipation of their needs as and when they partake in new activities*, which is similar to our findings regarding the stage-wise evolution of user scenarios.

On a tangent, of course, one has to realize that price sensitivity for most 'wearable' (or otherwise radically innovative) applications most likely will be relatively high, whilst allowances for such development continue to be moderate. Thus, deployment techniques must take into account rather restricted business models. Finger et al. describe how it is particularly important *and* difficult in ubiquitous and wearable computing to prototype rapidly and cost-effectively [14]. Our work in the NORMANS project clearly resonates with the work at CMU. We believe that properly managing compatibility issues will definitely be one way of achieving exactly the combination of reasonable costs with fast deployment and realistic user testing.

Conclusion

Based on the industrial case study of the NORMANS project, we can safely say that wearable computing (just like any other broadly scoped ubiquitous, networked system) will encounter some serious challenges. There will be shortcomings of technology, misunderstandings of requirements and defects in code. Thus, the technical artefacts that we can offer will not be perfect the first time around.

The project that we studied ended up concluding that even the selected set of COTS did not live up to the standards required for arctic operation by soldiers in the field. Much of the hardware needed to be improved, replaced or designed and implemented from scratch. Some of it did not work in the cold. This is something that one has to expect in a challenging environment.

At the same time, user will not forever accept to receive and test cumbersome and error-prone wearable computing systems, for which they can see no immediate useful usage. This is probably always the case to some extent for particularly innovative systems and therefore it becomes especially noticeable for wearable computing. One can hardly expect to be allowed to develop everything from scratch, and therefore COTS components will have to be somehow effectively embedded. This represents, on the other hand, a tremendous integration task, which will run throughout the entire life-cycle of a project.

Therefore we propose to conceive this class of systems as running on top of an innovation infrastructure, of which the "first property" is that it meets a set of compatibility requirements. These requirements are non-functional and intractable in terms of eliciting them using tradition systems development methods. It would be a great advantage for innovative projects if such 'compatibility management' could be built into the infrastructure in the future.

References

[1] Gellersen HW, Schmidt A, Beigl M (2002) Multi-Sensor Context-Awareness in Mobile Devices and Smart Artifacts. Mobile Network Applications, vol 7, no 5, pp 341-351

[2] Smailagic A, Siewiorek DP (2002) Application Design for Wearable and Context-Aware Computers. Pervasive Computing, vol 1, no 4, pp 20-29

[3] Kortuem G, Bauer M, Segall Z (1999) NETMAN: the Design of a Collaborative Wearable Computer System. Mob. Netw. Appl. vol 4, no 1, pp 49-58

[4] Starner T (2001) The Challenges of Wearable Computing Part 1. IEEE Micro

[5] Rensing NM, et al. (2002) Threat Response: A Compelling Application for Wearable Computing. In: ISWC. 2002

[6] Starner T (2001) The Challenges of Wearable Computing Part 2. IEEE Micro

[7] Thomas B, et al. (1998) A Wearable Computer System with Augmented Reality to Support Terrestrial Navigation. In: ISWC '98 (Second Int. Symp. on Wearable Computers). Pittsburgh PA

[8] Murray S (2001) Development of Wearable Tools for Mobile Task Support. In: Biennial Review. SSC San Diego

[9] Crabtree A (1998) Etnography in Participatory Design. In: Participatory Design Conference

[10] Silvermann D (1993) Interpreting Qualitative Data. Sage Publ London Thousand Oaks

[11] Tang JC (1992) Why Do Users Like Video? Studies of Multimedia-Supported Collaboration. Sun Microsystems Inc

[12] Zieniewicz MJ, et al. (2002) The Evolution of Army Wearable Computers. Pervasive Computing, vol 1, no 4, pp 30-14

[13] Davies N, Gellersen H-W (2002) Beyond Prototypes: Challenges in Deploying Ubiquitous Systems. IEEE Pervasive Computing, vol 1, no 1, pp 26-35

[14] Finger S, et al. (1996) Rapid Design and Manufacture of Wearable Computers. Communications of the ACM, vol 39, no 2, pp 63-70

Defining User Characteristics to Divide Layers in a Multi-Layered Context

Linn Gustavsson Christiernin

Department of Computer Science, University of Trollhättan, Sweden.
linn.gustavsson@htu.se

Introduction

Interaction design deals with the complexity arising in the interplay between humans and the interfaces of modern machines [5]. In the field of software development the complexity is often very high and the task frequently defined in an imprecise manner, or not even defined at all. It is further more common that neither the different users' roles nor the computer knowledge is taken into account when developing software [5, 13]. In this context it is crucial regardless of the choice of design method to be able to identify the different needs, knowledge, tasks and behaviors of the users [14, 15]. Many of the interfaces of common applications are rich or full interfaces where all functionality or features are available to the user at once; often with little guidance on where to start, how to best progress through the application and finally how to learn and get a deeper understanding of the functionality [12]. A large factor behind user frustration is the feeling of lack of control, misunderstandings and limitations, or overwhelming resources or options. The frustration triggers stress and creates unhealthy work environments [1, 2].

Lately the Multi-Layered Design (MLD) has been proven to provide a viable alternative for interface-design [3, 4, 6, 10-12] taking the user's knowledge and skills into careful consideration, providing the individual users with functionality organized in different layers to promote personal learning in steps. However, currently there exists no well defined method to identify and categorize the different design layers or structures based on the users' knowledge or needs. When using MLD one of the major problems is to identify the contents and decide the number of layers suited for the application at hand.

In this paper we present a first proposal for a user representation to define the layers in the Multi-Layered Design. First the different variations of MLD are presented, followed by how users can be mapped in a new sort of representation and how the users groups in that representation correlate to the standard variations of MLD. The layers in the MLD structure can then be identified and categorized. The presentation ends with an example of how the representation can be used for a real application.

Background

The concept of Multi-Layered Design [3, 4, 6, 10-12] is focused on the knowledge level of the users. The application is divided into layers which can be activated one by one, where each layer holds a set of functionality. A Multi-Layered interface is created to give the users control over which sets of functionality they need and when to work with them. When the users have gained confidence and learned the first layer they can progress to layers with more functionality. The learning plan in MLD is focused on the users' progress through task functionality, with new interface concepts only introduced when they are needed to support more complex tasks. For expert users a rapid progress is possible or they can start at the top level right from the beginning. The novice users on the other hand start at the first layer and when ready they move up through the layer structure. If the layers are carefully designed the structure can enable users to learn features or functions in a meaningful sequence, while limiting the complexity of the application [3, 11, 12].

Simple functions that everybody need are placed in the first layer and then the functions are divided between the rest of the layers. The last layer has full functionality and contains all functions the application holds. The simplicity should also be adapted in the layers; the first layers can have a more simple way to visualize the functions while the last layers must offer the expert users ways to perform quick tasks like shortcuts and commands.

Definitions of MLD Structure

In order to be able to treat the MLD on a more formal basis, it is necessary to define both the variety of structures possible in a Multi-Layered Design and what a proper design layer consists of.

The Multi-Layer structure can be varied in several ways to fit different learners and different types of users. In figure 1 four basic types of layered structures are illustrated (based on B. Shneidermans visual representation [12]). The small shapes in the layers represent a specific type of functionality while the color represents the level of difficulty; the darker the color is, the more difficult the function is. The number of shapes in each layer represents the amount of new functions added. The complexity in each layer is consequently determined by a combination of the number of new functions and the level of difficulty of the added functions, together with the functionality retained from all the earlier layers.

The most fundamental variation of the different illustrated divisions of layers in the MLD approach is the one depicted in figure 1a). Here each layer adds an equal number of new functions to the application and the level of difficulty grows slowly with the number of layers; the growth of complexity is linear and the functions provide a clear sequence of learning to the user. This basic form of MLD could in some cases be too restrictive and is not suitable for the application at hand. An alternative is then to use an expanding Multi-Layered Design where the first layer only holds a few functions and is followed by an exponentially increasing number of functions in each new layer, see fig. 1b). In the figure the level of difficulty of each function is equal in all layers, which implies that the complexity only increases by the number of functions. The number of layers in this type of MLD is often small and the growth exponent will increase rapidly if the complexity is influenced both by the number of functions and the level of difficulty. Sometimes the complexity of each new function grows so much that it is no longer possible to keep adding functionality at a steady pace though. In this case, the design in figure 1b) can be turned up-side-down and become a contracting MLD, where the number of new functions is decreasing with the added layers in order to counter balance the rapidly increasing difficulty of the functions. The result provides a controlled expansion of complexity of each layer, adapted to the users learning ability.

In many cases the users need or use the sets of functionality differently, for example could the users be divided into groups with specific tasks or roles. Some functions are then used by all users while others only are used by a few. In this case the layers have to be divided into another structure. In figure 1d a so called Multi-Layered Mushroom is illustrated to explain this type of structure. The complexity of the mushroom illustrated in 1d is rather low. The level of difficulty only increases in three steps and the number of functions for each user increase linear while the total number of functions in the application increases exponentially. Each group in the cap can also be divided into layers which would create a more complex model.

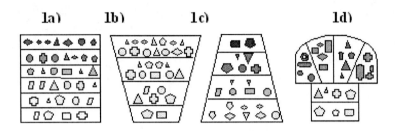

Fig. 1. Four ways to illustrate how an interface can be divided with MLD where each new layer retains all "lower" functionality while adding new functional and graphical objects. **1a)** shows a fundamental MLD structure with six layers while **1b)** is an expanding MLD. 1c) is an contracting MLD structure where the number of new functions decrease but the difficulty of the functionality increase. The last figure in **1d)** shows the structure for a differentiated user group illustrated with a Multi-Layer Mushroom. The shapes in the figure represent a type of functionality while the color represents level of difficulty: the darker the color, the more difficult the function is. The number represents complexity in each layer [4].

User Representation

Multi-Layered Design supports the knowledge level of the user, but to be able to design such a layer and to create a meaningful learning sequence we must have a way to identify and describe the intended users. We need to get an understanding of the user characteristics [9, 15, 16]. To do so we need to be able to create a user representation; a diagram, an image visualization or a model where the users and the characteristics are outlined [9, 15].

A common way to describe users or user groups is to use two dimensional graphs with shapes representing the user groups or the task they perform [7, 12]. This type of diagram shows very effectively an overview and if the types overlap or not. In figure 2a) a typical two dimensional graph is illustrated where four categories with different needs are represented. Some needs are overlapping while others are parted.

The first three categories in figure 2a have needs that partly overlap with a number of similar characteristics while the fourth category is very different from the others. This type of diagram is very well suited to visualize an overview of the user groups and gives a first indication of the level of complexity needed in the MLD structure. But on the other hand it is difficult in this user representation to see what kind of needs that are overlapping; a more detailed description is wanted in order to define the design. Only a few parameters can be illustrated through different size of the circles and how the circles overlap. The number of categories in such a model must also be low because the circles otherwise will hide and collide with each other (see 2b). If graded axes are added to figure 2a) the shape of the circles can represent a third parameter. In figure 2c) the horizontal axis could for example represent computer knowledge and the vertical axis usage frequency. The figure then gives a good overview of how much the users know about how to use computers and how often they use them.

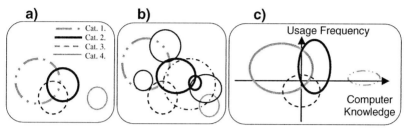

Fig. 2. Three types of a simple model of how user categories can be described with overlapping or not overlapping needs. The size of the circle illustrates the number of persons in each group. In 3b a scale is added and the shape of the circles represents how the users are distributed along the axis.

The relations between the illustrated parameters must be simple since the model otherwise will be too complex to read. In addition, the low dimensionality of the representation (i.e. the "flat" character of the diagram) does not support any further advanced user categorization.

To be able to describe a realistic situation with several different aspects such as computer knowledge, task frequencies, task experience, different security and access rights etc a substantially more complex description is needed. In principle this may be accomplished by using a variety of diagrams such as those above, all being related to each other by different aspects such as "rights vs. computer knowledge". But this type of relations is rarely straightforward and the representation will become highly abstract and risks to quickly become incomprehensible and impossible to represent in a good way. Hence there is a distinct need to either refine the current representation or develop a new one.

Creating a New Representation

The representation should guide the division of contents and the definition of the number of layers. To illustrate a more complex system we have to use a better representation then the simple model illustrated in figure 2. In a regular line chart diagram two parameters can be illustrated, but when more parameters are needed a more complex chart type, one with many axes, should be used. We therefore selected the radar diagram type to our user representation, a diagram type used in other applications to show complex relations [14].

The different characteristics measured should be essential parameters that influence the design of the interface and the interaction. Parameters like different knowledge levels, rights, and need for different functionality groups should be measured. Each axis in the radar diagram constitutes of one separate characteristic measured from 0 to 100 percent. The measured values of the characteristics are then plotted into the radar diagram to create a first visualization of the users.

Depending on the actual interface concept utilized in the design of any real-world system, one characteristic will constitute the main characteristics for which the system is optimized. This then becomes the dominating parameter since optimization normally can be done only with one focus at a time. This difficulty is parallel to the problem when software developers have to select if they are optimizing the software for speed, memory usage, performance, maintenance, or something else [8]. The designer then has to select the main focus of the interface design. The main focus can for example be knowledge of tasks, knowledge of operating system or knowledge of functionality.

When such a choice has been made, the users can be grouped depending on where they are located on the scale for the main characteristic (fig. 3). To identify the groups we start at the center of the radar diagram and follow it to the end of the specified axis. A level is defined for each point at the axis in the radar diagram where a group of users are detected (arrows in figure 3).

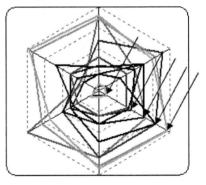

Figure 3. A radar diagram with plotted user characteristics and arrows marking each level of user groups

If the knowledge development should be linear the distance between each layer should be equal but if the development is exponential the distance should expand.

There is a gap between the first and the second level due to missing data or lack of users at that level. It is then important to remember to create layers with the same learning pattern independent of if there are users at that exact level, because the users below that level must have a logical path to follow to reach the higher levels. To get that logical development a new area is created and added in the radar diagram. The new area is created from a mean value of the smaller area before this level and the larger area after it.

When the levels are defined, the next step is to define the sequence of smallest common areas within that level. Figure 4 illustrates the flow for how the layers are determined from the complex diagram with all users (4a) to the structured diagram with defined layers (4d). Based on the levels found in figure 3 a simplified diagram is created (4b) as a first step. A mean value of each user group is used to create the new simplified diagram. To define the number of layers a sequence of "smallest common areas" ordered after the main characteristic is created.

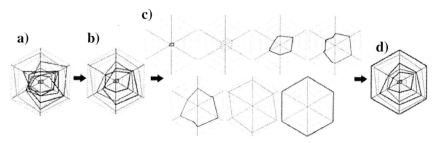

Figure 4. Work flow for definition of layers, from a complex diagram in a) to seven layers in d). c) constitutes of the six areas taken from the diagram in b) plus an extrapolated area marked with a dashed line in the second diagram from the left I c)

When creating the mean values for the groups at each level it is important to look at the topology of the diagram. If all areas of the group are more or less overlapping like they are in figure 4a) there will be no problems with creating mean values. If the diagram, on the other hand, has a butterfly-like shape the design of the application should be a Multi-Layered Mushroom (see figure 1).

Continuing by analyzing the topology we are looking for the standard patterns based on the four types of MLD described in figure 1. Based on variations of the four types, the layer structure can be built from the visualized radar diagram. In figure 5 four radar diagrams are visualized representing users distributed according to the four types of Multi-Layered structures visualized in figure 1.

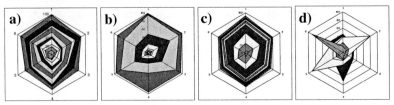

Fig. 5. Standard user groups distributed according to the four types of MLD (see fig. 1)

In the example in 4d) the new divided levels of layers are illustrated together with the last full knowledge level. Compared to figure 5 the distribution of levels is very similar to the one in 5a) and the application should therefore be structured as a regular MLD. The number of layers for the application in this example should be seven layers with a linear progress of the knowledge sequence.

Finally the developer has to translate the diagram back to functions and objects in the real interface and create a Multi-Layered Design in the application based on the user representation found in the diagram topology.

Practical Use of the Model

To properly understand how the user representation could be used we introduce a practical example to illustrate how an application can be divided into a layered design.

In the current example a new text editor is to be created and a Multi-Layered design is suggested. The example is based on a WIMP [5] environment. In the organization there are five user groups that are going to use the editor. The data is collected and then plotted in a radar diagram where the measured characteristics are marked on the different axes (see figure 6a). The selected main characteristic is to handle text and the users vary from good users to novice users. Next the mean values are calculated and a new layer visualization is defined based on the groups we can see in the diagram (6a). To give the users a good sequence of learning the layers are created from a series of smallest common areas representing the common difficulty the users at that level share. (See figure 6b).

The topology in the diagram is a centered homogeneous topology and the layer structure should then follow a linear growth of complexity in each new layer which means that the same amount of new functionality should be added to each layer and the level of difficulty should increase equally between the layers.

a)

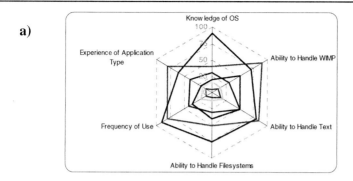

b)

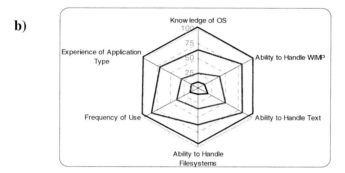

Fig. 6. In a) is a set of six user groups represented with characteristics. In b) is the new layer structure illustrated. Three layers based on the user groups and one full layer

The actual design of the text editor is then developed. In the first, smallest layer the interface offers a lot of help on how to save and edit texts. The graphical objects are adapted to users that do not use the system often and the text editing only holds the basic functionality. Next layer holds the same functionalities as in the first plus a number of new functions for text handling and window manipulation. The third layer has changed the file handling routines to allow more complex actions and the number of text editing tools has increased. The last layer holds all functionality the application has to offer.

How much the graphical representation in each layer should differ is a question of how difficult it is for the users to grasp a new representation of functions and objects. The users should have use of the knowledge earned in earlier layer and if the graphical representation changes too much it can bee confusing. On the other hand can a simpler representation in a low layer be easier to understand for a novice while childish for an expert. The final design of the graphical objects must therefore be adapted to the users and to the type of application at hand in each new case.

Conclusions and Discussion

When using a layered design, it becomes possible to allow the users to both choose their own set of functionality and at the same time create an individual learning path to the full interface of the application. This kind of design is not possible, however, without a good user representation of the different user groups and their knowledge. The representation should guide the number of layers as well as the contents of them, providing a suitable learning sequence for the user.

In this work we have utilized radar diagrams to describe a multitude of user characteristics, identify and categorize the layers and how much the complexity should increase for each layer. The radar diagram representation furthermore provides a good way to identify what kind of structure the design should have; which one of the four basic layered design types one should follow. It is also possible to use the radar diagrams for more complex structures and design choices, still giving a good overview. In the current representation the diagram is two dimensional but it would be possible to describe complexity with a three dimensional diagram in order to for example show a development of knowledge over time.

In larger software systems the combination of different requirements, functionalities, and users is often more irregular and complex than what the standard Multi Layered Design structures support though. If some users differ from the rest of the users there will be difficulties to get a correct representation of that group. The users might be divided into two or more user groups using completely different functionalities in the application or have completely different prerequisites. In many cases it is enough to create an MLD Mushroom, but in some cases even such a structure is too simple. The representation presented here must then be complemented with other diagrams and more data to be supportive. The layer structure is at that point not obvious and a more thorough analysis must be done of the diagrams, resulting in a layer-structure that is a mix of the four types. A fully expanded representation of such a design will require continued work on a more extensive model where characteristics are more formally measured and the development of layers completely covered.

The current representation is nevertheless an excellent tool when working with MLD but should bee seen as the first step in a bigger model and the next step of the user representation is to define the diagrams more formally and complement them with other diagrams to handle more complex systems and users.

A full model for the whole design process should then be created where the designer can follow a number of steps to create the MLD, from collecting user characteristics in a formal way to implementing the layer structure in the application. Such a model can also be complemented with a three dimensional representation technique to be able to illustrate e.g. the different users' learning curve.

Acknowledgements

The author would specially like to thank Stefan Christiernin, Andreas Boklund and Christian Jiresjö for editorial help and very interesting conversations about how to create and illustrate the diagrams and how to apply the representation.

References

[1] Bessiere K, Ceaparu I, Lazar J, Robinson J, Shneiderman B (2002) Social and Psychological Influences on Computer User Frustration. Newhagen Book Chapter Draft

[2] Ceaparu I, Lazar J, Bessiere K, Robinsson J, Shneiderman B (2004) Determining Causes and severity of End-User Frustration. International Journal of Human-Computer Interaction, vol 17, no 3, pp 333-356

[3] Christiernin LG, Lindahl F, Torgersson O (2004) Designing a Multi-Layered Image Viewer. Proc of the International Nordic Conference on Computer-Human Interaction (NordiCHI)

[4] Christiernin LG, Torgersson O (2005) Benefits of a Multi-Layer Design in Software with Multi-User Interfaces – Conclusions from a Three Level Case Study. Proc of IASTED International Conference on Software Engineering. Innsbruck Austria

[5] Dix A, Finlay J, Abowe GD, Beale R (2004) Human-Computer Interaction. 3d ed. Pearson & Prentice Hall Harlow England

[6] Kang H, Plaisant C, Shneiderman B (2003) New Approaches to Help Users Get Started with Visual Interfaces: Multi-Layered Interfaces and Integrated Initial Guidance. Proc Of the National Conference on Digital Government Research

[7] Kujala S, Kauppinen M (2004) Identifying and Selecting Users for User-Centered Design. Proc of the Nordic Conference on Human-Computer Interaction Tampere Finland

[8] Hägganger D (2001) Software Design Conflicts – Maintainabilities versus Performance and Availability. Dissertation Blekinge Institute of Technology

[9] Larm C (2005) Applying UML and Patterns – an Introduction to Object-Oriented Analysis and Design and Iterative development. 3d ed. Prentice Hall Upper Saddle River USA

[10] McGreenere J, Baecker RM, Booth KS (2002) An Evolution of a Multiple Interface Design Solution for Bloated Software. Proc of the Conference on Human Factors in Computing Systems (CHI2002). Minneapolis Minnesota USA, vol 4, no 1, pp 163-170

[11] Shneiderman B (1998) Designing the User Interface-Strategies for Effective Human-Computer Interaction. 3rd ed. Addison Wesley Longman Inc USA

[12] Shneiderman B (2003) Promoting Universal Usability with Multi-Layer Interface Design. Proc of 2003 Conference on Universal Usability. Vancouver British Columbia Canada

[13] Sommerville I (2001) Software Engineering. 6th edition. Addison Wesley Pearson Educational Limited Edinburgh Gate England

[14] Tähti M (2003) Framework for Evaluating Application Adaptivity. Proc of the Conference on Human Factors in Computing Systems (CHI2003). Florida USA

[15] Vicente KJ (1999) Cognitive Work Analysis – Toward Safe, Productive, and Healthy Computer-Based Work. Lawrence Erlbaum Associates Inc Publishers London England

[16] Wilson JR, Corlett EN (2002) Evaluation of Human Work – A Practical Ergonomics Methodology. 2nd ed. Taylor & Francis Ltd London England

Translating Metaphors into Design Patterns

Peter Rittgen

School of Business and Informatics, University College of Borås, Sweden.
peter.rittgen@hb.se

Introduction

Metaphors are powerful cognitive instruments that help us in making sense of the world around us. We start using them already as very small children and they accompany us throughout our lives. Some authors go as far as claiming that all knowledge is metaphorical (Indurkhya 1994). But even if we do not subscribe to that position we cannot but admit that metaphors are an important cornerstone of human creativity (Seitz 1997). It therefore stands to reason that they might be useful in highly creative undertakings such as the development of information systems. The latter activity in particular is fraught with a principal problem: Most stakeholders in the system are not knowledgeable in system design and they find it very difficult – if not impossible – to envision a system that does not yet exist. It is not there to look at or to play with and in early stages there is not even a rudimentary prototype that could be studied. To imagine how a future system might look like, what functions it will have and how it will support and shape my daily work is well beyond the powers of most potential users of such a system. In this context a metaphor can be a powerful device for building a bridge from the known to the unknown. It draws on ideas that people are familiar with from their everyday experience.

A simple example of a metaphor is that of a CD player. Most people have experience in operating a hardware player so that its design can be used as a template for that of the software player. The user interface of the latter will thus include images of the knobs, slides, dials, buttons, lamps, displays and all other devices found on a hardware player and the user will be able to operate it in a very similar way. This facilitates the use of the software player and a user manual is hardly required.

But the use of metaphors is not always as straightforward as that. In the case of more sophisticated information systems it can be hard to find a suitable metaphor and even harder to translate it into the system design. A common approach to facilitating the design of information systems is that of design patterns. A design pattern is a very general model of a system's architecture. It does not specify the design down to the smallest detail but only outlines the basic structure. It can be seen as a reusable solution to a commonly occuring problem. An example of such a design pattern is the Model-View-Controller architecture (MVC). The model component contains the business logic and data of the application. Views that are registered to the model can access its data and present it to the user in a suitable form. The controller component accepts user input and triggers the corresponding functions in the model. The model notifies the views of resulting changes in the data, which in turn update their displays accordingly. This architecture provides for a separation of concerns: The model is freed from dealing with the user interface and can instead focus on the functionality of the application domain.

Design patterns are typically not based on experiences from everyday life of users. They are often abstract and technology-oriented and do not appeal to intuition or common sense. That makes them unsuitable as a platform for communication between information system stakeholders. There metaphors perform better. But design patterns do have a place in system design where they make a valuable contribution to well-structured, reusable and less error-prone software. It is therefore worthwhile to investigate the question of how a metaphor can be translated into a design pattern in order to lower the communicative barriers between the stakeholders and to allow them to join in the co-design of "their" system. To this end we first introduce the Bunge-Wand-Weber ontology that is used to anchor both the metaphor language and the design pattern language; this facilitates the translation between the two languages. We then address the fundamental concepts of metaphors and design patterns and the respective languages. We proceed by specifying a translation based on structure-mapping theory and providing an example that employs the metaphor of the labour market to develop the architecture of an eService system.

Bunge-Wand-Weber Ontology

The Bunge-Wand-Weber ontology (BWW ontology) is an established tool for analyzing modeling languages. It is based on Mario Bunge's ontology (Bunge 1977, Bunge 1979) and was later adapted by Yair Wand and Ron Weber to the information systems field (Wand and Weber 1989, Wand and Weber 1995, Weber 1997). According to this ontology the world consists of *things* that possess *properties*. Both of them exist irrespective of the human observer. The observer can only witness attributes that he takes for the properties of the things he observes. The things themselves are not observable. In the BWW ontology an attribute is represented by a *property function* over time that maps onto a *property co-domain* containing the possible *property values*. An *intrinsic property* belongs to an individual thing, a *mutual property* to two or more things. A *whole-part relation* is a property of an *aggregate thing* and a *component thing*. A *resultant property* of an aggregate is derived from the components, an *emergent property* of an aggregate not (i.e. it is new). A *complex property* is made up of other properties. A *class* consists exactly of the things that share a set of *characteristic properties*. A *natural kind* is a class where all the characteristic properties are laws. "*Laws* reflect either natural or artificial constraints imposed upon things." (Wand and Weber 1990)

In the following sections we will use that ontology to anchor both the metaphor language and the design pattern language which facilitates the mapping between them.

Metaphors

A metaphor is a figure of speech that involves a transfer of meaning between seemingly unrelated terms. It has its origins in the rhetoric of ancient Greece where it was used to make a talk more interesting and easier to follow. When we say "The customer is king" we do not mean it literally. It is a metaphor that attributes to a customer many of the qualities that we typically associate with a king: influence, importance, power and so on. A metaphor can transfer complex meaning such as in that of a nation as "a ship of state" where the captain of the ship represents the government, the sea the flow of time, bad weather a crisis, lack of wind economic stagnation etc. An example of an information system metaphor is that of the desktop in windows environments. Metaphors are used in many disciplines such as organizational theory (Morgan 1997), architecture (Alexander et al. 1977), software development (Beck 2000), economics (McCloskey 1998) and information systems (Carroll et al. 1988, Gazendam 1999, Walsham 1991, Madsen 1994, Coyne 1995).

According to cognitive linguistics (Lakoff and Johnson 1980) a metaphor connects two conceptual spaces: the source (also called secondary system or vehicle) and the target (also called primary system or topic). The connection takes on the form of a mapping from source to target (see figure 1). As an example we might use the commonly known labour market with employers, job seekers, job announcements, applications etc. to explain the architecture of a yet-to-be-built eService market with eService providers, eService clients, eService offers, eService requests and so on.

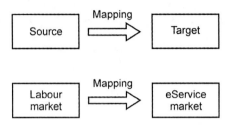

Fig. 1. Metaphor – concept and example

The Metaphor Language (ML) is used to express the vehicle with which we anchor the metaphor in the stakeholders' imagination (as well as the target). For this reason it must be a very simple language that closely resembles our "natural" or "intuitive" way of conceptualizing the world around us. A common and very basic approach is to view the world as a number of things that are related in some way. In the different modeling languages these things are called classes, objects, entities and so on. They can be on the instance or type level, i.e. they refer to individual things or sets of things, respectively. Likewise the relations between things can be termed links, associations, relations etc. Again we distinguish between type and instance level. For the Metaphor Language we make use of this rudimentary conceptualization: A metaphor model consists of *entity types* and *transfer types*. Entity types are sets of concrete things sharing common properties. Transfer types are ternary relation types where an entity of the second type is transfered from one of the first to one of the third. The first or third entity type must be *active*, i.e. its entities must be able to perform activities. These entities could be human beings, software artifacts or organizations. Using ternary relation types is a simple way of introducing a dynamic element into the language without encumbering it with additional constructs. An example of a transfer is an employer who makes a job offer to a job seeker (shown in figure 2, on the type level). Often transfer types can be compared to simple communicative transactions but they can also describe material acts. Table 1 shows how this language is anchored in the BWW ontology.

Figure 2 shows how the source of the labour market metaphor might look like. Job seekers register at the placement service by giving information on themselves and their qualifications. Employers hand in a description of each vacancy. It consists of a list of required qualifications. The placement service then compares required and provided qualifications and sends the employers the available information about matching candidates.

Based on that employers can then decide to make a job offer which the job seeker in turn can accept or decline.

Table 1. BWW ontology of the Metaphor Language (ML)

ML construct	BWW construct
ML-entity type	BWW-natural kind of things
ML-active entity type	BWW-natural kind of things that act on other things
ML-transfer type	BWW-characteristic mutual property of 3 things + BWW-transformation

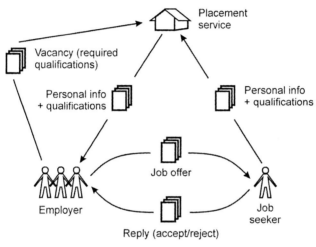

Fig. 2. The labour market metaphor (source)

Design Patterns

The design patterns used in the development of object-oriented software were introduced by Gamma et al. (1995). They have been influenced strongly by Alexander's architectural design patterns where each pattern is defined as a three-part rule, which expresses a relation between a certain context, a problem, and a solution (Alexander 1979). The context describes the conditions under which the pattern can be applied. The problem is a "system of forces" that the solution is supposed to balance. This definition is used in a slightly rephrased form also in software engineering: A design pattern is a solution to a recurring problem in a certain context. According to Trætteberg (2000) it involves:

1. a description of a problem and a possible solution,
2. examples of usages of the solution in actual designs,
3. reasons for why the solution actually solves the problem,
4. criteria for when to use and when to avoid this particular solution and
5. relations to other design patterns.

In object-oriented design the solution is often described as a class diagram that can be accompanied by some interaction diagram. Sometimes the term design pattern is used to refer to the solution alone.

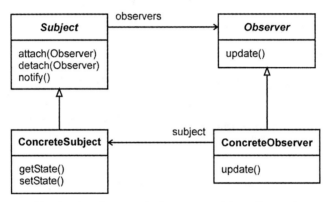

Fig. 3. The observer design pattern (class diagram)

An example of the (solution part of a) design pattern is given in figure 3. It addresses the problem of maintaining consistency between related objects: How can we make sure that dependants are updated when the state of the object they depend on is changed? Such a situation arises when we have multiple views on the same data, e.g. a pie and a bar chart representing the same numerical data. If the numbers change we want to make sure that the respective views are updated accordingly. The solution that the observer pattern offers involves an *Observer* and a *Subject* class. These classes are abstract, i.e. they have no instances. Instead they are specialized into *ConcreteObserver* and *ConcreteSubject*. Each dependant is an instance of the former, the object they depend on is an instance of the latter. An observer can register at a subject by sending it an *attach* message. All registered observers will be notified by the subject whenever its state changes. This is done by the *notify* operation that sends an *update* message to all attached observers which in turn send a *getState* message to the subject to find out about the new state.

We use the Unified Modeling Language (UML, OMG 2003) to express the solution part of design patterns, in particular the class and sequence diagrams of UML. Ontological evaluations of the UML based on BWW have been done by Evermann and Wand (2001) and Opdahl and Henderson-Sellers (2002). Table 2 lists the relevant constructs and their BWW equivalents according to Opdahl and Henderson-Sellers (2004).

Table 2. BWW ontology of some UML constructs

UML construct	BWW construct
UML-class	BWW-natural kind of things
UML-active class	BWW-natural kind of things that act on other things
UML-attribute [of a class]	BWW-characteristic intrinsic property [that defines a natural kind and] that is not a law or a whole-part relation, but can be either resultant or emergent
UML-object	BWW-thing
UML-property [of an object]	BWW-intrinsic property [of a thing] that is not a law or a whole-part relation, but can be either resultant or emergent BWW-intrinsic complex property (if the UML-property has a non-primitive type)
UML-association	BWW-characteristic mutual property
UML-multiplicity	BWW-characteristic state law about how many BWW-properties that a thing can possess
UML-object lifeline	BWW-segment of a history
UML-messsage	BWW-binding mutual property
UML-operation	BWW-transformation

Translating Metaphors into Design Patterns

The translation of metaphors into design patterns is based on structure-mapping theory. It has originally been developed to describe the nature of analogies (Gentner 1983) but has later been adapted to metaphors (Gentner et al. 1988). The central assumption of structure-mapping theory is that the likeness between the source and target domains of analogies or metaphors is not so much in the properties of the objects of each domain themselves but rather in the relations between them. In our example of the labour and eService markets an employer and an eService client have little in common but the relation between an employer and a job seeker on the one hand, and an eService client and an eService provider on the other hand is close: in both cases the second offers a service to the first. In structure-mapping we define interpretation rules that map knowledge about a source domain into a target domain by relying on the syntactic properties of the knowledge domain alone and not on the specific content of the domains.

The translation proceeds in two steps: metaphorical mapping and design mapping. In metaphorical mapping the terms of the source domain are translated into the corresponding terms of the target domain. In this step the structure of the source is largely conserved. The result is a model that is still expressed in ML but now refers to the target. It is therefore called the metaphor target model. The metaphorical mapping can be supported by a translation table that shows how source and target terms are related. In table 3 some of the labour market terms are translated into their eService market equivalents. The resulting metaphor target model is shown in fig 4.

Table 3. Translation of some of the labour market terms

Source term	Target term
Employer	eService client
Job seeker	eService provider
Placement service	eService broker
Vacancy	eService request

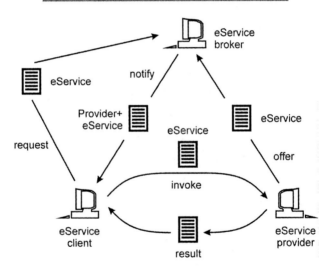

Fig. 4. Metaphor target model of the eService market

The second step, design mapping, translates the metaphor target model into the design pattern. The design pattern language is UML. As this step involves a mapping between different languages (i.e from ML to UML) it is more complex than metaphorical mapping. The ontological analysis of the two languages reveals that the constructs of the ML should be translated into UML as shown in table 4.

Table 4. Mapping ML constructs onto UML

ML construct	UML construct
ML-entity type	UML-class
ML-active entity type	UML-active class
ML-transfer type	UML-association (ternary) +
	UML-operation (message)

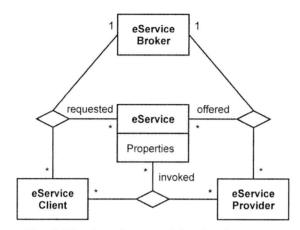

Fig. 5. The class diagram of the eService pattern

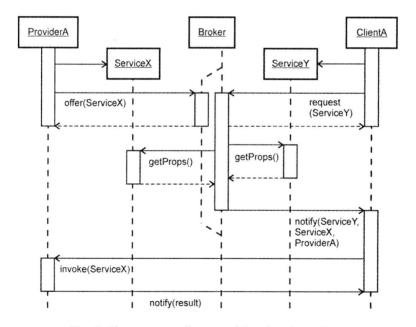

Fig. 6. The sequence diagram of the eService pattern

The mapping from ML to UML is not surjective (i.e. it does not cover all UML constructs) even if we restrict the UML to the subset of constructs that are required for class and sequence diagrams. This means that we have to supply additional information which is not present in the metaphor when we want to create the design pattern. In particular we need to provide the time order of messages, attributes of classes, multiplicities and objects for the sequence diagram. Figures 5 and 6 show the result of this step, the class and sequence diagrams, respectively.

Conclusion

Developing an information system is a very complex task that requires the active collaboration of a substantial number of people, called stakeholders, if the system is to be successful. These people have to understand each other (i.e. to speak the same language) and they have to agree on some common design for the system. This process is called co-design (Liu et al. 2002, Forsgren 1991). To really facilitate mutual understanding the common language we use must reflect the hetorogenity of the stakeholders' cultures, i.e. it must not be derived from any particular culture such as that of systems engineering. UML, for example, is not a suitable language for this task. But metaphors, on the other hand, provide the required features because they resort to knowledge that is rooted in common sense and therefore shared by everybody. We have introduced a simple language for expressing metaphors and suggested a way to translate them into patterns that can be used for system design. Finding a suitable metaphor is still a creative act (or maybe a stroke of genius) that can hardly be supported in a systematic way. But once it has been found we can provide some help in performing the ensuing steps.

References

Alexander C, Ishikawa S, Silverstein M, Jacobson M, Fiksdahl-King I, Angel S (1977) A Pattern Language: Towns, Buildings, Construction. Oxford University Press New York

Alexander C (1979) The Timeless Way of Building. Oxford University Press NY

Beck K (2000) Extreme Programming Explained. Addison-Wesley Longman Reading MA

Bunge M (1977) Ontology I: The Furniture of the World. Dordrecht Holland

Bunge M (1979) Ontology II: A World of Systems. Dordrecht Holland

Carroll JM, Mack RL, Kellogg WA (1988) Interface Metaphors and User Interface Design. In: Helander M (ed) Handbook of Human-Computer Interaction. Elsevier Science Publishers Amsterdam The Netherlands

Coyne R (1995) Designing Information Technology in the Postmodern Age: From Method to Metaphor. The MIT Press Cambridge MA

Evermann J, Wand Y (2001) Towards Ontologically Based Semantics for UML Constructs. Proc of the 20th International Conf on Conceptual Modeling: Conceptual Modeling – ER 2001. Yokohama Japan November 27-30 2001

Forsgren O (1991) Co-Constructive Computer Applications: Core Ideas and Some Complementary Strategies in the Development of a Humanistic Computer Science. In: Bazewicz M (ed) Information Systems Architecture and Technologies - ISAT'91. Politechnika Wroclawska Wroclaw

Gamma E, Helm R, Johnson R, Vlissides J (1995) Design Patterns: Elements of Reusable Object-Oriented Software. Addison-Wesley Reading MA

Gazendam HWM (1999) Information System Metaphors. Journal of Management and Economics, vol 3, no 3

Gentner D (1983) Structure Mapping: A Theoretical Framework for Analogy. Cognitive Science, vol 7, no 2, pp 155-170

Gentner D, Falkenhainer B, Skorstad J (1988) Viewing Metaphor as Analogy: The Good, The Bad and The Ugly. In: Helma DH (ed) Analogical Reasoning: Perspectives of Artificial Intelligence, Cognitive Science and Philosophy. Kluwer Dordrecht The Netherlands

Indurkhya B (1994) The Thesis That All Knowledge Is Metaphorical and Meanings of Metaphor. Metaphor and Symbolic Activity, vol 9, no 1, pp 61-63

Lakoff G, Johnson M (1980) Metaphors we Live By. The University of Chicago Press Chicago

Liu K, Sun L, Bennett K (2002) Co-Design of Business and IT Systems. Information Systems Frontiers, vol 4, no 3, pp 251-256

Madsen KH (1994) A Guide to Metaphorical Design. Communications of the ACM, vol 37, no 12, pp 57-62

McCloskey DN (1998) The Rhetoric of Economics. University of Wisconsin Press Madison WI

Morgan G (1997) Images of Organisation. 2nd ed. Sage Beverly Hills

OMG (2003) Unified Modeling Language Specification: Version 1.5. Object Management Group Needham MA USA. www.omg.org/docs/formal/03-03-01.pdf

Opdahl AL, Henderson-Sellers B (2002) Ontological Evaluation of the UML Using the Bunge-Wand-Weber Model. Software and Systems Modeling, vol 1, no 1, pp 43-67

Opdahl AL, Henderson-Sellers B (2004) A Template for Defining Enterprise Modeling Constructs. Journal of Database Management, vol 15, no 2, pp 39-73

Seitz JA (1997) The Development of Metaphoric Understanding: Implications for a Theory of Creativity. Creativity Research Journal, vol 10, no 4, pp 347-353

Trætteberg H (2000) Model Based Design Patterns. Position Paper Workshop on User Interface Design Patterns CHI'2000 The Netherlands

Walsham G (1991) Organizational Metaphors and Information Systems Research. European Journal of Information Systems, vol 1, no 2, pp 83-94

Wand Y, Weber R (1989) An Ontological Evaluation of Systems Analysis and Design Methods. In: Falkenberg ED, Lindgreen P (eds) Information Systems Concepts: An In-Depth Analysis. North-Holland

Wand Y, Weber R (1990) An Ontological Model of an Information System. IEEE Transactions on Software Engineering, vol 16, no 11, pp 1282-1292

Wand Y, Weber R (1995) On the Deep Structure of Information Systems. Information Systems Journal, no 5, pp 203-223

Weber R (1997) Ontological Foundations of Information Systems. Melbourne

Exploring the Feasibility of a Spatial User Interface Paradigm for Privacy-Enhancing Technology

Mike Bergmann[1], Martin Rost[2] and John Sören Pettersson[3]

[1] Technical University Dresden, Germany. mb41@inf.tu-dresden.de
[2] Independent Centre for Privacy Privacy Protection (ICPP), Germany. martin.rost@datenschutzzentrum.de
[3] Karlstad University, Sweden. john_soren.pettersson@kau.se

Introduction

Electronic devices get more and more involved in many of our communication processes for personal and professional activities. Each communication process may implicitly affect our privacy. An example may be the location trace of mobile phones. Experts present identity management systems to preserve the user's[1] privacy [2]. In digital correspondence users should decide about disclosure of personally identifiable information (in the following simply called "data"). However, identity management for Everyman is not yet a commonplace.

To address the whole area of identity management, it is necessary to find an easy to understand model similar to the usage of a phone or a debit card. We suppose that after the shell and command line solutions and the window-based interface, one now has to look for a new paradigm to provide more intuitive handling of the communication process and work flow.

In particular, we have been interested in how to facilitate for users to manage several preference settings, so that different communication partners are treated differently by the user's identity management tool without demanding the user to change settings during ordinary use of his communication devices. We refine the "Virtual City" idea, originally proposed by Andreas Pfitzmann and published in [7], using a town map as a user interface, to manage identity related processes regarding these devices. This interface could potentially allow users with various levels of education to manage their digital identities intuitively by transferring their existing ex-

---

[1] In the context of this paper, the term "user" describes the person who is using the digital equipment related to the identity management sensitive activities.

periences. We have let ordinary Internet users judge some features of this paradigm to gather results on spatial user interfaces for identity management. These results are presented in this paper together with a discussion on their implications for further elaboration both of the interface paradigm itself as well as of the conditions for user testing such a paradigm.

Immediately below some of the relevant publications in this field are summerized. Then the town map is introduced as a metaphor to visualize identity management related processes. We continue by presenting a test set-up based on animated screen mock-ups as a way to address the question of how to conduct user evaluation in the lack of an implemented town map user interface. We also discuss test results that derive from sessions including 34 test participants. Finally, the paper endeavours an outlook on the place in the 'computer' of user interfaces for privacy protection.

Related Work

An early work on users' interaction with identity management systems is found in [11] where also the term privacy-enhancing technology (PET) is introduced to refer to the "variety of technologies that safeguard personal privacy by minimizing or eliminating the collection of identifiable data". Identity management is an important part of such technology but beside identity management there are special techniques such as cryptography which are not in themselves related to identity management.

Still, usability issues are not very frequent in PET studies. This is in contrast to the public interest in, on the one hand, privacy in the information society, and, on the other hand, new user interface metaphors (e.g., [10] and [13]).

A statement about the significance of usable interfaces with respect to identity management we find in [1], where Acquisti et al. examine the cost of usability from the economic point of view. They state that "[...] Reducing options can lead to reduced usability, scaring away the users and leaving a useless anonymity system." We will discuss the question how to avoid this.

Wohlgemuth et al. [14], and earlier Gerd tom Markotten and Kaiser [6], develop the thesis about the necessity of a comfortable user interface to enable users to apply identity management. We agree with the authors' statements. Their suggestions are based on conventional window-based control elements such as lists, buttons etc. Also the integration of protection properties into user interfaces, as developed by Wolf and Pfitzmann [15], projects the identity management functionality to common window-based controls. We will extend this approach using a well-known graphical metaphor.

The idea to build a virtual city to manage identities and relations is mentioned by Hansen and Berlich [7]. However, the authors only raise the issue without drawing a concrete scenario. Rost [12] discussed this approach from a sociological point of view. We elaborate this idea further.

It should also be mentioned that leading design experts often bemoan metaphors in user interfaces. Setting out finding a new global metaphor one should consider the criticism launched by Cooper and Reimann against keeping a whole user interface within the confines of a single metaphor ([4], p. 253). They furthermore stress the utility of having controls easily utilized by users. As will be explained further on, we will introduce city districts in a rather metaphoric sense, but only to provide quick and clear access for the user. Indeed, what we will suggest here may not be the only user interface paradigm used within a computer system.

A suitable user interface should be comfortable for clueless and advanced users alike and should cover the complexity of the identity management in an appropriate manner. An identity management application should help the user to enforce his rights of informational self-determination in a complex digital environment [2]. Different studies document that users worry about their privacy [9]. Moreover, the very special security and privacy related terms regarding PET are difficult to understand for normal users. This incomprehensibility often brings negative effects to privacy and/or security, as outlined in [8] and [5].

Furthermore, in everyday life it is not acceptable for the user to have an explicit learning process to become familiar with the PET.

The wide spread desktop metaphor is not sufficient to make identity-related functions accessible. Communication is at the core of using computers nowadays, and privacy protection should thereby also be in the centre. We see the need to sketch a user interface "beyond the desktop".

Introducing the Town Map

As already mentioned, the core concept of the town map idea is to describe socially relevant communication relations using the topological information of the communication partners.

Two of the most significant benefits of the town map paradigm are first the richness of possible structure in the map to be applicable for most of the existing and further kinds of communication and second the intuitive perceptions across different cultures.

The town map as a spatial metaphor offers easily approachable hierarchies, e.g. using areal representation it is possible to visualize different environments (private, public, restricted, etc). With less distance it is possible to use the building analogy and inside the building the room analogy. Even in an office, we may have the "classical desk", a bank safe, etc. At the beginning the town map looks empty, there are symbols and signs, but no personal places.

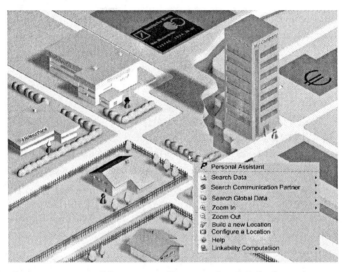

Fig. 1. A town map with some attributes and a simple drop-down menu

In particular, it provides an opportunity to deal with one user interface criterion not easily dealt within any program, namely the simultaneous use of several preference settings; in the present context it is the user's privacy preference settings that are in focus. While font size might be a thing that a user sets once and for all in his Internet browser, it is not that convenient to have only one privacy preference setting active in the browser. How anonymous one prefers to be varies very much according to what service provider one is in contact with or even for what kind of service one is up to. Some standard settings can be defined by (or for) the user, but explicitly switching between settings may be felt as an unnecessary burden for people who are used to browse the web by simply clicking links or entering addresses.

Because privacy protection is a secondary activity in digitally-based communication the identity management functions must not demand extra clicks and key-presses from the user. The question is how to integrate the town map paradigm for user interfaces with the primary activities. In the mock-up we demonstrated in the user test, we catered for three cases:

For the simple case of starting a privacy related application (like email, browser, etc.) and connecting to a communication partner, the town map is very suitable. The map will not emphasize the applications in contrast to the desktop of current PC systems but the communication partners; the corresponding policy settings are implied by location in the map. (In the user test we compromised this global design for a PC system by including the town map as a start page for the browser – it thus functioned as an elaborated bookmark list such as the 'Favorites' in Internet Explorer.)

A quite different case is when the user already is in contact with one service provider, but needs some side issue to be dealt with, such as paying via a pay-service company. Then our PET should be aware of this in order to check credentials for the partner in question. This also means that our PET can show the user what is going on, and we displayed this by a tilted town map introduced in the ordinary browser (cf. explanation to Figure 4).

Thirdly, when a user connects to a communication partner unfamiliar to his PET system (for instance, by clicking on a link on a web page or entering an address in the address field of his browser), then the identity management system should start with maximum privacy settings. If the user wants to bookmark the new site, the system asks for the concomitant policy settings by inviting the user to indicate an appropriate place in the map.

Living in the Town Map

The typical map contains different areas, districts and buildings, similar to residential areas, city center, business district, recreational parks, etc. These areas represent *different roles* the user can act on. Possibly, avatars at the bounding area of the map will represent corresponding *pseudonyms*.

Areas may be separated by topological borders like rivers and streets. At least four main areas should be defined. The *Public area* represents the anonymous part of the town and incorporates the different social organizations, the shopping area, the entertainment and wellness area etc. The *Business related area* represents the working zone with areas for the company, office, customers and competitors. The *"My Home"* area represents the personal part of the environment and is incorporated in the *Private area* with the different personal social contact partners like houses of friends, family and neighbours, and trusted e-serivces. An example of a town map with some predefined action places is shown in Figure 1.

The topological borders will demarcate different areas with different policies for communication, with different data sets, with different privacy rules and different levels of privacy protection. Entering these areas will change the privacy settings like "do not disclose e-mail address for marketing purpose", "do not disclose any payment information", "allow access to nick name" or "enforce unconditional unlinkability" for instance.

Imagine that the default predefined policy for communication in the public area is very restrictive with the lowest level of data disclosure, but around the community area, anonymous communication is not desired, because everybody knows each other. In comparison to this, the working area is characterized by a strong asymmetry between counterparts; the employer knows a lot of details about the employee – clients or customers in comparison know much less (hopefully).

Virtually walking through the town with the mouse pointer, the user's data policy changes automatically to the predefined set of privacy settings. Connectors between these areas, such as bridges, doors, gates, elevators etc., act as inspection points regarding the communication and privacy settings for the areas. These transition points can allow users to inspect or change the settings. Further domains, with special identity management requirements, could easily be defined. Buildings may contain rooms and areas with dedicated identity management functionality, or simply menu lists with such functions for users who prefer less graphics.

As mentioned above, the main areas include buildings, clustered by the similarity[2] of their privacy policies. In the public area, for instance, there are groups of buildings addressing the shopping context (supermarket, cinema, dry cleaning services), groups addressing the administration context (bank, assurance, e-government), groups for the education context (libraries, universities, school) and the religion context. The distance vs. closeness of the groups to each other could be visualized using different kinds of streets (small alleys, broad roads, avenues, motorways, or similar).

It might be sufficient to have a few predefined places with specific privacy attributes as foreseen in our town map, i.e. the public area, the private area, and the work area. Of course there is a need to offer the possibility to define other places within the map, but predefined places are in all likelihood needed to support novice users.

Attributes in the Town Map

Attributes are privacy-related policies and properties related to communication partners. Configuration of these attributes may be really complex

---

[2] It has to be defined how to use slightly different settings in one area and how to visualize the differences without loosing usability and comfortability.

and overburden the normal user. To project these properties intuitively into the town map metaphor we propose the usage of the distances between objects to describe their properties and to group these locations with the topmost level of provision[3] and place them around the other locations with respect to the closeness to other districts. It seems feasible to quarter the whole area into the districts mentioned in the previous section. If a user decides to go inside such a location (e.g., simply by clicking on it) the system may switch to a more detailed presentation, preserving the quartering with respect to the overall privacy settings. Here it opens up new possibilities to introduce associations to special places or direction of movements, similar to joystick-based mobile phone interfaces. The access is granted depending on the access policy of the object and the contingently existing reputation of the user.

Test Results

How people understand and feel about the town map was tested within the PRIME project (see Acknowledgement) by preference ranking of colour pictures shown in combination with animated user interface video clips.

Aims and Construction of the Test

The town map paradigm was compared to a traditionally styled browser enhanced with roles. In fact, in addition to the Figure 2 TownMap also the CrossRoad of Figure 3 was shown, which is a very simplified town map with the potential to be fitted in small displays. The traditionally styled browser and the more realistic TownMap were animated with a guiding native (= Swedish) voice explaining the actions of the 'user'. Before the test, participants were given a one-page English introduction to identity management and privacy protection. This written introduction also explained two icons appearing in the animations, viz. icons used to symbolise two pre-defined roles. Test sessions were held in lecture halls, allowing multiples of participants in each session.

The goal was not to see if a town map was better than a traditionally styled browser, because most test participants would probably prefer the

---

[3] From the sociological point of view the groups may be based on the classical four big systems: Economics, Law, Politics, Science. But the organizations are not differentiable by these criteria as far as they implement various connections and communication channels.

browser that looked as they expected, especially since the privacy-enhancement with its specific goals might not be fully comprehended. It must be remembered that people may have varying degrees of understanding of the purpose of identity management and therefore not readily understand the individual steps taken by the 'user' in the animations. Considering this, it would be only natural if they prefer a familiar user interface.

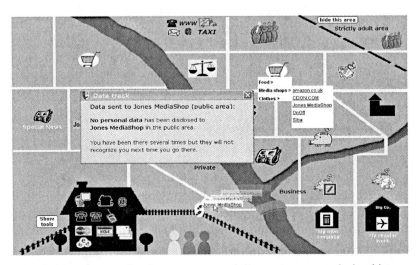

Fig. 2. User drags a shop's name to a track icon to get transmission history

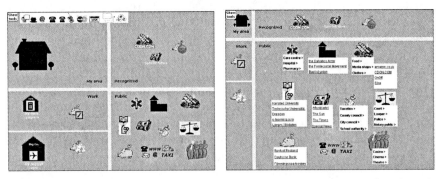

Fig. 3. Cross Road consists of four areas; to the right the Public area is enlarged

Thus, the goal was not to see if a town map was better than a traditionally styled browser. Instead, the purpose was to get a basis for discussions within the PRIME project, and of course with interested parties in the rest of the research community, about the semiotic dimension one should venture to play on in more costly prototyping. Especially, since the town map easily allows for demonstrations of data transactions between parties, this feature was included in the animation of the town map (only one of the maps was animated). The user dragged a name icon and a credit card icon to a pay service; his own house and two icons representing the relevant service providers were visible in a tilted town map shown in Figure 4. Later the user also inquired about who had received his name by dropping his name icon on a symbol for his data transactions database (Figure 2).

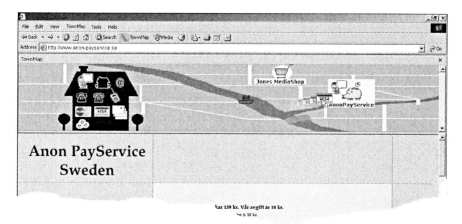

Fig. 4. The tested tilted town map (upper half of browser window)

Results

Thirty-four university students aged 20 and above, some being older than 45, participated in the preference test; all had used Internet Explorer and only some had used other browsers in addition. Our traditionally styled alternative was based on an Internet Explorer mock-up. As expected, the traditional-styled browser got in general a positive response. More than half of the answers gave positive descriptions of it. The maps, on the other hand, were considered by many to be messy.

On the question about their impression of the display of data and money transaction, 19 answered that it facilitates while 11 regarded it as superfluous. Nine of these eleven persons also thought that it looked childish; fifteen thought it looked OK.

When ranking the alternatives, 24 persons put the traditional browser as their primary choice; they also seemed to prefer the simple CrossRoad as a secondary choice. Seven preferred the realistic TownMap and three preferred the simplified CrossRoad, but there was no tendency for the secondary choice.

Two fifths of the participants answered that they would like to be able to switch between designs.

After this paper was submitted this test has been replicated in the USA with 27 university students: the results were in the main similar to the test conducted in Sweden, although a majority of the American subjects wanted to be able to toggle between designs. (The comparison between US and EU users concerned several tests and will be reported in the future.)

Discussion

In conclusion, even if the map designs were less favoured, there was some interest in this user interface paradigm. This in itself can motivate a further elaboration of this concept. As Allan Cooper explained about targeting a product to a receptive user group: "80% of people in focus groups hated the new Dodge Ram pickup. [Chrysler] went ahead with production, and made it into a bestseller because the other 20% *loved* it. Having people love your product, even if it is only a minority, is how you succeed." ([3] p. 125) But there are further topics of this test that can be discussed.

One should note that the TownMap demonstration film as well as the colour pictures showed maps that were already populated. This fact might have made them appear messier than if users had been introduced with empty maps (corresponding to an empty menu of bookmarks). The bookmarks menu in the Internet Explorer mock-up, on the other hand, contained only six items. In this case it made sense to have only a few items, because the menu did not look sparsely populated as there were simply no empty town districts to fill. The menu was of course short and there were no unmotivated empty spaces. This will have to be remembered for future tests of more elaborate TownMaps or similar user interfaces.

Obviously, there is a conflict between showing first-timers the working of a product and in the same time make him identify himself with the user of that product. In gauging the value of this test one must consider the difficulties of the alternative approach, i.e. of letting test subjects populate the map themselves. Such a test design would be time consuming for two reasons: (1) If participants are to work with the system they would have to do this one-by-one since it is only a mock-up; alternatively, one would have to spend time on producing a working prototype to be able to run it in a computer hall in order to have several participants in each session. (2) Each session takes longer time – to compare, before the preference test real usability tests had in fact been conducted with the traditionally styled mock-up, but these tests often took more than an hour and then it was only one paradigm that was tested. Thus, our preference test was quite cost-efficient even if we might have a "messiness" bias.

One should further note that more than half of the participants answered that animation of transactions "facilitates". This makes it meaningful to use town map-like formats also in traditionally styled browsers for informing the user of transactions going on. Moreover, it may indicate the utility of using such formats for getting input from the user on data releases. (As explained earlier, in the TownMap demonstration film used in this test some of the animations of transactions were done by the 'user'.)

In fact, a user may very well benefit from the graphical demonstration of different data disclosures and their effects if third party processors come into play. Possible side-channel attacks might also be easier to visualize than to explain in a text. Thus, the question of visualizing with a town map may not only be thought of as replacing the old desktop but may be introduced via the back door of tutorials and other help functions to become a familiar concept for future communication technology.

Outlook

This paper raises the question about the feasibility of a new approach to privacy friendly digital environments. It can be argued that by using well-known illustrations from the real world some important issues may be resolved. Currently, the above described system would typically be based on an existing conventional operating systems like Linux, MacOS or Windows. However, it seems conceivable that there is not only a need to create new classes of applications to address the need for managing and administrating the whole communication process with respect to privacy. Instead, this kind of functionality should be directly related to the operating system, or even better should be integrated into the operating system user interface. This guarantees a high level of security, connecting the system to trusted platforms.

Acknowledgment

We thank all our colleagues for helpful comments, especially Marit Hansen from ICPP, Andreas Pfitzmann, Rainer Böhme from TU Dresden. We thank Simone Fischer-Hübner and Ninni Danielsson, Karlstad University, and Rainer Groh, Katrin Borcea, TU Dresden, and all others for very helpful discussions. Special thanks to Jenny Nilsson, Karlstad University, and Kenneth Ray, TU Dresden, for graphical support. – The work reported in this paper was supported by the PRIME project which receives research funding from the European Community's Sixth Framework Program and the Swiss Federal Office for Education and Science.

References

[1]   Acquisti A, Dingledine R, Syverson P (2003) On the Economics of Anonymity. Proc of Financial Cryptography (FC '03) LNCS 2742.
      http://freehaven.net/doc/fc03/ econymics.pdf

[2]   Clauß S, Köhntopp M (2001) Identity Management and its Support of Multilateral Security. Computer Networks, no 37, pp 205-219

[3]   Cooper A (1999) The Inmates are Running the Asylum. SAMS

[4]   Cooper A, Reimann R (2003) About Face 2.0 The Essentials of Interaction Design. Wiley Publishing USA

[5]   Gerd tom Markotten D (2003) Benutzbare Sicherheit für informationstechnische Systeme. Dissertation an der Albert-Ludwigs-Universität Freiburg

[6]   Gerd tom Markotten D, Kaiser J (2000) Benutzbare Sicherheit – Herausforderungen und Modell für E-Commerce-Systeme. Wirtschaftsinformatik, vol 42, no 6, pp 531-538

[7]   Hansen M, Berlich P (2003) Identity Management Systems: Gateway and Guardian for Virtual Residences. EMTEL Conference New Media, Technology and Everyday Life in Europe Conference London

[8]   Pettersson JS, Fischer-Hübner S (eds) (2004) PRIME Deliverable D6.1.b Evaluation of Early Prototypes.
      www.prime-project.eu.org/public/prime_products/deliverables/

[9]   Leenes R, Lips M (2004) Social Evaluation of Early Prototypes. In: Pettersson JS, Fischer-Hübner S (eds) PRIME Deliverable D6.1.b; see [8].

[10] NN (2004) Metaphorically Speaking. The Economist 373 (8399) Survey of Information Technology. Oct. 28, pp 16-17

[11] van Rossum H, Gardeniers H, Borking J et al (1995) Privacy-Enhancing Technologies: The Path to Anonymity. Registrierkamer The Netherlands, and Information & Privacy Commissioner/Ontario Canada

[12] Rost M (2004) Leben mit der Landkarte – Make Identity-Management Easy.
      www.maroki.de/pub/privacy/tm.html

[13] Hillenbrand, Th (2004) Melindas Mutantenzoo. Spiegel Online.
      www.spiegel.de/netzwelt/netzkultur/0,1518,329307,00.html

[14] Wohlgemuth S, Jendricke U, Gerd tom Markotten D, Dorner F, Müller G (2003) Sicherheit und Benutzbarkeit durch Identitätsmanagement. Proc of Aktuelle Trends in der Softwareforschung – Tagungsband zum doITForschungstag 2003 IRB Verlag Stuttgart

[15] Wolf G, Pfitzmann A (2000) Properties of Protection Goals and their Integration into a User Interface. Computer Networks, no 32, pp 685-699

Database Level Honeytoken Modules for Active DBMS Protection

Antanas Čenys[1], Darius Rainys[2], Lukas Radvilavičius[3] and Nikolaj Goranin[4]

[1] Informtion Systems Laboratory, Semiconductor Physics Institute, Lithuania. cenys@uj.pfi.lt
[2] UAB "BlueBridge", Lithuania. darius.rainys@bluebridge.lt
[3][4] Vilnius Gediminas Technical University, Lithuania. (lukas, ngrnn)@fmf.vtu.lt

Introduction

Data and information are sometimes called the "crown jewels" of an organization [3]. Modern company cannot exist without flexible, fast and secure data management system. Insuring data security is of vital importance for any company.

To ensure data security various methods and tools are used. According to cyber-security specialist Bruce Schneier's definition given in his book, "Secrets and Lies"[5], security could break into three areas: prevention, detection, and reaction. Nowadays most of the companies use passive data protection mechanisms, i.e. firewalls, IDS and NIDS, and security audits. Internal and external audits can be used to detect "weak" places in company's security policy and its implementation. Firewall and IDS solutions are effective in detecting and preventing simple and/or well-known illegal access methods. Network level firewalls (generation I) usually use predefined rules blocking access to specific network ports from certain IP numbers or ranges and they correspond to a classical prevention method. IDS and generation II (program level) firewalls can detect, block and alarm on known exploits and attack mechanisms by the use of attack "signatures". These tools are quite effective for detection purposes. But on the other hand IDS have serious weaknesses such as a large number of false alarms, huge and difficult to maintain reports, disability to detect new attacks with unknown signature.

All above security tools and methods are passive by definition. More pro-active method is to prepare a special "traps" for an attacker known as honeypots. The first articles on honeypots were published in late 80-ies, early 90-ies [1,6]. A honeypot is defined as an information system resource whose only value lies in unauthorized or illicit use of that resource [7]. It can be used in different ways for prevention, detection and reaction. Different aspects of honeypot usage were described in [7-8] and "Honeypot Alliance" white papers. Traditionally honeypots for DBMS protection are described as real DBMS servers or DBMS server emulators installed as a part of honeynet – network of honeypots. "Classical" honeypot cannot help to detect legal database user trying to obtain information for which he does not have access permission. On the other hand detecting illegal activities of legal users is very important since according to recent statistics up to 80% of cyber-crimes are committed by employees. One of the solutions tackling this problem can be deployment of specific 'traps' – so called honeytokens. The term honeytoken was first coined by Augusto Paes de Barros in 2003 on the honeypots mailing list. Any interaction with a honeytoken most likely represents unauthorized or malicious activity [9]. Any data resource – DB, DB table, file or letter can be used as honeytoken. Honeytokens are not designed specifically to detect attackers or prevent attacks, but are a flexible and simple tool with multiple security applications. Pete Herzog, managing director of the Institute for Security and Open Methodologies, says that he has used honeytokens to detect when employees illicitly download forbidden material. For example, he has entered corporate memos with particular typos into private databases and then monitored company networks to see where those typos show up. Tracing these honeytokens, he says, often leads to catches of illegal materials stored on the network. [10].

In his article Mr. Lance Spitzner suggests one concept of honeytoken implementation in database.

"For example, the credit card number 4356974837584710 could be embedded into database, file server, or some other type of repository. The number is unique enough that there will be minimal, if any, false positives. An IDS tool, such as Snort, could be used to detect when that honeytoken is accessed. Such a simple signature could look as follows: alert ip any any -> any any (msg:"Honeytoken Access - Potential unauthorized Activity"; content:"4356974837584710";)"

It was the only publicly available solution of honeytoken usage for DBMS security we were able to find. Spitzner's idea is attractive due to its universality and versatility. However such simple version of honeytoken has some disadvantages: it won't work if SQL query output is provided in encrypted form, additional computer system is needed since running sniffer on the same machine as DBMS may look suspicious for hacker, DBMS log analysis for access to honeytoken may be misleading, since logs might be modified or polluted.

Presented in the paper concept for honeytoken implementation is platform specific (runs on DBMS Oracle 9i EE or higher), but does not possess disadvantages described above. It is based on Oracle FGA mechanism with some additional original modules.

Requirements to DB Level Honeytoken Module

Usually access to the database is organized through third-party applications made for accessing and managing data. When data is accessed in such a way, it is not too difficult for a malicious user to gain database usernames and passwords. After gaining login information of database an attacker can connect to the database through SQL client and try to view the data manually. Honeytoken strategy is to insert a table with "sweet" name able to attract malicious user. Any activity with such a table can be registered and an alert message sent to system administrator.

Particular structure of any honeytoken module depends on the aims and goals of the system. The initial requirements and suggestions on the structure of the honeypot module were presented in [2] It was proposed that the module should contain analysis and reaction subsystems. It was also proposed to use the SPIKE software package for connection emulation. Taking into consideration previous experience the following goals for the honeytoken module can be formulated: honeytoken module should be a simple and cheap tool to detect illegal activity at database level coming from the inside and outside of the company without decreasing existing level of security. It would be useful also to provide automatic reacting tools and to be able to log the malicious activity. Implementation of such q module would result in database security improvement. Honeytoken log may be used to analyze data stealing methods and be a base for further improvements and changes.

Above formulated goals as well as the general honeytoken strategy lead to specific requirements for the module:

- To be cheap, easy to implement and administrate the module should not be a dedicated system but an integrated part of DBMS able to monitor any type of database objects. The effort should be taken to ensure that the module produces few false-positives and false-negatives.
- For security reasons implementation of the module should not require DBMS to contain specially unpatched known security holes;
- Module should not look suspicious to the attacker and contain real-looking information. For example database table EMPLOYEES should

keep a large number of real names with corresponding unreal salaries and social insurance numbers;
- A care should be taken for the module implementation not to contradict national and international laws on provoking of criminal activities;

In addition database tables security settings containing sensitive information should be audited and list of users, accessing them, should be revised. It is also very important to store module's log files on a separate secure storage, since it is assumed that an attacker may have access not only to the DBMS, but to the operating system as well.

To meet the above requirements the following structure of the module consisting of four parts was chosen:

1. Database object (table, view, etc.) with real-like data and attractive ("sweet") name, for example, TABLE CREDIT_CARDS or VIEW EMPLOYEES_SALARY;
2. Object (function / library), monitoring access (insert, select, etc.) to honeytoken object;
3. Object (function / library) launching external software when monitored honeytoken is being accessed.
4. External software module, responsible for logging, administrator alerting and automatic reacting to incidents (for example blocking access). Testing variant of external software module was programmed to alert administrator by sending him e-mail with security violation descriptions and is based on a simple bash-script and open-source utilities. Additional functionality will be added after long-term honeytoken module tests.

Honeytoken module for DBMS Oracle

Implementation of honeytoken module for particular DBMS depends on its structure and communication with external processes. DBMS Oracle 9i EE has a possibility to launch external processes using Oracle native process (library) "extproc". "Listener" program is responsible for communication between Oracle DB server and client side applications. It is the only legal way Oracle developers have left for communication with external libraries.

We suggest three possible honeytoken module implementations:

- to use table-simulating pipelined function in combination with the external procedure.

- to use combination of triggers and external procedure. This solution is the most universal and fulfills the requirements above. The disadvantage of this method is its complexity.
- to use combination of Oracle Fine Grained Auditing (FGA) and external library. This method can be used only for DBMS Oracle versions from 9i EE and higher.

It should be pointed out that some specific DBMS Oracle features influenced realization of the module. Triggers in DBMS Oracle 9i EE can be activated only on "insert" and "update" transactions, but not on "select". This is a reason why special way-around for second implementation (combination of triggers and external library) is needed. In the third FGA case this limitation does not exist, however this implementation can be used only for DBMS Oracle 9i EE and higher.

Module Insertion Concept

General scheme of module insertion to Oracle 9i EE DBMS is shown in Fig.1. pseudo-connections are shown by the dashed arrows. The provided object links may be not exact, since real internal Oracle DBMS architecture is not in public domain.

To insert a honeytoken module to DBMS a chain of procedures is performed. DBMS Oracle can use specially prepared external libraries, but cannot start an external program. So we have to create a library (shell_lib):

```
void sh(char *);
int sh( char *cmd ) {
int num;
num = system(cmd); return num;}
```

This library is compiled with internal Oracle libraries as gcc compiler parameters.

DBMS Oracle has a library structure, similar to the Operating system. Because of that we have to create internal Oracle library with all the parameters necessary.

```
CREATE OR REPLACE LIBRARY shell_lib is
'/opt/oracle/product/9.2.0/lib/shelllib.so';
```

After this action we get shell_lib library. After successful ending we will get:

```
Library created.
```

Oracle configuration files TNSNAMES.ORA and LISTENER.ORA are modified so we could use external procedures.Now we can create an internal Oracle procedure shells. This procedure is called every time the "sweet" table is accessed.

```
CREATE or REPLACE procedure shellas(cmd IN char) as exter-
nal name "sh" library shell_lib language C parameters (cmd
string);
```

External alerting module is programmed. In our case it is a simple bash-script which sends a database administrator notification by e-mail if someone tries to access the monitored table. Finally we create a honeytoken table and fill it with real-like data.

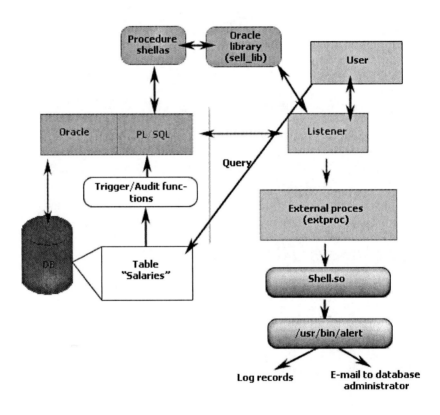

Fig. 1. General honeytoken module scheme

Pipelined Function Realization

Pipelined function is a special object, which can be used to emulate a database table. In this case triggers are not used, since the pipelined function can access the external process through the sequence of procedures and libraries. The problem is that pipelined function is not listed among database tables. To create the pipelined function one should use such a procedure:

- create object equivalent to the table:

```
CREATE OR REPLACE type tabview as object (Reg_Date Time-
stamp, Surname varchar2(20), Name varchar2(15), Per-
sonal_number varchar2(11));
```

- create tabview table

```
create type tabview_table as table of tabview;
```

- create the function

```
CREATE or REPLACE function Salaries
return tabview_table pipelined as
cursor c1 is select Reg_Date, Name, Surname, Per-
sonal_number from Salaries;
begin
for c1_row in c1 loop shellas('/usr/bin/aliarmas');
PIPE ROW    (tabview(c1_row.Reg_Date, c1_row.Name,
c1_row.Surname, c1_row.Personal_number));
end loop; return; end Salaries;
```

Now if the attacker tries to access the "Salaries" table, the corresponding pipelined function will be started and alerting script "aliarmas" will inform the DBMS administrator about the incident.

Combination of Triggers and External Procedure

Honeytoken+Trigger/External Procedure case is the most universal one and can be used on almost all DBMS Oracle versions. There are only several adjustments you have to do to the main conceptual model to create a honeytoken module of this type.

First of all, you have to create a table, called "Salaries_audit", where attempts to access the "sweet" table "Salaries" will be logged. The second step is to turn audit on for the "Salaries" table and to create triggers, which are activated when new records are added to the audit table "Salaries_audit". For example:

```
CREATE trigger danger
after insert on Salaries_audit for each row  begin shellas
('/usr/bin/alert');
end danger;
```

Now every time an attacker tries to select, modify or add data to the "Salaries" table the trigger "danger" is activated, as a new record is added to the audit table "Salaries_audit". It calls procedure "shellas", which is able to start an external alerting module "alert" with the help of the library "shell_lib".

Combination of Oracle FGA and External Library

Traditional Oracle Database auditing options let track the actions users perform on objects at the macro level. However it is not possible to detect what is selected.

In Oracle9i Database version a new feature called fine-grained auditing (FGA) was added. This feature allows to audit individual SELECT statements along with exact statements issued by users. In addition to simply tracking statements, FGA provides a way to simulate a trigger for SELECT statements by executing a code whenever a user selects a particular set of data. The power of FGA doesn't stop at merely recording events in audit trails; FGA can also optionally execute procedures. A procedure could perform an action such as sending an e-mail alert to an auditor when a user selects a certain row from a table, or it could write to a different audit trail. [4].

Reaction mechanism can be organized similarly to the triggers/external procedure case.

Conclusions

Possibilities to use honeytokens for DBMS security have been studied. We have developed, implemented, and tested three different honeytoken modules for DBMS Oracle 9i Enterprise Edition: a) honeytoken plus pipelined function; b) honeytoken plus trigers/external procedures; c) honeytoken plus FGA; all based on the same concept of module insertion. Implemented modules can monitor "sweet" objects in database, perform simple reaction procedures, such as e-mail sending to the DBMS administrator and log the malicious activity to external file or database table. All modules were created with the help of free software tools, implemented and tested at Vilnius Gediminas Technical University IT Laboratory. The tests performed at the IT laboratory have shown, that module usage does not increase the load on DBMS and Operating system. In the future we are going to perform tests on industrial DBMS and to evaluate system load for heavily used databases.

For the databases with a large number of records and users honeytoken modules can be very effective tools for early intrusion detection. It should be pointed out, however, that honeytoken type tools having many advantages such as simplicity of the concept and ability to detect local threats by no way can replace other security tools.

References

[1] Cheswick B (1991) An Evening with Berferd in which a Cracker is Lured, Endured, and Studied. www.tracking-hackers.com/papers/berferd.pdf

[2] Čenys A, Rainys D, Radvilavičius L, Bielko A (2004) Development of Honeypot System Emulating Functions of Database Server. Proc of the NATO "Symposium on Adaptive Defense in Unclassified Networks". Toulouse France April 19-20 2004. www.rta.nato.int/abstracts.asp

[3] Finnigan P (2003) Introduction to Simple Oracle Auditing, www.petefinnigan.com/

[4] Nanda A (2003) Fine-Grained Auditing for Real-World Problems. www.oracle.com/technology/oramag/webcolumns/2003/techarticles/nanda_f ga.html

[5] Schneier B, Wiley J (2000) Secrets and Lies: Digital Security in a Networked World. John Wiley & Sons New York

[6] Stoll C (1990), Cuckoo's Egg: Tracking a Spy through the Maze of Computer Espionage. Pocket Books New York

[7] Spitzner L (2002) Honeypots: Tracking Hackers. www.spitzner.net/

[8] Spitzner L (2003) Honeypots: Definitions and Value of Honeypots. www.tracking-hackers.com/papers/honeypots.html

[9] Spitzner L (2003) Honeytokens: The Other Honeypot. www.securityfocus.com/infocus /1713

[10] Thompson N (2003) New Economy. www.nytco.com/

Morally Successful Collaboration between Academia and Industry – A Case of a Project Course

Tero Vartiainen

Department of Computer Science and Information Systems, University of Jyväskylä, Finland. tvarti@cs.jyu.fi

Introduction

Academia-industry collaboration is common in the IT-field, and it includes training programs, research centre activities, and industry advisory boards (Watson and Huber 2000). For the industry, co-operation provides possibilities to acquire human resources and, for the academia, co-operation ensures that research and teaching activities are relevant. Regardless of its popularity little is known about moral issues relating to this phenomenon. This study intends to fill the gap in knowledge by determining the nature of moral conflicts perceived by clients, students, and instructors of a collaborative project course, and by formulating a framework to successfully getting grips with these conflicts. This article is a summary of the research the detailed description of which is found in Vartiainen (2005).

There are several definitions for a moral conflict (or a moral dilemma) (Audi 1995). Typically moral conflict is defined as a decision-making situation, in which two incompatible actions are morally required. In philosophical literature, distinction is made between solvable and insolvable moral conflicts, the latter ones being known as moral dilemmas (Hill 1996; Nagel 1987). In moral dilemmas the moral agent feels mental anguish about the situation, whereas in the case of a solvable moral conflict, s/he is able to produce a defendable solution. Predicaments of moral conflicts motivate us to organize our institutions and the society in such a way that the most severe moral conflicts would not emerge (Marcus 1987, 188).

In this study, a concept of moral success is introduced to tackle moral conflicts in project collaboration. Success/failure of projects is commonly investigated in project management and IS literature (Shenar and Levy

1997). The concept of moral success is adopted from the field[1] of moral psychology and from the work of James Rest (1994). James Rest (1994) organized existing research on the psychology of morality into four processes: moral sensitivity, judgment, motivation, and character. In these processes an individual may morally fail in his/her actions, or, if we take the opposite view as in the framework defined here, morally succeed. These processes aim to answer the question: "What must we suppose happens psychologically in order for moral behavior to take place?" Rest showed that it is possible that a moral agent may conceive having failed morally in his/her acts if s/he concludes that his/her deliberation might have been deficient. *Moral sensitivity* implies awareness of how our actions affect other people. It also implies being aware of alternative actions and of how those actions may affect other parties. For example, a teacher may not notice that he favours boys at the expense of girls, but if someone points this out to him, he may begin to observe his own behaviour in a new light. Moral sensitivity is a key component in recognizing moral conflicts – it is possible that an individual cannot see the moral relevance that the decision-making situation may have. However, being aware of morally significant issues is not enough: when confronting decision-making situations one needs to make decisions. *Moral judgment* is about judging which courses of action are the most justified. As moral judgment develops, a person's problem solving strategies become more in tune with others and more principled in nature. Kohlberg's (1981) six stages of moral development are based on the theory that people change their moral problem-solving strategies as they grow. People at higher stages can understand the principles they had used at the lower stages, although no longer preferring them. Moral judgment and sensitivity were observed to develop with the help of small-group discussions on moral issues (Rest 1994; McNeel 1994). *Moral motivation* refers to prioritizing moral values above non-moral values. Here a moral agent asks "why be moral?" It is possible that a moral agent is aware of an ethical issue (moral sensitivity) and knows what should be done (moral judgment) but is not fully motivated to do what s/he considers the right thing to do. For example, if by lying one can profit economically, one must select between an economical value (profit) and a moral value (honesty). If one chooses to lie, one has failed in moral motivation. Moral motivation, as well as moral character, connects knowledge to action. *Moral character* refers to the psychological strength to carry out a line of action. A person may be weak-willed, and if others put enough pressure on him to act immorally, he may fail in this component.

---

[1] Moral psychology can be perceived as a subfield of psychology tracing individuals' development of moral reasoning and opinions (Audi 1995, 510).

The framework for a morally successful project course is constructed as follows. First, to attain information about moral conflicts in a project course, a research design for gathering information about moral conflicts is presented, and then, the resulted abstractions of moral conflicts are introduced. After this, a framework utilizing the resulted abstractions is discussed before the final conclusions are presented.

Research Design

Studies on student project courses (Fielden 1999; Scott et al. 1994) show that the key players of these courses are students, instructors and agencies for which the projects are implemented. Therefore, the focus of this study is on determining moral conflicts perceived by these key players. For this an empirical qualitative research was conducted at the Department of Computer Science and Information Systems, at the University of Jyväskylä, in Finland. The Development Project (DP) course selected collaborates with local IT-firms and other organizations. The course has a long history starting from 1977. Typically, client organizations represent private IT-firms, which may be enterprises and computing departments of various sizes in, e.g., industrial plants. Client representatives are usually managers and specialists in their organizations. In the collaboration, the role of clients is to provide students with substance guidance (e.g., technical guidance), and the role of instructors is to guide the process (e.g., planning, reporting). The students are typically third-year-students in CS/IS, and they form groups of five members. Each student practices the role of a project manager for one month or so during the project, which takes from five to six months. Project tasks have varied from information systems development to business and research-oriented projects.

To identify moral conflicts perceived by each party of the course I chose the qualitative and interpretive research approach. To collect descriptions of moral conflicts the subjects were let to express themselves freely and openly. The clients who were interviewed about moral problems they confronted during the project course totaled 21. 13 individual students and 6 student groups wrote diaries, 17 students responded to a survey and 13 of them draw moral conflicts during an exercise. I conducted participant observation to identify moral conflicts which I and my colleagues confronted. The subjects' perceptions were analysed with the phenomenographical method (Marton 1986).

Empirical Results

The empirical results of the study are summarized in Figure 1. My experience of the course over five years confirms that the following examples of moral conflicts are typical of those confronted by the parties of the course.

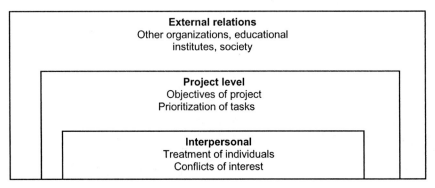

Fig. 1. Moral conflicts in project collaboration divided into external relations, project level, and interpersonal conflicts

External relations

In moral conflicts of external relations subjects deliberate about relations between organizations, educational institutes and private firms.

Instructors coordinating the collaboration confront moral conflicts relating to just treatment of local private IT-firms. The co-operation may cause instability in the markets at least in two ways: First, constant co-operation between particular IT-firms and the DP course may make the managing of the DP course easier, but it may be considered unfair by other IT-firms. The university might be seen as favouring their chosen IT-firms by offering them cheap work force. In addition, student groups can undertake projects producing services or products that could otherwise be bought from the local IT-firms. Thus, the course may invade the territory of some of the IT-firms.

Client representatives are concerned about implementation of corporate social responsibilities. Although clients may openly declare that their motives for co-operation with the university are based on beneficial objectives, they consider it as a moral problem whenever they need to decide whether they should fulfil certain, sometimes unforeseen, social responsibilities towards the university and local communities. These questions are brought up when a client considers the benefit to the society and educational institute when co-operating with an educational institute in a local community.

Project Level

In project level moral conflicts, the concern is on the objectives of the project and on prioritization and commitment questions. For the university, the primary objective is to teach project work skills to the students, and for the clients, the primary objective is to get the results of the project. For the students, the objectives are twofold: as they implement the project task, they are expected to reflect and develop project work skills. Conflicting objectives were considered as a moral conflict by all parties because it is possible to stress one objective in the expense of another.

Attaining beneficial objectives is of importance for the clients. In the following example, a client confronted a moral conflict between his duty for his employer and his demands on students:

"... I am responsible for getting value for the money. And this kind of internal discussion I had with myself about what should I do. Then I decided that, damn it, although they are students, they have to ... they are to practice this real project, how a real project is implemented in the real life. And after that I started to make higher demands and I really did it ..." (interview extract)

A university instructor confronts a role conflict between her roles as an assessor and coach. Guiding student's actions and assessing them conflict with each other in the way that the instructor is forced to choose his actions and words carefully because s/he needs accurate information about his/her groups while s/he is obliged to assess and grade her students. In other words, building trust requires consideration.

For all parties, commitment and prioritizing, for example, between project tasks and other things created a moral conflict. As an example, a student considered that, regarding her group, activities outside the project competed with some tasks of the project.

Interpersonal

In interpersonal moral conflicts, subjects deliberate about treatment of other individuals and conflicts of interest. Intervening with other individuals' actions was considered difficult because the intervention itself might make the situation worse, by, for example, offending the object of intervention. The intervention considered here consists of giving feedback, of making demands, and of the possibility to raise discussions about a group's ineffective functioning.

Instructors confronted moral conflicts in intervening with other individuals' actions, namely with students' and other instructors' actions. As an example of this, an instructor described a group including a deviant student. The deviance could, potentially, affect the whole project, but bringing the issue up might have worsened the situation by embarrassing the student.

In interaction with students, clients perceive moral problems relating to giving feedback to the students, employing them, and in treating them in an impartial or fair way. In addition to this, client representatives interact with other employees inside the client organization. Demanding that they should be working for the student project – along with their primary projects - may bring additional stress upon them. The clients had openly declared that the employment of the students had been an important objective of the collaboration. For a client, this created a moral conflict, because employing students often makes their studies last longer.

Typically students have not had any leadership experience, and therefore, conducting the role of a project manager is demanding and occasionally stressful for them. In that role, fellow-students' capabilities to complete assigned work tasks, and efficiency questions were of concern. As an example, a student confronted a moral conflict related to assigning a work task to a fellow-student whose ability to complete the task was in doubt. For the sake of honesty, she thought, she probably should tell the student about her concern, although telling the truth might wound him. On the other hand, if she assigned the work task to her without taking any precautions, she might endanger the project.

A Framework of a Morally Successful Project Course

A framework for a morally successful project course utilizes the Four Component Model (Rest 1994) and adopts content from the three abstractions of moral conflicts perceived by the parties of the course. Behavior of a moral agent, in this case, a client representative, a student, or an instructor, may be reflected and developed in terms of the components of the model.

Developing Moral Sensitivity and Judgment

The main themes of moral conflicts in a project course, external relations, project level, and interpersonal moral conflicts, function as guiding lights in sensitizing moral agents to morally relevant issues in collaborative project course and to making decisions in moral conflicts. External relations relate to the context of a project, and, according to Boddy (2002, 31) context includes the contemporary setting within and beyond the organization. In the case of a project course, the context consists of all parties (e.g., society, organizations, departments) outside the particular student project. The two other themes have similarities with managerial grid (Blake and Mouton 1978, referenced in Kast and Rosenzweig 1985, 352), a framework for organizational improvement programs, which include management (concern for production) and leadership (concern for people) orientations. In leadership, people are taken into account and in management they are used merely as a means (Maylor 2003, 264). The existence of a project is based on a task, which is to be completed. In project level conflicts (management) the concern is on managing the project, that is to say, in achieving the objectives of the project. Each student project is targeted to achieve two objectives, i.e., results for the client, and learning results for the students. In addition to conflicting objectives, when implementing the objectives, commitment and prioritization problems are likely to emerge. In interpersonal moral conflicts (leadership) the concern is on taking people into account, and as Kant (1993, 95) declared, a rational being should "treat himself and others never merely as a means, but always at the same time as an end in himself". Consequently, participants of a project should be taken into account as ends themselves in achieving the objectives of the project. For example, giving feedback to someone should be constructive rather than destructive.

In moral judgments a moral agent constructs and justifies a solution for a moral conflict s/he has become aware of. As the results of Kohlberg show, people mature in moral judgment as they grow. Therefore, students are likely to demonstrate lower capabilities in moral judgment (and in moral sensitivity) than client representatives and instructors. Development of moral judgment is fostered by providing the moral agents with ethical analysis skills (Ruggiero 1999; Collins and Miller 1992) and by exposing them to situations in which they are to solve moral conflicts in interaction with other parties. Nucci (1987, 90) expressed the three characteristics of effective moral discussion: 1) Conflict. Stage transition is likely to occur if in a discussion there are students who disagree about the solution for a given dilemma. 2) Stage disparity. One-half stage has been observed as the optimal distance in developmental levels between students.3) Transactive discussions. Moral development occurs if a listener in a discussion integrates the speaker's statements into her own framework before generating a response. To "transact" means that one aims to extend the logic, refute assumptions, or provide commonality or resolution to the speaker's positions.

To foster moral sensitivity and judgment the three main themes of moral conflicts should be used to sensitize moral agents to morally relevant themes, ethical analysis skills should be taught, and there should be opportunities for the moral agents to analyze and solve moral conflicts in small groups. Moral conflicts could be real life conflicts from the project collaboration or from the IT-field. Integrating client representatives into the discussion might create stage disparity and thus speed up development in both components.

Developing Moral Motivation: Values Analysis and Criticism

Success in moral motivation means prioritization of moral values above non-moral ones. Bebeau (2002, 285) states that in the context of professional practice career pressures, established relationships, idiosyncratic personal concerns, self-actualization, protecting one's self or organization may compete with what is morally right to do. He states that understanding the responsibility of one's acts bridges the gap between "knowing" and "doing". This understanding has to grow from inside a moral agent. Research on professional identity is concerned about instilling desired values, internalized standards and codes on entry-level pre-professionals (Bebeau 2002). However, socialization of students to pre-defined professional values raises serious questions about indoctrination, about teachers imposing their doctrines upon students who may receive them uncritically or on the basis of unquestioned authority (Warnock 1975; Lisman 1998). As a solution Morrill (1980) suggests values analysis, consciousness, and criticism, which aim to make moral agents aware of values and to change them, if needed, and to implement them. In practice, a values analysis may be questioning any situation about its characteristics such as relations between matters of facts and questions of value, and about which factors are given weight in the situation. Values analysis and consciousness go hand in hand, and according to Morrill (1980, 87) awareness of values may be developed through a process of comparison and contrast. Contrasting our experiences with those of others makes us aware of our values. The aim of values criticism (Morrill 1980, 91) is to develop capacity for constructive self-criticism and for choice and implementation of values without prescribing any specific answers. In this way knowledge and action may be linked. These methods aim to avoid indoctrination because they do not prescribe specific content of an individual's value system.

In the case of a project course in collaboration with industry, parties have a possibility to become aware of experiences and criticize values of each other. For example, students may consider professional values expressed by client representatives. However, the possibility of client representatives (along with instructors) instilling their professional values based of their authority should be taken into consideration.

Developing Moral Character: Just Community

Moral character refers to the psychological strength to carry out a line of action. Nucci (1997) uses the term "character" to describe the tendency to act in accordance with what one understands to be morally right. However, character building cannot rely only on development of moral reasoning, it also means habituating oneself to morally good virtues. Following the ideas of Aristotle (1994, 27) one becomes virtuous by practising a virtue. Singer (1994, 169) referred to two studies which suggest that Aristotle may be right. In those studies blood donors and their motives for donating blood were investigated and, according to the results, incentives of external forces (e.g., a friend was donating) were substituted by internal motivations (sense of personal responsibility towards ones community) as the donors continued donating. The studies thus suggest that practising a virtue may make us internally virtuous. And with this internal strength we may struggle against pressures from the outside to avoid acts we perceive immoral. A way to habituate individuals to morally desirable virtues is to be found in the just community approach put forward by Kohlberg (1985, 71). Research on just community programs supports the view that a communal environment, which supports the virtues of trust, care, participation, and responsibility are the best approaches in character development (Power 1997). Just community programs emphasize self-governance, democratic process in decision-making and abiding by the norms of the community (Morrill 1980, 31). Teachers in just community schools have to demonstrate their students how to participate in decision-making in a democratic way and how to build a community. The students are habituated in a controlled situation to take part in a democratic community. In this way, their sense of responsibility and abilities to generalize their behaviour are affected. Here, the problem of indoctrination is evident. According to Kohlberg (1985, 80), although ethics teachers aim to avoid indoctrination, which is possible in the case of hypothetical moral conflicts, when teaching in real life one has to take a stance on real life moral conflicts. In the case of the just community approach, indoctrination is avoided by establishing participatory democracy, in which teachers participate in terms of rationality and not in terms of authority and power. Students are to form rules and discipline the process, and they are to take the responsibility to implement them.

In its fullest form realization, the just community approach in a project course would require all parties to take part in the democratic process of decision-making and to abide by its norms. In this way, the sense of community and responsibility would grow in each party. As our experiences from the field show, after graduation, the students of the course may become future clients with the sense of belonging to their university. For example, in line with the main themes of moral conflicts, the following issues could be critically discussed: rules of collaboration between the academia and the industry (external relations), project objectives, and commitment and prioritization questions (project level), and how individuals should be treated (interpersonal). However, as our experiences from the field show, clients tend to emphasize beneficial objectives at the expense of learning, which is a fundamental value of any university. Therefore, participatory democracy as such at the inter-organizational level may not be the working method, instead, critical discussion between representatives of organizations about objectives and rules sustains the long-term collaboration.

To sum up, the framework defined here aims for moral success in each component regarding each party of a project course. The framework broadens the traditional idea of learning professional ethics in an educational institute with hypothetical moral conflicts to a form of experiential learning in which IT-professionals together with students critically deliberate about moral conflicts they have confronted in real life.

Conclusion

This article summarized the results of an empirical case study, which determined moral conflicts perceived by clients, students, and instructors of a project course in information systems education, and proposed a framework for morally successful project course in collaboration between academia and industry. The results show that subjects confront external relations, project level, and interpersonal moral conflicts. The framework suggests that the traditional practice of ethics teaching is broadened by integrating client representatives into the ethics education program. Ideally, clients, students, and instructors may be perceived as co-learners of professional ethics. All the three parties could reflect on moral issues in the cooperation and in the practice on the IT-field. Future research should test if the main themes are found in other project courses in computing.

For practical implementation the following issues should be considered. First, implementation of the framework as a whole requires resources, education, and motivation from each party. Parts of the framework could be implemented, for example, by concentrating on the development of moral sensitivity and judgment. Similarly, the framework could be implemented among certain parties, for example, moral argumentation among students or critical moral discussions about industry-academia relations between instructors and client representatives. Second, as profitability is a fundamental responsibility of business (Carroll 1999), the incentives for client representatives to participate in this kind of educational program have to emerge from their personal developmental aims. Third, the problem of indoctrination should be dealt with carefully in cases where clients without professional experience from teaching took part in this kind of educational intervention.

References

Aristotle (1994) Moral Virtue, How Produced. In: Singer P (ed) Ethics. Oxford University Press Oxford

Audi R (ed) (1995) The Cambridge Dictionary of Philosophy. Cambridge University Press Cambridge

Bebeau MJ (2002) The Defining Issues Test and the Four Component Model: Contributions to Professional Education. Journal of Moral Education, vol 31, no 3, pp 271-295

Blake RR, Mouton, JS (1978) The New Managerial Grid. Gulf Publishing Company, Houston. Rererenced in Kast FE, Rosenzweig JE (1985) Organization & Management, A Systems and Contingency Approach. McGraw-Hill, New York

Boddy D (2002) Managing Projects: Building and Leading the Team. Prentice Hall Harlow Essex

Carroll AB (1999) Ethics in Management. In: Frederick RE (ed) A Companion to Business Ethics. Blackwell Oxford

Collins WR, Miller KW (1992) Paramedic Ethics for Computer Professionals. Journal of Systems Software, vol 17, no 1, pp 23-38

Fielden K (1999) Starting Right: Ethical Education for Information Systems Developers. In: Simpson CR (ed) AICEC99 Conference Proc, 14-16 July 1999. Melbourne. Australian Institute of Computer Ethics. Brunswick East Victoria

Hill TE (1996) Moral Dilemmas, Gaps, and Residues: A Kantian Perspective. In: Mason HE (ed) Moral Dilemmas and Moral Theory. Oxford University Press New York

Kant I (1993) The Moral Law, Groundwork of the Metaphysic of Morals. Translated by Paton HJ. Routledge London

Kohlberg L (1981) The Philosophy of Moral Development, Moral Stages and the Idea of Justice. Harper & Row San Francisco

Lisman CD (1998) Ethics Education in Schools. In: Chadwick R (ed) Encyclopedia of Applied Ethics, vol 2. Academic Press San Diego California

Marcus RB (1987) Moral Dilemmas and Consistency. In: Gowans CW (ed) Moral Dilemmas. Oxford University Press New York

Marton F (1986) Phenomenography – a Research Approach to Investigating Different Understandings of Reality. Journal of Thought, vol 21, no 3, pp 28-49

Maylor H (2003) Project Management. Prentice Hall Harlow Essex

McNeel SP (1994) College Teaching and Student Moral Development. In: Rest JR, Narvaez D (eds) Moral Development in the Professions: Psychology and Applied Ethics. Lawrence Erlbaum Associates Mahwah

Morrill RL (1980) Teaching Values in College. Jossey-Bass Publishers San Francisco

Nagel T (1987) The Fragmentation of Value. In: Gowans CW (ed) Moral Dilemmas. Oxford University Press New York

Nucci L (1987) Synthesis of Research on Moral Development. Educational Leadership, vol 44, no 5, pp 86-92

Power FC (1997) Understanding the Character in Character Education. In: Nucci L (ed) Symposium of Developmental Perspectives and Approaches to Character Education. Symposium conducted at the meeting of the American Educational Research Association, Chicago, March 1997

Rest JR (1994) Background: Theory and Research. In: Rest JR, Narvaez D (eds) Moral Development in the Professions: Psychology and Applied Ethics. Lawrence Erlbaum Associates, Mahwah

Ruggiero VR (1997) Thinking Critically About Ethical Issues. Mayfield Publishing Company California

Scott TJ, Tichenor, LH, Bisland, RB Jr, Cross JH (1994) Team dynamics in student programing projects. SIGSCE, vol 26, no 1, pp 111-115

Singer P (1994) How Are We To Live? Ethics in an Age of Self-Interest. Mandarin London.

Shenhar AJ, Levy O (1997) Mapping the Dimensions of Project Success. Project Management Journal, vol 28, no 2, pp 5-13

Warnock M (1975) The Neutral Teacher. In: Taylor M (ed) Progress & problems in moral education. NFER Publishing Company Windsor

Vartiainen T (2005) Moral Conflicts in a Project Course in Information Systems Education. Jyväskylä University Printing House, Jyväskylä. Diss

Watson, HJ, Huber, MW (2000) Innovative Ways to Connect Information Systems Programs to the Business Community. Communications of the AIS 3, Article 11

Information Society Development in Latvia: Current State and Perspectives

Janis Grundspenkis

Department of Systems Theory and Design, Faculty of Computer Science and Information Technology, Riga Technical University, Latvia.
jgrun@cs.rtu.lv

Introduction

Nowadays we can observe the epochal evolution from the industrial age to the information age. The characteristic features of the industrial age are: production and consumption of material things; hierarchical, centralized distribution processes; re-use of pre-defined content, i.e., application of fixed procedures; compliance with standardized information schemes. By contrast, the information age, which starts since last decades of the 20th century, can be characterized by production and consumption of information; interpretation of non-standardized information for problem solving and decision making; decision making from bottom-up; and variable organizational networks [5].

The evolution towards the information age causes the rise of the information society in its diverse reality. The foundation of this society is "informationalism", which means that the defining activities in all realms of human practice are based on information technology organized in information networks and centered around information processing [3]. Moreover, these changes cause emerging of a new type of intellectual work called "a knowledge work". The essence of the knowledge work is turning information into knowledge through the interpretation of available non-standardized information for the purposes of problem solving and decision making. As it is noted in [8] "knowledge has become increasingly relevant for organizations since the shift from an industrial economy based on assembly lines and hierarchical control to a global, decentralized, co-operative, innovative, and information-driven economy". In this context the term "information society" is connected with the development of the new economy. Concurrently there are other processes of structural transformation towards informationalism that offer a contrast in terms of institutional foundations and social consequences, while reaching similar results in terms of technological innovation, productivity growth, and economic competitiveness [4]. As a consequence, the information society have some common structural features, and it is observed that the paths and outcomes of the structural transformation are extraordinary diverse [4].

The purpose of the paper is twofold. First, the overview of requirements dictated by the information age is presented, and structural features as well as different models of the information society are discussed. Second, the information society development in Latvia is analysed. The analysis, due to the expertise of the author, is based on the subset of characteristics of the information society, such as, technology and education (the full set of characteristics according with [4] includes four dimensions: technology, economics, welfare and social values).

The paper is organized as follows. In the second section new requirements, paradigms and technologies that are the basis for a new type of intellectual work, so called knowledge work, are outlined. In the third section characteristic features and models of the information society are discussed in brief. Issues of the information society development in Latvia are presented in the fourth section. The SWOT analysis of perspectives of the information society development in Latvia is given in this section, too. We conclude with some contradictions that cause serious challenges for the information society development in Latvia.

New Requirements, Paradigms and Technologies – The Driving Force for Information Society Development

If one looks back to the last two decades of the 20th century he/she can notice the focus on quality in the 1980s and reengineering in 1990s. While quality placed an emphasis on getting all employees to use their brainpower better, reengineering emphasized the use of technology to improve business processes. At the very beginning of the 21th century demand for skilled knowledge workers escalates around the world as a consequence of a shift from the industrial economy to the information driven economy. Thus entering the information age causes appearance of a new organization form of production and management. In this new system the labor force operates in the "network enterprise" as a constantly transforming network of decision-making and task implementation [4]. Jobs require not only the ability to use information technology and process information, but also the ability to learn new knowledge and to get new skills. This new type of intellectual work is called a knowledge work. Knowledge work is about making sense, i.e., information is converted into knowledge through human process of shared understanding and sense making at both a personal level and an organizational level.

Modern organizations realize that knowledge is their most important asset. Understanding and supporting knowledge work requires a paradigm shift in organizational thinking with respect to business process planning, control and reengineering. According to Peter Drucker "to make knowledge work productive is the great management task of this century, just as to make manual work productive was the great management task of the last century" [8]. Knowledge management has become a new way of capturing and efficiently managing organization's full experience and knowledge. Knowledge management may be considered as the ability to turn knowledge into action. Moreover, it may be considered as the expansion of individual's personal knowledge to knowledge of organization as a whole (a new direction in knowledge management called personal knowledge management emerged recently). Understanding and supporting knowledge management leads towards creation of knowledge environment and widespread usage of knowledge management tools in organization's everyday life. For both types of knowledge (personal and organizational) a knowledge environment contributes knowledge creation (development, acquisition, inference, generation), storage (representation, preservation), aggregation (creation of meta-knowledge), use/reuse (access, analysis, application) and transfer (distribution, sharing) [5]. Knowledge management tools and techniques afford effective technological solutions for acquisition, preservation and use of organization's knowledge, converting information to knowledge and connecting people to knowledge. Knowledge management tools may be supported by information technology infrastructure and/or artificial intelligence techniques. Information management tools such as, data warehouses, data search engines, data modelling and visualization, allow to generate, store, access and analyse data. Knowledge management tools (knowledge flow enablers; knowledge navigation systems and tools; corporate, organizational and enterprise memories; knowledge repositories and libraries) allow to develop, combine, distribute and secure knowledge. Knowledge identification, creation, supply, dissemination, reuse, storage and preservation in knowledge bases are supported by artificial intelligence techniques, such as decision support systems, expert systems, intelligent agents, multiagent systems and artificial life [5]. To summarize this short overview (more details may be found in [1, 5, 6]) we conclude that all tools and techniques provide the development and maintenance of high-quality knowledge based labor force. This labor force is the most important factor of production to win a competitive advantage in the informational economy.

New requirements, paradigms and technologies that crucially influence production and business also influence the whole society of every country that moves towards the information society. The information society have some common structural features: it is based on knowledge generation and dissemination, and information collection and processing, with the help of information technologies; it is organized in information network structures of different scale (global and local); and its main activities are networked and integrated on the global level, working as a whole in real time thanks to the infrastructure of communications and transportation. But there are other processes of structural transformation towards the information society and social consequences that should be taken into account, too.

Characteristic Features and Models of the Information Society

This section presents a brief discussion that mainly is based on characteristic indicators and models of the information society proposed in [4]. Castells and Himanen argue [4] that "the information society can exist, and indeed does exist, in a plurality of social and cultural models, in the same way that the industrial society developed in very different, and even antagonistic, models of modernity, for instance in the United States and the Soviet Union, as well as in Scandinavia or Japan". All societies evolve toward adapting the features characteristic of the information society. At the same time, however, it is observed that the paths and outcomes of transformations are extraordinary diverse. Countries around the world become informational at different speeds and in sharply divergent degrees, according to their level of development [4]. We may conclude that societies and economies can reach very similar levels of the information society starting from different histories and cultures, using a variety of institutions, and reaching distinct forms of social organization, i.e., there are various models of the information society. In [4] a comparison of three models of the information society, namely, Finland, United States and Singapore, is presented. Twenty four indicators grouped into four groups of dimensions (technology, economy, welfare and social values) have been chosen so that they can also be used to differentiate between various information societies. Authors state that one can call a society an information society if it is strong in information technology. Technology dimensions are infrastructure, production and knowledge. Infrastructure dimension has two indicators: Internet hosts and mobile phone subscriptions per 1000 population. Production is characterized by high-tech exports/total goods exports (%), and e-commerce (secure servers per 100000 population). Knowledge dimension also has two indicators: Internet users (%), and science, mathematics and engineering tertiary students (%). Economy is characterized by six indicators that belong to national, global and innovativeness dimensions, while welfare has six indicators that reflect education, health and welfare dimensions. At last, social values have six politics, civil society and globality indicators. The usage of listed dimensions and indicators allow to conclude that there are very different economically and technologically dynamic models of the information society: "the Silicon Valley Model" of a market-driven, open information society; "the Singapore Model" of an authoritarian information society; and "the Finnish Model" of an open, welfare information society [4].

The work of Castells and Himanen gave the impulse to analyse the current state and perspectives of the information society development in Latvia. Some results of this analysis are presented in the next section.

Information Society Development in Latvia

The restricted number of dimensions and indicators are used in this section due to the expertise of the author and the scope of the paper. More precisely, the information society development in Latvia is analysed using two dimensions (technology and education) and the following indicators: personal computer and mobile phone users per 100 population; percentage of enterprises which have at least one computer and Internet connections; production in information technology sector; structure of state investments in research and development; and number of information technology tertiary students and graduates.

Infrastructure is characterized by indicators that reflect penetration of information and communication technologies. Numbers given in Table 1 show that infrastructure in Latvia develops rather quickly.

The structure of information technology sector in Latvia in given in Fig. 1. In 2000, ICT products and services accounted for 4,5% of total GDP, and its share grew to 4,6% in 2001. Software production was 0,4% of GDP in 2000 and 0,5% in 2001. The software industry has been growing at a rate of 15% per anum and the ICT industry is regarded as the sector with the post potential for future development [7]. Economic activities related to production of goods and services of IT in 2002 equaled to approximately 5,2% of GDP (the share of software development – about 7,5%) [2].

Table 1. Penetration of ICT

Indicators	2002	2004	2005
PCs/100	19		33
Internet/100	6		25
Mobile Cell Phone/100	34,2		59
Enterprises that use computers (%)	51		53
Active enterprises that use computers (%)		85	
Enterprises with Internet connections (%)	36		41
Active enterprises with Internet connections (%)		72	

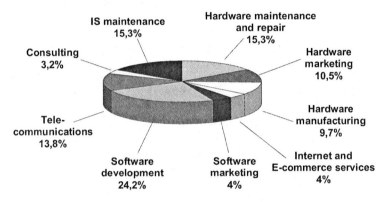

Fig. 1. The structure of information technology sector in Latvia (2002)

Research to the certain extent supports production in the ICT sector. It is worth to point out that research in Latvia, and in particular in the ICT, as a rule, is state financed. This is the weakest point in the information society development in Latvia because share of investments for research and development in only 0,18% within GDP (the lowest among all EU countries). Distribution of research areas financed by the state in 2005 is shown in Fig. 2.

The number of projects financed in 2005 by the Latvian Council of Science in computer science and information technology is too high compared with the amount of money invested in this area (45 projects and only 5,71% from total investments in research). As a consequence, the average money received for one project is too small for establishing strong scientific bodies. Results of the analysis of main research areas in informatics are given in Table 2.

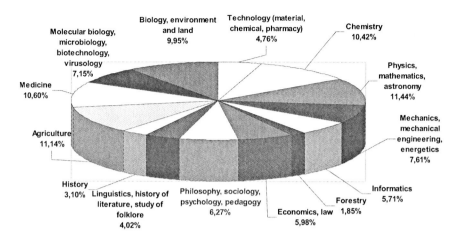

Fig. 2. State financing of research (2005)

Table 2. Projects financed by the Latvian Council of Science (2005)

No	Research area	Number of projects	Financing, %
1.	Applications of CS and IT	11	30,44
2.	Electronics	8	20,76
3.	Signal processing and communications	8	15,08
4.	Artificial intelligence and knowledge based systems	8	13,49
5.	System modelling and simulation	5	10,79
6.	Software engineering and information systems	5	9,44
	Total	45	

The general education trend in Latvia is the increase in the number of people acquiring education or improving their qualification. According to data of Central Statistics Bureau there were 55 students per 1000 inhabitants of Latvia in 2003/2004. It is one of the highest rates if compared with other European countries. Share of students within population 18-23 years old is 32,1%. Some other indicators of higher education in Latvia are the following: number of academic personnel – 3636; share of professors within academic personnel – 24%; number of students per one academic personnel – 28; share of expenditures for education and for higher education within GDP – 7,4% and 1,5%, respectively [2]. The total number of students in study year 2004/2005 is 130693, from them approximately 10% are computer science and information technology (CS&IT) students. There are around 1000 graduates yearly in CS&IT. At the same time distribution of students according to study programmes in study year 2003/2004 is unfavourable from the viewpoint of the information society development (see Fig. 3).

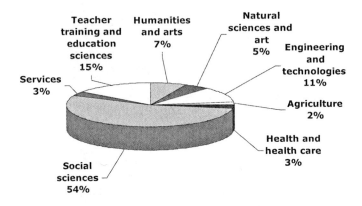

Fig. 3. Distribution of students according to study programmes (2003/2004)

There are 12 institutions of higher education that have study programmes in CS&IT. The total number of enrolled students and graduates in this sector is given in Table 3.

Table 3. The total number of enrolled students and graduates

Year	Number of enrolled	Number of graduates
2000	2079 / 800*	731
2001	2467 / 1043	757
2002	2421 / 1229	882
2003	2516 / 904	951
2004	2283 / 732	1148

* The first number denotes students whose studies are financed by the state, and the second number corresponds to those who pay for their education

In order to look at the way in which Latvia appears against the background of other countries in the world the World Bank Development Data Group assessments that highlight the ICT skills level may be used [2]. These assessments use ratings from 1 to 7 to measure the availability of highly-skilled technology workers in the industry. Latvia get 4,1 rating for highly skilled IT job market (Finland – 6,6, US – 6,7). Readiness for the network society has three components, and Latvia's ratings in 2002 are the following: network learning – 4,23 (Finland – 6,23; US – 5,97), ICT opportunities – 3,70 (Finland – 6,35, US – 6,65), social capital – 5,77 (Finland – 6,66, US – 6,04).

The current state and perspectives of the information society development are summarized in the SWOT Analysis (see Table 4).

Table 4. SWOT Analysis of perspectives of the information society development in Latvia

Strengths	Weaknesses
• Stable economic environment • High level of ICT skills • Well-trained and qualified specialists to develop high-quality software products • High standards of education • Relatively low labor and service costs • Literacy of foreign languages • Well-developed communications and logistics infrastructure	• Insufficiently low financing of research and development (funding practically only from the state budget and it is too small for establishing strong research groups) • Insufficient financing of higher education • Lack of financial support for IT start-up projects and lack of development support • Weak motivation, lack of time to submit proposals and lack of experience in international projects with EU funding
Opportunities	Threats
• Integration into the European Union • Number of applicants for studies in IT permanently is high • Large number of graduates attracted to IT sector • Number of doctoral students is growing • Possibility of expansion of IS cluster with low investments in infrastructure	• Lack of sufficient amount of investments (unfavourable governmental financial support) • Lack of research and development could lead to backwardness of industry • Age and overload of experienced researchers and teachers • High rate of drop outs from doctoral studies

Conclusion

The defining aspects of different models of the information society are the following: competitive economy and high level of technologies; the role of the state in the development of the information society and the welfare of the state; the relationship between globalization and national identity (the latest is complex and contradictory issue in Latvia). We need to take into account that all information societies also have their weaknesses. The most serious challenges in Latvian case are: the contradiction between the information society and the structures of government of the industrial age; the contradiction between a strong national identity and integration in a multi-cultural world; the rise of new inequalities; the conflict between current needs of the new economy of the industrial age and lack of sufficient amount of investments.

At the present moment it is hard to say which economical and technological model of the information society Latvia will follow. Definitely it will be an open information society. The main question is to which extent Latvia will be able to reach the needed level of technology, economy, welfare and social value dimensions. Answer to this open question strongly depends on willingness and skills of the government and society to take advantage of our strengths and opportunities as well as to overcome weaknesses and to prevent threats.

References

[1] Apshvalka D, Grundspenkis J (2003) Making Organization to Act More Intelligently in the Framework of the Organizational Knowledge Management System. In: Scientific Proc of Riga Technical University, 5th series, Computer Science, Applied Computer Systems, vol 17. Riga Technical University Publishing Riga Latvia, pp. 72-82
[2] Assessment Study: Potential of ICT Sector in Latvia (2003) Latvian Information Technology and Telecommunications Association (LITTA).
[3] Castells M (2000) The Information Age: Economy, Society and Culture. Blackwell Oxford.
[4] Castells M, Himanen P (2002) The Information Society and the Welfare State. The Finnish Model. University Press Oxford.
[5] Grundspenkis J (2001) Concepts of Organizations, Intelligent Agents, Knowledge, Learning and Memories: Towards an Inter-Disciplinary Knowledge Management. In: Wang K, Grundspenkis J, Yerofeev A (eds) Applied Computational Intelligence to Engineering and Business. Riga Technical University Publishing Riga Latvia, pp 172-191
[6] Grundspenkis J, Kirikova M (2004) Impact of the Intelligent Agent Paradigm on Knowledge Management. In: Leondes CT (ed) Intelligent Knowledge-Based Systems, vol 1. Kluwer Academic Press New York, pp 164-206
[7] Information and Communication Technology. Country Profile: Latvia (2003) Technical Paper of International Trade Centre UNCTAD/WTO. Geneva.
[8] Information Technology for Knowledge Management (1998) Borghoff UM, Pareschi R (eds) Springer-Verlag Berlin Heidelberg New York

Portalen Handelsplats Wermland – Practical E-commerce for Värmland's Businesses and Municipalities

Ulrika Obstfelder Peterson and Ulf Borg

Wermland Chamber of Commerce, Karlstad, Sweden.
(www.handelsplatswermland.se) (ulrika, ulf.borg)@wermland.cci.se

Abstract

Portalen Handelsplats Wermland (Portal Meetingpoint Wermland) offers a range of services designed by the Wermland Chamber of Commerce to permit the cost-effective exchange of electronic messages, including invoicing, ordering, certification and procurement. The portal meets the needs and expectations faced by businesses, both large and small, in the area of e-commerce. The portal also provides a way for businesses to share the cost of applications and equipment. As a result, they enjoy greater flexibility with their partners and more efficient internal procedures. Most importantly, the portal represents a local, impartial effort to strengthen Värmland's private sector and open up avenues that are beyond the financial means of individual businesses.

A series of packaged solutions furnish even small and medium-sized busi-nesses with simple, inexpensive options. The portal currently offers both EDI (Electronic Data Interchange) and Web EDI services. An electronic procurement service and a procurement supply center are also up and running. The objective of Wermland Chamber of Commerce is to promote e-commerce between municipalities and businesses, whether large, medium-sized or small. The portal strives to be the first place that a municipality or business will turn when it wants to engage in e-commerce – in other words, it is a regional hub for exchanging electronic messages. What makes the portal so special is its use of the latest technology to help sup-pliers meet the requirements of purchasers.

How Standard Are the Standard Barriers to E-commerce Adoption? Empirical Evidence from Australia, Sweden and the USA

Robert MacGregor[1], Lejla Vrazalic[2], Sten Carlsson[3], Jean Pratt[4] and Matthew Harris[5]

[1][2] Information Systems, University of Wollongong, Australia.
(rmacgreg, lejla)@uow.edu.au
[3] Information Systems, Karlstad University, Sweden. sten.carlsson@kau.se
[4][5] Business Information Systems, Utah State University, USA.
(jean.pratt, mattharris)@usu.edu

Introduction

Despite their size, small to medium enterprises (SMEs) are increasingly turning to global markets. This development has been enabled by the advent of electronic commerce technology. There are numerous definitions of e-commerce in the literature, however, fundamentally e-commerce can best be described as "the buying and selling of information, products, and services via computer networks" (Kalakota & Whinston, 1997, p.3). E-commerce has the potential to become a source of competitive advantage to the SME sector because it is a cost effective way of accessing customers and being 'wired to the global marketplace'.

Despite the exponential growth of e-commerce, it is mostly larger businesses that have reaped the benefits (Riquelme, 2002). In contrast, the rate of e-commerce adoption in the regional SME sector has remained relatively low (Van Akkeren & Cavaye, 1999). According to the National Research Council (2000), only 25% of SMEs had a web site in mid-1999. Of those that did have a web site, the revenue they generated via business-to-customer e-commerce was negligible.

The sluggish pace of e-commerce diffusion in the SME sector has been attributed to various adoption barriers that are faced by SMEs. These barriers have been well documented in numerous research studies. While several studies (MacGregor et al, 2004; MacGregor, 2004) have examined the correlation of barriers in an attempt to develop a simplified model, little has been done to discover whether, in fact, these barriers are universal to the small business sector, or how they differ from location to location. This paper presents three studies of regional SMEs located in Australia, Sweden and the USA to determine whether barriers to e-commerce adoption are perceived differently in different locations, and to identify any common underlying factors. The paper begins by examining the nature of SMEs. A brief discussion of barriers to e-commerce adoption is then presented. This is followed by a correlation and factor analysis of the two sets of data and a discussion of the results.

Small to Medium Enterprises

There are a number of definitions of what constitutes an SME. Some of these definitions are based on quantitative measures such as staffing levels, turnover or assets, while others employ a qualitative approach. Meredith (1994) suggests that any definition must include a quantitative component as well as a qualitative component that reflects how the business is organised and how it operates. In this paper, small businesses are defined as organizations employing less than 50 people, while medium enterprises have more than 50 but less than 250 employees.

Qualitatively, any description of an SME must be premised on the notion that they are not simply scaled down large businesses (Wynarczyk et al 1993) and although size is a major distinguishing factor, SMEs have a number of unique features that set them apart from larger businesses. SMEs tend to be more prone to risk than their larger counterparts (Delone, 1988), tend to be subject to higher failure rates (Cochran, 1981), and suffer from a lack of trained staff (Welsh and White, 1981). These traits are termed 'resource poverty' (*ibid*) and their net effect is to magnify the effects of environmental impacts, particularly where IT was involved. These early studies have been supported by more recent research (e.g. Barry & Milner, 2002; Raymond, 2001). SMEs located in regional areas have faced even more problems than their counterparts in major cities and metropolitan areas.

SMEs in Regional Areas

SMEs located in regional areas are affected by circumstances inherent to their location. Regional areas are defined as geographical areas located outside metropolitan centres and major cities. The Australian Bureau of Statistics (2001) classifies regional areas into inner and outer regions, remote and very remote areas. Determining the classification of a region is based on a formula which primarily relies on the measures of proximity to services. Rather than remote and rural areas (which are sparsely populated), the research presented in this paper focuses on inner and outer regional areas (which are more urbanised).

Regional areas are of particular interest to governments because they are characterised by high unemployment rates (Larsson et al, 2003), a shortage of skilled people, limited access to resources and a lack of infrastructure (Keniry et al, 2003). Yet, at the same time, businesses located in regional areas in Australia contribute 50% of the national export income (Keniry, 2003). This implies that small businesses have the potential to play a major role in developing regional areas. The European Union views small businesses as a catalyst for regional development (Europa, 2003). In 2001, the Swedish Parliament passed legislation that resulted in the creation of Regional Development Councils (Johansson, 2003). The Councils have a mandate to promote a positive business climate and sustainable growth in their respective regions. SMEs have been earmarked as playing an important role in promoting this growth because they are seen as a key source of jobs and employment prospects (Keniry et al, 2003; Larssen et al, 2003). Subsequently, government organisations have been heavily promoting the adoption of information and communication technology (ICT), including e-commerce, by SMEs. However, barriers to adoption still remain.

Barriers to E-commerce Adoption in SMEs

The slow paced uptake of e-commerce technologies in SMEs has been widely documented and researched. The barriers to e-commerce adoption can be classified as external or internal to the business. Hadjimanolis (1999) found that external barriers could be further categorised into supply barriers, demand barriers and environmental barriers. Internal barriers were further divided into resource barriers and system barriers. A brief summary of e-commerce adoption barriers in SMEs are offered in Table 1.

Table 1. Brief literature review of e-commerce adoption barriers

Barriers to e-commerce adoption	Reported by
High cost of e-commerce implementation	Quayle (2002)
E-commerce too complex to implement	Quayle (2002)
Lack of technical skills amongst employees	Quayle (2002)
Lack of time to implement e-commerce	Walczuch et al (2000)
Not suited to the way the SME does business	Poon & Swatman (1999)
Not suited to the SME's products/services	Walczuch et al (2000)

Table 1. (cont.)

Lack of awareness about benefits of e-commerce	Quayle (2002)
Lack of available information about e-commerce	Lawrence (1997)
Concern about security of e-commerce	Quayle (2002)
Lack of critical mass among customers/suppliers	Hadjimanolis (1999)
Lack of e-commerce standards	Tuunainen (1998)

Although extensive research has been undertaken to identify e-commerce adoption barriers, our understanding of these remains fragmented. Furthermore, there are few studies to compare results and establish whether there are any similarities between barriers faced by SMEs in different locations. The study presented in this paper aims to address this.

Methodology

Ten of the most commonly occurring barriers to e-commerce adoption were identified from the literature. A series of six in-depth interviews with regional small businesses was undertaken to determine whether the barriers were applicable and complete. All of the identified barriers were found to applicable and no additional barriers were forthcoming. Based on the six in-depth interviews, a survey instrument was developed to collect data about e-commerce adoption barriers (amongst other things). Respondents who had not adopted e-commerce were asked to rate the importance of each barrier to their decision not to adopt e-commerce (as shown in Table 2 below) using a standard 5 point Likert scale. The Likert scale responses were assumed to posses the characteristics of an interval measurement scale for data analysis purposes.

The study was primarily concerned with SMEs located in regional areas, especially since no other research has investigated e-commerce adoption barriers in these areas specifically. As a result, this study was conceived primarily as exploratory in nature. Sweden, Australia and USA were chosen to carry out the study for several reasons. All of the countries have a large number of SMEs located in regional areas and the governments of these countries are keen to promote e-commerce adoption by SMEs. Furthermore, all of the countries are classified by the World Bank Group as high income nations and are members of the OECD. A set of location guidelines was developed in order to choose a specific region in each country. These were: the location must be a large regional centre; a viable chamber of commerce must exist and be well patronised by SMEs; the location should have the full range of educational facilities; a cross-section of business ages, sizes, sectors and market foci must exist.

Table 2. Question about barriers to e-commerce adoption used in survey

23. This question relates to the reasons why your organisation is not be using e-commerce. Below is a list of statements indicating possible reasons. Based on your opinion, please rank each statement on a scale of 1 to 5 to indicate how important it was to your decision NOT to use e-commerce, where 1means the reason was very unimportant and 5 means the reason was very important.

1 E-commerce is not suited to our products/ services	1 2 3 4 5
2 E-commerce is not suited to our way of doing business	1 2 3 4 5
3 E-commerce is not suited to the ways our clients do business	1 2 3 4 5
4 E-commerce does not offer any advantages to our organisation	1 2 3 4 5
5 We don't have the technical knowledge to implement e-commerce	1 2 3 4 5
6 E-commerce is too complicated to implement	1 2 3 4 5
7 E-commerce is not secure	1 2 3 4 5
8 Financial investment required to implement e-comm is too high	1 2 3 4 5
9 We do not have time to implement e-commerce	1 2 3 4 5
10 Difficult to choose most suitable e-commerce standard with many different options	1 2 3 4 5

Based on these guidelines, three locations were chosen, Karlstad (Sweden), Wollongong (Australia), and Salt Lake City (Utah, USA). All three locations met the guidelines and each location contained personnel who could assist with the distribution and collection of the survey instrument. A total of 1170 surveys were distributed by post in four regional areas of Sweden: Karlstad, Filipstad, Saffle and Arvika. A total of 250 surveys were administered by telephone in Wollongong and a total of 150 surveys were administered by telephone in the USA. The mode of the data collection was selected based on previous research by de Heer (1999) which indicated that Scandinavian countries had historically high survey response rates (although he notes that this is declining). Therefore, a low cost mail survey was used in Sweden, while the more expensive mode was used in Australia and the USA to ensure higher levels of participation.

Results

Responses were obtained from 313 SMEs in Sweden giving an unexpectedly low response rate of 26.8%. (It is interesting to note that the low response rate confirms de Heer's (1999) findings that response rates in Sweden are falling.) Of these, 275 responses were considered to be valid and usable. The total number non-adopters was 123, representing 44.7% of the valid responses. The responses of these non-adopters were examined in detail and it was determined that 89 of them responded to every statement in the question regarding barriers to e-commerce adoption. Responses were obtained from 164 SMEs in Australia giving a higher response rate of 65.6% which is consistent with phone surveys (Frazer & Lawley, 2000). In Australia, the total number non-adopters was 139, representing 84.4% of the valid responses. The responses of the non-adopters were examined in detail and it was determined that all 139 responded to every statement in the question regarding barriers to e-commerce adoption. Responses were obtained from 116 small business organisations in the US giving a response rate of 77.3%. The total number non-adopters was 47, representing 40.5% of the valid responses. The responses of the non-adopters were examined in detail and it was determined that all 47 responded to every statement in the question regarding barriers to e-commerce adoption. The responses formed the basis for the statistical analysis carried out using SPSS. An inspection of the frequencies indicated, in all three locations, that the full range of the scale was utilised by the respondents (i.e. every barrier had at least one instance of each rating from 1 to 5).

The aim of the statistical analysis was to establish the correlations between e-commerce adoption barriers in the data set. The results are shown in Tables 3-5. The barriers have been numerically abbreviated as per Table 2. Correlations significant at the .001 level are shown in bold.

Table 3. Correlation Matrix of e-commerce adoption barriers – Sweden

	1	2	3	4	5	6	7	8	9
2	**.746**								
3	**.462**	**.530**							
4	**.482**	**.547**	.280						
5	-.030	.054	-.097	0.249*					
6	-.009	.059	.065	.106	**.544**				
7	0.184*	0.303**	.098	0.249*	0.277*	**.516**			
8	-0.51	-.138	.092	-.104	**.445**	**.481**	0.217*		
9	-0.245*	-0.261**	-.056	-0.195*	**.432**	**.587**	.174	**.448**	
10	-.056	-.005	-.033	.062	**.514**	**.579**	**.334**	**.494**	**.532**

Table 4. Correlation Matrix of e-commerce adoption barriers – Australia

	1	2	3	4	5	6	7	8	9
2	**.747**								
3	**.435**	**.804**							
4	**.654**	**.647**	**.413**						
5	.213*	.221**	.206*	.255**					
6	.039	.105	.155	.177**	**.708**				
7	-.047	.027	.101	.156	**.441**	**.554**			
8	.119	.140	.024	.201*	**.525**	**.537**	.357		
9	.011	.033	.106	.142	**.420**	**.510**	.299	**.556**	
10	.035	.075	-.047	.174*	**.415**	**.484**	**.366**	**.407**	**.603**

Table 5. Correlation Matrix of e-commerce adoption barriers – USA

	1	2	3	4	5	6	7	8	9
2	.415**								
3	.437**	.586							
4	.642	.355*	.344*						
5	-.023	.218	.115	-.061					
6	.067	.079	.034	.079	.679				
7	.119	.454**	-.073	.114	.371*	.383**			
8	.089	.193	.017	.001	.426**	.338*	.344*		
9	.123	.099	.179	.142	.762	.811	.259	.245	
10	.095	.156	.148	.200	.614	.873	.498	.361*	.686

* significant at 0.05 level   ** significant at 0.01 level

For all three countries, the first four barriers seem to all correlate with each other, but show weak or no correlations with the last set of barriers. Similarly, it appears that correlations exist between the last five barriers in the Correlation Matrix. For Australia and Sweden, two distinct groupings of results can be identified in the Correlation Matrix. In the first grouping, there is a strong positive correlation between the barriers "E-commerce is not suited to our products/services" and "E-commerce is not suited to our way of doing business" (Pearson's r = .747, p< .000). These two barriers also show moderately strong positive correlations with the barriers "E-commerce is not suited to the ways our clients do business" and "E-commerce does not offer any advantages to our organisation". In the second grouping, the barriers relating to the investment, time, number of options, complexity and security aspects of e-commerce adoption generally show moderately strong positive correlations with each other.

For the US respondents, two distinct groupings of results can be identified in the Correlation Matrix. In the first grouping there is a strong correlation between the barriers "E-commerce is not suited to our products/ services" and "We see no advantage in using E-commerce" (Pearson's r = .642, p< .000). These two barriers also show moderately strong positive correlations with the barriers "E-commerce is not suited to the ways our clients do business" and "E-commerce is not suited to our way of doing business". In the second grouping, the results are as per Sweden and Australia. However, the barriers within these two groupings appear to be unrelated to the barriers in the alternate group in all three locations, with the exception of very weak correlations for the security and time barriers.

These findings suggested the use of Factor Analysis to investigate any separate underlying factors and to reduce the redundancy of certain barriers indicated in the Correlation Matrices. The results of Kaiser-Meyer-Olkin MSA (.735 for Sweden, .905 for Australia and .530 for the US) and Bartlett's Test of Sphericity (χ^2 = 343, p = .000 for Sweden, χ^2 = 1395.670, p = .000 for Australia and χ^2 = 355.044, p = .000 for the US) indicated that the data set satisfied the assumptions for factorability. Principle Components Analysis was chosen as the method of extraction in order to account for maximum variance in the data using a minimum number of factors. A two-factor solution was extracted for Sweden and Australia. A three factor solution was extracted for the USA. This was supported by an inspection of the Scree Plots. The two factors accounted for 59.973% of the total variance in Sweden and 77.977% in Australia. The three factors accounted for 70.646% of the total variance in the US sample (Table 6).

Table 6. Total Variance Explained

Comp	Eigenvalue			% of Variance			Cumulative %		
	SW	AUS	USA	SW	AUS	USA	SW	AUS	USA
1	3.252	4.212	4.624	32.520	42.116	38.530	32.520	42.116	38.530
2	2.745	3.586	2.435	27.453	35.860	20.290	59.973	77.977	58.820
3			1.419			11.826			70.646

The resulting components were rotated using the Varimax procedure and a simple structure was achieved as shown in the Rotated Component Matrix (Table 7). Five barriers loaded highly on the first component. These barriers were related to e-commerce complexity, options, high cost and lack of knowledge and time. This component has been termed the "Too Difficult" factor. The barriers highly loaded on the second component are termed the "Unsuitable" factor and are related to the suitability of e-commerce to the respondent's business. For the US study, a third factor termed "Investment & Security" was extracted. Two barriers (high cost and security) loaded onto this factor. These factors are independent and uncorrelated, as an orthogonal rotation procedure was used.

Table 7. Rotated Component Matrix (Sweden, Australia & US)

Barrier	Component 1: Too Difficult			Component 2: Unsuitable			Comp. 3: Investment & Security
	Sweden	Australia	USA	Sweden	Australia	USA	USA
1	-.086	.209	.278	.844	.917	.721	.162
2	-.034	.271	.422	.909	.912	.563	.469
3	-.004	.262	.331	.643	.909	.694	-.146
4	.076	.355	.300	.731	.837	.689	.032
5	.743	.787	.840	.074	.349	-.272	-.253
6	.852	.869	.850	.102	.237	-.220	.507
7	.525	.767	.455	.385	.216	.052	.580
8	.703	.795	.485	-.092	.272	-.195	.580
9	.742	.813	.840	-.294	.205	-.136	-.344
10	.800	.802	.840	-.054	.217	-.104	-.168

Discussion

Before examining the groupings of factors in detail, a number of comments are appropriate. Firstly, while the groupings of barriers differ from one location to another, the results suggest that each of the ten barriers is applicable to SMEs in regional areas. Secondly, despite each of the three locations satisfying conditions for classification as regional, the uptake of e-commerce is vastly different from location to location. 53.3% of the regional Swedish SMEs surveyed had adopted e-commerce, 59.5% of the regional US SMEs had done likewise, while only 15.6% of the Australian SMEs had done so. A number of explanations are possible. One explanation is that there is a deliberate 'push' by some governments to develop professional and voluntary organisations and courses to 'ease small business into e-commerce'. This is supported by a number of recent studies (see for example Barry et al, 2003). A second explanation is supported by studies carried out in UK, US and Australia (see for example Gibb, 2000) who found that there is a willingness by SMEs in the US and UK to seek alternative approaches to marketing and technology. This was not found in Australia.

A number of authors (see for example Martin & Matlay, 2001) have noted that, among other factors, the location of the SME does have a bearing on the decision-making process when it comes to the adoption of e-commerce. The study results show that while barriers to e-commerce loaded onto two factors ('Unsuitable' and 'Too Difficult') in Sweden and Australia, a third factor ('Investment and Security') was clearly present in the US study. Thus where both the Swedish and Australian SMEs considered security to be a technical problem and cost to be an internal problem, the US respondents saw these two barriers as being aligned and an entirely different class of barrier to deal with.

As already indicated, there have been a number of criticisms levelled at government developed methodologies aimed at assisting SMEs to adopt e-commerce (see Martin & Matlay, 2001; MacGregor, 2004; MacGregor & Vrazalic, 2004). Foremost in these criticisms has been that most governments, and most methodologies developed by governments, view the SME sector as largely homogeneous. This research shows that in regard to regional SMEs, this is not the case. While three locations were deliberately chosen for their apparent similarity, not only was the uptake of e-commerce different, but the groupings of reasons for that lack of uptake differed as well.

Finally, although the relationship between the e-commerce barriers and SME characteristics was not empirically examined in this study, the barrier groupings are clearly linked to the underlying features of a typical SME. SMEs lack the knowledge and expertise of their larger counterparts and subsequently find e-commerce too difficult. SMEs have concerns about the security of e-commerce for the same reason. Furthemore, SMEs often have a short-term planning perspective and a preoccupation with day-to-day operations prevents them developing long-term strategies for business expansion, including the use of e-commerce which they deem to be unsuitable. Finally, the risk of failure in SMEs is higher than in larger organisations which implies a higher degree of caution when it comes to making investment decisions. Clearly, further research is required to investigate the relationship between e-commerce barriers and SME characteristics.

Limitations

It should be noted that the study presented here has several limitations. The data for the study was collected from various industry sectors so it is not possible to make sector specific conclusions. Also, the choice of variables selected for the study is somewhat problematic because of the complex nature of adoption barriers which change over time. Furthermore, according to Sohal and Ng (1998), the views expressed in the surveys are of a single individual from the responding organisation, and only those interested in the study are likely to complete and return the survey. Finally, this is a quantitative study, and further qualitative research is required to gain a better understanding of the key issues.

Conclusion

The main aim of this paper was to determine whether barriers to e-commerce adoption were standard and thus perceived in the same way by SME owner/managers in different, but inherently similar locations. A study of SMEs in regional Sweden, Australia and US was undertaken. The results showed that for Sweden and Australia barriers could be grouped under two factors, 'Unsuitable' and 'Too Difficult'. For the US a third barrier, termed 'Investment and Security' was required to fully factor the barriers. Despite the similarities between the three countries in terms of their economic development, SMEs have slightly different concerns in relation to e-commerce adoption barriers.

The implications of the study are significant for government organisations engaged in promoting e-commerce adoption, especially in regional

SMEs. This research suggests that SME variations exist depending on the location of the small business. This would suggest that any strategies developed to promote e-commerce in SMEs located in different areas should address barriers differently. Further research needs to take place, both to address the reasons behind the differences and possible solutions to alleviate the concerns of SMEs.

References

Australian Bureau of Statistics (2001) www.abs.gov.au (10.12.03)

Barry H, Milner B (2002) SMEs and Electronic Commerce: A Departure from the Traditional Prioritisation of Training? Journal of European Industrial Training, vol 25, no 7, pp 316-326

Barry J, Berg E, Chandler J (2003) Managing Intellectual Labour in Sweden and England. Cross Cultural Management, vol 10, no 3, pp 3-22

Cochran AB (1981) Small Business Mortality Rates: A review of the Literature. Journal of Small Business Management, vol 19, no 4, pp 50-59

de Heer W (1999) International Response Trends: Results of an International Survey. Journal of Official Statistics, vol 15, no 2, pp 129-142

DeLone WH (1988) Determinants for Success for Computer Usage in Small Business. MIS Quarterly

Europa (2003) SME Definition. europa.eu.int/comm/enterprise/enterprise_policy/sme_definition (15.12.03)

Frazer L, Lawley M (2000) Questionnaire Design and Administration. Wiley

Gibb A (1993) Small Business Development in Central and Eastern Europe – Opportunity for a Rethink. Journal of Business Venturing, vol 8, pp 461-486

Hadjimonolis A (1999) Barriers to Innovation for SMEs in a Small Less Developed Country (Cyprus). Technovation, vol 19, no 9, pp 561-570

Johansson U (2003) Regional Development in Sweden: October 2003. Svenska Kommunförbundet. (14.12.03) www.lf.svekom.se/tru/RSO/Regional_development_in_Sweden.pdf

Kalakota R, Whinston A (1997) Electronic Commerce: A Manager's Guide. Addison-Wesley

Keniry J, Blums A, Notter E, Radford E, Thomson S (2003) Regional Business – A Plan for Action. Department of Transport and Regional Services. www.rbda.gov.au/ action_plan (13.12.03)

Larsson E, Hedelin L, Gärling T (2003) Influence of Expert Advice on Expansion Goals of Small Businesses in Rural Sweden. Journal of Small Business Management, vol 41, no 2, pp 205-212

Lawrence KL (1997) Factors Inhibiting the Utilisation of Electronic Commerce Facilities in Tasmanian Small- to Medium- Sized Enterprises. Proc of the 8th Australasian Conference on Information Systems

MacGregor RC (2004) Factors Associated with Formal Networking in Regional Small Business: Some Findings from a Study of Swedish SMEs. Journal of Small Business and Enterprise Development, vol 11, no 1, pp 60-74

MacGregor RC, Vrazalic L (2004) The Effects of Strategic Alliance Membership on the Disadvantages of Electronic Commerce Adoption: A Comparative Study of Swedish and Australian Small Businesses. Journal of Global Information Management, vol 13, no 3, pp 1-19

MacGregor RC, Vrazalic L, Bunker DJ, Carlsson S, Magnusson M (2004) Comparison of Factors Pertaining to the Adoption and Non-Adoption of Electronic Commerce in Formally Networked and Non-Networked Regional SMEs: A Study of Swedish Small Businesses. In: Corbitt BJ, Al-Qirim NAY (eds) E-Business, E-Government & Small and Medium-Sized Enterprises: Opportunities and Challenges. Idea Publishing Group

Martin LM, Matlay H (2001) Blanket Approaches to Promoting ICT in Small Firms: Some Lessons from the DTI Ladder Adoption Model in the UK. Internet Research, vol 11, no 5, pp 399-410

Meredith GG (1994) Small Business Management in Australia. McGraw Hill

National Research Council (2000) Surviving Supply Chain Integration: Strategies for Small Manufacturers. http://books.nap.edu/books/0309068789 (02.06.03)

Poon S, Swatman PMC (1999) An Exploratory Study of Small Business Internet Commerce Issues. Information & Management, no 35, pp 9-18

Quayle M (2002) E-commerce: the Challenge for UK SMEs in the Twenty-First Century. International Journal of Operations and Production Management, vol 22, no 10, pp 1148-1161

Raymond L (2001) Determinants of Web Site Implementation in Small Business. Internet Research: Electronic Network Applications and Policy, vol 11, vol 5, pp 411-422

Riquelme H (2002) Commercial Internet Adoption in China: Comparing the Experience of Small, Medium and Large Businesses. Internet Research: Electronic Networking Applications and Policy, vol 12, no 3, pp 276-286

Sohal AS, Ng L (1998) The Role And Impact Of Information Technology In Australian Business. Journal of Information Technology, vol 13, no 3, pp 201-217

Tuunainen VK (1998) Opportunities for Effective Integration of EDI for Small Businesses in the Automotive Industry. Information & Management, vol 36, no 6, pp 361-375

Van Akkeren J, Cavaye ALM (1999) Factors Affecting Entry-Level Internet Technology Adoption by Small Business in Australia: An Empirical Study. Proc of the 10th Australasian Conference on Information Systems

Walczuch R, Van Braven G, Lundgren H (2000) Internet Adoption Barriers for Small Firms in the Netherlands. European Management Journal, vol 18, no 5, pp 561-572

Welsh JA, White JF (1981) A Small Business is not a Little Big Business. Harvard Business Review, vol 59, no 4, pp 46-58

Wynarczyk P, Watson R, Storey DJ, Short H, Keasey K (1993) The Managerial Labour Market in Small and Medium Sized Enterprises. Routledge

The Role of Change Agents in Technology Adoption Process

Regina Gyampoh-Vidogah and Robert Moreton

School of Computing and Information Technology, University of Wolverhampton, United Kingdom. (r.gyampoh-vidogah, r.moreton)@wlv.ac.uk

Introduction

Although the total or partial failure of Information Technology (IT) projects are well documented such failures are not entirely technical in nature
(Donohue et al, 2001). Project failures are often caused by lack of attention
to social factors. Oram and Headon (2002) identified ethical issues whilst
Glass (1999) and Procaccino *et al* (2002) point to human factors, which in
essence are the norms and culture of the implementation environment. On
the influence of culture on project success, Gardiner (2003) noted that, the
cultural problems are much bigger than the technical ones, adding: *"The
biggest hurdle is making people realise that information needs to be
shared. It is only with this ethos of sharing information that take-up of
technologies will be hastened."* Consequently, research and debate about
IT implementation is likely to continue until the development process is
under better control (Nolan 1999). This state of constant evaluation is crucial because aborted IT projects are still common place. According to
Glass, (1998), 31% of all corporate technology development projects resulted in cancellation. Although in broad terms, there seems to be ample
evidence of the influence of non-technical factors on project failure the
dynamics of how this happens is not widely discussed. There are some
pointers to the dynamics of the process in literature. The most common
reasons cited by analysts are: (i) high profile failures of costly system failures, technology hype from vendors keen to sell new technology and complexity of proposed systems (Todd, 2000; Warchus, 2001; Gyampoh-
Vidogah, 2002; Gardiner, 2003).

Impact of Costly System Failures

The impact of costly failures on technology take-up is illustrated by
Anderson's (2003) account of a Hospital Episode System (HES). The HES

is a central government database used for planning purposes which records the nature and cost of every episode of hospital care, whether inpatient or outpatient, in the NHS. At the time the HES was under development, health professionals raised concerns about the privacy of patient data. Even though senior managers and politicians gave assurances, the initial system failed to meet their concerns. However, the subsequent compromises made in order to make the system acceptable, led to data outputs that were widely regarded as inaccurate and misleading. It was further stated that, there are many other central systems under development, which pose similar problems that spurred the medical profession into open revolt during 1995 and 1996. This included a medical boycott of a data network that the NHS wanted to introduce for centralised data collection of personal health information for management and other purposes. This state of affairs is by no means limited to the public sector. The problems involving the life insurers Prudential and retailers the Co-op are examples of private sector failures. The net effect is to deter the implementation of new systems and or result in the significant scaling down of IT projects in general Anderson (ibid).

Hyped Up Technology

The issues of IT specialists 'talking up' the latest technology is an important non-technical factor. The result of hype is that unrealistic expectation of technology can hinder adoption and in some cases implementation failure. The recent assessment by Gyampoh-Vidogah, (2002) of the impact of extensible mark-up Language (XML) on Internet based systems is revealing. According to Gardiner (ibid) while all the major players now adopt the XML standard, it is yet to make a major impact upon the web. Initially XML was at the vanguard – a flag-waving technology, a must have for the big players. Even Microsoft went some way to making its support real through its .NET strategy based on XML protocols. But real adoption continues to be slow. So the question is, why are companies not already using XML-based software? The problem turns out to be that XML was never just a replacement for HTML. Hype had obscured the real benefits of XML because people made unsubstantiated claims.

Enterprise Resource Planning (ERP) software is another example. Todd (2000) reported in a survey that, two thirds of IT managers regard ERP as 'hype' and even higher proportion of other managers share their lack of expectation. ERP was widely regarded by respondents as an expensive, slow to install, risky strategy and best left to large companies that demand complex, integrated world-wide systems (Howard 2003). Also on the list of 'hyped up' technology that has been the subject of much criticism are Customer Relationship Management (CRM) software and web services. Another significant effect of IT hype is that, it obscures the need for the evolution of heterogeneous IT infrastructure of tools, technologies and business products with the aim of gaining competitive edge. The enormous growth of mergers and acquisitions whilst aspiring to provide a broader business base has also introduced further diversity and consequent complexity, in terms of integration and IT service provision.

Complexity of Proposed Systems

It has been suggested that in many IT projects, where the complexity of the implementation environments are ignored, the resulting system becomes unusable and unreliable (Simons, 2003). Further, Anderson (ibid) suggested that, because United Kingdom civil service tackles projects in a completely different way from private sector companies, the likelihood of failure of complex systems is higher. In his view in all cases of public sector projects that failed, considerations of social, economic, political and ethical environments were not taken into account when designing the systems because such issues are rarely seen to be of importance if at all in the system development process. Although techniques exist, satisfactory solutions have not been offered to address such issues (McCowan and Mohamed, 2003).

The cumulative effect of failure to address these issues is the general resistance to change scepticism of new technology and hence lack of innovation in technology adoption.

Research Approach and Background

The study involved a review of literature from a number of related studies. The review attempts to answer how change agents can influence IT adoption.

A change agent can be defined as a full time organisational development professional, a leader of an organisation, a manager or director charged with the responsibility of bringing about a change in his/her area. Anyone involved in helping a team achieve something new becomes an agent of change (Tearle, 2001; Covington, 2003).

These agents as champions of IT adoption need to be able to develop and integrate multiple strategic capabilities, yet at the same time, build and manage the complicated yet subtle development process and deliver co-ordinated action (Barlett and Ghosal, 1989). Consequently the change agent like most leaders require core knowledge, skills and abilities (Black and Gregersen, 1999). The research reported in this paper is part of an on-going research into the management qualities of change agents required for successful technology adoption process. This paper explores the key competencies required for fulfilling the role of a change agent based on preliminary research of leadership theory.

The Role of the Change Agent

Research on management styles such as those reported by Burns (1978) and House (1976) suggests that effective leaders are transformational. Burns (ibid) defines transformational leadership as a process where leaders and their subordinates raise one another to higher levels of motivation, morality leading to successful decision making. Transformational leaders act as strong role models, communicate high expectations and inspire through a shared vision and stimulate creativity (Howell and Avolio, 1993). Consequently, leadership theory suggested that change agents, to be transformational in their approach need to undertake a variety of roles. Based on our preliminary study, these roles are to act as educators, leaders, motivators, IT/IS experts and project managers.

The Change Agent as an Educator

The importance of education is highlighted by a recent Autodesk survey (Autodesk, 2003) of users and prospective customers which, found that, good firms scored 'organisation' as the most important success factor followed by quality, production and investment. The survey indicated that, computer aided design (CAD) with the least IT adoption saw 'culture' as the biggest drawback, followed by investment and organisation. Reinert, (1998) and Yukl, (2002) supports this view stating that, one of the key role of the change agent is to educate the workforce to initiate a serious discussion how adopting of new technology can increase productivity and efficiency. The change agent's goal in this educational drive is to develop the critical analytical, communication and problem solving skills required to succeed in a fast changing, technology driven workplace. This should focus mainly in the area of technology analysis, specification and evaluation for business managers. Failure in this task results in a reluctance to adopt innovative approaches in organisations regarding IT, which according to Vines and Egbu (2003), and Meek (1988) manifests as: (i) lack of expertise, experience and confidence (ii) un-considered cultural principles to identify issues directly affiliated to system development. Unfortunately, training in organisation on IT effectively may not be a high priority for most companies. Consequently, most organisations without a change agent do not have the trained workforce required to embrace IT and thus take advantage of 'cutting edge' technologies.

The Change Agent as a Leader

Change will happen if management and change agents involve everyone (Daft, 1999). Management and change agents should be an enabler and able to communicate clearly to all employees what IT means to the organisation (Black and Gregersen, 1999). Part of the change agent's role is to champion such programmes and steer the change strategically and facilitate implementation (Adler, 1997). However in order to be effective, a prerequisite for the change agent is the ability to demonstrate professionalism and leadership skills in computing information systems and IT and the ability to transfer such knowledge into a multidisciplinary capacity as suggested by (Wright, 1996) is the definition of effective leadership.

As such, the Change Agent should also be able to explain the benefits of IT adoption to the workforce and be the significant part of the process of changing the cultural environment of the organisation to IT adoption. The extent of the influence of culture in every organisation should be understood by the change agents in order to influence technology adoption. This is because a leader should be aware of the context within which implementation is being considered. This is according to leadership theory one of the key skills and abilities identified as core requirement in multifaceted or global interconnected environment (Black and Gregersen, ibid).

The Change Agent as a Motivator

The catalyst for the adoption of IT is the demonstration of success stories and best practice in other sectors to the organisation in order to prove the value of IT projects. The key is to persuade the employees to embrace the new technology. The change agent should explain to management the need to "rethink innovation" as a movement for radical change in organisations and institutions in the context of IT systems for the future (Gick and

Holyoak, 1987). As such the change agent should take every opportunity to challenge employees thinking. Meaningful examples should be given both from within and external to the organisation, in a challenging yet convincing way (Daft, ibid, Howell and Avolio ibid). In other to do this, the change agent should understand the latest technologies. For example, rapid application development tools, modelling of information processes and the effect on change to get the stamina in changing the culture of all employees' perception of IT adoption.

The Change Agent as an IS/IT Expert

Given that most enterprise IT implementations are seen at initiation as critical to business goals it is imperative that change agents are people of considerable knowledge. This is because the work of a number of re-searchers, Ford and Krainger (1995) suggested clearly that experts are more likely to understand task relevant information, more likely to cease solutions that are not likely to work. Experts are also more aware of the degree of difficulty of new problems.

Change agents as a consequence need to define and understand their or-ganisations IT environment or architecture in order to be able to propose systems that are realistic and attainable with reasonable resources and time frames. This is necessary because the primary purpose of enterprise sys-tems architecture is to provide a coherent platform for business (Bye, 2002). In most instances proposed systems have to provide a framework for implementing applications as well as connections to internal and exter-nal systems.

Obviously, given a clean sheet, most organisations would have some idea of the kind of IT environment that best suits their purpose. The reality is that, where new developments are being considered, there exists a het-erogeneous IT environment containing diverse hardware platforms and several operating systems. These systems host applications of different types and ages, which may be critical to business, and contain the accumu-lated wisdom of many years. These are not easily rewritten, as the statistics of project failure show. Existing systems have to be accommodated, and adapted or wrapped, to interface with new applications. Consequently, when change agents come to consider new applications, three important is-sues have to be understood in the analysis and evaluation of new technol-ogy. These pertain to levels of the nature and capacity of existing IT infra-structure, then implementation technologies available to realize the new system and lastly the interfaces required with existing systems. As figure 1 illustrates, target systems are simply the proposed information system areas to be implemented using a combination of one or more computing technologies. The computing technologies based on appropriated interfaces rely on existing information and software technology infrastructure.

When the business case is established within the context of existing infrastructure how deployment of the new system integrates with existing systems needs consideration. As Figure 1 illustrates, the change agent should establish alternative implementation technologies or models. This is to build a picture of the combination of software products that can fit the existing architecture. For example, where the proposed application involves access via the Internet, two competing technologies are available, J2EE implementations and Microsoft COM+ with .NET. This is where attitude can affect rational choice hence the role of the change agent is critical. Without a clear appreciation of the fundamentals of the technologies, these choices could tend to be based on fashion and/or trends, often based on exaggerated claims for particular technologies or products.

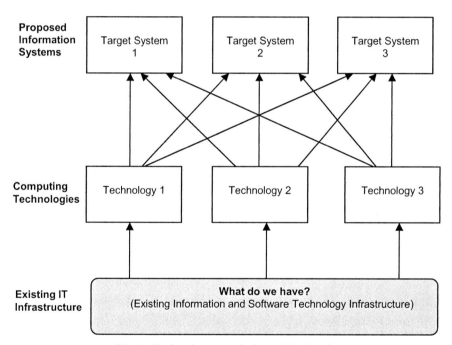

Fig. 1. Technology Analysis and Evaluation

For instance if the development team are Microsoft developers, there is no point in defining an advanced Java-based application. Similarly, if the

company IT infrastructure is of a particular design, it is important that prospective developers have experience of the technologies needed. This
avoids business critical project being used as a training ground for developers in new technology. In this respect the knowledge of the change agent
can make all the difference between success and total failure.

The Change Agent as a Project Director or Manager

In order to champion a project, the change agent should not try to follow
the precise technical intricacies of the project. Rather change agents should
focus on establishing why the project needs to be implemented, the exact
benefits in terms of workflow and process control and its predicted impact
on the bottom line (Hodgson, 2002). Obtaining definitive answers to these
questions will provide business managers with information they need to
view the project as a whole without getting into the technicalities. This
means that business managers aided by change agents can identify project
deliverables in a way that is clear and concise. The consequence is that to
start with, a technology specific project need to be based on a solid business case rather than being driven by emerging technology, or by a need to
keep up with trends. As a result developers will have to accept they do not
instinctively know what end users of the systems require. An issue here for
change agents is the question of whether the proposed system is achievable
using existing software technology. In order to arrive at a decision the
change agent should be able to produce a full application feature list.
Against this feature list, change agents can then ask developers or vendors
as the case may be to indicate how or whether their technology can support
the feature. For example, if the decision is to implement and host an e-
transaction site to provide sales and order processing using the Internet,
then a web or e-transaction server is required. As an illustrative purposes at
the moment, four candidate servers are available. These are NetWare 5.0,
Windows NT 4.0 server, Windows 2000 server and Windows 2003 server.
The feature list could be similar to that shown in Table 1 completed with
the aid of information from computer specialists (Table 1). For an e-
commerce site, three main features are paramount. First how web services
are to be provided, secondly how data will be made available to the end
user, language support for developers, and lastly the level of messaging
that will be provided for the transaction services.

Table 1. Application Feature List and Technology Options

Features/technology	Netware 5.0	Windows NT 4.0 Server	Windows 2000 server	Windows 2003 server
Web Services				
Server Side scripting	■	■	■	■
Java script Server scripting Support	■	■	■	■
Java Server Support	■			
Script debugger		■	■	■
XML Integration		■	■	■
Distributed data Access				
JDBC support	■			
ODBC support	■	■	■	■
Language Support				
Java language support	■	■	■	■
Java beans support	■			
Message Services				
Message queuing implementation available		■	■	■
E-mail services integration		■	■	■
Security Integration		■	■	■

By defining the role of technology in the context of the business requirements, change agents prevents organisations from adopting ad-hoc requirement features management which leads to ineffective software architecture and software complexity (Booch 1998).

Conclusion and Further Work

The lack of adoption to new IT as part of businesses drive to attain greater efficiency and profitability is the subject of many debates. Research suggests that this is partly due to the effect of issues such as failures of costly IT projects, vendors keen to sell new technology, fragmentation and complexity of proposed systems. The consequences are resistance to change, scepticism towards new technology and hence lack of innovation in technology adoption. This paper examined ways in which these issues can be overcome and the role of change agents to accelerate IT adoption in organisations' IS projects. Our conclusion is that the role of change agent is critical to the successful adoption of IT but the role of change agents are not fully appreciated and certainly not well defined. Therefore, further research work requires exploration including an empirical study in organisations using a combination of quantitative and qualitative research that will address social and cultural challenges relating to technology adoption. The research should focus on both technical and non-technical factors, which play an important role in IT and IS projects. The main focus will be based on UK and European companies and will look to incorporate appropriated cultural contexts. Taking these issues seriously is important because those companies that actively employ change agents to develop their information technology and communications now will be better positioned to 'win' by spotting or creating business opportunities. They will have awakened their employees to the potential of IT adoption, reinforced the importance of customer focus and built a platform for electronic systems.

References

Adler NJ (1997) Global Leadership: Women Leaders. Management International Review, vol 37 (1 Special issue), pp 171-196

Anderson RJ (2003) Information Technology in Medical Practice: Safety and Privacy Lessons from the United Kingdom.
www.cl.cam.ac.uk/users/rja14/policy11.html

Autodesk (2003) Manufacturing Control in Real Time. Organisation is Key to Succcess. Manufacturing Computer Solutions. The definitive IT guide for UK Manufacturers. February, 2003, p. 6

Bartlett CA, Ghosal S (1989) Managing Across Borders: The Transnational Solution. Harvard Business School Press Boston

Black JS, Gregersen HB (1999) The Right Way to Manage Expatriates. Harvard Business Review, vol 77, no 2, pp 52-63

Booch G (1998) The Unified Modelling Language User guide. Journal of database Management, vol 10, no 4, pp 51-52

Burns JM (1978) Leadership. Harper and Row New York

Bye P (2002) Avoiding Dogma. Conspectus
http//www.conspectus.com/2002 July/index.htm

Covington (2003) Rethinking Special Education and Behavior Disorders Symposium Hyatt Regency Crown Center Kansas City, Missouri February 20-22, 2003

Daft RL (1999) Leadership Theory and Practice. Dryden Press Harcourt Brace Publishers Orlando

Donohue A, Rochford C, Kinsellar J, Bryan (2001) The Cultural Implications on Management Accounting and Control Systems in Global firms.
http://www.realtimeclub.org.uk/publications/e-commerce/IT

Ford JK, Kraiger K (1995) The Application of Cognitive Constructs and Principles to the Instructional Systems Model of Training: Implications for Needs

Assessment, Design and Transfer. In: Cooper CL, Robertson IT (eds) International Review of Industrial and Organisational Psychology, vol 10, p 6. John Wiley & Sons West Sussex

Gardiner J (2003) Cultural Problems Holding Back a Killer Technology? CNET Network inc.

Gick ML, Holyoak KJ (1987) The Cognitive Basis of Knowledge Transfer. In: Cormier SM, Hagman JD (eds) Transfer of Learning. Academic Press San Diego

Glass RL (1998) Software Runaways. Prentice Hall New Jessey

Glass RL (1999) Evolving a New Theory of Project Success. Communications of ACM, vol 42, no 11, p 17

Graham D (2002) Why Technology Breeds Contempt. Conspectus, The IT Report for Directors and Decision Makers. E-Commerce Software, pp 14-15

Gyampoh-Vidogah R (2002) Improving Project Administration in the Construction Industry using EDMS: An integrated IS/IT solution. PhD Thesis, University of Wolverhampton UK

Hodgson OI (2002) Keeping your Head Above Water. Conspectus: The IT Report for Directors and Decision Makers. E-Commerce Software, May 2002, pp 30-31

House RJ (1976) A 1976 Theory of Charismatic Leadership. In: Hunt JG, Larson LI (eds) Leadership: Cutting Edge. South Illinois University Press Carbondale

Howard J (2003) Considering a New ERP System? Top Ten System Contract Mistakes? Manufacturing Computer Solutions. The Definitive IT Guide for UK Manufacturers. May 2003, pp 12-17

Howell JM, Avolio BJ (1993) Transformational Leadership, Transactional Leadership, Locus of Control, and Support Innovation: Key Predictors of Consolidated-Business-Unit Performance. American Psychology Association, vol 78, no 6, pp 891-902

Mangione C (2003) Software Project Failure: The Reasons, the Cost, CIO Information Network. USA viewed, August 2004

McCowan A, Mohamed S (2003) A Comparison of Risk Analysis Techniques in Construction Project Management. Proceedings of 2nd International Conference on Innovation in Architecture, Engineering and Construction. Loughborough University UK

Meek VL (1988) Organisational Culture: Origins and Weaknesses. Organisation Studies, vol 9, no 4, pp 453-73

Nolan P (1999) Instructor's Manual and Test Bank for Human Societies. 8th Ed. McGraw-Hill New York

Oram D, Headon M (2002) Conference Paper: Avoiding Information Systems Failure: Culturally Determined Ethical Approaches and their Practical Application in the New Economy. International Scientific Conference, 18-19 April 2002, Kaunas Lithuania

Procaccino JD, Verner JM, Overmyer SP, Darter ME (2002) Case Study: Factors for Early Prediction of Software Development Success. Journal of Information and Software Technology, vol 44, no 1, pp 53-62

Reinert JR (1998) Testimony on Educating our Workforce with Technology Skills Needed to Compete in the 21st Century. Report on Promoting Electrotechnology Careers and Public Policy Institute of Electrical and Electronics Engineers United States of America.

Simons M (2003) IT Strikes at Home Office. Stress Caused by Unworkable Computer System Sparks Staff Walkout. Computer Weekly, May 2003, p 1

Tearle R (2004) The Role of Change Master. From Change Agent to 'Change Master'n (Assessed 2004)
http://www. change designs. co.za/The_role_of_a_change%20master.htm

Thomas D (2004) Report Exposes Failure of IT Project Management. Computer Weekly, April 2004, p 8

Todd R (2000) Manufacturing in the Millennium. MAX International. White Paper – Axis Beta, Woodlands Almondsbury Bristol

Vines M, Egbu C (2003) Knowledge Management and e-Business Initiatives – Deriving an Appropriate Synergy for the Benefit of the Construction Industry. Proc of 2nd International Conference on Innovation in Architecture, Engineering and Construction. Loughborough University UK

Wachus J (2001) E-Construction: Technology to Rescue? The Growth of E-Construction Services. Business to Business collaboration.
www.4Project.com.

Wright P (1996) Management Leadership. Routledge London

Yukl G (2002) Leadership in Organisations. Printice Hall New Jessey

Zubialde JP (2001) MD Leading Change Versus Managing Care: The Role of Change Agent. Family Medicine Essays and Commentary, vol 33, no 2

Conceptual Model of Multidimensional Marketing Information System

Dalia Kriksciuniene[1] and Ruta Urbanskiene[2]

[1] Department of Informatics, Vilnius University, Lithuania.
dalia.kriksciuniene@vukhf.lt
[2] Department of Strategic Management, Kaunas University of Technology,
Lithuania. Ruta.Urbanskiene@ktu.lt

Introduction

This article is aimed to analyse, why the information systems at the enterprise not always satisfy the expectations of marketing management specialists. The computerized systems more and more successfully serve information needs of those areas of enterprise management, where they can create the information equivalent of real management processes. Yet their inability to effectively fulfill marketing needs indicate the gaps not only in ability to structure marketing processes, but in the conceptual development of marketing information systems (MkIS) as well.

Marketing managers need to be empowered by the system, able to apply information selection criteria at various dimensions of human reasoning, including objective and subjective judgments, theoretical and experience-based assumptions. The core capabilities of organization and the influences of market arc analysed at business logics dimension, the problems of finding reliable and timely information sources are solved at information dimension, the abilities to accomplish organizational goals are evaluated at strategic goals dimension.

This point of view is analyzed in the article, aimed to substantiate concept of MkIS creation, which could embody the multidimensional origin of information needs of marketing manager and to create information equivalent of marketing management process of the enterprise.

Classification scheme of existing MkIS models, related to synergy of the identified influence factors, is presented for substantiating limited possibility to adapt MkIS to multidimensional origin of information needs. Multidimensional MkIS concept is formulated and its ability to present solutions to the indicated drawbacks of current systems is revealed.

The structural element, named multidimensional marketing relationship, is introduced for creating the multidimensional structure of MkIS model. The functioning principle of multidimensional MkIS, based on decomposing marketing activities and management processes to MMR groups were suggested and structured by using UML notation. The results, summarizing empirical research, conducted at 23 enterprises are provided.

Keywords: Marketing information system, MkIS, multidimensional system, multidimensional MkIS model

Development Analysis of Marketing Information Systems

MkIS are generally defined as systems, designed to generate, store and distribute appropriate information to marketing decision-maker (Cox and Good, 1967; Kotler, 1985; McCarthy, 1985; O'Connor, 1999; McLeod and Schell, 2001). These MkIS definitions do not advise any MkIS structure, so the scientific literature offers the whole variety of specialized MkIS models with different functional abilities in sales, promotion, pricing, direct marketing, managing customer relationships, marketing in the internet, and other activities of marketing area (Talvinen, 1995; Dyche, 2001; Turban et al, 2002).

MkIS serves to marketing manager as a set of information processing tools, defined and selected by subjective judgment of the manager and used to meet his requirements for information in different steps of marketing decision-making, planning, control processes. High level of subjectivity create main difficulties to usage of MkIS, such as unpredictable information needs, and discontinuous information supply to MkIS, which serve as the criteria for evaluating MkIS models. The adaptation to changing needs problem is also preventing from wider usage of MkIS, as revealed by surveys at various types of organizations (Bessen, 1993; Amaravadi et al 1995; Li et al, 2000). The main premises, which create conditions for different functional structure of MkIS, are indicated in this article by comparative analysis of theoretical MkIS models.

The main factors influencing MkIS creation were identified. These factors are present in each MkIS and are expressed in different strength, marked as axes in Fig. 1:

- Specialization means that MkIS is aimed to fulfillment and analysis of the operations of specific business. MkIS in scientific literature range from highly specialized to cross-industry marketing-related systems.

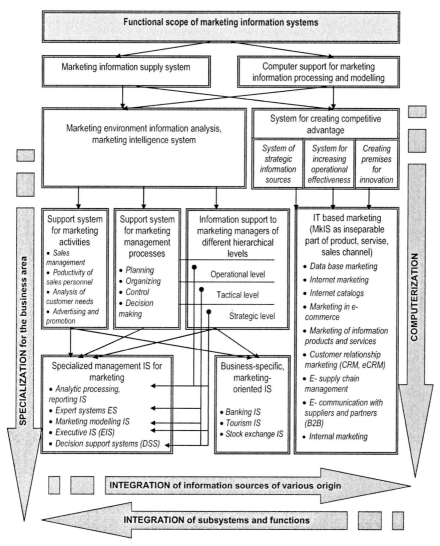

Fig. 1. Functional scope of marketing information systems

- Integration of information sources of various origins point to the important feature of MkIS, that it uses input information mainly created outside marketing department, including intentionally collected research information or structured tacit knowledge of marketing manager.
- The axis of integration of MkIS subsystems and functions indicates MkIS scope, which can vary from the specialized tools, serving separate

functions of marketing activities, to the integrated view of marketing management activities.

- Computerization of MkIS is the strong influence factor of MkIS. In most enterprises the computerization tools of various complexity coexist simultaneously. Surveys (Morris and Shiang, 1998; Li et al., 2000) reveal that the computer- based systems in marketing vary from general IT tools such as spreadsheets, graphic packages, word processing or electronic mail, to the advanced IT: data warehousing, OLAP, data mining, which enable to search for patterns in data, and handle queries.

The analysed MkIS can be applied for one or two levels of analysis (usually information and control levels) and only for partial presentation of marketing situation and dynamics. The most advanced systems from the multidimensional point of view are the CRM systems, created for enterprise relationships, directed to customers. They present possibility to map relationships, connected with related information created in various functional modules of integrated system (MS Axapta, Microstrategy, SAP). The software for balanced scorecard is created in several integrated systems (Axapta, SAP), which allows to calculate and relate scores for control. These parts exist separately and cannot express the marketing processes, situation and development in enterprise, but present possibility for their conceptual integration in a multidimensional MkIS.

Analysis of MkIS structure showed that most prevalent approach for its creation is the marketing mix theory (4P), yet marketing itself is developed by employing numerous modern theories. The differences of "4P" and **relationship marketing theory** (RM) suggest necessary changes in MkIS model. The core idea in 4P approach states that marketing decision-making areas are defined first, and the RM deal with relationships processes that have to be established, maintained and further enhanced, or terminated (Grönroos, 1996, Gummesson, 1996). In this case, MkIS model could be based not on instant marketing-related activities, but on continuous relationship processes. The integrated view to the processes of marketing management requires decision support ability to evaluate each activity according to the enterprise goals. The **balanced scorecard theory** (Kaplan and Norton 1996-2002), suggested including the qualitative and quantitative, future and past measures, which well conform to the nature of marketing activities. Importance of information sources of personal and enterprise knowledge and their intensive need for marketing requires applying theoretical achievements of **knowledge management** for MkIS. The requirement of technological support for processing "close-loop" decisions based on customer information (McKenna, 2003) increases need to register and use the experience information, owned by the managers. The new theoretical developments of relationship marketing, knowledge management, balanced scorecard have major influence for MkIS creation principles. Their integrated use enables the information processing in three levels- logical, informational and goals- and can serve as basis for multidimensional MkIS structure.

The Concept of Multidimensional MkIS and Model Formation

The premises for creating new framework of MkIS are based on research of MkIS models and influences of their theoretical development.

Multidimensional MkIS is defined as a system, created for providing information for marketing management processes (decision support, planning, control, organizing marketing activities), where the input information, describing the marketing-related phenomena, is transformed into multidimensional space, and analysed along the following dimensions: marketing relationships, knowledge and balanced scorecard.

The dimensions of MkIS conform to the levels of judgment, applied by marketing managers to the information analysis. The business logics level of information analysis is implemented at marketing relationships dimension. It is based on the assumption that the marketing-related phenomena of the business environment have to be analysed for making marketing decisions. The theoretical background is the relationship marketing.

The information level of analysis is implemented at the knowledge dimension of MkIS. It is formed by attaching sources of information related by context to the marketing relationships. The theoretical background for the knowledge dimension is knowledge management, that includes structuring and storage of the organizational memory, experience information, which enhance the intellectual capital of the enterprise.

The balanced scorecard dimension implements the goals level, created for feedback and control of the MkIS. It is based on the balanced scorecard theory, introduced and revealed by Kaplan and Norton (1996). This dimension uses the knowledge layer information, including the intellectual capital, to evaluate marketing relationships developed by the organization.

New conceptual element of MkIS structure is introduced by defining multidimensional marketing relationship (MMR). It is formed and parameterized at the three dimensions of MkIS. The MMR life cycle operations are: MMR is created in case the interaction among organization and market phenomena (or object) is identified; MMR development is registered in MkIS by indicating the relationship parameters, information sources and balanced scores; MMR is marked as disconnected from MkIS, if the relationship between organization and market object is stopped. The understanding of marketing information system as the entirety of relationships, which can be formed and adapted for each enterprise by set of MMR elements, is used for introduction of the vertical MkIS structure instead of traditional horizontal MkIS structure, combined of operational modules of various functionality. The functioning of MkIS is based on the decomposing principle, where all the marketing processes and activities are represented as groups of related MMR (Fig. 2).

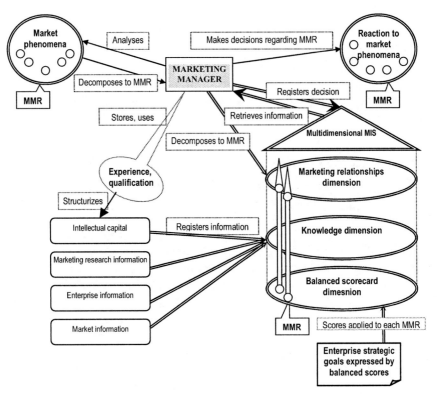

Fig. 2. Decision-making process in multidimensional MkIS

The compounds of the system are illustrated in UML diagram (Fig. 3).

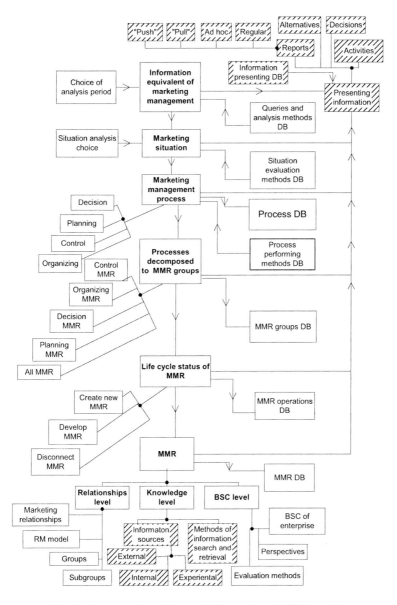

Fig. 3. Compounds of the multidimensional MkIS model

Decision-making process, planning or control starts with analysis of market phenomena, where the manager selects the phenomena-related marketing relationships, thus decomposing them to MMR.

The obtained group of MMR is supplied with information by means of the knowledge level and then is evaluated by the scores of the balanced scorecard level. It helps to register outcomes of the processes to DB and use for further analysis. The darker blocks mark the compounds which are used in existing MkIS models. The added blocks of core part of the suggested model is creation of three levels of MMR and registering them to DB. The top part of the model presents marketing situation and development, based on evaluation of all MMR and related processes. The outcome of using each MkIS compound is viewed by presenting information in selected format: reports, suggested alternatives, decisions or automated responses of MkIS, as activities.

The consistency of information supply is based on the retread of information sources registered in the knowledge level of enterprise. The multidimensional structure of MkIS can be adapted at each enterprise, as all of them can identify their marketing relationships, organize information flows and compose balanced scorecard, aligned to their strategy. Applying multidimensional MkIS concept for marketing creates the information equivalent of its processes in the information system, which was not possible by using existing MkIS models.

Empirical Research of the MkIS Multidimensional Concept and Model

Two stages of the research were set for testing the theoretical findings of MkIS analysis:

1. Explore the possibilities to apply the concept of multidimensional MkIS.
2. Testing the constructed MkIS model prototype for marketing activities.

The first stage was conducted for applying MkIS multidimensional concept at the 23 selected enterprises. The possibilities of analysing marketing situation, dynamics and meeting the criteria for MkIS creation were researched. For the second stage of the research the illustrative scenario of marketing processes were composed for real case of individualized travel product creation at the tourism agency, and the multidimensional MkIS model prototype was applied for activities of marketing managers.

Research methodology. Case study was selected for the research, as it is the most common qualitative method used in information systems (Orlikowski, 1993). The aim of case study research method selection is focused to presenting detailed description, thus suitable to reveal existing

MkIS drawbacks of enterprises and explore possibilities to apply concept of multidimensional MkIS.

Data collection. The 23 organizations were selected for the empirical research. The selection criteria was heterogeneity of the business area, which was different in all researched cases (tourism, sports goods, tele-communications, etc.), it fell to the following categories at similar proportions: manufacturing (17%), service (30%), sales (13%), combination of two categories (40%). The research took place in March- June, 2001, March – November, 2002 and has been updated in 2004 at the organizations of Kaunas and Vilnius.

Possibilities to apply concept for multidimensional MkIS were explored by using relationship marketing 30R model (Gummesson, 1999), knowledge management model (Sveiby, 1997) and the balanced scorecard (Kaplan, Downing, 2000).

Data analysis. The analysis of exploring the possibilities to apply the concept of multidimensional MkIS was made by analysing marketing management activities of enterprises from the point of dimensions of MkIS. Mapping structure of marketing relationships, creating knowledge and balanced scorecard dimensions was made by assigning research data to the most suitable categories found in the theoretical models, then analysing the interrelationships of dimensions.

All the organizations managed to map their marketing activities according to their influence to marketing relationships (average quantity of selected main relationship groups was 9.4), thus creating the relationships dimension of MkIS structure. Some types of relationships were present at most organizations, such as relationship R1 (according to Gummesson, 1999, it is the classic dyad: the relationship between the supplier and the customer), found at all 23 organizations or R4 (the classic triad: the customer-supplier-competitor relationship), which were important at 18 organizations. For analysis of knowledge dimension, the information sources, used by the enterprises, were assigned to each relationship. At least three information sources were selected for describing each marketing relationship, mostly combining external (22%) and internal sources (69%). Only 9% organizations assigned experience information of marketing manager as a source, as they had practice of registering it using specialized software.

The attempts to form balanced scorecard dimension showed that marketing activities in the researched organizations were hardly related to the strategic goals of the organization. Managers of the organizations managed to assign average number of 26 main scores to marketing relationships, including quantitative (mainly financial) scores (23%) and qualitative scores

(77%). The average number of scores assigned according each perspectives of the balanced scorecard: financial (6.5 scores), user (5.2 scores), internal processes perspective (10.1 scores), learning and growth perspective (3.8 scores).

While processing the illustrative scenario 12 marketing relationships were influenced: 8 of them were already developed in the enterprise and the remaining 4 were created. While using the procedures for MMR creation and development, the need to systematic arrangement of information sources in knowledge level was recognized, as the most valuable information of product features and customers was often obtained outside the system by direct communication and then found fragmented, recorded only by personal initiative of managers. New sources of experience information were registered in the system, which added to the intellectual capital of enterprise and could be used by all responsible persons. The measures of 6 balanced scores were agreed for evaluation of marketing activities. They were taken from the common practice of the agency and were effectively used to performing the scenario. The MkIS model prototype was used for management processes, such as planning, control, decision - making and organizing. After performing these activities, they were registered in the data bases (fig.3), thus using all functions of MkIS model.

Research results. The empirical testing of the possibilities to apply multidimensional MkIS confirmed the viability of the suggested MkIS multidimensional concept, as all the enterprises could adapt the suggested model for reflecting all their marketing activities. Relationship dimension helped to identify all the marketing relationships to which their efforts and attention have to be focussed, keeping the possibility to add and remove relationships without changing MkIS structure. The entirety of marketing relationships served as the prism for obtaining overall view of marketing activities of the firms, their current situation and change over time. The knowledge dimension was formed of information sources, arranged according to the context related to each marketing relationship, but not according to the origin of the information source, as in traditional MkIS. External, internal and experience information was interrelated for describing each marketing relationship. Otherwise, each information source could be processed in different ways and relate to several marketing relationships. The balanced scorecard, formed at each enterprise, helped organizations to add the feedback function to the system and align coordination of all marketing activities. Marketing managers agreed that the balanced scores fully describe the cause-effect impacts of marketing activities for reaching enterprise goals.

The illustrative scenario of the tourism organization was formed by registering marketing activities, related to new individual tourism creation and offering. The activities, included in real marketing scenario, were processed by using functions of multidimensional MkIS model. Marketing situation was expressed by the entirety of MMR, registered in the system. For evaluation of marketing performance, the databases were used to track changes in MMR development and analysing the marketing management processes performed by managers. The empirical research results encourage using the multidimensional MkIS concept for creating a structured multidimensional MkIS model, which could be adapted and parameterised at each organization, thus solving the adaptability criteria for creating MkIS. The interrelationship of MkIS dimensions increases the continuous information flow and decreases uncertainty of information requirements, which meets requirements applied for MkIS models creation.

Conclusions

1. The variety of structure and functions of MkIS conceptual models presented in the scientific literature is caused by synergy of the four factors which influence creation of MkIS models.
2. The new theoretical developments of relationship marketing, knowledge management, balanced scorecard have major influence for MkIS creation principles. Their integrated use enables the information processing in three levels- logical, informational and goals- and can serve as basis for multidimensional MkIS structure.
3. Multidimensional MkIS is defined as a system, created for providing information for marketing management processes, where the input information, describing the marketing-related phenomena, is analysed along the following dimensions: marketing relationships, knowledge and balanced scorecard. In contrast to existing systems, the multidimensional MkIS not only provides information to marketing processes, but provides means to reflect overall marketing situation and dynamics in three levels.
4. The vertical MkIS structure consisting of set of multidimensional elements is introduced, instead of traditional horizontal MkIS structure, which is combined of modules of various functionalities. The vertical element of the MkIS structure is defined as multidimensional marketing relationship (MMR), which is formed and parameterised at the three dimensions of MkIS.
5. The evaluation of the qualitative empirical research results at 23 diverse enterprises confirms that adaptable and parameterised multidimensional

MkIS is created at each enterprise independently of factors, creating uniqueness of MkIS structure of the existing MkIS models.

References

Cox DF, Good RE (1967) How to Build a Marketing Information System. Harvard Business Review, vol 45, no 3, pp 145-154

Dyche J (2001) The CRM Handbook: A Business Guide to Customer Relationship Management. Addison-Wesley Pub Co

Dyche J (2001) The CRM Handbook: A Business Guide to Customer Relationship Management. Addison-Wesley Pub Co

Grönroos C (1996) From Marketing Mix to Relationship Marketing: Towards a Paradigm Shift in Marketing. Management Decision Conference Background Paper. www.mcb.co.uk/services/conferen/feb96/

Gummesson E (1996) Relationship Marketing and Imaginary Organizations: a Synthesis. European Journal of Marketing, vol 30, Issue 2

Kaplan RS, Downing L (2000) Fast Tracking Your Balanced Scorecard. Netconferences Archive. www. bscol.com

Kotler P, Turner R (1985) Marketing Management: Analysis, Planning and Control. 5th ed. Prentice Hall Canada Inc Scarborough Ontario

McCarthy JE, Shapiro SJ, Perreault WD (1989) Basic Marketing. 5th ed. IRWIN Homewood IL Boston MA

McLeod RJr, Shell G (2001) Management Information Systems. 8th ed. Prentice-Hall Inc New Jersey USA

Morris H, Shiang D (1998) Unlocking Better Business Understanding: Hyperion's Analytic Applications. IDC (International Data Corporation)

O'Connor J, Galvin E (2001) Marketing in the Digital Age. Financial Times Harlow

Orlikowski WJ, Baroudi JJ (1991) Studying Information Technology in Organisations: Research Approaches and Assumptions. Information Systems Research, vol 2, no 1

Sveiby KE (1997) The New Wealth: Intangible Assets.

Talvinen JA (1995) Information Systems in Marketing. Identifying Opportunities for New Applications. European Journal of Marketing, vol 29, Issue 1

Turban E, King D, Lee J, Warkentin M, Chung MH (2002) Electronic Commerce. A Managerial Perspective. Pearson Education Upper Saddle River www.knowledgecreators.com.

A Distributed Workspace to Enable Engineering Inter-Company Collaboration: Validation and New Lessons Learnt from SIMNET

Kamel Rouibah and Samia Rouibah

Department of Quantitative Methods & Information Systems, College of Business Administration, Kuwait University, Kuwait.
krouibah@cba.edu.kw, samia_rouibah@hotmail.com

Introduction

Collaborative-complex product development is characterized by enormous quantity of engineering data, variety of complex engineering processes, process uncertainty and disturbances, much iteration due to its iterative nature and multiple levels of data maturity (Baldwin et al. 1995). Product design therefore does require changes. The ability of companies to better manage engineering processes and engineering changes can decrease cost, shorten development time, and produce higher quality products. Engineering changes refer to changes or modifications in form, representation, design, material, dimensions, functions of a product or component after an initial engineering decision has been made (Huang et al. 1999). Past studies have reported that engineering change is a costly and time-consuming problem (Maull et al. 1992, Boznak 1993). Accordingly companies use Product Data Management (PDM) systems. A PDM is a system that supports management of both engineering data and product development process during the whole product life cycle. PDM systems have several benefits that have been well addressed in previous researches (e.g. Liu et al., 2001). As the product development was expanded in 2000 to including suppliers, partners and customers, the PDM concept was transformed to Product LifeCycle Management and Collaborative Product Definition Management (www.cimdata.com, Abramovici et al. 2002). A PDM system includes a variety of functions (see Kumar et al. 2004 for a review of these functions). Over the last decade, focus was on different issues such as: methods to design PDM web-based (Chu et al. 1999), problems and issues related to PDM implementation (Siddiqui et al., 2004), integration of workflow and PDM systems (Kim et al. 2001), system integration and data exchange among heterogeneous systems (Yeh et al. 2002). Despite these efforts, PDM systems do not provide adequate support for data sharing when collaboration spans company borders (Rouibah et al., 2005, Noel et al., 2003).

This paper focuses on collaboration within an engineering community. We define this community as a network created by at least two independent organizations in order to jointly design a complex product. Since design is performed in a parallel way, concurrent engineering principles call partners to fulfill some requirements: (a) extensively share data hosted at different partners sites; (b) systems that host data must provide the location transparency, i.e. system supplying a user with request data, and the user does not need to know at which site those data are located; (c) provide easy access to product data of the partners if granted; (d) require a notification service to notify users about design progress and engineering changes; (e) monitor the progress being made. With regard to above requirements existing frameworks do offer partially support (Chen et al., 2000). They are based on: Collaboration through database sharing, Coordination through administrative workflow and Communication through e-mails. But in the engineering field, engineering tasks are ad-hoc and unstructured such as Engineering Change Management (ECM). If there is any change in any product items, it is hard to know who needs to be informed and how to propagate the changes. Furthermore, existing papers on ECM did focus and investigate the subject within single companies (Huang et al. 1999, Kim et al. 2001, Maull et al. 1992).

This paper contributes to this area through the description of a concept, it implementation as a PDM prototype and its test. These efforts have been done during an EC project EP26780 SIMNET, between 1999 and December 2001. The concepts were derived from a case study developed within two European companies (Rouibah et al., 2005). The proposed concepts were reviewed and refined in several workshops within the SIMNET consortium. The proposed enhancements were implemented as a prototype within the PDM axalant™ developed by Eigner & Partners (E+P).

The remaining of the paper is structured as follows. The next section presents the concept (framework) and the prototype. The section after describes the test and the main results. Finally the paper summarizes the findings and points out to some problems raised during the project.

The SIMNET Method and Prototype

The proposed method, to be illustrated in the following sections, is based on several concepts, derived from a case study (see fig. 1). These are: parameters, parameter list, hardness grade, user categories, activities, parameter network, parameter approval and release workflow, engineering change management, engineering change based on parameter propagations.

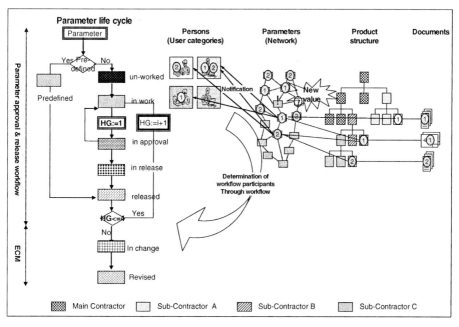

Fig. 1. Framework of the PBC-supported engineering change

The SIMNET Method

The case study shows that engineers' activities are unstructured. Engineers tend to view their work as assigning values to parameters and to affect relationships among parameters. Based on this finding, we developed the Parameter Based Collaboration (PBC) to structure the collaboration from the parameter perspective. The relationships between parameters and the people working with them capture the evolution of product design. This approach describes complex product development as a form of parameter processing that has input and output, and involves roles and constraints. We then approach engineering process as a network of activities that uses and produces parameters (see fig. 1). Parameters refer to dimensions, forces or movements. They share complex relationships represented in terms of functions. Evolution of parameters involves two kinds of workflows: administrative workflow (i.e. predefined processes) as well as ad-hoc workflow (i.e. processes that cannot be defined prior to their execution). The parameter evolution is based upon a single administrative process that includes eight activities: predefined, un-worked, in-work, in approval, in release and released, in change and revised (see fig.1).

The PBC is also based on the concept of parameter maturity, called hardness grades. This refers to the quality and stability of a parameter specification during design evolution. We defined five hardness grades (noted HG). When a parameter reaches HG 5 it cannot be changed until a demand of change is initiated, studied and approved. This is done by the ECM approach. The ad-hoc workflow is based on the relationship we establish between parameters, product structure items, and people who are assigned to these parameters (see fig.1).

Working on parameters involves many engineers and people, with different background from different partners. Therefore we specified five user categories to upgrade and work on parameters either inside the engineering area (Coordinator, Collaborators) as well as outside the engineering (Reviewers, Subscribers and Supervisor). Their duties and privileges were also specified.

Application of the PBC passes through several steps: instantiate a project container, define set of parameters independent from any project (i.e. parameter that are redundant in major projects); identify the five user categories within each partner and assign people to user categories; identify predefined parameter that are specified by the final customers; link parameters with product structure items; create values for the remaining parameters, apply the parameter approval and release workflow to upgrade parameters from HG1 to HG5. Parameters may be presented to end-users individually or grouped as a set (list) of parameters for possible upgrading. The ECM approach is applied to move parameters on the two other activities "*in change* and *revised*" (see fig.1). It consists to propagate change done a specific parameter through parameter network when such as parameter is released and reached HG 5. ECM evolves several steps: define interface parameter, i.e., parameters that are jointly defined by the partners; create the parameter networks (fig.1); identify parameters requiring changes; propagate the change by auditing parameters directly and indirectly affected; discuss potential parameters affected by reporting the change to others who may have interest; identify a list of parameters that effectively need changes; and apply a joint approval and release workflow for the parameter list. Both PBC and ECM require a notification mechanism. If there is any change in any product structure item, the notification mechanism is launched to notify users as well as to propagate changes over the parameter network (see fig.1).

The SIMNET Implementation

Based on the previous SIMNET method, we developed a distributed work-space prototype.

The Distributed Workspace

The workspace is used to publish a collection of useful data (parameters and associated objects and documents) that support collaboration in a controlled manner. Nodes represent link to remote objects hosted at a partner's site. Workspace enables efficient data management and avoids data duplication and data inconsistency. All project participants are able to access the workspace using either a PDM native client or a web client. The architecture is shown in fig 2a.

The distributed workspace enables online transactions and offline message exchanges. Online is the case when a native client program or web browser interacts with the SIMNET application server. Offline is the case when the notification service may use standard e-mail to dispatch information to users of the engineering community. The distributed workspace is managed by an Application Service Provider that acts as a central gateway to access project relevant data (Mission Critical, www.miscrit.be).

Fig 2.a illustrates collaboration between two companies A and B. They already published collaborative data (nodes) in the workspace. Nodes 1, 2 and 3 are under A while nodes 4, 5 and 6 are under B. Fig 2.b shows how a user from company A can request to access data from company B via the web client. First, he must logon on to the workspace in order to be recognized as a valid of the community. Second, user receives access to company B. Third he receives access to limited data hosted by B. For such purpose, the PDM system at B checks if access is granted to this user. If so, data is checked out and presented in the web-client.

In addition, the workspace server is used to store the mapping between data coming from different source systems in the PDM system of the main contractor and the suppliers. Changes on one of the sites are communicated via the workspace notification and users can react accordingly. All requests for approval are directed to the *workspace in-box* of the user. The current view of a parameter is presented by following the link provided in the work item. To retrieve additional information the user does not have to care where to get it from since it is handled by the workspace server. Requests are addressed to all servers that provide the needed information. Updates and modification done by the user at a specific server (e.g. at company A) are passed back to the workspace server.

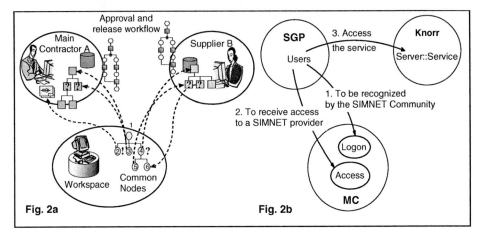

Fig. 2. Architecture of the SIMNET distributed workspace

Security is deployed and ensured based on CLAVIS™, a full security framework designed and developed by Mission Critical. It plays the role of management entity that is independent from any single organization and is trusted by all the members of community. The role of the ME is to implement the security policies decided by the community (e.g. encryption of messages, authentication of users, authorization of services, integrity and non-repudiation of messages). The SIMNET security solution is based on state of the art standards – Public Key Infrastructure. All partners of the engineering community are peers, except the Management Entity.

The main developments achieved during implementation include several modules of the workspace: the parameter module allows to define and manage several items associated with the PBC approach (e.g. parameters value creation, date of creation); the workflow module allows to define and execute administrative and ad-hoc workflow; the notification service module is used to link the workspace axalant™ with external e-mail systems; the security module is used to authenticate users of the workspace and secure data exchange.

Tests

The tests we carried out took place in the form of a pilot phase during six months. Tests consists to introduce the method (and its concepts) and the prototype to a limited area of two companies.

Product and Participants in the Pilot Phase

A real development project that integrates the magnetic track brake into a specific rail way bogie platform is chosen for the test. These bogies are designed for use on heavy weight metro vehicles. The test involves two European companies (SGP and Knorr). SGP manufactures the bogie frames and engine, while, Knorr manufactures the magnetic track brake. The magnetic track brake operates independently from the friction between wheel and rail. It is installed in the bogie frame.

Twelve people from SGP and two from Knorr were involved in the tests. These people belong to operational, management and strategic levels. People in the operational level refer to those directly involved in testing the pilot application. Persons in tactical level refer to those responsible for organizational matters (e.g. the appointment of meetings, setting of due dates). Persons in the strategic level refer to those responsible for strategic aspects and decision-making as well as the enhancements of the pilot. In addition, test evolves other persons who represent E+P, mission critical and another ICT company

Data Collection

During test, participants were asked to evaluate both the SIMNET method and the prototype. For this purpose, users were asked to test the systems, and two methods of data collections were used: survey questionnaire to collect quantitative method, and semi-structured interview to collect qualitative data.

Data were then analyzed using the *portfolio method* developed by Prof. Dr. Horst Wildemann[1]. It is based upon two criteria: *importance* of the concept to customer and level of *fulfillment*. We have selected this method because it serves to identify the need for improvement in a company sitting. It allows assessing the benefits in term of: (1) immediate action through a complete redesign of existing practices; (2) immediate improvement of existing practices, (3) step-by-step improvement of existing practices, (4) no need for actions, and (5) potential for rationalization.

The Wildemann's portfolio method has been customized to evaluate the *method*, the *implementation*, and also to point the *potential to improvements*. This customization is based on the *importance* and *maturity* of the SIMNET method. Importance refers to how participants perceive the method as important to their activities. Maturity refers to how participants

---

[1] www.bwl.wi.tum.de/contenido/cms/front_content.php?idcat=41

perceive the method as mature and doesn't need extra improvements. The customized portfolio for implementation is based on the *significance* and *fulfillment* of their implementation. Significance refers to how participants perceive the implementation as stable, quality-based and user friendliness. Fulfillment refers to how participants perceive the achievement during the implementation compare to their manual tasks. The customized portfolio for potential improvement is based on the *method achievement* as well *implementation fulfillment* in relation with the need to increase the maturity of the method.

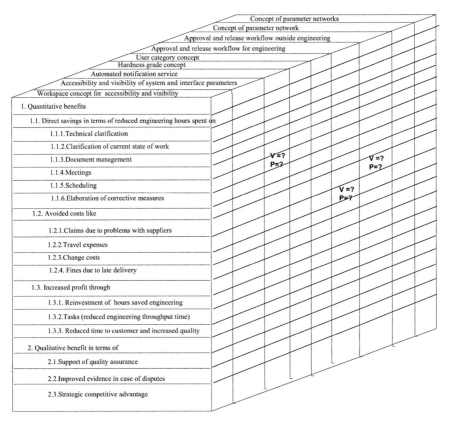

Fig. 3. Concepts, variables to measure benefits of SIMNET

The SIMNET method (including the nine concepts) and the prototype were evaluated against their expected quantitative and qualitative benefits (fig. 3). Participants need to create two matrixes (fig. 3) for SIMNET method evaluation: one matrix for potential achievement of benefits (represented by "P") and a second matrix to refer to the level of achievement (represented by "V"). These two matrixes enable to generate the portfolio method "potential vs achievement". Further participants need also to create two matrixes for SIMNET implementation: one represents significance (represented by "S", and another for the level fulfillment (represented by "V"). These two variables enable to generate the portfolios implementation "significance vs fulfillment". The Portfolios for follow-up actions is based on the *method fulfillment* and *implementation achievement*.

Test Results

Analysis of questionnaires shows the following results. Initial concept of composing parameter networks turned out to be too rigid. It was therefore replaced by a more flexible approach which allows the creation of user-specific parameter-sets. Scenarios with the parameter-based change management functionality revealed a need for significant changes of the underlying procedures and methods. With respect to quantitative benefits in terms of reduced engineering hours and avoided costs SIMNET methods were evaluated by the end-users very helpful, especially as far as the "clarification of the current state of work", "elaboration of corrective measures" and "change costs" are concerned. The qualitative benefits were seen in "support of quality assurance" and "improved evidence in case of disputes". Substantial conceptual changes were required regarding the way how parameter networks are defined (introduction of "parameter sets") as well as how the parameter-based change management was to be performed. The parameter-based change functionality was under continuous modifications and refinements until the very end of the pilot phase and the SIMNET runtime. In addition, the feedback obtained on parameter networks and change management are considered extremely useful to achieve a higher maturity of the entire SIMNET solution. With regard to perceived usefulness of SIMNET implementation, results show the following. The quality of implementation in general resulted in high rankings. Exceptions are the parameter-based change management functionality (which receives low ranking), the functionality based on the web client is ranked medium; and the functionality for the definition and management of parameter networks via sets is ranked medium.

With regard to interviews, participants did limit their reactions only to five concept solutions, among the nine, either positively or negatively. As for the first concept solution (the centralized management...), participant believe *"project container approach is easy to handle"*. They *"propose that parameter attributes defined at definition level should be selectable for instantiation from a menu"*. Participants believe the *"existence of the parameter definitions independent from a specific project is very useful and can be used like templates to facilitate initiating a new project"*. As for the hardness grades concepts, all participant *"agree to consider the five grades as convenient to control design progress and its quality"*. As for the user category concepts, participant believe the *"subscriber is useless since he may become a nuisance"*. For the concept of parameter network based on sets for the traceability of change propagation, participants think *"it is really hard and often difficult to distinguish between first degree relations and relation of nth degree"*. As for the method for parameter-based change management, participants think the *"parameter change management procedure is too simplified compare to the real life use in bogie design"*. Moreover, they found the *"parameter change procedure is facing problems especially if parameters candidate to change appear on more than one change list"*. In addition, two participants believe user interface of the change management functionality based on the web client is good, but unstable. Other quotations were made against the proposed SIMNET method. All participants agreed *"collaboration engineering is important and promising for senior managers and where savings may be generated"*. Other participants also state that parameter based collaboration approach is *"a way to structure collaboration and coordination among a community of partners"*. Another added *"this approach is helpful to better communication during collaboration engineering"*. Another added *"the PBC allows dynamic data sharing in a controlled manner but it needs further improvement"*.

Conclusion

This paper highlights the experience of an European engineering project in order to further knowledge about collaboration engineering. The overall conclusion of the pilot phase is that collaboration engineering is potentially important for senior managers and the end-users in the test were specifically attracted more by the concept itself rather than by the implementation. They consider the SIMNET results (method and prototype) very useful and of high quality. Except from the parameter-based change management, the functionality could be sufficiently tested. Accordingly the pilot phase itself can be evaluated as satisfactory for user categories, parameter lists without notification, parameter lists with notification and, approval and release workflow. But the pilot phase can be evaluated as unsatisfactory for phase parameter network and change management, while very useful feedback was obtained for the further development of the entire solution for parameter-based workflow management. These results reveal that inter-company engineering change management is very complex process.

Besides the above findings, SIMNET method and its implementation faced unexpected circumstances. The workspace implementation have suffered from a major setback by Siemens rejecting axalant™ as their PDM solution in favor of Winchill (www.ptc.com). This adverse decision demonstrates the fragility of one-to-one (SGP- E+P) developments when it comes to cross-enterprise collaboration. Interoperability between heterogeneous systems cannot be handled without careful assessment of political ramifications. This suggests several observations. First, technical competencies of E+P are not sufficient condition for inter-organizational information system development's success. Second, development of cross company strategic information system is a very complex to approach. Accordingly cross company information system design should be approached carefully. Third, rather IT competencies, it is the support of strategic management level (at SGP) that constitutes the critical success factor for the achievement especially for systems that cross company borders (Lederer and Sethi 1991). Fourth, the European Community sponsors projects that are of high quality and high innovativeness, within a period that ranged from one to three years. For such projects, it spends huge investment (the SIMNET project was sponsored around € 2.2. millions). Even a lot experience has been acquired, the results were wasted. Beside the Siemens decision, other factors have led to willingness to pursue the workspace implementation by E+P. With the emerging market of workspace, Eigner has been acquired by its competitor Agile, leaving the Partner alone. This unexpected event pushed Partner to abandon the workspace and to refocuses its entire business around the Enterprise Application Integration and, to incorporate some of the workspace functionality on it. Finally, this paper leaves the following research question as perspective: does our approach improve user ability to perform design tasks and whether the product (design result/development) becomes better?

References

Abramovici M, Sieg OC (2002) Status and Development Trends of Product Life-Cycle Management Systems. www.itm.rub.de/download/publikationen/Status _ and_Development_Trends_of_PLM.pdf

Baldwin RA, Chung MJ (1995) Managing Engineering Data for Complex Products. Research in Engineering Design. no 7, pp 215-231

Boznak RG (1993) Competitive Product Development. Business One Irwin /Quality Press, Milwaukee, WI

Chu X, Fan Y (1999) Product Data Management Based on Web Technology. Integrated Manufacturing Systems, vol 10, pp 84-88

Chen YM, Liang MW (2000) Design and Implementation of a Collaborative Engineering Information System for Allied Concurrent Engineering. International Journal of Computer Integrated Manufacturing, vol 13, no 1, pp 11-30

Huang GQ, Mak KL (1999) Current Practices of Engineering Change Management in UK Manufacturing Industries. International Journal of Operations & Production Management, vol 19, no 1, pp 21-37

Web-Based Support for Collaborative Product Design Review. Computers in Industry, vol 48, pp 71-88

Kim Y, Kang S, Lee S, Yoo S (2001) A Distributed Open Intelligent Product Data Management System. International Journal of Computer Integrated Manufacturing, vol 14, pp 224-235

Kumar R, Midha PS (2004) A QFD Methodology for Evaluating a Company's PDM Requirements for Collaborative Product Development. Industrial Management + Data Systems, vol 101, no 3/4, pp 126-132

Lederer AL, Sethi V (1991) Critical Dimensions of Strategic Information Systems Planning. Decision Sciences, vol 22, no 1, pp 104-119

Liu T, Xu XW (2001) A Review of Web-Based Product Data Management Systems. Computers in Industry, vol 44, pp 251-262

Maull R, Hughes D, Bennett J (1992) The Role of the Bill-of-Materials as a CAD/CAPM Interface and the Key Importance of Engineering Change Control. Computing and Control Engineering Journal, March, pp 63-70

Noel F, Brissaud D (2003) Dynamic Data Sharing in a Collaborative Design Environment. International Journal of Computer Integrated Manufacturing, vol 16, no 7-8, pp 546-556

Rouibah K, Caskey K (2005) Managing Concurrent Engineering Across Company Borders: a Case Study. Forthcoming in International Journal of Computer Integrated Manufacturing

Siddiqui QA, Burns ND, Backhouse CJ (2004) Implementing Product Management the First Time. International Journal of Computer Integrated Manufacturing, vol 17, no 6, pp 520-533

Yeh S, You C (2002) STEP-Based Data Schema for Implementing Product Data Management. International Journal of Computer-Integrated Manufacturing, vol 15, no 1, pp 1-17

Advances in
Information Systems Development

**Bridging the Gap between Academia
and Industry**

Volume 2

Advances in Information Systems Development

Bridging the Gap between Academia and Industry

Volume 2

Edited by

Anders G. Nilsson and Remigijus Gustas

Karlstad University
Karlstad, Sweden

Wita Wojtkowski and W. Gregory Wojtkowski

Boise State University
Boise, Idaho, USA

Stanisław Wrycza

University of Gdansk
Gdansk, Poland

Jože Zupančič

University of Maribor
Kranj, Slovenia

 Springer

Anders G. Nilsson
Karlstad University
Universitetsgatan 2
SE-651 88 Karlstad
Sweden
anders.nilsson@kau.se

Remigijus Gustas
Karlstad University
Universitetsgatan 2
SE-651 88 Karlstad
Sweden
remigijus.gustas@kau.se

Wita Wojtkowski
Boise State University
1910 University Drive
Boise, Idaho 83725
USA
wwojtkow@boisestate.edu

W. Gregory Wojtkowski
Boise State University
1910 University Drive
Boise, Idaho 83725
USA
gwojtkow@boisestate.edu

Stanisław Wrycza
University of Gdansk
ul. Armii Krajowej 119/121
PL-81-824 Sopot
Poland
swrycza@univ.gda.pl

Jože Zupančič
University of Maribor
Systems Development Laboratory
SI-6400 Presernova 11
Slovenia
joze.zupancic@fov.uni-mb.si

Proceedings of the 14th International Conference on Information Systems Development—Bridging the Gap between Academia and Industry (ISD 2005), held in Karlstad, Sweden, August 14–17, 2005.

Volume (2): Part 2 of a two-volume set.

Library of Congress Control Number: 2005937686

ISBN-10: 0-387-30834-2
ISBN-13: 978-0387-30834-0

Printed in the United States of America   (EB)

9 8 7 6 5 4 3 2 1

springer.com

Preface

This publication is an outcome of the Fourteenth International Conference on Information Systems Development, ISD'2005, held in Karlstad, Sweden during 14-17 August 2005. The theme for the ISD'2005 conference was "Advances in Information Systems Development: Bridging the Gap between Academia and Industry". This conference continues the fine tradition of the first Polish – Scandinavian Seminar on Current Trends in Information Systems Development Methodologies, held in 1988, Gdańsk, Poland. Through the years this seminar has evolved into the "International Conference on Information Systems Development (ISD)" as we know today. This ISD conference compliments the network of general Information Systems conferences, e.g. ICIS, ECIS, AMCIS, PACIS and ACIS.

Information Systems Development (ISD) progresses rapidly, continually creating new challenges for the professionals involved. New concepts, approaches and techniques of systems development emerge constantly in this field. Progress in ISD comes from research as well as from practice. The aim of the Conference is to provide an international forum for the exchange of ideas and experiences between academia and industry, and to stimulate exploration of new solutions. The Conference gives participants an opportunity to express ideas on the current state of the art in information systems development, and to discuss and exchange views about new methods, tools and applications. ISD as our professional and academic discipline has responded to these challenges. As a practice-based discipline, ISD has always promoted a close interaction between theory and practice that has been influential in setting the ISD agenda. This agenda has largely focused on the integration of people, business processes and information technology (IT) together with the context in which this occurs.

The ISD conference provides a meeting point or venue for researchers and practitioners. They are coming from over 30 countries representing all continents in the world. The main objective of the conference is to share scientific knowledge and interests and to establish strong professional ties among the participants. This year, the ISD'2005 conference provided an opportunity to bring participants to the newly established Karlstad University in Sweden. Karlstad University is well known for its multidisciplinary research and education programs as well as the close cooperation with the local industry of the Värmland region. The ISD'2005 conference was organised around seven research tracks. This Springer book of proceedings, published in two volumes, is organised after the following conference tracks including a variety of papers forming separate chapters of the book:

- Co-design of Business and IT
- Communication and Methods
- Human Values of Information Technology
- Service Development and IT
- Requirements Engineering (RE) in the IS Life-Cycle
- Semantic Web Approaches and Applications
- Management and IT (MIT)

Three invited keynote speeches were held during the ISD'2005 conference by very prominent authorities in the field: Prof Göran Goldkuhl, CEO Hans Karlander and Prof Bo Edvardsson. In parallel with the conference we held a practical Workshop for the ISD delegates including presentation of a professional E-portal from the Wermland Chamber of Commerce.

The conference call for papers attracted a high number of good quality contributions. Of the 130 submitted papers we finally accepted 81 for publication, representing an acceptance rate of approximately 60%. In addition we had a pre-conference opportunity for promoting and supporting researchers in their professional careers. The pre-conference comprised 25 papers which are published in separate proceedings from Karlstad University Press. We had a best paper award appointment of four papers from the pre-conference offered to join this Springer book of proceedings. All together we have 89 contributions (88 papers and one abstract) published as chapters in this book. The selection of papers for the whole ISD'2005 conference was based on reviews from the International Program Committee (IPC). All papers were reviewed following a "double blind" procedure by three independent senior academics from IPC. Papers were assessed and ranked from several criteria such as originality, relevance and presentation.

We would like to thank the authors of papers submitted to ISD'2005 conference for their efforts. We would like to express our thanks to all program chairs, track chairs and IPC members for their essential work. We would also like to thank and acknowledge the work of those behind the scenes, especially Niklas Johansson for managing the web-site and submission system MyReview and Jenny Nilsson for all valuable help with editing the papers according to the Springer book template. We are also grateful to Karlstad University in particular to Rector Christina Ullenius, Dean Stephen Hwang and Head of Division Stig Håkangård for their support with resources to be able to make the local arrangements.

Karlstad in August 2005

Anders G. Nilsson and **Remigijus Gustas**
Conference Chairs ISD'2005

Conference Organisation

General Chair

Anders G. Nilsson, Karlstad University, Sweden

Program Co-Chairs and Proceedings Editors

Anders G. Nilsson, Karlstad University, Sweden
Remigijus Gustas, Karlstad University, Sweden
Wita Wojtkowski, Boise State University, Idaho, USA
W. Gregory Wojtkowski, Boise State University, Idaho, USA
Stanisław Wrycza, University of Gdańsk, Poland
Jože Zupančič, University of Maribor, Kranj, Slovenia

Track Chairs

Sten Carlsson, Karlstad University, Sweden *(Workshops for Industry)*
Sven Carlsson, Lund University, Sweden *(Management and IT)*
Rodney Clarke, University of Wollongong, Australia *(Communication & Methods)*
Olov Forsgren, University College of Borås, Sweden *(Co-design)*
Odd Fredriksson, Karlstad University, Sweden *(Service Development)*
Göran Goldkuhl, Linköping University, Sweden *(Co-design)*
John Sören Pettersson, Karlstad University, Sweden *(Human Values of IT)*
Birger Rapp, Linköping University, Sweden *(Management and IT)*
William Song, University of Durham, United Kingdom *(Semantic Web)*
Benkt Wangler, University of Skövde, Sweden *(Requirements Engineering)*

International Program Committee (IPC)

Gary Allen, University of Huddersfield, United Kingdom
Erling S. Andersen, Norwegian School of Management, Oslo, Norway
Karin Axelsson, Linköping University, Sweden
Janis Barzdins, University of Latvia, Riga, Latvia
Juris Borzovs, University of Latvia and Riga Technical University, Latvia
Frada Burstein, Monash University, Melbourne, Australia
Rimantas Butleris, Kaunas Technical University, Lithuania
Albertas Caplinskas, Institute of Mathematics and Informatics, Vilnius, Lithuania
Antanas Cenys, Semiconductor Physics Institute, Vilnius, Lithuania

Deren Chen, Zhejiang University, Hangzhou, China
Heitor Augustus Xavier Costa, Universidade Federal de Lavras, Brazil
Stefan Cronholm, Linköping University, Sweden
Darren Dalcher, Middlesex University, London, United Kingdom
Dalé Dzemydiené, Law University, Vilnius, Lithuania
Owen Eriksson, Dalarna University College, Borlänge, Sweden
Jørgen Fischer Nilsson, Technical University of Denmark, Lyngby, Denmark
Julie Fisher, Monash University, Melbourne, Australia
Guy Fitzgerald, Brunel University, Middlesex, United Kingdom
Chris Freyberg, Massey University, Palmerston North, New Zealand
Janis Grundspenkis, Riga Technical University, Latvia
Hele-Mai Haav, Tallinn University of Technology, Estonia
G. Harindranath, University of London, United Kingdom
Igor Hawryszkiewycz, University of Technology, Sydney, Australia
Alfred Helmerich, Research Institute of Applied Technology, Munich, Germany
Joshua Huang, E-Business Technology Institute, Hong Kong, China
Juhani Iivari, University of Oulu, Finland
Mirjana Ivanovic, University of Novi Sad, Serbia and Montenegro
Marius A. Janson, University of Missouri - St. Louis, USA
Nimal Jayaratna, Curtin University, Perth, Australia
Roland Kaschek, Massey University, Palmerston North, New Zealand
Karlheinz Kautz, Copenhagen Business School, Denmark
Marite Kirikova, Riga Technical University, Latvia
Jerzy A. Kisielnicki, Warsaw University, Poland
Gábor Knapp, Budapest University of Technology and Economics, Hungary
John Krogstie, Norwegian University Science/Technology, Trondheim, Norway
Rein Kuusik, Tallinn University of Technology, Estonia
Sergei Kuznetsov, Russian Academy of Science, Moscow, Russia
Michael Lang, National University of Ireland, Galway, Ireland
Xiaoming Li, Peking University, Beijing, China
Mikael Lind, University College of Borås, Sweden
Henry Linger, Monash University, Melbourne, Australia
Björn Lundell, University of Skövde, Sweden
Audrone Lupeikiene, Institute of Mathematics and Informatics, Vilnius, Lithuania
Kalle Lyytinen, Case Western Reserve University, Cleveland, Ohio, USA
Leszek A. Maciaszek, Macquarie University, Sydney, Australia
Gábor Magyar, Budapest University of Technology and Economics, Hungary
Yannis Manolopoulos, Aristotle University, Thessaloniki, Greece
Majed Al-Mashari, King Saud University, Riyadh, Saudi Arabia
Heinrich C. Mayr, University of Klagenfurt, Austria
Ulf Melin, Linköping University, Sweden
Elisabeth Métais, CNAM University, Paris, France
Robert Moreton, University of Wolverhampton, United Kingdom
Pavol Navrat, Slovak University of Technology, Bratislava, Slovakia
Lina Nemuraite, Kaunas Technical University, Lithuania
Ovidiu Noran, Griffith University, Brisbane, Australia

Jacob Nørbjerg, Copenhagen Business School, Denmark
Eugene K. Ovsyannikov, The Academy of Sciences, St. Petersburg, Russia
Jari Palomäki, Technical University of Tampere/Pori, Finland
Malgorzata Pankowska, University of Economics in Katowice, Poland
George A. Papadopoulus, University of Cyprus, Nicosia, Cyprus
Anne Persson, University of Skövde, Sweden
Alain Pirotte, University of Louvain, Belgium
Jaroslav Pokorný, Charles University in Prague, Czech Republic
Boris Rachev, University of Rousse and Technical University of Varna, Bulgaria
Vaclav Repa, Prague University of Economics, Czech Republic
Kamel Rouibah, College of Business Administration, Safat, Kuwait University
David G. Schwartz, Bar-Ilan University, Ramat Gan, Israel
Zhongzhi Shi, Institute of Computing Technology, CAS, Beijing, China
Timothy K. Shih, Tamkang University, Tamsui, Taipeh Hsien, Taiwan
Klaas Sikkel, University of Twente, Netherlands
Guttorm Sindre, Norwegian University Science/Technology, Trondheim, Norway
Larry Stapleton, Waterford Institute of Technology, Republic of Ireland
Eberhard Stickel, Bonn University of Applied Sciences, Germany
Uldis Sukovskis, Riga Technical University, Latvia
Bo Sundgren, Statistics Sweden and Stockholm School of Economics, Sweden
Arne Sølvberg, Norwegian University Science/Technology, Trondheim, Norway
Janis Tenteris, Riga Technical University, Latvia
Jacek Unold, Wrowlaw University of Economics, Poland
Olegas Vasilecas, Vilnius Gediminas Technical University, Lithuania
Jiri Vorisek, Prague University of Economics, Czech Republic
Gottfried Vossen, University of Münster, Germany
Gert-Jan de Vreede, University of Nebraska at Omaha, USA
Roel Wieringa, University of Twente, Netherlands
Carson C. Woo, University of British Columbia, Vancouver, Canada
Aoying Zhou, Fudan University, Shanghai, China
Hai Zhuge, Institute of Computing Technology, CAS, Beijing, China

Organising Committee

Anders G. Nilsson, Karlstad University, Sweden *(Chair)*
Remigijus Gustas, Karlstad University, Sweden *(Movie Production)*
Niklas Johansson, Karlstad University, Sweden *(IT Resources)*
Ulrika Mollstedt, Karlstad University, Sweden *(Marketing)*
Jenny Nilsson, Karlstad University, Sweden *(Editing Work)*
Kurt Samuelsson, Karlstad University, Sweden *(Photographing)*
Maria Kull, Karlstad University, Sweden *(Conference Services)*
Helena Persson, Karlstad University, Sweden *(Conference Services)*
Ximena Dahlborn, Karlstad University, Sweden *(Communication)*
Nina Sundelin, Karlstad University, Sweden *(Accounting)*

Sponsors

The organisers would like to thank the following for their support:

Karlstad University
Rector's Office, Faculty Board, Division for Information Technology

City of Karlstad
Karlstads kommun

Compare Karlstad
Competence Area network for IT companies in Karlstad

Elite Hotels of Sweden
Stadshotellet Karlstad

Contents

Volume 1

Keynote Speeches

Co-design of Business and IT

Communication and Methods

Human Values of Information Technology

Service Development and IT

Volume 2

Service Development and IT (cont.)

Requirements Engineering (RE) in the IS Life-Cycle

Semantic Web Approaches and Applications

List of Authors

ISETTA: Service Orientation in the "Bologna Process" of a Large University

Gottfried Vossen and Gunnar Thies

European Research Center for Information Systems (ERCIS), University of Münster, Germany. (vossen, gunnart)@uni-muenster.de

Introduction

With the signing of the "Bologna Declaration" in June 1999 by 29 representatives of the European education ministries, a decision was made to introduce comparable educational structures among European universities based on a Bachelor-Master system until the year 2010. The process itself, collectively known as the "Bologna process,"[1] is now well-underway and has created both administrative as well as technical challenges. The ISETTA project at the University of Muenster in Germany aims at the development of an *Integrated Student, Exam, Test, and Teaching Application* that properly reflects the changes of the university's internal activities caused by the Bologna process. In this paper, we report on the specific requirements of the project, the approach that has been taken and the current status of ISETTA.

Several goals are pursued with the general restructuring of the European university landscape: First, a system of easy-to-understand and comparable degrees is to be created. In this context two degrees of higher education will generally be offered, a Bachelor degree with a three-year study duration and a Master degree with an additional one to two-year duration. For Germany, one of the implications is a complete elimination of "Diploma" degrees. Second, a credit point system in the style of the *European Credit Transfer System* (ECTS) is to be adopted, of which the basic idea is that students get credit points for every passed exam. Third, new courses developed in response to Bologna should not only have new names, but should also break new ground, including aspects such as modularity of content, intensified exploitation of new media, internationalization, clear orientation towards future job markets. Beyond this, universities are given

---

[1] www.bologna-bergen2005.no/

external and internal requirements, e.g., they are asked to advance cooperation within Europe or to introduce quality management tools.

For a traditional university such as our own, the introduction of consecutive Bachelor and Master degrees creates a major challenge, as it leads to a considerable restructuring of both study programs and the administrative processes that support these programs. In this paper, the impact of the "Bologna process" on a university's IT infrastructure is investigated. To this end, the current infrastructure, to a great extent given by various legacy systems as well as by a number of legal restrictions, is taken as a starting point. It is then shown how comprehensive process modeling followed by the development of a service-oriented architecture can help making "Bologna" a reality with reasonable effort. The paper concentrates on the exam and test administration of the University of Muenster and identifies a number of relevant customer processes whose realization clearly indicates how the process in general can be accomplished.

The remainder of this paper is organized as follows: In Section 2 we discuss prerequisites of the ISETTA project and briefly look at related work. We then outline, in Section 3, our approach, which is essentially a top-down one that starts from a major process modeling activity, and we take a closer look at several sample processes from the area of exam administration. In Section 4 we briefly discuss realization options, and in Section 5 we draw some conclusions and outline future work in this area.

Prerequisites

In this section we briefly discuss the prerequisites for our ISETTA project, and we also take a brief look at related work. The prerequisites fall into two major categories:

- Legal restrictions that are imposed by the federal or the state government, the latter of which has so far been in charge of the universities and their programs;
- local restrictions caused by the way university processes have been working until now and the software that is in use for supporting these processes.

With respect to legal restrictions, most striking is the fact that many German universities have recently started to charge tuition. While this is currently based on a fee students have to pay under certain circumstances (e.g., if they study "too long," whatever that means in a particular case), it will soon be based on an "allowance" that is managed like an account, and that has a certain initial filling and that is charged every time a student enrolls in a particular class; once the account hits zero, the student has to pay for further services he or she will make use of. It should be clear that the introduction of student accounts has a major impact on the IT support of a university, which up to now did not have to have this functionality. Moreover, a very flexible handling of student accounts will be needed, as debits to the account need to be legally valid.

With respect to local restrictions, many German universities employ a software system called HIS[2] (*Higher education Information System*) for large portions of their everyday business. HIS is a typical legacy system in that it comes with a hard-to-read database schema as well as an underlying database, a number of add-ons and components that sometimes interact in cryptic ways (and are therefore difficult, if not impossible to adapt to changes), and with serious deficiencies in usability. The HIS component most relevant to our project is called POS and deals with exam administration. There is a Web front-end for HIS in general, but that is also difficult to adapt to self-service functionality as is now intended for students.

A major challenge for HIS imposed by the Bologna process and its implementation is scalability. Indeed, with numerous new study programs, each with a reasonable number of modules and each module consisting of a number of individual lectures, seminars, or other forms of study, large universities such as our own (with currently around 38,000 students) are faced with bookings into student accounts that reach the millions every semester. Another challenge, equally important, is the fact that there is no way for universities as customers to modify HIS components or to adapt them to changes. In that sense, HIS is a proprietary legacy system that a user has to live with; the only chance for the creation of appropriate IT support for Bologna thus is to identify the spots and places where new components with new functionality can be added. Steps in this direction will be reported in the remainder of this paper.

Before we do so, we take a brief look at related work. As every university in Europe is part of the Bologna process, it does not come as a surprise that several other projects are underway through Europe in general and Germany in particular. We here mention only those that we have been able to identify in Germany, since these may be the ones we could benefit from most.

At the University of Ulm, the SASy project[3] aims at providing an information system for students that is particularly able to familiarize them with the formal aspects (e.g., exam regulations) of their chosen study program.

---

[2] www.his.de/English
[3] http://medien.informatik.uni-ulm.de/forschung/projekte/sasy.xml

Gottfried Vossen and Gunnar Thies

Thus, SASy's goal is different from ours. The HIS@TUM project[4] at the Technical University of Munich is similar to ISETTA in that it concentrates on exam administration; a major difference is that they try to introduce HIS in each department that needs to manage exams, while we are currently trying to identify the (business) processes that underlie an exam administration. Another recent effort is the KIM project[5] at the University of Karlsruhe in Germany, which even tries to go along similar lines as we do in ISETTA; however, KIM seems to have just started, so that a further comparison is difficult. We emphasize that these are definitely not all the activities within Germany or Europe regarding a modernization of the university IT infrastructures; however, some projects are still kept as a secret and others have a different focus.

The ISETTA Approach to Exam Administration

In this section, we outline the approach of ISETTA. To this end, we start from the following assertions:

- Both the administrative activities of a university and the student-related ones are best perceived as business processes or workflows [1, 6] in order to understand their details as well as their interactions.
- As a consequence, a process model is a reasonable approach to capture and specify the functionality of a system under development.
- Such a process model is best developed in a top-down manner and ultimately mapped to a service-oriented architecture [7].

As is well-known, top-down modeling generally provides a rough view of an application or a system which is then refined through various levels of granularity in a step-wise fashion. At each level, it makes sense to consider activities, objects to be handled by these activities, resources executing activities and organizational structures that provide these resources together, in order to be able to properly perceive their interactions, and to capture all relevant aspects of an application.

A method along the lines just described is the INCOME method, described in detail, for example, in [6]. This method is based on higher-level Petri nets [1] for describing processes and models organizational as well as object structures as the process models evolve. In a nutshell, a Petri net comprises activities and objects in a strictly alternating fashion, and can be

---

[4] www.his.tum.de
[5] www.kim.uni-karlsruhe.de/

organized hierarchically in order to capture various levels of abstraction or detail. INCOME first constructs a process map in which all major business processes are identified together with their relationships; in our case, this phase refers to core processes of an exam administration. Then each process is analyzed in detail, and its technological boundary conditions as well as the infrastructure it needs to rely upon are established.

Importantly, INCOME suggests to model the relevant object structures in parallel to the processes. For us, the consequence is the development of a reference database model [9] representing the relevant entities of a, say, Bachelor program regulation and their relationships. As has turned out, our database model even allows for a mapping of the examination regulations of a Bachelor program through a construction of views over the given legacy database.

In brief, our process modeling phase has so far concentrated on exam administration only, and has identified 13 core processes (out of a total of 23 processes) which are shown in Fig. 1.

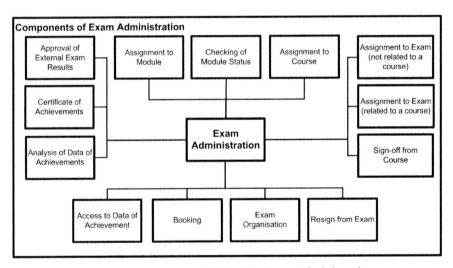

Fig. 1. Core Processes of ISETTA Exam Administration

These have so far been divided into five levels of abstraction for which granularity gets finer as you go deeper into the various levels. The lowest abstraction level (currently level 5) represents the processes of finest granularity, such as the test for number of trials of a specific exam. Figure 2 shows abstraction levels 0 and 1, which represent the upper portion of the process map we have developed.

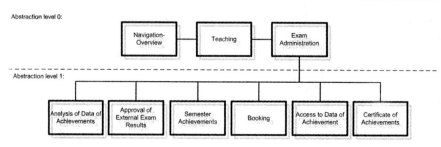

Fig. 2. Upper layers of the ISETTA process map

As can be seen in this figure, the highest abstraction level shows broad classes of processes, namely *Teaching* and *Exam administration*. The latter is refined into 6 lower level process categories, which allow analyzing exam data, approval of externally achieved credits, credits obtained during a semester, booking and recording of credits, access to credit data, and the creation of credit certificates.

In what follows we will present one of these processes in further detail, namely a possible workflow of the exam administration, or how it could look in the future. Nearly all the processes are optimized for use as Web components and are built for the use by students. Moreover, an examiner can record examination results by these processes over a Web component. Technical conditions are not considered here, with the exception of the specified database accesses that are needed to the underlying HIS database.

In Figure 3 an exam administration process model is shown that is geared towards future Bologna requirements and its implications for a university like Muenster. Notice that for all processes from level 1 Figure 3 shows how they interact. Basically, all activities originate from the HIS database, most of them by reading or writing a student's data record. Each action has assigned to it one or more roles, which means that only the assigned role can actually run the process. Hence, in Figure 3 the following roles are offered: *Student, Examiner, Examination Office,* and *Department Representative*. The left side of the model directly deals with semester achievements done by a student, while the right side shows supporting processes.

An important subprocess of the exam administration is the *Approval of External Exam Results*. These are course credits obtained at another university inside or outside the state. The approval can concern individual course achievements or entire modules. Either the external course credits are considered equivalent to local credits, or no correspondence to a local course can be established. The cycle involving *semester achievement* and *booking* is most frequently taken within a student's life. Here for each semester course credits (e.g., exams, oral examinations, papers) are obtained and then recorded by an examiner or teacher.

The supporting process *Certificate of Achievements* on the right side of Figure 3 renders it possible to print certificates or other documents. The goal is that this cannot only be done at the university but also over a self-service (Web) component from home; details can be found in [8].

A further process existing exclusively for students is *Access to Data of Achievements*. Here a student has the possibility to look at his or her standing, i.e., module results, course credits, or current registrations for upcoming exams and courses. This component will also be available over a Web component.

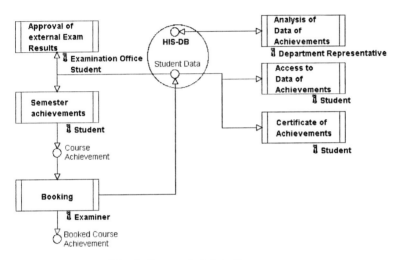

Fig. 3. Exam administration process

Finally, Figure 3 indicates another future process of the exam administration, the *Analysis of Data of Achievements*. So far the examination office has to offer raw statistical data. These are made available for the departments and the statistic national office. In the future, however, it will be possible to generate statistics over a Web component without dealing with the raw data at all.

As was briefly mentioned before, the processes we have modeled within the ISETTA project so far, which are documented in [8], need to be realized atop the legacy HIS database and within the general framework of HIS applications. To this end, the various documents that are handled by processes have been modeled in a way that allows us the creation of views [9] over the HIS database. These views can be materialized from a HIS database for answering queries efficiently, while all data is still stored within the HIS database. The former is important for the creation of Web interfaces, which typically generate database queries themselves. The latter is important so that ISETTA does not have to take care of database backups or recovery from crashes.

Realization Options

In this section we discuss realization options for ISETTA. In particular, we outline why service orientation appears to be the method of choice.

In order not to impair the operability of the legacy software currently in use, a hard requirement for ISETTA is not to touch existing database tables. We have accommodated this requirement in a reference database model [8] that consists of a number of views over the core database. This collection of views facilitates our goal of integrating the exam administration processes into the existing IT landscape. The core processes of the exam administration are generally optimized for use over the Web by students or staff. In particular, many processes represent services that are offered to students or staff by the system. Thus, a corresponding realization as software services appears feasible. As a result, the general four-layer architecture is as shown in Figure 4.

The user layer describes the Web components which are used by students or examiners in order to activate processes. Underneath is the process layer which comprises the processes that have been identified for the exam administration. Finally, the view layer is used to access the legacy data within HIS databases; note that also the program logic for a number of services (processes) is contained in this layer, since Web interfaces or underlying processes typically rely upon database functionality that is expressed in terms of view manipulation. The lowest layer describes the data retention layer of the legacy system.

Clearly, the core layers of this architecture are the Process and View Layers. In order to realize these, one approach could be to design a comprehensive software system that sits on top of the HIS application collection. Another would be an extension of HIS itself, which is, however, infeasible due to the legal and organizational construction of HIS. A third and most promising option then is to identify major processes as services, and to realize the entire scenario as a service-oriented architecture (SOA) [5, 7]. To this end, core processes would be made available as Web services [4, 2], which fits with other developments we have made in recent years, for example in the area of electronic learning [10].

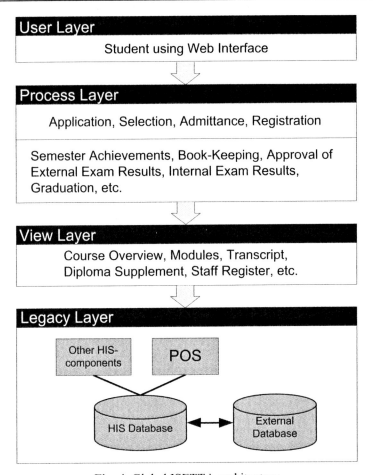

Fig. 4. Global ISETTA architecture

Conclusions and Outlook

The European "Bologna processes" is currently creating major IT challenges for a number of universities. In order to cope with these, process orientation, which has proven useful in numerous business applications, seems a reasonable approach. However, process orientation is new to most university administrations, and is at the same time confronted with a host of legacy applications. As has been indicated in this paper, a step-wise top-down approach to process modeling that identifies core applications and how they should work in the future can help making Bologna a reality. As it turns out, once process orientation is adopted and the process is started, it becomes apparent what the loop holes and deficiencies in current regulation proposals are, so that they can be clarified before any of this goes live.

From an implementation perspective, through the introduction of processes together with the reference database model it will be possible to keep realization costs for the "new" exam administration reasonable. Indeed, it could be shown with the help of the reference database model that the comprehensive changes, primarily the modularization of a course program, can be constructed using the existing legacy database. On the other hand, entering a complete module handbook manually is very time consuming, so that automating steps need to be taken here.

The four-layer architecture shown in Figure 4 has been implemented as a first prototype in order to provide a proof of concept and to show how the service-oriented target architecture can be put to work as a Web based system. Future steps will consist of modeling adjacent areas and of gradually going live with the system over the next year. As the implementation progresses, several interfaces will be acceptable at the user layer through suitably built XML interfaces [3].

References

[1] Aalst W vd, Hee K (2002) Workflow Management: Models, Methods, and Systems. MIT Press
[2] Alonso G, Casati F, Kuno H, Machiraju V (2004) Web Services – Concepts, Architectures and Applications. Springer-Verlag Berlin
[3] Harold ER, Means WS (2002) XML in a Nutshell (2nd ed). O'Reilly & Associates
[4] Hündling J, Weske M (2003) Web Services: Foundation and Composition. Electronic Markets, vol 13, no 2, pp 108-119
[5] Huhns MN, Singh MP (2005) Service-Oriented Computing: Key Concepts and Principles. IEEE Internet Computing Jan/Feb 2005, pp 75-81
[6] Richter-von Hagen C, Stucky W (2004) Business-Process und Workflow Management. Teubner
[7] Singh MP, Huhns MN (2005) Service-Oriented Computing – Semantics, Processes, Agents. John Wiley & Sons Ltd, Chichester England
[8] Thies G (2005) Process Modeling for Universities with the Example of Exam Administration. Diploma Thesis. In German. University of Münster Germany
[9] Vossen G (2000) Data Models, Database Languages, and Database Management Systems (4th ed). In German. R Oldenbourg Verlag Munich
[10] Vossen, G, Westerkamp P (2003) E-Learning as a Web Service. Proc 7th International Database Engineering and Application Symposium (IDEAS) Hong Kong China

The User Interface as a Supplier of Intertwined e-Services

Göran Hultgren and Owen Eriksson

Department of Culture, Media and Data, Dalarna University College
("Högskolan Dalarna") and the Research network VITS, Sweden.
(ghu, oer)@du.se

Introduction

Today, much of the world economy is focused on the service sector (Stafford and Saunders 2004). One of the changes driving service economic growth has been the rapid development in computer technology, mobile technology and the Internet (ibid.). There are e.g. mobile positioning services, traffic information services and intermediary services such as banking services on the Internet. With the help of channels such as the Internet and mobile telecommunications, information and functionalities are delivered by service providers, and are used by customers with the help of information technology (IT) systems. Many of these services have a characteristic where customers can meet and communicate with each other.

The focus of this paper is on services where the service provider and the customer(s) do not meet at the same time, and/or at the same place, i.e. the IT system acts as a service performer and medium in the service delivery process. This is an exciting new area of study which needs new perspectives and new methods which deal with the design, delivery and impact of these services, because they are likely to push the limits of software engineering in terms of analysis, design and testing (Chidambaram 2001). According to Dahlbom (2002) service thinking is focused upon individuals, actions, results and support. This implies a shift of context from the use of the IT system in order to improve the efficiency of routines and work processes of the organisation, to a focus on customers acting in a market receiving occasional services in a flexible way (ibid.).

We chose the term *e-service* to talk about the phenomenon where the IT system is used to offer services to customers in a market. A conceptualisation of the notion of e-service in such a context is presented in Hultgren and Eriksson (2005). This conceptualisation is theoretically based on a social interaction perspective (e.g. Habermas 1984), a view of IT systems as action systems (e.g. Ågerfalk 2003) and on Service Marketing (e.g. Grön-roos 1998; Edvardsson et.al. 2000). This theoretical base puts emphasis on the social aspects of e-services, i.e. that customers and service providers are communicating and acting through the IT system, and that this interaction is social and not only technical.

The social interaction is performed through the IT-systems *user interface*. This implies that the user interface is used to support the interaction between the service provider and the customer to produce the e-service. This user interface consists of a series of screen layouts providing different functionalities and messages.

It is important to recognise, as a consequence, the usability aspects in developing web interfaces (e.g. Nielsen 2000). These aspects are also closely related to the research on service quality in e-services (e.g. Grön-roos et.al. 2000; Santos 2003). One fundamental claim in web design research is the development of user interfaces informing the users both what to do and how by being consequent in the use of functionalities, colours, frames, messages, etc. One claim in service quality research is to be explicit in the service concept offered to the customer. Put in the context of e-services we claim that these usability aspects in designing good user interfaces should easily inform the customer about the e-service concept.

The problem is that there is not a one-to-one relation between a specific e-service and the user interface presenting it. Instead several e-services are *intertwined* with each other and presented by one or several user interfaces consisting of several screen layouts.

A user interface for an e-marketplace (Fig 1), consists (as we will show later in this paper) thus of several e-services and has to be seen as a service conglomerate hosting several e-services where the e-marketplace for 'advertisers' meeting 'readers' is *one* e-service. The 'service provider' view of the e-marketplace is also to benefit from the presence of the "visitors" and use them as resources in other e-services. From this viewpoint, we can see that the existing e-marketplace in Figure 1 also provides functionalities to search for new cars, to obtain financial and car insurance services, to receive information about recommended prices for a specific type of used car, to use search facilities and (to be a subject for) banner marketing (i.e. a "clickable" commercial message). This means that the 'service provider' in this example can use the presence of the 'advertisers' and the 'readers' as important subjects for *other* e-services. This also results in a user interface which hardly can be described as *one* e-service because of its complexity.

We claim that there is a need to be explicit in the design of what an e-service covers and how other e-services are related, in order to be able to design good web-based user interfaces. By having a distinct e-service design, the criteria laid out in web design research can be applied in order to make different, but intertwined, e-services apparent for the customers.

Fig. 1. One screen layout from the interface of an Internet based e-marketplace

The purpose of the paper is to present a framework for how intertwined e-services can be analysed as a base to design service apparent user interfaces. The paper is based on a qualitative research method built on both theoretical and empirical studies using the evolving framework for analysis and design of several e-services. The paper is structured as follows: In the next section, the notion of e-service from Hultgren and Eriksson (2005) is described and elaborated with additional aspects necessary for the analysis of intertwined e-services. Thereafter, the existing e-marketplace is presented more deeply and analysed in the following section. Finally, we discuss the analysis and conclude the paper.

The Notion of e-Service

In this section we first describe the notion of e-service presented in Hultgren and Eriksson (2005) in order to understand the fundamental aspects of e-services. Thereafter we present four complementary aspects required in order to analyse how the user interface presents different e-services.

The notion of e-service from Hultgren and Eriksson (2005) outlines three cornerstones when describing an e-service: the service concept, the relationships and the use situations. The first two cornerstones are necessary in order to define the e-service, while the third cornerstone describes how the involved actors use the IT system. The two first cornerstones are briefly described in this paper because they are needed as a base for delimiting different e-services from each other.

The *service concept* is the result from an e-service produced by the actors involved in the social interaction in order to be beneficial to the customer. The service concept is a product specification which the service provider is responsible for. The service concept can be divided into a description of core services and additional services; where the additional services are complementary to the core services in order to make the service more useful. Fundamental for e-services is that they are produced in the interaction between a service provider and a customer (or several customers) in order to fulfill customer needs, and that the IT system is used in a social interaction context which consists of actors, social relationships, norms, rules, values and expectations.

The *relationships* are created and maintained due to the communication performed between the service provider and the customer(s) mediated and performed by the IT system. It is also important to stress that these relationships are not only technical in character; they are also social, because they are based on interpretation of communication acts performed in a social context. The communication acts are used to create relationships based on information, commitments and expectations. Based on the actor roles, those of the service provider and the customer, there are two basic relationships in the e-service context: the service provider-to-customer relationship; and the customer-to-customer relationship.

The service concept and the relationships described above can be used to describe and understand *one* specific e-service. But in order to delimit one e-service from other intertwined e-services, we have to look closer to the user interface and introduce some further aspects.

The User Interface

The *user interface* for the customer consists of the functionality, the information and the screen layout. The functionalities can e.g. be what action possibilities are available in the user interface; the provided information e.g. about logotypes and other messages; and, the screen layout e.g. about different frames, colors and windows.

The user interface can be consisted by a series of screen layouts. Within web design research this series of screen layouts is recognised as important to keep together in the user interface in order to develop a usable IT system "telling" the user what to do and how (e.g. Nielsen 2000).

The Focused e-Service

As e-services are intertwined with each other we have to decide from which e-service, i.e. service concept, we are starting our analyses. We use the term of *focused e-service* to talk about a certain e-service. A focused e-service consists of several core- and additional services, i.e. a service concept provided by a service provider. A focused e-service can be presented by several screen layouts and it is therefore important to distinguish between screen layouts which are related to each other and which are not, because this regulates what commitments the involved actors make and determines the usability of the IT system and the e-service.

The Service Environment

It is common that the series of screen layouts presented to the customer in order to use a focused e-service provides several other functionalities and messages out of the scope of the focused e-service. We use the term *service environment* in order to talk about messages and functionalities, i.e. links to other e-services out of the scope of the focused e-service.

Three Types of e-Services

We have to understand that there are *three different types* of e-services co-existing in the user interface:

1. The *focused e-service* (already discussed);
2. *Related e-services* to the focused e-service;
3. *Interrelating e-services* which provide linking facilities from the focused e-service or its service environment to related e-services.

Figure 2 describes how the used terms in this section relate to each other and that the interrelating e-services are used in two different ways: a) to link from the focused e-service to related e-services; and b) to link from the service environment to related e-services.

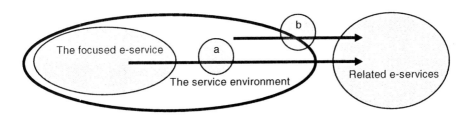

Fig. 2. The two ways of using the interrelating e-services

Example: The User Interface for the e-Marketplace

In this section we describe the user interface for an existing e-marketplace (www.autos.yahoo.com). The e-marketplace is open for 'advertisers' to buy or sell used cars. The 'advertiser' provides a textual message and, as an option, one or several pictures of the car for sale. The 'service provider' for the web based marketplace charges a fee for this service by using credit card payment facilities. After payment the advertisement is published on the Internet. The 'reader' can then be made aware of the advertisement interactively by using search facilities. If a 'reader' is interested in buying or selling a specific car, he can contact the 'advertiser' via the website or externally by telephone.

Fig. 3. The list of used cars   **Fig. 4.** The description of a specific car

The start page for the e-marketplace was shown in Figure 1. From this page the possibility to search for a used car and to sell a used car can be chosen. This page renders also the possibility to link several other functionalities, e.g. to search for a new car, to obtain financial and car insurance services, to receive information about recommended prices for a specific type of used car and to be subject to banner marketing. The 'reader' can use the search facilities in order to obtain a list of cars (as in Fig. 3). The 'reader' can click on a specific advertisement in the list in Figure 3 and a more detailed presentation of the car is shown (Fig. 4). This page also renders the possibility to contact the 'advertiser'.

If the option to click on the "Finance" button is chosen, a list of possible financial companies are presented (Fig. 5). After choosing one specific financial company, the layout given in Figure 6 is presented. If we use the option to click on the "Blue Book Pricing" button in order to get a recommended price for a specific type of used car, the information shown in Figure 7 appears after choosing a specific car type and answering some questions. Clicking on a banner results for example in Figure 8.

Fig. 5. A list of financial companies   **Fig. 6.** A specific financial company

Fig. 7. "Blue Book Pricing"

Fig. 8. "Banner" marketing

Example: The e-Services Intertwined in the e-Marketplace

In this section we illustrate how the perspective on e-services can help us to analyse the user interface for the existing e-marketplace.

The Focused e-Service and its Service Concept

The focused e-service is an e-marketplace for 'advertisers' of used cars to expose "for sale" or "want to buy" items searchable by potential 'readers'. The aim of the e-service is to let 'advertisers' and 'readers' meet. This means that the e-service has both 'advertisers' and 'readers' as customers. The core service for the 'advertiser' is to publish advertisements which he wants to buy or sell and to make contact with 'readers'. The core service for the 'reader' is to search for advertisements, access them and to make contact with the 'advertisers'. There are also additional services such as the presentation of a list of financial institutions (the 'Finance' button). The reason for describing the service concept in this way is that it represents a thematic wholeness building on a complete set of relationships.

The Focused e-Service and its Basic Relationships

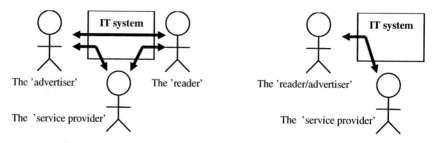

Fig. 9. Relationships within the e-Marketplace's core- and additional services

The relationships for the core services are built on three actor roles – the 'advertiser', the 'reader' and the 'service provider'. The social interaction performed through the IT system between those actors creates three basic social relationships (Fig. 9, left). The additional service (the lists of financial and insurance institutions) is built on the social relationship between the 'reader/advertiser' and the 'service provider' (Fig. 9, right).

The relationships between the 'service provider' and the 'advertiser', and between the 'service provider' and the 'reader' is based on information, social commitments and expectations. The relationship between the 'advertisers' and the 'readers' is important because the real value of the e-service is that it acts as a meeting place for customers. The relationship for the additional service between the 'service provider' and the 'reader/advertiser' is, in this analysis, built on the interpretation that the list is an impartial list of *recommended* financial or insurance companies.

The Service Environment to the Focused e-Service

Figures 1, 3, 4 and 5 describe the user interface, i.e. the series of screen layouts for the focused e-service. In all the figures the layout is similar: similar functionalities, the same service provider and similar colors, buttons, frames, etc. The layout tells the user that they are using one e-service. The layout also includes several functionalities out of the scope of the described service concept, such as banner marketing, the "Blue Book Pricing" button and the "New Cars" button. These possibilities are closely related to the focused e-service, belonging to its *service environment* and representing intertwined e-services.

The Focused e-Service and the Intertwined e-Services

The focused e-service and its service environment depict several intertwined e-services, which are of two types:

1. *Related e-services*, e.g. the 'Blue Book Pricing', e-services provided by the banner marketing companies and the financial offering e-service;
2. *Interrelating e-services*, e.g. the clickable banner marketing messages and the logotypes of the financial companies presented in the list of recommended institutions.

Related e-Services

The 'Blue Book Pricing' e-service is an example of an *related* e-service. After clicking on the "Blue Book Pricing" button in Figures 1, 3, 4 and 5, the e-service renders the possibility for the 'reader' to get information on the recommended price levels for used cars. Yahoo takes no responsibility for what Kelly, as the 'service provider' of this e-service, offers. This e-service is presented outside the focused e-service environment (Fig. 7) and a new relationship is created between the Kelly company as 'service provider' and the 'reader'. The service concept for the customer is to obtain information regarding the price level for a specified car. The layout for this e-service also informs the user that it is another e-service.

E-services provided by the banner marketing companies are also related to the focused e-service via the service environment. Such e-services provided by actors other than Yahoo are easily viewed as related e-services. The e-service in Figure 8 is provided by Yahoo, but is viewed in a new layout indicating the offer of another service concept out of the theme for the focused e-service concept. The 'reader' is linked to the banner marketing company's e-service outside the focused e-service environment and a new relationship is created between the 'company' as service provider and the 'reader' as a 'customer'. The service concept for the 'reader' is to get more information from the company.

The financial service (after a specific company has been chosen from the list of appropriate companies in Figure 5) is a new e-service provided by the chosen 'financial company'. This e-service is presented by the 'financial company' outside the focused e-service environment and another relationship is created between the 'financial company' as service provider and the 'customer' (the former 'reader'). The service concept for the customer is to obtain a financial offer. The layout also informs that it is another e-service.

Interrelating e-Services

Yahoo Autos provides also several *interrelating e-services* intertwined with the focused e-service and its service environment. All the interrelating e-services are building on a set of relationships where Yahoo is the 'service provider', and the 'advertiser/reader' and the companies are the customers. The service concepts for those e-services are to allow the customers to come into contact with each other by linking visitors to the companies. The clickable banner messages and the 'Blue Book Pricing' button are interrelating e-services linking from the service environment to related e-services. The clickable financial companies in the list of appropriate companies presented in the additional financial e-service are interrelating e-services linking from the focused e-service to other e-services.

Discussion

Both the focused e-service and its service environment determine the quality of the focused e-service from the customers' point of view. This means that the actual mix of both the focused e-service and its intertwined e-services provided by the user interface can lead to an improved or a deteriorated customer experience of the focused e-service as a whole. We claim that in order to design the focused e-service it is important also to design the service environment presented by the same user interface.

Evaluating the exemplified e-marketplace we can easily recognise the focused e-service concept which is offered. The layout is consistently designed (Fig. 1, 3, 4 and 5) and the messages regulate the commitments made by the involved actors (the 'advertiser', the 'reader' and the 'service provider'). However, the status of the list of appropriate financial companies provided by the additional financial e-service is unclear. Is the list impartial or is it is more to be seen as an e-service for the (paying) companies to get in contact with potential customers (like conventional banners)?

The interrelating e-services like the clickable banner messages and the 'Blue Book Pricing' button are easily recognised as intertwined e-services, where Yahoo as the 'service provider' mediates contact between the visitors and the companies. The interrelating e-services result in the start of other e-services out of the scope of the focused e-service and its environment. E-services provided by the banner marketing companies are opened in new windows indicating that they are other e-services. The user interface for the 'Blue Book Pricing' e-service provided by Kelly could, as an example, be improved because it does not open in a new window.

The two cornerstones defining the e-service according to Hultgren and Eriksson (2005): the service concept and the relationships, can be used when discussing how existing e-services can be developed. In the exemplified e-marketplace we described the "Blue Book Pricing" e-service as an related e-service because of its different interface and that another service provider (the company Kelly) was responsible for the e-service and not Yahoo Autos. There is a potential to enhance the value of the focused e-service concept in the example by *internalising* the "Blue Book Pricing" e-service as an additional e-service. To do this, Yahoo would have to take responsibility for the service as the service provider instead of Kelly and to develop the interface in Figure 7 in a way similar to the series of interfaces shown in Figures 1, 3, 4 and 5.

Conclusions

Designing e-services is about designing IT systems and their user interfaces. However in a service context customers occasionally use the e-service navigating through the IT system if it is beneficial in some sense. The main problem facing the IT system's design in a service context is to design the user interface, i.e. the series of layouts, informing the customer what e-services, i.e. which value adding activities, the IT system at the moment is delivering and which commitments and responsibility the involved actors have; both the service provider and the customers.

When designing e-services there are various possibilities to intertwine several e-services to each other and obtain advantages in different settings; both for the service providers and the customers. However, it is important to make these intertwined e-services explicit via the design of the service concepts and the user interfaces. To design *good* IT systems interfaces which present *distinct* e-services, we have to have ideas of what e-services the service provider offers and takes responsibility for and how the offer of other e-services can be related and provided by other service providers without creating confusion, irritation etc for the customers.

We claim that the framework presented in this paper combined with established web design criteria can be used in order to analyse and design user interfaces for the focused e-service, its service environment and the intertwined e-services. We also claim that the framework can be used as a tool in e-service development, analysing e.g. how to internalise intertwined e-services into the focused e-service and enhance the value for customers.

References

Ågerfalk PJ (2003) Information Systems Actability: Understanding Information Technology as a Tool for Business Action and Communication. Department of Computer and Information Science Linköping University Sweden

Chidambaram L (2001) The Editor's Column. E-Service Journal, vol 1, no 1

Dahlbom B (2002) From Systems to Services. www.viktoria.se/ ~dahlbom/

Edvardsson B, Gustafsson A, Johnson MD, Sandén B (2000) New Service Development and Innovation in the New Economy. Studentlitteratur Lund Sweden.

Grönroos C (1998) Service Marketing Theory – Back to Basics. Swedish School of Economics and Business Administration Helsingfors Finland

Grönroos C, Helnomen F, Isoniemi K, Lindholm M (2000) The NetOffer Model: a Case Example From the Virtual Market Space. Management Decision, vol 38, no 4, pp 243-252

Habermas J (1984) The Theory of Communicative Action. Vol One. Reason and the Rationalization of Society Beacon Press Boston

Hultgren G, Eriksson O (2005) The Concept of e-Service from a Social Interaction Perspective. Proc of the Action in Language, Organisations and Information Systems, Limerick Ireland

Nielsen J (2000) Designing Web Usability: the Practice of Simplicity. New Riders

Santos J (2003) E-service Quality: a Model of Virtual Service Quality Dimensions. Managing Service Quality, vol 13, no 3, pp 233-246

Stafford TF, Saunders C (2004) Introduction. E-Service Journal, vol 3, no 1

Selecting Processes for Co-designing eGovernment Services

Jörg Becker, Björn Niehaves, Lars Algermissen, Thorsten Falk and Patrick Delfmann

European Research Center for Information Systems (ERCIS), University of Münster, Germany. (becker, bjoern.niehaves, lars.algermissen, thorsten.falk, patrick.delfmann)@ercis.de

The Potential for Reorganisation Through eGovernment

Public administration has been confronted by a series of new demands on the one hand and has been forced to cost and staff cuttings on the other hand. There is a conspicuous trend towards growing individualization, whereby there are increasing demands by individuals on the state, to provide solutions to a variety of problems. Simultaneously, in the context of national and international competition, efficient and effective state activity and support for entrepreneurial activities in a region or country are becoming an increasingly decisive factor in location decisions. For some years, the term 'eGovernment' has been universally proposed as a way of closing the public administrations' modernization and performance gap (Budäus and Schwiering 1999).

Hence many public administrations started with eGovernment initiatives. Most of them deal with an improvement of their websites to so-called "Virtual Town Halls". However, most of the administrations just focus on an enhanced information quality and do not take into account the reorganization potential of communication and transaction processes. Our approach is a process oriented one and hence we define the core of eGovernment as the execution of administrative processes (Langkabel 2000): eGovernment entails the simplification and implementation of information, communication and transaction processes, in order to achieve, by means of information and communication technology, an administrative service, within and between authorities and, likewise, between authorities and private individuals or companies (Becker et al. 2005).

To find out whether eGovernment already had a broad impact in restructuring public administrations we conducted an empirical study. The study takes into account two different perspectives to measure and benchmark the degree of utilization of eGovernment activities. To ensure a representative sample in terms of demographic and sociological structure all investigated public administrations are settled in the same region – the "Muensterland".

On the one hand an external perspective was examined which deals with the citizen and industry perception of eGovernment activities. With a catalogue of criteria the internet portals of all 66 municipality and four county administrations were analyzed. The focus of this evaluation was the "Virtual Town Hall" which is the area of the portal where the regarded public services are offered. Beside the scope of these offered services the overall impression (e.g. graphical design and structured layout) of the website, the amount and quality of offered information and the navigation concepts to and within the public services were evaluated (Becker et al. 2005). The results show that the degree of interaction of most services does not reach the level of transaction. The majority of the municipalities only describes the services (information) or provides contact information (communication). However significant benefits can only be realized when a public service offers the chance for transactions and hence becomes an eService. Before classic public services can be offered as eServices it is advisable to reorganize the underlying processes and organizational structure in the back office. To evaluate the current state of reorganization activities the study includes the second perspective.

The internal perspective deals with the self-assessment of the local public administrations. The data collection was made by the use of a questionnaire which was structured into five categories concerning the following thematic scopes:

- Status-quo of eGovernment activities
- Scope of the internet portal
- Used domain specific software applications
- Perspective of future eGovernment activities
- Organizational and technical environment concerning eGovernment activities

The questionnaire was sent to all municipality and county administrations and after two weeks of process time 51 of 70 questionnaires had been answered which results in a representative 73 % rate of return. The evaluation indicated that the questionnaires were answered by the organizational units which are responsible for eGovernment activities in the regarded administration and therefore own the essential knowledge regarding the questionnaire. This concludes adequate data-quality of the self-assessment in this empirical study.

The most important question in the described context we asked was: What impact had eGovernment initiatives on your organizational structure and your processes to date?

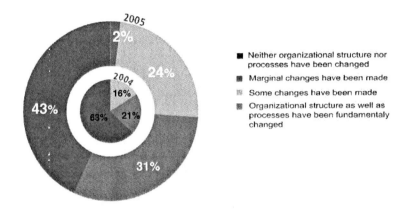

Fig. 1. Impact of eGovernment initiatives on organizational structure (n=51)

The results validate our thesis as in 2005 74 % (2004: 84%) of the public administrations eGovernment have conducted none or only marginal changes in the processes and the organizational structure in the context of eGovernment.

To enforce a structured approach towards process oriented reorganization and hence to improve the diffusion of transaction enabled eServices in virtual town halls we propose a procedural model for process-oriented reorganization projects.

Procedural Model for Process-Oriented Reorganization

Business process orientation is a paradigm of organizational design that has been established as a dictum in the praxis of organizational design since the early 90s (Davenport and Short 1990, Davenport 1993, Hammer 1990, Hammer and Champy 1993). Business process management (process management) provides methods for the realization of business process orientation. The following procedural model partitions the life cycle of a process management project and enunciate target recommendations concerning stages for the project implementation (Becker et al. 2005a). It consists of seven consecutive phases as well as the task of project management that covers the entire project (see figure 2).

1. **Phase I:** Project management is the foundation for the successful realization of any project. Subtasks as well as the use of personnel and resources have to be organized, planned, managed and controlled in a target-oriented manner (Becker et al. 2005a). Project goals must be defined regarding to content as well as formally (with respect to cost, time and quality). Their attainment has to be backed up by an appropriate project controlling.
2. **Phase II:** Preparation of process modelling is necessary due to the high complexity of process management projects within which usually numerous process models have to be produced. Thus, the modelling purpose ("why" shall we model), the model receiver ("for whom" shall we model) and modelling methods and tools ("how" shall we model) must be determined beforehand (Rosemann et al. 2005).
3. **Phase III:** The development of a strategy and an organizational framework helps to reduce the complexity which results from the fact that models are located on several hierarchy levels and linked among each other in different ways. This framework contains the company's essential tasks on the highest level and serves as a super ordinate model. It puts existing sub models into over-all coherence and allows for navigation through the different processes.
4. **Phase IV:** In the course of actual modelling or "As-is modelling" and analysis, the current state of the processes is recorded, analyzed and evaluated with regard to the accomplishment of the business objectives (Schwegmann and Laske 2005). This helps to create transparency within the company that facilitates the comprehension of technical interrelations and problems and to identify existing weak points.
5. **Phase V:** Process optimization aims at developing new processes by a "To-be modelling" work. The weak spots pointed out by actual modelling ("As-is modelling") have to be analyzed and eliminated if possible.
6. **Phase VI:** The development of process-oriented organizational structure is the consequential and necessary continuation of the business process redesign (Kugeler 2000, Kugeler and Vieting 2005). Thereby, the process-oriented organizational structure aims at enabling the adequate implementation of the optimized processes.
7. **Phase VII:** The introduction of the new organization deals with the implementation of the compiled process improvements (Hansmann et al. 2005). There is not just one possible way for implementation of new processes (or roll-out). In fact, appropriate measures have to be chosen and combined wisely considering factual, political and cultural factors

as well as the existing organization and the extent of the reorganization project.

For different reasons (e. g. new products, new staff, and changes in law) some processes turn out to be inefficient or ineffective after having been introduced. This requires a continuous adjustment of the processes of a company. Therefore, in addition to the monitoring of process implementation, the major task of a continuous process management is the constant, incremental improvement of the process organization. This process can be broken down into the four phases accomplishment, analysis, objective-redefinition and modelling (Neumann et al. 2005). These phases compose a cycle that helps to ensure a continuous alignment of the processes to changing business objectives and environmental conditions.

Prioritization of Processes with a Potential for Reorganization

The application of the presented procedural model in eGovernment projects requires its concretion, especially in the phase of actual modelling (Phase IV). Common product catalogues of municipal administrations prove that the range of services offered by public administrations presently comprises more than 1000 individual services, which are all represented by unique business processes. The number of processes implies that their reorganization will not bring about a significant rationalization for every single one of them. Therefore, it is advisable to pass through a stage of selection before beginning with the detailed cost and time extensive modelling of the present situation to select only those processes where the expected results of streamlining measures will exceed the modelling costs by far (Meffert and Bruhn 2000). An efficient way to select the processes with the highest potential for reorganization is by dividing the process of prioritization into different steps, which reduce the number of candidates for reorganization measures amongst the total number of processes (Schwegmann and Laske 2005). This method allows for the usage of straightforward assessment criteria to accelerate the selection in the early steps, whereas a more detailed analysis of the processes will further diminish the number of processes in the later steps. Only after applying this method the necessary modelling activities for the purpose of reorganization should be started.

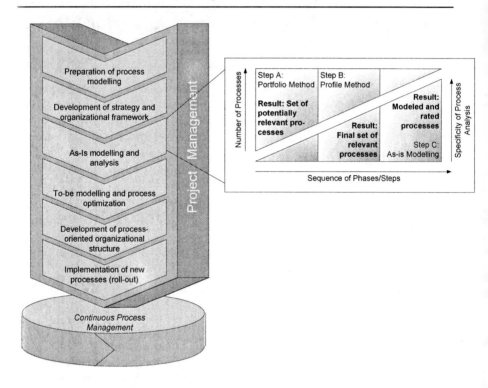

Fig. 2. Process-prioritization-phases in the context of the procedural model for process-oriented reorganization

We introduced a reference procedural model for process-oriented reorganization (see section 2). The phase of selecting high-potential processes for rationalization can be substantiated as shown in fig. 2. The phase of actual modelling or "As-is modelling" and analysis can be divided into three steps; the first and second being responsible for the selection of the processes that ought to be modeled in the third step.

Step A: Portfolio Method. After the identification of services provided by administrations, the expected number of related processes is comparatively high. Therefore, there is an obvious need for a tool that can provide a basic overview of the most important qualitative features of a service at minimal cost whilst conveying its potential for a modelling project. We have chosen a portfolio method, based on two pairs of criteria (Boller and Beuchat 2001, Gisler 2001, Isselhorst 2001).

The pair of criteria technical development determines the processes' penetration by information technology. It is specified by the technically feasible degree of interaction with the customer/citizen, and by the integration of information technology. For example, a mainly paper-based internal processing of information combined with missing online transaction facilities for the citizen is a strong indicator for a need for reorganizing measures. The criterion interaction intensity can have the values:

- Information: The value Information describes the mere unilateral technical provision of information like opening hours of the city hall on a website.
- Communication: The exchange of information between citizen and administration can be performed in a bidirectional manner. Besides, there is a possibility of interactive information retrieval (e. g., communication via email)
- Transaction: The citizen is given the possibility to handle entire administrative transactions, e. g. tax declaration, vehicle registration etc. via the internet.

The criterion integration intensity can adopt the following values:

- Media break: The execution of a service can be supported by means of modern information technology, but its fulfilment includes at least one discontinuity in the use of media (e. g. the manual submission of an order form).
- Without media breaks: The performance of the service is almost entirely supported by information technology, i. e. the fulfilment is realized without media discontinuities. Still, individual decisions, which impede the automated workflows, mark the action of the institution.
- Automated: Services are supplied by an information system without any need for further human action. This automation is particularly suitable for procedures, which do not require any scope of discretion or individual consideration.

After having clustered the processes by the pair of criteria technical development, a first impression of the processes' need for reorganization can be obtained and a first prioritization can be established. Additionally, services that do not require reorganization can be identified and implemented immediately. This applies especially in those cases, where services are comprehensively supported by information technology, but the online access for the citizen is still missing.

The second pair of criteria (intensity of execution) sheds light on the cost intensity of the inspected processes (Hagen 2000). As a result, the potential for rationalization measures becomes obvious. This portfolio focuses on the following two criteria:

- Number of cases: The number of cases of a process indicates the number of instances of one process within a certain period of time, i. e. how many times a process is executed in that period.
- Share of power users: Customers, who trigger the instances of service processes with an above-average frequency, are called power users. For example car dealers usually register a certain number of vehicles on behalf of their customers.

Having clustered the processes by the criteria number of cases and share of power users, further decisions on the prioritization can be made. A process with just a small number of executions for instance does not cause an immense effort and should therefore be put on hold.

Criterion	Values		
Organizational Complexity		**Technical complexity**	
Number of involved employees	☑ One ☑ Two ☑ More than two: _____ (Number)	Number and type of used applications	☑ None ☑ One: _____ (Producer) ☑ Several: _____ (Number, producer)
Person in charge to approve the results of a service	☑ Nobody ☑ Officials ☑ Head of department ☑ Mayor / District chief executive	Number of proprietary developments involved	☑ None ☑ One ☑ More than one
Number of involved entities	☑ One ☑ Two ☑ More than two: _____ (Number)	Further usage of service data	☑ Data is treated confidentially ☑ Data is used internally ☑ Data is forwarded to external institutions
Cooperation with other institutions of public administration	☑ None ☑ One ☑ Several: _____ (Number)	Hosting of procedures	☑ Desktop PC ☑ Internal server ☑ External server ☑ Internal and external servers
Number of changes of responsibility	☑ None ☑ One ☑ Several: _____ (Number)	**Formalities**	
		Existence of rules for the execution of processes	☑ No ☑ Instruction ☑ Law
Average processing time	☑ Hours ☑ Days ☑ Weeks ☑ Months	Form of usage	☑ Informal ☑ Written form is required ☑ Physical presence of applicant is required
Degree of complexity	☑ Mainly routine processes ☑ Mainly in... ☐ ...th	Scope of discretion in the supply of a service	...ope of discretion ...one of discretion

Fig. 3. Criteria and values of the profile

Step B: Profile Method. The portfolio of the processes has been reduced by the preceding analysis. In a second step it is now possible to assess the remaining processes on a more detailed level. To enable the evaluation of the processes' potential for reorganization, we propose to determine their organizational as well as technical complexity. Additionally, the degree of citizen integration into the provision of a service and the existence of formalities have to be taken into consideration (Eiffert 2000). Especially the latter aspect determines the feasibility of a mere electronically processing of public administration services. The application for identification documents for instance requires the physical presence of the applicant, which makes the process unsuitable for online handling.

Organizational and technical complexity, degree of citizen integration and formalities add up to a profile which allows to further reduce the amount of candidates for reorganization. The processes have to be analyzed according to the defined criteria and their possible values. Those values should be defined explicitly in advance to permit the comparison of the results. Figure 3 shows some of the criteria and their possible values. Based on the obtained results, the final choice of processes, which will be modelled in the next stage, can be achieved by using selection methods such as the Value Benefit Analysis (Zangenmeister 1970). At the end of this phase the number of candidates should have reduced to a level where a detailed modelling of the current situation seems economical.

Step C: Modelling of current situation and analysis of weaknesses. The application of the portfolio and profile method has resulted in the identification of the processes with the highest potential for reorganization. Those processes will be modeled in detail in this step in order to discover weak spots, which in return will form the basis for the creation of nominal processes. The decision concerning the modelling technique for this phase has already been made in the preparation of the activities. By means of interviews not only with officials, but also with managerial staff members, the "state of play" can be captured and transferred into process models.

The presented prioritization procedure does not only select processes with high reorganization potential but does also rank all other processes with respect to their potential. The results can be used for future projects to select the next processes to be reorganized and offered as transactional eServices within the "Virtual Town Hall". Further the fine granular separation of selection phases will result in a well and easy to understand documentation of the selection process to justify the selections made with respect to the project goals set by the project management.

Conclusions and Further Research

The term 'eGovernment' has been proposed as a way of closing the public administrations' modernization and performance gap. To measure the status-quo of eGovernment activities and their impact in restructuring public administrations an empirical study containing two perspectives was conducted. The external perspective examined the status-quo of eGovernment activities by analyzing the offered public services within the "Virtual Town Hall" of the administrations' internet portals. The results show that most of the administrations just focus on an enhanced information quality and that most of them don't offer fully transactional eServices. The second perspective which represents the internal perception of public administrations examined the made efforts to reorganize internal processes and organizational structures to enable classic public services to become fully transactional eServices. The results validate our thesis as in 2005 74 % of the public administrations eGovernment have conducted none or only marginal changes in the processes and the organizational structure. To structure the process of reorganization activities and to prioritize adequate processes to be reorganized an established procedural model has been presented and has been extended by a prioritization schema.

The presented procedural models have proven their usability in a real world projects however fields of activity can be identified.

- Advancement of the 3-step-model for selecting business processes with a potential for reorganization: e.g., the selection criteria could be adopted with regards to the national specifics of the context of application.
- Application of the phase model in other administrations (for instance, Algermissen et al. 2005) and further domains: especially the 3-step-model for prioritizing business processes was developed for and applied in the domain of public administration. Some experiences from practical applications can be found at www.regio-komm.de. Thus, it should be evaluated, for example, in other service oriented domains, e.g. insurance.
- Implementation of tool-support.
- The gained knowledge from modelled classic public service processes and reorganized processes should be used for formulation of reference models for administrational processes. These reference process models should be usable by a broad range of other administrations to fasten and enhance their reorganization projects within eGovernment activities.

References

Algermissen L, Delfmann P, Falk T, Niehaves B (2005) Priorisierung von Geschäftsprozessen für die prozessorientierte Reorganisation in öffentlichen Verwaltungen. In: Becker J, Kugeler M, Rosemann M (eds) Prozessmanagement. Ein Leitfaden zur prozessorientierten Organisationsgestaltung. 5th ed. Berlin

Becker J, Algermissen L, Niehaves B (2003) E-Government – State of the Art and Development Perspectives. Working Report No. 94 of the Department of Information Systems University of Muenster Muenster

Becker J, Algermissen L, Delfmann P, Falk T, Niehaves B (2005) Virtuelles Rathaus Münsterland 2005. Status quo und Entwicklungsperspektiven Muenster

Becker J, Berning W, Kahn D (2005a) Projektmanagement. In: Becker J, Kugeler M, Rosemann M (eds) Prozessmanagement. Ein Leitfaden zur prozessorientierten Organisationsgestaltung. 5th ed. Berlin

Boller R, Beuchat A (2001) Vertrauen und Sicherheit im Netz. In: Gisler M, Spahni D (eds) eGovernment. 2nd ed. Bern

Budäus D, Schwiering K (1999) Die Rolle der Informations- und Kommunikationstechnologien im Modernisierungsprozeß öffentlicher Verwaltungen. In: Scheer A-W (ed) Electronic Business und Knowledge Management. Heidelberg

Davenport TH (1993) Process Innovation: Reengineering Work through Information Technology. Boston

Davenport TH, Short JE (1990) The New Industrial Engineering: Information Technology and Business Process Redesign. Sloan Management Review, vol 31, no 4, pp 11-27

Eifert M (2000) Online-Verwaltung und Schriftform im Verwaltungsrecht. Kommunikation und Recht. O. Jg. 10, pp 11-20

Gisler M (2001) Einführung in die Begriffswelt des eGovernment. In: Gisler M, Spahni D (eds) eGovernment. 2nd ed. Bern

Hagen M (2000) Die Auswahl online-geeigneter Dienstleistungen. In: Reinermann H (ed) Regieren und Verwalten im Informationszeitalter. Heidelberg

Hammer M (1990) Re-Engineering Work: Don't Automate – Obliterate. Harvard Business Review, vol 68, no 4, pp 104-112

Hammer M, Champy J (1993) Reengineering the Corporation: A Manifesto for Business Revolution. New York

Hansmann H, Laske M, Luxem R (2005) Einführung der Prozesse – Prozess-Roll-out. In: Becker J, Kugeler M, Rosemann M (eds) Prozessmanagement. Ein Leitfaden zur prozessorientierten Organisationsgestaltung. 5th ed. Berlin

Isselhorst H (2001) Klassifikationsschema für E-Government-Verfahren. In: BSI (ed) E-Government-Handbuch. Bonn

Kugeler M (2000) Informationsmodellbasierte Organisationsgestaltung. Modellierungskonventionen und Referenzvorgehensmodell zur prozessorientierten Reorganisation. Berlin

Kugeler M, Vieting M (2005) Gestaltung einer prozessorientiert(er)en Aufbauorganisation. In: Becker J, Kugeler M, Rosemann M (eds) Prozessmanagement. Ein Leitfaden zur prozessorientierten Organisationsgestaltung. 5th ed. Berlin

Langkabel T (2000) e-Government – Der Weg ist das Ziel. V.O.P., Sonderheft 2, pp 6-8

Meffert H, Bruhn M (2000) Dienstleistungsmarketing. Grundlagen – Konzepte – Methoden. 3rd ed. Wiesbaden

Neumann S, Probst C, Wernsmann C (2005) Kontinuierliches Prozessmanagement. In: Becker J, Kugeler M, Rosemann M (eds) Prozessmanagement. Ein Leitfaden zur prozessorientierten Organisationsgestaltung. 5th ed. Berlin

Rosemann M, Schwegmann A, Delfmann P (2005) Vorbereitung der Prozessmodellierung. In: Becker J, Kugeler M, Rosemann M (eds) Prozessmanagement. Ein Leitfaden zur prozessorientierten Organisationsgestaltung. 5th ed. Berlin

Schwegmann A, Laske M (2005) Istmodellierung und Istanalyse. In: Becker J, Kugeler M, Rosemann M (eds) Prozessmanagement. Ein Leitfaden zur prozessorientierten Organisationsgestaltung. 5th ed. Berlin

Zangemeister C (1970) Nutzwertanalyse in der Systemtechnik. Eine Methodik zur multidimensionalen Bewertung und Auswahl von Projektalternativen. München

Infusing Technology into Customer Relationships: Balancing High-Tech and High-Touch

Harald Salomann, Lutz Kolbe and Walter Brenner

Institute of Information Management, University of St. Gallen, Switzerland. (Harald.Salomann, Lutz.Kolbe, Walter.Brenner)@unisg.ch

Introduction

In today's business environment, self-service is becoming increasingly important. In order to promote their self-service activities, banks have created online-only products and airlines offer exclusive discounts for passengers booking online. Self-service technologies' practical applications demonstrate this approach's potential. For example, Amtrak introduced an IVR (Interactive Voice Response) system, allowing cost savings of $13m; likewise Royal Mail installed an IVR system leading to a reduction of its customer service costs by 25% (Economist 2004).

On the other hand, the substitution of human contact with self-service technology is not always as successful as expected. For example, a study conducted by the market research company Forrester, in which 110 large companies were surveyed, shows that IVR systems meet customers' needs only 18% of the time, which is less than any other type of customer contact (Temkin et al. 2004).

These contradicting facts motivated the authors to examine self-services in customer relationships from companies' perspective. The research questions derived from the above outlined observations are as follows: Firstly, what is the actual status quo of the self-service domain? Secondly, how can self-services be successfully designed and implemented in practice if based on the findings regarding the status quo?

In order to address these research questions, a survey was conducted of renowned companies' CRM (Customer Relationship Management) executives in the German-speaking countries. Prior to this survey, the authors had conducted an extensive literature review. This also served as the basis of the survey's questionnaire.

The paper starts by presenting the theoretical concepts of self-services and self-service technology (SST) in the context of customer relationships. After this the research methodology and the survey design are outlined. The following section discusses self-services' status quo in customer relationships. The research findings culminate in a framework for the successful design and implementation of self-services. Finally, the paper concludes with a few remarks highlighting the limitations of as well as the contributions to further research stemming from this effort.

Theoretical Background

From Transactions to Relationships

Ever increasing competition and a simultaneous decrease in customer loyalty have led to the emergence of concepts that focus on the establishment and nurturing of relationships with customers. Customer relationship management emerged as a combination of different management and information systems approaches, in particular relationship marketing and technology-oriented approaches such as computer-aided selling and sales force automation.

Relationship marketing was the first systematic approach to the development of buyer-seller relationships. It can be defined as an integrated effort to identify, build up and maintain a network with individual customers and to continuously strengthen the network through interactive, individualized and value-added contacts for both sides' mutual benefit over a long period of time (Shani/Chalasani 1992).

The concept of CRM and its different perspectives and implications (i.e. process, strategy, philosophy, capability and technology) have been widely discussed by marketing practitioners and scholars alike. For our research purposes, we follow a process-oriented approach by Shaw and Reed (Shaw/Reed 1999), who define CRM as an interactive process achieving the optimum balance between corporate investments and the satisfaction of customer needs to generate the maximum profit.

Self-Service Concept

Characteristics of Self-Service

In a self-service system, the degree of a consumer's direct and active involvement in the service process is higher than that in other service systems. For example, Wikström refers to self-service as "a sort of joint venture in the marketplace, in which the consumer increasingly assumes the role of co-producer." (Wikström 1996) Consequently, the component 'self' in the term 'self-service' points to two important aspects:

In the context of a service's process dimension, the consumer's increased involvement in and integration into a service's workflow characterize self-service in comparison to 'traditional' service systems. The customer is involved "in tasks once done for her or him by others." (Toffler 1970)

In the context of self-service interactions between the consumer and service provider, the human element is eliminated from the service provider's side. Consequently, the interaction type 'human-human' is not part of the self-service concept. The 'high-touch' that usually characterizes services is replaced with 'high-tech'. In the current literature, technology is considered an enabler of self-service offerings. It is becoming ever more important. This development is demonstrated by the increased use of terms such as 'technology-based self-service' (Dabholkar 1996) and 'self-service technology' (Meuter et al. 2000).

Self-Services in Customer Relationships

The current literature in the self-service domain emphasizes the realization of potential cost savings as a prominent motive for companies to introduce self-services into customer relationships (e.g., Meuter et al. 2000). Since self-services enable non-human service interactions, personal care is substituted with technological solutions, which makes tremendous labor cost savings possible.

Furthermore, an ever-growing number of customers demand, and even expect, a self-service alternative. The targeting of this customer segment is therefore a main driver of the increasing importance of self-services in customer relationships. For example, one key element of Wells Fargo's strategy is to provide its customers with alternative delivery channels (Bitner et al. 2002). Consequently, Wells Fargo was the first bank in the U.S. to offer online banking to its customers. Wells Fargo's findings show that their online customers are the most satisfied and most loyal customer group.

Studies examining self-services in customer relationships also show that self-services are particularly appealing to a tech-savvy customer segment asking for more control over the service process and higher flexibility in terms of time (e.g., Bateson 1985). This aspect is also reflected in current self-service strategies in practice. For example, Blue Shield of California, a U.S.-based insurance company, offered online self-services after conducting research with focus groups composed of customers as well as potential health customers ('mylifepath.com') (Gallagher 2002).

Research Methodology

The authors of this paper conducted a survey aimed at examining the current status quo and future challenges in the CRM area with particular regard to critical success factors and common pitfalls. In addition to a more general CRM part, the survey also included a part that was specifically dedicated to self-services in customer relationships. The overall goal of this particular part of the survey was to identify and document the actual status quo in this area. In order to address these objectives, a questionnaire, aimed at eliciting a detailed description of the current activities in the self-service domain, was developed specifically for this focus topic's requirements.

The survey was carried out in the second half of 2004. 1,000 decision makers in the German-speaking regions (i.e. Germany, Austria and Switzerland), who are in charge of their companies' CRM activities, were invited to participate. An individually addressed email invitation explained the purpose of the research and included a link to the survey's online platform. Finally, this yielded a total of 89 responses for the general CRM study, equaling a return rate of approximately 9%. Of the 89 respondents, 44 actually utilize self-services. The details described in the following only refer to the self-service part of the survey.

The survey participants, who offer self-services to their customers, belong to a variety of different industries. The industry represented most often is "Banking/Financial Services" at 39%, followed by "Insurance" (20%) and "Telecommunications" (11%). Although this can be partially traced to the composition of the CRM survey's overall sample, it also allows the conclusion to be drawn that these industries, which represent approximately 59% of the self-service sample size, are currently placing most emphasis on self-services and the application of SST in customer relationships.

The majority of the participating companies (i.e. 26 of 44) are located in Germany. Fourteen companies are based in Switzerland and four firms are from Austria. The respondents are mainly representatives of large-scale enterprises in terms of number of employees as well as turnover per year.

Status Quo of Self-Services in Customer Relationships

Direction of Current Self-Service Activities

Currently, many companies (about 55%) refer to self-services as a matter of separate, divisional or channel-specific initiatives. Similarly, 20% of the companies described their self-service activities as single projects with no interaction with other projects. Only approximately 25% of the firms initiate coordinated, enterprise-wide self-service projects.

Companies mentioned cost reduction most often when asked about their motivation for the introduction of self-services in customer relationships. This goal adds up to a total percentage of around 86%, which highlights companies' widespread belief that self-service is an efficiency tool facilitating processes' streamlining through the elimination of media conversions and the reduction of idle time. Approximately 77% of the companies in our survey maintained that increasing customer satisfaction and loyalty are also motivations for the utilization of self-services. Compared to these figures, only about 32% of the companies declared deploying SST in order to reach new customer segments.

Furthermore, about 86% of the polled companies maintained that they offer retail customers self-services, whereas approximately 73% provide business customers with a self-service option. Many companies also consider service management employees as an attractive target group for self-service offerings. The majority of the respondents (around 64%) offer self-services to this group of employees in order to support the interaction with the customer.

The survey results show that self-services are most often used in the areas of transactions and customer service. Approximately 70% of the polled firms stated that they deploy self-service offerings in order to support transactions directed towards the interaction with an individual customer. Around 66% of the companies utilize SST for customer service concerning interactions that are one way or another related to supporting a company's core product.

Usage of Technology

As already pointed out before, the application of technology is a typical characteristic of self-service systems. The survey's results indicate that Internet technology plays a key role in the self-services context. Almost all companies (around 96%) maintained that they utilize the Internet as an interface for offering their customers self-services. According to our survey, popular applications of this SST are FAQs (Frequently Asked Questions) on websites and online tracking and tracing services.

The telephone/voice interface is ranked second in respect of the remaining SSTs. Exactly 50% of the firms participating in the survey use telephone self-services. The examples most frequently mentioned by the participants were fax-on-demand, IVR and voice recognition technologies.

Only approximately 32% of the companies utilize interactive kiosks as an SST. This result emphasizes the fact that the usage of kiosks in service management is decreasing due to Internet technology's popularity and diffusion in recent years.

Lastly, around 16% of the polled companies use video/CD technology in the context of self-service offerings. Video and TV-based training for customers is a common application of this self-service interface.

Benefits and Shortcomings

The majority of companies (around 84%) refer to the realization of cost reductions as the biggest benefit of self-services. The reduction of process cycle time is almost as important as cost savings. This benefit was named by 36 of 44 companies (equaling approximately 82%). Furthermore, the elimination of media conversion is regarded as yet another benefit by approximately 43% of the companies. These results underpin the prevalent argument that efficiency gains in terms of time and money are the main advantages of SST.

However, besides these benefits listed above, 25% of the companies referred to other advantages. These comprise aspects such as an increased freedom of choice for customers, generation of leads, identification of prospects, and the positioning of the company as an innovation leader. These benefits demonstrate that self-service is not only about 'reducing' time and costs. It is also about 'enhancing' a company's strategic options and capabilities.

As far as the shortcomings of SST are concerned, 30 of 44 companies (equaling about 68%) characterize customers' lack of acceptance of SST as the main shortcoming. The causes of this lack of acceptance as based on the firms' experiences were also cited. One reason is the shifting of tasks formerly performed by the company to customers. Many customers are not willing to accept this shift of tasks. Consequently, they refuse to make use of SST. Another frequently mentioned reason is that self-services usually only appeal to a certain, tech-savvy customer segment.

Another disadvantage closely related to insufficient acceptance is the lack of personal contact with customers which results in weak social bonds. This shortcoming was mentioned by 24 companies, equaling approximately 55%. A further consequence of this lack of personal contact is the severely limited advisory service. Since this advisory service is missing in self-service interactions, it is also almost impossible to identify the same degree of cross- and up-selling potential as would be possible in a face-to-face meeting.

Discussion of the Status Quo

The empirical findings (see also Fig 1) reveal that about half of the polled companies actually offer their customers self-services (i.e. 44 out of 89 companies). Therefore, although self-service is on many companies' agenda, there is still a considerable potential for growth, which leads to the conclusion that self-service is here to stay. Currently, however, self-services are primarily offered by financial services, banking and insurance companies.

Self-Services in Customer Relationships			
Organizational alignment	Divisional, channel-specific	Enterprise-wide program of projects	Single project
Ranking (Percentage)	1 (55%)	2 (25%)	3 (20%)
Motivation for introduction	Cost reduction	Increase customer satisfaction and loyalty	Reach new customer segments
Ranking (Percentage)	1 (86%)	2 (77%)	3 (32%)
Scope	Transactions	Customer service	Education
Ranking (Percentage)	1 (71%)	2 (66%)	3 (39%)
Deployed technology	Internet	Telephone	Interactive Kiosks	Video/CD
Ranking (Percentage)	1 (96%)	2 (50%)	3 (23%)	4 (16%)

Fig. 1. Status Quo of Self-Services in Customer Relationships

Furthermore, companies are beginning to realize that the self-service approach is not just about cutting costs and improving efficiency. Although this is still the motive that was most frequently mentioned by the participating firms, increasing customer satisfaction and loyalty is almost equally important. A few participants explicitly referred to self-services as a way of enhancing a company's strategic options.

The results of our survey point towards one key challenge: SST constitutes a 'double-edged sword' for companies that are unable to find the right balance between high-tech and high-touch. This is caused by the fact that self-services' strengths are simultaneously their main weaknesses. On the one hand, utilization of SST makes tremendous cost savings possible. The downside of service automation is, however, a lack of customer acceptance, weak social bonds and a loss of personal contact and client control.

A Framework for Self-Services in Customer Relationships

Within the scope of our study we also asked the participants what they considered important for self-services' design and implementation, be it good ('best practice') or bad ('lessons learned'). For this reason, we included a section in the questionnaire were participants had the opportunity to comment on their first-hand experience with self-service technology. Based on these comments, we identify four critical factors that should be considered for self-services in customer relationships.

Development of a Focused Self-Service Strategy

Most companies commenting on unsuccessful self-service initiatives put the blame on a diffuse strategic impetus resulting in a lack of focused self-service activities. Our survey findings reveal that successful firms focus their self-service activities in terms of their goals and scope. They gear their self-service strategy towards one primary goal aligned with their particular business strategy. The primary goal of a focused self-service strategy is typically one of the following: cost reduction, increased customer satisfaction and loyalty, or development of new customer segments.

Furthermore, companies focus their self-service offerings within a certain scope instead of covering the whole range. According to our survey results, two main directions can be differentiated: transaction orientation and knowledge seeking.

The first direction aims at supporting customers' transactions by means of SST. This transaction-driven self-service is directed towards an individual's relationship with the company and follows a specific objective. It is only, however, relevant at a particular moment in time. This type of self-service requires standardized processes with real-time information and contextual knowledge delivery. Examples are completing an order online, changing an address and the tracking and tracing of an order's status.

The second direction is geared towards knowledge-seeking interactions aimed at providing and exchanging knowledge between a company and its customers. This knowledge-driven self-service concerns generalized information about the company's products and procedures such as inquiries concerning product usage, troubleshooting, warranty information and store locations. This type of self-service interaction requires extensive search and retrieval functionalities as well as logic to identify the appropriate knowledge required for the customer's inquiry.

Change and Awareness within the Organization

Self-services are affecting and changing companies on an organizational level. Very often companies underestimate this fact and consider self-services as a solely technological challenge, or something that can be left to a single department within the organization. Our survey findings emphasize the fact that the majority of companies perform self-service activities as a matter of separate, divisional or channel-specific initiatives.

Only a small number of companies are fully aware of the enterprise-wide implications of self-service activities. However, these are the ones that are achieving success in the self-service domain. Our research shows that successful firms sensitize the whole organization by spanning their self-services activities across departmental boundaries instead of limiting them to organizational 'silos'. In this context, the launch of enterprise-wide projects and the integration of efforts across all customer touch points pave the way for the successful design and implementation of self-services.

Internet Technology as a Self-Service Enabler

Technology is a key enabler of the creation of a compelling self-service experience for customers. Following our survey findings, we conclude that successful companies fully grasp technological advances' limits and benefits with regard to their suitability for self-service environments. The technology most appropriate for the successful design of self-services is the Internet (although the Internet is more than a self-service technology). The diffusion of the Internet and its 'anytime, anywhere' characteristics ensure a company's accessibility by turning it into a 'virtual store' that is permanently accessible from (almost) anywhere.

Internet technology also allows firms to identify customers' needs and to tailor self-services to meet a customer's needs throughout his/her individual customer process phases. The Internet's technological enhancements furthermore enable service providers to personalize their self-services. According to the survey participants, personalized self-services have a positive impact on customer relationships because customers feel that they are truly known and individually acknowledged by a firm along the customer process. The survey participants' comments indicated that this personalization of self-services is more important than the offering of price discounts as incentives. The survey results show, moreover, that companies are also not willing to allow price discounts, as this would diminish the potential cost savings they are hoping for.

Our research findings indicate that other SSTs are less likely to match the specific needs of self-service systems due to their restrictions in terms of time and location. Kiosks can, for example, only be accessed at certain locations, whereas the Internet is not as limited in this regard.

Integration of Self-Service Activities

Another critical success factor that has to be considered in self-service design is the integration of the self-service world into traditional channels. According to our research results, companies excelling at this discipline do so by leveraging their self-service activities by means of running a common platform for self-services as well as all other customer interactions. Integrated systems are a prerequisite for such a strategy.

In this context, successful companies consider the self-service channel as complementary to, rather than a substitute for, other channels. For example, if a user opts out of a self-service channel, companies that successfully integrated self-service channels with their 'traditional' channels are able to pass the self-service channel's information to the call center agent in real-time. Consequently, the customer always has the choice to resort to a 'traditional' channel without going through repetitive authentication procedures and answering redundant questions concerning his/her inquiry.

The integration of self-service activities also includes making the self-service platform available to both customers and to contact center employees as a tool for helping customers. This assists companies in ensuring consistency of information across all interfaces and channels. Such an approach avoids the sending of 'mixed messages' to customers.

A Framework for Self-Service Design

Based on our findings outlined in the sections above, we propose a framework as is illustrated in Fig 2. This proposed self-service framework is based on an earlier framework describing the necessary elements for successful CRM initiatives. The initial CRM framework was the result of ongoing research that combines theoretical conceptualization efforts with practical application. The theoretical findings of this research, which have been introduced to the research community, elaborate on eight years of case study and action research in conjunction with quantitative research methods (e.g., Gebert et al. 2003; Bueren et al. 2005). The research results have also been discussed and validated in practice through collaboration with research partners.

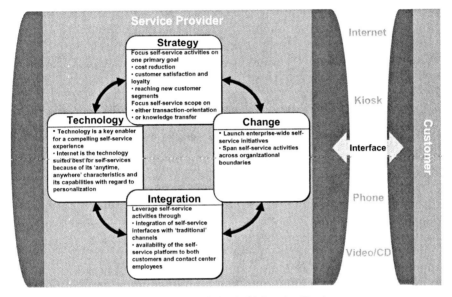

Fig. 2. Framework for Self-Service Design

Limitations and Directions for Future Research

The authors did not intend to investigate self-services in customer relationships in any hypothetic-deductive way at this point. Nevertheless, the survey's results should support the development of future theory and models in this field with particular reference to the successful use of technology in self-service systems. The proposed framework will be further refined and substantiated by means of in-depth industry case studies.

The sample size for the empirical study is relatively small, although within the range found in many other studies in this area (e.g., Xue et al. 2005). The study is also limited to the German-speaking area and lacks generalizability within a specific industry. Future research can shed light on the analysis of self-services outside the German-speaking area and may focus on a specific industry. The internationalization of research in this field may also give rise to cultural issues as an emerging theme in the area of self-services in customer relationships.

References

Bateson, JEG (1985) Self-Service Consumer: An Exploratory Study. Journal of Retailing, vol 61, no 3, pp 49-76

Bitner MJ, Ostrom, AL, Meuter ML (2002) Implementing successful self-service technologies. In: Academy of Management Executive, vol 16, no 4, pp 96-109

Bueren A, Schierholz R, Kolbe L, Brenner W (Forthcoming) Improving Performance of Customer Processes with Knowledge Management. In: Business Process Management Journal

Dabholkar PA (1996) Consumer Evaluations of New Technology-Based Self-Service Options: An Investigation of Alternative Models of Service Quality. In: International Journal of Research in Marketing, vol 13, pp 29-51

Economist (2004) You're hired, September 16th

Gallagher J (2002) Balancing between High-Tech & High-Touch. In: Insurance & Technology, vol 27, no 3, pp 22-27

Gebert H, Geib M, Kolbe LM, Brenner W (2003) Knowledge-Enabled Customer Relationship Management. Journal of Knowledge Management, vol 7, no 5, pp 107-123

Meuter ML, Ostrom A, Roundtree RI, Bitner MJ (2000) Self-Service Technologies: Understanding Customer Satisfaction with Technology-Based Service Encounters. Journal of Marketing, vol 64, no. 3, pp 50-64

Shani D, Chalasani S (1992) Exploiting Niches Using Relationship Marketing. The Journal of Consumer Marketing, vol 9, no 3, pp 33-42

Shaw R, Reed D (1999) Measuring and Valuing Customer Relationships: How to Develop the Measures that Drive Profitable CRM Strategies. Business Intelligence, London

Temkin BD, Manning H, Sonderegger P, Amato M (2004) Scenario Design: A Disciplined Approach to Customer Experience. Forrester

Toffler A (1970) Future Shock. Amereon Ltd., New York

Wikström S (1996) Value Creation by Company-Consumer Interaction. Journal of Marketing Management, vol 12, no 5, pp 359-374

Xue M, Hein GR, Harker PT (2005) Consumer and Co-Producer Roles in e-Service: Analysing Efficiency and Effectiveness of e-Service Designs. International Journal of Electronic Business, vol 3, no 2, pp 174-197

Prerequisites and Effects of CRM Systems Use in Poland

Dorota Buchnowska and Stanislaw Wrycza

Department of Information Systems, University of Gdańsk, Poland.
grzywka@panda.bg.univ.gda.pl, swrycza@univ.gda.pl

Introduction

It has been demonstrated in numerous studies that CRM implementation is beneficial in terms of higher revenues and lower costs (Aberdeen Group 2004: Thompson 2004) However, many potential CRM users in Poland are discouraged by high implementation costs and a high proportion of abortive implementations. Managers complain about lack of best practices that might convince them about the advisability of their strategy. The high failure rate in CRM implementation (Hellweg 2002) is often the result of the fact that the firms responsible for implementation lack an adequate and proven methodology.

Most information on CRM concept and supporting it systems, especially on benefits of CRM applications, comes from CRM vendors. Companies do not trust the suppliers and their assurances about the gains that can be achieved owing to CRM system introduction. There has been a need, therefore, for a methodologically objective, academic study that would provide reliable results. This drove the authors to embark on a study, the main goal of which is to analyse and assess economically how useful CRM software is in supporting customer relations management in various business organisations in Poland. The classical statistical analysis of structure has been used.

The first part of the paper presents the scope of the research and the methodology. The second part is a study of benefits brought by CRM system implementation. CRM success factors identified in this way are described in the third part.

Research Method

The way the goal has been formulated indicates that the study focused on business entities which have implemented systems of the CRM class. In order to avoid ambiguity in identifying statistical units, the following permanent attributes have been determined that decide the inclusion of an organisation in the population studied:

- *material attribute* – CRM class system implementation and operation;
- *time attribute* – determined by the study period (June – August 2003);
- *space attribute* – the territory of Poland.

There are several dozen CRM class systems on offer in Poland. They vary a lot in terms of both functionality and implementation cost. Besides, the use of CRM label by software suppliers is on the increase. For this reason, only those business entities have been analysed which use a system that, beyond any doubt, can efficiently support the strategy of customer relations management. The list of such applications includes CRM systems which:

- are recognised as the quality products by research institutions of world renown, dealing with CRM issues (ISM Inc (ISM 2002: ISM 2003), Gartner Group (Bona and Davies 2002; Thompson 2003)) and are available on the Polish market;
- are most commonly used in Poland (according to Process4E report (Stanusch 2002)) and perform sales, marketing and customer service functions.

On the whole, 23 CRM applications were eligible for the study, including: Siebel, modern.marketing, mySAP, Oracle, Claryfy, Amdocs, Pivotal, SAS, Goldmine FrontOffice, Vantive, Peoplesoft, iBAAN, Clientele, Logotec CRM9000, Exact, Teta, IFS, Impuls BPSC, Simple CRM, Insoft CRM, M2Net CRM, Taktikos, Aurum and EuroCRM

When the list of systems to be studied and analysed was completed, the list of business entities – users of the selected CRM systems was made. This was done on the basis of reference lists of the manufacturers, the implementation companies and the firms doing CRM systems pre-implementation studies. Information provided by magazines and vortals dealing with CRM issues was also used.

The use of these sources led to the creation of a preliminary list of respondents, consisting of 155 business organisations. The list was then validated by checking if all the entities actually used one of the previously selected CRM class systems.

It turned out that only 73 per cent of previously chosen organisations actually used customer relations management supporting systems. The remaining 27 per cent should not have been included in the population – most commonly because CRM implementation had not been completed (41%) or because the companies did not confirm that implementation had been completed or was in progress (29%). Other reasons for rejection were that the system was used for other purposes than customer relations management, the company was non-existent, or the system was used in a way which made it impossible to evaluate implementation process and results. In conclusion, the general population of the survey consisted of 116 business entities, further referred to as „CRM application users", which operated in Poland between June and August 2003 and were using one of the previously defined CRM class systems.

The basic form of data collection was *Computer Assisted Telephone Interviewing – CATI* using a questionnaire of 57 questions covering three basic areas:

- company profile;
- description of the changes that had taken place in the company as a result of CRM system implementation;
- description of system implementation.

In order to obtain all this data, interviews were often conducted with several people from one company (mostly people who were responsible for CRM system implementation). Finally, meaningful data was obtained from eighty-five companies, giving a return rate of 73%.

Benefits of Implementing a CRM Class Application

Expected Benefits

Implementation of an application supporting customer relations management is to give the company long-term gains, both quantifiable and non-quantifiable. Aware of the high implementation cost, companies expect proportionate effects. Expectations of the technology are high, the more so as suppliers promise gains that will outweigh the expenditure. Such promises are often supported by studies conducted by independent research organisations. The chart in Figure 1 shows basic benefits that can be derived from the implementation of a CRM class application. It also illustrates how the effects are interrelated.

The benefits presented in the figure have been grouped in four basic categories, which also show the sequence in which they occur. The basic function of CRM systems is to collect all relevant customer and business environment information. Owing to this, the information is accessible on a current basis to all authorised personnel (sometimes also to partners or suppliers).

The first effect of CRM implementation that is observed is the rearrangement of the knowledge of the customers, which results in improved communications. CRM implementation gives every employee a holistic view of the client. The buyer, on the other hand, owing to the integration of all communication channels, can use the communication form of their choice and be sure of getting good service.

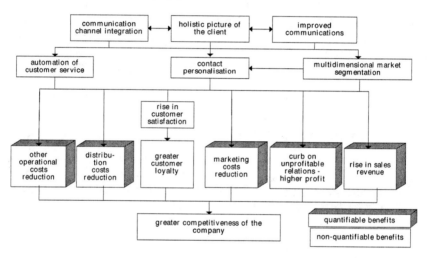

Fig. 1. Benefits of implementing CRM application

The rearranged, overall knowledge determines how useful the software is and is indispensable for customer service automation as well as for the use of functionalities designed to improve individual customer relations management. It is only then that quantifiable benefits emerge, like higher revenues, lower operational costs, contributing to higher competitiveness of the company.

Table 1 shows what benefits the businesses surveyed in this study meant to achieve through the implementation of technology supporting customer relations management. Respondents could choose several of listed gains. List of these benefits was prepared on basis of studies of literature (Dyche

2001; Burnett 2000; Bergeron 2002). Respondents had also the possibility of addition their own, not listed benefits.

Most of Polish CRM users recognized that by implementing CRM they wanted to improve in-house communications and get a holistic picture of the client. In view of the fact that the two are elementary benefits of CRM implementation, the percentage of companies that mentioned them was not high. All other benefits are derived from them and depend on the implemented functionality of the system and the degree of its integration with the other management supporting applications. 82% of the surveyed organisations hoped that the implementation of CRM strategy supporting tools would automate the customer service process boosting the productivity of the personnel involved. How useful the technology actually is depends on the data stored in the system and how much it concentrates on the properly designed processes.

Table 1. Expected and achieved benefits of implementing CRM system

Benefit type	% of CRM users which expected this type of benefit	% of CRM users which achieved this type of benefit
improved in-house communications	91	90
getting a holistic picture of the customer	84	76
customer service automation and standardization	82	74
greater competitiveness	78	57
getting rid of lost information costs	75	67
lower distribution costs	74	47
lower marketing costs	72	44
market segmentation (buyers)	71	56
greater customer satisfaction – better quality of service	71	55
higher loyalty /customer retention rate	65	47
other operational and administrative costs reduction	63	40
higher sales revenue	62	44
customer communication channels integration	62	48
higher profit – less investment in no-profit customers	60	40
personalization	54	43

At every stage, CRM systems make adequate customer information available as well as system information guiding the user through its subsequent stages. Work automation helps to reduce costs and improve quality, therefore to raise customer satisfaction, thus leading to the emergence of subsequent benefits – this time quantifiable.

After process automation, higher competitiveness of the organisation is the second most frequently mentioned positive effect that the surveyed companies wanted to achieve through CRM implementation. It should be noted that it is the most frequently identified „real" long-term benefit (in view of results that are a source of other quantifiable benefits). One may, therefore, conclude that higher competitiveness of the organisation is the main objective of implementing a CRM application. All the other quantifiable benefits expected by the organisations are but tools – used to a varying degree – in the pursuit of the main objective of maintaining good standing in the competitive market.

Achieved Benefits

The previous section presented what was expected of the CRM technology. Subsequent analysis is to confront these expectations with the results actually achieved. Table 1 shows data which allow us to identify the benefits of implementing a CRM class system that were achieved by the statistically surveyed business organisations.

The data obtained from the respondents indicate that improved communications within the company is the most frequently perceived benefit of implementing technology which supports customer relationship management. Owing to CRM software implementation, more than three quarters of the organisations obtained an overall, uniform picture of the customer. The two benefits mentioned are closely related, as they result from systemising the knowledge contained in the information held by the company. It should be stressed that the two benefits were most frequently mentioned as expected effects of CRM implementation by the users and were achieved by the greatest number of companies. Improved communications were materialized (achieved by the organisations that had expected it) by 95% of CRM users, while 89% of the businesses expecting to get a holistic picture of their customer through CRM implementation did achieve this objective (Table 2).

By examining the data contained in the table, we may say that the surveyed organisations see the non-quantifiable effects of the CRM project. The quantifiable ones are perceived much less frequently. This is due to the fact that they are difficult to quantify. While the former can easily be seen „with the naked eye", the occurrence of the latter has to be substantiated by work-consuming calculations. Their estimation is usually a costly undertaking and, as such, is frequently abandoned, especially in small projects. Therefore, it is not always possible to determine the extent to which individual effects are an immediate outcome of the CRM project. For this reason, most companies do not even try to quantify the financial gains of CRM implementation, expected or achieved.

Table 2. The extent to which benefits of CRM implementation have materialized

Benefit type	% of CRM users which materialized this type of benefit
Non-quantifiable benefits	
improved in-house communications	95
customer service automation and standardization	89
getting a holistic picture of the customer	89
getting rid of lost information costs	85
customer communication channels integration	77
personalization	76
market segmentation (buyers)	75
greater customer satisfaction – better quality of service	74
greater competitiveness	73
higher loyalty /customer retention rate	71
Benefit type	% of CRM users which materialized this type of benefit
Quantifiable benefits	
higher sales revenue	70
higher profit – less investment in no-profit customers	66
other operational and administrative costs reduction	63
lower distribution costs	63
lower marketing costs	60

Quantifiable Benefits of Implementing a CRM Application

The difficulty in estimating economic effects of CRM project can be seen through the pattern of replies to the closed question: „What quantifiable benefits has the company achieved owing to the implementation of a CRM application?" The pattern is presented in Table 3.

As seen in this table, most users of CRM systems are not able to determine if and/or to what extent software implementation has brought about specific gains. The proportion of organisations which observed no change is similar for all of the quantifiable benefits. It has to be stressed, though, that the purpose of the question was to define the level of change of selected values. The way the question was asked did not preclude the "no change" reply if the change was not supported by relevant calculations. For this reason, further analysis will focus on those organisations which observed a given benefit and were able to quantify it.

Table 3. Quantifiable benefits of implementing a CRM application

Benefit type Reply	Higher profit	Higher sales revenue	Lower opera- tional costs	Higher customer satisfaction index
Difficult to say	78%	68%	68%	64%
Change in %	10%	19%	18%	24%
No change	12%	13%	14%	12%

The data from the Table 3 indicate that higher profit was shown in the calculations of only 10% of the organisations. The highest proportion of companies observed and quantified the growth in customer satisfaction index. It means, organizations begin to perceive, that the decided, about the company position on competitive market, factor is customers' satisfaction. In order to raise the level of satisfaction, indispensable it is however her measurement. Thanks to use of quantitative techniques of satisfaction measurement it is possible not only establish current level of the customers' satisfaction, but also recognize, what influences on her growth.

The chart contained in Figure 2 presents the measures describing the mean level of quantifiable benefits of CRM implementation (annually) in those organisations that were able to determine it.

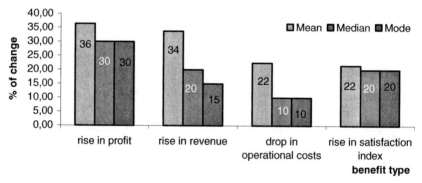

Fig. 2. Level of quantifiable effects of CRM implementation

The mean rise in profit resulting from CRM implementation among the companies that were able to define it was 36%. The rise varied from 15% to 100%, in the greatest number of cases (56%) it reached 30%. The companies analysed in this part of the study achieved, on the average, a 34% rise in sales revenue. The rise varied from 10 to 100 per cent, so the disparity is greater than for the rise in profit. The distribution is also more uneven, and its bias to the right indicates that the majority of organisations (83%) recorded a rise in sales revenue below the mean of 34%.

Variations in the distribution are even greater when it comes to the drop in operational costs. The companies that observed and quantified it quoted values ranging from 5 to 100 per cent. The mean reduction of operational costs stood at 22%, yet in 79% of the companies it was lower than average. One half of the organisations fixed it at between 10 and 20 per cent.

For greater satisfaction resulting from CRM implementation, the distribution is marked by smallest range of variations (10-50%) and smallest variations within the distribution in absolute terms. The use of the system raised the level of satisfaction (in the group of companies here analysed) by an average of 22%. The largest group of companies (30%) recorded a 20% rise of this indicator.

The data presented above demonstrate that the use of CRM system may give a organisation significant, quantifiable gains. It should be added that the effects achieved by Polish companies do not differ much from those achieved by organisations operating in America. A study done in 1998 by Insight Technology Group, for instance, showed that 21% of the companies surveyed after they had introduced IT supporting a CRM strategy had, on the average, a 42% rise in profit, a 35% drop in distribution costs and a 20% rise in consumer satisfaction index. (Dickie and Hayes 2002)

Success Factors of CRM Project

Implementation of CRM software in a company is a difficult undertaking. The task of the system of this class is to support the strategy adopted by the company. Therefore, implementation is a project affecting the whole organisation and the risk involved is high[1]. The fact is supported by studies done by analytical firms, according to which 50 to 70 per cent of CRM projects do not bring the expected results (Gartner Group 2001). In order to mitigate the risk involved in an IT project, one should make use of the

---

[1] Statistics show that 65% of very large IT projects are abandoned. (Capers 1996)

experiences of the organisations which completed a similar initiative and can see the success factors in perspective.

Figure 3 shows data that can be an indication of what affects the success of a CRM implementation project, from the point of view of Polish users. The chart shows what proportion of companies considered individual of listed factors to be very important in the process of CRM implementation. The list of critical factors of success was established on basis of a survey of literature (Dickie and Hayes 2002; Myron and Ganeshram 2002; Gobel, Schulz-Klein and Stender 2003).

Most of the organisations think that the success is primarily determined by the commitment of the employees and none of the respondents said that a pro-active attitude of project participants does not affect the success of the implementation, while only 2.5% considered this to be of minor importance for the final success. We may, therefore, acknowledge that the users of CRM application realise that without the cooperation of the employees and their positive attitude a CRM initiative is bound to fail. There will be no employee commitment without the support and the commitment of the management. It is their task to motivate the staff and to demonstrate through their own attitudes how important the project is. Project participants must be convinced that the results will be proportionate to their efforts. This is why a significant proportion of the respondents (44%) have decided that support and commitment of the management is a factor significantly affecting the CRM success.

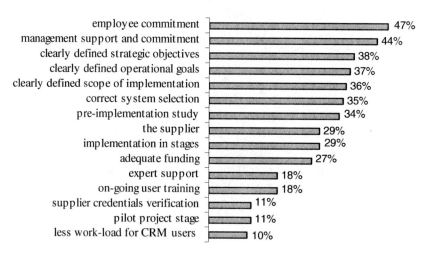

Fig. 3. Success factors in implementing a CRM application

Apart from motivating the staff, the management is also responsible for project coordination. CRM covers various areas of company operations (sales, marketing, post-sale customer service). Employees of various departments may have various needs and expectations of the new technology. If differences hindering work progress are to be avoided, strategic objectives and operational goals of implementation must be clearly formulated. Precisely identified objectives are, therefore, another key to success of a CRM project.

Further examination has shown that the success factors described above are the most important ones for the buyer of the CRM technology. Each scored at least four points in a scale of five, where 1 meant "no impact" and 5 meant "heavy impact" on the success of the project.

The factors identified by Polish users of CRM applications differ considerably from those identified by CRM projects participants in the USA. The chart in Figure 4 shows the results of a relevant study conducted by Insight Technology Group (ITG) (Dickie and Hayes 2002).

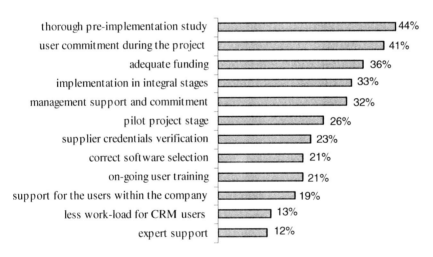

Fig. 4. CRM initiative success factors according to American organisations
Prepared after Dickie and Hayes (2002)

These data show that the largest proportion of American users of CRM applications consider a pre-implementation study of business processes to be a prerequisite for success. In comparison with Polish organisations, ten per cent more companies surveyed by ITG considered it a very important CRM success factor. American respondents more often than their Polish counterparts stressed the importance of other pre-implementation work, notably of pilot project stage (15% more) and of verifying the credentials of the supplier (12% more). The pilot stage and credentials verification were, according to the survey done by the author, considered irrelevant for CRM success by Polish respondents. Polish users, more often than American ones, mentioned the support and commitment of the management (12% more) and the selection of adequate software (13% more).

Conclusion

In conclusion, we may say that according to business organisations in Poland, the success of a project implementing CRM system primarily depends on the company culture, i.e. a homogenous system of shared corporate values (Stachowich-Stanusch 2000). Factors connected with the implementation process or the application itself are important, but they will not "save" the project in the absence of an adequate human factor involvement and a clearly defined strategy of the company.

References

Aberdeen Group (2004) What Works: Ten Significant CRM Implementations 2003. www.aberdeen.com (20.07.2004)

Bergeron B (2002) Essentials of CRM: A Guide to Customer Relationship Management. Wiley New York

Bona A, Davies J (2002) EMEA CSS Magic Quadrant 4Q02. Gartner Research. www4.gartner.com/ (06.12.2002)

Burnett K (2000) Handbook of Key Customer Relationship Management, The: The Definitive Guide to Winning, Managing and Developing Key Account Business. Financial Times/Prentice Hall

Capers J (1996) Patterns of Software Systems Failure and Success. International Thomson Computer Press

Brown SA (ed) (2000) Customer Relationship Management. Wiley Canada

Dickie J, Hayes L (2002) The Sales & Marketing Excellence Challenge Study Results. Insight Technology Group & CRM Insights Research. www.csoinsights.com, 20.10.2003.

Dyche J (2001) The CRM Handbook: A Business Guide to Customer Relationship Management. Addison-Wesley Professional

Gartner Group (2001) Gartner Says More than 50 Percent of CRM Implementations Considered Failures from Customer's Point of View. (09.11.2002) www4.gartner.com/5_about/press_releases/2001/pr20010912b.html

Gobel S, Schulz-Klein E, Stender M (2003) CRM Implementation Practices in Europe. Fraunhofer Institute for Industrial Engineering University of Stuttgart Stuttgart

Hellweg E (2002) CRM Success: Still the Exception, Not the Rule. www.business2.com/articles/web/0,1653,42051,FF.html (29.10.2002)

ISM (2002) ISM Unveils the 2002 Top 30 CRM Software Packages. www.ismguide.com/ (13.02.2002)

ISM (2003) ISM Announces the 2003 Top 30 CRM Software Packages. www.ismguide.com/ (15.03.2003)

Myron D, Ganeshram R (2002) The Truth About CRM Success & Failure. CRM Magazine July

Stachowicz-Stanusch A (2000) Kultura marketingowa przedsiębiorstw. PWN Warszawa

Stanusch M (2002) Raport - Wdrożenia CRM w Polsce. Process4E Warszawa

Thompson E (2003) EMEA Sales Applications Magic Quadrant 1H03. Gartner Research 28.02.2003

Thompson B (2004) Successful CRM: Turning Customer Loyalty into Profitability. RighNow Technologies Publication

Understanding Enterprise Systems' Impact(s) on Business Relationships

Peter Ekman and Peter Thilenius

School of Business, Mälardalen University, Sweden.
(peter.ekman, peter.thilenius)@mdh.se

Introduction

Enterprise systems (ESs), i.e. standardized applications supplied from software vendors such as SAP or Oracle, have been extensively employed by companies during the last decade. Today all *Fortune 500* companies have, or are in the process of installing, this kind of information system (Seddon et al. 2003). A wide-spread denotation for these applications is enterprise resource planning (ERP) systems. But the broad utilization use of these software packages in business is rendering this labelling too narrow (Davenport 2000).

A central aspect of ESs is their multi-dimensional characteristics. Based upon a (virtual) common database, ESs allow all business activities to be observed throughout the company (i.e. an operation performed by marketing may be displayed in finance; purchasing; supply functions, and so forth, in real-time). But with this high visibility and extensive information processing capacity comes the drawback that the information system as a whole may be hard to grasp (Markus 2004, Davenport 1998).

When implementing an ES package, the company can select from different industry-adapted modules providing core functionalities (i.e. that support processes such as production, supply chain management, and R&D), as well among complementary modules to be used in support processes (such as finance, HR, marketing, etc). In fact, along with Internet, ESs can be seen as the most important technology to have attained widespread use during the last decade (Seddon et al. 2003). For a company this means that the integration of an ES into its business operations by necessity will, to a greater or lesser extent, affect the business activities that are carried out. For companies, these business activities have been observed by researchers to take place within relatively stable, long-term oriented business relationships with specific well-known counterparts (Håkansson and Snehota 1995). This means that ESs, especially with the high level of usage in companies (Seddon et al. 2003), become an interesting research object not only from a company-focused perspective, but also from a broader perspective, allowing business relationships to unique suppliers and customers to be included.

But how can ESs be captured and understood in this setting? This question will be discussed and elaborated on in the following sections, leading to some recommendations on relevant issues

The Nature of Enterprise Systems

Enterprise systems can briefly be described as information systems available 'off-the-shelf' (Nilsson 1991, Davenport 1998), offering companies 'ready to use' best practice through their wide industry coverage. Other characteristics, described by Hedman (2003), are the wide organizational scope and coverage of an ES, although this is based on generic functionality allowing for limited competitive advantages. Important features are also the integrated data, the process-oriented functionality and the enabling of e-commerce solutions (Hedman 2003, Davenport 2000, O'Leary 2000). The effects on a company can be divided into; [1] *tangible benefits* such as inventory and personnel reduction, productivity and order management improvements, and better financial control; and [2] *intangible benefits* such as information visibility, improved and new processes, a higher customer responsiveness, and other aspects such as standardization, flexibility, perceived business performance, and so forth (Sandoe et al. 2001).

But enterprise systems also bring along obstacles and downsides. When companies started to implement these software packages, Davenport (1998) warned managers of only seeing the opportunities with enterprise systems: 'An enterprise system imposes its own logic on a company's strategy, culture, and organization' (p. 127), which in turn means that 'enterprise systems can deliver great rewards but the risks they carry are equally important' (p. 128). Therefore, the effects of an ES on a company's operation must not be underrated. An illustrative example is professor Lynne Markus' description that the adoption and use of ESs 'promise major strategic benefits and business improvements from cross-functional integration and business process streamlining, but they are now notorious for their implementation challenges and problematic organizational consequences' (Markus 2004, p. 5). ESs are, thus, potential sources of organizational and business disturbances but, at the same time, they provide an opportunity for business enhancement for the adopting company in its day-to-day businesses activities.

Enterprise System Implementation Process

An enterprise system is *a dynamic research object*, and to capture its impact(s) three different aspects may be considered: (1) at what phase of the life cycle is the ES studied; (2) how extensive is the ES's scope, i.e. how wide-spread is its functionality in relation to the organization's structure and though the activities supported by it and; (3) to what degree is the ES modified to fit the specific company?

The *life cycle phases* of an ES may be labelled [1] project phase, [2] shakedown phase, and [3] onward and upward phase. In the project phase the business effects of the ES may be hard to trace, due to its novelty in the organization. In this phase, the implementation team may have the authority and the individuals that use the new ES may be participating in training. This in turn means that the full functionality of the ES is still to be discovered. During the shakedown phase, the system 'go-live', and in this phase the first short-term impacts on operations may be seen. During this phase, the customers and suppliers may notice disturbances in interactions with the company due to the adjustments of the personnel to new routines. After the ES's uses have been internalised into the company, the ES moves into the onward and upward phase where the personnel uses the fundamental functionalities of the adopted ES package(s). During this phase, there will also be the complementary adoption of other packages and modules as well as upgrades, but with a less stressful impact on the organization than in the project phase. (Markus et al. 2003)

But the ES phases may not be as easily conceptualised, as described by Markus et al. (2003). Following the results from Davenport et al. (2004), the adoption of an ES is an ongoing process. 'We found that contrary to popular opinion and research treating implementation as complete [...] most organizations that we studied are still implementing ES functionality' (p. 17). Their study indicates that managers continue to consolidate and integrate data into the ES. This imposes standardized data and processes beyond what can be considered to be part of the implementation phase.

Besides the phase aspect, ESs are used to varying degrees. This can be labelled the *ES scope*, which is described as 'the degree to which the [ES] will change managerial autonomy, task coordination, and process integration in the business units of the enterprise.' (Markus et al. 2000, p. 43) As an example, an enterprise system that is used to handle the financial flows between business units may have less of an impact on day-to-day business than a fully-integrated ES package with both supply chain management (SCM) and customer relationship management (CRM) functionalities.

Finally, the *degree of ES modification* may affect what kind of impact(s) the ES may cause. An important aspect of the ESs' adoption is that they come as standard software packages (Davenport 1998). This means that the adopting company must considerer whether to follow the built-in logic of the ES or whether to modify and adjust (through so-called 'parameters') the ES. A less successful implementation may be filled with different workarounds, the use of complementary software ('bolt-ons'), a mix of different 'best of breeds' or a heftily modified and customized ES package. (Markus et al. 2003, O'Leary 2000, Soh et al. 2000) The companies that have chosen to adapt to the standard functionality of the selected ESs have followed a 'vanilla implementation' (Sumner 2005). With such an implementation, the technical solution may be stable, but the price for this is re-engineering and organizational change.

Summarizing the Nature of Enterprise Systems

To describe and understand an enterprise system in studies that try to capture its business implications may be difficult, based upon its characteristics. As mentioned, ES comes with both tangible and intangible effects, and these can also be traced to the use (or perhaps non-use or even misuse) of the system. This means that the ES cannot be described as a monolith or a black box. Instead, it is a highly dynamic IS solution that may span the whole company, offering information visibility and integrated data handling as well as being able to 'lock' employees into standardized processes and routines. But the ES adoption may also be described as a continuous 'implementation phase' with periods of both minor and major changes spread over time (cf. Davenport et al. 2004). To understand the state of an adopted enterprise system, it is relevant to capture three aspects: [1] the prevailing ES life cycle phase, [2] the ES scope, and [3] the degree of ES modification. The three suggested aspects may be used to capture the ES coverage in studies aiming to understand the organizational impacts. But to fully understand the implications of the ES from a focal company's point of view, an inclusion of the prevailing situation of the company's business activities is necessary. This will be addressed in the next section.

Theories on Business Relationships

To be able to trace the business effects of enterprise systems, a theoretical approach explaining day-to-day business is needed. To capture this complex IS, both physical (technological) and social factors have to be considered. As described by Orlikowski and Barley (2001): 'technologies are simultaneously social and physical artefacts' (p. 149). To capture the ES impact(s) on a company's business, the 'markets-as-networks' (MAN) approach is suggested.

A couple of decades ago, sociologist Mark Granovetter declared that the field of business may also be an interesting area for sociologists (Granovetter 1985). A legacy from this article is the description of *embeddedness*, i.e. that business market activities are about more than products or services in exchange for money. It also involves social bonds and inter-personal commitments. This aspect has been considered in later theorizing within marketing, where approaches such as relationship marketing (RM) and marketing-as-networks (MAN) (Mattsson 1997, Grönroos 1994) have been developed.

The MAN approach has been inductively developed since the 70s, e.g. before Mark Granovetter's discussions on social aspects of business. Since its start, the MAN approach (manifested by the IMP group, see www.imp-group.org) has studied over 1000 business relationships, and an important lesson is that business-to-business (B2B) affairs are not a question of action (from the seller) and reaction (from the buyer), but rather a question of *interaction* (Ford et al. 2002).

This social and mutually oriented view of business may also be found in later studies within the IS discipline. As an example, Walsham (2001) describes how company representatives were affected by different ESs and how this affected their behaviour towards customers. Another example is offered by Schultze & Orlikowski (2004) who have followed the use of self-service technologies (SST) in a service context and learnt that: 'Because network relations are enacted through the work practices and interactions of customers and providers, the use of self-service technology by customers led to arm's-length relations at the firm level. For a firm relying on embedded relationships and social capital to generate revenue, such an enactment raised serious challenges for the viability of its business model' (p. 105). Following the research of members in the IMP group, it seems that most business relationships have different levels of social embeddedness, something that works like a governing mechanism reducing uncertainties and opportunistic behaviour (cf. Håkansson and Snehota 1995). To summarize, business is made up of individuals (humans) that are social entities with interpersonal linkages and bonds.

The IMP Approach to Business Relationships

As a description of how business can be understood and theorized, an early theory within the MAN approach was the *interaction model* (Håkansson

(1982). The interaction model indicates the mutual interest of both buyer and seller, and highlights how both parties have an interest in the business exchange. In a short-term perspective, it describes different exchanges (products and/or services, financial means, information, and social) that can be seen as the activities constituting business relations between the involved partners. In a longer-term perspective, the supplier and customer may adapt to each other's behaviour as well as developing unique ways of acting in their business relationship. The short-term and long-term aspects form an atmosphere of the business relationship which can be described in terms of power/dependence, degrees of cooperation and closeness, as well as the parties' expectations. (Ibid.)

In the interaction model's most elementary form, two business partners, i.e. a dyad, and their business relationship can be described by the ongoing exchanges that takes place. These exchanges involve products and/or services as well as financial exchange, but it can also involve information exchange (i.e. product features, transport possibilities, and so forth) plus social exchange similar to one between friends (cf. Ford et al. 2002). In the long run, these exchanges may be altered to accommodate both business partners' way of acting. This in turn means that their mutual behaviour is institutionalized and that there have been adaptations made by both business partners. Through time, this also affects the products and/or services that the supplier develops and also what the customer needs and demands. (Ford et al. 2002, Ford et al. 2003, Håkansson et al. 2004)

Later research by the IMP group has lead to several theoretical models and descriptions. These models show that *business-to-business activities are best described as business relationships between several partners in a network setting*. Due to the network characteristics, business appears different depending on the starting-point taken. The common approach is to start from a focal company, in this setting a company that has implemented an enterprise system. With a markets-as-networks approach, we employ ideas from the interaction model (that the business exchange holds more than mere product and service exchanges), thereby expanding the picture to include both customers and suppliers (and when it seems relevant, also other interest groups interacting with the focal company).

As illustrated in figure 1, both customers and suppliers of the focal company may have relationships with other partners, as end-customer and 2-tier suppliers. In this article, the perspective is delimited to include only two business relationships illustrated as a single black line. In practice, business relationships involve the interaction between several individuals at each company, that have different functional roles and spanning different hierarchal levels.

Fig. 1. The smallest 'network'

The *network approach* offers several ways of approaching the pheno-menon. Basically, the network can be traced by identifying the resources (e.g. what is offered; a product, a service, knowledge, etc.), the activities that surround this resource, and by following the actors that are involved in these activities. (Håkansson and Snehota 1995) Another approach is to use different aspects of embeddedness (i.e. different parts that are integrated into the business relationships) such as social, technical, spatial, temporal, political, and market embeddedness (Halinen and Törnroos 1998). A third way of approaching this phenomenon is to select what could be described as the primary or core business processes, such as: customer relationship management (CRM), customer service management, demand management, order fulfillment, manufacturing flow management, procurement, product development (R&D) and commercialization, and returns (Lambert and Cooper 2000).

Enterprise Usage in a Business Network Perspective

When approaching enterprise systems with a network perspective, two as-pects need to be considered when trying to grasp the business impact(s) of ES. The first issue is where the effects may be traced, and the second issue is how to treat the IS users, i.e. those who are directly affected by the en-terprise system.

Where to Trace the Effects

To view the individuals studied as having multiple roles, both as business actors and IS users simultaneously, offers analytical opportunities at an in-dividual, group or even organizational level. But to grasp the impact(s) of an ES on a focal company's business, the perspective must go beyond the focal company's organizational boundary. One way of describing this is to address different areas of analysis.

The first area of analysis when studying an enterprise system (#1 in figure 2) concerns the impact and utilization within *the focal company*. This implies an intra-organizational perspective, and business aspects like issues of storage needs, re-engineering possibilities and personnel reduction, efficiency gains, and so forth may be the focus of study. The interest of organizational effects has a strong position within the IS discipline (cf. Orlikowski and Barley 2001). With an interest in business, the opportunities or obstacles for 'business actors' (i.e. the individuals) to perform their function with the support of the ES becomes a central issue.

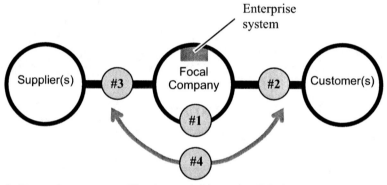

Fig. 2. Enterprise system utilization and where possible impacts on a focal company may be traced

The second area of analysis (#2 in figure 2) deals with how *the customer relationships* are affected. A relationship can be viewed as an entity between two partners. With a perspective such as this, questions addressing how the focal company's and the customer's needs are communicated become central. Questions like; can the resources be exchanged more efficiently and, in businesses where social embeddedness is considered important, can the inter-personal linkages be upheld and enhanced, are examples of relevance.

A third effect can be seen in *the supplier relationships* (#3 in figure 2) where issues of how to develop the relationship, to the benefit of both partners, are of interest. To what degree may the focal company's ES support cross-organizational production and/or services, and how are the different business processes handled?

The fourth, and perhaps the most interesting, area is the one that can be described as spanning *the focal company's business relationships* (#4 in figure 2). When focusing on this analytical area, factors internal to the focal company, as well as the relationships between customers and suppliers, are considered. For example, how might the focal company's enterprise system support the customer's requests by providing information about the suppliers' stocks? Can the internal ES's use (#1) be interpreted when it comes to the focal company's business relationships (#2 and #3) as well as how it is doing business (#4)? By reflecting on all these analytical areas, the impact(s) of the ES on the focal company's business may be captured and understood.

IS Users as Business Actors

Finally, when studying enterprise systems it is important to understand that the ES users hardly regard themselves as users (Lamb and Kling 2003), but rather as business actors (i.e. as a salesman, a purchase manager, and so forth). Within both the information systems and marketing discipline, the social aspects of business and technology have received attention and recognition. As an example from the IS domain, Kling & Scacchi (1982) described how the individuals' use of information systems was dependent on their social context through their 'web of computing'. Within marketing, the description of Granovetter (1985), where business actors also have a social dimension, has been mentioned.

One approach that captures the social dimension of both business and IS use is to trace the *representational role* of the individuals. 'The representational role means that in themselves and through their actions, business actors (companies or individuals) represent their country, industry, company or department in the eyes of other network members at a specific point in time. They also represent certain assets, knowledge, information, experience and credibility acquired in the past and present.' (Halinen and Törnroos 1998, p. 198) Each individual strives to uphold and develop the processes (i.e. the resource exchange as well as the mutual activities affecting the involved business partners) needed to fulfil its obligations towards both inter-organizational standards as well as intra-organizational demands. In this operation, the individual can be seen; (a) as a *business actor* representative trying to adapt to the contingencies that doing business means and at the same time (b) as an *IS user*, affected by the opportunities and limitations of the enterprise system that he or she is using.

Concluding Remarks

Enterprise systems are, by to their nature, difficult to capture and conceptualise when trying to grasp their wider implications for companies and their business relationships. A basic reason is the introduction and impact of an ES on the organization. Usually the ES is modified to fit the ongoing day-to-day operations, but the modifications are replaced later on with standard solutions that affect the business processes. Even when approaching a case where the ES may be considered to be "stable", the impact can be found on a variety of places in the company, i.e. in different departments and at different hierarchal levels. Furthermore, the ES is rarely separated from other information system resources; it is more or less integrated with other (both legacy and novel) information systems providing support for the ongoing business activities.

To reach an understanding about what an ES means for a company from a business point of view, an interaction and network approach stemming from the field of business-to-business marketing has been proposed. The effect on a company's business relationships can thereby be captured and understood. In the discussion, different areas of analysis to deal with the impact(s) caused by an enterprise system were suggested. There has also been reasoning about how individuals, performing the business activities, act as business actors but also (simultaneously) as IS users. By combining these perspectives on ES utilization, implications on how the focal company is affected by its ES can be made. By expanding the traditional focus of the IS field, i.e. on a single organization, to include important customers and suppliers may provide a broader understanding on the implications of ESs on business.

Within the field of marketing, a debate regarding the threats of overly simplistic models and theories when trying to understand how companies do business is taking place. One alternative can be seen in theories like relationship marketing (RM) and markets as networks (MAN) where knowledge on how companies actually interact can be turned into managerial implications on how the single company needs to act. To deepen the knowledge on enterprise systems and fully understand their impact(s), similar reasoning has to be brought into the IS discipline. Trying to capture ES as it is actually used by companies, calls for the perspective of the business situation to be revised from enclosed to relational.

References

Davenport TH (1998) Putting the Enterprise into the Enterprise System. Harvard Business Review, vol 77, pp 106-116

Davenport TH (2000) Mission Critical - Realizing the Promise of Enterprise Systems. Harvard Business School Press Boston MA

Davenport TH et al (2004) Enterprise Systems and Ongoing Process Change. Business Process Management Journal, vol 10, pp 16-26

Ford D et al (eds) (2002) The Business Marketing Course - Managing in Complex Networks. John Wiley & Sons Ltd Chichester

Ford D et al (eds) (2003) Managing Business Relationship. John Wiley & Sons Chichester West Sussex UK

Granovetter M (1985) Economic Action and Social Structure: The Problem of Embeddedness. American Journal of Sociology, vol 91, pp 481-510

Grönroos C (1994) Quo Vadis, Marketing? Toward a Relationship Marketing Paradigm. Journal of Marketing Management, vol 10, pp 347-360

Halinen A, Törnroos J-Å (1998) The Role of Embeddedness in the Evolution of Business Networks. Scandinavian Journal of Management, vol 14, pp 187-205.

Hedman J (2003) On Enterprise Systems Artifacts: Changes in Information Systems Development and Evaluation. Ph D Thesis, Lund University Lund

Håkansson H (ed) (1982) International Marketing and Purchasing of Industrial Goods: an Interaction Approach. John Wiley & Sons Chichester

Håkansson H et al (2004) Introduction: Rethinking Marketing. In: Håkansson H et al (eds) Rethinking Marketing. John Wiley & Sons Chichester West Sussex UK

Håkansson H, Snehota I (eds) (1995) Developing Relationships in Business Networks. Routledge London

Kling R, Scacchi W (1982) The Web of Computing: Computer Technology as Social Organization. Advances in Computers, vol 21, pp 2-90

Lamb R, Kling R (2003) Reconceptualizing Users as Social Actors in Information Systems Research. MIS Quarterly, vol 27, pp 197-235

Lambert DM, Cooper MC (2000) Issues in Supply Chain Management. Industrial Marketing Management, vol 29, pp 65-83

Markus LM (2004) Technochange Management: Using IT to Drive Organizational Change. Journal of Information Technology, vol 19, pp 4-20

Markus LM et al (2003) Learning from Experiences with ERP: Problems Encountered and Success Achieved. In: Shanks G et al (eds) Second-Wave Enterprise Resource Planning Systems - Implementing for Effectiveness. Cambridge University Press New York

Markus LM et al (2000) Multiple ERP Implementations. Communications of the ACM, vol 43, pp 42-46

Mattsson L-G (1997) Relationship Marketing and the Markets-as-Networks Approach - A comparative analysis of two evolving streams of research. Journal of Marketing Management, vol 13, pp 447-461

Nilsson AG (1991) Anskaffning av standardsystem för att utveckla verksamheter: Utveckling och prövning av SIV-metoden. Ph D Thesis, Handelshögskolan i Stockholm Stockholm

O'Leary DE (2000) Enterprise Resource Planning Systems - Systems, Life Cycle, Electronic Commerce, and Risk. Cambridge University Press New York

Orlikowski WJ, Barley SR (2001) Technology and Institutions: What Can Research in Information Technology and research on Organizations Learn from Each Other? MIS Quarterly, vol 25, pp 145-165

Sandoe K et al (2001) Enterprise Integration. John Wiley & Sons New York

Schultze U, Orlikowski WJ (2004) A Practice Perspective on Technology-Mediated Network Relations: The Use of Internet-Based Self-Service Technologies. Information Systems Research, vol 15, pp 87-106

Seddon P et al (2003) ERP - The Quiet Revolution. In: Shanks G et al (eds) Second-Wave Enterprise Resource Planning Systems - Implementing for Effectiveness. Cambirdge University Press New York

Soh C et al (2000) Cultural Fits and Misfits: Is ERP a Universal Solution? Communications of the ACM, vol 43, pp 47-51

Sumner M (2005) Enterprise Resource Planning. Pearson Prentice Hall Upper Saddle River NJ

Walsham G (2001) Making a World of Difference - IT in a Global Context. John Wiley & Sons Ltd Chichester

Personalized Faculty Support from Central IT Geo-Teams

Samuel Scalise

Sonoma State University, USA. scalise@sonoma.edu

Introduction

Great professors focus on the core competencies of their discipline, not on Information Technology support. Meanwhile, information technology has become an integral part of their instruction and research. Professors cannot depend solely on generic, campus-wide IT service offerings. Each professor has unique information technology needs. As technology has become more complex and security risks have grown, each professor requires personalized information technology support.

Sonoma State University has begun a program to assign specific Central IT consultants to provide personalized support for professors and their computing needs. The consultants draw upon the range of Central IT service staff in various units – web design, instructional design, programming, database design, computer and server support, etc. – combined with Library resources, to fulfill the research and teaching-related information technology needs of individual professors.

The consultants work in "Geo-Teams" providing pro-active support that is geographically close and in which consultants are familiar with specific professors, their discipline, and their work. The Geo-Teams perform service in a consistent manner across campus. The collective of all Geo-Teams meets weekly to discuss the kinds of work they will be performing for faculty and the technical problems they have encountered. Geo-Team consultants proactively schedule faculty visits to fix small problems before they become emergencies. They secure proactive computer maintenance to prevent security and compatibility problems. Most importantly, at the behest of each professor, they coordinate the information technology needs of their research and instruction.

Traditional Models of IT Support

Traditional models of supporting faculty's use of information technology usually fall into a combination of the following methods:

1. Support from a central IT shop
2. Support form a department-based IT shop
3. Support from a faculty member's research staff
4. Self-support
5. No support

Support from a Central IT Shop

Central IT Shop models usually evolved from computer support organizations of the 1960s. Their focus was usually on some core administrative functions and/or supporting a few key faculty with computer-centric research. The staff interactions with faculty were very limited and computer-technical.

As computers extended themselves in the 1970s and early 1980s, the Central IT Shops evolved to support more computers (usually mini computers), remote terminals, and the network. However, the applications were still fairly dependent on computer-savvy faculty. When the technology need was too much for an individual faculty member, they often depended on some computer-savvy graduate students who worked for them.

When personal computers came out, many Central IT shops avoided providing support. Indeed, personal computers were touted as providing an alternative to the Central IT shop. The early adopters of personal computers tended to be computer-savvy faculty or their graduate students.

Today, Central IT shops have picked up some of the responsibilities of supporting personal computers, but it tends to be in areas of communications support (hooking the computer to the network) and in operating system management. Some central IT shops also provide training services to various campus groups.

Central IT support tends to be cost effective, production-level quality, and secure. But it usually is not discipline specific, nor is it focused on the particular computing needs of an individual faculty member.

Support from a Department-Based IT Shop

As the opportunities from minicomputers grew in the late 1970s and early 1980s, some departments purchased the increasingly affordable computers, freeing themselves from Central IT restrictions on mainframe computers. These departments tended to be those steeped in traditional calculation-intensive research, such as statistics, physics, and economics. Such departments developed small computer support staffs, usually managed by a computer-savvy faculty member or two, and operated by graduate students. Still, in order to use the systems, a professor was pretty much left to his or her own devices.

When personal computers arrived, those departments with Department-Based IT shops already supporting minicomputers quickly took advantage of the limited capabilities of the small processors.

As personal computer-based applications became more useful to the classical professor, they were adopted in departments that hadn't made much use of computing. Sometimes frustration with the Central IT Shop began on campuses where expectations for personal computer support were assumed, but not provided centrally by the campus and not funded. This resulted in the creation of more department-based IT Shops on campus, generally developed from computer savvy graduate students and a handful of interested faculty members.

Personal Computers became an increasing part of the curriculum, as faculty shared creative solutions in their discipline with students and contemporaries. This resulted in computer labs, often funded with one-time grant money, or fashioned from castaway computers that still worked.

By the late 80s and early 90s, the Central IT shop's role became more clearly defined as maintaining the infrastructure, mainframe, and server-based applications that provided campus-wide utility. Central IT shops eventually assumed the email and network operations as they grew more complex and as 7x24 production level support became critical.

In parallel, nearly every department or school had its own IT shop, providing support for faculty and staff using personal computers for word processing and spreadsheets. Many Department-based IT shops also got into the email and network business, providing these services to their employees. Departmental consultants doing the support were often knowledgeable about the discipline and could provide relevant help. Also, they were down the hall, so support was more timely.

One problem in some Department-Based Computer Support organizations was that assertive and computer-inquisitive faculty got more support than other faculty members. Computer-passive faculty often got hand-me-down equipment, for instance. There was a somewhat inaccurate assumption that some faculty's work was more conducive to computing than others, and that the power of the computer should be distributed accordingly.

Support from a Professor's Research Staff

In contrast to other the central campus IT services model or the Departmental IT shops, some faculty continued to base their computing support on their own research staff and programmers, usually part-time or students, that they hired. Of course, not all faculty have research staff capable of doing computer support. But those who do have benefited by having staff dedicated to their computing needs. Indeed, the faculty and research staff share similar goals. Computer support from research staff knowledge about the faculty discipline has some great advantages over support from department and Central IT Shop. And, graduate students have a reputation of putting in long hours to complete their work, usually at modest pay compared to professional staff programmers.

However, such research staff rarely receive professional training in computer technology – they are rarely familiar with standard programming algorithms, or the details of the network, authentication, and databases. And any time they spend on computer support is time they cannot focus on the discipline-specific research, so such drawbacks are implicit in the research staff computing support approach.

Self Support

The first time anybody directly uses computer technology, they usually provide their own support. As an undergrad or grad student, they quickly learn clever tools and see the value of computer technology for their research. Some use this as a springboard to dig deeply into self-support.

Self-support is valuable, especially if it results in the eventual use of support teams. Faculty who have done self-support at some point know what services they are looking for in their support staff.

Students in the 1970s often learned Fortran and SPSS, and that was enough to be effective self-supporters in many computing environments of that era. But as information technology became more complex, the number and complexity of computer tools became more challenging for any one faculty member to master. As with the research staff support approach, self-support also may be a substantial drain on the use of time that otherwise might go toward discipline-specific research, and self-support may detract from the discipline focus.

IT Support Characteristics

The weakness in all of the traditional models of IT-support is that they do not maximize the totality of IT support characteristics, leaving a marginalized result. In some cases, support is discipline specific and may be well tailored to the needs of individual faculty members and research projects, such as in the self-support and research group support models. However, these approaches often suffer from lack of range and depth of expertise, continuity of support, security needs, timeliness, cost efficiency and many other challenges. If the goal is to get the most productivity out of IT support of faculty research, then it is important to understand the characteristics of IT support and to put together a model that maximizes the totality of these characteristics, given the support situation under consideration in a given situation. This is the goal of the Geo-Team model.

The list of IT support characteristics are nearly endless, see table 1.

Table 1. IT support characteristics

Faculty Projects	Discipline-Specific
General Contractor Access to Computer Skills	Personalized Interest in Faculty's Work
Range of Expertise	Depth of Expertise
Staff Backup	Continuity
Security	Timeliness
Production Quality	Equitable Support
Parallel (Team) Support	Tested Technology
Cost	Cost Effectiveness
Opportunity Costs	Emergencies
Computer Maintenance	Regular Faculty Visits
Training	Courseware Development

Geo-Team Model

Geo-Team Support was first started at UC Berkeley in 1994 to address the diverse and extensive needs of faculty and staff doing world-class research. Each faculty member has a unique set of IT needs. If resources were unlimited, every faculty member could have a production-level IT staff doing everything from programming, to network management, to accessible web page development. But, even the wealthiest universities don't have enough resources for each faculty member to have such an IT staff.

In the Geo-Team model, each faculty member has a centrally-coordinated IT consultant stationed within their building or a neighboring building, with discipline specific IT expertise, as a one-stop shopping contact for local IT needs. At the same time, consultants work in teams across buildings, for instance in quadrants or other larger areas, such that the teams represent a much broader range of expertise than any one consultant would be able to provide. Teams are carefully organized and selected to contain individuals with complementary skill sets, interlinking to cover the vast IT needs of contemporary research and instruction. Each local Geo-Team consultant can call on any other members of their Geo-Team for expertise as needed. This ensures a close relationships between faculty members and a single IT staff member who "speaks their language" and is always available, but allows a much broader range of expertise to come into play within the team as needed. Strong professional relationships and well-structured training programs within the team help ensure the quality of work across the range of IT challenges, and lead to successful interactions across the IT spectrum, while discipline-specific expertise is addressed with the local component. Geo-Teams can be balanced to reflect an effective combination for each research and instructional setting, leading to an effective support model that is well received by faculty members.

The Geo-Team Model maximizes IT resources, regardless of their abundance. It is a model designed to distribute the IT resources in an efficient, cost-effective, and equitable manner. Support is provided by consultants who:

- Are dedicated to specific faculty.
- Arrange for all computer support.
- Are sufficient in number.
- Work in teams.
- Have the best interest of the faculty member uppermost in mind.

  Producing the following benefits:

- Timely Support
- Provide expertise in all areas of computer technology.
- Provide coordinated support (the network works with the database people, etc.)
- Continuity of support is ensured.

Geo-Team support is the concept of pro-active support from a small consultant team that is geographically close and familiar with each faculty member and their work, yet performs service in professionally consistent manner like all of the other Geo-Teams. Geo-Team consultants act as IT general contractors, working with centralized support providers in a professional manner to secure the specific needs of each faculty member. The collective of all Geo-Teams meet weekly to discuss the kinds of work they will be performing for faculty and the technical problems they have encountered. Geo-Team consultants know what their work is, and all customers receive their support that consists of scheduled visits with faculty members, computer maintenance, faculty projects, and of course emergency response.

Regular proactive visits with faculty enable consultants to stay on top of all computer projects and to fix "small" problems before they are big enough to report. Perhaps a faculty member is having trouble printing a letterhead, but hasn't reported it because it hasn't become an emergency. That same problem will become an emergency if the President is waiting for a report. With proactive visits, faculty are more likely to report these problems before they get big.

Geo-Team consultants provide tested, proactive computer maintenance, so that emergency services are rarely needed. The Geo-Teams collectively provide the same maintenance to all computers on campus, ensuring reliability everywhere. Operating system patches and virus protection updates are almost a daily activity. Most of this is done through the network. But, a key part of maintenance is following up to make sure that everything was installed and configured appropriately, and that no applications broke.

Projects are the meat and potatoes of what a faculty member uses his computer for. In Physics, it may be a complex computer program using parallel processing. In Music, it may be the design of a web page that interacts with music files. The Geo-Team consultants may do some of the work themselves. Or, they will secure the appropriate professionals to do the work for which they do not have the right skills, or when a different skill level is appropriate. Why have a high-end programmer do operating system maintenance?

Emergencies are anything that the faculty member says is an emergency. Geo-Teams have very few of them, but response must be timely. So, it is important that Geo-Teams have 7x24 backup. If the primary consultant is away on vacation, and a faculty member's project has a problem, other members of the Geo-Team are already familiar with the project, and can help out.

Measurement

A key success factor is to measure, report, and evaluate IT services being provided. Faculty and departments need an itemization of the computer work being done. When computer support is good, it is a challenge to be aware of, and appreciate the work being done. So, it is important to provide a list of these services. Reporting also ensures that support is being provided equitably to all faculty. Evaluations help identify support problem areas, and act as a feedforward mechanism for future IT support planning.

Summary

Today's faculty computer needs are complex. A faculty member needs comprehensive support. More and more faculty are using complex tools such as meeting and collaboration software, learning management systems, and custom research software. These require appropriate security and management to work well in different environments. While some faculty may feel comfortable configuring the complex components that integrate computer, network, and server – other faculty need assistance with this. Providing support in Geo-Teams ensures high-quality, consistent, professional support customized to the unique needs of each professor.

Verifying Information Content Containment of Conceptual Data Schemata by Using Channel Theory

Yang Wang and JunKang Feng

Database Research Group, School of Computing, University of Paisley, Scotland, UK and eBusiness Research Institutes, Business College, Beijing Union University, China. (yang.wang, junkang.feng)@paisley.ac.uk

Introduction

To obtain a satisfactory information system is the goal pursued by every system designer. Conceptual modelling using, for example, the 'entity-relationship model' is crucial for achieve this goal (Batini et al.1992, Chen 1999).Although number of researchers concentrate on information and semantic information in high conceptual level of abstraction, for instances, Relative Information Capacity (Hull 1986; Miller 1993 and 1994), Proposition-based logical Information Capacity (Duzi 1992), it would seem that fundamental questions of 'what enables the conceptual models to be what they are, and why they are capable of providing required information', have not been answered convincingly. To just say that it is because entities and their relationships provided by the model are meaningful to the user is not adequate, as it has been argued that the information embodied in a signal (linguistic or otherwise) is only incidentally related to the meaning (if any) of that signal (Dretske 1981). A semantic information theory, might provide one avenue to investigating such problems by distinguishing essential concepts of 'information' and 'data', formulating flow of information, and in particular connecting 'real world' objects with concepts in conceptual models, which would give us a foundation for exploring the information content of a conceptual model.

Following this line of thinking, we put forward a notion called the 'Information Bearing Capability' (IBC) of a data schema (Feng 1999), and subsequently identified four conditions that would enable a data construct to bear a particular piece of information (Feng 2005). The Principle is a result of our observations through many years of working in the IS area, and it does seem to make sense.

To verify whether the four conditions hold of a particular system is difficult. To this end, we have found that employing a sophisticated theory of information flow within a notional distributed system, namely the Channel Theory presented by Barwise and Seligman (1997), introduces much needed rigor into this work and can serve as a systemic and mathematically sound means for verifying whether the 'Information Content Containment' condition of the IBC Principle is satisfied over *any* given pair of elements: one is a data construct and the other a piece of information. In this paper we describe our approach by using an example, and avoid any lengthy description of the CT *per se*.

The rest of the paper is organized as follows. In the next section, the 'information content containment' condition of the IBC Principle is briefly introduced. After that, the reasons why we choose the CT as our intellectual tool for the job at hand are given. Then, we describe our approach and show the details on how we verify the 'Information Content Containment' condition by using the CT in conceptual modeling. Finally, we give conclusions and indicate directions for further work.

The 'Information Content Containment' Condition

The notion of IBC and the work around it were developed over a number of years by Feng and his colleagues (Feng 2005, Xu and Feng 2002, Hu and Feng 2002). The version of it that we discuss here is that which takes into account the three major parties that are involved in information flow, namely information source (S), information bearer (B), and information receiver (R). We call such a thought the framework of SBR for convenience. The IBC Principle (Feng 2005) is now specified as four basic conditions. The first condition is known as the 'Information Content Containment' condition, i.e.,

'For an instance level data construct (or a 'media construct' in general), say t, to be capable of representing an individual real world object or an individual relationship between some real world objects (or a 'referent construct' in general), say s, which is neither necessarily true nor necessarily false (Floridi 2002), the information content of t when it is considered in isolation must include s, the simplest case of which is that the literal or conventional meaning of t is part of its information content, and the literal or conventional meaning of t is s.'

Reasons for Using 'CT' Within the OS Framework to Verify 'IBC'

For information systems (IS), information flow plays an important role. As stated by Stowell and West (1994), an information system is a notional system regarding the information aspect of a problem domain, without the creation and transmission of information being explicitly expressed; the notional system would not be complete.

Dretske's (1981) semantic theory of information and Devlin's theory (1991) on information flow help us formulate our ideas, but Channel Theory (Barwise and Seligman 1997) seems an applicable tool for verifying whether a given data construct satisfies aforementioned 'information content containment condition'. More detailed reasons for this are summarised below.

In general, saying that 'B bears information about S' is the same as saying 'there is information flow from S to B'. And the latter is in the language of CT. With CT, information flow is possible only because what is involved in the information flow can be seen as components of a distributed system. Within a 'distributed system', 'information channels' can be constructed within which information flows.

Information flow requires the existence of certain 'connections' (which may be abstract or concrete) among components. Following Dretske (1981, p.65), such a 'connection' is primarily made possible by the notion of 'conditional probability' where the condition is the 'Bearer'. However, this is perhaps only a particular way for 'connections' to be established. It would be desirable to see in general how a connection becomes possible. The notion of 'information channel' in CT helps here. In CT terms, information flow is captured by 'local logics' (which can be seen as conditionals between 'sets of types') within a distributed system. Normally, connections lie with 'partial alignments' (Kalfoglou and Schorlemmer 2003) between components. CT is capable of formulating such alignments by using concepts such as 'infomorphisms', 'state space', and 'event classification'. The property of 'state space' enables *every* instance and state relevant to the problem to be captured. We ask our readers, who are not familiar with CT, to bear with us here as we will use an example to show the basics of CT shortly.

A Method for Verifying Information Content Containment

We have developed a method for the task at hand, which consists of the following steps:

- Identify component *classifications*[1] relevant to the task at hand and then use them to construct a distributed system;
- Validate the existence of *infomorphisms*[2] between the classifications and construct an *information channel*[3] relevant to the task at hand;
- Construct the *core of the channel* by identifying those parts of the component classifications (including *normal tokens*[4]) that contribute to the desired information flow;
- Find the *local logic*[5] on the core, i.e., the entailment relationships between types of the classification for the 'core' that is directly relevant to the information flow, i.e., the information content containment at hand;
- Arrive at a *theory*[6] that is desired on the level of components by applying the *f-Elim rule*[7] on the local logic on the core.

Verifying 'Information Content Containment Condition'

Inspired by the ideas of Organisational Semiotics (Stamper 1997, Liu 2000, Anderson 1990) the conditions of the IBC Principle are examined on the levels of 'syntactic' and 'semantic'. We use the following diagram (Fig.1.) to show our points.

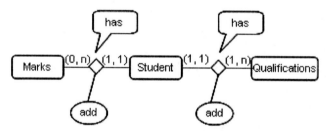

Fig. 1. Topological connection t

Semantic Level

On this level, the problem being addressed is 'meaning, propositions, validity, signification, denotations,...' (Stamper 1997, p.276). Accordingly, what should be looked at is how a topological connection (also called 'topological relation') is able to represent a real world relationship.

In the world of CT, information flow is considered in the context of distributed systems. Within such a system, 'what' flows is captured by the notion of 'local logics' and 'why' information can flow is explained by the concept of 'information channel'. Therefore, it is essential to construct relevant and appropriate 'distributed systems'. Considering the job at hand under the SBR framework, the components of the required justifiable system includes the information source that is the 'individual real world object or individual relationship between some real world objects (or a 'semantic relation' in general) s', and the information bearer that is the 'topological relation t'. To make sure that such a system supports information flow between these two different types of things, the connections between them are crucial.

We view the process of constructing a conceptual schema for representing some particular real world as a 'notional system' (Checkland 1981). It is interesting to note that the notion of 'distributed system' in CT is similar to the concept of 'notional system' in Soft Systems Methodology (SSM). Also, if we treat the whole system as our channel classification, the core of it will model the actual process of 'constructing' practice'. The connections are consequently causal links between our conceptual model (i.e., the schema) and what it models for. The types are ways of classifying these links. The logic on this classification models the understanding of users on putting information content (namely the semantic relations) to the model. Therefore, the *constraints* of the system represent the way users make use of the links between the conceptual model and what it models for. The *normal tokens* of the logic are the links that must satisfy the constraints, among all possible tokens of the system.

Now let us use Figure 1 to illustrate our ideas. Assume that there is a semantic relation s, say 'After successfully achieving all the marks, a student receives a new qualification (a degree or diploma)'. We show how the topological relation t (as shown in Fig.1.), represents the semantic relation s. The information channel and infomorphisms for justifying this are shown as following (Fig.2.).

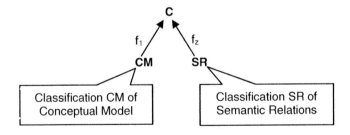

Fig. 2. Information channel diagram 1

In this diagram, **C** is the 'core' of the information channel; **CM** and **SR** are classifications corresponding to the conceptual model and the real world objects respectively. Infomorphisms $\mathbf{f_1}$: $\mathbf{CM} \leftrightarrows \mathbf{C}$ and $\mathbf{f_2}$: $\mathbf{SR} \leftrightarrows \mathbf{C}$ enable the part-whole relations between these two component classifications and the core, which is also a classification. Combining these two infomorphisms, we obtain an infomorphism $\mathbf{f} = \mathbf{f_1} + \mathbf{f_2}$ from **CM+SR** to **C**. In the example, the business rule or norm that 'if a student has passed all required modules, he/she is awarded a new qualification' can be captured as part of the local logic ζ on the core, namely

f_1 (topological connection between 'student', 'marks' and 'qualifications') $\vdash \zeta_C$
f_2 (semantic relation between 'student', 'marks' and 'qualifications')

Then the **f-Elim** Rule allows us to move from this constraint in the local logic on the core of the channel to the component level of theory, and thus we have:

topological connection between 'student', 'marks' and 'qualifications' $\vdash_{CM+SR}$
semantic relation between 'student', 'marks' and 'qualifications'.

Note that this move is only valid for those tokens that are actually connected by the channel. This is determined by the properties of the **f-Elim** Rule, namely it preserves nonvalidity but not validity (Barwise and Seligman 1997, p.39).

Syntactic Level

This level deals with possible information flow between different parts of the conceptual model (schema) *per se*. This is concerned with how a conceptual schema works as a whole thereby to be capable of representing something in the real world. The job mainly involves the construction of an appropriate 'distributed system' at the syntactic level (namely the schema) and the associated information channel that would support the desired local logics. We will use the same aforementioned example (Fig.1.). But this time, we will look at the entities in the schema separately rather than as a whole topological connection. That is, how the entity 'mark' actually provides information about entity 'qualifications' by both connecting to the entity of 'student'. At this level, the relationship 'marks-student' is now the information bearer, t, while the relationship 'student-qualification' is the information source, s. The relevant distributed system will be constructed by using these two relationships accordingly.

Barwise and Seligman (1997, p.43) point out: 'there are many ways to analyze a particular system as an information channel', and 'if one changes the channel, one typically gets different constraints and so different information flow'. We will use entity 'student' to illustrate how to construct a distributed system and information channel for a particular purpose. To help this, the schema is now extended as shown in Figure 3.

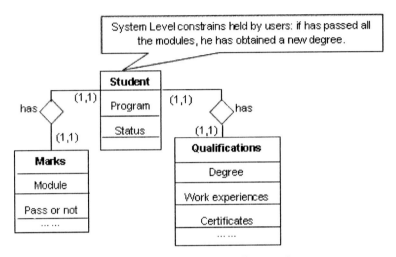

Fig. 3. Information channel diagram 1

Now, we can define the 'classifications' involved.

Classification A: for relationship 'mark-student'. The tokens **a**, **a'**....of **A** consist of individual 'mark-student' relationships at various times. There are many ways to classify the tokens. The way adopted here is 'a student receives his/her final mark for a module'. For example, there are marks for 'SPM' ('Software Project Management' module), 'ISTP' ('Information Systems Theory and Practice'), etc. These then become the types of the classification.

Classification B: for relationship 'student-qualification'. Like Classification **A**, the tokens **b**, **b'** ...of **B** consist of individual 'student-qualification' relationships at various times. To classify these tokens we use types like 'a student is awarded a particular qualification'. Examples of the qualifications are 'BSc IT', 'BA BA', etc.

State space [8] S_A: for classification A. The tokens **x**, **x'**... of S_A consist of individual 'mark-student' relationships at various times. The states consist of 0 and 1 for each model. The state of s_i (i is the name of a model.) is 1, if 'a student receives his/her final mark that is no less than 50 for a module'. Otherwise it is 0. For example, if $M_{SPM} \geq 50$, then $s_{SPM} = 1_{SPM}$, otherwise $s_{SPM} = 0_{SPM}$. Consequently, the set of state r_A for S_A should consist of each state of every included module, namely $r_A = \{\{0_{SPM}, 0_{ISTP}, ...,$

$0_{OAD}\}$, ..., $\{1_{SPM}, 1_{ISTP}, ...1_{OAD}\}\}$. If there are altogether 8 modules, the cardinality of r_A is $2^8 = 64$.

Event classification [9] **Evt(S_A).** The event Classification **A** associated with S_A, namely **Evt(S_A)** has the same tokens as S_A, but the types of it will be all the subsets of r_A, for instances, $\{\Phi\}$, $\{0_{SPM}, 0_{ISTP},..., 0_{OAD}\}$, ..., $\{\{0_{SPM}, 0_{ISTP},..., 0_{OAD}\}, \{0_{SPM}, 0_{ISTP},..., 1_{OAD}\}\},...,$ $\{\{0_{SPM}, 0_{ISTP},..., 0_{OAD}\}$, $\{0_{SPM}, 0_{ISTP},..., 1_{OAD}\}$, ..., $\{1_{SPM}, 1_{ISTP},..., 1_{OAD}\}\}$. That is, **Evt($S_A$)** is the power set of S_A. The total number of types of **Evt(S_A)** is therefore 2^{64}. The relationships between the types and the tokens of **A** and **Evt(S_A)** follow the token-identical infomorphism g_A: **A** $\leftrightarrows$ **Evt(S_A)** (Barwise and Seligman 1997, p.55).

State space S_B: for classification B. The tokens **y, y'**... of S_B consist of individual 'student-qualification' relationships at various times. Like S_A, the states are also 0 and 1 for each qualification. The state of s_j (j is the name of a qualification.) is 1, if the 'degree' attribute of 'student-qualification' is set to an appropriate degree name. The state of s_j is 0 if there is no new degree is added. For example, if degree, BSc BIT, is added, the state $S_{BSc\ BIT} = 1$, otherwise, $S_{BSc\ BIT} = 0$. Therefore, the set of state r_B for S_B should consist of each state of every added degree, such as $r_B = \{1_{BSc\ BIT}, 0_{BA\ BA}, ...\}$. If there are altogether two possible added degrees, the cardinality of r_B is $2^2 = 4$.

Event Classification Evt(S_B). The same tokens are present in the event classification **Evt(S_B)**. Similarly, the types of it are also all the possible subsets of r_B. For example, $\{\Phi\}$, $\{0_{BSc\ BIT} \}$, $\{0_{BA\ BA} \}$, ..., $\{0_{BSc\ BIT}, 1_{BA\ BA} \},..., \{1_{BSc\ BIT}, 0_{BA\ BA}\},..., \{0_{BSc\ BIT}, 0_{BA\ BA}, 1_{BSc\ BIT}, 1_{BA\ BA}\}$. If there are totally two degrees, the number of types for **Evt(S_B)** will be 2^4. Also, there is a natural infomorphism g_B: **B** $\leftrightarrows$ **Evt(S_B)**.

We define a classification, say **W**, on which a desired local logic lives, which is the *sum*[10] of Classification **A** and Classification **B**, namely **W** = **A** + **B**. Any token of this classification consists of two parts, <**a, b**>, where **a** and **b** are instances of the 'mark-student' relationship, and the 'student-qualification' relationship respectively. The types of **W** are the disjoint union of the types of classification **A** and **B**. It is important to notice that there are no one-to-one relationships between tokens of classifications **A** and **B**. Although **W** connects them, not all tokens of **W** represent meaningful and useful connections between their tokens. For example, a student might have marks, which will not relate to a certain degree if he changes his stream of a course in the middle of a semester. That is to say, only part of the tokens of **W** actually participate in the actual information flow. Therefore, classification **W** is not the information channel that we require. Our aim is to find the *partial alignment* (Kalfoglou and Schorlemmer 2003) for the core of channel.

To this end, we define state space **S** for classification **W**. The tokens **c**, **c'**.... of **S** are arbitrary instances of the classification **W** at various times. The set of states of **S** is $\{r_A, r_B\}$. An instance, say w, of classification **W** is in state $<r_{A1}, r_{B1}>$, if the state of w's 'mark for a module' part is r_{A1}, and the state of w's 'qualification awarding' part is r_{B1}. There are natural projections associated with state space **S**, i.e., $p_A: S \rightrightarrows S_A$, $p_B: S \rightrightarrows S_B$. In order to find the real informational relationship, i.e., that a student has passed all required modules for a course bears the information that the student is awarded a certain degree, we need to restrict the state space by eliminating those invalid states, such as $<\{0_{SPM}, 1_{ISTP}, \ldots 1_{OAD}\}, \{1_{BSc\ BIT}\}>$. This is the subspace **S***of **S**. This subspace inherits all the properties of space **S** including the natural projections.

As we did above regarding **Evt(S$_A$)** and **Evt(S$_B$)**, we can find the event classification **Evt(S*)** for **S***. Such an event classification enables the existence of partial relationships between tokens of **Evt(S$_A$)** and **Evt(S$_B$)**. This is what we want to model as the core of the information channel. According to a proven proposition, i.e., **Proposition 8.17** (Barwise and Seligman 1997, p.109), there are infomorphisms between event classifications **Evt(S$_A$)**, **Evt(S$_B$)** and **Evt(S*)** on inverse directions of the natural projections between them.

The infomorphisms from the component classifications to the core of the information channel **C** are defined as follows.

The infomorphism $f_A: A \leftrightarrows C$ is the composition of the infomorphisms $g_A: A \leftrightarrows Evt(S_A)$ and $Evt(p_A): Evt(S_A) \leftrightarrows C$.

The infomorphism $f_B: B \leftrightarrows C$ is the composition of the infomorphisms $g_B: B \leftrightarrows Evt(S_B)$ and $Evt(p_B): Evt(S_B) \leftrightarrows C$.

The relationship between information channel **C**, component classifications **A** and **B** can now be seen in Figure 4.

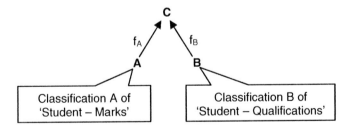

Fig. 4. Information channel diagram 2

The core Classification **C** supports a local logic L_C, which is concerned with entailment relations between sets of states of state space **S**. Here, as shown in the conceptual schema diagram, following a regulation in this particular organisation, there is a system level constraint, namely 'if having passed all required modules like SPM, ISTP $\ldots_{(5),}$ OAD , the student obtains a new degree, BSc BIT'. Resulted from this, there should be a *constraint* supported by the L_C:

f_A (a student gets final marks that are no less than 50 for SPM, ISTP $\ldots_{(5)},$OAD) $\vdash_{Lc} f_B$ (a student is awarded BSc BIT degree)

If we apply the **f-Elim** Rule on infomorphisms, f_A and f_B, this logic can be moved (translated) from the core to the component level theory about classifications **A** and **B**:

a student gets final marks that are no less than 50 for SPM, ISTP $\ldots_{(5),}$ OAD $\vdash_{Ls}$ a student is awarded BSc BIT degree

This constraint is valid only under the condition that relationships 'marks-student' and 'student-qualification' are satisfied through the channel **C**.

Conclusions and Future Work

This work is carried out in the context of the development of the IBC Principle and research around it. The intellectual tool used for verifying the IBC Principle is Channel Theory. The aspiration of doing so and our approach have been described in this paper. Due to space constraints, we are unable to present our work on other conditions under the IBC Principle. The main conclusion through this work is that the ideas embodied by the IBC Principle make sense, helpful, and moreover justifiable not only by using Dretske's theory (1981) and Devlin's theory (1991), on which the Principle is based, but also by using Channel Theory (Barwise and Seligman 1997), a sophisticated mathematical theory of information flow. This work also extends the application scope of Channel Theory from knowledge organization to conceptual modeling. We will continue our investigation along this line to further develop our theoretical thinking and to consolidate and further explore its practical relevance, for example, in the areas of schema optimization and query answering capability of a schema.

References

Anderson P B (1990) A Theory of Computer Semiotics: Semiotic Approaches to Construction and Assessment of Computer Systems. Cambridge University Press Cambridge

Barwise J, Seligman J (1997) Information Flow: the Logic of Distributed Systems. Cambridge University Press Cambridge

Batini C, Ceri S, Navathe SB (1992) Conceptual Database Design: An Entity-Relationship Approach. The Benjamin/Cummings Publishing Company Inc. Redwood City California

Checkland P (1981) Systems Thinking, Systems Practice. John Wiley & Sons Chichester

Chen P Peter (1999) Conceptual Modeling: Current Issues and Future Directions. Springer Verlag Berlin

Devlin K (1991) Logic and Information. Cambridge

Dretske F (1981) Knowledge and the Flow of Information. Basil Blackwell Oxford

Duzí M (1992) Semantic Information Connected with Data. Proc Database Theory – ICDT'92 Lecture Notes in Computer Science. Springer-Verlag Berlin

Feng J (1999) An Information and Meaning Oriented Approach to the Construction of a Conceptual Data Schema. PhD Thesis University of Paisley UK

Feng J (2005) Conditions for Information Bearing Capability. Computing and Information Systems Technical Reports No 28 University of Paisley UK

Floridi L (2002) What is the Philosophy of Information? Mataphilosophy, vol 33, no 1-2, pp 123-45.

Hu W, Feng J (2002) Some Considerations for a Semantic Analysis of Conceptual Data Schemata. In: Systems Theory and Practice in the Knowledge Age. Kluwer Academic/Plenum Publishers New York

Hull R (1986) Relative Information Capacity of Simple Relational Database Schemata. SIAM Journal of Computing, vol 15, no 3, pp 856-886

Kalfoglou Y, Schorlemmer (2003) Using Information Flow Theory to Enable Semantic Interoperability. Proc of the 6th Catalan Conference on Artificial Intelligence (CCIA '03) Palma de Mallorca Spain October 2003

Liu K C (2000) Semiotics in Information Systems Engineering. Cambridge Press

Miller RJ, Ioannidis YE, Ramakrishnan R (1993) The Use of Information Capacity in Schema Integration and Translation. Proc of the 19th International Conference on Very Large Data Base San Francisco

Miller RJ, Ioannidis YE, Ramakrishnan R (1994) Schema Equivalence in Heterogeneous Systems: Bridging Theory and Practice. Information Systems, vol 19, no 1, pp 3-31

Stamper R (1997) Organizational Semiotics. In: Mingers J, Stowell FA (eds) Information Systems: An Emerging Discipline? McGraw-Hill London

Stowell F, West D (1994) Client-Led Design. McGraw-Hill London

Xu H, Feng J (2002) The "How" Aspect of Information Bearing Capability of a Conceptual Schema at the Path Level. Proc of the 7th Annual Conference of the UK Academy for Information Systems UKAIS'2002 Leeds

Appendix

1. A *classification* is a structure $A = <U, \sum_A, \vdash_A>$ where U is the tokens of A, $\sum_A$ the types of A used to classify the tokens, and $\vdash_A$ is their binary relations.

2. Let A and C to be two *classifications*. An *infomorphism* between them is a pair $f = <f^\vee,$ $f^\wedge>$ of functions. For all tokens c of C and all types α of A, it is true that

$$f^\vee(c) \vdash_A \alpha \ iff \ c \vdash_C f^\wedge(\alpha)$$

3. *Information channel* consists of an indexed family $C = \{f_i: A_i \rightleftarrows C\}_{i \in I}$ of infomorphisms with a common co-domain C, the core of the channel.

4. A subset of tokens that really participate in the information flow are called *normal tokens*.

5. A *local logic* $L = <A, \vdash_L, N_L>$ consists of a classification A, a set of sequent $\vdash_L$ involving the types of A, the constraints of L, and a subset N_L as the normal tokens of L, which satisfy $\vdash_L$.

6. *Theory* $T = <typ(T), \vdash>$ consist of a set $typ(T)$ of types, and a binary relation $\vdash$ between subsets of $typ(T)$. Pairs $<\Gamma, \Delta>$ of subsets of $typ(T)$ are called sequents. If $\Gamma \vdash \Delta$, for $\Gamma, \Delta \subseteq type(T)$, then the sequent $\Gamma \vdash \Delta$ is a constraint. T is regular if for all $\alpha \in typ(T)$ and all sets $\Gamma, \Gamma', \Delta, \Delta', \sum', \sum_0, \sum_1$ of type:

   Identity: $\alpha \vdash \alpha$,
   Weakening: if $\Gamma \vdash \Delta$, then $\Gamma, \Gamma' \vdash \Delta, \Delta'$,
   Global Cut: if $\Gamma, \sum_0 \vdash \Delta, \sum_1$ for each partition $<\sum_0, \sum_1> (\sum_0 \cup \sum_1 = \sum'$ and $\sum_0 \cap \sum_1 = \Phi)$, then $\Gamma \vdash \Delta$.

7.

$$f\text{-Intro:} \quad \frac{\Gamma^\uparrow \vdash_A \Delta^\uparrow}{\Gamma \vdash_B \Delta}$$

$$f\text{-Elim:} \quad \frac{\Gamma^\uparrow \vdash_B \Delta^\uparrow}{\Gamma \vdash_A \Delta}$$

These rules consider mappings of types. *f-Intro* preserves validity but not non-validity. *f-Elim* does not preserve validity but preserves non-validity.

8. *State Space* is a classification **S** for which each token is of exactly one type. The types of a state space are called states, and we say that **a** is in state δ if $a \vdash_S \delta$. The state space **S** is complete if every state is the state of some token.

9. *Event Classification Evt(S)* associated with a state space **S** has as tokens the tokens of **S**. its types are arbitrary sets of states of **S**. The classification relation is given by $a \vdash_{Evt(S)} \alpha$, if and only if $state_S(a) \in \alpha$.

10. *Sum A+B* of classification has as set of tokens the Cartesian product of $tok(A)$ and $tok(B)$ and as set of types the disjoint union of $type(A)$ and $typ(B)$, such that for $\alpha \in typ(A)$ and $\beta \in typ(B)$, $<a, b> \vdash_{A+B} \alpha$ iff $a \vdash_A \alpha$, and $<a, b> \vdash_{A+B} \beta$ iff $b \vdash_B \beta$.

Integration of Schemas on the Pre-Design Level Using the KCPM-Approach

Jürgen Vöhringer and Heinrich C. Mayr

Institute of Business Informatics and Application Systems, University of Klagenfurt, Austria. (juergen, heinrich)@ifit.uni-klu.ac.at

Introduction[1]

Integration is a central research and operational issue in information system design and development. It can be conducted on the system, schema, and view or data level. On the *system level*, integration deals with the progressive linking and testing of system components to merge their functional and technical characteristics and behavior into a comprehensive, interoperable system. *Schema integration* comprises the comparison and merging of two or more schemas, usually conceptual database schemas. The *integration of data* deals with merging the contents of multiple sources of related data. *View integration* is similar to schema integration, however focuses on views and queries on these instead of schemas. All these types of integration have in common, that two or more sources are merged and previously compared, in order to identify matches and mismatches as well as conflicts and inconsistencies. The sources may stem from heterogeneous companies, organizational units or projects. Integration enables the reuse and combined use of source components.

The main problem comes with the fact, that the sources often have heterogeneous structures, so that the conflicts between these sources have to be resolved first. Often integration is done in relationship to a global (domain) ontology, which determines the domain terminology, its interdependencies and the way of naming source objects.

This paper introduces an approach that handles schema integration on the pre-design level. It will be shown that such an approach comes with a number of advantages, in particular reduced structural conflicts and enhanced user communication, thus maximizing feedback for further requirements engineering. Both advantages result from the orientation at

---

[1] The work underlying that paper has been financed partly by the Klaus-Tschira-Stiftung Heidelberg

domain notions rather than at design oriented categories as used in other conceptual modeling languages like UML.

The paper proceeds as follows: Section 2 gives an overview of the current state of the art in the field of schema integration. Current research directions are mentioned, in particular those affecting or influencing our own work. Section 3 outlines KCPM, the conceptual pre-design model we are using, and shows its usage for ontology representation, and requirements modeling. Section 4 discusses KCPM schema integration in detail. Section 5 concludes the paper by a short summary and an outlook on future work to be done.

Previous Work

When performing schema integration certain constraints have to be met, namely the four main conditions completeness, correctness, minimality and understandability. *Completeness* requires that all information is preserved. *Correctness* means that an integrated schema is not in contradiction to the original sub-schemas. A schema is *minimal* if it contains no redundancy. Integrated schemas should also be *understandable* and comprehensible. Possible conflicts in the integration process include naming-, semantic-, structural-, data model- and data conflicts. *Naming conflicts* deal with the assignment of different names to the same real world entities (synonyms). *Semantic conflicts* occur when two schemas contain the same concept names without representing the same real world data (homonyms). *Structural conflicts* appear when different data structures represent similar concepts, e.g. the same concept is modeled as an entity type in one sub-schema and as a value type in another. *Data model conflicts* occur when heterogeneous data models, like a relational and a hierarchical data model, are integrated.

Recent integration research focuses on automating the integration and resolution of conflicts. Parent and Spaccapietra (1998) give an overview over the integration process and mention the use of ontologies and other linguistic tools as a prerequisite for automatic schema integration. Bouzeghoub et al. (1996) describe structural and semantic ontologies that contain information about schema concepts. Such ontologies are also used by Comyn-Wattiau and Mètais (1997), who advise the use of canonical graphs and concept hierarchies in order to store additional semantic knowledge. Storey (2000) proposes the development of ontologies that allow the classification of relationship verb-phrases. The RADD-NLI-approach addresses the definition of antonyms in ontologies as an aid for automatically deriving contrastive or opposite relationships between verb phrases (Buchholz et al. 1996). Ekenberg and Johannesson (1996) discuss the use of inter-schema correspondence assertions for defining similarities of schema entities. Gal and Trombetta (2003) describe probabilistic and fuzzy methods, which can be utilized for the calculation of confidence measures for similarity. Schema discrepancy conflicts are another important issue of integration – they occur when the same information is modeled explicitly as data in one schema and implicitly as metadata in another. He and Ling (2004) propose to resolve the problem by transforming schema context into entity types. Martins and Pinto (2001) describe the ontology integration process and identify the required process steps. Other researchers define formal frameworks for ontology integration (Calí et al. 2001). Winiwarter and Zillner (2004) show how ontologies can be used for semantic multimedia modeling, and therefore mark the way for the integration of multimedia knowledge-bases.

All these approaches have in common that they deal with schema integration issues on the conceptual level. This is mostly due to the fact that a variety of conceptual models has emerged in the last two decades shifting design and integration issues up from the logical level of concrete database data models to a more semantic one, thus allowing for developing a global integrated schema before mapping it to a concrete implementation oriented level. By this way, also the perspective has widened from the data centered view to a more general one including also functionality and dynamics. However, as will be shown in the next sections, most conceptual models still suffer from some deficiencies which also impede the integration task and could be avoided by a more general modeling approach.

KCPM as a Domain Ontology

Motivation

The need for the Klagenfurt Conceptual Pre-design Model (KCPM) originates from insufficient or imprecise communication between clients and software engineers that may happen because of the complexity that is inherent to most conceptual models. Such models may correctly represent the system designer's idea of the system, but still are not suitable for getting the desired client feedback. Business-owners, who are the typical clients of software development projects, are in the majority of cases not skilled in interpreting conceptual models and lack the intuitive understanding of their graphical representations. The system designers on the other hand have the necessary technical knowledge but lack a deep understanding of the corresponding domain. Conceptual pre-design models are a way to escape from this predicament, because they intend to improve the communication between the parties that are involved in the system analysis and design process. This is achieved by a more general representation of the domain, concentrating on the essentials instead of on unnecessary design details that ultimately confuse customers. Thus the partial informality of the pre-design approach is exploited to facilitate end-user communication.

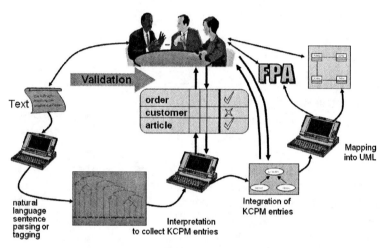

Fig. 1. The NIBA process (Fliedl et al. 2002)

KCPM is a pre-design model that was developed as part of the project NIBA (Figure 1) by adopting concepts of the NIAM Object-Role Model (Nijssen and Halpin 1989). NIBA deals with the pre-processing and interpreting of natural language, from which KCPM schemas can be derived. The extraction of KCPM-schemas from natural language text is described in detail in (Fliedl et al. 2000) and (Kop 2002). KCPM schemas can be used to model static as well as dynamic aspects of a Universe of Discourse (UoD). KCPM acts as a conceptual Interlingua between natural language texts and state-of-the-art conceptual models (i.e. UML, Petri-nets). We have developed an extensive prototype for the maintenance of static and dynamic KCPM schemas, which contains a component for mapping pre-design KCPM schemas on more formal conceptual design schemas. Currently the target schemas are UML static models and UML activity diagrams respectively. The mapping from KCPM models to conceptual schemas is described in (Kop and Mayr 2002) and (Kop 2002).

The Main Elements of KCPM

The key modeling notions for capturing static UoD aspects are thing-type, connection-type and perspective, while the dynamic aspects of a domain are described by operation-types, cooperation-types and conditions.

Thing-types correlate to classes, attributes, values or types in common conceptual modeling. Simple nouns, proper nouns and noun phrases are mapped to thing-types. *Connection-types* depict relationships between thing-types. They are commonly represented by a verb or verb phrase. For each binary connection, two *perspectives* exist, i.e. one perspective for the point of view of each related thing-type (see, e.g. the NIAM Object-Role model (Nijssen and Halpin 1989)). Perspectives may have cardinalities or multiplicities. It should be clear that by introducing only two main modeling notions for capturing UoD aspects and their interrelationships the business-owner can concentrate on the domain specific aspects and terminology and is not forced to make technical decisions between concepts like classes and values, associations and attributes. This facilitates user interpretation and validation of KCPM schemas substantially and in addition, avoids frequent re-definitions (conceptual changes) as usual in conceptual model development. Since from KCPM schemas more formal ones may be derived automatically based on a set of heuristic rules (Kop and Mayr 2002), its use does not hamper the design process.

Operation-types model system functions and are related to thing-types modeling the caller, executor and parameters of the respective function. *Cooperation-types* aggregate operation-types that can be executed concurrently and describe the related pre- and/or post-*conditions*. Each cooperation-type has at least one pre- and post-condition, and each dynamic KCPM-schema must have one start- and one end-condition. Logical terms may be defined for cooperation-types that contain additional information about the way concatenations of associated pre- and post-conditions should be resolved. Dynamic KCPM schemas specify hierarchical structures by the means of operation- and cooperation-types. An operation-type can be interpreted as a use case or an atomic activity. On the top level, operation types are generally use cases. A use case describes a process, which is modeled as a series of cooperation-types, that are sequentially ordered by pre- and post-conditions. Cooperation-types in turn contain one or more operation-types which may again be either atomic activities or use cases. In the latter case they contain another cooperation-type/condition-schema. We do not impose an explicit restriction to the depth of dynamic KCPM-hierarchies.

Ontologies in the KCPM Approach

Ontologies mirror a domain with the help of a standardized vocabulary. They can be classified on a scale from highly informal to rigorously formal. Depending on its formality an ontology can be interpreted manually or automatically. Highly informal ontologies are plain, unstructured documents of natural language text, while semi-formal ontologies contain a limited set of predefined categories and relationships and therefore limited capabilities for automatic inference and reasoning. Formal ontologies are declarative, heavily structured and can describe any arbitrary domain.

The terms of an ontology vocabulary are called *concepts*. Concepts consist of *slots*, describing their features. *Facets* are defined for slots and restrict slot value ranges or put other constraints on their contents. *Taxonomies* describe hierarchical structures, i.e. generalizations and aggregations, of concepts. *Facts* and *rules* are used especially in formal ontologies to describe additional constraints or relationships between concepts.

Ontologies are not restricted to single projects or organizational units. On the contrary they endorse the collective reuse of shared knowledge, i.e. they should be reusable among different task areas and organizational units and possibly even among companies. Knowledge reuse is possible because ontologies store universally valid domain-terminologies and –relationships instead of implementation-specific knowledge. The use of ontologies is reasonable whenever access to knowledge about the problem domain is needed. This is the case throughout the requirements engineering and system development process, specifically whenever people communicate and risk using blurry notions instead of well-defined terms.

By ensuring that all schemas that are related to a certain domain adhere to a common ontology, their integration is facilitated substantially since ontological relationships may be used for identifying similarities and conflicts. Clearly such an ontology can be kept dynamic in the sense that it can be extended in cases where schema elements are detected that are not yet elements of that ontology.

KCPM is basically a domain-independent semi-formal (meta-)ontology classifying words as thing-types, connection-types, etc. On the other hand, integrated and generalized KCPM schema may be seen as a domain ontology of the respective UoD (and thus be re-used in subsequent design and integration projects). Actually, we are working on the definition of rules for mapping KCPM to a formal ontology (Kop et al. 2004).

The Integration Methodology

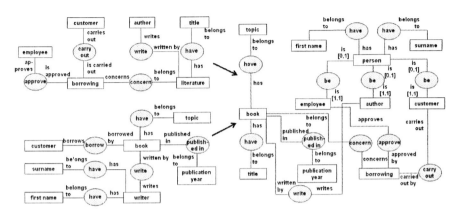

Fig. 2. Static KCPM integration

Motivation for Performing Pre-Design KCPM Integration

As had been said in the introduction, one of the main advantages of KCPM schema integration is to circumvent certain types of integration conflicts that appear on the design level. In particular, structural conflicts can be widely neglected due to the fact that KCPM does not differentiate between entities and attribute types. Also, data model conflicts are reduced to a minimum because of the leanness of the model. Another advantage comes with the user centeredness of KCPM which allows the users to take part in the integration process, give authentic feedback on conflict resolution decisions, and validate integration results. Finally, since an integrated pre-design schema can be mapped to a more detailed conceptual one automatically, no further integration is necessary on the conceptual design level.

For example, consider the integration of two UML static schemas. The first model consists of one class "borrowing" that contains all the relevant information as attributes. The other model contains the same semantic information in the form of multiple classes that are all connected to a central class "borrowing". An integration of those models is tricky. It has to be decided, which concepts are equivalent and whether to model the similar concepts as attributes or as classes in the target schema. Implementation details like keys and null-values are also to be considered and increase the complexity of the integration. On the pre-design level the complexity is lower, since only thing- and connection-types exist. Therefore, on the pre-design level we can concentrate on integrating models themselves without worrying about subtleties of implementation, thus simplifying the whole integration process – which in turn helps to involve the customers in the process – and separating it from technical decisions by deferring these to the design stage.

Manual Integration of KCPM Models

Figure 2 shows an example for the integration of static KCPM schemas, with two source schemas on the left-hand side and an integrated schema on the right-hand side. Since our approach is in an early research phase and no tool exists yet, the process was performed manually in order to demonstrate the possible outcome of pre-design integration. Nevertheless, it should become clear, that the integration steps can be automated easily. The static KCPM source schemas describe the structure of a library system. The upper sub-schema describes an employee's perspective on the system, while the lower sub-schema is modeled from the customer's perspective. Since the sub-schemas have a different focus they use partly differently named and structured concepts.

The principal procedure in the manual integration of static and dynamic schemas is identical, though problems exist in the latter case that will be discussed subsequently. The expert, who carries out the manual integration, compares all concepts of one schema with all the concepts from the other one:

- If two concepts have the same name they may be merged if they are not homonyms (e.g. the expert identifies the thing-type "customer" in both sub-schemas of Fig. 2, decides it has the same meaning in both cases and creates a thing-type "customer" in the integrated schema, that inherits its properties from the corresponding concept of the source-schemas).
- If two concepts have different names, and the expert does not notice any similarities or dependencies, then he accepts both of them as part of the integrated schema (e.g. the thing-types "borrowing" and "publication year" are not similar, therefore both are transferred to the target schema).
- If two concepts are different, but the expert thinks that they model similar real world constructs, then he evaluates the differences and tries to resolve them by deciding intuitively which parts to change, which ones to keep and how to represent the merged concepts in the integrated schema (e.g. the thing-types "book" and "literature" are synonyms and thus represented as one thing-type "book" in the target schema).

An expert bases his matching-decisions not solely on the naming of concepts; he also evaluates the adjacent concepts. Similar environments can indicate a connection between concepts that would go unnoticed otherwise. The expert continues the matching and merging actions until the integrated schema is complete.

Static and dynamic schemas are treated as independent in regard to integration since they have only thing-types in common: callers, executors or parameters of operations. Contrary to thing-types, operation-types are more difficult to integrate. Apart from atomic operations which can be recognized easily as being similar, this may be intricate in the case of more complex operations. Also, different dynamic schemas often lack common conditions at which they could be reasonably joined. Dynamic integration is therefore highly dependent on user-feedback.

Semi-Automatic Integration of KCPM Models

Semi-automatic KCPM schema integration consists of two major steps. Firstly the *concept matching* takes place, which will be achieved by a linguistic analysis of the concept names. Secondly formal *integration rules* must be applied, that enable conflict resolution and schema merging.

We will use ontologies to maintain a vocabulary about KCPM schemas that will contain valid terms of the domain and additional information about them. Consider the following example, which shows the advantages of using separate linguistic and domain ontologies, as proposed by Comyn-Wattiau and Mètais (1997) and Bouzeghoub et al. (1996): Let

- "if student(X) then person(X)"
- "if student(X) then attends(X,Y) and university(Y)"

be entries of a linguistic ontology. In contrast to that, the domain ontology for the domain "university library" might contain the concept *"student"*, classified as a synonym of the term *"customer"* and with the semantic description *"person that lends books"*.

Moreover, the concept *"student"* in this ontology might be defined as generalization of the concepts *"regular student"* and *"PhD student"*, the latter granting additional lending rights.

The example shows how domain ontologies offer domain-specific semantic knowledge that is valuable in the current domain but can not be universally used outside of it. The general linguistic ontology contains domain-independent knowledge, like general classifications, taxonomies, synonym- and homonym-relationships, that can be referenced when no suitable matches are found in the domain-ontology and that has the advantage that it can be reused without restrictions.

In the first step of semi-automatic integration of static schemas the concepts of the source-schemas are compared one after another. This is easy for thing-types, because they usually consist of base forms of simple nouns. Since connection-types consist in most cases of simple infinitive verbs, they are also easy to compare. However, in order to decide if connection-types are equal one has to compare the adjacent thing-types too. Concept matching has three possible results: the matched concepts are equal, different or similar. *Equality* means that the base forms of the concepts correspond. When direct keyword matching is not sufficient, the *Similarity* between two concepts is determined. Two concepts are similar, if their base forms do not correspond, but they are part of a common fact, rule, classification or taxonomy in the ontology (e.g. the words are synonymous, one word is the generalization of the other, or a probabilistic similarity-relationship is defined between two words). *Difference* means that the base forms of the concepts do not correspond, and they are not defined as similar in the ontology. We will analyze a promising approach for enhancing the significance of connection-type matching, which consists of the definition of semantic classifications for generic verbs like "have" or "do" (Storey 2000).

In the second step the conflicts are resolved by consulting a formal rule set, which controls the automatic adaptation of the source schemas' terms and structures to those of the ontology if needed. If two concepts are equal, they are merged in the resulting schema. If they are different, both are accepted in the integrated schema. If the concepts are similar, then one of them has to be renamed according to the ontology before the concepts are merged. A client may also be involved in the process by accepting or declining resolve-proposals for specific conflicts.

The approach to semi-automatic integration of dynamic KCPM schemas is mostly analogous to the static integration, although there are specific problems. Firstly, operation-types, cooperation-types and conditions may consist of *complex linguistic terms* like phrases or sentence fragments. To resolve these terms and make them comparable to each other, they have to be decomposed and their elements have to be reduced to their base form. In order to make this process easier we consider defining naming rules for dynamic KCPM concepts that must be followed when such concepts are added or edited. Secondly, the potential problem of *state overlapping* (Eder and Frank 1997) is a major obstacle for dynamic integration. State overlapping occurs when two state diagrams contain similar states that are not directly comparable, because one state is a subset of the other one, or because one state corresponds to a number of states in the second diagram.

Such problems cannot be solved automatically and are in fact even for expert users hard to recognize and resolve. State overlapping is relevant for KCPM integration, because conditions are largely equivalent to states and may therefore also overlap. All similar operation-type pairs, with similar but non equal neighborhood, i.e. assigned conditions, may potentially overlap. In dynamic integration we will frequently fall back on user feedback, in the hope to prevent or resolve overlapping conditions.

Summary and Future Work

In this paper we gave an overview on our approach to integrate schemas on the pre-design level. We described the potential benefits, presented a general methodology for performing KCPM-integration using ontology knowledge and argued the use of KCPM for the implementation of the approach. Our research will be prosecuted, particularized and implemented, beginning with the identification of necessary ontology extensions or supplements. We will then continue by detailing a palpable ontology matching algorithm. One major goal of our research project will be the definition of formal integration rules, for KCPM schema integration.

Another recent branch of research in the NIBA project focuses on adapting KCPM as an ontology language for describing business process fragments on a pre-design level, which can be represented by KCPM. In this context we will research the integration of KCPM business processes, which is a special case of KCPM schema integration. As part of the latter project we also plan to develop a new version of our current KCPM visualization tool, which will then allow the editing and maintenance of graphically represented KCPM business process schemas and also contain the integration component.

References

Bouzeghoub M, Comyn-Wattiau I, Kedad Z, Métais E (1996) Implementation of a Third Generation View Integration Tool. Proc of the 2nd International Workshop on Applications of Natural Language to Data Bases

Buchholz E, Düsterhöft A, Thalheim B (1996) Capturing Information on Behaviour with the RADD-NLI: A Linguistic and Knowledge Based Approach. Applications of Natural Language to Information Systems. Proc of the Second International Workshop

Calí A, Calvanese D, De Giacomo G, Lenzerini M (2001) A Framework for Ontology Integration. Proc of the 1st Semantic Web Working Symposium

Comyn-Wattiau I, Mètais E (1997) View Integration as a Way to Build a Semantic Dictionary for a Data Warehouse. Proc of the 3rd NLDB Workshop, NLDB'97

Eder J, Frank H (1997) Integration of Behaviour Models. ER'97 Workshop on Behavioural Models and Design Transformations

Ekenberg L, Johannesson P (1996) A Formal Basis for Dynamic Schema Integration. Proc of ER 96, 15th International Conference on Conceptual Modeling

Fliedl G, Kop C, Mayr HC, Mayerthaler W, Winkler C (2000) From Natural Language to Conceptual Predesign (Static and Dynamic Aspects of Language Engineering). ÖGAI Journal, vol 20, no 1

Fliedl G, Kop C, Mayr HC (2002) The NIBA Workflow. ICSSEA'2002 International Conference "Software & Systems Engineering and their Applications"

Gal A, Trombetta A (2003) A Model for Schema Integration in Heterogeneous Databases. Proc of IDEAS 2003

He Q, Ling TW (2004) Resolving Schematic Discrepancy in the Integration of Entity-Relationship Schemas. Proc of the 23rd International Conference on Conceptual Modeling ER 2004

Kop C (2002) Rechnergestützte Katalogisierung von Anforderungsspezifikationen und deren Transformation in ein konzeptuelles Modell. Doctoral Thesis

Kop C, Mayr HC (2002) Mapping Functional Requirements: from Natural Language to Conceptual Schemata. Proc of the 6th IASTED International Conference on Software Engineering and Applications

Kop C, Mayr HC, Zavinska T (2004) Using KCPM for Defining and Integrating Domain Ontologies. Proc of the International Workshop on Fragmentation versus Integration - Perspectives of the Web Information Systems Discipline

Nijssen GM, Halpin TA (1989) Conceptual Schema and Relational Database Design – A Fact Oriented Approach. Prentice Hall Publ Comp

Martins JP, Pinto HS (2001) Ontology Integration: How to Perform the Process. Proc of IJCAI2001, Workshop on Ontologies and Information Sharing

Parent C, Spaccapietra S (1998) Issues and Approaches of Database Integration. Communications of the ACM, vol 41, no 5, pp 166-178

Storey VC (2000) Understanding and Representing Relationship Semantics in Database Design. Proc of the 5th International Conference on Applications of Natural Language to Information Systems

Winiwarter W, Zillner S (2004) Integrating Ontology Knowledge into a Query Algebra for Multimedia Meta Objects. Proc of the 5th International Conference on Web Information Systems Engineering WISE 2004

Towards a Generic and Integrated Enterprise Modeling Approach to Designing Databases and Software Components

Peter Bellström and Lars Jakobsson

Department of Information Systems, Karlstad University, Sweden.
(Peter.Bellstrom, Lars.Jakobsson)@kau.se

Introduction

In order to design databases and software components that are fulfilling the customers requirements, modeling languages that define them at a high level of abstraction are needed e.g. [2, 12, 15, 18]. Several modeling languages and methods have been proposed but most of them put focus on the implementation level and the technical parts of the future information system [15].

For conceptual database design, the entity-relationship (ER) model is almost seen as a de facto standard [22] because it is one of the most popular and commonly used model today [10, 23]. ER was originally proposed by [7] in the mid seventies and has since that been extended (generally termed EER) and used in several methods (e.g. [9, 25]). Although the ER has been widely used it has been criticized for its general use of the relationship concept [9]. For software components, the Unified Modeling Language (UML) has almost reached the same position, accommodating for software components by alterations suggested by various authors [6, 24]. UML is intended for requirements engineering and information system modeling [5]. It provides twelve standard diagram types to analyze a technical system solution. Nevertheless, the current UML foundation has some inherent integrity problems of static and behavioral aspects [12]. One problem is the absence of a complete agreement on how to control the integrity and consistency between various diagrams [15]. In this paper, the Enterprise Modeling (EM) approach is applied in the context of being a generic and integrated modeling technique for conceptual design of databases and software components. It is argued that EM is to be used as a generic and integrated modeling approach for design of databases and software components. This paper is organized as described in Fig. 1.

Design Procedure and System Specification

To be able to present a comprehensible description of the design procedure and the system specification that is used in this paper, Fig. 1 is included and described. Fig. 1 should be interpreted starting with the Customer Requirements (CR1, CR2).

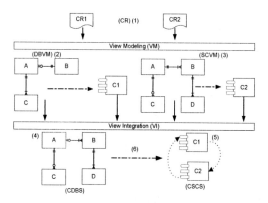

Fig. 1. Database Design and Software Components

The numbers inside the parenthesis are references to the numbers illustrated in Fig. 1. CR (1) includes a specification about what the future database is to store and a specification for what services future software components are to provide. The design scenario in this paper deals with a sale (CR1) and a warehouse (CR2) department. After the designers have studied and interpreted CR, the Database View Modeling (DBVM) and the Software Component View Modeling (SCVM) are carried out during the View Modeling (VM) phase. DBVM (2) is based on the information that the CR has to offer, and the SCVM (3) is based on both the database views and the CR information. During these two tasks, DBVM and SCVM views are developed for each of the two mentioned departments.

The local views are thereafter integrated into global schemata during the View Integration (VI) phase, resulting in global schemata, one for conceptual database design (4) and one for conceptual software component design (5). During this phase, the interaction between the two components unfolds, which reveals some integrity problems. The last step, (6) point out that there is a need to study the connection between the designed conceptual database views and schema, and the designed conceptual software component views and schema. This approach can be used to validate the database design during the dynamic component design process, whenever a classical bottom-up perspective on IS-design is used.

Database Design

In order to design a database that is correct according to the perspective of both the end users and the database designers a method has to be used. In [2] it is pointed out that a database design method is composed of at least three main phases: *conceptual database design, logical database design,* and *physical database design.* This chapter put focus on the first of these three phases since it influences the rest of the design and therefore is the most important phase.

Conceptual Database Design

The main task in this design phase is to identify concepts, dependencies between the concepts and finally illustrate these in a conceptual schema. One big challenge during conceptual database design is to define a global schema that is semantically correct, complete, easy to use and comprehensive [21] using the chosen modeling language [23]. Many methods and models have been proposed during the last thirty years. One of the first modeling techniques which has been one of the most popular and commonly used [10, 23] is the entity-relationship (ER) model [7] proposed by Chen in mid seventies. There are at least three things that have contributed to its popularity: 1) ER has been extended (generally termed EER) and used in several database design methods (e.g. [9, 25]), 2) the concepts used in ER are naturally occurring in database design [17] and finally 3) ER is useful for communicating with end users [25]. It has also been proven that the EER is useful when defining unary and ternary relationships [21] but it has been criticized for its general use of the relationship construct [9]. In this paper a modeling approach, that classifies a relationship as association, composition, aggregation, specialization, generalization or instance of is applied. This approach, EM, gives the designer an opportunity to define detailed dependencies between the concepts. The static dependencies adapted from EM are illustrated in Fig. 2.

One way to capture how the concepts are defined and named is to involve the end users in the view modeling process. In this design step, smaller schemata, views, are defined for each end user or user group. View modeling in conceptual database design is important since a global schema can mask differences on how different end users view their organization [20]. During view modeling, each end user or user group describes their view of the organization resulting in a graphical illustration, a view. The organization can be defined and graphically illustrated in many different ways. One concept can for instance be modeled at different levels of abstraction or even using different modeling constructs [16]. Another aspect to consider is that different end users or user groups can have different focus while defining their view. This aspect is also illustrated in Fig. 3a and Fig. 3b where sales and warehouse department are graphically illustrated using the primitives in Fig. 2. In Fig. 3a the concepts: *Customer, Order,* and *Article* are focused and in Fig. 3b the concepts: *Product* and *Order*.

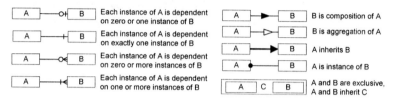

Fig. 2. Adapted and modified representation of static dependencies in EM ([15])

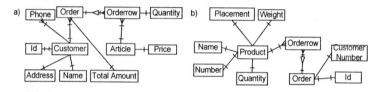

Fig. 3. Database views for Sales Department (a) and Warehouse Department (b)

In Fig. 3a and 3b there are two kinds of relationships that need to be addressed. First of all, between *Customer* and *Id* (3a), *Product* and *Number* (3b), and *Order* and *Id* (3b) there exists a one-to-one relationship that indicates that for each of the mentioned concepts there only exists one match, e.g. between *Customer* and *Id*. Secondly, between *Order* and *Orderrow* (3a and 3b) there exists an aggregate relationship which indicates that each *Order* is aggregated from one or several *Orderrows*.

After view modeling the static local views are integrated into one conceptual schema, which will be used as documentation and template for the future database. To be able to integrate the views, conflicts that exist between them have to be identified and resolved.

Designing Software Components

The use of software components in software development has not been a feasible way to improve the development process until recently, since a systematic component-based approach is needed to achieve this [8].

Since software developed today is very complex, descriptions in a high level of abstraction are needed to aid in requirements analysis for the system. It is imperative that these representations are useable throughout the software development process for the system. This means that the descriptions have to be comprehendible for all interest groups throughout the entire software development process [14]. Three dimensions of the system must be addressed to accommodate for this; pragmatic level, semantic level and syntactic level modeling [11].

All of the three levels mentioned above need a comprehensive modeling technique with the possibility to address the gap between programmers and system designers. Understanding the intention of the system to be developed and interactions between parts of the system are essential for successful end results [13]. A model well suited for this is the EM technique, since it addresses all of the levels (pragmatic, semantic and syntactic) [14]. This paper focus is on the semantic aspects of an integrated approach.

A comprehensive modeling technique can support the development process by providing the essential descriptiveness of the models used for analysis of the information system requirements [14].

Semantic Dependencies in the EM Approach

Semantic dependencies in EM are of two kinds: static and dynamic. Descriptions of organizational *activities* as well as *actors* are based on the dynamic dependencies. The dynamic part of EM can be represented by actions that are using and producing communication flows and by actors that are responsible for initiation of those actions. The dynamic relations are state dependencies and communication dependencies. Actions are represented by an ellipse. Dynamic constituents in the extended communication flow and action dependency are represented in Fig. 4. State dependencies are represented by solid arrows, defining semantic relationships between states (see states A and B).

Unfortunately, many communication-based approaches often neglect behavioral aspects of the state transition and vice versa, many software engineering approaches disregard communication dependencies [15].

Dynamic dependencies are used to define relations between different actors, their actions and communication flows. If concept A is connected to B by a communication dependency, then A is an agent and B is a recipient. Depending on whether there is a physical flow in the action or not, the communication flows can be information, material or decision.

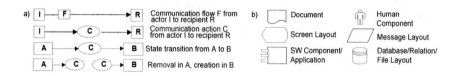

Fig. 4. Dynamic dependencies (a) and Syntactic Elements (b) [15]

Modeling primitives of the syntactic level are considered as the implementation perspective or CASE tool dependent [15]. This means that the list of symbols is not exhaustive; other symbols can be added on demand.

Combinations of the notations shown in Fig. 2 and Fig. 4 make it possible to describe syntactic and semantic aspects of a system using the same diagram type. This means that it is possible to keep track of ambiguities and inconsistencies in the model and to capture the potential problems before actually starting to implement the system. Recent studies indicate that it is more confusing for the developer as well as for the user to switch between different diagram types than keeping everything in a larger, well-organized model with the possibility to integrate more specific or more abstract views [26].

Designing component interaction loops only based on static database views may result in incomplete component views. This is illustrated in Fig. 5, which corresponds to the database view shown in Fig. 3a.

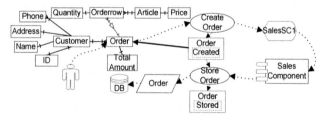

Fig. 5. Component View - Sales Department

However, it is difficult, if not impossible, to create complete component views only based on database views and customer requirements, since local views may lack in describing dependencies which are only apparent when a local view integration process has been performed.

The view shown in Fig. 5 is incomplete, since it is not clear what data is stored in the database. If we study the local database views, we can conclude that both views probably contain data that should be stored, but it is only after view integration we can determine the data to be stored. The component view for the warehouse department, shown in Fig. 6, is designed based on the database view shown in Fig. 3b. The representation of the dynamic parts of the system incorporates the static properties from the two database views (Fig. 3a and Fig. 3b).

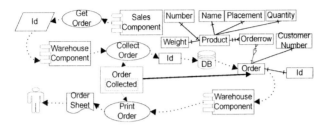

Fig. 6. Component View - Warehouse Department

The view shown in Fig. 6 is incomplete, since it would be impossible to retrieve any data about a specific order from the database unless the order is created first. This implies that we do not have sufficient data in the first two database views separately, to create complete component views. Thus, for a complete system specification schema, we need to integrate the different views. Integration of the component views into one schema should be performed after the corresponding database views have been integrated into one schema. Using this approach will make it possible to capture certain conflicts before designing the dynamic models.

Integration

After the end users have defined the local views they should be integrated into one global conceptual schema, defined by [1] as "[…] the activity of integrating the schemas of existing or proposed databases into one global, unified schema." Several methods (e.g. [17, 19, 22]) have been proposed during the last twenty years and a comprehensive survey of methods is found in [1]. In the survey performed by [1] it was found that each integration method is composed of a mixture of the following four phases: 1) *preintegration*, 2) *comparison of the schemas*, 3) *conforming the schemas*, and 4) *merging and restructuring*. To avoid ambiguity regarding the names of the phases these are hereafter named *preintegration, comparison of the view, conforming the views, and merging* and *restructuring*.

In this paper, the three last phases are emphasized. The reason for this is that phase two and three identifies and resolves conflicts between the views, while phase four superimpose and restructure them. Conflicts appear because different end users use different vocabulary and different ways to define the same concept, a phenomenon also called semantic relativism [22]. Several conflicts that need to be resolved can be detected while *comparing the views*. What types of conflicts that can occur depends on the chosen modeling language (e.g. ER, UML, EM) and which level the integration is performed at (e.g. conceptual or logical level). In this paper a study at the conceptual level using EM is conducted and therefore the conflict classification used in [1] is adapted. The conflicts in [1] are classified as either name or structural conflicts. Name conflicts are further divided into *synonyms* and *homonyms* [1]. A deeper analysis on identification and resolution of homonym conflicts in the context of EM is found in [3]. Structural conflicts are further divided into *type conflicts*, *dependency conflicts*, *key conflicts*, and *behavioral conflicts* [1]. During *conforming the views* all the conflicts are resolved and finally, during *merging and restructuring* the views are superimposed into one schema and thereafter restructured according to eight quality criterions [2].

Database View Integration

To successfully use the view integration approach for the views found in Fig. 3a and 3b, three phases have to be applied starting with *comparison of the views*. While comparing the sales department view (3a) and the warehouse department view (3b), five conflicts; three homonyms, one synonym, and one key conflict, are identified. Homonyms are: *Name, Quantity* and *Id*, synonyms are *Product* and *Article* and the key conflict is identified between *CustomerNumber* and *Id*. The second phase is *conforming the views* and it is during this phase that the conflicts are resolved. For the synonym, identified between the Sales and the Warehouse department views the following reasoning can be applied **Product ⟶▶ Article, Article ⟶▶ Product if and only if Product ◀—▶ Article** [3, 11]. The single arrow '⟶▶' represents inheritance and the double arrow '◀—▶' represents mutual inheritance also used for representing synonyms. For the homonyms another reasoning can be applied as follows: **if Customer → Name (0,1; 1,1) then Customer.Name ⟵→→ Customer (1,1; 1,*), Customer.Name ⟶▶ Name** [11] **and if Order ⟵→ Id (1,1; 1,1) then Order.Id ⟵→ Order (1,1; 1,1), Order.Id ⟶▶ Id**. The '.' dot notation, prefixing, is used for compound concepts to unambiguously identify a concept in a schema. In this case, it is used to solve homonyms. One conflict still exist which needs to be resolved. The resolution technique is to include both concepts and leave the decision about which one to use as the primary key to the logical database designer since this is a task conducted during the logical database design. By using the illustrated conflict resolution technique all concept names are retained for both homonyms and synonyms. This is a strength since otherwise the language used in the views can impoverish, a problem criticized in [4]. This means that an over specification for the solved name conflicts exists. Fig. 7 illustrates the final static integrated schema where the mentioned conflicts have been resolved.

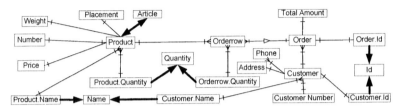

Fig. 7. Integrated Database Schema

Component View Integration

In order to make a complete component schema, the local database views were integrated into a global database schema. To achieve a complete component schema, the dynamic views must be merged based on the integrated database schema, shown in Fig. 7 and thereafter restructured according to the quality criterions described by [2]. The integrated component schema, Fig. 8, illustrates the necessity for schema integration, by the detailed specification of the *Order* object created by the *Create Order* action.

Since the composition of *Order* is only possible by deriving data from the integrated global database schema, shown in Fig. 7, we can conclude that it is only possible to create a complete and correct component schema when the local database views are integrated into one global schema, and when the component views have been integrated into one schema, based on the integrated database schema. Furthermore, we can avoid homonyms and synonyms if we perform view integration on the static parts of the system, as shown in the previous section.

In the integrated component schema, we can see the composition of a stored order, as well as the complete interaction between the involved software components and human actors. It is also possible to identify the slight over specification of Fig. 7, since only specified concepts (e.g. *Product.Name* and *Customer.Name*) are used, and not more general ones (e.g. *Name*).

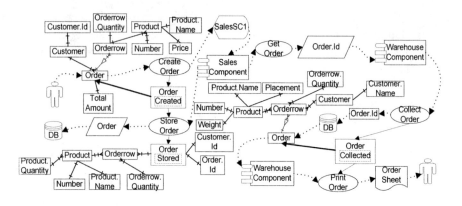

Fig. 8. Integrated Component Schema

Summary and Conclusion

Several important aspects for a generic and integrated modeling approach have been detected in this work. Static design problems can be resolved by analyzing the local views and integrating them into one global schema. Thus, it is important to have a consistent use of concept names. If a concept is named *Order* in the database schema, it should be named *Order* in the software component schema.

Dynamic or behavioral conflicts are best resolved by analyzing the dynamic views, but normally we also need to analyze the static schema for a complete understanding of what is needed for the dynamic schema. In the dynamic views, we can identify pre- and post conditions for each action in the system, but we need the integrated static schema to be able to describe the contents of the conditions for the actions more completely. The dynamic views also provide a means to analyze the completeness of the static views, since the systems dynamic behavior may result in additional states being created, as well as identification of over specification in database views.

The conceptual database schema is developed as specification of the entire future database. The conceptual software component schema is developed according to given scenarios – what the software components are to carry out in a specified situation. By using the view approach to database and software component design, the complexity increase, but at the same time it is controlled. The integration of views results in one schema that illustrates the complete database and all components working together. This integration of the views is needed since the global schema contain additional information that is needed by the IS.

Based on the results in the previous sections of this paper, we can identify a design process, shown in Fig. 1, for integrating static and dynamic modeling of software systems. It has been shown that in order to create complete static and dynamic schemata of an information system, local views must be integrated into larger global schemata. This is because of the dependency that dynamic behaviors create, is linking different parts of a system together. By integrating the static views first, and basing the dynamic schema on the integrated database schema, we can avoid naming conflicts although over specification still exist to some extent. Furthermore, we can identify composition of pre- and post conditions for the dynamic schema. Thus, we can eliminate unnecessary problems before trying to implement the information system.

References

[1] Batini C, Lenzerini M, Navathe BL (1986) A Comparative Analysis of Methodologies for Database Schema Integration. ACM Computing Surveys, vol 18, no 4, pp 323-363

[2] Batini C, Ceri S, Navathe S (1992) Conceptuel Database Design – An Entity-Relationship Approach. Benjamin-Cummings, Redwood City California

[3] Bellström P (2005) Using Enterprise Modeling for Identification and Resolution of Homonym Conflicts in View Integration. In: Vasilecas O, Caplinskas A, Wojtkowski W, Wojtkowski G, Zupancic J, Wrycza S (eds) Information Systems Development Advances in Theory, Practice, and Education. Springer, pp 265-276

[4] Bellström P, Carlsson S (2004) Towards an Understanding of the Meaning and the Contents of a Database through Design and Reconstruction. In: Vasilecas O, Caplinskas A, Wojtkowski W, Wojtkowski G, Zupancic J, Wrycza S (eds) Proc of ISD'2004, pp 283-293

[5] Booch G, Rumbaugh J, Jacobsson I (1999) The Unified Modelling Language User Guide. Addison Wesley Longman Inc Massachusetts

[6] Cheesman J, Daniels J (2001) UML Components: A Simple Process for Specifying Component Based Software, Addison-Wesley

[7] Chen P (1976) The Entity-Relationship Model – Toward a Unified View of Data. ACM Transactions on Database Systems, vol 1, no 1, pp 9-36

[8] Crnkovic I, Larsson M (2000) A Case Study: Demands on Component Based Development. In: Proc of the 22nd International Conference in Software Engineering. Limerick Ireland

[9] Engels G, Gogolla M, Hohenstein U, Hulsmann K, Lohr-Richter P, Saake G, Ehrich HD (1992) Concepual Modelling of Database Applications Using an Extended ER Model. Data & Knowledge Engineering, vol 9, pp 157-204

[10] Fahrner C, Vossen G (1995) A Survey of Database Design Transformations Based on the Entity-Relationship Model. Data & Knowledge Engineering, vol 15, pp 213-250

[11] Gustas R (1994) Towards Understanding and Formal Definition of Conceptual Constraints. In: Kangassalo H, Jaakola H, Oshuga S, Wangler B (eds) Information Modelling and Knowledge Bases VI, IOS Press, pp 381-399

[12] Gustas R, Jakobsson L (2004) Enterprise Modelling of Component Oriented Information System Architectures. In: Fujita H, Gruhn V (eds) Proc of SoMeT_W04, IOS Press, pp 88-102

[13] Jakobsson L (2002) Extending Process Route Diagrams for Use With Software Components. In: Fujita H, Johannesson P (eds) Frontiers in Artificial Intelligence and Applications, IOS Press, Amsterdam, pp 289-300

[14] Jakobsson L (2004) Component Based Software – Implications on the Development Process and Modeling Yechniques. Licentiate thesis, Karlstad University Press

[15] Jakobsson L, Gustas R (2004) Towards a Systematic Modeling of Component Based Software Architectures. International SSCCII-2004, Amalfi, Italy

[16] Johannesson P (1993) Schema Integration, Schema Translation, and Interoperability in Federated Information Systems. PhD thesis, Dept of Computer & Systems Sciences, Stockholm Uni, Royal Inst of Technology, 93-010-DSV

[17] Lee ML, Ling TW (2003) A Methodology for Structural Conflict Resolution in the Integration of Entity-Relationship Schemas. Knowledge and Information System, vol 5, no 2, pp 225-247

[18] Martin J, Odell JJ (1998) Object-Oriented Methods: A Foundation (UML edition). Prentice-Hall, Englewood Cliffs, New Jersey

[19] Navathe S, Elmasri R, Larson J (1986) Integrating User Views in Database Design. IEEE Computer, vol 19, no. 1, pp 50-62

[20] Parsons J (2002) Effects on Local Versus Global Schema Diagrams on Verification and Communication in Conceptual Data Modeling. Journal of Management Information Systems, vol 19, no 3, pp 155-183

[21] Shoval P, Shiran S (1997) Entity-Relationship and Object-Oriented Data Modeling – An Experimental Comparison of Design Quality. Data & Knowledge Engineering, vol 21, pp 297-315

[22] Spaccapietra S, Parent C (1994) View Integration: a Step Forward in Solving Structural Conflicts. IEEE Transactions on Knowledge and Data Engineering, vol 6, no 2, pp 258-274

[23] Storey VC, Thompson CB, Ram S (1995) Understanding Database Design Expertise. Data & Knowledge Engineering, vol 16, pp 97-124

[24] Szyperski C (1998) Component Software – Beyond Object-Oriented Programming. Reading MA Addison-Wesley

[25] Teorey TJ, Yang D, Fry JP (1986) A Logical Design Methodology for Relational Databases Using the Extended Entity-Relationship Model. Computing Surveys, vol 18, no 2, pp 197-222

[26] Turetken O, Schuff D (2002) The Use of Fisheye View Visualizations in Understanding Business Process. In: Wrycza, S (ed) Proc of ECIS2002, Gdansk, Poland, pp. 322-330

A Synthesis Approach to Deriving Object-Based Specifications from Object Interaction Scenarios

King-Sing Cheung[1] and Kai-On Chow[2]

[1] Hong Kong Baptist University, Kowloon, Hong Kong.
cheungks@hkbu.edu.hk
[2] City University of Hong Kong, Kowloon, Hong Kong.
cspchow@cityu.edu.hk

Introduction

Object orientation has been an influential approach in software engineering. Basically, an object is regarded as an entity that encapsulates states and behaviours. A system is a collection of objects which interact with others to accomplish some functionalities. Objects with the same attributes and behaviours are abstracted into a class. Classes with common attributes and behaviours are generalised to form an inheritance hierarchy. An object-oriented system is designed in accordance with these principles of encapsulation, inheritance and object interactions.

In object-oriented system design, the designer has to create from a set of object interaction scenarios an object-based specification delineating the individual object behaviours. The task is difficult as different levels of abstraction are concerned. The former is concerned with interobject behaviour while the latter is concerned with intraobject behaviour In this paper, we propose method to solve this problem effectively. Based on a synthesis approach, our method involves the following three steps :

1. Each object interaction scenario is specified as a labelled Petri net or labelled net (Reisig 1985, Murata 1989, Desel & Reisig 1998). These labelled nets are then synthesised into an integrated labelled net.
2. Duplicate labels are eliminated from the integrated net, while preserving the firing sequences (event sequences).
3. Individual object-based specifications are obtained as projections of the integrated net on to the individual objects.

The rest of this paper is structured as follows. After discussing the major problems of deriving an object-based specification, we describe the synthesis method and illustrate it with an example. Finally, we conclude our results and highlight the features of our method. It should be noted that readers of this paper are expected to have knowledge on Petri nets (Reisig 1985, Murata 1989, Desel & Reisig 1998).

Problems in Object-Oriented System Design

In object-oriented system design, objects are analysed and specified in dual-aspects, namely, structure and behaviour (Arlow & Neustadt 2002, Bennet et al. 2002, Booch et al. 1999, Breu et al. 1998, Cheung & Chow 1996, Cheung et al. 1997a, Cheung et al. 1997b, Cheung et al. 1999, Fowler 2000, Graham 2001, Iivari 1995, Rumbaugh et al. 1999, Yourdon 1994). The former refers to the structural characteristics whereas the latter concerns how individual objects behave in interacting with others for accomplishing the system's functionalities.

This paper focus on the behavioural aspects of the design specification. Basically, use cases are first elaborated as object interaction scenarios and specified as UML sequence diagrams and collaboration diagrams (Jacobson et al. 1992, Jacobson et al. 1999, Kruchten 1999, Rosenberg 1999, Rosenberg & Scott 2001, Schneider & Winters 1998). From these scenarios, the specifications for individual objects are obtained as statechart diagrams. The specifications are then verified on correctness and consistency with respect to the interaction scenarios.

There are at least the following three problems in deriving an object-based design specification.

First, the specification constructs for object interaction scenarios are too primitive. The sequence diagrams and collaboration diagrams lacks the formality for representing the pre-conditions and post-conditions of every event occurrence in an object interaction scenario. These are however needed in deriving a design specification.

Second, there are different abstractions between intra-object lifecycle and inter-object interaction. It is difficult to derive individual object behaviours (within the object lifecycle) from the object interaction scenarios because of the difference in abstraction (single objects versus multiple objects). In the literature, there is a lack of rigorous approaches for this problem.

Third, there are difficulties in verifying the correctness of the design specification. There is no effective way for analysing the properties of the system. It is also difficult to ensure that the objects will exhibit behaviours consistent with the given object interaction scenarios (Cheung et al. 1998a, Cheung et al. 1998b, Glinz 2000). In practice, the designer need to go through all possible scenarios and make sure that there are no unrealistic scenarios and no unintended scenarios. The process is very time-consuming.

The Proposed Synthesis Method

This section describes the details of our synthesis method using the following example.

It is an Office Access Control System used in a high-tech company for controlling staff access to its 30+ offices. In the company, some offices can be accessed by all staff while others by authorised staff only and/or during specified time periods. Every office entrance is implemented with a card-reader, an emergency switch and an electronic lock, all controlled by a central server.

There are three possible scenarios (use cases) in order for one to gain access to an office.

- Successful access (U_1): A staff member presents his/her staff card via a card-reader. Access is then granted. The door is unlocked for five seconds and then re-locked.
- Unsuccessful access (U_2): A staff member presents his/her staff card via a card-reader. It is found that the access is not authorised, and the access is not granted. The door remains locked.
- Emergency access (U_3): A staff member presses the emergency key, and the door is unlocked immediately. After resetting by a security officer, the door is re-locked.

The system will keep a transaction log for recording transactions of the above scenarios.

From the object-oriented perspective, the central server and the doors are the objects of the system. The above scenarios or use cases are then elaborated as the possible object interaction scenarios between the server object (s : Server) and the door object (d : Door), and are specified as UML sequence diagrams and collaboration diagrams as shown in Figure 1. It should be noted that, for precise specification, condition labels are appended to these diagrams to denote the pre-conditions and post-conditions for each event occurrence.

Step 1 is to specify these object interaction scenarios U_1, U_2 and U_3 as labelled nets (N_1, M_{10}), (N_2, M_{20}) and (N_3, M_{30}), as shown in Figure 2. These labelled nets are synthesised into an integrated labelled net (N, M_0), by fusing those places which refer to the same initial states or conditions:

p_{11}, p_{21} and p_{31} are fused into one place p_{41}, and p_{15}, p_{24} and p_{34} into p_{42}. Figure 3 show the integrated net. The net contains some duplicate labels. As for example, place p_{12} and p_{22} have the same condition label $s.c_{12}$ and transitions t_{11} and t_{21} have the same event label e_1.

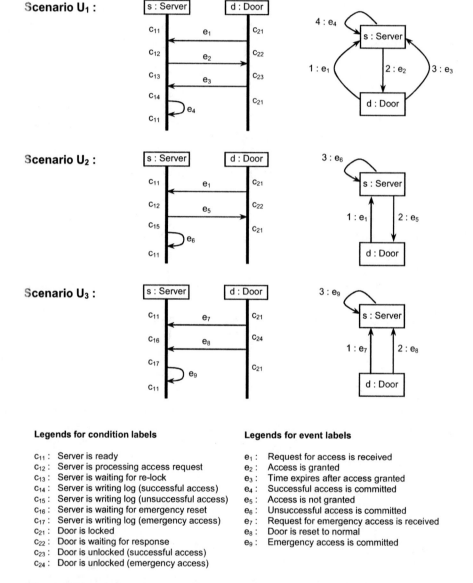

Legends for condition labels

c_{11} : Server is ready
c_{12} : Server is processing access request
c_{13} : Server is waiting for re-lock
c_{14} : Server is writing log (successful access)
c_{15} : Server is writing log (unsuccessful access)
c_{16} : Server is waiting for emergency reset
c_{17} : Server is writing log (emergency access)
c_{21} : Door is locked
c_{22} : Door is waiting for response
c_{23} : Door is unlocked (successful access)
c_{24} : Door is unlocked (emergency access)

Legends for event labels

e_1 : Request for access is received
e_2 : Access is granted
e_3 : Time expires after access granted
e_4 : Successful access is committed
e_5 : Access is not granted
e_6 : Unsuccessful access is committed
e_7 : Request for emergency access is received
e_8 : Door is reset to normal
e_9 : Emergency access is committed

Fig. 1. Object interaction scenarios as sequence diagrams (left) and collaboration diagrams (right)

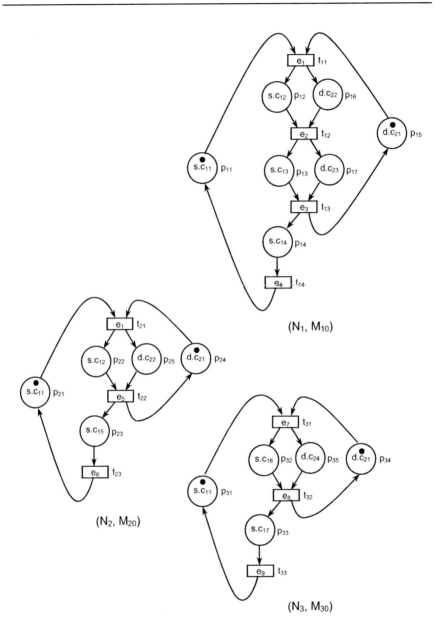

Fig. 2. Labelled nets representing the object interaction scenarios in Figure 1

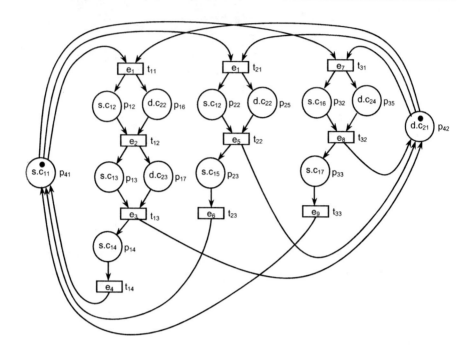

Fig. 3. The integrated net obtained by synthesising the labelled nets in Figure 2

Step 2 is to eliminate the duplicate labels from the integrated net. This is attained by refining the nets through the fusion of common places and/or transitions. The firing sequences (event sequences) must be preserved so as not to alter the system behaviour. For the purpose of preserving firing sequences, dummy places (φ) and transitions (ε) are appended, and colour labels are assigned, based on coloured Petri nets (Jensen 1992). Figure 4 shows the refined integrated net where duplicate labels are eliminated.

Step 3 is to obtain projections of the refined integrated net for individual objects. This is simply made by ignoring those places, transitions and arcs which are irrelevant to the object concerned. For object s (the server object), we keep those places with object label s (including dummy places) and those transitions having at least one input place or output place labelled by s. For object d (the door object), we keep those places with object label d (including dummy places) and those transitions having at least one input place or output place labelled by d. Figure 5 shows the projections (N_s, M_{s0}) and (N_d, M_{d0}) obtained by projecting the net (N', M_0') on to objects s and d, respectively. They serve as the specification for individual objects s and d.

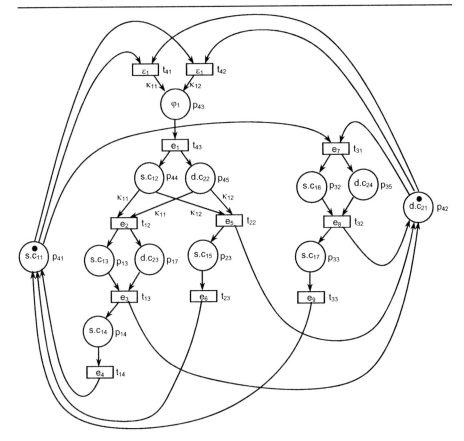

Fig. 4. The refined integrated net obtained by eliminating the duplicate labels from the integrated net in Figure 3

Conclusion

In this paper, we proposed a synthesis method for deriving an object-based design specification from a given set of object interaction scenarios, and illustrated it with a real-life example. Our method offers the following distinctive features.

First, our method provides formal specification of object interaction scenarios. Labelled Petri nets are used for specifying the object interaction scenarios. By making use of the Petri net constructs, the specification is unambiguous and semantically rich.

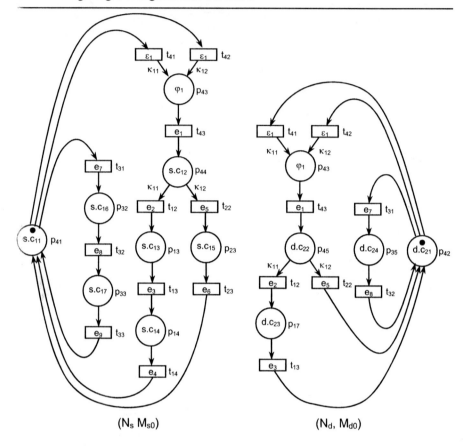

Fig. 5. Projections (N_s, M_{s0}) and (N_d, M_{d0}) from the integrated nets

Second, our method provides a rigorous synthesis process for deriving a correct and consistent design specification. The specification so obtained reflects exactly the functionalities of the object interaction scenarios.

Third, our method obtains a design specification readily for implementation. Since the same event or condition may appear in many object interaction scenarios, duplicate labels may exist in the initial specification. Yet a condition is eventually implemented as a state and an event as an action or activity. In our method, all duplicate labels are eliminated.

Our method can be effectively used in object-oriented system design for deriving an object-based specification from a given set of object interaction scenarios. As a further step, it can be implemented in CASE tools for object-oriented system design.

References

Arlow J, Neustadt I (2002) UML and the Unified Process: Practical Object-Oriented Analysis and Design. Addison-Wesley

Bennet S et al (2002) Object-Oriented Systems Analysis and Design Using UML. McGraw Hill

Booch G et al (1999) The Unified Modeling Language: User Guide. Addison-Wesley

Breu B et al (1998) Systems, Views and Models of UML. In: Schader M, Korthaus A (eds) The Unified Modeling Language: Technical Aspects and Applications. Physica-Verlag

Cheung KS, Chow, KO (1996) Comparison of Object-Oriented Models by Views and Abstraction Constructs. Proc of the International Conference on Intelligent Technologies in Human-Related Sciences (ITHRS 1996). Leon Spain

Cheung KS et al (1997a) Towards an Integration of Syntactic Constructs and Structural Features for Formalised Object-Oriented Methods. Proc of the International Conference on Reliable Software Technologies (Ada Europe 1997). Lecture Notes in Computer Science, vol 1251, pp 173-184. Springer-Verlag

Cheung KS et al (1997b) A Feature-Based Approach for Consistent Object-Oriented Requirements Specifications. In: Wojtkowshi WG et al (eds) Systems Development Methods for the Next Century. Plenum Publishing

Cheung KS et al (1998a) Consistency Analysis on Lifecycle Model and Interaction Model. Proc of the International Conference on Object-Oriented Information Systems (OOIS 1998). Springer

Cheung KS et al (1998b) Deriving Scenarios of Object Interaction through Petri Nets. Proc of the International Conference on Technology of Object Oriented Languages and Systems (TOOL 27). IEEE Computer Society Press

Cheung KS et al (1999) Extending Formal Specification to Object-Oriented Models through Level-View Structured Schemas. Proc of the International Conference on Technology of Object Oriented Languages and Systems (TOOL 31). IEEE Computer Society Press

Desel J, Reisig W (1998) Place Transition Petri Nets. In: Reisig W, Rozenberg G (eds) Lectures on Petri Nets I: Basic Models. Lecture Notes in Computer Science, vol 1491, pp 122-173. Springer-Verlag

Fowler M (2000) UML Distilled: A Brief Guide to the Standard Object Modeling Language. Addison-Wesley

Glinz M (2000) A Lightweight Approach to Consistency of Scenarios and Class Models. Proc of the IEEE International Conference on Requirements Engineering. Schaumburg USA

Graham I (2001) Object-Oriented Methods: Principles and Practice. Addison-Wesley

Iivari J (1995) Object Orientation as Structural, Functional and Behavioural Modelling: A Comparison of Six Methods for Object-Oriented Analysis. Information and Software Technology, vol 37, no 3, pp 155-163

Jacobson I et al (1992) Object-Oriented Software Engineering: A Use-Case-Driven Approach. Addison-Wesley

Jacobson I et al (1999) The Unified Software Development Process. Addison-Wesley

Jensen K (1992) Coloured Petri Nets: Basic Concepts, Analysis Methods and Practical Use. Vol 1. Springer-Verlag

Kruchten P (1999) The Rational Unified Process: An Introduction. Addison-Wesley

Murata T (1989) Petri Nets: Properties, Analysis and Applications. Proc of the IEEE, vol 77, no 4

Reisig W (1985) Petri Nets: An Introduction. Springer-Verlag

Rosenberg D (1999) Use Case Driven Object Modeling with UML: A Practical Approach. Addison-Wesley

Rosenberg D, Scott K (2001) Applying Use Case Driven Object Modeling with UML. Addison-Wesley

Rumbaugh J et al (1999) The Unified Modeling Language: Reference Manual. Addison-Wesley

Schneider G, Winters JP (1998) Applying Use Cases. Addison-Wesley

Yourdon E (1994) Object-Oriented Systems Design: An Integrated Approach. Yourdon Press

Formalizing Constraints for Geographic Information

Jesper Vinther Christensen[1] and Mads Johnsen[2]

[1] National Survey & Cadastre, Denmark and Informatics and Mathematical Modelling, Technical University of Denmark. jvc@kms.dk
[2] Informatics and Mathematical Modelling, Technical University of Denmark. m@ds-johnsen.dk

Introduction

An important aspect when producing geographic information is to ensure that the produced information is consistent and homogeneous. Data content specifications are used to describe objects that should be included in a data collection, and to evaluate if the quality of the produced information is acceptable. Product specialists, under consideration of the requirements from the various users and customers, write specifications in natural languages. Parts of these specifications can be implemented as constraints in production systems, and used to evaluate if the produced information has the intended content.

Constraints for geographic information are specified by e.g. cartographers and topographers using natural language, and afterward hard-coded into the production software by programmers. There are several reasons why this approach is hard to maintain. Firstly products are defined or redefined at a regular basis, resulting in changes in the content and number of constraints. This requires a programmer each time a new constraint is needed, or an existing should be changed. Secondly the sources to information are changing from only being collected from aerial photos, to include a variety of new sources e.g. administrative updates from municipalities, and changes posted at web pages. Information from new sources are delivered in multiple structures and content, which makes it impossible, or at least very difficult, to require that all information must pass through a single application for validation. Thirdly the existing approach requires the constraints to be defined at implementation level, meaning that they have to be redefined if changes to the database schema are introduced.

In this paper we introduce a language called High Level Constraint Language (HLCL). HLCL has three important properties, making it capable to solve the problems listed above: 1) it has a syntax close to natural language, which makes it easy to use, 2) it can be parsed and translated automatically into SQL, which enables validation of information, and 3) the constrains are formulated on the basis of conceptual models, and is therefore loosely coupled to the actual database implementation.

Constraints and integrity constraints are a well-established topic within research on domain modeling and databases. Several other attempts for creating a constraint language can be fund in the literature. The COLAN language (Bassiliades and Gray 1995) has properties similar to HLCL, but works on a data model called "P/FDM", which is a functional data model built on Prolog, and therefore seems to be lacking a clear correspondence to the relational data model. UML has an extension called the object constraint language, OCL (Object Management Group 2003). Like HLCL, OCL, builds on conceptual models, but OCL has syntax with a programming language style, which makes it difficult to use for product specialists. OCL has been tested for its capabilities for writing constraints for geographic information. The conclusion of this work was that OCL has to be extended to meet the requirements (Casanova, 2000). In some geographic information systems (GIS) constraints can be specified. The ArcGIS software family has some capabilities of specifying topological rules (Hoel et. Al. 2003), but only a predefined number of topologic relations can be included in the constraints, and the distinction between the conceptual model and the implementation model is somewhat unclear.

In the next section we discuss the requirements to specify constraints for geographic information. In section 1.3 the properties of the High Level Constraint Language are described. HLCL is a well-formed language, and has a well defined semantic and syntax. We will not present the mathematical foundation in this paper, but leave this to another paper already under preparation (Fischer and Johnsen, forthcoming). Section 1.4 is an elaborated example that goes through the process of describing a conceptual model, writing constraints in HLCL, mapping the conceptual model to an implementation model, and how constraints are translated into SQL. The paper is finalized with some concluding remarks and directions for the future work on and application of HLCL.

Specifying Geographic Information

A geographic entity is a real world phenomenon with spatial properties that in a given context can be distinguished from all other geographic entities. Geographic entities can be represented as geographic objects stored in computable data structures. A set of geographic objects is often denoted as a data collection or as geographic information. The intention of geographic information is to establish a model that simulates properties and behaviors of geographic entities and the relations among these.

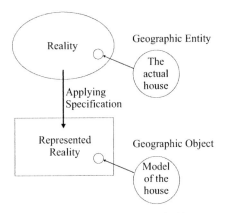

Fig. 1. Geographic entities and objects

Specifications of geographic information are developed to describe how reality must be interpreted to instantiate geographic objects. A specification can be regarded as a collection of constraints that describe how geographic entities are identified, which one should have a representation, and how this representation should be. These constraints are statements build over two sets of vocabularies, one used for denoting geographic entities and their properties, and one for denoting geographic objects and their properties. Constraint in this sense has a wider meaning than within the domain of database constraints (Mustiére 2003)

Some of the constraints in a specification can be formalized and implemented in a production system, and thereby used to evaluate if produced information conforms to the formulated constraints. Only constraints that include terms from the conceptual model that can be related to objects in the implementation model, have the potential for being implemented, and used to validate produced information.

High Level Constraint Language

The High Level Constraint Language (HLCL) (Johnsen 2005) is developed to bridge the gap between constraints or business rules formulated in natural language and their implementation using e.g. SQL. HLCL is a constraint specification language, which is designed to have a syntax as close to natural language as possible, but still with a clear and unambiguous underlying semantic model. HLCL expressions are formulated in the context of a conceptual model. Therefore the HLCL compiler needs to have access to a database specification that consists of the conceptual model, a description of the low-level database schema and a mapping between the two. By introducing a map between the conceptual model and the logical model, changes in the low-level database schema can be accommodated in the map, thereby leaving the conceptual model and ultimately the HLCL constraints unchanged. The constraints can be updated by recompiling the constraints in the context of the new mapping and schema.

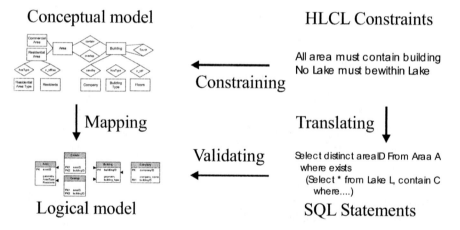

Fig. 2. The principle of using HLCL

The basic construct in HLCL involves two classes in an **"all-must"** structure as seen below:

* **All house must building:** The constraint specifies that "*all houses should be buildings*". In general the left-hand side of the "**must**" specifies which class the constraint applies to and the right-hand side specifies limitation on the class. Using paths as seen below, we can extend the class-expressions:

- **No lake may contain building:** The constraint expresses that *"no lake may contain any building"*. In the above example the inverse top-construction **"no-may"** is used to express class disjointness. The **"contain building"** fragment specifies a relational path in the conceptual model. Relational paths are expressed by a series of relations and classes; they are implicit existentially quantified in HLCL, such that the path above is understood as *"contain at least one building"*. Paths can be of any length, one simply adds more relations and classes, and multiple paths can be bundled together by the **"or"** disjunction and the **"and"** conjunction operator. Other quantifications can also be used in relational paths, but these need to be defined explicitly as seen below:
- **All residentialArea must contain solely building type residential:** The constraint expresses that *"all residential areas must contain solely residential buildings"*. This constraint makes use of an even longer relational path on the right-hand side of the expression. The **"solely"** keyword expresses that residentialArea should only contain residential buldings and nothing else. Similar to the **"solely"** keyword, HLCL has an **"all"** keyword, which expresses that the relational path should be fulfilled for all the classes, e.g. "contain all building" expresses that all buildings should be contained. Finally there is the option using a numerical quantifier **"at least/at most/exactly n"**, e.g. "contain at least 5 building" expresses that at least five buildings should be contained.

HLCL makes use of user-defined variables to express equality of sets. Variables are represented by capital letters, which are put immediately after a class, an example of their usage can be seen below:

- **All building B must contain building B:** The constraint expresses that: "all buildings must contain themselves". In order to express this constraint we must use a user-defined variable **"B"**, to express that the two buildings mentioned in the constraint must be the same. Finally HLCL allows user-defined functions, which typically express various arithmetical relationships.

Using HLCL for Specifying Constraints

In this section we introduce an example that illustrates the capabilities of the High Level Constraint Language described in the last section. The example is inspired by a conceptual model and constraints taken from the TOP10DK specification (National Survey & Cadastre - Denmark, 2002). We will show how the natural language based specification can be translated into HLCL statements, and how a mapping between the conceptual model and an implementation model is specified to enable a translation from HLCL to SQL. The example also constitutes a framework or best practice for how HLCL is used. The framework includes the following steps:

1. Developing a conceptual model
2. Specifying the conceptual model in HLCL
3. Writing constraints in HLCL
4. Developing a logical model
5. Specifying the logical model in HLCL
6. Mapping the conceptual and logical model
7. Translating HLCL constraints to SQL

This framework has proven that the knowledge the participants posses about the data collection at hand evolves as steps in the framework are concluded, i.e. existing requirements can be reformulated so that they more precisely express requirements to produced information, and requirements that have been implicitly given or not expressed by mistakes surfaces. Therefore, in reality, the process of writing HLCL statements is iterative, changing between improving the conceptual model, specifying constraints in HLCL, and mapping these to the logical model.

Conceptual Model

The first step in using HLCL to specify formal constraints is to develop a conceptual model that includes the concepts and relations that exist between these. In our examples the conceptual model has four classes: Area, Residential Area, Commercial Area, and Building. Area is the super class of Residential Area and Commercial Area. Residential Area has two attributes: Residential Area Type and numbers of residents. Building also has attributes: Building Type and number of floors. There are two topologic relations between Area and Building: contain and overlap. The contain relation indicates which buildings are contained in an area, and overlap indicates if there is an overlap between the boundary of an Area and the boundary of a building.

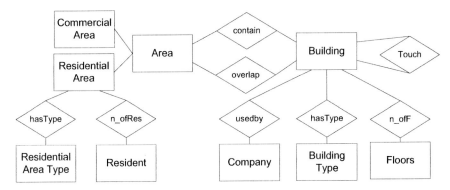

Fig. 3. Conceptual model

The HLCL system has a number of requirements to the conceptual model. Attributes must be modeled as entities, relations must be binary, and inverse relations must be explicitly defined. To enable the HLCL system to get access to the conceptual model it has to be specified in the syntax illustrated on the example below.

```
class(Building)              relation(Building,touch,Building)
class(Area)                  relation(Building,usedby,Company)
class(ResidentialArea)       relation(Building,hasType,Building Type)
class(CommercialArea)        relation(Building,n_ofF,Floors)
class(Company)               relation(ResidentialArea,n_ofRes,Resident)
relation(Area,contain,Building)
relation(ResidentialArea,hasType,Residential Area Type)
isa(area,[ResidentialArea,CommercialArea])
```

Constraints

Having a conceptual model, the constraints that are not already present in the model, can be formulated using the classes and relations present in model. In table 1, some constraints in natural language are listed in the left column and their HLCL equivalent in the right. The constraints are inspired by the TOP10DK data content specification (National Survey & Cadastre - Denmark, 2002). As seen the names on classes and relations can be used in combination with HLCL keywords to form formal constraints with syntax that has a natural language look and feel.

Table 1. Example constraints

Natural Language	High Level Constraint Language
Residential Area must contain at most 1 Commercial Building	all Residential Areas must contain at most 1Building hasType Commercial
All Residential Buildings within Low Residential Areas must have at most 3 floors	all building hastype residential and within Residential Area hastype lowresidential must n_ofF at most 3 Floor
If two buildings of the same type are neighbors then the z-difference between the two building must be larger than 5 meters	all Building A hastype T neighbor Building B hastype T must havezdifferencebiggerthan(A,B,5)
Two buildings of the same type touching each other, must either be within or outside an area	all Building hastype T and containedin Area A must touch building hastype T and containedin Area A ornot touch Building type T
	all Building hastype T and outside area A must touch Building hastype T and outside area A ornot touch Building hastype T
Buildings of type commercial that are containted In Commercial Areas must be used by at least 1 company	all building of hastype commercial and within Commercial Area must usedby Company
No building must overlap an area	no Building must overlap Area
Buildings can be of type Commercial, high residential or low residential	all Building must type commercial or type highresidential or type lowresidential

Logical Data Model

One of the major advantages of HLCL is that constraints can be automatically translated into SQL. To do so a logical model and a map between the conceptual and logical model must be specified. In this section we introduce a logical model, a specification of this in HLCL, and a mapping between the two models. These steps are step number 4, 5, and 6 in the suggested procedure.

Figure 4 shows the table layout for the suggested logical model. In the present version of HLCL relations must be tables or views on tables, but in the next version, which is already under development, foreign keys and functional relationships, like spatial relations, will be supported directly. Below the HLCL statements describing the logical model are listed.

```
table(Area, [areaID,geometry,areatype,residents])
table(Building, [buildingID,numoffloors,geometry,building_type])
table(Company, [companyID,company_name])
table(Contain, [areaID,buildingID])
```

```
table(Overlap, [areaID,buildingID])
table(RelBuildingCompany, [companyID,buildingID]
```

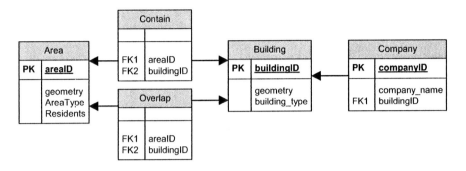

Fig. 4. Logical model

To be able to translate HLCL constraints into SQL a mapping between the conceptual and logical model must be supplied. The list below defines this mapping for our example.

```
classmap(commercialArea, Area, [], [areaID])
classmap(residentialArea, Area, [], [areaID])
classmap(company,company, [], [companyID])
relmap(building,usedby,company,relBuildingCompany, [buildingID],
[companyID])
valuemap(building,numoffloors,floors,numoffloors,integertype)
valuemap(building,isType,buildingtype,building_type,buildingtype)
valuemap(Area,n_ofRes,residents,num_of_residents,residents)
valuemap(residentialArea,hasType,residentialAreaType,residential_
type, stringtype)
```

Generating SQL

The constraints formulated in HLCL can be translated to SQL using a parser. This parser is described in (Johnsen 2005), where it is shown that HLCL is a "safe" language, meaning that translation into SQL does not pose any problems regarding termination and recursiveness.

The translated constraints are built up as SQL statements in such a way that if a constraint is fulfilled, the execution of the translated query will return no rows. In this section we show how a few of the constraints in HLCL are translated to SQL. The first example is the "No building must overlap area" constraint, which is translated into the following SQL query shown below:

```
SELECT *
FROM building a
WHERE EXISTS(
```

```
SELECT *
FROM overlap b
WHERE b.buildingID = a.buildingID
AND EXISTS(
        SELECT *
        FROM area c
        WHERE c.areaID = b.areaID
```

The general idea is that every class and relation in the conceptual model corresponds to a table in the underlying database. The SQL expressions are built up as nested SELECT-FROM-WHERE clauses. As seen, classes and relations are no longer referred to as their names in the conceptual model; instead the actual table names in the database model are used. Comparison is done with the set of attributes that constitutes the primary key.

Let us look at a more advanced query, namely the one corresponding to the constraint: "all buildings must type commercial or type highresidential or type lowresidential". The corresponding SQL query to the constraint is:

```
SELECT *
FROM building a
WHERE NOT(
      a.building_type = 'commercial'
      OR
      a.building_type = 'highresidential'
      OR
      a.building_type = 'lowresidential')
```

As seen, the general structure is the same as in the first query. The translation of the operators in HLCL is straightforward, since the used operators are available in SQL. The relational paths are not parsed into any "EXISTS" statements, since the relational paths are actually properties of the building class, resulting in much simpler SQL.

Let us look at one final example with user-defined constraints, namely the constraint stating: "all building A type T neighbour building B type T must havez(A,B,5)". In SQL this would look as seen below:

```
SELECT *
FROM building a
WHERE EXISTS
      SELECT   *
      FROM building b
      WHERE b.buildingID != a.buildingID
      AND b.building_type = a.building_type
      AND NOT (zdifferencelargerthan(a.geometry,b.geometry,5))
```

The SQL follows the same structure as the other examples, although there are some extra clauses in the innermost WHERE clause. The first of those expresses that the two buildings should be different, this is due to the different variables used in the HLCL. The next clause expresses that the two buildings should have the same type. This is the translation of the "T" variable. The third and final clause is the translation of the user-defined predicate, we can see how the user-defined predicate is translated straight into SQL.

Conclusion and Continuation

The aim of the presented work is to enable product and production specialists to write formal constraints that can automatically be implemented in production software. We conclude that it is possible to define a language in which constraints can be formulated using a syntax that has resemblance to natural language. We believe what HLCL has an expressiveness that can fulfill most requirements on writing constraints, and have illustrated how fairly complex constraints for geographic information can be specified using HLCL and translated into SQL. Even though HLCL is quit easy to understand, it still requires some basic knowledge about the syntax and what actually can be done using HLCL. Currently a work on developing a graphic user interface that helps the users to develop conceptual models, and to formulate HLCL statement, is under development. The intention is that this interface will make HLCL even more accessible to non-programmers. Other research that has to be carried out before HLCL can be used in large scale production systems, is a strategy for executing the SQL statements in a efficient way, and a support for different kind of standard database implementations.

References

Bassiliades N, Gray P (1995) Colan: A Functional Constraint Language and its Implementation. Data Knowledge Eng. no 14, pp 203-249

Casanova M, Wallet T, D'Hondt M (2000) Ensuring Quality of Geographic Data with UML and OCL. Proc of the 3rd International Conference on the Unified Modeling Language. Vol 1939 of Lecture Notes in Computer Science. Springer

Hoel E, Menon S, Morehouse S (2003) Building a Robust Relational Implementation of Topology. International Symposium on Spatial and Temporal Databases, no 8

Johnsen M (2005) A High Level Interface to Databases, with Application to GIS (2005). Danish Technical University of Denmark

Mustiére S, Gesbert N, Sheeren D. (2003) A Formal Model for the Specification of Geographic Databases. International Workshop on Sematic Processing of Spatial Data

National Survey & Cadastre – Denmark (2003) TOP10DK Data Content Specification Version 3.2. In Danish

Nilsson JF, Johnsen M. (Forthcoming) A High Level Logical-Algebraic Constraint Checking Language Compiling into Database Queries

Object Management Group (2004) UML 2.0 OCL Specification

A Practical Approach of Web System Testing

Javier Jesús Gutierrez, María José Escalona, Manuel Mejías and
Jesús Torres

Department of Computer Languages and Systems. University of Seville,
Spain. (javierj, escalona, risoto, jtorres)@lsi.us.es

Introduction

The process of testing software system is gaining more importance every
day [6]. Software applications are growing in size and complexity quickly.
It makes more necessary to dispose techniques to assure quality of the systems and that the result satisfied initial specifications [1].

Assure the quality of the system is very important in web engineering.
First web systems, at the beginning of nineties, had a simple design based
on static HTML pages. Nowadays, web systems are built applying heterogeneous technologies like client-side scripting languages included into
HTML, client-side components like Java applets, server-side scripting languages like PHP or PERL, server-side components like Java Servlets, web
services, databases servers, etc. All these heterogeneous technologies have
to work together, in order to obtain a multi-user and multi-platform application. The design, maintenance and test of the modern web applications
have many challenges to developers and software engineers [7][13].

Internet and web systems also bring to developers a new and innovative
way to build software. Internet allows millions of users to access to an application [7]. Thus, problems in a web application can affect to millions of
users, cause many costs to the business [13] and destroy a commercial image. For all these reasons, quality assurance and software testing acquire a
vital importance in the web system development.

This work introduces theory and practice about the generation and implementation of system test cases in web applications. This work presents
a complete vision of system testing showing how to put in practice the
ideas exposed. Section 2 defines the process of software testing and studies
in depth system testing process and how it can be applied to web development. Section 3 shows a practical case of generation and implementation
of system test cases. Finally, section 4 resumes conclusions and future
works.

System Testing over Web Systems

This section describes the process of software testing, studies the process of system testing in depth, from the point of view of web engineering and, finally, describes briefly a proposal to generate system test cases in a systematic way. This approach will be applied in the practical case described in section 3.

An Overview of Software Testing Process

The process of software testing cannot be done at the end of the construction of the system, neither expecting to test the whole system ant one time [2]. The process of software testing has to be divided into sub-process. Every sub-process indicates which elements must be tested and the moment to perform every test. The sub-process might be applied when first elements under test are available. One possible division in sub-process widely accepted is showed in figure 1 [9].

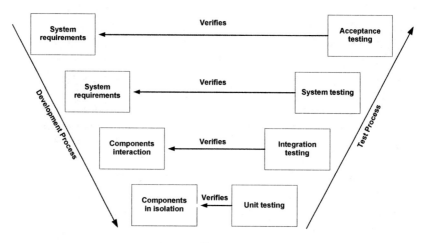

Fig. 1. Software testing process

Unit testing is done during building of software system [8]. Their objectives are the verification of the design and the functionality of every component in the system. Integration testing is done during the building of software system. Their objectives are the verification of the union among system components through their interfaces and their functionality. System testing is done after building of software system. System testing answer the question: is the entire system working to deliver the user goals? [17]. Acceptance testing is done after software system implantation. Their objectives are the verification that system covers all requirements expected and satisfies the needs of the users.

In figure 1 another kind of testing, regression testing, is lost. It was not included because they are not performed during the development of the system. Regression testing are applied during the maintenance of the system to accurate that the changes does not introduces unexpected errors in unmodified elements.

Testing process described in figure 1 might be applied to all types of software system: desktop applications, client-server applications, mobile applications, etc. In the specific case of web systems, it is needed to arrange specific techniques, like separate client-side and server-side components, and specific tools, like HTML validation tool, to web applications that allows to apply this process.

Next section describes in depth the process of the software system testing and how it must be applied in web projects.

System Test Process

Unit and integration testing guarantees an error-free code, or, at least, that the code has not the most important or common errors, due of the fact that it is impossible to test the whole code in depth [2]. However, unit and integration testing are not enough to assure the quality of the system. It is possible to have an error-free code that does not satisfy the expectative or the needed of the system final users. This one makes necessary a system test phase. This phase will be performed after unit and integration test phases, and when first system requirements are completely implemented.

An important rule that can be applied in all phases of software testing process is that testing must begin as soon as possible [12]. Due the cost of time and resources needed to correct an error increases at same time than time between the apparition and the detection of that error, it is vital to detect all errors as soon as possible. In system test cases, system is verified like a black box. Thus, system tester have to wait until the system is built, or, at least, until some requirements are fully implemented. An implemented requirement means that all elements needed to perform that requirements from the user point of view, like user interfaces, persistent layers, databases, etc, are implemented. However it is possible to advance definition and design of system test cases to early development phases.

In [4] a group of representative proposals of early testing are described, analyzed and compared.

The process of generation of system test cases from functional requirements consists in build a use model of the system from its requirements, and, later, to generate a set of input values, a set of events or interactions among system and users or actors, and the expected results [5]. The evolution of methodological proposals to drive this process has been focused in how to build and represent the use model.

There are works, like [11], that propose new kinds of requirements specific for web development, like actors' requirements, adaptability requirements or navigational requirements. However, functional requirements are still playing a very important role in web systems, but must be complemented with other types of requirements like navigational or information requirements.

Functional requirements should be independent of the implemented platform or the architecture of the system in early development phases. Thus functional requirements must not include any reference to any platform, like web or standalone platform. Due this fact, methodologies to generate system test cases from requirements are also applied in web systems. An example of integration of a process to generate system cases into a web development methodology can be found in [9]. Test cases are, also, independence of the complexity of web interfaces.

Next section describes a possible approach to generate automatically system test cases. This process is applied in the practical example in section 3.

A Proposal to Generate System Test Cases from Requirements

Descriptions of functional requirements are the main artifact to the design of system test cases [5]. Nowadays, there are a big number of proposals to systematize this process. A complete survey about these proposals is presented in [4].

This section introduces briefly the fundaments of a systematic proposal to generation of system test cases from use cases. This proposal has been development from the conclusions of comparative studios and analyzes of several existing proposals, like [4]. The generation of test cases is showed in figure 2 with an activity diagram [14]. It starts with the enumeration and the description of the **observable results**. An observable result is anything that can be automatically or manual checked, like a system screen, a new stored, modified or deleted record, a received message by other computer or server, etc. In conclusion,

In second step, all possible **execution paths** are identified. An execution path is a description of the interactions among system and one or more actors to obtain one of the results identified in previous activity.

After identifying all the execution paths, all needed values for each path must be identified. A valid value is a data or precondition that applied to an execution path allows obtaining the expected result.

In the last step, all **redundant execution paths** must be removed. An execution path is redundant when there is other equal path or when it is included into other path, with the same values, and the same results are obtained.

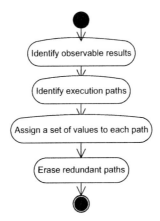

Fig. 2. Activity diagram to generate system test cases

This proposal can be applied in parallel with identification and definition of requirements. In the next section, we are going to put in practise this proposal in order to generate a set of system test cases for a simple example.

A Case Study

In order to explain in a detail way the approach presented in the previous section, in this section we are going to apply it in a real project.

System Description

This section describes a simplified web application that we use like a simple example in next sections to apply the presented approach. The objective of this web system is to manage the information about customers in a business. Concretely, the selected example is the functional requirement: "System must allow that one registered user inserts new customers into customers database". It indicates that the system has to allow to add new costumers.

This requirement is too basic and ambiguous to be directly implemented. Thus, the requirement has been refined and splitters in two use cases. The first use case describes the process to access into the system and the second one offers the way to insert a new customer. Both use cases are graphically showed in the UML use case diagram [14] in figure 3 and described textually in table 2 and 3.

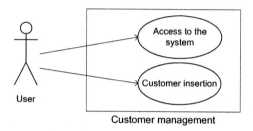

Fig. 3. Use cases to insert new customers

In order to describe deeply each requirements. We will use a patterns, that is a special template, described by the proposals NDT (Navigational Development Techniques) [11]. NDT is a methodological proposal to drive the requirements and analysis phases in a web system development. NDT also includes a support tool called NDT-Tool [10]. For instance, the pattern for the firs use cases is presented in table 2.

Using a similar pattern for the other use case, the requirements can be implemented in a web application. In our wor, Technologies used in the implementation were HTML and JavaScript, to define the user interfaces, and PHP to define the business logic and data access. This web application is composed of two main forms: the first one controls the access to the system, and the other one inserts new customers. Figures 4 shows the first one.

Table 1. Textual description for the use case "Access to the system"

FR-01	Access to the system
Description	The system has to manage the access to the system and verify the identity of each doctor. For that, it has to play like it is describe in this use case.
Normal execution	Step Action
	1 An user tries to access to the system
	2 System asks for identifier and password.
	3 User gives the system this information.
	4 If this information is correct, the system allows the user the access, and its continue with use case FR-02.
Post-condition	None
Exceptions	Step Action
	3 If identifies does not exist and the number of attempts is less than 3, system shows a message telling that user name does not exists and asks it again.
	3 If password does not match with the user password and the number of attempts is less than 3, system shows a message telling that password is invalid and asks it again.
	3 If identifier does not exist or password does not match and the number of attempts is 3 or bigger, system shows a message and denied access to the system.

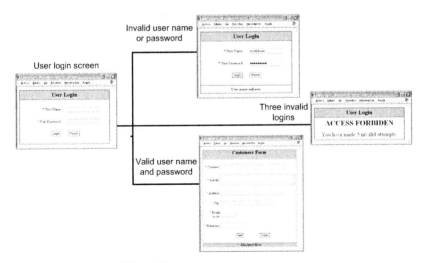

Fig. 4. Access to system screens

Unit and integration testing have already been successfully performed. Next section shows how to generate a set of test cases from the requirements of this application.

System Test Cases Generation

Previous section has showed a proposal to generate system test case from functional requirements expressed like use cases. In this section, that proposal will be applied to generate test cases from use cases described. These test cases will verify the success implementation of the requirement described in table 1 into the web application.

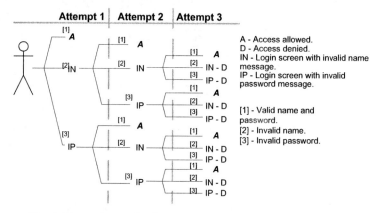

Fig. 5. Execution paths from "Access to system" use case

The simplest way to find execution paths is to explore all combinations among steps described in a use case. Figures 5, for instance, shows execution paths that cover all combinations of steps. They include the normal execution sequence and the alternative execution sequences. From the "Access to system" use case, twenty-one execution paths are generated.

It is more difficult to study the number of possible combinations in the "Insert customer" use case. In theory, an infinite number of executions paths are possible, for instance, "do not writing a mandatory field". In our example, we are going to suppose that this scenario can appear just one time, in order words, a mandatory field could be empty just the first time. Applying this supposition, from the "Insert customer" use case, , seven execution paths are generated.

Calculating all possible combinations between both use cases, 21 x 7 = 147 execution paths are generated. This number is too high in order to implement one test from each possible execution path. We will choose a representative subset of paths only to be implemented as system test cases. It is out of the scope of this work to show the criterions to select the adequate paths to be implemented as test cases. Several algorithms for select paths can be found in [15] and [16]. Some heuristics and guides can be applied in order to sure the quality of the election. Next paragraphs describe the chosen paths.

The objective of system test cases is to verify the success insertion of a new customer. The only way to access to insertion customer form is from user login screen. So, the entire test includes a valid login, in other words, a success path through the use case in table 2.

Table 3. Executions paths

Execution path description	Observable result.
1 Write a valid name and password. Write a valid customer.	Customer inserted screen.
2 Write a valid name and password. Write a valid customer without a mandatory field. Write the mandatory field.	Customer inserted screen.
3 Write a valid name and password. Write an existing customer.	Customer error screen.

Table 4. Test values

Path	Values set	Concrete values.
1 2, 3	Valid login.	Name: validname Password: validpassword.
1, 3	Valid customer.	Customer : customer_name Activity : customer_activity Address : customer_address City : customer_city Postal code : customer_postalcode Telephone : customer_telephone
2	Valid customer without a mandatory field.	Customer : customer_name Activity : customer_activity Address : <empty> City : customer_city Postal code : customer_postalcode Telephone : customer_telephone

Database server is an external component to web system, but it is also need to perform the requirement. Thus, to accurate that any error is provoked just only into the system and not into external components, all test cases assume that database server components is always running and always process successfully the operations requested.

Execution paths selected to be implemented as system test cases are showed and described in table 3 and table 4.

To study in depth all possible combinations of every use case separately from other uses cases is useful in order to verify the implementation of every use case in isolation. However, at the time to verify a requirement composed of several use cases, it is better to choose a subset that verifies the whole functionality of that requirement.

Test Case Implementation

This section shows how to implement the test generated in section 3.2. to be executed over the example web application. We have searched for an open-source tool that facilities the implementation task. The characteristics searched in the tool were: possibility to describe the operations performed in every test case and possibility to compare the results with the expected results.

There are two kind of testing tools. Tools that record and replay a sequence of actions and tools that offers an API to write code that simulates a user interaction.

API tools are more flexible, minimize the maintenance of test cases and allow easily testing web system that returns big, dynamic or complex web pages. We have chosen HttpUnit [3] from all available tools. It is out of the scope of this work to explain how to implement a test with HttpUnit.

The code implements the first execution path in table 4 will have the next steps: 1. Connect to web server, 2. Ask for login page. 3. Verify that received page is login page. 4. Write a valid user and password and press submit button. 5. Verify that received page is customer form. 6. Write a new valid customer and press submit button. 7. Verify that received page is ok page.

Conclusions

This work has described the process of software testing, applying over web applications. This work has also showed the needs that become necessary to perform system testing. A methodological proposal to generate system test cases from functional requirements has been briefly described.

System test cases are written from functional requirements. Thus, system test cases are independent of the type of system or architecture under development. All proposals to generate system test cases from requirements might be applied to web systems. Design of software testing can also start as soon as first requirements are available. Planning and design of software test cases in early development phases performs and additional validation over the system requirements, allowing to detect errors, omissions, incongruences and even overspecification or, in other words, too much requirements. Correcting errors detected in early development phases are easy and economic because the cost of correct errors increases in the same way that time between apparition and detecting increases [4].

All the ideas exposed in first sections of this work, have been applied in a practical case of study. In this case of study, a set of system test cases have been generated and implemented from a real web application. This example also shows how is possible to use different technologies and languages in the development of web applications without integration problems. Concretely, languages used in web application example have been: JavaScript, HTML and PHP, and language of the tool to test the application has been Java.

System testing can be completed with another types of tests, like performance, reliability [17] and navigability [18] tests.

An investigation line open is to study the integration of the generation of system test cases into a web development process. First ideas can be found in [9]. Another line of investigation is to automate the generation process and integrate it into a CASE tool like [10]. Construction of web system involves many types of non-functional requirements very important, like navigation requirements [11]. Another line of investigation open is to develop another generation process to be applied over non-functional requirements.

References

[1] Ash L (2003) The Web Testing Companion: The Insider's Guide to Efficient and Effective Tests. John Wiley & Sons, Hoboken, USA
[2] Binder Rober V (1999) Testing Object-Oriented Systems. Addison Wesley
[3] HttpUnit. http://httpunit.sourceforge.net/
[4] Gutiérrez, JJ, Escalona MJ et-al. (2004) Comparative Analysis Of Methodological Proposes to Systematic Generation Of System Test Cases From System Requisites. SE'04 Workshop, Paris France
[5] Jacobs F (2004) Automatic Generation of Test Cases From Use Cases. ICSTEST'04. Bilbao Spain

[6] Pankaj J (2002) Software Project Management in Practice. Addison Wesley USA
[7] Offutt J et-al. (2004) Web Application Bypass Testing. 15th IEEE International Symposium on Software Reliability Engineering ISSRE. Saint-Malo France
[8] Link J, Frohlich P (2003) Testing in Java: How Tests Drive the Code. Morgan Kaufmann Publishers USA
[9] Escalona MJ et-al. (2004) Testing Methods Applied In Web Requirement Engineering with NDT. IADIS WWW/Internet 2.004. 353-360
[10] Escalona MJ et-al. (2003) NDT-Tool: A Case Tool to Deal with Requirements in Web Information Systems. ICWE'03. Oviedo Spain
[11] Escalona MJ (2004) Models and Techniques to Specify and Analyze Navigation in Software Systems. Ph. European Thesis. Department of Computer Languages and Systems. University of Seville. Seville Spain
     www.lsi.us.es/~escalona/files/reports /tesis. rar
[12] Magro B, Garbajosa J et-al. (2004) Automated Support for Requirements and Validation Tests as Development Drivers. Proc of the 3rd workshop on System Testing and Validation. pp 9-18. Paris France
[13] Wu Y, Offutt J, Du X (2004) Modelling and Testing of Dynamic Aspects of Web Applications. Submitted for journal publication
[14] 2003. OMG Unified Modelling Language Specification 2.0
[15] Nebut C et-al. (2003) Requirements by Contract Allow Automated System Testing. Proc of the 14th International symposium of Software Reliability Engineering (ISSRE'03). Denver Colorado EEUU
[16] Nebut C et-al. (2004) A Requirement-Based Approach to Test Product Families. LNCS. pp 198-210
[17] Cohen F (2004) Java Testing and Design. Prentice Hall USA
[18] Ricca F, Tonella P (2001) Analysis and Testing of Web Applications. 23rd International Conference on Software Engineering. Toronto Canada

Overview of the Evaluation Approaches and Frameworks for Requirements Engineering Tools

Raimundas Matulevičius and Guttorm Sindre

Department of Computer and Information Science, Norwegian University of Science and Technology, Norway. (raimunda, guttors)@idi.ntnu.no

Introduction

The requirements engineering (RE) process is described as a sequence of actions, where requirements for a new system are elicited, analysed, validated, and documented into a formal, complete and agreed requirements specification [23]. For such a complex process, a powerful tool support is clearly useful [11], but, the mainstream of RE practice relies on office rather than RE-tools (e.g., DOORS, RequisitePro, and CaliberRM) provided by various companies. Part of the problem is the difficulty to assess the RE-tools in terms of their impact on an organisation, and in an experimental situation, because it is difficult to control the variation in users' capabilities. RE-tools provide the greatest benefit for large projects, while a controlled experiment requires prescribed tasks of a fairly limited size. Hence, to support the completeness of the RE-tool assessment, it should be grounded in a sound framework providing methodological guidelines.

RE-tools can be seen as (Commercial-Off-The-Shelf) products. RE-tools are ready made products and users can select them from vendor product lists [21]. RE-tools are sold in many copies and users are neither controlling the tools' specifications nor development [24]. Finally, tool users do not get access to the RE-tool source code (except in case of open source tools), and vendors are responsible for the maintenance [1].

This paper makes an analytical overview and comparison of the RE-tool frameworks and assessment approaches. Such a survey might be useful for the practitioners who are in a process of the RE-tool selection. The overview could also be of use to researchers working on improved RE-tools, or improved ways to evaluate RE-tools.

The second and third sections of this paper survey the RE-tool evaluation approaches and frameworks. The fourth section makes comparison and suggests guidelines for the RE-tool evaluation methodology.

General COTS Evaluation Approaches

General COTS product selection approaches are applicable for RE-tool comparison. The process consists of four phases [4]: requirements specification, understanding of available tools, assessment of the tool compatibility with the requirements, and selection of the "best" tool (fig. 1).

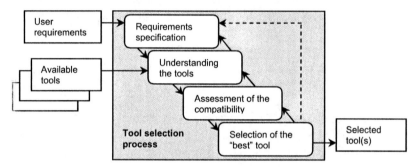

Fig. 1. Tool Selection Process

Requirements specification is based on the working domain knowledge and existing manual tools. *Understanding of the available tools* involves the consideration of the functionality and relating it to the known processes from the user's experience. During the *assessment of the tool compatibility* the user has to assess the extent to which tools satisfy the requirements. *Selection of the "best" available tool(s)* depends on the compatibility with the requirements and the prioritisation of these requirements. The user may have to compromise on requirements not satisfied by any of the tools. Then the user reconsiders the requirements and iterates the selection or reorganizes work practices in order to fit the "best" tool.

This section makes a survey of general COTS evaluation approaches. They are PORE [18], OTSO [10], CAP [22], scenario-based selection [3], STACE [13], ISO/IEC 9126 quality-based selection [5], and R-TEA [20].

PORE (Procurement-Oriented Requirements Engineering) advocates a parallel and iterative requirements acquisition and tool-candidate selection/rejection based on the templates [18], which include guidelines over the vendor data, tool demonstration, hands-on tool evaluation, and user trial of emerge properties. The PORE application has been demonstrated in the banking domain and the SCARLET (Selecting Components against Requirements) approach [16, 17] which guides through the tool selection.

OTSO (Off-The-Shelf Option) describes a way to incorporate COTS tools into the systems used in an organisation [10]. OTSO includes entry and exit parameters and advocates hierarchical criteria definition. OTSO ignores the definition of the user requirements specification, thus giving little support in evaluating whether a tool fits the organisational needs.

CAP (COTS Acquisition Process) consists of three parts [22]. *Initialization* describes measurement plans. *Execution* comprises the activities to identify possible tool candidates, measure them, and decide on their selection. *Reuse* comprises the packing activities for future information use.

The **scenario-based COTS selection** [3] proposes a comparison between *baseline scenarios* which describe how an organisation operates and *tool scenarios* which projects baseline scenario into a future, where a tool is applied. Analyst rewrites the baseline scenarios adapting it to scenarios when using the tools. The scenario selection does not analyse specific tool requirements, interoperability with other systems, vendor's ability to support the tool. These criteria are defined during the tool selection (fig. 1).

STACE (social-technical approach to COTS evaluation) consists of [13] 1) requirements elicitation; 2) social-technical criteria definition; 3) alternatives identification; and 4) evaluation. In the *elicitation*, requirements are discovered through consultations with users and domain analysis. In the *social-technical criteria* definition the requirements are decomposed into a hierarchy, and each branch of this hierarchy ends in a measure or metric. *Alternative identification* includes searching for tool candidates. *Evaluation* involves ranking of identified tools against the social-technical criteria by examining capabilities, documentation, and experimentation.

The **ISO/IEC 9126 quality-based** approach [5] constructs a quality model for a targeted tool domain. Following the ISO/IEC 9126 [9] standard, attributes and relations are structured to criteria and metrics. Next the general process (fig. 1) is used to select the "best" tool. The approach has been tested for several tool domains (mail servers [5], and RE-tools [2]).

R-TEA (RE-tool evaluation approach) may support tool selection in general (fig. 1), but is designed principally for the RE-tool domain and uses two requirements frameworks [19, 20]. R-TEA consists of six steps. 1) Preparation of a requirements specification according to the frameworks; 2) Selection of business parties and the RE-tool candidates; 3) Investigation of the functional requirements contributes with the RE-tool functionality assessment; 4) Non-functional process requirements are analysed in correspondence to the functionality; 5) Product requirements are evaluated applying tests and analysing the vendor abilities to support the RE-tools; 6) Decision about the RE-tool selection is made after summarising the results which select a tool(s) with the highest score, or conclude about evaluation iteration if none of the RE-tools is good enough.

Evaluation Frameworks Specifically for RE-tools

This section surveys frameworks specifically targeted towards the evaluation of the RE-tools. These include: the Lang and Duggan requirements [14], the INCOSE [8], priority-based [6], role-based [7] frameworks, and the frameworks for functional [19] and non-functional [20] requirements.

The **Lang and Duggan requirements** [14] characterize a requirement management, communication and cooperative work tools. They are:

Req.1   Maintain uniquely identifiable description of all requirements;
Req.2   Classify requirements into logical user-defined groupings;
Req.3   Specify requirements using textual, graphical, and model-based descriptions, with support for rich media description (such as images and animated simulations);
Req.4   Define traceable associations between requirements;
Req.5   Verify the assignments of user requirements to technical design specifications;
Req.6   Maintain an audit trail of changes, archive baseline versions; and engage a mechanism to authenticate and approve change requests;
Req.7   Support secure, concurrent cooperative work between members of a multidisciplinary team, which may be geographically distributed;
Req.8   Support standard system modelling techniques and notations;
Req.9   Maintain a comprehensive data dictionary of all project components and requirements in a shared repository;
Req.10 Generate predefined and ad hoc reports;
Req.11 Generate documents that comply with standard industrial templates, with support for presentation-quality output, WYSIWYG preview, and built-in document quality controls;
Req.12 Connect seamlessly with other tools and systems, by supporting interoperable protocols and standards.

While all stated requirements are clearly useful, the list can be criticised for being somewhat unsystematic. Req.5 deals with requirements and design traceability, but it partly duplicates Req.1, Req.3, Req.4, and Req.8. Req.1 speaks about the unique description, but does not consider the specification language. Req.8 covers modelling techniques, which can be both semiformal and formal. Req.4 deals with requirement-requirement traces, but neglects source-requirement and requirement-design traceability. Req.10 and Req.11 overlap since both deal with the reports and views.

The **INCOSE framework** [8] suggested by the INCOSE working group, classifies 52 requirements into 14 categories. Based on the vendors' information, INCOSE provides a RE-tool survey, too. But the terminology is not defined, so the survey obtained some strange results when vendors interpreted features in an unintended way, making their tools look fully compliant, but if one takes a closer look this is not necessarily the case.

The **priority-based evaluation framework** [6] was created in consultations with practitioners. It classifies 53 requirements according to three priority levels (fig. 2) – *high* (essential), *medium* (useful) and *low* (desirable, but not essential). But organisations are not homogeneous environments, and priorities depend on various objective and subjective circumstances. The framework does not have guidelines for how to analyse the RE-tool if user priorities vary in different environments.

The **role-based framework** [7] suggests 93 requirements (fig. 3), which are grouped according to *developer*, *project administrator* and *RE-tool administrator* roles. The separation reduces the amount of text users have to read to get an idea of an RE-tool. However, requirements are not perfectly disjunctive, as one user may have several roles in a project.

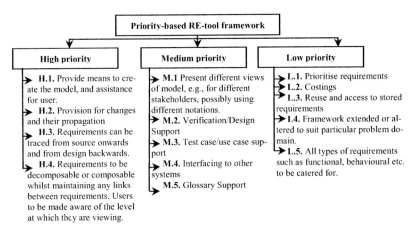

Fig. 2. Priority-based Framework

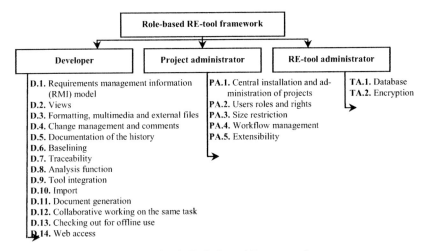

Fig. 3. Role-based Framework

The role-based framework does not consider guidelines for the application depending on the context. Also the authors do not provide empirical evidence of the framework's validity. The framework is only focused on functional RE-tool requirements, ignoring non-functional issues.

Two frameworks, one for functional and one for non-functional requirements are combined and used in the R-TEA method.

The **framework [19] for functional RE-tool requirements** (fig. 4) consists of three requirements dimensions [23]. The *representation* dimension deals with the degree of formality, where requirements are described using informal, semiformal and formal languages. The *agreement* dimension deals with the degree of agreement among project participants by communication, collaborative means and maintenance of rationale. The *specification* dimension deals with the completeness of specification and the degree of requirements understanding at a given time moment. The framework categories are reconsidered according to the Lang and Duggan [14] requirements, and are expanded with RE activities. The framework supports the evaluation by distinguishing between the goals to be reached and the means used to reach them, as done in the semiotic framework [15].

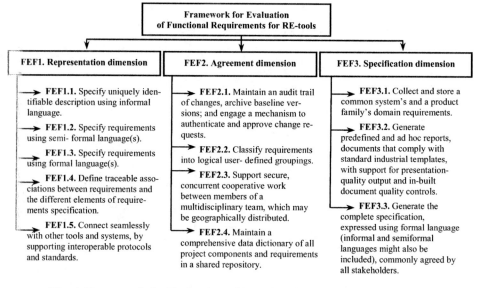

Fig. 4. Framework for Evaluation of Functional RE-tool Requirements

The **framework [20] for non-functional RE-tool requirements** (fig. 5) separates process, product and external requirements as suggested in [11]. *Process requirements* are constraints placed upon the user's work practice. *Product requirements* specify the desired RE-tool qualities (e.g., usability, performance, reliability, and maintenance). *External requirements* are divided into organisational requirements and requirements to business parties. *Organisational requirements* comprise direct and indirect costs and business practice. *Requirements to business parties* deal with the vendor performance, reliability, customer base and track records.

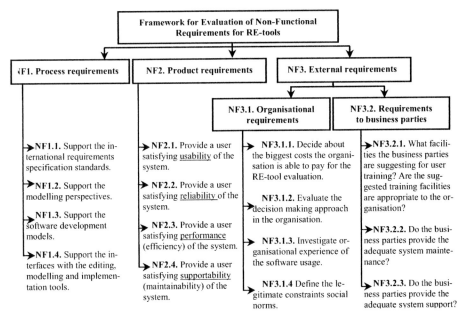

Fig. 5. Framework for Evaluation of Non-functional RE-tool Requirements

Discussion and Conclusions

Comparison of evaluation approaches

Table 1a and Table 1b shows comparison of approaches according to activity focus, material required, detail of guidelines, evaluation criteria, and maturity. All approaches correspond to the general COTS selection process in fig. 1. But each of them highlights different techniques. PORE describes template-based procurement. The scenario-based selection maps baseline scenario and tool scenario. The quality-based approach constructs a quality model for tool domain. R-TEA supports framework-based evaluation. OTSO, CAP, scenario-based selection and STACE assume that evaluation criteria are defined in advance.

The *one-round* and *multi-round* evaluations could be separated. The one-round evaluation is executed one time with all the candidate tools. After each step, the tool list is reduced and the user requirements are expanded (e.g. PORE). But most of the approaches (OTSO, CAP, scenario-based, STACE, and R-TEA) apply the multi-round evaluation, when the full evaluation cycle is repeated with each individual tool. The decision about tool suitability is made after testing all tools.

PORE, quality-based, and STACE are criticised for labour-intensive activities to define evaluation criteria. The approaches are not specifically targeted towards RE-tools, so the evaluation criteria and process definition are time consuming and domain knowledge demanding. R-TEA targets the RE-tool domain and supports the evaluation process using the two mentioned evaluation frameworks [19, 20].

Table 1a. Comparison of evaluation approaches

	PORE	OTSO	CAP	Scenario-based
Activity focus	Requirements specification, assessment the compatibility	Criteria definition, assessment the compatibility	Criteria definition	Determination how organisation works.
Material required	Test cases, Vendor demonstration	Templates for criteria construction, Initial criteria taxonomy.	Requirements specification, phase outputs.	Stakeholder work scenarios
How detail guidelines are?	Detail templates guide the process.	6 phases (search, screen, evaluate, analyse, deploy, assess)	Detail guidelines, describing inputs, steps, and outputs	Detail guidelines how to write scenario.
Evaluation criteria	Not specifically defined, depends on the domain and templates.	General criteria, goal/question/ metric plan.	General taxonomy, based on ISO/IEC 9126 standard.	No evaluation criteria. Focus on scenario writing.
Maturity	Reported 1998, case study (RE-tools), BANK-SEC project and SCARLET approach.	Reported 1995, case studies (map application, hypertext browsers).	Reported 2000, case study (administrative task tools).	Reported 1998, teaching seminar.

Table 1b. Comparison of evaluation approaches (cont.)

	STACE	Quality-based	R-TEA
Activity focus	Criteria definition	Criteria definition	Assessment of the compatibility
Material required	Documents, domain knowledge, market studies.	ISO/IEC 9126 standard, literature review, web page analysis.	Specification exemplar, RE-tool tutorials, evaluation scenarios.
How detail guidelines	Guidelines include 5 general phases	7 guidelines for construction quality models.	Guidelines include 6 general phases.
Evaluation criteria	General categories, adapted to a domain	Quality model, based on ISO/IEC 9126 standard.	Two evaluation frameworks.
Maturity	Reported 1999, case study (GIS).	Reported 2002, case studies (mail servers, RE-tools).	Reported 2004, academic case studies without purpose to select a tool.

Comparison of evaluation framework

Frameworks describe RE-tool functionality, and only some of them analyse non-functional requirements, like costs [6, 8, 20], tool performance,
usability, reliability [7, 20] and vendor characteristics [20]. The common
functional requirements are:

- *Requirements model representation* using different representation paradigms and languages, like requirements Req.1, Req.3, and Req.8 [14];
  capturing requirements/identification and capturing element structure
  [8]; means to create the model (H.1) [6]; requirements management information model (D.1); multimedia and external files (D.3) [7]; and requirements representation using informal (FEF1.1), semiformal
  (FEF1.2) and formal languages (FEF1.3) [19].
- *Requirements traceability*, like requirements Req.4 and Req.5 [14]; requirements flow-down and traceability analysis [8]; requirements traces
  from source onwards and from design backwards (H.3) [6]; traceability
  (D.7) [7]; and traceable associations (FEF1.4) [19].
- *RE-tool association and interfaces with other tools*, like requirement
  Req.12 [14]; FEF1.5 [19]; interface to tools [8], verification and design

support (M.2), and interfacing to other systems (M.4) [6]; and tool integration (D.9), and import (D.10) [7];

- *User and user group definition*, like user roles and rights (PA.2) [7] and some activities of features FEF2.1 [19];
- Maintenance of requirements *history*, *views* and *baseline*, like requirement Req.6 [14]; activities of FEF2.1 [19]; configuration management, and groupware [8]; requirements (de)composition (H.4) and model views (M.1) [6]; and views (D.2), baselining (D.6), and documentation on the history (D5) [7];
- Requirements *attributes* and requirements *prioritisation*, like requirements Req.2 [14]; FEF2.2 [19]; and L.1 [6];
- *Collaborative work support*, and requirements model *change propagation*, like requirement Req.7 [14]; FEF2.3 [19]; change management and comments (D.4), collaborative working on the same task (D.12), and Web access (D.13) [7];
- *Assistance for RE-tool users*, like requirements Req.8 [14]; FEF2.4 [19]; workflow management [7]; training [8]; assistance for users and glossary support (M.5) [6].
- *Requirements repository functionality*, like FEF3.1 [19]; reuse and access to stored requirements (L.3) [6]; and size restriction (PA.3) and database (TA.1) [7];
- *Report printing* according to different system and requirements views, like requirements Req.10, LDReq.11 [15]; FEF3.2 [19]; documents and other output media [8]; and document generation (D.11) [7].

Three frameworks [6, 7, 19] prioritise requirements according to their importance (high, medium, and low). But none of the frameworks (except [19] and [20]) specify traceability between RE-tool functionality and usability. Lack of traceability could result in poor consistency during the RE-tool evaluation and/or development. None of the frameworks provide terminology explanation, and, therefore, they could mislead during the evaluation, especially, if RE-tools are considered by different evaluators.

Guidelines for RE-tool evaluation methodology
The working hypothesis is that if a qualitative methodology is to be used for RE-tool acquisition, it would contribute with an RE-tool, which would yield prepare a high-quality specification. Composition of both evaluation approach and framework (e.g., the quality-based and INCOSE framework [2], PORE and role-based framework [7]) could contribute with a RE-tool selection methodology. However, only R-TEA combines and guides two frameworks [19, 20] and gives an account to a stepwise assessment of RE-tools.

A proper methodology saves time, helps to highlight the criteria and guides through evaluation. Here, the guidelines for methodology are suggested, according to a framework proposed by Krogstie and Sølvberg [12]:

Apply a constructivistic world-view. An objectivistic world-view describes an organisation, where stakeholders can map the required RE-tool without changing the organisational processes. In comparison to this, a constructivistic approach supports stakeholder knowledge externalization and internalization processes, and makes the organisational environment part of the individual understanding. Therefore, the methodology should support the constructivistic world-view (e.g., PORE [18], R-TEA [20])[1].

Be ready to change work processes. It is important to consider the organisational maturity before the tool acquisition to environment. RE-tools may lead to process improvement, but only if the organisation is able to take advantage of the tools. If the organisation has an immature process, there are probably other improvement steps that should be taken before considering the tool acquisition (e.g., [6, 7, 19, 20]).

Evaluate the software already available in the organisation. Usually the RE-tool will not be a stand-alone application in the organisation, but will be used together with other development tools. Hence, the RE-tool ability to interoperate with other tools should be a part of the general tool evaluation (e.g., [6, 7, 8, 19, 20]).

Involve users in the RE-tool evaluation. The users have different experiences arising from work and other activities; however, they are the true evaluators and can describe lacking points of automated support (e.g., PORE [18], R-TEA [20]).

Teach users the tool functionality. Surveys [14, 19] report about RE-tool complexity. In order the tool selection to be successful, the methodology should comprise the teaching. The users should perform themselves the evaluation, and the evaluation team should help them during the RE-tool testing (e.g., R-TEA [20]).

Evaluate the maturity. The methodology maturity could be evaluated by methodology usage time (used for a long time or new), awareness (used in many places, or only by one company or research group), and application (tried out in practice) (e.g., PORE [18], quality-based selection [5]).

Reuse the collected information could be divided to several cases. 1) Reuse of the same type of tool evaluation by the same organisation. The case could happen if the tool versions change. 2) Reuse of other type of tool evaluation by the same organisation. This reuse contributes with environment description; however a new tools and new needs should be de-

---

[1] This and other examples suggest the some methods as examples; however, sample is not limited, as the approach selection and application depend on the context.

fined. 3) Reuse of the same tool type but by a different organisation could happen if the organisations have similar needs. The gathered information should be also packaged for the future needs (e.g., CAP [22]).

There is no clearly "best" solution for the RE-tool evaluation methodology. The guidelines show that a methodology depends on the organisational profile and goals.

References

[1]   Basili VR, Boehm B (2001) COTS-Based Systems Top 10. IEEE Computer, vol 34, no 5, pp 91-93

[2]   Carvallo JP, Franch X, Quer C (2004) A Quality Model for Requirements Management Tools. In: Requirements Engineering for Sociotechnical Systems. Idea Group Publishing

[3]   Feblowitz MD, Greenspan SJ (1998) Scenario-Based Analysis of COTS Acquisition Impacts. Requirements Engineering, vol 3, pp 182-201

[4]   Finkelstein A, Spanoudakis G, Ryan M (1996) Software Package Requirements and Procurement. Proc of the 8th International Workshop Software Specification and Design USA

[5]   Franch X, Carvallo I (2002) A Quality-Model-Based Approach for Describing and Evaluating Software Packages. Proc of the International Conference on Requirements Engineering (RE'02) Essen Germany

[6]   Haywood E, Dart P (1997) Towards Requirements for Requirements Modelling Tools. Proc of the 2nd Australian Workshop on Requirements Engineering, Australia

[7]   Hoffmann M, Kuhn N, Weber M, Bittner M (1997) Requirements for Requirements Management Tools. Proc of the International Conference on Requirements Engineering (RE'04) Japan

[8]   INCOSE: Tools Survey: Requirements Management (RM) Tools by International Council on Systems Engineering (INCOSE). www.incose.org/

[9]   ISO/IEC 9126 (1991) Information Technology – Software Product Evaluation– Quality Characteristics and Guide Lines for their Use. Switzerland

[10] Kontio J (1996) A Case Study in Applying a Systematic Method for COTS Selection. Proc of the 18th Int Conf on Software Engineering (ICSE'96)

[11] Kotonya G, Sommerville I (1998) Requirements Engineering: Process and Techniques. Wiley

[12] Krogstie J, Sølvberg A (1996) A Classification of Methodology Frameworks for Computerized Information Systems Support in Organisations. Proc of the IFIP8.1/8.2 Conference on Method Engineering: Principles of Method Construction and Tool Support USA

[13] Kunda D (2003) STACE: Social Technical Approach to COTS Software Selection. In: Cechich A, Piattini M, Vallecillo A (eds) Component-Based Software Quality – Methods and Techniques. Lecture Notes in Computer Science Springer-Verlag

[14] Lang M, Duggan J (2001) A Tool to Support Collaborative Software Requirements Management. Requirement Engineering, vol 6, no 3, pp 161-172

[15] Lindland OI, Sindre G, Sølvberg A (1994) Understanding Quality in Conceptual Modelling. IEEE Software, vol 11, no 2, pp 42-49

[16] Maiden NA, Kim H (2002) SCARLET: Light-Weight Component Selection in BANKSEC. In: Barbier F (ed) Business Computer-based Software Engineering. Kluwer Academic Publishers

[17] Maiden NA, Kim H, Ncube C (2002) Rethinking Process Guidelines for Selecting Software Components. Proc of the 1st International Conference on COTS-Based Software Systems. Lecture Notes in Computer Science Springer-Verlag

[18] Maiden NA, Ncube C (1998) Acquiring COTS Software Selection Requirements. IEEE Software, pp 46-56

[19] Matulevičius R (2004) Validating an Evaluation Framework for Requirement Engineering Tools. In: Krogstie J, Halpin T, Siau K (eds) Information Modeling Methods and Methodologies. Idea Group Publishing

[20] Matulevičius R, Sindre G (2004) Requirements Specification for RE-tool Evaluation: Towards a Specification Exemplar. Proc of the 17th International Conference Software and Systems Engineering and their Applications (ICSSEA 2004) France

[21] Oberndorf T (1997) COTS and Open Systems – an Overview.

[22] www.sei.cmu.edu/str/descriptions/cots.html#ndi

[23] Ochs MA, Pfahl D, Chrobok-Diening G, Nothhelfer-Kolb B (2000) A COTS Acquisition Process: Definition and Application Experience. Proc of the 11th ESCOM Conference

[24] Pohl K (1994) The Three Dimensions of Requirements Engineering: a Framework and its Applications. Information systems, vol 19, no 3, pp 243-258

[25] Vigder MR, Dean J (1997) An Architectural Approach to Building Systems from COTS Software Components. Proc of the 1997 Center for Advanced Studies Conference (CASCON 97) Toronto

Requirements Engineering Tool Evaluation Approach

Raimundas Matulevičius and Guttorm Sindre

Department of Computer and Information Science, Norwegian University of Science and Technology, Norway. (raimunda, guttors)@idi.ntnu.no

Introduction

Requirements engineering (RE) is a complex activity, potentially involving stakeholders participating in the elicitation, documentation, validation and management of system requirements. For such a complex activity, powerful tool support is clearly useful [10, 12]; however, the mainstream of RE practice relies on office and modelling tools rather than targeted RE-tools (e.g. DOORS, CaliberRM, and RequisitePro). Reasons for not using the RE-tools include financial causes, like high RE-tool price and low return on investment. Hofmann and Lehner [8] stress that a lack of well-defined RE process and a lack of team training in the selected tools cause the insufficient RE support. An infrastructure must be set for tool acquisition, and a company must be willing to invest in putting such an infrastructure [2]. However, the management of such companies usually has the unrealistic expectations, e.g., immediate pay-off.

A part of the reason might be that it is difficult to evaluate the RE-tools available. Because of their limited use in practice it is difficult to evaluate them in terms of their impact on an organisation's processes. Similarly, it is difficult to examine tools in an experiment, as it is difficult to control for the variation in system developers' capabilities. Moreover, RE-tools provide the greatest benefit for large projects with real stakeholders who frequently change their minds about requirements, while a controlled experiment normally requires prescribed tasks of a fairly limited size. It would thus be hard to create experimental tests that would provide a realistic evaluation of the tools, and for small- and medium-size organisations the cost of thus evaluating several RE-tools empirically might be prohibitive. There is also a need for a cheaper kind of evaluation that can be done analytically rather than empirically. A potential problem of such evaluation, however, is that they easily become ad hoc and subjective. Hence, to support the completeness and effectiveness of such evaluations, it should be grounded in a sound evaluation frameworks providing methodological support to the evaluators. This work analyses a research question: *How to evaluate and acquire software tools for the RE process support according to organisation's needs in order to improve the RE process?*

In the second section of this paper an RE-tool evaluation approach (R-TEA) is presented. R-TEA is a systematic way to assess RE-tools using two evaluation frameworks [17, 18]. In the third section a case study is considered in order to test the approach. The fourth section analyses the related work. Finally, the conclusions and future work is discussed in the last section.

RE-Tool Evaluation Approach

A common way to investigate tools is to define categories and requirements, where requirements are used as measures or metrics. Such organisation could be considered as the *evaluation framework* which provides a skeleton structure for the tool comparison. RE-tool frameworks [6, 7, 9] specify different RE-tool requirements. However, the frameworks are development-oriented and lack application for the evaluation purposes.

The RE-tool evaluation approach (R-TEA) starts with a specification exemplar which is based on two evaluation frameworks [17] and [18]. This section characterises the frameworks, exemplar and the R-TEA method.

The **framework [17] for functional RE-tool requirements** (fig. 1) consists of three requirements dimensions, inspired by Pohl's work in the NATURE project [21]. The requirements *representation* dimension deals with the degree of formality, where requirements are described using informal, semiformal and formal languages. The requirements *agreement* dimension deals with the degree of agreement among project participants by communication, collaborative means and maintenance of rationale. The requirements *specification* dimension deals with the completeness of requirements specification and the degree of requirements understanding at a given time moment. The framework supports the evaluation by distinguishing between the goals to be reached and the means used to reach them, as done in the semiotic quality framework [13].

The **framework [18] for non-functional RE-tool requirements** (fig. 2) separates process, product and external requirements as suggested in [12]. *Process requirements* are constraints placed upon the user's work practice (but not upon developing or evaluating the RE-tools).

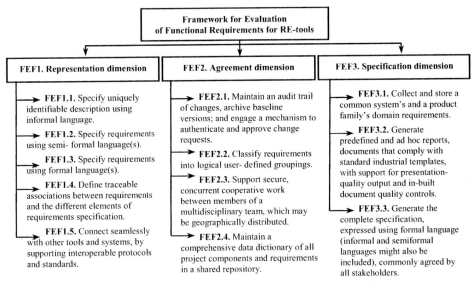

Fig. 1. Framework for Evaluation of Functional RE-tool Requirements

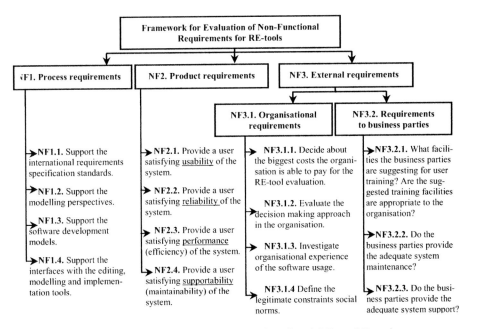

Fig. 2. Framework for Evaluation of Non-functional RE-tool Requirements

Product requirements specify the desired RE-tool qualities (e.g., usability, performance, reliability, and maintenance). *External requirements* are divided into organisational requirements and requirements to business parties. *Organisational requirements* comprise direct and indirect costs and business practice. *Requirements to business parties* deal with the vendor performance, reliability, customer base and track records.

The **specification exemplar** [18] **for RE-tool evaluation** is constructed from evaluation frameworks. The exemplar supports the RE-tool evaluation in two ways: 1) it provides the evaluation criteria; 2) it is used as the try-on instrument. The exemplar is not made to favour one particular RE-tool or tool vendor. It allows evaluation of limited tool functionality. The exemplar does not specify whether the task must be done automatically or manually. The exemplar contains steps modifying requirements, analysing conflicts and restructuring the whole specification. Its application results the RE-tool evaluation approach (R-TEA) shown in fig. 3.

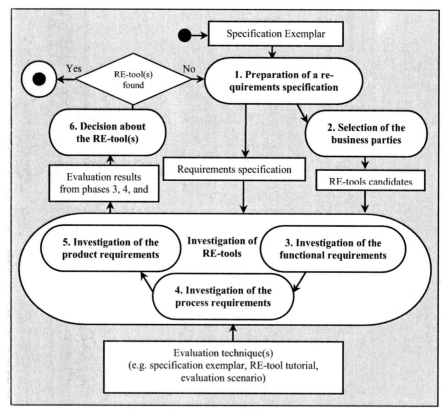

Fig. 3. RE-tools Evaluation Approach

R-TEA involves two actor groups: *evaluation team* which manages the process, and *users*, who perform the activities. R-TEA has six phases:

1. *Preparation of a requirements specification* for the RE-tool selection consists of analysing the specification exemplar and adapting it to the user needs. The evaluation team performs elicitation and highlights the environment's needs. The prioritisation has to determine the most important requirements. The evaluation team could apply different methods (e.g., Analytic Hierarchy Process (AHP) in [22], and weighted scoring method (WSM) in [11]). Based on elicitation and prioritisation, the evaluation team prepares the specification containing the requirements listed according to priorities.

2. *Selection of business parties* involves the investigation of the RE-tool market according to the external requirements. The evaluation team requests trial and demonstration RE-tool versions from the business parties. Next, phases 3, 4, and 5 evaluate each of the RE-tools selected in phase 2.

3. *Investigation of the functional requirements* contributes with the functionality evaluation of the RE-tool candidate. An evaluation technique(s) from table 1 is used to test tool functionality. The combination of several techniques could help to get more detail tool evaluation, but the evaluation itself takes more time than using one evaluation technique. When the users perform the RE-tool tests, the evaluation team should maintain observation. The evaluation team could react to the problems arising during tool tests. Observation could also provide the useful information about RE-tool usability, reliability, and performance.

4. *Investigation of the process requirements* is performed in correspondence with the functionality analysis. The phase results with inadequacies between the user activities and the RE-tool support for these activities. The inadequacies are considered in phase 5 as the maintainability requirements.

5. *Investigation of the product requirements* is performed as the usability, performance and reliability tests. The evaluation team should also investigate which maintainability requirements could be fulfilled by the tool users internally, and which should be redirected to the RE-tool vendors.

6. *Decision about the RE-tool selection* is made after summarising the results from phases 3, 4 and 5. One of three decisions should be made: *i*) the users adapt the "best-evaluated" RE-tool without changing the RE process; *ii*) the users start using the "best-evaluated" RE-tool, but they have to reconsider the RE process; or *iii*) the "best-evaluated" tool is not suitable for the users and they need to repeat the RE-tool evaluation (reconsider requirements, and/or search for other RE-tool candidates).

Table 1. Evaluation techniques

Technique	Advantages	Disadvantages
Requirements specification	Prepared in phase 1 according to the specification exemplar and according to user familiar domain; Emphasises the same evaluation issues.	No guidance during the RE-tool assessment.
RE-tool tutorial	Emphasises on teaching the RE-tool functions; Is received together with RE-tools; Provides guidance during the RE-tool assessment.	Evaluation is not comparable if tutorials emphasize different functionality.
Evaluation scenario	Emphasises on teaching the RE-tool functions; Emphasises the same functions for all RE-tools; Provides guidance during RE-tool assessment; Prepared for all RE-tools on the same problem; Problem could be related to the user work.	Preparation is time demanding; Preparation is problem domain knowledge demanding.

Case Study

A case study was executed at the Norwegian University of Science and Technology. 44 students were divided into ten groups of 4-5 persons. The main purpose of the case study was to investigate whether R-TEA helps to select tools, which yield high-quality requirements specifications.

The **problem** used in the experiment is a natural language case description of the information system dealing with network fault handling. The problem statement also included a list of requirements which should be maintained in requirements specifications.

Tasks. The case study comprised three tasks. In the *first* RE-tools and office tools are used to prepare three requirements specifications for the problem. The first specification is prepared using RE-tool #1 and the evaluation scenario. The second specification is prepared with RE-tool #2 and the RE-tool tutorial. The third specification is prepared using office tools chosen by the group. In the *second* task the participants used the prototype tool which supports R-TEA, and assessed the RE-tool functionality. The *third* task comprised the survey, where the semiotic quality framework [13] is applied to evaluate the specification quality.

The **post-evaluation** helps to reduce the evaluation subjectivity. Four teaching assistants evaluated the group performance and the specification quality. First, the assistants inspected the specifications individually; next they agreed about the "best-quality" specifications for each group.

The **result analysis** method comprises correlation analysis. In table 2 the correspondence between the tool functionality and SRS quality are displayed. The *tool functionality* is calculated as a sum of all framework activity evaluations:

$$Tool\ functionality = \sum_{i}^{n}\sum_{j}^{m} p_{i,j} e_{i,j}, \qquad (1)$$

where n – group size, m - number of activities, $p_{i,j}$ – the priority of activity j, and $e_{i,j}$ – evaluation of activity j, evaluated by group member i.

The *SRS quality* evaluation is calculated as a sum of all quality type (as described in [13]) evaluations:

$$SRS\ quality = \sum_{i}^{n}\sum_{j}^{t} q_{i,j}, \qquad (2)$$

where t – the number of quality types, and $q_{i,j}$ – the evaluation of the quality type j, evaluated by group member i. *Correlation coefficients* are calculated between tool functionality and SRS quality.

Results. In table 2 the correlation coefficients between the tool functionality and specification quality show a direct dependency in seven groups (I, IV, V, VII, VIII, IX, and X). The post-evaluation selects the same seven specifications. In groups II, III, and VI the correlation coefficient is negative which does not mean that there is no dependency. It rather defines that there are other factors; e.g. low tool usability or participants' inexperience, which might have caused a low quality of specifications.

Validity. The participants had basic knowledge but limited experience in RE practice. However, they all were following the same course (essentially the same study program for 3,5 years), i.e., the participants were quite homogeneous regarding age and background. Since the participants were in their fourth year, they had only one year left of their studies, their knowledge were quite close at least to practitioners who just graduated.

External validity is influenced by the number of requirements, which was relatively small. Therefore many participants preferred office tools instead of RE-tools. The situation could be different if dealing with a large number of requirements changing over time, where the usefulness of advanced tools would be more evident.

Conclusions. The R-TEA method helps to select RE-tools which yield high-quality specifications. However the evaluation is subjective and much affected by the user experience with tools. The findings show that tool tutorials introduce the RE-tool functionality, and the evaluation scenarios help to assess the RE-tool performance according to the same problem.

Table 2. Evaluation of tool functionality and requirements specification quality

Cir. No	Tools	Evaluation technique	Tool function-ality score	Specifi-cation quality score	Cor-relation coeffi-cient	Post-evaluation
I	RDT	Eval. scenario	3603	119	0,9674	Requisite-PRO
	RequisitePRO	RE-tool tutorial	3672	128		
	Office tools	-	2370	98		
II	CORE	Eval. scenario	4844	101	-0,7450	CORE and MS Office
	CaliberRM	RE-tool tutorial	5583	102		
	Office tools	-	4448	127		
III	CORE	Eval. scenario	4155	96	-0,6549	CORE
	CaliberRM	RE-tool tutorial	5378	81		
	Office tools	-	2933	91		
IV	CORE	Eval. scenario	1396	105	0,8811	CORE
	RequisitePRO	RE-tool tutorial	1466	98		
	Office tools	-	805	87		
V	CORE	Eval. scenario	2165	85	0,7060	Office tools
	CaliberRM	RE-tool tutorial	1850	83		
	Office tools	-	2238	105		
VI	RequisitePRO	Eval. scenario	3571	110	-0,7626	Requisite-PRO
	CaliberRM	RE-tool tutorial	4536	109		
	Office tools	-	3167	126		
VII	RDT	Eval. scenario	1338	99	0,8765	CORE and Office tools
	CORE	RE-tool tutorial	1496	136		
	Office tools	-	1620	134		
VIII	RDT	Eval. scenario	1626	70	0,2849	RDT, CORE and Office tools
	CORE	RE-tool tutorial	1656	87		
	Office tools	-	1173	75		
IX	RDT	Eval. scenario	3168	114	0,4881	Requisite-PRO
	RequisitePRO	RE-tool tutorial	4255	148		
	Office tools	-	2460	135		
X	RDT	Eval. scenario	4208	90	0,9926	CaliberRM and RDT
	CaliberRM	RE-tool tutorial	5108	93		
	Office tools	-	2133	77		

A RE-tool selection depends not only on functional features but also on tool non-functional characteristics which were assessed in an additional questionnaire but not analysed here. The results indicated poor usability of RE-tools, although the functionality is higher than office tools. RE-tools are designed for the skilled users [10, 12, 17] proficient in engineering methods and the tool functionality. But this is not always the case when assessing the RE-tools where users have different working experience.

Related Work

The literature suggests a number of evaluation approaches [3, 5, 11, 15, 16, 20]. Matulevičius and Sindre in [19] presented an overview of the existing tools selection approaches and frameworks specifically designed for the RE-tools. In this section an analytical comparison of R-TEA and these approaches is performed.

PORE *vs.* **R-TEA.** PORE (Procurement Oriented Requirements Engineering) integrates requirements acquisition and tool selection with process guidance using templates [16]. R-TEA is guided using two evaluation frameworks. PORE and R-TEA involve the potential tool users. In PORE users are 'spectators' and requirements providers. In R-TEA users are tool evaluators, at the same time they learn how to use the RE-tool. PORE involves of the tool vendors; however they might provide the promotion information. R-TEA suggests involvement of domain experts, who could act as evaluation team which manage the evaluation activities.

OTSO *vs.* **R-TEA.** OTSO (Off-The-Shelf Option) [11] consists of search, screening, evaluation, analysis, deployment and assessment. The search and screening correspond to the second R-TEA phase. The evaluation corresponds to the third, fourth and fifth phases of R-TEA. OTSO does not support any particular domain; therefore the criteria are defined each time when the method is applied. The OTSO analysis and deployment correspond to the sixth phase of R-TEA. The OTSO assessment describes reuse and improvement of the next OTSO process. This activity is not directly supported in R-TEA.

CAP *vs.* **R-TEA.** CAP (COTS Acquisition Process) [20] constructs criteria according to predefined specification and the ISO/IEC 9126 standard. As the R-TEA requirements specification is prepared according to a specification exemplar, the main R-TEA focus is on the RE-tool compatibility assessment. CAP maintains a four-level general criteria hierarchy. R-TEA uses two RE-tool frameworks. CAP defines process inputs, steps to perform and the outputs. R-TEA provides general guidelines for the evaluation process.

Scenario-based Selection *vs.* **R-TEA.** The scenario-based selection [3] proposes a comparison between baseline scenarios which describe how the organisation operates, and tool scenarios which projects a baseline scenario into a future where a tool is applied. This corresponds to the R-TEA fourth phase which considers the work process requirements. Scenario-based selection does not analyse tool functionality, product requirements, and requirements to business parties. In R-TEA the way organisation is (and will be) working, is directly related to tool functionality, maintainability, and vendor capabilities to support the RE-tool.

STACE *vs.* **R-TEA.** STACE (social-technical approach to COTS evaluation) comprises four interrelated processes [15]: requirements elicitation, social-technical criteria definition alternatives identification, and evaluation. The requirements elicitation resembles the preparation of the requirements specification in R-TEA. In the STACE social-technical criteria definition, the criteria are constructed for the particular tool domain. In R-TEA the criteria are provided by two frameworks which include tool functionality, quality characteristics (product requirements) and social-economic factors (external requirements). The STACE alternative identification corresponds to the second phase of R-TEA. The STACE evaluation or assessment investigates the tool compatibility to the organisational environment. R-TEA has three phases (third, fourth, and fifth) which describe the RE-tool assessment. In the sixth phase R-TEA summarises makes decision about the RE-tool selection.

Quality-based Selection *vs.* **R-TEA.** The *quality-based* approach [5] constructs a quality model following the ISO/IEC 9126 standard. R-TEA starts with the exemplar which is transformed to the requirements specification for the RE-tool selection. The quality-based selection is described by the COSTUME method [1]. The R-TEA method describes the RE-tool assessment according to six phases shown in figure 3.

Conclusions and Future Work

Coming back to the research question formulated in the introduction, this work proposes an RE-tool evaluation approach (R-TEA) which guides application of two evaluation frameworks. In comparison to the existing RE-tool frameworks [6, 7, 9], the described frameworks [17, 18] are evaluation-oriented and define relationships between requirements. In comparison to the COTS selection approaches [3, 5, 11, 15, 16, 20] which generally lack evaluation criteria, R-TEA reduces an evaluation time and improves the RE-tool assessment as the criteria are defined by the frameworks. R-TEA recognises the importance of the requirements specification, which contributes with the basis for the architecture, design, implementation and maintenance of the RE-tools.

The concluding R-TEA evaluation is done following the methodological framework suggested by Krogstie and Sølvberg [14]:

• R-TEA supports a *constructivistic* world-view. Users externalise their knowledge throughout the evaluation. The internalisability activities involve the maintenance of the requirements specification and analysis of the tool selection results.

- R-TEA suggests how to assess the RE-tools and to adapt them to the RE process. The organisation should determine its maturity level and be ready for changes before starting the RE-tool assessment.
- It is important to consider the information interoperability between the RE-tool(s) and other tools. R-TEA provides requirements for relationships between the RE-tool and other tools used in the organisation.
- R-TEA suggests several evaluation techniques which tend to teach potential tool users the tool functionality.
- R-TEA do not analyses the information reuse activities. However, the knowledge collected during requirement specification and tool evaluation, could be easily reused for further purposes.
- R-TEA is a new method. The case study described here, concludes with a positive method performance. However the study involved students as the research objects and had no purpose to acquire an RE-tool.

In order to validate the R-TEA method and its frameworks, case studies have to involve practitioners. Especially it would be useful to apply the method in an organisation that has decided to adapt an RE-tool to its practice. The experimental investigation should also determine the R-TEA usefulness against other evaluation approaches. The future work involves studies where several approaches would be tested under similar settings.

References

[1]   Carvallo JP, Franch X, Quer C (2004) A Quality Model for Requirements Management Tools. In: Requirements Engineering for Sociotechnical Systems, Idea Group Publishing

[2]   El Emam K, Madhavji NH (1995) A Field Study of Requirements Engineering Practice in Information Systems Development. Proc of the 2nd IEEE International Symposium on Requirements Engineering, pp 68-80

[3]   Feblowitz MD, Greenspan SJ (1998) Scenario-Based Analysis of COTS Acquisition Impacts. Requirements Engineering, vol 3, pp 182-201

[4]   Finkelstein A, Spanoudakis G, Ryan M (1996) Software Package Requirements and Procurement. Proc of the 8th International Workshop Software Specification and Design, pp 141-145

[5]   Franch X, Carvallo I (2002) A Quality-model-based Approach for Describing and Evaluating Software Packages. Proc of the International Conference on Requirements Engineering (RE'02), Essen Germany, pp 104-111

[6] Haywood E, Dart P (1997) Towards Requirements for Requirements Model-
     ling Tools. Proc of the 2nd Australian Workshop on Requirements Engineer-
     ing, Australia, pp 61-69
[7] Hoffmann M, Kuhn N, Weber M, Bittner M (1997) Requirements for Re-
     quirements Management Tools, Proc of the International Conference on Re-
     quirements Engineering (RE'04), Kioto Japan, pp 301-308
[8] Hofmann HF, Lehner F (2001) Requirements Engineering as a Success Fac-
     tor in Software Projects. IEEE Software, pp 58-66
[9] INCOSE, Tools Survey: Requirements Management (RM) Tools by Interna-
     tional Council on Systems Engineering (INCOSE) www.incose.org/
[10] Kaindl H, Brinkkemper S, Bubenko J jr, Farbey B, Greenspan SJ, Heitmeyer
     CL, do Prado Leite JCS, Mead NR, Mylopoulos J, Siddiqi J (2002) Require-
     ments Engineering and Technology Transfer: Obstacles, Incentives, and Im-
     provement Agenda. Requirements Engineering, vol 7, pp 113-123
[11] Kontio J (1996) A Case Study in Applying a Systematic Method for COTS
     Selection. Proc of the 18th International Conference on Software Engineering
[12] Kotonya G, Sommerville I (1998) Requirements Engineering: Process and
     Techniques. Wiley
[13] Krogstie J (2001) A Semiotic Approach to Quality in Requirements Specifi-
     cations. Proc IFIP 8.1 Working Conference on Organisational Semiotics
[14] Krogstie J, Sølvberg A (1996) A Classification of Methodology Frameworks
     for Computerized Information Systems Support in Organizations. Proc of the
     IFIP8.1/8.2 Conference on Method Engineering: Principles of Method Con-
     struction and Tool Support, USA
[15] Kunda D (2003) STACE: Social Technical Approach to COTS Software Se-
     lection. In: Cechich A, Piattini M, Vallecillo A (eds) Component-Based
     Software Quality - Methods and Techniques. Lecture Notes in Computer Sci-
     ence, Springer-Verlag, pp 85-98
[16] Maiden NA, Ncube C (1998) Acquiring COTS Software Selection Require-
     ments. IEEE Software, pp 46-56
[17] Matulevičius R (2004) Validating an Evaluation Framework for Requirement
     Engineering Tools, In: Krogstie J, Halpin T, Siau K (eds) Information Mod-
     eling Methods and Methodologies, Idea Group Publishing, pp. 148-174
[18] Matulevičius R, Sindre G (2004) Requirements Specification for RE-tool
     Evaluation: Towards a Specification Exemplar. Proc of the 17th International
     Conference Software and Systems Engineering and their Applications
[19] Matulevičius R, Sindre G (2005) Overview of the Evaluation Approaches
     and Frameworks for Requirements Engineering Tools, published in this book
[20] Ochs MA, Pfahl D, Chrobok-Diening G, Nothhelfer-Kolb B (2000) A COTS
     Acquisition Process: Definition and Application Experience. Proc of the 11th
     ESCOM Conference, pp 335-343
[21] Pohl K (1994) The Three Dimensions of Requirements Engineering:
     a Framework and its Applications. Information Systems, vol 19, no 3, pp
     243-258
[22] Saaty TL (1980) The Analytic Hierarchy Process. McGraw-Hill New York

Decision-Making Activities in Requirements Engineering Decision Processes: A Case Study

Beatrice Alenljung and Anne Persson

School of Humanities and Informatics, University of Skövde, Sweden.
(beatrice.alenljung, anne.persson)@his.se

Introduction

Decisions are made at all steps in information systems development (ISD), for example with regard to requirements, architecture, components, project planning, validation etc. (Kotonya and Sommerville 1998; Ruhe 2003). In the same way the requirements engineering (RE) process can be viewed as a decision-making process (Aurum and Wholin 2003; Regnell et al. 2001).

Decision-making in the RE process is far from straightforward. It involves the difficulties that characterize decision-making in natural settings, e.g. uncertain and dynamic environment; shifting, ill-defined, or competing goals or values; time stress; and multiple players (Orasanu and Connolly 1993). This implies that decision-makers in the RE process need decision support. In order to assist RE decision-makers and to increase the effectiveness and efficiency of RE decision-making activities, several aspects need to be emphasized, such as identifying the stakeholders who participate in each RE activity and accordingly consider specific decision aids for each type of stakeholder; identifying the decision types and its actions in each RE phase; identifying the information needed in each phase; as well as providing decision support tools (Aurum and Wohlin 2003).

One of many challenges when developing decision support is to properly understand the actual decision situation in which the decision-maker acts, so that decision-making can be supported from the decision-maker's perspective. Properly means that attention has to be paid to the very nature of the decision-making situation. Otherwise we risk supporting what does not need to be supported or we risk providing support in an inappropriate way. A support system is only useful in relation to the characteristics of the target users, the tasks that are supposed to be carried out, and the context in which the system is going to be used (e.g. Maguire 2001). This means that adopting a user-centred design approach to obtain a successful decision support is reasonable (Parker and Sinclair 2001). The target users in the case of RE decision-making are the requirements engineers.

Decision situations can be highly complex (Alenljung and Persson 2004), which is shown in Fig. 1. The framework is the result of a thorough analysis of decision-making literature and it describes important perspectives related to any type of decision-maker. In this paper we focus on the decision processes of requirements engineers, the decision-making activities that are conducted in these processes and the decision matters that they manage. A decision matter is viewed as the subject matter that is dealt with in a decision process. A decision process is viewed as a number of phases or steps related to each other that result in a decision and the implementation of the decision. Decision-making is considered to be activities, mentally or physically, carried out by a decision-maker.

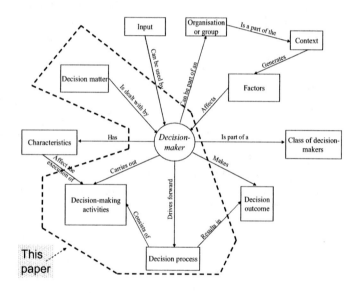

Fig. 1. This framework describes aspects of the decision-maker's situation (Alenljung and Persson 2004)

The aim of our research project is to propose how better decision support can be provided to requirements engineers, for instance through decision-maker centred improvements of requirements management tools. A first step towards this aim is to study RE decision-making processes in order to understand the actual decision situations of requirements engineers. This has been done in a case study involving a mature software development organisation in Sweden. This paper reports on the findings from this case study and discusses the implication of the findings for RE decision-making support. The remainder of the paper is organized as follows. Section 2 presents the research method. In section 3 we describe the RE decision-making processes discovered in the case study and compare these processes. We also discuss the implications of our findings for RE decision support. In section 4 we make some concluding remarks.

Research Method

The case study was carried out at Ericsson Microwave Systems (EMW) in Sweden. EMW has several products, e.g. military radar systems, which all may be subject to tailoring according to customer requests. Development projects at EMW are long and expensive and only a few units of each product are delivered. A project in which a product is tailored to a customer's needs involves between 3000 and 6000 requirements depending on the type of product. Such a project typically runs for 2-4 years and consists of about 25 000 man hours. When a new product is developed the project typically runs for 5-10 years and consists of about 250 000 man hours.

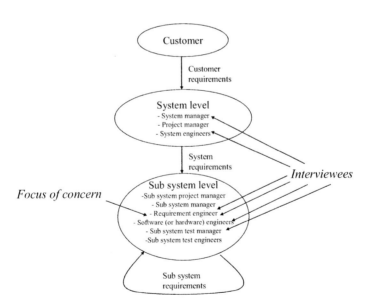

Fig. 2. Requirements flow within a project and actors that have been interviewed

As seen in Fig. 2, a project begins when a contract has been signed with a customer. The product is sometimes to be integrated with the customer's existing products, which results in several "folders" of customer requirements. The requirements are then transformed to requirements on the system level. The system requirements are then allocated to different sub systems. The requirements engineers then create sub system requirements based on the allocated system requirements. A sub system involves 700-1300 requirements. Some functions, and thereby also requirements, are used by two or more projects at the same time.

The approach in the case study is human-centred and focuses on the experiences of the requirements engineers and the actors in the development process that are closely related to requirements engineers. The purpose of the case study was to investigate the actual decision situations of requirements engineers. The study involved three stages:

1. Five requirements engineers were interviewed. They had worked between 4 and 25 years at EMW and had been requirements engineers for between 1 and 10 years. Open-ended interviews, inspired by the HCI methods contextual inquiry (Holtzblatt and Jones 1993) and analysis of information utilization (Gulliksen et al. 1997), were used. The interviews were conducted at the workplace of the interviewees and lasted between 1.5 and 4 hours. Two of the interviewees were interviewed together, according to their wishes.
2. A focus group session was held at the company with nine participants. Two of the interviewed requirements engineers were present. The other participants were system engineers, a product manager, a system manager, requirements engineers, and sub system test engineers. In the first part of the session the results from the interviews were presented and in the second part the participants discussed the results. The discussion was recorded and later analysed together with the material from stage 3.
3. Five persons, whose roles were related to requirements engineers, were interviewed. Two of them had participated in the focus group. It was a system manager, a sub system test manager, a sub system manager, who also worked as a software engineer, and two system engineers, one of whom also worked as a software engineer. Open-ended interviews, inspired by contextual inquiry, were used. Interviews were conducted at the workplace of the interviewees and lasted between 1 and 1.5 hours. Two interviewees were interviewed together, according to their wishes. All interviewees were first asked to describe their own work and then to discuss the work carried out by the requirements engineers, as well as problems and difficulties related to that.

Two persons were interviewed at the same time at their own discretion, which may mean that they influenced each other. However, they did not appear to avoid discussing somewhat delicate matters, and they did not always agree. It was rather the opposite, they triggered each other and the discussion was rich. Neither was one of the two particularly dominant. Two of the interviewees in the third stage of the research process had participated in the focus group. This may have influenced their answers, but we did not explicitly discuss the preliminary results that had been presented in the focus group session. However, the interviewees did relate to the results a couple of times.

Results

Two separate decision processes in the studied RE process have been found. The first decision process concerns the *establishment of requirements in a new project*, and the second decision process concerns *management of requirement changes*. These two processes have similarities, but also important differences from a decision-making perspective. Both processes include many decision-making activities in different decision phases. Both are highly iterative and embrace several sub-decisions. These sub-decisions are both work-related and system-related, and affect the efficiency of the ISD process as well as the quality of the system.

The decision-making activities in the two identified decision processes in RE have been structured using the phases and routines in the decision process model of Mintzberg et al. (1976), which have been complemented with the last two phases of Power's (2002) decision process model, implementation and follow up, as can be seen in Fig. 4.

Mintzberg's model also includes three sets of supporting routines: a) decision control routines, e.g. allocating organisational resources, b) decision communication routines, and c) political routines, e.g. clarifying power relationships in the organisation. In the empirical findings there are no activities that can be categorised as decision control and political, at least not in the way Mintzberg et al. (1976) describe them. However, activities that can be categorised as decision communication frequently occur in the empirical findings, and are therefore included in the presentation below. There are three decision communication routines: a) the exploration routine, i.e. "general scanning for information and passive review of what comes unsolicited", b) the investigation routine, i.e. "focused search and research for special-purpose information", and c) the dissemination routine, i.e. disseminating information of the progress of the decision process and the decision outcome (Mintzberg et al. 1976, p 261).

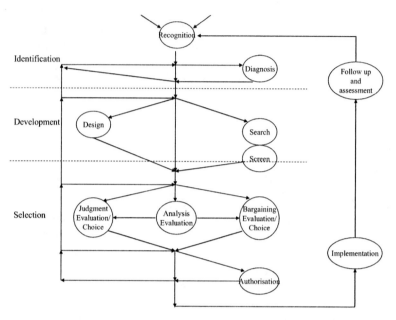

Fig. 4 Decision process model (adapted from Mintzberg et al. 1976; Power 2002)

Establishment of Requirements in a New Project

The Identification Phase

The decision process begins with the *decision recognition routine*. The decision process called 'establishment of requirements in a new project' is activated when the sub system requirements engineer receives new customer and system requirements.

In the *diagnosis routine* the decision-maker "is faced with an array of partially ordered data and a novel situation" (Mintzberg et al. 1976, p 254). In this routine, the requirements engineers conduct several decision-making activities. They find out what the customer requirements and system requirements mean. They investigate of ambiguities in system requirements. They initiate themselves into interfaces provided by the customer. They analyse what is important for the sub system and they do a basic analysis of the functionality. All of these activities are system-related. However, there is also a process-related activity, in which they create a general view of the needs and problems in the process to come.

Two decision communication activities are identified in the diagnosis routine. The requirements engineers conduct investigations trying to understand the problem by searching documents and talking to relevant stakeholders e.g. the customer. The dissemination that takes place is to notify those who are responsible for the entire system when there are problems in the customer requirements.

The Development Phase

In the *search routine* decision-makers seek ready-made solutions and in the closely related *screen routine* these alternatives are reduced to a few feasible ones (Mintzberg et al. 1976). In these routines the requirements engineers compare the new requirements with existing components and find out if something can be reused.

In the *design routine* custom-made solutions are developed and ready-made solutions are modified (Mintzberg et al. 1976). The requirements engineers create use cases and write requirements, such as internal requirements and requirements that specify the interface between the subsystems. Dependences between use cases are also drawn in this routine.

Three decision communication activities are identified. All three are categorized as belonging to the investigation routine. The requirements engineers discuss ideas and solutions with those who are responsible for the entire system. They also discuss with other actors responsible for sub system requirements. Each person documents the result of discussions in their "own" use cases. They also have to stay alert on the customer requirements and system requirements, so that they are covered in the sub system requirements.

The Selection Phase

The *evaluation-choice routine* consists of three different modes: analysis, bargaining, and judgement. In the *analysis mode* the alternatives are evaluated (Mintzberg et al., 1976). In this mode, the requirements engineers trace the requirements to higher level requirements. They check the requirements together with other stakeholders, and also analyse risks together with others. The decision communication that is carried out is to call everyone together for a requirements check.

In the *bargaining mode*, there are several decision-makers with different goals that make the choice (Mintzberg et al. 1976). Two system-related decision matters are dealt with by the requirements engineers:

- Which system requirements belong to which subsystem?
- Which actors are there?

In the *judgement mode*, an individual makes the choice (Mintzberg et al. 1976). Three system-related decision matters are handled by the requirements engineers:

- Can the requirements be settled?
- How is the sub system going to behave and what is it going to look like?
- Which use cases are needed?

There are also work-related decisions that the requirements engineers make. These are:

- Which level of detail is relevant for the requirements and which type of content should they have?
- In which order should the requirements be implemented, i.e. which is the priority of the requirements?
- Which level of effort should an investigation have?

There is also an *authorization routine* in the decision process model of Mintzberg et al. (1976), in which the decision is approved by someone in order to commit the organization to this course of action. We have not found any specific authorizing decision-making activities in our case study.

The Implementation Phase

Decisions trigger actions, and in the implementation phase several decision activities are performed, such as communicating decisions, plan actions, and track performance (Power 2002). In this phase the requirements engineers set up the requirements document that is to be used. They document trade offs, decisions and rationale for decisions together with the functionality. They check design specifications, support the persons who verify and construct the software to interpret the requirements and functions as a service point for all requirements stakeholders. The decision communication that is carried out is dissemination, i.e. the requirements engineers inform others of decisions made.

The Follow-Up and Assessment Phase

In the last phase the consequences of decisions are checked. This may lead to the identification of new problems (Power 2002). In this phase the requirements engineers check the verification and test specifications. They also have user group meetings in order to validate the outcome with the users.

Management of Requirement Changes

The Identification Phase

There are three different ways that requirements engineers *recognise* problems that initiate the decision process called management of requirements changes. There can be error reports from verification or construction, or there can be direct requirement change proposals that get the process going. Requirements errors can also be discovered by the requirements engineer and in such cases he or she carries out dissemination activities in writing an error report.

In the *diagnosis routine*, the requirements engineer check change proposals, investigate error reports, and initiate themselves into input from the customer, depending on what initiated the decision process.

The Development Phase

In the *design routine* the requirements engineers solve error reports, and change/add requirements. We have not identified specific activities that can be categorised as belonging to the search routine or the screen routine.

The Selection Phase

In the *analysis mode* in the *evaluation-choice routine*, the requirements engineers check that a change proposal is not going to become a problem for other sub systems.

In the *bargaining mode*, there is one system-related decision matter. This decision matter is negotiated when the requirement in question is shared with other projects:

- Is a requirement change proposal going to be approved or not?

There are also two work-related decision matters managed here:

- When is the requirement change going to be current?
- When is the requirement change going to be implemented?

In the *judgement mode*, there is one system-related decision matter, dealt with by the individual requirements engineer when the requirement in question is project unique.

- Is a requirement change proposal going to be approved or not?

There is also one work-related decision matter to handle:

- How shall requirements changes be managed?

As in the previously described decision process, we have not identified authorization activities in the requirements change decision process.

The Implementation Phase

In this phase the requirements engineers generate requirements documents and generate documents to the verifiers and constructors that show the differences between former and current requirements documents.

The Follow-Up and Assessment Phase

We have not identified any specific activities in this decision process that can be categorised as belonging to the follow-up and assessment phase.

Comparison and Consequences

In our study we have found two different RE decision processes: a) establishment of requirements in a new project and b) management of requirements changes. Although they have similarities, there are also important differences. Both processes are highly iterative and include several sub-decisions. The first decision process occurs once in the lifetime of a project, while the second decision process occurs frequently. The first process embraces more decision-making activities than the second one. Some of the decision-making activities are shared by the two processes, and some activities are unique to each process. The nature of the tasks conducted by the requirements engineers within these two different decision processes is different. These differences imply that the requirements engineers need different types of decision support depending on which decision process he or she works in. Below, we give two examples of such differences.

The process of establishing requirements includes many creative challenges for the requirements engineer. He or she has to a higher extent than in the process of managing requirements changes to generate ideas. This may need support. Such decision support can be directed towards reducing the effects of human decision-making weaknesses or cognitive limitations in general and stimulate the perception, imagination, and creative insights of the decision-maker (Holsapple and Whinston 1996; Silver 1991).

The process of managing requirements changes is more of a routine process compared to establishing requirements. The stimuli that initiate the process of requirements changes is requirements errors and change proposals. Consequently, the nature of the task is idea evaluation and problem solving. In order to support the problem solving, the ability of a decision-maker to tackle large-scale, time-consuming, complex problems can be extended (Marakas 1999). The quality of problem solving can be enhanced through e.g. better abilities to see relationships between variables and through increased depth and sophistication of analysis (Keen 1989).

Concluding Remarks and Future Research

In this paper, we describe two different RE decision processes: a) establishment of requirements in a new project, and b) management of requirements changes. There are similarities between the processes, but more importantly there are differences. The nature of the differing tasks implies that different decision support is needed within the two processes.

We assume that these two decision processes exist in most, if not all, ISD projects. However, the specific decision-making activities may be unique for each project. At this stage of our research we do not claim to have a complete set of decision-making activities. More research is needed to determine which activities occur in most RE decision processes as well as which activities vary.

The results presented in this paper take us towards our aim to improve decision support to requirements engineers. RE decision-making is complex and can also be project specific. Therefore, future enhancements of RE tools need to focus on improving decision support by concentrating on certain decision matters or a certain activities in a certain decision process. In our future research we will investigate how different RE tools support the processes described in this paper.

References

Alenljung B, Persson A (2004) Supporting Requirement-Based Decision-Making in the Software Engineering Process: A Position Paper. In: Proc of the Tenth International Workshop on Requirements Engineering: Foundation for Software Quality (REFSQ 2004), 7-8 June 2004, Riga Latvia, pp 63-68

Aurum A, Wohlin C (2003) The Fundamental Nature of Requirements Engineering Activities as a Decision-Making Process. Information and Software Technology, vol 45, pp 945-954

Gulliksen J, Lif M, Lind M, Nygren E, Sandblad B (1997) Analysis of Information Utilization (AIU). International Journal of Human-Computer Interaction, vol 9, no 3, pp 255-282

Holsapple CW, Whinston AB (1996) Decision Support Systems: A Knowledge-Based Approach. West Publishing Company, Minneapolis/St. Paul

Holtzblatt K, Jones S (1993) Contextual Inquiry: A Participatory Technique for System Design. In: Schuler D, Namioka A (eds) Participatory Design: Principles and Practices. Lawrence Erlbaum Hillsdale NJ, pp 177-210

Keen PGW (1989) Value Analysis: Justifying Decision Support Systems. In: Sprague RH, Watson HJ (eds) Decision Support Systems: Putting Theory into Practice (2nd ed) Prentice Hall Englewood Cliffs New Jersey, pp 9-35

Kotonya G, Sommerville I (1998) Requirements engineering: Processes and techniques. John Wiley and Sons, Chichester, England

Maguire M (2001) Context of Use within Usability Activities. International Journal of Human-Computer Studies, vol 55, pp 453-483

Marakas GM (1999) Decision Support Systems in the 21st Century. Prentice Hall Upper Saddle River New Jersey

Mintzberg H, Raisinghani D, Théorêt A (1976) The Structure of "Unstructured" Decision Processes. Administrative Science Quarterly, vol 21, pp 246-275

Orasanu J, Connolly T (1993) The Reinvention of Decision Making. In: Klein GA, Orasanu J, Calderwood R, Zsambok CE (eds) Decision Making in Action: Models and Methods. Ablex Publishing Norwood New Jersey, pp 3-20

Parker C, Sinclair M (2001) User-Centred Design Does Make a Difference: The Case of Decision Supports Systems in Crop Production. Behaviour and Information Technology, vol 20, no 6, pp 449-460

Power DJ (2002) Decision Support Systems: Concepts and Resources for Managers. Quorum Books Westport Connecticut

Regnell B, Paech B, Aurum C, Wohlin C, Dutoit A, Natt och Dag J (2001) Requirements Means Decision! - Research Issues for Understanding and Supporting Decision Making in Requirements Engineering. 1st Swedish Conf on Software Engineering Research and Practice Ronneby Sweden, pp 49-52

Ruhe G (2003) Software Engineering Decision Support: A New Paradigm for Learning Software Organizations. Lecture Notes in Computer Science 2640, pp 104-113

Silver MS (1991) Systems That Support Decision Makers: Description and Analysis. John Wiley and Sons Chichester England

Requirements Practices: A Comparative Industrial Survey

June M. Verner[1], Steven J. Bleistein[2], Narciso Cerpa[3] and Karl A. Cox[4]

[1][2][4] Empirical Software Engineering, National ICT Australia Ltd., Sydney, Australia and CSE, University of New South Wales (UNSW), Australia. stevenb@cse.unsw.edu.au, (june.verner, karl.cox)@nicta.com.au
[3] Departamento de Ingeniería de Sistemas, Universidad de Talca, Chile. ncerpa@utalca.cl

Introduction

Evidence suggests that some of the most common and serious problems associated with developing software can be traced back to requirements management [12]. Organizations that implement effective requirements engineering (RE) practices reap multiple benefits, with great rewards coming from the reduction of rework during later development stages and throughout maintenance [26]. We believe that it is important to examine what RE practices are actually used and which of these practices lead to good requirements. If we know what is really going on we are able to position our research within an appropriate context [5]. A survey, developed by Verner and Cerpa was used to describe requirements and project management practices in organizations in the United States and Australia [21, 22, 23, 24]. The survey was originally developed as a result of discussions held with U.S. developers and includes factors they considered important for project success. The Verner and Cerpa survey is used here to provide data on Chilean practitioners' views regarding software project success and failure, and the practices they consider important to software development projects. We compare the Chilean practices with those from the U.S. to help in understanding which practices are universal and which may be culturally dependent.

Our Study

Our survey was conducted with project managers (PMs) both in commercial organizations that develop in-house software and organizations developing software for external clients. Respondents were asked if they considered the project they referenced when answering the questionnaire, 1) to be a success and 2) if it had good requirements at some stage during the development process. We define good requirements as those that are complete and fully understood by the development team and the customers/users [16]. Only questions relating to the development of good requirements are considered here (see Table 1 for the questions asked). Our paper is organized as follows: in the next section we describe our study and discuss some details of the questionnaire responses; we then compare, in Section 4, the results with the U.S. data set described in Verner et al. [25]. The final section presents some conclusions.

Results and Analysis

We received completed questionnaires from 133 respondents, reporting on 133 projects. Our sample is not random but rather a convenience sample of practitioners known to us. Fifty percent of our respondents were developers involved with software for use within their own organizations and fifty percent were practitioners developing software for external clients (i.e., software companies). The organizations developing third party software belong to an association of software companies; several export software products to the rest of Latin America. Overall 76% of projects were regarded as successful and 24% unsuccessful, 91% of projects were development projects (76% successful), and 9% of the projects were small (in terms of effort) maintenance/enhancement projects (75% successful). The percentage of projects by number of full-time IT employees is 1-4 = 52%; 5-9 = 32%; 10-19 = 8%; 20-29 = 1%; 30-39 = 2.5%; 40-99 = 4.5%; (range 1-81, mean 7, median 4). The Chilean projects are much smaller than the U. S. sample described in [25]; they are approximately half the size (U. S. mean was 13 and median 7). We performed chi square tests to determine the degree of association between variables, and correlation analyses to provide the direction of that association. If a pair of variables is significantly associated (<0.05) and positively correlated, we refer to them as *significantly associated*. We mention negative association explicitly when it occurs. In Table 1, our questions are classified as follows: "S" refers to questions that deal with the project sponsor/senior management, "C" to customers and users, "R" to questions directly related to specific requirements issues, and "M" to questions related to the PM and project management.

Project Sponsor/Senior Management

A powerful political sponsor can assure that a project is adequately re-sourced, and that customers and users make sufficient time available for requirements gathering. A high level of sponsor participation can prevent unrealistic schedules, schedule changes or other undermining changes [13, 14]. Loss or failure to properly establish sponsorship can indicate that the project is in jeopardy [13, 16]. The only variable significantly associated with project success was S4 *senior management negatively impacted the project* and using logistic regression with the responses to "S" questions, none of the "S" variables on its own was a useful predictor of projects with good requirements. This section of the questionnaire needs revision in or-der to differentiate between the support given by different kinds of spon-sors and the effects that the support has on good requirements and project success. Effectively we believe that in analysing software projects we need to differentiate between development of software in-house and those or-ganizations whose core business is to produce software for third parties.

Customer/Users

Unrealistic customer and user expectations can arise because projects start with incomplete requirements [23]. Hence, we need an explicit user-inclusion strategy for effective requirements gathering as user support and enlightened involvement are important for ownership [8, 13, 15, 18, 20]. Evidence shows that a high level of customer/user involvement throughout the project, from requirements elicitation to acceptance testing, is neces-sary for project success, and helps with "buy in" to the project [19]. Cus-tomer/user participation can reflect confidence in the development team, positive expectations, and the desire to contribute knowledge of their busi-ness needs. Of course, if there are a large number of customers/users rep-resentative groups of customers/users must be carefully identified. User participation supports more realistic expectations, which reduces conflict [8] although stakeholders often see requirements effort as a disruption to their work [17].

We found a high degree of multi co-linearity among C1, C2, C3, C4, and C5 suggesting that (C1), a high level of customer/user involvement, may result in (C4), commitment and involvement of other stakeholders, (C2), customers and users having a high level of confidence in the devel-opment team, and (C3), involved customers and users will then stay right through the project. Our analysis also suggests that C1 is very important as a high level of customer/user involvement may lead to (C5), they will make adequate time available for requirements gathering, thus implying good requirements. The importance of user involvement in requirements gathering (C5) supports observations of both Clavadetscher [4] and Glass [7]. We did not find that large numbers of customers and users impacted the development of good requirements.

Table 1. Significant Relationships with Good Requirements (133 cases)

Category	Question	Significance
S1	Project began with a committed sponsor	Ns
S2	Sponsor commitment lasted through the project	Ns
S3	Sponsor was involved in project decisions	Ns
S4	Senior management negatively impacted the project	0.008
C1	High level of customer/user involvement	Ns
C2	Other stakeholders were committed and involved	0.045
C3	Involved customers/users stayed right through project	ns
C4	Customers/users had high level of confidence in development team	0.022
C5	Adequate time made available by customers/users for requirements gathering	0.001
C6	Customers/users had realistic expectations	0.006
C7	Customer/user's expectations managed throughout	Ns
C8	Problems caused by large numbers of customers/users	Ns
R1	There was a central repository for requirements	Ns
R2	Project size impacted elicitation of requirements	0.003
R3	Requirements gathered using specific methodology	Ns
R4	Project had a well-defined scope	0.006
R5	Project scope increased during the project	-0.018
R6	Requirements were managed effectively	ns
M1	PM given full authority to manage project	0.050
M2	PM was above average	0.026
M4	PM had a clear vision of the project	0.000
M5	PM really understood the customers problem	Ns
M6	PM communicated well with staff	0.028
M7	PM was experienced in the application area	Ns
M8	Years of experience of the PM < 10	Ns
M9	PM's background (IT, Business, other)	Ns
M10	Risks identified at the beginning of the project	0.005
M11	Risks incorporated into the project plan	0.021
M12	Risks controlled and managed by the PM	Ns

Using logistic regression with the responses to the "C" questions, the best predictor of good requirements was C5 (adequate time was made available by customers and users for requirements gathering) with C6 (customers/users had realistic expectations) which predicted 90% of projects with good requirements, 32% of projects without good requirements, and 77% correctly overall. In summary:

- We were surprised that large numbers of customers and users did not impact upon the establishment of good requirements. This may reflect the relatively small size of the projects in our sample or suggest that there was no difficulty in identifying representative customers and users. Further research will clarify the effects of large numbers of customers and users on the requirements elicitation process.
- Our research supports, as an important requirements determinant, one of the most frequently identified factors for the development of good requirements, the importance of customers/users making adequate time available for requirements gathering.

Requirements Issues

Definition of a requirements development process at the start of a project will normally include the use of a RE methodology [26]. We found that gathering requirements with a specific methodology (R3) was not significantly associated with good requirements. Fifty-six percent of projects had no defined requirements gathering methodology, 13% used only interviews, 4 projects used prototyping, 10 used JAD, and 7 projects used UML to document requirements. Though a central requirements repository is thought to be essential for managing requirements throughout the development process [26] we found that R1, *there was a central repository for requirements,* was not significantly associated with good requirements. This may be because 78% of the projects used a central repository making this variable useless for differentiation between projects. Practitioners had earlier suggested that large projects are less likely to be successful than smaller projects [25]. R2, *project size impacted elicitation of requirements,* was significantly negatively associated with good requirements. This result agrees with [9], suggesting that project size hampers requirements gathering. Wiegers [26] addresses a number of good RE practices including the need for a well-defined project scope. R4, *the project had a well-defined scope,* and R5, *project scope increased during the project,* were both significantly associated with good requirements, R5 negatively. R5, *project scope increased during the project,* was significantly associated (0.000) with R2, *project size impacted elicitation of requirements*. An increase in scope and creeping requirements pose major risks to software projects [11]. If a PM has a sufficient vision of the project and begins with a well-defined scope then this is a first step in managing scope creep [26]. R4, the *project had a well-defined scope,* was significantly associated with M4, the *PM had a clear vision of the project* (0.006), and associated negatively with R5 (*project scope increased during the project*). There is a high degree of multi co-linearity between most of the "R" variables. Analysis suggests that a project with good requirements is a *project that is not so big that requirements elicitation is affected (R2), has a well-defined scope* (R4), *that did not increase during the project* (R5). This means essentially that the PM must understand the problem boundaries. Using logistic regression with the responses to the "R" questions, the best predictor of good requirements was R4 (*the project had a well-defined scope*) with R2 (*project size impacted elicitation of requirements*) which predicted 90% of projects with good requirements, 17% of projects without good requirements, and 73% correctly overall. In summary:

- Our results reinforce research that identifies the importance of a well-defined scope, emphasizing that understanding the problem context and its boundaries is critical to good requirements.
- The importance of a central repository as an aid in the development of good requirements is frequently underestimated. The Chilean organizations appear to understand that this is central to RE contributing to good requirements and ultimately project success.

Project Manager and Project Management

There is a significant relationship between M1, *PM was given full authority to manage the project,* and good requirements. We were puzzled that a good PM suffered as much from interference as a poor PM. M2, *PM was above average*, is significantly associated with good requirements (even when the project suffered from interference). This result is not surprising since "poor management can increase software costs more rapidly than any other factor" [3]. The quality of software project management is characterized by active risk management [9]. This observation is supported by the correlation between responses to questions M10, *risks were identified at the beginning of the project*, M11, *risks were incorporated into the project plan* and M12, *risks were controlled and managed by the PM*, and M2, *the PM was above average*. Even though risk management practices are significantly associated with good requirements [1], most developers and

PMs perceive risk management activities as extra work and expense [10]. However, just identifying the risks without doing something about them is not enough. While 51% of projects had their risks identified, 49% had the risks incorporated into the project plan and the same number had their risks controlled and managed by the PM. Lack of a clear vision leads to poorly defined goals, requirements and specifications, insufficient time planning the project, lack of a project plan, and unrealistic deadlines and budgets [6]. This underscores the importance of understanding requirements beyond micro-level user needs [18]. M4, *PM had a clear vision of the project*, is significantly associated with M5, *the PM really understood the customer's problem*, (0.000), and both are significantly associated with good requirements. Project success is dependent on the quality and effectiveness of communication channels established within the development team [2]. M5, the *PM communicated well with staff*, was significantly associated with good requirements. Common wisdom suggests that M7, *the PM is experienced in the application area*, will increase the chances of a project's success. However, our data did not support this. M7 was not significantly associated with either project success or good requirements. Although practitioners have suggested that an experienced PM is more likely to be associated with a successful project [25] the data did not support this as M8, *PM's years of experience,* was not significantly associated with either project success or good requirements. Practitioners have suggested [25] that a PM with an IT background was more likely to be associated with a successful project [24, 25]. However, our results did not support this as M9, the *background of the PM*, was not significantly associated with either project success or good requirements. There was a high degree of multi co-linearity between most "M" variables. Analysis suggests that a project with a *PM who is given full authority to manage the project* (M1*), who is above average* (M2*), relates well to staff* (M3*), has a clear vision of the project (*M4*), really understands the customer's problems* (M5), and/or *communicates well with staff* (M6), is likely to have good requirements. These results show that, for PMs, vision, communication and relationships with team members are more important than any particular background, underscoring research that stresses the need for a PM to have good interpersonal skills [6, 7]. Using logistic regression with the responses to the "M" questions, the best predictor of good requirements was M4 (*PM had a clear vision of the project*) which predicted 88% of projects with good requirements, 53% of projects without good requirements, and 80% correctly overall. In summary:

- More than one quarter of projects was subjected to interference. When interference occurred, it was mainly related to staffing issues, and adequate staffing is significantly associated with good requirements.
- The importance of M4, *PM had a clear vision of the project*, reinforces the importance of project scope, but includes an extra dimension; the importance of knowing expected business outcomes.
- Effective communication is frequently suggested as a key to good requirements, and our analysis supports this.
- Because M12, *risks were controlled and managed by the PM*, was not significantly associated with project success we suspect that much of the risk management for these relatively small projects was relatively informal.

Comparison of U.S. and Chilean Data

With respect to the "C" questions, our Chilean respondents agreed with the U.S. respondents [25] regarding the importance of committed and involved stakeholders, customers/users having a high level of confidence in the development team, adequate time being made available by the customers/users for requirements gathering, and customers/users with realistic expectations. Our respondents also agreed with the U.S. respondents that large numbers of customers and users did not cause them requirements problems. They disagreed with the U.S. respondents when it comes to the involvement of customers/users, and the importance of managing customer/user expectations; however, this may be explained by the fact that 50% of the Chilean projects were for third parties in which the primary point of contact may not be a customer and a number of users but rather a sales or account manager. With respect to the "R" questions our respondents agreed with the U.S. respondents that to get good requirements important factors are: project size, and a well-defined scope, that does not increase during the project for good requirements. However, they disagreed on the importance of a central repository and effective requirements management. Interestingly, the majority of Chilean projects used a central repository suggesting that in this case this variable is not a useful differentiator between projects with good requirements and those without. Further research using a more targeted question on requirements management, suited to third party development, may clarify this issue. Neither group of respondents considered that the use of a specific requirements elicitation methodology was significant for good requirements. With respect to the "M" questions both groups of respondents agreed that to get good requirements we need: a PM with full authority to manage the project, who is above average and has a clear vision of the project, who communicates well with staff, and identifies risks at the start of the project. They also agreed that a PM's experience in the application area, number of years of experience, and background were not important to getting good requirements. However, they disagreed on the importance of a PM really understanding the customer's problem, control of risks, and incorporating risks into the project plan. To clarify the importance of the latter three factors requires further research with both in-house and third party development projects. The best prediction equation for good requirements using the Chilean data is M4 the *PM had a clear vision of the project.* This variable predicted 88% of projects with good requirements, 53% of projects without good requirements, and 80% of projects correctly overall. The best prediction equation for the U.S. data used C4 (*customers/users had high level of confidence in development team*), R4 (*project had a well-defined scope*), and M12 (*risks were controlled and managed by the PM*). Using this equation to predict the state of the requirements in the Chilean data we obtain predictions of 94% of projects with good requirements, 42% of projects without good requirements, and 81% of projects correctly overall. The Chilean data set had fewer failed projects than the U.S. data set resulting in less satisfactory prediction of projects without good requirements. We recognize some limitations of this study. Surveys are based on self-reported data which reflects people's perceptions, not what might have actually happened. Because we surveyed software developers our results are limited to their knowledge, attitudes, and beliefs regarding the projects and PMs with which they were involved. The dominance of small projects may have biased our results with the Chilean projects smaller than the U.S. projects in terms of the number of personnel employed [25].

Conclusions and Further Research

The questionnaire designed by Verner and Cerpa was specifically designed to investigate practices for in-house software development. As such, the questions regarding *sponsors* may not be appropriate for software projects that are developing software for other organizations. This is because the *sponsor* was assumed to be *internal* to the organization, supporting an *internal* project. In the case of organizations that supply software to other organizations the dynamics of a sponsor are different. A software project for a customer may have an *internal* sponsor. At the same time, an *external* sponsor, who is likely to be important for requirements elicitation, may be present within the client organization. Because the questionnaire used was designed elsewhere specifically for in-house software projects the questions regarding sponsorship may have solicited responses difficult to interpret in this study. As about half of the Chilean projects are outsourced, and the outsourcing company may be part of a supply chain, there is less opportunity for our developers to understand the customers' problem and to interact with them. Analysis of the data from both groups of respondents supports research that suggests the following factors lead to good requirements: 1) the importance of committed and involved stakeholders, 2) customers/users with a high level of confidence in the development team, 3) adequate time being made available by the customers/user for requirements gathering, 4) customers/users with realistic expectations, 5) a PM with full authority to manage the project, 6) a PM who is above average, 7) a PM with a clear vision of the project, 8) a PM who communicates well with staff, and 9) a PM who identifies risks at the start of the project. Contrary to suggestions made by developers and/or cited in the literature, analysis of both groups of data suggests that the following factors are not important for good requirements: 1) large numbers of customers/users, 2) use of a specific requirements elicitation methodology, 3) PMs experience in the application area, 4) PMs years of experience, and 5) PMs background. There was disagreement on 1) the involvement of customers/users, 2) the importance of managing customer/user expectations, 3) the importance of a central repository and 4) effective requirements management. However, further research on these factors should clarify which factors are culturally dependent, and which depend on the type of development (in-house or third party) undertaken. Overall, these results underscore research suggesting PMs vision, and communication with team members are more important than any particular background, or requirements engineering methodology they may use.

Acknowledgement

This research was supported by a FONDECYT grant (project 1030785) from CONICYT Chile.

References

[1]   Addison T, Vellabh S (2002) Controlling Software Project Risks – An Empirical Study of Methods Used by Experienced Project Managers. Proc. of SAICSIT, pp 128-140

[2] Bandinetti S, Di Nitto E, Fuggetta A (1996) Supporting Co-Operation in the SPADE-1 Environment. IEEE TSE, vol 22, no 12, pp 841-865

[3] Boehm BW, Basili VR (2001) Software Defect Reduction: Top 10 List. IEEE Computer, vol 34, no 1, pp 135-137

[4] Clavadetscher C (1998) User Involvement: Key to Success. IEEE Software, vol 15, Issue 2, p 30, 32

[5] Davis, A, Hickey A (2002) Requirements Researchers: Do We Practice What We Preach? Requirements Engineering Journal, vol 7, pp 107-111

[6] DeMarco T, Lister T (2003) Waltzing With Bears. Dorset House Publishing New York NY

[7] DeMarco and Lister Peopleware (1987) Productive Projects and Teams. Dorset House Publishing Co NY

[8] Gause D, Weinberg G (1989) Exploring Requirements: Quality before Design. Dorset House NY

[9] Glass RL (1998) How Not To Prepare For A Consulting Assignment And Other Ugly Consultancy Truths. Communications of the ACM, vol 41, issue 12, pp 11-13

[10] Glass RL (2001) Frequently Forgotten Fundamental Facts about Software Engineering. IEEE Software, May/June, pp 112, 110, 111

[11] Jones TC (1994) Assessment and Control of Software Risks. Prentice Hall Englewood Cliffs NJ

[12] Leffingwell D, Widrig D (2000) Managing Software Requirements: A Unified Approach. Addison-Wesley

[13] McConnell S (1996) Rapid Development. Microsoft Press Redmond Washington

[14] McKeen JD, Guimares T (1997) Successful Strategies for User Participation in Systems Development. Journal of Management Information Systems, vol 14, no 2, pp 133-150

[15] Paulk M, Curtis B, Chrissis M, Webster C (1993) Capability Maturity Model for Software. Technical Report, CMU/SEI-93-TR-024, Software Engineering Institute, Carnegie Mellon

[16] Pressman R (2000) Software Engineering: A Practitioners Approach. Adapted by Darryl Ince, 5th edition, McGraw Hill London

[17] Robertson J, Robertson S (2000) Requirements Management: A Cinderella Story. Requirements Engineering Journal, vol 5, no 2, pp 134-136

[18] Roy V, Aubert B (2003) A Dream Project Turns Nightmare: How Flawless Software Never Got Implemented. Annals of cases on Information technology Idea Group Publishing, pp 98-111

[19] Standish Group (1999) Chaos: A Recipe for Success. Standish Group International

[20] Tackett B, van Doren B (1999) Process Control for Error-Free Software: A Software Success Story. IEEE Software, vol 16, no 3, pp 24-29

[21] Verner JM, Evanco WM (2005) In–house Software Development: What Software Project Management Practices Lead to Success? IEEE Software, vol 22, issue 1, pp 86-93

[22] Verner JM, Cox K, Bleistein S, Cerpa N (2004) Requirements Engineering and Software Project Success: An Industrial Survey in Australia and the U.S. Proc of AWRE, Adelaide Australia

[23] Verner JM, Overmyer SP, McCain KW (1999) In the 25 Years Since the Mythical Man-Month What Have We Learned About Project Management? Information and Software Technology, vol 41, no 14, pp 1021-1026

[24] Verner JM, Cerpa N (2005) Australian Software Development: What Software Project Management Practices Lead to Success? IEEE Proc of ASWEC, Ed Paul Strooper, Brisbane Australia, March 29-31, pp 70-77

[25] Verner JM, Cox KA, Bannerman PL, Bleistein SJ (2005) How Do You Get Good Requirements: An Empirical Study. Submitted to TSE March 2005

[26] Wiegers K (2003) Software Requirements, Second Edition. Microsoft Press Redmond WA

An Empirical Study Identifying High Perceived Value Requirements Engineering Practices

Mahmood Niazi, Karl A. Cox and June M. Verner

Empirical Software Engineering, National ICT Australia Ltd., Sydney, Australia and CSE, University of New South Wales (UNSW), Australia. (mahmood.niazi, karl.cox, june.verner)@nicta.com.au

Introduction

In order to reduce requirements problems many Requirements Engineering (RE) practices have been suggested [1]. Though there have already been many surveys identifying requirements problems (e.g. [2], [3]), as researchers, we need to be constantly aware of what is really going on in practice and to understand what RE practices are perceived to be useful by practitioners. This will enable us to position our research within an appropriate context [4]. It is important to discover which practices will benefit an organization, as research has shown that effective RE practices provide multiple benefits including help in keeping delivery times and product quality under control [1; 5].

Sommerville et al [1] proposed a number of practices that lead to RE process improvement and that ultimately should lead to business benefits [6]. Because these practices are derived from existing standards, studies of requirements processes and from practical experience [1], we investigate their impact on the software development process to see if they really have a perceived value.

Sommerville et al [1] suggest that RE practices can be divided into several broad RE process categories. In order to test our thesis we investigate three of their categories: requirements documentation, requirements elicitation and requirements management. We begin our research with these particular categories because they typically receive less attention in the RE literature than the more technology-driven categories such as analysis, modeling and specification.

We conducted a study with ten Australian software development companies; an understanding the perceived value of each RE practice across different companies may help with more effective RE process improvement. We believe that where respondents from different companies identify a practice as having a high perceived value then that practice should be seriously considered for its importance in process improvement. If different software development companies use the same practice, it is obviously important to the practitioners involved. If practitioners perceive that a practice has value they are more likely to use it.

In order to improve the RE process Sommerville et al. [7; 8] have suggested a requirements maturity model. This model is based upon 66 good requirements practices, classified as basic, intermediate and advanced. There are 36 basic practices that are concerned with fundamental activities that are required to gain control of the RE process. The 21 intermediate practices are mostly concerned with the use of methodical approaches and tools. The 9 advanced practices are concerned with methods such as formal specification used typically for critical systems development.

Thus far, little research has been conducted in order to validate the requirements maturity model. Niazi and Shastry [9] conducted an empirical study of requirements problems as identified by 22 requirements practitioners. The results indicated that there were no significant differences in the numbers of problems faced by companies with mature and immature RE processes. However, it was found that the problems cited by mature companies were related to organizational issues, e.g. lack of training, complexity of application and communications etc. The type of problems cited within immature companies were related to the technical aspects of the RE process, e.g. undefined requirements process.

More recently, Sommerville and Ransom [6] conducted an empirical study with 9 companies in order to evaluate the requirements maturity model [7] and to assess if requirements process improvement leads to business improvement. They concluded that the "RE process maturity model is useful in supporting maturity assessment and in identifying process improvements and there is some evidence to suggest that process improvement leads to business benefits. However, whether these business benefits were a consequence of the changes to the RE process or whether these benefits resulted from side-effects of the study such as greater self-awareness of business processes remain an open question" [6]. However, no studies have been conducted to investigate the practices suggested in the requirements maturity model and if these practices are those that practitioners commonly use in their companies, i.e., are perceived by practitioners as having a high value. Three research questions have motivated the research reported here:

RQ1. What requirements documentation, elicitation and management practices do companies commonly use in their projects?
RQ2. What practices have the highest perceived value?

RQ3. Are Sommerville's classifications of Basic, Intermediate and Advanced practices appropriate?

The contribution of this work is to identify what practices are perceived as useful and should be considered when designing RE improvement processes. If we identify what are the most commonly used practices in the software industry we will be able to build a better understanding of the relative perceived value of the set of RE practices we have investigated. This will assist us in validating Sommerville's list of RE categories and provide an initial assessment of the appropriateness of his three classification levels.

This paper is organised as follows: Section 2 discusses the definition of perceived value. Section 3 describes the design of our study. In Section 4 our findings are presented, analysed and discussed. Section 5 discusses threats to validity. Section 6 presents conclusions and suggested future research.

Perceived Value

In this particular study we define 'perceived value' to mean the extent to which a RE practice is used because it is perceived by practitioners to bring benefit either to the project, or to the organization. This may be considered to be a subjective view as it provided by the respondents we interviewed. However, our respondents are considered to be requirements experts within their organizations. As such, we can assume that their opinion is grounded in significant experience of real world RE practices.

In order to describe the notion of perceived value within RE practices, it is important to decide on the "criticality" of a perceived value. For this purpose, we have used the following criterion:

- If a perceived value of a RE practice is cited in the interviews with a frequency of >=50%, then we treat it as critical.

A similar approach has been used in the literature [10; 11]. Rainer and Hall [10] identified important factors in software process improvement with the criterion that "if the majority of respondents (>=50%) thought that the factor had a major impact then we treat that factor as having a major impact".

The perceived values of RE practices can act as a guide for RE practitioners when designing RE processes because it will be easier to encourage the use of practices that are commonly used elsewhere and hence have higher perceived values. It will be more difficult to convince practitioners that practices with low perceived values are useful.

Study Design

Interviews were conducted with 10 Australian software development companies with one interview per company. The respondent chosen from each organisation was considered to be the organization's most expert requirements engineer and hence was the most appropriate person to answer questions about requirements practices. Thus the sample is not random but a convenience sample because we sought a response from a person with a specific role within the organization. The target population in this research consists of software-producing organizations that produce both in-house software and software for third parties. It is important to note that our data was collected from practitioners who were tackling RE issues on a daily basis; therefore we have high confidence that they accurately reported what was happening in their organization. In the interviews we asked practitioners to choose from four types of assessment for each practice investigated [1]:

- Standardized: A practice has a documented standard and is always followed as part of the organization's software development process i.e., it is mandatory. We refer to this practice as having a 'high' perceived value.
- Normal use: This means that the practice is widely followed in the organization but is not mandatory. We refer to this practice as having a 'medium' perceived value.
- Used at the discretion of the project manager (PM): Some PMs may have introduced the practice only for that project. This practice is described as 'low' perceived value.
- Never used: The practice is never or rarely applied and is a 'zero' perceived value.

In order to analyse the perceived value of each requirements practice, the occurrence of a perceived value (high, medium, low, zero) in each interview transcript was recorded. The frequency of each data variable was then included in frequency tables. By comparing the occurrences of one requirements practice's perceived values obtained from the interview transcripts against the occurrences of other requirements practices perceived value, the relative importance of each requirements practice can be calculated. This methodology has been successfully used in previous research [11; 12].

Findings

Requirements Documentation Practices

Table 1 presents the list of requirements documentation practices discussed in the interviews. The most common standardised requirements documentation practice (7 out of 10) is to state a business case for a project (RD4). Often, the accounting department and/or the CIO will insist that a project will not be funded unless a business case is made for the system, i.e., the system must meet an organizational business goal. What is surprising is that two organizations did not do this at all. We consider this activity should be required for every project. Senior sponsor support and customer/user participation have been shown to be important for software project success [13]. A senior sponsor is likely to exert him or herself to provide ongoing support for a system that will meet an important business goal.

The majority of companies in our sample have *defined standard structures for requirements documents* (RD1). As Table 1 shows, many companies include an overview section in the requirements document that *summarizes the purpose of the system and principal system requirements* (RD3). RD4, RD1 and RD3 were most often found to be standardized practices and can be considered to be high-perceived value practices.

Table 1. Requirements documents practices identified through the empirical study

ID	Type	Practice	Type of Assessment			
			SU	NU	DU	NE
RD1	Basic	Define a standard document structure	5	3	1	1
RD2	Basic	Explain how to use the document	3	3	1	3
RD3	Basic	Include a summary of the requirements	5	3	1	1
RD4	Basic	Make a business case for the system	7	1	0	2
RD5	Basic	Define specialized terms	3	5	2	0
RD6	Basic	Make document layout readable	4	5	1	0
RD7	Basic	Help readers find information	3	4	2	1
RD8	Basic	Make the document easy to change	4	5	0	1

SU = Standardized use, NU = Normal use, DU = Discretion use, NE = Never use

The practices RD5, RD6 and RD8 can be considered to be 'normal use' practices. This means that these practices are widely followed in the companies but are not mandatory. We did not find any RE practices with high percentages for 'discretionary use' and 'never used' categories.

We find it strange that there are organizations that do not *define a standard document structure* (RD1), do not *provide guidance for readers* (RD7), and do not *make the document easy to change* (RD8) as standard. Documents that present an unfamiliar structure can be difficult to read, follow and update.

Using the criterion described in Section 3, we have identified three requirements documents practices (RD1, RD3 and RD4) as having a 'high' perceived value. We have also identified three requirements documents practices (RD5, RD6 and RD8) as having a 'medium' perceived value. All these practices are considered *basic* by Sommerville. Our results indicate that the organizations questioned have reasonable control over their requirements documentation processes.

Requirements Elicitation Practices

Table 2 shows that the state of RE elicitation practice is still fair at best, confirming previous findings [14]. Sixty per cent of respondents stated that their organization carries out a feasibility study (RE1) as mandatory before investing resources in eliciting requirements. 30% of respondents stated this was normal practice. Many companies define the proposed system's operating environment (RE5) during or before requirements elicitation. It is critical to determine the scope of the environment where the system is to have its effect [15]. However, it is also critical to manage that scope, as more about the problem is understood, and more requirements are elicited [14]. We were surprised that only half the respondents stated their organization identifies abstract high-level business goals, i.e. use business concerns to drive requirements elicitation (RE6) and then uses them as drivers for requirements elicitation as standard practice. This is critical for business-IT alignment, something that has proven time and again to be the biggest IT concern for CIOs [16]. These findings do not agree with those in section 5.1 where the majority of respondents state that they include a business case for the system in their documents. It might be the case that these business cases are not always acting as the drivers for requirements elicitation. We speculate this might be because the business case does not clearly express business goals or objectives but only considers financial implications – what savings can be made irrespective of whether this meets the business objectives of the organization. Since business objectives and goals drive requirements elicitation, we view failure to standardise this practice as a serious concern.

Although it is not mandatory, many *companies identify and consult anyone who benefits directly or indirectly from the system being developed* (RE3). This is 'normal' practice. The risk of not getting the requirements right are amplified if key stakeholders are not consulted [14]. The organizations we sampled also *record requirements sources* (RE4) and *record requirements rationale* (RE8) as "Normal Use" requirements elicitation practices.

Table 2. Requirements elicitation practices as identified through an empirical study

ID	Type	Practice	Type of Assessment			
			SU	NU	DU	NE
RE1	Basic	Assess System Feasibility	6	3	0	1
RE2	Basic	Be sensitive to organizational and political consideration	4	4	0	2
RE3	Basic	Identify and consult system stakeholders	2	7	1	0
RE4	Basic	Record requirements sources	3	5	1	1
RE5	Basic	Define the system's operating environment	5	2	2	1
RE6	Basic	Use business concerns to drive requirements elicitation	5	2	3	0
RE7	Intermediate	Look for domain constraints	2	4	1	3
RE8	Intermediate	Record requirements rationale	1	5	2	2
RE9	Intermediate	Collect requirements from multiple viewpoints	1	4	4	1
RE10	Intermediate	Prototype poorly understood requirements	1	4	3	2
RE11	Intermediate	Use scenarios to elicit requirements	0	4	5	1
RE12	Intermediate	Define operational processes	4	2	3	1
RE13	Advanced	Reuse requirements	2	2	5	1

The two other requirements elicitation practices, i.e. *use scenarios to elicit requirements* (RE11) and *reuse requirements* (RE13) are used at the discretion of project manager in many companies. We found it strange that scenarios are used mainly at the discretion of the project manager – none use scenarios are standard practice. Though the context of each project should determine what requirements tool is useful [15], the RE research community has invested a great deal of effort promoting the role scenarios play in requirements elicitation, e.g. [17; 18]. If this survey is a reasonable reflection on RE practice, it appears that there is still a wide gap between research and practice.

We are not surprised at the low standardized or normal levels for the re-use of requirements. It is difficult to reuse a requirement unless one's context is the same. For organizations conducting product line development or packaged software, reuse is fundamentally important; standard features can be re-applied in the next product release. However, for organizations engaging in new development projects, reuse is not as straightforward, especially smaller organizations who do not typically have processes and process repositories in place [19].

We are concerned that only 60% of respondents say their organization attempts to *identify domain constraints* (RE7) as a matter of normal or standardized practice. Defining the boundary of one's problem, either physical or technical, has been shown to be fundamental to software project success, e.g. [5; 14; 15]. Failure to determine one's boundary will almost certainly lead to scope creep or technical failure.

Three elicitation practices have a 'high' perceived value. Clearly a feasibility study is important to all projects (RE1), as is defining the system's operating environment (RE5) and using the business objectives to drive requirements elicitation (RE6). These are all basic practices and are fundamental to success. Three practices have 'medium' perceived value (RE3, RE4 and RE8). Though identification and consultation with stakeholders (RE3) is only considered a medium value practice, we view it as fundamental that all key stakeholders be consulted. This should be a mandatory practice and be of high value. Two requirements elicitation practices have a 'low' perceived value (R11 and R13).

Our survey shows that it is the basic practices that are done reasonably well. The only intermediate or advanced practice that is relatively common is *define operational processes* (RE12). Perhaps this should be considered a basic practice.

Requirements Management Practices

The majority of organizations in our sample (see table 3) define policies for requirements change management (RM6). Properly organized requirements change management is a critical factor for successful project outcomes. Ad hoc change management can lead to escalating requirements, uncontrolled scope creep and potentially uncontrolled system development. Global system requirements (RM7) set out desirable or essential properties of the system as a whole. They were identified by the 50% of our sample as standardized, with 30% as normal use. Requirements management practices identify volatile requirements (RM8) is used in the majority of organizations but is not mandatory though inability to manage changing and/or volatile requirements is recognised as a leading cause of project failure [18]. The majority of rejected requirements are recorded (RM9) at the discretion of the project manager in many companies. This is curious considering that requirements typically change [5] and discarded requirements are often reused in later product releases or increments, particularly in product line development.

Thirty percent of organizations do not *use a requirements management database* (RM5). This research finding agrees with [14] who found that 40% of organizations did not use a requirements management database (RMDB). Despite the fact that RMDBs are widely available and simple to use, organizations are still prepared to risk poorly managed requirements. We believe that a RMDB should be mandatory for every project, no matter how simple it might appear to be and we would classify this as basic practice. Without a repository of any kind, change management, for instance, becomes far more difficult to manage though Sommerville rates this a basic practice. The fact that only 30% of respondents reported that a RMDB was standardized in their organization indicates that the message is failing to get through.

We have identified two requirements management practices (RM6, RM7) to have 'high' perceived value. It is recognised that *defining a change management policy* (RM6) is a critical success factor [13; 14] and we view this as such a fundamental practice we would label it Basic. *Identifying volatile requirements* (RM8) has a 'medium' perceived value. However, identifying volatile requirements is important since project failure due to inability to manage unstable requirements is recognised [20]. We note that the requirements management practice, *record rejected requirements* (RM9), has 'low' perceived value and that Sommerville considers this an advanced practice. We believe it is important to keep a repository of discarded requirements as the RE process is often iterative, new requirements can be those that were previously discarded. Keeping a record of these will no doubt save effort and money. Of course, a repository or requirements database is fundamental to the success of this practice.

Table 3. Requirements management practices as identified through an empirical study

ID	Type	Practice	Type of Assessment			
			SU	NU	DU	NE
RM1	Basic	Uniquely identify each requirement	4	2	2	2
RM2	Basic	Define policies for requirements management	1	4	2	3
RM3	Basic	Define traceability policies	2	2	3	3
RM4	Basic	Maintain a traceability manual	2	3	3	2
RM5	Intermediate	Use a database to manage requirements	3	4	0	3
RM6	Intermediate	Define change management policies	6	2	1	1
RM7	Intermediate	Identify global system requirements	5	3	1	1
RM8	Advanced	Identify volatile requirements	2	5	2	1
RM9	Advanced	Record rejected requirements	2	2	5	1

Validity

Construct validity is concerned with whether or not the measurement scales represent the attributes being measured. The attributes are taken from a substantial body of previous research [1; 7] and further studies [21]. The responses from the practitioners interviewed show that all the attributes considered (the questions) were relevant to their workspace, even if some practices were not conducted. The practices discussed are perceived as important in the day-to-day activities of real projects. External validity is concerned with the generalization of the results to other environments than the one in which the initial study was conducted [22]. External validity was examined by interviewing practitioners from ten different environments. Though a sample of ten is small and generalizability to the whole software engineering community is problematic, our findings confirm results found in other surveys, such as 30 percent of organizations do not use a repository to manage requirements [14].

We recognize some limitations of the study. Interviews are based on self-reported data that reflects what people say happened, not necessarily what they actually did or experienced. Our results are limited to the respondents' knowledge, attitudes, and beliefs regarding the projects with which they are involved. However, 4 organizations had fewer than 5 people in their RE teams, 4 had 6 on average and 2 had between 8 and 15. As such, we believe that the respondents were well informed on most RE activities carried out within their organizations.

Conclusions

We reported on an empirical study of RE practices in ten Australian organizations that develop software. Four types of RE practice usage were identified that have led us to the notion of a 'perceived value' associated with each RE practice (from high value to no value). To have a perceived high value, we refer to a practice that is used as standard across all projects, as opposed to a very successful practice that was used on just one project. Our survey reviewed the practices recommended by Sommerville et al. [1; 6].

We believe companies use RE practices on the basis of the perceived value of that practice. This focus on perceived value associated with each RE practice, offers RE practitioners opportunities for implementing practices to improve a company's requirements development capabilities. By analysing the degree to which companies use each of the RE practices, we can identify a number of critical RE practices for RE practitioners. Our results provide advice to RE managers on what practices to consider when designing RE process improvement.

Another research goal is to explore if Sommerville's categorization of practices (basic, intermediate, advanced) are reflected in actual use. We focus specifically requirements documentation, elicitation and management practices. Most organisations perceived their documentation practices to be of high value. They recognised the need for a business case and an overview of the system's requirements. In terms of elicitation, most organisations conducted feasibility studies as mandatory or normal practice. But only half used business concerns to drive the requirements elicitation process as mandatory. Use of scenarios is not considered a high-value practice despite the emphasis the RE research community has placed on scenarios [1; 6]. In terms of management, organisations established change management policies and identified global requirements as the most important practices. We find it surprising that use of a requirements repository or database is not mandatory in 70% of the organizations surveyed. Evidence shows that such use is a significant project success factor, e.g. [13; 14]. It seems that industry is not learning why projects succeed or fail. Failure to conduct post-mortem reviews is one reason for this [13]. We consider use of a repository to be so fundamental that it can only be considered a basic practice. Without a database it becomes much more difficult to implement change management, to track volatile requirements, to manage version control, to produce documents. We suggest a re-examination of Sommerville's classification of basic, intermediate and advanced practices to bring them into line with evidence of current practices. In summary, we found,

- Requirements documentation practice was either standardised or normal practice, and at a basic level, in agreement with Sommerville.
- Elicitation practices are only fair, at best. Most basic practices were standard or normal. Surprisingly, few practices were considered mandatory.
- Requirements management practices are poor. Though Sommerville views change management policy definition and use of a requirements database as intermediate practices, we view both as basic because they are fundamental to project success.

Acknowledgements

Acknowledgements to MS Sudha Shastry for her contribution to this paper.

References

[1]   Sommerville I, Sawyer P (1997) Requirements Engineering - A good Practice Guide. Wiley
[2]   Neill CJ, Laplante PA (2003) Requirements Engineering: State of the Practice. IEEE Software November/December, pp 40-45
[3]   Hall T, Beecham S, Rainer A (2002) Requirements Problems in Twelve Software Companies: An Empirical Analysis. IEE Proc Software, pp 153-160
[4]   Davis A, Hickey A (2002) Requirements Researchers: Do We Practice What We Preach? Requirements Engineering Journal, vol 7, pp 107-111
[5]   Wiegers KE (2003) Software Requirements, Second Edition. Microsoft Press, Redmond WA
[6]   Sommerville I, Jane R (2005) An Empirical Study of Industrial Requirements Engineering Process Assessment and Improvement. ACM Transactions on Software Engineering and Methodology, vol 14, no 1, pp 85-117
[7]   Sommerville I, Sawyer P, Viller S (1997) Requirements Process Improvement Through the Phased Introduction of Good Practice. Software Process-Improvement and Practice, vol 3, pp 19-34

[8] Sommerville I, Sawyer P, Viller S (1998) Improving the Requirements Process. Fourth International Workshop on Requirements Engineering: Foundation of Software Quality, pp 71-84

[9] Niazi M, Shastry S (2003) Role of Requirements Engineering in Software Development Process: An empirical study. IEEE International Multi-Topic Conference (INMIC03), pp 402-407

[10] Rainer A, Hall T (2002) Key Success Factors for Implementing Software Process Improvement: a Maturity-Based Analysis. Journal of Systems & Software, vol 62, pp 71-84

[11] Niazi M, Wilson D, Zowghi D (2005) A Maturity Model for the Implementation of Software Process Improvement: An empirical study. Journal of Systems and Software, vol 74, no 2, pp 155-172

[12] Niazi M, Wilson D, Zowghi D (2005) A Framework for Assisting the Design of Effective Software Process Improvement Implementation Strategies. Accepted for publication: Journal of Systems and Software

[13] Verner J, M EW (2005) In-house Software Development: What Software Project Management Practices Lead to Success? IEEE Software, vol 22, no 1, pp 86-93

[14] Verner J, Cox K, Bleistein S, Cerpa N (2005) Requirements Engineering and Software Project Success: An Industrial Survey in Australia and the US. Australian Journal of Information Systems (to appear Sept 2005)

[15] Jackson M (1995) Software Requirements and Specifications. Addison-Wesley/ACM Press

[16] Luftman J, Maclean E (2004) Key Issues for IT Executives. MIS Quarterly Executive, vol 3, pp 89-104

[17] Alexander I, Maiden NE (2004) Scenarios, Stories, Use Cases. Wiley

[18] Carroll JE (1995) Scenario-Based Design: Envisioning Work and Technology in System Development. Wiley

[19] Kamsties E, Hormann K, Schlich M (1998) Requirements Engineering in Small and Medium Enterprises. Requirements Engineering, vol 3, no 2, pp 84-90

[20] Briand L, Wust J, Lounis H (2001) Replicated Case Studies for Investigating Quality Factors in Object Oriented Designs. Empirical Software Engineering, vol 6, no 1, pp 11-58

[21] Niazi M (2005) An Instrument to Measure the Maturity of Requirements Engineering Process. PROFES. Oulu Finland

[22] Regnell B, Runeson P, Thelin T (2000) Are the Perspectives Really Different-Further Experimentation on Scenario-Based Reading of Requirements. Empirical Software Engineering, vol 5, no 4, pp 331-356

A First Step towards General Quality Requirements for e-Records

Erik Borglund

Department of Information Technology and Media, Mid Sweden University, Sweden. erik.borglund@miun.se

Introduction

Medical journals, police reports, and company registrations are example of records, recorded information. There is a widespread changeover from paper based records towards electronic records (e-records) in many organizations. Records in general should be reliable and authentic, i.e. be trustworthy. According to Duranti (2001) e-records have difficulties to be trustworthy dependent on the lack of use of both archival and record requirements.

E-records may be preserved for ever, this raises a question of how should information systems that are going to create, and manage e-records, be designed and developed to maintain the trustworthiness of e-records during long term preservation. There have been attempt to design and develop information systems managing e-records that have been less successful. Grimson (2001) gives examples of electronic healthcare records which have proven that it is problematic to build a workable information system, managing e-records. Access over time and preservation are issues, which have been of limited interest when designing electronic healthcare record systems. Records vary in type and the uses of records also are varying, and are difficult to predict, which makes development of information systems managing e-records difficult. According to Holgersson (2001) some of the information systems managing records in the Swedish police, filter information which negatively influence possibilities to trust and make correct decisions based on those e-records.

During system and software development requirements are vital component for a successful development process (e.g. Pressman & Ince, 2000). Requirements can be divided into functional and non-functional requirements (Borg, 2004; Carlshamre, 2001; Kotonya & Sommerville, 1998). Non functional requirements are about quality dimensions of the system and the software. The question of interest in this research is what quality requirements are needed to maintain trustworthiness of e-records? e-records can due to the preservation need, be compelled to last longer than the information system managing the e-record. This makes it difficult to separate quality requirements for e-records, and the information system/software where the e-records are created or managed.

Both the Swedish Emergency Management Agency and The Swedish Agency for Public Management have found that there are no guidelines for design and development of information system that enable long term preservation of e-records (Krisberedskapsmyndigheten, 2005; Statskontoret, 2003). Such guidelines could involve general quality requirements for e-records.

This purpose of this paper is to present a set of quality requirements aimed to maintain the trustworthiness of e-records, results from a case study of the development project of an electronic archive system at Swedish Companies Registration Office (SCRO). The quality requirements are a first step towards general quality requirements for e-records.

Research Site and Research Method

The organisation where the study was performed is Swedish Companies Registration Office (SCRO), an agency under the Ministry of Industry. The SCRO keep records over every company in Sweden, which include new registration of companies (trade and industry records), changes within companies, decision-making of liquidations, received annual reports, and a register of corporate mortgages (Bolagsverket, 2004). The SCRO is also responsible for making the information in the trade and industry records available for the public.

The trade and industry records are archives of SCRO. There is a large case flow at the SCRO, they handle 600000 cases each year, register more than 50000 new companies, and have more than 960000 business enterprises in their archives. The physical archive consists of more than 20000 running meters of records (Bolagsverket, 2004).

Since 2004 the SCRO are scanning all incoming records, and transform them into TIFF[1] pictures. The SCRO have an implemented e-service for registration of private companies. People can register private business companies using Internet, the service will be developed further to cover all possible communication between people/companies and the SCRO. This e-service only produces e-records. The archives of the SCRO are one of their

---

[1] TIFF is an approved format for digital objects by the Swedish National Archives.

main business and need to be managed correct. The e-records, both the ones that have been transformed and those that are electronic in original are managed in an own developed electronic archives solution. Due to regulations from Swedish National Archives, all records in the main archives should be kept forever.

The SCRO aim to make a changeover from their hybrid usage of both e-records and paper based records to a fully use of e-records. During the autumn of 2004 the SCRO started a development project, BILLY, which aimed to develop a durable electronic archive solution. The project was initiated by the need to change storage medium for the existent electronic archive solution. SCRO also needed to follow the recommendations given by the Swedish National Archives to order the archive following a archive description standard called ISAD(G) and in suitable parts implement the OAIS model. The OAIS model is a reference model for electronic archives (CCSDS, 2002).

The selection of this organisation can be described as an adapted selection process (Hartman, 1998) where the organization was one of very few organizations starting such project during the autumn of 2004. Another criteria for choosing SCRO as place to perform a case study was the minor complexity of different record types at SCRO. SCRO deals with many records, but the variety of the records within BILLY is of intelligible variety and complexity.

Method

This study was performed as a seven month case study, with an underlying inductive approach (Walsham, 2002). During the case study different data collection methods were used, a characteristic for case studies (Eisenhardt, 1989; Yin, 2003). The data was collected and analyzed in an iterative process, with similarities to the research approach presented by Walsham (2002) and Strauss & Corbin (1998).

The study began in September 2004 when the SCRO started a preliminary study concerning an electronic archive system. Empirical data was collected during the autumn of 2004, by participation during project meetings. The SCRO core businesses were also studied by using observations and interviews as data collection methods. The purpose for the later was to increase the knowledge of what role records were playing in the SCRO business. In January and February of 2005 the uniqueness of the record both electronic and paper based were studied by physical use and reading of records. Observations and interviews were used to collect data in order to understand how the SCROs old e-record management system was working, and how that managed trustworthiness in e-records. In April of 2005 interviews were held with people involved in the BILLY project.

The analysis process of the empirical material describes in below, where the results are presented.

Theoretical Framework

Records

Records and archives are the two concepts which make archival science. Records are physical, have a content, a structure/form and are created in a context (Hofman, 1998), and are process bound information (Thomassen, 2001). International Council on Archives (2000, p. 11) defines records as: "Recorded information in any form or medium, created or received and maintaine d, by an organization or person in the transaction of business or the conduct of affairs." According to Thomassen (2001) a record has several characteristics, which makes the record unique in relation to other types of information. Records should serve as evidence over actions and transactions (1). Records should support accountability (2). Records are related to processes (3), i.e. "information that is generated by and linked to work processes" (Thomassen, 2001, p 374). Records are going to be preserved, some even for eternity (4). In an organisation records are part of the organisational memory and are used to support operational management. Cox (2001) stated that the evidential value of a record can only exist if the content, structure, and context are preserved. The context is the link between different records that belongs together and also to the process where the record was created. There is no difference in expected functions between paper based records and e-records, but there are differences in structure and form. A paper based record is a physical entity, often a document (Thomassen, 2001). The e-record is more of a logical entity, which integral parts can be managed at different places within an information system, or even in different information systems (Dollar, 1992). In this paper an e-record is a record in electronic form, i.e. a record created by a computer based information system or transformed to an electronic form.

According to Duranti (2001) trustworthy and trustworthiness are generic terms for reliability of the e-records content and authenticity of the e-record itself, an interpretation also valid for this paper. An e-record must be trustworthy in order to maintain its evidential value, and the possibility to use an old e-record as evidence is related to trustworthiness of that record (Gladney, 2004).

Quality Requirements

In this paper the quality requirements are of interest, a type of non-functional requirements. Non-functional requirements are about how the software or system will deal with specific tasks, often quality related (Borg, 2004; Carlshamre, 2001; Kotonya & Sommerville, 1998). According to Chirinos et al. (2004, p. 18) quality requirements have its origin in the ISO 9126-1 standard, which defines quality: "an entity's set of attributes that are characteristic of its ability to satisfy established and implied needs". For the research presented in this paper are for both quality requirements for e-records, and for the information system/software of interest. More precise are quality requirements that enable long term preservation of trustworthy e-records in focus.

Related Research

When e-government services are going to be developed, management of e-records within such services is necessary. E-government services often use information technology to increase quality on services and efficiency for the potential users. The solutions are rather complex, and imaginable users are many (Bresciani *et al.*, 2003; Donzelli & Bresciani, 2003). Donzelli & Bresciani and Bresciani *et al* have in their research not focused on requirements for e-records. Instead their research is about finding suitable models and techniques for requirements engineering in development of e-government services. They propose a goal and an actor orientated approach in the requirement engineering process of an e-record management system (ERMS). They state that an ERMS is a complex system with many potential users and system related tasks, which make traditional requirements engineering techniques less suitable. According to Grimson (2001) is e-record management systems, complex and the use is difficult to predict, which affect the success of implementation.

There are two archival science initiated projects for functional requirements one is MoReq (European Commission, 2002) and the other is the Pittsburg project (Barata, 1997). Those two projects have identified functional requirements for e-record management systems, functional requirements following international archival standards. None of those projects cover Non functional requirements.

Empirical Result

This section begins with a brief explanation of the new electronic archive at the SCRO, named BILLY, an explanation which not has a purpose to cover the real complexity of BILLY, it only aims to support the results that presents below.

BILLY consists of one database, one storage unit, and an interface. Outside Billy there is a journal management system called UniReg, which only communicate with BILLY through the interface/system (fig 1). Users can communicate with BILLY through that interface. Their communication with UniReg is independent of BILLY.

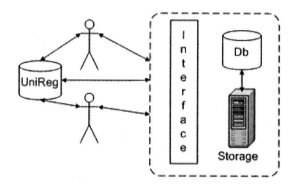

Fig. 1. The electronic archive named BILLY at the SCRO

New records are stored in storage solution from EMC[2] called Centera. each record is labeled with Metadata. The records can not be changed, or manipulated. Each record gets a unique auto generated id-number from storage solution (not to be mixed up with registration number) which is stored in the database.

Quality Requirements Identified and Engineered During Development of BILLY

The SCRO have worked with requirements in a rather unstructured way. The requirements come from both the business, future user of BILLY, and from the SCRO's archivist. The requirements have evolved in an iterative

---

[2] EMC is a World-Wide enterprise with products and services for information storage and management

process within the BILLY project. Functional requirements have been the type of requirements of interest in the BILLY project, a phenomenon also identified by Borg (2004). Quality requirements have not been an issue of priority, and are not even documented.

Dependent on the non existing work with quality requirements in the BILLY project, the analysis of the collected empirical data have focused on implemented and planned functionality and solutions within BILLY. Functionality and solutions that in some way affect reliability and authenticity of e-records have been highlighted in the transcriptions from interviews and observations. These highlighted areas have been categorized into six different categories that could be described as dimensions of quality that make e-records trustworthy. Each category is named in a descriptive manner. The names of the categories have been influenced by dimensions of information quality as: accessibility, accuracy, and format (Holmes, 1996) and data quality as: accessibility, accuracy, consistent representation, and interpretability (Pipino et al., 2002; Wang & Strong, 1996).

Below do the e-record quality categories be presented, they should implicit be interpreted quality requirements for e-records.

Originality and Interpretability

The SCRO has chosen to preserve every record, the scanned ones, those created within the SCRO, and those received and created in the SCRO's e-service in a form and structure as corresponding to how the record looked like when they were created. The scanned records are stored as TIFF pictures, which make them photographic copies of the original. SCRO have discussed to separate the form from the content within their e-service to save storage space, but they have chosen to store every record with content and structure/form united.

This way, to preserve each record as they looked liked when they were created increases the possibility for future user to interpret the record correct. The SCRO have in their forms descriptive information of how to fill in the form correct, and for what purpose some information must be added. This information clarifies much of which rules and regulations affect the process, action, or transaction the form is meant for. E.g. the form for registration of companies is informative and describes in detail why and what information needed for a successful registration. With the preservation of a record as close to how it looked like at creation stage as possible, a future user may also be able to understand how the record was interpreted when it was created by a historical user.

Moveability and Portability

In BILLY the storage separated from the internal management of the records, and the BILLY storage only store e-records. Each record gets a unique id number, and is labeled with some Metadata. More detailed information of each record is to be found in the database, physical separated from storage, see fig. 1. The separation between storage and the database creates independence between those two units. SCRO have chosen this structure for both security reasons but mainly to enable change of storage solution, as well as change of database. All e-records and its related information must be able to be moved to newer storage and database solutions without losses. A needed functionality, if the records should last the technical solutions.

Accuracy through Identification

The SCRO's implemented e-service is using electronic ID, to create an electronic signature attached to each record. The electronic signature provides accuracy for the records by guaranteeing that the content is reliable and correct according to the creator of the record (the person with the electronic ID). The identification is a necessary component to fulfill legal demands. The SCRO has planned to implement an organizational electronic ID for communications between the SCRO and individuals or other organizations as well as other more advanced electronic ID solutions e.g. electronic certificate of company registrations.

Standardization of File Formats i.e. Consistent Representation

The SCRO is following the recommendations and regulations provided by Swedish National Archives for e-records file formats. The SCRO uses TIFF as format for the records that are transformed from paper (original) to electronic forms, and XML for records that are created electronic in e-services or by business action in the SCRO. PDF/A is a format that will be used as soon as the format have been standardized and fully documented. By using approved file formats, the SCRO follow best practice of record management in Sweden, which increase trustworthiness. The use of standardized file formats also make migration of the file formats to new formats easier to perform, if those are needed in the future.

Storage Accuracy and Authenticity

The chosen storage solution has an embedded functionality where the storage product guarantees storage accuracy, availability for stored records, and authenticity of stored records. The storage solution provides function-ality of non-overwriteable, and non-erasable content, seamless content mi-gration, and self healing. The SCRO has made the choice of solution upon the accuracy and authenticity provided by the solution. A secure storage is necessary for trustworthy management of e-records.

Accessibility

BILLY was developed by the SCRO to increase the accessibility of re-cords, and to reduce the lost of records. Paper based records have been lost and misplaced in the physical archives at SCRO. A paper based record can also only be used by one person in original form. E-records can be used by many and are difficult to loose. With BILLY, accessibility, and search ability increases, which makes BILLY more trustworthy than the paper based systems for record management. If an e-record is lost anyway BILLY makes it easier to recover by the embedded search options infor-mation systems have.

Discussion

The identified quality categories are possible to interpret as implemented and fulfilled quality requirements. The categories are both valid for the electronic archive and for the e-records. From the empirical data of this re-search it is not possible to separate what quality requirements are valid for both the electronic archive and e-records, or for only one of them. The pre-sented quality categories implicit prove that quality requirements for an e-record management systems/electronic archive system can not be identi-fied without also identifying quality requirements for e-records.

Archival theory state that records should be able to serve as evidence over actions and transactions (Thomassen, 2001). In this study this have not been found and identified as quality categories or requirements. By preserving each record as close to the original form as possible, the con-nection to actions and transactions in some cases can be cleared anyway. This is totally dependent on how informative the form of the record is, and not dependent of BILLY as an electronic archive solution. According to the theoretical description of a record, both an e-record and an electronic archive should have quality requirements guaranteeing a visible connec-tion to the action, transaction, or process where the record was created. This also holds for cases where a record is part of a larger business process or transaction. The businesses of SCRO are not process oriented. The variation of actions and transactions possible for a record to be part of, is limited and employees at SCRO have no problem to relate a record to a specific type of transaction within a process. A future user might though have difficulties for understand this relationship between records and transactions/actions. This might be the reason for the non existence of connection to actions and transactions.

Concluding Remarks

The purpose of this paper was to present a set of quality requirements aimed to maintain the trustworthiness of e-records, results derived from a case study of an electronic archive system development project at SCRO. This research has identified a set of quality requirements, presented as six categories, identified during the development of electronic archive system, BILLY.

The result presented in this paper is based on one single case study, which makes the results only valid within SCRO and far away from general and applicable results in other organizations. SCRO have a minor complex variety of e-records which also makes a generalization more difficult. Though can these quality requirements be used as basis for future research where different solutions of e-archives are going to be studied. The presented results are supposed to be seen as a first step towards a set of general quality requirements that could support the development of information systems to manage e-records trustworthy.

The rather unstructured way SCRO dealt with the requirements engineering process is not recommendable. The evidential value of a record is too high to be dealt in that careless manner. Requirements engineering for e-record systems and electronic archives must be performed with precision and accuracy, though it is a too important part of the development process.

References

Barata KJ (1997) Functional Requirements for Evidence in Recordkeeping: Further Developments at the University of Pittsburgh. Bulletin of the American Society for Information Science and Technology, vol 23, no 5

Bolagsverket (2004) Bolagsverket at Your Service as Business Owner. www.bolagsverket.se/dokument/pdf/infomtrl_eng/90e.pdf (Retrieved 2 Mars, 2005)

Borg A (2004). Contributions to Management and Validation of Non-Functional Requirements. Linköpings Universitet Sweden

Bresciani P, Donzelli P, Forte A (2003) Requirements Engineering for Knowledge Management in Egovernment. Paper presented at the 4th Working Conference on Knowledge Management in Electronic Government (KMGov03) Rhodes Island Greece

Carlshamre P (2001) A Usability Perspective on Requirements Engineering: From Methodology to Product Development. Linköping University Linköping

CCSDS (2002) Reference Model for an Open Archival Information System (oais). http://ssdoo.gsfc.nasa.gov/nost/wwwclassic/documents/pdf/CCSDS-650.0-B-1.pdf (Retrieved 24 mars 2005)

Chirinos L, Losavio F, Matteo A (2004) Identifying Quality-Based Requirements. Information Systems Management, vol 21, no 1, pp 15-26

Cox RJ (2001) Managing Records as Evidence and Information. Quorum Books Westport Conn London

Dollar CM (1992) Archival Theory and Information Technologies: The Impact of Information Technologies in Archival Principles and Methods. University of Macerata Macerata

Donzelli P, Bresciani P (2003) Goal-Oriented Requirements Engineering: A Case Study in e-Government. Paper presented at the 15th Conference on Advanced Information Systems Engineering (CAiSE 03) Klagenfurt/Velden Austria

Duranti L (2001) Concepts, Principles, and Methods for the Management of Electronic Records. The Information Society, vol 17, pp 271-279

Eisenhardt KM (1989) Building Theories from Case Study Research. Academy of Management Review, vol 14, no 4, pp 532-550

European Commission (2002) Model Requirements for the Management of Electronic Records. Office for Official Publications of the European Communities Luxembourg

Gladney HM (2004) Trustworthy 100-Year Digital Objects: Evidence after Every Witness is Dead. ACM Transactions on Information Systems, vol 22, no 3, pp 406-436

Grimson J (2001) Delivering the Electronic Healthcare Record for the 21st Century. International Journal of Medical Informatics, vol 64, no 2-3, pp 111-127

Hartman J (1998) Vetenskapligt tänkande: Från kunskapsteori till metodteori. Studentlitteratur Lund

Hofman H (1998). Lost in Cyberspace: Where is the Record? In: Abukhanfusa K (ed) The Concept of Record: Report from the Second Stockholm Conference on Archival Science and the Concept of Record. Swedish National Archives Stockholm 30-31 May 1996

Holgersson S (2001) It-system och filtrering av verksamhetskunskap: Kvalitetsproblem vid analyser och beslutsfattande som bygger på uppgifter hämtade från polisens it-system. Institutionen för datavetenskap Linköping University Sweden

Holmes M (1996) The Multiple Dimensions of Information Quality. Information Systems Management, vol 13, no 2, pp 79-82

International Council on Archives (2000) Isad(g): General International Standard Archival Description: Adopted by the Committee on Descriptive Standards,

Stockholm Sweden 19-22 September 1999 (2. ed) Subdirección General de Archivos Estatales Madrid

Kotonya G, Sommerville I (1998) Requirements Engineering: Processes and Techniques. John Wiley Chichester

Krisberedskapsmyndigheten (2005) Samhällets informationssäkerhet - läges-bedömning 2005. Krisberedskapsmyndigheten

Pipino LL, Lee YW, Wang RY (2002) Data Quality Assessment. Communications of the ACM, vol 45, no 4, pp 211-218

Pressman RS, Ince D (2000) Software Engineering: A Practitioner's Approach (5. ed) McGraw-Hill London

Statskontoret (2003) Förstudierapport om framtidens elektroniska arkiv. No 2003/67

Strauss AL, Corbin JM (1998) Basics of Qualitative Research: Techniques and Procedures for Developing Grounded Theory (2. ed) SAGE Thousand Oaks California

Thomassen T (2001) A First Introduction to Archival Science. Archival Science, vol 1, pp 373-385

Walsham G (2002) Interpretative Case Studies in is Research: Nature and Method. In: Myers MD, Avison DE (eds) Qualitative Research in Information Systems: A Reader. SAGE London

Wang RY, Strong DM (1996) Beyond Accuracy: What Data Quality Means to Data Consumers? Journal of Management Information Systems, vol 12, no 4, pp 5-34

Yin RK (2003) Case Study Research: Design and Methods (3. ed) Sage Publications Thousand Oaks California

Handling Instable Requirements by Concern-Based Versioning

Zoltan Fazekas

Institute of Informatics and Software Engineering, Faculty of Informatics and Information Technologies, Slovak University of Technology, Bratislava, Slovakia. fazekas@fiit.stuba.sk

Scattered Requirements

Handling instable requirements is an evergreen challenge in software engineering. Instability can involve both reformulation and invalidation of existing requirements. Both cases require modifications to the corresponding fragments of code, whereas the latter one is rather simple, as code fragments "only" have to be removed in a non-invasive way. In both cases, however, we face a time-consuming and error-prone task. In the rest of this section we explore some of the reasons for this complexity and briefly overview the research areas involved in addressing them.

Although we used the term requirement, we actually had a particular kind of requirements – features – in mind. We understand features intuitively as a set of logically related functional requirements providing a capability to a user and enabling satisfaction of a business objective. Common examples of features are e.g. user management or access control. The implementation of features usually involves modifications to multiple modules of a program, depending among others on the design being used. A typical example is the usage of the model-view-controller pattern [1], which leads to dispersed implementation of features such as user management in at least three modules. Although approaches like [18] can improve the manageability of software design, the more sophisticated the design, the more dispersed the implementation of features will be. Persistence, logging and access control are also typical examples of features implemented in multiple modules. The reason in this case is, however, primarily not in the design, rather in the semantics of these features: they are orthogonal to the features determining the structure of the software. Consequently, they are even more dispersed and are usually present in almost each module of the program. Thus, in addition to scattering, they are also tangled with other features.

The above described problem of scattering and tangling has been studied extensively by the growing community involved in the aspect-oriented software development research. They call the problem described above the crosscutting of concerns. As concerns can, in general, refer to any goals and interests involved in the development of software, their notion is much broader than the one of features. The problem of scattering and tangling of features is therefore a special case of the same problem with concerns. AspectJ [2], Composition Filters [3] and Hyper/J [4], just to mention a few of the mainstream approaches proposed in the past decade, enable the programmer to capture such concerns in a modularized way. However, aspect-oriented software development still involves several challenges (see [5]) and is not yet generally available. As an alternative to the language-oriented approaches listed above, tool-oriented approaches such as Software Plans [6], Spotlight [7] and the Feature Selector [8] evolved to enable addressing of crosscutting concerns in classical programs as well. These provide for manual demarcation of concerns in the source code. Another category of tool-oriented approaches including JQuery [9], FEAT [10], SNIAFL [11], Aspect Browser [12], Aspect Mining Tool [13], Software Reconnaissance [14] and TraceGraph [15] facilitates static and dynamic location of concerns in the source code. In general, both language-oriented as well as tool-oriented approaches facilitate understanding, extension, maintenance and reuse of software to some extent. However, their support with respect to variability is limited. Language-oriented approaches impose restrictions on the kinds of join points and the granularity of aspects that can be composed. Feature-location approaches, on the other side, rely on techniques accepting some uncertainty about the actual contribution of code fragments to concerns. In addition, direct removal of the code fragments located by them is usually invasive with respect to the integrity of the involved modules and results in code that can not be compiled.

Variability involves issues addressed by software configuration management and in particular by version control. Different versioning models [16] provide for different grades of flexibility in configuration construction. From the version description point of view, we distinguish state-oriented and change-oriented versioning. State-oriented versioning describes versions in terms of variants and revisions, whereas change-oriented versioning defines versions as combination of changes. From the version selection perspective, which is actually orthogonal to version description perspective, we can differentiate between extensional and intensional versioning. Extensional versioning is rather used for reconstructing explicitly defined versions, whereas intensional versioning provides for constructing arbitrary versions, usually based on attribute / value pairs. Configurations are defined in terms of configuration rules. Stored configuration rules constrain the combination of versions or changes, whereas submitted configuration rules serve for the selection of intended variants, revisions or changes. Now let us explore some combinability issues related to versioning models. Extensional versioning is known for being rigid, as it only allows for construction of configurations from a fixed set of predefined versions. However, intensional (change-oriented) versioning has also limitations with respect to combinability. For instance, even changes treated as atomic can contribute to multiple concerns (Fig. 1).

Before:
```
public static Vector find ( )
```

After change:
```
public static Vector find ( String name , String street )
```

Fig. 1. Concerns glued together because of a change involving multiple concerns

As the change shown on Fig. 1 contributes both to the customer name as well as to the customer street concern, it is not possible to split it later into two individual changes contributing to one concern only. Consequently, it will not be possible to select a configuration which compromises only one of these concerns.

Before:
```
public static Vector find ( )
```

After first change:
```
public static Vector find ( String name )
```

After second change:
```
public static Vector find ( String name , String street )
```

Fig. 2. Changes glued together because of the order of changes

Let us suppose the above presented change is split in two separate changes, each contributing to one of the two concerns as presented on Fig. 2. In this case, we can select a configuration compromising the customer name concern and another one compromising both the customer name as well as the customer street concern. However, selecting a configuration compromising the customer street concern without the customer name concern would result in syntactically incorrect code as shown on Fig. 3.

```
public static Vector find ( , String street )
```

Fig. 3. Syntactical incorrectness caused by hidden dependencies between changes

The rest of this paper is structured as follows. First we propose a versioning approach based on concerns addressing the shortcomings of intensional versioning described above. Then we provide a brief overview of CHAT, a tool supporting the usage of the proposed concern-based versioning approach and present some empirical results gained from a case study. After this we shortly compare or approach with others. And finally we draw conclusions and point out the direction of further work on our approach.

Concern-Based Versioning

In this section we propose a solution for addressing shortcomings of versioning models presented above that have to do with the granularity and the immutability of changes. Our approach provides for better combinability of changes using fine-grained change-oriented versioning based on concerns. First of all, let us discuss some requirements the proposed approach is supposed to meet.

Overall Goals

The main goal of our approach is to enable on-demand (re-)configuration of software with minimal effort. We want to avoid any kind of manual adjustments of the source code of a configuration, but at the same time, we also want to allow any meaningful combination of changes without the limitations introduced at the of this paper. To ensure their meaningfulness, our approach offers consistency control of configurations on both the syntactic and the semantic level. We will discuss this topic in more detail later in this paper.

Improving variability is not the only goal of or approach. It also aims at facilitating software maintenance and reuse using concerns. It helps programmers to understand individual instructions as well as entire program units by pointing out their semantics in terms of concerns. Highlighting all changes involved in the implementation of a concern helps programmers to maintain that particular concern. Our approach also helps in reusing complex changes. Highlighting a previously captured set of changes used for implementing a concern eases the reuse of these changes for implementing and integrating similar concerns.

Our approach is applicable to any kind of text-based artefacts. As for source code, the approach is paradigm and programming language independent. It preserves the source code in its original, readable form to enable other tools to operate on it as well.

The usage of the proposed approach requires moderate effort. Our first experiences showed, that this effort is comparable with the effort necessary for commenting individual lines of code. In order to minimize this additional effort, the approach does not require the specification of concerns for all changes. Instead of that, concerns that should be variable, maintainable and reusable are defined and traced along the evolution of the software. In addition, it is also not necessary to use this approach from the beginning of a software development activity. Its usage can be incremental and iterative, i.e. additional concerns can be defined at any time and can be assigned to changes even at a later time after performing the changes. Thus, the approach can be used with legacy systems as well if their source code is available.

Tracking Changes by Concerns

The main principle of our approach is to demarcate all physical changes that were done in order to implement a particular concern and should be undone (removed) again if the concern were not desirable any more. In our approach, changes are very fine-grained: they correspond to insertions, deletions and modifications of individual tokens.

We distinguish three kinds of insertions. The first kind of insertions – insertions of tokens that are crucial for the implementation of one of the defined concerns – should be assigned to the corresponding concern. The second kind of insertions involves tokens that do not influence the implementation of concerns directly, but are indispensable for the syntactical correctness of a code fragment incorporating insertions of the first kind. For such changes we have to define appropriate change-based configuration rules as described in the next section. The third kind of insertions includes all other insertions that are neither relevant for the implementation of concerns nor necessary for ensuring the syntactical correctness of the source code.

Deletions of tokens can be subdivided into two categories. Deletions of the first kind arise during maintenance and result in a new revision. In this case, tokens originating from earlier insertions can be simply deleted without any additional actions. The resulting revision will not contain the removed tokens any more, the same which variant is selected. The second kind of deletions occurs, if some variant contains tokens by mistake which have not been properly assigned to concerns. In this case, it is not appropriate to delete these tokens; rather their assignment to concerns has to be revisited. After they get assigned to concerns properly, they will disappear from variants they do not belong to.

Modifications to individual tokens, i.e. replacements of tokens with other tokens, should be handled as follows. If the modification does not influence the assignment of the token to concerns, i.e. its semantics does not change, modifications can be done within the token, but the token should never be removed completely (i.e. at least one character should remain in place), since otherwise it loses its assignment to concerns. If the modification, however, affects which concerns should be assigned to the token, i.e. the token gets a different substance, it should be removed completely and a new token should be inserted in its place.

Ensuring Meaningfulness and Syntactical Correctness of Configurations

A concern-based configuration is the product of the combination of all changes that are associated with some selected concerns and all other changes that are not associated with any concern at all. Of course, not all concern combinations lead to a meaningful configuration. In order to describe meaningful combinations, our approach uses concern-based stored configuration rules. Currently our approach considers two kinds of concern-based configuration rules: requires and contradicts. Both are defined on pairs of concerns. If concern c_1 requires concern c_2, no configuration compromising c_1 but not c_2 is valid. If concern c_1 contradicts c_2, no valid configuration compromising c_1 may contain c_2 as well.

Without rules constraining the syntactically correct combination of changes, however, not even the source code of meaningful configurations would be compilable. A typical example is shown on Fig. 4.

Configuration compromising the customer name (concern):
```
public static Vector find ( String name , String street )
```

Configuration omitting the customer name (concern):
```
public static Vector find ( , String street )
```

Fig. 4. Reconfiguration resulting in not compilable code

The first formal parameter of the find method is assigned to the customer name concern. If this is not included in a particular configuration, the first formal parameter will be omitted. This, however, results in syntactically incorrect code. To come around this, our approach uses change-based stored configuration rules describing when particular changes should be omitted. They can be defined for any change as a propositional formula in the conjunctive normal form referring to other changes that have to be included into the configuration too if the concerned change should be included in it. In case of Fig. 4 the configuration rule defined for the change inserting the comma between the two formal parameters would be *"String name"* ∧ *"String street"*.

Change-based configuration rules, however, can only help to ensure syntactical correctness, if the source code makes it possible. Fig. 5 shows a typical example where the code has to be adapted to make use of change-based configuration rules.

```
public String getMessage() {
    return error ;
}
```

Fig. 5. Removal of the error control concern (i.e. the corresponding highlighted change) leads to syntactically incorrect code

Our approach encompasses recommendations for a coding convention that eliminates cases like the one presented in Fig. 5, however, these go beyond the extent of this paper.

Case Study

Overview of CHAT

CHAT is a research prototype developed to demonstrate the advantages of our approach. It is available as a plug-in for Eclipse (see Fig. 6). It offers an extended source code editor highlighting changes corresponding to individual concerns, a concern editor serving for defining concerns and assigning them to changes, configuration rule editors for defining stored configuration rules restricting the combination of changes and concerns and last but not least a configuration selector for constructing configurations corresponding to a selected set of concerns.

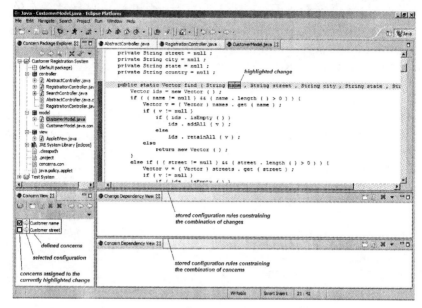

Fig. 6. Views and editors offered by CHAT

Some of the current restrictions of CHAT include the missing ability to handle revisions and the lack of tool-supported concern location.

First Experiences with CHAT

In this section we report on experiences with CHAT during a case study based on Customer Registration System (CRS), a small application with two major features: registering of customers and searching for registered customers. A customer record consist in CRS of a few fields as shown on Fig. 7.

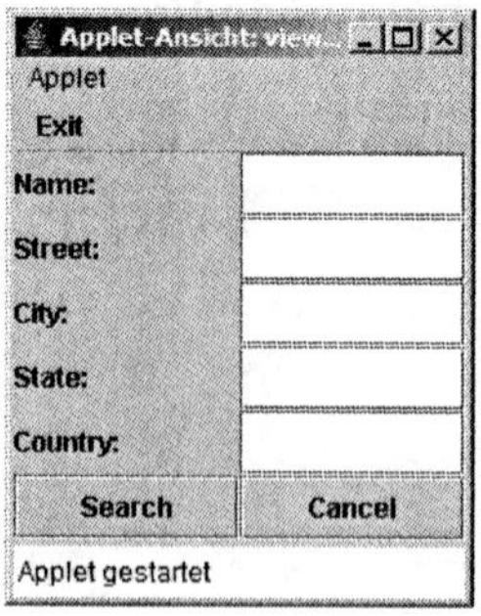

Fig. 7. Searching for customers in the CRS application

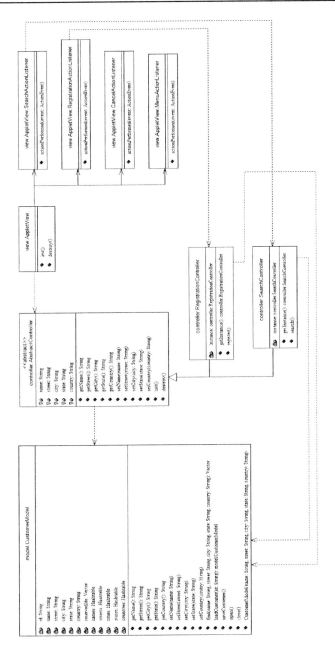

Fig. 8. Class model of the CRS application

The class model on Figure 8 reflects the design of CRS based on the initial requirements. In the case study we considered the following change requests:

1. The name of a customer should consist of a first name and a last name
2. The state should not be part of the address (suitable for non-US users) or the country should not be part of the address (suitable for users operating in one country only)
3. Neither the state nor the country should be part of the address (suitable for users operating in one non-US country only)
4. The post code should be separated from the city
5. The state and the country should be restored in the customer address
6. The post code should be an integer instead of a string.

All change requests involved modifications in more than the half of all classes shown on Fig. 8. We performed the required modifications both with and without using our approach. Table 1 shows a comparison of the times we needed to accomplish the modifications in both cases.

Table 2 shows the overhead resulting from the usage of our approach in case of using it continuously from the beginning of the software development and in case of using it only after the code has already been written.

Table 1. Comparing the effort made to make some modifications to the CRS application in case of using and not using the proposed approach

Modification	Without our approach	With our approach
Split name into first name and last name	23 minutes	11 minutes
Remove either state or country from the customer address	9 minutes	0 minutes
Remove state and country from the customer address	12 minutes	0 minutes
Add post code to the customer address	19 minutes	6 minutes
Re-add state and country to the customer address	26 minutes	0 minutes
Modify the type of the post code from string to integer	11 minutes	4 minutes

When we used the proposed approach consequently throughout the whole development task, we managed to perform the required modifications in 33 minutes including the overhead related to the definition of concerns and their assignment to all related changes. Without using the proposed approach, the same modifications took about 100 minutes.

Table 2. Comparing the overhead involved in using the proposed approach during coding and afterwards

Demarcation of all changes	During coding	After coding
involved in the implementation of one concern (e.g. customer name)	3 minutes	10 minutes
involved in the implementation of all four concerns	12 minutes	18 minutes

Related Work

Our approach is complementary to both aspect-oriented programming as well as to feature location and can be combined with them to achieve even higher efficiency. Feature location has its strength in discovering concerns in the code. Thus it can help to make use of our approach on legacy code and in all other cases, where changes were not assigned to concerns during coding. If our approach is used on aspect-oriented programs, concerns can be directly derived from existing aspects. The entire code of individual aspects can then be assigned to the corresponding concerns. Our approach is quite similar to Software Plans [6], Spotlight [7] or Feature Selection [8]. Its advantage is, however, in the (re-)configuration software based on concerns, while others concentrate on providing mechanisms easing comprehension of the code. On the other side, our approach lacks more sophisticated concern visualization as known e.g. from Aspect Browser [12].

Conclusions

We described a simple but powerful method enhancing traceability and variability of features in the source code using very fine-grained intensional change-oriented versioning extended with the notion of concerns, allowing for flexible reaction to changing requirements. In the future we aim to focus on factors limiting the usability of our approach such as the organization and management of a large number of concerns, closer integration with software development environments for supporting concern-based re-factoring, the adaptation of our approach for other software artefacts (e.g. user documentation) and last but not least the investigation of synergies of the combination of our results with model-driven approaches such as the one described in [17].

Acknowledgements

The work reported here was partially supported by Slovak Scientific Agency, grant No. VG 1/0162/03, and by the Science and Technology Assistance Agency under grant APVT-51-024604.

References

[1] Gamma E, Helm R, Johnson R, Vlissides J (1995) Design Patterns: Elements of Reusable Object-Oriented Software. Addison-Wesley
[2] Kiczales G, Hilsdale E, Hugunin J, Kersten M, Palm J, Griswold W (2001) Getting Started with ASPECTJ. Communications of the ACM, vol 44, Issue 10, pp 59-65
[3] Bergmans L, Aksits M (2001) Composing Crosscutting Concerns Using Composition Filters. Comm of the ACM, vol 44, Issue 10, pp 51-57
[4] Ossher H, Tarr P (2000) Hyper/J: Multi-Dimensional Separation of Concerns for Java. Proc of the 22nd International Conference on Software Engineering. Limerick Ireland
[5] Tarr PL, D'Hondt M, Bergmans L, Lopes CV (2000) Workshop on Aspects and Dimensions of Concerns: Requirements on, and Challenge Problems for Advanced Separation of Concerns. Lecture Notes in Computer Science. Vol 1964. Proc of the Workshops, Panels, and Posters on Object-Oriented Technology. Springer-Verlag
[6] Coppit D, Cox B (2004) Software Plans for Separation of Concerns. Proc of the Third AOSD Workshop on Aspects, Components, and Patterns for Infrastructure Software. Lancaster UK, March 22 2004
[7] Revelle M, Broadbent T, Coppit D (2005) Understanding Concerns in Software: Insights Gained from Two Case Studies. Proc of the 13th International Workshop on Program Comprehension. Vol 00
[8] Lai A, Murphy GC (1999) The Structure of Features in Java Code: An Exploratory Investigation. In OOPSLA'99 Workshop on Multi-Dimensional Separation of Concerns
[9] McCormick E, De Volder K (2004) JQuery: Finding Your Way Through Tangled Code. Conference on Object Oriented Programming Systems Languages and Applications. Vancouver Canada
[10] Robillard MP, Murphy GC (2003) FEAT: a Tool for Locating, Describing, and Analyzing Concerns in Source Code. Proc of the 25th International Conference on Software Engineering. Portland Oregon
[11] Zhao W, Zhang L, Liu Y, Sun J, Yang F (2004) SNIAFL: Towards a Static Non-Interactive Approach to Feature Location. Proc of the 26th International Conference on Software Engineering (ICSE'04). Edinburgh UK

[12] Griswold WG, Kato Y, Yuan J (1999) Aspect Browser: Tool Support for Managing Dispersed Aspects. First Workshop on Multi-Dimensional Separation of Concerns in Object-oriented Systems, OOPSLA

[13] Hannemann J, Kiczales G (2001) Overcoming the Prevalent Decomposition in Legacy Code. Proc of Advanced Separation of Concerns Workshop

[14] Wilde N, Scully M (1995) Software Reconnaissance: Mapping Program Features to Code. Journal of Software Maintenance: Research and Practice, vol 7, pp 49-62

[15] Lukoit K, Wilde N, Stowell S, Hennessey T (2000) TraceGraph: Immediate Visual Location of Software Features. Proc of the International Conference on Software Maintenance (ICSM'00)

[16] Conradi R, Westfechtel B (1998) Version Models for Software Configuration Management. ACM Computing Surveys (CSUR), vol 30, Issue 2, pp 232-282

[17] Filkorn R, Navrat P (2005) An Approach for Integrating Analysis Patterns and Feature Diagrams into Model Driven Architecture. Proc of the 31st International Conference on Current Trends in Theory and Practice of Informatics (SOFSEM'05). Liptovsky Jan Slovakia

[18] Marko V (2005) Describing Structural Properties of Object-Oriented Design Patterns. Proc of the 31st International Conference on Current Trends in Theory and Practice of Informatics (SOFSEM'05). Liptovsky Jan Slovakia

Domain Knowledge-Based Reconciliation of Model Fragments

Darijus Strasunskas[1], Yun Lin[2] and Sari Hakkarainen[3]

[1] Norwegian University of Science and Technology, Norway and Vilnius University, Lithuania. Darijus.Strasunskas@idi.ntnu.no
[2][3] Norwegian University of Science and Technology, Norway. (Yun.Lin, Sari.Hakkarainen)@idi.ntnu.no

Introduction

Modelling is the activity of formally describing some aspects of the physical and social world around us for the purposes of understanding and communication [5] that often is applied in the early phases of systems development: analysis and design. However, different people usually present different models even when given the same domain and the same problem. Same information about a system can be modelled on various levels of abstraction, from different viewpoints, and consider different aspects. Model heterogeneity generally arises due to the creative nature of the modelling activity. Other factors such as the richness of the modelling language [4], and the ambiguities of modelling grammars typically strengthen model heterogeneity.

Modelling is usually cooperative activity among several developers/ analysts, where a final model must be composed from different intermediate model fragments. The challenge in modelling is to arrive at a coherent, complete and consistent description of the problem in a particular domain. In this paper, we seek to answer the questions: "How can we relate different views and aspects in modelling?" and: "How can we manage the changes in a distributed modelling environment?"

Ontologies have been used in various roles for different types of consolidation purposes, e.g. [2, 3, 12] for data integration, or schema and ontology integration through upper level ontology. Similarly to conceptual models, ontologies are built with the aim of sharing knowledge, or definitions, with other people. In addition, they are created to support automatic reasoning. Here, we elaborate on how ontologies could be used as an intermediate medium for model consolidation. The focus is on end-user support for the individual developers. Their views and perceptions of the Universe of Discourse (UoD) are integrated based on some explicit basic knowledge about the domain. Ontology is used as a reference point and built with the sole intention to share knowledge with others. We use ontology to define and formalize basic knowledge and the main objects in the domain. Below settings and an illustration of the problem are discussed, followed by a section presenting our approach in detail. Before concluding the paper, our approach is compared to the current state of the art.

The Complex Activity of Distributed Modelling

In general, modelling is a complex and difficult task. It is usually a creative and collaborative process, during which different stakeholders are expressing them at different levels of abstraction, focusing on different aspects, and producing different variants of each model. Thus, the problem here is how to support the management of logically and/or geographically distributed modelling tasks. The problem can be illustrated by the following scenario which will be used throughout the paper.

Consider a process of designing an offshore platform at an oil company. Different (groups of) engineers are responsible for modelling different parts and aspects of a new oil platform. One group is responsible for the pipeline system design, i.e. the technological equipment; another is modelling the platform on which all equipment will stand; and yet another is dealing with the capacity of oil extraction and production, i.e. the drilling and pumping devices.

Developers (groups) work separately having only weekly meetings to align and reconcile their models. During the meetings every developer goes through the changes and decisions made after the last meeting. Other developers know, based on previous experience and common knowledge, what impact those changes have on their own models. For instance, if the production engineer decides to increase the oil pumping production by a certain amount, the engineer responsible for pipe lines knows that some of the pipes should be changed to wider and thicker ones to support the increased pressure. Meanwhile, the engineer designing a platform can see an impact to her part of the work as the platform will need to carry heavier constructions built on it. The problem here is how to support this kind of collaboration activity by at least partially computerizing and automating this troublesome task of model reconciliation.

Such rough impact assessments are based on ad-hoc expertise shared by all developers engaged in this project. They are aware of the dependencies that hold between model elements, even if the parts are not explicitly or directly related. The dependency type considered here is the impact relationship where, if one element is modified, then the other is impacted by this modification, yet the elements are not otherwise physically or logically related. Other types of dependency are (but not restricted to) derived-from, composed-of, and based-on relationships.

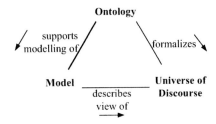

Fig. 1. Abstract view of our approach

Ontology as Intermediate Model

In order to relate the variety of model fragments we need to have common reference point. Our basic assumptions consider ontology, model and UoD as depicted in Fig.1. The approach is inspired by one of the linguistics' methods for describing the meaning of objects – the so called semiotic triangle [6].

UoD is basic knowledge about a particular domain. Ontology is used to represent (a portion of) UoD and to transform it into a man/machine understandable format. Ontology captures main concepts from a domain and represents relationships among the concepts in a machine readable and reasoning-able way. The goal is to capture common knowledge about which entities and what kind of dependency relationships they have in particular UoD. A model is instantiation of the ontology, where the basic theory supports representation of a particular problem. Consequently, our framework has two layers: an ontology layer for representing and formalizing a given UoD; and a model layer for modelling a problem (solution to the problem) within that UoD.

The advantage of this framework is that it separates the basic knowledge as the most reusable knowledge and places this in an ontology layer, keeping the layer of models separately. Ontology layer is composed of a set of concepts representing abstract entities in the real world, and relations among them that are normally based on the external and functional properties of the concepts. Model layer is instantiated abstract entities. To return to our scenario, each modelling of a variant of the oil platform is based on knowledge already captured in the ontology. Thus, ontology layer is used to reason about dependencies among modelled objects based on their properties and model layer is used for reconciliation of the situated model fragments. Relationships between the properties set a foundation for reasoning about the behaviour of objects in a domain.

Functional View

The model layer provides an environment where all model fragments are stored and managed. In order to achieve this there is one prerequisite for the distributed modelling activity and three iterative execution steps. Our approach consists of the following steps.

step 0 – Ontology development. This step is run only the first time when entering into new domain, when the knowledge about that domain is not yet formally described. The abstract objects, their properties and relationships are defined.

step 1 – Properties mapping. Mappings between function and external properties based on particular domain are produced.

step 2 – Collaborative modelling. During this step, models to solve the problem in question are developed, distributed and assessed. While modelling, the developers instantiate (decompose) the abstract concepts from the ontology layer.

step 3 – Model reconciliation. This step deals with model integration, change notification, i.e., the information captured in previous steps is used to reason about the dependencies among model fragments.

Model fragments are at different abstraction levels within the same domain. Therefore, certain concepts in the model fragments may be referred as being sub-class concepts of the concepts in ontology layer. These relationships, depicted as 'kind_of', and other formalized relationships among the concepts in the ontology layer are used to reason about the dependency between model fragments.

Functional and External Properties

In order to formalize the relationships, functional and external properties need to be defined for any ontology, in our scenario the oil drilling domain. A functional property of a thing is significant only when the function is used in a relationship with another thing. For example, the load limit of a platform needs to be mentioned only when the platform is expected to support things (constructions) put on it. Usually, external properties constrain the value of a thing's functional property. An external property of a thing is present visibly even when the thing stands alone. The length, width, height and weight are external properties of a platform. Thus, a functional property is a property of an entity that denotes the main function of object in a particular UoD. An external property is a property of entity that denotes physically distinguishing features. Both properties are intrinsic properties in the sense of [13].

A contract holds between two things if they have a relationship, where some functional property of one thing and some external property of the other thing are mapped. Functional properties and external properties are mapped under certain conditions, which define a rule in an ontology as follows.

$$\text{Rule}: Func(x) \xrightarrow{\ map\ } Ext(y) \tag{1}$$

Recall the oil platform scenario. We demonstrate implementation of our approach in the next section. The external and functional[1] properties and the mappings are explained. We discuss a limited set of concepts, namely, `Platform`, `Oil`, `Pipe` and `PipeSystem`. The ontology is built in OWL using Protégé 3.0.

Ontology Building and Rules Definition

The ontology layer is used to capture the functional and external properties of entities in a UoD, and to represent the relationship between them. In the ontology fragment depicted in Fig. 2 in UML. `Platform` and `PipeSystem` are both defined as subclass of `Facility`. `PipeSystem` is composed of `Pipe` and `Oil`.

OWL distinguishes two types of properties, datatype property and object property. The former is an attribute of an object. The latter is a relationship between two objects. A datatype property can be regarded both as an external property and a functional property in our approach. For example, a `Platform` has a `support` relationship with `PipeSystem`, a functional `load` property with `Platform` and an external `weight` property of `Platform`.

An ontology model does not explicitly distinguish between external and functional properties. OWL is used to annotate them. A vocabulary **semAnn** is used to distinguish between them. The following is an OWL representation of the functional `load` property and the external `weight` property.

---

[1] Our definition of functional property is different from the OWL functional property.

```
<owl:DatatypeProperty rdf:ID="load">
   <rdfs:domain rdf:resource="#Platform"/>
   <rdfs:range
rdf:resource="http://www.w3.org/2001/XMLSchema#float"/>
   <SemAnn:functional_property rdf:ID="load"/>
</owl:DatatypeProperty>

<owl:DatatypeProperty rdf:ID="weight">
  <rdfs:domain>
    <owl:Class>
      <owl:unionOf rdf:parseType="Collection">
        <owl:Class rdf:about="#Pipe"/>
        <owl:Class rdf:about="#Facility"/>
      </owl:unionOf>
    </owl:Class>
  </rdfs:domain>
  <rdfs:range
rdf:resource="http://www.w3.org/2001/XMLSchema#float"/>
   <SemAnn:external_property rdf:ID="weight"/>
</owl:DatatypeProperty>
```

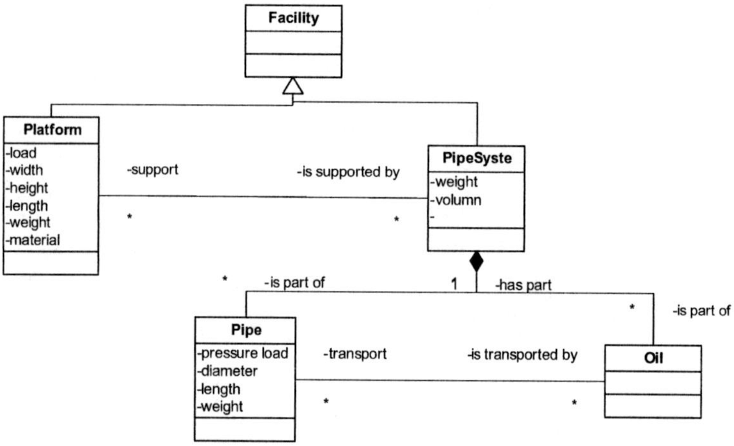

Fig. 2. Ontology fragment

In this domain ontology, we define the relationship between `Platform` and `PipeSystem` and assign them the related functional and external properties, followed by an example. Let r be a relationship (r' is a reverse relationship of r), f be a function, EP be a set of external properties, and v be value of a property. Then, fp^f is a functional property of a thing related to the function, ep^f is an external property of a thing constraining the function of another thing and ep_i is an external property. Finally, ct is a contract between two things and cs is a constraint of properties. Example:

```
r(Platform, PipeSystem) = 'support'
r'(PipeSystem, Platform) = 'is_supported_by'
```

```
f(Platform) = 'supporting'
EP(Platform)={epᵢ(Platform)| (i=1,2,…,v)}={Length, Width, Height,
                                        Material, Weight, …}
fpsupporting(Platform)=Platform.load
epsupporting(PipeSystem)=PipeSystem.weight
fpsupporting(Platform)→epsupporting(PipeSystem)=ct(Platform, PipeSystem)
v(Platform.load) <= v(PipeSystem.weight)
v(Platform.load) = cs(Platform.length, Platfrom.width, …)
```

Collaboration and Model Reconciliation

Model fragments in the model layer refer the knowledge that is stored in the ontology layer in order to 1) consolidate concepts, 2) find connection points, and 3) apply constraints when reconciling and integrating the distributed model fragments. Thus, a method for impact prediction and change propagation is needed.

The vocabulary **semAnn** is used to link the model instances to the abstract concepts that are defined on the ontology level. These concepts, including the relations, external and functional properties annotate the corresponding model fragments in local models as follows.

```
<semAnn:concept/relation/property
        rdf:resource="REFERENCE_ONTO:CONCEPT/
        OBJECT PROPERTY/DATATYPE PROPERTY" >
    MODEL FRAGMENT
</semAnn:concept/relation/property>
```

As two distributed models are connected, the relationships between models are built automatically. If one relationship in the model reflects a relationship in the ontology and a functional property is related to that relation, then there must be a functional property in one model and an external property in another. These two properties build an interface for the two models and they are expressed in constraints. If the functional property already is defined in the model and annotated as a property, then it is denoted a functional property. If the functional property is not defined in the model, it can be added referring to the functional property in the ontology. The related function and value of the functional property are annotated using `Rule:function` and `Rule:value`. The square brackets indicate optional statements in the annotation structure below.

```
<semAnn:property rdf:resource="REFERENCE_ONTO:DATATYPE
  PROPERTY">
    [MODEL FRAGMENT]
    <semAnn:functional_property/external_property>
    <Rule:function rdf:resource="RULE#FUNCTION"/>
    [<Rule:value>VALUE</Rule:value>]
    </semAnn:functional_property/external_property>
</semAnn:property>
```

Consider again the oil platform scenario in the OWL representation below. The `platformmodel` is built by an expert on platform engineering, and the `pipesystemmodel` is designed by another engineer. When two models are integrated to a `connectedmodel`, local concepts are aligned with common concepts.

```
<semAnn:property rdf:resource="uri://domonto#length">
    <platformmodel:platform_length id="id2">
        ...
    </platformmodel:platform_length>
<semAnn:external_property>
    <Rule:value>580m</Rule:value>
    <Rule:cs rdf:resource="uri://rule#cs">
    </semAnn:external_property>
</semAnn:property>

<semAnn:property rdf:resource="uri://domonto#load">
    <platformmodel:carrying_capacity id="id6">
        ...
    </platformmodel:carrying_capacity >
<semAnn:functional_property>
    <Rule:function
      rdf:resource=" uri://rule#supporting"/>
    <Rule:value>500ton</Rule:value>
    <Rule:cs rdf:resource="uri://rule#CS">
    </semAnn:functional_property>
</semAnn:property>

<semAnn:property rdf:resource="uri://domonto#weight">
    <pipesystemmodel:weight id="id9">
    ...
    </pipesystemmodel:weight>
<semAnn:external_property>
    <Rule:function    rdf:resource="uri://rule#supporting"/>
    <Rule:value>200ton</Rule:value>
    </semAnn:external_property>
</semAnn:property>

<semAnn:relation rdf:resource="uri://domonto#support">
    <connectedmodel:hold id="cid5"/>
    <Rule:function    rdf:resource="uri://rule#supporting"/>
    <Rule:ct rdf:resource="uri://rule#CT">
</semAnn:relation>
```

`Platform` can support `PipeSystem`; thus the properties of `PipeSystem` in the model should satisfy the limits of `load` of platform represented in another model. When an external property, e.g. `length` in the platform model is changed, the functional property `load` will be impacted according to the constraints defined in the rules. Since two models are connected, the contract between two models should be checked. Because the `weight` of `PipeSystem` is involved in the contract, the model fragments referring to the `PipeSystem` concept have to make corresponding changes. The changes can be traced using the annotation information in local models.

Two-Layered Approach Revisited – Semantic Reconciliation

In distributed models concepts as they are used may vary in a way they are denoted and represented. Those same-concepts-in-different-models need to be reconciled according to the ontology when models are to be integrated. Lets assume that context similarity has already been considered during the agreement and identification of the same concepts, as described in [9]. Here, distributed local models adjust their semantics referring to the ontology. The local models – `platformmodel` and `pipesystemmodel` – locate corresponding concepts in ontology. The relationships between the objects in ontology provide a clue for integrating the models. In the ontology of the scenario, OWL object `support` property is related to the functional `load` property and connects two objects – `Platform` and `PipeSystem`. That indicates how the `platformmodel` is to be integrated with the `pipesystemmodel`.

The rules, which contain the two functional properties, should be applied during the integration. These rules constrain the changes of models and are also used to check change impact on consolidated models. Three possible impacts are: 1) changes on the functional property may impact other models (e.g., changes on the range of `load` of `Platform` will impact the maximum `weight` of `PipeSystem`), 2) changes on external property of one object may impact its functional property (e.g., changes on `length` of `Platform` will impact its `load`), and 3) changes on external properties may impact other models (e.g., changes on `length` of `Platform` will impact maximum `weight` of `PipeSystem`). The procedure of checking for change of property is as follows.

```
if one property in a local model is changed
{ check the property in ontology level;
  if the property is functional property
     if the functional property is related with
        Object_Property
        { if the functional property is involved in con-
           tract-rules
              check changes on the other object which is
              involved in the contract-rules;
        else
              check changes on the other object which is
              involved in this Object_property;}
  else
        if the property is involved in constraint-rules
        { check changes impacting other properties involved
           in the constraint-rules;}
}
```

Our preliminary prototype is implemented in Python. The main interface window consists of 5 panels: 1) a panel listing of model fragments stored in a repository; 2) a modelling panel for editing instantiated (related or associated) abstract entities; 3) a panel for ontology browsing; 4) a notification panel for listing changes and their impacts; and in addition 5) a chat panel for discussion between team members.

Related Work

Ontology is commonly defined being an explicit (formal) specification of a conceptualization [1] in the recent literature. Therefore, application of ontologies is in resolving semantic heterogeneity. With respect to the integration of data sources, ontologies can be used for the identification and association of semantically corresponding information concepts [12]. Ontologies are previously used to provide semantic interoperability in information sharing e.g., [2, 3, 12]. The semantics of a resource in a particular domain can be explicitly defined by associating concepts, terms and various information resources with concepts in an ontology.

Further, ontologies can be used as means to abstract from different representation formats and to relate various product fragments at different abstraction levels. Ontologies (domain models) are used in [8] to relate various fragments of system specification to establish dependency relationships for change impact prediction. The end product of system development is seen as a collection of loosely coupled product (specification) fragments from various perspectives that focus on different aspects. The co-ordination of the development process and integration of different product fragments utilizes a common reference layer, i.e. ontology.

An on-going research project [7] is looking at supporting requirements elicitation and composing software from re-usable architectures, frameworks, components and software packages. The use of ontology and its reasoning mechanism helps to maintain semantic consistency. Ontology system there has two layers; one for requirements elicitation and the other for re-usable parts. The ontology system bridges gaps between a requirements specification and an architectural design at a semantic level by establishing relationships between the two layers [7].

An interesting approach is described in [14], where knowledge is organized in knowledge grid. They separate between epistemology and ontology treating both as inseparable profiles of the unified human cognition process. The epistemology mechanism used as a semantic description tool to reflect human subjective cognition. The mechanism helps humans understand and relate their knowledge to the one captured in ontology. Ontology reflects people's consensus on semantics [14].

The work that has been done so far in the area of development and maintenance of ontologies mainly has focused on one ontology, which is edited by the developer. On another hand, there are some tools which allow collaborative ontology creation. For instance, Hozo [10] environment for distributed ontology development is based on splitting ontology into component ontology and establishing dependency between them. The target ontology is obtained by compiling the component ontologies, based on predefined links between them.

In summary, there are different application areas for ontology usage. We find our approach novel as ontologies are used as supervising guidelines during modelling activity. The approach allows checking models under development whether they are semantically correct within particular domain, i.e., how a model corresponds to basic domain knowledge captured in ontology.

Concluding Remarks and Future Works

A vision of a methodological approach to facilitate management of collaborative logically or geographically distributed modelling activities is presented. The approach is based on distinguishing two main layers: an ontology layer; and a model layer. Ontologies are used as a medium for common knowledge representation and as a guide for models reconciliation. The ontology layer contains a set of predefined valid relationships for the creation of situated models. Further, it provides reasoning about relationships between model fragments. We capture two types of object properties in ontology – functional and external property. Relationship between those properties is the foundation for reasoning about the behaviour of objects in a particular domain, e.g., how change of one property influences the change of another. We provide the motivation for our research, discuss the settings and provide conceptual description of the approach followed by scenario that illustrates the applicability of our approach.

There are some remaining challenges to our approach and to the current version of our prototype, however. One is to create an algorithm for automatic update of the models based on both observed changes in the model fragments and on formalized relationships in the ontological layer. Further, description of the rules in a related web-based syntax would be an advantage for the approach as it will allow usage of the same reasoning mechanism as in the ontology layer. The proposal for *Semantic Web Rule Language* (SWRL) [11], whose syntax is based on a combination of OWL DL and the Datalog sublanguage of RuleML, is a good candidate for the further implementation.

References

[1] Gruber TR (1993) A Translation Approach to Portable Ontology Specifications. Knowledge Acquisition, vol 5, no 2, pp 199-220
[2] Gruber TR (1991) The Role of Common Ontology in Achieving Sharable, Reusable Knowledge Bases. In: Allen JA, Fikes R, Sandewall E (eds) Principles of Knowledge Representation and Reasoning. Morgan Kaufman
[3] Kashyap V, Sheth A (1994) Semantics-Based Information Brokering. Proc of the 3rd Intl. Conf on Information and Knowledge Management
[4] Moriarty T (2000) The Importance of Names. The Data Administration Newsletter 15
[5] Mylopoulos J (1992) Conceptual Modeling and Telos. In: Loucopoulos, Zicari (eds) Conceptual Modeling, Databases, and CASE. Wiley
[6] Ogden CK, Richards IA (1923) The Meaning of Meaning. 8th ed. Harcourt, Brace & World Inc. New York
[7] Saeki M (2004) Ontology-Based Software Development Techniques. ERCIM News, no 58, p 14
[8] Strasunskas D, Hakkarainen S (2003) Process of Product Fragments Management in Distributed Development. Proc of the (CoopIS'2003), Springer, LNCS2888
[9] Strasunskas D, Lin Y (2004) Model and Knowledge Management in Distributed Development: Agreement Based Approach. Proc of the 13th Intl. Conf. on Information Systems Development (ISD'2004) Vilnius Lithuania
[10] Sunagawa E, Kozaki K, Kitamura Y, Mizoguchi R (2003) An Environment for Distributed Ontology Development Based on Dependency Management. In: Fensel D et al (eds) LNCS 2870. Springer
[11] Horrocks I, Patel-Schneider PF, Boley H, Tabet S, Grosof B, Dean M (2004) SWRL: A Semantic Web Rule Language Combining OWL and RuleML
[12] Wache H, Vogele T, Visser U, Stuckenschmidt H, Schuster G, Neumann H, Hubner S (2001) Ontology-Based Integration of Information – A Survey of Existing Approaches. In: Stuckenschmidt H (ed) IJCAI-01 Workshop: Ontologies and Information Sharing
[13] Wand Y, Weber R (1995) On the Deep Structure of Information Systems. Information Systems Journal, vol 5, pp 203-223
[14] Zhuge H (2004) China's e-Science Knowledge Grid Environment. IEEE Intelligent Systems, vol 19, no 1, pp 13-17

Using Ontologies for Business and Application Integration in Enterprise Quality Management

Alexandra Galatescu and Taisia Greceanu

National Institute for R&D in Informatics, Romania. (agal, gresta)@ici.ro

Introduction and Motivation

Among the requirements and solutions for the overall quality improvement in an enterprise, this paper approaches only those referring to the continuous improvement of the process quality (e.g. processes for product manufacturing, service providing, marketing, etc) inside or cross organizations. Process quality improvement (PQI) is necessary when the resulted products or services do not comply with the customer's requirements, when the processes are unstable, when new types of products are required, etc. For the continuous PQI, the enterprise processes and the IT applications which support them must be periodically analyzed and dynamically maintained.

Main functions of a software for PQI are the analysis of an existing process, according to an improvement objective and the decision on the process change. Additional functions are team organization and the collection and organization (during brainstorming sessions) of ideas on the process to analyze, on the improvement objectives, on the representation of the existing process and on the data collection points, on the quality characteristics, on the changes to apply, etc.

The technologies for Total Quality Management (TQM) [1, 2] and for Taguchi experiments [3] aim at the incremental and continuous PQI. They unify conceptual tools for building process flowcharts, verbal structures (e.g cause-effect diagrams, structures with ideas), data collection sheets, graphical charts, experiment matrices, brainstorming, decision tools (e.g. ideas grouping and voting). These types of structures can already be built with existing software products like: Pathmaker [4], Memory Jogger [5], Solutions-PROSPER and PRO-QMS [6], Qualitek [3], Microsoft Visio, etc. However, these tools have *limits and remaining problems* still unsolved for PQI automation. The most important ones are with respect to: (1) *process improvement:* they implement either TQM methodology or Taguchi method. There is no tool which integrates them both, although they are complementary. (2) *system accesibility:* lack of guidance for users who are forced to be specialists in TQM or Taguchi method and in mathematical statistics; (3) *mutual understanding in the PQI team*: lack of a common vocabulary during the brainstorming sessions, for members with different specializations (e.g.technical, management, marketing, etc). (4) *integration of the PQI conceptual tools*: the symbolic interface of the tools forces the users to manage many symbols with an informal semantics that cannot be compared or transferred between different types of diagrams and structures. (5) *representation completeness*: lack of description and automatic use of explicit (outside the code) correlations between activities (which compose the process) and the objects which describe them or participate in their execution. Also, they do not allow explicit correlations between objects and their quality characteristics, statistically analyzed. These correlations are in the user's mind. This paper shows how these problems have been solved using ontologies and how the integration of the ontologies resulted in the integration of the PQI system (our target application) with the analyzed business/ domain.

PQI system described in the paper was conceived as a personal assistant for process analysis and for decision making on the process quality improvement. Each assistant can be used stand-alone or in a virtual team of assistants. It integrates operations for creation and analysis of domain-specific information, data collection sheets, diagrams, ideas, reports, computation results etc, needed for member's tasks and decisions; and operations for guidance throughout the improvement methodology.

The types of ontologies in the PQI system and the main requirements for their building are described in the next Section. The last Section exemplifies the integration of the application and domain ontologies for PQI.

Uniform Representation of PQI and Domain Ontologies

The system which automates the PQI methodology, basically relies on: (1) a predefined *PQI ontology* describing the TQM and Taguchi methodologies and, implicitly, the interface of the system; (2) a *domain ontology*, created by the user and describing the enterprise business processes, the analyzed objects, the characteristics of the objects, the technical factors that impact on object (product) quality, etc. In this system, the PQI ontology stands for the 'application ontology'.

For the creation and integration of the two ontologies, the following *requirements* have been identified and implemented in the PQI system: (1) a *uniform representation of the two ontologies* in order to facilitate their integration and to diminish the user's time for learning the system (because both infrastructures, for user interface (relying on the PQI ontology) and for the domain ontology, are composed of the same categories of concepts and relationships); (2) a *process-oriented representation* of the two ontologies, with capabilities for describing processes, activities and the objects involved in their execution; (3) *explicit decomposition of both PQI and domain-specific processes* into activities, possibly conditionally executed and correlated by procedural means in order to represent their sequential, parallel or alternative execution, their grouping, their mandatory or optional execution, etc; (4) *explicit and, posssibly, dynamic description of the operations* in either ontology (by their attributes and by the objects which participate in their execution); (5) a *common vocabulary between the members of the team*, implemented as domain ontology and used for defining the process flowchart, sheets, diagrams, ideas, etc.

Main *benefits from ontologies* in the PQI system came from their features: (1) the ontology specification is explicit (outside the code) and given at the analysis and design time [7]. This is the case of PQI ontology which describes, categorizes and constrains concepts and relationships of the PQI process, before its execution; (2) the explicit semantics of the concepts in the domain and PQI ontologies facilitate the semantics-based analysis of the domain processes and execution of the PQI process; (3) the repository with data to be analyzed is accessed by means of concepts in the domain ontology, shared by all steps and operations in the PQI system; (4) the encoded reasoning of the PQI system is minimized.

Previous applications of ontologies to enterprise process management already exist (e.g. the ontologies described in [8-13]). Lately, ontologies are used for managing Web service-oriented processes (e.g. in [14]). For the representation of the enterprise dynamics and for the enterprise conceptual integration and interoperability, the existing ontologies borrow features from object-oriented models. As business process ontology, PSL (Process Specification Language) [15], initiated by NIST, is recommended, because it can be logically integrated with KIF (Knowledge Interchange Format), proposed for knowledge description and exchange.

Most existing ontologies today are built and managed with existing ontology editors and management tools (e.g. Protégé, OilEd, OntoBroker/ OntoEdit, KAON, Ontolingua, OntoWeb, OntoSaurus, etc) which are not process-oriented, i.e. do not have capabilities for the explicit and standard representation, decomposition and interpretation of the processes. The semantic separation of the process and activity-like concepts from the object (entity)-like concepts involved in the process execution is usually encoded. If the designers want their explicit separation, they must devise their own types of concepts and relationships for process description, sometimes complying with a process-oriented language (e.g. PSL, BPEL).

The implicit type of semantic relationships defined with the existing editors is the specialization/ generalization. The composition/ decomposition of objects or of processes and activities should be defined and interpreted by the builder of a domain specific ontology or of an upper-level ontology (e.g. one of the upper-level ontologies described in [16-19]). The builder of a process-oriented ontology should develop a specific reasoner and management functionality for his ontology.

In consequence, for the process-oriented ontologies in PQI system, specific types of concepts and relationships have been introduced and a specific reasoner on them has been built. These ontologies explicitly correlate operations and objects in operation description structures (similarly to the operation signatures in the programming languages). They also represent explicit relationships for process decomposition, with additional information on the operation sequential order and on the operation preconditions.

Basic types of concepts in a process-oriented upper-level ontology. The conceptual, syntactic and semantic differences between the models and languages for business representation and application implementation made the researchers think of a unifying language for their conceptual integration and interoperability (e.g. [20]), including the ontology-based interoperability [21]. On the other hand, the analysis of the requirements above for PQI led the authors to the conclusion that it is necessary a process-oriented *upper-level ontology* (UO), able to represent several types of relationships between concepts. For the ontology integration, an alternative solution to the upper-level ontology is a *translation algorithm* between the concepts and rules in the two ontologies. The main disadvantages are that this algorithm is mostly encoded and the conceptual integration is accomplished only at the run time of the PQI system.

The first alternative was adopted and used for implementing the PQI system, as summarized in Fig. 1 (the implemented functions are represented by thick arrows). In short, for the process quality improvement, the concepts, relationships and axioms in a process-oriented UO (detailed in [22-23]) are used for the definition of both the PQI (application) ontology and a business/ domain ontology. The interface of the PQI system is dynamically built relying on the PQI ontology. Business/ domain ontology describes the enterprise (organization) processes and stands for the common vocabulary of the members in the PQI team.

Using the same conceptual background (provided by UO), the application ontology can be extended or new application ontologies can be integrated with the existing ones.

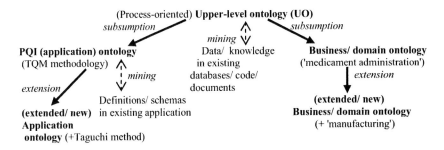

Fig. 1 Types of ontologies and operations for business and application integration in PQI system (thick arrows: already implemented functions)

In the PQI system described in this paper, the authors have first built the ontology for the implementation of the TQM methodology and, then, they extended it for the integration of the Taguchi method. Similarly, an initial domain ontology can be extended with other domains, analyzed using the same PQI software and repository. For instance, TQM methodology has been tested for 'medicament administration' domain and Taguchi method for the 'manufacturing' domain. The ontologies for both domains coexist in the same repository. Besides its direct subsumption from UO, an application ontology can also be built by mining the existing applications for definitions and schemas (according to the concepts and axioms of UO). Similarly, the business ontology could be created by mining the existing databases, code, documents and by the conversion of the extracted information/ knowledge according to the concepts and axioms in UO. These are further objectives for the PQI system.

The vocabulary of UO, instantiated in the two ontologies, is composed of the following *basic concept types*: (1) *process*: a controlled sequence of operations (e.g. the operations that compose the process 'medicament administration' in the domain ontology); (2) atomic or complex (decomposable) *operation*: an action or a sequence of actions, e.g atomic actions in the domain ontology are 'order', 'check', 'supervise', etc; (3) *object*: an entity, e.g. 'patient', 'medicament'; (4) *characteristic* of an object (e.g. an attribute like 'patient age') or of an operation (e.g. an object standing for the operation's determiner like in 'med order', 'pharmacy check' or an operation attribute like in 'wrong order', 'failed check'); (5) *factor*, element which impacts on the values of one or more characteristics of an object (used only in the implementation of Taguchi method and represented only in the domain ontology). The two ontologies differ by the instances of these basic concept types (by particular processes, operations, objects, characteristics).

Excepting the concept type 'factor', the semantics of the other types of concepts ('object', 'operation', 'characteristic') in UO is inspired from the semantics (linguistic meaning) of the basic syntactic categories in natural language (NL): nouns, verbs, adjectives (attributes of nouns) and adverbs (attributes of verbs). Their meaning contribute to the meaning of the ontological sentences, inspired from the simple/ compound sentences in NL. *'Ontological sentence'* represents a part of a process or a part of idea. Other syntactic elements in the two ontologies, with impact on their semantics, are: (1) (universal and existential) *quantifiers* of objects and the object's *plural*; (2) elements for the procedural description of processes: operation *'modality'* (e.g. 'must', 'may'), operation *'pre-conditions'*, inter-operation *'connector'* (e.g. 'case', 'then', 'must repeat', etc).

The quantifiers, modalities, pre-conditions and connectors in the PQI ontology are used for both visual guidance and automatic verification of the user's actions. The automatic verification consists in checking the operation precondition, the operation obligativity in each step, the obligativity of the object selection before the operation execution, the existance of the selected objects in the repository, etc. Figures 2 and 3 reveal the basic types of concepts in UO, instantiated in the PQI and domain ontologies. They also reveal the following types of semantic relationships in UO, instantiated between concepts in PQI or domain ontology: (1) *(de)composition* (part-of) relationship, which correlates a concept (aggregate) with other concepts standing for its parts (components); (2) *description* relationship, which correlates the described concept with the concepts which describe it (e.g for *identification*, using immutable attributes of the concept or for *qualification*, using dynamically added attributes to concept description); (3) *impact* relationship, which correlates a characteristic of a domain-specific object with the factors which impact on its values.

PQI ontology. The basic concept types and the relationships between them in the PQI ontology are organized as in Fig. 2. The concepts needed for the representation of the PQI process are correlated by explicit *(de)-composition* (part-of) relationships or by explicit *description* ones.

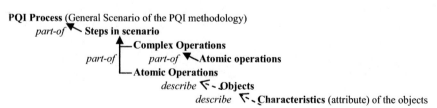

Fig. 2 Basic types of concepts and relationships in the PQI ontology

PQI process is described by a general scenario, composed of PQI steps. The steps are composed of complex or atomic operations. Each atomic operation is described by objects which participate in its execution (similarly to the nouns which describe the action of a verb in NL). The objects are described by their characteristics. The steps and operations are controlled by pre-conditions and inter-operation connectors that can state their sequential or parallel execution, obligatory or optional execution, alternation, repetition, etc (e.g must, may, case, must repeat, etc).

Domain ontology. The concepts in this ontology are user-defined instances of the concept types organized as in Fig. 3. PQI system provides the infrastructure for ontology building. The basic relationships between concepts are *(de)composition* (part-of), operation or object *description* relationships and *impact* relationships.

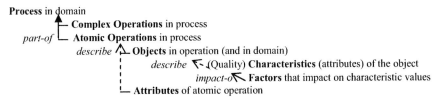

Fig. 3 Basic types of concepts and relationships in the domain ontology

The process description (in the domain ontology and in the process flowcharts) implicitly refers to descriptions of the component (complex or atomic) operations. The operation description unifies the objects involved in the operation execution during the analyzed process. The objects are described by their characteristics (mainly, the characteristics which are subject to analysis). The attributes of the domain-specific operations are specified in the domain ontology and, also, in the definition of the process flowchart (e.g operation goal, precondition, responsible person, if the operation is selected for data collection, etc). For the domain ontology, in addition to the relationships in Fig. 3, the user is allowed to specify *synonymy relationships*, between domain-specific operations or objects. The synonymy relationships are used in the PQI system for the comparison of the ideas collected from the members of the team.

Ontology implementation. The two ontologies have been stored in a relational database (Microsoft Access). A part of the reasoning on them is external, in macros, and another part is internal, encoded using Visual Basic for Applications. The preconditions on the PQI steps and operations are also external, in the PQI ontology.

Ontology manager is an intrinsic component of each PQI assistant supporting a member in the virtual team. It facilitates: (1) dynamic creation of the system interface, based on PQI ontology; (2) definition, navigation, extension of the domain ontology; (3) automatic classification and retrieval of the domain-specific concepts, according to the working context; (4) communication between the members of the team, relying on PQI and domain ontologies; (5) correlation, comparison and inference on members' ideas expressed using concepts in the domain ontology.

The two ontologies exist in each assistant which shares them with the intrinsic ontology manager. Practically, the assistant's actions are driven by the ontology manager. The automatic *reasoning* on the PQI and domain ontologies is mainly for: the dynamic creation of the system interface; the guidance and verification of the user's actions; the dynamic creation of the schema for the data collection sheets (based on the domain ontology); the statistical analysis of the collected data; the comparison and concatenation of the process flowcharts; the comparison and grouping of the ideas; the customization of the PQI assistant.

Ontology Use and Integration for Process Quality Improvement

This section gives examples on the use and integration of ontologies in the PQI system (see also [22-23]). It reveals the ontology-based solutions to the unsolved problems in the existing tools for PQI (see Introduction) and to the requirements for the creation and integration of the two ontologies (see the second Section). The examples are for the 'medicament administration' process in the domain 'patient administration'. The improvement objective is 'reducing the medication errors and costs'.

The interface of the system is dynamically created according to the user's choices on the PQI steps and operations and on the analyzed objects or characteristics. All elements of the user interface are described in the PQI ontology, integrated in this interface. The users are first guided visually, e.g. by inter-operation connectors which implicitly suggest the operation modality ('must', 'may') or by the preconditions on the step execution (see Fig. 4). On demand, the system also provides automated guidance and verification of the user's actions. Each step chosen by the user expands into a complex operation (e.g. in Fig. 4, for Step 4 – Create AS-IS Process Diagram). The operations in this step are described in the PQI ontology.

After the user has defined the domain ontology (in Step 2 and 3 of the general scenario), the concepts in this ontology are used in the next steps of the PQI methodology, for the creation and integration of diagrams, data collection sheets, statistical charts, Taguchi experiments and analyses, ideas expression. E.g., the operations defined in domain ontology appear in the flowchart in Fig. 5 and also in a cause-effect diagram, built in Step 8.

eck Condition	Mode	Operation Name
	MUST	SELECT current Domain and Process
	MAY	MANAGE Structure
Selected AS-IS process	MAY	Add/ Modify/ Delete the Flowchart for current AS-IS Process
Selected Flowchart	MAY	Interpret Flowchart
Selected AS-IS and TO-BE process	MAY	Flowchart comparison
Selected domain and process	MAY	Create final flowchart and merge with it a collected flowchart
Selected process	MAY	Replace flowchart for current AS-IS process with the flowchart in a selected/ nan
	MAY	Replace/Delete structures with ideas/ diagrams

Fig. 4 Operations for Step 4 (described in PQI ontology)

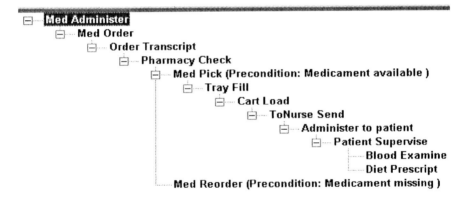

Fig. 5 Flowchart with operations of the process 'Med Administer' (described in domain ontology)

Another example for the integration of PQI operations using the domain ontology is for the analysis of the quality characteristic 'medicine_cost' for the object 'patient'. The data collection sheet for this characteristic (see Fig. 6) was dynamically built in Step 5. The schema of the sheet is composed of three characteristics of the object 'patient' defined by the user in the domain ontology. The result of the statistical analysis on the collected values in the sheet is in the control chart in Fig. 7 (composed of X-Bar and R charts). The parameters for chart creation are the same characteristics which compose the schema of the sheet in Fig. 6.

In PQI ontology, the integration of the operations with the objects which participate in their execution is performed by ontological sentences, like the sentence in Fig. 8, for the description of the operation 'add/modify/delete AS-IS flowchart'. One may notice the existential quantifiers of the objects (mandatory or optional existance).

Month	Medicine_cost	Hospital_department
1/30/2002	2378	Dep1
1/30/2002	2094	Dep2
1/30/2002	1137	Dep3
1/30/2002	1389	Dep4
2/28/2002	2078	Dep1
2/28/2002	1954	Dep2
2/28/2002	1789	Dep3
2/28/2002	986	Dep4

Schema dynamically created with concepts in the domain ontology

Data used in the analysis of the characteristic 'medicine cost' in the charts in Fig. 8

Fig. 6 Part of the sheet for data collection on the characteristic 'medicine_cost' of the object 'patient' described in the domain ontology

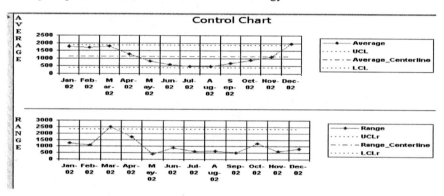

Fig. 7 Example of X-Bar and R charts for the characteristic 'medicine_cost' of the object 'patient' described in the domain ontology. LCL and UCL (lower and upper control limit) are located at three standard deviations from the centerline.

Operation Name	Object Name	Object Quantifier Execute
Add/ Modify/ Delete AS-IS Flowchart	Current Domain	MUST EXIST
Add/ Modify/ Delete AS-IS Flowchart	Current Process	MUST EXIST
Add/ Modify/ Delete AS-IS Flowchart	Flowchart General Description	MUST EXIST
Add/ Modify/ Delete AS-IS Flowchart	Flowchart for current AS-IS process	MAY EXIST

Fig. 8 Description of the operation 'add/modify/delete AS-IS flowchart' using objects in PQI ontology

The integration of an operation in the domain ontology with the objects that describe it is exemplified in Fig. 9, where the operation 'med order' is described by four objects in the domain ontology and by their quantification and plural values. PQI ontology provides the infrastructure (meta-schema) of the table. The rows represent domain-specific operations and objects, provided by the user in the domain ontology. So, the structure in Fig. 9 is another example of ontology integration (PQI ontology and domain ontology).

Domain	Operation Type	Object	Object Quantifier	Object Plural
Medicament admini	Med Order	Patient	MUST EXIST	just one
Medicament admini	Med Order	Medicament	MUST EXIST	several together
Medicament admini	Med Order	Physician	MUST EXIST	several distinct
Medicament admini	Med Order	Dose	MUST EXIST	just one

Fig. 9 Description of operation 'med order' using objects in domain ontology. The schema of the table is defined in the PQI ontology

The integration of TQM and Taguchi methodologies relies on the extension of the initial PQI ontology (for TQM) with steps, operations and objects specific to Taguchi method. The interface for both methodologies is dynamically built using the same reasoning algorithm, but different concepts in the PQI ontology. Also, the same algorithm is used for the automatic guidance and verification of the user's actions throughout both methodologies. The two methodologies share the ontology manager and the infrastructure (predefined in PQI ontology) for the domain ontology. They also share the utility steps (for scenario customization, project scheduling and brainstorming).

Conclusions

The main goal of the paper was to reveal the use of ontologies for the automation of the process quality improvement in an organization. The paper described and exemplified the representation and integration of the PQI and domain ontologies, relying on concepts and relationships provided in a process-oriented upper-level ontology. The experience described in this paper led to the conclusion that the developers of applications can benefit from ontologies not only for the description of the business (e.g. 'patient administration'), but also for the description of their applications (e.g. a PQI system) and for their interfaces. Most part of the code for the application interface (and, also, a part of the code for its execution) can be reused for other applications, by changing/ extending the application ontology. In this case, the PQI ontology for TQM methodology has been extended for the integration of Taguchi method.

References

[1] Pollock R (2003) On-line Resources about Quality Management and Performance Excellence. www.gslis.utexas.edu/~rpollock/tqm.html
[2] DON (1996) Handbook for Process Improvement. Department of Navy, USA
[3] NUTEK (2001) Design of experiments (DOE) and the Taguchi Approach. Nutek, Inc. www.rkroy.com/wp-doe.html
[4] SKYMARK (2002) PathMaker 3.0. Software.www.skymark.com/pathmaker/
[5] GOALQPC (2003) Memory Jogger Software. www.goalqpc.com
[6] DSS Infotech (2000) Solutions Prosper & PROQMS. DSS Infotech Pvt. Ltd
[7] Guarino N, Welty C (2000) Tutorial on Conceptual Modeling and Ontological Analysis. www.cs.vassar.edu/faculty/welty/aaai-2000/
[8] Uschold M, King M, Moralee S, Zorgios Y (1998) The Enterprise Ontology. Knowledge Engineering Review, vol 13
[9] Schlenoff C, Ivester R, Knutilla A (1998) A robust process ontology for manufacturing systems integration. CommerceNet ECO Framework. www.ontology.org/ main/papers/psl.html
[10] Scacchi W, Valente A (1999) Developing a Knowledege Web for Business Process Redesign. www1.ics.uci.edu/~wscacchi/Papers/KnowledgeWeb
[11] Kim H, Tham D (2002) Designing Business Processes and Communication Infrastructures for e-Business Using Ontology-based Enterprise Models with Mathematical Models. Enterprise Information System. Kluwer Acad. Publ.
[12] Guizzardi G, Wagner G (2004) A Unified Foundational Ontology and some Applications of it in Business Modelling. Proc on Ws on Enterprise Modelling and Ontologies for Interoperability (EMOI-INTEROP)
[13] Jenz D (2003) Speeding-up Business Process Design. www.jenzundpartner.de/Resources/RE_BuPrOntology/
[14] Sivashanmugam K, Miller J, Sheth A, Verma K (2003) Framework for Semantic Web process Composition. TR 03-008, LSDIS, Univ. of Georgia
[15] Gruninger M et al. (2003) Process Specification Language for Project Information Exchange. Intl. Journal of IT in Architecture, Eng. & Constr.
[16] Suggested Upper Merged Ontology (2004) http://ontology.teknowledge.com/
[17] Masolo C, Borgo S, Gangemi A et al. (2003) Ontology Library. Deliverable D18, IST Project 'WonderWeb', ISTC-CNR, Italy
[18] OpenCyc Documentation (2004). www.opencyc.org/doc/
[19] Sowa JF (2000) Knowledge Representation – Logical, Philosophical and Computational Foundation. Brooks Cole Publishing Co., Pacific Grove
[20] Berio G, Anaya V, Benali K et al.(2003) Unified Enterprise Modelling Language - Deliverable D 3.1 (Requirements analysis). www.ueml.org
[21] Anastasiou M, Missikof M (2003) Ontology State of the Art. Deliv. D1.1, IDEAS Project. www.ideas-roadmap.net
[22] Galatescu A, Greceanu T (2002) Ontologies Supporting Business Process Reengineering. Enterprise Information Systems IV, Kluwer Acad. Publ.
[23] Galatescu A, Greceanu T (2004) Ontologies for Analysis and Improvement of Business Process Quality in a Virtual Enterprise. Ws on Enterprise Modelling and Ontologies for Interoperability (EMOI-INTEROP)

Ontology-Based Elicitation of Business Rules

Olegas Vasilecas and Diana Bugaite

Department of Information Systems, Vilnius Gediminas Technical University, Lithuania. Olegas.Vasilecas@fm.vtu.lt, diana@isl.vtu.lt

Introduction

Information systems are central to any business because they capture and store the information required to support business operations and help to execute these business operations. Modern information systems are much more complex in every dimension (human, organizational and technical) than the ones constructed just a decade ago. Rapidly changing requirements raise the problem in creating and/or modifying the applications. Most of these requirements are in the form of or related to business rules.

Business rules control and constrain the behaviour of systems in the organization. Business rules are derived from business policies, and these in turn are the direct implementation of business goals and objectives. The process of determining which rules apply to a particular business situation often involves an open-ended search through multiple sources [1]. The consensus from all the business stakeholders should be obtained on the problem of what the rules should be used. Therefore, it is vital to determine the rules and ensure that the rules are appropriate. When the business changes the rules should be properly adapted to new conditions. Capturing, documenting and retaining of the business rules prevent the loss of knowledge, when employees leave an enterprise [2].

Since ontology represents the real-world domain knowledge and business rules making a specific part of all domain knowledge, ontology can be used to form a set of business rules. The constraints, which are found in ontology, can be mapped to the business rules in the application domain [3].

The objective of this paper is to show how the domain ontology can be used to elicit and to form a set of business rules.

Related Work on the Development of Business Rules and Ontology

Since this paper is addressed to an interdisciplinary audience, it is necessary to define some terms to be used.

Definition of a business rule depends on the context in which it is used. From the business perspective, a business rule is a statement that defines or constrains some aspects of a particular business. They are intended to assert the business structure, or to control or influence the behaviour of the business [4, 5]. At the business system level, business rules are statements expressing business policies in a declarative manner [6].

The final set of business rules should comprise only atomic business rules. The atomic business rules are such business rules that cannot be broken down or decomposed into more detailed business rules because some important information about the business can be lost. [2]

From the perspective of information systems, a business rule is a statement, which define the major rules of information processing using a rule-based language [6].

Different taxonomies of business rules are presented in [2]. However, from the implementation perspective, all business rules can be classified into [2]:

- Structural assertions, which introduce the definitions of business entities and describe the connection between them;
- Dynamic assertions (like dynamic constraints, derivation rules and reaction rules).

Dynamic assertions smoothly map to the ECA paradigm (when *event* occurs, if *condition* is true, then *action*). Business rules, which belong to dynamic assertions, operate on data and are triggered by data state transitions. Some of them have an explicit condition, while others do not. All dynamic assertions have a defined action. Dynamic constraints may have no explicit action since they can state what kind of transition from one data state to another is not admissible.

This taxonomy is used because dynamic assertions enable us to implement the active behaviour of business systems. Firstly, it is necessary to form a set of business rules to use them in an information system, which supports a business system by processing all necessary information.

The following business rule elicitation from the application domain problems may be defined:

1. Business representatives do not use any expert systems or program languages to define business rules. Business representatives express busi-

ness rules in "business speak". Therefore, it is difficult to identify business rules from the "speak" and documents used in business. [5]

2. Since some terms used in business have a double meaning, it is necessary to clearly understand and define terms used in business [7]. A simple example of a business rule can be: "An order must be placed by a customer."

3. Terms *"order"* and *"customer"* have to be clearly and unambiguously defined by a sentence [1].

4. It is difficult to form a consistent, integral, correct and complete set of business rules [1, 7].

Using domain ontology in information system development may solve the defined above problems.

The importance of ontology is recognized in a wide range of research fields and application areas, including knowledge engineering, because ontology represents the real-world domain knowledge. Business rules are part of domain knowledge. Therefore, the domain ontology can be used to elicit business rules.

The term "ontology" is borrowed from philosophy, where Ontology means a systematic account of Existence. The most popular is T. Gruber's definition of ontology, where in the context of knowledge sharing the term ontology means a *specification of a conceptualisation* [8]. In other words, ontology is a description (like a formal specification of a program) of the concepts and relationships that are typical of an agent or a community of agents [8].

The subject of ontology is the study of the categories of things that exist or may exist in some domain [9].

Any information system has its own ontology, since it ascribes some meaning to the symbols used according to the particular view of the world, e.g. ontology defines a specific fragment of business [10]. The role of ontology is to provide a comprehensive set of terms, definitions, relationships and constraints for a domain [3], e.g. the domain ontology is used as the domain model in information system engineering [3, 11].

We will use the following definition of ontology:

Ontology defines the basic terms and their relationships comprising the vocabulary of an application domain and the axioms for constraining the relationships among terms.

Classifications of ontologies are analysed below to determine which of them are used in information system engineering and development.

There are formal, informal and semi-formal ontologies. An example of informal ontology can be the ontology specified by a catalogue of types presenting definitions stated in a natural language. An example of formal ontology is the ontology specified by axioms and definitions stated in a formal language [9, 11]. The more formal the ontology, for more different purposes it can be used in information system development.

According to their applications, the ontologies can be terminological, informational and others.

In information system engineering, a classification of ontologies according to their level of generalisation is usually used. At the top level there is *general ontology*, which is independent of a particular problem or domain. It describes very general concepts, such as space, time, object, event, action, etc. At an intermediate level, there are *domain or task ontologies*, which describe the vocabulary related to a generic domain (e.g. medicine, automobiles, or business) or a generic task or activity (e.g. diagnosing or selling), by specializing the terms introduced in the general ontology. Finally, at the lowest level, there are *highly specialised domain ontologies* which specify the domain or task ontologies [10, 11, 12]. Such ontologies are used for the development of single applications, so-called microworlds. The principal advantage of this ontology is easiness of design and implementation. However, it is difficult to reuse the highly specialised domain ontology in other micro-worlds. Thus, enterprise engineering requires even more generic shared ontologies that can support applications across many domains, e.g. across all areas of the enterprise business [11].

The domain ontology, which specifies conceptualisations specific to the domain, is directly related to information systems development [3].

An information system is ontology-driven, if the ontology plays the central role in the life cycle of the information system [13].

An information system consists of the following main components:

- Application programs,
- Information resources, such as databases, knowledge bases, and
- User interfaces.

These components are integrated so as to be used for a business purpose.

When an ontological approach is applied to information system development, the ontology becomes a separate component of an information system. This component can be used by other information system components for different purposes [10, 13]. The impact of ontology on information system can be observed at the *development time* (*for* an information system) and at the *run time* (*within* an information system) [10]. In this paper, we focus on the first case.

First, information system development based on the ontological approach depends on what kind of ontology domain or generic is used. If we deal with the domain ontology, then the result obtained at the development phase will be a highly specialised domain ontology (application ontology). It enables the developer to reuse knowledge rather than software and shares the application domain knowledge using a common vocabulary across heterogeneous software platforms. If we have the generic ontology, we can develop a highly specialised domain ontology without necessarily having the domain ontology [10].

Second, each of the components of the information system can use the ontology in its own specific way [10]:

- Database component:
  - Ontology can be used in the analysis of requirements.
  - Ontology can suggest missing entities and the relationships among them for the application domain [3].
  - Ontology can be compared with the database conceptual model. It can be represented as a computer-processable ontology and from there mapped to concrete target platforms [10].
  - This conceptual model (computer-processable ontology) can be used in mapping heterogeneous conceptual schemes (information integration) [3, 10].
- User interface component – semantic information embodied in ontology can be used to generate form-based interfaces. It was successfully implemented in the Protégé Project [3].
- Application program component – ontology can be used to generate static (type or class declarations) and procedural (e.g. business rules) parts of a program [3, 10].

The more formal the ontology is, the more suitable it is for automatic generation of the information system components. The use of ontology is demonstrated in Figure 1.

In the related works, no explicit explanation is provided about the relationship of ontology with business rules and methods of generating a set of business rules.

In the present paper, an assumption is made that the use of ontology in information system development helps to solve the problems of eliciting the business rules defined above. In particular, since the domain ontology represents the real-world domain knowledge and business rules make a specific part of all domain knowledge, ontology can be used for eliciting business rules that are very common for particular domain. The domain ontology clearly and unambiguously defines the basic terms and their relationships which are used in business rules.

For this purpose, it is necessary to determine how the domain ontology is related to business rules.

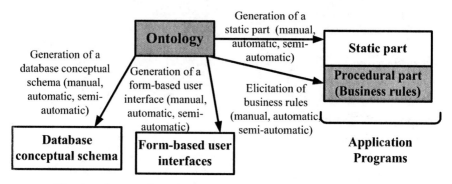

Fig. 1. Using ontology for the development of information system

Using Ontology for Eliciting Business Rules

Business rules are part of the domain ontology and the latter can be used to elicit business rules in the following way:

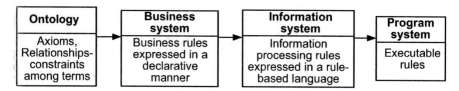

Fig. 2. From ontology axioms to executable rules

The business rules are captured in ontology by axioms and constrains of relationships among terms. Therefore, ontology axioms (and ontology as a whole) represented in a formal way can be used to elicit business rules. The ontology axioms can be transformed into business rules, while the business rules can be transformed into information processing rules and the information processing rules can be transformed into executable rules (like SQL triggers in active DBMS). And, vice versa, business rules expressed in a formal way (for example, using predicate logic [20]) can be transformed into axioms.

The mathematical models of ontology and business rules need to be created to determine the relationship between ontology and business rules.

A number of ontology definitions and models [14, 15, 16, 17, 18] were analysed and it was determined that ontology could be expressed in the following way:

$$\Psi =< \{\Psi_i \mid i = 1,...,k\}, A >, \tag{1}$$

where Ψ_i is the ontology element which can be expressed by triplet:

$$< v_i, R'_i, I_i > \text{ with } v_i \in V \wedge R'_i \in R' \wedge I_i \in I, \tag{2}$$

where $V = \{v_0, v_1,...,v_n\}$ is a universal set of atomic terms, $R = \{r_0, r_1,...,r_m\}$ is a universal set of relationships (e.g. *is-a, synonym, related-to, part-of*, etc.) between the terms and $I = \{I_i \mid i = 1,...,n\}$ is a set of term definitions. A stands for the axioms expressing other relationships between terms and limiting their intended interpretation [10] (see below).

Business rules – structural assertions can be expressed as follows:

$$< v_i, v_j, c_i > \text{ with } v_i, v_j \in V \wedge c_i \in C, \tag{3}$$

where v_i and v_j are terms used in structural assertions and c_i is a relationship-constraint, such as *must, must not, should, should not* or *prerequisite relationship* (for example, *an order must have an order-data), temporal* (for example, *reservation precedes tour), mutually-inclusive* (for example, *to travel to a foreign country a VISA is required, based upon citizenship), mutually-exclusive* (for example, *a cruise cannot be listed as being sold out and have availability at the same time*) etc.

The analysis of formulas (1-3) allows us to state that terms and relationships expressing constraints which are used in structural assertions are adopted from sets of ontology terms and relationships. Therefore, we can assume that structural assertions are part of ontology.

Then, if $T_1(t_1,...,t_n)$ is a set of structural assertions, consisting of two terms and the relationship between terms, the ontology element Ψ_i can be expressed by the twain:

$$< t_i, I_i >. \tag{4}$$

The other part containing the rules is more complex, consisting of more than two terms and relationships between them. For example:

A customer must not place more than three rush orders charged to its credit account.

These business rules are captured and fixed in the domain ontology by *axioms* (*A*).

The axioms define the constraints and business rules on terms and other horizontal relationships between them. The theory of axioms is based on situation calculus and predicate calculus to represent the dynamically changing world [13]. The situation theory views the domain as having a state. When the state is changed, it is necessary to take an action. The predicate theory defines the conditions under which the specific actions can be taken.

A simple example of formal representation of axioms states that, if there is a product, the demand for it should exist. It is provided below [13]:

Exist (demand/product).

The axioms represent the intension of concept types and relation types and, generally speaking, knowledge which is not strictly terminological. The axioms specify the way the terminological primitives must be manipulated [19].

A Case Study of Business Rule Elicitation from the Domain Ontology

The ontology for a particular business enterprise was created using Protégé-2000 ontology development tool to support the statement of the authors that business rules can be elicited from the domain ontology. We chose Protégé-2000 to develop the ontology because it allows the open source software to be installed locally. A free version of the software provides all features and capabilities required for the present research as well as being user-friendly. It also maintains multiple inheritances, provides exhaustive decomposition, disjoint decomposition and constraints writing as well as being Java-based [20].

The axioms are implemented in Protégé-2000 ontology by the Protégé Axiom Language (PAL) constraints. PAL is a superset of the first-order logic which is used for writing strong logical constraints [21].

The schema of PAL constraints was analysed to enable their transformation into business rules.

PAL provides a set of special-purpose frames to hold the constraints that are added to a Protégé-2000 knowledge base, respectively the *:PAL-CONSTRAINT* class. A PAL constraint is an instance of the *:PAL-CONSTRAINT* class. The class has the following slots [22]:

- *:PAL-name*, which holds a label for the constraint;
- *:PAL-documentation*, which holds a natural language description of the constraint;

- *:PAL-range*, which holds the definition of local and global variables that appear in the statement;
- *:PAL-statement*, which holds the sentence of the constraint.

The main part of the PAL constraint is the *PAL-statement*, which can be mapped to the business rule and consequently to the ECA rule. The PAL-statement *has* clearly defined *action* and, sometimes, *condition* parts. *Event* part is not defined because the user triggers constraints represented by PAL manually, when it is necessary. All constraints written by PAL define the state in which the domain should be. However, no information is provided about what should be done to implement a desirable state. Therefore, it is necessary to develop some rules for transforming PAL constraints into ECA rules.

An example of the PAL constraint is as follows:

```
(defrange ?contract_product :FRAME Contract_Product)
(forall ?contract_product
        (and (=> (and (> (quantity ?contract_product) 10.0)
                      (< (quantity ?contract_product) 19.0))
                 (= (discount ?contract_product) 0.03))
             (=> (and (> (quantity ?contract_product) 20.0)
                      (< (quantity ?contract_product) 49.0))
                 (= (discount ?contract_product) 0.05))
             (=> (and (> (quantity ?contract_product) 50.0)
                      (< (quantity ?contract_product) 100.0))
                 (= (discount ?contract_product) 0.1))
             (=> (> (quantity ?contract_product) 100.0)
                 (= (discount ?contract_product) 0.15))))
```

The non-formal interpretation is: The discount of a contract product depends on quantity of units of a contract product customer buys per time. If quantity is 10-19, discount is 3 %. If quantity is 20-49, discount is 5%. If quantity is 50-100, discount is 10%. If quantity is more then 100, discount is 15%.

Event triggering this rule arises when you are updating the existing data related to the contract product or creating new data. *Conditions* are *if* (=> in PAL) parts. This constraint has few explicit *action* parts. For example, one *action* part sets the discount value which depends on the condition that is evaluated as true. The ECA rule is described as follows:

When the instance of the contract product is created, or updated,
If the quantity is < 10 and > 20,
Then set discount equal to 3 %...

Conclusions and Further Developments

The analysis of the related works on knowledge-based information system development using the domain ontology shows that the business rules are part of knowledge represented by the ontology. Business rules are captured in ontology by axioms and relationships-constraints of the terms.

The ontology-based approach for eliciting business rules from the ontology constraints or axioms which are the integral part of ontology was offered. We argue that the ontology constraints or axioms can be used to create a set of business rules. They can be transformed into ECA rules and then to active DBMS triggers.

The example provided shows that the suggested approach can be used to elicit business rules from ontology axioms described in a formal way. For this transformation, a suitable tool was needed and Protégé-2000 was chosen.

The analysis has shown that this tool can be used for the purposes pursued in this study. However, it is not provided with a suitable plug-in for PAL constraints transformation into ECA rules. Therefore, PAL constraints can be transformed into ECA rules only manually at the moment. The plug-in for automatic transformation of constraints is under development now.

References

[1] Ross RG (2003) Principles of the Business Rule Approach. Addison Wesley
[2] Valatkaite I, Vasilecas O (2004) On Business Rules Approach to the Information Systems Development. Proc of the Twelfth International Conference on Information Systems Development. Constructing the Infrastructure for the Knowledge Economy. Melbourne Australia
[3] Sugumaran V, Storey VC(2002) Ontologies for Conceptual Modeling: Their Creation, Use, and Management. Data Knowl Eng, vol 42, no 3, pp 251-271
[4] Zachman JA, Sowa JF (1992) Extending and Formalizing the Framework for Information Systems Architecture. IBM Systems Journal, vol 31, no 3, pp 590-616
[5] Role Machines Corporation (2003) Why Use Rules? www.rulemachines.com/VRS/whyrules.htm
[6] Perrin O, Godart C (2004) An Approach to Implement Contracts as Trusted Intermediaries. Proc of the First International Workshop on Electronic Contracting (WEC'04)
[7] Appleton DS (2004) Business Rules: The Missing Link. www.defenselink.mil/nii/bpr/bprcd/5001.htm

[8]   Gruber T (2004) What is an Ontology?
      www.ksl.stanford.edu/kst/what-is-an-ontology.html
[9]   Sowa JF (2000) Knowledge Representation: Logical, Philosophical, and
      Computational Foundation. Brooks/Cole Thomson Learning CA
[10] Guarino N (1998) Formal Ontology and Information Systems. Proc of
      FOIS'98 Trento Italy 6-8 June 1998
[11] Caplinskas A, Lupeikiene A, Vasilecas O (2003) The Role of Ontologies in
      Reusing Domain and Enterprise Engineering Assets. INFORMATICA 2003,
      vol 14, no 4, pp 455-470
[12] Ciuksys D, Caplinskas A (2003) Overview of Ontology-Based Approach to
      Domain Engineering. Information Sciences. vol 26, pp 94-97 (In Lithuanian)
[13] Chandra C, Tumanyan A (2004) Supply Chain System Analysis and Model-
      ing Using Ontology Engineering. Proc of the Tenth Americas Conference on
      Information Systems August 2004 New York
[14] Zacharias V (2002) Kaon – Towards a Large Scale Semantic Web. Proc of
      EC-Web 2002 LNCS pp 304-313
[15] Goncalves MA, Watson LT, Fox EA (2004) Towards a Digital Library The-
      ory: A Formal Digital Library Ontology. Virginia Polytechnic Institute and
      State University. www.dcs.vein.hu/CIR/cikkek/MFIR_DLOntology4.pdf
[16] Culmone R, Rossi G, Merelli E (2002) An Ontology Similarity Algorithm for
      BioAgent in NETTAB Workshop on Agents and Bioinformtics. Bologna.
      www.bioagent.net/WWWPublications/Download/NETTAB02P1.pdf
[17] Hu Z, Kruse E, Draws L (2003) Intelligent Binding in the Engineering of
      Automation Systems Using Ontology and Web Services. IEEE Transactions
      on Systems, Man, and Cybernetics – Part C: Applications and Reviewes, vol
      33, no 3, pp 403-412.
      http://ieeexplore.ieee.org/iel5/5326/27780/01238682.pdf
[18] Lin S, Miller LL, Tsai H-J, Xu J (2001) Integrating a Heterogeneous Distrib-
      uted Data Environment with a Database Specific Ontology. The International
      Conference on Parallel and Distributed Systems.
      http://dg.statlab.iastate.edu/dg/papers_presentations/pdfs/lin_miller_et_al_20
      01_pdcs.pdf
[19] Fürst F, Leclère M, Trichet F (2003) TooCoM: a Tool to Operationalize an
      Ontology with the Conceptual Graphs Model. http://sunsite.informatik.rwth-
      aachen.de/Publications/CEUR-WS//Vol-87/EON2003_Fuerst.pdf.
[20] Jakkilinki R, Sharda N, Georgievski M (2004) Developing an Ontology for
      Teaching Multimedia Design and Planning.
      http://sci.vu.edu.au/~nalin/MUDPYOntologyPreprintV2.pdf
[21] Crubézy M (2002) The Protégé Axiom Language and Toolset ("PAL").
      http://protege.stanford.edu/plugins/paltabs/pal-documentation/index.html
[22] PAL Conceptual Framework (2005) http://protege.stanford.edu/plugins/
      altabs/pal-documentation/lang_ramework.htm

Exporting Relational Data into a Native XML Store

Jaroslav Pokorný and Jakub Reschke

Department of Software Engineering, Faculty of Mathematics and Physics, Charles University, Czech Republic. pokorny@ksi.ms.mff.cuni.cz, jakub.reschke@centrum.cz

Introduction

XML, see Bray et al. (2004), has thoroughly established itself as the standard format for data interchange between heterogeneous systems. Its significant role is also in the vision of so-called Semantic web specified in W3C (2001) where it contributes to low-level representation of information. As most of the enterprise's data is stored in relational database systems, conversion problems of relational data into XML should be studied in details. The publishing scenario can be twofold: relational data has to be visible as XML data independently from how the data is stored or, and it is more important today, relational data has to reside in a native XML store. The former scenario is simple because the resulting structure mirrors the original relational tables' flat structure. The latter requires more advanced techniques, for example preserving at least a part of integrity constraints applied in the original relational database or ensuring non-redundant storing the database as XML data. Generally, it means to convert relational database schemes into schemes expressed in XML Schema language (Fallside and Walmsley 2004).

Commercial RDBMS partially support these facilities mainly through the XML features of the standard SQL:2003, see ISO (2003), particularly its part SQL/XML (XML-Related Specifications) given in ISO (2004). SQL/XML (hereinafter called "the standard") has been embraced by most major relational database vendors. Anyhow, there are many previously released proprietal solutions in their RDBMSs as well.

The standard treats not only XML publishing functions, but also mapping rules for transformations from the extended relational data model (RDM) to XML Schema. By "extended" we mean mainly a possibility to nest relations, which distinguishes the model from the original flat relations. According to usual terminology we call a description of XML data expressed in XML Schema as *XSD* (*XML Schema Definition*). This paper offers an algorithm doing this task and respecting recommendations of the standard. It covers also some integrity constrains. A prototype implementation by Reschke (2005) enables to generate an XSD, a conversion of relational data into an XML document, and its validation against the XSD.

The paper starts with a brief introduction to XML Schema and a relevant part of the standard. After this we describe some existing algorithms, particularly NeReFT developed by Liu et al. (2004). Then we introduce a new algorithm, called XMLConversion here, which is based on NeReFT. XMLConversion provides a number of improvements and keeps the rules proposed in the standard. We also mention shortly its implementation and conclude the paper.

XML Schema

We mention only the features of XML Schema that are important for the transformation algorithms. Figure 1 shows the hierarchy of data types used in the language.

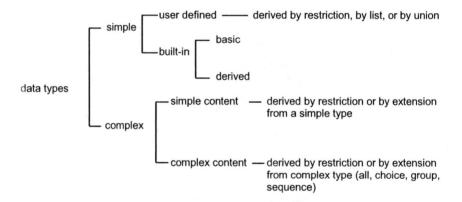

Fig. 1. Taxonomy of data types in XML Schema

As usually, simple data types include Boolean, string, float, etc. as well as various time and date types. Among types derived from built-in string types we can find e.g. ID, IDREF, and IDREFS. For expressing XML structures of relational data, the complex types are of great importance.

Clauses unique, key, a keyref are useful for expressing identities. Each identity constraint is expressed by an expression in XPath, see Clark and DeRose (1999). We can express referential integrity similarly to relational databases with these clauses. A unique element contains exactly one selector subelement and at lest one field subelement. The se-

`lector` determines a set of items (elements or attributes) inside of which the items determined by element(s) `field` must be unique. By key element we denote relational attributes or their combination whose resulted value must be in a given area unique and always defined. The value of `keyref` attribute must be a value of a `key` or `unique` element.

SQL: 2003

Recently INCITS, ANSI, and ISO have added XML publishing functions to SQL:2003. We refer here to the version FCD (Final Committee Draft). It is expected that a movement from FCD to DIS (Draft Information Standard) should bring no significant changes influencing the approach used in our transformation algorithm.

New Data Types

Comparing to the version SQL:1999, focused mainly on the object-relational data model, the new standard contains the following extensions:

- data types `BIGINT`, `MULTISET`, and `XML`,
- functions for publishing XML data,
- mapping rules for description of XSD schemes and valid transformed relational data that conforms these schemes.

For our paper we will consider as relevant only the data structures of non-XML data, i.e. typed tables together with nesting via `ARRAY` and `MULTISET`, and omit the repertoire of associated predicates and operations usable in SQL queries.

XML Publishing Functions

The standard introduces a set of functions applicable directly in the `SELECT` statement which make it possible to generate data of XML type.

- `XMLELEMENT` – creates an XML element of given name with optional specification of namespaces (parameter `XMLNAMESPACES`) and attributes (parameter `ATTRIBUTES`).
- `XMLATTRIBUTES` - lists XML attributes to be placed in the XML element created by enclosing call of `XMLELEMENT`.

- XMLFOREST – is a shortcut function for generating a forest of elements with only columnar content. It takes as its arguments a set of column names or aliased column names.
- XMLCONCAT – based on a list of independently constructed XML expressions (for example via XMLELEMENT) constructs one value as a concatenation of values of these expressions.
- XMLAGG – aggregates a set of rows in the result set, emitting the XML that is specified as the XMLAgg function's argument for each row that is processed. It enables to express relationships with cardinality 1:N in XML.

For example, the statement

```
SELECT e.id,XMLELEMENT(NAME "Employee",
   XMLELEMENT(NAME "Name",e.first_n||''||e.last_n),
   XMLELEMENT(NAME "Subordinates",
     (SELECT COUNT (*) FROM Subordinates s
         WHERE s.chief = e.id ) ) AS Description
         FROM Employees e WHERE ...
```

can generate the table

```
ID                      Description
154                     <Employee>
                            <Name>John Smith</Name>
                            <Subordinates>3</Subordinates>
                        </Employee>
```

Mapping Rules

The standard introduces mapping rules for tables, schemes, and catalogues to XML. Mapping rules include also coding data, NULL value representation, etc. They enable to express also simple integrity constraints allowing to describe better the value set for a given simple or derived simple type.

Mapping tables to XML documents: The standard defines how to map tables to an XML document. The source can be a single table, all tables, all tables in a schema, or all tables in a catalogue. As a result of the mapping we obtain two documents, the first one contains data from tables and the second one the associated XSD. The data document is valid against the XSD. Although there is more possibilities for a table representation in XML, the standard supports the one in which values of table columns are mapped to subelements of a <row> element. Notice that with subelements we fix an order of columns, which is not required in RDM. Modelling columns by XML attributes would determine no order.

A database with more than one table can be mapped into XML by two methods. Figure 2 represents two tables, `Reader(R1, R2)` and `Books(B1 ,B2)`, from a relational schema `Library`.

Which mapping is chosen depends fully on a user. Consequently, any tool doing these transformations should be interactive or at least parameterizable.

```
<Library>                      <Library>
<Readers>                      <Readers>
<row>                            <R1>1</R1>
  <R1>1</R1>                     <R2>Kate</R2>
  <R2>Kate</R2>                </Readers>
</row>                         <Readers>
...                             <R1>2</R1>
</Readers>                       <R2>John</R2>
<Books>                        </Readers>
<row>                          ...
  <B1>1</B1>                   <Books>
  <B2>Wings</B2>                <B1>1</B1>
</row>                          <B2>Wings</B2>
...                            </Books>
</Books>                       ...
</Library>                     </Library>
```

Fig. 2. Two possibilities how to represent relations in XML Schema

Mapping NULL values: A user has two flavours in the standard how to map NULL values. In the first one, the attribute `xsi:nil="true"` indicates that the column value is NULL. The person with NULL value of `Birth_date` looks in XML as

```
<row>
  <Id>1</Id>
  <First_n>John</First_n>
  <Last_n>Smith</Last_n>
  <Birth_date xsi:nil="true"></Birth_date>
  <Degree xsi:nil="true"/>
</row>
```

In the second case, the relational representation of columns with NULL value is omitted.

Mapping Data Types: The standard provides rules for transformation of particular types. For example, SQL types based on strings are mapped on XML Schema type `xsd:string` with subelements `xsd:length` or `xsd:maxLength` specifying the string length and maximal length, respectively. The "xsd" namespace prefix is used to indicate the XML Schema namespace.

For example, the SQL type CHAR restricted to 25 symbols has the following representation:

```
<xsd:simpleType name="CHAR_25">
  <xsd:restriction base="xsd:string">
  <xsd:length value="25"/>
  </xsd:restriction>
</xsd:simpleType>
```

Unfortunately, SMALLINT, INTEGER, and BIGINT are mapped in the standard to types with the same name. This leads to inconsistencies in situations when we have various constraints on values, e.g. of SMALLINT. We correctly resolve this problem by renaming new types.

SQL ARRAY a MULTISET types are mapped to complex types. The basic data type, whose values are stored into an array/multiset, is mapped to a simple type. For example,

```
<xsd:complexType name="Array_5.Array_5.VARCH_10">
  <xsd:sequence>
    <xsd:element name="element" minOccurs="0"
          maxOccurs="25" nillable="true"
          type="VARCHAR_10"/>
    </xsd:element>
  </xsd:sequence>
</xsd:complexType>
```

maps a two-dimensional array of 5×5 strings with maximum length equal to 10.

SQL XML type is mapped to a complex type. The structure of values stored in the XML type is not processed. An XML value is considered as a plain text without a meaning. To forbid processing such value during a validation, it is necessary to use the attribute processContents with the value "skip".

```
<xsd:complexType name="XML" mixed="true">
  <xsd:sequence>
    <xsd:any name="element" minOccurs="0"
      maxOccurs="unbounded"
      processContents="skip"/>
    </xsd:sequence>
</xsd:complexType>
```

Generating Schema in the Language XML Schema: There are many possibilities how to generate XSD describing relational database schemes composed from particular table schemes. The standard considers generating for each type and a table, own global type. These types are then used in more complex definitions.

Related Works

We will overview shortly existing algorithms for conversion of the relational database schema to the languages DTD and XML Schema. We suppose a relational database schema $R = (R_1,...,R_K, K\geq1;$ IC), where R_i are relation schemes and IC is a set of integrity constraints. By R^* we mean a relation associated to R.

Target Language – DTD: In FT (Flat Translation) Lee et al. (2001) transform relation schemes from R to elements of an XSD and attributes of relation schemes to attributes or elements of the XSD. A usage of attributes or elements depends on a user, since the algorithm can work in both modes. IC is not considered in the algorithm. The approach also does not exploit non-flat features of XML model, e.g. regular expressions specifying a number of element occurrences, and hierarchical nesting of elements.

NeT (*Nesting-based Translation*) algorithm presented in the same paper tries to overcome drawbacks of FT using an operator *Nest*. The main idea is to describe a structure of nested elements by Kleene operators. Unlike NeT the CoT algorithm (*Constraints-based Translation*) by Lee et al. (2002) considers also a referential integrity.

Target Language – XML Schema: The ConvRel (*Relationship Conversion*) algorithm by Duta (2003) considers referential integrity and constraints expressed by UNIQUE and NULL. The author classifies cardinalities 1:1, 1:N and M:N between rows of associated relations to determine a nesting of elements. A key problem is to determine which relation will create the outer element and which one its subelement.

ConvRel considers only simple links between two relations, while the relations are actually connected by more complex links. Each table can refer to or is referenced from more other tables. In the algorithm Conv2XML Duta considers links among three tables.

NeReFT Algorithm: Li et al. (2003) approach the problem with rules that are applicable for relation schemes of various types. These rules are driven by referential integrity associations between schemes. NeReFT (Nested Redundancy Free Translation) works also simply with NULL/NOT NULL constraints by properly setting minOccurs attribute in XML elements. UNIQUE constraints have a straightforward representation with unique mechanism in XML Schema. The strategy of NeReFT is to reach nested XML structures and minimum redundancy in XML data. By redundancy we mean here repeating data in the resulting XML data document[1].

---

[1] Problems of redundancy are discussed in details by Vincent et al. (2004).

Thus, IC include primary keys, referential integrities, NULL/NOT NULL, and UNIQUE constraints. As an output we obtain an XSD describing non-redundant XML documents.

Suppose a schema $R(K_1,...,K_n,A_{n+1},...,A_{n+m})$, where $K_1,...,K_n$ compose the primary key (PK$_R$) of R. For a referential integrity between relations R and P, where a foreign key (FK) from R references to P, we denote this fact as FK$_R \to P$. Referential integrity naturally induces a digraph G_R. Schemes R and P are called *child* and *parent*, respectively. Each R from $\boldsymbol{R}$ is classified into one of four categories dependent of PK$_R$:

- *regular* – no FK occurs among $K_1,...,K_n$.
- *component* – there is K_i which references to P. The rest of PK$_R$ serves to local identification of rows under one K_i value.
- *supplementary* – the PK$_R$ is also an FK$_R$, FK$_R \to P$, for a P.
- *association* – the PK$_R$ contains more FK$_R$S.

In practice, regular and component relations correspond to entity and weak entity types, respectively. Supplementary relations correspond often to members of an ISA hierarchy or a vertical decomposition of relation. Finally, association relations are transformed relationship types.

The algorithm core:

1. For a schema $\boldsymbol{R}$ the algorithm creates a root element in the target XSD.
2. For a regular or an association relation R, it creates an element with the name R and puts it under the root element. The created element may be moved down later depending on some constraints.
3. For a component or a supplementary R, an element is created and placed as a child element of the element for its parent relation. The representations of both relation types differ only in the value of maxOccurs attribute.
4. For each single attribute PK of a regular R, an attribute of the element for R is created with ID data type. For each multiple attribute PK of a regular, a component or an association R, an attribute of the element for R is created for each PK attribute with its corresponding data type; a key element is defined with a selector to select the element for R and several fields to identify all PK attributes.
5. For each FK of a relation R, where FK $\not\subset$ PK of a component or a supplementary relation, if it is a single attribute FK, an attribute of the element for R is created with IDREF data type; otherwise, an attribute is created for each FK attribute with its corresponding data type, a keyref element is defined with a selector to select the element for R and several fields to identify FK attributes.

6. For a non-key attribute of *R*, an element is created under the element for *R*.

7. To achieve higher level of nesting, if a relation *R* has a NOT NULL FK_R, $FK_R \rightarrow P$, and there is no loop between *R* and *P* in G_R, we can move the element for *R* under the *P* element. This rule reflects N:1 cardinality among rows of *R* and *P*.

XML Conversion Algorithm

SQL data types are categorized into built-in and user defined types (UDT). Built-in data types are further differentiated into simple and complex data types. Simple (e.g. numeric or string) data types are straightforward translated into simple types in XSD.

Complex data types (as ARRAY, MULTISET, ROW) are processed in a different way. ARRAY or MULTISET is a collection of the same basic type. This basic type can be repeatedly complex data type, so the translation recursively generates all necessary definitions according mapping rules given by SQL: 2003. Data type ROW is translated into complex type containing record for every simple item, which this data type ROW contains. Simple items can be of complex data type, so they must be recursively processed as well. These definitions result in a nested structure.

Let *N* be a type ARRAY, MULTISET, or ROW used in ***R***. For purposes of this paper we denote the nearest supertype of *N* in ***R*** as *owner* of *N*. Clearly, there can be more such owners. These additional definitions are used in more complex XSD definitions.

Processing of UDTs depends on their complexity. In the case of UDT founded on a simple data type, a simple type is created in XSD. Otherwise, a complex data type is created, as well as by complex data types.

As the standard uses as key constructs key, keyref clauses and does not prefer combination ID and IDREF in the case of single-attribute keys, we use in our algorithm key, keyref for all keys. Relation attributes are transformed to elements in all cases.

Phase I – Preparation: For nested types (tables) (see MULTISET, ARRAY, and ROW possibilities) their owner types (tables) are determined. In this case, the definition of a new complex type describing such a nested table has to be introduced first in the resulted XSD. Then the definition of its owner relation can be introduced. It will contain the definition of the nested table as an element.

Suppose that all information about ***R*** were analyzed and stored. The following steps are performed:

1. Each schema R from $\boldsymbol{R}$ receives a type according to the NeReFT classification. This type depends on the number of FK_Rs in PK_R and whether the FK_R is entire the PK_R. In the case, if R is a component or a supplementary relation, its parent relation is determined.
2. An order is assigned to all schemes of $\boldsymbol{R}$. According to the order the R_i will be processed. This order is implied by mapping rules (1) – (6).
    a. First, regular relations are processed. For each such R the component and supplementary relations dependent of R are preferred. They obtain lower order and will be processed earlier. This process is done recursively because these dependent relations can be parents for other dependent relations. After processing all dependent component and supplementary relations the R is incorporated into the ordered list of relations.
    b. For each remaining (association) relation R an order is set. It follows the order in which the metadata concerning R is stored in the XMLConversion implementation.
    c. There are created records about the explicit nested relations.
3. Based of the rule (7) the order of relations to be processed is changed. For each R is tested if the condition in (7) is fulfilled. If yes, then (7) can be applied. The order is modified in this way that the parent relation of R will be processed later than the child relation.

Phase II – Generating XSD:

1. XML declaration is generated and information about namespaces is put into tags `<xsd:schema>` and `<xsd:import>`.
2. All relations are processed in the given order according to the mapping rules included in the standard. If a relation depends on a currently processed relation R (or other relations are nested in R), in the definition of complex type describing R a new element is included. The type of this element was defined earlier in Phase II. This means, that explicit nested relations are processed too and definitions of their types are used for new elements included in R.
3. After creating the types defining structures of all relations, a new type T_R describing the entire schema $\boldsymbol{R}$ is created. T_R contains elements whose types are the types describing particular R_i. Only the types are used that are not nested and do not occur in other types.
4. A new element is created, whose type is T_R. This element will contain all definitions of keys and references to keys via elements `<xsd:key>`, `<xsd:unique>` and `<xsd:keyref>`. The XSD is closed with `</xsd:schema>`.

Phase III – Generating XML document:

1. XML declaration is generated. In the start tag of the root element, with name corresponding to **R**, attributes with information about namespaces are stored.
2. According to the predefined order of the relations, processing all un-nested tables are consecutively taken. For each relation R^* all its nested relations are determined. The relation R^* is then processed in the following way:
   a. For each row of R^*, a part of XML document containing row's data is generated. Then the associated nested data follows. Values of FK attributes of rows of nested data match values of PK attributes in this part of XML document.
   b. When input of nested data is finished, the part of XML document associated to one row from R^* is closed. The closing depends on a way how the tables are mapped to the document.
3. According to the given order all yet non-processed R are consecutively chosen. Data of each R^* is processed according to the mapping rules. The entire XML document is closed by the end tag of the root element.

Implementation

For implementation it is necessary to gain all important about **R**. This information is stored in the system tables in a way which differs in various RDBMSs. A lot of special parameterized SQL queries have to be constructed for this purpose. For our implementation the Interbase RDBMS has been used and application development environment Delphi 6. Any transfer of the system to another RDBMS would require a change of this part.

Generating schemes is completely independent on RDBMS. As a parser and validator of XML documents we used Altova XMLSpy 2005 tool.

Conclusions

The problem addressed in this paper is related to exporting relational data in a native XML store. Our algorithm is designed with respect to the rules recommended by the specification SQL/XML. In implementation we had to change some details of this specification, as it not followed through. In opposite case, the generated XML documents could be not valid against the generated XSD.

An open problem is how to preserve more integrity constraints in XSD, i.e. these ones contained in the CHECK clause of CREAT TABLE statement of SQL. As yet this case is not tackled in a satisfactory way.

Acknowledgement

This research was supported in part by the National programme of research (Information society project 1ET100300419).

References

Bray T, Paoli J, Sperberg-McQueen CM, Maler E (2004) Extensible Markup Language (XML) 1.0 (Second Edition). W3C. www.w3.org/TR/REC-xml

Clark J, DeRose S (1999) XML Path Language (XPath) Version 1.0. W3C November. www.w3.org/TR/xpath

Duta C (2003) Conversion from Relational Schema to XML Nested-Based Schema. MSc Thesis. Calgary Canada.

Fallside DC, Walmsley P (2004) XML Schema Part 0: Primer. W3C. www.w3.org/TR/xmlschema-0/

ISO (2004) Information Technology – Database Languages – SQL – Part 14: XML-Related Specifications (SQL/XML). ISO/IEC 9075-14:2004

ISO (2003) Information Technology – Database Languages – SQL – Part 2: Foundation (SQL/Foundation). ISO/IEC 9075-2:2003

Lee D, Mani M, Chiu F, Chu WW (2001) Nesting-Based Relational to XML Schema Translation. Int'l Workshop on the Web and Databases (WebDB) Santa Barbara CA

Lee D, Mani M, Chiu F, Chu WW (2002) Effective Schema Conversions between XML and Relational Models. Proc. of European Conf on Artificial Intelligence Knowledge Transformation Workshop (ECAI-OT) Lyon France

Liu Ch, Liu J, Guo M (2003) On Transformation to Redundancy Free XML Schema from Relational Database Schema. Proc of APWeb 2003 LNCS 2642

Reschke J (2005) Transformations of Relational Database Schemes to XML Schemes. MSc. Thesis Charles University Prague (in Czech)

Vincent MW, Liu J, Liu Ch (2004) Redundancy Free Mappings from Relations to XML. Proc of WAIM 2004 LNCS 3129

W3C (2001) Semantic Web. www.w3.org/2001/sw/

The XSD-Builder Specification Language – Toward a Semantic View of XML Schema Definition

Joseph Fong and San Kuen Cheung

Department of Computer Science, City University of Hong Kong, Hong Kong. csjfong@cityu.edu.hk, joe.c@student.cityu.edu.hk

Introduction

In the present database market, XML database model is a main structure for the forthcoming database system in the Internet environment. As a conceptual schema of XML database, XML Model has its limitation on presenting its data semantics. System analyst has no toolset for modeling and analyzing XML system. We apply XML Tree Model (shown in Figure 2) as a conceptual schema of XML database to model and analyze the structure of an XML database. It is important not only for visualizing, specifying, and documenting structural models, but also for constructing executable systems. The tree model represents inter-relationship among elements inside different logical schema such as XML Schema Definition (XSD), DTD, Schematron, XDR, SOX, and DSD (shown in Figure 1, an explanation of the terms in the figure are shown in Table 1). The XSD-Builder consists of XML Tree Model, source language, translator, and XSD. The source language is called XSD-Source which is mainly for providing an environment with concept of user friendliness while writing an XSD. The source language will consequently be translated by XSD-Translator. Output of XSD-Translator is an XSD which is our target and is called as an object language.

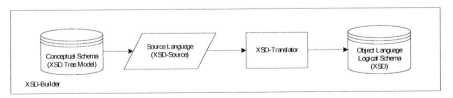

Fig. 1. Architecture for XSD-Builder

Table 1. Explanation of the terms of in figure 1

Term	Description
XSD-Builder	It consists of XML Tree Model, XSD-Source, XSD-Translator, and XSD for providing a toolset to generate XSD from source language.
XML Tree Model	It is a name of the conceptual schema of XML Model for providing a modeling, visualizing, and documenting structural model. A tree diagram view presents inter-relationship of XML DB.
XSD-Source	It is a name of our source language for providing a native environment of human thinking on creating XSD. The language is user friendly and is data-semantic-oriented.
XSD-Translator	It is a name of our host language for translating from source language (i.e. XSD-Source) to object language (i.e. XSD). The language internally cooperates with lexing (i.e. scanning), parsing, recovering, optimizing, and generating.
XSD	It is a name of our object language for executing logical schema of XML Model on a database management system. The language is recommended by W3C and is widely accepted as a logical schema of XML Model.

Related Work

R. Conrad et al [6] considered designing Object-oriented software (UML) with the XML structure (DTD). They addressed that the DTD lacked clarity and readability. C. Kleiner and U. Lipeck [7] introduced an automatic generator for translating from conceptual schema (ER model) to XML DTD. However, some data semantics cannot be presented on their paper. FIXT [8] used the Structural Graph to extract index and sub index for efficient XML transformation for producing a graphical structure as a conceptual view. XTABLES [9] used the DTD Graph that mirrored the structure of DTD. The graph consisted of elements, attributes, and operator. The function of DTD Graph is for constructing the desired relational schema. However, they did not mention about the data semantics on their graph. R. S. Chen [5] used XML Schema hierarchical tree to construct a toolkit of enterprise model-based software development and application framework.

XML Tree Model

Many researchers elaborated their view on conceptual schema of XML Model such as XML tree [2, 3, 4], DTD Graph [5], and so on. Most papers used the XML tree to visualize elements, attributes and data. The DTD Graph proposed by IBM's XTABLE [5] is a conceptual schema for XML Model but it cannot show data semantics. Our model can be used to show data semantics and it is simple to reader for comparing with XML document.

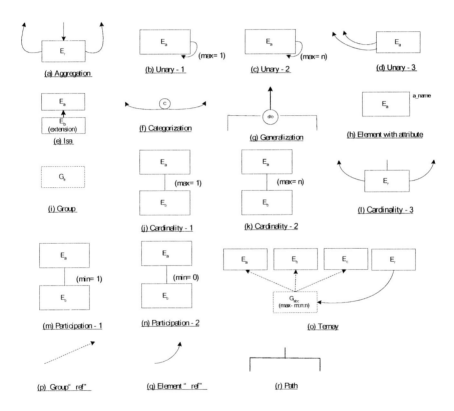

Fig. 2. Legend for XML Tree Model

Table 2. Description of Figure 2

Item	Description
(a)	Sub-element E_r that is an aggregate element points to two elements for creating a binary relationship in "m:n" cardinality.
(b)	E_a that is in "1:1" and "1:n" cardinalities points to itself for creating unary relationship.
(c)	E_a that is in "m:n" cardinality constructs two links pointing to the same element for creating unary relationship.
(d)	E_b with "extension" keyword inherits all properties of E_a for showing "isa" relationship.
(e)	Sub-element with "c" circle that is a subset in union operation of relational algebra links up with two group elements by using "choice" keyword.
(f)	Two or more sub-elements with "d" or "o" circle can be generalized from element for showing disjoint or overlap generalization.
(g)	E_a represents an element with an attribute declaration.
(h)	G_a represents a group declaration.
(i)	E_b is a sub-element belonging to an element E_a. E_b has "1:1" or "1:n" cardinality relationship in connection with E_a.
(j)	E_r that is a sub-element points to two elements for creating "m:n" cardinality relationship.
(k)	E_b with "min=1" keyword that is a sub-element links up with an element E_a for showing total participation relationship.
(l)	E_b with "min=0" keyword that is a sub-element links up with an element E_a for showing partial participation relationship.
(m)	Three elements named E_a, E_b and E_c are pointed by a group named G_{abc} with "m:n:n" keyword also pointed by a element named E_r for showing "m:n:n" ternary relationship.
(n)	Broken line with arrow represents a "ref" keyword within a group declaration.
(o)	Concrete Line with arrow represents a "ref" keyword within an element declaration.
(p)	Hierarchy path shows one top element with two sub-elements.

Source Language

XSD-Builder includes source, host, and object languages. The host language deals with an XSD-Translator (T). The object language deals with an XSD which is denoted as S(X). The source language deals with an XSD-Source which is composed by symbols and block-structured declarations, and denoted as S(S). In the declarations, we define two parts constructed by component and constraint declarations assisted by symbol and keyword tables. In the component declaration, we distinguish four types of declarations in which we find element, group, complex type, and simple type. A schema of XSD-Source is transformed to a schema of XSD through the XSD-Translator (T). Let S(S), S(X) and T denote a set of source code of the schema (XSD-Source), a set of object code of the schema (XSD), and a set of transformation code of the XSD-Translator respectively. If S(S) is mapped to S(X) without any loss of information by T, then T' is a reverse transformation from S(X) to S(S). It is shown that T(T'(S(S))) = S(S) where S(S) is a source language before transformation. To achieve our goal, S(S) → S(X) is equivalent via transformation T, denoted S(S) ≡ S(X) [12].

Component Declaration

In our methodology, the users have to declare a framework of XSD. It includes not only all elements, group elements, complex types, and simple types, but also all attributes. In this stage, users have no need to define data constraints. The workflow of constructing a hierarchy of XSD is in constraint declaration in which users can group specified components to form data semantic. The following is syntax of component declaration:

```
create <el | gp | ct | st>
<element_name> has <attribute_name_1 type>[, <attrib-
   ute_name_2 type>, ....]
<sub-element_name_1> has <attribute_name_1 type>[, <attrib-
   ute_name_2 type>, ....]
[<sub-element_name_2> has <attribute_name_1 type>][, <at-
   tribute_name_2 type>, ....];
```

Constraint Declaration

There are 14 constraint declarations. Users can map constraint symbols to corresponding constraint declarations. In this stage, users encounter on designing relationships among elements. They have to deal with several terms such as aggregation, generalization, and categorization. Using an XSD-Source, they can construct these terms without difficulties. The general syntax for the constraint declaration is as follow:

```
create <is| dg | og | ag | ca | tp | pp | cl | cn | cm | te
   | ul | un | um>
<element_name>[ has <sub-element_name_1 minOccurs maxOc-
   curs>, <sub-element_name_2 minOccurs maxOccurs>, ....]
[<group_name_1>, <group_name_2>]
[<sub-element_name minOccurs maxOccurs> add <ref_name_1> ...]
[<child_element_name> add <ref_name_1> ...]
[<keyref_name> link <ref_name>]
```

```
[<group_name> has <sub-element_name_1 minOccurs maxOccurs>
   add <ref_name_1> …]
[<sub-element_name> add <ref_name>];
```

Table 3. The constraint types by using constraint declaration

Constraint	Syntax
Isa	create \<is\>
	\<parent_element_name\> has \<child_element_name\> add \<ref_name\>;
Disjoint Generalization	create \<dg\>
	\<parent_element_name\> has \<child_element_name\> add \<ref_name_1\> \<ref_name_2\> …;
Overlap Generalization	create \<og\>
	\<parent_element_name\> has \<child_element_name\> add \<ref_name_1\> \<ref_name_2\> …;
Aggregation	create \<ag\>
	\<element_name\> has \<sub-element_name minOccurs maxOccurs\>
	\<element_name\> has \<sub-element_name minOccurs maxOccurs\> add \<ref_name_1\> \<ref_name_2\>;
Categorization	create \<ca\>
	\<element_name\> has \<group_name_1\>, \<group_name_2\>;
Total Participation	create \<tp\>
	\<element_name\> has \<sub-element_name minOccurs maxOccurs\>;
Partial Participation	create \<pp\>
	\<element_name\> has \<sub-element_name_1 minOccurs maxOccurs\> add \<keyref_attribute_name_1\>, \<sub-element_name_2 minOccurs maxOccurs\> add \<keyref_attribute_name_2\> \<keyref_name\> link \<ref_name\>;
Cardinality in 1:1 and 1:n	create \<c1|cn\>
	\<element_name\> has \<sub-element_name minOccurs maxOccurs\>;
Cardinality in m:n	create \<cm\>
	\<element_name\> has \<sub-element_name minOccurs maxOccurs\> add \<ref_name_1\> \<ref_name_2\>;
Unary in 1:1 and 1:n	create \<u1|un\>
	\<element_name\> has \<sub-element_name ref_type minOccurs maxOccurs\>;
Unary in m:n	create \<um\>
	\<element_name\> has \<sub-element_name minOccurs maxOccurs\> add \<ref_name_1\> \<ref_name_2\>;

XSD-Translator

Translator uses for translating from source language (i.e. XSD-Source) to object language (i.e. XSD). The methodology of XSD-Translator is similar to a compiler except for object language. We focus on XSD instead of machine language. The architecture of XSD-Translator is grouped by 5 steps: Lexing, Parsing, Recovering, Optimizing, and Generating [10, 11] (as shown in Figure 3).

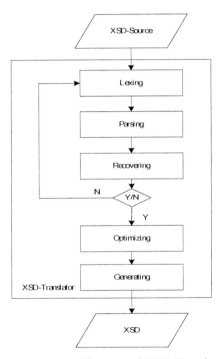

Fig. 3. Architecture of XSD-Translator

Lexing

Lexing is also called lexical analysis [11]. In general, an analyzer scans XSD-Source and lists them as XSD-Type and XSD-Attributes. The generic type is called XSD-Type and specific instances of the generic type are named XSD-Attributes. The following is an example XSD-Source of declaring a disjoint generalization relationship among a, A, b, c, and d elements.

```
create <dg>
<a> has <A> add <b> <c> <d>;
```

Parsing

Parsing is syntactic analysis [11]. We construct concrete syntax tree to show structure, order of keywords, and XSD-Type in a sentence. This tree is used in stages of optimizing and generating. Two parsing methods are used for this analysis. The first is top-down parsing and the second is bottom-up parsing. We apply a Left to Right (LR) parsing programming algorithm which is a bottom-up execution for searching typical grammars in an efficient way. The semantic analysis is recognized by a parser and took place with the syntactic analysis at the same time. This process is a syntax-directed translation. In this approach, when we execute a simple element phrase, we parse it into "identifier" + "keyword" + "identifier + symbol" (i.e. <element_name> has <attribute_name attribute_type>). This is a bottom-up parsing methodology in syntactic analysis. And also, we interpret the grammar as ("id"→"ky"→"id"→"sy") in semantic analysis.

Syntactic Analysis of Component Declaration

```
create <el>
<element_name> has <attribute_name_1 type>, <attrib-
   ute_name_2 type>
<sub-element_name_1> has <attribute_name_1 type>, <attrib-
   ute_name_2 type>;
```

In the above syntax, we see identifier, component symbols, keyword attributes, separator, and terminator. Grammar of this component declaration is that the "create" keyword attribute is defined as the core of sentence and placed at the first position of the declaration. The "el" component symbol is placed at the second position. After that, we can locate identifiers "element_name", "attribute_name", and "type" followed by the component symbol. A "has" keyword attribute may also be located if an element contains attribute. Otherwise, other identifiers as "sub-element", "attribute_name", and "type" are placed and a "has" keyword may be located in between "sub-element" and "attribute_name" if sub-element contains attribute.

Syntactic Analysis of Constraint Declaration

We apply the above theory for creating a constraint declaration in which we have 14 types of constraint symbols. The following is the example syntax for disjoint generalization.

```
create <dg>
<parent_element_name> has <child_element_name> add <sub-
    element_name_1>  <sub-element_name_2>;
```

The above syntax of constraint declaration is very close to the syntax of component declaration in which all elements and attributes are created. The aim of constraint declaration is to group all elements for forming a tree (i.e. creating relationship among elements). We find keywords, constraint symbol, identifiers, constant, unbounded, separator, and terminator. The "create" keyword attribute is defined as a starter and placed at the first position of declaration. The "dg" constraint symbol is placed at the second position. The rest of statement is used for defining facilities while constructing the "dg" constraint. The "parent_element_name" identifier and the "has" keyword attribute must be in this sequence. After that, we find a sub-element phrase containing an "element name" identifier. In the sub-element phrases, we find a keyword named "add" which is followed by the "element name" identifier. At the last sub-element phrase, we find several identifiers and a terminator.

Recovering

An automatic Error Recovering (AER) is used before a source language (i.e. XSD-Source) is optimized by XSD-Translator. The AER prompts users with error code found incorporate with line number of source language. A possible solution appears after the error code. Recovering works together with parsing. A set of criteria is used for proceeding error recovering from source language using "must/should" statement. The "must" statement means that AER must find in source code. The "should" statement means that AER should find in source code so that this statement is optional.

Optimizing

Optimizing analyzes organization of source language itself at intermediate level. The process will start at each declaration individually for implementing a global optimization. We search according to syntax of each declaration so as to link up all elements to provide a tree view. We work for a data semantics optimization. Each data semantic has a set of elements, subelements, group elements, complex type, or simple type. We have to organize and to manage those accessories for reducing redundancy occurring in semantic declaration. We apply self optimization on each set of component lists. For instance, if we find duplicated elements on an element list, then we erase others for implementing a unique name on the element list.

Otherwise, we add as a new element on the list. We also use compound optimization in referring element and referring attribute located in one of lists as element, complex type, simple type, and group.

Generating

The generator (i.e. XSD-Translator) is not for generating a source language into machine language. An object language generated by XSD-Translator is XSD. After examining the XSD-Source through several processes as parsing, recovering, and optimizing, it reaches a final stage to be translated into an XSD. The following is a rudimentary code segment for generating an XSD.

Element, Group, ComplexType, SimpleType	Appearing in the second level of tree
Sub-element, Ref-element Ref-attribute, Ref-group, Attribute	Appearing in the third or higher level of tree

Case Study for XSD from XML Tree Model

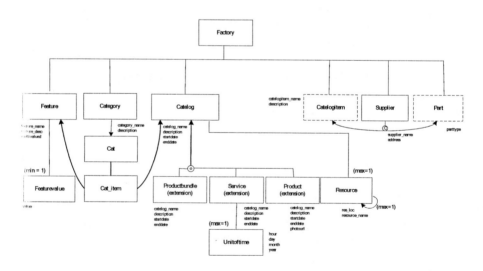

Fig. 4. XML Tree Model for the "factory" Case

Prototype of XSD-Builder

When we click on our prototype, we can see an opening screen. In that screen, there are several dialog-boxes such as component declaration, constraint declaration, error message, tree view, and XSD view. Firstly, we must input all components using the component dialog-box. And then, we can click on the transferring button near the component dialog-box. A tree view relating to the input will be displayed on the tree view dialog-box as shown in Fig. 5.

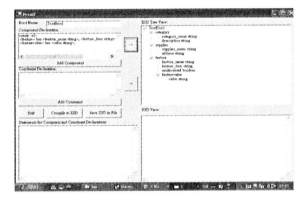

Fig. 5. Component Declaration and Tree View

Secondly, after loading the constraint declarations using the constraint dialog-box, the tree view will automatically be updated by the system. Eventually, if we do not have error message listed on the error dialog-box, we can generate XSD by pressing the compiling button as shown in Fig. 6.

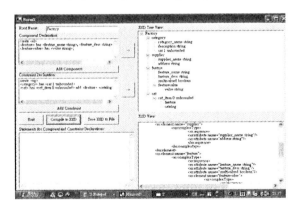

Fig. 6. Compiling XSD from Source Language

Conclusion

The main contribution of the paper is to create an XML Tree Model and an XSD-Builder specification language for XML Model. The XML Tree Model is initiated as a conceptual schema with data semantics preservation. User can design an XSD from an XML Tree Model by using our XSD-Builder. The data semantics can be confirmed by comparing with an XML document according to the data requirements. The prototype of XSD-Builder proves our algorithm is feasible and the proposed algorithm is effective and practical.

References

[1] Fong J, Huang S (1997) Information Systems Reengineering Chapter 7. Springer, Hong Kong
[2] Biron PV, Malhotra A (2001) XML Schema Part 2: Datatypes W3C Recommendation
[3] Nicolle C, Yetongnon K, Simon JC (2003) XML Integration and Toolkit for B2B Applications. J. of Database Management, vol 14, no 4, pp 33-58
[4] Fong J, Wong HK, Fong A (2003) Converting Relational Database into XML Documents with DOM. Journal of IST, vol 45, pp 335-355.
[5] Vlist EVD (2001) Using W3C XML Schema.
[6] Conrad R, Scheffner D, Freytag JC (2000) XML Conceptual Modeling Using UML. 19th I.C. on Conceptual Modeling, USA
[7] Kleiner C, Lipeck U (2001) Automatic Generation of XML DTDs from Conceptual Database Schemas. Workshop "Web Databases", Conf of German and Austrian Computer Societies, Session III, Vienna
[8] Xiao J, Wang Q, Li M, Zhou A (2003) FIXT: A Flexible Index for XML Transformation. 5th APWeb Conference, Springer, pp 144-149
[9] Funderburk JE, Kiernan G, Shanmugasundaram J, Shekita E, Wei C (2002) XTABLES: Bridging Relational Technology and XML. IBM Systems Journal, vol 41, no 4, pp 616-641
[10] Barrett WA, Couch JD (1979) Compiler Construction: Theory and Practice. Science Research Associates Ltd, pp 1-319
[11] Teufel B, Schmidt S, Teufel T (1993) Compiler Concepts. Springer-Verlag
[12] Miller RJ, Ioannidis YE, Ramakrishnan R (1993) The Use of Information Capacity in Schema Integration and Translation. Proc of the 19th VLDB Conference, Dublin Ireland

Challenges in Developing XML-Based Learning Repositories

Jerzy Auksztol and Tomasz Przechlewski

Department of Information Systems, University of Gdańsk, Poland.
(jerzya, ekotp)@univ.gda.pl

Introduction

There is no doubt that modular design has many advantages, including the most important ones: reusability and cost-effectiveness. In an e-learning community parlance the modules are determined as Learning Objects (LOs) [11]. An increasing amount of learning objects have been created and published online, several standards has been established and multiple repositories developed for them. For example Cisco Systems, Inc., "recognizes a need to move from creating and delivering large inflexible training courses, to database-driven objects that can be reused, searched, and modified independent of their delivery media" [6]. The learning object paradigm of education resources authoring is promoted mainly to reduce the cost of the content development and to increase its quality. A frequently used metaphor of Learning Objects paradigm compares them to Lego Logs or objects in Object-Oriented program design [25]. However a metaphor is only an abstract idea, which should be turned to something more concrete to be usable. The problem is that many papers on LOs end up solely in metaphors. In our opinion Lego or OO metaphors are gross oversimplificatation of the problem as there is much easier to develop Lego set or design objects in OO program than develop truly interoperable, context-free learning content[1].

The paper discusses in detail technical challenges of developing learning content in a modular way with XML-based technologies. In particular various approaches to XML schema design are presented. Next, authoring, storage, and management of structured documents as well as formatting and publishing problems are described. The concluding section contains

---

[1] Some authors strongly neglect the LO concept claiming that it is only motivated in cost-reduction obsessions and is not equally concerned with the pedagogical soundness of the instructions generated which results in low quality content [19].

a short description of Istyar—a small LCMS system based on XML and Java developed at the Gdańsk University.

The Concept of Reusable Learning Objects

There are several definitions what is a Learning Object. According to IEEE Learning Technology Standards Committee, the LO is: "any entity, digital or non-digital, that can be used or referenced during technology-supported learning" [16]. Obviously the above definition is next to useless for any practical use due to its vast generality. Thus in several other definitions the notion of Learning Object is limited only to "any *digital* entity that can be used to support learning" [25] but even those definitions of LOs lack details necessary for any practical application.

To implement LOs the definitions known to us are useless as they do not define precisely their content and structure. For example the most popular suite of e-learning "standards" SCORM defines LOs in a rather informal fashion: "The SCORM Content Model is made up of Assets, Sharable Content Objects (SCOs, SCO is a collection of one or more Assets) and Content Organization. Assets are an electronic representation of media, such as text, images, sound, assessment objects or any other piece of data that can be rendered by a Web client and presented to a learner"[2]. In our opinion the above definition, which describes data resources not formally but rather through "experiment" [renders by a Web client[2]] can be regarded only as a curiosity.

To sum up, although it is quite unclear what exactly a LO is, there is no doubt about the merits of a Learning Object. The key features of "perfect" LOs are: interoperability[3], adaptability[4], reusability[5], durability[6], and granularity[7]. A unit of a learning object can be a computer application (program), a course, a module, a lesson, a part of a lesson, or a binary object. Generally, finer level of granularity promotes reusability by allowing exploitation in multiple contexts. Of course the greater number of (smaller) objects the more efforts are required to search/discover and assemble LOs

---

[2] There are dozens of Web clients in use.
[3] The ability of two or more systems or components to exchange information and to use the information that has been exchanged [16].
[4] The ability of LO to match individual and/or contextual needs.
[5] Denotes the degree to which a software module or other work product can be used in more than one computing program or software system [16].
[6] Denotes LO's resistance to IT changes.
[7] Denotes the size and level of complexity of a learning resource.

into complete courses. With extremely high granularity the burden of assembling the content from very small pieces can surpass profits from information reuse [19].

Although resource content is generally undefined in various e-learning "standards", there are specifications defining metadata descriptions, such as LOM specification proposed by IEEE and incorporated by SCORM suite of specifications [2] (see also [15] for interesting critical review of LOs standardization efforts). It is envisaged that properly cataloged LOs can be easily searched and combined into modules regardless of its data format. However the quality of LOs publicly available in such repositories as ARIADNE (http://www.ariadne-eu.org/) clearly demonstrates that the above approach may be not feasible in practice. As granularity of ARIADNE content is rather low and metadata description very coarse, the re-use possibilities are very limited. It seems like a paradox that it is much easier to find and reuse educational content via general-purpose search engine, like Google than searching dedicated educational repository [22].

Developing Reusable Resources with XML

In traditional paper-based publishing environment cooperation between an author, an editor, and a graphic designer was required to achieve high quality output. An author was responsible for content delivery, an editor was taking care about structural consistency while a designer was preparing the presentation layout. The introduction of word-processors and DTP programs did not change the above process very much. Authors usually deliver content using some sort of office applications (like MS Word), later the content is edited and finally typeset. The fundamental obstacle is that at different stages of publishing process the parties involved usually use different, proprietary and incompatible document formats. Typically authors/editors use MS Words while the final layout is done in QuarkXPress, Adobe FrameMaker or similar. Any feedback is next to impossible as requires costly conversions.

To break the deadlock all involved parties should use one common *source format*, which separates the content of the document from its presentation layout. Such an approach allows *presentation layouts* for various requirements and/or different media to be generated automatically from the information contained in the source document. Further, it allows the content to be reused for additional purposes, not necessarily related to the original purpose of publishing or even foreseen when setting up the publishing system.

The eXtensible Markup Language (XML) [3] is widely regarded as a feasible approach for single-source publishing. Key features of the XML approach are logically-oriented, schema-driven authoring and automatic stylesheets-driven conversion to presentation formats. As the content of document can be precisely and in detail defined (and subsequently verified with appropriate software) its role is similar to the editor's job. To achieve this goal the logical structure of document should be carefully defined. It is the *structure-based editing*, not XML data format *per se*[8] which creates added value of easy reuse.

On the other hand stylesheets-driven document production substitutes graphic designer's job. Such documents can be easily processed to produce various presentational effects. These effects are displayed to the user or reader using new or previously existing technologies, including, but not limited to, HTML and PDF. Figure 1 depicts data flow in XML-based document management system.

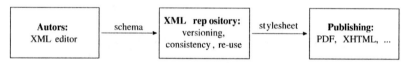

Fig. 1. Data flow in XML-based document management system

Approaches to Schema Development

There are several languages for developing XML schemas. The most popular ones are: Document Type Definition (DTD) [3], XML Schema (XSD) [13], and Relax NG [9]. DTD is the oldest schema language, originated from SGML. It has several drawbacks as non-XML syntax, weak datatyping of the content of leaf elements and attributes, or lack of any documentation facility which we consider its the most important shortcoming. As semantics of elements and attributes cannot be expressed in DTD it requires distinct sets of documentation to be developed, which is cumbersome. The advantage of DTD is its relative simplicity and availability of many applications, which support this standard.

XML Schema's key features include: strong typing for elements and attributes, enhanced integrity constraints (i.e. links between nodes within

---

[8] XML schema may define flat structured, visually oriented, documents (for example XHTML). Such documents do not offer almost any possibilities for reuse and multi-output presentation.

a document or between documents), namespaces support (essential for ex-tensibility), XML syntax, object-oriented design (i.e. schemas can extend or restrict a type) and documenting facility build-in. However one should note that almost all merits mentioned above are not particularly essential for document authoring and are rather targeted to such domains as data-base integration (for example Web Services, EDI, etc.). Moreover, XSD is complex, there are a few applications supporting it, and some of them im-plement XSD standard only partially.

The last standard seems to be the best trade-off between functionality and complexity. The Relax NG specification is the work of the OASIS Re-lax NG Technical Committee. OASIS, the Organization for the Advance-ment of Structured Information Standards, is an international, not-for-profit consortium that designs and develops industry standard specifica-tions for interoperability based on XML. Relax NG is supported by a fast growing number of tools and applications. Finally, it is possible to convert between different schema languages using such application as J. Clark's trang [7].

While it is certainly possible to create a fully customized schema for learning materials, the costs involved in creating and maintaining the schema, along with associated stylesheets, make this approach cost inef-fective. As XML-based solutions depend on open standards and are sup-ported by a huge number of free applications the strategy employed was to reuse what is available in the public. It have appeared that there are only a few widely used XML schemas, namely: XHTML [23], DocBook [24], and TEI [4][9] . There are some more, like Too-to-Matic used for authoring content at IBM developers site, but these are much less popular[10].

Docbook [24] is not only a schema, but a complete publishing frame-work, i.e. schemas plus stylesheets for conversion to presentation formats, actively developed and maintained. It is de facto standard for documenting many Open Source projects and as such it is widely known and used. Docbook schemas are available in DTD, XSD and Relax NG syntax. The drawbacks of Docbook are: 1) it is an extensive schema containing almost 400 elements, 2) the document structure is relatively loose (to fit various needs) and oriented towards technical documentation manuals and similar documents.

---

[9] Specialized, domain-oriented vocabularies like SVG [14] for vector graphics and MathML [5] for math formulas describe terminal nodes of XML-tree and thus its is easy—using XML namespaces—to embed them in other languages.

[10] On the other hand initiatives like *The Educational Modeling Language* (EML) are targeted to describe complex pedagogical models, not to define course re-sources structures.

The Text Encoding Initiative (TEI) Guidelines [4] are an international and interdisciplinary standard that facilitates libraries, museums, and publishers represent a variety of literary and linguistic texts online. It is not as popular as DocBook, used mainly in the academia. TEI schemas are available in DTD, XSD and Relax NG syntax.

All above mentioned schemas have appeared to be unsuitable for authoring of e-learning content for various reasons. Docbook and TEI are too complicated, while XHTML completely is unsuitable as a visually oriented application of XML.

To avoid developing yet another XML schema a technique of using different schemas at different stages of editorial process[11] may be considered. In this model the hub may be DocBook or TEI schema. Using common, widely used document format (Docbook/TEI) should enhance data interoperability and avoid locking in specific data format. The translation of documents from authoring schema into the reference schema may be easily performed with XSLT stylesheets.

Challenges of XML-based Authoring

The best way of authoring XML documents is with the help of dedicated schema-driven editors (aka XML editors)[12] , which have the following features: on-the-fly document validation, context-sensitive editing, tree view, syntax-highlighting or/and markup-hiding. There are however at least two problems with XML editors:

1. At present most authors are accustomed with "Office" like applications which are simply unsuitable for authoring complex-structured XML documents;
2. There are only a few full-functional XML editors, most of them are simple applications with limited functionality.

Many XML editors limit their support to syntax highlighting and cannot validate the document content. Many applications lack support for mixed content, which is a crucial feature for document authoring. There are no

---

[11] Following Maler (cf. [17]) we will call the schema common to a group of users within an interest group as *reference* schema while those used solely for editing purposes as *authoring* schema

[12] The other way is to produce content with office applications (like MS Office or Open Office) using styles and then converted it to XML. It is however only feasible for simple documents as styles have flat structure and there is no facility to verify authoring consistency.

applications supporting such advanced functions as: visual table editing, easy authoring of mathematical formulas (MathML support), point-and-click interface for inserting pictures. There are problems with spell checkers/thesauruses etc., particularly in non-English environment.

To enhance content reuse, the documents have to be managed in a central database—such as CVS or Subversion repository—or accessed by Webdav protocol. XML document can be easily assembled from separated parts using either XML entities or newer XInclude standard. W3C XInclude [18] standard defines a simple mechanism for creating use-by-reference links within XML documents. Both, entire external documents or parts of them can be included. Moreover, the XInclude fallback element can be used to provide some form of fallback content in case that the inclusion cannot be resolved. It is however unrealistic to expect authors to specify Xinclude references with Xpoiner [12] attributes. Some sort of user interface enabling simple selection via "point and click" interface is needed. Currently however none of the available XML authoring applications provide the XInclude support.

The authoring with access control, versioning, and consistency enforced with schemas has clear advantages over the collaboration of users based on standard word processors.

Formatting with XSLT

Traditionally a document is regarded as a self-contained unit of information, intended solely for human interpretation. With XML it is no longer true, and often some extensive processing is needed before formatting content. The problem is addressed with several W3C's recommendations, namely XPath[13], XSLT[14], and XSL-FO[15]. There are numerous high-quality implementations of XPath and XSLT languages both at a server as well as a browser side (including MSIE and Mozilla/Firefox browsers). Moreover, it is expected that support for XML-encoded information will become ubiquitous and several standards will be added to next-generation web browsers[16].

---

[13] A language for addressing parts of an XML document tree.
[14] A language for transforming XML documents into other XML documents, HTML, or text.
[15] Defines an XML vocabulary for specifying formatting semantics.
[16] Like SVG for vector graphics, MathML for math formulas and (perhaps) XML-FO for high quality graphical layout.

XSLT is commonly regarded as a perfect solution for transforming XML into HTML. However, production-quality paginated output from the XML content is a much harder problem, which is addressed by the XSL-FO (or shortly FO) W3C's specification. A FO document describes the details of the presentation, such as page size, margins, fonts, colors, etc. using XML syntax. To obtain a hard-copy output some FO-aware application is needed. Today the most common application of FO is to produce Adobe PDF documents from the source XML files. However, there are only a few FO implementations available, including Open Source fop processor from Apache Project. Implementation of FO specification by fop is incomplete, with substantial parts unsupported; for example there are some problems with rendering tables, widows/orphans control or positioning of floating elements such as figures. The typographical quality of PDF documents produced with fop processor is rather poor.

Using DocBook schema as a hub format ready-available DocBook XSL stylesheets (http://sourceforge.net/projects/docbook/) can be used to translate XML document to XHTML or FO [21]. Such an approach can greatly reduce development costs and improve quality. As they are written in a modular fashion they can be easily customized and localized. To publish XHTML from XML documents an XSLT engine is needed. With just a few customizations, the translation from XML to XHTML presents no problems. For hard copy output two step process is used. First, the XSLT engine produces formatting objects, which later must be processed with a formatting object processor for PDF output.

Managing Content with Istyar

The framework of e-learning content publishing at Gdańsk University is based on traditional publishing workflow [20]. Potential projects are firstly reviewed and only those accepted are published (with IBM Lotus LMS). The content delivered by authors is converted and processed by professional editors and designers. As it is expected the authors will deliver their content in "office" applications without strict requirements concerning its format. It causes great amount of editorial costs. Thus, due to financial restrictions only limited number of projects can be published. Moreover, the reuse of the content is difficult as author's documents and finally published content are "incompatible".

Certainly, the infrastructure is designed for high-quality projects—similar to traditional textbooks—but not for smaller ones, like tutorials, deliverables, students projects, etc. These documents are very often built collaboratively, by various authors and have to be updated pretty frequently[17].

The common practice is to develop a content with the help of office applications and publish them in a native format or converted to HTML or PDF. While simple, such an approach impedes interoperability: the content is developed virtually for the personal usage of the limited number of users. Valuable resources are often not reused for nobody knows about their existence or publication format does not allow any modifications.

To support authoring and publishing content within the scenario described above Istyar (cf. http://www.istyar.org), a small LCMS based on the ideas and technologies described in the previous sections was developed. The main design assumption is to use XML standards in order to separate content form presentation, facilitate collaborative authoring, storage, search/discovery and reuse of simple learning content.

Istyar was inspired by Toot-o-matic framework (ie. schema, stylesheets and software for processing automation) developed at IBM for authoring IT-related tutorials (cf. http://www-130.ibm.com/developerworks/). Toot-o-matic is simple yet powerful and clearly demonstrates the advantages of using open standards. The process of building learning content in Istyar was completely redesigned. In particular, Toot-o-matic schema lacks important elements (like authors name and publishing date for example) and formatting stylesheets are only suitable for publishing at IBM site. The figure 2 shows the phases of transformation from schema oriented XML documents to presentation formats such as HTMLs and PDFs.

The technology used to transform learning content is based on various packages from Jakarta project, namely: ant for process automation, batik for conversion of various graphics formats, fop for converting FO files to PDF and Xalan/Xerces for transforming XML files via XSLT stylesheets.

The findings of Istyar project are twofold. The positive aspects relate to the separation of the content and the presentation. The system can be extended to some new forms of presentation, for example Braille's documents, without changing any elements in the XML learning content base. On the other hand, the project shows the limitations of some of the tools used. The authoring/transformation of complex content—like tables and math formulas—is difficult and cumbersome. This leads to the conclusion that developing an "advanced" content such as assessment objects, graphics or multimedia in a reusable way should be carefully evaluated.

---

[17] Particularly, those concerned with IT are subject to frequent updates due to new version of software installed in computer labs, new hardware available etc.

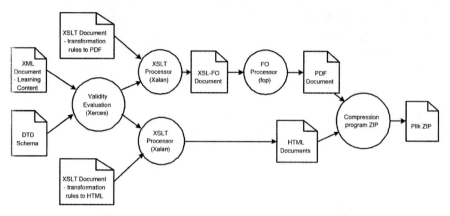

Fig. 2. Transformation process in Istyar project

Summary

The paper presents the concept of electronic archive of learning content based on XML and related standards. It is argued that structured documents are the best format for storing/retrieving documents as they are not tied to any presentation medium. They also enable efficient workflow and retrieval of documents. XSLT stylesheets enables efficient formatting on different presentation media. In our paper the outline of a complete XML-based system for electronic documents publishing and storing is described as well as the successes and challenges encountered in implementing it.

References

[1] Adler S et al. (2001) Extensible Stylesheet Language (XSL) version 1.0. http://www.w3.org/TR/xsl/
[2] ADL Initiative (2004) SCORM Content Aggregation Model version 1.3.1. http://www.adlnet.org
[3] Bray T, Paoli J, Sperberg-McQueen CM (1998) Extensible Markup Language (XML) 1.0. http://www.w3.org/TR/1998/REC-xml-19980210/
[4] Burnard L, Sperberg-McQueen CM (2002) TEI Lite: An Introduction to Text Encoding for Intechange. http://www.tei-c.org/Lite/
[5] Carlisle D et al. (2003) Mathematical Markup Language (MathML) Version 2.0. http://www.w3.org/TR/2003/REC-MathML2-20031021/
[6] Cisco Systems Reusable Information Object Strategy: Definition, Creation, Overview and Guidelines (1999) http://www.cisco.com/

[7] Clark J (2003) Trang—Multi-Format Schema Converter Based on RELAX NG. http://www.thaiopensource.com/relaxng/trang.html
[8] Clark J (undated) XSL Transformations (XSLT) Version 1.0. www.w3.org/TR/xslt/.
[9] Clark J, Murata M (2001) Relax NG Specification. www.relaxng.org/
[10] De Rose S, Maler E, Orchard D (2001) XML Linking Language (Xlink). www.w3.org/TR/xlink
[11] Downes S (2003) Design and Reusability of Learning Objects in an Academic Context: a New Economy of Education? USDLA Journal, vol 17, no 1. www.usdla.org/html/journal/JAN03_Issue/
[12] Grosso P, Maler E, Marsh J, Walsh N (2003) XPointer Framework. W3C. http://www.w3.org/TR/xptr-framework/
[13] Fallside DC, Walmsley P (2004) XML Schema Part 0: Primer Second Edition. W3C. www.w3.org/TR/xmlschema-0/
[14] Ferraiolo J (red) (2001) Scalable Vector Graphics (SVG) 1.0 Specification. www.w3.org/TR/SVG/
[15] Friesen N (2004) Three Objections to Learning Objects and E-learning Standards. In: McGreal R (ed) Online Education Using Learning Objects. Routledge London. www.learningspaces.org/n/papers/objections.html
[16] IEEE Standard Computer Dictionary: A Compilation of IEEE Standard Computer Glossaries (1999) IEEE New York
[17] Maler E, El Andaloussi J (1995) Developing SGML DTDs. From Text to Model to Markup. Prentice Hall PTR
[18] Marsh J, Orchard D (2004) XML Inclusions (XInclude) Version 1.0. W3C. www.w3.org/TR/2004/REC-xinclude-20041220/
[19] Mohan P, Greer J (2003) Reusable Learning Objects: Current Status and Future Directions. www.campussaskatchewan.ca/pdf.asp?pdf=PMohanEdMedia03.pdf
[20] Penkowska G (2005) Wybrane elementy e-edukacji na Uniwersytecie Gdanskim, e-Mentor, 2/2005
[21] Stayton R (2003) Using the DocBook XSL Stylesheets. Sagehill Enterprises, www.sagehill.net/docbookxsl/index.html
[22] Verhaart M (2004) Learning Object Repositories: How useful are they? In: Mann S, Clear T (eds) Proc of the 17th Annual Conference of the National Advisory Committee on Computing Qualifications Conference, Christchurch New Zealand, July 6-9 2004. www25.brinkster.com/verhaart/mvcv.htm.
[23] W3C (2002) XHTML 1.0 The Extensible HyperText Markup Language. www.w3.org/TR/xhtml1/.
[24] Walsh N, Muelner L (1999) Docbook: the Definitive Guide. O'Reilly. www.docbook.org/tdg/en/html/docbook.html.
[25] Wiley DA (2000) Connecting Learning Objects to Instructional Design Theory: A Definition, a Metaphor, and a Taxonomy. In: Wiley DA (ed) The Instructional Use of Learning Objects. http://reusability.org/

Semantic Modeling for Virtual Organization: A Case for Virtual Course

William Song[1] and Xiaoming Li[2]

[1] Computer Science, University of Durham, United Kingdom.
w.w.song@durham.ac.uk
[2] Information School, Peking University, China. lxm@pku.edu.cn

Introduction[1]

Current researches on the World Wide Web and the Grid, as well as Web Services, have come to a consensus issue. That is, how to extract and represent semantics for the web information and the Grid recourses. As known to us, the World Wide Web provides an infrastructure for information exchange and interoperation and the Grid provides an infrastructure for resource sharing and cooperation. The interoperability and collaboration requires common understanding of information about resources and the understanding requires canonical and well-formed semantic description. The semantic description is used both for human and machine to understand each other.

It is known to us, in the grid computing environment, there are many resources, such as university or governmental departments, and courses or software components as well, which we call nodes in the context of the virtual organizations. A virtual organization can be seen as "a temporary alliance of contracted individuals or companies linked together by information and communication technologies, which assembles for the purpose of a specific business task" (ICENI). These nodes are connected to each other, exchanging information, sharing their resources, and collaborating on certain tasks. Usually, for a given purpose or task, a collection of nodes can be temporarily and dynamically organized together to form a virtual organization, while each node in the virtual organization plays different roles and performs different activities and these nodes are coordinate and cooperate so that the different roles and activities are integrated to achieve the assigned goal.

[1] The work is partially supported by the ChinaGrid project and the 973 project (2004CB318204).

Because these nodes in the grid are usually heterogeneous, autonomous, have different structures, and possess different characteristics and ontologies, it is indispensable for the nodes to experience a painful process of communications and mutual understanding before reaching a consensus and forming an organization (virtual and dynamic). During this process, commonalities and distinctions in information and organizational structure, domain problems, community terminologies, and business strategies and domain ontologies are analyzed, described, and represented.

Key Issues in Modeling for Virtual Organization

In the investigation of the concept "virtual organization", we find ourselves facing three great difficulties in the description, structuring, and integration of the nodes to produce a virtual organization (Song 2003). The first one is how to capture and understand each single node in terms of its structure, functionality, resource distribution and assignment, etc. The second one is how to build up a semantic description framework suitable for the understanding, description, representation, and validation of the nodes as well as their integration. The third one is how to coordinate and integrate all the nodes (their structures, semantics, functionalities, processes, etc.) in the organization and to produce a global virtual organization with all the requirements met and all the features maintained.

Corresponding to the three difficulties, there are three aspects of issues concerning a virtual organization: the enterprise issue, semantic issue, and integration issue. The **enterprise issue** concerns the motivations or objectives of a virtual organization. An enterprise model can support to describe the characteristics of a virtual organization in terms of its objectives. The enterprise model indicates how different components work together. This part of the description framework attempts to state the strategic activities among the organization.

The **semantic issue** mainly concerns the concepts to be defined. The concepts and related ideas are defined in a way that all the partners in the organization can understand and agree with them. This requires first of all a semantic perception of all the terms and concepts used in the organization, including actors, roles, processes, ontologies, etc.

The definition of these terms and their interrelations provide the domain knowledge for the organization. The information sharing and exchange is extremely important for the organization. Good semantic capturing and representation for the concepts and components in the organization paves a way toward a good integration.

Regarding the **integration issue**, the properties of two nodes in a virtual organization are compared with each other to determine a set of interdependencies between them. The interdependencies can be logic ones if the fulfillment of node A is a condition for the fulfillment of node B. The interdependencies can be structural ones where each node plays a particular role in the virtual organization and all these roles make up the virtual organization. The interdependencies can be semantic ones where one node semantically implies other nodes.

Realcourse: an Application Case

University Course Online (in short, *realcourse*), composed of 20 servers, is a Course service supported by a collection of physical servers distributed on CERNET all over China (Zhang and Li 2004). Besides the servers that share the single URL (http://realcourse.grids.cn), there are more than 2000 hours of quality course services available. These services are from different universities, uploaded to different servers with a permanent backup copy created in a server other than the original one, and flow from one server to another. If one server is down, its duty is automatically taken up by some other server.

In this circumstance, each server provides a number of resources for a course (usually all the resources required for a course are in one server). However, with the fast growing capacity of resources and variation of courses, it will be difficult and unreasonable for one server to contain all the required resources for a "single" course.

We propose the metadata model to provide semantic description for resources and courses. Other than the elements, similar to the Dublin Core elements, the metadata model also provides pre-condition and post-condition for resources so that it is possible to integrate a number of resources to form a "virtual" course. The description for a course is more complicated. For example, a course may consist of a lot of resources, which include a few training materials such as video clips and sound clips, a dozen of presentations (in PPT or PDF form), many research papers, articles, standards specifications documents, and other textual materials, some tools with the user manuals and reference books. Therefore we use the enterprise model for the description of courses and requirements.

In order to describe and manage all these resources (physically distributed) and make them well organized and available on demand (on requirements), we propose the method of "virtual organization" (in this circumstance, a virtual course) for the purpose. The proposed concept attempts to contain semantic description for resources and enterprise analysis for course search, matching, and integration.

Overview

The paper is organized as follows. In the next section we discuss some basic concepts for virtual organization and virtual course, where we focus on the concept of resources. Then we propose a semantic description framework for description of physical and logical resources in section 3. The framework contains an ontology model, a metadata model and an enterprise model. Using the enterprise modeling facility to support search and match in the virtual course is a key issue addressed in this paper, in particular, for the users' requirements and goals. In section 4, we discuss how to construct goals and other factors for object search and match. We propose the design architecture for building up a virtual course in section 5 and finally in section 6 we conclude the paper by discussing our next research work.

Basic Concepts

In this section, we attempt to informally define some basic concepts. Generally speaking, a "virtual organization" is a temporary grouping of physically distributed resources, semantically linked together in a certain information infrastructure, which serves the purpose of a specific task. The main concept to be discussed is "resource".

We distinguish two kinds of resources, i.e., physical resources and logical resources. A physical resource is an object physically existing in a server, for example, CPU time. A typical property of such physical resources is its status, i.e., whether it is connected or disconnected to the internet. Usually a physical resource has, as its attributes, a name, an identifier, a visit address, a size, etc.

A logical resource usually represents a set of distributed physical resources. A logical resource has, as its attributes, a name, an address, a location, a type, and other metadata such as subject. A logical resource usually has relationships with other logic resources, for example, having the same subject or being similar.

A virtual organization is a set of interrelated resources likely from different servers. A virtual organization is usually involved in a number of logic structures. On the server side, each server provides a set of physical resources forming a logical structure. For example, the virtual course "Protégé" takes a demo system from Stanford, a series of tutorials from Manchester, and so on.

The logic structure for the set of resources on the server is described by the semantic modeling methodology, consisting of metadata model, ontology model, and enterprise model.

Semantic Modeling for Virtual Organization

There are many resources available on the web but most of them are less described and structured. Web resources such as electronic documents, images, movies, sounds, and their interrelations and links, all are quite complicated. As the web information is explosively growing, this complexity must be effectively managed. Semantic modeling is an effective means to manage complexity in information construction.

Semantic models help us to understand the web resources by simplifying some of details (Conallen 1999). Semantic modeling also helps us to represent main features and main structures of the web resources and their management and exchange. Modeling has two benefits in support of web resource management. One is to understand and represent application domains and map them to information systems. The other is to abstract the existing web information for re-organization.

Physical Resources

As we previously described, each server provides a set of physical resources and a virtual organization consists of resources from many servers. For a given virtual organization, there are a collection of servers to support the virtual organization to operate, which are denoted to be $S = \{s_1, s_2, ..., s_m\}$. Each server contains a collection of resources, denoted to be $R = \{R_1, R_2, ..., R_m\}$, where $R_i = \{r_1, r_2, ..., r_n\}$, r_j is a single resource and R_i is the set of resources in the server s_i.

We define a resource to be a quadruple: $r_j = \{$**id, name, type, ps**$\}$, where **id** is the internal representation of the resource, **name** is the name of the resource, **type** is the type of the resource, and **ps** is the physical structure of the resource.

The **type** element indicates the type of a resource. The types contain multimedia type, textual type, and executable file type. A multimedia type can be mpg, rm, etc. A textual type can be doc, ppt, etc. The physical structure, **ps**, is used to organize the resources in a server. For each resource, there is a path from the server root to the folder which directly contains the resource. In this path, a non-leave node represents a folder (represented by its name). The root node is the server (i.e. server name) and the leave node is the resource.

Maintaining these paths (forming a hierarchy for all the resources) aims at acquiring the original and natural information of how the users organize their resources. This organization embodies the users' understanding of the structure of the resources in the servers.

Semantic Model

The semantic model provides a semantic description for a resource. The semantic description includes the attributes of the resource, the relationships of the resource with other resources, some special structure of the resource, and so on. As we know, the major purpose for a virtual organization is to find a suitable set of interrelated resources to fulfill the requirements for a given task. Therefore the semantic modeling should target at resource description, resource integration, and requirement description. The semantic description for resources includes a metadata model and an ontology model. The semantic description for requirements or the users queries is an enterprise modeling. The constructs of these models are based on the basic concepts defined in the basic semantic model.

The **basic semantic model** contains three constructs: object type, relationship type, and attribute type. An object of the **Object type** represents any static or dynamic resource, or a grouping of the resources. It can be simply viewed as a logic resource. A relationship of the **Relationship type** represents any connection between objects. An attribute of the **Attribute type** represents any descriptive characteristics for an object.

The **ontology model** is a special structure for a set of objects, where only a special relationship between the objects is maintained, for example, generalization (is-a). From the point of view of concepts, an ontology model is a tree, where all the nodes are concepts. There is one special node, called the root, which is the most generalization concept in the tree. A parent concept of a number of concepts is the generalization of their children concepts.

The purpose of defining the ontology model is to provide a referencing conceptual framework for the virtual organization, which we use to reason about, e.g., whether two resources (teacher A and lecturer B) belong to the same concept. In the reality, we can obtain this kind of ontology from the standards or conventions. For example, an ordinary library subject category (LSC) is this kind of ontology model for learning domain

The **metadata model** is a set of standardized metadata descriptions for an object. Each metadata represents an object attribute in the metadata model. In the application domain, the metadata model contains these attributes: object name (also representing its concept), subjects (associating with its ontology model), keywords, physical structure (a logic mapping of its resource physical structure), and pre-conditions and post-conditions. All the attributes for physical resource description are naturally included in the metadata model.

Among others, the pre-conditions and post-condition attributes of an object are two sets of special attributes, which are used for finding suitable objects as the context of this object. The statements of pre-conditions and post-conditions are used in enterprise analysis. In this application, we propose the association graph, a directed graph, to describe the relations between objects. Due to the paper size, we will not discuss this in detail.

Enterprise Modeling and User Requirements

The process to form a virtual organization is a complex one. Other than building up the structures for resources on the distributed servers using the semantic model, it is crucial to capture and formulate the end users requirements, as that is the ultimate goal of the virtual organization.

The user requirements come from two aspects: a set of general requirements that we collect from the end users and a set of specific queries. To analyze the users' requirements the enterprise modeling and analysis is a very effective method. An enterprise model contains as its constructs goal type, process type, actor type, and concept type (Bubenko and Kirikova 98). The **goal type** indicates the "why" that the users want the objects or course. The **process type** indicates that the "how" the users would consider it can be performed. Some of the process type issues have already been discussed above in the dynamic aspects. The **actor type** indicates the "who" that will perform the processes. The **concept type** provides the definitions of objects. Most of the concerns about the concepts are mainly dealt with in the semantic modeling.

Enterprise Analysis for Search

Search for required objects is important in the virtual organization system. Although many search methods have been proposed, little attention is paid to a synthetic representation of information from the end users (or actors), such as preferences. Furthermore, if we view the users' requirements as a set of goals, the process of search is that of goal matching. In the following we explain the goal driven search for a virtual organization system.

Object search is not a blind search when we search for a certain object for a course. Usually when proposing a virtual course, the users have already some expectations in mind. Some expectations are quite clear but others may be vague. No matter how unclear, incomplete, and ambiguous these expectations are, they are considered search goals. In addition, we can collect the users' preferences and profiles for search. In the following we discuss what the forms of goals driven search are, how preferences and profiles are represented, and what search paths are used.

Search Structure

As discussed previously, the first important element in a search goal is **goal**. This element is expressed explicitly by the user. The element can be a statement or one word for the subject to search. Since we allow search goals to be vague, so a goal statement can be in the form of one word or a set of words, about subjects or topics. The second element assigned is **carrier** (for example, the server or the folder to the user's knowledge that holds the object) of the objects. We allow "null" as default value for the element. The third and fourth elements are users' **preferences** and **profiles**. The preferences and profiles are mainly used for tuning the goal matching process.

Therefore, a search goal structure is: <[Goal-statement], [Carrier], [Preference], [Profile]> where a) goal-statement is a list of subjects or a statement of search goal; b) carrier is the server of the object; c) preference is a list of statements that the user specifies; and d) profile is a set of related information about the user.

For example, a university student wants to find some courses on Java. He or she may be aware of its carrier being server A and the course is for the beginners. Then the goal he or she will write is: <[Programming, Java], [Server A], [beginner], [university student]>.

Another example is a search goal for a marketing department manager. She hopes to know *what the trend for electronic commerce on the market is*. This goal needs some analysis first before fitting in the search goal structure. The goal needs to be decomposed into a number of sub-goals, e.g. electronic commerce, products, market, economic situation, etc. Here two goals are defined as follows: <[electronic commerce, products], [any], [trend], [marketing department, manager]>, and <[marketing, electronic commerce], [e-Business], [positive], [--]>.

More important is a formal construction for goal descriptions because goals will find their places when a set of exact descriptions for various goals are well specified (Song 1997).

Search Goal Matching

The search goal match deals with the users' goal structure, e.g., what she or he would like. The goal match process contains comparing the user's requirements with the description items (metadata) of the objects stored and maintained in the repository (remember that the Web is a huge repository for the Grid resources). Once a goal match is found, either the matched object is presented to the user, or a further match is expected if there are a number of decomposed goals. Under this circumstance, we call search goal match contains search paths.

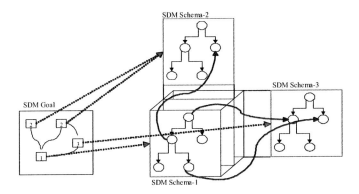

Fig. 1. Goal match and search paths. A SDM schema is a semantic description of a physical server or logic structure of the requirements for a virtual course

Search paths mean that a collection of goal driven requirements, preferences and profiles, is associated to different aspects in the semantic model schemas for an application domain, see Fig.1. In the figure, the cubic, multi-layered box at the center is a semantic description of the virtual organization objects on an application domain. Each layer is a semantic description model (SDM) schema with a hierarchical description of objects on e.g. a subject or a user preference. Here we show three layers, called respectively SDM Schema-1, SDM Schema-2, and SDM Schema-3. The objects in different layer schemas are connected as e.g. neighbor relationship, displayed by the curved arrowed lines. To the left of the figure, a flat box represents a search goal structure, where search goal statements, carriers, the user preferences, and profiles are included in the numbered smaller boxes. Search paths are these dotted arrow lines from the search goal box to the SDM Schemas. This accomplishes the whole process of search goal matching.

The search process is an integration process since different search elements in a search goal structure are directed toward different SDM schemas first. After the goal matches, these search paths are synthesized to form a meaningful search result. For example, consider this goal, <[marketing, electronic commerce], [e-Business], [general], [manager]>. The goal statement contains two sub-goals, marketing and electronic commerce. These sub-goals are analyzed in the SDM Schema-2 and then the results will be further compared with the other results from the SDM schemas, Schema-1 and Schema-3.

Design Architecture for Virtual Organization

A virtual organization system concerns three kinds of places: servers, clients, and ontology suppliers, see Fig. 2. First, at the server side, all resources are physically maintained. We need to use the semantic modeling facilities to supply semantics to modify the resources and build semantic properties to the resources and semantic relationships among the resources as well. Hence we obtain a logic representation and semantic representation for the resource set. Since there are many such servers containing lots of resources available, this semantic modeling process is indispensable to automatic or semi-automatic discover what resources from which server are semantically meeting our demands.

Second, at the client side, we analyze the real users' requirements and transform the requirements into a formal representation. To establish a virtual organization, the users provide their serious considerations and demands. The proposed system also provides an interactive mechanism, so that at run time, the users can still supply their queries based on the current results from the virtual organization.

Third, the ontology knowledge and metadata knowledge are from the application domain experts. For example, a librarian possesses much rich knowledge on how a library subject category is structured and meant. So it is more professional and authoritative to connect to these places for gaining the ontology and metadata standards. Both the resource providers (the nodes in a grid) and the virtual organization users require these knowledge repositories for their modeling processes.

Based on the analysis of the user's requirements (objectives and demands), a formal structure for search is generated and the user's personal agent will broadcast the search information to the Web/Grid. The results searched will be collected and sent to the client side for matching.

Finally we briefly discuss the architecture for the virtual course integration. The core of the architecture consists of a semantic dictionary that maintains the properties (formal definitions) of the nodes in the virtual organization, a set of integration rules that put together the nodes, and a set of functions that the virtual organization is going to perform (Song 2004).

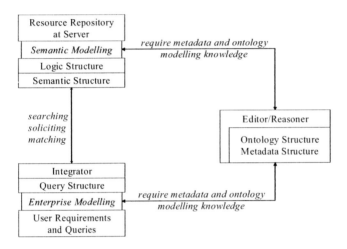

Fig. 2. Design architecture of virtual organization for *Realcourse*

This set of functions is a means to measure how the virtual organization works as well as its performance. For each set of functions, the semantic dictionary and the integration rules will dynamically produce a set of nodes to form a virtual organization.

In addition, a language processor is designed for the XML documents, RDF/S documents, and ontology structures. An inference engine will perform the reasoning tasks for comparison, match, and integration of nodes. A node database is used to manage all the data about the nodes in the grid.

Conclusion

"Virtual organization" has become an important issue in many application areas, such as semantic grid computing, semantic web, e-Learning, e-Government, and e-Business. It is a key step to best make use of the resources distributed over the web and grid environment, i.e., to find the most suitable resources, to best meet the users' requirements, to efficiently integrate the resources to form the virtual organization on demand. The first step toward the objective is to develop a resource based semantic description model.

In this paper, we used *Realcourse* as a virtual course, to realize some important aspects of a virtual organization, including semantic extraction and modeling from resources, user requirements description and modeling, the requirements search and match.

Our next step is to formalize the semantic description model for virtual organization components. Then based on the model, we will realize, on top of *Realcourse*, a resource representation structure and a user query formation, and hence make the high-level goal search available over the web.

References

Bubenko JA, Kirikova M (1998) Improving the Quality of Requirements Specifications by Enterprise Modelling. In: Nilsson, AG, Tolis C, Nellborn C (eds) Perspectives on Business Modelling. Spriger Verlag

Conallen J (1999) Modeling Web Application Architectures with UML. Communications of the ACM, vol 42, no 10

Introna L, Moore H, Cushman M (1999) The Virtual Organisation – Technical or Social Innovation? Lessons from the Film Industry. Working Paper Series 72, Department of Information Systems London School of Economics and Political Science UK

Song W (1997) OFEM: An Approach towards Detection and Reduction of Objectives Inconsistencies. Proc of the International Database Engineering and Applications Symposium (IDEAS'97) Montreal Canada

Song W (2003) Semantic Issues in the Grid computing and Web Services. Proc of International Conference on Management of e-Commerce and e-Government Nanchang China

Song W (2004) An Investigation of Semantic Web Services in the Context of Virtual Organization. Dept. Report Computer Science University of Durham

Zhang J-Y, Li X-M (2004) The Model, Architecture and Mechanism Behind Realcourse. Proc of International Symposium on Parallel and Distributed Applications (ISPA04)

ICENI Virtual Organisation Management. London e-Science Centre UK

semiBlog – Semantic Publishing of Desktop Data

Knud Möller, John Breslin and Stefan Decker

DERI, National University of Ireland, Galway, Republic of Ireland.
(knud.moeller, john.breslin, stefan.decker)@deri.org

Introduction

A number of approaches have been suggested to solve the chicken-and-egg problem that the Semantic Web faces; one of the most prominent among them being the automatic generation of formal data from text and other sources through the use of various Information Extraction (IE) techniques. In this paper, however, we will not take that approach, but instead follow the suggestion to build applications that would produce formal, Semantic Web (SW)-conformant data as a by-product of processes that users might already be performing on a regular basis [6].

A typical user will often have a vast amount of data available on their desktop[1], such as entries in an electronic address book, bibliographic metadata in formats like BibTeX, or MP3 metadata. This data might either have been entered manually by the users themselves, or collected externally (e.g. through sources like Bibster [5] or Gracenote's CDDB[2]). Such data is already formal data, and can in principle be transformed into a SW format like the Resource Description Framework (RDF). However, while this transformation is theoretically a simple enough process, in the absence of easy-to-use tools it is time consuming and tiresome for an ordinary user to perform. This leads to the situation that there is usually little to no motivation to actually produce and publish SW data. The data remains locked within the user's computer.

At the same time, the recent phenomenon of weblogging (or "blogging") [14] has made it possible for ordinary users to publish on the Web, and thus become content producers instead of content consumers. A number of blogging platforms such as Blogger[3] or Movable Type[4] allow users to pub-

---

[1] We use the term *desktop* as a metaphor for the entire working environment within a computer.

[2] CDDB: www.gracenote.com/music/

[3] Blogger: www.blogger.com

[4] Movable Type: www.sixapart.com/movabletype/

lish almost any kind of data (mostly text and pictures). Blog authors manage their own content in their own blog, structure it through time in the form of discrete blog entries and are able to categorise these entries. It is also possible to comment on other people's entries or refer to them through links (trackbacks[5], pingbacks[6]). Most blogs provide a so-called newsfeed, which acts as a syndicated table of contents. These feeds are usually published alongside the blog at a separate URL and can contain various kinds of metadata for each entry (e.g. a title, short description, date, author, link, etc.). Feeds are used by blog or news readers and aggregators to allow subscription to and aggregation of different blogs. Various kinds of dialects for newsfeeds are currently in use, the most prominent being the RSS family of feed languages. Of these, versions 0.9x and 2.0 are implemented in XML, while the 1.0 strand (RDF Site Summary (RSS 1.0) [1]) uses RDF[7].

Semantic Blogging

We believe that it will be possible to utilise the blogging phenomenon to unlock the data on a user's desktop and make it easy to publish it on the SW. The result would be what we call "semantic blogging" – blogs enriched with semantic, machine-understandable metadata. Whenever a user publishes an entry that relates to or discusses some entity that has a formal representation on his desktop, they could add an RDF version of this representation to the blog entry. For example, an entry mentioning one or more persons might be enriched with RDF versions of the respective address book entries, and entries about papers or other documents would then contain an RDF version of the corresponding BibTeX metadata. In this way, semantic metadata can be made available with little or no overhead. We can also assume that the user has a strong motivation for publishing a blog to begin with, so that as a result of these factors, the problem of motivation for creating SW data would disappear.

Semantic blogging has two main advantages: *(i)* the addition of semantic metadata would make content published in a user's blog easier to find and browse through, and *(ii)* this would help to solve the chicken-and-egg problem of the SW.

Building a semantic blog in the way described above would require software that integrates tightly with the user's desktop environment. In this pa-

---

[5] Trackbacks: www.movabletype.org/trackback/
[6] Pingbacks: www.hixie.ch/specs/pingback/pingback/
[7] The situation in the RSS world is a little complicated. Please refer to [10] for a more in-depth explanation of the various versions and strands.

per we describe the *semiBlog* system. semiBlog is similar to other software like MarsEdit[8] in that it allows a user to write blog entries, structure them through time, and add pictures to them – in short, to produce their own blog. However, semiBlog goes beyond the capabilities of existing software in that it allows the user to easily tap the data that exists on their computer, transform it into SW-conformant data and add it to the blog, thus producing a semantic blog.

Outline of the Paper

The remainder of this paper is structured as follows. We will begin by presenting some other recent approaches to semantic blogging. After this, we will discuss a number of possibilities as to how and where semantic metadata can actually be represented in a blog. This discussion is followed by an overview of the semiBlog prototype itself. We will describe a short example session of the editor, present in detail the architecture of semiBlog, and close with some thoughts concerning future work.

Other Approaches to Semantic Blogging

The concept of Semantic Blogging is not our invention; a number of recent papers have investigated the topic from different angles. [7] discusses a semantic blogging prototype built on top of the SW browser Haystack [12]. They interpret blog entries mainly as annotations of other blog entries and web resources in general, and devise a platform to realise this in terms of the SW. We extend the scope of this interpretation and include the possibility of annotating resources that originally do not exist on the Web, but only on a user's desktop. The paper also underlines the inherent semantic structure of blogs and their entries as such, and presents a way of formalising these semantics in a SW fashion. This point is also made (on a more general level, encompassing various kinds of web based information exchange such as e-mail, bulletin boards, etc.) by [2] and [11]. [4] puts a strong emphasis on the use of semantic technologies to enhance the possibilities of blog consumption, by allowing viewing, navigation and querying with respect to semantics. The paper describes a prototype for both creation and browsing of semantic blogs, which was developed as part of the SWAD-E project[9]. While the prototype only deals with bibliographic

---

[8] MarsEdit: http://ranchero.com/marsedit/
[9] SWAD-E: www.w3.org/2001/sw/Europe/

metadata as annotations to blog entries, the authors point out that the same technologies can be used for any kind of metadata. [8] describes a platform called Semblog, which uses the Friend of a Friend (FOAF) ontology [3] as an integral part. FOAF descriptions of blog authors are linked to their blogs. In this way, the blog as a whole is annotated with metadata about its author. On a more fine-grained level individual blog entries are classified by linking them to personalised ontology. To implement their platform, the authors provide both a Perl CGI-based tool called RNA and a standalone Windows-based tool called Glucose.

Where to Put the Semantics

When trying to answer the general question of how to actually add semantic metadata to blogs and thus turn them into semantic blogs, two problems have to be addressed: *(i)* the choice of format to express the semantics and *(ii)* the physical location for placing the metadata. From a SW perspective, the answer to the first problem is straightforward: since the fundamental data model and language for the SW is RDF, semantic metadata for blogs should use this format. However, we also generally believe that the graph structure of RDF makes it an excellent choice for expressing semantic relations and metadata, as opposed to the tree structure of simpler formats like XML. As to the second problem, there are two basic options, defined by the two publication channels which blogs usually use: the HTML rendered version and the syndicated feed. The HTML rendering is the main channel, which can be viewed by readers in a web browser. The newsfeed usually has the function of augmenting the HTML, and mostly acts as a summary or table of contents. As we have already mentioned, these feeds contain metadata about the blog and its entries and are implemented in either XML or RDF.

The first option for placing the metadata would then be to bind it to the HTML pages. Several approaches for achieving this have been discussed; a good overview is given by Palmer [9]. However, Palmer also mentions that many approaches seem to suffer from inherent disadvantages: embedding the RDF might either lead to invalid HTML or require long and complex DTDs. Also, the problem of conflicting fragment identifiers arises. Another approach for binding to HTML is to link to external RDF resources, by using the <link> tag (in the head of the document) or the <a> tag (in the body of the document). However, the first possibility will restrict the author to only have metadata relating to the whole HTML document, while the second might lead to confusing hyperlinks in the browser rendering of the document. A number of other approaches are mentioned, but they all require significant implementation efforts in the form of specialised parsers, etc.

```
<rdf:RDF
  <!-- ... metadata about the blog in general, etc. -->>
  <rss:item rdf:about=
    "http://www.example.org/blog#YARSMeeting">
    <rss:title>YARS and Space Travel</rss:title>
    <rss:link>http://www.example.org/blog#YARSMeeting
    </rss:link>
    <rss:description>
      Today I had a meeting with Andreas. We went over his
      paper and talked about possibilities of using his
      YARS RDF store for a manned mission to Alpha Centauri
    </rss:description>
    <dc:date>2005-04-06</dc:date>
    <dc:subject>
      <foaf:Person rdf:ID="andreas">
        <foaf:homepage
          rdf:resource="http://sw.deri.org/~aharth/"/>
        <foaf:surname>Harth</foaf:surname>
        <foaf:firstName>Andreas</foaf:firstName>
        <!-- ... more properties ... -->
        <rdf:value>Andreas Harth</rdf:value>
      </foaf:Person>
    </dc:subject>
    <dc:subject>
      <bibtex:InProceedings>
        <bibtex:title>Yet Another RDF Store: Perfect Index
          Structures for Storing Semantic Web Data With
          Contexts
        </bibtex:title>
        <bibtex:author rdf:resource="#andreas"/>
        <!-- ... more properties ... -->
        <rdf:value>YARS Paper</rdf:value>
      </bibtex:InProceedings>
    </dc:subject>
  </rss:item>
  <!-- ... more entries ... -->
</rdf:RDF>
```

Fig. 1. Example of an RSS 1.0 feed, enriched with additional metadata

Another option – and in fact the option chosen by all approaches towards semantic blogging listed in the section on other approaches – is to place the semantics into the news feed. Using this option, the most natural choice of feed dialect is RSS 1.0. As one of the various RSS dialects, its most obvious purpose is to act as a simple table of contents for the blog. However, since it is based on RDF, it can easily be extended to accommodate arbitrary additional RDF metadata. As noted by [7] one problem of embedding metadata in newsfeeds is that they often only contain the *n* most recent entries. The authors of this paper also note that the solution to this problem can be archives of newsfeeds. Despite possible problems, we chose to adopt this approach, mainly because it does not have any of the inherent problems of binding to HTML and will be compatible with ordinary RDF crawlers without any modification.

Figure 1 shows an example of an RSS 1.0 feed with additional metadata, using the RDF/XML syntax[10]. The <rss:item> tag indicates an instance of the item class and represents an individual blog entry; all enclosed elements represent properties of this entry. Properties in the rss namespace are defined in the core RSS 1.0 specification, while the dc namespace is reserved for the Dublin Core[11] extension module[12]. The foaf and bibtex namespaces are not part of the specification at all and represent examples of arbitrary additional metadata added to the RSS feed.

Due to the nature of RDF there are various possibilities to associate arbitrary metadata with a blog entry in RSS 1.0 , e.g. [4] defines a contains property, and [8] adopt the foaf:topic property for the same purpose. However, we chose to use the dc:subject property already included in the Dublin Core module. While the only valid values currently defined for this property are flat string literals, the specification also suggests the possibility of using richer semantics, by allowing complex resources instead of strings. We follow this suggestion, as illustrated in Fig. 1. In this example, the user has written a blog entry about a meeting he had with his colleague Andreas, concerning a paper written by him. Since the entry is therefore relating to Andreas and his paper (amongst other things), complex metadata about these two entities has been added to the blog's RSS feed. More specifically, it has been added as the entry's dc:subject. A "dumbed down" representation of the resources is also provided, using the rdf:value property.

semiBlog Application

The main focus in the creation of semiBlog was to make the authoring of a semantic blog as easy as possible. In particular, we wanted to allow the user to easily add semantic metadata to the blog about entities that already exist on their desktop. This led to the early design decision to make semiBlog a desktop-based application, rather than web-based. Access to

---

[10] RDF/XML: www.w3.org/TR/rdf-syntax-grammar/
[11] Dublin Core: http://dublincore.org
[12] For details on RSS 1.0 and modules, see
   http://web.resource.org/rss/1.0/modules/

other desktop applications and their data (e.g. through their public APIs), control of the clipboard, and techniques like drag-and-drop are difficult or impossible to implement in a web-based environment. Another design decision was to make the first prototype a native, platform-dependent application – this was chosen for similar reasons (access to application APIs, etc.), but also because it allowed for a much easier and quicker development process. For these reasons, semiBlog is currently only available for the Mac OS X operating system. Future versions of semiBlog could be more platform independent, particularly the components comprising the *semiBlog Core* block in Fig. 3. However, we believe that for an application that wants to interface directly to existing desktop data, a certain degree of platform dependence is always necessary.

Example Scenario

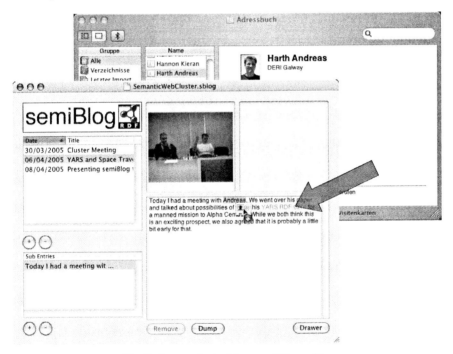

Fig. 2. Screenshot of the semiBlog editor

A screenshot of an example session in semiBlog is shown in Fig. 2. The user has just had a meeting with his colleague Andreas, where they went over an academic paper discussing one of Andreas' projects, named

"YARS". He creates a new entry for this in his blog, adds some text and a picture. Then he decides to annotate the entry with some semantic metadata. To do so, he simply selects the name of his colleague, drags the corresponding card from his address book and drops it onto the text field.

The entry (or rather a part of it) is now linked to a piece of data on the user's desktop. In a similar fashion he drags and drops the URL of the YARS project page from his web browser, as well as the BibTeX entry for the paper from his bibliography tool. Once a piece of text has been annotated, it is highlighted in the editor, so that each type of data is represented by a different colour.

Architecture and Flow of Data

Figure 3 gives an abstract overview of the architecture and flow of data in semiBlog. The left-hand side of the figure shows some examples of desktop data that a user might have. We show address book entries, bibliographical metadata and web pages, but any other kind of data is conceivable as well. semiBlog's architecture allows custom wrapper plug-ins for each data source, which take the object information from the various desktop applications and transform it into RDF metadata form. Together with the textual entry provided by the user, this metadata is then combined into an intermediate XML representation. To generate the actual blog, the XML is transformed into the various publication channels (currently a non-semantic HTML rendering and the semantic RSS 1.0 feed, which links to the HTML). The blog is now ready for publication on the web.

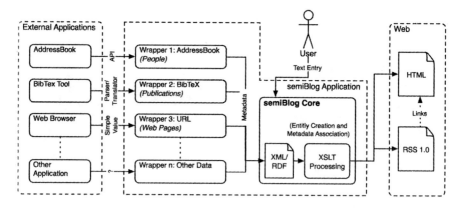

Fig. 3. semiBlog architecture and flow of data

Wrappers

For each individual wrapper, access to the data can be handled in a different way: if the data is tied to a specific application (e.g. the AddressBook application for Mac OS X), then access via an application API might be possible. Other, more generic data (e.g. BibTeX) will be handled by appropriate parsers/translators. Wrappers are implemented as plug-ins to the platform, which makes it easy to add new functionality and cover more data sources as the need arises. Plug-ins are basically implementations of an abstract `AnnotationType` class, which defines the basic API each plug-in has to provide. Parts of this API are getter and setter methods for the supported data types (objects in a drag-and-drop operation provide their data in various types or data flavors); colours for highlighting in the editor; a method `annotationFromData` to generate RDF; and a method `mainAnchorFromData` to generate a hyperlink reference for the HTML rendering of the blog.

Intermediate XML

semiBlog uses XML as an intermediate data format. Each entry is represented by an `entry` element, the textual content is contained in a `text` element. This element allows mixed content of text and `annotation` elements, which provides the possibility to add metadata to individual substrings of an entry. We chose this inline annotation technique over external annotation by reference, because it makes the XSLT transformations in the next step easier to accomplish. Each annotation contains a `mainAnchor` to be used in the HTML rendering of the blog (or in any other non-semantic representation), the RDF metadata and the actual substring of the entry to be annotated.

```
<!-- ... -->
<text>
  Today I had a meeting with
  <annotation>
    <mainAnchor>http://sw.deri.org/~aharth</mainAnchor>
    <metadata>
      <foaf:Person>
        <foaf:name>Andreas Harth</foaf:name>
        <!-- ... other properties -->
      </foaf:Person>
    </metadata>
    <content>Andreas</content>
  </annotation>.
  We went over his
  <annotation>
    <mainAnchor>
      http://sw.deri.org/2004/06/yars/doc/summary
    </mainAnchor>
```

```
<metadata>
  <bibtex:InProceedings>
    <bibtex:title>
      Yet Another RDF Store:...
    </bibtex:title>
    <!-- ... other properties -->
  </bibtex:InProceedings>
</metadata>
<content>paper</content>
</annotation>
and talked about possibilities of using his YARS RDF
store for a manned mission to Alpha Centauri. ...
</text>
<!-- ... -->
```

Fig. 4. Intermediate XML

XSLT Transformation

Once the user's textual entry and the semantic metadata have been combined into the intermediate XML format, we can use XSLT to transform it into arbitrary publication channels. This is a rather straight-forward process: there is one XSLT stylesheet per channel, and each one picks those elements out of the XML, which are appropriate for the corresponding publication channel. For example, the XML → HTML stylesheet will ignore the metadata element and instead pick the content and mainAnchor tags to produce a hyperlink for specific substrings of the entry. The XML → RSS stylesheet will only look at the metadata element and annotate the entry as a whole. Once this is done, the blog (now consisting of various files) can be uploaded to a server.

Future Work

Although the full chain of steps involved in publishing a semantic blog – writing a textual entry, adding pictures, annotating the entry with semantic metadata and transforming the internal data format into the actual components of the blog – is implemented and can be performed within semiBlog, the software is still very much a prototype and can be improved in many areas. Since the main focus was on the interaction between semiBlog and other desktop applications, we have so far neglected aspects such as layout capabilities. As a result, the user is currently bound to a static layout scheme for the blog. In future versions, we will have to address this and perhaps allow the user to choose between different Cascading Style Sheets (CSS) templates. Also, it is currently not possible to add metadata other than that provided by the wrapper plug-ins. Users should have the option to manually annotate entries with arbitrary metadata, if they wish to do so (however, since we were interested in *easy* drag-and-drop based annotation, this was of no concern to us for the prototype). Also, by using an ontology like SIOC [2], more semantic metadata could be generated easily by making use of the internal semantic structure of the blog.

Future versions of the editor will allow integration with generic Semantic Desktop solutions like Gnowsis [13]. This would eliminate the need for application specific data wrappers as they are currently used in semiBlog.

Conclusion

In this paper, we have shown that the recent phenomenon of blogging, combined with a tool to easily generate SW data from existing formal desktop data, can result in a form of semantic blogging. We discussed various ways of representing semantic metadata in a blog and decided to apply indirect annotation through RSS 1.0 feeds. We presented a prototype of the *semiBlog* editor, which was created with the purpose of semantic blogging in mind. We argued that such a semantic blog editor should integrate tightly with a user's desktop environment, as this allows direct API access to external applications and user interface idioms such as drag-and-drop and makes integration of existing data into the blog as easy as possible. We believe that by providing such a tool, we will increase the motivation to add to and to help realise the vision of the Semantic Web.

Acknowledgement

This material is based upon works supported by the Science Foundation Ireland under Grant No. SFI/02/CE1/I131.

References

[1] Beged-Dov G, Brickley D, Dornfest R, Davis I, Dodds L, Eisenzopf J, Galbraith D, Guha R, MacLeod K, Miller E, Swartz A, van der Vlist E (2001) RDF Site Summary (RSS) 1.0. http://web.resource.org/rss/ 1.0/spec
[2] Breslin JG, Harth A, Bojars U, Decker S (2005) Towards Semantically Interlinked Online Communities. Proc of the 2nd European Semantic Web Conference (ESWC '05) Heraklion Greece May 2005
[3] Brickley D, Miller L (2005) FOAF Vocabulary Specification. http://xmlns.com/foaf/0.1/.

[4] Cayzer S (2004) Semantic Blogging: Spreading the Semantic Web Meme. Proc of XML Europe 2004 Amsterdam Netherlands April 2004

[5] Haase P, Broekstra J, Ehrig M, Menken M, Mika P, Plechawski M, Pyszlak P, Schnizler B, Siebes R, Staab S, Tempich C (2004) Bibster - A Semantics-Based Bibliographic Peer-to-Peer System. Proc of the Third International Semantic Web Conference (ISWC2004) Hiroshima Japan November 2004

[6] Hendler J (2001) Agents and the Semantic Web. IEEE Intelligent Systems, vol 16, no 2, pp 30–37

[7] Karger DR, Quan D (2004) What Would It Mean to Blog on the Semantic Web? Proc of the Third International Semantic Web Conference (ISWC2004) Hiroshima Japan November 2004

[8] Ohmukai I, Takeda H (2004) Semblog: Personal Publishing Platform with RSS and FOAF. Proc of the 1st Workshop on Friend of a Friend Social Networking and the (Semantic) Web Galway September 2004

[9] Palmer SB (2002) RDF in HTML: Approaches. http://infomesh.net/ 2002/rdfinhtml/.

[10] Pilgrim M (2002) What is RSS? www.xml.com/pub/a/2002/ 12/18/dive-into-xml.html.

[11] Quan D, Bakshi K, Karger DR (2003) A Unified Abstraction for Messaging on the Semantic Web. Proc of the Twelfth International World Wide Web Conference (WWW2003) Budapest Hungary May 2003

[12] Quan D, Huynh D, Karger DR (2003) Haystack: A Platform for Authoring End User Semantic Web Applications. Proc of the Second International Semantic Web Conference (ISWC2003)

[13] Sauermann L (2003) The Gnowsis — Using Semantic Web Technologies to build a Semantic Desktop. Master's Thesis Technische Universität Wien

[14] Walker J (2005) Weblog. In: Routledge Encyclopedia of Narrative Theory. Routledge London and New York

WEB Services Networks and Technological Hybrids – The Integration Challenges of WAN Distributed Computing for ASP Providers

Pawel Mroczkiewicz

Department of Information Systems, University of Gdańsk, Poland.
mroczkiewiczp@poczta.onet.pl

Introduction

A necessity of integration of both information systems and office software existing in organizations has had a long history. The beginning of this kind of solutions reaches back to the old generation of network protocols called EDI (Electronic Data Interchange) and EDIFACT standard, which was initiated in 1988 and has dynamically evolved ever since (S. Michalski, M. Suskiewicz, 1995). The mentioned protocol was usually used for converting documents into natural formats processed by applications. It caused problems with binary files and, furthermore, the communication mechanisms had to be modified each time new documents or applications were added. When we compare EDI with the previously used communication mechanisms, EDI was a great step forward as it was the first, big scale attempt to define standards of data interchange between the applications in business transactions (V. Leyland, 1995, p. 47).

As EDI and its based on the newer technologies successors' popularity was growing, the integration of systems and applications (as a service and software) has been quickly adapted by software vendors, consulting and outsourcing companies. This gave birth to "value-added oriented networks" (VAN – Value-Added Network), also named VADS (Value-Added Data Services) (V. Leyland, 1995, p. 213).

VAN network is defined as „an outside service provider, which allows exchange of digital data – documents and transaction information – between the members of the merchant society" (B. Lheureux, F. Kenney, 2002). Today, thanks to the development of the open standards like XML or TCP/IP, VAN networks allow widening a spectrum of offered services, what results in a growing interest from business customers.

WEB Services Networks and Technological Hybrids

When a concept of web services emerged, it caused a new trend in the application development and information support of business processes. A component model of system development was generalized within a local range to a network where a service becomes the main component. Delivering functionality to a customer, as a combination of the services located on the network, has also influenced modern approaches to B2BAI integration. A number of solutions have emerged as an effect of these conditions. They base on the dynamic approach with the use of service architectures and web services (G. Samtani, D. Sadhwani, 2001). In practice it means that it is possible to reconfigure an integrated solution as needed without redesigning a whole communication mechanism. This class' solutions are called Web Services Networks (WSN) (B. Lheureux, 2002). Additionally WSN allow creating systems that base directly on processes. A system in this approach is a process supported by IT and the world of systems within an organization consists of process applications, which handle particular processes in an aggregated form in End-to-End perspective. An integration of the business processes into larger structures, which are easier to manage in a rational way, is called Business Process Fusion (BPF) (D. Flint, 2003).

Providers' solutions can be created within the area of integration on basis of the modern network technologies, like the mentioned above web services, semantic webs, BPM, or Grid Computing. These solutions allow BPF postulates realization or assure a process approach to the integration where a dynamic configuration of the resources available on the network has been considered. The flexible use of the services requires processing of the meaning (interpretation) of their public interface by the machines, scalability adjusted to the changing number of customers and mechanisms for billing between a user and a service provider. Using network technologies alone (within today architecture) does not give expected results. It is, therefore, necessary to get a synergy by combining functionalities of the described above technologies'. A model of architecture used by an ASP vendor is presented in Fig. 1. It shows network technologies positioning and their interdependences.

As shown on Fig. 1 an integration vendor is an organization that works as a broker of data transfer between applications (in the traditional meaning) and services, which are available in the network. Some of these services may be located on the vendor's repositories. It causes that a proper execution environment can assure access to a GRID solution (make a GRID solution available) (which are scaled both in a range of inside and outside resources of a provider, assuming there are subjects that share resources and have a compatible GRID solution) and allows sustaining a controlled efficiency without a need of buying additional hardware.

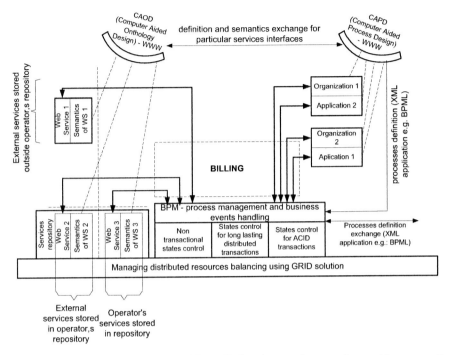

Fig. 1. A model of an ASP provider offering integration services with a use of modern network technologies.

A key component of an integration solution is a BPM process engine, which coordinates data flow between applications and web services, according to the previously built scenarios. This approach allows avoiding both information desynchronization in systems and services and activity desynchronization. A well designed process should, therefore, distribute entered data and effects of the activities into other systems, so there don't appear contradictions between them. The key stage of a properly working integration mechanism design is defining a process, which includes defining required system ends, service ends, and manual ends, based on the dedicated CAPD (Computer Aided Process Design) module. The defined processes can be exchanged between customers with use of XML, where they are saved in a chosen standard. The process engine, which calls particular applications and services, actually refers to the defined interfaces within them. A possibility of using them is conditioned with availability of the actual semantic (meaning) and functionality. A semantic and syntactic wrap of web services is a big help in this situation. Despite they have self-defined elements of the WSDL language, they don't represent any semantics of particular methods, which could be interpreted by machines. This interpretation is important due to a need of dynamic flow reconfiguration when the services are not available or a growing usage costs. Additionally it has to be noticed that a possibility of so called "orchestration" in the BPM engine can use semantic descriptions for moving around the network. An orchestration allows the engine making decisions about the flow due to business events (some of the paths in a process may not be defined; a process may make decisions about itself on basis of events).

Another aspect is scalability and billing of the services. Since services are dedicated functionality providers, many customers may have access to them. Therefore, assuring a proper reaction to the changing load is a must. The classic approach allows using a simple calculation to define resources that are necessary for servicing the software. New network technologies allow treating this problem in a different way. A GRID net together with web services can be a technological hybrid, which main advantage is auto-scalability of the service on basis of the inside and outside resources. The usage of the services according to the functionality and load should be cleared. Therefore, there is a need of using appropriate billing modules, which allow realization of these requirements.

Other components of the vendor's architecture are distributed transactions controllers. It is worth to remember that processing in WAN network, is a huge challenge for transaction processing. Newly created network protocols, which can become standards for communication between services (e.g. SOAP), base on "not warranted" protocols of a lower layer of TCP/IP, like HTTP. It causes problems with a control of data delivery and retransmission as it is not in case of "warranted" transport systems MOM. MOM protocols' disadvantage is that they require "runtime" environment installation on both ends of a transfer. So it excludes a possibility of a standard thin client, which communicates with a service. However, if there is a requirement of full atomicity, the only reliable solution is MOM. There are, however, other conditions of WAN distributed processing development. It should be flexible and independent of a platform and dedicated (producer's) protocols. Considering that a wide area network usually slows down data transfer and people may take part in process activities (manual activities or people working with systems), it is very important to build transaction monitors, which cooperate with BPM engines and fulfill the mentioned requirements. This approach is called LLDT (Long Lasting Distributed Transactions) in this work and is an extension of the BTP specification (Business Transaction Protocol) provided by OASIS (A. Ceponkus, S. Dalal, T. Fletcher, P. Furniss, A. Green, B. Pope, 2002). Table 1 shows main goals of building the technological hybrids and their limitations. Use of LLTD will be discussed in the latter part of this article.

Table 1. Goals and limitations of technological hybrids in integration solutions of ASP providers.

Hybrid name	Goals	Main disadvantages and limitations or dangers
Web services supported by semantics	- Quick identification of web services functionality based on a semantic model (using the semantis to execute services by interpretation of service range semantics). A properly created semantic model eliminates problems with the interpretation of an offer that is realized by a service - Detection of syntactic mistakes in queries to the semantic web, wrapping a web service.	- Wrong definition of semantics in ontology - The syntactic similarity detection algorithm is not effective
Web services based on Grid Computing	- Assures auto-scalability of web services (with respect to the indicators' levels defined in SLA) - Assures flexible clearing model to calculate usage of particular application options and for clearings with outside vendors of resources, based on billing functionality included in web services	- The need of including additional logic in services for servicing billing functionality (implementation of billing classes according to the pattern)

Web Services Supported by Semantics

Web services make an interface available for the environment. This interface allows calling appropriate methods within a service, which provide required, at the time, functionalities. The interfaces are usually described with WSDL language and placed in UDDI registries, which allow archiving information about them. Additionally web services have to provide a possibility of automatic search of required functionalities and an access to these functionalities with standard network protocols (SOAP is usually used in web services). It's connected to some basic risks, which refer to semantic identification that are offered outside the access mechanisms. Despite WSDL language syntactic defines rules of using particular interfaces, an automat (machine or network protocol) is not able to identify whether a provided functionality is the one it requires or not. These problems are addressed with a functionality offered by semantic webs. A semantic web allows creating a model of semantic (meaning) dependences of particular definitions and activities, which describe service performing rules. A semantic model should be implemented in a web service on two levels (layers):

- definitions semantic level (generic model)
- methods semantic level (detailed model)

Definitions Semantic Level

Definitions semantics in a model of web service hybrid supported by semantics provides generic information about a range of functionalities offered by a web service to a searching mechanism. In practice it mainly concerns on providing a semantic model that copies white and yellow pages of UDDI registry (a similar function at a provider is played by a services repository). This approach allows eliminating services that don't fulfill the chosen criteria, which are described in a semantic oriented query, at the stage of subject range search. As an effect of starting a search engine, the results, after an appropriate semantic connections analysis, are displayed. These results are referred to semantics on basis of ontology graphs. This assures that methods semantic models, which are made accessible by certain services as interfaces, are not searched through straight away. It limits a number of operations required for starting chosen mechanisms.

Methods Semantic Level

A methods semantic is a second and final step in identifying an appropriate mechanism (or mechanisms), which should be called, in order to reach the goal. A typical example of a problem, which would appear in case of using "pure" web services technology, is a machine interpretation of, so called, "call signature" – a method syntactic and its parameters. Supposing we have a method: String( ) getClientsNames(String date), it would be easy for a human to interpret its meaning (most probably this method returns a table with clients names, which made transactions on a particular day). It is misleading though, because an interpretation of this method's performing rules can vary without defining additional parameters. Entering a description stating that the method has to get clients, which signed a contract on a particular day, would be explicitly interpreted by a human but it could be hard to interpret for a search machine. Implementing a semantic model based on ontology can help search mechanism to automate a choice of an appropriate method and interpretation of its parameters meanings. In effect this method could be called with parameters, which values would be defined on basis of mapping the semantic model on available information resources (e.g. a defined field of a database record). A result of the method *(in a similar way)* would be interpreted and transferred for further processing.

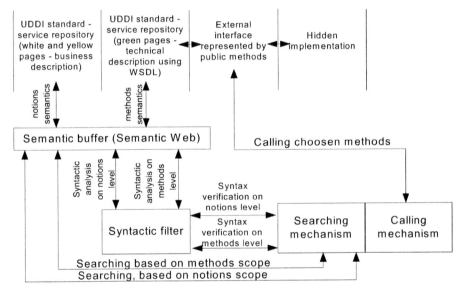

Fig. 2. A model of semantic supported web service architecture with use of syntactic filters

Semantic webs have series of definitions and their relationships within the range of ontological graphs. They are not, however, resistant to syntactic mistakes (because of the function that has been assigned to them). It needs to be noticed, therefore, that processing a syntax that has a (syntactic) mistake can result in rejecting a string by the semantic web and the search result (even though some other components are consistent) can be inadequate or be not generated at all. The solution for this problem is use of so called syntactic filter, which conducts syntactic analysis with a reference to appropriate dictionaries for definitions that are not mapped in the ontology. The filter will suggest changing inappropriate words (from onto-logical point of view) with words that can be found in the semantic graph. Semantic filter can be constructed on basis of windows methods of com-paring strings. These methods allow estimating a probability that two strings are intended to be the same (Q.X. Yang, S.S. Yuan, L. Zhao, L. Chun, S. Peng, 2001). Fig. 2 presents a scheme of architecture of a whole solution of a semantic supported web service with use of syntactic filter.

Grid Based Web Services

The main goal of providing web services supported by Grid Computing is assuring a solution that is easily scalable. This solution, while realizes cus-tomers' functionality needs, allows accepting increasing load, in a smooth way, and at the same time sustaining or even decreasing usage costs. A web service based on Grid Computing uses a virtual machine, which al-lows seeing resources available for software as continuous. Main resources used by a web service are hard disks, processor calculating time, and oper-ating memory. These resources may be owned by a provider or be avail-able through the network with the use of GRID module. Scaling within self owned resources is fully predictable as a provider is conscious of the pur-chase costs of these resources. A situation with an outside grid is different. Availability of the resources may change over time and their costs may evolve (Availability and costs of the resources may change over time). Use of the outside resources depends on number of users (including processes and applications) that use particular interfaces of the web services on the provider's side. Customers of integration services provider, who decide to use an integration mechanism and its supporting services, which are pro-vided by a net, want to get a warranty that a service level won't be lower than indicators defined by the limit values. The level of the mentioned in-dicators should be, therefore, monitored and available for control. Main indicators that can be constantly (continuously) controlled are efficiency indicators. A so called SLA (Services Level Agreement) should usually be prepared on the basis of the assumed levels. This agreement warranties a client a safe use of services and puts a risk of lowering services' level on providers side. A monitoring of the chosen indicators should be conducted with the use of the dedicated network applications, which analyze proto-cols' behavior during data transmission through the net. This allows both abnormalities registration and simulation/numeric extrapolation of the sys-tem's behavior in a short period of time. This approach allows reporting a need for autoscaling to a GRID mechanism before levels of the indicators go below the levels described in the SLA agreement what causes additional costs to a provider. Architecture of web services based on Grid Computing with use of SLM (Services Level Management) balancing is shown on Fig. 3.

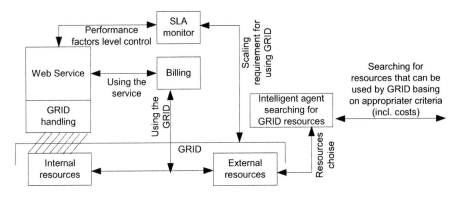

Fig. 3. Architecture of a web service based on Grid Computing

In the presented approach a special task is assigned to a billing mechanism. This mechanism allows clearing the service use; also in terms of costs, which are the result of using outside resources. Billing that regards customers accounts related to the started services can be a powerful tool in cost analysis in terms of usage of inside and outside resources. Resources and services billing configuration can be a base for a provider to create tariffs suited to a customer.

In a web service supported by a GRID net we can distinguish two main types of calculations:

- Billing of network functions (realized as a class billing)
- Billing of network efficiency and scalability parameters (GRID billing as interconnect billing between a service provider and outside resources vendors).

Billing of Network Functions (Class Billing)

These clearings (calculations) should be based on web service definition and implementation. On a web service level mechanisms should be sewed up, which can appropriately calculate use of particular functions, threads or overall usage time. This way a client is given a detailed billing about the network usage degree, with a list of called methods or load of data structures. It allows a customer to decrease extra costs, which are created in a form of lump sum payments for providers' services, where a risk is balanced by an excessive price. In the described case a client receives a very detailed calculation.

Billing of Network Efficiency and Scalability Parameters (GRID Billing)

The resources that are used mutually by providers should be calculated in this case. These resources, which include processor capability, operational memory, or hard disk space, can be excessive for some players and grid machines can make use of this situation. This dependence is bi-directional. All parties can dynamically manipulate the resources they share outside depending on a load of own processes. This way a net of connections is created and a split of usage costs has to be assured. This functionality is provided by a GRID billing. Well-chosen resources should allow integration providers full scalability; this solution can also be cheaper than buying own hardware.

Model of Long Lasting Distributed Transactions with Events Management (LLTD – Long Lasting Distributed Transactions)

As mentioned before distributed processing may require controlling of interdependences between results of the operations realized in the network on process's components. In many situations an important part is to determine a range of activities that have to be completed. Other way certain repair steps can be taken, which require, however, that ACID assumptions have to be loosen as a possibility of rolling back all activities is highly uncertain. New approach (LLTD) should be based on intermediate states, which assure stability of a whole system and at the same time are not, as a requirement, equivalents of atomic states, i.e. completion confirmation – assumed state or complete rollback – primary state. Additionally it has to be noticed that long lasting transactions dynamics should also be based on an event model, which conditions, to a certain degree, operation progress with outside impulses (where outside impulses condition, to a certain degree, operation progress).

The presented above approach allows managing long lasting distributed transactions by creating a certain number of states' sets on objects that are used in a transaction, in a way that their combinations establish an integral state. In effect, LLDT transactions are able to search for intermediate states in case of failures of both processing and rolling back an operation. Lack of information about an object's state, after an operation on it has started, has to be treated, in all cases, as a critical error and to be logged into a manual solution of a problem. Ending a transaction with a critical error may also happen in a situation when the transaction cannot go into any of the states that are recognized as stable, i.e. primary state, assumed state or intermediate – coherent state. An LLTD process can be presented as a sequence of steps:

Transaction start -> Executing steps of a transaction -> If all steps were successful, finishing and committing a transaction -> If some steps were unsuccessful, starting a full transaction rollback -> If rolling back was successful, finishing a transaction -> If rolling back was unsuccessful, further trials are started in order to achieve a coherent state -> If a coherent state was achieved, a transaction is ended -> A transaction tries to achieve compact states until there are none left on the list -> If a compact state was not achieved, a transaction ends with a critical error.

A probability of a successful transaction ending depends on a number of defined intermediate states and a probability of achieving them. A range of possible definitions of intermediate states is called "Coherence Area". A coherence area is a field that can be used by an organization to set restrictions for its transactions executed in a wide area network environment. A model of a transaction, which oscillates around particular compact states, together with trials of achieving compact states is named in this article "a model of transaction convergence". Its main characteristic is tending to a steady state in a number of iterations. A steady state is, in LLTD monitor (physical implementation) interpretation, compactness.

It is worth noticing that despite using a convergence model when using a BPM system as a process management engine there is a potential probability of modification of a whole steps sequence by an incoming business event (a reaction takes place during processing a transaction only, not after a transaction is ended). In this situation a return to previous steps can take place, which can result in both a successful ending of operations that have not been processed and unsuccessful ending of operations that have already been completed. A transaction event model adjust them to an environment better but makes management harder. A result of an event may be a transaction knocked out of a coherent state, which could be achieved without the event on one hand, and on the other hand a transaction that achieved a coherent state, which couldn't be achieved without the event. In order to make event handling possible within a transaction, an event handling has to be defined with use of separate listening threads, which enable appropriate reaction for outside impulses. In conclusion, LLDT transactions have to be multithreaded. Incoming events can cause making steps forward and back within a transaction. After a transaction is ended a listening thread is eliminated by the monitor, what eliminates further influence of business events.

The presented above discussion treats about interdependences between the modern network technologies and model of long lasting transactions, which can be components of integration solutions within a VAN network generation called WSN. It's been shown that integration solutions require making use of an effect of synergy of particular technologies as these technologies alone are not able to fulfill the goals in this area.

References

Andrews W (2003) Web Services Offer Path to Real-Time Enterprise Benefits, Gartner Research. www.gartner.com

Andrews W, Hostman B (2002) Web Services Catalyze Data Analysis, Gartner Research. www.gartner.com

Berman D (2002) Web Services: Will Anything Really Change. EAI Journal

Ceponkus A, Dalal S, Fletcher T, Furniss P, Green A, Pope B (2002) Business Transaction Protocol. An OASIS Committee Specification

Delphi Group (2002) Taxonomy & Content Classification Market Milestone Report. www.delphigroup.com, Boston

Flint D (2003) Managing Business Process Fusion: Why, How, What's Next. Gartner Research. www.gartner.com

Hayward S (2003) BPM: A Key Ingerdient in Business Process Fusion. Gartner Research. www.gartner.com

Leyland V (1995) EDI: Elektroniczna wymiana dokumentacji; Wydawnictwo naukowo techniczne, Warszawa

Lheureux B (2002) Flamenco Networks-Facilitating Web Services, P2P Style. Artner Research. www.gartner.com

Lheureux B (2002) Grand Central: The First WSN-Managed Service Provider. Gartner Research. www.gartner.com

Lheureux B (2002) Web Services Networks Secure a New Web Technology. Gartner Research. www.gartner.com

Lheureux B, Kenny F (2002) The "Value" in Value-Addeed Network Services. Gartner Research. www.gartner.com

Michalski S, Suskiewicz M (1995) Usługi EDI, jako nowa forma przesyłania wiadomości w sieciach TPSA; Łączność

Plummer D, Smith D, Andrews W (2002) What Web Services Will and Won't Do. Gartner Research. www.gartner.com

Samtani G, Sadhwani D (2001) EAI and Web Services-Easier Enterprise Application Integration, Web Services Architect

Yang QX, Yuan SS, Zhao L, Chun L, Peng S (2001) Faster Algorithm of String Comparison. Institute of High Performance of Computing, School of Computing, National University of Singapore, Singapore

Named Entity Recognition in a Hungarian NL Based QA System

Domonkos Tikk[1], P. Ferenc Szidarovszky[2], Zsolt T. Kardkovács[3] and Gábor Magyar[4]

[1][3][4] Department of Telecommunications & Media Informatics, University of Technology and Economics, Budapest, Hungary.
(tikk, kardkovacs, magyar)@tmit.bme.hu
[2] Szidarovszky Ltd., Hungary. ferenc.szidarovszky@szidarovszky.com

Introduction[1]

In WoW project our purpose is to create a complex search interface with the following features: search in the deep web content of contracted partners' databases, processing Hungarian natural language (NL) questions and transforming them to SQL queries for database access, image search supported by a visual thesaurus that describes in a structural form the visual content of images (also in Hungarian). This paper primarily focuses on a particular problem of question processing task: the entity recognition. Before going into details we give a short overview of the project's aims.

The Deep Web

The deep web (DW) is content that resides in searchable and online accessible databases, whose results can only be discovered by a direct query[2]. Without the directed query, the database does not publish the result. Result pages are posted as dynamic web pages as answer to direct queries. Incorporating DW access in the internet search engines is a very important issue. Studies about the internet [2] show among other facts that: (1) the size of DW is about 400 times larger than that of the surface web that is accessible to traditional keyword-based search engines; (2) the size of DW is growing much faster than the surface web; (3) DW is the category where new information appears the fastest on the web; (4) DW sites tend to be narrower and deeper than conventional surface web sites; (5) DW sites

[1] This research was supported by NKFP 0019/2002.
[2] www.brightplanet.com

typically reside topic specific databases, therefore the quality of the information stored on these sites are usually more adequate in the given topic than the one accessible through conventional pages.

Our Solution to DW Based Search

One of the bottlenecks of traditional search engines is that they keep keyword-based catalogued information about web pages; therefore they retrieve only the keywords from users' queries and display pages with matched ones. This matching method neglects important information granules of a natural language query, such as the focus of the query, the semantic information and linguistic connections between various terms, etc. Traditional searchers retrieve the same pages for *"When does the president of the United States visit Russia"* and *"Why does the president of Russia visit the United States"*, though the requested information is quite different.

There has been a lot of work in recent years on both natural language processing and web-based queries. A non-exhaustive list of projects: Practice [16][16], START [11][13][8], NL for Cindi [20], Masque/SQL [1], Chat-80 [22] or Team [7] provide solutions for English, Spanish NLQ [18], Sylvia-NLQ [9] for Spanish, Phoenix [3] for Swedish, Edite [19], LIL/SQL [6], JaVaLI! [5] for Portuguese, NChiql [15] for Chinese and KID [4][14] for Korean languages. Although several ideas and techniques has been adapted from these systems to WoW, none of them can be applied directly to our purpose, both because of the peculiarity of DW search and that of the language.

In order to alleviate the shortcomings of keyword based search, in our DWS we enable the user to formulate his/her information need by NL question. Processing of arbitrary NL question is generally an extremely complicated problem for all languages, and Hungarian is not an exception. In fact, due to the agglutinative nature of the language even dictionary based search algorithms have to be equipped with intelligent functionality because, e.g.,

1. The stem of words can change;
2. Additional suffixes can modify the form of previous suffixes.

In this paper we deal with the natural language module of our DWS (depicted in Figure 1) with a special focus on the particular important issue of entity recognition. First, a brief description is given about the NL module, then the entity recognition problem is treated in details.

Here we remark that, though, NL processing is always language-dependent but the non-language specific part of the operation, e.g. the structure of our system can directly be adapted for question processing in other languages.

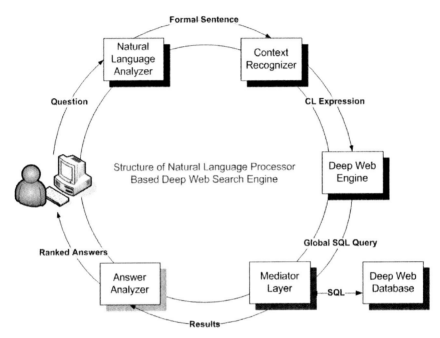

Fig. 1. Structure of our DWS enabling NL querying

Description of NL Module

We apply several restrictions on input questions of the system, which are originated from different reasons. First, DWS attempts to answer user queries on the basis of the content of a collection of topic-specific DW sites. The information stored at DW sites are typically factual ones, therefore we do not allow questions focusing on casuality (*"Why did the Allies win WW2?"*), intension (*"Would you like a cup of coffee "*), subjective (*"How am I "*) or other type of non-factual information. Second, there are grammatical limitations on input question in order to make NL question processing feasible: the system accepts only simple (only one tensed verb is allowed), well-formulated and -spelled interrogative sentences starting with a question word from a given list.

A basic tool that helps the operation of the module is the HunMorph morphological parser (MP) [10].

Definition of Entity

The knowledge base of the NL module contains various dictionaries storing the lexical information of special tokens (proper names, interrogatives, lists of some significant words, dates, URLs etc.). These tokens are called together *entities*. Entities can be single or multi-word expressions. Entities are of two basic types:

1. Dictionary based: the entity has a fixed form that is stored in the dictionary (e.g. proper names, interrogatives, special words). Such entities are inserted to the dictionary on the basis of the content of partner DW sites. At insertion context information can also be linked to entities.
2. Pattern based: only the possible patterns of the entity is given (e.g. URL, date, e-mail address). A candidate text is matched against the pattern when checking identity. A pattern consists of a set of simple rules, which is given for each pattern manually.

Operation of NL Module

NL module consists of two submodules: the tokenizer and the bracketing module. The input question is first passed to the *tokenizer*. Its first task is to identify tokens (syntactically relevant units) of the sentence. Tokens are one-word or multi-word expressions whose internal structures are irrelevant for the syntactic parsing of the sentence. Multi-word tokens are entities, such as personal names, institution, proprietary and company names, titles, addresses, etc. As Hungarian is a highly agglutinative language where major semantic/syntactic relations are signalled by a series of "stackable" suffixes, the identification of entities is a more complex task than simple pattern recognition and requires the support of a morphological parser [10] (described later). MP assigns *part of speech* labels to tokens and provides their morphological analysis. This information is the basis of the subsequent bracketing phase. One of the characteristics of the morphological system of the Hungarian language is that many morphologically complex word forms are ambiguous in terms of their morphological structure. Such ambiguous tokens are disambiguated in parsed alternatives.

The bracketing module groups related tokens in brackets. The module has several submodules for recognizing: (1) adverbs and participles; (2) adjective groups; (3) conjunctions (logical operators); (4) genitive and; (5) postposition structures. Submodules use the morphological annotation of tokens: stem, part of speech, suffixes (entities are labelled by their type as "part of speech"). The operation of bracketing is not detailed in this paper, for further details see [21] .

The Entity Recognizer

The entire algorithm of tokenizer relies on entity recognition. The entity recognizer (ER) has two main tasks:

- *Searching*: determining the entities in the sentence;
- *Annotating*: specifying the morphological characters of the entity.

The searching and annotating tasks are usually connected and cannot be performed separately.

In what follows we describe the algorithm of ER for fixed form *dictionary based* entities. The recognition of the pattern based entities is performed by Smart Tag Detector (STD), and is not detailed here.

Because an entity can consist of several words, theoretically all segment of an input question is a possible candidate. The number of segments in a sentence of size n is $n(n+1)/2$. The average size of an input sentence is 7–10 words, while the size of the dictionary containing entities can be of order 10^6. Therefore it is much more efficient to search on the basis of sentence segments than on the basis of dictionary entries. The search of an expression in the dictionary can be optimized by organizing dictionary entries into hash table. Segments of a sentence are checked against the dictionary entries by decreasing size.

Another problem of entity recognition is that an entity can be a part of another one (see e.g. *The New York Times* is a newspaper). While in [22], the Blitz NL processor selects a unique entity among the recognized ones based on confidence values, we intend to recognize all entities of a sentence, and generate different parsed sentence alternatives. Consequently, regardless from the success of a search each subsegment is checked again for shorter entities.

The order of segment checks are the following:

1. We start with the entire sentence: $[1,...,n]$.
2. Each subsegment of the sentence is examined by decreasing size: $[1,...,j]$, where $j = n-1,...,1$.
3. Segments starting with the second word are examined: $[2,...,j]$, where $j = n,...,2$.
4. Systematically all segments are examined first ordered by the index of the first word and then by the length of the segment: $[i,...,j]$, where $j = n,...,i, i = 3,...,n$.

Remark 1. It is obvious that not all the $n(n + 1)/2$ segments are valid entity candidate. Considering that the first word of the sentence must be an interrogative, one may start from segment [2,..., n] and thus reducing the number of segments to $n(n - 1)/2$.

In what follows we describe the entity recognition of a particular segment of the input question, called *candidate*. In Hungarian, the stem of a word can be modified when adding certain suffixes to it. In most cases only the last two letters of the word stem may change (*tűz* → *tüzet*[3] ; *álom* → *álmot*[4]). Also, the previous suffix can be changed when an additional suffix is put at the end of a word (this case only happens when the entity itself is of inflected form that is further declined in the sentence: *Vissza a jövőbe* → *Vissza a jövőbét*[5]). In this case only the last letter may change. These considerations are reflected in the searching phase of ER.

A significant part of the entities are not Hungarian expression, and hence MP is not able to parse them. Nevertheless, when processing such an entity, the ER has to annotate them with morphological characters. We assume that for each entity a substitution word is given that is a morphologically parsable word having the same inflection as the last word of the entity. It is often the last word of the entity (if it is a nominative Hungarian word), or is generated algorithmically when inserting the entity entry into the dictionary. The substitution word plays role in the determination of the entity's suffixes.

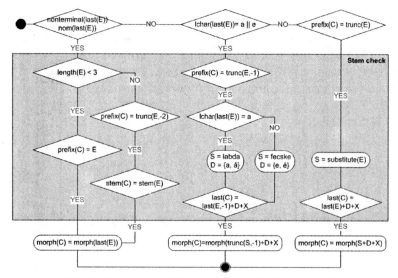

Fig. 2. Flowchart of the algorithm of entity recognizer

---

[3] fire [NOM] → fire [ACC]
[4] dream [NOM] → dream [ACC]
[5] Back to the future [NOM] → [ACC]

We will use the following denotation:

- last(x) denotes the last word of an expression x.
- length(x) is the size of the word x in characters.
- trunc(x,i) the word x truncated by i characters from the end.
- lchar(x) the last character of x.

Further we use abbreviation C (candidate), S (substitution word) and E (entity). The flowchart of the algorithm is depicted on Figure 2.

1. If last(E) is variable in form (i.e. can be inflected), nominative, Hungarian word (i.e. recognized by MP)
   1.1 searching
      1.1.a If length(last(E))≥3 then it is checked whether trunc(E,2) is a prefix of C.
      1.1.b If length(last(E))<3 then it is checked whether E is a prefix of C.
   1.2 stem check: If 1.1.a is successful, that is trunc(E,2) is a prefix of C, then it should be examined whether the stem of last(C) and last(E) are identical. The reason of this is that after truncation there may be several words that match the prefix of last(E). This step can be skipped when 1.1.b is valid.
   1.3 annotation: If the stems in 1.2 are identical then C is the entity E that is annotated with morphological characters of last(C). If both E and C have some non-terminal morpheme, that is discarded at annotation (see also Example 4).
2. If last(E) does not meet the condition of (1), i.e. it is either not recognized by MP, or invariable in form (i.e. cannot be inflected), or can be inflected but not nominative word.
   2.1 searching
      2.1.a If lchar(last(E)) = a or = e then the prefix matching is performed with trunc(E,1).
      2.1.b If lchar(last(E)) ≠ a or ≠e then the prefix matching is performed with E.
   2.2 determination of substitution word
      2.2.a If 2.1.a is successful and lchar(last(E)) = a then S = *labda*; and when lchar(last(E)) = e then S = *fecske*.
      2.2.b If 2.1.b is successful then we take the provided S of the E.
   2.3 annotation
      2.3.a The last word of the C has the following form: [trunc(*last*(E,1)){a,e}rest], where rest is the remaining characters (if any) at the end of last(c). The following strings are created and passed to MP: [trunk(*last*(S,1)){a,á}rest]([trunk (*last*(S,1)){e,é}rest]) if lchar(E) = a (lchar(E) = e), resp. Only

one of the strings is a valid word, and hence will be recognized by the MP. The annotation of *C* will be the morphological characters of the valid words.

2.3.b The last word of the *C* has the following form: [*E*rest]. The following string is created and passed to MP: [*S*rest]. The annotation of *C* will be the morphological characters of the compounded word [*S*rest].

Remark 2. One can observe that the first case of the algorithm is more complicated at searching, because the matching is more complex when word of variable form are concerned. In contrast, the second case of the algorithm is more complicated at annotating because the suffixes of the entity can be determined only by a proper substitution word.

Remark 3. We apply a semi-heuristic algorithm when assigning the substitution word S to each entity of case 2.2.b. S is selected from a table based on the last consonant and the vowels in the last of word of the entity. It is not perfect but assigns good words in the majority of case (over 98%).

Remark 4. At 2.3 if length(*rest*) = 0 then one can omit calling MP, because it means that there are no suffixes on the entity, so it can be considered a nominative noun.

Examples

Here we present some example to illustrate the algorithm of ER. The questions are taken from the sample inputs used for testing NL module.

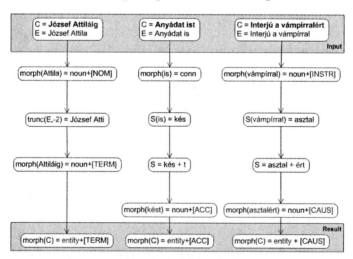

Fig. 3. Illustration of ER's algorithm on examples 1–3

Example 1. See also Figure 3.

Milyen költők vannak Arany Jánostól József Attiláig?[6]

E = *József Attila, last(E)* is recognized by MP as

`Attila[noun_prs] + [NOM]`

therefore 1) is the actual case. The matching is performed with search form *"József Atti"*, and is successful when matched against segment C = *József Attiláig* (because the right choice of C is trivial in these examples, we will not specify it explicitly in the next). The result of MP for last(C) is

`Attila[noun_prs] + [TERM]`

It means that the entity E is found in C and it is annotated as [TERM].

Example 2. See also Figure 3.

Ki rendezte az Anyádat ist?[7]

E = *Anyádat is*. This is the case 2 (b), because the part of speech of *is* is conjunction that cannot be inflected. Let S be *kés*[8], hence *kést* is passed to MP. The result is `kés[noun] + [ACC]` so the recognized entity is: *Anyádat is* $_{entity}$ +[ACC].

Example 3. See also Figure 3.

Mennyit kell fizetnem az Interjú a vámpírralért?[9]

E = *Interjú a vámpírral* . This is also case 2, because last(E) is an inflected word: `vámpír[noun] + [INSTR]`. Let S be *asztal*[10], and so *asztalért* is passed to MP that returns: `asztal[noun] + [CAUS/FIN]`. The final result of ER will be *Interjú a vámpírral* $_{entity}$ +[CAUS/FIN].

Example 4. and 5. Refer to the Figure 4 for the explanation of the algorithm on below two sentences.

Ki rendezte Az én kis mosodámat?[11]

Hol játsszák az Aidát?[12]

---

[6] What poets are between János Arany and Attila József? (e.g. concerning alphabetical order)
[7] Who directed And Your Mother Too?
[8] knife
[9] How much I should pay for the Interview with the Vampire?
[10] table
[11] Who directed My beautiful launderette?
[12] Where Aida is played?

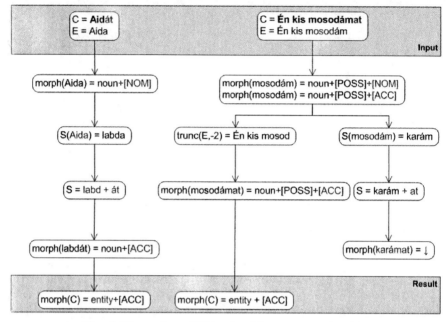

Fig. 4. Illustration of ER's algorithm on examples 4–5

Evaluation

Our algorithm is not a (supervised) learning method that is trained to recognize unknown entities in free text. Its purpose is to recognize *known entities* from a collected data base in free text even if they are in inflected form. These entities are stored in a local data base and are extracted from databases of our contracted content providers. The method was tested on a small test set of entities (248) and sentences (75) of various kind. The recognition rate was 100%, however, we expect that on larger corpora this success rate will decrease a few (1–2) percent.

Algorithm of the Tokenizer

The algorithm of the tokenizer is straightforward based on ER. It processes each segment of the question in the order specified above. If there are no entities starting with a given word *W* of the question, then a token is created from *W* itself and annotated with the respective output of MP. Whenever a single word is not recognized by MP, it is treated as a nominative noun.

Conclusions

In this paper we presented some results of the "In the web of words" (WoW) project that aimed to create a complex search interface that incorporates deep web search, Hungarian natural language question processing, image search support by visual thesaurus. The paper was focused on the processing of Hungarian questions and with special focus on the entity recognizer algorithm. Its goal is to recognized known entities in all possible inflected form. By means of a morphological parser we also determine morphological characteristics of recognized entities. The success rate of our algorithm was 100% on a small but diverse test set, and we expect that this rate falls only with a few percent on larger corpora.

References

[1] Androutsopoulos I, Ritchie GD, Thanisch P (1993) Masque/SQL – an Efficient and Portable Natural Language Query Interface for Relational Databases. Proc of IEA/AIE 93 Conference Edinburgh UK

[2] Bergman MK (2001) The Deep Web: Surfacing Hidden Value. Journal of Electronic Publishing, no 7. www.press.umich.edu/jep/07-01/bergman.html

[3] Cedermark P (2003) Swedish Noun and Adjective Morphology in a Natural Language Interface to Databases. Master Thesis Department of Linguistics Uppsala University Sweden

[4] Chae J, Lee S (1998) Frame-Based Decomposition Method for Korean Natural Language Query Processing. International Journal of Computer Processing of Oriental Languages, no 11, pp. 213-232

[5] Coheur L, Batista F, Paulo J (2003) JaVaLi!: Understanding Real Questions. Proc of the Student Workshop on Applied Natural Language Processing (EUROLAN 2003) Universitat Hamburg

[6] Filipe PP, Mamede NJ (2000) Databases and Natural Language Interfaces. Proc of 5th Jornada de Engenharia de Software e Bases de Dados (JISBD) Valladolid Spain

[7] Grosz BJ, Appelt DE, Martin PA, Pereira FC (1987) Team: An Experiment in the Design of Transportable Natural-Language Interfaces. Artifical Intelligence, no 32, pp 173-243

[8] www.ai.mit.edu/projects/infolab/

[9] www.lllf.uam.es/proyectos/sylvia.html

[10] Hunmorph (2004) http://mokk.bme.hu/resources/hunmorph/

[11] Katz B, Lin JL (2002) Start and Beyond. Proc of World Multiconference on Systemics Cybernetics and Informatics (SCI02) vol XVI. Orlando FL USA

[12] Katz B, Yuret D, Lin J, Felshin S, Schulman R, Ilik A (1998) Blitz: A Preprocessor for Detecting Context-Independent Linguistic Structures. Proc of

the 5th Pacific Rim Conference on Artificial Intelligence (PRICAI '98). Singapore

[13] Katz B (1990) Using English for Indexing and Retrieving. In: Winston P, Shellard S (eds) Artificial Intelligence at MIT: Expanding Frontiers. Vol 1. MIT Press, pp 134-165

[14] Lee H, Park JC (2002) Interpretation of Natural Language Queries for Relational Database Access with Combinatory Categorical Grammar. Int Journal of Computer Processing of Oriental Languages, no 15, pp 281-303

[15] Meng X, Wang S (2001) Overview of a Chinese Natural Language Interface to Databases: Nchiql. International Journal of Computer Processing of Oriental Languages, no 14, pp 213-232

[16] Popescu AM, Armanasu A, Etzioni O, Ko D, Yates A (2004) Modern Natural Language Interfaces to Databases: Composing Statistical Parsing with Semantic Tractability. Proc of the International Conference on Computational Linguistics (COLING04). Geneva Switzerland

[17] Popescu AM, Etzioni O, Kautz H (2003) Towards a Theory of Natural Language Interfaces to Databases. Proc of the 8th International Conference on Intelligent User Interfaces (IUI03). Miami FL USA

[18] Rangel RAP, Gelbukh AF, Barbosa JJG, Ruiz EA, Mejía AM, Sánchez APD (2002) Spanish Natural Language Interface for a Relational Database Querying System. Proc of TSD 2002. Vol 2448 of Lecture Notes in Computer Science. Springer-Verlag Brno Czech Republic

[19] Reis P, Matias J, Mamede N (1997) Edite: A Natural Language Interface to Databases – a New Perspective for an Old Approach. Proc of ENTER'97 Information and Communication Technologies in Tourism. Edinburgh UK

[20] Stratica N, Kosseim L, Desai BC (2002) A Natural Language Processor for Querying Cindi. Proc of SSGRR 2002. L'Aquila Italy

[21] Tikk D, Kardkovács ZT, Andriska Z, Magyar G, Babarczy A, Szakadát I (2004) Natural Language Question Processing for Hungarian Deep Web Searcher. Proc of IEEE International Conference on Computational Cybernetics (ICCC04). Wien Austria

[22] Warren D, Pereira F (1982) An Efficient Easily Adaptable System for Interpreting Natural Language Queries. Computational Linguistics, no 8, pp 110-122

Mobile Agents Architecture in Data Presentation Domain

Algirdas Laukaitis and Olegas Vasilecas

Department of Information Systems, Gediminas Technical University, Lithuania. algirdas@isl.vtu.lt, olegas.vasilecas@fm.vtu.lt

Introduction

Data environments are becoming more and more complex as the amount of information a company manages continues to grow. Information delivery web portals have emerged as the preferred way to bring together information resources. Using information delivery web portal, your organization's employees, customers, suppliers, business partners, and other interested parties can have a customized, integrated, personalized, and secure view of all information with which they need to interact. But one big challenge remains for organization: how to teach employees or customers to use and understand complex database environment without involving experts and IT resources which are costly and time consuming. One of the solutions use natural language database interfaces.

From the early 80's and 90's there was many efforts involved in the research of natural language use for information extraction from data base management systems (DBMS). NLDBIS have received particular attention within the natural language processing community (see [2] for reviews of the field), and they constitute one of the first areas of natural language technology that have given rise to commercial applications. Some successes have been achieved and some commercial applications emerged but the NLP techniques have not become a popular approach for DBMS interfaces. As mentioned by researchers in [2, 3, 7, 8, 22, 33] this is due to:

Graphical and menu driven interfaces achieved the level of sophistication that many data analyst can do analysis without deep knowledge of some data queering language (e.g. SQL), on the other side NLP techniques has not been able to deliver interfaces of adequate sophistication.

Most research and achieved results reports on the possibility to generate only one data queering script (in most cases this was one SQL sentence) generated from one natural language sentence. They do not support complex dialog, which is the most usual case in real life when we want interactively to build adequate request. We think that resent advances is building personal assistants in such fields like an adaptive information research from internet [5] or personalized learning knowledge maps [24] will renew researches interest in (NLDBIS) field.

Our approach in this paper was the use of dialog instead of one sentence and on the other hand we do not look at NLP techniques as the one exclusive solution to query databases, instead we look at it as supplementary technique and as a part of multi-modal interfaces. To tackle mentioned problems we propose our system JminingDialog, which is constituent part of our open source information delivery web portal JMining. Figure 1 shows main blocks in our system. White block represents our research concerning information delivery portal and has been reported in [15] and [16]. For NLP modules we propose an architecture that is based on mobile intelligent agents. The use of mobile agents in architecture is reasoned by the approach, which argues that knowledge consists largely of a personal, stored locally data files. Mobile agents can travel to various hosts where local knowledge is stored and gather necessary information that meets user request. The paradigm of agents is a very promising approach to overcome some of the problems connected with heterogeneity on the side of the data sources as well as on the side of the users. As agents should operate autonomously and can be loosely coupled, they are well suited for the integration of distributed heterogeneous data sources. This becomes especially beneficial, if agents can learn to extract information from an information source automatically (see for example [10] and [25]). On the side of the users, the paradigm of personal information agents offers a way to encapsulate the interests, the knowledge as well as the preferences of individual users. Personal agents can take the role of mediators between users and information sources, as well as between users among each other (see also [10]). Furthermore we present an agent architecture consisting of a set of asynchronously operating agents. This architecture enables us to perform sophisticated data and interaction analysis, without loosing the property of short respond times essential for interactive work in real-time. Based on the paradigm of mobile agents, we present a model for expressing knowledge that has been acquired continuously by individuals and groups of users and for using this as a means for semantic identification of various elements to build necessary web applications.

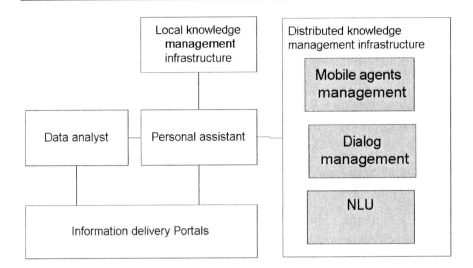

Fig. 1. JminingDialog main modules

In our architectural implementation we used several well established between academic and industry institutions toolboxes. For natural language understanding we used IBM NLU toolbox [11], [12] as an example of an agent, which represents some kind of black box, i.e. we give input for an agent and get the answer without knowing algorithm and other implementation methods. As supplement to the NLU agent based on IBM NLU toolbox we build second type of NLU agents that are based completely on open source projects: general natural language architecture GATE [6] and JOONE neural networks toolbox [14]. Both technologies combined implements hybrid neural network NLU agents.

General Architecture

The architecture supports coordinated distribution of natural language dialog management and understanding agents and their integration with information delivery web portal components. Figure 2 shows basic components of this architecture. Below follows description of those components and their interconnection.

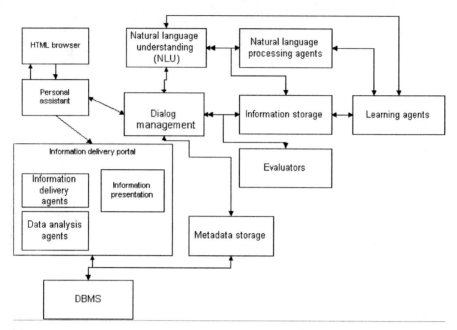

Fig. 2. General architecture of information delivery portal natural language interface

Personal assistant – it is an agent that hides all infrastructures behind information delivery portal and it's NLP components and uses multi-modal interface to communicate with the user. At presents architectural implementation it is possible to use HTML input forms with active hyperlinks and in addition forms with standard natural language dialog interface. At its present implementation personal assistant is far away from passing Turing test but we see it evolution in the future as becoming more intelligent and with ability to communicate with the user in more like human-expert way. Currently the most research in personal assistants has been done to help users search and gather information from unstructured data sources [5], [24] i.e. Internet, papers collections etc.

Dialog management – represents two sets of agents: state space dialog management agents and form based dialog management agents. The *state space* dialogue strategy is a mapping from a set of states (which summarize the entire dialogue) to a set of actions (such as identification of tables and database queries). The *state space* is defined by the collection of all variables that characterize the state of the dialogue system at a certain point in time. To avoid combinatorial explosion the designer of the system must consider how on the one hand to limit number of variables and the number of values assigned to variables and on the other hand how to use enough variables so that to cover particular domain with various dialog flow possible paths. The *set of actions* describes what the system can do, i.e. the set of functions the system can invoke at any time (e.g. play a certain prompt, query a database, hang up, etc.). The *strategy* is a mapping between the state space and the action set. For any possible state the strategy prescribes what is the next action to perform. As a result of the action and its interaction with the external environment (e.g. user, database, etc.) the system gets some new observations (e.g. database entities, attributes, etc.). The new observations are registered and modify the state of the system. This process continues until a final state is reached (e.g. the state with legitimate SQL,XML script) [20]. The frame-based systems use templates, i.e., collections of information as a basis for dialogue management. The purpose of the dialogue is to fill necessary information slots, i.e., to find values for the required variables and then perform a query or similar operation on the basis of the frame. We use frame based approach when we identify entities and the system ask the user to fill entities attributes. The dialog manager communicates with two other modules from the system: natural language understanding agents to get semantic representation of user utterance (e.g. identify entities, attributes, relationships between entities i.e. to cover all elements from entities relationships diagram) and with metadata module where databases metadata and the information delivery portal knowledge base are stored.

Natural language understanding (NLU) agents – Agent receives text input entered by user and produces the set of possible actions (identified entities) with weights that represents the probability of correct (by means of user understanding) entity identification. We identify two types of agents by their entities identification possibilities: one type of agents uses only current text input without using dialog history another one uses all information of current dialog state i.e. it uses all history of current dialog. In our current implementation first type of agents is IBM NLU toolbox and the second one is hybrid neural network NLU agent.

Information delivery portal – is the Internet/Intranet based system for queering corporate databases, analysing retrieved data and presenting results to the user in graphical and textual templates. Information delivery web portal can be used without NLP techniques but in this paper we concentrate on natural language user interface modalities and their integration with IDP. In our system NLU components are able to map user utterance to semantic concepts that represents three types of scripts: SQL script for queering relational databases, simple script for manipulating with generated by IDP HTML and XML documents. There are many commercially successful information delivery web portal products that are available in the market. Architecture of IDP implemented by our previous project JMining [15], [16] and many IDP providers implement similar three tier architecture. We have no intention to describe this architecture in details and for details about used in this paper IDP JMining we refer to [16], Microsoft [23], Information builders [13], etc for details of some commercial implementations.

Information storage – is a black board for storing various information units that are used later by other system modules. It is used as the communication media between agents. In our implementation we used a hashmap object type container to store all objects by various agents.

Natural language processing agents – implements various elements from natural language processing area: named entities recognition, coreference resolution, tokenisation, sentence splitting, gazetteer lookup, etc.

Learning agents – ensures that the system learns from data presented for learning as well as from dialogs with users.

Evaluators - are used for the particular type of agents. This means that different evaluators evaluate different aspects of agents from different viewpoints. For example, an evaluator may use the dialogue history to determine which dialogue strategy should be used (i.e. which kind of dialogue agent should be selected), while another evaluator may establish which agents is more suited to bring the answer for the user. Like in [26] our evaluators give scores for agents using a scale between [0,1].

Dialog Supporting Agents

The agent architecture approach to dialogue management makes it possible to use different dialogue control models, such as state-machines and forms inside the same system. The combination of different control models is useful when sub-dialogues are implemented in different ways. For example, most database retrieval tasks can be modelled efficiently by using forms, while more open-ended dialogues, such as entities identification in corporate databases may be implemented more efficiently using state-machines.

Below we describe state variables and variables values in our dialog management system for data retrieval, analysis and presentations tasks. Because the system is user centric orientated the values of some state space variables are nor fixed as in [21] but has some range of flexibility.

Table 1. The state space variables

agenda	System after the greeting of the user presents agenda. Each item of the agenda is associated with some number.
objects	0- no object under current dialog state, 1- database name, 2- user name, 3- user password, 4- system, etc.
obj_con	1 – if the object under current dialog management has been established, 0 -if not.
appobject	0- if no atomic application objects, 1-SQL, 2-HTML, 3-XML, 4-visualization template. This variable is redundant but we find that it helps control dialog flow.
confidence	like in [21] represents the confidence that the dialog management system has after obtaining a value for an attribute. The values 0, 1, and 2 represent the lowest, middle and highest confidence values. The values 3 and 4 are set when system receives "yes" or "no" after a confirmation question.
value_track	Tracks whether the system has obtained a value for the attribute (no=0, yes=1).
num_times	Tracks the number of times that the dialog manager has asked the user about the attribute.

Both types of dialog management agents can use all presented variables. Agents that uses state space representation method uses variable to trigger next action and move to the next state. Strategies for moving can be established from learning data. We established 94 dialogs and used reinforcement learning (RL) [21] algorithm to learn strategies for actions triggering.

Next we present simple dialog between human and our system example end shortly discuss how the system responds.

Table 2. Human-Machine multi-modal dialog example

Dialog	Description of actions
C: Hello. I am an expert in the following areas (the content of the metadata is provided in the form of hyperlinks). What you want to do now? H: Assessment type.	Personal assistant brings all answers by all agents participated at the established session. Returned page contains direct answer from dialog manager (it can be retrieved data or request for some information from the user).
C: 8 items associated with Assessment type. Can you chose from the list.(the list is presented in separate HTML frame). H: Clients with the assessment type Operational Risk.	System identifies the answer with the biggest confident variable value and shows table content in separate frame. In addition system provides the list of hyperlinks of other possible actions.

Table 2. (cont.)

C: Request from tables "Involved Party", "Assessment". Filtering on table "Assessment" column "Assessment Type" = "Operational Risk Assessment"? Say "yes" to confirm you request. H: yes.	NLU agents returns semantic objects: tables, columns, filtering values. Representation agent builds question for the system and tries to ask confirmation. After the confirmation the system retrieves request results to the separate frame.
C: What do you want do next. H: Change the colour to the red.	NLU agents return semantic objects: HTML page, action "colour", value – "red". Representation agent changes the colour of HTML page.
C: What do you want do next. H: Save it.	NLU agents return semantic objects: action – "save atomic application".Representation agent sends the message to information delivery portal to save atomic application.

JMiningDialog Architecture

In this section we present more details on our dialog management that we implemented on the general architecture described above. Figure 3 shows basic structure of the system.

In the rest of this section we will concentrate mainly on natural language understanding layer. As mentioned above we implemented two types of agents. The first set of agents utilizes technologies proposed by IBM corporation: Aglets – a framework for building mobile (and stationary but we used only mobile concept) agents and IBM NLU toolbox for natural language applications. The system works as follows. The master aglet sends mobile agents to remote hosts where mobile agents gather information stored locally in IBM NLU toolbox internal storage. Each agent then returns to master agent and store returned results. Results comprises of the list of action and level of confidence for each action. Each IBM toolbox is presented as a black box where you put you request and get the answer. Putting in the special IBM NLU toolbox sentences with associated actions does the learning process. The methods of IBM NLU statistical processing are not known.

Mobile Agents Role

Mobile agents are computational software processes capable of roaming wide area networks (WANs) such as the WWW, interacting with foreign hosts, gathering information on behalf of its owner and coming 'back home' having performed the duties set by its user. Mobile agents may co-operate or communicate by one agent making the location of some of its internal objects and methods known to other agents. By doing this, an agent exchanges data or information with other agents without necessarily giving all its information away [1]. The idea is that there are significant benefits to be accrued, in certain applications, by putting away static agents in favour of their mobile counterparts. These benefits are largely *non-functional*, i.e. we could do without mobile agents, and only have static ones but the costs of such a move are high. For example, in our case consider the scenario when mobile agent is requested to find some knowledge structures related to the words *arrangement and accounts* from several users computers. A static single-agent program would need to request for all files residing on the remote knowledge sharing host, which may total to several gigabytes. Each of these actions involves sifting through plenty of extraneous information which could/would clog up the network.

And consider the alternative. JMiningDialog NLU module encapsulates, user sentences to the entire program within an agent which consumes may be only several kilobytes which roams the other hosts included in the knowledge sharing network, arrive safely and queries these hosts locally, and returns ultimately to the home computer. This alternative obviates the high communications costs of shifting, possibly, gigabytes of information to user local computer.

We have used aglets mobile agents framework in our implementation. They are Java objects that can move from one host on the network to another and have all features mentioned above. More on this techniques can be found in [18].

As the second type of NLU agents we used stationary hybrid neural networks NLU agents that we build on JOONE neural network toolbox [14] and GATE general natural language processing toolbox. Gate has been used as NLP pre-processor and the results converted into binary string have been presented to the neural network. More on this techniques can be found in [17].

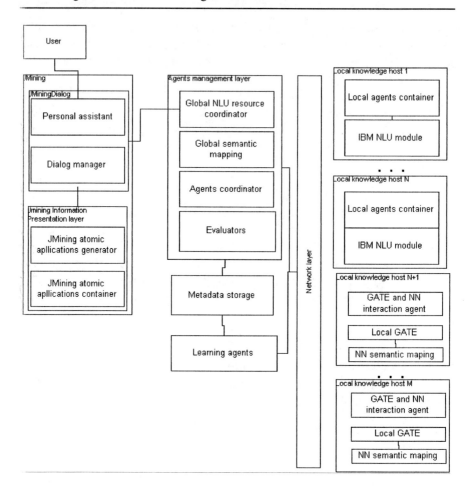

Fig. 3. NLP modules

Conclusions and Future Work

We presented agent based natural language dialog and understanding architecture for data querying from database management systems and presenting it to the user. We presented reasons why it is important to have in the future, solutions based on mobile agent approach even if now our data amount can be solved by stationary agents approach. Our experience showed that even if we have limited amount of data for teaching process, the right strategies can be found. We believe that integration between agents that extract information from Internet and others unstructured information sources and information delivery software brings optimal solution for companies data analysts.

Our research shows that distributed knowledge architecture is more flexible and adaptable for such tasks then centralised solutions.

References

[1] Oshima M, Karjoth G (1997) Aglets Specification.
www.trl.ibm.com/aglets/spec10.htm

[2] Androutsopoulos I, Ritchie GD, Thanisch P (1995) Natural Language Interfaces to Databases – An Introduction. Natural Language Engineering, vol 1, no 1, pp 29-8

[3] Androutsopoulos I, Ritchie GD, Thanisch P (1995) Experience Using TSQL2 in a Natural Language Interface. In: Clifford J, Tuzhilin A (eds) Recent Advances in Temporal Databases. Proc of the International Workshop on Temporal Databases Zurich Switzerland Workshops in Computing. Springer-Verlag, Berlin

[4] Atzeni P, Mecca G, Merialdo P (1998) Design and Maintenance of Data-Intensive Web Sites. Proc EDBT'98

[5] Bottraud JC, Bisson G, Bruandet MF (2003) An Adaptive Information Research Personal Assistant. White paper.
www.dimi.uniud.it/workshop/ai2ia/cameraready/bottraud.pdf

[6] Cunningham H, Maynard D, Bontcheva K, Tablan V, Wilks Y (2000) Experience of Using GATE for NLP R/D. Proc of the Workshop on Using Toolsets References 200 and Architectures To Build NLP Systems at COLING-2000, Luxembourg. http://gate.ac.uk/

[7] ELF Software Co. www.elf-software.com

[8] Esposito D (1999) Talk to Your Data. White paper. http://msdn.microsoft.com/library/default.asp?url=/library/en-us/dnenq/html/mseq75.asp.

[9] Fuggetta A (2003) Open Source Software – An Evaluation. Journal of Systems and Software, vol 66, no 1, pp 77-90

[10] Huhns MN, Stephens LM (1999) Intelligent Agents. In: Weiss G (ed) Multiagent Systems: A Modern Approach to Distributed Artificial Intelligence. MIT Press Cambridge MA

[11] IBM (2003) An Introduction to IBM Natural Language Understanding. An IBM White Paper

[12] IBM Voice Toolkit V5.1 for WebSphere® Studio.
www-306.ibm.com/software/pervasive/voice_toolkit/ 2004.

[13] Information Builders (2004) Leveraging Your Data Architecture for Enterprise Business Intelligence. White Paper.
www.informationbuilders.com

[14] Joone – Java Object Oriented Neural Engine. http://www.jooneworld.com/

[15] Laukaitis A, Vasilecas O, Berniunas R (2005) JMining – Information Delivery Web Portal Architecture and Open Source Implementation. In: Vasilecas

O et al (eds) Information Systems Development: Advances in Theory, Practice and Education. To appear. Springer

[16] Gedimino Technical University (2004) JMining project.
http://fmisl-09.vtu.lt/Portal

[17] Laukaitis A, Augilius E (2005) Hybrid Neural Network Architecture for DBMS Entities Identification in a Natural Language Dialog. Information Technologies – Lithuanian Science and Industry

[18] Laukaitis A, Berniunas R, Vasilecas O (2005) Natural Language Understanding by Means of Mobile Agents Architecture. Information Technologies – Lithuanian Science and Industry

[19] Levin E, Pieraccini R, Eckert W (1998) Using Markov Decision Process for Learning Dialogue Strategies. Proc ICASSP 98, Seattle WA

[20] Levin E, Pieraccini R, Eckert W, DiFabbrizio G, Narayanan S (1999) Spoken Language Dialogue: From Theory to Practice. IEEE Automatic Speech Recognition and Understanding Workshop, Keystone Colorado

[21] Litman DJ, Kearns MS, Walker MA (1998) Automatic Optimization of Dialogue Management. White paper

[22] Microsoft Corporation (2003) SQL Server and English Query.
http://msdn.microsoft.com/library/default.asp?url=/library/enus/architec/8_ar_ad_0hyx.asp

[23] Microsoft Corporation (2001) Building a Corporate Portal using Microsoft Office XP and Microsoft SharePoint Portal Server. White Paper

[24] Novak J, Wurst M, Fleischmann1 M, Strauss W (2002) Discovering, Visualizing, and Sharing Knowledge through Personalized Learning Knowledge Maps. White paper

[25] Nwana HS (1996) The Potential Benefits of Software Agent Technology to BT. Internal Technical Report Project NOMADS Intelligent Systems Research AA&T BT Labs UK

[26] Turunen M, Hakulinen J (2000) Jaspis – A Framework for Multilingual Adaptive Speech Applications. Proc of 6th International Conference of Spoken Language Processing (ICSLP 2000)

Active Extensions in a Visual Interface to Databases

Mariusz Trzaska and Kazimierz Subieta

Polish-Japanese Institute of IT and Institute of Computer Science, Poland.
(mtrzaska, subieta)@pjwstk.edu.pl

Introduction

The retrieval capabilities of the visual information retrieval system Mavigator have been designed for a naive user, typically a computer non-professional. In contrast to retrieval engines on raw text (such as Google), Mavigator addresses structured data (e.g. XML repositories). For such data a query language is proper, however naive users cannot deal with sophisticated retrieval methods and metaphors, especially using keyboard-oriented languages a la SQL and script languages for formatting retrieval output. There are two options: some generic output format (e.g. a table), which is usually too restrictive for the users, or some attractive visual form (e.g. a function chart), which in turn must be specialized to a particular application and retrieval kind. Some tradeoff between these extremes is necessary.

The Active Extensions module, which is a part of the Mavigator proto-type [1], allows extending its existing functionalities by professional pro-grammers. In contrast to Visage [2], which uses a dedicated script lan-guage, Active Extensions are based on a fully-fledged programming language (C#). Such a solution does not restrict the form of output, execution speed or algorithmic complexity of output formatting functions.

A disadvantage of our solution is that end users asking for a new output format need cooperation with a professional programmer. We believe that this solution is inevitable if we do not want to sacrifice the expressive power of the visual interface. In majority of visual retrieval tasks such a mode of making changes to end user interfaces is acceptable regarding the time, cost and convenience.

The paper is organized as follows. In next section we discuss related work. Then we give detailed description of our proposal concerning new functionalities. After this, Mavigator's information retrieval capabilities are presented. Next section concerns implementation and architecture of a working prototype and the last one concludes.

Related Work

The related solutions could be analysed from two points of views: methods of modifying application's functionalities and the way of information retrieval. There are not so many applications, which could be assigned to the both mentioned groups. Hence we present them in two separate subsections.

Methods of Modifying Application's Functionalities

DRIVE [3] is an example of a user interface to a database development environment. The system dynamically interprets a conceptual object-oriented data language with active constructs. Specification of the interface is made in a textual language called NOODL. The framework includes the following main classes: user, data, interface, and visualisation. Due to separation of data and interfaces, each data item could have associated multiple interface components. Each user could have own set of user-specific views and access privileges. Visual programming facilities help in creating queries, constraints, and other retrieval options. Although DRIVE has been designed as an easy-to-use graphical development system, it is disputable if every user kind (especially a naive one) will be ready to accept it.

Teallach [4] employs the idea of a Model-Based User Interface Development Environment (MB-UIDE). It particularly supports specification of Domain, Task and Presentation Models. A domain model is extracted from a database scheme. Then, using a graphical editor, the user builds an interface by linking together appropriate items from presentation and task models. Teallach does not introduce built-in information retrieval capabilities, thus all retrieval methods should be designed by the user. From one point of view it is an advantage because the user has full freedom in employing various retrieval metaphors. On the other hand, it could be a disadvantage, because there is no common and coherent basis of information retrieval methods.

Visage [2] is an example of another approach. A user interface itself contains some navigational methods for retrieval. Moreover, each data visualization component, called *frame*, could be modified by attaching a special script. Similarly to Mavigator, scripts are written by programmers.

However, in contrast to our approach, Visage utilizes a scripting language similar to Basic. Unfortunately the interpretation overhead limits the dataset size that can be manipulated with no speed constraint. That is one of the reasons for using in Mavigator a fully-fledged programming language.

Visual Tools for Information Retrieval

Roughly speaking, visual metaphors for information retrieval can be subdivided into two groups: based on a graphical query language and based on browsing. Some systems combine features from both groups. An example is Pesto [5] having possibilities to browse through objects from a database. Unlike Mavigator, browsing is performed from one object to a next one. Besides browsing, Pesto supports quite powerful query capabilities. It utilizes a query-in-place feature, which enables the user to access nested objects, e.g. courses of particular students, but still in the one-by-one mode. Another advantage concerns complex queries with the use of existential and universal quantification, however, not very usable for less professional users.

An essential issue behind such interfaces is how the user uses and accumulates information during querying. In particular, the user may see all the attributes even those, which are not required for the current task. Otherwise, the user can hide non-interesting attributes, but this requires from him/her some extra action. Therefore, from the user point of view, there is some tradeoff between actions preparing the information for querying and actions of further querying. To accomplish complex queries the system should support combinations of both types of actions.

Typical visual querying systems are Kaleidoscape [6], based on its language Kaleidoquery, and VOODOO [7]. Both are declared to be visual counterparts of ODMG OQL thus graphical queries are translated to their textual counterparts and then processed by an already implemented query engine.

An example of a browsing system is GOOVI [8]. A strong point of the system is the ability to work with heterogeneous data sources. Another interesting browser is presented in [9], which is dedicated to Criminal Intelligence Analysis. It is based on an object graph and provides facilities to make various analyses. Some of them are: retrieving all objects connected directly/indirectly to specified objects (i.e. e. all people, who are connected to a suspected man), finding similar objects, etc. Querying capabilities include filtering based on attributes and filter patterns. The latter allow filtering links in a valid path by their name, associated type, direction or combination of these methods. The browsing style is similar to our *extensional navigation*.

Active Extensions

When we started to develop methods of extending existing functionalities two different approaches come to our minds:

- Utilizing some kind of a graphical metaphor like in [3] or [4]. Both of them are tradeoffs between the power and easy-to-use. They are claimed to be easy enough for the target user. In our opinion, however, for our target user they are still too complex. Moreover, the metaphors seriously restrict the field of user retrieval activities.
- Using a programming language. Depending on a language kind, limitations can be reduced partly or at all. We have assumed that a Mavigator's user is not a programmer and will not be able to use such extensions. Hence the support from a professional programmer is required.

Mavigator already employs some information retrieval metaphors (see next section), which are powerful and yet easy-to-use, so we have decided to provide a way to add new functionalities operating only on a query result. The approach does not complicate the entire application's architecture, but guarantees sufficient flexibility.

Mavigator is our second prototype. The first one, called Structural Knowledge Graph Navigator (SKGN), has been designed and implemented (in Java) for the European project ICONS, thus we have gathered some practical experience of its use by computer non-professionals [10], [11], [1]. The current prototype uses Microsoft C# as a language for active extensions. A programmer is aware of the Mavigator meta-data environment, which allows him/her to write a source code of the required functionality in C#. Writing an Active Extension source code is possible through a Mavigator's special editor. Once programmer compiles the code, a particular Active Extension is ready to use (without stopping Mavigator). Then the end user is supported with one click button causing execution of the written code. The code processes a query result or objects recorded in a user basket. The functionality of such programs is unlimited. Next three sub-sections present its particular applications.

Simple Active Extensions

A simplest type of Active Extensions may perform some calculations. In Mavigator we have implemented popular aggregate functions, such as the minimal attribute's value, maximum attribute's value and average attribute's value. All are very easy for use. The user has to select a particular type of calculation and then to select a particular attribute in a query result. Then the result of the calculation is shown to the user.

Active Projections

Fig. 1. Active projections

Another application of the Active Extensions module is an active projection (Fig 1) which allows the user to visualize a set of objects. The x, y coordinates of icons representing objects are determined by values of objects' attributes. The current implementation uses two axes (2D), which allow visualizing dependencies of two attributes. Fig. 1 shows objects of the class Product and theirs dependencies between unit's price and units in stock.

An active projection makes it possible to perform some data mining investigations, in particular, to identify some groups of objects. For instance it is easy to see in Fig. 1 two groups, where one includes cheap products with a higher stock and the second one (right-bottom corner) more expensive products with a smaller stock. One can also observe that there are more cheap products than expensive ones.

Besides the visual analysis of objects dependencies it is also possible to utilize projections in more active fashion. Object taken from a basket can be dropped on projection's surface, which cause right (based on attributes values) placement. It is also possible to perform reverse action: drag an object from the surface onto the basket (which cause recording object in a basket).

Objects Exporters

Objects exporters allow cooperating with other software systems. Having a query result, it is possible to send it to other programs, such as Excel, Crystal Reports, etc. That approach makes it possible a subsequent processing of Mavigator's results of querying/browsing. The current prototype exports to XML files, which could be post-processed by a number of modern software tools.

Information Retrieval Capabilities

Mavigator is made up of three metaphors utilized for information retrieval: intensional navigation, extensional navigation and persistent baskets. The subdivision of graphical querying to "intensional" and "extensional" can be found in [12]. We have adopted these terms for the paradigm based on navigation in a graph. The user can combine these metaphors in an arbitrary way to accomplish a specific task.

Intensional and extensional navigation are based on navigation in a graph according to semantic associations among objects. Because a schema graph (usually dozens of nodes) is much smaller than a corresponding object graph (possibly millions of nodes), we anticipate that intensional navigation will be used as a basic retrieval method, while extensional navigation will be auxiliary and used primarily to refine the results.

Next subsections contain short description of the methods (for detailed one see [1]).

Intensional Navigation

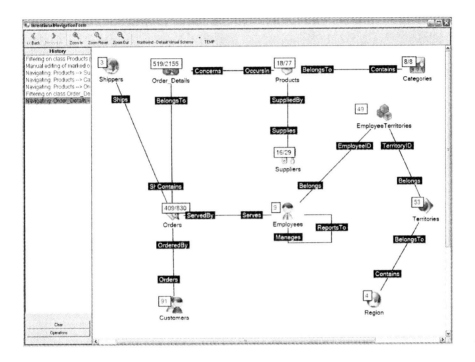

Fig. 2. Intensional navigation window

Intensional navigation utilizes a database schema graph. Fig 2 shows a window containing a database schema graph of the Northwind sample (shipped with the MS SQL Server). A graph consists of the following primitives:

- Vertices, which represent classes or collections of objects. With each of them we associate two numbers: the number of objects that are marked by the user (see further) and the number of all objects in the class,
- Edges, which represent semantic associations among objects (in the UML terms),
- Labels with names of association roles. They are understood as pointers from objects to objects (like in the ODMG standard, C++ binding).

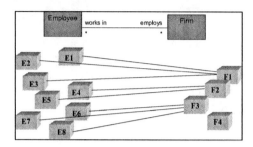

Fig. 3. Explanation of marking objects using intensional navigation

The user can navigate through vertices via edges. Objects that are relevant for the user (candidates to the search result) can be marked, i.e. added to the group of marked objects. There are a number of actions, which cause objects to be marked:

- Filtering through a predicate based on objects' attributes. The action causes marking those objects for which the corresponding predicate is true.
- Manual selection. Using values of special attributes from objects (identifying objects by comprehensive phrases) it is possible to mark particular objects manually. It is especially useful when the number of objects is not too large and there are no common properties among them.
- Navigation (Fig 3) from marked objects of one class, through a selected association role, to objects of another class. An object from a target class is marked if there is an association link to the object from a marked object in the source class. Fig 3 explains the idea. Let's assume that the *Firm* set of marked objects has four marked objects: *F1,...,F4*. Than, navigating from *Firm* via *employs* causes marking eight objects: *E1,...,E8*. This activity is similar to using path expressions in query languages. A new set of marked objects (the result of navigation) replaces an existing one. It is also possible to perform a union or intersection of new marked objects with the old ones.
- Basket activities – see section about baskets.
- Active extensions. In principle, this capability is introduced to process marked objects rather than to mark objects. However, because all the information on marked objects is accessible from an Active Extension source code, the capability can also be used to mark objects.

Intensional navigation and its features allow the user to receive (in many steps but in a simple way) the same effects as through complex, nested queries. Integrating these methods with extensional navigation, manual selection and other options supports the user even with the power not available in typical query languages.

An open issue concerns functionalities that are available in typical query languages, such as queries involving joins and aggregate functions. There are no technical problems to introduce them to Mavigator (except some extra implementation effort) but we want to avoid situation when excess options will cause our interface to be too complex for the users. We hope that during evaluation we will find answers on such questions.

Extensional Navigation

Extensional navigation takes place inside extensions of classes. Graph's vertices represent objects, and graph's edges represent links. When the user double clicks on a vertex, an appropriate neighborhood (objects and links) is downloaded from the database, which means "growing" of the graph.

Extensional navigation is useful when there are no common rules (or they are hard to define) among required objects. In such a situation the user can start navigation from any related object, and then follow the links. It is possible to use basket for storing temporary objects or to use them as starting points for the navigation.

Baskets

Baskets are persistent storages of search results. They store two kinds of entities: unique object identifiers (OIDs) and sub-baskets. The hierarchy of baskets is especially useful for information categorization and keeping order. Each basket has its name that is typed in by the user during its creation. The user is also not aware of OIDs, because special objects labels are used. During both kinds of navigation, it is possible to drag an object (or a set of marked objects) and to drop them onto a basket. The main basket (holding all the OIDs and sub-baskets) is assigned to a particular user. At the end of a user session, all baskets are stored in the database.

Basket activities include: creating a new basket, removing selected items (sub-baskets or objects), performing operations on two baskets (sum of baskets, intersection of baskets, and set-theoretic difference of baskets; the operation result can be stored in one of the participating baskets or in a new one). There are also two more advanced operations:

- Drag an object and drop it onto an extensional navigation frame. As the result, the neighborhood (other objects and links) of a dropped object will be downloaded from the database.
- Drag a basket and drop it onto class's visualization in the intensional navigation window. As the result, a new set of marked object can be created. Only objects of that class are considered.

Software Architecture and Implementation

The Mavigator prototype is implemented as a Windows Form Application in the C# language. Its architecture (Fig 4) consists of the following elements:

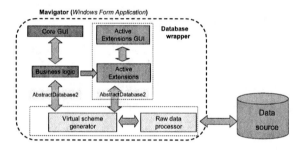

Fig. 4. Architecture of the Mavigator prototype

- Core GUI – contains implementation of the core user interface elements like intensional navigation window, basket window, etc.,
- Business logic – includes implementation of the Mavigator retrieval metaphors and some additional routines,
- Active Extensions GUI – GUI elements being a part of Active Extensions like an Active Projections window,
- Active Extensions – elements compiled from a source code written by an Active Extensions programmer. The arrow, which comes from the business logic block, symbolizes query results processed by AE,
- A database wrapper – ensures communication, via the defined AbstractDatabase2 interface, with any data source. We note that all internal data processing (including Active Extensions) works on an abstract data model (independent of implementation), which ensures that an entire application can work in the same manner aside of the current (possibly,

heterogeneous) data sources. Moreover, an entire application works with virtual schemas. They allow to redefine (using the SBQL query language [[13]]) a physically database scheme. This option can be useful for security, hiding some parts of data, changing data names, and so on.

• Data sources. Currently we are working with an ODRA prototype database, however after implementing a dedicated wrapper it is possible to work with any kind of data source, including object/relational databases, XML/RDF files and repositories, ODBC, JDBC, etc.

The Mavigator prototype utilizes active extensions written in Microsoft C#. The functionality requires compiling and running a source code (which implements a particular extension) during execution (runtime) of the Mavigator. Our first idea was to define some programming interface implemented by a particular C# class created by the programmer. However, finally we have found that such a solution would be too heavy with respect to the goal. The programmer developing a particular Active Extension has to create only one method (in a special class): public, static, with two parameters: an instance of a data wrapper and a collection containing OIDs of the objects being processed. Of course, inside the method could be any valid C# code including calling other modules, creating objects, etc. After successful compilation, the system adds this method to the list of created extensions. When the user wishes to run a particular Active Extension, the system runs an associated method, passing an instance of the data wrapper and a collection of objects' OIDs as parameters.

Conclusions and Future Work

We have presented Mavigator, which offers new qualities in extending existing application's functionalities. The Active Extensions, which use a fully-fledged programming language, make it possible to create any kind of additions to the Mavigator's core functions. The designed architecture is flexible and allows the users to work with any kind of a data source. The utilized data retrieval metaphors are easy to understand for casual (naive) users.

We plan to conduct a formal usability test on a group of users. We have some, generally positive, informal input coming from the users of the ICONS prototype. We also plan investigations concerning new visual functionalities and metaphors, which will make our tool more powerful and easy-to-use.

References

[1] Trzaska M, Subieta K (2004) Usability of Visual Information Retrieval Metaphors for Object-Oriented Databases. Proc of the On The Move Federated Conferences and Workshops (DOA, ODBASE, CoopIS, PhD Symposium) Springer Lecture Notes in Computer Science (LNCS 3292)

[2] Roth F, Chuah M, Kerpedjiev S, Kolojejchick J, Lucas P (1997) Towards an Information Visualization Workspace: Combining Multiple Means of Expression. Human-Computer Interaction Journal, vol 12, no 1 & 2, pp 131-185

[3] Mitchell K, Kennedy J (1996) DRIVE: An Environment for the Organised Construction of User Interfaces to Databases. 3rd International Workshop on Interfaces to Databases. Springer-Verlag Electronic WIC

[4] Barclay PJ, Griffiths T, McKirdy J, Kennedy J, Cooper R, Paton NW, Gray P (2003) Teallach – A Flexible User-Interface Development Environment for Object Database Applications. Journal of Visual Languages and Computing, vol 14, no 1, pp 47-77

[5] Carey MJ, Haas LM, Maganty V, Williams JH (1996) PESTO: An Integrated Query/Browser for Object Databases. Proc of VLDB

[6] Murray N, Goble C, Paton N (1998) Kaleidoscape: A 3D Environment for Querying ODMG Compliant Databases. Proc of Visual Databases 4 L'Aquila Italy 27-29 May

[7] Fegaras L (1999) VOODOO: A Visual Object-Oriented Database Language for ODMG OQL. ECOOP Workshop on Object-Oriented Databases 1999

[8] Cassel K, Risch T (2001) An Object-Oriented Multi-Mediator Browser. 2nd International Workshop on User Interfaces to Data Intensive Systems. Zürich Switzerland

[9] Smith M, King P (2002) The Exploratory Construction Of Database Views. Research Report BBKCS-02-02 School of CS and IS Birkbeck College University of London

[10] Trzaska M, Subieta K (2004) Structural Knowledge Graph Navigator for the Icons Prototype. Proc of the IASTED International Conference on Databases and Applications (DBA 2004)

[11] Trzaska M, Subieta K (2004) The User as Navigator. Proc of the 8th East-European Conference on Advances in Databases and Information Systems (ADBIS) September 2004 Budapest Hungary

[12] Batini C, Catarci T, Costabile MF, Levialdi S (1991) Visual Strategies for Querying Databases. Proc of the IEEE International Workshop on Visual Languages. Japan

[13] Subieta K, Beeri C, Matthes F, Schmidt JW (1995) A Stack-Based Approach to Query Languages. Proc of the 2nd East-West Database Workshop, Springer Workshops in Computing

Information Management in Small Enterprises – Construction of a Tool with a Holistic Perspective

Carina Helmersson and Theresia Olsson Neve

School of Business, Mälardalen University, Sweden.
(carina.helmersson, theresia.olsson.neve)@mdh.se

Introduction

Governmental and regional efforts in Sweden regarding information in small enterprises (SEs) were, the years before 2000, mainly focused on increasing the use of information technology. The project "IT @ small enterprises" was financed by the Swedish Business Development Agency (NUTEK 1999). The objectives of the project were to get a general view of activities promoting the use of IT in SEs, and to suggest measures that will favour that progress. From a report of 120 projects of IT efforts and regional development, a large number of the projects just emphasize the increase in IT use (IT-kommissionens rapport 1/98). There was little discussion in these projects on how the SE would benefit from increased IT and there was little attention paid to the role of IT in the SEs.

In advance of a procurement of IT a SE would benefit from investigating its entire information environment. The solution to information problems within the enterprise is not necessarily new IT. The solution might instead be to reorganize work routines, to build a culture in order to promote information and knowledge exchange with an individual perspective, see for example Olsson Neve (2003), to organize information in such a way that information sharing among all personnel is made possible, or to educate and encourage staff to use IT-systems already in use.

To choose what factors to take into consideration for reaching effective use of information, this paper relies on evidence from research of Marchand, Kettinger and Rollins (2000). The concept *Information Orientation* (IO), measures a company's capability to effectively manage and use information. IO is made up of three components: IT practices, management of information and information behaviour. All three components must be strong and working together if superior business performance is to be achieved. Marchand et al. (ibid) showed in an international study conducted during a period of two and a half years the positive relation between IO and superior business performance. They claim that "IO indeed predicts business performance. From a practical perspective, therefore, IO represents a measure of how effectively a company manages and uses information" (ibid, p. 70).

The information ecology model, developed by Davenport (1997), includes the components of IO. Information ecology emphasizes the use of an organization's entire *information environment* from a holistic view. The following six components are to be examined when using an information ecology perspective on the information environment:

- Information strategy is answering questions like "What do we want to do with the information within this organization?"
- Information culture and behavior deals with the values and beliefs about information, how to behave on information sharing, and the information culture.
- Information processes surveys how information work gets done: the work processes and in what actions information is used.
- Information politics deals with the pitfalls that can interfere with information sharing. This factor involves the power information provides, the governance responsibilities for its management and use, and the politics for information sharing.
- Information staff is people who interpret, categorize, filter and integrate information.
- Information architecture constitutes the IT-systems already in place.

The information environment also affects and is affected by *the organizational environment* and *the external environment* of the marketplace.

The interplay between these three environments needs to be taken into consideration. The concept external environment is easy to interpret as other researchers also use this denotation of the world outside the enterprise. The concept environment together with information and organizational might be confusing. In these two cases the concept environment does not imply the outside. Our interpretation is that Davenport uses the concept environment as a synonym for system in these two combinations (Davenport, 1997).The three environments and the six components of the information environment are shown in Figure 1 (see next page).The latest report on SEs from NUTEK is a report concerning regional differences in the use of IT in Swedish SEs (NUTEK, 2004). That report concludes that efficient IT structure is not sufficient to achieve regional development (ibid.). This conclusion differs from earlier development efforts where increased access to IT was the dominant issue. Furthermore, this conclusion interplays with the argumentation that a SE would benefit from investigating its entire information environment in advance of a procurement of IT. The purpose of the research presented in this paper was to create a tool to investigate information management in SEs from a holistic perspective. The holistic perspective of the tool is derived from applying the holistic perspective of the information ecology model. The contribution of this research is to adapt the information ecology model in purpose of making it applicable to SEs.

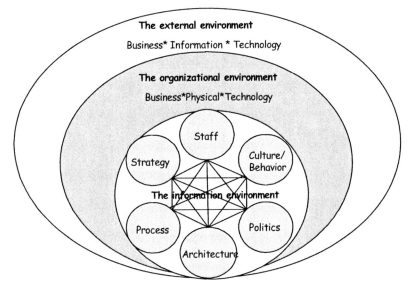

Fig. 1. The information ecology model (Davenport, 1997, p. 34)

To name the tool, the acronym TIMS is made up of *T*ool for investigating *I*nformation *M*anagement within *S*mall enterprises.

TIMS is made up of three parts:

1. *Questions* to capture how the investigated SE manages information.
2. *Guidelines* how to analyze the gathered description of information management within the SE.
3. *Demands* on the performance of the investigation as such. Examples of demands are number of interview occasions and involvement expectations on the participating SE.

The tool is meant to be used by consultants giving advice to SEs or in a development and research project aiming at supporting SEs in their management and use of information. A person using the tool is referred to as an investigator. TIMS is further explained in section "Constructing TIMS".

Findings on IT-Systems and Organizational Characteristics of SEs

Research concerning IT practices in SEs is relatively widespread. There is no research in the area of SEs that addresses all three components of IO (Helmersson, 2005).

SEs use, commonly, IT for operational support and transaction processing (Andersson 1999). Almost all SEs in Sweden (96% of the enterprises have 10 – 49 employees), use some sort of IT equipment (NUTEK 2004). In the development of new products and services the use of IT as a strategic tool has a considerably lower rating: 36% for all branches investigated; 30% for the manufacturing industry; and only 9% for the building industry. Levy et al. (1998) found SEs where IT was being used strategically, but these SEs were rare. The use of IT was rather characterized with that "there is no recognition of the role of information in supporting the achievement of business strategy" (ibid, p. 5) for more than half of the SEs in their sample.

To explore the role of IT-systems an analytical model, the Focus-Dominance model, is suggested by Levy et al. (2001). They say that SEs investments and use of IT-systems are influenced by the SEs strategic context, defined as a function of two dimensions: 1) the strategic focus for IT investments, cost reduction or value adding, and 2) the market positioning of the SE where the enterprise either relies on few customers or strives at a market position with many customers. (Levy et al. 2001)

The results from studies examining what factors lead to successful IT-system implementation are not fully consistent. The similarities and differences in those results will be exemplified with findings from Thong (2000), Hussin, King and Cragg (2002) and Burgess (2002). The SEs having highly effective external experts, adequate IT-system investment, high users' IT-system knowledge, high user involvement, and high CEO support get successful IT-systems according to Thong (2000). Hussin et al. (2002) point out that aligning IT strategy to business strategy will strengthen the performance of the enterprise. IT alignment, in turn, is positively related to the SEs level of IT maturity and the level of the CEOs software knowledge. The CEOs personal involvement in IT planning, personal IT usage, and different forms of external expertise, has little influence on IT alignment (ibid).

Burgess (2002, p. 5) summarizes barriers to successful implementation of IT within SEs with the following list:

- The cost of IT
- Lack of time to devote to the implementation and maintenance of IT

- A lack of IT knowledge combined with difficulty in finding useful, impartial advise
- Lack of use of external consultants and vendors
- Short-range management perspectives
- A lack of understanding the benefits that IT can provide, and how to measure those benefits
- A lack of formal planning or control procedures

Research, clearly fitting the two other components; information management and information behaviour, is rare. Tools for quality assessment have been formed to suite SEs. These tools cover the component information management but are poor on IT practice (Craig, 2002).

The need for research where all three components of IO; IT practices, information management, and information behaviour, are considered is motivated of this brief review.

Method and Outline of the Paper

TIMS has been created with the purpose to improve information handling within SEs. This goes along with *design science* which has the purpose to create things that serve human purposes – i.e. constructing an artifact (March & Smith, 1995; Järvinen, 2000). Research activities in design science consist of two main activities: to *construct* the artifact and to *evaluate* the artifact. This paper mainly concerns the construction phase.

This construction phase includes: a) the interpretation and adjustment of the information ecology model when constructing the interview questions, b) using the tool in a pilot study, c) constructing guidelines for analysis, and d) performing demands for information management investigation. The process is described in greater detail in section "Constructing TIMS" together with examples of questions and considerations. TIMS has been used in four different SEs within the manufacturing industry when investigating their routines and use of information. This usage gave an opportunity to a preliminary evaluation of the tool. The evaluation criteria for the tool as a whole are presented in section "Using the tool". The evaluation of the interview questions is presented as well.

Theoretical Basis

In this section the characteristics of SEs used in the paper are presented. Also the perspectives on information systems and information management that have influenced the design of the guidelines on how to analyze the gathered description of information management in the SE are shown.

Characteristics of SEs

There is a great heterogeneity among SEs. Not only due to the number of employees, ranging from self-employed persons to companies of up to 500 employees, but also differences between different sectors such as; manufacturing, trade and services, or "craft" companies. In spite of this, Julien (1998) suggests six characteristics to define the concept of small business:

1. Small size (number of employees, turnover)
2. Management centralization. Management is almost always concentrated in the person of the owner-manager.
3. Low level of specialization, from the point of view of management, employees and equipment
4. An intuitive informal strategy
5. An uncomplicated or unorganized internal information system
6. A simple external information system

These characteristics has been used as guide when constructing the TIMS-tool and especially the interview questions.

In this work SEs with 10 to 49 employees was used. Amongst the enterprises in this research the core business is not in the sector of information management or information technology. Further, there is a low grade of specialization and the enterprise lack expertise on information management or information technology. TIMS is generic within the limits mentioned above.

Perspectives Used for Analyzing Information Management

In this paper the concept IT-system is used if an information system includes IT. Thus an information system is a more general concept which not necessarily embraces IT. An information system certainly manages information. The notion "information management" includes not only the design of the information system of an enterprise but also how effectively IT, if any, is used and to what degree humans in the enterprise share information with each other. To analyse and summarize information management within an investigated SE, the investigator is instructed to focus on central parts among the findings on information management. The analysis of the information management in the SE should pay attention to the interplay between formal and informal information (Andersen, 1994) and to external versus internal information (Kreps, 1990). The enterprises capability of innovation opposed to stability should be mapped (Kreps, 1990). Walsham (1993) arguments that research on information systems should deal with context and processes. The context may include the organizational units or the organization as a whole and various social structures. Human affairs are in constant state of change. The process of transformation and change has to be taken into consideration.

The analysis part of TIMS is primarily focusing on a) how the context, in a number of different forms, influences the IT-system(s) within a SE, and b) how the use of an IT-system, for example work routines, influences the context. The investigator should focus on for what actions information and IT-systems are used (Goldkuhl, 1996; Checkland & Holwell, 1998).

Constructing TIMS

In this section, the process of constructing the TIMS-tool, including forming the interview questions (QIMS), guidelines for analysis (GAIMS), and procedure for investigating information management (PIMS) will be accounted for.

Creating the Questions for Investigating Information Management in Small enterprises, QIMS

The major parts of the information ecology model should be applicable to SEs except for the component *Information Staff*. The SEs at hand does not have special staff to manage information. The tasks that the information staff manages within larger enterprises should be managed by the owner or some other central administrator within a SE. Since the factor Information Staff was excluded the model used here consists of the following components:

Information environment
- Information Strategy
- Information Politics
- Information Behaviour and Culture
- Information Processes
- Information Architecture

Organizational environment
- Business Situation
- Technology Investment
- Physical Arrangement

External environment
- Business Markets
- Technology Markets
- Information Market

Davenport (1997) described these different components in text together with examples from his scattered empirical findings from 48 different large enterprises. He also suggested measuring to what degree enterprises work in an ecological way. Davenport presented a number of statements for the reader to use for this purpose. The statements are meant to be judged, on a scale from agree to disagree, by respondents from an enterprise. Agreement to the different statements means that the enterprise works in an ecological way.

Initially, in our study, we used 60 statements. Each statement was judged if it was applicable to a SE or not. If so, a number of questions were formulated to explore the issue at hand. This gave a number of preliminary questions that were applied in a pilot study. The experience from the pilot study resulted in reconstruction of some of the questions. The final outcome resulted in 32 questions. These interview questions should be used by the investigator that uses the TIMS-tool. To exemplify, an interview question from the component Information Behavior and Culture in the Information Environment is shown:

1. What does the enterprise do to encourage employees to share information and knowledge among each other?

Using the Guidelines of how to Analyze Information Management in Small enterprises, GAIMS

The experience from the pilot study called for a systematic way to analyse the answers of the questions. This led to the creation of guidelines for analysis (GAIMS). To be able to analyze and summarize information management in an investigated SE, central issues of each of the components in the information ecology model were chosen. For each issue, the guidelines consist of instructions on how to analyze and illustrate the issue using selected perspectives on information management. Here is an example from our study concerning the factor Technology Investment in the Organizational Environment component. The following issues were chosen:

1. The visions and needs of change of technology in the nearby future
2. Planning for introduction of new technology

In order to use GAIMS, i.e. to analyze and illustrate these issues, the investigator should bear in mind the reasoning from theoretical perspectives central to this research. For issue 1 this concerns:

- Stability versus innovation
- How the context influences the IT-system

- What actions are supported of the information use

In our study when developing GAIMS, the guide to issue 1 was formulated in the following way:

☁ The investigator should note if the owner/manager considers the need for change of information technology to emanate from a wish to achieve a higher degree of stability or a wish to make the enterprise more innovative. What drives a possible request for change? The change could be initiated from personnel, the possibilities of technology or demands from customers or suppliers.

The following perspective should be applied to issue 2:

- How the IT-system influences the context
  The guide to issue 2 was formulated:

☁ The investigator should note if the owner/manager is aware of, and has taken measures to manage the impact new technology causes. The impact could consist of increased knowledge for the personnel, change of working tasks and other routines.

Creating the Procedure for Investigating Information Management in Small Enterprises, PIMS

a) The procedure for the investigation was designed mainly according to experiences from the pilot study. The procedure for investigating information management in small enterprises consists of written:*demands,* such as allocating time and discussing the results of the investigation, for the participating small enterprise, and
b) *instructions* to the investigator on the procedure of how to carryout the investigation.

It is important that the investigator is aware of the fact that the investigation is a qualitative study. The investigator should be able to reflect on the findings obtained when visiting the enterprise and when interviewing the employees. The interview of a person in a leading position in the enterprise, often the owner, should take part on two different occasions. On the first occasion questions from the external and the internal environments are to be asked. After about a week the investigator continues with the questions from the information environment. This gives the investigator an opportunity to meet the enterprise on at least two occasions and also time to reflect on answers given in the first interview.

To get a second opinion on information management in the enterprise an additional interview with another employee, else than the owner/manager, should be made. The questions in this interview mainly covers the issues in the information environment and concern what type of information he/she uses and produce in his/her work and if the information is easy to find and appropriate for the task.

Enterprises that agree to participate in the investigation have to accept to read and discuss the description of information management in the enterprise with the investigator.

Using the Tool

Evaluating an artifact means answering the question: "How well does it work?" (March & Smith 1995). The tool, TIMS, can't be judged on any absolute and objective criteria. It is also impossible to say that the tool is ready and not possible to improve further. The construction phase can go on as long as the tool is used. The preliminary evaluation in this research also encouraged some further improvements. Construction and evaluation can be viewed as an iterative process[1].

TIMS is to be considered as useful if it illustrates the problems and the abilities the SE possesses within the area of information management. To be able to judge if this criteria was fulfilled the tool was used in four different SEs within the manufacturing industry. In this paper it is only possible to give some examples from the result of the four investigations.

A separate evaluation of QIMS was carried through after the interviews were completed. The investigator, in this case the authors, carried through the evaluation after listening to and reading the literal written texts from the interviews from all four investigations. The desirable criteria for each question were that:

- The interviewer should feel that the question was appropriate and possible for the respondent to answer
- The interviewer should be able to explain the intention with the question if the respondent wished complementary explanation of the meaning of the question
- The answer of the question should not repeat answers of earlier asked questions
- The range of the question should be suitable, not a simple answer and not an answer that covered a life history.

---

[1] See: www.eki.mdh.se/personal/chn01/IMSE/ for presentation of the tool

This evaluation revealed some possibilities of improvement of the questions.

Conclusions

The conclusion of the research reported in this paper is that it was possible to use the holistic approach of the information ecology model as a basis for the tool. SEs showed to have both problems and abilities within IT practices, management of information, and information behaviour. By using the tool it was possible to distinguish problems for and abilities in each SE in the area of information handling. Typical examples of problems found are:

- The goal of the enterprise is vague and the enterprise lacks a plan to reach the goal.
- The enterprise uses different IT-systems. They are not compatible. This leads to redundant data and information that is hard to grasp.
- The IT-systems in use are not compatible. The business executive doesn't use the IT-systems in the enterprise. This gives duplication of work.
- The business executive possesses a lot of information him/herself.
- External information is not collected systematically, but often informal and owned by the owner/manager.
  Example of abilities shown is:
- Informal information is often successfully used, for example in unplanned meetings in the SE and in planned recurrent meetings.

When a SE gets aware of its problems and abilities in the area of information management this gives the SE a foundation to improve problematic areas. This in turn will enhance information management and increase performance.

References

Andersen ES (1994) Systemutveckling – principer, metoder och tekniker. Andra upplagan. Studentlitteratur Lund
Andersson J (1999) Business Process Development and Information Technology in Small and Medium-Sized Companies. In: Nilsson AG, Tolis C, Nellborn C (eds) Perspectives on Business Modeling, Understanding and Changing organizations. Springer

Burgess S (2002) Managing Information Technology in Small Business: Challenges & Solutions. Idea Group Publishing

Checkland P, Holwell S (1998) Information, Systems and Information Systems – Making Sense of the Field. John Wiley & Son's Ltd

Cragg PB (2002) Benchmarking Information Technology Practices in Small Firms. European Journal of Information Systems, no 11, pp 267-282

Davenport TH (1997) Information Ecology. Oxford University Press

Goldkuhl G (1996) Handlingsteoretisk definition av informationssystem. Presented in Swedish at VITS Höstkonferens Systemarkitekturer 1996-11-21

Helmersson C (2005) Investigating Information Handling in Small Businesses – a Review of Current Research. Proc of the Fifth Conference for the Promotion of Research in IT at New Universities and University Colleges in Sweden 11-13 May Borlänge Sweden

Hussin H, King M, Cragg P (2002) IT Alignment in Small Firms. European Journal of Information Systems, no 11, pp 108-127

IT-kommissionens rapport (1/1998) Statens offentliga utredningar 1998:19. IT och regional utveckling -120 exempel från Sveriges län. Kommunikationsdepartementet

Julien P-A (ed) (1998) The State of the Art in Small Business and Entrepreneurship. Ashgate

Järvinen PH (2000) Research Questions Guiding Selection of an Appropriate Research Method. Proc of the 8th European Conference on Information Systems

Kreps GL (1990) Organizational Communication. Second ed. Longman

Levy M, Powell P, Yetton P (2001) SME:s Aligning IS and the Strategic Context. Journal of Information Technology, vol 16, pp 133-144

Levy M, Powell P, Yetton P (1998) SME:s and the Gains from IS: from Cost Reduction to Value Added. Proc IFIP 8.2/8.6 Helsinki

Marchand DA, Kettinger WJ, Rollins JD (2000) Information Orientation: People, Technology and the Bottom Line. Sloan Management Review, Summer 2000, pp 69-80

March ST, Smith GF (1995) Design and Natural Science Research on Information Technology. Decision Support Systems, no 15, pp 251-266

NUTEK (1999) Nyttan av IT – i småföretagarens ögon. Nutek

NUTEK (2004) IT i småföretag: regionala skillnader i användningen av IT. Nutek

Olsson Neve T (2003) A Cognitive Narrative Approach to Individual Learning and Personal Development within Organisations. Licentiate Thesis Stockholm University Sweden

Thong JYL (2001) Resource Constraints and Information Systems Implementation in Singaporean Small Businesses. Omega, no 29, pp 143-156

Walsham G (1993) Interpreting Information Systems in Organizations. John Wiley & Sons Chichester

Improving ICT Governance by Reorganizing Operation of ICT and Software Applications: The First Step to Outsource

Björn Johansson

Jönköping International Business School, Jönköping University, Sweden and Faculty of Information Technology, Monash University, Australia.
bjorn.johansson@jibs.hj.se

Introduction

During recent years great attention has been paid to outsourcing as well as to the reverse, insourcing (Dibbern et al., 2004). There has been a strong focus on how the management of software applications and information and communication technology (ICT), expressed as ICT management versus ICT governance, should be carried out (Grembergen, 2004). The maintenance and operation of software applications and ICT use a lot of the resources spent on ICT in organizations today (Bearingpoint, 2004), and managers are asked to increase the business benefits of these investments (Weill & Ross, 2004). That is, they are asked to improve the usage of ICT and to develop new business critical solutions supported by ICT. It also means that investments in ICT and software applications need to be shown to be worthwhile. Basically there are two considerations to take into account with ICT usage: cost reduction and improving business value. How the governance and management of ICT and software applications are organized is important. This means that the improvement of the control of maintenance and operation may be of interest to executives of organizations. It can be stated that usage is dependent on how it is organized. So, if an increase of ICT governance is the same as having well-organized ICT resources, could this be seen as the first step in organizations striving for external provision of ICT? This question is dealt with to some degree in this paper. However, the aim is to describe how and why the decision-making in an organization that has an ideology of decentralization, makes the decision to centralize its operation of software applications and ICT.

The rest of the paper is organized as follows: the second section describes ICT governance and ICT management and the differences between these concepts; Section 3 describes a retrospective study of the Municipality that acts as empirical evidence of the findings that are outlined in Section 4 which discusses how and why the decision was made in the Municipality and why the outcome of the decision turned out as it did. The final, section summarises the paper and give some conclusions that can be drawn from the study.

Governance and Management of ICT

According to Weill & Ross (2004), effective ICT governance is important in order to be able to handle ICT management in an effective way. They claim that, by implementing effective governance, top-performing organizations following the same strategy generate 20 per cent higher profit than firms with poor governance. They also state that top-performing organizations with effective governance have a return on investment of ICT 40 per cent higher than that of their competitors. If this is the case, why do not all organizations implement effective governance? To answer that question one has to define governance. It could, to a great extent, be defined as "authority" as defined by Simon (1997) or "politics and power" as defined by Pettigrew (1973) or strictly as "decision-rights". So the question is what these "decision-rights" are about. Weill & Ross (2004) describe ICT governance as decision-rights regarding ICT Management. They (2004, p. 8) define ICT governance as *"specifying the decision rights and accountability framework to encourage desirable behaviour in the use of ICT"*. This indicates that ICT governance, to a great extent, is about how resources are organized, and in that way it is related to decision-making about sourcing options. However, they claim that ICT governance is not about making specific ICT decisions; instead they state that making specific ICT decisions is about ICT management. According to Weill & Ross there are three questions that need to be answered to determine whether the implemented governance is effective. These are: What decisions must be taken to ensure effective use and management of ICT? Who should make these decisions, and how will the decisions be made and monitored? However, in this author's view these questions further blur the concepts of management and governance. Governance could be compared with strategy. However, Weill & Ross's (2004) claim is contradictory since they say that it differs between organizations with the same strategy. It then must be asked what they mean by strategy in relation to governance. The distinction they make between governance and management indicates that governance could be seen as a strategy to execute management. But, what is the relation between governance and strategy? According to Weill & Ross there are five distinctive areas, expressed as major ICT decisions, which are managed in the governance work: ICT principles, ICT architecture, ICT infrastructure strategies, business applications needs and ICT investments. The question now is: What is left for ICT management?

However, from the discussion above it can be concluded that governance determines who should make the decisions while management is the process of making and implementing them. The description of ICT governance by Weill & Ross emphasises that there are two sides of governance: a behavioural side and a normative side. This paper argues that the behavioural side of governance is closely related to strategy while the normative side is more closely related to management. At least two possible explanations can be found for why organizations do not implement effective ICT governance: first, Weill & Ross (2004) conclude that difficulties in explaining ICT governance is the most serious barrier to effective implementation; second it could be that there is effective governance but it is not labelled as such or that the activities of managers are not as governance.

Weill & Ross describe ICT governance as a function of two things: the tight link between ICT and business processes, and the attempt by the organization's stakeholders to get more value from ICT investments. According to Weill & Ross, organizations get more value from ICT by clarifying their strategy and the role of ICT in fulfilling their strategy. They also do it by increasing the measurement and management of ICT spending. And, according to Weill & Ross, implementing effective ICT governance is the way to do that.

How then is implementing of ICT governance related to decision-making and management? According to Simon (1960) decision-making and management are almost the same. However, there are many views of what constitutes management. According to Easterby-Smith et al. (2002) there are two different uses of the word that describe management either as an activity or as a group of people. The latter description represents the people called managers and implies that management is something that is done in hierarchical levels. Relating this to governance, it could be claimed that governance is something that is done at the highest level in organizations. Simon (1960) claims that all organizations could be seen as a three-layered cake. The bottom layer consists of the basic work processes; the middle consists of decision-makers making programmed decisions aimed at governing the day-to-day operations in the bottom layer; in the top layer, non-programmed decisions are made aimed at designing and redesigning the entire organization and support it with its basic goals and objectives and monitor and control the performance of the organization. According to Simon (1960), organizations are systems of behaviour designed as a joint function of human characteristics and the nature of the work environment, expressed in a hierarchical structure of departments and sub-departments. In a specific organization, the issue is about the optimal size of its departments. Simon puts this as a question of centralisation or decentralization. Another question is about the relations between the departments and management authority. This indicates that governance is about non-programmed decisions made with a high degree of formal authority. It also suggests that implementing effective ICT governance is about centralized decision-making authority in organizations.

Easterby-Smith et al. (2002) and Simon (1960) put forward the idea of management as an activity. They argue that this view has evolved into a perspective that sees management as something that everyone does and must be skilled in. Using this description makes it harder to distinguish between governance and management. It therefore is not that clear that centralisation is the best way of implementing effective governance or that governance is the same as formal authority. Andersen (1986) describes management and decision-making as almost the same. He claims that decision-making is an essential part of management. The major decision-making activities can, according to Andersen (1986), and Easterby-Smith et al. (2002) referring to Taylor and Fayol, be grouped into the following four activities: planning for future activities; organising and deciding how to link the organization with its environment; coordinating activities that aim at improving the effectiveness of the organization; and controlling the use of resources in the organization.

Earl (1989) describes ICT management as consisting of three distinct activities: The first, planning, is the one that receives most attention in organizations which means that the question about what applications we need is answered. The second activity is organization in which questions about how an organization should structure its resources are answered. The third is labelled control which means that the organization tries to have control over its resources. A typical question here is: What is the costs of our ICT? According to Earl, the three activities are interdependent, but dependent on and affected by the overall management practice of the organization. In the description by Earl (1989) the activity control was reported as the area activity which receive least attention from ICT managers in his 1982/83 study. According to Earl this indicated that the control was enough at that time. However, general managers gave a higher priority to the control activity. This paper argues that this low attention to control means not that, as Earl claims that, ICT is under good control. Instead it could be explained by the productivity paradox (Brynjolfsson, 1993). The fact that it has been stated as extremely difficult to evaluate ICT and ICT costs has meant that the control activity has been avoided. And even if the manager tries to emphasise having control over ICT costs, the development and evolution of ICT has more or less made it impossible. The conclusion thus far is that governance to a great extent is about controlling what happens in organizations and especially about how they use ICT and software applications in the best way. The decision-making processes case, when a Municipality decides which sourcing option to use for its operation of software applications and ICT, illustrates this.

The Municipality Case

This section reports on a retrospective study of a decision-making process done in a Swedish Municipality, which in 2002 started an investigation about how it should organize its ICT operation. The study of this process consists of 11 tape-recorded semi-structured interviews. The material under investigation includes documented materials in the form of meeting protocols and reports on investigations made by the participants in the decision-making process. It also includes a consultancy report by an external consultant.

The history of the Municipality can, to a great extent, be described by its ideology, which is to strive for decentralization. The Municipality's administrative unit consists of eleven different committees, six of which are organized into one group, the Municipal executive committee. The other five are self organized committees which are supposed to be supervised by the Municipal executive committee. However, as the ideology of the Municipality focuses on decentralization, these committees have the authority to make decisions. The basic ideology of both the political unit and the administrative unit is to decentralize as much as possible. The effects of this ideology are very clearly shown in how the Municipality has organized its ICT operation. Each of the committees has developed its own organization of ICT. However, the municipal executive committee has overall responsibility for the Municipality's general ICT infrastructure. To illustrate the effect of this decentralization and the evolvement of software applications and ICT in the Municipality, it can be mentioned that it uses a great diversity of software and ICT. For example, there are 9 different office products, 11 different database systems, 16 different operative systems, 5 different e-mail software and 66 different software applications that are identified as critical for the Municipality. In addition to the 66 software applications there are an unidentified number of software applications used. This could to a great extent describe the reason for the sourcing decision-making process. As described by the CEO in the municipal executive committee *"the wilderness of the Municipality's software applications and ICT has to be controlled"*. This could probably be seen as the starting point of the decision-making process and the project *"ICT and telephony coordination"*.

The Sourcing Decision-Making Process

The process started in March 2002, when a standing committee, consisting of the five municipal commissioners and the CEO of the municipal executive committee, gave the municipal executive committee the task of investigating the common ICT infrastructure in the Municipality. The reason for why this investigation should be done was the expansion of ICT used in the Municipality. The direction was to review the Municipality's general ICT infrastructure. The investigation was to define the municipal executive committee's responsibilities of development, operation and maintenance and to describe the need for competence development and how this could be arranged. The municipal executive committee engaged a consultant to make the investigation. The consultant interviewed employees on different committees including some with responsibilities for the different committees' ICT. The consultant stated that the organization of ICT was distinguished to a great extent by decentralization, and that there should be a long-term plan for how ICT should be developed.

The consultancy report revealed a need to increase strategic management in the Municipality. The controlling role of the municipal executive committee also needed to be improved. The report outlined 15 reflections that, further on, were expressed as 12 recommendations. These were summarised by the CEO of the municipal executive committee and discussed at the standing committee. The standing committee suggested that the municipal executive board make a decision about giving the municipal executive committee seven work tasks. One of them was to investigate the possibilities of coordinate operation of the Municipality's entire ICT in a planned new data centre. Another was to establish the position of a new CIO at the municipal executive committee, who should have the authority for the entire Municipality. In December 2002, the municipal executive board gave the commission to the municipal executive committee to investigate, in cooperation with involved committees, the possibility of coordinating the operation of software applications to the planned data centre.

The next step in this decision-making process and the one that probably had most impact on the decisions outcome, was the employment of the new CIO who began to work on this matter in 2003 and immediately organized the decision-making process as a project with five sub-projects:

communication, premises, telephony, system technical platforms and customer service. The representatives involved in the project were organized into five groups; 1) a steering group, 2) a reference group consisting of employees with responsibility for software applications, 3) a reference group with representatives from the union, 4) a group of sub-project leaders and 5) a project leader group. The main work was done by the sub-project leader group and the project leader group. However, the steering group had the overall decision-making authority, and was the last instance of decision-making among the administrative units.

In October 2004 the CIO reported to the municipal executive board, on the results of the project. He stated that it was necessary to position the Municipality for its future development. He then described the decision as choosing between two different options which were to *"continue with the ICT infrastructure that historically has been built up at the different committees with a very low grade of coordination"* or *"to coordinate the ICT function and telephony for better usage of existing resources making the Municipality prepared to meet future challenges and possibilities to increased effectiveness".*

The material provided as basic data for the decision-making was a report from the project work a register of investments necessary for 2005 to 2007 and a compilation of costs for the operation of ICT after the reorganization. The municipal executive board decided on the latter option aimed at restructuring and coordinating. Though this decision demanded investments that go beyond the decided budget it needed to be discussed and decided on in the municipal council. This was done in November 2004, and the decision was to coordinate the operation of ICT in the planned new data centre. The municipal council accepted this decision unanimously.

Discussion

The structure of the software applications and ICT in the Municipality is overgrown and unwieldy. To some extent, it could be claimed that it is well controlled, though each committee controls its own resources. However, from an overall perspective, there are weak controls. The municipal executive committee that is supposed to have the overall control and who also should coordinate the ICT has a hard time doing so. That ICT resources not are well controlled was shown in the statement by the municipality's CIO that nobody could say how many different systems there were. He stated that there were somewhere between 300 to 400 different software applications used in the Municipality. The structure of operation follows the decentralization ideology. It can be claimed that ICT management is well done at the different committees. But, it certainly would be claimed that the ICT governance is weak if governance is seen as the centralisation of control. The main reason for the investigation of the coordination of operations was that it was found that the ICT governance needed to be improved. This could be seen as a divergence from the common ideology of the Municipality.

Making Decisions that Diverge from the Municipalities Ideology

According to Brunsson (1985), decisions that diverge from the main ideology of an organization are especially hard to make. When it comes to political organizations such as the Municipality the basic idea is that they would have different ideologies. Brunsson claims that, quite often, different ideologies exist between the political unit and the administrative unit. This is not the case in the Municipality. This means that so long as decisions are proposed and taken that do not disturb the ideology the more likely it is that they will be accepted. But, if something is proposed that disturbs the ideology, harmony is also disturbed. Brunsson describes this kind of decision as the hardest to get motivation for and therefore the hardest to get commitment to. This is clearly shown in the consultancy report that states that *"there is a very strong scepticism letting someone outside the committee manage operation and maintenance of software applications and servers"*. The expressed motive for this scepticism is that an external partner could not be sufficiently knowledgeable. What the respondents expressed to the consultant is that the development and implementation must be carried out by internal employees of the committees. This shows first, that other committees in the Municipality are seen as outsiders and second, that the respondents mix up operation, maintenance and development. It is possible to claim that though the question from the beginning was to investigate if operation of ICT could be coordinated among the different committees, the confusion about operation and maintenance makes the decision-making hard to manage.

It can clearly be stated that had the proposal that the Municipality should coordinate all operations in one data centre after the initial investigation, there would have been great resistance. Brunsson (1985) claims that, if decisions should result in organizational action, high commitment is needed from those that are affected of the decision is needed. To receive high commitment there are four rationalities in the decision-making process that are important: risks, uncertainty, motivation and expectations.

How did then the Municipality and its decision-makers manage this? Here, Simon's (1960) decision-making model could be useful. It describes decision-making as rational and consisting of the following three steps: intelligence, design and choice. In the first step the environment is searched by the decision-makers in order to be acquainted with what goes on in it. This was decided mainly by the CIO of the Municipality who then discussed how other Municipalities had implemented the coordination and centralization of their ICT operations. This can be described as part of irrational decision-making (Brunsson, 1985) though the presented alternatives were in line with what the decision-maker, in this case the CIO, wanted the decision to be. The second step aims at inventing, developing and analyzing possible courses of action (Simon, 1960) which means that, after identifying the problem in the first step possible solutions for the problem are identified. This second step then answers the question about what alternatives there were for solving the problem. In the Municipality's decision-making process this step can be related to Brunsson's description of irrational decision-making, though it was presented with alternatives that were not relevant, aiming at increasing commitment among stakeholders. At the beginning of the decision-making process, it was quite clear that something has to be done. The alternative to just continue was unrealistic but the final decision was presented as choosing between two alternatives, do nothing or coordinate. In the last step, the selection of a particular action was made. Here, the decision authority of the CIO was used; there were some questions raised about other alternatives but they were never investigated. The description of this decision-making process can to a great extent be described by the statement Simon (1960) made, when he said that the last step is often decided first. He claims that it is common that the selected action in the last step is made in advance and that directs what happens in the first two.

Why the Decision-Making Process Started

The reason for why the decision-making process aimed at restructuring the operation of software applications started in the Municipality can be described in two ways. First, the Municipality need to increase the control over its ICT costs. The cost for the management of ICT has probably increased considerably. The reason for using the word "probably" is that the Municipality does not know how much its ICT operation costs. Each of the committees has, according to the CEO, at each of the units a good grasp of its own costs. But, when it comes to the overall control of costs the control is weak. Cost control is emphasised as one area that must improve. Weak cost control is also given as one reason why not outsourcing is a possible alternative at this stage. However, the attempt at coordinating and increasing control is described as aiming to give the possibility of having an external partner to compete with the internal data centre. Second, security is raised as an important factor for starting the process. In the current structure the operation of a lot of critical software applications is dependent on only one person. This is described as an effect of the decentralization and the only way to solve it is to centralize the operation. The other security concern is that some of the committees do not have suitable premises for their servers. Both cost and security reasons could be described as a wish to increase control and could therefore be seen as an attempt to increase governance of the operation of software applications and ICT in the Municipality.

To increase control can therefore be seen as the reason for the initial directive from the standing committee in March 2002 which was to investigate the Municipality's general ICT infrastructure. It is not clear how the directive to the consultant was formulated. However, from his report, is it obvious that he investigated more than was stated in the original directive. Although he was not asked to investigate the different committees ICT infrastructure he did and he also gave some advice that a total investigation should be carried out aiming at centralising all operation to a central data centre. Nor it is clear whom the consultant interviewed. This author's interviews gave the understanding that it was mostly the employees at the municipal executive committee that were interviewed. In that way the investigation seems to be a little unjust. This was also indicated in my interviews where representatives in the decision-making process claimed that the outcome of the process was already decided on before it started. They also say that they were not involved in the first investigation made by the consultant despite the fact that the investigation involved their work to a great extent. However, the consultant's report has one very interesting point that reflects the results of the entire decision-making process in an interesting way. He states that the development of broadband connections in the Municipality put forward the question of a coordinated operation of the entire collection of the Municipality's servers. This indicates that an understanding of the history of an organization is important to the understanding of why decisions are made. This is something that Pettigrew (1973) emphasises. This goes back to the start of the investigation and the question of power and politics in the decision-making process. In my study it has become clear that there are a group of five persons that, on a more or regular basis, meets every week. This group consists of CIOs from different committees and the CEO of the Municipality. They have no formal decision authority but they do have the possibility of discuss and propose what should be done to a great extent. This can be compared with Petti-grew's statement that organizational decision-making should generally be understood as a political process that balances various power vectors.

It could be argued that one reason for the Municipality to start the sourc-ing decision was that it had decentralized too far. As Simon described it, decentralization is not something on which the organization has to decide. Instead, is it a question of how far the decentralization should go. In the Municipality, the decentralization of ICT resources had gone too far at least from the entire organization's perspective. It had evolved and built up a structure in each department which means that the operation and mainte-nance work of its software applications have increased in complexity.

Conclusions

The decision-making model presented by Simon (1960) and the presenta-tion by Brunsson (1985) regarding irrational decision-making describe very well how the decision-making process was carried out in the Munici-pality. It can be described as an irrational decision-making process aiming at organizational action. The decision that was taken in the Municipality differs considerably from its ideology. To make such a decision the deci-sion-makers must have high commitment from those who are affected by it. The decision-making process in the Municipality was successfully man-aged and finalised the first step of the decision.

It is claimed that the Municipality has strong management of its ICT at the separate committees. However, the governance of ICT-related re-sources is weak and seen as the main reason why the Municipality needs to centralize its operation of software applications and ICT. It can be con-cluded that strong ICT governance is needed to manage software applica-tions and ICT successful. Centralisation of operations is one way to in-crease control and thereby improve governance.

This paper concludes that organizations that have decentralized their operation of software applications and ICT are weak in their ICT govern-ance. It argues that strong governance is needed to first evaluate and make a judgement about whether outsourcing is a reasonable option for an or-ganization. It suggests that improving ICT governance involves increasing control over ICT-related resources. This increased control was seen as necessary for the Municipality in order to have efficient and effective ICT management. Therefore, improving ICT governance can be seen as the first step in considering outsourcing.

References

Andersen R (1986) Management, Information Systems and Computers: An Introduction. Macmillan Education Ltd. London

BearingPoint (2004) IT-Benchmark 2003/2004. White paper from BearingPoint, Inc. www.bearingpoint.com

Brunsson N (1985) The Irrational Organization: Irrationality as a Basis for Organizational Action and Change. John Wiley & Sons Ltd. Chichester

Brynjolfsson E (1993) The Productivity Paradox of Information Technology: Review and Assessment. Research paper from MIT Sloan School of Management. http://ccs.mit.edu/papers/CCSWP130/CCSWP130.html

Dibbern J, Goles T, Hirschheim R, Jayatilaka B (2004) Information Systems Outsourcing: A Survey and Analysis of the Literature. The DATA BASE for Advances in Information Systems, vol 35, no 4, pp 6-102

Earl MJ (1989) Management Strategies for Information Technology. Prentice Hall Europe Harlow England

Easterby-Smith M, Thorpe R, Lowe A (2002) Management Research: An Introduction 2ed. SAGE Publications Ltd. London

Grembergen WV (2004) Strategies for Information Technology Governance. Idea Group Publishing Hershey Pa London

Pettigrew AM (1973) The Politics of OrganizationalDecision-making. Tavistock Publications Ltd. London

Simon HA (1997) Administrative Behavior: A Study of Decision-Making Processes in Administrative Organization 4ed. The Free Press New York

Simon HA (1960) The New Science of Management Decision. Harper & Row, Publishers Inc. New York

Weill P, Roos JW (2004) IT Governance: How Top Performers Manage IT Decision Rights for Superior Results. Harvard Business School Press Boston Massachusetts

Beliefs and Attitudes Associated with ERP Adoption Behaviours: A Grounded Theory Study from IT Manager and End-user Perspectives

Santipat Arunthari and Helen Hasan

School of Economics and Information Systems, University of Wollongong, Australia. (sa83, hasan)@uow.edu.au

Introduction

Davenport (1998, p.121) defines an Enterprise Resource Planning (ERP) system as an enterprise system that promises seamless integration of all information flowing through a company, including financial and accounting information, human resource information, supply chain information, customer information. ERP systems came on the scene in the early 1990s as a response to the proliferation of standalone business applications to service these separate information needs in most large organisations. Enterprise wide projects, such as data warehousing, requiring integrated approaches to organisational operations and information management were inhibited through a proliferation of incompatible off-the-shelf packages, in-house developments and aging legacy systems.

While ERP systems had become commonplace by the late 1990s with considerable impact, both positive and negative, on organisations they are only recently becoming objects of interest to IS researchers. They are considered to be a high complex technology. Installing it requires large investments of money, time, and expertise, and involves coordination requirements across multi-adopters at different organisational levels. Based on this concern, ERP system adoption needs special consideration. However, a review of the literature reveals that there is a lack of research on the adoption of ERP systems and selection of ERP system vendors. Although the concept of complete integration has been pursued for more than two decades (Klaus, 2000), published research on the topic of ERP has only recently emerged and mainly focuses on issues related to the implementation phase of the ERP lifecycle (Esteves & Pastor, 2001; Al-Mashari, 2002).

There is limited knowledge on ERP system adoption and users' attitudes towards ERP systems that have been conducted in developing Asian countries. Only a few studies attempted to explain the relationship between user beliefs, attitude, and behavioral intention to adopt and use an ERP system. Furthermore, most of them have been conducted in developed countries (Abdinnour-Helm et al, 2002; Amoako-Gyampah & Salam, 2004). It is apparent that an ERP system created for and working in developed Western countries may not be a perfect fit in organisations in different countries. Problems that companies in developed countries face may not be presented in the context of developing countries (in this case, Thailand), which may in turn have unique issues of their own. It is also arguable that there may not be difference between organisations in Thailand and those in other places, but also a distinction between Thai-owned and multinational companies (MNCs) operating in Thailand.

This paper presents the findings of a study, which aimed to examine the attitudes of IT managers and end-users towards ERP systems. We believed that attitude and behavioural intention towards ERP system adoption are correlated. Positive (negative) attitude can increase (decrease) the intention to adopt an ERP system. Although in most cases the use of an ERP system is mandatory, variations exist in the intentions of users (Amoako-Gyampah & Salam, 2004). Thus, it is important to examine behavioral intention to adopt a new technology and to change their responsibilities, which leads to implementation success and effective usage. The findings will help ERP system project leaders to recognise the importance of attitudes towards ERP systems, and lead to better planning. This paper begins with an overview of the relevant literature to provide a theoretical background for the study. Thereafter, the research methodology is described, followed by the findings from the study. The paper concludes with a discussion of the practical implications of the findings and identifies areas for possible future research.

The Theoretical Framework

Attitude in simplest terms may be defined as a predisposition that determines how a person behave or does not behave in a particular way. However, this definition may be insufficient to understand how attitude could be related to behaviour in this type of study. In the 1970s in the field of social psychology, Ajzen and Fishbein (1975, 1980) developed the Theory of Reasoned Action (TRA) in an attempt to provide a model to understand how a person's attitude impacts their behaviour (Severin & Tankard, 2001). The TRA model has been adapted for use in many fields. For example, using TRA as a theoretical basis, Davis (1986, 1989) developed the

Technology Acceptance Model (TAM), which is widely used by information system (IS) researchers.

The TRA operates on the assumption that human beings are rational animals who are able to systematically process and use the information available to them. People consider the implications of their actions or outcomes before they decide to engage or not engage in a given behaviour (Ajzen & Fishbein, 1980, p.5). According to TRA, there are two main components that explain intention. They include the attitude towards performing the behaviour and the perceived social pressure, or the subjective norms. In this study, the focus is on the former.

Attitude is regarded as the primary predictor of intention, and is perceived as "a latent or underlying variable that is assumed to guide or influence behaviour" (Fishbein & Ajzen, 1975, p.8). Attitude is determined by a set of behavioural beliefs about the outcome of behaviour. It refers to the person's evaluation or judgement that the potential outcome will be 'positive or negative' or 'good or bad' and the probability or likelihood that performing a given behaviour will result in a given outcome. Figure 1 shows the flowchart of TRA with an emphasis on attitude, and illustrates the transmission of belief into behaviour.

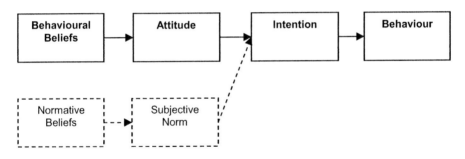

Fig. 1. A Flowchart of the Theory of Reasoned Action (TRA)

Fishbein and Ajzen (1975, p.8) further point out the importance of attitude: "Knowledge of a person's attitude, therefore, permits prediction of one or more specific behaviours". In other words, a positive attitude would lead to the performance of positive behaviours and a negative attitude to the performance of negative behaviours (Fishbein & Ajzen, ibid, p.9). Accordingly, in an ERP case, if an employee perceives that positive benefits are due to implementing an ERP system, he or she will be motivated and intend to be co-operative, which leads to the success of ERP system implementation.

Methodology

In order not to preclude any issues that may not be initially considered by the researchers and to canvas as many diverse views on the topic as possible, findings of this study were allowed to emerge from raw data, collected through interviews, and there was no attempt to test hypotheses or forced the data into a fixed framework. Thus, grounded theory was deemed the most appropriate methodology for the study. This allowed categories and a theory of facts to emerge from collected data. To be specific, it allowed the IT managers and end users to freely explain what their perceptions or attitudes were from their own perspective.

Thirty-two companies were selected and included in the study as follows: 1) eight Thai-owned companies that implemented an ERP system, 2) eight Thai-owned companies that did not implement an ERP system, 3) eight MNCs that implemented an ERP system, and 4) eight MNCs that did not implement an ERP system. The MNCs were randomly selected from lists supplied from foreign Chambers of Commerce in Thailand. At the same time, the Thai-owned companies, which have the largest turnover of all companies in Thailand, were drawn from the database of the Revenue Department of Thailand. All IT managers were contacted by telephone, in order to determine their willingness to participate. In each case, at least one IT manager and one end-user participated in the interviews. Each IT manager was allowed to decide which end-users would be subsequently interviewed. In those companies not implementing ERP systems, the chosen end-users at least had heard about ERP systems known about the concept. The interviews were conducted at each company, taking place at either the participant's office or the conference room and during normal working days.

All the qualitative data collected from the interviews were analysed by using a grounded theory method. As defined by Glaser (1992, p.16), grounded theory is "a general methodology of analysis linked with data collection that uses a systematically applied set of methods to generate an inductive theory about a substantive area". Thus, a grounded theory method provides a practical guide to managing and analysing data systematically. Undertaking the constant comparative method of analysis and coding procedures in grounded theory, the quantity of data was reduced, the empirical nature of the data was transcended, and as a result a condensed, abstract view scope of the data was obtained (Glaser, 1978, p.55). The results of this reduction were a set of categories whose properties and attributes reflect the content of the data. Those relating to the topic of this paper are now presented.

Findings

Attitudes

Many IT managers and end-users in both Thai-owned and multinational companies expressed their positive and negative attitudes. As Fishbein and Ajzen (1975, p.131) argue, "attitudes are usually measured by assessing a person's belief". We thus identified a number of beliefs that influences these attitudes. The positive attitude consisted of 7 beliefs while the negative attitude included 3 beliefs, as shown in Table 1.

Table 1. Attitudes and Beliefs

Positive attitude	*Belief 1:* Inventory accuracy and visibility *Belief 2:* Cost saving *Belief 3:* Personnel reduction *Belief 4:* Improved internal integration between Systems *Belief 5:* Enhanced visibility of data and greater accessibility to data *Belief 6:* New or improved business processes *Belief 7:* Increased responsiveness
Negative attitude	*Belief 1:* Suspicion *Belief 2:* Resistance to change *Belief 3:* Difficulty

We found there to be no obvious distinction between the Thai-owned and multinational companies. However, as anticipated, companies that did not have an ERP system in place had more negative attitudes and expectations than the ERP-adopting companies. The attitudes and associated beliefs are presented as follows.

The positive attitude

Belief 1: Inventory accuracy and visibility
ERP evolved from MRP (Materials Requirements Planning) and subsequently MRPII, which were initially designed for manufacturing operations. Therefore, the capability of inventory management throughout the supply chain is recognised by interviewees. An ERP system could increase accuracy in tracking and managing repair and new inventories as well as raw materials. At the same time, it could plan and schedule inventory flow

throughout the entire procurement process, which in turn leads to reducing excess inventories and costs to manage them.

Belief 2: Cost saving

An ERP system could save costs in many business areas. Many interviewees agreed that their companies could reduce purchasing costs by improving procurement activities. Furthermore, an ERP system could hold down administrative burdens and lower paperwork.

Belief 3: Personnel reduction

Business process reengineering, which often accompanies an ERP system implementation, could improve processes and eliminate some non value-adding activities, thereby reducing the risk of human error. As many business functions could be automated in this process -covering a significant amount of clerical work at the same time, companies adopting an ERP system could reduce staff costs.

Belief 4: Improved internal integration between systems

As most companies are organised and operated in a decentralised manner, different departments, business units or even branches of companies deploy different computer systems and software that sometimes operate under different platforms, with separate users' interfaces, databases and maintenance requirements. These different systems do not easily communicate with one another, and data is stored and processed separately. There is a necessity for interfaces among systems to transfer data across system boundaries. An ERP system could replace these disparate aging systems, centralising them into one comprehensive multi-module software system that integrates all (or many) fundamental business activities across departments or even across regions, and serves the entire company.

Belief 5: Enhanced visibility of data and greater accessibility to data

With one common database, users at all levels could have convenient access to truly accurate, real-time and consolidated information. With a real-time integration environment, information is updated and exchanged immediately and continuously. Once data are entered into an ERP system from one department, all other departments can view it. With an integrated ERP system, all (or many) disconnected functional areas can electronically communicate among themselves. Employees can share the same information horizonontally and even vertically. Because of this, according to most employees concerned with data entry in both Thai-owned and multinational companies, data entry time, duplicate information and redundant jobs can reduced.

Belief 6: New or improved business processes

The architecture of an ERP system introduces new ways of thinking (e.g., about how employees do work, and how they think about work), and in most cases forces a company to switch from a functional (or departmental) to a process-driven model. Nearly all interviewees saw the opportunity to review, and alter their business processes and organisational structure, which are based on recognised theories or best business practices.

Belief 7: Increased responsiveness

In the interviewees' views, an ERP system could help to improve their company's ability to respond to customer inquiries by delivering just the information that customers want about their manufactured goods. Their companies could coordinate plant assets and resources to deliver goods to customers more quickly.

The negative attitude

Belief 1: Suspicion

During interviewing, some questions as well as doubts were raised by several ERP end-users, and even IT managers: 'How long does it take to implement ERP?', 'How can we know for sure that it is worth investing?', and 'How can we implement and use ERP to maximise a return on investment?'. An IT manager of a non-ERP-adopting Thai-owned company argued that since end-users would not see the benefits of an ERP system in a short-time period, it is not easy to convince them of the value of investing an ERP system. Another IT manager of an ERP adopting MNC agreed by saying that it was difficult to measure ROI (the Return on Investment) of an ERP system implementation, and therefore it was impossible to see the value of an ERP system as soon as it was installed. In addition, nearly all ERP end-users interviewed were worried that an ERP implementation project might create extra workload, and that there were difficulties waiting ahead.

Belief 2: Resistance to change

Most interviewees were keen to stress that massive changes in existing processes and organisational structure would inevitably occur, which might have an adverse impact on their jobs. There was no evidence that employees were afraid of losing their jobs, since in Thailand employees are normally guaranteed job security. However, most ERP end-users did not want to see any change in their job description, and feared unwanted job assignments. They did not want to have to learn new skills, and accept new responsibilities. Furthermore, they did not want to experience a loss of certainty.

Belief 3: Difficulty

Apart from the high cost of software itself and implementation, a majority of IT managers were more concerned with the complexity of implementation and difficulty of configuration, modification and maintenance. An IT manager of a non-ERP-adopting Thai-owned company believed that, ERP system implementation was not simply about buying cutting-edge technology. Another IT manager of another non-ERP-adopting Thai-owned company commented that an ERP system was difficult to install and configure by his staff and himself. Approximately 40% of the IT managers interviewed were also afraid for any number of reasons that there was not a good functional fit for their organization. However, there is no concrete evidence on technical matters from ERP end-users, partly because they could not evaluate an ERP system technically. They had no idea how an ERP system worked, and how application modules were integrated. Some of them saw the demonstrations, but still could not make a judgement. However, from the ERP end-users' view, an ERP system was not easy to learn and use.

It is reasonable to conclude that these above beliefs that we have found can be categories into two groups: shared and individual. Shared beliefs occurred when most employees perceived relative advantage of an ERP system for their company. In other word, employees believed that an ERP system would benefit their companies. They could be motivated and intend to be co-operative. These beliefs had an influence on a positive attitude towards ERP systems. Consequently, this attitude can increase the intention of ERP system adoption, and lead to the success of ERP system implementation.

Individual beliefs were formed when employees were suspicious and concerned that ERP system adoption would cause them a problem. Organisational change surrounding ERP system implementation and difficulty of ERP system configuration and use are consistent with the innovative characteristics of Rogers. These beliefs or perceived characteristics of an ERP system had an influence on negative attitudes, and could cause ERP system implementation failure.

Based on the above discussion, we refined the existing TRA model to shows the impact of both shared and individual beliefs and intention on ERP system adoption and usage. It should be noted again that subjective norm was not the focus of our study. Figure 2 shows the transmission of shared and individual beliefs into the adoption and use of an ERP system.

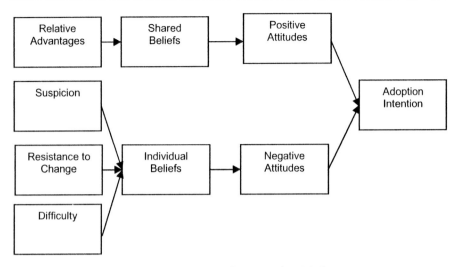

Fig. 2. A Model of Attitudes towards ERP Systems

The Different Attitudes towards ERP Systems in Thai-Owned and Multinational Companies

Organisational culture can influence attitudes towards ERP system adoption. Whereas in Thai-owned companies this is local and homogeneous, in global MNCs the culture of the local branch may be quite different from that of the company origin. In most cases, the adoption and use of IT applications of MNCs (especially a large package application like an ERP system) is mandatory. Decisions on new IT adoption are normally made at the corporate headquarters which in the case of most MNCs in the US or European countries. The consequential changes cannot be resisted by local managers and employees. However, the findings revealed that employees of MNCs seemed to have a greater degree of organisational commitment and a strong confidence in their organisation's decision. They appreciate the overall benefits that could be gained to their organization, and so they seem to have positive attitudes towards their ERP system.

On the other hand, Thai-owned companies seemed to have more problems of user resistance to change than MNCs. Most Thai-owned companies allowed their employees to be involved in an ERP project, and employees could express their likes or dislikes in regard to the implementation. In some Thai-owned companies, employees even had some influence on ERP system adoption and vendor selection. Although they did not completely reject a new system, they still wanted it to be customised to be familiar with the ways they were accustomed to working.

Many IS authors (e.g., Laudon & Laudon, 2004) argue that user participation and involvement in implementation activities can overcome user resistance. However, the findings revealed that employees in Thai-owned companies felt that they had an option and chose to avoid using their ERP system where possible. Bring a new system into their company required them to learn new skills, and accepted new responsibilities. They seemed pessimistic, and had negative attitudes towards their ERP system.

The Difference of Attitudes towards ERP Systems between IT Managers and End Users

IT managers and end-users reacted differently to the changes brought upon them by the ERP systems. IT managers seemed to have a more positive attitude towards change, and were more willing to adopt an ERP system. They seemed to understand more the value of adopting the system as they knew how an ERP system works and could foresee the promised benefits that their companies would gain from an ERP system. On the other hand, end-users, who are at a relatively low level in the organisation, felt that they had no choice. In most cases, they were not given any opportunity to learn the usefulness of an ERP system before the decision was made to adopt it, but they must accept the ERP system, as their managers wanted them to do so. They were then required to adjust themselves to new ways of doing their jobs with little help or understanding from management. Thus, end-users seemed to be more reluctant to accept change.

Discussion, Conclusion and Future Research

From the findings of this study in locally-owned and multinational companies in Thailand, the research model shown in Figure 2 is proposed to represent the breadth of attitudes influencing the behavioural intention to adopt an ERP system. The interviewees indicated positive and negative attitudes towards ERP systems, and identified a set of beliefs were identified as significant. Our general interpretation of the findings leading to the model were that shared beliefs of an ERP system were associated with a more positive attitude towards adopting an ERP system, while individual beliefs were associated with a more negative attitude. This shared belief and hence more positive attitude seemed to be more prevalent in MNCs than in Thai-owned companies and also more likely to exist among IT staff than general employees.

These findings seem to point to aspects of organisational and professional culture were likely to influence attitudes towards ERP system adoption. From the findings, employees of the MNCs seemed to have positive attitudes towards an ERP system, while employees of Thai-owned companies seemed pessimistic, and had negative attitudes towards an ERP system. This may indicate that their organisational culture is such that managers in MNCs place greater value on a shared vision and expected some effort into building and maintaining this. The importance of this effort may not be appreciated in locally-owned companies, and there may be an assumption that it automatically exists without the need to foster it. On the other hand, IT managers in both groups of companies seemed to have a more positive attitude towards the change brought on by the ERP system implementation than end-users who felt that they had no choice, and must accept an ERP system as their managers wanted them to do so. This could be explained in two ways: firstly, that they naturally have an shared professional culture and set of beliefs or secondly, that their greater knowledge of IT makes them more comfortable with the demands of a package such as an ERP system.

To deal with negative attitudes associated with difficulty, the findings suggest that management should provide information and training to their users. Users should not only be trained individually to understand how an ERP system works, but also to appreciate how their work co-ordinates with that of other to create a shared set of beliefs. Intense resistance to change should be reduced, and suspicion should be dispelled if users could have a clear idea of how an ERP system would have a collective impact on their work. It is also important that management takes an active part in managing change and will be part of the process of creating a shared vision. Their role is critical, and their contribution can make an ERP system implementation project successful through convincing users of the value of their ERP system. Management should share information with them, help them to build an understanding, and to recognise the potential benefits of their ERP system together.

Some limitations or the study are inherent in that it was inductive in nature, and the findings allowed the generation of a number of theories that emerges from the experiences of participants in the substantive area of research, but are not necessarily generalisable. We suggest that future research could seek to test the research model of attitudes towards EPR systems, using either quantitative or qualitative data or both. In addition, a similar study could be conducted in other countries.

References

Abdinnour-Helm S, Lengnick-Hall ML, Lengick-Hall CA (2003) Pre-Imprementation Attitudes and Organizational Readiness for Implementing and Enterprise Resource Planning System. European Journal of Operational Research, vol 146, pp 258-273

Ajzen I, Fishbein M (1980) Understanding Attitudes and Predicting Social Behaviour. Prentice-Hall New Jersey

Al-Mashari M (2002) Enterprise Resource Planning (ERP) Systems: a Research Agnea. Industrial Management & Data Systems, vol 102, no 3, pp 165-170

Amoako-Gyampah K, Salam AF (2004) An Extension of the Technology Acceptance Model in an ERP Implementation Environment. Information and Management, vol 41, no 6, pp 731-745

Davenport TH (1998) Putting the Enterprise into Enterprise Systems. Harvard Business Review, vol 76, no 4, pp 121-131

Esteves J, Paster J (2001) Enterprise Resource Planning Systems Research: An Annotated Bibliography. Communications of the Association for Information Systems (CAIS), vol 7, article 8. (Retrieved January 25, 2005)
http://cais.isworld.org/articles/7-8/default.asp?View=html&x=64 &y=12

Fishbein M, Ajzen I (1975) Belief, Attitude, Intention and Behavior: An Introduction to Theory and Research. Addison-Wesley CA

Glaser BG (1978) Theoretical Sensitivity: Advances in the Methodology of Grounded Theory. Sociology Press CA

Klaus H, Rosemann M, Gabel GG (2000) What is ERP? Information Systems Frontiers, vol 2, no 2, pp 141-162

Laudon KC, Laudon JP (2004) Management Information Systems: Managing the Digital Firm (8th ed). Prentice Hall NJ

Severin, WJ, Tankard JW Jr (2001) Communication Theories: Origins, Methods and Uses in the Mass Media (5th ed.). Longman NY

Supporting Knowledge Transfer in IS Deployment Projects

Mikael Schönström

Department of Informatics, School of Economics and Management, Lund University, Sweden. mikael_schonstrom@hermes.ics.lu.se

Introduction

To deploy new information systems is an expensive and complex task, and does seldom result in successful usage where the system adds strategic value to the firm (e.g. Sharma et al. 2003). It has been argued that innovation diffusion is a knowledge integration problem (Newell et al. 2000). Knowledge about business processes, deployment processes, information systems and technology are needed in a large-scale deployment of a corporate IS. These deployments can therefore to a large extent be argued to be a knowledge management (KM) problem. An effective deployment requires that knowledge about the system is effectively transferred to the target organization (Ko et al. 2005).

This paper reports an empirical study of a corporate IS deployment project in a global industrial firm. An example of corporate IS would be enterprise systems like SAP, or as in this case an enterprise document management system (EDMS). Deployment in this context means the activities that are needed to bring the system to the users. It includes e.g. the set up of a maintenance organization, training, and deployment project coordination. The research aims to further explore knowledge transfer in deployment contexts. Existing research has not addressed to any significant degree how the deployment organization and the deployment process impact the transfer of IS product knowledge and deployment process knowledge.

The purpose of this article is to study the deployment of large-scale systems in terms of how methods and the deployment organization can be managed to improve knowledge transfer throughout the deployment. The following research question was formulated: how do the deployment organization and the process used impact the knowledge transfer in a deployment program?

The reminder of the paper is organized as follows; the subsequent section presents theories related to knowledge management, IT adoption and innovation diffusion. Section three presents the research approach. Section four presents the case. Section five presents the major findings. The findings are further discussed in section six, which also includes concluding remarks.

Theoretical Framework

The introduction of new information systems in organizations is a common research topic where much research exists. IS deployment relates to the areas of IT adoption and technology diffusion because a successful deployment requires that the system is in the end used by the organization. The phenomenon has been researched from many perspectives e.g. information systems, psychology and sociology (Venkatesh et al. 2003). Major factors that have been identified to support technology use are management support (e.g. Sharma et al. 2003), training, beliefs and expectations on technology (Venkatesh et al. 2003). These factors have in common a focus on the end-user and their use of the IT artefact. IT adoption studies have not to the same degree studied the management of complex deployment programs and how knowledge about the new system and the deployment processes is transferred in these programs.

Knowledge – There have been several attempts made to define knowledge. Nonaka & Takeuchi (1995) defines knowledge as "justified true belief". Knowledge is a complex concept and various dimensions have been used to discuss knowledge in the literature. The explicit/ tacit dichotomy has been commonly used in the KM literature (e.g. Nonaka et al. 1995). Explicit knowledge is codified knowledge which is easy to communicate. Tacit knowledge is more difficult to codify and therefore harder to transfer. An additional epistemology presented in the literature is that of knowing which includes an activity or action dimension. Knowing is argued to be a type of knowledge, which includes action (Cook et al. 1999).

Knowledge transfer - In a deployment project context knowledge about the system and deployment processes are important to transfer in order to reduce project time and cost. IS product knowledge is important because it is required by the organization to use the system accordingly. IS deployment knowledge is important because large deployments generate many subprojects and best practices for how to manage the local deployment projects is important from an efficiency perspective. Knowledge transfer is facilitated by a shared language and a common system of meaning (Boland et al. 1995). Ko et al. (2005) studied what factors that support knowledge transfer in an ERP implementation context. They studied knowledge transfer among consultants and clients in an ERP implementation context and they found that communication factors such as communication encoding/ decoding and source credibility played a significant role in supporting knowledge transfer. They also found that knowledge factors such as absorptive capacity, shared understanding and arduous relationship supported knowledge transfer. Regarding motivational factors they found only support for intrinsic motivation. Extrinsic motivation was found to play only a marginal role. In this paper knowledge transfer is defined as "...the communication of knowledge from a source so that it is learned and applied by a recipient" Ko et al. (2005).

Deployment process – The deployment process is a key factor in a deployment project. I make a distinction between a process and a method, and in this paper I define process as a "...a specific ordering of work activities across time and place, with a beginning, and end, and clearly identiifed inputs and outputs: a structure for action." (Davenport 1993). The relationship between a process and method is that the method give guidance to the process. Earlier research has pointed out that methods can function as a platform for communication and knowledge sharing (Hirschheim et al. 1996, Rossi et al. 2000). Other presented reasons for using methods throughout a project-based organization are that methods are assumed to facilitate change and transfer of staff from project to project without retraining. The use of methods is believed to facilitate reuse of knowledge and experiences (Nandhakumar et al. 1999). However, KM related research indicate that a method's ability to function as a platform for best practice transfer should be limited. Research suggest that what is learned in a project environment is often tacit, intangible and context dependent (Bresenen et al. 2003). Best practices have also been argued to be "sticky" (Szulanski 1996), thus they are not easily moved to other parts of the organization. However common methods define the language used for different activities and support the development of shared mental models. Language and mental models play an important role in knowledge creation and sharing (Ko et al. 2005).

Deployment organization – Another important factor in IS deployments is how the deployment is organized. Organizational structures have been found to play a key role in knowledge transfer processes. Recent research on knowledge transfer and organizational structures suggest that knowledge transfer is impeded by centralization, that formal hierarchical structures have a negative impact on intra-firm knowledge transfer (Tsai 2002). A possible explanation is that centralization does not facilitate and encourage social interaction which is important to knowledge transfer. Knowledge transferring is a complex social process that demands collaborative efforts and informal lateral relations have therefore showed a significant positive effect on inter-unit knowledge transfer. Social interactions in the knowledge transfer process create trust and foster cooperation according to Tsai (2002). Hansen (2002) has similarly found that lateral network relations supports inter-unit knowledge sharing in multiunit firms. Knowledge networks have been suggested to be important when disseminating tacit knowledge. Knowledge networks and networking support knowledge creation and innovation as they enable cross-fertilization of tacit knowledge between groups (Seufert et al. 1999).

Using the existing theories that cover knowledge transfer the following research model is presented (figure 1).

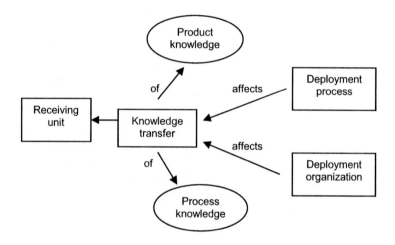

Fig. 1. Research framework

Research Methodology

A case study approach was used and the data collection methods were observations, semi-structured interviews and project documentation (minutes of meeting, final reports, method documentation). The observational study was in the form of participant observation; the observation data was then complemented with data from the semi-structured interviews. The role I played as observer was complete-member researcher (Adler et al. 1994). I studied the deployment activities during two periods of time. The first study took place in 2000, and that study was followed up by a smaller study in 2003.

The first study (in 2000) involved observations, interviews and project documentation. Two local deployment projects were observed. The first unit was a patent support organization of about 20 employees, which worked with filing patents covering the European market. The second unit worked with expatriates and their contracts. The unit employed 30 people at the headquarters. In addition to the observations a number of semi-structured interviews were also made with people working at other units. In total eight people were interviewed in 2000. The interviews spanned from 1 hour to 1,5 hours.

In the second study (in 2003) interviews and documents were used as data collection methods. The interviews involved two key people who had been working with DocSystem since the start, the product manager and the application strategist. These were the only two people left from the group that had worked with the system since it was launched in 1999. The interviews focused on how the central deployment unit had perceived the knowledge build up regarding the new system during the last 3 years and how knowledge about the system were disseminated to the rest of the company. The interviews were unstructured and were about 2 hours in length.

The interviews were tape recorded and transcribed into protocols. Using the research model (figure 1) the data was coded with respect to two general categories: (1) deployment process and (2) deployment organization. A second analysis was done with the aim to study the knowledge transfer characteristics of the deployment process and the deployment organization. The observational data were analysed in a similar way as the interview data. The categories became the backbone of the analysis and of the presented findings in section five.

Case Presentation

The studied case was a deployment program with the goal to rollout a document management system to approximately 80,000 users within TeleGroup worldwide (in 1999). TeleGroup is a today a global telecom equipment producer with almost 50.000 employees (in 2004) in 120 countries. Currently, deployment activities have stopped due to significant reductions of the IT budget, layoffs, and outsourcing. The company has moved from 120 000 employees (in 1999 when the study started) to under 50.000 employees (in 2004) thus there has been a dramatic change since 1999 when the study started. When most of the observations and interviews were done (in 2000) the deployment was ongoing on a large scale, and had reached a point where approximately 40 local deployment projects around the world were simultaneously conducted.

The DocSystem initiative started in mid 1998. Corporate IT, the group's central IS/IT unit, had identified a major problem with the current heterogeneous system landscape for document management within the group which resulted in high costs for administration and maintenance. Due to the amount of systems and their incompatibility it was also hard to find and share information. To improve the situation Corporate IT decided to deploy one common system for document management within the whole group. The goals for the new system were of a technical character and formulated from a CorporateIT perspective.

The deployment was organized in several local deployment projects. All local deployment projects were coordinated and/or followed up by the DocSystem centre. Whether to deploy the system or not was a local decision of the local units. Thus the IS/IT department of the group could not force anyone to start using the system.

The stakeholders that were involved in the project during the first study were: *Users* – The users were of all types of employees from executive managers to assistants. *Deployment managers* – A central role in the DocSystem initiative was the deployment managers, which had the responsibility for deploying the system in the local units. *Coach* – The Coach was a role that was introduced some time after the deployment started. It was found out that a complementary role was needed to the deployment manager. In the projects where the deployment manager had limited skills in document management and the system a coach was hired. Coaches were offered as a service provided by the Doc System centre until 2001. *Product manager-* The product manager's responsibility was initially to set up the infrastructure and to build the support plus the maintenance functions for the system. *Corporate IT* – The Corporate IT department was the unit within TeleGroup headquarters that had the responsibility for all major IS/IT investments and related strategies that were of strategic importance for the group as a whole. *DocSystem Centre* – At the DocSystem centre some of the central functions such as support, application development, and application strategies, deployment support were grouped. Resources that worked in the DocSystem centre was significantly reduced after 2001, from about 20 people to about 6 at the end of 2002. *Coordination manager* – The coordination manager's most important role was to facilitate the communication between the deployment projects and the DocSystem centre, and between deployment projects.

The DocSystem Deployment

Deployment Process

To facilitate the deployment of the system and to help deployment managers to structure their work a deployment method was developed by the DocSystem centre. The method was mainly a reuse from the deployment of SAP and MS Exchange within TeleGroup, and it was based on the company's general project management method. The method was introduced to deployment managers via courses. The first version of the method was ambitious and described all activities to be performed and planned by the deployment manager. The method emphasized activities such as business process mapping, communication planning, change management planning, and the creation of business cases for local deployment projects. The method contained also links to examples and templates for the different documents that should be produced, such as project specification, strategic fit analysis, migration plan, and so forth. The knowledge exploitation approach used to develop the method had some negative effects. The deployment managers did not think that the method helped them in their job, since it had weak relation to how things actually worked. Or as one deployment manager said: *"There is no connection between the process and the real world, how things really work. It is also too complex with too many documents that should be developed."* Systems like SAP or MS Exchange have different characteristics and other aspects of the deployment are therefore focused in these deployment processes.

Related to the mentioned issue above it is interesting to comment on how the method was initially developed. One person was given the assignment to create the method. That person contacted people which had experience from other large scale deployments (i.e. SAP and MS Exchange), with the purpose to re-use existing methods as much as possible. Unfortunately the new method was not verified with the earlier pilot projects or others that had some pre experiences with the deployment of the DocSystem. Thus the method development became essentially a document production activity. Three years later in the follow up study it was also expressed that the failure of the method could be described to the fact that it lacked a connection to the context of this particular deployment. Even if the method was changed based on some feed back from practice the changes only resulted in a reduction of activities and documents to be produced.

Deployment Organization

There were several organizational units in the deployment organization that supported knowledge transfer. These units were the DocSystem centre, the coaches and the coordination manager.

The DocSystem centre: The DocSystem centre had an important role to play, a) they had most of the knowledge of how the system worked (functionality) b) they knew what deployment projects were going on within the organization c) they had the major contacts to other knowledge resources, such as the vendor itself d) they had a coordination role regarding resources and support to deployment projects e) they received all requests for changes in the system, and they also received information on deployment problems. A major problem to the DocSystem center in the beginning of the project was that it became overwhelmed with urgent technical problems in the system itself due to an unstable system. After 2001 the DocSystem centre ceased to exist due to budget cuts and a reduction in deployment activities.

The Coach: The coach had good knowledge about the system and the company's document management rules. He or she worked also in some occasions as trainer holding courses in DocSystem. These persons spent one or more days per week with the deployment projects to assist solving technical or process related issues. The coach worked normally with several deployment projects at a time and thus gained insights about other projects' issues and solutions. The coaches were perceived as a very good way to transfer knowledge about the system to the local units. The deployment managers had a positive view of the coaches as they could assist with in-depth knowledge about the system and inform on similar issues in other projects. The coaches were enthusiastic about the system and its potential, which encouraged the projects to continue implementations despite many deployment issues.

The coordination manager: At the DocSystem centre there was one person whose role was to coordinate the ongoing projects (the coordination manager). This person organized meetings for the deployment managers across the organization, known as coordination meetings. During these two-hour meetings that were scheduled once every two months the project managers and coaches had the possibility to meet and to exchange ideas and issues. These meetings provided an opportunity for deployment managers to know each other informally so they could easily talk to each other about issues when needed. The coordination manager had thus an overview regarding the activities related to the DocSystem deployment and was as such a strategic resource to the DocSystem centre. Having this position the coordination manager also functioned as a mediator of DocSystem knowledge.

Discussions and Conclusions

The goals provided by corporate IT that should explain why the system was deployed related more to an infrastructure deployment with the purpose to cut cost for document management rather than that the system should support business processes. Comparing corporate IT's goals with what was emphasized in the method, that DocSystem should not just be a new IT system, but a new way of working indicates a clear mismatch between corporate IT's goals and the method's design. The inconsistent message created uncertainty as to why the system was deployed. As stressed in the KM literature, the corporate strategy is the most important context for KM (Zack 1999). A better link to the corporate strategy and its environment could have made it easier for the project to develop a shared understanding for what and how the system should be used. From a knowledge transfer perspective a shared understanding is an important enabling factor (Ko et al. 2005). A shared vision could have been formulated, which in turn could have supported the alignment of methods and networking activities within the deployment.

The study showed that methods in large deployment projects has limited role in knowledge transferring if it has not been designed with the purpose to support practice and the knowledge processes. The method in this study was not designed to support the deployment of this particular system. These findings regarding the use of the method correspond well with the critical IS method literature (e.g. Fitzgerald 1997, Truex et al. 2000)

If a common deployment method is developed it must be designed for the specific project. The case showed that it is ineffective to only reuse methods from similar application deployments. Each application affects the business processes differently and thus the method must take these special characteristics of the application into account. The problems with the method further strengthens earlier research that point at the context dependency of knowledge and the difficulty of transferring best-practice (Szulanski 1996).

The inability to create and implement a common method that supported the deployment projects created a situation where no common processes were followed. Much time in the deployment projects were spent on method related issues. Every project had to create their method and the common method provided by the deployment program was of limited help in this regard.

The organizational structure worked better from a knowledge transfer perspective as it supported knowledge networking. The coaches helped to combine knowledge from different sources. The coach worked as a form of knowledge broker (Davenport et al. 1998). The coach can be characterized as a human networking strategy (Swan et al. 1999). The network structure worked as a flexible way to disseminate knowledge and to support problem solving in the local projects. It was able to disseminate tacit knowledge which is important in learning processes (Nonaka et al. 1995). The network structure that facilitated networking was represented by: coaches, DocSystem centre and the coordination manager.

The DocSystem Center could have played an even more central role in knowledge transfer. It became however overwhelmed with technical issues. The problems the DocSystem centre encountered with an immature system in the beginning made it too focused on solving technical issues instead of planning and supporting the deployment. A separation of the technical development activities and the deployment activities could have reduced this issue. The DocSystem centre would probably have been more successful if it was not directly responsible for development and maintenance of the system. If the systems management was some other unit's responsibility it could instead focus on supporting the deployment with knowledge management instead of using all resources internally to fix technical problems.

The support structures for knowledge networking could have been even further explored and strengthened. DocSystem centre coordinated projects and gathered deployment managers regularly to discuss project and system issues. Increased networking between communities could maybe not only have strengthened knowledge transfer further on an operational level but also solved some issues of strategic nature. Many of the problems originated from poor management on the strategic level. If representatives from CorpIT were part of the deployment organization better strategies for the system could probably have been jointly developed as knowledge from the two communities could have been more efficiently exchanged. Now, as the CorpIT did not take an active role in the deployment important knowledge were missing and thus could not be transferred. Instead that knowledge gap was filled by new knowledge created by actors when needed, which had some unwanted consequences. Unfortunately the limited understanding for knowledge transfer and the importance of knowledge in this project reduced the efficiency of the deployment.

This research studied deployment activities and how the deployment organization and the deployment process supported the dissemination of knowledge regarding DocSystem and deployment processes. From a deployment organization perspective the study showed that knowledge networking play an important role in knowledge transferring when deploying a corporate IS. Knowledge networking enables communication and knowledge diffusion regarding the system and solutions to issues. Knowledge networking played a more important role in knowledge transferring than methods in this case and this is an important lesson for future large-scale deployment of corporate IS. Deployment coaches, coordination centers, and coordination managers showed in this case to be a successful approach to support large-scale deployment from a knowledge transfer perspective. Methods on the contrary played a limited role in this case mainly due to its poor design. Based on this research I suggest that methods in the future should focus more on how to enable knowledge creation and diffusion, e.g. how a networking structure (like the one in this case) is set up and focus less on specifying how traditional activities like gap analysis, business case development are performed in sequence.

Limitations of this research relates to the limited secondary study which only included two interviews (mainly due to access issues). One should also have in mind that the studied company went through some really turbulent times during this study. Generalizbility of the findings may therefore be limited but they give an indication for how large-scale deployment projects of corporate IS can be improved with KM.

I suggest that future research should further focus on how deployment methods can be designed to incorporate guidelines on how knowledge creation and dissemination is enabled via networking.

References

Adler P, Adler P (1994) Observational techniques. In: Denzin NK, Lincoln YS (eds) Handbook of Qualitative Research. Sage, Thousand Oaks

Boland RJ, Tenkasi RV (1995) Perspective Making and Perspective Taking in Communities of Knowing. Organization Science, vol 6, no. 4, pp 350-372

Bresnen M, Edelman L, Newell S, Scarbrough H, Swan J (2003) Social Practices and the Management of Knowledge in Project Environments. International Journal of Project Management, vol 21, no 3, pp 157-166

Cook SDN, Brown JS (1999) Bridging Epistemologies: the Generative Dance between Organizational Knowledge and Organizational Knowing. Organization Science, vol 10, no 4, pp 382-400

Davenport T (1993) Process Innovation – Reengineering Work trough Information Technology. Harvard Business School Press Boston

Davenport T, Prusak L (1998) Working Knowledge – how Organizations Manage What They Know. Harvard Business School Press Boston

Fitzgerald B (1997) The Use of Systems Development Methodologies in Practice: a Field Study. Information Systems Journal, vol 7, pp 201-212

Hansen MT (2002) Knowledge Networks: Explaining Knowledge Sharing in Multiunit Companies. Organization Science, vol 13, no 3, pp 232-248

Hirschheim R, Klein KH, Lyytinen K (1996) Exploring the Intellectual Structures of Information Systems Development: a Social Action Theoretic Analysis. Accounting, Management & Information Technology, vol 6, no 1-2, pp 1-64

Ko D-G, Kirsch LJ, King WR (2005) Antecedents of Knowledge Transfer from Consultants to Clients in Enterprise System Implementations. MIS Quarterly, vol 29, no 1, pp 59-86

Nandhakumar J, Avison DE (1999) The Fiction of Methodological Development: a Field Study of Information Systems Development. Information Technology & People, vol 12, no 2, pp 176-191

Newell S, Swan JA, Galliers RD (2000) A Knowledge-Focused Perspective on the Diffusion and Adoption of Complex Information Technologies: the BPR Example. Information Systems Journal, vol 10, pp 239-259

Nonaka I, Takeuchi H (1995) The Knowledge Creating Company – how Japanese Companies Create the Dynamics of Innovation. Oxford University Press New York

Rossi M, Tolvanen JP, Ramesh B, Lyytinen K, Kaipala J (2000) Method Rationale in Method Engineering. Proc of the 33rd Hawaii International Conference on Systems Sciences Hawaii

Seufert A, von Krogh G, Bach A (1999) Towards Knowledge Networking. Journal of Knowledge Management, vol 3, no 3, pp 180-190

Sharma R, Yetton P (2003) The Contingent Effects of Management Support and Task Interdependence on Successful Information Systems Implementation. MIS Quarterly, vol 27, no 4, pp 533-555

Swan J, Newell S, Scarbrough H, Hislop D (1999) Knowledge Management and Innovation: Networks and Networking. Journal of Knowledge Management, vol 3, no 4, pp 262-275

Szulanski G (1996) Exploring Internal Stickiness: Impediments to the Transfer of Best Practice within the Firm. Strategic Management Journal, vol 17, Winter – Special Issue, pp 27-43

Truex D, Baskerville R, Travis J (2000) Amethodical Systems Development: the Deferred Meaning of Systems Development Methods. Accounting, Management & Information Technology, vol 10, pp 53-79

Tsai W (2002) Social Structure of "Coopetition" within a Multiunit Organization: Coordination, Competition, and Intraorganizational Knowledge Sharing. Organization Science, vol 13, no 2, pp 179-190

Zack MH (1999) Developing a Knowledge Strategy. California Management Review, vol 41, no 3, pp 125-145

Venkatesh V, Morris MG, Davis GB, Davis FD (2003) User Acceptance of Information Technology: Toward a Unified View. MIS Quarterly, vol 27, no 3, pp 425-478

IT Enabled Enterprise Transformation: Perspectives Using Product Data Management

Erisa K. Hines and Jayakanth Srinivasan

Lean Aerospace Initiative, Massachusetts Institute of Technology (MIT), USA. (erisak, jksrini)@mit.edu

Introduction

Information and Communication technologies (ICT) have radically altered the way enterprises operate in today's turbulent environment. They not only contribute in part to this environment through increased information availability to customers but also provide a means of ameliorating the uncertainty associated with a fast-clock speed operational environment by facilitating the integration of suppliers and partners across the enterprise. There are two aspects that need to be considered when an IT system is implemented across an enterprise: the ability of the system to meet current and future enterprise needs, and the ability of the enterprise to adapt to and leverage the capabilities of the implemented IT system. Both aspects have to be addressed synergistically to realize the benefits of the investment at the enterprise level.

It has been widely documented that large-scale IT projects fail for reasons unrelated to the technical feasibility of the system or due to the reliability of its implementation (ST 1995, MK 1994). Additionally, it has been noted that good technology implementation, coupled with change management techniques, can substantially increase the probability of success (BL 1993). Markus and Benjamin (MB 1997) advance the *Magic Bullet Theory of IT and Organization Change,* in which enterprise change is seen as an expected outcome of the implementation of a powerful technology, only to highlight the fundamentally flawed nature of this theory; consequently, they identify alternative roles for IT change agents. Brynjolfsson and Hitt (BH 2000) argue that a significant component of the value of an IT system arises from the ability to enable complementary organizational investments, such as business processes and work practices. Our paper provides further case-based validation for that argument.

CIMdata (CIM 2003) defines Product Lifecycle Management (PLM), from the perspective of a provider of PDM technology, as "a strategic business approach that applies a consistent set of business solutions in support of the use of product definition information across an extended enterprise from concept to end of life – integrating people, process, business systems, and information". The conceptual mapping of the evolution of PLM to the levels of enterprise transformation is shown in Figure 1. The figure follows the Venkataraman framework (VM 1994) for the enterprise reconfiguration that happens when IT systems are adopted. The historical roots of PLM can be traced to computer-aided design (CAD) data management, which enables an enterprise to gain cost savings through the use of a centralized data vault. The impact of CAD-related data management was felt only within the design process. The PDM technology that followed had the potential to enable better design data flow across the enterprise. Its potential impact encompasses both evolutionary change involving work flow improvements during the design phase and revolutionary change through integration of design and manufacturing processes. PLM as it is currently defined requires revolutionary change to enable the seamless flow of product data across the entire lifecycle from design, all the way through product retirement.

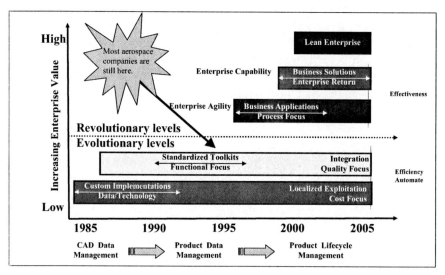

Fig. 1. PDM in the context of enterprise transformation

Unlike other industries in which product data flows only up to the distribution stage, aerospace requires product data to be managed through a system's lifecycle, until its retirement. There are three motivating factors for PLM in aerospace:

- Products have long lifecycles (up to 90+ years) and sustainment is often carried out not by the original manufacturer but other organizations specializing in sustainment activities.
- Customer and/or government agency visibility throughout the product lifecycle is often required.
- Potential cost savings in process and tool standardization, and seamless integration between IT systems.

There has been significant research into DM and its associated technologies. Abramovici and Sieg (AS 2001), and Hameri and Nihitilä (HN 1998) both provide an overview of the evolution of PDM/PLM. However, there has been little research highlighting the current state of PDM/PLM within the aerospace industry. The question of what impediments, if any, were faced by specific companies in implementing the system and how they were overcome in accomplishing ultimately successful implementation has remained an open question. This paper attempts to bridge that gap, providing insight into both the current state of DM within the US aerospace industry, and the expected trajectory of change based on the survey findings. The case-based narratives of IT-enabled change provide insight into the cultural and organizational challenges that lie ahead.

Research Design

The key research questions were identified through a one-day workshop at MIT, involving LAI consortium members. The workshop participants were selected to represent both prime contractors and suppliers of PDM technologies and services. In addition, the participants had PDM implementation initiatives at various stages of progress and maturity. This was done to get an accurate picture of the challenges faced at various phases of PDM implementation. During the workshop, a focused and representative list of the most pressing questions faced by the industry framed the research agenda. The questions included:

- What are the high-level requirements for PDM and how are they implemented?
- What are the success factors in implementing PDM at various stages of the implementation process?

Given the questions and relevant literature, the research lent itself to an exploratory and descriptive methodology. It was decided that a two-phase approach should be taken. Phase one would consist of a structured interview process to gather initial data. Case studies would comprise phase two, an opportunity to further explore specific questions identified in phase one.

Phase One

Overall, nine company sites representing six different companies were visited. Sites were chosen based on having current or recent PDM-implementation activities. A broad range of company types was desired in order to represent the aerospace industry so prime contractors, suppliers and federally funded research and development centers (FFRDC) were present in the sample. Structured interviews were administered at each location at both the site and program level. More than 50 questions were asked each interviewee, covering a broad range of topics related to their PDM system's capabilities, implementation approaches and experiences with the technology and user communities. The questions were developed from the workshop proceedings, reviewed by the team, and piloted at two sites prior to data collection. Interviewees at the site level were exclusively directors and senior managers in the engineering or IT organization. Interviewees at the program level were predominantly program managers and chief engineers.

Phase Two

Based on the findings from the initial interview data, two new questions were posed for exploration using the case studies. These were:

1. What was the initial tool selection process?
2. How are the technology and organization evolving over time?

Two companies were chosen for the case studies, based on their disparate experiences and company type. The two companies highlighted very different patterns of progress in terms of both the initial selection decision processes and the subsequent evolution of the implementation processes, as well as in terms of degrees of eventual implementation success achieved. The results reported here highlight interim findings.

Phase One Survey Findings

For each site, at least one interview was at the site level and up to three at the program level. Some of the results highlight patterns of PDM implementation within the companies surveyed. Several interesting patterns also emerged regarding the approach taken to major PDM implementation efforts and how the outcome seemed to be shaped by both the context and various challenges faced during the implementation process.

The data presented in Figure 2 and Figure 3 were collected from the twenty programs interviewed. These two figures capture the four main approaches employed to product data management: only PDM, PDM and some additional method, configuration management (CM), or without any formal configuration management. Figure 2 illustrates the state of product data management prior to the implementation of a new PDM system. The use of PDM in the surveyed programs covered less than thirty percent of the total data managed beyond the creation of the Manufacturing Bill of Materials. This highlights the disconnect that existed between the engineering and manufacturing phases of system development.

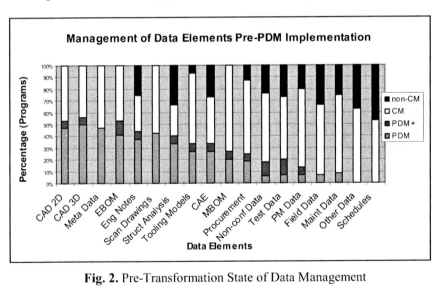

Fig. 2. Pre-Transformation State of Data Management

Figure 3 illustrates the expected state of product data management after the implementation of a new PDM system. A key finding from the survey is the increased use of PDM in managing engineering design data. The flow of data to the manufacturing and support phases through the use of PDM still remains largely unexploited. Even in the case of new PDM implementation efforts, the scope of data management in terms of encompassing other functions beyond engineering seems to be seriously limited. Therefore, future PDM implementation initiatives should focus more attention to the ability of transferring data to other downstream enterprise functions. Figure 3 indicates a potential shift over the next few years to data management covering more of the downstream enterprise functions including manufacturing and sustainment.

One of the implementation-related questions posed at the site level covered the approaches used to training the site personnel and how success was perceived. Although six out of eight responses answered "yes" and one answered "functional" when asked whether the interviewees considered their training to have been successful, the "yes" response was always accompanied by a "sort of" or a candid "no." A clear pattern emerging from the interviews indicated that more effort needs to be spent in communicating the significance to the user community of what they are about to experience. As described by a director of design engineering, "Where [training] has been a success, it was because the people understood the impact. This isn't just a PDM – it's their new job. In other instances, some heard but didn't listen." Others commented as well, saying that making the transition more 'real' to the user community would have lessened the resistance.

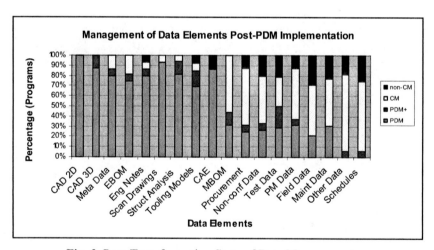

Fig. 3. Post-Transformation State of Data Management

From the interviews, there were several themes like those above describing typical implementation processes that tend to be very challenging to execute. The challenges cited raised some questions about how the software selected for implementation was chosen in the first place. They further raised other questions, such as whether certain changes were forced upon the organization or whether these changes were the results of software system being implemented. These and related early questions led to the case studies.

Phase Two Case Study Findings

The two companies selected for the case studies were based on their different approaches to PDM, the different sectors within which they operated, and the changes enabled by PDM. Company Aero is a business unit of an aerospace company that has been in the weapon platforms business dating back to the 1960s. Company Space is a research and development establishment, specializing in spacecraft, space systems and mission operations, dating back to the early 1940s.

Successful Enterprise Transformation Case Study

Aero's history of mergers, acquisitions and an arguably unstable stream of government contracts had placed it in the threatened position of being shut down. For political reasons, shutting down was not an option for the corporation, hence Aero as a business unit was challenged to reduce its operating costs by 20%. Facing a 'burning platform', Aero's leadership supplemented its organization with an experienced team from a sister business unit. The management of Aero's bill of material (BOM) was identified by the experienced outsiders as the focal point of concern. Process change enabled through PDM technology was prescribed as the solution Aero needed.

The team understood that the transition would not simply be a new IT system. Led within the engineering organization, the processes were fundamentally re-evaluated and redesigned; interfaces across functional disciplines and external stakeholders were identified and addressed; users were required to use the new system, they avoided any training and found loopholes to continue using the legacy system. Perhaps most important, the leadership at the "burning platform" site was given the budgetary support and authoritative backing to make drastic changes.

After a series of three incremental implementation efforts, Aero had transformed the way it did business. It went from a loss center to the top-performing center within its line of business across the parent company. Its major customer now has complete visibility into Aero's processes and has instituted having such a capability as a requirement in its other contracts. Aero is able to share digital data across the company as well as with its supplier network and customers. Most important, it now can track its cost and schedule drivers as a reconcilable, fully managed BOM drives the company's product lifecycle. Aero is currently transferring its knowledge and expertise to a remote design center to enable a similar transformation.

Aero continues to make improvements in its processes and capabilities. It also continues to change its existing culture as it strives to make further progress with its PDM-implementation related efforts. These implementation efforts have nevertheless fundamentally changed Aero for the better and enabled it to be prepared to address the challenges ahead.

Struggling Enterprise Transformation Case Study

Space's culture has remained fairly static over its history. It quickly established its place in the industry as a strong research and development center, producing small quantities of specialized products. Space is mostly comprised of master's- and PhD-level employees who are largely self-driven and motivated. However, it has a diluted management culture, perhaps resulting from its distributed leadership structure. Its business needs also differ sufficiently from others in the aerospace industry, such that having a robust DM capability has not been seen as a high priority.

Space's initial PDM efforts were driven by the need to replace the retiring director of its DM group, framing its 'burning platform'. The decision was made to automate configuration management of drawings. The assignment continued to reside in the IT organization, with little attention paid to it by upper management. The initial implementation consisted of the IT team selecting a PDM solution that could not only manage drawings but also automate many additional processes. It launched the solution without involving any of the users or entertaining their input. Given Space's culture, the users essentially boycotted the system.

Over a period of six years, Space's PDM efforts struggled due to management changes, reorganizations, and an undefined internal IT mandate. Five years ago, Space declared that IT was not a core competency, its IT/PDM management stabilized, and a new, defined PDM effort emerged. Since then, it has successfully piloted its new system, involved the participation of the affected programs within the company, and begun rolling out the new IT/PDM capability. As Space's environment has become more competitive as well as more collaborative, its PDM capabilities have helped the company to meet these emerging.

Space continues to struggle, however, with its culture. It is a long way from obtaining the gains made by Aero, mainly due to the lack of value placed on the capability by upper management. Space's transformation efforts as an enterprise will continue to be restrained/inhibited as long as the culture is given free reign over its programs' IT choices and management does not provide stronger budgetary and authoritative support for the effort.

Conclusions

The enterprises studied here still have a way to go before product data can be used successfully across the entire lifecycle. PDM/PLM systems can provide strategic capabilities to the enterprise in terms of enabling faster responses to customer needs, and providing product knowledge capture within the enterprise. Successful leveraging of these capabilities arises from understanding the need for product data management, assessing the current internal enterprise capabilities and those provided by vendors, managing the process change that results from implementing the system, and keeping the implementation current. There are technical, organizational and cultural challenges that arise from implementing a new IT system; PDM systems provide an excellent illustrative example of these challenges.

Our survey data reflects the increased adoption of product data management within the aerospace industry, and highlights the expected change trajectory over the next five years. A snapshot from nominal data regarding training experience helps to illustrate one of the typical but highly critical decision points. This and others such as the composition of the PDM development and implementation team have the potential to cripple an otherwise well-planned implementation strategy. The two cases presented represent different contexts and progressions in enterprise IT adoption. The main findings from the cases were:

• One size does not fit all: The two cases presented used contrasting IT implementation approaches. Their strategies were a function of resource availability, management commitment and system understanding. The approach adopted must reflect limitations imposed by the organization, technology and culture.

- Authority to transform the enterprise: The team given responsibility for designing and implementing the system must be given authority and the requisite budget to drive change.
- Gaining user commitment: Not communicating the criticality of transitioning to the new system is a common stumbling block in gaining user commitment. This requires user involvement in the process redesign as well as training of end users in the process changes and in using the tool itself.
- Managing process evolution: A successful execution requires management of process changes before, during and after system implementation.

References

Abramovici M, Sieg O (2002) Status and Development Trends of Product Lifecycle Management Systems. Proc of IPPD Nov 21-22 2002 Wroclaw Poland

Benjamin RI, Levinson E (1993) A Framework for Managing IT-Enabled Change. Sloan Management Review, vol 34 pp 23-33

Brynjolfsson E, Hitt L (2000) Beyond Computation: Information Technology, Organizational Transformation and Business Performance. Journal of Economic Perspectives, vol 14, no 4, pp 23-48

CIMdata (2003) PDM to PLM: Growth of an Industry

Hameri, A-P, Nihtilä J (1998) Product Data Management – Exploratory Study on State-of-the-Art in One-of-a-Kind Industry. Computers in Industry, vol 35, no 3, pp 195-206

Liu, DT, Xu XW (2001) A Review of Web-Based Product Data Management Systems. Computers in Industry, vol 44, no 3, pp 251-262

Markus ML, Benjamin RI (1997) The Magic Bullet Theory in IT-Enabled Transformation. Sloan Management Review, vol 38, no 2, pp 55-68

Markus ML, Keil M (1994) If We Build It, They Will Come: Designing Information Systems That Users Want to Use. Sloan Management Review, vol 35, pp 11-25

Robey D, Boudreau M-C (1999) Accounting for the Contradictory Organizational Consequences of Information Technology: Theoretical Directions and Methodological Implications. Information Systems Research, vol 10, no 2, pp 167-185

Standish Group (1995) The CHAOS Report into Project Failure, The Standish Group International Inc. www.standishgroup.com/visitor/chaos.html

Venkataraman N (1994) IT-Enabled Business Transformation: From Automation to Business Scope Redefinition. Sloan Management Review, vol 35, no 2, pp 73-87

Integration of Text- and Data-Mining Technologies for Use in Banking Applications

Jacek Maslankowski

Department of Information Systems, University of Gdańsk, Poland.
jacek@univ.gda.pl

Introduction

Unstructured data, most of it in the form of text files, typically accounts for 85% of an organization's knowledge stores, but it's not always easy to find, access, analyze or use (Robb 2004). That is why it is important to use solutions based on text and data mining. This solution is known as duo mining. This leads to improve management based on knowledge owned in organization. The results are interesting. Data mining provides to lead with structuralized data, usually powered from data warehouses. Text mining, sometimes called web mining, looks for patterns in unstructured data – memos, document and www. Integrating text-based information with structured data enriches predictive modeling capabilities and provides new stores of insightful and valuable information for driving business and research initiatives forward.

Methods for Integration Data- and Text-Mining

Progress in digital data acquisition and storage technology has resulted in the growth of huge databases (Hand et al. 2001). Data mining has become useful over past decade in business to gain more information, to have a better understanding of running a business, and to find a new ways and ideas to extrapolate a business to other markets (Bargain et al. 2002). Data mining involves extraction, transformation and presentation of data in useful form. Creating a mining model can be compared to manufacturing process - from data by the algorithm towards the mining model (Paul et al.2002). Integrate methods of text analysis with methods for data analysis may take more profits to organizations. Data and text mining is the element of business Intelligence system, which contains software for supporting decisions. Business Intelligence means using data assets to make better business decisions. It is about access, analysis, and uncovering new opportunities (Almeida et al. 1999). The source to powered Business Intelligence systems is metadata. Several factors have triggered the need for metadata in businesses today. These include the following:

- Current systems are inflexible and nonintegrated.
- Existing data warehouses and data marts need to grow.
- Business users needs are not being fulfilled.
- Companies need to reduce the impact of employee turnover.
- Businesses need to increase user confidence in data (Marco 2000).

A major difficulty with the dataset usually used in the data mining model is its relational structure (Grant 2003). The problem has been solved by leading with dimensional structures. The data mining model describes where the source of data is that is used to train the model is stored. This source can be an OLAP cube in which the model is called MOLAP (Multidimensional OLAP). The second type is called ROLAP (Relational OLAP). A third option which attempts to take the best of each is called HOLAP (Hybrid OLAP). Data Mining model algorithms include classification, clustering, descriptive and predictive models (Bain et al.2001). The heart of data mining systems is the data warehouse. OLAP allows users to view information from many angles, drill down to atomic data, or roll up into aggregations to see trends and historical information. It is the final and arguably most important piece of the data warehouse architecture (Moeller 2001). A data warehouse is subject-oriented, integrated, nonvolatile, and time-variant collection of data in support of management's decision (Inmon 2002). Subject areas are major grouping of physical items, concepts, events, people, and places of interest to the enterprise (Imhoff 2003).The data warehouse contains fact and dimension tables. Facts represents a business measure, while the dimension tables contain the textual descriptors of the business (Kimball and Ross 2002). The results of requirements analysis and source system audit serve as inputs to the design of the warehouse schema. The schema details all fact and dimension tables and fields, as well as data sources for each warehouse field (Humphries et al. 2001). The design of the data warehouse includes star and snowflake schemas (Scalzo 2003). Functions in text analysis are to select features for further processing. Text mining is needed to process text into a form that data mining procedures can use (Weiss 2004). This usually contains language identification, feature extraction, clustering and categorization. The language identification tool can automatically discover the language in which a document is written. Feature extraction recognizes significant vocabulary items in text. Clustering is a process which divides a collection of documents into groups. Categorization tools assign documents to preexisting categories, sometimes called "topics" or "themes" (Tkach 1998). A document warehousing is a technology which leads with text documents. It is characterized by following attributes: there is no single document structure or document type, documents are drawn form multiple sources, essential features of documents are automatically extracted and explicitly stored in the document warehouse, which are designed to integrated semantically related documents (Sullivan 2001).

Data preparation is one of the most important step in the model development process. From the simplest analysis to the most complex model, the quality of the data going in is key of success of the project (Rud 2001).

DEA (Data Envelopment Analysis) is the mathematical programming approach developed to evaluate the relative efficiency of a set of units that have multiple performance measures – inputs and outputs. DEA is particularly useful when the relationships among the multiple performance measures are unknown (Wang 2003).

Research Method

There are three main aspects of the text- and data- mining integration. First aspect concerns source of data. The data warehouse is the best source used for integration data from various OLTP systems and for using to transform into business information easily understood by tools and decision workers. This leads to create a source for data mining application. Document warehouse can be used as the source for text mining tools. Second aspect is to find a logical model, which integrates both technologies and provides useful information for decision workers. Vendors, such as SAS Institute, provides solutions to build data mining models in its enterprise miner, and text mining models in text miner. There is no simple solution to join both applications. Third aspect is how to build the presentation layer, which can visualize data taken from both sources.

The data warehouse build for using in banking organizations should cover all aspects of its organizational structure. In it's operating with data mining model particularly static activity should be included. The next step should begin process of determining sources for document warehouse. These sources are often documents, applications and any notes from clients. The most important thing is that the warehouse must properly process the documents. The least efficient warehouse contains errors in its data. Research leads by The Data Warehousing Institute has argued that bad quality of data in USA wasted about 600 milliards dollars per year. The proposal is to implement methods to prevent data errors in warehouses in this first layer of data- and text- mining integration.

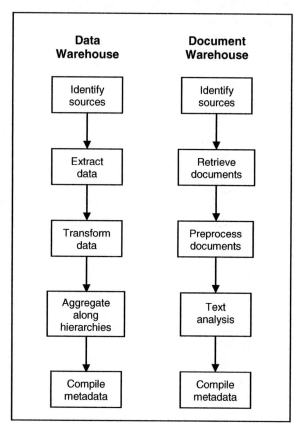

Fig. 1. Steps in document warehouse construction compared to data warehousing

As showed in figure above, the last step in building data and document warehouses is compiling metadata. In banking applications metadata used with both warehouses are similar. It is important that metadata types used in document warehouse should be similar to data warehouse. This can improve process of modeling integration tools for supporting both technologies. Using common description for metadata can provide a model which can be split by external application.

The next step is to build a solution for supporting both data- and text mining technology. The main task is to find a pattern in data or text and then use it to provide to upper layers of this proposal. This model should support reporting based on both technologies. In authors' opinion, the best way is to use external application. It can safe from losing coherence in data and document warehouses. This model has been tested based on SAS 9.1.3 software. For data mining technology was used SAS Enterprise Miner, text mining was supported by SAS Text Miner. Both technologies were split based on Sun Java architecture, supported by SAS application. In this solution there has been added indexing table, which split indexing tables from text and data mining and a search engine has been developed.

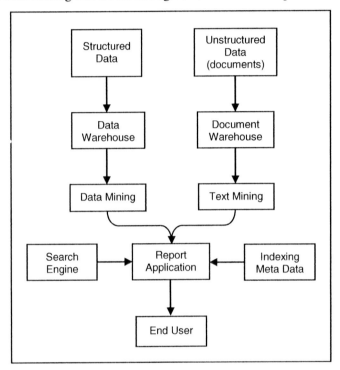

Fig. 2. Integration of data- and text-mining technologies on upper layer

The last step is to provide visualization layer for this technologies. The technology used in this model was Java Swing, based on Sun Microsystems applications. End user can request for any data from any criteria.

Results

The result is that there is a multiplier effect going on. By using data mining and text mining together, enterprises have been able to improve its functioning to around 20 percent, with the range being from 5 to 50 percent

(Creese 2004). The effect is particularly visible while loan analysis. The documents from customer can be used as a pattern for text mining tools, while his credit account can be analyzed by using data mining technology. For example a customer cannot pay rate because of a random accident. He could write a document with explaining this situation. By using only data mining tools it will not be as simple to discover the problem in payment. By using both technologies the system can compare these two patterns and discover why the client cannot pay this payment. It can take small amount of time to do this, while using only one technology can lead to necessary analyze both documents by the person.

Conclusion

The present paper has identified aspects in modeling text- and data mining technologies in tandem. Nowadays duo mining technologies are not widely used in organization. There is no literature and experience for using this technology in organizations of all kinds. In authors' opinion, this will be increasing. This requires a new approach to develop text and data mining tools. The banking organization is the best practice for using the solutions proposed by author. The application for this solution has been developed and tested in SAS 9.1.3 system.

References

Almeida M, Ishikawa M, Reinschmidt J, Roeber T (1999) Getting Started with Data Warehouse and Business Intelligence. IBM Press San Jose

Bain T, Benkovich M, Dewson R, Ferguson S, Graves C, Joubert TJ, Lee D, Scott M, Skoglund R, Turley P, Youness S (2001) Professional SQL Server 2000 Data Warehousing with Analysis Services. Wrox Press Ltd

Baragoin C, Chan R, Gottschalk H, Meyer G, Pereira P, Verhees J (2002) Enhance Your Business Applications. IBM Redbooks

Berry MW (ed) (2004) Survey of Text Mining. Springer

Creese G (2004) Volume Analytics: Duo-mining: Combining Data and Text Mining. DMReview September 2004

Grant G (2003) ERP & Data Warehousing in Organizations: Issues and Challenges. Idea Group Publishing

Hand D, Mannila H, Smyth P (2001) Principles of Data Mining. The MIT Press Cambridge

Humphries M, Hawkins MW, Dy MC (2001) Data Warehousing: Architecture and Implementation. Pearson

Imhoff C, Galemmo N, Geiger J (2003) Mastering Data Warehouse Design: Relational and Dimensional Techniques. John Wiley & Sons

Inmon WH (2002) Building the Data Warehouse. Third Edition. John Wiley & Sons

Kimball R, Ross M (2002) The Data Warehouse Toolkit: The Complete Guide to Dimensional Modeling. Second ed. John Wiley & Sons

Marco D (2000) Building and Managing the Metadata Repository: A Full Lifecycle Guide. John Wiley & Sons

Moeller RA (2001) Distributed Data Warehousing using Web Technology: How to Build a More Cost-Effective and Flexible Warehouse. Amacom

Paul S, Guatam N, Balint R (2002) Preparing and Mining Data with Microsoft® SQL Server™ 2000 and Analysis Services. MS Press

Rob D (2004) Text Mining Tools Take on Unstructured Data. Computerworld June 21 2004

Rud OP (2001) Data Mining Cookbook: Modeling Data for Marketing, Risk, and Customer Relationship Management. John Wiley & Sons

Scalzo B (2003) Oracle DBA Guide to Data Warehousing and Star Schemas. Prentice Hall

Sullivan D (2001) Document Warehousing and Text Mining. Wiley

Tkach D (1998) Text Mining Technology: Turning Information into Knowledge. IBM Corporation

Wang J (ed) (2003) Data Mining: Opportunities and Challenges. Idea Publishing Group

Weiss SM, Indurkhya N, Zhang T, Damerau F (2004) Predictive Methods for Analyzing Unstructured Information. Axel Springer

Syndicate Data Incorporation into Data Warehouses: A Categorization and Verification of Problems

Mattias Strand, Benkt Wangler, Björn Lundell and Markus Niklasson

School of Humanities and Informatics, University of Skövde, Sweden.
(mattias.strand, benkt.wangler, bjorn.lundell, markus.niklasson)@his.se

Introduction

Organizations experience problems when incorporating external data into data warehouses (DWs), e.g. (Adelman, 1998; Damato, 1999; Devlin, 1997; Kimball, 1996; Oglesby, 1999) and therefore, they are not able to fully exploit the potential thereof (Strand & Wangler, 2004). In alignment, the need for developing a support that may assist organizations in better exploiting the potential of the incorporated external data has been emphasized by DW consultants (Strand and Wangler, 2004), as well as banking organizations (Strand et al., 2004b).

However, for being able to develop such support, one must have a thorough understanding of the reasons for why organizations fail in fully exploiting their external data investments, i.e. one must understand the problems they experience.

Therefore, to create a foundation for a future development of some kind of support, the work reported on here aimed at identifying, describing, categorizing, and verifying common problems. We focus on problems related to syndicate data, which is the most common subcategory of external data being incorporated into DWs (Strand & Wangler, 2004; Strand et al., 2004b).

The work was conducted in two steps: 1) the identification, description, and categorization of syndicate data incorporation problems accounted for in the literature, and 2) a verification, via an interview study, that the problems are industry-independent. Verifying that the problems are broadly experienced was deemed important, since the support has a general purpose and should not be directed towards a particular industry.

The result of the work provides a categorization of 22 industry-independent problems. The problems are, for example, difficulties in selecting the most appropriate data supplier, missing metadata, laws that restrict how they may use the data, and missing data identifiers.

Background

The literature lacks for any definition of syndicate data. Kimball (1996) provides the first instance of the concept, but does not define it. He only accounts for it as data acquired from syndicate data suppliers (SDSs), i.e. organizations specialized in collecting, compiling, and selling data to other organizations. Therefore, in order to define syndicate data, we suggest the following definition: Syndicate data is business data (and its associated metadata), purchased from an organization specialized in collecting, compiling, and selling data, and targeted towards the strategic and/or the tactic decision making processes of the incorporating organization. The definition is based upon the work of Devlin (1997), Kelly (1996), and Kimball (1996), indicating that the data is organizationally external (Devlin, 1997), there is always a monetary cost associated with external data incorporated from specialized suppliers (Kelly, 1996) and syndicate data is primarily applied at strategic and tactical levels of organizations (Kimball, 1996).

External data (and thereby syndicate data) incorporation is a process comprising the following four activities; 1) identification, 2) acquisition, 3) integration, and 4) usage (Strand & Wangler, 2004). Hence-fourth, this process will be referred to as the external data incorporation process (EDIP). The activities are not unique for external or syndicate data, since they appear in general data warehouse development processes (e.g. Damato, 1999; Hammer, 1997; Hessinger, 1997) and thus may be considered as generic. Still, the process of incorporating external data in general and syndicate data in particular differs from the process of integrating internal data in that the data is acquired from outside the organization and thereby crosses organizational boundaries, which may cause other types of problems than those experienced with internal data (Strand & Wangler, 2004).

Research Approach

The research approach of this work was divided into two steps. Firstly, an inclusive literature review was undertaken, aimed at identifying, describing, and categorizing problems accounted for in the literature. Secondly, the literature review was complemented with an interview study, which aimed at verifying which problems that are industry-independent.

The implementation of the literature review was guided by the structured approach according to Webster & Watson (2002). Initially, leading journals, conference proceedings, and books were examined, covering DWs, business intelligence systems, executive information systems, environmental scanning, decision support systems, and knowledge management systems. The literature review thus became inclusive, in accordance with the advice of Webster & Watson (2002, pp. xv-xvi) who suggest that a literature review should "not be confined to one research methodology, one set of journals, or one geographical region".

Although relevant literature was also derived from forward and backward citations of the identified articles, few articles were obtained. To illustrate, a search of the following strings in the library database INSPEC resulted in: 19 papers for "external data AND data warehouse", 11 papers for "external data source", and 0 papers for "syndicate data". The search scope was therefore extended to also include DW-resource web pages (e.g. www.dmreview.com and www.dw-institute.com). Although one might question the quality of such resources, they were included, since the literature review aimed at identifying as many problems as possible.

Once the search for the relevant literature was completed, the material obtained was reviewed from a concept-centric angle (Webster & Watson, 2002), which in our case were the problems. For each problem, we analyzed phrases or words from the literature that contributed with details. The initial analysis resulted in 38 different problems. However, focusing on syndicate data caused a concept problem, since some authors use the term external data, while indicating that the data is bought from SDSs or are not referring to any type of source at all. Consequently, we had to determine whether a problem was relevant or not, from a syndicate data perspective. This relevance check excluded 14 of the initial 38 problems. For example, Zhu (1999) and Zhu et al. (2000) address the problem of dynamic data sources. After a thorough analysis, it became evident that they referred to web pages. Since the Internet is another type of source/supplier of external data unconnected to syndicate data, this particular problem was excluded. The remaining 24 problems were consequently described and categorized according to the activities of the EDIP, which were the units of analysis.

The interview study initially identified large companies via purposeful sampling (Patton, 2002), in which different types of industries were a key consideration, in order to verify that the problems are broadly experienced. The decision to contact large organizations was informed by the fact that DW solutions and syndicate data are expensive and that large organizations were assumed to have sufficient resources for investing in these. The appropriateness of this sampling decision is supported by the results of Hwang et al. (2004). Their study shows that larger sized banks are keener on adopting DW technology than smaller sized ones.

In the initial contacts, it was also verified that the companies, as well as the respondents, had been working on syndicate data incorporation for a number of years, since a more extensive experience should increase the probability that they had been exposed to a richer flora of problems. In addition, the experience was also deemed necessary for the respondents to be able to understand and explicitly express the problems, their causes and impacts, and possible solutions.

The final sample resulted in 5 respondents (R1-R5), comprising: R1 employed by a newspaper with 950 employees and a turnover of €173M; R2 who works for a car manufacturer with 28.000 employees (turnover N/A); R3 employed by a grocery retailer with 40.000 employees and a turnover of €7800M; R4 who works for a petroleum refiner with 4000 employees and a turnover of €3600M; and R5 employed by a medical company with 60.000 employees and a turnover of €2100M.

As the sampling progressed, the interview questions were developed. Each categorized problem in Table 1 had a corresponding question, which aimed to identify if the company had experienced it. In addition, follow-up questions regarding the problems' causes and impacts, and their solutions were also specified. Hence, the five interviews were semi-structured (Williamson, 2002) and conducted over the telephone, since the respondents were unable to spare more than the actual time for the interview. The interviews lasted for approximately one hour during which notes were taken. Following the completion of each interview, these notes were checked for spelling and sometimes restructured, e.g. if the respondent had further in the interview complemented an answer. The notes of each interview were returned to the respective respondents for approval and to enable them to make corrections, additions or removals.

Analysis and Results

The problems resulting from the literature review are provided in Table 1.

Table 1. The problems categorization resulting from the literature review

Identification problems
1.1 Identifying new entrants – Organizations find in difficult to identify new entrants, since established SDSs rigorously promote their data and services. Identifying new entrants is important, as they may be cheaper or able to offer different data (Strand et al, 2004b).
1.2 Overlapping suppliers' capabilities – Selecting the most appropriate supplier for data acquisition is problematic. Often several data suppliers provide the same data, but in different formats or via different services or products (Strand et al, 2004b).
1.3 Overlapping data or products/services – Organizations experience difficulties identifying the most appropriate syndicate data, even from a specific supplier, since a supplier may deliver different standardized data sets that overlap (Strand et al, 2004b; Zhu & Buchman, 2002).

Acquisition problems
2.1 Employing under-dimensioned distribution channels – Suppliers employ various data distribution techniques, such as CD-ROMs or email attachments which may cause problems when delivering larger data sets, since these techniques are not able to accommodate the distribution of large data sets (Oglesby, 1999; Strand et al., 2004a).
2.2 Acquiring incomplete data sets – Organizations that acquire incomplete data sets from the SDSs usually end up with problems. For example, if an address update is incomplete, the organization might send out information to out-dated addresses which results in costly postal returns (Strand et al., 2004a).
2.3 Varying data source stability – The stability of the syndicate data sources may vary, thereby causing acquisition and integration problems for the user organizations (Strand et al., 2003; Zhu & Buchmann, 2002).
2.4 Purchasing expensive syndicate data – Many organizations consider syndicate data expensive and consequently, some hesitate in undertaking such initiatives (Oglesby, 1999; Strand et al., 2004a; Strand et al, 2004b; Stedman, 1998).

Integration problems
3.1 Demanding to design & maintain transformation processes – It is demanding to transform and integrate syndicate data into DWs, since the transformation processes are both time-consuming and costly to design and maintain, due to less control of the data (Adelman, 1998).
3.2 Diverging data representations and structures – Syndicate data does usually not follow the standards of the acquiring organization (Adelman, 1998). The differences between the internal and syndicate data structures are the most common problems of such initiatives (Kimball, 1996; Strand et al., 2004a).
3.3 Assuring data consistency – Organizations experience problems assuring that all the components and storages related to the DW are updated when new syndicate data is integrated. Problems arise when decisions are based on inconsistent data (Strand et al, 2004b).

Table 1. (cont.)

3.4 Missing data identifiers – If unique data identifiers are not provided by the SDSs, resource-demanding work is required, when organizations try (if possible) to integrate the syndicate data with the internal data accurately (Adelman, 1998; Strand et al., 2004a).

3.5 Diverging time-stamps – Organizations recognize integration problems that are related to diverging time-stamps of the data, i.e. the data may be time-stamped from an integration perspective rather than the real time perspective, which organizations need in order to map the syndicate data to the internal data (Damato, 1999; Strand et al., 2004a).

3.6 Conflicting data from multiple sources – Integrating data from several SDSs may lead to problems with conflicting data. This may, in turn, cause problems when organizations integrate the different syndicate data sets with the internal data (Damato, 1999).

3.7 Hiding data quality issues in commercial ETL-tools – Commercial ETL (Extraction, Transformation, and Load)-tools conceal data quality issues in a black-box manner when the syndicate data is automatically integrated with the internal data any errors in the data caused by poorly designed ETL-processes are hidden from the users (Strand et al., 2004a).

Usage problems

4.1 Misunderstanding the meaning of syndicate data – The meaning of the syndicate data acquired by organizations may be difficult to understand and causes problems, when interpreted incorrectly (Damato, 1999; Strand & Wangler, 2004; Strand et al, 2004b).

4.2 Missing metadata – Syndicate data is sometimes stored without any related metadata that explains the relationships with other internal or syndicate data (Adelman, 1998; Damato, 1999).

4.3 Lacking routines for data quality assurance – Syndicate data is not as carefully examined, reviewed or filtered as regular internal data sources, and may therefore be of poorer quality (Strand et al., 2004a; Zhu & Buchmann, 2002).

4.4 Making decisions on out-dated data – Data acquired from SDSs may be out of date, resulting in decisions based on inaccurate data (Bischoff, 1997; Strand et al., 2004a).

4.5 Using data that is biased – Syndicate data may be biased, e.g. some information is excluded or incorrect (Strand et al., 2004a; Zhu & Buchmann, 2002). Furthermore, the syndicate data can be biased due to supplier problems, false assumptions made by the organization, or different political and cultural contexts (Zhu et al., 2000).

4.6 Trusting the data – The origin of the data contributes to its perceived reliability (Zhu & Buchmann, 2002). If the source of the data is external its trustworthiness may be questionable, perhaps resulting in data that is not used and thus wasting resources (Strand & Wangler, 2004; Strand et al, 2004b).

Table 1. (cont.)

4.7 Contradicting data from multiple sources – Using data from several SDSs can result in conflicting data, as suppliers may deliver different data values for the same corresponding internal record. Ultimately, organizations must choose which data they trust the most, and base their decisions on that data (Damato, 1999).

4.8 Ignoring syndicate data for DW purposes – If syndicate data is present in a company, but not integrated into the data warehouse, it may not be taken into consideration when decisions are made (Damato, 1999; Kimball, 1996; Strand & Wangler, 2004).

4.9 Restricting laws and regulations – Laws restrict how companies are allowed to use the syndicate data. It is therefore important that organizations understand these laws and ensure that their data use is legal (Strand et al, 2004b).

4.10 Conflicting ethics views – Syndicate data use may conflict with the users' or organizations' ethical views and influence how the data is adopted in the work-routines (Strand et al, 2004b).

The analysis of the material from the interview study aimed at verifying if the problems in Table 1 are industry-independent. The following problems were experienced by a majority of the respondents and were therefore considered industry-independent and included in the verified categorization without further motivation: *1.1 Identifying new entrants*; *1.3 Overlapping data or products/services*; *2.4 Purchasing expensive syndicate data*; *3.1 Demanding to design & maintain transformation processes*; *3.2 Diverging data representations and structures*; *3.3 Assuring data consistency*; *3.7 Hiding data quality issues in commercial ETL-tools*; *4.1 Misunderstanding the meaning of the data*; *4.2 Missing metadata*; *4.3 Lacking routines for data quality assurance*; *4.4 Making decisions on out-dated data*; and *4.9 Restricting laws and regulations*.

In the following, the remaining problems from Table 1 will be analyzed with respect to whether they should be considered industry-independent or not.

Problem 1.2 – Overlapping suppliers' capabilities

Three respondents (R2, R3, and R5) commented in terms of experiencing this problem or that it might become a problem. In fact only R2 had experienced it, since R3 and R5 were acquiring data from a SDS in a monopoly situation. Still, R3 and R5 acknowledged that it might become a problem, if their SDSs lost their monopoly. R2 claimed that some of their suppliers could not maintain a certain level of data quality and therefore they had changed supplier. The problem remained in the categorization due to its occurrence in the literature and among the respondents.

Problem 2.1 – Employing under-dimensioned distribution channels

This problem was excluded since none of the respondents had experienced it. However, they did state that it was an inconvenience to acquire data via e-mails or CD-ROMs, rather than an actual problem. In addition, they claimed that such distribution techniques were only complements to other technologies e.g. FTP.

Problem 2.2 – Acquiring incomplete data sets.

This problem was only experience by R3, indicating that aggregation levels were sometimes missing, but such deficiencies were worked around with the query tools. The problem remained in the categorization, since it was indicated in the literature and by R3, and the fact that should an organization's query tool not enable a work around, the problem would occur. Furthermore, since syndicate data is expensive, it should be complete.

Problem 2.3 – Varying data source stability

This problem was divided into two separate problems, of which one remained an acquisition problem, accounted for in this paragraph and the other became an integration problem (Problem 3.8 – Varying source content). R1 and R2 had experienced problems with varying data source stability and R5 avoided it by not acquiring anything from their suppliers without a notification that the expected data set was uploaded and the supplier's source was operational. R1 and R2 indicated that the source of the problem was the program-to-program connections from which they automatically download the data from the SDS. R5 exemplified that they had selected their suppliers based upon the service they offered, with respect to e.g. source notifications. The problem remained in the categorization due to its multiple occurrences in literature and among practitioners.

Problem 3.4 – Missing data identifiers

The problem of incomplete data mappings was encountered by two respondents (R2 and R5). R2 explained that this problem originates from missing data identifiers in the syndicate data. R5 also claimed missing data identifiers as a key problem when mapping the syndicate data to the internal data. R2 and R5 indicated that they solved their problems by simply contacting their SDS and acquiring complementary data or new data sets. The problem remained in the categorization due to its multiple occurrences in literature and among practitioners.

Problem 3.5 – Diverging time-stamps

Respondents R2 and R5 had experienced problems with diverging time-stamps. According to R2, this problem rarely occurs, but when it arises, it causes major disturbance. The reason for the divergences was due to unsynchronized dates, since R2's organization and its SDS have different periodical classifications. The supplier bases its time classification of the data on 13 periods a year, whereas R2 bases the data on weeks and months. To solve this problem, R2 manually transforms the timestamps of the syndicate data to the organization's own system. Respondent 5 claimed that since they acquire the data on a monthly basis, all the data has the same timestamp. As a consequence, they may not drill-down and conduct analyses on week levels. The problem remained due to its multiple occurrences in literature and among practitioners.

Problem 3.6 - Conflicting data from multiple sources
The problem of conflicting data was only acknowledged by R2, who indicated that data packages from different SDSs sometimes overlap, causing integration problems. R2's solution was to manually examine the data and decide which source to use. R1 also indicated that this could have been a problem, but they had established contracts with their SDS, assuring completely separate data sets. Although the problem was only expressed by R2, it remained in the categorization, since it is also discussed by Damato (1999) who states that integrating data from several SDSs is a major problem, due to the diversities of the data formats or structures.

Problem 3.8 – Varying source content
As indicated previously, this problem was added as a result of the interviews. R2 indicated that sometimes the SDSs failed to notify them when they changed the structure or format of the data. Since the ETL-processes are designed to manage data in specific formats and predefined structures, problems arise. Although only expressed by one respondent and not previously identified in literature, the problem was added to the categorization, since it was deemed interesting enough for further elaboration in the forthcoming study with the SDSs (accounted for in the next section).

Problem 4.5 – Using data that is biased
The problem with biased syndicate data was only indicated by R3 and did not seem to be an actual problem. Instead, R3 explained that it was probably due to misunderstandings between them and their suppliers. Since the problem was only vaguely mentioned by one respondent, it was excluded from the categorization.

Problem 4.6 – Trusting the data
R2 and R4 expressed problems with trusting the data. Occasionally key measures were miscalculated (or misinterpreted), making the users hesitate to apply the data. However, both respondents strongly emphasized that trust is very much related to data quality. R2 also indicated that trust is something that must be built, both with respect to the collaboration with a particular SDS and internally in trying to make the user trust the data. This

is also supported by Devlin (1997) stating that all external data must undergo an acceptance process before it may be fully exploited. In addition, also Strand et al. (2004b) and Zhu & Buchmann (2002) acknowledge the lack of trust as a possible problem, but they also point out that it is most likely to become a problem if the source/supplier of the data is unknown or not established in the market. The problem remained in the categorization due to its multiple occurrences in literature and among practitioners.

Problem 4.7 – Contradicting data from multiple sources

This problem was experienced by R2 and R5. R5 indicated that they experienced this problem when address data from several suppliers diverged. The problem was solved by assessing which of the SDSs was considered the most trustworthy. R2 claimed that it all comes down to whether you trust a supplier or not. R2 also indicated that they are increasingly working with the selection of the suppliers as a solution to the problem. The problem remained due to its multiple occurrences in literature and among practitioners.

Problem 4.8 – Ignoring syndicate data for DW purposes

This problem was only experienced by R5, who explained that they have contractual limitations with the suppliers, which disallows them to apply the data for whatever purpose they want. R5 also indicated that it is frustrating having the data and being able to see powerful analysis opportunities and not being allowed to explore them. As both literature and R5 emphasize the problem, it remained in the categorization.

Problem 4.10 – The usage of the data may conflict with various ethical aspects

None of the respondents had experienced this problem, or acknowledged that it could become a problem. In addition, since the problem is only vaguely expressed in Strand et al. (2004b), it was excluded from the categorization.

In summary, Table 2 provides the updated categorization of industry-independent problems.

Table 2. The updated categorization of industry-independent problems (the problems are renumbered to maintain sequential numbering)

Problems Categorization		Old nr.
Id.1	Identifying new entrants	1.1
Id.2	Overlapping suppliers' capabilities	1.2
Id.3	Overlapping data or products/services	1.3
Ac.1	Acquiring incomplete data sets	2.2
Ac.2	Varying data source stability	2.3
Ac.3	The syndicate data is expensive	2.4
In.1	Demanding to design & maintain transformation processes	3.1
In.2	Diverging data representations and structures	3.2
In.3	Assuring data consistency	3.3
In.4	Missing data identifiers	3.4
In.5	Diverging time-stamps	3.5
In.6	Conflicting data from multiple sources	3.6
In.7	Hiding data quality issues in commercial ETL-tools	3.7
In.8	Varying source content	New
Us.1	Misunderstanding the meaning of the syndicate data	4.1
Us.2	Missing metadata	4.2
Us.3	Lacking routines for data quality assurance	4.3
Us.4	Making decisions on out-dated data	4.4
Us.5	Trusting the data	4.6
Us.6	Contradicting data from multiple sources	4.7
Us.7	Ignoring syndicate data for DW purposes	4.8
Us.8	Restricting laws and regulations	4.9

Conclusions and Future Work

The results show that all participating organizations had experienced problems when incorporating syndicate data into DWs. In addition, the respondents gave very few concrete examples on how these problems may be avoided or solved. Often, solutions were manual and time-consuming work-arounds or focused on adapting to the suppliers' standards. The absence of concrete solutions further stresses the need for developing a support that may assist organizations. In developing such a support, the updated categorization constitutes a firm foundation, since it indicates common problems that must be avoided or solved. In addition, to the best of our knowledge, this is the first time the problems related to syndicate data incorporation have been compiled and categorized.

Furthermore, the participating organizations represented different industries and had been applying incorporation initiatives for several years. Still, only one new problem was identified during the interviews. Therefore, we argue that the updated categorization covers most of the syndicate data incorporation problems that organizations experience.

Finally, the results of this work further emphasize that the syndicate data suppliers are an important stakeholder group, as an important collaborator for the user organizations, but also as the root to some of the problems. We will therefore undertake a study with these suppliers, aimed at characterizing the industry and contrasting the problems to the opinions and experiences of the suppliers. The results of such a study would balance the description of syndicate data incorporation problems from multiple, empirical perspectives.

References

Adelman S (1998) Estimating a Data Warehouse Pilot Project? DM Review. www.dmreview.com/ (Accessed 04.03.21)

Bischoff J (1997) Physical Design. In: Bischoff J, Alexander T (eds) Practical Advice from the Experts. Prentice Hall New Jersey

Damato GM (1999) Strategic Information from External Sources: a Broader Picture of Business Reality for the Data Warehouse. http://www.dwway.com (Accessed 03.02.20)

Devlin B (1997) Data Warehouse: from Architecture to Implementation. Addison Wesley Longman Harlow

Hammer K (1997) Migrating Data from Legacy Systems. In: Barquin R, Edelstein H (eds) Building, Using, and Managing the Data Warehouse. Prentice Hall PTR New Jersey

Hessinger P (1997) A Renaissance for Information Technology. In: Bischoff J, Alexander T (eds) Data Warehouse Practical Advice from the Experts. Prentice Hall PTR New Jersey

Hwang H-G, Ku C-Y, Yen DC, Cheng C-C (2004) Critical Factors Influencing the Adoption of Data Warehouse Technology: a Study of the Banking Industry in Taiwan. Decision Support Systems, vol 37, no 1, pp 1-21

Kelly S (1996) Data Warehousing: the Route to Mass Customization. John Wiley & Sons New York

Kimball R (1996) The Data Warehouse Toolkit. John Wiley & Sons New York

Oglesby WE (1999) Using External Data Sources and Warehouses to Enhance Your Direct Marketing Effort. DM Review. www.dmreview.com/ (Accessed 03.02.21)

Patton MQ (2002) Qualitative Research and Evaluation Methods. 3rd edition. Sage Publications Thousand Oaks

Strand M, Wangler B (2004) Incorporating External Data into Data Warehouses – Problems Identified and Contextualized. Proc of the 7th International Conference on Information Fusion (Fusion'04), vol. 1

Strand M, Wangler B, Lauren C-F (2004a) Acquiring and Integrating External Data into Data Warehouses: Are You Familiar with the Most Common Process? Proc of the 6th International Conference on Enterprise Information Systems (ICEIS'2004), vol 1

Strand M, Wangler B, Niklasson M (2004b) External Data Incorporation into Data Warehouses: An Exploratory Study of Identification and Usage Practices in Banking Organizations. Proc of the CAiSE Forum at the 16th International Conference on Advanced Information Systems Engineering (CAiSE'04)

Strand M, Wangler B, Olsson M (2003) Incorporating External Data into Data Warehouses: Characterizing and Categorizing Suppliers and Types of External Data. Proc of the Americas Conference on Information Systems (AMCIS'03)

Stedman C (1998) Scaling the Warehouse Wall. Computerworld, March 02, www.computerworld.com/ (Accessed August, 2003)

Webster J, Watson RT (2002) Analyzing the Past to Prepare for the Future: Writing a Literature Review. MIS Quarterly, vol 26, no 2, pp xiii-xxiii

Williamson K (2002) Research Methods for Students, Academics and Professionals. 2nd edition. Sage Publications Thousand Oaks

Zhu Y (1999) A Framework for Warehousing the Web Contents. Proc of the 5th International Computer Science Conference on Internet Applications (ICSC99)

Zhu Y, Bornhövd C, Sautner D, Buchmann AP (2000) Materializing Web Data for OLAP and DSS. Proc of the 1st International Conference on Web-Age Information Management (WAIM00)

Zhu Y, Buchmann A (2002) Evaluating and Selecting Web Sources as External Information Resources of a Data Warehouse. Proc of the 3rd International Conference on Web Information Systems Engineering (WISE'00)

Reflections on the Body of Knowledge in Software Engineering

Dace Apshvalka[1] and Peter Wendorff[2]

[1] Faculty of Computer Science and Information Technology, Riga Technical University, Latvia. Dace.Apshvalka@gmail.com
[2] ASSET GmbH, Germany. Peter.Wendorff@integrative-paradigm.com

Introduction

Software engineering (SE) is a discipline with an enormous and complex body of knowledge (BoK). Bourque et al. (1999) note: "Articulating a body of knowledge is an essential step toward developing a profession because it represents a broad consensus regarding the contents of the discipline" (p. 35). But what exactly is a BoK in SE?

For example, IEEE (2004) is a recent attempt to define a BoK in SE, called "SWEBOK". In its foreword the following characterisation is given:

"In this Guide, the IEEE Computer Society establishes for the first time a baseline for the body of knowledge for the field of software engineering, [...]. It should be noted that the Guide does not purport to define the body of knowledge but rather to serve as a compendium and guide to the body of knowledge that has been developing and evolving over the past four decades. Furthermore, this body of knowledge is not static. The Guide must, necessarily, develop and evolve as software engineering matures. It nevertheless constitutes a valuable element of the software engineering infrastructure." (p. vii)

Two major objectives of the SWEBOK project have been to "characterize the contents of the software engineering discipline" and to "promote a consistent view of software engineering worldwide" (Bourque et al. 1999, p. 36). The result is a voluminous document that provides topical access to an enormous body of literature. In Bourque et al. (1999) the authors, who represent the SWEBOK editorial team, give the following rationale for their selection of material:

"From the outset, the question arose as to the depth of treatment the Guide should provide. After substantial discussion, we adopted a concept of *generally accepted knowledge*, [...]. The generally accepted knowledge applies to most projects most of the time, and widespread consensus validates its value and effectiveness." (p. 37)

If a BoK in SE is based on "widespread consensus", then the following question arises: How can any BoK in SE address controversial issues in the discipline?

Our paper provides a discussion of this question. To illustrate our position, we look at the recent dispute between supporters of plan-driven and agile software development methods in this paper. We will now argue for the practical importance of this discussion.

A number of competing plan-driven and agile methods exist, and usually their definitions are clearly given in textbooks, etc. The inclusion of this sort of knowledge in a BoK is obviously no challenge. The challenge is, however, to include knowledge necessary to choose the most suitable method in a given situation. Currently, as Boehm and Turner (2004) point out, proponents of plan-driven and agile approaches make conflicting claims of superiority in favour of their preferred methods. We agree with Glass (2004) that the failure of researchers to address the issue of method selection conclusively has led to much disappointment among practitioners, contributing to the gap between theory and practice in SE.

This creates a dilemma for the editors of any BoK in SE, as they have two basic options. Firstly, they can choose to include material, only, where a widespread consensus exists. Secondly, they can include material, too, for which no widespread consensus exists.

The first option has the disadvantage that the BoK would not cover some issues of immense interest for practitioners, and that would make it less useful. As an advantage it would provide clear, unambiguous guidance on the issues covered.

The second option has the disadvantage that the BoK would not only contain knowledge, but also beliefs, opinions, etc., eventually making the very term "body of knowledge" appear as a misnomer. As an advantage it could cover a broader range of issues relevant to practitioners.

We start our discussion in the second section with a look at the nature of belief and knowledge in SE from a philosophical point of view. In the third section we focus on scientific enquiry as a way for the acquisition of knowledge. In the fourth section we address human perception and observation as essential prerequisites for scientific enquiry. In the fifth section we introduce two general research paradigms that are used in SE and point to implications for any BoK in the discipline. In the sixth section we look closer at the recent method war between supporters of plan-driven and agile methods in SE.

Belief and Knowledge

The controversy about agile methods is a clear example of disagreement among experts in SE. It is important to realise that expert opinion represents belief, but not necessarily knowledge.

Indeed philosophers have tried for the last two millennia to define the difference between knowledge and belief, but there is no universal consensus (Jashapara 2004). Ladyman (2002) points out that knowledge is often characterised as justified true belief. This pragmatic characterisation indicates that human knowledge usually satisfies three conditions:

- It is justified, i.e., it results from sound enquiry
- It is true, i.e., it describes some aspects of reality
- It is belief, i.e., it describes an actionable mental state

Here knowledge is characterised as belief with additional, desirable properties. A claim to knowledge implies that, in addition to a belief, these properties are demonstrably present.

If a person holds a belief, that does not imply that another person holding a conflicting belief is wrong, because beliefs are not necessarily true. However, a claim that a specific belief qualifies as knowledge implies that the belief is true, and it means that a person holding a conflicting belief is wrong. While the expression of a belief does not say anything about the quality of beliefs held by others, the expression of knowledge represents a judgement of beliefs held by others as right or wrong. In that sense the expression of a belief as a mere belief may be less controversial than the expression of that belief as if it were knowledge.

The terms "sound enquiry" and "aspects of reality" are obviously in need of elaboration. Graziano and Raulin (2004) point out that historically there have been many mechanisms of belief justification in human societies, for example:

- tradition: beliefs that are inherent in a culture
- intuition: beliefs that mainly result from emotions
- authority: beliefs that are based on trust in the discoverer

These mechanisms have a long history as justifications for beliefs, and thereby as sources of knowledge. Unfortunately they have suffered from a high failure rate due to their inherent subjectivity and arbitrariness. Glass (2003) presents many examples of fallacies in SE resulting from this.

As a consequence another way of belief justification has been developed: scientific enquiry.

Scientific Enquiry

Scientific enquiry is a means to establish the justification and truth of beliefs within a framework of specified procedures that are based on objectivity and logic (Ladyman 2002). That framework defines what sound enquiry means and what the observable aspects of reality are. These common standards shared within the community ensure that knowledge can hardly be controversial.

Graziano and Raulin (2004, p. 37) characterise scientific enquiry: "Indeed, the entire scientific research enterprise can be seen as the development of a framework within which scientists can carry out inductive and deductive reasoning under the most precise conditions. [...] the essence of science is its process of thinking, a process that entails systematic inductive-deductive logic. Science, more than any other way of gaining knowledge, bases its inductive reasoning on carefully observed facts."

There are at least four problems that can make an inductive argument dubious. To illustrate this we assume that a SE method M has been used on 11 projects by its creator C. Of these, 10 were successfully completed, 1 was cancelled by the sponsors due to a reorganisation. A possible inductive inference might be: "Projects where M is used are successful". However, there are problems with this argument:

- Many experts would probably regard 10 observations as insufficient for a convincing inductive argument. However, there is no generally accepted standard regarding the required number of observations for convincing inductive arguments.
- It is likely to assume that the inventor of M was involved in all projects, e.g., in a management role. Therefore, an alternative, equally plausible inductive inference is: "Projects where C has a management role are usually successful."
- An inductive argument is possible only, if there are no contradicting observations. The cancelled project was an application of M, therefore an inductive argument requires to assess its success. Assessment of success for a cancelled project seems to be a dubious idea.
- An inductive argument uses past observations to justify beliefs about the future. Any inductive argument rests on the auxiliary assumption that regularities in the past will continue to exist in the future. But this assumption is particularly questionable in SE, because it is an area with a high rate of technological change.

From these examples we conclude that it can be difficult to make compelling inductive arguments for methods in SE. The same can be said of general theories in SE.

Typical problems with deductive reasoning in SE can be illustrated with the following example. Assumed there are two general "best practices" P1 and P2 in software development. Then it is tempting to create a SE method M comprising P1 and P2. The typical deductive argument in SE can be expressed as follows: "P1 and P2 are 'best practices' individually. M combines P1 and P2, therefore M is a superior method."

For example, Beck (2000) and Jacobson et al. (1999) use this argument as rationale for their SE methods. This sort of thinking is problematic, for the following reasons:

- P1 and P2 may be successful individually, but there is no logical rule to infer that their combination is successful. If each practice works in isolation, it may well be that their combination results in a superior method, but it may equally well be that the result is an inferior method.
- P1 and P2 may be part of M, but there is no logical rule to infer that they cause the performance of M. When M is used to carry out a real software project, then other factors, e.g., strong and effective leadership, etc., may be much more important.
- The notion of "best practice" is one of the most obscure and questionable ideas in SE (Harrison 2004). Therefore, P1 and P2 are obscure and questionable premises, and naturally this applies to any conclusion drawn from them.

A slightly different sort of thinking is used by Beck (2000), p. xv, who gives the following rationale for his SE method called "XP": "To some folks, XP seems like just good common sense. So why the 'extreme' in the name? XP takes commonsense principles and practices to extreme levels." This may seem to be a valid logical argument: If something is commonsense, then taking it to an extreme level should result in extreme commonsense.

The deductive fallacy here is the omission of a central premise in the argument: It is implicitly assumed that scaling up does not reach a point beyond which inefficiencies set in. This assumption is questionable for a complex artefact like a software development method.

The preceding discussion has shown that there are many fundamental problems with scientific enquiry in SE. Additional problems arise from the reliance of scientific enquiry on human perception and observation.

Perception and Observation

Scientific enquiry is based on observations, that are the result of human perception. As Bernstein et al. (1997) note, human perception is not totally objective:

"Perception is the process through which sensations are interpreted, using knowledge and understanding of the world, so that they become meaningful experiences. Thus perception is not a passive process of simply absorbing and decoding incoming sensations. [...] Instead, our brains take sensations and create a coherent world, often by filling in missing information and using past experience to give meaning to what we see, hear, or touch." (p. 126)

Therefore, observations are not fully objective, too.

Three fundamental problems with observations in empirical SE can be illustrated with a simple example of a software project P where a development method M is used. To evaluate M it is straightforward to ask the following questions:

1. Was M properly applied in P?
2. Was P successful?
3. Was M causative of the outcome?

To answer the first question, one would have to assess the complete history of P, and the assessor would need to have a thorough understanding of M. It is obvious that any such assessment would be difficult. It would also be subjective because it would depend on the knowledge, skill, bias and preferences of the assessor.

To answer the second question, a definition of success would be required. However, there is no single, straightforward definition of software project success. Wateridge (1998) looks at different stakeholders in IS/IT projects and points out that many different criteria for project success are used in SE. The adoption of a specific set of criteria is arbitrary to some degree, and as a result the second question can only be answered with some subjectivity.

An answer to the third question relates to one of the most difficult areas in the philosophy of science: causation. Basically causation can never be conclusively proved, and it is a subject of ongoing philosophical debate (Ladyman 2002). Naturally this creates potential for disagreement, particularly in the light of a statement by Pfleeger (2005, p. 68), who claims: "Sometimes researchers are eager to show a positive result, even when they're trying hard to design an objective study. This situation is particularly true for doctoral candidates and for creators of a new technology, who prefer a positive rather than negative result." Wishful thinking, personal aims, economic interests, and ideological affiliation can occasionally compromise observations in SE.

Graziano and Raulin (2004) highlight another factor that can undermine the validity of observations, namely "the phenomenon of participants behaving differently than they might normally because they know that they are being observed" (pp. 136). Their remark illustrates that scientific observation is never entirely passive, instead, in order to make observations, researchers must interact with the subjects under observation in some way. Referring to the famous "Hawthorne studies", Babbie (2001) illustrates the tremendous confounding influence these observer effects can have on scientific enquiry.

We conclude that knowledge gained through scientific enquiry in SE is subjective to some degree, because totally objective and valid data cannot be obtained. To that extent discovery and validation of knowledge remain a unique, personal experience of the individual.

Research Paradigms

In the philosophy of science several general research paradigms have been identified. Two of the most widespread are logical positivism and social constructivism (Klee 1997).

Logical positivism rests on the assumption that knowledge can be isolated from the social context in which it emanates. According to this view objective knowledge can be gained through the rigorous use of the scientific method.

Social constructivism, on the other hand, rests on the assumption that the experience of the world by human beings is their personal construction in relation to their social context. Social constructivists usually deny the existence of completely objective knowledge and believe that human knowledge is intrinsically personal, resulting from subjective interpretations of unique interactions with the environment.

We now refer to Jacobson et al. (1999) on plan-driven software development and Cockburn (2002) on agile software development to show that the positions of logical positivism and social constructivism are both present in SE.

In their book Jacobson et al. (1999) voice the belief that a single "best process" for software development can be found: "We need such a process [...]. Any old process will not do; we need one that will be the *best* process the industry is capable of putting together at this point in its history" (p. xviii). Clearly this reflects a logical positivist attitude to knowledge generation in SE: A best process can be found. This suggests that the SE community should try hard to find it, and it should be included in the SE BoK under the label "The Best Software Development Process". Alternative software development processes should only be mentioned for their historical role, and their use should be discouraged.

Cockburn (2002) voices a quite different attitude towards software development processes: "A methodology is the conventions that your group agrees to. The conventions your group agrees to is a social construction. It is also a construction that you can and should revisit from time to time" (p. 115). This remark reveals a social constructivist position. Later Cockburn (2002) gives this advice to users of methodologies: "Beware the methodology author. Your experiences with a methodology may have a lot to do with how well your personal habits align with those of the methodology author" (p. 148). This ouvert social constructivist attitude to knowledge generation in SE implies: A best process cannot be found. Different processes are more or less useful dependent on personal, social, cultural and a diversity of other factors. Due to differing personal opinions within the SE community, any such BoK would be contentious to a degree. It would be a body of beliefs and knowledge, rather than a pure BoK. Such a body of beliefs and knowledge should include all relevant software development processes together with information regarding their applicability. To some extent this body of beliefs and knowledge would be diverse, complex, incomplete, ambiguous and inconsistent.

It is not difficult to imagine that such a body of beliefs and knowledge, whether it is explicitly documented or implicitly held in the community, can result in controversy, for example, the infamous SE method wars.

Method Wars

The area of software development methods is characterised by diversity, change and disagreement. Anecdotal evidence of success as well as failure can be found for any method, while scientific evidence for their effectiveness or efficiency is almost non-existent, and there exists little reliable guidance on choosing an appropriate method in a given situation (Avison and Fitzgerald 2003).

Glass (2001) rightly notes that the "method wars" between advocates of agile and plan-driven methods are largely based on conflicting beliefs. He points out that many principles of plan-driven methods are simply beliefs. He also notes that the "Manifesto for Agile Software Development" (Agile Alliance 2001) is mainly a collection of beliefs.

These two sets of beliefs are clearly different, but currently there is no compelling evidence in favour of one over the other (Baskerville et al. 2003; Boehm and Turner 2004).

Unfortunately many people in SE present their beliefs as if they were knowledge. For example, the Manifesto for Agile Software Development starts with the claim, "We are uncovering better ways of developing software by doing it and helping others do it. [...]", and under the label "Principles behind the Agile Manifesto" it contains the following statements:

- "The most efficient and effective method of conveying information to and within a development team is face-to-face conversation."
- "The best architectures, requirements, and designs emerge from self-organizing teams."

We regard these claims as very contentious. To us they do not sound like humble expressions of belief, but bold claims to knowledge. At least the presentation in the Manifesto appears ambiguous and provocative.

It should be noted that the Manifesto does not refer to any clear evidence to justify the claims expressed in it, and we are not aware of the existence of convincing evidence to support these claims.

We share the opinion of Boehm and Turner (2004) that unjustified claims to knowledge in the debate about plan-driven and agile methods are sources of perplexity that have led to confusion and acrimony in the SE community. Given the ambiguous and provocative style of the Manifesto it does not come as a surprise that it is a source of controversy in the SE community.

In our opinion there is a clear lesson to be learned from the debate about plan-driven and agile methods: The members of the community should more clearly distinguish between beliefs and knowledge. Inappropriate claims to knowledge, ambiguous statements and provocative language are certainly effective rhetorical techniques for method marketing, but they are not necessarily signs of serious and respectful discourse.

At present the discussion of plan-driven and agile methods is one of the most relevant and most controversial issues in SE, with profound implications for professional practice (Boehm and Turner 2004).

That clearly illustrates the dilemma that editors of any BoK in this discipline face: the trade-offs between scope and reliability of the included material. If they choose to include material, only, for which there is a widespread consensus, then the resulting BoK may be reliable, but there is a danger that its scope is reduced considerably, potentially resulting in an incomplete representation of highly relevant issues. If, on the other hand, they include material, too, for which there is no widespread consensus, then the resulting BoK may have a broader scope, but there is a danger that its contents is arbitrary to a degree, making it vulnerable to political manipulation and criticism.

In the SWEBOK (IEEE 2004), for example, selection between plan-driven and agile methods is barely covered. Indeed the keyword "agile" is only found four times in the entire document. Obviously the editors avoid a highly controversial issue that way, but the result is a BoK that does not provide guidance on an important contemporary issue.

Conclusion

SE is a discipline with an enormous and complex BoK. Most of that knowledge has been arrived at through careful research following respectable scientific standards. In parallel to that knowledge, an influential body of beliefs operates, often justified by tradition, intuition or authority.

There exist no clear, universal criteria to distinguish knowledge from belief in a completely objective way, but the pragmatic definition of knowledge as justified true belief provides some useful criteria. These criteria suggest to distinguish knowledge from belief in discourse very carefully. If a belief is expressed as knowledge, this implies a judgement of the quality of beliefs held by others. To that extent claims to knowledge are potentially more controversial than clear expressions of belief.

Tradition, intuition or authority as mechanisms of belief justification are highly subjective and fallible. To avoid these problems scientific enquiry offers an alternative way of knowledge generation based on objectivity and logic. However, a closer examination reveals problems.

Apart from some particular problems with induction and deduction in SE, the reliance of any scientific enquiry on potentially fallible and subjective human perception and observation makes it vulnerable to subjectivity and manipulation to some extent.

Causation is one of the most critical areas in the philosophy of science. Basically causation can never be conclusively proved or disproved in any scientific field. This leaves much room for speculation, and in SE there is a rich culture of anecdotal success stories making claims that the use of a specific method led to the success of a particular project. Claims of that sort cannot be confirmed or ruled out within the framework of scientific enquiry, but they should be regarded with a certain amount of scepticism, because of their dubious nature.

SE is a human activity, and observation of subjects is part of almost all empirical research in the field. Observer effects on the subjects under study can have confounding influence on observations and constitute a possible source of distortion.

Our analysis in this paper suggests that scientific enquiry in SE suffers from some fundamental problems that make it subjective and fallible to a degree. Therefore, research in SE sometimes does not result in general, clear, absolute statements. Inevitably the result is a BoK that is not completely objective, but includes some contentious issues on which there is disagreement among experts. In these cases software engineers will have to base their decisions on tradition, intuition, authority, etc., rather than compelling scientific evidence.

While the traditional account of objective science is still widely in use, many contributors to the philosophy of science question the possibility of total objectivity in general. Instead they suggest that scientific knowledge is often influenced by social and political processes and not only the pure result of objective scientific evidence. This diversity is reflected in the positions of logical positivism and social constructivism, that are widespread in SE. These research paradigms are based on conflicting assumptions about the nature of knowledge, enquiry and reality. Different research paradigms imply very different bodies of knowledge in SE. Therefore, it is important to be aware of their assumptions and implications.

In our opinion there is a clear lesson to be learned from the debate about plan-driven and agile methods: The members of the community need to distinguish more clearly between beliefs and knowledge. We regard the Manifesto for Agile Software Development as a collection of beliefs that are presented as if these beliefs were knowledge. Given this ambiguity it does not come as a surprise that the Manifesto has become a source of controversy in the SE community.

Our investigation in this paper has revealed some reasons to suggest that a certain level of disagreement in SE is inevitable, and these reasons are there to stay in the future. Most of these reasons are inherent in any form of scientific enquiry, and they should not be mistaken as indicators of specific immaturity of SE as a discipline.

The editors of any BoK in SE face a dilemma: the trade-offs between scope and reliability of the included material. Our investigation shows that decisions regarding these trade-offs are arbitrary to some degree, and a balanced decision is necessary to arrive at a useful BoK with sufficient scope and reliability to bridge the gap between theory and practice successfully. However, any BoK in SE will be imperfect in some way, and we regard it as desirable to promote a culture of critical thinking in the field to prepare software engineers to deal with these shortcomings effectively.

References

Agile Alliance (2001) Manifesto for Agile Software Development. www.AgileAlliance.org (accessed June 26, 2005)

Avison DE, Fitzgerald G (2003) Where Now for Development Methodologies? Communications of the ACM, vol 46, no 1, pp 78-82

Babbie E (2001) The Practice of Social Research. Wadsworth.

Baskerville R, Balasubramaniam R, Levine L, Pries-Heje J, Slaughter S (2003) Is Internet-Speed Software Development Different? IEEE Software, November/December, pp 70-77

Beck K (2000) Extreme Programming Explained. Addison-Wesley

Bernstein DA, Clarke-Stewart A, Roy EJ, Wickens CD (1997) Psychology. Houghton Mifflin

Boehm B, Turner R (2004) Balancing Agility and Discipline. Addison-Wesley

Bourque P, Dupuis R, Abran A, Moore JW, Tripp L (1999) The Guide to the Software Engineering Body of Knowledge. IEEE Software, November/December, pp 35-44

Cockburn A (2002) Agile Software Development. Addison-Wesley

Glass RL (2001) Agile Versus Traditional: Make Love, Not War. Cutter IT Journal, vol 14, no 12, pp 12-18

Glass RL (2003) Facts and Fallacies of Software Engineering. Addison-Wesley

Glass RL (2004) Matching Methodology to Problem Domain. Communications of the ACM, vol 47, no 5, pp 19-21

Graziano AM, Raulin ML (2004) Research Methods. Pearson

Harrison W (2004) Best Practices: Who Says? IEEE Software, January/February, pp 8-9

IEEE (2004) Guide to the Software Engineering Body of Knowledge (SWEBOK, 2004 Version). Institute of Electrical and Electronics Engineers (IEEE). www.swebok.org (accessed June 26, 2005)

Jacobson I, Booch G, Rumbaugh J (1999) The Unified Software Development Process. Addison-Wesley

Jashapara A (2004) Knowledge Management. Prentice Hall

Klee R (1997) Introduction to the Philosophy of Science. Oxford University Press

Ladyman J (2002) Understanding Philosophy of Science. Routledge

Pfleeger SL (2005) The Role of Evidential Force in Empirical Software Engineering. IEEE Software, January/February, pp 66-73

Wateridge J (1998) How can IS/IT projects be measured for success? International Journal of Project Management, vol 16, no 1, pp. 59-63

A Relational Perspective on Knowledge Integration between Self-Contained Work Groups: A Case Study in the Health Care Sector

May Wismén[1] and Sven Carlsson[2]

[1] Department of Informatics, Jönköping International Business School, Sweden. may.wismen@jibs.hj.se
[2] Department of Informatics, School of Economics and Management, Lund University, Sweden. sven.carlsson@.ics.lu.se

Introduction

For many organizations, their abilities to create, share, exchange, integrate, and use knowledge have major impacts on their performance (Nonaka and Takeuchi 1995; von Krogh et al. 2000); and organizations are increasingly dependent on different types of intra- and inter-organizational collaborations (Malone 2004). This paper focuses on intra-organizational collaboration between different self-contained work groups. A self-contained work group has specific goals and the primary resources it needs to perform its tasks, but since it is part of an organization it also needs to have different types of intra- and inter-organizational relationships. Information systems (IS), which can be manual, digital, or a combination, can play different roles in the transfer of information between individuals and groups. Since information transferred between collaborating self-contained work groups must be interpreted, it can be fruitful to explore the collaboration process from a knowledge and knowledge integration perspective. An increased understanding of this area can enhance explaining and designing of such processes. The overall research questions are: how knowledge integration between self-contained work groups is performed, and if there are inaccuracies in the process, how can we explain why the integration is less than successful.

The context selected for the study is a public medical service, more specifically, a microbiology laboratory and four of its customers. To provide good medical treatment, specialists and occupational groups must develop knowledge internally, but they must also exchange information and knowledge with other groups. When a patient sees a physician, for example, knowledge are compiled about the patient's problems and possible treatment. Clinical laboratories are one type of service units that physicians might use as further external information and knowledge sources. Physicians and nurses may be seen as customers who request analyses from the laboratories who consequently receive laboratory reports. For this to work, customers and laboratory personnel must have deep knowledge about the analyses and what information should be transferred. This brief presentation of the case context illustrates why it is a good context for studying knowledge integration between self-contained work groups.

Next we present our key concepts related to knowledge and knowledge perspectives. This is followed by a presentation of our analytical knowledge integration model, which has been used to guide the empirical study and in the analysis. Thereafter three sections with presentations of the research approach, the case and the case analysis. The analysis is organised according to three sub-questions followed by our main research questions. The three sub-questions are: 1) how is knowledge integrated between laboratory and customers, 2) how is the integrated knowledge created, and 3) how is the integrated knowledge used. The final section presents conclusions and suggests further research.

Knowledge and Knowledge Perspective

Knowledge may be seen both from an individual level and a group level. Tsoukas and Vlademirou (2001) define individual knowledge as "...the individual ability to draw distinctions within a collective domain of action, based on appreciation of context or theory, or both" (p. 979); knowledge becomes organisational when "...as well as drawing distinctions in the course of their work by taking into account the contextuallity of their actions, *individuals draw and act upon a corpus of generalizations in the form of generic rules produced by the organization*" (p. 979). The definitions illustrate how we may say that different work groups have knowledge as a result of established ways of working. The definitions highlight *contextualization* and that knowledge, even if it is seen as an individual capability, is created and used in a *social environment*. To these two critical concepts, contextualization and socialization, we add a third concept: *process* thinking. There are two dominating perspectives within the knowledge management field: 1) knowledge as an object which can be codified, stored, and distributed, and 2) knowledge as a knowing process (Blackler 1995; Hayes and Walsham 2003). The latter perspective emphasizes social relationships as knowledge development structures and mechanisms. Knowledge is situated in people's heads, but as a result of social interactions also in a group of people (community) who share a common interest. Hayes and Walsham's (2003) concept for this perspective is the *relational perspective*, with which they also bring out knowledge as a context dependent process. Knowing represents a process of acquiring knowledge, which is situated and relational. Spender (2003) argues that an organization is an instrument for integrating knowledge and activities, and should not be seen as a stock of knowledge.

There are different concepts which are used to describe how knowledge flows between individuals and between groups (i.e. Bechky 2003). Following Grant (1996), we use the concept *integration*. The essence of integration is well illustrated by a quotation: "If Grant and Spender wish to write a joint paper together, efficiency is maximized not by Grant learning everything that Spender knows (and vice versa), but by establishing a mode of interaction such that Grant's knowledge of economics is integrated with Spender's knowledge of philosophy, psychology and technology, while minimizing the time spent transferring knowledge between them." (Grant 1996, p. 114).

An Analytical Knowledge Integration Model

One knowledge theory that is founded on a relational perspective is Communities of Practice (COP), which is a social theory about situated learning (Lave and Wenger 1991). A COP is a group of connected people who share engagement, have a common meaning of what they are doing and how they are doing it (Wenger 1998). Learning in a COP, is a continuous process, as a movement from peripheral participation to full membership in a group. This learning process is often messy and partly "invisible". Participation, identity, experience and practice are important factors in the theory. When you participate in a group of people, you create your identity and get more and more experienced. Practice is all the social activities in which we participate. When we do things, we use language, tools, explicit and implicit rules, roles, and tacit knowledge. The creation of meaning is an important component in practice, which takes place through two processes: *participation* and *reification* (ibid.). Participation refers to the situations when we are active in social situations; we talk, think and have both positive and negative feelings. Reification refers to methods for creating shortcuts in our communication; examples of reifications are laws, procedures, categorizations, or tools.

Collective Knowledge

We focus on knowledge integration processes between self-contained work groups. Hence, we focus on what happens between the recognition of needing knowledge and the point when that need is satisfied. Holsapple and Joshi's (2003) model for knowledge processes (knowledge management episodes) captures this process. An episode is a collection of different activities and these involve a number of knowledge resources. Knowledge management episodes can result in learning, i.e. change in the organization's knowledge resources, and projection, i.e. knowledge embedded in products or services.

The knowledge resources are purpose (the organization's goals, and objectives), strategy (plans for achieving the purpose), culture (values, principles, norms, and unwritten rules), infrastructure (roles and relationships between the roles), artifacts (i.e. videotapes, books, memory notes, manuals, and products), and participants' knowledge.

Within an episode, several activities may take place. When a need for knowledge is identified, internal or external knowledge may be used and therefore, one activity is to select knowledge from previously developed knowledge resources and another is to acquire knowledge from external sources. Both types of knowledge may be used immediately or be stored for later knowledge management episodes. A using activity is divided into two sub-activities: *generating* and *externalizing*. Generating refers to an internal process where the knowledge used is evaluated and synthesized to new knowledge. Externalizing takes place when knowledge becomes available outside the own organization (or unit) and includes projection in products or physical activities. From the using activity new knowledge is internalized in the organization and includes value estimating the new knowledge, and decisions about which of the existing knowledge resources that shall be influenced. Accordingly, it should be determined within this activity whether the new knowledge shall disseminate within the group, if it shall be formalized in routine descriptions, etc.

An Analytical Model of Knowledge Integration between Groups

Since we shall describe and explain knowledge integration between self-contained work groups, we need to take a closer look at how knowledge is acquired. The theory of COP includes means for knowledge integration between groups: *boundary objects*[1] and *brokers*. A boundary object, e.g. an

---

[1] The boundary object concept originates from Star & Griesemer (1989)

IS, is a reification that can be viewed from different group perspectives. Brokers refer to human beings having a kind of multi-membership and having working roles comprising integration of knowledge between groups.

Figure 1 depicts our model of knowledge integration between self-contained work groups (incl. COPs). It is a combination and integration of the two main theories presented above. In the combined model, which is thoroughly discussed in Wismén (2004), the external sources as well as internal knowledge resources may be captured in different COPs (here exemplified with two overlapping COPs). There may exist common COPs between internal and external work groups, which can function as knowledge integration mechanisms (COP with dotted boundary line). As complements, or instead of a common COP, boundary objects and/or brokers may handle the knowledge integration.

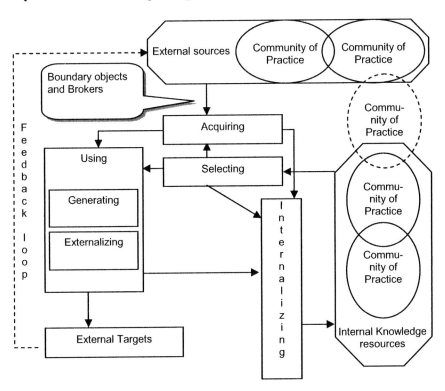

Fig. 1. An analytical model of knowledge integration between and within work groups and COPs (modified from Holsapple and Joshi 2003, p. 105)

Background and Method for the Case Study

The empirical data was collected in the Swedish health care sector and we focused on knowledge integration between a microbiology laboratory and four of its customers. The communication between laboratories and customers has traditionally been made using paper-based orders (referrals) and paper-based answers (laboratory reports). Information transfer in the Swedish medical service is now changing rapidly, and the ordering-reporting process is to be digitalized in 2005. This study, which is one part of a large longitudinal study focusing on changing working practices and routines as a result of computerisation, examines the use of the current paper-based ordering-reporting IS. (The first author has extensive microbiology education and microbiology laboratory work experience.)

The microbiology laboratory is a county comprehensive specialty that diagnoses diseases caused by bacteria, viruses, fungi, parasites, and immunological reactions. Two of the customers are primary care centers and the other two are hospital wards. In the laboratory, two observations and two interviews (laboratory instructor and laboratory physician) were carried out. The observations consisted of participating in laboratory technicians' ongoing analysis work. The customer interviews were done with two to five individuals (physicians, nurses, local laboratory technicians and assistant nurse) from each centre. All materials from the observations and the interviews were written down and analysed using our research questions and model. Internal knowledge resources and external knowledge sources were identified, and the different integration activities were studied to identify common COPs, boundary objects and brokers.

Case Analysis

How is Knowledge Integrated between Laboratory and Customers?

The customer makes an analysis order (referral), taking a specimen and sending the referral together with the specimen to the laboratory. The laboratory technicians choose the analysis method, analyse the specimen and make a laboratory report to the customer. The customer receives the laboratory report and makes an interpretation of its information.

In the analysis model this referral, specimen and laboratory report are externalized knowledge in the *using* activity. This externalizing is done against the laboratory's respective the customers' external targets. The referrals consist of a number of predefined text fields where the customer shall write, for example, patient identity and name, clinical data, diagnosis and expected laboratory findings. Furthermore, there are small checkboxes that customers may tick for analysis or telling the laboratory which type of specimen they have taken. The laboratory tries to elicit all the necessary information through the predefined fields and checkboxes, but the study showed many examples where the customers gave insufficient or wrong information. For example, if the referral did not include information about how deep an ulcer is, some important bacteria may be overlooked.

The specimens that are sent to the laboratory can be all types of body fluids or secretions. To perform an analysis, the laboratory must get specimens that were taken correctly, but our study showed several examples where the specimens were taken incorrectly or were unsuitable. When the analysis is finalized, the laboratory sends the laboratory report to the customer. This answer may consist of preprinted text that tells the customer what the analysis has showed, or numbers (measurements) together with a short interpretation guideline. If the preprinted alternatives do not cover the result of an analysis, laboratory personnel may write an adjusted answer or explanation.

How is the Integrated Knowledge Created?

The creation of integrated knowledge in the model is represented by the *acquiring*, *selecting*, and *generating* activities. Both acquiring and selecting may be done through *COPs*, which can be internal, external or shared between laboratory and customers. External knowledge may also be acquired by means of *boundary objects* and/or *brokers*.

Different internal *COPs* are identified. Both the customers and the laboratory expressed, for example, a clear picture of how less experienced employees were learning from the more experienced. Some also stressed the learning between different occupational groups, e.g. nurses and local laboratory technicians who learn from physicians, but the closeness of the occupational groups varied which affected the learning extent. It was difficult to identify COPs that were shared between customers and the laboratory. This indicates that the major knowledge integration is done through boundary objects or brokers.

Three main *boundary objects* were identified. Referrals may be seen as a boundary object since they are a kind of communication document between the customers and the laboratory. Some fields on the referral are easy for the customer to interpret, e.g. where to specify concrete facts about the patient, while others are more demanding, e.g. fields which shall contain clinical data, diagnosis and expected laboratory findings. The rules say that all ordering shall be done by a physician, but they often leave the active writing of the referral to nurses or other personnel. In one of the units some referrals were written by the local laboratory technicians, and they had no access to the patient record system, which means that they could not provide the referral with all the relevant information.

Another type of boundary object is the laboratory reports that are sent back to the customers. Physicians shall interpret the reports, but in all the studied units, nurses make the first interpretation and give signals to physicians if there are some acute actions that must be taken. The laboratory is creating the reports with physicians' medical knowledge and responsibility in mind and when nurses handle the reports they must obtain this knowledge, but in some cases, the nurses have difficulties with the interpretation.

The third type of boundary object is instructions for specimen taking and specimen handling. These instructions are, since summer 2001, published on the county council's intranet and are constantly updated. Only two of the customers interviewed (employees at the same unit) say that they use the intranet for this purpose. The other respondents use an old version of the instructions, which is published in book form and has not been updated since 1994.

Individuals that work as *brokers* can be seen both at the laboratory and at the customers units. In the laboratory, the physicians and a laboratory technician who is employed as instructor have these roles since their work tasks comprise informing customers and answering their queries. The instructor is known by the customers' local laboratory technicians, but not by other occupational groups. The laboratory physicians are more widely known, but several of the customers say that they hardly ever spoke to them. The most mentioned name is instead one of the secretaries at the laboratory, because she is the first person they speak to when they call the laboratory. She often is able to answer customer queries.

On the customers' side, some individuals with more knowledge about microbiological analyses than others are identified. Their extra knowledge comes from special education, special interest or special work tasks. These customer brokers spread their knowledge in their work groups, but they are not known as resources by the laboratory.

Besides acquiring external knowledge sources, *internal knowledge resources* are selected. The knowledge that resides in the individuals, internal group or organization affects the integration process since people have established certain ways of working. The internal knowledge resources - purpose, strategy, culture, infrastructure, participants' knowledge, and artefacts – may all be disseminated within COP. In most cases the resources are the first input in knowledge episodes, and they are often unconscious.

The four customer units and the laboratory belong to the same county council and have several knowledge resources in common. In this council overall purpose, strategies, infrastructure and artefacts are defined, but local adaptations seem to be more important for the daily work. Local adaptations could be identified in formal documents like vision documents, goal descriptions, work descriptions and job definitions. However, the most important adaptations seem to be the informal and unwritten rules that guide the work activities. Participants' knowledge may also to a certain extent be predefined and formalised. Positions in health care require specially trained personnel, but the study shows that individual interests and experiences vary. In the knowledge process the individual knowledge resources seem to be more important than formal education, position or job description.

How is the Integrated Knowledge Used?

The use of integrated knowledge includes generating new knowledge and the externalizing activity. An additional activity, *internalizing*, is crucial. In this activity the new knowledge becomes available for coming knowledge processes. The COP-theory emphasizes internalizing, especially how tacit knowledge is shared between people in a group. Internalization concerns participants' knowledge, but also other knowledge resources.

The total knowledge process implies that every situation where knowledge is used is a new knowledge management episode: taking a specimen, ordering an analysis, interpreting a referral, analysing the specimen, creating the laboratory report and interpreting the report. Previous knowledge resources are selected for the new situation, if it is necessary external sources are added, and new knowledge is created. Even if no external knowledge is added, successive learning takes place in the COP, due to the individuals' increased experiences, and that will influence the next knowledge episode.

Problems in the Knowledge Integration

The first part of our research question – how is knowledge integration between self-contained work groups performed – was addressed above. We identified some problems that may occur in the process. For example, referrals can be provided with insufficient or inadequate information and specimens may be wrongly taken, which may result in non-relevant analyses. Nurses may have problems interpreting laboratory reports, which can result in uncertainty about the importance of the laboratory finding.

Using the analysis model, some explanations for the problems can be identified and remedies suggested. If the external targets shall be known by the knowledge senders, there must exist some knowledge integration mediators. There are internal COPs in the different units, but it was difficult to find COP that cross the boundary between the laboratory and customers. Another possibility is boundary objects, which were identified as referrals, laboratory reports and instructions for specimen taking and specimen handling. Because of the inaccurate or missing information in the referrals, we can suggest that they are not always adequate as boundary objects. This may depend on the design of the referrals or ignorance of the person who ordered it. The same reasoning can be applied to the laboratory reports. Instructions are available on the intranet about how to take a specimen and how to order an analysis. However, there was a clear tendency to use an old version of these instructions which means that the laboratory has difficulties to disseminate any changes and news.

The third knowledge mediators are brokers. Even if brokers are identified, their brokering role is not complete. Brokers have a sort of double membership, because they belong to different COP at the same time (Wenger 1998). The brokers identified in this study belong to one setting; therefore their full potential is not utilized. Since they are not known by the different COPs, their knowledge integration capacity is limited.

The analysis of this knowledge integration also shows some potential problems in the internalizing activity. There is no consistent routine at the laboratory, which implies that customers do not get feedback if information at referral is insufficient or inadequate. If the customers do not know, and if they do not actively check the laboratory report against the information they send to the laboratory, they probably will internalise the knowledge that the whole process was successful, even if it was not. If the specimens are obviously wrong, the laboratory can contact the customer, but if the laboratory personnel are not able to see the errors, for instance, if a specimen that must be kept in the refrigerator has been stored at room temperature, the laboratory reports may contain information that is not relevant for the patient. In the same way, personnel in the laboratory do not normally get any feedback from the customers after receiving their laboratory reports. Consequently the laboratory personnel do not know how the customers interpret the given information and whether the report is relevant or if it could have been done better.

Other important factors in this integration process are the internal knowledge resources in the shape of organization purpose, strategies, etc.. Because of the local adoptions there are large differences between the customers. If the laboratory gives information to customers, they will interpret it through their previous knowledge resources. This means that there may be difficulties for the laboratory to treat all customers in the same way. This also means that the IS, as a boundary object, must be able to handle all different customers in a way that is appropriate for both the laboratory and the customers. The study suggests that this is questionable.

Conclusion and Further Research

El Sawy et al. (2001) identify three modes of shared knowledge creation (in this study knowledge integration): informing, coordinating and collaborating. Our analytical model and the empirical study, focusing on the less well-researched collaborating mode (view), have enhanced our understanding of knowledge integration between self-contained work groups. Based on the study, we draw some conclusions and identify a number of interesting issues to explore further.

One conclusion is that if knowledge integration between groups shall be successful, knowledge intermediaries as shared COP, boundary objects or brokers must be functioning well. Interesting questions related to the relationships between intermediaries can be generated. For example, can we design computerized IS which handle knowledge integration without changing other boundary objects, brokers and shared COP?

Another conclusion is the importance of feedback. When knowledge is integrated the receiving group internalizes new knowledge in its internal knowledge resources. If feedback is missing, wrong knowledge may be internalized, and successively strengthened. This conclusion leads to the research question: How can we design computerized IS to get good feedback?

The third conclusion is that the internal knowledge resources, like organizational purpose, strategy, culture and infrastructure, are important in the internal integration process, but the variations and local adjustments affect the knowledge integration between the self-contained work groups. The study shows that IS are mutually dependent on other knowledge resources. This leads to the research question: how is a computerized IS, having a built in standardization, affecting and being affected by varying internal resources? Boudreau and Robey (2005) showed in their study of an ERP system that users first avoided the new system and tried to keep their old working routines, and then found ways to work around what they thought were limitations in the system. Will the laboratory customers respond in the same way?

References

Bechky BA (2003) Sharing Meaning Across Occupational Communities: The Transformation of Understanding on a Production Floor. Organization Science, vol 14, no 3, pp 312-330

Blackler F (1995) Knowledge, Knowledge Work and Organizations: An Overview and Interpretation. Organization Studies, vol 16, no 6, pp 1021-1046

Boudreau M-C, Robey D (2005) Enacting Integrated Information Technology: A Human Agency Perspective. Organization Science, vol 16, no 1, pp 3-18

El Sawy OA, Eriksson I, Raven A, Carlsson, S (2001) Understanding Shared Knowledge Creation Spaces around Business Processes: Precursors to Process Innovation Implementation. International Journal of Technology Management, vol 22, no 1/2/3, pp 149-173

Grant RM (1996) Toward a Knowledge-based Theory of the Firm. Strategic Management Journal, vol 17 (Special Issue: Knowledge and the Firm), pp 109-122

Hayes N, Walsham G (2003) Knowledge Sharing and ICTs: A relational Perspective. In: Easterby-Smith M, Lyles MA (eds) The Blackwell Handbook of Organizational Learning and Knowledge Management. Blackwell Publishing USA

Holsapple CW, Joshi KD (2003) A Knowledge Management Ontology. In: Holsapple CW (ed) Handbook on Knowledge Management 1. Spinger-Verlag Berlin

Lave J, Wenger E (1991) Situated Learning. Legitimate Peripheral Participation, Cambridge University Press Cambridge

Malone TW (2004) The Future of Work. Harvard Business School Press Boston

Nonaka I, Takeuchi H (1995) The Knowledge-Creating Company. Oxford University Press New York

Spender J-C (2003) Knowledge Fields: Some Post-9/11 Thoughts about the Knowledge-Based Theory of the Firm. In: Holsapple CW (ed) Handbook on Knowledge Management 1. Spinger-Verlag Berlin

Star SL, Griesemer JR (1989) Institutional Ecology, 'Translations' and Boundary Objects: Amateurs and Professionals in Berkely's Museum of Vertebrate Zoology, 1907-39. Social Studies of Science, no 19, pp 387-420

Tsoukas H, Vlademinrou E (2001) What is Organizational Knowledge? Journal of Management Studies, vol 38, no 7, pp 973-993

von Krogh G, Nonaka I, Nishiguchi T (eds) (2000) Knowledge Creation: A Source of Value. Macmillan Press London

Wenger E (1998) Communities of Practice: Learning, Meaning, and Identity. Cambridge University Press Cambridge

Wismén M (2004) Knowledge Transformation between Different Working Groups: a Model for Description and Analysis. Proc of the 27th Information Systems Research Seminar in Scandinavia

The Birth, Death, and Resurrection of an SPI Project

Sven Carlsson and Mikael Schönström

Department of Informatics, School of Economics and Management, Lund University, Sweden.
sven.carlsson@ics.lu.se, mikael_schonstrom@hermes.ics.lu.se

Introduction

Commentators on contemporary themes of strategic management and firm competitiveness stress that a firm's competitive advantage flows from its unique knowledge and how it manages knowledge, and for many firms their ability to create, share, exchange, and use knowledge have a major impact on their competitiveness (Nonaka & Teece 2001). In software development, knowledge management (KM) plays an increasingly important role. It has been argued that the KM-field is an important source for creating new perspectives on the software development process (Iivari 2000). Several Software Process Improvement (SPI) approaches stress the importance of managing knowledge and experiences as a way for improving software processes (Ahern et al. 2001). Another SPI-trend is the use of ideas from process management like in the Capability Maturity Model (CMM). Unfortunately, little research on the effects of the use of process management ideas in SPI exists. Given the influx of process management ideas to SPI, the impact of these ideas should be addressed.

This paper presents and discusses an SPI project in a high-technology company. The case illustrates how two common KM approaches—networking and codification—were used in the SPI project. It also illustrates how process management ideas were to be implemented in the SPI project and the advantages and disadvantages of these process management ideas. The purpose of this paper is twofold. First, *to present and discuss an SPI initiative that used two completely different approaches through its different stages and went through some problematic times.* Second, based on the case, theories, frameworks, and concepts, discuss a critical SPI-issue: *how to strike a balance between exploitation and exploration in software development and SPI and how the use of ambidextrous organizational forms can provide a means for striking this balance.*

The next section presents KM, process management, and SPI. It is followed by a presentation of the firm studied (called GAMMA) and its business context. GAMMA is a software company within a large telecommunication equipment company (ALPHA). The fourth section focuses on the SPI-initiative at GAMMA. It presents the rise, death, and resurrection of the initiative. The fifth section discusses what we can learn from GAMMA's SPI-initiative. The section raises one issue neglected in the SPI-literature—exploitation versus exploration—and discusses an organizational form for striking a balance between exploitation and exploration. The final section presents conclusion and discusses future research.

KM, Process Management, and SPI

The core business process chosen for this study is software development in a high-technology company—a telecommunication equipment company. In GAMMA, software development is a new product development (NPD) process. There are several reasons for choosing NPD and software development as study object. First, NPD is a business process that is highly knowledge-intensive and one of the key business processes for creating new organizational knowledge. Second, software development is in most cases done through projects. To learn from previous projects and to share knowledge between projects are critical.

The products developed and marketed by ALPHA consist mainly of software. Of the average product cost, 70% is related to software costs and 30% to hardware costs. High costs related to software development and a limited success ratio in software development projects make the case for KM within software processes even stronger. In software development, as well as in other core business processes, KM plays a critical role in the generation and implementation of innovations, and thus provides both an interesting area for KM-research and an excellent leverage point for project improvements (El Sawy et al. 2001). Although this study focuses on SPI, its results and learning are likely to be applicable to other core business processes and projects where KM is a critical capability.

SPI is an approach to systematic and continuous improvement of a software producing organisation's ability to produce and deliver quality software within time and budget constraints. SPI emphasises incremental and cumulative improvements and addresses all aspects of the software process; i.e. the practices of the software professionals, planning and production procedures, documentation, organisation, and management (Humphrey 1995; Paulk et al. 1993). The CMM principles have been extended to other areas, like software acquisition and product management. These have been integrated in CMM Integrated (Ahern et al. 2001). The SPI "movement" has been heavily influenced by ideas, models, measures, etc. from the process management field and especially of ideas for process management improvement. Unfortunately, the use of these ideas, models, measures, etc. in SPI have not been scrutinized.

GAMMA and its Business Context

GAMMA is a company within a large telecommunication equipment company (ALPHA). GAMMA designs and develops software for management systems for mobile phone systems and telephony and data communication switches. GAMMA, in part, establishes product requirements for the software it designs and develops. This can be based on agreements with customers as well as based on ideas for new products and services. GAMMA is located at several places in Sweden. It is organized in business centers and each business center consists of several business units. A business unit is working with one to three products and has about 20-30 employees.

Within GAMMA, as well as within other ALPHA-companies, there is an understanding of how critical it is to improve software development capabilities. ALPHA has to increasingly be able to deliver new products and services satisfying the markets (current customer sets as well as new customer sets); and this at an increased pace. As for many other companies, speed (Fine 1998)—primarily measured as time-to-market—and knowledge are the keys to success for ALPHA. Increasingly, GAMMA's products and services have shorter life span and are more complex.

The Rise, Death and Resurrection of an SPI Initiative

A couple of years ago GAMMA decided that it should start an SPI project. The goal was to design, develop, and implement a knowledge management system (KMS) to better and in a more formalized way capture software experiences for redeployment and software process improvement. Hence, the project has also a process management improvement perspective. This section presents GAMMA's SPI initiative; the different approaches used and the turns the project took. The primary sources for the case were interviews with members of the SPI-project, software project leaders, and software project members. Secondary sources were also used.

The Rise and Death of GAMMA's Experience Base

GAMMA decided that it should, based on the Experience Factory (Basili 1993, 1994, Basili et al. 1992), design and implement a computer-based knowledge repository aiming at the collective knowledge of GAMMA's software engineers (a computer-based knowledge repository is one type of KMS).

The Experience Factory is an experiential learning SPI approach (Basili et al. 1992). It deals with the reuse of software development knowledge and experience (Figure 1). The Experience Factory can either be a logical and/or physical organisation, but it should be separated from the project organisation (Basili et al. 1992). The Experience Base (a knowledge repository) is a critical component of the Experience Factory. The idea with the Experience Factory is to take the products from the software projects, like plans and data (e.g. error measures) gathered during development and to transform these into reusable units. The units are stored in the Experience Base. From a KM perspective the Experience Factory is primarily based on a knowledge codification strategy and focuses on explicit knowledge.

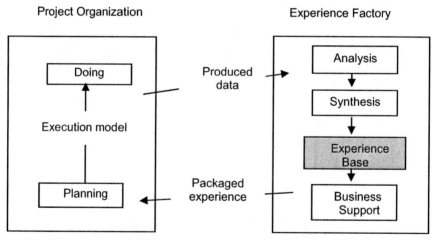

Fig. 1. The experience factory model (adapted from Basili et al., 1992b)

The Experience Factory "…deals with the reuse of all kinds of software engineering knowledge and experience. It can package resource models and baselines, change and defect baselines and models, product tracking models and baselines, process definitions and models, method and technique models and evaluations, products and products parts, quality models and various lessons learned. These packages can take a variety of forms, e.g. equations defining the relationship between variables, ... , histograms or pie charts of raw or analyzed data, ... , or graphs defining ranges of "normal". ... They can be in the form of specific lessons learned, associated with project types, phases, activities, e.g., reading by stepwise abstraction is most effective for finding interface faults, or in the form of risks or recommendations ... They can be in the form of models or algorithms specifying the processes, methods, or techniques" (Basili 1994). (For more information on the Experience Factory see: http://sel.gsfc.nasa.gov/website/exp-factory.htm) The Experience Base is a critical component of the Experience Factory. The goal is that an Experience Base should contain an organization's software engineering experience of value and software engineering core competence. GAMMA's Experience Factory project should develop an Experience Base which should be possible to use to collect, analyze, generalize, formalize, and packet experiences from GAMMA's software development projects. (Henceforth, GAMMA's knowledge management project is called KNOWIT and the GAMMA Experience Base is called EXPBASE.) Hence, the project started with a traditional codification strategy to knowledge management (Hansen et al. 1999).

KNOWIT spent more than 1,000 person-hours designing EXPBASE. The project estimated that EXPBASE would be quite large and complex. It should contain information on productivity, measurements of software correctness and fault, lead-time data, etc. After the initial design, EXPBASE was presented to its intended users. Based on the reactions of the intended users it was decided that the project should be halted. The intended users expressed that EXPBASE would not solve the problems encountered in GAMMA's software processes and that it would not be a good means to improve software processes.

In parallel with the design and development of EXPBASE, the project decided to increase its understanding of how experiences were really exchanged within and between GAMMA's software projects. The KNOWIT-manager was supervising a student-thesis focusing on GAMMA's software development. The student tracked and described how knowledge was exchanged and distributed within and between projects. The student also tracked and described what types of knowledge different software project members really needed and used. Software project leaders and members were followed over a number of working days. In parallel with the thesis-study, members of KNOWIT conducted a number of interviews with software project leaders and members. The interviews were focusing on how knowledge was sought and exchanged within and between projects. The results from the two studies showed how experiences were exchanged within projects and between projects. The studies showed major discrepancies between how people were seeking knowledge and exchanging experiences and what EXPBASE would require people to do to seek knowledge and exchange experiences. Although GAMMA had invested more than 1,000 person-hours in designing EXPBASE, it decided, based on the two studies, to stop the development of EXPBASE.

The two studies suggested that KNOWIT and the EXPBASE was missing two important dimensions found in the studies. First, the lack of physical spaces for knowledge exchanges. As noted in the literature, in many cases it is not enough to have virtual spaces for knowledge exchanges; spatial design can be as crucial in improving knowledge exchanges (Brown & Duguid 2000). Second, EXPBASE did not seem to be a good way for handling spontaneous and ad hoc needs for knowledge. For example, the two studies found that during meetings knowledge needs were strongly related to how different issues emerged. EXPBASE would in these cases not be a suitable support.

The studies also showed that spontaneous and informal knowledge exchanges were frequently used for knowledge exchange. The exchange in these situations was directed towards specific problems that had to be solved "right away". Spontaneous and informal knowledge exchanges were of two types. The first type was networking where a reference was made to a source of knowledge (e.g., a project, person, or a document). The second type involved actual exchange of substantive knowledge and experiences. EXPBASE could have been useful in these situations, but it was assessed that it was unlikely that it should be used. It was likely that the intended users would find EXPBASE too cumbersome to use compared to face-to-face exchange—the latter was also pointed out as the preferred exchange mode for spontaneous and informal knowledge exchanges.

Resurrection of the SPI Initiative

Although EXPBASE was stopped, KNOWIT thought KNOWIT's primary goal—to improve knowledge management within and between software projects—was still a goal to pursue. Based on the EXPBASE failure and the two studies, the knowledge management initiative was redirected. KNOWIT decided that a less technology-based and more behavioral approach was needed. It was decided that an Experience Engine should be designed and that the primary "engine" for knowledge exchange should be humans. Hence, the Experience Engine can be characterized as a personalization or networking strategy to KM (Hansen et al. 2002). Henceforth, the GAMMA Experience Engine is called EXPENG.

To design EXPENG, a study was carried out by KNOWIT. It studied over 100 knowledge exchange occasions. The study indicated that to improve knowledge exchange, informal knowledge exchange processes have to be supported and strengthen by formal roles. At the core of EXPENG are two centrally created formal roles: experience broker and experience communicator.

A primary goal of the experience broker is to be a human "yellow pages". The role is focusing lateral relations (Galbraith 1973). The experience broker must have broad and "holistic" knowledge and also have a well-developed network. The experience broker can be characterized as a human networking strategy (Swan et al. 1999). The experience broker should spend most of his time wandering around in the organization; moving between different teams, meetings, and joining ad hoc meetings. The experience broker should also spend time hanging around, for example, in coffee rooms, copying rooms, etc.

The experience communicator transfers knowledge and experiences and must be able to present and communicate the experiences in such a way that it helps a software developer solving a specific problem. The idea is that an experience communicator should transfer knowledge that will help a software developer solve a problem in such a way that the software developer increases his knowledge and will be able to deploy this knowledge in further projects.

KNOWIT characterizes EXPENG as "knowledge management by wandering and hanging around". EXPENG illustrates well how to implement a knowledge management systems without using ICT. EXPENG is currently being implemented throughout GAMMA—time will tell if the case is a success or not.

KNOWIT is aware of some drawbacks and potential problems of EXPENG. For example, when a person with considerable knowledge leaves the organization, a lot of knowledge also leaves unless the person's knowledge has been documented or structurally implemented in processes and activities. One way KNOWIT addresses the problems is through the development of a culture where it is natural to share knowledge and experiences, for example, by encouraging software developers to establish contacts outside their natural group. Another way is to invite an experience communicator in the start-up of a new software project.

Another problem is related to how knowledge is redeployed in EXPENG. The main means to redeploy knowledge in EXPENG, is to redeploy experts. This approach obviously has its limitations: you can only time-slice the experience brokers and experience communicators so thin.

An obvious step would be to find ways knowledge could be acquired and exchanged independently from the experience brokers and experience communicators.

Learning from the GAMMA Case

GAMMA's SPI initiative went through some troubled times, which meant some major changes in the approaches used. It can be argued that the development of EXPBASE was another KM-project forgetting the people, or that the project started with a "silver bullet" or a "if we build it, they will come" assumption. We think the case illustrates more than this. Hansen et al. (2004) after reviewing 322 contributions to the SPI literature suggest that researcher should use theoretical analysis of SPI descriptions using theories from related disciplines. Using the case and theories and concepts from related disciplines this section discusses one critical issue which to a large extent is neglected in the software development and SPI literature: exploitation and exploration in software development and SPI.

Software Development and SPI: a Focus on Exploitation and/or Exploration

An issue in the innovation, organizational learning, and strategic management literature is how to strike a good balance between exploitation and exploration. March in discussing organizational learning points out that a "*... central concern of studies of adaptive processes is the relation between the exploration of new possibilities and the exploitation of old certainties.*" (March 1991). Broadly, exploration "*...includes things captured by terms such as search, variation, risk taking, experimentation, play, flexibility, discovery, innovation*" and exploitation "*...includes such things as refinement, choice, production, efficiency, selection, implementation, execution.*" (March 1991). An organization must engage itself in both exploration and exploitation to survive in the long run. An organization has scarce resources; exploration and exploitation compete for these scarce resources. An organization's members make more or less conscious choices between exploration and exploitation. Said March, "*...maintaining an appropriate balance between exploration and exploitation is a primary factor in system survival and prosperity*". In discussing the pros and cons of exploration and exploitation, March points out that "*...adaptive processes characteristically improve exploitation more rapidly than exploration. These advantages for exploitation cumulate. Each increase in competence at an activity* *increases the likelihood of rewards for engaging in that activity, thereby further increasing the competence and the likelihood."* (March 1991). Still, for an organization, it is critical to sustain a reasonable level of exploration. According to organizational learning theories, the tendencies to increase exploitation and reduce exploration are likely to become effective in the short run but potentially self-destructive in the long run (March 1991).

If we take March's words on the relationship between exploration and exploitation seriously, the tendency to use KM or SPI for exploitation, ceteris paribus, can be a disadvantage to an organization in the long run. It consumes resources that should have been used for exploration. The approach taken in EXPBASE was primarily for strengthening exploitation. Through EXPBASE it would be possible to map and "streamline" the software processes. According to Benner & Tushman (2003) this will primarily lead to incremental innovations and a lower level of architectural innovations. The innovations will be primarily for the current customer base.

EXPENG can be viewed as a different KM and SPI approach. It can be characterized as an anchoring and adjustment approach. Anchoring and adjustment means that the formal ways to KM and SPI tend to be the result of minor adjustments of the current ways to KM and SPI (the anchor points). A major problem of this approach is that it might lead to a "usability trap": the design and implementation of KM and SPI roles, processes, and activities being useable and used but not very useful. Designing EXPENG was based on studies of how knowledge management in software development was done—the anchor point. Through the two roles, minor adjustments were made. There were no serious discussion in KNOWIT related to the exploration/exploitation problem. It might be that EXPENG is successful in the short run, but that it in the long run makes exploration difficult.

Using the organizational learning literature, we suggest that from an organizational point of view KM and SPI as exploitation might in the long run for GAMMA and similar software development organizations lead to some unwanted consequences. Under what condition this might be the case will be discussed next.

Software Development and SPI in Different Environments

In implementing and evaluating knowledge management and SPI initiatives, the external environment of the firm has to be considered. In general the SPI literature lacks this external view. It has an internal process focus. As said above, GAMMA's environment can be characterized as being ambiguous, having occurrence of frequent and unpredictable events with non-incremental technological changes; these events have clear and critical implications for the future of GAMMA. It should also be noted that some of GAMMA's product/service areas are quite stable with primarily incremental technological changes. Hence, GAMMA is working in turbulent or high-velocity environments as well as in more stable environments.

Using the literature on strategic management (Eisenhardt & Santos 2001) and dynamic capabilities (Teece et al. 1997, Eisenhardt & Martin 2000), we can evaluate KNOWIT's KM and SPI approaches in relation to GAMMA's environments. The literature suggests that in turbulent and high-velocity environments knowledge-management processes have to be rather simple and flexible to be effective and efficient. Knowledge management should be characterized as rather simple experiential routines; relying on newly created knowledge specific to situations. On the other hand in stable environments the processes can be rather stable and detailed and relying extensively on existing knowledge. There are primarily linear execution of processes with feedback. This leads to "frequent" and nearby variation (anchor and adjust) to perfect the processes.

Using the literature we can conclude that GAMMA's environment as well as the exploration/exploitation issue require an organizational form different from what is stressed in the SPI-literature as well as different from the organizational forms GAMMA tried to implement.

Organizational Forms for SPI Supporting Exploitation and Exploration in Different Environments

Using the productivity and innovation literature we can highlight the inconsistency between SPI initiatives focused on productivity improvements and cost reductions and those SPI initiatives focused on innovation and flexibility. The organizational forms suggested in the literature for enabling and enhancing exploitation or exploration are quite different. As discussed above the process working well in stable environments are quite different from the ones working well in turbulent and high-velocity environments. In situation like this, the literature suggests that both tight and loose couplings are needed. Ambidextrous or dual organizational forms are architectures that build in these coupling simultaneously (Sutcliffe et al. 2000).

The literature gives support for formulating the hypothesis that good SPI is depending on finding a balanced ambidextrous form for software development and SPI. For software projects that can be characterized as exploitation projects (stable environments) increasing process management, through traditional SPI activities like CMM and Experience Factory can increase performance and speed up organizational responsiveness. For software projects that can be characterized as exploration (turbulent environments and technological ferment) increasing process management can lead to a decrease in performance and responsiveness.

Conclusion and Further Research

The paper has presented and discussed an SPI initiative in a high-technology company. The project used two common approaches to KM, codification and networking, but with special twists. Using the case and the literature, we discussed one critical issue not treated well in the SPI literature. We suggested that the software development and SPI field could be informed by literature from other fields. Using the literature we suggested that a key issue in SPI is to find a striking balance between initiatives supporting exploitation and exploration. We suggested also that ambidextrous or dual organizational forms are worth exploring for striking a balance between exploration and exploitation.

References

Ahern DM, Clouse A, Turner R (2001) CMMI Distilled: An Introduction to Multi-discipline Process Improvement. Addison-Wesley Reading MA

Basili VR (1993) The Experience Factory and its Relationship to other Improvements Paradigms. Proc of the 4th European Software Engineering Conference ESEC '93, pp 68-83

Basili VR (1994) A Quantitative Approach to Software Management and Engineering. CMSC 735 Institute for Advanced Computer Studies and Department of Computer Science University of Maryland College Park

Basili VR, Caldiera G, Canone G (1992) A Reference Architecture for the Component Factory. ACM Transactions on Software Engineering and Methodology, vol 1, no 1, pp 53-80

Benner MJ, Tushman ML (2003) Exploitation, Exploration, and Process Management: the Productivity Dilemma Revisited. Academy of Management Review, vol 28, no 2, pp 238-256

Brown JS, Duguid P (2000) The Social Life of Information. Harvard Business School Press Boston

Eisenhardt KM, Martin JA (2000) Dynamic Capabilities: What are they? Strategic Management Journal, vol 21, pp 1105-1121

Eisenhardt KM, Santos FM (2001) Knowledge-Based View: A New Theory of Strategy? In: Pettigrew A, Thomas H, Whittington R (eds) Handbook of Strategy and Management. Sage Thousand Oaks

El Sawy OA, Eriksson I, Raven A, Carlsson S (2001) Understanding Shared Knowledge Creation Spaces around Business Processes: Precursors to Process Innovation Implementation. International Journal of Technology Management, vol 22, no 1-3, pp 149-173

Fine C (1998) Clockspeed. Perseus Books Bosto

Galbraith J (1973) Designing Complex Organizations. Addison-Wesley Reading

Hansen MT, Nohria N, Tierney T (1999) What's Your Strategy for Managing Knowledge? Harvard Business Review, vol 77, no 2, pp 106-116

Hansen MT (2002) Knowledge Networks: Explaining Effective Knowledge Sharing in Multiunit Companies. Organization Science, vol 13, no 3, pp 232-248

Hansen B, Rose J, Tjornehoj G (2004) Prescription, Description, Reflection: the Shape of the Software Improvement Field. International Journal of Information Management, vol 24, pp 457-472

Humphrey WS (1995) A Discipline for Software Engineering. Addison-Wesley Reading

Iivari J (2000) Information Systems Development as Knowledge Work: The Body of Systems Development Process Knowledge. Proc of the Xth Conference on Information Modelling and Knowledge Bases

March JG (1991) Exploration and Exploitation in Organizational Learning. Organization Science, vol 2, no 1, pp 71-87

Nonaka I, Teece DJ (eds) (2001) Managing Industrial Knowledge: Creation, Transfer and Utilization. Sage London

Paulk MC, Curtis B, Chrissis MB, Weber CV (1993) Capability Maturity Model for Software (Version1.1). SEI/CMU-93-TR-24 Software Engineering Institute Carnegie Mellon University Pittsburgh

Sutcliffe K, Sitkin S, Browning L (2000) Tailoring Process Management to Situational Requirements. In: Cole R, Scott W (eds) The Quality Movement & Organization Theory. Sage London

Swan J, Newell S, Scarbrough H, Hislop D (1999) Knowledge Management and Innovation: Networks and Networking. Journal of Knowledge Management, vol 3, no 4, pp 262-275

Teece DJ, Pisano G, Schuen A (1997) Dynamic Capabilities and Strategic Management. Strategic Management Journal, vol 18, no 7, pp 509-533

Developing Organisational Knowledge Management Initiatives: A Collaborative Research Approach

Henry Linger

Knowledge Management Research Program, Faculty of Information Technology, Monash University, Australia.
henry.linger@infotech.monash.edu.au

Background

The articulation of the knowledge management (KM) concept has occurred in the context of a radical shift away from goods and services to an information-based economy (Porter and Millar, 1985; Drucker, 1993; Boisot, 1995; 1998). The organisational response to this shift has been a move towards global enterprises with very flat structures that, in principle, enable enterprises to react rapidly to changes in their operating environments (Drucker, 1988; Scott Morton, 1991; Galliers and Baets, 1998). Organisations that operate in the information economy require an ability to generate, access and utilise the volumes of information that are now readily available without the constraint of media, geography or time (Boisot, 1995). A critical factor is the speed at which they are able to productively process such information.

This emerging economic reality, coupled with social and industrial restructuring, have instigated the current corporate interest in KM. There is a widespread realisation that a more rigorous approach to the exploitation of knowledge as an organisational resource is required. Thus KM assumes a pragmatic orientation that reflects organisational realities. In this context, the overlay of knowledge and technology assumes that KM is a construct that stores, manipulates and disseminates knowledge that is codified and commodified (Whitley, 2000). Furthermore, it implies that organisations are rational and that codified knowledge represents a rational explanation of events. These are necessary assumptions that enable the management of knowledge to be directed to the productive function of the organisation (Day, 2001). It is this need to appropriate knowledge for production that is the fundamental rationale of corporate knowledge management.

Further, the shift from information to knowledge is an acknowledgment of the significant role of the human actor in the process of transforming information into organisational outcomes (Quinn et al. 1996; Lesser 2000). It is these outcomes that address the organisation's ability to adapt to the changing environment over time. It also means that organisations must operate effectively as well as efficiently.

There are however contradictions in this position. On the one hand organisations need to maintain a high degree of flexibility to ensure its capacity to adapt. In this context flexibility refers to efficiency often achieved by reducing staff as the largest single cost factor in any organisation (Hammer and Champy, 1993; Sveiby, 1997).

On the other hand, long-term effectiveness relates to the organisation's ability to anticipate the market and deliver appropriate products or services. It relies on innovation that depends on the organisation's creative capability as well as its knowledge and understanding of the market (van de Van et al. 1989; Dougherty, 1996). Innovation is knowledge intensive, relying on staff experience, their understanding of the history and culture of the organisation and published information (Cohen and Levinthal, 1990; Burns and Stalker, 1961). One important aspect of innovation is process improvement; the ability of the organisation to improve its means of production. Thus innovation addresses both the organisation's internal functioning as well as its external engagement (Takeuchi and Nonaka, 1986) and its long-term viability.

Innovation implies that individuals, and the organisation itself, are engaged in a continuous learning process (Brown and Duguid, 1991; Senge, 1990). For learning to be effective, actors need to draw on their experience of performing their work in order to reflect on that activity (Kim, 1993). Innovation implies actors take responsibility, and have the authority, to to implement what they have learnt. Such work organisation is consistent with the concept of post-Fordist work (Amin, 1994).

The dilemma is to find the dynamic balance between the demands for innovation and the requirement for operational efficiency. Thus the overt goal of KM is organisational outcomes that meet external demands, while the underlying goal is organisational transformation to meet the need for internal changes. As John Seely Brown states (1991; p154), "the most important invention that will come out of the corporate research lab in the future will be the corporation itself". KM is at the core of this process of corporate re-invention.

The granularity of KM extends the complexity of KM beyond the dichotomies of internal/external innovation and the effectiveness/efficiency of operations. The KM focus on innovation reveals the need to understand work practices and the personal, social and organisational dimensions that are necessary to support that work. KM is therefore concerned with constructing inscriptions (Latour, 1986) that reflect the work task.

Utilising information and communications technologies (ICT) for these inscriptions provides the basis for sharing this knowledge, constructing a memory of past instances of the work task and exploiting this memory to learn and innovate. Sharing also reveals the important interactions that serve to define the authority and responsibility and the organising principles that allow diverse and disparate individuals, groups and organisational units to be melded into an effective organisation.

Published case studies (eg Schultz, 1999) and my own research, show that KM can only be understood when it is grounded in the workplace and complexity is the focus of study. This is a strong argument to adopt an action research approach to study KM phenomena. In this paper I present a model of collaborative research that adapts the action research approach to the contingencies of KM. The following section is an overview of action research to identify areas that need to be adapted for KM research. The next section presents the collaborative research model followed by an illustrative case study. The paper concludes with some reflective remarks regarding the collaborative research approach in practice.

The Action Research Paradigm

Action research emerged in the 1940's from the work of Kurt Lewin on group dynamics and general theory of how social change occurs (Lewin, 1947). His concern was with the study of general laws and diagnosis of specific situations, with particular concern about measuring outcomes and controlling contextual variables, particularly given ill-structured data. His focus on the relationship between perception and action allowed the researcher to be visible and to have an explicit impact on the situation. His work was adapted into the socio-technical systems approach in the UK especially in the work of Mumford (Mumford and Weir, 1987) and Checkland (1981). The Scandinavian adaption was framed by interventions to democratise the workplace (Baskerville and Wood-Harper, 1998).

Action research as understood in Information Systems research is a form of qualitative research in which a researcher intervenes in a problematic situation. The resolution of the problem is based on that interventionwithout challenging the dominant managerial ideology. Action research is therefore problem solving rather than transformative. Other approaches to action research focus on developing effective professional practice, such as educational practice, and Argyris and Schön's "action science" (1978), where the researcher is investigator, subject and consumer.

The organisation, as a complex social system cannot be simplified for the purpose of study. Intervention is premised on an interpretivist viewpoint that the subject of the study is socially constructed (Berger and Luckmann, 1966). The researcher and her co-participants, are engaged in the development of a shared understanding of the problem so as to construct the cognitive framework to will inform action; their "Weltanschauung" (Checkland, 1981). This is cyclical as action needs to be based on understanding while understanding arises from action.

In action research the goals of both the researcher and client must overlap in order for each to learn from the situation. In this sense, action research involves a commitment to learning and theory building and this distinguishes it from consultancy practice and its predefined solutions.

Action research can be generalised as a cyclic process of diagnosis, action planning, action taking, evaluation and learning. McKay and Marshall (2001) however propose that there are in fact two concurrent process cycles – a problem-solving cycle and a research interest cycle. The implications of this more reflective analysis addresses the quality of both research and problem outcomes.

From a KM perspective action research needs to be adapted in a number of significant ways. The first issue is the choice of the intervention setting. In the problem solving cycle, a KM initiative has the potential to change not only products or services, but also the means of their production. This implies that the changes go beyond the existing managerial ideology. Thus setting that already acknowledge knowledge work, including learning and reflection, reduce the need for radical organisational transformation.

A second issue is the subject of the intervention. KM is usually applied to intractable, systemic problems that do not lend themselves to usual organisational responses. The complexity and broad agenda of KM require distance from the subject and reflection. This requires a negotiation process that defines what facet of KM the intervention will address while maintaining the integrity of the KM enterprise.

A third issue is the nature of the intervention itself. In terms of McKay and Marshall's dual loops, the intervention also needs to have a clear research focus. But aligning research and organisational goals is potentially problematic. This is compounded by the complexity of KM initiatives as it can overwhelm a rigorous research practice. The complexity of KM also means that organisational goals are difficult to define at the outset of the intervention and are more likely to be contingent on the intervention itself. Further, the scope of KM brings into question the time frame of the intervention. Typically, organisational problem solving has a shorter time scale than the research cycle. But both are shorter than the organisational transformation implicit in KM.

Collaborative Research: Extending the Action Research Approach

From a KM perspective, the issues identified above need to be addressed in a way that is consistent with the general principles and structures of action research since this approach maps well with the character of KM. The proposed adaptation of action research is based on a KM research program conducted over the past 10 years as shown in Table 1. The research program is based on the application of KM to tasks that are unambiguously knowledge work, conducted in collegial environments where professionals are expected to perform most of the productive work themselves.

An important prerequisite for each research project was that the Head of unit who hosted the intervention recognised an intractable problem that was not amenable to be solved through existing approaches and had a commitment to exploring innovative uses of ICT. This led to close collaboration between the academic researchers and clients who were also usually researchers or professionals.

The creation of a collaborative space allows all participants, clients and academic researchers, to assume the role of action researchers. The subject of the research was negotiated between the collaborators, drawing on both the operational problems and theoretical frameworks contributed by the academics. However, the outcomes of this collaborative research was limited to a proof-of-concept and/or a framework or model to demonstrate the utility of a particular theoretical construct to a specific work situation. These outcomes provide the participants in the collaborative space with tangible artefacts that can be reinterpreted back to their primary constituency. For the academic researcher, the collaboration results in refinements to theory development within the academy. Since the collaborative outcomes are grounded in a concrete situation, they ensure that the evolving theory remains relevant. For the client, the outcomes can also be transformed into specific projects and/or strategies that have specific, but broad, relevance to the host organisation (Kock et al. 2002). A model of such collaborative research is shown in Figure 1 below.

From an action research perspective, the research model presented in Figure 1 suggests that there are in fact three process cycles that are not concurrent but do have temporal dependencies. The research interest cycle is addressed by the potential of the collaborative research to support theory development. The operational problem-solving cycle arises when projects and/or strategy that emerge from the collaboration are implemented. Reflecting on the model, it is apparent that neither theory refinement nor organisational initiatives are a necessary outcome of collaboration. Thus the willingness of the organisation to adopt any project or strategy limits the utility of collaborative research but this limitation is often imposed by external factors or internal political considerations. Importantly, it is not the problem solving cycle that directly impacts the research cycle but the outcomes of the research conducted in the collaborative space. Similarly, problem solving is also only directly influenced by the outcomes of collaborative research rather than the direct influence of academic research.

Table 1. Issues and applications of task based KM (Burstein and Linger, 2003)

Application Area	Task	Issues Investigated	Reference
Lexicography	Bilingual dictionary construction from anthropological field notes	Social and cultural aspects of data	Austin et al., 1994
Biology	Modelling molecular and cellular biology of HIV	Exploring boundaries of known facts	McPhee et al., 1994
Immunology	Simulation modelling of the immune response to HIV infection	Testing competing paradigms to explain observed data	Linger et al., 1994
Epidemiology	Survey design	Discontinuity in knowledge and data	Linger et al., 1998
Banking	Creation of strategy	Creating processes for organizational learning	Clayton and Linger, 1998
Meteorology	Weather forecasting	Managing large data holding and resolving contradictions in a distributed e nvironment	Linger and Burstein, 2001
Defence	Strategic and tactical HQ operations of army, navy and air force	Learning and knowledge work in a dynamic environment	Linger and Warne, 2001

The importance of the collaborative space derives from the various perspectives of the collaboration as shown in Figure 1. From inside the collaborative space, the academic researcher views collaborative research as an opportunity for theory testing, while the industry participant is engaged in reflective practice. The external view of collaborative research is a form of 'skunk works' for the organisation and applied research for the academy. All these perspectives are valuable to the stakeholders as the collaboration provides an important forum for learning by the participants. For the organisation the collaboration provides a relatively low-cost exploration of relevant issues and a forum for productive engagement with academics, and in particular, an opportunity to be exposed to current academic theory. For those actors who actually participate in collaborative research, it is an opportunity for learning, including an exploration of their theory in use (Argyris and Schön, 1978). These aspects of collaboration contribute to the human and intellectual capital of the organisation. For the academy, the collaboration provides the means to apply theory to practice, to gain knowledge of current practices, identify issues within an industry sector and establish links with industry partners. These aspects of collaboration go some way towards ensuring that both research and teaching within the academy remain relevant to, and broadens the academy's engagement with, industry and the wider society.

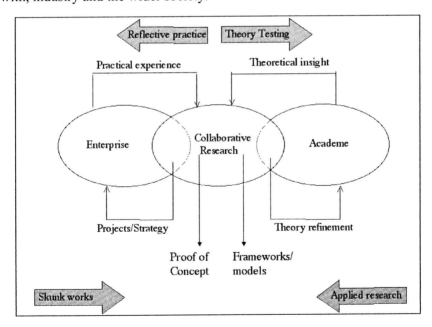

Fig. 1. The collaboration research model

A further justification for the creation of the collaborative space arises from the nature of the issues that are considered. In most cases, a KM initiative is of such magnitude that it is not feasible to consider its implementation in the context of a research program. The collaboration is an opportunity to identify and explore pertinent aspect of such KM initiatives without any commitment to those initiatives. The collaborative space provides the necessary resources, space, time and people to reflect and learn without overt operational constraints. It provides an opportunity to be creative and innovative.

Collaborative research shares some characteristics with participatory action research in that some members of the organisation are active researchers rather than subjects (Whyte, 1991). This establishes a two-way relationship between the academic researchers and the organisation. However participatory action research is motivated by an emancipatory interest and seeks to establish change and/or learning as a self-maintaining process (Argyris and Schön, 1991). Collaborative research on the other hand is much more oriented to sensemaking both from an organisational and a theoretical perspective (Weick, 1995).

The collaborative research model is essentially a process of reinterpreting a theoretical framework in a specific situation that is itself defined by the reinterpretation of organisational practice. This mutuality defines the research agenda within the collaborative space and requires an innovative interpretation of theory to match the creative articulation of practice. It is this process, coupled with the negotiations that define the collaborative space, that has the potential to make an independent contribution to theory and practice. The research in the collaborative space often surfaced issues that not only refined theory but take it into new territory to meet the complexity and variety that emerged when practice was deconstructed.

Collaborative Research in Action: an Illustrative Case Study

The Australian Bureau of Meteorology (BoM) has used IT, particularly in numerical weather modelling and data visualisation. This approach is comptutationally intensive and relies on large volumes of data. Advances in the scientific understanding of atmospheric dynamics and improved algorithms have resulted in models that are able to produce more accurate long-term weather prediction. The limitation of these forecasts is that they are more suited to a macro scale, continental or hemispheric forecasts, rather than the meso or regional scale where the influence of local topology and micro factors influence the local weather. These localised forecasts represent the major workload of the BoM forecasting effort.

Within the collaborative space, KM was proposed so as to allow meteorologists to focus on their professional work while reducing the administrative components of their workload. Our initial involvement was based on student projects that provided a forum for Bureau staff and researcher to come together to explore their mutual interests: BoM could learn about KM and how it might support the forecast process; the academics assessed BoM as a venue for our intervention and forecasting as a KM task.

The student projects were carefully and subtly guided by both sides. The result was a number of very successful proof-of-concept applications that were implemented as operational tools for forecasters. The development of these tools provided the Bureau with an opportunity to ascertain whether the KM principles embedded in the proof-of-concept could be translated into production systems.

These efforts, as well as external political, legal and operational factors combined to focus BoM management on the need to improve the forecast process resulting in a proposal for a "Forecast Streamlining and Enhancement Program (FSEP)" as a major Bureau initiative (Bell, 2003, Kelly et al. 2004). In this context, we formulated a four-year research project, in partnership with the BoM that was jointly funded by the Australian Research Council and BoM.

FSEP aims to completely redevelop all aspects of the forecasting support systems (excluding the numerical modelling). This is a massive undertaking requiring governmental authority and additional resource allocation over many years. Our collaborative research project is designed to provide input into FSEP regarding the nature of forecasting work, information and technology architectures, intelligent ICT tools to support and computerise the procedural and administrative aspect of forecasting.

The academics used the collaboration to explore the procedural aspects of our theoretical framework of KM. During this project we became aware that the nature of the forecasting task had not been explored. This led us to embark on an inter-disciplinary research project with philosophy to investigate the social epistemology of knowledge use. This in turn encouraged us to reopen our investigations into the nature of knowledge work.

Concluding Remarks

The collaborative research model represents an extension of action research that accommodates the specific character of knowledge management. It establishes a defined space where practitioners and researchers can engage productively to jointly explore aspects of knowledge management through an innovative application of a theoretical framework applied to a creative conceptualisation of work practices. The model provides the participants with an opportunity to conduct research without the constraints of operational imperatives or theoretical restrictions but the results contribute to both the theory and practice of knowledge management. Importantly such collaborative research provides the means to study knowledge management without the need for simplification thus maintaining the focus on complexity as its intrinsic characteristic.

But perhaps the most significant aspect of the collaborative research model is that it identifies how industry and the academy can engage productively for mutual benefit while maintaining their integrity.

References

Amin A (ed) (1994) Post-Fordism: a Reader. Oxford Blackwell P/L

Argyris C, Schön D (1991) Participatory Action Research and Action Science Compared. In: Whyte WF (ed.) Participatory Action Research. Sage Newbury Park NJ

Argyris C, Schön DA (1978) Organizational Learning: A Theory of Action Perspective. Addision-Wesley Reading MA

Austin P, Linger H, Nathan D (1994) Computer-aided Lexicography: From Characters to Lexicographic Concepts. Australex'94: Lexicography and Computers. Melbourne Australia

Baskerville R, Wood-Harper T (1998) Diversity in Information Systems Action Research Methods. European Journal of Information Systems, vol 7, no 2, pp 90-107

Checkland P, Scholes J (1990) Soft Systems Methodology in Practice. J Wiley Chichester UK

Bell I (2003) FSEP Principles. Bureau of Meteorology – Internal Technical Report

Berger P, Luckmann T (1966) The Social Construction of Reality: A Treatise in the Sociology of Knowledge. Anchor Press New York

Boisot MH (1995) Information Space: A Framework for Learning in Organisations, Institutions and Culture. Routledge London

Boisot MH (1998) Knowledge Assets: Securing Competitive Advantage in the Information Economy. Oxford University Press Oxford UK

Brown JS, Duguid P (1991) Organizational Learning and Communities-of-Practice: Toward a Unified View of Working, Learning, and Innovation. Organization Science, vol 2, no 1, pp 40-57

Burns T, Stalker GM (1961) The Management of Innovation. Tavistock London

Burstein F, Linger H (2003) Supporting Post-Fordist Work Practices: A Knowledge Management Framework for Dynamic Intelligent Decision Support. Journal of IT&P Special Issue on KM, vol 16, no 3, pp 289-305

Checkland P (1991) From Framework through Experience to Learning: The Essential Nature of Action Research. In: Enissen H, Klien HK, Hirschheim R (eds) Information Systems Research: Contemporary Approaches and Emergent Traditions. North-Holland Amsterdam

Clayton J, Linger H (1998) The Role of Methods in Strategy Development and Implementation: A Finance Industry Case Study. Proc of ISD'98 Bled Slovenia

Cohen WM, Levinthal D (1990) Absorptive Capacity: a New Perspective on Learning and Innovation. Administrative Science Quarterly, no 35, pp 128-152

Day RE (2001) Totality and Representation: A History of Knowledge Management through European Documentation, Critical Modernity, and Post-Fordism. Journal of the American Society for Information Science and Technology, vol 52, no 9, pp 725-735

Dougherty D (1996) Organising for Innovation. In: Clegg et al (1991)

Drucker PF (1993) Post-Capitalist Society. Harper Business New York

Drucker PF (1988) The Coming of the New Organisation. In: Harvard Business Review on Knowledge Management (1998). Harvard Business School Press Boston MA

Galliers RD, Baets WRJ (1998) Information Technology and Organisational Transformation. John Wiley & Sons Chichester England

Hammer M, Champy J (1993) Reengineering the Corporation: a Manifesto for Business Revolution. Nicholas Brealey Publishing London

Hammer M (1990) Re-engineering Work: Don't Automate, Obliterate. Harvard Business Review, vol 68, no 4, pp 104-111

Kelly J, Donaldson A, Ryan CJ, Bally J, Wilson J, Potts RJ (2004) The Australian Bureau of Meteorology's Next Generation Forecasting System. Proc of the 20th International Conference on Interactive Information and Processing Systems (IIPS) for Meteorology, Oceanography, and Hydrology

Kim DH (1993) The Link Between Individual and Organisational Learning. Sloan Management Review, fall, pp 37-50

Kock N, Gray P, Hoving R, Klein H, Myers M, Rockart J (2002) IS Research Relevance Revisited: Subtle Accomplishment, Unfulfilled Promise, or Serial Hypocrisy? CAIS, vol 8, art 23

Latour B (1986) Visualisation and Cognition: Thinking with Eyes and Hands. Knowledge and Society: Studies in the Sociology of Culture Past and Present, no 6, pp 1-40

Lesser EL (ed) (2000) Knowledge and Social Captial: Foundations and Applications. Butterworth-Heinemann Boston MA

Lewin K (1947) Frontiers in Group Dynamics. Human Relations, vol 1, no 1, pp 5-41

Linger H, Burstein F (2001) From Computation to Knowledge Management: The Changing Paradigm of Decision Support for Meteorological Forecasting.

Journal of Decision Systems Special Issue on Decision Support Systems in Action. Hermes Science Publishing Ltd Oxford, vol 10, no 2, pp 195-216

Linger H, Warne L (2001) Making the Invisible Visible: Social Learning in a Knowledge Management Context. Australian Journal of Information Systems Special Issue on Knowledge Management, pp 56-66

Linger H, Burstein F, Zaslavsky A, Aitkin C, Crofts N (1998) An Innovative Organizational Tool for Epidemiological Research. European Journal of Epidemiology, vol 14, pp 587-593

Linger H, Newnham J, Deacon N, McPhee D, Komleva N (1994) The Construction of a System for Biological Experimentation: Computer Simulation of HIV-1 Infection. Proc of the 1st World Congress on Computational Medicine: Public Health and Biotechnology. Austin Texas

McKay J, Marshall P (2001) The Dual Imperatives of Action Research. Information Technology and People, vol 14, no 1, pp 46-59

McPhee D, Deacon N, Newnham J, Linger H (1994) Modelling the HIV-1 Infection Cycle. Working Paper 26/94 Department of Information Systems Monash University

Mumford E, Weir M (1979) Computer Systems Work Design: The ETHICS Method. Associated Business Press London

Nonaka I, Takeuchi H (1995) The Knowledge Creating Company. Oxford University Press New York

Porter M, Millar VE (1985) How Information Gives Competitive Advantage. Harvard Business Review, vol 63, no 4, pp 110-118

Quinn JB, Anderson P, Finkelstein S (1996) Managing Professional Intellect: Making the Most of the Best. In: Harvard Business Review on Knowledge Management (1998). Harvard Business School Press Boston MA

Scott Morton M (ed) (1991) The Corporation of the 1990's: Information Technology and Organisational Transformation. Oxford University Press New York

Schultze U (1999) A Confessional Account of an Ethnography about Knowledge Work. MISQ, vol 24, no 1, pp 3-41

Senge P (1990) The Fifth Discipline: The art and Practice of the Learning Organisation. Nicholas Brealey Publishing London

Sveiby K (1997) The New Organisational Wealth: Managing and Measuring Knowledge-Based Assets. Berrett-Koehler Publishers San Francisco CA

Takeuchi H, Nonaka I (1986) The New Product Development Game. Harvard Business Review, no 64, pp 137-146

van de Ven, AH, Angle HL, Poole MS (eds) (1989) Research on the Management of Innovation: The Minnesota Studies. Harper & Row New York

Weick KE (1995) Sensemaking in Organizations. Sage Publications London

Whitley EA (2000) Tacit and Explicit Knowledge: Conceptual Confusion around the Commodification of Knowledge. Working Papers Series WP90 Department of Information Systems London School of Economics

Whyte WF (ed) (1991) Participatory Action Research. Sage Newbury Park NJ

Challenges in System Testing – An Interview Study

Åsa Dahlstedt

School of Humanities and Informatics, University of Skövde, Sweden.
asa.dahlsetdt@his.se.

Introduction

One of the major quality criteria of a software system is how well it fulfils the customers' and users' needs and expectations. This criterion makes both requirements engineering (RE) and software testing into crucial tasks within software engineering. RE since it concerns the identification and specification of these needs and expectations, and software testing since it ensures that the software system really fulfills these requirements.

Generally speaking, software testing is about ensuring that the software system fulfils the requirements posed on it (Sommerville 1996). This is made by comparing the actual behaviour of the software, with the specified behaviour as described by the requirements (Leung and Wong 1997). There are usually different levels of software testing (Abran et al. 2004, Sommerville 1996). In this paper, we focus on system testing, which is concerned with the behaviour of the system as a whole, and ensures that the requirements of the system have been met.

Even though this relationship between RE and testing is strong (Gramham 2002; Leung and Wong 1997; Lausen and Vinter 2001), it is often missing in practice (Graham 2002). We are about to start up a research project focused on supporting the integration of these two activities within software engineering. We have performed a pre-study to this project in form of a minor interview study, where testers' requirements on the RE practices and its results are explored[1]. In order to provide a context to these requirements, the study also included questions about how system testing is conducted at each company as well as major challenges. This paper pre-

---

[1] The result focused on the testers requirements on RE is presented in Dahlstedt, Å (2005) Guidelines regarding the requirements engineering practices in order to facilitate system testing. The 11th International Workshop on Requirements Engineering: Foundations for Software Quality, 13-14 June, Porto, Portugal.

sents a discussion on the major challenges within system testing experienced by the respondents within this interview study.

The paper continues with a section on our way of working regarding the interview study, followed by the third section where the results from the inter-view study are presented. The paper ends with some concluding remarks.

Way of Working

The aim of the interview study was to get some initial insights into system testing, its relationship to RE and challenges related to this. We therefore chose to concentrate our interviews on persons involved and experienced in system testing. Due to the explorative nature of this study, we also chose open-ended interviews in order to get an overview of the testing practices and its relation to and needs regarding the requirements work in a number of organizations.

The interview study presented here includes six interviews. They are all involved in and experienced in testing. Four interviewees as testing managers, one as a knowledgeable project leader with much involvement in testing, and one as an educator, mentor, and process engineer related to testing. Three of the interviewees are consultants, and have answered the questions from a generic perspective as well as discuss common problems due to their broad experience in varying projects. The other three respondents work with testing in a particular organisation. One of them have been involved in large projects which includes many testers and last over several years. The other two have been involved in smaller projects. We can therefore conclude that despite this small sample, there is a good spread in knowledge and experiences within the group. The interviewees are presented in more detail in Appendix A.

The interviews lasted between one and one and a half hour. Extensive notes were taken during the interviews, and they were also recorded. The analysis of the interviews is performed mainly through a qualitative content analysis (Patton 2002). It was concentrated on finding themes regarding challenges within system testing, in particular how it is related to RE. This was made by reading through the notes and carefully listen to the tapes, while documenting all statements related to current practices or challenges within system testing and its relationship to RE. These notes were compared in order to identified themes or patterns regarding these advises or requirements. The study is hence performed based on a hermeneutic approach.

Challenges within System Testing

We have identified six areas of challenges experienced by the interviewees. These areas are described within this section.

Quality of the Requirements

The fact that the quality of the requirements influences the effectiveness and efficiency of software testing is no news. However, several of our interviewees discuss problems related to this issue and also emphasises the importance of the requirements' quality. This hence indicates that this issue is still a problem in industry. This section includes a discussion on how low quality of the requirements influences system testing according to our interviewees.

Incomplete and ambiguous requirements are considered as a problem to software testers.

"The most difficult thing without competition is that requirements or the specifications that we start working with are not equivalent with the whole system. There are in other words gaps and room for interpretation, and we are trying to understand and guessing what is expected to happen." (A[2])

This is also explicitly stated by Interviewee F, who also mentions the problem with gaps and room for interpretation amongst the requirements. Interviewee E indirectly agrees, when arguing about the importance of involving testers within requirements analysis in order discover problems such as gaps among the requirements or conflicting requirements at an early stage. The consequence of these problems is that the testers are forced to guess or estimate the correct behaviour of the software, which unfortunately is a more insecure way of ensuring that the system behaves according to the plan. Mistakes regarding the interpretation of the requirements may result in costly and unnecessary rework of the test specifications and test cases.

Interviewee A discusses this further by emphasising that the **expected outcome** of a certain takes must be easily and clearly identifiable within the requirements. This should be fundamental criterion when formulating your requirements, but in A's experience it is a common shortage during the requirements work. Sometimes testers have to explore whether a detected error is due to a software defect or to a test case defect, i.e. if the

---

[2] Shows which interviewee that made the statement

identified problem is really an unwanted behaviour of the software or if it is an erroneous test case due to a misinterpretation of the requirements.

The interviews also indicate that it is not only criteria such as requirements completeness and unambiguity that influences testing, but also how **the requirements are structured and presented**. A well-structured requirements specification, with clear headings and where the requirements are intelligently grouped increases the understandability, according to Interviewee C. Interviewee B state that a clear view of the requirements hierarchy is a valuable support when designing test cases, since it allow you to explore the motive of the actual requirement (in high level requirements) and more details about the it (within the lower level requirements). Interviewee D structures their requirement specification in scenarios in order to increase the requirements understandability and support tests design. These ways of working are about placing the requirements into a context in order to facilitate interpreting them the correct way.

Changing Requirements

Changing requirements obviously influences system testing, and is also mentioned as a common problem by Interviewee A, B, C, and E. E.g.

"We also have had a significant problem where the requirements set have changed very much and very late. This has caused problems." (B)

"The most important property of a requirements specification, in order for me as a tested to do my job, is that it is stable. The worst thing you can have is constant requirements changes." (C)

Changes to the requirements may cause test cases to be rewritten or updated, as well as re-execution of test cases if changes affect test cases already executed. Both these are resulting in the situation that the resources are spent on redoing work already made.

Of course, the interviewees are well aware that requirements may be changed for a good reason. However, it is important to be aware of the effect that the requirements changes has on test design and execution already made within testing. In addition, interviewee A and E emphasise that exploring the impact of a proposed change and based on that deciding whether to implement a change or not is only one part of the problem. In case of approving the change, you must also have routines to ensure that all affected documentation and other related information is updated. Furthermore, the changes must be communicated to all the other affected developers.

Requirements changes must hence be managed in a controlled way, where a good overview of your test information (as well as all other information developed during software engineering) and good communication routines are necessary to cope with changing requirements (see also the two following sections).

Managing Test Related Information

Another problem area is related to **maintaining the testing related information**. Examples of such information are test cases and their relation to the requirements, which test cases that have been executed, the results of those, which test cases that should be re-executed when an new release have been made from the programmers, etc. Managing this information is about keeping control of your testing situation and also easily communicating relevant information to project members. An issue that is especially important when the requirements are changing (see the previous section).

Our interviewees mention several examples of projects were lack of management routines have caused severe problems, resulting in project delays and costly rework. For example: not basing your test case design on the right version of the requirements specification, communicating changes to the requirements to the testers, and keeping control of trouble reports so you know which test cases to re-execute when the new version arrives.

Even though few of our interviewees use tools (besides word processors), most of them have at least some procedures regarding how to manage testing related information. Interviewee A, B, C and D stores information in some way about which requirements a certain test case is aimed to ensure. Interviewee W and E also state that the requirements preferably should be autonomous i.e. that one requirements only covered one function/action. This enables the testers to pinpoint exactly where potential errors belong, which facilitate fixing the defect and reexecuting the necessary test cases. Interviewee B uses the links between the high level requirements and the more detail requirements to fully understand how to test the high level requirements. Interviewee E emphasise the need to prioritise both the requirements and the test cases to support downsizing of the test suite if, or rather when, the project are running out of time.

Interviewee C states that **regression testing** is one of the most difficult parts of testing. To be able to choose the right test cases to be re-executed, in order to quickly verify that changes have not influenced those parts of the software already tested. Interviewee A have the same problem and would like to have the ability to identify related tests e.g. in case of regression test, via the requirements.

"Well, which requirements are related? Here you wish to have the possibility to pose that question to a requirements tool, e.g. –Well, suppose that this requirement have been incorrectly implemented, which other requirements are dependent on this requirement or influence by this requirement?"

Furthermore, test cases can (or at least should) not be done in an ad hoc order. Due to **dependencies** between test cases, there may be some tests that can not be executed before another one has passed. Especially Interviewee B has experienced this problem.

"… in order to verify this requirements, this and this and this must have been verified. In addition, we shall use data from the verification of this and this and this requirement. This posed rather high demands on how test cases were written on this level. […] Trying to sort this nest of dependencies out, it took time."

Even though most other interviewees acknowledge the impact of requirements interdependencies on testing, the projects in interviewee B's company are much larger which makes the issue more severe.

Finally, Interviewee B emphasises a related problem which is **requirements coverage**. How to decide whether a test case really covers a certain requirements well enough?

Co-operation and Co-ordination

Co-ordinating your development team(s), and **facilitate co-operation between teams and members** is important during the whole software engineering process. Testing is no exception, and we have already mentioned some issues regarding this in relation to managing requirements change in the above section. Our interviews also mention some other problems related to this issue when asked to describe their major challenges.

In one of Interviewee B's project, it is not the same people who write the test cases and who execute them due to the huge amount of requirements within that project. However, there are large drawbacks with this way of working since it is difficult to get an overview and control of the testing activity. Especially knowing that all requirements have been tested and that all test cases really ensures that the system as a whole works according to plan. *"This is a huge problem"*. This way of working, which probably is rather usual in large projects as in B's company, most likely requires more careful co-ordination between developers.

Another situation which requires good co-operation is emphasised by Interviewee E. In E's company many errors found during system testing, is of such a characteristic that the developers constructing the software did not have the possibility to find those in their limited testing environment.

In order to identify and describe the actual problem, the testers sometimes need to invite the responsible developer to the testing environment to show what is happening during test execution. This requires a good cooperation and working climate between testers and developers, which is sometimes missing.

Non-functional Aspects

A testing dilemma, according to Interviewee A, is that **performance** usually cannot be measured until rather late during testing. The functionality of the software must be more or less at place before you can run the performance tests, since those usually is about conducting these function many times and very fast during a period of time. At the same time, errors related to performance tend to include major changes as they are corrected. So, you would like to do performance testing rather early, but it is usually not possible. This issue is related to design for testability, i.e. that some kind of support functions could be installed in order to facilitate rudimentary performance testing.

Interviewee E views this as a more general problem since it is common that **non-functional requirements** are not considered at all.

Furthermore, Interviewee D and E, finds **the test environment** problematic some times. Interviewee D uses simulators when conducting their system tests. This requires that the right versions of these simulators are used every time, and that they are actually working together. Setting up the test environment could sometimes be rather tricky. Interviewee E emphasises the importance to start this set up in time. When the first release is made from the developers to the testers, the test environment must be up and running. Many testers have made the mistake of starting the environmental set up to late and wasted valuable testing time due to this.

Enough Time for Testing

According to Interviewee E, one of the major troubles for software testing is its place as the final phase in the development life cycle. When earlier phases are getting a little late, the cumulative delay may be severe for testing. There are usually not much time left to conduct testing as well as the testers would like. Even though time is an issue in many phases in the development process, our interviewees emphasises their frustration. The **time available for testing** gets too short and you got to downsize your testing ambitions. Therefore, prioritisation of test cases is important. Which functions to we have to test now and which ones can we do later? Which ones are most important and which ones should we exclude first? This problem is also experienced by Interviewee D and F.

Concluding Remarks and Future Work

This paper includes a discussion on challenges regarding system testing, identified during a minor interview study including six interviewees. The challenges are grouped into six problem areas, which are a) quality of the requirements, b) changing requirements, c) managing testing information, d) co-operation and co-ordination, e) non-functional aspects and f) enough time for testing.

Due to the minor sample within this study, we cannot draw any firm conclusions. However, there are some indications. Firstly, the requirements engineering practices do influence system testing, and poor requirements quality poses challenges in system testing. Secondly, there are not many challenges that are related to the actual execution of tests. Most challenges are related to planning, test design, and social issues. This may be influenced on the focus on the interview study, which are on the relationship between RE and testing.

Furthermore, the problems are fairly generally described and a more thorough investigation of these problems needs to be made. The first study within our requirements-testing project is to further explore the testers needs on RE and its results. This includes more closely investigating problems regarding the relations between RE and testing, mainly related to the first three problem areas, the quality of the requirements, changing requirements and managing testing information. The plan is to continue the project with evaluate RE tools based on the requirements identified within the first study.

References

Abran A, Moore JW, Bourque P, Dupuis R (2004) Guide to the Software Engineering Body of Knowledge – SWEBOK (2004 Version). A Project of the Software Engineering Coordinating Committee. IEEE Computer Society, Los Alamitos California. www.swebok.org/
Graham D (2002) Requirements and Testing: Seven Missing-Link Myths. IEEE Software, vol 19, p 15-18
Lausen S, Vinter O (2001) Preventing Requirements Defects: An Experiment in Process Improvement. Requirements Engineering, vol 6, p 37-50

Leung HKN, Wong PWL (1997) A Study of User Acceptance Tests. Software Quality Journal, vol 6, p 137-149

Lutz RR, Mikulski IC (2004) Ongoing Requirements Discovery in High-Integrity Systems. IEEE Software, vol 21, p 19-26

Patton MQ (2002) Qualitative Research and Evaluation Methods. Sage Publications Inc, California USA

Sommerville I (1996) Software Engineering. Addison-Wesley

Appendix A: Presentation of the Interviewees

This appendix presents an overview of the four interviewees involved in the interview study on testing and its requirements on the RE process.

Interviewee A: Works at a consultancy company, with over 300 employees where about 45 of them are working with testing related issues. The interviewee has over 10 years of experience within testing and is nowadays involved in educations within testing, evaluation and development of testing procedures, and has a mentor role for those working with testing within the projects. The respondent has been involved in very varying projects, from one man projects to large projects involving several thousands developers.

Interviewee B: Works at the software engineering department within a defence related company. The company has over 400 employees, of which 100 are at the software engineering department and about ten of them are working with testing. The interviewee works as a testing manager, but is also involved in writing test cases for the projects. The interviewee has mainly been involved in two projects. One project where a pure software part was developed, which include 30 – 60 persons and have lingered for 5-6 years. The other is a considerably larger project which includes both hardware and software (no specific numbers could be mentioned).

Interviewee C: Works at another defence related company, which develops communication solutions. This department is focused on radar solutions, and involves 80 persons. The interviewee works as a testing manager, and is both working with test planning as well as writing and executing test cases. The current project includes about 10 persons, where 3 of them are involved in testing.

Interviewee D: Works at the same company as interviewee C but at another department, which develops the user interface and the functionality which the radar operator is about to use. The department involves about 70 employees. The interviewee works as a testing manager at his/hers department, and as for interviewee 3 this includes planning the testing as well as writing and executing test cases. A project typically involves about 20-25 persons, where 2-5 persons are involved in the testing part.

Interviewee E: Works at the same consultancy company as interviewee A. The interviewee have been involved in testing issues for over 20 years, and the working tasks include project management, quality issues such as auditing, test management, and education related to testing. The interviewee has worked in many different types of projects, from large rigorous ones to smaller more flexible.

Interviewee F: Works at the same consultancy company as interviewee A and E. The interviewee has been a software developer for over 40 years and worked with testing related issues for over 15 year. The interviewee works as a testing manager and tester, and has mainly been involved in smaller project with both system testing and acceptance testing.